Diana Forsythe

READER IN
COMPARATIVE
RELIGION

D0621283

READER IN COMPARATIVE RELIGION *An Anthropological Approach*

THIRD EDITION

William A. Lessa
Professor Emeritus
UNIVERSITY OF CALIFORNIA, LOS ANGELES

Evon Z. Vogt
HARVARD UNIVERSITY

HARPER & ROW, PUBLISHERS
New York   Evanston   San Francisco   London

CONTENTS

FOREWORD

Three things appear to distinguish man from all other living creatures: the systematic making of tools, the use of abstract language, and religion. Some observers think they have detected among certain birds, mammals, and even other organisms the analogues of ritual. But no one has seriously suggested the presence of myth or theology. For these, another of the three distinctively human phenomena —abstract language—is surely a precondition.

Until the emergence of Communist societies we know of no human groups without religion. Even the Communists, as has often been said, have their "secular religion." While they repudiate the supernatural, they give allegiance in feeling as well as in thought to a body of doctrine that purports to provide life with a fairly immediate meaning. Nor is communism without its ritual and ceremonial side.

The universality of religion (in the broadest sense) suggests that it corresponds to some deep and probably inescapable human needs. All of these are repeatedly discussed in this book. There is the need for a moral order. Human life is necessarily a moral life precisely because it is a social life, and in the case of the human animal the minimum requirements for predictability of social behavior that will ensure some stability and continuity are not taken care of automatically by biologically inherited instincts, as is the case with the bees and the ants. Hence there must be generally accepted standards of conduct, and these values are more compelling if they are invested with divine authority and continually symbolized in rites that appeal to the senses. But no religion is solely a system of ethics. All religions also represent a response to the wonder and the terror of the ineluctable process of nature. They supply some answer to the profound uncertainties of experience, most especially to the homogeneity of death— even though some religions make a pure acknowledgment of death and erectly, carelessly, undauntedly admit nothingness.

The needs met by religion are not, however, by any means limited to those of constituting or bolstering a social order or of providing cognitive "explanations." Man is a symbolic as well as a tool-making creature. Cassirer understandably considers myth as an autonomous form of symbolism comparable to language, art, and science. In many and varied respects religion is an expressive activity: an outlet in drama, poetry, dance, and the plastic and graphic arts for the diverse temperaments of individuals, for particular subgroups, for the total community or society. My teacher, R. R. Marett, used to say "primitive religion is danced, not believed."

He did not intend, of course, that this aphorism should be taken literally. And one of the strong points of this book is that Professors Lessa and Vogt have resolutely emphasized the continuity of all religious phenomena. Yet there is one matter on which the equivocal word "primitive" gives us a useful reminder. In so-called primitive societies religion encompasses philosophy, theater, "science," ethics, diversion, and other behavior spheres which recent Western civilization has tended to segregate. The student must be aware of this fact, though the adjective "comparative" in the title of this book is altogether factual.

Indeed this reader is more genuinely comparative than any volume I know. Careful study of it should free any student from a narrow and culture-bound conception of religion. And it will become quite apparent that at least the symbolic forms of all religions derive from the particular nature and specific experience of the peoples that created these forms. As Xenophanes (560–475 B.C.) wrote:

Yes, and if oxen and horses or lions had hands, and could paint with their hands, and produce works of art as men do, horses would paint the forms of their gods like horses, and oxen like oxen, and make their bodies in the image of their several kinds. . . . The Ethiopians make their gods black and snub-nosed; the Thracians say theirs have blue eyes and red hair.

All religious systems—in practice if not in theory—have had to make some concessions to the frailties of human nature.

Because religious beliefs and practices, learned so early in contexts intimately associated with the most intense human experiences, are the targets of strong positive and negative feelings on the part of both participants and observers and because religion embraces such a wide and such a complex area of human life, the scientific study of religion is peculiarly difficult. The most honest and best course is the one which the editors have followed with great sensitivity and skill: achieve a decent balance between data and interpretation; present opposing points of view fairly and in historical depth; be as wide-ranging and comprehensive as space will allow. Nevertheless, thanks to the introductions to each chapter and the paragraphs linking the selections, the editors have succeeded in making judicious contributions to the establishment of regularities, to general theory. At the same time, the rich bibliographic aids make it easy for teacher and student to check and control the inductive generalizations which Professors Lessa and Vogt set forth on all the major topical areas of religion.

This, surely, is no parochial book. There are passages from the sacred texts of many religions. These passages and the descriptive accounts swing through the centuries and all the continents. The authors represent many nationalities and professions. We have bishops and anthropologists, literary critics and sociologists, psychiatrists and clergymen, administrators and psychologists. And the full gamut of the religious experience merges in the materials: rationality and passion; the supplication of bliss and of dread; a lurking, snakelike fear; the carrion gobbling of the garbage of sensations; mistrust and lurking insolence, insolence against a higher creation; the drift of spent souls; the striving for a center to life; the wheeling upon a dark void; the unquenched desire to worship.

CLYDE KLUCKHOHN

ACKNOWLEDGMENT

The third edition of this volume has been made possible by the reception given the first and second, and so we must reaffirm the help given us in the past before we can go on to express our new indebtedness.

When the editors first contemplated the compilation of a book of readings that would be useful to them and possibly to others in teaching comparative and primitive religion, they received much encouragement and many significant suggestions from their friends and associates, particularly the late Clyde Kluckhohn, Robert N. Bellah, Clifford Geertz, and Melford E. Spiro, whose advice was gratefully absorbed in molding the form and content of the *Reader*. The junior editor, while at the Center for Advanced Study in the Behavioral Sciences during 1956 and 1957, received further reinforcement through stimulating discussions with E. E. Evans-Pritchard, Morris E. Opler, and John M. Roberts. When it came time to put words on paper, Robert B. Edgerton and Roger C. Owen skillfully assisted in preparing some of the introductions to the selections and generally served as intellectual sounding boards, while Barbara Metzger wrote most of the original notes for the monographs on non-Western religious systems.

The second edition turned once more to some of its old supporters and at the same time added new names to its roster of collaborating colleagues, these being John W. M. Whiting, Michael G. Smith, and Philip L. Newman. We were also indebted to Jack Stauder for comments on the second edition.

The student assistants at the University of California, Los Angeles, who helped prepare the manuscript of the second edition for presentation to the publisher should also be given the recognition that belongs to them. Building on the foundation laid by Carol Romer Jones, who almost single-handedly worked on the first edition, Claudia Stevens, Carol Swartout, and Judy Wiseman collaborated on the second, which, strange to say, made more demands on time, patience, and ingenuity than one would have imagined necessary.

The work for the third edition was almost all done at Harvard University where the junior editor had the expert and devoted assistance of Kirk M. Endicott, Gary H. Gossen, Priscilla Rachun Linn, Michelle Zimbalist Rosaldo, and Renato I. Rosaldo, Jr., who collaborated with him from the beginning in selecting new materials, abridging the selections, and drafting the introductions for chapters and articles. Without their competent help, this third edition would never have appeared in print on schedule. Throughout the process of planning the third edition, we also profited from the research assistance of Catherine C. Vogt and from the bibliographic suggestions and advice of James J. Fox. The technical task of typing and assembling the manuscript for the third edition was efficiently accomplished by Mrs. Dolores Vidal Dale. We are deeply indebted to all the members of this talented staff who worked together so productively to meet our deadlines.

Finally, we must express our gratitude to the publishers, editors, and authors whose selections appear in this latest edition. Indeed, in several instances they offered to substitute, add, or revise selections. A number of them suggested that they were flattered to be included, although of course we look at this the other way around. There would have been no *Reader* without their contributions.

W.A.L.
E.Z.V.

READER IN COMPARATIVE RELIGION

GENERAL INTRODUCTION

I

Religion may be described as a system of beliefs and practices directed toward the "ultimate concern" of a society. "Ultimate concern," a concept used by Paul Tillich, has two aspects—meaning and power. It has meaning in the sense of ultimate meaning of the central values of a society, and it has power in the sense of ultimate, sacred, or supernatural power which stands behind those values.

Viewed in this way, religion is concerned with the explanation and expression of the ultimate values of a society; in other words, it has important *integrative* functions for groups and for individual personalities. At the same time religion is concerned with the threats to these central values, or to social or individual existence; it has important *defense* functions in providing ways of managing tensions and anxieties. Thus, religion both maintains the ultimate values of a society and manages tensions in the personalities of individual members of a society.

The religious beliefs and practices that provide this double-barreled function are of course almost infinitely varied from culture to culture, and are developed and tailored with symbols, myths and rituals that fit the varying cultural contexts. But the basic functions, and the concept of an "ultimate concern" with meaning and power, are probably found universally in human societies.

Although the problem of the nature of religion has for centuries absorbed the imagination and energies of scholars in different cultures, the detached comparative approach to the matter is a relatively recent experience in history. Indeed, the first sustained and systematic efforts to understand and interpret the phenomenon stem from the works of nineteenth- and early twentieth-century British scholars, especially Sir Edward B. Tylor, William Robertson Smith, Andrew Lang, Sir James Frazer, and R. R. Marett. Many of these men were merely amateur or quasiprofessional anthropologists, but they were endowed with inquiring minds and fine intellects.

These writers were for the most part influenced by the Darwinian concept of biological evolution and were interested in describing what they conceived to be the stages in cultural evolution. They turned to the study of "primitive" peoples living in the far corners of the world because they believed that these cultures represented what amounted to an earlier evolutionary stage in our own cultural development. They were motivated by a basic question: What are the origins of religion in mankind's development? By careful study of the accounts of missionaries and travelers among primitive peoples—they did no field work themselves—they attempted to reconstruct what the earlier stages of religion were like and to answer such questions as: How did man first create myths and develop ritual? Was animism the first form of religion, or was there a preanimistic religion? Did an age of magic precede an age of religion?

A special problem related to this question of "origins" involved the inquiry into whether or not the most primitive peoples, such as the Ona and Yahgan of Tierra del Fuego, the Eskimo, or the Ainu of Japan, worshiped a "primitive high god" or "Supreme Being." The implication was that perhaps mankind developed polytheistic religions only later in history, and did not return to monotheism until the development of the great religions in the Near East. Father Wilhelm Schmidt was one of the principal investigators of this problem.

Another major trend of thought is found in the works of the so-called French sociological school, and particularly in the work of Émile Durkheim. Some of Durkheim's ideas were foreshadowed by Fustel de Coulanges' *The Ancient City*, and we have added some selections from this classic to provide background information. In the work of Durkheim the emphasis is upon treating religion as an integral part of a society, but interestingly enough the question of origins still persists. Witness, for example, how Durkheim selects the case of the Australian aborigines to work out his theory that the reality underlying religion is society itself; he is interested in the origin of religious emotion and therefore selects a primitive culture. The works of this school are of crucial importance in that they form a kind of historical bridge between the earlier interests in "origins" and the later interests in the "functions" of religion, whatever their origin. The French school has exerted considerable influence outside its own national boundaries, thanks mostly to the prestige and international experience of an Englishman, Radcliffe-Brown.

A third major theoretical strand also coming from sociology is found in the works of Max Weber, especially in his explorations of the relationships between religious and economic institutions and his clear recognition of the fundamental importance of the problem of "meaning." This latter problem has two aspects: One is the difficulty of answers to the question of why unpredictable, unfortunate events occur in human life. This interest continues and is dealt with very perceptively in a selection from Evans-Pritchard, who shows with incisive clarity how witchcraft explains unfortunate events in Azande life. The second aspect has to do with the relationship between major institutional forms in a society. That is, the economic system must have some meaning in terms of the religious system and vice versa. Although we have not included a selection from Weber, his influence is evident in the writings of Talcott Parsons, and the questions we raise are clearly dealt with in the selection entitled "Religious Perspectives in Sociology and Social Psychology."

A fourth major theoretical thread was injected into the comparative study of religion by Sigmund Freud, who has been a crucial influence in thinking about the nature of religion, especially the relationship of religious thought and emotions to unconscious motivation and the treatment of religion as a projective system. Again it is significant that the interest in origins is also found here; witness how Freud concerned himself with the origin of the incest taboo in *Totem and Taboo*. Other writers have carried on the tradition, especially Géza Róheim and Bruno Bettelheim.

Meanwhile, influenced in part by the French sociological school and by their own firsthand field researches with primitive peoples, two major figures emerged who were to have a lasting impact on the anthropological treatment of religion: Malinowski and Radcliffe-Brown. In their "functional" approach to religion the question of origins in the older classical sense has shifted to a different question: What is the function of religion, whatever its origin, in any society and in particular societies? In other words, what does religion *do* for people and for social groups? There are great similarities but also important differences in the theoretical approach of these two scholars; Homans attempts to resolve the differences.

In recent decades the study of religion by anthropologists has been more sporadic, but there is evidence that interest and research in the field is quickening both in the United States and in Europe, as well as in Australia. A number of works by the American anthropologists A. Irving Hallowell, Morris Opler, and the late Clyde Kluckhohn favor a synthesis of the functional and psychoanalytic approaches to religion. We have included papers by Kluckhohn and Opler but not by Hallowell, since most of the latter's important papers have been reprinted in *Culture and Experience* (1955). Other American and some British anthropologists have been busy studying the religions that have emerged in the acculturation situation, such as the Ghost Dance, Peyote Cult, and Cargo Cults, and have produced a number of remarkable publications like Anthony Wallace's "Revitalization Movements" (1956), which is reprinted in Chapter 10. Other American scholars have been applying anthropological concepts to the study of the religions of the high cultures of the Far East, India, and Southeast Asia, and to the analysis of certain aspects of ritual in our own culture. There has also been a recent revival of interest in evolution in the religious aspects of societies, as exemplified in Bellah's interesting paper "Religious Evolution" (1964), which has been included in Chapter 1.

The recent British publications on religion have included both a variety of stimulating papers and a number of excellent monographs which we cite in various chapters of the *Reader*. Of special note are the two monographs of the Association of Social Anthropologists of the Commonwealth: *Anthropological Approaches to the Study of Religion*, edited by Michael Banton (1966), and *The Structural Study of Myth and Totemism*, edited by Edmund R. Leach (1967).

In France the most important development has been the stimulating publications by Claude Lévi-Strauss on myth and various aspects of ritual. Two of his articles, "The Bear and the Barber" (1963) and "The Structural Study of Myth" (1955; revised 1963), have been included in the *Reader*. But the student should read his other publications that contain materials on religion, especially *Totemism* (1963), *Structural Anthropology* (1963), *The Savage Mind* (1966), *The Raw and the Cooked* (1969), *Mythologiques: Du Miel aux cendres* (1966), and *Mythologiques: L'Origine des Manières de table* (1969), as well as the Festschrift in his honor entitled *Échanges et communications*, edited by Jean Pouillon and Pierre Maranda (1970).

Among the recent general trends in the study of religion by anthropologists we have noted especially an upsurge of interest in "symbolic analysis" of both rituals and myths, including the interesting problems involved in "symbolic classification." There are many scholars currently working in these fast-developing areas, especially Mary Douglas, Edmund Leach, John Middleton, Rodney Needham, and Victor Turner, as well as a number of younger anthropologists, both in the United States and in Europe; and we have attempted to include a sample of

their writings in this new edition of the *Reader*.

But it is still apparent that progress in theoretical treatment and methodological sophistication still lags behind the study of other aspects of culture (e.g., social structure, kinship, language), and we hope that this volume will stimulate younger generations of students to inquire further into the nature and function of religion.

II

At this point it may be appropriate to explain to some readers our seeming brashness in appropriating to our own use the term "comparative religion," in view of the fact that it has had different connotations for older students of religion as well as for modern theologians. Actually, the editors are not giving a special meaning to the term. It reflects a whole point of view in anthropology, and accordingly there occurs in the anthropological literature a series of related expressions, such as "comparative law," "comparative art," "comparative folklore," and "comparative institutions." The philosophy behind these terms will shortly be explained, but for the moment it will be well to examine the older and more traditional meaning of comparative religion.

Earlier studies of religion purported to be comparative—and indeed they often were—but these early studies used comparison as a sort of apologetics for the dominant Judaic-Christian religions.[1] During the latter stages of the nineteenth century several factors were combining to emancipate the comparative study of religion from this earlier goal of providing data for the validation of the origins and authority of Judaism or Christianity. One such factor was the accreting store of knowledge about primitive religions that was being collected by travelers, soldiers, missionaries, and administrators. Another was the Darwinian theory of biological evolution, which led to studies of other forms of evolution—among them that of religion. Several scholarly disciplines began to contribute stimuli to objective comparative

[1] In recent years theologians and others working in this more traditional and restricted field have veered away from the term "comparative religion" and substituted "history of religions" and "phenomenology of religions"—terms growing out of the general body of knowledge originally known as *Allgemeine Religionswissenschaft* (see Joseph M. Kitagawa, "The Nature and Program of the History of Religions Field," *Divinity School News*, November, 1957, pp. 13–25).

studies; sociology, anthropology, philology, mythology, folk psychology, and history all began to eschew apologetics for science.

The new comparative religion as represented by the anthropological approach makes no effort to evaluate, and it encompasses all the religions of the world, past and present, about which there is any information. By going beyond the complex cults of the great contemporary civilizations it is possible to gain not only a wider range of variation but also a greater degree of detachment. For example, those who are close to Christianity cannot always divorce themselves from the cultural and emotional associations that they entertain toward it. And they are apt to have preconceived notions regarding religions, such as Judaism and Islam, which have had intimate historical relationships with it. It is much more possible to retain an objective point of view when treating of the belief of the Koryak, Betsimisarka, Kankanay, Witoto, or Ewe. In addition,. the religions of the simpler societies have the advantage of being divested of the complex trappings characteristic of the faiths of civilized groups. They are more internally consistent, possessed of fewer alternatives of dogma, less complicated by sophisticated metaphysics, and freer of hierarchical superstructure. In short, they permit one to get down to the core—the fundamentals—of religion and its place in human life.

But what is the comparative method? Unfortunately, since it has meant many things to different people, the answer is not simple. Essentially, it is a method that attempts to achieve generalization through comparison of similar kinds of phenomena. It seeks to extract common denominators from a mass of variants. But the methods for which comparison has been utilized and the goals toward which these methods have been directed have not always been the same. The most comprehensive and fruitful effort to bring order out of the chaotic state into which the meaning of the expression has fallen is one made by Oscar Lewis in an article entitled "Comparisons in Cultural Anthropology" (1955). We shall take the liberty of reviewing some of his analysis.

According to Professor Lewis, there are two broad types of comparative studies in anthropology. The first examines societies that are historically related. Their common culture provides controls against which variables may be tested. This type, which has been given little recognition as an aspect of the comparative method, may involve either comparisons within a single culture or community, within a single culture area, or within a single nation. There are many advantages to comparative studies of this more limited kind. The data are more intensively studied, usually along comparable lines, so there is greater assurance of comparability. The culture is seen as a whole and not in fractions, so that all aspects of the culture appear in context. Moreover, a large number of variables can be studied functionally. The objectives are usually modest and the research designs closer to those made in truly experimental studies. It is here that we find the greater proportion of recent studies based on comparative field research. The greatest drawback to the limited approach is that it has narrow vistas.

The second broad type of comparative study compares historically unrelated societies, taking a broader and more ambitious approach, often of a holistic character. It may make comparisons within a continent, between continents or nations, or on a random or global scale. The purpose is to utilize similarities in form, structure, and process as a basis for deriving typologies or establishing causal relationships among various aspects of culture. It might be observed parenthetically that in this case we are dealing with headier wine. This kind of comparison looks for universals, worldwide typologies, or evolutionary sequences. Here is where the work of men such as Tylor, Freud, Durkheim, and Radcliffe-Brown fits in. The weakness of this overall approach is that it does not have many of the controls possible in the more limited studies described in the previous paragraph. Moreover, when statistics are used they often artificially quantify the culture elements and control only a few of the variables. Recently there have been more sophisticated comparative studies along these lines in the "cross-cultural" works of Murdock, Whiting, and others who have used the Human Relations Area Files as a basis for careful samples of the world's societies and have successfully arrived at generalizations with high validity, as for example in Murdock's *Social Structure* (1949). Whiting's helpful paper "The Cross-Cultural Method" (1954) provides an excellent description of the general approach.

Evans-Pritchard ("Religion," 1956) has in effect advocated a combination of these two approaches if we are to retain the objectivity necessary to reach general and significant conclusions regarding the nature of primitive religions as a whole. He says that we must, for example, first investigate the religion of one Melanesian people, then compare the religion of that group with several other Melanesian societies that are nearest to it in their culture. After that would come a comparative study of all Melanesian groups, and only then could one say something about Melanesian religion in general. This laborious kind of research is the only hope for eventually achieving broader conclusions about religion. This newer stress on careful comparisons on a smaller scale has also been emphasized by others, especially Eggan, who writes, "My own preference is for the utilization of the comparative method on a smaller scale and with as much control over the frame of comparison as it is possible to secure" ("Social Anthropology and the Method of Controlled Comparison," 1954). Eggan's masterful discussion of controlled comparisons shows that he is aware that there is much work ahead, and that no one approach is sufficient—the anthropological concepts of structure and function can and should be combined with the ethnological concepts of process and history.

More than mere painstaking labor is needed for valid comparisons. We must be sure that a comparative analysis is based on comparable data. Franz Boas' old warning on this score it still valid and has been eloquently renewed by Clyde Kluckhohn in a paper entitled "Universal Categories of Culture" (1953). As one of his examples he makes specific mention of the field of religion, which he says is a recurring pattern but not a uniform phenomenon, as evidenced by the lack of a clear-cut distinction between magic and religion. These concepts, he says, have heuristic usefulness in given situations but are not sufficiently distinct to serve as units from which larger concepts can be built up.

As for the aims which anthropologists have in their comparisons, Lewis (*op. cit.*) says that there are several: to establish general laws or regularities; to document the range of variation in the phenomena studied; to document the distribution of traits or aspects of culture; to reconstruct culture history; to test hypotheses derived from non-Western societies. This is a broad range, and it should be noted that it covers all

the approaches in cultural anthropology, whether functional, diffusionist, *kulturkreis*, or evolutionary. The difference lies both in the ways in which they are used and in the objectives toward which they are directed.

The present volume is not concerned with documenting distributions or reconstructing history. Rather, as a work of science, it is concerned with comparison only insofar as it helps to establish regularities in religious phenomena. Of course, this would presuppose the testing of hypotheses in different cultural contexts. Some of the articles in the pages that follow do not explicitly state their aims, but these can be interpreted with reasonable accuracy. Many of the articles seem to be essentially descriptive or historical, but our purpose has been to use them as contributions to general theory and not as particular and discrete facts.

We can conclude by warning that anthropology cannot claim comparison as its brain child. Aside from the impressionistic comparisons of the layman, there are the systematic and controlled ones of all scientific disciplines, which use correlation and covariation in their study of similarities and differences. If we may at this point venture an opinion, it would be to the effect that anthropology can at least take pride in the fact that of all the social sciences it has most expanded the possibilities of comparison by adding to the general pool the thousands of case histories made available by its study of tribal societies. Moreover, some of the claims for exclusiveness were undoubtedly derived from the very special use of comparison made by the classical evolutionists of the last century—a specious method that employed a circular type of reasoning, but which nonetheless commanded considerable support in its time.

III

The basic purpose of this book of readings is to provide the student with a guide to the literature concerning what anthropologists have found out about religion in the last 100 years. In a few cases we have included selections from the pens of sociologists, historians, and others, and particularly from scholars in these related fields whose works have especially influenced anthropological thinking or who have dealt with data from primitive cultures.

The book grew out of a need felt by the two editors as they attempted to teach courses in comparative and primitive religion at the University of California at Los Angeles and at Harvard University and discovered that many of the best materials were published in obscure journals or were inaccessible to large numbers of our students.

There are a number of interesting introductory texts on primitive religion, including Annemarie De Waal Malefijt's *Religion and Culture: An Introduction to Anthropology of Religion*, William J. Goode's *Religion Among the Primitives*, W. W. Howells' *The Heathens*, Robert H. Lowie's *Primitive Religion*, Edward Norbeck's *Religion in Primitive Society*, Paul Radin's *Primitive Religion*, Anthony F. C. Wallace's *Religion: An Anthropological View*, J. Milton Yinger's two books *Religion, Society, and the Individual* and *The Scientific Study of Religion*. But after students have read one of these texts in the opening weeks of a school term, there is then little for them to do except turn to the long, specialized monographs, or some of the smaller monographs such as "Case Studies in Cultural Anthropology," edited by George and Louise Spindler. It is hoped that this collection of readings will fill the gap between the introductory texts and the monographs and will give the student a significant overview of the anthropological literature. Additional useful collections of readings may be found in the recent books edited by John Middleton, including *Myth and Cosmos* (1967), *Gods and Rituals* (1967), and *Magic, Witchcraft, and Curing* (1967). The teaching procedure that we recommend is, first, an introductory text; second, this volume; and third, exposure of the students to one or more of the monographs. We have included a selected list of the longer, specialized monographs on religion that we have found useful.

IV

Throughout the present collection we have attempted to strike a balance between the general and theoretical and the descriptive and concrete. The more general, theoretical selections on the origins and functions of religion have been placed in Chapters 1 and 2. This third edition then includes almost completely new Chapters 3, 4, 5, and 6, which emphasize the new trends in symbolic analysis and classification and the new and promising attempts to decode the symbolic meanings found in myths and rituals. Chapter 7 deals with shamanism, with two new selections. Chapters 8 and 9 focus, respectively, on magic, witchcraft, and divination and on death, ghosts, and ancestor worship, with some deletions and additions to those selections we utilized in the second edition. The final Chapter 10 deals with the dynamics of religion, again with some revisions for this third edition. Since the size of the *Reader* had to be reduced because of rising publication costs, we have reluctantly deleted three substantive chapters—on mana and taboo, on totemism, and on the magical treatment of illness—which were included in the second edition. For students interested in these traditional areas in the study of primitive religion we would like to recommend Franz Steiner's classic study *Taboo* (1956) and Claude Lévi-Strauss' book *Totemism* (1963), which contains a useful review of earlier theories as well as a good exposition of Lévi-Strauss' ideas about the phenomena. These can be supplemented by also reading Meyer Fortes' excellent recent paper "Totem and Taboo" (1966). The selections we have retained on the curing of illness can be found in Chapter 7 on shamanism; other relevant materials on this subject are found in various other chapters in this edition. The reader will note that we also deleted the chapter on new methods of analysis which appeared in the second edition; actually most of the selections have been retained in this third edition, but by now most of these methods are in use by anthropologists and hence a special chapter was no longer necessary.

The introductions to each chapter and introductory paragraphs for each selection are designed to place the material in context and to provide bibliographic and teaching aids.

1
THE ORIGIN AND DEVELOPMENT OF RELIGION

Introduction

The origins of religion can only be speculated upon; they can never be discovered. Theories with enormous "documentation" and nimble imagination may temporarily delude the impressionable reader into believing that answers have been found, but sober reflection will always show the futility of accepting any one of them as constituting more than a scholarly guess. Should we on this account turn away from such speculations? Not at all. The better and more responsible of these hypotheses have pointed the way to rewarding lines of investigation. Not only have they caused an immense amount of field data to be collected and studied, but they have been ultimately responsible for analytic contributions of lasting value. Even scholars who have consciously renounced historical interests in religion owe a great debt to others who have had such interests and helped found a science of religion.

One might ask what gave these early students the courage to proceed with reconstructions in the face of our inability to recover the past from actual documentary evidence. What did they substitute for fact? The answer is, schemes, analogies, and assumptions, all overlaid with rich imagination. One method of approach was through the so-called comparative method. "Evidences" from tribes all over the world were taken out of context and arranged in a sequential scheme. But this was done only

according to a preconceived plan and was justified on the grounds that it arranged the data in such a way that they conformed to the scheme and therefore proved its validity. Another method was through the use of so-called survivals—"processes, customs, opinions, and so forth, which have been carried on by force of habit into a new state of society different from that in which they had their original home, and thus they remain proofs and examples of an older condition of culture out of which a newer had been evolved" (Tylor). In brief, existing survivals throw light on the history of the past. But in the absence of written records there is no way of knowing that a custom is actually a vestigial remnant of a formerly widespread condition. Again, reliance was firmly placed on the principle of the psychic unity of mankind—human nature is basically uniform, therefore similar results have come independently from the same causes. The implication of such panhumanism is that processes and reactions which we can study and understand today can be used to reconstruct the past because man's mind always reacts in the same way to similar external stimuli. Although anthropologists admit the great force of such psychic unity, they feel that the evolutionists did not take sufficient cognizance of the even greater effects of diffusion in producing cultural similarity. Thus specific religious phenomena with which we are acquainted through firsthand experience may not be used to project back into the past, because religious traits may be borrowed instead of developed independently. Such borrowing can disturb any picture of uniform development. Some evolutionists, notably Herbert Spencer, were guided by the principle of progress—society keeps advancing from a less desirable state to a better and better one. The way in which this principle operates is to regard the civilization of western Europe as the acme of man's achievements and to assume that the situation in the childhood of mankind must for each human institution have been exactly the opposite, with intermediate stages grading off from the one to the other. Thus if monotheism prevails today in western Europe, the belief in many spirits must have been a very early condition, polytheism being a less enlightened stage than belief in one God. Since progress is a matter of opinion and merely begs the question as to what is a desirable kind of change, such a theoretical plan rests on a tenuous base; it cannot tell us what the situation was like in primeval times. Moreover, the principle of progress as used by Spencer demands that it be regarded as an irresistible trend, an assumption that finds many objections. To reconstruct the past the surest evidences must come from archaeology; valuable leads have indeed been suggested by the study of old cultural remains. The burials of Neanderthal man and Cro-Magnon man have strong implications for the theory that they indicate an ancient belief in the soul and the afterworld. But since archaeological interpretations must so often rely on analogies with contemporary primitives they are not always conclusive. There is justifiable reason for being cautious in using archaeological data to say that the art of the Upper Paleolithic is magico-religious in nature.

The articles selected for this chapter, except for the last, consist of both theories of origins and critiques of such theories. It will be noticed that for the most part they do not bear a recent date, a reflection of the fact that the problem of origins is not a pressing current issue. But one should not minimize the value of these ideas, for they command serious attention as exploratory efforts and have had far-reaching and often fruitful effects. The first article is by Tylor, and represents the earliest of the major anthropological hypotheses of origins; it views religion as being rooted in the idea of the soul, and argues that out of this rational creation by primeval man came the subsequent belief that a plurality of spirits is associated with various spheres of nature, human activities, and so on. Tylor's basic position was challenged by Father Wilhelm Schmidt of the *Kulturkreis* school of anthropological thought that developed especially in Vienna. Schmidt (1931) maintained that in the beginning man had belief in one Spirit and that the multiplicity of gods we see in some contemporary societies is a degeneration from the earliest position. Another approach to the problem of origins was offered by W. Robertson Smith (1889; reprinted in paperback, 1956), who wrote especially on the origin of sacrifice. He was influential in shaping the ideas of many subsequent writers, among them Freud, whose views in *Totem and Taboo* (paperback edition, 1952) are here represented only indirectly through two articles by Kroeber, who was at variance with the psychoanalytic interpretation of the origin not only of sacrifice but of religion in general. Durkheim's provocative theory of the origin of religion, which has had a strong and lasting influence in contemporary thinking, is presented in the form of selections from *The Elementary Forms of the Religious Life* (the most recent paperback edition was issued in 1954).

One important historical theory is not represented in the selections and deserves special notice. It is the naturism explanation originally offered in 1856 by F. Max Müller and subsequently expanded by him and other students of Sanskrit. The discovery of the ancient Vedas of the Hindus influenced Müller's ideas. The impulse to religious thought and language, he maintained, arises in the first instance from sensuous experience—from the influence of external nature on man. Nature contains surprise, terror, marvels, miracles. This vast domain of the unknown and infinite, rather than the known and finite, is what provided the sensation from which religions are derived. Fire, for example, could create such an impression on the mind of man. So could the sun and rivers and the wind, to name but a few phenomena. Religions only came into being, however, when the forces of nature were transformed by man from abstract forces to personal agents, that is, spirits. This came about through a "disease of language." Language influences the way in which people classify newly learned things. Natural phenomena came to be compared to human acts, and expressions originally used for human acts came to be applied to natural objects. A thunderbolt was called Something that tears up the soil or spreads fire, the wind Something that sighs or whistles, a river Something that flows, and so on. After this had been done, spirits had to be invented to account for the acts attributed to them by their names, and so arose pantheons of gods. The myth-making process then took hold and carried matters still further by endowing each god with a biography. Thus religion is really a fabric of errors. The supernatural world was composed of beings created out of nothing. In this developmental scheme Müller did not ignore Tylor's later theory of the origin of the soul, but he felt that it was a secondary idea. His chief error was in explaining primitive personalism about nature as if it were some sort of cognitive mistake—a disease of language—as if the primitive first saw the world in coldly objective and scientific terms and then through cognitive error lost this view. But the primitive never had such a world view, which was itself the product of cultural development. Müller's other error was in supposing that he could take ancient historic records from India and attribute religious developments there to the whole world. Writing is, after all, a recent phenomenon and does not even approach the antiquity ascribed to religion.

The final article, by Bellah, is the only one representing neoevolutionism.

Edward B. Tylor

ANIMISM

More than any other anthropologist, Sir Edward B. Tylor stressed the importance of the soul both in defining religion and in understanding the evolutionary stages through which religious phenomena have passed. To him, the belief in spirit beings—animism—constitutes the minimum definition of religion.

The present passage from Tylor's extensive account of animism does not clearly reveal his evolutionary position, but it is apparent that he is concerned with origin and development. First he delves into the question of how men came to create the concept of the soul, and finds the answer in men's efforts to interpret dreams, hallucinations, and other aberrant psychic phenomena which puzzle them. Tylor adduces what he considers to be evidences from primitive peoples that the idea of the soul is not only universal but is also consistent with his dream theory. Along the way he accounts for the origin of human sacrifice by asserting that it is a way of freeing the soul from the body and putting it into the service of the dead. It is only a reasonable step that early man should next extend the idea of the soul to animals, and then to plants, for they too live and die, enjoy health and suffer disease. This accounts for animal sacrifice, which is designed to aid the dead in the afterlife; however, there does not exist a counterpart among plants, for they are are not sacrificed for the purpose of enlisting their souls for the service of the dead. Continuing to reason by analogy, says Tylor, early man extended the theory of the soul to stones, weapons, food, ornaments, and other objects which we who are civilized would endow with neither a soul nor life.

The portions of Tylor's theory of animism which have not been included in the accompanying article are lengthy, constituting six chapters of his *Primitive Culture*. They deal with such matters as transmigration and the future life; the expanding of the original theory of souls into a wider doctrine of spirits, that is, an animistic theory of nature; the development of the view that spirits are personal causes of phenomena of the world; the origin of guardian spirits and nature spirits; the origin of polytheism; and, finally, the development of the idea of

Reprinted in abridged form from Edward B. Tylor, *Primitive Culture* (2 vols.; 2d ed.; London: John Murray, 1873), Chap. 11, by permission of the publishers.

monotheism as the completion of the polytheistic system and the outcome of the animistic philosophy. All these are fitted into an unsystematic unilinear scheme of development, in which certain inevitable stages are passed through.

The first aspect of Tylor's theory, which is contained in the article that follows, has been attacked with far less severity than the evolutionary aspect, and even today it continues to impress scholars with its plausibility. The usual criticism is that it is an intellectualistic explanation, and that a rational need to explain the physiological phenomena of such unusual psychic states as dreams not only does not concern the primitive but fails to produce the emotional quality necessary for religion. It is for this reason that some theorists have substituted the criterion of supernaturalism for that of animism as a minimum requirement for religion. Another criticism is that primitive man could not have developed the concept of the soul through dreams because it would have been too easy for him to be contradicted when trying to check with his tribal mates on his hallucinatory experiences. Nevertheless, Tylor's theory has its admirers. Lowie remarks that it not only has a "high degree of probability" but to his knowledge has no serious competitor among rival theories. Even Marett, who put forth the theory that animatism preceded animism, expressed appreciation of Tylor's hypothesis and asserted that he himself was "no irreconcilable foe who has a rival theory to put forward concerning the origin of religion."

Greater vulnerability attaches to the second aspect of Tylor's theory, for when he attempts to show that out of the concept of the soul there evolved the concept of animism, then polydaemonism, then polytheism, and finally monotheism, he falls into most of the fallacies of the evolutionists of his time. In treating primitive man as primeval he had to assume that over a period of hundreds of thousands of years some of the simpler peoples of the world had retained religious beliefs unchanged. One could argue that religion shows a remarkable tenacity and indeed undergoes less alteration than other aspects of culture; but in this case it is asking too much. And, one could argue, too, as did the irrepressible Andrew Lang, that among the simplest peoples of the world there frequently appears a high god; therefore, while the idea of the soul as outlined by Tylor might itself be valid, it need not be supposed that it evolved into the concept of the high god. Other deficiencies in Tylor's chronological scheme could be mentioned, but they are mostly reducible to the use he made of survivals and the faulty comparative method of contemporary evolutionists.

Notwithstanding these limitations, there can be no doubt that Tylor made a challenging attempt to describe the origin of the soul and the general history of religion, and it stimulated subsequent and more sophisticated efforts.

The first requisite in a systematic study of the religions of the lower races is to lay down a rudimentary definition of religion. By requiring in this definition the belief in a supreme deity or of a judgment after death, the adoration of idols or the practice of sacrifice, or other partially diffused doctrines or rites, no doubt many tribes may be excluded from the category of religious. But such narrow definition has the fault of identifying religion rather with particular developments than with the deeper motive which underlies them. It seems best to fall back at once on this essential source, and simply to claim, as a minimum definition of religion, the belief in Spiritual Beings. So far as I can judge from the immense mass of accessible evidence, we have to admit that the belief in spiritual beings appears among all low races with whom we have attained to thoroughly intimate acquaintance; whereas the assertion of absence of such belief must apply either to ancient tribes, or to more or less imperfectly described modern ones.

I purpose here, under the name of Animism, to investigate the deep-lying doctrine of Spiritual Beings, which embodies the very essence of Spiritualistic as opposed to Materialistic philosophy. Animism is not a new technical term, though now seldom used. From its special relation to the doctrine of the soul, it will be seen to have a peculiar appropriateness to the view here taken of the mode in which theological ideas have been developed among mankind. The word "Spiritualism," though it may be, and sometimes is, used in a general sense, has this obvious defect to us, that it has become the designation of a particular modern sect, who indeed hold extreme spiritualistic views, but cannot be taken as typical representatives of these views in the world at large. The sense of

Spiritualism in its wider acceptation, the general belief in spiritual beings, is here given to Animism.

Animism characterizes tribes very low in the scale of humanity, and thence ascends, deeply modified in its transmission, but from first to last preserving an unbroken continuity, into the midst of high modern culture. Doctrines adverse to it, so largely held by individuals or schools, are usually due not to early lowness of civilization, but to later changes in the intellectual course, to divergence from, or rejection of, ancestral faiths; and such newer developments do not affect the present inquiry as to the fundamental religious condition of mankind. Animism is, in fact, the groundwork of the Philosophy of Religion, from that of savages up to that of civilized men. And although it may at first sight seem to afford but a bare and meager definition of a minimum of religion, it will be found practically sufficient; for where the root is, the branches will generally be produced. It is habitually found that the theory of Animism divides into two great dogmas, forming parts of one consistent doctrine; first concerning souls of individual creatures, capable of continued existence after the death or destruction of the body; second, concerning other spirits, upward to the rank of powerful deities. Spiritual beings are held to affect or control the events of the material world, and man's life here and hereafter; and it being considered that they hold intercourse with men, and receive pleasure or displeasure from human actions, the belief in their existence leads naturally, and it might almost be said inevitably, sooner or later to active reverence and propitiation. Thus Animism, in its full development, includes the belief in souls and in a future state, in controlling deities and subordinate spirits, these doctrines practically resulting in some kind of active worship. One great element of religion, that moral element which among the higher nations forms its most vital part, is indeed little represented in the religion of the lower races. It is not that these races have no moral sense or no moral standard, for both are strongly marked among them, if not in formal precept, at least in that traditional consensus of society which we call public opinion, according to which certain actions are held to be good or bad, right or wrong. It is that the conjunction of ethics and Animistic philosophy, so intimate and powerful in the higher culture, seems scarcely yet to

have begun in the lower. I propose here hardly to touch upon the purely moral aspects of religion, but rather to study the animism of the world so far as it constitutes, as unquestionably it does constitute, an ancient and world-wide philosophy, of which belief is the theory and worship is the practice. Endeavoring to shape the materials for an inquiry hitherto strangely undervalued and neglected, it will now be my task to bring as clearly as may be into view the fundamental animism of the lower races, and in some slight and broken outline to trace its course into higher regions of civilization. Here let me state once and for all two principal conditions under which the present research is carried on. First, as to the religious doctrines and practices examined, these are treated as belonging to theological systems devised by human reason, without supernatural aid or revelation; in other words, as being developments of Natural Religion. Second, as to the connection between similar ideas and rites in the religions of the savage and the civilized world. While dwelling at some length on doctrines and ceremonies of the lower races, and sometimes particularizing for special reasons the related doctines and ceremonies of the higher nations, it has not seemed my proper task to work out in detail the problems thus suggested among the philosophies and creeds of Christendom. Such applications, extending farthest from the direct scope of a work on primitive culture, are briefly stated in general terms, or touched in slight allusion, or taken for granted without remark. Educated readers possess the information required to work out their general bearing on theology, while more technical discussion is left to philosophers and theologians specially occupied with such arguments.

The first branch of the subject to be considered is the doctrine of human and other souls, an examination of which will occupy the rest of the present theory of its development. It seems as though thinking men, as yet at a low level of culture, were deeply impressed by two groups of biological problems. In the first place, what is it that makes the difference between a living body and a dead one; what causes waking, sleep, trance, disease, death? In the second place, what are those human shapes which appear in dreams and visions? Looking at these two groups of phenomena, the ancient savage philosophers probably made their first step by the obvious inference that every man has two things belonging to him, namely, a life and a phantom. These two are evidently in close connection with the body, the life as enabling it to feel and think and act, the phantom as being its image or second self; both, also, are perceived to be things separable from the body, the life as able to go away and leave it insensible or dead, the phantom as appearing to people at a distance from it. The second step would seem also easy for savages to make, seeing how extremely difficult civilized men have found it to unmake. It is merely to combine the life and the phantom. As both belong to the body, why should they not also belong to one another, and be manifestations of one and the same soul? Let them then be considered as united, and the result is that well-known conception which may be described as an apparitional soul, a ghost-soul. This, at any rate, corresponds with the actual conception of the personal soul or spirit among the lower races, which may be defined as follows: It is a thin unsubstantial human image, in its nature a sort of vapor, film, or shadow; the cause of life and thought in the individual it animates; independently possessing the personal consciousness and volition of its corporeal owner, past or present; capable of leaving the body far behind, to flash swiftly from place to place; mostly impalpable and invisible, yet also manifesting physical power, and especially appearing to men waking or asleep as a phantasm separate from the body of which it bears the likeness; continuing to exist and appear to men after the death of that body; able to enter into, possess, and act in the bodies of other men, of animals, and even of things. Though this definition is by no means of universal application, it has sufficient generality to be taken as a standard, modified by more or less divergence among any particular people. Far from these worldwide opinions being arbitrary or conventional products, it is seldom even justifiable to consider their uniformity among distant races as proving communication of any sort. They are doctrines answering in the most forcible way to the plain evidence of men's senses, as interpreted by a fairly consistent and rational primitive philosophy. So well, indeed, does primitive animism account for the facts of nature, that it has held its place into the higher levels of education. Though classic and medieval philosophy modified it much, and modern philosophy has handled it yet more unsparingly, it has so

far retained the traces of its original character, that heirlooms of primitive ages may be claimed in the existing psychology of the civilized world. Out of the vast mass of evidence, collected among the most various and distant races of mankind, typical details may now be selected to display the earlier theory of the soul, the relations of the parts of this theory, and the manner in which these parts have been abandoned, modified, or kept up, along the course of culture.

To understand the popular conceptions of the human soul or spirit, it is instructive to notice the words which have been found suitable to express it. The ghost or phantasm seen by the dreamer or the visionary is an unsubstantial form, like a shadow, and thus the familiar term of the *shade* comes in to express the soul. Thus the Tasmanian word for the shadow is also that for the spirit; the Algonquin Indians describe a man's soul as *otahchuk*, "his shadow," the Quiché language uses *natub* for "shadow, soul"; the Arawac *ueja* means "shadow, soul, image"; the Abipones made the one word *loákal* serve for "shadow, soul, echo, image." The Zulus not only use the word *tunzi* for "shadow, spirit, ghost," but they consider that at death the shadow of a man will in some way depart from the corpse, to become an ancestral spirit. The Basutos not only call the spirit remaining after death the *seriti* or "shadow," but they think that if a man walks on the river bank a crocodile may seize his shadow in the water and draw him in; while in Old Calabar there is found the same identification of the spirit with the *ukpon* or "shadow," for a man to lose which is fatal. There are thus found among the lower races not only the types of those familiar classic terms, the *skia* and *umbra*, but also what seems the fundamental thought of the stories of shadowless men still current in the folklore of Europe, and familiar to modern readers in Chamisso's tale of Peter Schlemihl. Thus the dead in Purgatory knew that Dante was alive when they saw that, unlike theirs, his fingers cast a shadow on the ground. Other attributes are taken into the notion of soul or spirit, with especial regard to its being the cause of life. Thus the Caribs, connecting the pulses with spiritual beings, and especially considering that in the heart dwells man's chief soul, destined to a future heavenly life, could reasonably use the one word *iouanni* for "soul, life, heart." The Tongans supposed the soul to exist throughout the whole extension of the body, but particularly in the heart. On one occasion, the natives were declaring to a European that a man buried months ago was nevertheless still alive. "And one, endeavoring to make me understand what he meant, took hold of my hand, and squeezing it, said, 'This will die, but the life that is within you will never die'; with his other hand pointing to my heart." So the Basutos say of a dead man that his heart is gone, and of one recovering from sickness that his heart is coming back. This corresponds to the familiar Old World view of the heart as the prime mover in life, thought, and passion. The connection of soul and blood, familiar to the Karens and Papuas, appears prominently in Jewish and Arabic philosophy.

The act of breathing, so characteristic of the high animals during life, and coinciding so closely with life in its departure, has been repeatedly and naturally identified with the life or soul itself. It is thus that West Australians used one word *waug* for "breath, spirit, soul"; that in the Netela language of California, *piuts* means "life, breath, soul"; that certain Greenlanders reckoned two souls to man, namely, his shadow and his breath; that the Malays say the soul of the dying man escapes through his nostrils, and in Java use the same word *nawa* for "breath, life, soul." The conception of the soul as breath may be followed up through Semitic and Aryan etymology, and thus into the main streams of the philosophy of the world. Hebrew shows *nephesh*, "breath" passing into all the meanings of "life, soul, mind, animal," while *ruach* and *neshamah* make the like transition from "breath" to "spirit"; and to these the Arabic *nefs* and *ruh* correspond. The same is the history of Sanskrit *atman* and *prana*, of Greek *psyche* and *pneuma*, of Latin *animus, anima, spiritus*. German *geist* and English *ghost*, too, may possibly have the same original sense of breath. And if any should think such expressions due to mere metaphor, they may judge the strength of the implied connection between breath and spirit by cases of most unequivocal significance. Among the Seminoles of Florida, when a woman died in childbirth, the infant was held over her face to receive her parting spirit, and thus acquire strength and knowledge for its future use. These Indians could have well understood why at the deathbed of an ancient Roman, the nearest kinsman leant over to inhale the last breath of the departing (*ex excipies hanc animan ore pio*). Their state of mind is kept up to this day among Tyrolese peasants, who can still fancy a good man's soul to issue from his mouth at death like a little white cloud.

Among rude races, the original conception of the human soul seems to have been that of ethereality, or vaporous materiality, which has held so large a place in human thought ever since. In fact, the later metaphysical notion of immateriality could scarcely have conveyed any meaning to a savage. It is moreover to be noticed that, as to the whole nature and action of apparitional souls, the lower philosophy escapes various difficulties which down to modern times have perplexed metaphysicians and theologians of the civilized world. Considering the thin ethereal body of the soul to be itself sufficient and suitable for visibility, movement, and speech, the primitive animists had no need of additional hypotheses to account for these manifestations, theological theories such as we may find detailed by Calmet, as that immaterial souls have their own vaporous bodies provided for them by supernatural means to enable them to appear as specters, or that they possess the power of condensing the circumambient air into phantomlike bodies to invest themselves in, or of forming from it vocal instruments. It appears to have been within systematic schools of civilized philosophy that the transcendental definitions of the immaterial soul were obtained, by abstraction from the primitive conception of the ethereal-material soul, so as to reduce it from a physical to a metaphysical entity.

Departing from the body at the time of death, the soul or spirit is considered set free to linger near the tomb, to wander on earth or flit in the air, or to travel to the proper region of spirits—the world beyond the grave. The principal conceptions of the lower psychology as to a Future Life will be considered in the following chapters, but for the present purpose of investigating the theory of souls in general, it will be well to enter here upon one department of the subject. Men do not stop short at the persuasion that death releases the soul to a free and active existence, but they quite logically proceed to assist nature, by slaying men in order to liberate their souls for ghostly uses. Thus there arises one of the most widespread, distinct, and intelligible rites of animistic religion—that of funeral human sacrifice for the service of the dead. When a man of rank dies and his soul departs to its own place, wherever and whatever that place may be, it is a rational inference of early philosophy that the souls of attendants, slaves, and wives, put to death at his funeral, will make the same journey and continue their service in the next life, and the argument is frequently stretched further, to include the souls of new victims sacrificed in order that they may enter upon the same ghostly servitude. It will appear from the ethnography of this rite that it is not strongly marked in the very lowest levels of culture, but that, arising in the higher savagery, it develops itself in the barbaric stage, and thenceforth continues or dwindles in survival.

Of the murderous practices to which this opinion leads, remarkably distinct accounts may be cited from among tribes of the Indian Archipelago. The following account is given of the funerals of great men among the savage Kayans of Borneo: "Slaves are killed in order that they may follow the deceased and attend upon him. Before they are killed the relations who surround them enjoin them to take great care of their master when they join him, to watch and shampoo him when he is indisposed, to be always near him, and to obey all his behests. The female relatives of the deceased then takes a spear and slightly wound the victims, after which the males spear them to death." Again, the opinion of the Idaan is "that all whom they kill in this world shall attend them as slaves after death. This notion of further interest in the destruction of the human species is a great impediment to an intercourse with them, as murder goes further than present advantage or resentment. From the same principle they will purchase a slave, guilty of any capital crime, at fourfold his value, that they may be his executioners." With the same idea is connected the ferocious custom of "head-hunting," so prevalent among the Dayaks before Rajah Brooke's time. They considered that the owner of every human head they could procure would serve them in the next world, where, indeed, a man's rank would be according to his number of heads in this. They would continue the mourning for a dead man till a head was brought in, to provide him with a slave to accompany him to the "habitation of souls"; a father who lost his child would go out and kill the first man he met, as a funeral ceremony; a young man might not marry till he had procured a head, and some tribes would bury with a

dead man the first head he had taken, together with spears, cloth, rice, and betel. Waylaying and murdering men for their heads became, in fact, the Dayaks' national sport, and they remarked "the white men read books, we hunt heads instead." Of such rites in the Pacific islands, the most hideously purposeful accounts reach us from the Fiji group. Till lately, a main part of the ceremony of a great man's funeral was the strangling of wives, friends, and slaves, for the distinct purpose of attending him into the world of spirits. Ordinarily the first victim was the wife of the deceased, and more than one if he had several, and their corpses, oiled as for a feast, clothed with new fringed girdles, with heads dressed and ornamented, and vermilion and turmeric powder spread on their faces and bosoms, were laid by the side of the dead warrior. Associates and inferior attendants were likewise slain, and these bodies were spoken of as "grass for bedding the grave." When Ra Mbithi, the pride of Somosomo, was lost at sea, seventeen of his wives were killed; and after the news of the massacre of the Namena people, in 1839, eighty women were strangled to accompany the spirits of their murdered husbands.

In now passing from the consideration of the souls of men to that of the souls of the lower animals, we have first to inform ourselves as to the savage man's idea, which is very different from the civilized man's, of the nature of these lower animals. A remarkable group of observances customary among rude tribes will bring this distinction sharply into view. Savages talk quite seriously to beasts alive or dead as they would to men alive or dead, offer them homage, ask pardon when it is their painful duty to hunt and kill them. A North American Indian will reason with a horse as if rational. Some will spare the rattlesnake, fearing the vengeance of its spirit if slain; others will salute the creature reverently, bid it welcome as a friend from the land of spirits, sprinkle a pinch of tobacco on its head for an offering, catch it by the tail and dispatch it with extreme dexterity, and carry off its skin as a trophy. If an Indian is attacked and torn by a bear, it is that the beast fell upon him intentionally in anger, perhaps to revenge the hurt done to another bear. When a bear is killed, they will beg pardon of him, or even make him condone the offense by smoking the peace-pipe with his murderers, who put the pipe in his mouth and blow down it, begging his spirit not to take revenge. So in Africa, the Kafirs will hunt the elephant, begging him not to tread on them and kill them, and when he is dead they will assure him that they did not kill him on purpose, and they will bury his trunk, for the elephant is a mighty chief, and his trunk is his hand that he may hurt withal. The Congo people will even avenge such a murder by a pretended attack on the hunters who did the deed. Such customs are common among the lower Asiatic tribes. The Stiens of Kambodia ask pardon of the beast they have killed; the Ainos of Yesso kill the bear, offer obeisance and salutation to him, and cut up his carcase. The Koriaks, if they have slain a bear or wolf, will flay him, dress one of their people in the skin, and dance round him, chanting excuses that they did not do it, and especially laying the blame on a Russian. But if it is a fox, they take his skin, wrap his dead body in hay, and sneering tell him to go to his own people and say what famous hospitality he has had, and how they gave him a new coat instead of his old one. The Samoyeds excuse themselves to the slain bear, telling him that it was the Russian who did it, and that a Russian knife will cut him up. The Goldi will set up the slain bear, call him "my lord" and do ironical homage to him, or taking him alive will fatten him in a cage, call him "son" and "brother," and kill and eat him as a sacrifice at a solemn festival. In Borneo, the Dayaks, when they have caught an alligator with a baited hook and rope, address him with respect and soothing till they have his legs fast, and then mocking call him "rajah" and "grandfather." Thus when the savage gets over his fears, he still keeps up in ironical merriment the reverence which had its origin in trembling sincerity. Even now the Norse hunter will say with horror of a bear that will attack man, that he can be "no Christian bear."

The sense of an absolute psychical distinction between man and beast, so prevalent in the civilized world, is hardly to be found among the lower races. Men to whom the cries of beasts and birds seem like human language, and their actions guided as it were by human thought, logically enough allow the existence of souls to beasts, birds, and reptiles, as to men. The lower psychology cannot but recognize in beasts the very characteristic which it attributes to the human soul, namely, the phenomena of life and death, will and judgment, and the phantom seen in vision or in dream. As for believers, savage or civilized, in the great doctrine of metempsychosis, these not only consider that an animal may have a soul, but that this soul may have inhabited a human being, and thus the creature may be in fact their own ancestor or once familiar friend. A line of facts, arranged as waymarks along the course of civilization, will serve to indicate the history of opinion from savagery onward, as to the souls of animals during life and after death. North American Indians held every animal to have its spirit, and these spirits their future life; the soul of the Canadian dog went to serve his master in the other world; among the Sioux, the prerogative of having four souls was not confined to man, but belonged also to the bear, the most human of animals. The Greenlanders considered that a sick human soul might be replaced by the sorcerer with a fresh healthy soul of a hare, reindeer, or a young child. Maori taletellers have heard of the road by which the spirits of dogs descend to Reinga, the Hades of the departed; the Hovas of Madagascar know that the ghosts of beasts and men, dwelling in a great mountain in the south called Ambondromble, come out occasionally to walk among the tombs or execution-places of criminals. The Kamchadals held that every creature, even the smallest fry, would live again in the underworld. The Kukis of Assam think that the ghost of every animal a Kuki kills in the chase or for the feast will belong to him in the next life, even as the enemy he slays in the field will then become his slave. The Karens apply the doctrine of the spirit or personal life-phantom, which is apt to wander from the body and thus suffer injury, equally to men and to animals. The Zulus say the cattle they kill come to life again, and become the property of the dwellers in the world beneath. The Siamese butcher, when in defiance of the very principles of his Buddhism he slaughters an ox, before he kills the creature has at least the grace to beseech its spirit to seek a happier abode. In connection with such transmigration, Pythagorean and Platonic philosophy gives to the lower animals undying souls, while other classic opinion may recognize in beasts only an inferior order of soul, only the "anima" but not the human "animus" besides. Thus Juvenal:

Principio indulsit communis conditor illis
Tantum animas; nobis animum quoque. . .

Through the middle ages, controversy as to the psychology of brutes has lasted on into our own times, ranging between two extremes; on the one the theory of Descartes which reduced animals to mere machines, on the other what Mr. Alger defines as "the faith that animals have immaterial and deathless souls." Among modern speculations may be instanced that of Wesley, who thought that in the next life animals will be raised even above their bodily and mental state at the creation, "the horridness of their appearance will be exchanged for their primeval beauty," and it even may be that they will be made what men are now, creatures capable of religion. Adam Clarke's argument for the future life of animals rests on abstract justice: whereas they did not sin, but yet are involved in the sufferings of sinful man, and cannot have in the present state the happiness designed for them, it is reasonable that they must have it in another. Although, however, the primitive belief in the souls of animals still survives to some extent in serious philosophy, it is obvious that the tendency of educated opinion on the question whether brutes have soul, as distinguished from life and mind, has for ages been in a negative and skeptical direction.

Animals being thus considered in the primitive psychology to have souls like human beings, it follows as the simplest matter of course that tribes who kill wives and slaves, to dispatch their souls on errands of duty with their departed lords, may also kill animals in order that their spirits may do such service as is proper to them. The Pawnee warrior's horse is slain on his grave to be ready for him to mount again, and the Comanche's best horses are buried with his favorite weapons and his pipe, all alike to be used in the distant happy hunting-grounds. In South America not only do such rites occur, but they reach a practically disastrous extreme. Patagonian tribes, says D'Orbigny, believe in another life, where they are to enjoy perfect happiness, therefore they bury with the deceased his arms and ornaments, and even kill on his tomb all the animals which belonged to him, that he may find them in the abode of bliss; and this opposes an insurmountable barrier to all civilization, by preventing them from accumulating property and fixing their habitations. Not only do Pope's now hackneyed lines express a real motive with which the Indian's dog is buried with him, but in the North American

continent the spirit of the dog has another remarkable office to perform. Certain Eskimos, as Cranz relates, would lay a dog's head in a child's grave, that the soul of the dog, who ever finds his home, may guide the helpless infant to the land of souls. In accordance with this, Captain Scoresby in Jameson's Land found a dog's skull in a small grave, probably a child's. Again, in the distant region of the Aztecs, one of the principal ceremonies was to slaughter a techichi, or native dog; it was burnt or buried with the corpse, with a cotton thread fastened to its neck, and its office was to convey the deceased across the deep waters of Chiuhnahuapan, on the way to the Land of the Dead. The dead Buraet's favorite horse, led saddled to the grave, killed, and flung in, may serve for a Tartar example. In Tonquin, even wild animals have been customarily drowned at funeral ceremonies of princes, to be at the service of the departed in the next world. Among Semitic tribes, an instance of the custom may be found in the Arab sacrifice of a camel on the grave, for the dead man's spirit to ride upon. Among the nations of the Aryan race in Europe, the prevalence of such rites is deep, wide, and full of purpose. Thus warriors were provided in death with horses and housings, with hounds and falcons. Customs thus described in chronicle and legend are vouched for in our own time by the opening of old barbaric burial places. How clear a relic of savage meaning lies here may be judged from a Livonian account as late as the fourteenth century, which relates how men and women, slaves, sheep, and oxen, with other things, were burnt with the dead, who, it was believed, would reach some region of the living, and find there, with the multitude of cattle and slaves, a country of life and happiness. As usual, these rites may be traced onward in survival. The Mongols, who formerly slaughtered camels and horses at their owner's burial, have been induced to replace the actual sacrifice by a gift of the cattle to the Lamas. The Hindus offer a black cow to the Brahmans, in order to secure their passage across the Vaitarani, the river of death, and will often die grasping the cow's tail as if to swim across in herdsman's fashion, holding on to the cow. It is mentioned as a belief in Northern Europe that he who has given a cow to the poor will find a cow to take him over the bridge of the dead, and a custom of leading a cow in the funeral procession is said to have been kept up to modern times. All these rites probably belong together as connected with ancient funeral sacrifice, and the survival of the custom of sacrificing the warrior's horse at his tomb is yet more striking. Saint-Foix long ago put the French evidence very forcibly. Mentioning the horse led at the funeral of Charles VI, with the four valets-de-pied in black, and bareheaded, holding the corners of its caparison, he recalls the horses and servants killed and buried with pre-Christian kings.

Plants, partaking with animals the phenomena of life and death, health and sickness, not unnaturally have some kind of soul ascribed to them. In fact, the notion of a vegetable soul, common to plants and to the higher organisms possessing an animal soul in addition, was familiar to medieval philosophy, and is not yet forgotten by naturalists. But in the lower ranges of culture, at least within one wide district of the world, the souls of plants are much more fully identified with the souls of animals. The Society Islanders seem to have attributed "varua," i.e., surviving soul or spirit, not to men only but to animals and plants. The Dayaks of Borneo not only consider men and animals to have a spirit of living principle, whose departure from the body causes sickness and eventually death, but they also give to the rice its "samangat padi," or "spirit of the paddy," and they hold feasts to retain this soul securely, lest the crops should decay. The Karens say that plants as well as men and animals have their "la" ("kelah"), and the spirit of sickly rice is here also called back like the human spirit considered to have left the body. There is reason to think that the doctrine of the spirits of plants lay deep in the intellectual history of South-East Asia, but was in great measure superseded under Buddhist influence. The Buddhist books show that in the early days of their religion it was a matter of controversy whether trees had souls, and therefore whether they might lawfully be injured. Orthodox Buddhism decided against the tree-souls, and consequently against the scruple to harm them, declaring trees to have no mind nor sentient principle, though admitting that certain dewas or spirits do reside in the body of trees, and speak from within them. Buddhists also relate that a heterodox sect kept up the early doctrine of the actual animate life of trees, in connection with which may be remembered Marco Polo's somewhat doubtful statement as to certain austere Indians objecting to green herbs for such a reason, and some other passages from later writers. Generally speaking, the subject of the spirits of plants is an obscure one, whether from the lower races not having definite opinions, or from our not finding it easy to trace them. The evidence from funeral sacrifices, so valuable as to most departments of early psychology, fails us here, from plants not being thought suitable to send for the service of the dead. Yet, as we shall see more fully elsewhere, there are two topics which bear closely on the matter. On the one hand, the doctrine of transmigration widely and clearly recognizes the idea of trees or smaller plants being animated by human souls; on the other the belief in tree-spirits and the practice of tree-worship involve notions more or less closely coinciding with that of tree-souls, as when the classic hamadryad dies with her tree, or when the Talein of South-East Asia, considering every tree to have a demon or spirit, offers prayers before he cuts one down.

Thus far the details of the lower animistic philosophy are not very unfamiliar to modern students. The primitive view of the souls of men and beasts as asserted or acted on in the lower and middle levels of culture, so far belongs to current civilized thought, that those who hold the doctrine to be false, and the practices based upon it futile, can nevertheless understand and sympathize with the lower nations to whom they are matters of the most sober and serious conviction. Nor is even the notion of a separable spirit or soul as the cause of life in plants too incongruous with ordinary ideas to be readily appreciable. But the theory of souls in the lower culture stretches beyond this limit, to take in a conception much stranger to modern thought. Certain high savage races distinctly hold, and a large proportion of other savage and barbarian races make a more or less close approach to, a theory of separable and surviving souls or spirits belonging to stocks and stones, weapons, boats, food, clothes, ornaments, and other objects which to us are not merely soulless but lifeless.

Yet, strange as such a notion may seem to us at first sight, if we place ourselves by an effort in the intellectual position of an uncultured tribe, and examine the theory of object souls from their point of view, we shall hardly pronounce it irrational. In discussing the origin of myth, some account has been already given of the primitive stage of thought in which personality and life are ascribed not to men and beasts only, but to things. It has been shown how what we call inanimate objects—rivers, stones, trees, weapons, and so forth—are treated as living intelligent beings, talked to, propitiated, punished for the harm they do. Hume, whose *Natural History of Religion* is perhaps more than any other work the source of modern opinions as to the development of religion, comments on the influence of this personifying stage of thought. "There is a universal tendency among mankind to conceive all beings like themselves, and to transfer to every object those qualities with which they are familiarly acquainted, and of which they are intimately conscious. . . . The *unknown causes*, which continually employ their thought, appearing always in the same aspect, are all apprehended to be of the same kind or species. Nor is it long before we ascribe to them thought and reason, and passion, and sometimes even the limbs and figures of men, in order to bring them nearer to a resemblance with ourselves." Auguste Comte has ventured to bring such a state of thought under terms of strict definition in his conception of the primary mental condition of mankind—a state of "pure fetishism, constantly characterized by the free and direct exercise of our primitive tendency to conceive all external bodies soever, natural or artificial, as animated by a life essentially analogous to our own, with mere differences of intensity." Our comprehension of the lower stages of mental culture depends much on the thoroughness with which we can appreciate this primitive, childlike conception, and in this our best guide may be the memory of our own childish days. He who recollects when there was still personality to him in posts and sticks, chairs and toys, may well understand how the infant philosophy of mankind could extend the notion of vitality to what modern science only recognizes as lifeless things; thus one main part of the lower animistic doctrine as to souls of objects is accounted for. The doctrine requires for its full conception of a soul not only life, but also a phantom or apparitional spirit; this development, however, follows without difficulty, for the evidence of dreams and visions applies to the spirits of objects in much the same manner as to human ghosts. Everyone who has seen visions while lightheaded in fever, everyone who has ever

dreamt a dream, has seen the phantoms of objects as well as of persons. How then can we charge the savage with farfetched absurdity for taking into his philosophy and religion an opinion which rests on the very evidence of his senses? The notion is implicitly recognized in his accounts of ghosts, which do not come naked, but clothed, and even armed; of course there must be spirits of garments and weapons, seeing that the spirits of men come bearing them. It will indeed place savage philosophy in no unfavorable light, if we compare this extreme animistic development of it with the popular opinion still surviving in civilized countries, as to ghosts and the nature of the human soul as connected with them. When the ghost of Hamlet's father appeared armed cap-a-pie,

Such was the very armour he had on,
When he the ambitious Norway combated.

And thus it is a habitual feature of the ghost stories of the civilized, as of the savage world, that the ghost comes dressed, and even dressed in well-known clothing worn in life. Hearing as well as sight testifies to the phantoms of objects: the clanking of ghostly chains and the rustling of ghostly dresses are described in the literature of apparitions. Now by the savage theory, according to which the ghost and his clothes are alike imaginary and subjective, the facts of apparitions are rationally met. But the modern vulgar who ignore or repudiate the notion of ghosts of things, while retaining the notion of ghosts of persons, have fallen into a hybrid state of opinion which has neither the logic of the savage nor of the civilized philosopher.

It remains to sum up in a few words the doctrine of souls, in the various phases it has assumed from first to last among mankind. In the attempt to trace its main course through the successive grades of man's intellectual history, the evidence seems to accord best with a theory of its development, somewhat to the following effect. At the lowest levels of culture of which we have clear knowledge, the notion of a ghost-soul animating man while in the body, is found deeply ingrained. There is no reason to think that this belief was learnt by savage tribes from contact with higher races, nor that it is a relic of higher culture from which the savage tribes have degenerated: for what is here treated as the primitive animistic doctrine is thoroughly at home among savages, who appear to hold it on the very evidence of their senses, interpreted on the biological principle which seems to them most reasonable. We may now and then hear the savage doctrines and practices concerning souls claimed as relic of a high religious culture pervading the primeval race of man. They are said to be traces of remote ancestral religion, kept up in scanty and perverted memory by tribes degraded from a nobler state. It is easy to see that such an explanation of some few facts, sundered from their connection with the general array, may seem plausible to certain minds. But a large view of the subject can hardly leave such argument in possession. The animism of savages stands for and by itself; it explains its own origin. The animism of civilized men, while more appropriate to advanced knowledge, is in great measure only explicable as a developed product of the older and ruder system. It is the doctrines and rites of the lower races which are, according to their philosophy, results of point-blank natural evidence and acts of straightforward practical purpose. It is the doctrines and rites of the higher races which show survival of the old in the midst of the new, modification of the old to bring it into conformity with the new, abandonment of the old because it is no longer compatible with the new. Let us see at a glance in what general relation the doctrine of souls among savage tribes stands to the doctrine of souls among barbaric and cultured nations. Among races within the limits of savagery, the general doctrine of souls is found worked out with remarkable breadth and consistency. The souls of animals are recognized by a natural extension from the theory of human souls; the souls of trees and plants follow in some vague partial way; and the souls of inanimate objects expand the general category to its extremest boundary. Thenceforth, as we explore human thought onward from savage into barbarian and civilized life, we find a state of theory more conformed to positive science, but in itself less complete and consistent. Far on into civilization, men still act as though in some half-meant way they believed in souls or ghosts of objects, while nevertheless their knowledge of physical science is beyond so crude a philosophy. As to the doctrine of souls of plants, fragmentary evidence of the history of its breaking down in Asia has reached us. In our own day and country, the notion of souls of beasts is to be seen dying out. Animism, indeed, seems to be drawing in its outposts, and concentrating itself on its first and main position, the doctrine of the human soul. This doctrine has undergone extreme modification in the course of culture. It has outlived the almost total loss of one great argument attached to it—the objective reality of apparitional souls or ghosts seen in dreams and visions. The soul has given up its ethereal substance, and become an immaterial entity, "the shadow of a shade." Its theory is becoming separated from the investigations of biology and mental science, which now discuss the phenomena of life and thought, the sense and the intellect, the emotions and the will, on a groundwork of pure experience. There has arisen an intellectual product whose very existence is of the deepest significance, a "psychology" which has no longer anything to do with "soul." The soul's place in modern thought is in the metaphysics of religion, and its especial office there is that of furnishing an intellectual side to the religious doctrine of the future life. Such are the alterations which have differenced the fundamental animistic belief in its course through successive periods of the world's culture. Yet it is evidence that, notwithstanding all this profound change, the conception of the human soul is, as to its most essential nature, continuous from the philosophy of the savage thinker to that of the modern professor of theology. Its definition has remained from the first that of an animating, separable, surviving entity, the vehicle of individual personal existence. The theory of the soul is one principal part of a system of religious philosophy, which unites, in an unbroken line of mental connection, the savage fetish-worshiper and the civilized Christian. The divisions which have separated the great religions of the world into intolerant and hostile sects are for the most part superficial in comparison with the deepest of all religious schisms, that which divides Animism from Materialism.

Alfred L. Kroeber

TOTEM AND TABOO:
AN ETHNOLOGIC PSYCHOANALYSIS

In lieu of an abridgment of Freud's *Totem and Taboo* a critique has been offered instead, because while Freud's theory of the origin of sacrifice is well known and his book is available in reprinted forms, not too much is known of the anthropological reservations which have been made regarding it. Kroeber was admirably qualified to comment on the work, not only because of his regnant position in historical anthropology but also because of his experience as a practicing psychoanalyst from 1920 to 1923.

Freud's theory may be sharply different from that of others, but it was not derived out of thin air or psychoanalysis alone. He drew upon ideas from Bachofen, Atkinson, and Robertson Smith, to mention but a few. His "evidences" came from myth, totemic practices, and psychoanalysis, none of them documentary sources of the kind that historians or even anthropologists use to reconstruct the past. As a work of history, which it purports to be, Freud's reconstruction of the primal horde and the events which led to the slaying of the father and the instituting of commemorative sacrificial rites is the work of a fertile imagination. Prehistory is usually a reconstruction of a very tentative sort and all we can do is judge its plausibility. In this case the plausibility is low indeed.

Totem and Taboo, then, really falls back on whatever support it can derive from psychoanalytic theory. It is based on the assumption that the Oedipus complex is innate and universal. It is normal for the child to wish to have a sexual relationship with the mother and unwittingly will the death of its rival, the father, and this is often achieved vicariously through fantasy. In the primal horde, sexual gratification with their mothers was never consummated after the father had been slain by his sons; in fact, the sons set up specific taboos against sexual relations with their mothers, thus denying themselves the rewards of victory over the old man. The ritual slaughtering of an animal was instituted in order to commemorate the original parricide, says Freud, and in support of his view he points out that in the child's unconscious he frequently identifies his father with some animal. After the primal father had been killed, his sons felt some remorse for their action because they had felt some degree of admiration for his strength and protection. This ambivalent attitude is seen in the sacrificial ritual, which expresses not only the death-wish but *rapprochement* as well. The symbolism of the totem feast, then, is that it not only reenacts the original act of parricide, but establishes communion and reconciliation with the father through the father-substitute. Freud went so far as to say that all culture originated from the first sacrificial ritual.

Neo-Freudians discount the hereditary implications of the events in the primal horde. They feel that the Oedipus complex arises anew each time out of a familial configuration. Some even doubt that it is universal. The British psychoanalyst Money-Kyrle (*The Meaning of Sacrifice*, 1930) has modified Freud's position and attempted to make it more palatable by denying the implications of a racial mind and the inheritance of acquired memory; instead, he says, sacrifice should be viewed as the symbolic expression of an unconscious desire for parricide that each individual has acquired for himself. Malinowski, the ethnologist (*Sex and Repression in Savage Society*, 1927), long ago showed that the complex was modifiable in terms of social structure. More recently Lessa ("Oedipus-Type Tales in Oceania," 1956) has indicated that Oedipus stories not only reflect such modifications, but apparently are not universal, being present only in a contiguous band extending eastward from Europe to the south-west Pacific. As Kroeber and many others have insisted, Freud was brilliant in his insights into psychological motivation, but his attempt to explain sacrifice as the result of an historic incident does not bear up under scrutiny. In all fairness, it should be pointed out that at least some have interpreted the "historical" description in *Totem and Taboo* as a brilliant image not to be taken literally as an historical event.

Reprinted from *American Anthropologist*, XXII (1920), 48–55, by permission of the author and the American Anthropological Association.

The recent translation into English of Freud's interpretation of a number of ethnic phenomena[1] offers an occasion to review the startling series of essays which first appeared in *Imago* a number of years ago. There is the more reason for this because, little as this particular work of Freud has been noticed by anthropologists, the vogue of the psycho-analytic movement founded by him is now so strong that the book is certain to make an impression in many intelligent circles.

Freud's principal thesis emerges formally only toward the end of his book, but evidently has controlled his reasoning from the beginning, although perhaps unconsciously. This thesis is (p. 258) "that the beginnings of religion, ethics, society, and art meet in the Oedipus complex." He commences with the inference of Darwin, developed farther by Atkinson, that at a very early period man lived in small communities consisting of an adult male and a number of females and immature individuals, the males among the latter being driven off by the head of the group as they became old enough to evoke his jealousy. To this Freud adds the Robertson Smith theory that sacrifice at the altar is the essential element in every ancient cult, and that such sacrifice goes back to a killing and eating by the clan of its totem animal, which was regarded as of kin with the clan and its god, and whose killing at ordinary times was therefore strictly forbidden. The Oedipus complex directed upon these two hypotheses welds them into a mechanism with which it is possible to explain most of the essentials of human civilization, as follows. The expelled sons of the primal horde finally banded together and slew their father, ate him, and appropriated the females. In this they satisfied the same hate impulse that is a normal infantile trait and the basis of most neuroses, but which often leads to unconscious "displacement" of feelings, especially upon animals. At this point, however, the ambivalence of emotions proved decisive. The tender feelings which had always persisted by the side of the brothers' hate for their father, gained the upper hand as soon as this hate was satisfied, and took the form of remorse and sense of guilt. "What the father's presence had formerly prevented they themselves now prohibited in

the psychic situation of 'subsequent obedience' which we know so well from psychoanalysis. They undid their deed by declaring that the killing of the father substitute, the totem, was not allowed, and renounced the fruits of their deed by denying themselves the liberated women. Thus they created the two fundamental taboos of totemism" (p. 236). These are "the oldest and most important taboos" of mankind: "namely not to kill the totem animal and to avoid sexual intercourse with totem companions of the other sex." (p. 53), alongside which many if not all other taboos are "secondary, displaced and distorted." The renunciation of the women or incest prohibition had also this practical foundation: that any attempt to divide the spoils, when each member of the band really wished to emulate the father and possess all the women, would have disrupted the organization which had made the brothers strong (p. 237). The totem sacrifice and feast reflected the killing and eating of the father, assuaged "the burning sense of guilt," and brought about "a kind of reconciliation" or agreement by which the father-totem granted all wishes of his sons in return for their pledge to honor his life (p. 238). "All later religions prove to be . . . reactions aiming at the same great event with which culture began and which ever since has not let mankind come to rest" (p. 239).

This mere extrication and presentation of the framework of the Freudian hypothesis on the origin of socio-religious civilization is probably sufficient to prevent its acceptance; but a formal examination is only just.

First, the Darwin–Atkinson supposition is of course only hypothetical. It is a mere guess that the earliest organization of man resembled that of the gorilla rather than that of trooping monkeys.

Second, Robertson Smith's allegation that blood sacrifice is central in ancient cult holds chiefly or only for the Mediterranoid cultures of a certain period—say the last two thousand years B.C.—and cultures then or subsequently influenced by them. It does not apply to regions outside the sphere of affection by these cultures.

Third, it is at best problematical whether blood sacrifice goes back to a totemic observance. It is not established that totemism is an original possession of Semitic culture.

Fourth, coming to the Freudian theory proper, it is only conjecture that the sons would kill, let alone devour, the father.

[1] Sigmund Freud, *Totem and Taboo: Resemblances Between the Psychic Life of Savages and Neurotics.* Authorized English Translation, with Introduction, by A. A. Brill (New York: Moffat Yard & Co., 1918).

Fifth, the fact that a child sometimes displaces its father-hatred upon an animal—we are not told in what percentage of cases—is no proof that the sons did so.

Sixth, if they "displaced," would they retain enough of the original hate impulse to slay the father; and if so, would the slaying not resolve and evaporate the displacements? Psychoanalysts may affirm both questions; others will require more examination before they accept the affirmation.

Seventh, granting the sons' remorse and resolve no longer to kill the father-displacement-totem, it seems exceedingly dubious whether this resolve could be powerful and enduring enough to suppress permanently the gratification of the sexual impulses which was now possible. Again there may be psychoanalytic evidence sufficient to allay the doubt; but it will take a deal of evidence to convince "unanalytic" psychologists, ethnologists, and laymen.

Eighth, if the band of brothers allowed strangers—perhaps expelled by their jealous fathers—to have access to the women whom they had renounced, and matrilinear or matriarchal institutions thus came into existence, what would be left for the brothers (unless they were able to be content with lifelong celibacy or homosexuality), other than individual attachments to other clans; which would mean the disintegration of the very solidarity that they are pictured as so anxious to preserve, even by denying their physiological instincts?

Ninth, it is far from established that exogamy and totem abstinence are the two fundamental prohibitions of totemism. Freud refers (p. 180) to Goldenweiser's study of the subject, which is certainly both analytical and conducted from a psychological point of view even though not psychoanalytical; but he fails to either accept or refute this author's carefully substantiated finding that these two features cannot be designated as primary in the totemic complex.

Tenth, that these two totemic taboos are the oldest of all taboos is pure assertion. If all other taboos are derived from them by displacement or distortion, some presentation of the nature and operation and sequence of these displacements is in order. An astronomer who casually said that he believed Sirius to be the center of the stellar universe and then proceeded to weave this opinion into the fabric of a still broader hypothesis, would get little hearing from other astronomers.

A final criticism—that the persistence into modern society and religion of this first "great event with which culture began" is an unexplained process—will not be pressed here, because Freud has anticipated it with a *tu quoque* (pp. 259–261): social psychologists assume a "continuity in the psychic life of succeeding generations" without in general concerning themselves much with the manner in which this continuity is established.

No doubt still other challenges of fact or interpretation will occur to every careful reader of the book. The above enumeration has been compiled only far enough to prove the essential method of the work; which is to evade the painful process of arriving at a large certainty by the positive determination of smaller certainties and their unwavering addition irrespective of whether each augments or diminishes the sum total of conclusion arrived at. For this method the author substitutes a plan for multiplying into one another, as it were, fractional certainties—that is, more or less remote possibilities—without recognition that the multiplicity of factors must successively decrease the probability of their product. It is the old expedient of pyramiding hypotheses; which if theories had to be paid for like stocks or gaming cards, would be less frequently indulged in. Lest this criticism be construed as unnecessarily harsh upon a gallant and stimulating adventurer into ethnology, let it be added that it applies with equal stricture upon the majority of ethnologists from whom Freud has drawn an account of the renown or interest of their books: Reinach, Wundt, Spencer and Gillen, Lang, Robertson Smith, Durkheim and his school, Keane, Spencer, Avebury; and his special vade mecum Frazer.

There is another criticism that can be leveled against the plan of Freud's book: that of insidiousness, though evidently only as the result of the gradual growth of his thesis during its writing. The first chapter or essay, on the Savage's Dread of Incest, merely makes a case for the applicability of psychoanalysis to certain special social phenomena such as the mother-in-law taboo. In the second, the psychoanalytic doctrine of the ambivalence of emotions is very neatly and it seems justly brought to bear on the dual nature of taboo as at once holy and defiling. Concurrently a foundation is laid, though not revealed, for the push to the ultimate thesis. The third chapter on Animism, Magic, and the Omnipotence of Thought refrains from directly advancing the argument, but strengthens its future hold on the reader by emphasizing the parallelism between the thought systems of savages and neurotics. The last chapter is not, in the main, a discussion of the Infantile Recurrence of Totemism, as it is designated, but an analysis of current ethnological theories as to the origin of totemism in society and the presentation of the theory of the author. This hypothesis, toward which everything has been tending, does not however begin to be divulged until page 233; after which, except for tentative claims to a wide extensibility of the principle arrived at and some distinctly fair admissions of weakness, the book promptly closes without any re-examination or testing of its proposition. The explanation of taboo on pages 52–58 is an essential part of the theory developed on pages 233 *seq.*, without any indication being given that it is so. Then, when the parallelism of savage and neurotic thought has been driven home by material largely irrelevant to the final and quite specific thesis, this is suddenly sprung. Freud cannot be charged with more than a propagandist's zeal and perhaps haste of composition; but the consequence is that this book is keen without orderliness, intricately rather than closely reasoned, and endowed with an unsubstantiated convincingness. The critical reader will ascertain these qualities; but the book will fall into the hands of many who are lacking either in care or independence of judgment and who, under the influence of a great name and in the presence of a bewilderingly fertile imagination, will be carried into an illusory belief. Again there is palliation—but nothing more—in the fact that the literature of theoretical anthropology consists largely of bad precedent.

But, with all the essential failure of its finally avowed purpose, the book is an important and valuable contribution. However much cultural anthropology may come to lean more on the historical instead of the psychological method, it can never ultimately free itself, nor should it wish to, from the psychology that underlies it. To this psychology the psychoanalytic movement initiated by Freud has made an indubitably significant contribution, which every ethnologist must sooner or later take into consideration. For instance, the correspondences between taboo customs and "compulsion neuroses" as developed on pages 43–48 are unquestionable, as are also the parallelism between the two aspects of taboo and the ambivalence of emotions under an accepted prohibition (p. 112). Again the strange combination of mourning for the dead with the fear of them and taboos against them is certainly illumined if not explained by this theory of ambivalence (pp. 87–107).

It is even possible to extend Freud's point of view. Where the taboo on the name of the dead is in force we find not only the fear that utterance will recall the soul to the hurt of the living, but also actual shock at the utterance as a slight or manifestation of hostility to the dead. It is a fair question whether this shock may not be construed as a reaction from the unconscious hate carried toward the dead during their life, as if speaking of them were an admission of satisfaction at their going. The shock is certainly greatest where affection was deepest; persons who were indifferent were mentioned without emotional reluctance if circumstances permit, whereas enemies, that is individuals toward whom hate was avowed instead of repressed, may have the utterance of their names gloated over.

Of very broad interest is the problem raised by Freud's conjecture that the psychic impulses of primitive people possessed more ambivalence than our own except in the case of neurotics: that their mental life, like that of neurotics, is more sexualized and contains fewer social components than ours (pp. 111, 121, 148). Neurosis would therefore usually represent an atavistic constitution. Whatever its complete significance, there exists no doubt a remarkable similarity between the phenomena of magic, taboo, animism, and primitive religion in general, and neurotic manifestations. In both a creation that has only psychic validity is given greater or less preference over reality. As Freud says, the two are of course not the same, and the ultimate difference lies in the fact that neuroses are asocial creations due to a flight from dissatisfying reality (p. 123). This is certainly not to be denied on any ethnological grounds; yet the implication that savages are essentially more neurotic than civilized men may well be challenged, although it cannot be dismissed offhand.

The experience of firsthand observers will probably be unanimous that primitive communities, like peasant populations, contain very few individuals that can be put into a class with the numerous neurotics of our civilization. The reason seems to be that primitive societies have institutionalized such impulses as with us lead to neuroses. The individual of neurotic tendency finds an approved and therefore harmless outlet in taboo, magic, myth, and the like, whereas the non-neurotic, who at heart remains attached to reality, accepts these activities as forms which do not seriously disturb him. In accord with this interpretation is the fact that neurotics appear to become numerous and characteristic in populations among whom religion has become decadent and "enlightenment" active, as in the Hellenistic, Roman Imperial, and recent eras; whereas in the Middle Ages, when "superstition" and taboo were firmly established, there were social aberrations indeed, like the flagellants and children's crusade, but few neurotics. Much the same with homosexuality, which the North American and Siberian natives have socialized. Its acceptance as an institution may be a departure from normality, but has certainly saved countless individuals from the heavy strain which definite homosexualists undergo in our civilization. It would be unfitting to go into these matters further here: they are mentioned as an illustration of the importance of the problems which Freud raises. However precipitate his entry into anthropology and however flimsy some of his syntheses, he brings to bear keen insight, a fecund imagination, and above all a point of view which henceforth can never be ignored without stultification.

While the book thus is one that no ethnologist can afford to neglect, one remark may be extended to psychologists of the unconscious who propose to follow in Freud's footsteps: there really is a great deal of ethnology not at all represented by the authors whom Freud discusses. To students of this side of the science the line of work initiated by Tylor and developed and most notably represented among the living by Frazer, is not so much ethnology as an attempt to psychologize with ethnological data. The cause of Freud's leaning so heavily on Frazer is clear. The latter knows nothing of psychoanalysis and with all acumen his efforts are prevailingly a dilettantish playing; but in the last analysis they are psychology, and as history only a pleasing fabrication. If psychoanalysts wish to establish serious contacts with historical ethnology, they must first learn to know that such an ethnology exists. It is easy enough to say, as Freud does on page 179, that the nature of totemism and exogamy could be most readily grasped if we could get into closer touch with their origins, but that as we cannot we must depend on hypotheses. Such a remark rings a bit naïve to students who have long since made up their minds that ethnology, like every other branch of science, is work and not a game in which lucky guesses score; and who therefore hold that since we know nothing directly about the origin of totemism or other social phenomena but have information on these phenomena as they exist at present, our business is first to understand as thoroughly as possible the nature of these existing phenomena; in the hope that such understanding may gradually lead to a partial reconstruction of origins—without undue guessing.

Alfred L. Kroeber

TOTEM AND TABOO
IN RETROSPECT

Almost two decades after writing the foregoing critique, Kroeber, in an issue of the *American Journal of Sociology* that was devoted to Freud in appreciation rather than in criticism of his contributions, again criticizes Freud's historical fantasies. He was writing at a time when anthropology was reaching the apex of psychoanalytic interest. In 1948 (*Anthropology*) he maintained perhaps an even stronger position, saying "the psychoanalytic explanation of culture is intuitive,

Reprinted from the *American Journal of Sociology*, XLV (1939), 446–451, by permission of the author and The University of Chicago Press. Copyright 1939 by The University of Chicago.

dogmatic, and wholly unhistorical." In even more recent years he reiterated his disillusionment with the possibility of using psychoanalysis for historical reconstruction and was especially caustic concerning Freud's failure to advance beyond outmoded materials and approaches: "Freud preferred to forage in Frazer rather than to read the intellectually sophisticated works of his own age-mate Boas" (*The Nature of Culture*, 1952).

Nearly twenty years ago I wrote an analysis of *Totem and Taboo*—that brain child of Freud which was to be the precursor of a long series of psychoanalytic books and articles explaining this or that aspect of culture, or the whole of it.[1] It seems an appropriate time to return to the subject.

I see no reason to waver over my critical analysis of Freud's book. There is no indication that the consensus of anthropologists during these twenty years has moved even an inch nearer acceptance of Freud's central thesis. But I found myself somewhat conscience-stricken when, perhaps a decade later, I listened to a student in Sapir's seminar in Chicago making his report on *Totem and Taboo*, who, like myself, first spread out its gossamer texture and then laboriously tore it to shreds. It is a procedure too suggestive of breaking a butterfly on the wheel. An iridescent fantasy deserves a more delicate touch even in the act of demonstration of its unreality.

Freud himself has said of my review that it characterized his book as a *Just So* story. It is a felicitous phrase, coming from himself. Many a tale by Kipling or Andersen contains a profound psychological truth. One does not need therefore to cite and try it in the stern court of evidential confrontation.

However, the fault is not wholly mine. Freud does speak of the "great event with which culture began." And therewith he enters history. Events are historical and beginnings are historical, and human culture is appreciable historically. It is difficult to say how far he realized his vacillation between historic truth and abstract truth expressed through intuitive imagination. A historic finding calls for some specification of place and time and order; instead of which, he offers a finding of unique cardinality, such as history feels it cannot deal with.

Freud is reported subsequently to have said that his "event" is to be construed as "typical." Herewith we begin to approach a basis of possible agreement. A typical event, historically speaking, is a recurrent one.

[1] "Totem and Taboo: An Ethnologic Psychoanalysis," *American Anthropologist*, XXII (1920), 48–55.

This can hardly be admitted for the father-slaying, eating, and guilt sense. At any rate, there is no profit in discussing the recurrence of an event which we do not even know to have occurred once. But there is no need sticking fast on the word "event" because Freud used it. His argument is evidently ambiguous as between historical thinking and psychological thinking. If we omit the fatal concept of event, of an act as it happens in history, we have left over the concept of the psychologically potential. Psychological insight may legitimately hope to attain to the realization and definition of such a potentiality; and to this, Freud should have confined himself. We may accordingly properly disregard any seeming claim, or half-claim, to historic authenticity of the suggested actual happening, as being beside the real point, and consider whether Freud's theory contains any possibility of being a generic, timeless explanation of the psychology that underlies certain recurrent historic phenomena or institutions like totemism and taboo.

Here we obviously are on better ground. It becomes better yet if we disregard certain gratuitous and really irrelevant assumptions, such as that the self-imposed taboo following the father-slaying is the original of all taboos, these deriving from it as secondary displacements or distortions. Stripped down in this way, Freud's thesis would reduce to the proposition that certain psychic processes tend always to be operative and to find expression in wide-spread human institutions. Among these processes would be the incest drive and incest repression, filial ambivalence, and the like; in short, if one likes, the kernel of the Oedipus situation. After all, if ten modern anthropologists were asked to designate one universal human institution, nine would be likely to name the incest prohibition; some have expressly named it as the only universal one. Anything so constant as this, at least as regards its nucleus, in the notoriously fluctuating universe of culture, can hardly be the result of a "mere" historical accident devoid of psychological significance. If there is accordingly an underlying factor which keeps reproducing the phenomenon in an unstable world, this factor must be something in the human constitution—in other words, a psychic factor. Therewith the door is open not for an acceptance *in toto* of Freud's explanation but at any rate for its serious consideration as a scientific hypothesis. Moreover, it is an explanation certainly marked by deeper insight and supportable by more parallel evidence from personal psychology than the older views, such as that familiarity breeds sexual indifference, or recourse to a supposed "instinct" which is merely a verbal restatement of the observed behavior.

Totemism, which is a much rarer phenomenon than incest taboo, might then well be the joint product of the incest-drive-and-repression process and of some other less compelling factor. Nonsexual taboo, on the other hand, which rears itself in so many protean forms over the whole field of culture, might be due to a set of still different but analogous psychic factors. Anthropologists and sociologists have certainly long been groping for something underlying which would help them explain both the repetitions and the variations in culture, provided the explanation were evidential, extensible by further analysis, and neither too simplistic nor too one-sided. Put in some such form as this, Freud's hypothesis might long before this have proved fertile in the realm of cultural understanding instead of being mainly rejected or ignored as a brilliant fantasy.

What has stood in the way of such a fruitful restatement or transposition? There seem to be at least three factors: one due to Freud himself, another jointly to himself and his followers, the third mainly to the Freudians.

The first of these is Freud's already mentioned ambiguity which leads him to state a timeless psychological explanation as if it were also a historical one. This tendency is evident elsewhere in his thinking. It appears to be the counterpart of an extraordinarily explorative imagination, constantly impelled to penetrate into new intellectual terrain. One consequence is a curious analogy to what he himself has discovered in regard to the manifest and the latent in dreams. The manifest is there, but it is ambiguous; a deeper meaning lies below; from the point of view of this latent lower content, the manifest is accidental and inconsequential. Much like this, it seems to me, is the historical dress which Freud gives his psychological

insight. He does not repudiate it; he does not stand by it as integral. It is really irrelevant; but his insight having manifested itself in the dress, he cannot divest himself of this "manifest" form. His view is over-determined like a dream.

A second factor is the curious indifference which Freud has always shown as to whether his conclusions do or do not integrate with the totality of science. This led him at one time to accept the inheritance of acquired traits as if it did not clash with standard scientific attitude. Here again we have the complete explorer who forgets in his quest, or represses, knowledge of what he started from or left behind. In Freud himself one is inclined not to quarrel too hard with this tendency; without it, he might have opened fewer and shorter vistas. Of his disciples, however, who have so largely merely followed, more liaison might be expected. I recall Rank, while still a Freudian, after expounding his views to a critically sympathetic audience, being pressed to reconcile certain of them to the findings of science at large and, after an hour, conceding that psychoanalysts held that there might be more than one truth, each on its own level and independent of the other. And he made the admission without appearing to realize its import.

A third element in the situation is the all-or-none attitude of most avowed psychoanalysts. They insist on operating within a closed system. At any rate, if not wholly closed, it grows only from within; it is not open to influence from without. A classical example is Ernest Jones's resistance to Malinowski's finding that among the matrilineal Melanesians the effects directed toward the father in our civilization are largely displaced upon the mother's brother, the relation of father and children being rather one of simple and relatively univalent affection. Therewith Malinowski had really vindicated the mechanism of the Oedipus relation. He showed that the mechanism remained operative even in a changed family situation; a minor modification of it, in its direction, conforming to the change in given condition. Jones, however, could not see this, and resisted tooth and nail. Because Freud in the culture of Vienna had determined that ambivalence was directed toward the father, ambivalence had to remain directed to him universally, even where primary authority resided in an uncle.

The same tendency appears in Roheim, whose "Psycho-analysis of Primitive Cultural Types" contains a mass of psychological observations most valuable to cultural anthropologists, but so organized as to be unusable by them. None have used it, so far as I know. This is not due to lack of interest on the part of anthropologists in psychological behavior within cultures, for in recent years a whole series of them have begun avowedly to deal with such behavior. Nor is it due to any deficiency of quality in Roheim's data: these are rich, vivid, novel, and valuable. But the data are so presented as to possess organization only from the point of view of orthodox psychoanalytic theory. With reference to the culture in which they occur, or to the consecutive life histories of personalities, they are inchoate. The closing sentence of the monograph—following immediately on some illuminative material—is typical: "We see then, that the sexual practices of a people are indeed prototypical and that from their posture in coitus their whole psychic attitude may be inferred." Can a conclusion be imagined which would appear more arbitrarily dogmatic than this to any psychologist, psychiatrist, anthropologist, or sociologist?

The fundamental concepts which Freud formulated—repression, regression and infantile persistences, dream symbolism and overdetermination, guilt sense, the effects toward members of the family—have gradually seeped into general science and become an integral and important part of it. If one assumes that our science forms some kind of larger unit because its basic orientation and method are uniform, these concepts constitute the permanent contribution of Freud and psychoanalysis to general science; and the contribution is large. Beyond, there is a further set of concepts which in the main have not found their way into science: the censor, the superego, the castration complex, the explanation of specific cultural phenomena. To these concepts the several relevant branches of science—sociology, anthropology, psychology, and medicine alike—remain impervious about as consistently as when the concepts were first developed. It may therefore be inferred that science is likely to remain negative to them. To the

psychoanalysts, on the contrary, the two classes of concepts remain on the same level, of much the same value, and inseparably interwoven into one system. In this quality of nondifferentiation between what the scientific world accepts as reality and rejects as fantasy, between what is essential and what is incidental, the orthodox psychoanalytic movement reveals itself as partaking of the nature of a religion—a system of mysticism; even, it might be said, it shows certain of the qualities of a delusional system. It has appropriated to itself such of the data of science—the cumulative representative of reality—as were digestible to it and has ignored the larger remainder. It has sought little integration with the totality of science, and only on its own terms. By contrast, science, while also of course a system, has shown itself a relatively open one: it has accepted and already largely absorbed a considerable part of the concepts of psychoanalysis. It is indicative of the largeness of Freud's mind that, although the sole founder of the movement and the originator of most of its ideas, his very ambiguities in the more doubtful areas carry a stamp of tolerance. He may persist in certain interpretations; he does not insist on them; they remain more or less fruitful suggestions. Of this class is his theory of the primary determination of culture. As a construct, neither science nor history can use it; but it would seem that they can both accept and utilize some of the process concepts that are involved in the construct.

I trust that this reformulation may be construed not only as an *amende honorable* but as a tribute to one of the great minds of our day.

Note.—Since the above was written and submitted, Freud has published *Der Mann Moses und die monotheistische Religion.* The thesis of *Totem and Taboo* is reaffirmed: "Ich halte an diesen Aufbau noch heute fest" (p. 231). One concession in the direction of my argument is made: the father-killing was not a unique event but "hat sich in Wirklichkeit über Jahrtausende erstreckt" (p. 146). Of his stimulator, Robertson Smith, Freud says superbly: "Mit seinen Gegnern traf ich nie zusammen" (p. 232). We, on our part, if I may speak for ethnologists, though remaining unconverted, have met Freud, recognize the encounter as memorable, and herewith resalute him.

Émile Durkheim

THE ELEMENTARY FORMS OF THE RELIGIOUS LIFE

Few books on the science of religion stand out as powerfully as Émile Durkheim's *The Elementary Forms of the Religious Life*, published originally in 1912 in France under the title *Les Formes élémentaires de la vie religieuse: Le Système totémique en Australie*. The author had already foreshadowed his views on religion in his *Le Suicide* (1897) and an article in the *Année Sociologique* (1899), and had even published some of the first portions of his forthcoming book. What Durkheim had to say has had a deep impact on subsequent theoreticians, particularly Radcliffe-Brown, Evans-Pritchard, and Warner. Durkheim's realization that religion plays a vital part in social life was impressed upon him by the writings of Robertson Smith and those British anthropologists who had been concerned with the subject of religion. While Durkheim was in Paris in 1885 for the purpose of rounding out his training, Lucien Herr, the librarian of the École Normale, guided him toward Frazer's articles on totemism, and from then on he made it his concern to study primitive religion so that he could understand the role of religion in general.

Durkheim became convinced that in order to understand this role one must examine religion in its simplest and original form, totemism; therefore he used materials from Australia to make his analysis. Totemism, he maintained, embodies all the essential aspects of religion: the division of things into sacred and profane; the notion of the soul, spirits, mythical personalities, and divinity; a negative cult with ascetic practices; rites of oblation and communion; imitative rites; commemorative rites; and expiatory rites. The sacred attitude necessary for religion is to be seen in the totem, which derives its sacredness from the fact that it is essentially the symbol of society. The totem represents the clan, which to the aborigine is virtually society itself. Primitive man, especially as a consequence of the social environment that results when he meets in large ceremonial gatherings, realizes, however unconsciously, that as a member of society he can survive but that as a lone individual he cannot. He comes to view society as something sacred because he is utterly dependent on it as a source of strength and culture. But it is easier for him to visualize and direct his feeling of awe and respect toward a symbol than toward so complex a thing as a clan. The totem becomes the object of the sacred attitude. It is virtually God. Society, in effect, deifies itself. Durkheim equates Society with God. Not only are the members of society sacred, but so are all things which stand for society: the totemic plants and animals and the images of such totems. They become the object of a cult because they possess mana. As Lowie (*Primitive Religion*, 1948) has so aptly put it, "In this interpretation of totemism there is something like an anticipation of the Freudian interpretation of dreams. Things are not what they seem on the surface but have a hidden meaning."

His preoccupation with origins was merely incidental to Durkheim's main goal, which was to study the role of religion. In effect, Durkheim saw religion as a vast symbolic system which made social life possible by expressing and maintaining the sentiments or values of the society. He especially analyzed the role of ceremonial and ritualistic institutions, and concluded that they are disciplinary, integrating, vitalizing, and euphoric forces. His method was what only in later years came to be labeled "functional." It stemmed from such predecessors as Fustel de Coulanges (who was one of his professors at the École Normale and whose *La Cité antique* [1864] linked religion with political organization and other institutions in a complex of interdependent relations) and Robertson Smith.

Reprinted in abridged form from Emile Durkheim, *The Elementary Forms of the Religious Life*, trans. Joseph Ward Swain (London: George Allen & Unwin, Ltd., 1915), by permission of the publishers.

Religious phenomena are naturally arranged into two fundamental categories: beliefs and rites. The first are states of opinion, and consist in representations; the second are determined modes of action. Between these two classes of facts there is all the difference which separates thought from action.

The rites can be defined and distinguished from other human practices, moral practices, for example, only by the special nature of their object. A moral rule prescribes certain manners of acting to us, just as a rite does, but which are addressed to a different class of objects. So it is the object of the rite which must be characterized, if we are to characterize the rite itself. Now it is in the beliefs that the special nature of this object is expressed. It is possible to define the rite only after we have defined the belief.

All known religious beliefs, whether simple or complex, present one common characteristic: they presuppose a classification of all the things, real and ideal, of which men think, into two classes or opposed groups, generally designated by two distinct terms which are translated well enough by the words *profane* and *sacred* (*profane, sacré*). This division of the world into two domains, the one containing all that is sacred, the other all that is profane, is the distinctive trait of religious thought; the beliefs, myths, dogmas, and legends are either representations or systems of representations which express the nature of sacred things, the virtues and powers which are attributed to them, or their relations with each other and with profane things. But by sacred things one must not understand simply those personal beings which are called gods or spirits; a rock, a tree, a spring, a pebble, a piece of wood, a house, in a word, anything can be sacred. A rite can have this character; in fact, the rite does not exist which does not have it to a certain degree. There are words, expressions, and formulae which can be pronounced only by the mouths of consecrated persons; there are gestures and movements which everybody cannot perform. If the Vedic sacrifice has had such an efficacy that, according to mythology, it was the creator of the gods, and not merely a means of winning their favor, it is because it possessed a virtue comparable to that of the most sacred beings. The circle of sacred objects cannot be determined, then, once for all. Its extent varies infinitely, according to the different religions. That is how Buddhism

is a religion: in default of gods, it admits the existence of sacred things, namely, the four noble truths and the practices derived from them.

. . .

. . . The real characteristic of religious phenomena is that they always suppose a bipartite division of the whole universe, known and knowable, into two classes which embrace all that exists, but which radically exclude each other. Sacred things are those which the interdictions protect and isolate; profane things, those to which these interdictions are applied and which must remain at a distance from the first. Religious beliefs are the representations which express the nature of sacred things and the relations which they sustain, either with each other or with profane things. Finally, rites are the rules of conduct which prescribe how a man should comport himself in the presence of these sacred objects.

. . .

The really religious beliefs are always common to a determined group, which makes profession of adhering to them and of practicing the rites connected with them. They are not merely received individually by all the members of this group; they are something belonging to the group, and they make its unity. The individuals which compose it feel themselves united to each other by the simple fact that they have a common faith A society whose members are united by the fact that they think in the same way in regard to the sacred world and its relations with the profane world, and by the fact that they translate these common ideas into common practices, is what is called a "Church." In all history, we do not find a single religion without a Church. Sometimes the Church is strictly national, sometimes it passes the frontiers; sometimes it embraces an entire people (Rome, Athens, the Hebrews), sometimes it embraces only a part of them (the Christian societies since the advent of Protestantism); sometimes it is directed by a corps of priests, sometimes it is almost completely devoid of any official directing body. But wherever we observe the religious life, we find that it has a definite group as its foundation. Even the so-called "private" cults, such as the domestic cult or the cult of a corporation, satisfy this condition; for they are always celebrated by a group, the family, or the corporation. Moreover, even these particular religions are ordinarily only special forms of a more general religion which embraces all; these restricted Churches are in reality only chapels of a vaster Church which, by reason of this very extent, merits this name still more.

It is quite another matter with magic. To be sure, the belief in magic is always more or less general; it is very frequently diffused in large masses of the population, and there are even peoples where it has as many adherents as the real religion. But it does not result in binding together those who adhere to it, nor in uniting them into a group leading a common life. *There is no Church of magic.* Between the magician and the individuals who consult him, as between these individuals themselves, there are no lasting bonds which make them members of the same moral community, comparable to that formed by the believers in the same god or the observers of the same cult. The magician has a clientele and not a Church, and it is very possible that his clients have no other relations between each other, or even do not know each other; even the relations which they have with him are generally accidental and transient; they are just like those of a sick man with his physician. The official and public character with which he is sometimes invested changes nothing in this situation; the fact that he works openly does not unite him more regularly or more durably to those who have recourse to his services.

Thus we arrive at the following definition: *A religion is a unified system of beliefs and practices relative to sacred things, that is to say, things set apart and forbidden—beliefs and practices which unite into one single moral community called a Church, all those who adhere to them.* The second element which thus finds a place in our definition is no less essential than the first; for by showing that the idea of religion is inseparable from that of the Church, it makes it clear that religion should be an eminently collective thing.

. . .

LEADING CONCEPTIONS OF THE ELEMENTARY RELIGION

Even the crudest religions with which history and ethnology make us acquainted are already of a complexity which corresponds badly with the idea sometimes held of primitive mentality. One finds there not only a confused system of beliefs and rites, but also such a plurality of different principles, and such a richness of essential notions, that it seems impossible to see in them anything but the late product of a rather long evolution. Hence it has been concluded that to discover the truly original form of religious life, it is necessary to descend by analysis beyond these observable religions, to resolve them into their common and fundamental elements, and then to seek among these latter some one from which the others were derived.

To the problem thus stated, two contrary solutions have been given.

There is no religious system, ancient or recent, where one does not meet, under different forms, two religions, as it were, side by side, which, though being united closely and mutually penetrating each other, do not cease, nevertheless, to be distinct. The one addresses itself to the phenomena of nature, either the great cosmic forces, such as winds, rivers, stars, or the sky, etc., or else the objects of various sorts which cover the surface of the earth, such as plants, animals, rocks, etc.; for this reason it has been given the name of *naturism*. The other has spiritual beings as its object, spirits, souls, geniuses, demons, divinities properly so-called, animated and conscious agents like man, but distinguished from him, nevertheless, by the nature of their powers and especially by the peculiar characteristic that they do not affect the senses in the same way: ordinarily they are not visible to human eyes. This religion of spirits is called *animism*. Now, to explain the universal coexistence of these two sorts of cults, two contradictory theories have been proposed. For some, animism is the primitive religion, of which naturism is only a secondary and derived form. For the others, on the contrary, it is the nature cult which was the point of departure for religious evolution; the cult of spirits is only a peculiar case of that.

These two theories are, up to the present, the only ones by which the attempt has been made to explain rationally the origins of religious thought.

. . .

Finally, the animistic theory implies a consequence which is perhaps its best refutation.

If it were true, it would be necessary to admit that religious beliefs are so many hallucinatory representations, without any objective foundation whatsoever. It is supposed that they are all derived from the idea of the soul because one sees only a magnified soul in the spirits and gods. But according to Tylor and his disciples, the idea of the soul is itself constructed entirely out of the vague and inconsistent images which occupy our attention during sleep: for the soul is the double, and the double is merely a man as he appears to himself while he sleeps. From this point of view, then, sacred beings are only the imaginary conceptions which men have produced during a sort of delirium which regularly overtakes them every day, though it is quite impossible to see what useful ends these conceptions serve, nor what they answer to in reality. If a man prays, if he makes sacrifices and offerings, if he submits to the multiple privations which the ritual prescribes, it is because a sort of constitutional eccentricity has made him take his dreams for perceptions, death for a prolonged sleep, and dead bodies for living and thinking beings. Thus not only is it true, as many have held, that the forms under which religious powers have been represented to the mind do not express them exactly, and that the symbols with the aid of which they have been thought of partially hide their real nature, but more than that, behind these images and figures there exists nothing but the nightmares of private minds. In fine, religion is nothing but a dream, systematized and lived, but without any foundation in reality. Thence it comes about that the theorists of animism, when looking for the origins of religious thought, content themselves with a small outlay of energy When they think that they have explained how men have been induced to imagine beings of a strange, vaporous form, such as those they see in their dreams, they think the problem is resolved.

In reality, it is not even approached. It is inadmissible that systems of ideas like religions, which have held so considerable a place in history, and from which, in all times, men have come to receive the energy which they must have to live, should be made up of a tissue of illusions. Today we are beginning to realize that law, morals, and even scientific thought itself were born of religion, were for a long time confounded with it, and have remained penetrated with its spirit. How could a vain fantasy have been able to fashion the human consciousness so strongly and so durably? Surely it ought to be a principle of the science of religions that religion expresses nothing which does not exist in nature; for there are sciences only of natural phenomena.

. . .

The spirit of the naturistic school is quite different.

. . .

They talk about the marvel which men should feel as they discover the world. But really, that which characterizes the life of nature is a regularity which approaches monotony. Every morning the sun mounts in the horizon, every evening it sets; every month the moon goes through the same cycle; the river flows in an uninterrupted manner in its bed; the same seasons periodically bring back the same sensations. To be sure, here and there an unexpected event sometimes happens: the sun is eclipsed, the moon is hidden behind clouds, the river overflows. But these momentary variations could only give birth to equally momentary impressions, the remembrance of which is gone after a little while; they could not serve as a basis for these stable and permanent systems of ideas and practices which constitute religions. Normally, the course of nature is uniform, and uniformity could never produce strong emotions. Representing the savage as filled with admiration before these marvels transports much more recent sentiments to the beginnings of history. He is much too accustomed to it to be greatly surprised by it. It requires culture and reflection to shake off this yoke of habit and to discover how marvellous this regularity itself is. Besides, as we have already remarked, admiring an object is not enough to make it appear sacred to us, that is to say, to mark it with those characteristics which make all direct contact with it appear a sacrilege and a profanation. We misunderstand what the religious sentiment really is, if we confound it with every impression of admiration and surprise.

But, they say, even if it is not admiration, there is a certain impression which men cannot help feeling in the presence of nature. He cannot come in contact with it, without realizing that it is greater than he. It overwhelms him by its immensity. This sensation of an infinite space which surrounds him, of an infinite time which has preceded and will follow the present moment, and of forces infinitely superior to those of which he is master, cannot fail, as it seems, to awaken within him the idea that outside of him there exists an infinite power upon which he depends. And this idea enters as an essential element into our conception of the divine.

But let us bear in mind what the question is. We are trying to find out how men came to think that there are in reality two categories of things, radically heterogeneous and incomparable to each other. Now how could the spectacle of nature give rise to the idea of this duality? Nature is always and everywhere of the same sort. It matters little that it extends to infinity: beyond the extreme limit to which my eyes can reach, it is not different from what it is here. The space which I imagine beyond the horizon is still space, identical with that which I see. The time which flows without end is made up of moments identical with those which I have passed through. Extension, like duration, repeats itself indefinitely; if the portions which I touch have of themselves no sacred character, where did the others get theirs? The fact that I do not see them directly, is not enough to transform them. A world of profane things may well be unlimited; but it remains a profane world. Do they say that the physical forces with which we come in contact exceed our own? Sacred forces are not to be distinguished from profane ones simply by their great intensity, they are different; they have special qualities which the others do not have. Quite on the contrary, all the forces manifested in the universe are of the same nature, those that are within us just as those that are outside of us. And especially, there is no reason which could have allowed giving a sort of pre-eminent dignity to some in relation to others. Then if religion really was born because of the need of assigning causes to physical phenomena, the forces thus imagined would have been no more sacred than those conceived by the scientist today to account for the same facts. This is as much as to say that there would have been no sacred beings and therefore no religion.

. . .

TOTEMISM AS AN ELEMENTARY RELIGION
Since neither man nor nature have of themselves a sacred character, they must get it from another source. Aside from the human individual and the physical world, there should be some other reality, in relation to which this variety of delirium which all religion is in a sense, has a significance and an objective value. In other words, beyond those which we have called animistic and naturistic, there should be another sort of cult, more fundamental and more primitive, of which the first are only derived forms or particular aspects.

In fact, this cult does exist: it is the one to which ethnologists have given the name of *totemism*.

With one reservation which will be indicated below, we propose to limit our research to Australian societies. They are perfectly homogeneous, for though it is possible to distinguish varieties among them, they all belong to one common type. This homogeneity is even so great that the forms of social organization are not only the same, but that they are even designated by identical or equivalent names in multitude of tribes, sometimes very distant from each other. Also, Australian totemism is the variety for which our documents are the most complete. Finally, that which we propose to study in this work is the most primitive and simple religion which it is possible to find. It is therefore natural that to discover it, we address ourselves to societies as slightly evolved as possible, for it is evidently there that we have the greatest chance of finding it and studying it well. Now there are no societies which present this characteristic to a higher degree than the Australian ones. Not only is their civilization most rudimentary—the house and even the hut are still unknown—but also their organization is the most primitive and simple which is actually known; it is that which we have elsewhere called *organization on basis of clans*.

. . .

Among the beliefs upon which totemism rests, the most important are naturally those concerning the totem; it is with these that we must begin.

At the basis of nearly all the Australian tribes we find a group which holds a preponderating place in the collective life: this is the clan. Two essential traits characterize it.

In the first place, the individuals who compose it consider themselves united by a bond of kinship, but one which is of a very special nature. This relationship does not come from the fact that they have definite blood connections with one another; they are relatives from the mere fact that they have the same name. They are not fathers and mothers, sons or daughters, uncles or nephews of one another in the sense which we now give these words; yet they think of themselves as forming a single family, which is large or small according to the dimensions of the clan, merely because they are collectively designated by the same word. When we say that they regard themselves as a single family, we do so because they recognize duties toward each other which are identical with those which have always been incumbent upon kindred: such duties as aid, vengeance, mourning, the obligations not to marry among themselves, etc.

. . .

The species of things which serves to designate the clan collectively is called its *totem*. The totem of the clan is also that of each of its members.

Each clan has its totem, which belongs to it alone; two different clans of the same tribe cannot have the same. In fact, one is a member of a clan merely because he has a certain name. All who bear this name are members of it for that very reason; in whatever manner they may be spread over the tribal territory, they all have the same relations of kinship with one another. Consequently, two groups having the same totem can only be two sections of the same clan. Undoubtedly, it frequently happens that all of a clan does not reside in the same locality, but has representatives in several different places. However, this lack of a geographical basis does not cause its unity to be the less keenly felt.

. . .

In a very large proportion of the cases, the objects which serve as totems belong either to the animal or the vegetable kingdom, but especially to the former. Inanimate things are much more rarely employed. Out of more than 500 totemic names collected by Howitt among the tribes of southeastern Australia, there are scarcely forty which are not the names of plants or animals; these are the clouds, rain, hail, frost, the moon, the sun, the wind, the autumn, the summer, the winter, certain stars, thunder, fire, smoke, water, or the sea. It is noticeable how small a place is given to celestial bodies and, more generally, to the great cosmic phenomena, which were destined to so great a fortune in later religious development.

. . .

But the totem is not merely a name; it is an emblem, a veritable coat-of-arms whose analogies with the arms of heraldry have often been remarked. In speaking of the Australians, Grey says, "each family adopt an animal or vegetable as their crest and sign," and what Grey calls a family is incontestably a clan. Also Fison and Howitt say, "the Australian divisions show that the totem is, in the first place, the badge of a group."

. . .

These totemic decorations enable us to see that the totem is not merely a name and an emblem. It is in the course of the religious ceremonies that they are employed; they are a part of the liturgy; so while the totem is a collective label, it also has a religious character. In fact, it is in connection with it, that things are classified as sacred or profane. It is the very type of sacred thing.

The tribes of Central Australia, especially the Arunta, the Loritja, the Kaitish, the Unmatjera, and the Ilpirra, make constant use of certain instruments in their rites which are called the *churinga* by the Arunta according to Spencer and Gillen, or the *tjurunga*, according to Strehlow. They are pieces of wood or bits of polished stone, of a great variety of forms, but generally oval or oblong. Each totemic group has a more or less important collection of these. *Upon each of these is engraved a design representing the totem of this same group.* A certain number of the churinga have a hole at one end, through which goes a thread made of human hair or that of an opossum. Those which are made of wood and are pierced in this way serve for exactly the same purposes as those instruments of the cult to which English ethnographers have given the name of "bull-roarers." By means of the thread by which they are suspended, they are whirled rapidly in the air in such a way as to produce a sort of humming identical with that made by the toys of this name still used by our children; this deafening noise has a ritual significance and accompanies all ceremonies of any importance. These sorts of churinga are real bull-roarers. But there are others which are not made of wood and are not pierced; consequently they cannot be employed in this way. Nevertheless, they inspire the same religious sentiments.

In fact, every churinga, for whatever purpose it may be employed, is counted among the eminently sacred things; there are none which surpass it in religious dignity. This is indicated even by the word which is used to designate them. It is not only a substantive but also an adjective meaning sacred. Also, among the several names which each Arunta has, there is one so sacred that it must not be revealed to a stranger; it is pronounced but rarely, and then in a low voice and a sort of mysterious murmur.

. . .

Now in themselves, the churinga are objects of wood and stone like all others; they are distinguished from profane things of the same sort by only one particularity; this is that the totemic mark is drawn or engraved upon them. So it is this mark and this alone which gives them their sacred character.

. . .

But totemic images are not the only sacred things. There are real things which are also the object of rites, because of the relations which they have with the totem: before all others, are the beings of the totemic species and the members of the clan.

. . .

Every member of the clan is invested with a sacred character which is not materially inferior to that which we just observed in the animal. This personal sacredness is due to the fact that the man believes that while he is a man in the usual sense of the word, he is also an animal or plant of the totemic species.

In fact, he bears its name; this identity of name is therefore supposed to imply an identity of nature The first is not merely considered as an outward sign of the second; it supposes it logically. This is because the name, for a primitive, is not merely a word or a combination of sounds; it is a part of the being, and even something essential to it. A member of the Kangaroo clan calls himself a kangaroo; he is therefore, in one sense, an animal of this species.

. .

We have seen that totemism places the figured representations of the totem in the first rank of the things it considers sacred; next come the animals or vegetables whose name the clan bears, and finally the members of the clan. Since all these things are sacred in the same way, though to different degrees, their religious character can be due to none of the special attributes distinguishing them from each other. If a certain species of animal or vegetable is the object of a reverential fear, this is not because of its special properties, for the human members of the clan enjoy the same privilege, though to a slightly inferior degree, while the mere image of this same plant or animal inspires an even more pronounced respect. The similar sentiments inspired by these different sorts of things in the mind of the believer, which give them their sacred character, can evidently come only from some common principle partaken of alike by the totemic emblems, the men of the clan and the individuals of the species serving as totem. In reality, it is to this common principle that the cult is addressed. In other words, totemism is the religion, not of such and such animals or men or images, but of an anonymous and impersonal force, found in each of these beings but not to be confounded with any of them. No one possesses it entirely and all participate in it. It is so completely independent of the particular subjects in whom it incarnates itself, that it precedes them and survives them. Individuals die, generations pass and are replaced by others; but this force always remains actual, living, and the same. It animates the generations of today as it animated those of yesterday and as it will animate those of tomorrow.

. . .

Thus the totem is before all a symbol, a material expression of something else. But of what?

From the analysis to which we have been giving our attention, it is evident that it expresses and symbolizes two different sorts of things. In the first place, it is the outward and visible form of what we have called the totemic principle or god. But it is also the symbol of the determined society called the clan. It is its flag; it is the sign by which each clan distinguishes itself from the others, the visible mark of its personality, a mark borne by everything which is a part of the clan under any title whatsoever, men, beasts, or things. So if it is at once the symbol of the god and of the society, is that not because the god and the society are only one? How could the emblem of the group have been able to become the figure of this quasi-divinity, if the group and the divinity were two distinct realities? The god of the clan, the totemic principle, can therefore be nothing else than the clan itself, personified and represented to the imagination under the visible form of the animal or vegetable which serves as totem.

But how has this apotheosis been possible, and how did it happen to take place in this fashion?

In a general way, it is unquestionable that a society has all that is necessary to arouse the sensation of the divine in minds, merely by the power that it has over them; for to its members it is what a god is to his worshipers. In fact, a god is, first of all, a being whom men think of as superior to themselves, and upon whom they feel that they depend. Whether it be a conscious personality, such as Zeus or Jahveh, or merely abstract forces such as those in play in totemism, the worshiper, in the one case as in the other, believes himself held to certain manners of acting which are imposed upon him by the nature of the sacred principle with which he feels that he is in communion. Now society also gives us the sensation of a perpetual dependence. Since it has a nature which is peculiar to itself and different from our individual nature, it pursues ends which are likewise special to it; but, as it cannot attain them except through our intermediacy, it imperiously demands our aid. It requires that, forgetful of our own interests, we make ourselves its servitors, and it submits us to every sort of inconvenience, privation, and sacrifice, without which social life would be impossible. It is because of this that at every instant we are obliged to submit ourselves to rules of conduct and of thought which we have neither made nor desired, and which are sometimes even contrary to our most fundamental inclinations and instincts.

Since religious force is nothing other than the collective and anonymous force of the clan, and since this can be represented in the mind only in the form of the totem, the totemic emblem is like the visible body of the god. Therefore, it is from it that those kindly or dreadful actions seem to emanate, which the cult seeks to provoke and prevent; consequently, it is to it that the cult is addressed.

This is the explanation of why it holds the first place in the series of sacred things.

But the clan, like every other sort of society, can live only in and through the individual consciousnesses that compose it. So if religious force, in so far as it is conceived as incorporated in the totemic emblem, appears to be outside of the individuals and to be endowed with a sort of trancendence over them, it, like the clan of which it is the symbol, can be realized only in and through them; in this sense, it is immanent in them and they necessarily represent it as such. They feel it present and active within them, for it is this which raises them to a superior life. This is why men have believed that they contain within them a principle comparable to the one residing in the totem, and consequently, why they have attributed a sacred character to themselves, but one less marked than that of the emblem. It is because the emblem is the pre-eminent source of the religious life; the man participates in it only indirectly, as he is well aware; he takes into account the fact that the force that transports him into the world of sacred things is not inherent in him, but comes to him from the outside.

But for still another reason, the animals or vegetables of the totemic species should have the same character, and even to a higher degree. If the totemic principal is nothing else than the clan, it is the clan thought of under the material form of the totemic emblem; now this form is also that of the concrete beings whose name the clan bears. Owing to this resemblance, they could not fail to evoke sentiments analogous to those aroused by the emblem itself. Since the latter is the object of a religious respect, they too should inspire respect of the same sort and appear to be sacred. Having external forms so nearly identical, it would be impossible for the native not to attribute to them forces of the same nature. It is therefore forbidden to kill or eat the totemic animal, since its flesh is believed to have the positive virtues resulting from the rites; it is because it resembles the emblem of the clan, that is to say, it is in its own image. And since the animal naturally resembles the emblem more than the man does, it is placed on a superior rank in the hierarchy of sacred things. Between these two beings there is undoubtedly a close relationship, for they both partake of the same essence: both incarnate something of the totemic principle. However, since the principle itself is conceived under an animal form, the animal seems to incarnate it more fully than the man. Therefore, if men consider it and treat it as a brother, it is at least as an elder brother.

But even if the totemic principle has its preferred seat in a determined species of animal or vegetable, it cannot remain localized there. A sacred character is to a high degree contagious; it therefore spreads out from the totemic being to everything that is closely or remotely connected with it. The religious sentiments inspired by the animal are communicated to the substances upon which it is nourished and which serve to make or remake its flesh and blood, to the things that resemble it, and to the different beings with which it has constant relations. Thus, little by little, subtotems are attached to the totems and from the cosmological systems expressed by the primitive classifications. At last, the whole world is divided up among the totemic principles of each tribe.

We are now able to explain the origin of the ambiguity of religious forces as they appear in history, and how they are physical as well as human, moral as well as material. They are moral powers because they are made up entirely of the impressions this moral being, the group, arouses in those other moral beings, its individual members; they do not translate the manner in which physical things affect our senses, but the way in which the collective consciousness acts upon individual consciousnesses. Their authority is only one form of the moral ascendancy of society over its members. But, on the other hand, since they are conceived of under material forms, they could not fail to be regarded as closely related to material things. Therefore they dominate the two worlds. Their residence is in men, but at the same time they are the vital principles of things. They animate minds and discipline them, but it is also they who make plants grow and animals reproduce. It is this double nature which has enabled religion to be like the womb from which come all the leading germs of human civilization. Since it has been made to embrace all of reality, the physical world as well as the moral one, the forces that move bodies as well as those that move minds have been conceived in a religious form. That is how the most diverse methods and practices, both those that make possible the continuation of the moral life (laws, morals, beaux-arts) and those serving the material life (the natural, technical, and practical sciences), are either directly or indirectly derived from religion.

Robert N. Bellah

RELIGIOUS EVOLUTION

In recent years little intellectual effort has been devoted to the construction of an evolutionary interpretation of religion. This sophisticated new article by Bellah, much of which emerged from a seminar given together with Talcott Parsons and S. N. Eisenstadt, is not only almost unique, but courageous as well. Cautiously assuming that contemporary preliterates and their religions represent earlier phases, and utilizing historical materials, Bellah proposes a sequence of five ideal typical stages of development: primitive, archaic, historic, early modern, and modern. He examines each of these states in terms of their religious symbol systems, religious actions, religious organizations, and social implications. Basically, he is interested in demonstrating that religious symbol systems have evolved from compact to complex ones; that religious collectivities have become increasingly differentiated from other social structures; and that consciousness of the self as a religious subject develops increasingly after its emergence in the historic stage. He is careful, however, to indicate that his stages are not inevitable,

Reprinted from *American Sociological Review*, XXIX (1964), 358–374, by permission of the American Sociological Association and the author.

that there is a wide variety of types within each stage, and that actual cases present important features which cannot be neatly characterized in terms of any one stage.

Anticipated here to some extent is the interpretation of symbolism contained in Chapter 3, especially in the article by Geertz. Thus, Bellah views religion as symbolizing one's identity as well as concerning itself with imaging the ultimate conditions of man's existence.

There are of course other ways of looking at the broad sweep of change in religion, as Bellah explicitly reminds us. More conventional efforts at describing religious trends in industrial societies have stressed the diminishing importance of belief in the supernatural in the face of scientific advances and the intensification of the moral aspects of religious systems. But in our judgment, Bellah moves well beyond this simple generalization and formulates some propositions about religious evolution that will provoke controversy but will also stimulate further thinking and research along productive lines.

Time in its aging course teaches all things.
—Aeschylus: *Prometheus Bound*

Though one can name precursors as far back as Herodotus, the systematically scientific study of religions begins only in the second half of the 19th century. According to Chantepie de la Saussaye, the two preconditions for this emergence were that religion had become by the time of Hegel the object of comprehensive philosophical speculation and that history by the time of Buckle had been enlarged to include the history of civilization and culture in general. In its early phases, partly under the influence of Darwinism, the science of religion was dominated by an evolutionary tendency already implicit in Hegelian philosophy and early 19th century historiography. The grandfathers of modern sociology, Comte and Spencer, contributed to the strongly evolutionary approach to the study of religion as, with many reservations, did Durkheim and Weber.

But by the third decade of the 20th century the evolutionary wave was in full retreat both in the general field of science of religion and in the sociology of religion in particular. Of course, this was only one aspect of the general retreat of evolutionary thought in social science, but nowhere did the retreat go further nor the intensity of the opposition to evolution go deeper than in the field of religion. An attempt to explain the vicissitudes of evolutionary conceptions in the field of religion would be an interesting study in the sociology of knowledge but beyond the scope of this brief paper. Here I can only say that I hope that the present attempt to apply the evolutionary idea to religion evidences a serious appreciation of both 19th century evolutionary theories and 20th century criticisms of them.

Evolution at any system level I define as a process of increasing differentiation and complexity of organization which endows the organism, social system or whatever the unit in question may be, with greater capacity to adapt to its environment so that it is in some sense more autonomous relative to its environment than were its less complex ancestors. I do not assume that evolution is inevitable, irreversible or must follow any single particular course. Nor do I assume that simpler forms cannot prosper and survive alongside more complex forms. What I mean by evolution, then, is nothing metaphysical but the simple empirical generalization that more complex forms develop from less complex forms and that the properties and possibilities of more complex forms differ from those of less complex forms.

A brief handy definition of religion is considerably more difficult than a definition of evolution. An attempt at an adequate definition would, as Clifford Geertz has recently demonstrated, take a paper in itself for adequate explanation. So, for limited purposes only, let me define religion as a set of symbolic forms and acts which relate man to the ultimate conditions of his existence. The purpose of this definition is to indicate exactly what I claim has evolved. It is not the ultimate conditions, nor, in traditional language, God that has evolved, nor is it man in the broadest sense of *homo religiosus*. I am inclined to agree with Eliade when he holds that primitive man is as fully religious as man at any stage of existence, though I am not ready to go along with him when he implies *more* fully.

Neither religious man nor the structure of man's ultimate religious situation evolves, then, but rather religion as symbol system.

Erich Voegelin, who I suspect shares Eliade's basic philosophical position, speaks of a development from compact to differentiated symbolization. Everything already exists in some sense in the religious symbol system of the most primitive man; it would be hard to find anything later that is not "foreshadowed" there, as, for example, the monotheistic God is foreshadowed in the high gods of some primitive peoples. Yet just as obviously the two cannot be equated. Not only in their idea of God but in many other ways the monotheistic religions of Judaism, Christianity and Islam involve a much more differentiated symbolization of, and produce a much more complex relation to, the ultimate conditions of human existence than do primitive religions. At least the existence of that kind of difference is the thesis I wish to develop. I hope it is clear that there are a number of other possible meanings of the term "religious evolution" with which I am not concerned. I hope it is also clear that a complex and differentiated religious symbolization is not therefore a better or a truer or a more beautiful one than a compact religious symbolization. I am not a relativist and I do think judgments of value can reasonably be made between religions, societies or personalities. But the axis of that judgment is not provided by social evolution and if progress is used in an essentially ethical sense, then I for one will not speak of religious progress.

Having defined the ground rules under which I am operating let me now step back from the subject of religious evolution and look first at a few of the massive facts of human religious history. The first of these facts is the emergence in the first millennium B.C. all across the Old World, at least in centers of high culture, of the phenomenon of religious rejection of the world characterized by an extremely negative evaluation of man and society and the exaltation of another realm of reality as alone true and infinitely valuable. This theme emerges in Greece through a long development into Plato's classic formulation in the Phaedo that the body is the tomb or prison of the soul and that only by disentanglement from the body and all things worldly can the soul unify itself with the unimaginably different world of the divine. A very different formulation is found in Israel, but there too the world is profoundly devalued in the face of the transcendent God with whom alone is there any refuge or comfort. In India we find perhaps the most radical of all versions of world rejection, culminating in the great image of the Buddha, that the world is a burning house and man's urgent need is a way to escape from it. In China, Taoist ascetics urged the transvaluation of all the accepted values and withdrawal from human society, which they condemned as unnatural and perverse.

Nor was this a brief or passing phenomenon. For over 2000 years great pulses of world rejection spread over the civilized world. The *Qur'an* compares this present world to vegetation after rain, whose growth rejoices the unbeliever, but it quickly withers away and becomes as straw. Men prefer life in the present world but the life to come is infinitely superior—it alone is everlasting. Even in Japan, usually so innocently world accepting, Shōtoku Taishi declared that the world is a lie and only the Buddha is true, and in the Kamakura period the conviction that the world is hell led to orgies of religious suicide by seekers after Amida's paradise. And it is hardly necessary to quote Revelations or Augustine for comparable Christian sentiments. I do not deny that there are profound differences among these various rejections of the world; Max Weber has written a great essay on the different directions of world rejection and their consequences for human action. But for the moment I want to concentrate on the fact that they were all in some sense rejections and that world rejection is characteristic of a long and important period of religious history. I want to insist on this fact because I want to contrast it with an equally striking fact—namely the virtual absence of world rejection in primitive religions, in religion prior to the first millennium B.C., and in the modern world.

Primitive religions are on the whole oriented to a single cosmos—they know nothing of a wholly different world relative to which the actual world is utterly devoid of value. They are concerned with the maintenance of personal, social and cosmic harmony and with attaining specific goods—rain, harvest, children, health—as men have always been. But the overriding goal of salvation that dominates the world rejecting religions is almost absent in primitive religion, and life after death tends to be a shadowy semi-existence in some vaguely designated place in the single world.

World rejection is no more characteristic of the modern world than it is of primitive religion. Not only in the United States but through much of Asia there is at the moment something of a religious revival, but nowhere is this associated with a great new outburst of world rejection. In Asia apologists, even for religions with a long tradition of world rejection, are much more interested in showing the compatibility of their religions with the developing modern world than in totally rejecting it. And it is hardly necessary to point out that the American religious revival stems from motives quite opposite to world rejection.

One could attempt to account for this sequence of presence and absence of world rejection as a dominant religious theme without ever raising the issue of religious evolution, but I think I can account for these and many other facts of the historical development of religion in terms of a scheme of religious evolution. An extended rationale for the scheme and its broad empirical application must await publication in book form. Here all I can attempt is a very condensed overview.

The scheme is based on several presuppositions, the most basic of which I have already referred to: namely, that religious symbolization of what Geertz calls "the general order of existence" tends to change over time, at least in some instances, in the direction of more differentiated, comprehensive, and in Weber's sense, more rationalized formulations. A second assumption is that conceptions of religious action, of the nature of the religious actor, of religious organization and of the place of religion in the society tend to change in ways systematically related to the changes in symbolization. A third assumption is that these several changes in the sphere of religion, which constitute what I mean by religious evolution, are related to a variety of other dimensions of change in other social spheres which define the general process of sociocultural evolution.

Now, for heuristic purposes at least, it is also useful to assume a series of stages which may be regarded as relatively stable crystallizations of roughly the same order of complexity along a number of different dimensions. I shall use five stages which, for want of better terminology, I shall call primitive, archaic, historic, early modern and modern. These stages are ideal types derived from a theoretical formulation of the most generally observable historical regularities; they are

meant to have a temporal reference but only in a very general sense.

Of course the scheme itself is not intended as an adequate description of historical reality. Particular lines of religious development cannot simply be forced into the terms of the scheme. In reality there may be compromise formations involving elements from two stages which I have for theoretical reasons discriminated; earlier stages may, as I have already suggested, strikingly foreshadow later developments; and more developed may regress to less developed stages. And of course no stage is ever completely abandoned; all earlier stages continue to coexist with and often within later ones. So what I shall present is not intended as a procrustean bed into which the facts of history are to be forced but a theoretical construction against which historical facts may be illuminated. The logic is much the same as that involved in conceptualizing stages of the life cycle in personality development.

PRIMITIVE RELIGION

Before turning to the specific features of primitive religion let us go back to the definition of religion as a set of symbolic forms and acts relating man to the ultimate conditions of his existence. Lienhardt, in his book on Dinka religion, spells out this process of symbolization in a most interesting way:

I have suggested that the Powers may be understood as images corresponding to complex and various combinations of Dinka experience which are contingent upon their particular social and physical environment. For the Dinka they are the grounds of those experiences; in our analysis we have shown them to be grounded in them, for to a European the experiences are more readily understood than the Powers, and the existence of the latter cannot be posited as a condition of the former. Without these Powers or images or an alternative to them there would be for the Dinka no differentiation between experience of the self and of the world which acts upon it. Suffering, for example, could be merely "lived" or endured. With the imaging of the grounds of suffering in a particular Power, the Dinka can grasp its nature intellectually in a way which satisfies them, and thus to some extent transcend and dominate it in this act of knowledge. With this knowledge, this separation of a subject and an object in experience, there arises for them also the possibility of creating a form of experience they desire, and of freeing themselves symbolically from what they must otherwise passively endure.

If we take this as a description of religious symbolization in general, and I think we can, then it is clear that in terms of the conception of evolution used here the existence of even the simplest religion is an evolutionary advance. Animals or pre-religious men could only "passively endure" suffering or other limitations imposed by the conditions of their existence, but religious man can to some extent "transcend and dominate" them through his capacity for symbolization and thus attain a degree of freedom relative to his environment that was not previously possible.

Now though Lienhardt points out that the Dinka religious images make possible a "differentiation between experience of the self and of the world which acts upon it" he also points out earlier that the Dinka lack anything closely resembling our conception of the " 'mind,' as mediating and, as it were, storing up the experiences of the self." In fact, aspects of what we would attribute to the self are "imaged" among the divine Powers. Again if Lienhardt is describing something rather general, and I think there is every reason to believe he is, then religious symbolization relating man to the ultimate conditions of his existence is also involved in relating him to himself and in symbolizing his own identity.

Granted then that religious symbolization is concerned with imaging the ultimate conditions of existence, whether external or internal, we should examine at each stage the kind of symbol system involved, the kind of religious action it stimulates, the kind of social organization in which this religious action occurs and the implications for social action in general that the religious action contains.

Marcel Mauss, criticizing the heterogeneous sources from which Lévy-Bruhl had constructed the notion of primitive thought, suggested that the word primitive be restricted to Australia, which was the only major culture area largely unaffected by the neolithic. That was in 1923. In 1935 Lévy-Bruhl, heeding Mauss's stricture, published a book called *La Mythologie Primitive* in which the data are drawn almost exclusively from Australia and immediately adjacent islands. While Lévy-Bruhl finds material similar to his Australian data in all parts of the world, nowhere else does he find it in as pure a form. The differences between the Australian material and that of other areas are so great

that Lévy-Bruhl is tempted to disagree with Durkheim that Australian religion is an elementary form of religion and term it rather "pre-religion," a temptation which for reasons already indicated I would firmly reject. At any rate, W. E. H. Stanner, by far the most brilliant interpreter of Australian religion in recent years, goes far to confirm the main lines of Lévy-Bruhl's position, without committing himself on the more broadly controversial aspects of the assertions of either Mauss or Lévy-Bruhl (indeed without so much as mentioning them). My description of a primitive stage of religion is a theoretical abstraction, but it is heavily indebted to the work of Lévy-Bruhl and Stanner for its main features.

The *religious symbol system* at the primitive level is characterized by Lévy-Bruhl as *"le monde mythique,"* and Stanner directly translates the Australians' own word for it as "the Dreaming." The Dreaming is a time out of time, or in Stanner's words, "everywhen," inhabited by ancestral figures, some human, some animal. Though they are often of heroic proportions and have capacities beyond those of ordinary men as well as being the progenitors and creators of many particular things in the world, they are not gods, for they do not control the world and are not worshipped.

Two main features of this mythical world of primitive religion are important for the purposes of the present theoretical scheme. The first is the very high degree to which the mythical world is related to the detailed features of the actual world. Not only is every clan and local group defined in terms of the ancestral progenitors and the mythical events of settlement, but virtually every mountain, rock and tree is explained in terms of the actions of mythical beings. All human action is prefigured in the Dreaming, including crimes and folly, so that actual existence and the paradigmatic myths are related in the most intimate possible way. The second main feature, not unrelated to the extreme particularity of the mythical material, is the fluidity of its organization. Lienhardt, though describing a religion of a somewhat different type, catches the essentially free-associational nature of primitive myth when he says, "We meet here the typical lack of precise definition of the Dinka when they speak of divinities. As Garang, which is the name of the first man, is sometimes associated with the first man and sometimes said to be quite different, so Deng may in some sense be associated with anyone called Deng, and the Dinka connect or do not connect usages of the same name in different contexts according to their individual lights and to what they consider appropriate at any given moment." The fluid structure of the myth is almost consciously indicated by the Australians in their use of the word Dreaming: this is not purely metaphorical, for as Ronald Berndt has shown in a careful study, men do actually have a propensity to dream during the periods of cult performance. Through the dreams they reshape the cult symbolism for private psychic ends and what is even more interesting, dreams may actually lead to a reinterpretation in myth which in turn causes a ritual innovation. Both the particularity and the fluidity, then, help account for the hovering closeness of the world of myth to the actual world. A sense of gap, that things are not all they might be, is there but it is hardly experienced as tragic and is indeed on the verge of being comic.

Primitive *religious action* is characterized not, as we have said, by worship, nor, as we shall see, by sacrifice, but by identification, "participation," acting-out. Just as the primitive symbol system is myth *par excellence*, so primitive religious action is ritual *par excellence*. In the ritual the participants become identified with the mythical beings they represent. The mythical beings are not addressed or propitiated or beseeched. The distance between man and mythical being, which was at best slight, disappears altogether in the moment of ritual when every-when becomes now. There are no priests and no congregation, no mediating representative roles and no spectators. All present are involved in the ritual action itself and have become one with the myth.

The underlying structure of ritual, which in Australia always has themes related to initiation, is remarkably similar to that of sacrifice. The four basic movements of the ritual as analyzed by Stanner are offering, destruction, transformation, and return-communion. Through acting out of the mistakes and sufferings of the paradigmatic mythical hero, the new initiates come to terms symbolically with, again in Stanner's words, the "immemorial misdirection" of human life. Their former innocence is destroyed and they are transformed into new identities now more able to "assent to life, as it is, without morbidity." In a sense the whole gamut of the spiritual life is already visible in the Australian ritual. Yet the symbolism is so compact that there is almost no element of choice, will or responsibility. The religious life is as given and as fixed as the routines of daily living.

At the primitive level *religious organization* as a separate social structure does not exist. Church and society are one. Religious roles tend to be fused with other roles, and differentiations along lines of age, sex and kin group are important. While women are not as excluded from the religious life as male ethnographers once believed, their ritual life is to some degree separate and focused on particularly feminine life crises. In most primitive societies age is an important criterion for leadership in the ceremonial life. Ceremonies are often handed down in particular moieties and clans, as is only natural when the myths are so largely concerned with ancestors. Specialized shamans or medicine men are found in some tribes but are not a necessary feature of primitive religion.

As for the *social implications* of primitive religion, Durkheim's analysis seems still to be largely acceptable. The ritual life does reinforce the solidarity of the society and serves to induct the young into the norms of tribal behavior. We should not forget the innovative aspects of primitive religion, that particular myths and ceremonies are in a process of constant revision and alteration, and that in the face of severe historic crisis rather remarkable reformulations of primitive material can be made. Yet on the whole the religious life is the strongest reinforcement of the basic tenet of Australian philosophy, namely that life, as Stanner puts it, is a "one possibility thing." The very fluidity and flexibility of primitive religion is a barrier to radical innovation. Primitive religion gives little leverage from which to change the world.

ARCHAIC RELIGION

For purposes of the present conceptual scheme, as I have indicated, I am using primitive religion in an unusually restricted sense. Much that is usually classified as primitive religion would fall in my second category, archaic religion, which includes the religious systems of much of Africa and Polynesia and some of the New World, as well as the earliest religious systems of the ancient Middle East, India and China. The characteristic feature of archaic religion is the emergence of true cult with the complex of gods, priests, worship, sacrifice and in some cases divine or priestly kingship. The myth and ritual complex characteristic of primitive religion continues within the structure of archaic religion, but it is systematized and elaborated in new ways.

In the archaic *religious symbol system* mythical beings are much more definitely characterized. Instead of being great paradigmatic figures with whom men in ritual identify but with whom they do not really interact, the mythical beings are more objectified, conceived as actively and sometimes willfully controlling the natural and human world, and as beings with whom men must deal in a definite and purposive way—in a word they have become gods. Relations among the gods are a matter of considerable speculation and systematization, so that definite principles of organization, especially hierarchies of control, are established. The basic world view is still, like the primitives', monistic. There is still only one world with gods dominating particular parts of it, especially important being the high gods of the heavenly regions whose vision, knowledge and power may be conceived as very extensive indeed. But though the world is one it is far more differentiated, especially in a hierarchical way, than was the monistic world view of the primitives: archaic religions tend to elaborate a vast cosmology in which all things divine and natural have a place. Much of the particularity and fluidity characteristic of primitive myth is still to be found in archaic religious thinking. But where priestly roles have become well established a relatively stable symbolic structure may be worked out and transmitted over an extended period of time. Especially where at least craft literacy has been attained, the mythical tradition may become the object of critical reflection and innovative speculation which can lead to new developments beyond the nature of archaic religion.

Archaic *religious action* takes the form of cult in which the distinction between men as subjects and gods as objects is much more definite than in primitive religion. Because the division is sharper the need for a communication system through which gods and men can interact is much more acute. Worship and especially sacrifice are precisely such communication systems, as Henri Hubert and Marcel Mauss so brilliantly estab-

lished in their great essay on sacrifice. There is no space here for a technical analysis of the sacrificial process; suffice it to say that a double identification of priest and victim with both gods and men effects a transformation of motives comparable to that referred to in the discussion of primitive religious action. The main difference is that instead of a relatively passive identification in an all-encompassing ritual action, the sacrificial process, no matter how stereotyped, permits the human communicants a greater element of intentionality and entails more uncertainty relative to the divine response. Through this more differentiated form of religious action a new degree of freedom as well, perhaps, as an increased burden of anxiety enters the relations between man and the ultimate conditions of his existence.

Archaic *religious organization* is still by and large merged with other social structures, but the proliferation of functionally and hierarchically differentiated groups leads to a multiplication of cults, since every group in archaic society tends to have its cultic aspect. The emergence of a two-class system, itself related to the increasing density of population made possible by agriculture, has its religious aspect. The upper-status group, which tends to monopolize political and military power, usually claims a superior religious status as well. Noble families are proud of their divine descent and often have special priestly functions. The divine king who is the chief link between his people and the gods is only the extreme case of the general tendency of archaic societies. Specialized priesthoods attached to cult centers may differentiate out but are usually kept subordinate to the political elite, which at this stage never completely divests itself of religious leadership. Occasionally priesthoods at cult centers located interstitially relative to political units—for example, Delphi in ancient Greece—may come to exercise a certain independence.

The most significant limitation on archaic religious organization is the failure to develop differentiated religious collectivities including adherents as well as priests. The cult centers provide facilities for sacrifice and worship to an essentially transient clientele which is not itself organized as a collectivity, even though the priesthood itself may be rather tightly organized. The appearance of mystery cults and related religious confraternities in the ancient world is usually related to a reorganization of the religious symbol and action systems which indicates a transition to the next main type of religious structure.

The *social implications* of archaic religion are to some extent similar to those of primitive religion. The individual and his society are seen as merged in a natural-divine cosmos. Traditional social structures and social practices are considered to be grounded in the divinely instituted cosmic order and there is little tension between religious demand and social conformity. Indeed, social conformity is at every point reinforced with religious sanction. Nevertheless the very notion of well characterized gods acting over against men with a certain freedom introduces an element of openness that is less apparent at the primitive level. The struggle between rival groups may be interpreted as the struggle between rival deities or as a deity's change of favor from one group to another. Through the problems posed by religious rationalization of political change new modes of religious thinking may open up. This is clearly an important aspect of the early history of Israel, and it occurred in many other cases as well. The Greek preoccupation with the relation of the gods to the events of the Trojan War gave rise to a continuous deepening of religious thought from Homer to Euripides. In ancient China the attempt of the Chou to rationalize their conquest of the Shang led to an entirely new conception of the relation between human merit and divine favor. The breakdown of internal order led to messianic expectations of the coming of a savior king in such distant areas as Egypt on the one hand and Chou-period China on the other. These are but a few of the ways in which the problems of maintaining archaic religious symbolization in increasingly complex societies drove toward solutions that began to place the archaic pattern itself in jeopardy.

HISTORIC RELIGION

The next stage in this theoretical scheme is called historic simply because the religions included are all relatively recent; they emerged in societies that were more or less literate and so have fallen chiefly under the discipline of history rather than that of archaeology or ethnography. The criterion that distinguishes the historic religions from the archaic is that the historic religions are all in some sense transcendental. The cos-

mological monism of the earlier stage is now more or less completely broken through and an entirely different realm of universal reality, having for religious man the highest value, is proclaimed. The discovery of an entirely different realm of religious reality seems to imply a derogation of the value of the given empirical cosmos: at any rate the world rejection discussed above is, in this stage for the first time, a general characteristic of the religious system.

The *symbol systems* of the historic religions differ greatly among themselves but share the element of transcendentalism which sets them off from the archaic religions; in this sense they are all dualistic. The strong emphasis on hierarchical ordering characteristic of archaic religions continues to be stressed in most of the historic religions. Not only is the supernatural realm "above" this world in terms of both value and control but both the supernatural and earthly worlds are themselves organized in terms of a religiously legitimated hierarchy. For the masses, at least, the new dualism is above all expressed in the difference between this world and the life after death. Religious concern, focused on this life in primitive and archaic religions, now tends to focus on life in the other realm, which may be either infinitely superior or, under certain circumstances, with the emergence of various conceptions of hell, infinitely worse. Under these circumstances the religious goal of salvation (or enlightenment, release and so forth) is for the first time the central religious preoccupation.

In one sense historic religions represent a great "demythologization" relative to archaic religions. The notion of the one God who has neither court nor relatives, who has no myth himself and who is the sole creator and ruler of the universe, the notion of self subsistent being, or of release from the cycle of birth and rebirth, are all enormous simplifications of the ramified cosmologies of archaic religions. Yet all the historic religions have, to use Voegelin's term, mortgages imposed on them by the historical circumstances of their origin. All of them contain, in suspension as it were, elements of archaic cosmology alongside their transcendental assertions. Nonetheless, relative to earlier forms the historic religions are all universalistic. From the point of view of these religions a man is no longer defined chiefly in terms of what tribe or clan he comes from or what particular god he serves but rather as a being capable of salvation. That is to say that it is for the first time possible to conceive of man as such.

Religious action in the historic religions is thus above all action necessary for salvation. Even where elements of ritual and sacrifice remain prominent they take on a new significance. In primitive ritual the individual is put in harmony with the natural divine cosmos. His mistakes are overcome through symbolization as part of the total pattern. Through sacrifice archaic man can make up for his failures to fulfill his obligations to men or gods. He can atone for particular acts of unfaithfulness. But historic religion convicts man of a basic flaw far more serious than those conceived of by earlier religions. According to Buddhism, man's very nature is greed and anger from which he must seek a total escape. For the Hebrew prophets, man's sin is not particular wicked deeds but his profound heedlessness of God, and only a turn to complete obedience will be acceptable to the Lord. For Muhammad the *kafir* is not, as we usually translate, the "unbeliever" but rather the ungrateful man who is careless of the divine compassion. For him, only Islam, willing submission to the will of God, can bring salvation.

The identity diffusion characteristic of both primitive and archaic religions is radically challenged by the historic religious symbolization, which leads for the first time to a clearly structured conception of the self. Devaluation of the empirical world and the empirical self highlights the conception of a responsible self, a core self or a true self, deeper than the flux of everyday experience, facing a reality over against itself, a reality which has a consistency belied by the fluctuations of mere sensory impressions. Primitive man can only accept the world in its manifold givenness. Archaic man can through sacrifice fulfill his religious obligations and attain peace with the gods. But the historic religions promise man for the first time that he can understand the fundamental structure of reality and through salvation participate actively in it. The opportunity is far greater than before but so is the risk of failure.

Perhaps partly because of the profound risks involved the ideal of the religious life in the historic religions tends to be one of separation from the world. Even when, as in the case of Judaism and Islam, the religion enjoins types of worldly participation that are considered unacceptable or at least doubtful in some other historic religions, the devout are still set apart from ordinary worldlings by the massive collections of rules and obligations to which they must adhere. The early Christian solution, which, unlike the Buddhist, did allow the full possibility of salvation to the layman, nevertheless in its notion of a special state of religious perfection idealized religious withdrawal from the world. In fact the standard for lay piety tended to be closeness of approximation to the life of the religious.

Historic religion is associated with the emergence of differentiated religious collectivities as the chief characteristic of its *religious organization*. The profound dualism with respect to the conception of reality is also expressed in the social realm. The single religio-political hierarchy of archaic society tends to split into two at least partially independent hierarchies, one political and one religious. Together with the notion of a transcendent realm beyond the natural cosmos comes a new religious elite that claims direct relation to the transmundane world. Even though notions of divine kingship linger on for a very long time in various compromise forms, it is no longer possible for a divine king to monopolize religious leadership. With the emergence of a religious elite alongside the political one the problem of legitimizing political power enters a new phase. Legitimation now rests upon a delicate balance of forces between the political and religious leadership. But the differentiation between religious and political that exists most clearly at the level of leadership tends also to be pushed down into the masses so that the roles of believer and subject become distinct. Even where, as in the case of Islam, this distinction was not supported by religious norms, it was soon recognized as an actuality.

The emergence of the historic religions is part of a general shift from the two-class system of the archaic period to the four-class system characteristic of all the great historic civilizations up to modern times: a political-military elite, a cultural-religious elite, a rural lower-status group (peasantry) and an urban lower-status group (merchants and artisans). Closely associated with the new religious developments was the growth of literacy among the elite groups and in the upper segments of the urban lower class. Other social changes, such as the growth in the market resulting from the first widespread use of coinage, the development of bureaucracy and law as well as new levels of urbanization, are less directly associated with religion but are part of the same great transformation that got underway in the first millennium B.C. The distinction between religious and political elites applies to some extent to the two great lower strata. From the point of view of the historic religions the peasantry long remained relatively intractable and were often considered religiously second-class citizens, their predilection for cosmological symbolization rendering them always to some degree religiously suspect. The notion of the peasant as truly religious is a fairly modern idea. On the contrary it was the townsman who was much more likely to be numbered among the devout, and Max Weber has pointed out the great fecundity of the urban middle strata in religious innovations throughout the several great historical traditions. Such groups developed new symbolizations that sometimes threatened the structure of the historic religions in their early form, and in the one case where a new stage of religious symbolization was finally achieved they made important contributions.

The *social implications* of the historic religions are implicit in the remarks on religious organization. The differentiation of a religious elite brought a new level of tension and a new possibility of conflict and change onto the social scene. Whether the confrontation was between Israelite prophet and king, Islamic ulama and sultan, Christian pope and emperor or even between Confucian scholar-official and his ruler, it implied that political acts could be judged in terms of standards that the political authorities could not finally control. The degree to which these confrontations had serious social consequences of course depended on the degree to which the religious group was structurally independent and could exert real pressure. S. N. Eisenstadt has made a comprehensive survey of these differences; for our purposes it is enough to note that they were nowhere entirely absent. Religion, then, provided the ideology and social cohesion for many rebellions and reform movements in the historic civilizations, and consequently played a more dynamic and especially a more purposive role in social change than had previously been possible. On the other hand, we should not forget that in most of the

historic civilizations for long periods of time religion performed the functions we have noted from the beginning: legitimation and reinforcement of the existing social order.

EARLY MODERN RELIGION

In all previous stages the ideal type was based on a variety of actual cases. Now for the first time it derives from a single case or at best a congeries of related cases, namely, the Protestant Reformation. The defining characteristic of early modern religion is the collapse of the hierarchical structuring of both this and the other world. The dualism of the historic religions remains as a feature of early modern religion but takes on a new significance in the context of more direct confrontation between the two worlds. Under the new circumstances salvation is not to be found in any kind of withdrawal from the world but in the midst of worldly activities. Of course elements of this existed in the historic religions from the beginning, but on the whole the historic religions as institutionalized had offered a mediated salvation. Either conformity to religious law, or participation in a sacramental system or performance of mystical exercises was necessary for salvation. All of these to some extent involved a turning away from the world. Further, in the religious two-class systems characteristic of the institutionalized historic religions the upper-status groups, the Christian monks or Sufi shaykhs or Buddhist ascetics, could through their pure acts and personal charisma store up a fund of grace that could then be shared with the less worthy. In this way too salvation was mediated rather than immediate. What the Reformation did was in principle, with the usual reservations and mortgages to the past, break through the whole mediated system of salvation and declare salvation potentially available to any man no matter what his station or calling might be.

Since immediate salvation seems implicit in all the historic religions it is not surprising that similar reform movements exist in other traditions, notably Shinran Shonin's version of Pure Land Buddhism but also certain tendencies in Islam, Buddhism, Taoism and Confucianism. But the Protestant Reformation is the only attempt that was successfully institutionalized. In the case of Taoism and Confucianism the mortgage of archaic symbolization was so heavy that what seemed a new breakthrough easily became regressive. In the other cases, notably in the case of the Jōdo Shinshū, the radical implications were not sustained and a religion of mediated salvation soon reasserted itself. Religious movements of early modern type may be emerging in a number of the great traditions today, perhaps even in the Vatican Council, and there are also secular movements with features strongly analogous to what I call early modern religion. But all of these tendencies are too uncertain to rely on in constructing an ideal type.

Early modern *religious symbolism* concentrates on the direct relation between the individual and transcendent reality. A great deal of the cosmological baggage of medieval Christianity is dropped as superstition. The fundamentally ritualist interpretation of the sacrament of the Eucharist as a re-enactment of the paradigmatic sacrifice is replaced with the anti-ritualist interpretation of the Eucharist as a commemoration of a once-and-for-all historical event. Even though in one sense the world is more devalued in early Protestantism than in medieval Christianity, since the reformers re-emphasized the adical separation between divine and human, still by proclaiming the world as the theater of God's glory and the place wherein to fulfill his command, the Reformation reinforced positive autonomous action in the world instead of a relatively passive acceptance of it.

Religious action was now conceived to be identical with the whole of life. Special ascetic and devotional practices were dropped as well as the monastic roles that specialized in them and instead the service of God became a total demand in every walk of life. The stress was on faith, an internal quality of the person, rather than on particular acts clearly marked "religious." In this respect the process of identity unification that I have designated as a central feature of the historic religions advanced still further. The complex requirements for the attainment of salvation in the historic religions, though ideally they encouraged identity unification, could themselves become a new form of identity diffusion, as Luther and Shinran were aware. Assertion of the capacity for faith as an already received gift made it possible to undercut that difficulty. It also made it necessary to accept the ambiguity of human ethical life and the fact that salvation comes in spite of sin, not in its absolute absence. With the acceptance of the world not as it is but as a valid arena in which to work out the divine command, and with the acceptance of the self as capable of faith in spite of sin, the Reformation made it possible to turn away from world rejection in a way not possible in the historic religions. All of this was possible, however, only within the structure of a rigid orthodoxy and a tight though voluntaristic religious group.

I have already noted that early modern religion abandoned hierarchy as an essential dimension of its religious symbol system. It did the same in its *religious organization*. Not only did it reject papal authority, but it also rejected the old form of the religious distinction between two levels of relative religious perfection. This was replaced with a new kind of religious two-class system: the division between elect and reprobates. The new form differed from the old one in that the elect were really a vanguard group in the fulfillment of the divine plan rather than a qualitative religious elite. The political implications of Protestantism had much to do with the overthrow of the old conception of hierarchy in the secular field as well. Where Calvinistic Protestantism was powerful, hereditary aristocracy and kingship were either greatly weakened or abandoned. In fact the Reformation is part of the general process of social change in which the four-class system of peasant societies began to break up in Europe. Especially in the Anglo-Saxon world, Protestantism greatly contributed to its replacement by a more flexible multi-centered mode of social organization based more on contract and voluntary association. Both church and state lost some of the reified significance they had in medieval times and later on the continent. The roles of church member and citizen were but two among several. Both church and state had their delimited spheres of authority, but with the full institutionalization of the common law neither had a right to dominate each other or the whole of society. Nonetheless, the church acted for a long time as a sort of cultural and ethical holding company, and many developments in philosophy, literature and social welfare took their initiative from clerical or church groups.

The *social implications* of the Protestant Reformation are among the more debated subjects of contemporary social science. Lacking space to defend my assertions, let me simply say that I stand with Weber, Merton, *et al.*, in attributing very great significance to the Reformation, especially in its Calvinistic wing, in a whole series of developments from economics to science, from education to law. Whereas in most of the historic civilizations religion stands as virtually the only stable challenger to the dominance of the political elite, in the emerging early modern society religious impulses give rise to a variety of institutional structures, from the beginning or very soon becoming fully secular, which stand beside and to some extent compete with and limit the state. The direct religious response to political and moral problems does not disappear but the impact of religious orientations on society is also mediated by a variety of worldly institutions in which religious values have been expressed. Weber's critics, frequently assuming a pre-modern model of the relation between religion and society, have often failed to understand the subtle interconnections he was tracing. But the contrast with the historic stage, when pressures toward social change in the direction of value realization were sporadic and often utopian, is decisive.

In the early modern stage for the first time pressures to social change in the direction of greater realization of religious values are actually institutionalized as part of the structure of the society itself. The self-revising social order expressed in a voluntaristic and democratic society can be seen as just such an outcome. The earliest phase of this development, especially the several examples of Calvinist commonwealths, was voluntaristic only within the elect vanguard group and otherwise was often illiberal and even dictatorial. The transition toward a more completely democratic society was complex and subject to many blockages. Close analogies to the early modern situation occur in many of the contemporary developing countries, which are trying for the first time to construct social systems with a built-in tendency to change in the direction of greater value realization. The leadership of these countries varies widely between several kinds of vanguard revolutionary movements with distinctly illiberal proclivities to elites committed to the implementation of a later, more democratic, model of Western political society.

MODERN RELIGION

I am not sure whether in the long run what I call early modern religion will appear as a stage with the same degree of distinctness as the others I have distinguished or whether it will appear only as a transitional phase, but I am reasonably sure that, even though we must speak from the midst of it, the modern situation represents a stage of religious development in many ways profoundly different from that of historic religion. The central feature of the change is the collapse of the dualism that was so crucial to all the historic religions.

It is difficult to speak of a *modern religious symbol system*. It is indeed an open question whether there can be a religious symbol system analogous to any of the preceding ones in the modern situation, which is characterized by a deepening analysis of the very nature of symbolization itself. At the highest intellectual level I would trace the fundamental break with traditional historic symbolization to the work of Kant. By revealing the problematic nature of the traditional metaphysical basis of all the religions and by indicating that it is not so much a question of two worlds as it is of as many worlds as there are modes of apprehending them, he placed the whole religious problem in a new light. However simple the immediate result of his grounding religion in the structure of ethical life rather than in a metaphysics claiming cognitive adequacy, it nonetheless pointed decisively in the direction that modern religion would go. The entire modern analysis of religion, including much of the most important recent theology, though rejecting Kant's narrowly rational ethics, has been forced to ground religion in the structure of the human situation itself. In this respect the present paper is a symptom of the modern religious situation as well as an analysis of it. In the world view that has emerged from the tremendous intellectual advances of the last two centuries there is simply no room for a hierarchic dualistic religious symbol system of the classical historic type. This is not to be interpreted as a return to primitive monism: it is not that a single world has replaced a double one but that an infinitely multiplex one has replaced the simple duplex structure. It is not that life has become again a "one possibility thing" but that it has become an infinite possibility thing. The analysis of modern man as secular, materialistic, dehumanized and in the deepest sense areligious seems to me fundamentally misguided, for such a judgment is based on standards that cannot adequately gauge the modern temper.

Though it is central to the problems of modern religion, space forbids a review of the development of the modern analysis of religion on its scholarly and scientific side. I shall confine myself to some brief comments on directions of development within Protestant theology. In many respects Schliermacher is the key figure in early 19th century theology who saw the deeper implications of the Kantian breakthrough. The development of "liberal theology" in the later 19th century, partly on the basis of Schliermacher's beginnings, tended to fall back into Kant's overly rational limitations. Against this, Barth's reassertion of the power of the traditional symbolism was bound to produce a vigorous response, but unfortunately, due to Barth's own profound ambiguity on the ultimate status of dogma, the consequences were in part simply a regressive reassertion of the adequacy of the early modern theological formulation. By the middle of the 20th century, however, the deeper implications of Schliermacher's attempt were being developed in various ways by such diverse figures as Tillich, Bultmann and Bonhoeffer. Tillich's assertion of "ecstatic naturalism," Bultmann's program of "demythologization" and Bonhoeffer's search for a "religionless Christianity," though they cannot be simply equated with each other are efforts to come to terms with the modern situation. Even on the Catholic side the situation is beginning to be recognized.

Interestingly enough, indications of the same general search for an entirely new mode of religious symbolization, though mostly confined to the Protestant West, also appear in that most developed of the non-Western countries, Japan. Uchimura Kanzō's non-church Christianity was a relatively early indication of a search for new directions and is being developed even further today. Even more interesting perhaps is the emergence of a similar development out of the Jōdo Shinshū tradition, at least in the person of Ienaga Saburo. This example indeed suggests that highly "modern" implications exist in more than one strand of Mahayana Buddhism and perhaps several of the other great traditions as well. Although in my opinion these implications were never developed sufficiently to dominate a historical epoch as they did in the West in the last two centuries, they

may well prove decisive in the future of these religions.

So far what I have been saying applies mainly to intellectuals, but at least some evidence indicates that changes are also occurring at the level of mass religiosity. Behind the 96 per cent of Americans who claim to believe in God there are many instances of a massive reinterpretation that leaves Tillich, Bultmann and Bonhoeffer far behind. In fact, for many churchgoers the obligation of doctrinal orthodoxy sits lightly indeed, and the idea that all creedal statements must receive a personal reinterpretation is widely accepted. The dualistic world view certainly persists in the minds of many of the devout, but just as surely many others have developed elaborate and often pseudo-scientific rationalizations to bring their faith in its experienced validity into some kind of cognitive harmony with the 20th century world. The wave of popular response that some of the newer theology seems to be eliciting is another indication that not only the intellectuals find themselves in a new religious situation.

To concentrate on the church in a discussion of the modern religious situation is already misleading, for it is precisely the characteristic of the new situation that the great problem of religion as I have defined it, the symbolization of man's relation to the ultimate conditions of his existence, is no longer the monopoly of any groups explicitly labeled religious. However much the development of Western Christianity may have led up to and in a sense created the modern religious situation, it just as obviously is no longer in control of it. Not only has any obligation of doctrinal orthodoxy been abandoned by the leading edge of modern culture, but every fixed position has become open to question in the process of making sense out of man and his situation. This involves a profounder commitment to the process I have been calling religious symbolization than ever before. The historic religions discovered the self; the early modern religion found a doctrinal basis on which to accept the self in all its empirical ambiguity; modern religion is beginning to understand the laws of the self's own existence and so to help man take responsibility for his own fate.

This statement is not intended to imply a simple liberal optimism, for the modern analysis of man has also disclosed the depths of the limitations imposed by man's situation. Nevertheless, the fundamental symbolization of modern man and his situation is that of a dynamic multi-dimensional self capable, within limits, of continual self-transformation and capable, again within limits, of remaking the world including the very symbolic forms with which he deals with it, even the forms that state the unalterable conditions of his own existence. Such a statement should not be taken to mean that I expect, even less that I advocate, some ghastly religion of social science. Rather I expect traditional religious symbolism to be maintained and developed in new directions, but with growing awareness that it is symbolism and that man in the last analysis is responsible for the choice of his symbolism. Naturally, continuation of the symbolization characteristic of earlier stages without any reinterpretation is to be expected among many in the modern world, just as it has occurred in every previous period.

Religious action in the modern period is, I think, clearly a continuation of tendencies already evident in the early modern stage. Now less than ever can man's search for meaning be confined to the church. But with the collapse of a clearly defined doctrinal orthodoxy and a religiously supported objective system of moral standards, religious action in the world becomes more demanding than ever. The search for adequate standards of action, which is at the same time a search for personal maturity and social relevance, is in itself the heart of the modern quest for salvation, if I may divest that word of its dualistic associations. How the specifically religious bodies are to adjust their time honored practices of worship and devotion to modern conditions is of growing concern in religious circles. Such diverse movements as the liturgical revival, pastoral psychology and renewed emphasis on social action are all efforts to meet the present need. Few of these trends have gotten much beyond the experimental but we can expect the experiments to continue.

In the modern situation as I have defined it, one might almost be tempted to see in Thomas Paine's "My mind is my church," or Thomas Jefferson's "I am a sect myself" the typical expression of *religious organization* in the near future. Nonetheless it seems unlikely that collective symbolization of the great inescapabilities of life will soon disappear. Of course the "free intellectual" will continue to exist as he has for millennia but such a solution can hardly be very general. Private voluntary religious association in the

West achieved full legitimation for the first time in the early modern situation, but in the early stages especially, discipline and control within these groups was very intense. The tendency in more recent periods has been to continue the basic pattern but with a much more open and flexible pattern of membership. In accord with general trends I have already discussed, standards of doctrinal orthodoxy and attempts to enforce moral purity have largely been dropped. The assumption in most of the major Protestant denominations is that the church member can be considered responsible for himself. This trend seems likely to continue, with an increasingly fluid type of organization in which many special purpose sub-groups form and disband. Rather than interpreting these trends as significant of indifference and secularization, I see in them the increasing acceptance of the notion that each individual must work out his own ultimate solutions and that the most the church can do is provide him a favorable environment for doing so, without imposing on him a prefabricated set of answers. And it will be increasingly realized that answers to religious questions can validly be sought in various spheres of "secular" art and thought.

Here I can only suggest what I take to be the main *social implication* of the modern religious situation. Early modern society, to a considerable degree under religious pressure, developed, as we have seen, the notion of a self-revising social system in the form of a democratic society. But at least in the early phase of that development social flexibility was balanced against doctrinal (Protestant orthodoxy) and characterological (Puritan personality) rigidities. In a sense those rigidities were necessary to allow the flexibility to emerge in the social system, but it is the chief characteristic of the more recent modern phase that culture and personality themselves have come to be viewed as endlessly revisable. This has been characterized as a collapse of meaning and a failure of moral standards. No doubt the possibilities for pathological distortion in the modern situation are enormous. It remains to be seen whether the freedom modern society implies at the cultural and personality as well as the social level can be stably institutionalized in large-scale societies. Yet the very situation that has been characterized as one of the collapse of meaning and the failure of moral standards can also, and I would argue more fruitfully, be viewed as one offering unprecedented opportunities for creative innovation in every sphere of human action.

CONCLUSION

The schematic presentation of the stages of religious evolution just concluded is based on the proposition that at each stage the freedom of personality and society has increased relative to the environing conditions. Freedom has increased because at each successive stage the relation of man to the conditions of his existence has been conceived as more complex, more open and more subject to change and development. The distinction between conditions that are really ultimate and those that are alterable becomes increasingly clear though never complete. Of course this scheme of religious evolution has implied at almost every point a general theory of social evolution, which has had to remain largely implicit.

Let me suggest in closing, as a modest effort at empirical testing, how the evolutionary scheme may help to explain the facts of alternating world acceptance and rejection which were noted near the beginning of the paper. I have argued that the world acceptance of the primitive and archaic levels is largely to be explained as the only possible response to a reality that invades the self to such an extent that the symbolizations of self and world are only very partially separate. The great wave of world rejection of the historic religions I have interpreted as a major advance in what Lienhardt calls "the differ-entiation between experience of the self and of the world which acts upon it." Only by withdrawing cathexis from the myriad objects of empirical reality could consciousness of a centered self in relation to an encompassing reality emerge. Early modern religion made it possible to maintain the centered self without denying the multifold empirical reality and so made world rejection in the classical sense unnecessary. In the modern phase knowledge of the laws of the formation of the self, as well as much more about the structure of the world, has opened up almost unlimited new directions of exploration and development. World rejection marks the beginning of a clear objectification of the social order and sharp criticism of it. In the earlier world-accepting phases religious conceptions and social order were so fused that it was almost impossible to criticize the latter from the point of view of the former. In the later phases the possibility of remaking the world to conform to value demands has served in a very different way to mute the extremes of world rejection. The world acceptance of the last two stages is shown in this analysis to have a profoundly different significance from that of the first two.

Construction of a wide-ranging evolutionary scheme like the one presented in this paper is an extremely risky enterprise. Nevertheless such efforts are justifiable if, by throwing light on perplexing developmental problems they contribute to modern man's efforts at self interpretation.

2

THE FUNCTION
OF RELIGION
IN HUMAN SOCIETY

Introduction

While the earlier scholars, especially the writers on comparative religion in the nineteenth century, were concerned with the basic question of how various forms of religion originated in human history, the emphasis shifted in the twentieth century to the basic question of what functions religion has in human society. This shift of interest is well expressed by Radcliffe-Brown when he contrasts his own position with that of Sir James Frazer. He writes that

Sir James accounted for the taboos of savage tribes as the application in practice of beliefs arrived at by erroneous processes of reasoning, and he seems to have thought of the effect of these beliefs in creating or maintaining a stable orderly society as being accidental. My own view is that the negative and positive rites of savages exist and persist because they are part of the mechanism by which an orderly society maintains itself in existence, serving as they do to establish certain fundamental social values....I would suggest that what Sir James Frazer seems to regard as the accidental results of magical and religious beliefs really constitute their essential function and the ultimate reason for their existence [Taboo].

In other words, scholars began to be less concerned with the question of how religious beliefs and practices arose out of human experience, and more concerned with the study of what these beliefs and practices *do* for individuals and societies, whatever their origins. When the question was posed in this fashion, there began to be less disposition to study historical origins and stages of development, and less tendency to become embroiled in theological arguments. Instead, the student of comparative religion could start with the fundamental hypothesis that given the biological and social nature of man on this planet, some kind of religious system is a cultural universal; no human society can get along without a religion any more than it can survive without an economic system. The actual cultural content found in the religions of different societies may vary enormously, but underlying this diversity there may be impressive similarities in basic functions, involving the culturally prescribed solutions of human social and psychological problems and the ways of expressing and reaffirming the central values of a society. Viewed in this light, religion appears to be an essential ingredient of society.

To start with this position and to pose these questions, then, is a call for cross-cultural research and theoretical thinking that will lead both to a clear specification of those aspects of the human situation that require religious patterns and to a precise delineation of the functions religion does perform. We want to know what social and psychological problems are solved by religious beliefs and practices and how. We want to know to what extent and how a religious system helps to express, codify, and reaffirm the central values of a society in such a way as to maintain the social fabric of that society.

The following selections are from writers who have established landmarks in the development of functional thinking about the nature of religion and associated beliefs and practices. The first, by Fustel de Coulanges, represents the seminal stage in such thinking. The works of Malinowski and Radcliffe-Brown are clearly classics in this development of functionalism, and their publications have sparked a stimulating controversy over the concept of function as well as a disagreement over the relationships of anxiety to ritual. Malinowski's use of the concept of function revolved around the question: What human needs (individual and social) are fulfilled by cultural patterns? Radcliffe-Brown's use of the concept was based upon his "organismic analogy"; that is, just as an organ of the body has a function in preserving the successful maintenance of the body as a whole, so does a social custom or usage have a function in preserving the maintenance of a society as a whole. This conceptual difference led to the disagreements between Malinowski and Radcliffe-Brown over the relationship of anxiety to ritual—a disagreement which Homans later attempted to resolve in his paper.

Drawing upon these theories of the functions of religion, as well as upon the earlier work of Émile Durkheim, Max Weber, Vilfredo Pareto, and others, the selection from Talcott Parsons represents a recent synthesis of our theoretical knowledge concerning the role and functions of religion in human society. Finally, the selection by Clyde Kluckhohn, "Myths and Rituals: A General Theory," has been added as another theoretical synthesis on the functions of religion.

Numa-Denys Fustel de Coulanges
THE ANCIENT CITY

It is always rewarding to search for the antecedents of ideas and influences which in the course of time have come to be accepted almost as if they had burst upon us full-blown from out of the blue. The functionalist approach in social anthropology is an excellent example of the manner in which a younger generation without knowledge of the past history of a theory may erroneously assume it to have originated at a particular time with a particular scholar. Without attempting to trace the entire history of the functional concept of society, it is worthwhile to call attention to the influence of a single man, Fustel de Coulanges, on subsequent generations of anthropologists and sociologists. This great historian had as his pupil at the École Normal Supérieure in Paris the young Émile Durkheim, on whom he exerted an immediate and strong influence; the latter in turn attracted eventually a number of important scholars who either directly or indirectly came to adopt his approach. In his great work, *La Cité antique*, first published in 1864 and now available in a paperback edition in English, it is at once obvious that the author's goal was to single out and trace the dynamic role of religion in ancient Greek and Roman life, and to demonstrate its interrelatedness with the laws and institutions of the Greeks and Romans. He maintained that changes in the history of these peoples were due directly to changes in religious beliefs. While the causal sequence which he traced in the development of the city from its beginnings in the family can be challenged, as can his assertion that religion is the source of mores and institutions, he succeeded in elucidating the extent to which religious beliefs and institutions saturated Graeco-Roman social and political organization, especially in the family, marriage, property, morals, law, political authority, social class, and citizenship. *La Cité antique* tells us much

Excerpted from [Numa-Denys] Fustel de Coulanges, *The Ancient City*, trans. Willard Small (3d ed.; Boston: Lee and Shepard, 1877), by permission of Lothrop, Lee & Shepard.

more about the historical development of the ancient religion from familial ancestor worship (with the sacred fire as its principal symbol) to the worship of gods whom he says were a deification of nature. But for our purposes the essential value of the book is not as a work of history but as a force in developing a point of view towards religion that gave expression to the emancipated spirit of nineteenth century thought.

INTRODUCTION

It is proposed here to show upon what principles and by what rules Greek and Roman society was governed. We unite in the same study both the Greeks and Romans, because these two peoples, who were two branches of a single race, and who spoke two idioms of a single language, had also the same institutions and the same principles of government, and passed through a series of similar revolutions.

. .

The history of Greece and Rome is a witness and an example of the intimate relation which always exists between men's ideas and their social state. Examine the institutions of the ancients without thinking of their religious notions, and you find them obscure, whimsical, and inexplicable. Why were there patricians and plebeians, patrons and clients, eupatrids and thetes; and whence came the native and ineffaceable differences which we find between these classes? What was the meaning of those Lacedæmonian institutions which appear to us so contrary to nature? How are we to explain those unjust caprices of ancient private law; at Corinth and at Thebes, the sale of land prohibited; at Athens and at Rome, an inequality in the succession between brother and sister? What did the jurists understand by *agnation*, and by *gens*? Why those revolutions in the laws, those political revolutions? What was that singular patriotism which sometimes effaced every natural sentiment? What did they understand by that liberty of which they were always talking? How did it happen that institutions so very different from anything of which we have an idea to-day, could become established and reign for so long a time? What is the superior principle which gave them authority over the minds of men?

But by the side of these institutions and laws place the religious ideas of those times, and the facts at once become clear, and their explanation is no longer doubtful. If, on going back to the first ages of this race—that is to say, to the time when its institutions were founded—we observe the idea which it had of human existence, of life, of death, of a second life, of the divine principle, we perceive a close relation between these opinions and the ancient rules of private law; between the rites which spring from these opinions and their political institutions.

A comparison of beliefs and laws shows that a primitive religion constituted the Greek and Roman family, established marriage and paternal authority, fixed the order of relationship, and consecrated the right of property, and the right of inheritance. This same religion, after having enlarged and extended the family, formed a still larger association, the city, and reigned in that as it had reigned in the family. From it came all the institutions, as well as all the private law, of the ancients. It was from this that the city received all its principles, its rules, its usages, and its magistracies. But, in the course of time, this ancient religion became modified or effaced, and private law and political institutions were modified with it. Then came a series of revolutions, and social changes regularly followed the development of knowledge.

THE CITY FORMED

The tribe, like the family and phratry, was established as an independent body, since it had a special worship from which the stranger was excluded. Once formed, no new family could be admitted to it. No more could two tribes be fused into one; their religion was opposed to this. But just as several phratries were united in a tribe, several tribes might associate together, on condition that the religion of each should be respected. The day on which this alliance took place the city existed.

It is of little account to seek the cause which determined several neighboring tribes to unite. Sometimes it was voluntary; sometimes it was imposed by the superior force of a tribe, or by the powerful will of a man.

What is certain, is that the bond of the new association was still a religion. The tribes that united to form a city never failed to light a sacred fire, and to adopt a common religion.

Thus human society, in this race, did not enlarge like a circle, which increases on all sides, gaining little by little. There were, on the contrary, small groups, which, having been long established, were finally joined together in larger ones. Several families formed the phratry, several phratries the tribe, several tribes the city. Family, phratry, tribe, city, were, moreover, societies exactly similar to each other, which were formed one after the other by a series of federations.

We must remark, also, that when the different groups became thus associated, none of them lost its individuality, or its independence. Although several families were united in a phratry, each one of them remained constituted just as it had been when separate. Nothing was changed in it, neither worship nor priesthood, nor property nor internal justice. Curies afterwards became associated, but each retained its worship, its assemblies, its festivals, its chief. From the tribe men passed to the city; but the tribe was not dissolved on that account, and each of them continued to form a body, very much as if the city had not existed. In religion there subsisted a multitude of subordinate worships, above which was established one common to all; in politics, numerous little governments continued to act, while above them a common government was founded.

The city was a confederation. Hence it was obliged, at least for several centuries, to respect the religious and civil independence of the tribes, curies, and families, and had not the right, at first, to interfere in the private affairs of each of these little bodies. It had nothing to do in the interior of a family; it was not the judge of what passed there; it left to the father the right and duty of judging his wife, his son, and his client. It is for this reason that private law, which had been fixed at the time when families were isolated, could subsist in the city, and was modified only at a very late period.

The mode of founding ancient cities is attested by usages which continued for a very long time.

If we examine the army of the city in primitive times, we find it distributed into tribes, curies, and families, "in such a way," says one of the ancients, "that the warrior has for a neighbor in the combat one with whom, in time of peace, he has offered the libation and sacrifice at the same altar." If we look at the people when assembled, in the early ages of Rome, we see them voting by curies and by *gentes*. If we look at the worship, we see at Rome six Vestals, two for each tribe. At Athens, the archon offers the sacrifice in the name of the entire city, but he has in the religious part of the ceremony as many assistants as there are tribes.

Thus the city was not an assemblage of individuals; it was a confederation of several groups, which were established before it, and which it permitted to remain. We see, in the Athenian orators, that every Athenian formed a portion of four distinct societies at the same time; he was a member of a family, of a phratry, of a tribe, and of a city. He did not enter at the same time and the same day into all these four, like a Frenchman, who at the moment of his birth belongs at once to a family, a commune, a department, and a country. The phratry and the tribe are not administrative divisions. A man enters at different times into these four societies, and ascends, so to speak, from one to the other. First, the child is admitted into the family by the religious ceremony, which takes place six days after his birth. Some years later he enters the phratry by a new ceremony, which we have already described. Finally, at the age of sixteen or eighteen, he is presented for admission into the city. On that day, in the presence of an altar, and before the smoking flesh of a victim, he pronounces an oath, by which he binds himself, among other things, always to respect the religion of the city. From that day he is initiated into the public worship, and becomes a citizen. If we observe this young Athenian rising, step by step, from worship to worship, we have a symbol of the degrees through which human association has passed. The course which this young man is constrained to follow, is that which society first followed.

We should not lose sight of the excessive difficulty which, in primitive times, opposed the foundation of regular societies. The social tie was not easy to establish between those human beings who were so diverse, so free, so inconstant. To bring them under the rules of a community, to institute commandments and insure obedience, to cause passion to give way to reason, and individual right to public right, there certainly was something necessary, stronger than material force, more respectable than interest, surer than a philosophical theory, more unchangeable than a convention; something that should dwell equally in all hearts, and should be all-powerful there.

This power was a belief. Nothing has more power over the soul. A belief is the work of our mind, but we are not on that account free to modify it at will. It is our own creation, but we do not know it. It is human, and we believe it a god. It is the effect of our power, and is stronger than we are. It is in us; it does not quit us: it speaks to us at every moment. If it tells us to obey, we obey; if it traces duties for us, we submit. Man may, indeed, subdue nature, but he is subdued by his own thoughts.

Now, an ancient belief commanded a man to honor his ancestor; the worship of the ancestor grouped a family around an altar. Thus arose the first religion, the first prayers, the first ideas of duty, and of morals. Thus, too, was the right of property established, and the order of succession fixed. Thus, in fine, arose all private law, and all the rules of domestic organization. Later the belief grew, and human society grew at the same time. When men begin to perceive that there are common divinities for them, they unite in larger groups. The same rules, invented and established for the family, are applied successively to the phratry, the tribe, and the city.

Let us take in at a glance the road over which man has passed. In the beginning the family lived isolated, and man knew only the domestic gods—θεοι πάτρωοι, *dii gentiles*. Above the family was formed the phratry with its god—θεὸς φράτριος, *Juno curialis*. Then came the tribe, and the god of the tribe —θεὸς φύλιος. Finally came the city, and men conceived a god whose providence embraced this entire city—θεὸς πολιεύς, *penates publici*; a hierarchy of creeds, and a hierarchy of association. The religious idea was, among the ancients, the inspiring breath and organizer of society.

· ·

THE CITIZEN AND THE STRANGER

The citizen was recognized by the fact that he had a part in the religion of the city, and it was from this participation that he derived all his civil and political rights. If he renounced the worship, he renounced the rights. We have already spoken of the public meals, which were the principal ceremony of the national worship. Now, at Sparta, one who did not join in these, even if it was not his fault, ceased at once to be counted among the citizens. At Athens, one who did not take part in the festivals of the national gods lost the rights of a citizen. At Rome, it was necessary to have been present at the sacred ceremony of the lustration, in order to enjoy political rights. The man who had not taken part in this—that is to say, who had not joined in the common prayer and the sacrifice—lost his citizenship until the next lustration.

If we wished to give an exact definition of a citizen, we should say that it was a man who had the religion of the city. The stranger, on the contrary, is one who has not access to the worship, one whom gods of the city do not protect, and who has not even the right to invoke them. For these national gods do not wish to receive prayers and offering except from citizens; they repulse the stranger; entrance into their temples is forbidden to him, and his presence during the sacrifice is a sacrilege. Evidence of this ancient sentiment of repulsion has remained in one of the principal rites of Roman worship. The pontiff, when he sacrifices in the open air, must have his head veiled: "For before the sacred fires in the religious act which is offered to the national gods, the face of a stranger must not appear to the pontiff; the auspices would be disturbed." A sacred object which fell for a moment into the hands of a stranger at once became profane. It could not recover its religious character except by an expiatory ceremony. If the enemy seized upon a city, and the citizens succeeded in recovering it, above all things it was important that the temples should be purified and all the fires extinguished and rekindled. The presence of the stranger had defiled them.

Thus religion established between the citizen and the stranger a profound and ineffaceable distinction. This same religion, so long as it held its sway over the minds of men, forbade the right of citizenship to be granted to a stranger. In the time of Herodotus, Sparta had accorded it to no one except a prophet; and even for this the formal command of the oracle was necessary. Athens granted it sometimes; but with what precautions! First, it was necessary that the united people should vote by secret ballot for the admission of the stranger. Even this was nothing as yet; nine days afterwards a second assembly had to confirm the previous vote, and in this second case six thousand votes were required in favor of the admission— a number which will appear enormous when we recollect that it was very rare for an Athenian assembly to comprise so many citizens. After this a vote of the senate was required to confirm the decision of this double assembly. Finally, any citizen could oppose a sort of veto, and attack the decree as contrary to the ancient laws. Certainly there was no other public act where the legislator was surrounded with so many difficulties and precautions as that which conferred upon a stranger the title of citizen. The formalities to go through were not near so great in declaring war, or in passing a new law. Why should these men oppose so many obstacles to a stranger who wished to become a citizen? Assuredly they did not fear that in the political assemblies his vote would turn the balance. Demosthenes gives us the true motive and the true thought of the Athenians: "It is because the purity of the sacrifices must be preserved." To exclude the stranger was to "watch over the sacred ceremonies." To admit a stranger among the citizens was "to give him a part in the religion and in the sacrifices." Now, for such an act the people did not consider themselves entirely free, and were seized with religious scruples; for they knew that the national gods were disposed to repulse the stranger, and that the sacrifices would perhaps be rendered useless by the presence of the newcomer. The gift of the rights of a citizen to a stranger was a real violation of the fundamental principles of the national religion; and it is for this reason that, in the beginning, the city was so sparing of it. We must also note that the man admitted to citizenship with so much difficulty could be neither archon nor priest. The city, indeed, permitted him to take part in its worship, but as to presiding at it, that would have been too much.

No one could become a citizen at Athens if he was a citizen in another city; for it was a religious impossibility to be at the same time a member of two cities, as it also was to be a member of two families. One could not have two religions at the same time.

The participation in the worship carried with it the possession of rights. As the citizen might assist in the sacrifice which preceded the assembly, he could also vote at the assembly. As he could perform the sacrifices in the name of the city, he might be a prytane and an archon. Having the religion of the city, he might claim rights under its laws, and perform all the ceremonies of legal procedure.

The stranger, on the contrary, having no part in the religion, had none in the law. If he entered the sacred enclosure which the priests had traced for the assembly, he was punished with death. The laws of the city did not exist for him. If he had committed a crime, he was treated as a slave, and punished without process of law, the city owing him no legal protection. When men arrived at that stage that they felt the need of having laws for the stranger, it was necessary to establish an exceptional tribunal. At Rome, in order to judge the alien, the praetor had to become an alien himself—*praetor pere grinus*. At Athens the judge of foreigners was the polemarch—that is to say, the magistrate who was charged with the cares of war, and of all transactions with the enemy.

Neither at Rome nor at Athens could a foreigner be a proprietor. He could not marry; or, if he married, his marriage was not recognized, and his children were reputed illegitimate. He could not make a contract with a citizen; at any rate, the law did not recognize such a contract as valid. At first he could take no part in commerce. The Roman law forbade him to inherit from a citizen, and even forbade a citizen to inherit from him. They pushed this principle so far, that if a foreigner obtained the rights of a citizen without his son, born before this event, obtaining the same favor, the son became a foreigner in regard to his father, and could not inherit from him. The distinction between citizen and foreigner was stronger than the natural tie between father and son.

At first blush it would seem as if the aim had been to establish a system that should be vexatious towards foreigners; but there was nothing of this. Athens and Rome, on the contrary, gave him a good reception, both for commercial and political reasons. But neither their good will nor their interest could abolish the ancient laws which religion had established. This religion did not permit the stranger to become a proprietor, because he could not have any part in the religious soil of the city. It permitted neither the foreigner to inherit from the citizen, nor the citizen to inherit from the foreigner; because every transmission of property carried with it the transmission of a worship, and it was as impossible for the citizen to perform the foreigner's worship as for the foreigner to perform the citizen's.

Citizens could welcome the foreigner, watch over him, even esteem him if he was rich and honorable; but they could give him no part in their religion or their laws. The slave in certain respects was better treated than he was, because the slave, being a member of the family whose worship he shared, was connected with the city through his master; the gods protected him. The Roman religion taught, therefore, that the tomb of the slave was sacred, but that the foreigner's was not.

A foreigner, to be of any account in the eyes of the law, to be enabled to engage in trade, to make contracts, to enjoy his property securely, to have the benefit of the laws of the city to protect him, must become the client of a citizen. Rome and Athens required every foreigner to adopt a patron. By choosing a citizen as a patron the foreigner became connected with the city. Thenceforth he participated in some of the benefits of the civil law, and its protection was secured.

. . .

PATRICIANS AND CLIENTS

Thus far we have not spoken of the lower classes, because we have had no occasion to speak of them. For we have been attempting to describe the primitive organization of the city; and the lower classes counted absolutely for nothing in that organism. The city was constituted as if these classes had not existed. We were able therefore to defer the study of these till we had arrived at the period of the revolutions.

The ancient city, like all human society, had ranks, distinctions, and inequalities. We know the distinction originally made at Athens between the Eupatrids and the Thetes; at Sparta we find the class of Equals and that of the Inferiors; and in Eubœa, that of the Knights and that of the People. The history of Rome is full of the struggles between the Patricians and Plebeians, struggles that we find in all the Sabine, Latin, and Etruscan cities. We can even remark that the higher we ascend in the history of Greece and Italy, the more profound and the more strongly marked the distinction appears—a positive proof that the inequality did not grow up with time, but that it existed from

the beginning, and that it was contemporary with the birth of cities.

It is worth while to inquire upon what principles this division of classes rested. We can thus the more easily see by virtue of what ideas or what needs the struggles commenced, what the inferior classes claimed, and on what principles the superior classes defended their empire.

We have seen above that the city grew out of the confederation of families and tribes. Now, before the day on which the city was founded, the family already contained within itself this distinction of classes. Indeed, the family was never dismembered; it was indivisible, like the primitive religion of the hearth. The oldest son alone, succeeding the father, took possession of the priesthood, the property, and the authority, and his brothers were to him what they had been to their father. From generation to generation, from first-born to first-born, there was never but one family chief. He presided at the sacrifice, repeated the prayer, pronounced judgment, and governed. To him alone originally belonged the title of *pater*; for this word which signified power and not paternity, could be applied only to the chief of the family. His sons, his brothers, his servants, all called him by this title.

Here, then, in the inner constitution of the family is the first principle of inequality. The oldest is the privileged one for the worship, for the succession, and for command. After several centuries, there were naturally formed, in each of these great families, younger branches, that were, according to religion and by custom, inferior to the older branch, and who, living under its protection, submitted to its authority.

This family, then, had servants, who did not leave it, who were hereditarily attached to it, and upon whom the *pater*, or *patron*, exercised the triple authority of master, magistrate, and priest. They were called by names that varied with the locality: the more common names were Clients and Thetes.

Here was another inferior class. The client was inferior not only to the supreme chief of the family, but to the younger branches also. Between him and them there was this difference, that a member of a younger branch, by ascending the series of his ancestors, always arrived at a *pater*, that is to say, a family chief, one of those divine ancestors, whom the family invoked in its prayers. As he was descended from a *pater*, they called him in Latin *patricius*. The son of a client, on the contrary, however high he might ascend in his genealogy, never arrived at anything but a client or a slave. There was no *pater* among his ancestors. Hence came for him a state of inferiority from which there was no escape.

The distinction between these two classes of men was manifest in what concerned material interests. The property of the family belonged entirely to the chief, who, however, shared the enjoyment of it with the younger branches, and even with the clients. But while the younger branch had at least an eventual right to this property, in case of the extinction of the elder branch, the client could never become a proprietor. The land that he cultivated he had only in trust; if he died, it returned to his patron; Roman law of the later ages preserved a vestige of this ancient rule in what was called *jus applicationis*. The client's money, even, did not belong to him; the patron was the true owner of it, and could take it for his own needs. It was by virtue of this ancient rule that the Roman law required the client to endow the daughter of the patron, to pay the patron's fine, and to furnish his ransom, or contribute to the expenses of his magistracy.

The distinction is still more manifest in religion. The descendant of the *pater* alone can perform the ceremonies of the family worship. The client takes a part in it; a sacrifice is offered for him; he does not offer it for himself. Between him and the domestic divinity there is always a mediator. He cannot even replace the absent family. If this family becomes extinct, the clients do not continue the worship; they are dispersed. For the religion is not their patrimony; it is not of their blood, it does not come from their own ancestors. It is a borrowed religion; they have not the enjoyment or the ownership of it.

Let us keep in mind that according to the ideas of ancient generations, the right to have a god and to pray was hereditary. The sacred tradition, the rites, the sacramental words, the powerful formulas which determined the gods to act—all this was transmitted only with the blood. It was therefore very natural that in each of these ancient families, the free person who was really descended from the first ancestor, was alone in possession of the sacerdotal character. The Patricians or Eupatrids had the privilege of being priests, and of having a religion that belonged to them alone.

Thus, even before men left the family state, there existed a distinction of classes; the old domestic religion had established ranks. Afterwards, when the city was formed, nothing was changed in the inner constitution of the family. We have already shown that originally the city was not an association of individuals, but a confederation of tribes, curies, and families, and that in this sort of alliance each of these bodies remained what it had been before. The chiefs of these little groups united with each other, but each remained master in the little society of which he was already chief. This explains why the Roman law so long left to the *pater* the absolute authority over his family, and the control of and the right of judging his clients. The distinction of classes, born in the family, was continued therefore in the city.

The city in its first age was no more than an alliance of the heads of families. There are numerous evidences of a time when they alone were citizens. This rule was kept up at Sparta, where the younger sons had no political rights. We may still see vestiges of it in an ancient law of Athens, which declared that to be a citizen one must have a domestic god. Aristotle remarks that anciently, in many cities, it was the rule that the son was not a citizen during the life of his father, and that, the father being dead, the oldest son alone enjoyed political rights. The law then counted in the city neither the younger branches of the family, nor, for still stronger reason, the clients. Aristotle also adds that the real citizens were at that time very few.

We must not picture to ourselves the city of these ancient ages as an agglomeration of men living mingled together within the enclosure of the same walls. In the earliest times the city was hardly the place of habitation; it was the sanctuary where the gods of the community were; it was the fortress which defended them, and which their presence sanctified; it was the center of the association, the residence of the king and the priests, the place where justice was administered; but the people did not live there. For several generations yet men continued to live outside the city, in isolated families, that divided the soil among them. Each of these families occupied its canton, where it had its domestic sanctuary, and where it formed, under the authority of its *pater*, an indivisible group. Then, on certain days, if the interests of the city or the obligations of the common worship called, the chiefs of these families repaired to the city and assembled around the king, either to deliberate or to assist at a sacrifice. If it was a question of war, each of these chiefs arrived, followed by his family and his servants (*sua manus*): they were grouped by phratries, or curies, and formed the army of the city, under the command of the king.

THE PLEBEIANS

We must now point out another element of the population, which was below the clients themselves, and which, originally low, insensibly acquired strength enough to break the ancient social organization. This class, which became more numerous at Rome than in any other city, was there called the *plebs*. We must understand the origin and character of this class to understand the part it played in the history of the city, and of the family, among the ancients. The plebeians were not the clients; the historians of antiquity do not confound these two classes.

What constituted the peculiar character of the plebs was, that they were foreign to the religious organization of the city, and even to that of the family. By this we recognize the plebeian, and distinguish him from the client. The client shared at least in the worship of his patron, and made a part of the family and of the gens. The plebeian, at first, had no worship, and knew nothing of the sacred family.

What we have already seen of the social and religious state of ancient times explains to us how this class took its rise. Religion was not propagated; born in a family, it remained, as it were, shut in there; each family was forced to create its creed, its gods, and its worship. But there must have been, in those times, so distant from us, a great number of families in which the mind had not the power to create gods, to arrange a doctrine, to institute a worship, to invent hymns, and the rhythm of the prayer. These families naturally found themselves in a state of inferiority compared with those who had a religion, and could not make a part of society with them; they entered neither into the curies nor into the city. In the course of time it even happened that families which had a religion lost it either by negligence, forgetting the rites, or by one of those crimes which prevented a man from approaching his hearth and continuing his worship. It must have happened, also, that clients, on account of crime or bad treatment, quitted the family and renounced its religion. The son, too, who was born of a marriage in which the rites had not been performed, was reputed a bastard, like one who had been born of adultery, and the family religion did not exist for him. All these men, excluded from the family and from the worship, fell into the class of men without a sacred fire—that is to say, became plebeians.

We find this class around almost all the ancient cities, but separated by a line of demarcation. Originally a Greek city was double; there was the city, properly so called—πόλις, which was built ordinarily on the summit of some hill; it had been built with the religious rites, and enclosed the sanctuary of the national gods. At the foot of the hill was found an agglomeration of houses, which were built without any religious ceremony, and without a sacred enclosure. These were the dwellings of the plebeians, who could not live in the sacred city.

At Rome the difference between the two classes was striking. The city of the patricians and their clients was the one that Romulus founded, according to the rites, on the Palatine. The dwellings of the plebs were in the asylum, a species of enclosure situated on the slope of the Capitoline Hill, where Romulus admitted people without hearth or home, whom he could not admit into his city. Later, when new plebeians came to Rome, as they were strangers to the religion of the city, they were established on the Aventine—that is to say, without the pomœrium, or religious city.

One word characterizes these plebeians— they were without a hearth; they did not possess, in the beginning, at least, any domestic altars. Their adversaries were always reproaching them with having no ancestors, which certainly meant that they had not the worship of ancestors, and had no family tomb where they could carry their funeral repast. They had no father—*pater*; that is to say, they ascended the series of their ascendants in vain; they never arrived at a religious family chief. They had no family—*gentem non habent*; that is to say, they had only the natural family; as to the one which religion formed and constituted, they had not that.

The sacred marriage did not exist for them; they knew not its rites. Having no hearth, the union that the hearth established was forbidden to them; therefore the patricians, who knew no other regular union than that which united husband and wife in presence of the domestic divinity, could say, in speaking of the plebeians, "*Connubia promiscua habent more ferarum.*" There was no family for them, no paternal authority. They had the power over their children which strength gave them; but that sacred authority with which religion clothed the father, they had not.

For them there was no right of property; for all property was established and consecrated by a hearth, a tomb, and termini— that is to say, by all the elements of the domestic worship. If the plebeian possessed land, that land had no sacred character; it was profane, and had no boundaries. But could he hold land in the earliest times? We know that at Rome no one could exercise the right of property if he was not a citizen; and the plebeian, in the first ages of Rome, was not a citizen. According to the juris-consult, one could not be a proprietor except by quiritary right; but the plebeians were not counted at first among the Quirites. At the foundation of Rome the *ager Romanus* was divided up among the tribes, the curies, and the gentes. Now, the plebeians, who belonged to none of these groups, certainly did not share in the division. These plebeians, who had no religion, had not the qualification which enabled a man to make a portion of the soil his own. We know that they long inhabited the Aventine, and built houses there; but it was only after three centuries, and many struggles, that they finally obtained the ownership of this territory.

For the plebeians there was no law, no justice, since the law was the decision of religion, and the procedure was a body of rites. The client had the benefit of the Roman franchise through his patron; but for the plebeian this right did not exist. An ancient historian says formally that the sixth king of Rome was the first to make laws for the plebs, whilst the patricians had had theirs for a long time. It appears even that these laws were afterwards withdrawn from the plebs, or that, not being founded upon religion, the patricians refused to pay any attention to them. For we see in the historian that, when tribunes were created, a special law was required to protect their lives and liberty, and that this law was worded thus: "Let no one undertake to strike or kill a tribune as he would one of the plebs." It

seems, therefore, that any one had a right to strike or to kill a plebeian; or, at least, that this misdeed committed against a man who was beyond the pale of the law was not punished.

The plebeians had no political rights. They were not at first citizens, and no one among them could be a magistrate. For two centuries there was no other assembly at Rome than that of the curies; and the curies did not include the plebeians. The plebs did not even enter into the composition of the army so long as that was distributed by curies.

But what manifestly separated the plebeian from the patrician was, that the plebeian had no part in the religion of the city. It was impossible for him to fill the priestly office. We may even suppose that in the earliest ages prayer was forbidden him, and that the rites could not be revealed to him. It was as in India where "the Sudra should always be ignorant of the sacred formulas." He was a foreigner, and consequently his presence alone defiled the sacrifice. He was repulsed by the gods. Between him and the patrician there was all the distance that religion could place between two men. The plebs were a despised and abject class, beyond the pale of religion, law, society, and the family. The patrician could compare such an existence only with that of the brutes—*more ferarum*. The touch of the plebeian was impure. The decemvirs, in their first ten tables, had forgotten to interdict marriage between the two orders; for these first decemvirs were all patricians, and it never entered the mind of one of them that such a marriage was possible.

We see how many classes in the primitive age of the cities were superposed one above another. At the head was the aristocracy of family chiefs, those whom the official language of Rome called *patres*, whom the clients called *reges*, whom the Odyssey names βασιλεύς or ἄνακτες. Below were the younger branches of the families; still lower were the clients; and lowest were the plebs.

This distinction of classes came from religion. For at the time when the ancestors of the Greeks, the Italians, and Hindus still lived together in Central Asia, religion had said, "The oldest shall offer prayer." From this came the pre-eminence of the oldest in everything; the oldest branch in every family had been the sacerdotal and dominant branch. Still religion made great account of the younger branches, who were a species of reserve, to replace the older branch some day, if it should become extinct, and to save the worship. It also made some account of the client, and even of the slave, because they assisted in the religious acts. But the plebeian, who had no part in the worship, it reckoned as absolutely of no account. The ranks had been thus fixed.

But none of the social arrangements which man studies out and establishes is unchangeable. This carried in itself the germ of disease and death, which was too great an inequality. Many men had an interest in destroying a social organization that had no benefits for them.

NEW PRINCIPLES OF GOVERNMENT: THE PUBLIC INTEREST AND THE SUFFRAGE

The revolution which overthrew the rule of the sacerdotal class, and raised the lower class to a level with the ancient chiefs of gentes, marked a new period in the history of cities. A sort of social reconstruction was accomplished. It was not simply replacing one class of men in power by another. Old principles had been thrust aside, and new rules adopted that were to govern human societies. The new city, it is true, preserved the exterior forms of the preceding period. The republican system remained; almost everywhere the magistrates preserved their ancient names. Athens still had its archons, and Rome its consuls. Nor was anything changed in the ceremonies of the public religion; the repasts of the prytaneum, the sacrifices at the opening of the public assembly, the auspices and the prayers—all were preserved. It is quite common with man, when he rejects old institutions, to wish to preserve their exterior forms.

In reality all was changed. Neither institutions, nor laws, nor beliefs, nor manners were in this new period what they had been in the preceding. The old system disappeared, carrying with it the rigorous rules which it had established in all things; a new order of things was established, and human life changed its aspect.

During long ages religion had been the sole principle of government. Another principle had to be found capable of replacing it, and which, like it, might govern human institutions, and keep them as much as possible clear of fluctuations and conflicts. The principle upon which the governments of cities were founded thenceforth was public interest.

We must observe this new dogma which then made its appearance in the minds of men and history. Heretofore the superior rule whence social order was derived was not interest, but religion. The duty of performing the rites of worship had been the social bond. From this religious necessity were derived, for some the right to command, for others the obligation to obey. From this had come the rules of justice and of legal procedure, those of public deliberations and those of war. Cities did not ask if the institutions which they adopted were useful; these institutions were adopted because religion had wished it thus. Neither interest nor convenience had contributed to establish them. And if the sacerdotal class had tried to defend them, it was not in the name of the public interest; it was in the name of religious tradition. But in the period which we now enter, tradition no longer holds empire, and religion no longer governs. The regulating principle from which all institutions now derive their authority—the only one which is above individual wills, and which obliges them all to submit—is public interest.

. . .

The precepts of public interest are not so absolute, so clear, so manifest, as are those of religion. We may always discuss them; they are not perceived at once. The way that appeared the simplest and surest to know what the public interest demanded was to assemble the citizens, and consult them. This course was thought to be necessary, and was almost daily employed. In the preceding period the auspices had borne the chief weight of the deliberations; the opinion of the priest, of the king, of the sacred magistrate was all-powerful. Men voted little, and then rather as a formality than to express an opinion. After that time they voted on every question; the opinion of all was needed in order to know what was for the interest of all. The suffrage became the great means of government. It was the source of institutions and the rule of right; it decided what was useful and even what was just. It was above the magistrates and above the laws; it was sovereign in the city.

The nature of government was also changed. Its essential function was no longer the regular performance of religious ceremonies. It was especially constituted to maintain order and peace within and dignity and power without. What had before been of secondary importance was now of the first. Politics took precedence of religion, and the government of men became a human affair.

. . .

CHRISTIANITY CHANGES THE CONDITIONS OF GOVERNMENT

The victory of Christianity marks the end of ancient society. With the new religion this social transformation, which we saw begun six or seven centuries earlier, was completed.

With Christianity not only was the religious sentiment revived, but it assumed a higher and less material expression. Whilst previously men had made for themselves gods of the human soul, or of the great forces of nature, they now began to look upon God as really foreign by his essence, from human nature on the one hand, and from the world on the other. The divine Being was placed outside and above physical nature. Whilst previously every man had made a god for himself, and there were as many of them as there were families and cities, God now appeared as a unique, immense, universal being, alone animating the worlds, alone able to supply the need of adoration that is in man. Religion, instead of being, as formerly among the nations of Greece and Italy, little more than an assemblage of practices, a series of rites which men repeated without having any idea of them, a succession of formulas which often were no longer understood because the language had grown old, a tradition which had been transmitted from age to age, and which owed its sacred character to its antiquity alone—was now a collection of doctrines, and a great object proposed to faith. It was no longer exterior; it took up its abode especially in the thoughts of men. It was no longer matter; it became spirit. Christianity changed the nature and the form of adoration. Man no longer offered God food and drink. Prayer was no longer a form of incantation; it was an act of faith and a humble petition. The soul sustained another relation with the divinity; the fear of the gods was replaced by the love of God.

Christianity introduced other new ideas. It was not the domestic religion of any family, the national religion of any city, or of any race. It belonged neither to a caste nor to a corporation. From its first appearance it called to itself the whole human race. Christ said to his disciples, "Go ye into all the world, and preach the gospel to every creature."

In all this there was something new. For, everywhere, in the first ages of humanity, the divinity had been imagined as attaching himself especially to one race. The Jews had believed in the God of the Jews; the Athenians in the Athenian Pallas; the Romans in Jupiter Capitolinus. The right to practise a worship had been a privilege.

For this God there were no longer strangers. The stranger no longer profaned the temple, no longer tainted the sacrifice by his presence. The temple was open to all who believed in God. The priesthood ceased to be hereditary, because religion was no longer a patrimony. The worship was no longer kept secret; the rites, the prayers, the dogmas were no longer concealed. On the contrary, there was thenceforth religious instruction, which was not only given, but which was offered, which was carried to those who were the farthest away, and which sought out the most indifferent. The spirit of propagandism replaced the law of exclusion.

From this great consequences flowed, as well for the relations between nations as for the government of states.

Thus, by the single fact that the family no longer had its domestic religion, its constitution and its laws were transformed; so, too, from the single fact that the state no longer had its official religion, the rules for the government of men were forever changed.

Our study must end at this limit, which separates ancient from modern politics. We have written the history of a belief. It was established, and human society was constituted. It was modified, and society underwent a series of revolutions. It disappeared, and society changed its character. Such was the law of ancient times.

Bronislaw Malinowski

THE ROLE OF
MAGIC AND RELIGION

Few writers in modern times have written as lucidly and with as much firsthand field experience on the subject of magic and religion as has Bronislaw Malinowski. His classic paper on the subject is "Magic, Science, and Religion," which was first published in James Needham (ed.), *Science, Religion and Reality*, in 1925. But since this famous paper was reprinted by the Free Press in a book by the same name in 1948, and then in 1954 became available in a Doubleday Anchor Book edition, we are presenting a briefer statement of most of the same theoretical ground drawn from his article, "Culture," which appeared in the *Encyclopedia of the Social Sciences*. For a more detailed version of the argument, the reader may turn to the readily available Anchor Book entitled *Magic, Science, and Religion*.

To understand Malinowski's thesis that every society, even the most primitive, has perfectly sound empirical knowledge to carry out many of its practical activities; that "magic is to be expected and generally to be found whenever man comes to an unbridgeable gap, a hiatus in his knowledge or in his powers of practical control, and yet has to continue in his pursuit"; and that "religion is not born out of speculation or reflection, still less out of illusion or misapprehension, but rather out of the real tragedies of human life, out of the conflict between human plans and realities," one has to understand some of the thinking that was current about primitive religion at the time he wrote. Tylor had made primitive man into a kind of rational philosopher who tried to find answers to such problems as the difference between the living and the dead, and had developed the belief in animistic spirits which he regarded as the basis for primitive religion; Frazer had been concerned with showing that magic was a kind of "false science" and that an age of magic preceded an age of religion; Lévy-Bruhl had been engaging in brilliant speculations concerning the prelogical and mystical character of primitive thought. Into this cluster of ideas Malinowski brought some new insights—insights that were based for the first time on extensive, firsthand field experience. He was able to invite his readers "to step outside the closed study of the theorist into the open air of the Anthropological field," in this case the Trobriand Islands.

In addition to clarifying the relationships among magic, science, and religion, Malinowski clearly showed that the myths of primitive peoples also have important functions in social life. Thus he writes in the following article that "the function of myth is to strengthen tradition and to endow it with a greater value and prestige by tracing it back to a higher, better, more supernatural and more effective reality of initial events." For a more detailed version of his thesis on myths, and his classification of the oral literature into myths, legends, and folk tales, the reader may turn to his book *Myth in Primitive Psychology* (1926), which is also reprinted in the Anchor Book edition of *Magic, Science, and Religion*.

Excerpted from "Culture" by Bronislaw Malinowski. Reprinted with permission of the publisher from *Encyclopedia of the Social Sciences*, Seligman and Johnson, editors. Volume IV, 634–642. Copyright 1931 by The Macmillan Company, renewed 1959 by The Macmillan Company.

In spite of the various theories about a specific non-empirical and prelogical character of primitive mentality there can be no doubt that as soon as man developed the mastery of environment by the use of implements, and as soon as language came into being, there must also have existed primitive knowledge of an essentially scientific character. No culture could survive if its arts and crafts, its weapons and economic pursuits were based on mystical, non-empirical conceptions and doctrines. When human culture is approached from the pragmatic, technological side, it is found that primitive man is capable of exact observation, of sound generalizations and of logical reasoning in all those matters which affect his normal activities and are at the basis of his production. Knowledge is then an absolute derived necessity of culture. It is more, however, than a means to an end, and it was not classed therefore with the instrumental imperatives. Its place in culture, its function, is slightly different from that of production, of law, or of education. Systems of knowledge serve to connect various types of behavior; they carry over the results of past experiences into future enterprise and they bring together elements of human experience and allow man to co-ordinate and integrate his activities. Knowledge is a mental attitude, a diathesis of the nervous system, which allows man to carry on the work which culture makes him do. Its function is to organize and integrate the indispensable activities of culture.

The material embodiment of knowledge consists in the body of arts and crafts, of technical processes and rules of craftsmanship. More specifically, in most primitive cultures and certainly in higher ones there are special implements of knowledge—diagrams, topographical models, measures, aids to orientation or to counting.

The connection between native thought and language opens important problems of function. Linguistic abstraction, categories of space, time and relationship, and logical means of expressing the concatenation of ideas are extremely important matters, and the study of how thought works through language in any culture is still a virgin field of cultural linguistics. How primitive language works, where it is embodied, how it is related to social organization, to primitive religion and magic, are important problems of functional anthropology.

By the very forethought and foresight which it gives, the integrative function of knowledge creates new needs, that is, imposes new imperatives. Knowledge gives man the possibility of planning ahead, of embracing vast spaces of time and distance; it allows a wide range to his hopes and desires. But however much knowledge and science help man in allowing him to obtain what he wants, they are unable completely to control change, to eliminate accidents, to foresee the unexpected turn of natural events, or to make human handiwork reliable and adequate to all practical requirements. In this field, much more practical, definite, and circumscribed than that of religion, there develops a special type of ritual activities which anthropology labels collectively as magic.

The most hazardous of all human enterprises known to primitive man is sailing. In the preparation of his sailing craft and the laying out of his plans the savage turns to his science. The painstaking work as well as the intelligently organized labor in construction and in navigation bears witness to the savage's trust in science and submission to it. But adverse wind or no wind at all, rough weather, currents and reefs are always liable to upset his best plans and most careful preparations. He must admit that neither his knowledge nor his most painstaking efforts are a guaranty of success. Something unaccountable usually enters and baffles his anticipations. But although unaccountable it yet appears to have a deep meaning, to act or behave with a purpose. The sequence, the significant concatenation of events, seems to contain some inner logical consistency. Man feels that he can do something to wrestle with that mysterious element or force, to help and abet his luck. There are therefore always systems of superstition, of more or less developed ritual, associated with sailing, and in primitive communities the magic of sailing craft is highly developed. Those who are well acquainted with some good magic have, in virtue of that, courage and confidence. When the canoes are used for fishing, the accidents and the good or bad luck may refer not only to transport but also to the appearance of fish and to the conditions under which they are caught. In trading, whether overseas or with near neighbors, chance may favor or thwart the ends and desires of man. As a result both fishing and trading magic are very well developed.

Likewise in war, man, however primitive, knows that well-made weapons of attack and defense, strategy, the force of numbers, and the strength of the individuals ensure victory. Yet with all this the unforeseen and accidental help even the weaker to victory when the fray happens under the cover of night, when ambushes are possible, when the conditions of the encounter obviously favor one side at the expense of the other. Magic is used as something which over and above man's equipment and his force helps him to master accident and to ensnare luck. In love also a mysterious, unaccountable quality of success or else a predestination to failure seems to be accompanied by some force independent of ostensible attraction and of the best laid plans and arrangements. Magic enters to insure something which counts over and above the visible and accountable qualifications.

Primitive man depends on his economic pursuits for his welfare in a manner which makes him realize bad luck very painfully and directly. Among people who rely on their fields or gardens what might be called agricultural knowledge is invariably well developed. The natives know the properties of the soil, the need of a thorough clearing from bush and weed, fertilizing with ashes and appropriate planting. But however well chosen the site and well worked the gardens, mishaps occur. Drought or deluge coming at most inappropriate seasons destroys the crops altogether, or some blights, insects, or wild animals diminish them. Or some other year, when man is conscious that he deserves but a poor crop, everything runs so smoothly and prosperously that an unexpectedly good return rewards the undeserving gardener. The dreaded elements of rain and sunshine, pests and fertility seem to be controlled by a force which is beyond ordinary human experience and knowledge, and man repairs once more to magic.

In all these examples the same factors are involved. Experience and logic teach man that within definite limits knowledge is supreme; but beyond them nothing can be done by rationally founded practical exertions. Yet he rebels against inaction because although he realizes his impotence he is yet driven to action by intense desire and strong emotions. Nor is inaction at all possible. Once he has embarked on a distant voyage or finds himself in the middle of a fray or halfway through the cycle of garden growing, the native tries to make his frail canoe more seaworthy by charms or to drive away locusts and wild animals by ritual or to vanquish his enemies by dancing.

Magic changes its forms; it shifts its ground; but it exists everywhere. In modern societies magic is associated with the third cigarette lit by the same match, with spilled salt and the need of throwing it over the left shoulder, with broken mirrors, with passing under a ladder, with the new moon seen through glass or on the left hand, with the number thirteen or with Friday. These are minor superstitions which seem merely to vegetate among the intelligentsia of the western world. But these superstitions and much more developed systems also persist tenaciously and are given serious consideration among modern urban populations. Black magic is practiced in the slums of London by the classical method of destroying

the picture of the enemy. At marriage ceremonies good luck for the married couple is obtained by the strictest observance of several magical methods such as the throwing of the slipper and the spilling of rice. Among the peasants of central and eastern Europe elaborate magic still flourishes and children are treated by witches and warlocks. People are thought to have the power to prevent cows from giving milk, to induce cattle to multiply unduly, to produce rain and sunshine and to make people love or hate each other. The saints of the Roman Catholic Church become in popular practice passive accomplices of magic. They are beaten, cajoled and carried about. They can give rain by being placed in the field, stop flows of lava by confronting them and stop the progress of a disease, of a blight or of a plague of insects. The crude practical use made of certain religious rituals or objects makes their function magical. For magic is distinguished from religion in that the latter creates values and attains ends directly, whereas magic consists of acts which have a practical utilitarian value and are effective only as a means to an end. Thus a strictly utilitarian subject matter or issue of an act and its direct, instrumental function make it magic, and most modern established religions harbor within their ritual and even their ethics a good deal which really belongs to magic. But modern magic survives not only in the forms of minor superstitions or within the body of religious systems. Wherever there is danger, uncertainty, great incidence of chance and accident, even in entirely modern forms of enterprise, magic crops up. The gambler at Monte Carlo, on the turf, or in a continental state lottery develops systems. Motoring and modern sailing demand mascots and develop superstitions. Around every sensational sea tragedy there has formed a myth showing some mysterious magical indications or giving magical reasons for the catastrophe. Aviation is developing its superstitions and magic. Many pilots refuse to take up a passenger who is wearing anything green, to start a journey on a Friday, or to light three cigarettes with a match when in the air, and their sensitiveness to superstition seems to increase with altitude. In all large cities of Europe and America magic can be purchased from palmists, clairvoyants, and other soothsayers, who forecast the future, give practical advice as to lucky conduct, and retail ritual apparatus such as amulets, mascots, and talismans. The richest domain of magic, however, is, in civilization as in savagery, that of health. Here again the old venerable religions lend themselves readily to magic. Roman Catholicism opens its sacred shrines and places of worship to the ailing pilgrim, and faith healing flourishes also in other churches. The main function of Christian Science is the thinking away of illness and decay; its metaphysics are very strongly pragmatic and utilitarian and its ritual is essentially a means to the end of health and happiness. The unlimited range of universal remedies and blessings, osteopathy and chiropractic, dietetics and curing by sun, cold water, grape or lemon juice, raw food, starvation, alcohol or its prohibition —one and all shade invariably into magic. Intellectuals still submit to Coué and Freud, to Jaeger and Kneipp, to sun worship, either direct or through the mercury-vapor lamp—not to mention the bedside manner of the highly paid specialist. It is very difficult to discover where common sense ends and where magic begins.

The savage is not more rational than modern man nor is he more superstitious. He is more limited, less liable to free imaginings and to the confidence trick of new inventions. His magic is traditional and he has his stronghold of knowledge, his empirical and rational tradition of science. Since the superstitious or prelogical character of primitive man has been so much emphasized, it is necessary to draw clearly the dividing line between primitive science and magic. There are domains on which magic never encroaches. The making of fire, basketry, the actual production of stone implements, the making of strings or mats, cooking and all minor domestic activities although extremely important are never associated with magic. Some of them become the center of religious practices and of mythology, as, for example, fire or cooking or stone implements; but magic is never connected with their production. The reason is that ordinary skill guided by sound knowledge is sufficient to set man on the right path and to give him certainty of correct and complete control of these activities.

In some pursuits magic is used under certain conditions and is absent under others. In a maritime community depending on the products of the sea there is never magic connected with the collecting of shellfish or with fishing by poison, weirs, and fish traps, so long as these are completely reliable. On the other hand, any dangerous, hazardous, and uncertain type of fishing is surrounded by ritual. In hunting, the simple and reliable ways of trapping or killing are controlled by knowledge and skill alone; but let there be any danger or any uncertainty connected with an important supply of game and magic immediately appears. Coastal sailing as long as it is perfectly safe and easy commands no magic. Overseas expeditions are invariably bound up with ceremonies and ritual. Man resorts to magic only where chance and circumstances are not fully controlled by knowledge.

This is best seen in what might be called systems of magic. Magic may be but loosely and capriciously connected with its practical setting. One hunter may use certain formulae and rites, and another ignore them; or the same man may apply his conjurings on one occasion and not on another. But there are forms of enterprise in which magic must be used. In a big tribal adventure, such as war, or a hazardous sailing expedition or seasonal travel or an undertaking such as a big hunt or a perilous fishing expedition or the normal round of gardening, which as a rule is vital to the whole community, magic is often obligatory. It runs in a fixed sequence concatenated with the practical events, and the two orders, magical and practical, depend on one another and form a system. Such systems of magic appear at first sight an inextricable mixture of efficient work and superstitious practices and so seem to provide an unanswerable argument in favor of the theories that magic and science are under primitive conditions so fused as not to be separable. Fuller analysis, however, shows that magic and practical work are entirely independent and never fuse.

But magic is never used to replace work. In gardening the digging or the clearing of the ground or the strength of the fences or quality of the supports is never scamped because stronger magic has been used over them. The native knows well that mechanical construction must be produced by human labor according to strict rules of craft. He knows that all the processes which have been in the soil can be controlled by human effort to a certain extent but not beyond, and it is only this beyond which he tries to influence by magic. For his experience and his reason tell him that in certain matters his efforts and his intelligence are of no avail whatever. On the other hand, magic has been known to help; so at least his tradition tells him.

In the magic of war and of love, of trading expeditions and of fishing, of sailing and of canoe making, the rules of experience and logic are likewise strictly adhered to as regards technique, and knowledge and technique received due credit in all the good results which can be attributed to them. It is only the unaccountable results, which an outside observer would attribute to luck, to the knack of doing things successfully, to chance or to fortune, that the savage attempts to control by magic.

Magic therefore, far from being primitive science, is the outgrowth of clear recognition that science has its limits and that a human mind and human skill are at times impotent. For all its appearances of megalomania, for all that it seems to be the declaration of the "omnipotence of thought," as it has recently been defined by Freud, magic has greater affinity with an emotional outburst, with daydreaming, with strong, unrealizable desire.

To affirm with Frazer that magic is a psuedo-science would be to recognize that magic is not really primitive science. It would imply that magic has an affinity with science or at least that it is the raw material out of which science develops—implications which are untenable. The ritual of magic shows certain striking characteristics which have made it quite plausible for most writers from Grimm and Tylor to Freud and Lévy-Bruhl to affirm that magic takes the place of primitive science.

Magic unquestionably is dominated by the sympathetic principle: like produces like; the whole is affected if the sorcerer acts on a part of it; occult influences can be imparted by contagion. If one concentrates on the form of the ritual only, he can legitimately conclude with Frazer that the analogy between the magical and the scientific conceptions of the world is close and that the various cases of sympathetic magic are mistaken applications of one or the other of two great fundamental laws of thought, namely, the association of ideas by similarity and the association of ideas by contiguity in space or time.

But a study of the function of science and the function of magic casts a doubt on the sufficiency of these conclusions. Sympathy is not the basis of pragmatic science, even under the most primitive conditions. The savage knows scientifically that a small pointed stick of hard wood rubbed or drilled against a piece of soft, brittle wood, provided they are both dry, gives fire. He also knows that strong, energetic, increasingly swift motion has to be employed, that tinder must be produced in the action, the wind kept off, and the spark fanned immediately into a glow and this into a flame. There is no sympathy, no similarity, no taking the part instead of the legitimate whole, no contagion. The only association or connection is the empirical, correctly observed and correctly framed concatenation of natural events. The savage knows that a strong bow well handled releases a swift arrow, that a broad beam makes for stability and a light, well-shaped hull for swiftness in his canoe. There is here no association of ideas by similarity or contagion or *pars pro toto*. The native puts a yam or a banana sprout into an appropriate piece of ground. He waters or irrigates it unless it be well drenched by rain. He weeds the ground round it, and he knows quite well that barring unexpected calamities the plant will grow. Again there is no principle akin to that of sympathy contained in this activity. He creates conditions which are perfectly scientific and rational and lets nature do its work. Therefore in so far as magic consists in the enactment of sympathy, in so far as it is governed by an association of ideas, it radically differs from science; and on analysis the similarity of form between magic and science is revealed as merely apparent, not real.

The sympathetic rite although a very prominent element in magic functions always in the context of other elements. Its main purpose always consists in the generation and transference of magical force and accordingly it is performed in the atmosphere of the supernatural. As Hubert and Mauss have shown, acts of magic are always set apart, regarded as different, conceived and carried out under distinct conditions. The time when magic is performed is often determined by tradition rather than by the sympathetic principle, and the place where it is performed is only partly determined by sympathy or contagion and more by supernatural and mythological associations. Many of the substances used in magic are largely sympathetic but they are often used primarily for the physiological and emotional reaction which they elicit in man. The dramatic emotional elements in ritual enactment incorporate, in magic, factors which go far beyond sympathy or any scientific or pseudo-scientific principle. Mythology and tradition are everywhere embedded, especially in the performance of the magical spell, which must be repeated with absolute faithfulness to the traditional original and during which mythological events are recounted in which the power of the prototype is invoked. The supernatural character of magic is also expressed in the abnormal character of the magician and by the temporary taboos which surround its execution.

In brief, there exists a sympathetic principle: the ritual of magic contains usually some reference to the results to be achieved; it foreshadows them, anticipates the desired events. The magician is haunted by imagery, by symbolism, by associations of the result to follow. But he is quite as definitely haunted by the emotional obsession of the situation which has forced him to resort to magic. These facts do not fit into the simple scheme of sympathy conceived as misapplication of crude observations and half-logical deductions. The various apparently disjointed elements of magical ritual—the dramatic features, the emotional side, the mythological allusions, and the anticipation of the end—make it impossible to consider magic a sober scientific practice based on an empirical theory. Nor can magic be guided by experience and at the same time be constantly harking back to myth.

The fixed time, the determined spot, the preliminary isolating conditions of magic, the taboos to be observed by the performer, as well as his physiological and sociological nature, place the magical act in an atmosphere of the supernatural. Within this context of the supernatural the rite consists, functionally speaking, in the production of a specific virtue or force and of the launching, directing, or impelling of this force to the desired object. The production of magical force takes place by spell, manual and bodily gesticulation, and the proper condition of the officiating magician. All these elements exhibit a tendency to a formal assimilation toward the desired end or toward the ordinary means of producing this end. This formal resemblance is probably best defined in the statement that the whole ritual is dominated by the emotions of hate, fear, anger, or erotic passion, or by the desire to obtain a definite practical end.

The magical force or virtue is not conceived as a natural force. Hence the theories propounded by Preuss, Marett, and Hubert and Mauss, which would make the Melanesian mana or the similar North American concepts the clue to the understanding of all magic, are not satisfactory. The mana concept embraces personal power, natural force, excellence and efficiency alongside the specific virtue of magic. It is a force regarded as absolutely *sui generis*, different either from natural forces or from the normal faculties of man.

The force of magic can be produced only and exclusively within traditionally prescribed rites. It can be received and learned only by due initiation into the craft and by the taking over of the rigidly defined system of conditions, acts, and observances. Even when magic is discovered or invented it is invariably conceived as true revelation from the supernatural. Magic is an intrinsic, specific quality of a situation and of an object or phenomenon within the situation, consisting in the object being amenable to human control by means which are specifically and uniquely connected with the object and which can be handled only by appropriate people. Magic therefore is always conceived as something which does not reside in nature, that is, outside man, but in the relation between man and nature. Only those objects and forces in nature which are very important to man, on which he depends and which he cannot yet normally control elicit magic.

A functional explanation of magic may be stated in terms of individual psychology and of the cultural and social value of magic. Magic is to be expected and generally to be found whenever man comes to an unbridgeable gap, a hiatus in his knowledge or in his powers of practical control, and yet has to continue in his pursuit. Forsaken by his knowledge, baffled by the results of his experience, unable to apply any effective technical skill, he realizes his impotence. Yet his desire grips him only the more strongly. His fears and hopes, his general anxiety, produce a state of unstable equilibrium in his organism, by which he is driven to some sort of vicarious activity. In the natural human reaction to frustrated hate and impotent anger is found the *materia prima* of black magic. Unrequited love provokes spontaneous acts of prototype magic. Fear moves every human being to aimless but compulsory acts; in the presence of an ordeal one always has recourse to obsessive daydreaming.

The natural flow of ideas under the influence of emotions and desires thwarted in their full practical satisfaction leads one inevitably to the anticipation of the positive results. But the experience upon which this anticipatory or sympathetic attitude rests is not the ordinary experience of science. It is much more akin to daydreaming, to what the psychoanalysts call wish fulfillment. When the emotional state reaches the breaking point at which man loses control over himself, the words which he utters, the gestures to which he gives way, and the physiological processes within his organism which accompany all this allow the pent-up tension to flow over. Over all such outbursts of emotion, over such acts of prototype magic, there presides the obsessive image of the desired end. The substitute action in which the physiological crisis finds its expression has a subjective value: the desired end seems nearer satisfaction.

Standardized, traditional magic is nothing else but an institution which fixes, organizes and imposes upon the members of a society the positive solution in those inevitable conflicts which arise out of human impotence in dealing with all hazardous issues by mere knowledge and technical ability. The spontaneous, natural reaction of man to such situations supplies the raw material of magic. This raw material implies the sympathetic principle in that man has to dwell both on the desired end and on the best means of obtaining it. The expression of emotions in verbal utterances, in gestures, in an almost mystical belief that such words and gestures have a power, crops up naturally as a normal, physiological reaction. The elements which do not exist in the *materia prima* of magic but are to be found in the developed systems are the traditional, mythological elements. Human culture everywhere integrates a raw material of human interests and pursuits into standardized, traditional customs. In all human tradition a definite choice is made from within a variety of possibilities. In magic also the raw material supplies a number of possible ways of behavior. Tradition chooses from among them, fixes a special type and endues it with a hallmark of social value.

Tradition also reinforces the belief in magical efficacy by the context of special experience. Magic is so deeply believed in because its pragmatic truth is vouched for by its psychological or even physiological efficacy, since in its form and in its ideology and structure magic corresponds to the natural processes of the human organism. The conviction which is implied in these processes extends obviously to standardized magic. This conviction is useful because it raises the efficiency of the person who submits to it. Magic possesses therefore a functional truth or a pragmatic truth, since it arises always under conditions where the human organism is disintegrated. Magic corresponds to a real physiological need.

The seal of social approval given to the standardized reactions, selected traditionally out of the raw material of magic, gives it an additional backing. The general conviction that this and only this rite, spell or personal preparation enables the magician to control chance makes every individual believe in it through the ordinary mechanism of molding or conditioning. The public enactment of certain ceremonies, on the one hand, and the secrecy and esoteric atmosphere in which others are shrouded add again to their credibility. The fact also that magic usually is associated with intelligence and strong personality raises its credit in the eyes of any community. Thus a conviction that man can control by a special, traditional, standardized handling the forces of nature and human beings is not merely subjectively true through its physiological foundations, not merely pragmatically true in that it contributes to the reintegration of the individual, but it carries an additional evidence due to its sociological function.

Magic serves not only as an integrative force to the individual but also as an organizing force to society. The fact that the magician by the nature of his secret and esoteric lore has also the control of the associated practical activities causes him usually to be a person of the greatest importance in the community. The discovery of this was one of the great contributions of Frazer to anthropology. Magic, however, is of social importance not only because it gives power and thus raises a man to a high position. It is a real organizing force. In Australia the constitution of the tribe, of the clan, of the local group, is based on a system of totemic ideas. The main ceremonial expression of this system consists in the rites of magical multiplication of plants and animals and in the ceremonies of initiation into manhood. Both of these rites underlie the tribal framework and they are both the expression of a magical order of ideas based on totemic mythology. The leaders who arrange the tribal meetings, who conduct them, who direct the initiation and are the protagonists in dramatic representations of myth and in the public magical ceremonies, play this part because of their traditional magical filiation. The totemic magic of these tribes is their main organizing system.

To a large extent this is also true of the Papuan tribes of New Guinea, of the Melanesians and of the people of the Indonesian archipelagoes, where magical rites and ideas definitely supply the organizing principle in practical activities. The secret societies of the Bismarck Archipelago and West Africa, the rain makers of the Sudan, the medicine men of the North American Indians—all combine magical power with political and economic influence. Sufficient details to assess the extent and the mechanism by which magic enters and controls secular and ordinary life are often lacking. But among the Masai or Nandi in East Africa the evidence reveals that the military organization of the tribe is associated with war magic and that the guidance in political affairs and general tribal concerns depends on rain magic. In New Guinea garden magic, overseas trading expeditions, fishing and hunting on a big scale show that the ceremonial significance of magic supplies the moral and legal framework by which all practical activities are held together.

Sorcery in its major forms is usually specialized and institutionalized; that is, either the sorcerer is a professional whose services can be bought or commanded or sorcery is vested in a secret society or special organization. In all cases sorcery is either in the same hands as political power, prestige and wealth or else it can be purchased or demanded by those who can afford to do so. Sorcery thus is invariably a conservative force used at times for intimidation but usually for the enforcement of customary law or of the wishes of those in power. It is always a safeguard for the vested interests, for the organized, established privileges. The sorcerer who has behind him the chief or a powerful secret society can make his art felt more poignantly than if he were working against them or on his own.

The individual and sociological function of magic is thus made more efficient by the very mechanisms through which it works. In this and in the subjective aspect of the calculus of probability, which makes success overshadow failure, while failure again can be explained by countermagic, it is clear that the belief is not so ill founded nor due to such extravagant superstitiousness of the primitive mind as might at first appear. A strong belief in magic finds its public expression in the running mythology of magical miracles which is always found in company with all important types of magic. The competitive boasting of one community against another, the fame of outstanding magical success, the conviction that extraordinary good luck has probably been due to magic, create an ever nascent tradition which always surrounds famous magicians or famous systems of magic with a halo of supernatural reputation. This running tradition usually culminates retrospectively in a primeval myth, which gives the charter and credentials to the whole magical system. Myth of magic is definitely a warrant of its truth, a pedigree of its filiation, a charter of its claims to validity.

This is true not only of magical mythology. Myth in general is not an idle speculation about the origins of things or institutions. Nor is it the outcome of the contemplation of nature and rhapsodical interpretation of its laws. The function of myth is neither explanatory nor symbolic. It is the statement of an extraordinary event, the occurrence of which once for all had established the social order of a tribe or some of its economic pursuits, its arts and crafts or its religious or magical beliefs and ceremonies. Myth is not simply a piece of attractive fiction which is kept alive by the literary interest in the story. It is a statement of primeval reality which lives in the institutions and pursuits of a community. It justifies by precedent the existing order and it supplies a retrospective pattern of moral values, of sociological discriminations and burdens and of magical belief. In this consists its main cultural function. For all its similarity of form myth is neither a mere tale or prototype of literature or of science nor a branch of art or history nor an explanatory pseudo-theory. It fulfills a function *sui generis* closely connected with the nature of tradition and belief, with the continuity of culture, with the relation between age and youth and with the human attitude toward the past. The function of myth is to strengthen tradition and to endow it with a greater value and prestige by tracing it back to a higher, better, more supernatural and more effective reality of initial events.

The place of religion must be considered in the scheme of culture as a complex satisfaction of highly derived needs. The various theories of religion ascribe it to either a religious "instinct" or a specific religious sense (McDougall, Hauer) or else explain it as a primitive theory of animism (Tylor) or pre-animism (Marett) or ascribe it to the emotions of fear (Wundt) or to aesthetic raptures and lapses of speech (Max Müller) or the self-revelation of society (Durkheim). These theories make religion something superimposed on the whole structure of human culture, satisfying some needs perhaps, but needs which are entirely autonomous and have nothing to do with the hard-worked reality of human existence. Religion, however, can be shown to be intrinsically although indirectly connected with man's fundamental, that is, biological, needs. Like magic it comes from the curse of forethought and imagination, which fall on man once he rises above brute animal nature. Here there enter even wider issues of personal and social integration than those arising out of the practical necessity of hazardous action and dangerous enterprise. A whole range of anxieties, forebodings and problems concerning human destinies and man's place in the universe opens up once man begins to act in common not only with his fellow citizens but also with the past and future generations. Religion is not born out of speculation or reflection, still less out of illusion or misapprehension, but rather out of the real tragedies of human life, out of the conflict between human plans and realities.

Culture entails deep changes in man's personality; among other things it makes man surrender some of his self-love and self-seeking. For human relations do not rest merely or even mainly on constraint coming from without. Men can only work with and for one another by the moral forces which grow out of personal attachments and loyalties. These are primarily formed in the processes of parenthood and kinship but become inevitably widened and enriched. The love of parents for children and of children for their parents, that between husband and wife and between brothers and sisters, serve as prototypes and also as a nucleus for the loyalties of clanship, of neighborly feeling, and of

tribal citizenship. Co-operation and mutual assistance are based, in savage and civilized societies, on permanent sentiments.

The existence of strong personal attachments and the fact of death, which of all human events is the most upsetting and disorganizing to man's calculations, are perhaps the main sources of religious belief. The affirmation that death is not real, that man has a soul and that this is immortal, arises out of a deep need to deny personal destruction, a need which is not a pyschological instinct but is determined by culture, by co-operation and by the growth of human sentiments. To the individual who faces death the belief in immortality and the ritual of extreme unction, or last comforts (which in one form or another is almost universal), confirm his hope that there is a hereafter, that it is perhaps not worse than the present life and may be better. Thus the ritual before death confirms the emotional outlook which a dying man has come to need in his supreme conflict. After death the bereaved are thrown into a chaos of emotion, which might become dangerous to each of them individually and to the community as a whole were it not for the ritual of mortuary duties. The religious rites of wake and burial—all the assistance given to the departed soul—are acts expressing the dogma of continuity after death and of communion between dead and living. Any survivor who has gone through a number of mortuary ceremonials for others becomes prepared for his own death. The belief in immortality, which he has lived through ritually and practiced in the case of his mother or father, of his brothers and friends, makes him cherish more firmly the belief in his own future life. The belief in human immortality therefore, which is the foundation of ancestor worship, of domestic cults, or mortuary ritual and of animism, grows out of the constitution of human society.

Most of the other forms of religion when analyzed in their functional character correspond to deep although derived needs of the individual and of the community. Totemism, for example, when related to its wider setting affirms the existence of an intimate kinship between man and his surrounding world. The ritual side of totemism and nature worship consists to a large extent in rites of multiplication or of propitiation of animals or in rites of enhancing the fertility of vegetable nature which also establish links between man and his environment. Primitive religion is largely concerned with the sacralization of the crises of human life. Conception, birth, puberty, marriage, as well as the supreme crisis death, all give rise to sacramental acts. The fact of conception is surrounded by such beliefs as that in reincarnation, spirit entry and magical impregnation. At birth a wealth of animistic ideas concerning the formation of the human soul, the value of the individual to his community, the development of his moral powers, the possibility of forecasting his fate, become associated with and expressed in birth ritual. Initiation ceremonies, prevalent in puberty, have a developed mythological and dogmatic context. Guardian spirits, tutelary divinities, culture heroes, or a tribal All-Father are associated with initiation ceremonies. The contractual sacraments, such as marriage, entry into an age grade, or acceptance into a magical or religious fraternity, entail primarily ethical views but very often are also the expression of myths and dogmas.

Every important crisis of human life implies a strong emotional upheaval, mental conflict and possible disintegration. The hopes of a favorable issue have to struggle with anxieties and forebodings. Religious belief consists in the traditional standardization of the positive side in the mental conflict and therefore satisfies a definite individual need arising out of the psychological concomitants of social organization. On the other hand, religious belief and ritual, by making the critical acts and the social contracts of human life public, traditionally standardized, and subject to supernatural sanctions, strengthen the bonds of human cohesion.

Religion in its ethics sanctifies human life and conduct and becomes perhaps the most powerful force of social control. In its dogmatics it supplies man with strong cohesive forces. It grows out of every culture, because knowledge which gives foresight fails to overcome fate; because lifelong bonds of cooperation and mutual interest create sentiments, and sentiments rebel against death and dissolution. The cultural call for religion is highly derived and indirect but is finally rooted in the way in which the primary needs of man are satisfied in culture.

A. R. Radcliffe-Brown

TABOO

Another anthropological scholar whose writings on the function of religion in primitive society have been of major significance is Radcliffe-Brown. His three most important works on this subject are portions of his book, *The Andaman Islanders* (1922), his Frazer Lecture, *Taboo* (which is herewith reprinted), and a later paper, "Religion and Society" (1945).

Radcliffe-Brown's central thesis, that religious and magical rituals exist and persist because they are part of the mechanism by which society maintains itself in existence by establishing certain fundamental social values, should be understood in the wider context of his contributions toward the concepts and methods needed to pursue a systematic comparative study of societies, and especially of his thinking about the concept of "function." His series of papers reprinted in *Structure and Function in Primitive Society* (1952) are particularly useful.

In this paper on taboo Radcliffe-Brown begins by discussing the nature of one of the classic ideas in the primitive religions of Polynesia, but goes on to expound his thoughts on ritual and ritual values and their relationship to the essential constitution of a society. He reaches the conclusion that "the primary basis of ritual is the attribution of ritual value to objects and occasions which are

Reprinted from A. R. Radcliffe-Brown, *Taboo* ("The Frazer Lecture," 1939). Cambridge: At the University Press, 1939. Reprinted by permission of Professor E. E. Evans-Pritchard, literary executor of the late Professor Radcliffe-Brown.

either themselves objects of important common interests linking together the persons of a community or are symbolically representative of such objects." He then argues that men are more likely to experience concern and anxiety when a customary ritual is not performed than they are to turn to ritual procedures when they feel anxious.

The purpose of this lecture, which you have done me the honor of inviting me to deliver, is to commemorate the work of Sir James Frazer, as an example of lifelong, single-minded devotion to scientific investigation and as having contributed, in as large a measure as that of any man, to laying the foundations of the science of social anthropology. It therefore seems to me appropriate to select as the subject of my discourse one which Sir James was the first to investigate systematically half a century ago, when he wrote the article on "Taboo" for the ninth edition of the *Encyclopaedia Britannica*, and to the elucidation of which he has made many successive contributions in his writings since that time.

The English word "taboo" is derived from the Polynesian word "tabu" (with the accent on the first syllable). In the languages of Polynesia the word means simply "to forbid," "forbidden," and can be applied to any sort of prohibition. A rule of etiquette, an order issued by a chief, an injunction to children not to meddle with the possessions of their elders, may all be expressed by the use of the word "tabu."

The early voyagers in Polynesia adopted the word to refer to prohibitions of a special kind, which may be illustrated by an example. Certain things such as a newly born infant, a corpse or the person of a chief are said to be tabu. This means that one should, as far as possible, avoid touching them. A man who does touch one of these tabu objects immediately becomes tabu himself. This means two things. In the first place, a man who is tabu in this sense must observe a number of special restrictions on his behavior; for example, he may not use his hands to feed himself. He is regarded as being in a state of danger, and this is generally stated by saying that if he fails to observe the customary precautions he will be ill and perhaps die. In the second place he is also dangerous to other persons—he is tabu in the same sense as the thing he has touched. If he should come in contact with utensils in which, or the fire at which, food is cooked, the dangerous influence would be communicated to the food and so injure anyone who

partook of it. A person who is tabu in this way, as by touching a corpse, can be restored to his normal condition by rites of purification or desacralization. He is then said to be *noa* again, this term being the contrary of tabu.

Sir James Frazer has told us that when he took up the study of taboo in 1886 the current view of anthropologists at the time was that the institution in question was confined to the brown and black races of the Pacific, but that as a result of his investigations he came to the conclusion that the Polynesian body of practices and beliefs "is only one of a number of similar systems of superstition which among many, perhaps all the races of men have contributed in large measure, under many different names and with many variations of detail, to build up the complex fabric of society in all the various sides or elements of it which we describe as religious, social, political, moral, and economic."

The use of the word taboo in anthropology for customs all over the world which resemble in essentials the example given from Polynesia seems to me undesirable and inconvenient. There is the fact already mentioned that in the Polynesian language the word tabu has a much wider meaning, equivalent to our own word "forbidden." This has produced a good deal of confusion in the literature relating to Polynesia owing to the ambiguity resulting from two different uses of the same word. You will have noticed that I have used the word "taboo" (with the English spelling and pronunciation) in the meaning that it has for anthropologists, and "tabu" (with the Polynesian spelling and pronunciation) in special reference to Polynesia and in the Polynesian sense. But this is not entirely satisfactory.

I propose to refer to the customs we are considering as "ritual avoidances" or "ritual prohibitions" and to define them by reference to two fundamental concepts for which I have been in the habit of using the terms "ritual status" and "ritual value." I am not suggesting that these are the best terms to be found; they are merely the best that I have been able to find up to the present. In such a science as ours words are the instruments of analysis and we should always be prepared to discard inferior tools for superior when opportunity arises.

A ritual prohibition is a rule of behavior which is associated with a belief that an infraction will result in an undesirable change in the ritual status of the person who fails to keep to the rule. This change of ritual status is conceived in many different ways in different societies, but everywhere there is the idea that it involves the likelihood of some minor or major misfortune which will befall the person concerned.

We have already considered one example. The Polynesian who touches a corpse has, according to Polynesian belief, undergone what I am calling an undesirable change of ritual status. The misfortune of which he is considered to be in danger is illness, and he therefore takes precautions and goes through a ritual in order that he may escape the danger and be restored to his former ritual status.

Let us consider two examples of different kinds from contemporary England. There are some people who think that one should avoid spilling salt. The person who spills salt will have bad luck. But he can avoid this by throwing a pinch of the spilled salt over his shoulder. Putting this in my terminology, it can be said that spilling salt produces an undesirable change in the ritual status of the person who does so, and that he is restored to his normal or previous ritual status by the positive rite of throwing salt over his shoulder.

A member of the Roman Catholic Church, unless granted a dispensation, is required by his religion to abstain from eating meat on Fridays and during Lent. If he fails to observe the rule he sins, and must proceed, as in any other sin, to confess and obtain absolution. Different as this is in important ways from the rule about spilling salt, it can and must for scientific purposes be regarded as belonging to the same general class. Eating meat on Friday produces in the person who does so an undesirable change of ritual status which requires to be remedied by fixed appropriate means.

We may add to these examples two others from other societies. If you turn to the fifth chapter of Leviticus you will find that amongst the Hebrews if a "soul" touch the carcase of an unclean beast or of unclean cattle, or of unclean creeping things, even if he is unaware that he does so, then he is unclean and guilty and has sinned. When he

becomes aware of his sin he must confess that he has sinned and must take a trespass offering—a female from the flock, a lamb, or a kid of the goats—which the priest shall sacrifice to make an atonement for the sin so that it shall be forgiven him. Here the change in ritual status through touching an unclean carcase is described by the terms "sin," "unclean," and "guilty."

In the Kikuyu tribe of East Africa the word *thahu* denotes the undesirable ritual status that results from failure to observe rules of ritual avoidance. It is believed that a person who is *thahu* will be ill and will probably die unless he removes the *thahu* by the appropriate ritual remedies, which in all serious cases require the services of a priest or medicine man. Actions which produce this condition are touching or carrying a corpse, stepping over a corpse, eating food from a cracked pot, coming in contact with a woman's menstrual discharge, and many others. Just as amongst the Hebrews a soul may unwittingly be guilty of sin by touching in ignorance the carcase of an unclean animal, so amongst the Kikuyu a man may become *thahu* without any voluntary act on his part. If an elder or a woman when coming out of the hut slips and falls down on the ground, he or she is *thahu* and lies there until some of the elders of the neighborhood come and sacrifice a sheep. If the side-pole of a bedstead breaks, the person lying on it is *thahu* and must be purified. If the droppings of a kite or crow fall on a person he is *thahu*, and if a hyena defecates in a village, or a jackal barks therein, the village and its inhabitants are *thahu*.

I have purposely chosen from our own society two examples of ritual avoidances which are of very different kinds. The rule against eating meat on Friday or in Lent is a rule of religion, as is the rule, where it is recognized, against playing golf or tennis on Sunday. The rule against spilling salt, I suppose it will be agreed, is nonreligious. Our language permits us to make this distinction very clearly, for infractions of the rules of religion are sins, while the nonreligious avoidances are concerned with good and bad luck. Since this distinction is so obvious to us it might be thought that we should find it in other societies. My own experience is that in some of the societies with which I am acquainted this distinction between sinful acts and acts that bring bad luck cannot be made. Several anthropologists, however, have attempted to classify rites into two classes, religious rites and magical rites.

For Émile Durkheim the essential distinction is that religious rites are obligatory within a religious society or church, while magical rites are optional. A person who fails in religious observances is guilty of wrongdoing, whereas one who does not observe the precautions of magic or those relating to luck is simply acting foolishly. This distinction is of considerable theoretical importance. It is difficult to apply in the study of the rites of simple societies.

Sir James Frazer defines religion as "a propitiation or conciliation of superhuman powers which are believed to control nature and man," and regards magic as the erroneous application of the notion of causality. If we apply this to ritual prohibitions we may regard as belonging to religion those rules the infraction of which produces a change of ritual status in the individual by offending the superhuman powers, whereas the infraction of a rule of magic would be regarded as resulting immediately in a change of ritual status, or in the misfortune that follows, by a process of hidden causation. Spilling salt, by Sir James Frazer's definition, is a question of magic, while eating meat on Friday is a question of religion.

An attempt to apply this distinction systematically meets with certain difficulties. Thus with regard to the Maori, Sir James Frazer states that "the ultimate sanction of the taboo, in other words, that which engaged the people to observe its commandments, was a firm persuasion that any breach of those commandments would surely and speedily be punished by an *atua* or ghost, who would afflict the sinner with a painful malady till he died." This would seem to make the Polynesian taboo a matter of religion, not of magic. But my own observation of the Polynesians suggests to me that in general the native conceives of the change in his ritual status as taking place as the immediate result of such an act as touching a corpse, and that it is only when he proceeds to rationalize the whole system of taboos that he thinks of the gods and spirits— the *atua*—as being concerned. Incidentally, it should not be assumed that the Polynesian word *atua* or *otua* always refer to a personal spiritual being.

Of the various ways of distinguishing magic and religion I will mention only one

more. For Professor Malinowski a rite is magical when "it has a definite practical purpose which is known to all who practice it and can be easily elicited from any native informant," while a rite is religious if it is simply expressive and has no purpose, being not a means to an end but an end in itself. A difficulty in applying this criterion is due to uncertainty as to what is meant by "definite practical purpose." To avoid the bad luck which results from spilling salt is, I suppose, a practical purpose though not very definite. The desire to please God in all our actions and thus escape some period of Purgatory is perhaps definite enough, but Professor Malinowski may regard it as not practical What shall we say of the desire of the Polynesian to avoid sickness and possible death which he gives as his reason for not touching chiefs, corpses, and newly born babies?

Seeing that there is this absence of agreement as to the definitions of magic and religion and the nature of the distinction between them, and seeing that in many instances whether we call a particular rite magical or religious depends on which of the various proposed definitions we accept, the only sound procedure, at any rate in the present state of anthropological knowledge, is to avoid as far as possible the use of the terms in question until there is some general agreement about them. Certainly the distinctions made by Durkheim and Frazer and Malinowski may be theoretically significant, even though they are difficult to apply universally. Certainly, also, there is need for a systematic classification of rites, but a satisfactory classification will be fairly complex and a simple dichotomy between magic and religion does not carry us very far toward it.

Another distinction which we make in our own society within the field of ritual avoidances is between the holy and the unclean. Certain things must be treated with respect because they are holy, others because they are unclean. But, as Robertson Smith and Sir James Frazer have shown, there are many societies in which this distinction is entirely unrecognized. The Polynesian, for example, does not think of a chief or a temple as holy and a corpse as unclean. He thinks of them all as things dangerous. An example from Hawai'i will illustrate this fundamental identity of holiness and uncleanness. There, in former times, if a commoner committed incest with his sister he became *kapu* (the Hawai'ian form of tabu).

His presence was dangerous in the extreme for the whole community, and since he could not be purified he was put to death. But if a chief of high rank, who, by reason of his rank was, of course, sacred (*kapu*), married his sister he became still more so. An extreme sanctity or untouchability attached to a chief born of a brother and sister who were themselves the children of a brother and sister. The sanctity of such a chief and the uncleanness of the person put to death for incest have the same source and are the same thing. They are both denoted by saying that the person is *kapu*. In studying the simpler societies it is essential that we should carefully avoid thinking of their behavior and ideas in terms of our own ideas of holiness and uncleanness. Since most people find this difficult it is desirable to have terms which we can use that do not convey this connotation. Durkheim and others have used the word "sacred" as an inclusive term for the holy and the unclean together. This is easier to do in French than in English, and has some justification in the fact that the Latin *sacer* did apply to holy things such as the gods and also to accursed things such as persons guilty of certain crimes. But there is certainly a tendency in English to identify sacred with holy. I think that it will greatly aid clear thinking if we adopt some wide inclusive term which does not have any undesirable connotation. I venture to propose the term "ritual value."

Anything—a person, a material thing, a place, a word or name, an occasion or event, a day of the week or a period of the year— which is the object of a ritual avoidance or taboo can be said to have ritual value. Thus in Polynesia chiefs, corpses, and newly born babies have ritual value. For some people in England salt has ritual value. For Christians all Sundays and Good Friday have ritual value, and for Jews all Saturdays and the Day of Atonement. The ritual value is exhibited in the behavior adopted towards the object or occasion in question. Ritual values are exhibited not only in negative ritual but also in positive ritual, being possessed by the objects towards which positive rites are directed and also by objects, words, or places used in the rites. A large class of positive rites, those of consecration or sacralization, have for their purpose to endow objects with ritual value. It may be noted that in general anything that has value in positive ritual is also the object of some sort of ritual avoidance or at the very least of ritual respect.

The word "value," as I am using it, always refers to a relation between a subject and an object. The relation can be stated in two ways by saying either that the object has a value for the subject, or that the subject has an interest in the object. We can use the terms in this way to refer to any act of behavior towards an object. The relation is exhibited in and defined by the behavior. The words "interest" and "value" provide a convenient shorthand by which we can describe the reality, which consists of acts of behavior and the actual relations between subjects and objects which those acts of behavior reveal. If Jack loves Jill, then Jill has the value of a loved object for Jack, and Jack has a recognizable interest in Jill. When I am hungry I have an interest in food, and a good meal has an immediate value for me that it does not have at other times. My toothache has a value to me as something that I am interested in getting rid of as quickly as possible.

A social system can be conceived and studied as a system of values. A society consists of a number of individuals bound together in a network of social relations. A social relation exists between two or more persons when there is some harmonization of their individual interests, by some convergence of interest and by limitation or adjustment of divergent interests. An interest is always the interest of an individual. Two individuals may have similar interests. Similar interests do not in themselves constitute a social relation; two dogs may have a similar interest in the same bone and the result may be a dogfight. But a society cannot exist except on the basis of a certain measure of similarity in the interests of its members. Putting this in terms of value, the first necessary condition of the existence of a society is that the individual members shall agree in some measure in the values that they recognize.

Any particular society is characterized by a certain set of values—moral, aesthetic, economic, etc. In a simple society there is a fair amount of agreement amongst the members in their evaluations, though of course the agreement is never absolute. In a complex modern society we find much more disagreement if we consider the society as a whole, but we may find a closer measure of agreement amongst the members of a group or class within the society.

While some measure of agreement about values, some similarity of interests, is a prerequisite of a social system, social relations involve more than this. They require the existence of common interests and of social values. When two or more persons have a common interest in the same object and are aware of their community of interest a social relation is established. They form, whether for a moment or for a long period, an association, and the object may be said to have a social value. For a man and his wife the birth of a child, the child itself and its well-being and happiness or its death, are objects of a common interest which binds them together and they thus have, for the association formed by the two persons, social value. By this definition an object can only have a social value for an association of persons. In the simplest possible instance we have a triadic relation; Subject 1 and Subject 2 are both interested in the same way in the Object and each of the Subjects has an interest in the other, or at any rate in certain items of the behavior of the other, namely those directed toward the object. To avoid cumbersome circumlocutions it is convenient to speak of the object as having a social value for any one subject involved in such a relation, but it must be remembered that this is a loose way of speaking.

It is perhaps necessary for the avoidance of misunderstanding to add that a social system also requires that persons should be objects of interest to other persons. In relations of friendship or love each of two persons has a value for the other. In certain kinds of groups each member is an object of interest for all the others, and each member therefore has a social value for the groups as a whole. Further, since there are negative values as well as positive, persons may be united or associated by their antagonism to other persons. For the members of an anti-Comintern pact the Comintern has a specific social value.

Amongst the members of a society we find a certain measure of agreement as to the ritual value they attribute to objects of different kinds. We also find that most of these ritual values are social values as defined above. Thus for a local totemic clan in Australia the totem-centers, the natural species associated with them, i.e., the totems, and the myths and rites that relate thereto, have a specific social value for the clan; the common interest in them binds the individuals together into a firm and lasting association.

Ritual values exist in every known society, and show an immense diversity as we pass from one society to another. The problem of a natural science of society (and it is as such that I regard social anthropology) is to discover the deeper, not immediately perceptible, uniformities beneath the superficial differences. This is, of course, a highly complex problem which will require the studies begun by Sir James Frazer and others to be continued by many investigators over many years. The ultimate aim should be, I think, to find some relatively adequate answer to the question, *What is the relation of ritual and ritual values to the essential constitution of human society*? I have chosen a particular approach to this study which I believe to be promising—to investigate in a few societies studied as thoroughly as possible the relations of ritual values to other values including moral and aesthetic values. In the present lecture, however, it is only one small part of this study in which I seek to interest you—the question of a relation between ritual values and social values.

One way of approaching the study of ritual is by the consideration of the purposes or reasons for the rites. If one examines the literature of anthropology one finds this approach very frequently adopted. It is by far the least profitable, though the one that appeals most to common sense. Sometimes the purpose of a rite is obvious, or a reason may be volunteered by those who practice it. Sometimes the anthropologist has to ask the reason, and in such circumstances it may happen that different reasons are given by different informants. What is fundamentally the same rite in two different societies may have different purposes or reasons in the one and in the other. The reasons given by the members of a community for any custom they observe are important data for the anthropologist. But it is to fall into grievous error to suppose that they give a valid explanation of the custom. What is entirely inexcusable is for the anthropologist, when he cannot get from the people themselves a reason for their behavior which seems to him satisfactory, to attribute to them some purpose or reason on the basis of his own preconceptions about human motives. I could adduce many instances of this from the literature of ethnography, but I prefer to illustrate what I mean by an anecdote.

A Queenslander met a Chinese who was taking a bowl of cooked rice to place on his brother's grave. The Australian in jocular tones asked if he supposed that his brother would come and eat the rice. The reply was "No! We offer rice to people as an expression of friendship and affection. But since you speak as you do I suppose that you in this country place flowers on the graves of your dead in the belief that they will enjoy looking at them and smelling their sweet perfume."

So far as ritual avoidances are concerned the reasons for them may vary from a very vague idea that some sort of misfortune or ill-luck, not defined as to its kind, is likely to befall anyone who fails to observe the taboo, to a belief that nonobservance will produce some quite specific and undesirable result. Thus an Australian aborigine told me that if he spoke to any woman who stood in the relation of mother-in-law to him his hair would turn gray.

The very common tendency to look for the explanation of ritual actions in their purpose is the result of a false assimilation of them to what may be called technical acts. In any technical activity an adequate statement of the purpose of any particular act or series of acts constitutes by itself a sufficient explanation. But ritual acts differ from technical acts in having in all instances some expressive or symbolic element in them.

A second approach to the study of ritual is therefore by a consideration not of their purpose or reason, but of their meaning. I am here using the words "symbol" and "meaning" as coincident. Whatever has a meaning is a symbol and the meaning is whatever is expressed by the symbol.

But how are we to discover meanings? They do not lie on the surface. There is a sense in which people always know the meaning of their own symbols, but they do so intuitively and can rarely express their understanding in words. Shall we therefore be reduced to guessing at meanings as some anthropologists have guessed at reasons and purposes? I think not. For as long as we admit guesswork of any kind social anthropology cannot be a science. There are, I believe, methods of determining, with some fair degree of probability, the meanings of rites and other symbols.

There is still a third approach to the study of rites. We can consider the effects of the rite—not the effects that it is supposed to produce by the people who practice it but the effects that it does actually produce. A rite has immediate or direct effects on the persons who are in any way directly concerned in it, which we may call, for lack of a better term, the psychological effects. But there are also secondary effects upon the social structure, i.e., the network of social relations binding individuals together in an ordered life. These we may call the "social effects." By considering the psychological effects of a rite we may succeed in defining its psychological function; by considering the social effects we may discover its social function. Clearly it is impossible to discover the social function of a rite without taking into account its usual or average psychological effects. But it is possible to discuss the psychological effects while more or less completely ignoring the more remote sociological effects, and this is often done in what is called "functional anthropology."

Let us suppose that we wish to investigate in Australian tribes the totemic rites of a kind widely distributed over a large part of the continent. The ostensible purpose of these rites, as stated by the natives themselves, is to renew or maintain some part of nature, such as a species of animal or plant, or rain, or hot or cold weather. With reference to this purpose we have to say that from our point of view the natives are mistaken, that the rites do not actually do what they are believed to do. The rainmaking ceremony does not, we think, actually bring rain. In so far as the rites are performed for a purpose they are futile, based on erroneous belief. I do not believe that there is any scientific value in attempts to conjecture processes of reasoning which might be supposed to have led to these errors.

The rites are easily perceived to be symbolic, and we may therefore investigate their meaning. To do this we have to examine a considerable number of them and we then discover that there is a certain body of ritual idiom extending from the west coast of the continent to the east coast with some local variations. Since each rite has a myth associated with it we have similarly to investigate the meanings of the myths. As a result we find that the meaning of any single rite becomes clear in the light of a cosmology, a body of ideas and beliefs about nature and human society, which, so far as its most general features are concerned, is current in all Australian tribes.

The immediate psychological effects of the rites can be to some extent observed by watching and talking to the performers. The ostensible purpose of the rite is certainly present in their minds, but so also is that complex set of cosmological beliefs by reference to which the rite has a meaning. Certainly a person performing the rite, even if, as sometimes happens, he performs it alone, derives therefrom a definite feeling of satisfaction, but it would be entirely false to imagine that this is simply because he believes that he has helped to provide a more abundant supply of food for himself and his fellow tribesmen. His satisfaction is in having performed a ritual duty, we might say a religious duty. Putting in my own words what I judge, from my own observations, to express what the native feels, I would say that in the performance of the rite he has made that small contribution, which it is both his privilege and his duty to do, to the maintenance of that order of the universe of which man and nature are interdependent parts. The satisfaction which he thus receives gives the rite a special value for him. In some instances with which I am acquainted of the last survivor of a totemic group who still continues to perform the totemic rites by himself, it is this satisfaction that constitutes apparently the sole motive for his action.

To discover the social function of the totemic rites we have to consider the whole body of cosmological ideas of which each rite is a partial expression. I believe that it is possible to show that the social structure of an Australian tribe is connected in a very special way with these cosmological ideas and that the maintenance of its continuity depends on keeping them alive, by their regular expression in myth and rite.

Thus any satisfactory study of the totemic rites of Australia must be based not simply on the consideration of their ostensible purpose and their psychological function, or on an analysis of the motives of the individuals who perform the rites, but on the discovery of their meaning and of their social function.

It may be that some rites have no social function. This may be the case with such taboos as that against spilling salt in our own society. Nevertheless, the method of investigating rites and ritual values that I have found most profitable during work extending over more than thirty years is to study rites as symbolic expressions and to seek to discover their social functions. This method is not new except in so far as it is applied to the comparative study of many societies of diverse types. It was applied by Chinese thinkers to their own ritual more than twenty centuries ago.

In China, in the fifth and sixth centuries B.C., Confucius and his followers insisted on the great importance of the proper performance of ritual, such as funeral and mourning rites and sacrifices. After Confucius there came the reformer Mo Ti who taught a combination of altruism—love for all men—and utilitarianism. He held that funeral and mourning rites were useless and interfered with useful activities and should therefore be abolished or reduced to a minimum. In the third and second centuries B.C. the Confucians, Hsün Tze and the compilers of the *Li Chi* (Book of Rites), replied to Mo Ti to the effect that though these rites might have no utilitarian purpose they none the less had a very important social function. Briefly the theory is that the rites are the orderly (the *Li Chi* says the beautified) expression of feelings appropriate to a social situation. They thus serve to regulate and refine human emotions. We may say that partaking in the performance of rites serves to cultivate in the individual sentiments on whose existence the social order itself depends.

Let us consider the meaning and social function of an extremely simple example of ritual. In the Andaman Islands when a woman is expecting a baby a name is given to it while it is still in the womb. From that time until some weeks after the baby is born nobody is allowed to use the personal name of either the father or the mother; they can be referred to by teknonymy, i.e., in terms of their relation to the child. During this period both the parents are required to abstain from eating certain foods which they may freely eat at other times.

I did not obtain from the Andamanese any statement of the purpose or reason for this avoidance of names. Assuming that the act is symbolic, what method, other than that of guessing, is there of arriving at the meaning? I suggest that we may start with a general working hypothesis that when, in a single society, the same symbol is used in different contexts or on different kinds of occasions there is some common element of meaning, and that by comparing together the various uses of the symbol we may be able to discover what the common element is. This is precisely the method that we adopt in studying an unrecorded spoken language in order to discover the meanings of words and morphemes.

In the Andamans the name of a dead person is avoided from the occurrence of the death to the conclusion of mourning; the name of a person mourning for a dead relative is not used; there is avoidance of the name of a youth or girl who is passing through the ceremonies that take place at adolescence; a bride or bridegroom is not spoken of or to by his or her own name for a short time after the marriage. For the Andamanese the personal name is a symbol of the social personality, i.e., of the position that an individual occupies in the social structure and the social life. The avoidance of a personal name is a symbolic recognition of the fact that at the time the person is not occupying a normal position in the social life. It may be added that a person whose name is thus temporarily out of use is regarded as having for the time an abnormal ritual status.

Turning now to the rule as to avoiding certain foods, if the Andaman Islanders are asked what would happen if the father or mother broke this taboo the usual answer is that he or she would be ill, though one or two of my informants thought it might perhaps also affect the child. This is simply one instance of a standard formula which applies to a number of ritual prohibitions. Thus a person in mourning for a relative may not eat pork and turtle, the most important flesh foods, and the reason given is that if they did they would be ill.

To discover the meaning of the avoidance of foods by the parents we can apply the same method as in reference to the avoidance of their names. There are similar rules for mourners, for women during menstruation, and for youths and girls during the period of adolescence. But for a full demonstration we have to consider the place of foods in Andamanese ritual as a whole, and for an examination of this I must refer to what I have already written on the subject.

I should like to draw your attention to another point in the method by which it is possible to test our hypotheses as to the meanings of rites. We take the different occasions on which two rites are associated together, for example the association of the avoidance of a person's name with the avoidance by that person of certain foods,

which we find in the instance of mourners on the one hand and the expectant mother and father on the other. We must assume that for the Andamanese there is some important similarity between these two kinds of occasions—birth and death—by virtue of which they have similar ritual values. We cannot rest content with any interpretation of the taboos at childbirth unless there is a parallel interpretation of those relating to mourners. In the terms I am using here we can say that in the Andamans the relatives of a recently dead person, and the father and mother of a child that is about to be, or has recently been, born, are in an abnormal ritual status. This is recognized or indicated by the avoidance of their names. They are regarded as likely to suffer some misfortune, some bad luck, if you will, unless they observe certain prescribed ritual precautions of which the avoidance of certain foods is one. In the Andaman Islands the danger in such instances is thought of as the danger of illness. This is the case also with the Polynesian belief about the ritual status of anyone who has touched a corpse or a newly born baby. It is to be noted that for the Polynesians as well as for the Andamanese the occasion of a birth has a similar ritual value to that of a death.

The interpretation of the taboos at childbirth at which we arrive by studying it in relation to the whole system of ritual values of the Andamanese is too complex to be stated here in full. Clearly, however, they express, in accordance with Andamanese ritual idiom, a common concern in the event. The parents show their concern by avoiding certain foods; their friends show theirs by avoiding the parents' personal names. By virtue of these taboos the occasion acquires a certain social value, as that term has been defined above.

There is one theory that might seem to be applicable to our example. It is based on a hypothesis as to the psychological function of a class of rites. The theory is that in certain circumstances the individual human being is anxious about the outcome of some event or activity because it depends to some extent on conditions that he cannot control by any technical means. He therefore observes some rite which, since he believes that it will ensure good luck, serves to reassure him. Thus an aeronaut takes with him in a plane a mascot which he believes will protect him from accident and thus carries out his flight with confidence.

The theory has a respectable antiquity. It was perhaps implied in the *Primus in orbe deos fecit timor* of Petronius and Statius. It has taken various forms from Hume's explanation of religion to Malinowski's explanation of Trobriand magic. It can be made so plausible by a suitable selection of illustrations that it is necessary to examine it with particular care and treat it with reasonable skepticism. For there is always the danger that we may be taken in by the plausibility of a theory that ultimately proves to be unsound.

I think that for certain rites it would be easy to maintain with equal plausibility an exactly contrary theory, namely, that if it were not for the existence of the rite and the beliefs associated with it the individual would feel no anxiety, and that the psychological effect of the rite is to create in him a sense of insecurity or danger. It seems very unlikely that an Andaman Islander would think that it is dangerous to eat dugong or pork or turtle meat if it were not for the existence of a specific body of ritual the ostensible purpose of which is to protect him from those dangers. Many hundreds of similar instances could be mentioned from all over the world.

Thus, while one anthropological theory is that magic and religion give men confidence, comfort, and a sense of security, it could equally well be argued that they give men fears and anxieties from which they would otherwise be free—the fear of black magic or of spirits, fear of God, of the Devil, of Hell.

Actually in our fears or anxieties as well as in our hopes we are conditioned (as the phrase goes) by the community in which we live. And it is largely by the sharing of hopes and fears, by what I have called common concern in events or eventualities, that human beings are linked together in temporary or permanent associations.

To return to the Andamanese taboos at childbirth, there are difficulties in supposing that they are means by which parents reassure themselves against the accidents that may interfere with a successful delivery. If the prospective father fails to observe the food taboo it is he who will be sick, according to the general Andamanese opinion. Moreover, he must continue to observe the taboos after the child is safely delivered. Further, how are we to provide a parallel explanation of the similar taboos observed by a person mourning for a dead relative?

The taboos associated with pregnancy and parturition are often explained in terms of the hypothesis I have mentioned. A father, naturally anxious at the outcome of an event over which he does not have a technical control and which is subject to hazard, reassures himself by observing some taboo or carrying out some magical action. He may avoid certain foods. He may avoid making nets or tying knots, or he may go round the house untying all knots and opening any locked or closed boxes or containers.

I wish to arouse in your minds, if it is not already there, a suspicion that both the general theory and this special application of it do not give the whole truth and indeed may not be true at all. Skepticism of plausible but unproved hypotheses is essential in every science. There is at least good ground for suspicion in the fact that the theory has so far been considered in reference to facts that seem to fit it, and no systematic attempt has been made, so far as I am aware, to look for facts that do not fit. That there are many such I am satisfied from my own studies.

The alternative hypothesis which I am presenting for consideration is as follows. In a given community it is appropriate that an expectant father should feel concern or at least should make an appearance of doing so. Some suitable symbolic expression of his concern is found in terms of the general ritual or symbolic idiom of the society, and it is felt generally that a man in that situation ought to carry out the symbolic or ritual actions or abstentions. For every rule that *ought* to be observed there must be some sort of sanction or reason. For acts that patently affect other persons the moral and legal sanctions provide a generally sufficient controlling force upon the individual. For ritual obligations conformity and rationalization are provided by the ritual sanctions. The simplest form of ritual sanction is an accepted belief that if rules of ritual are not observed some undefined misfortune is likely to occur. In many societies the expected danger is somewhat more definitely conceived as a danger of sickness or, in extreme cases, death. In the more specialized forms of ritual sanction the good results to be hoped for or the bad results to be feared are more specifically defined in reference to the occasion or meaning of the ritual.

The theory is not concerned with the historical origin of ritual, nor is it another attempt to explain ritual in terms of human psychology; it is a hypothesis as to the relation of ritual and ritual values to the essential constitution of human society, i.e., to those invariant general characters which belong to all human societies, past, present, and future. It rests on the recognition of the fact that while in animal societies social coaptation depends on instinct, in human societies it depends upon the efficacy of symbols of many different kinds. The theory I am advancing must therefore, for a just estimation of its value, be considered in its place in a general theory of symbols and their social efficacy.

By this theory the Andamanese taboos relating to childbirth are the obligatory recognition in a standardized symbolic form of the significance and importance of the event to the parents and to the community at large. They thus serve to fix the social value of occasions of this kind. Similarly I have argued in another place that the Andamanese taboos relating to the animals and plants used for food are means of affixing a definite social value to food, based on its social importance. The social importance of food is not that it satisfies hunger, but that in such a community as an Andamanese camp or village an enormously large proportion of the activities are concerned with the getting and consuming of food, and that in these activities, with their daily instances of collaboration and mutual aid, there continuously occur those interrelations of interests which bind the individual men, women, and children into a society.

I believe that this theory can be generalized and with suitable modifications will be found to apply to a vast number of the taboos of different societies. My theory would go further for I would hold, as a reasonable working hypothesis, that we have here the primary basis of all ritual and therefore of religion and magic, however those may be distinguished. The primary basis of ritual, so the formulation would run, is the attribution of ritual value to objects and occasions which are either themselves objects of important common interests linking together the persons of a community or are symbolically representative of such objects. To illustrate what is meant by the last part of this statement two illustrations may be offered. In the Andamans ritual value is attributed to the cicada, not because it has any social importance itself but because it symbolically represents the seasons of the year which do have

importance. In some tribes of Eastern Australia the god Baiame is the personification, i.e., the symbolical representative, of the moral law of the tribe, and the rainbow-serpent (the Australian equivalent of the Chinese dragon) is a symbol representing growth and fertility in nature. Baiame and the rainbow-serpent in their turn are represented by the figures of earth which are made on the sacred ceremonial ground of the initiation ceremonies and at which rites are performed. The reverence that the Australian shows to the image of Baiame or towards his name is the symbolic method of fixing the social value of the moral law, particularly the laws relating to marriage.

In conclusion let me return once more to the work of the anthropologist whom we are here to honor. Sir James Frazer, in his *Psyche's Task* and in his other works, set himself to show how, in his own words, taboos have contributed to build up the complex fabric of society. He thus initiated that functional study of ritual to which I have in this lecture and elsewhere attempted to make some contribution. But there has been a shift of emphasis. Sir James accounted for the taboos of savage tribes as the application in practice of beliefs arrived at by erroneous processes of reasoning, and he seems to have thought of the effects of these beliefs in creating or maintaining a stable orderly society as being accidental. My own view is that the negative and positive rites of savages exist and persist because they are part of the mechanism by which an orderly society maintains itself in existence, serving as they do to establish certain fundamental social values. The beliefs by which the rites themselves are justified and given some sort of consistency are the rationalizations of symbolic actions and of the sentiments associated with them. I would suggest that what Sir James Frazer seems to regard as the accidental results of magical and religious beliefs really constitute their essential function and the ultimate reason for their existence.

Note.—The theory of ritual outlined in this lecture was first worked out in 1908 in a thesis on the Andaman Islanders. It was written out again in a revised and extended form in 1913 and appeared in print in 1922. Unfortunately the exposition contained in *The Andaman Islanders* is evidently not clear, since some of my critics have failed to understand what the theory is. For example, it has been assumed that by "social value" I mean "utility."

The best treatment of the subject of value with which I am acquainted is Ralph Barton Perry's *General Theory of Value*, 1926. For the Chinese theory of ritual the most easily accessible account is in Chapter XIV of Fung Yu-lan's *History of Chinese Philosophy*, 1937. The third chapter, on the uses of symbolism, of Whitehead's *Symbolism: Its Meaning and Effect*, is an admirable brief introduction to the sociological theory of symbolism.

One very important point that could not be dealt with in the lecture is that indicated by Whitehead in the following sentence: "No account of the uses of symbolism is complete without the recognition that the symbolic elements in life have a tendency to run wild, like the vegetation in a tropical forest."

George C. Homans

ANXIETY AND RITUAL: THE THEORIES OF MALINOWSKI AND RADCLIFFE-BROWN

With the publication of Malinowski's various books and papers on the function of ritual in allaying anxiety and inspiring confidence in men faced with an unbridgeable gap in their empirical knowledge, and of Radcliffe-Brown's lecture *Taboo*, which presents the thesis that anxiety is frequently experienced when a customary ritual is *not* performed, students of religion and magic were confronted by a theoretical dilemma of how to resolve these two essentially opposing theories.

In this brief but penetrating paper Homans suggests a resolution by introducing the concepts of "primary" and "secondary" anxieties and rituals and by clarifying the relationship between the individual and societal level of analysis. His use of the term "rationalization" for the native's justification of his ritual may be misleading to some readers. This is rationalization not from the native's point of view—he *believes* in his rituals and thinks they are efficacious—but from the outside observer's point of view.

Reprinted from *American Anthropologist*, XLIII (1941), 164–172, by permission of the author and the American Anthropological Association.

In his Frazer Lecture for the year 1939, recently published as a pamphlet under the title *Taboo*, Professor A. R. Radcliffe-Brown restates certain of his views on magic and religion.[1] At the same time, he makes certain criticisms of Professor Malinowski's theories on the subject. The appearance of *Taboo*, therefore, offers the anthropologist an occasion for examining the present status of the theory of ritual by means of a study of a controversy between what are perhaps its two most important experts. Incidentally, the reader will find illustrated a type of behavior common in disputes in the world of science.

Malinowski's theory of magic is well known and has been widely accepted.[2] He holds that any primitive people has a body of empirical knowledge, comparable to modern scientific knowledge, as to the behavior of nature and the means of controlling it to meet man's needs. This knowledge the primitives apply in a thoroughly practical manner to get the results they desire—a crop of tubers, a catch of fish, and so forth. But their techniques are seldom so powerful that the accomplishment of these results is a matter of certainty. When the tiller of the soil has done the best he can to see that his

[1] Elsewhere most prominently stated in *The Andaman Islanders* (new ed., 1933).

[2] See "Magic, Science, and Religion," in J. Needham (ed.), *Science, Religion and Reality; Coral Gardens and Their Magic;* and *Foundations of Faith and Morals* ("Riddell Memorial Lectures").

fields are properly planted and tended, a drought or a blight may overwhelm him. Under these circumstances the primitives feel a sentiment which we call "anxiety"[3] and they perform magical rites which they say will ensure good luck. These rites give them the confidence which allows them to attack their practical work with energy and determination.

Malinowski clinches his argument with an observation made in the course of his field work:

An interesting and crucial test is provided by fishing in the Trobriand Islands and its magic. While in the villages on the inner Lagoon fishing is done in an easy and absolutely reliable manner by the method of poisoning, yielding abundant results without danger and uncertainty, there are on the shores of the open sea dangerous modes of fishing and also certain types in which the yield varies greatly according to whether shoals of fish appear beforehand or not. It is most significant that in the Lagoon fishing, where man can rely completely upon his knowledge and skill, magic does not exist, while in the open-sea fishing, full of danger and uncertainty, there is extensive magical ritual to secure safety and good results.[4]

On this understanding of magic, Malinowski bases a distinction between magical and religious ritual. A magical rite, he says,

has a definite practical purpose which is known to all who practice it and can be easily elicited from any native informant.

This is not true of a religious rite.

While in the magical act the underlying idea and aim is always clear, straightforward, and definite, in the religious ceremony there is no purpose directed towards a subsequent event. It is only possible for the sociologist to establish the function, the sociological raison d'être *of the act. The native can always state the end of the magical rite, but he will say of a religious ceremony that it is done because such is the usage, or he will narrate an explanatory myth.*[5]

This argument is the first with which Professor Radcliffe-Brown takes issue, and his criticism seems to the writer justified. He points out that the difficulty in applying this distinction between magic and religion lies in uncertainty as to what is meant by "definite,

practical purpose." What is, in fact, the definite, practical purpose of a magical rite? To an anthropologist from western civilization, a magical rite and a religious rite are equally devoid of definite, practical results, in the usual sense of the phrase. The distinction between them must be based on other grounds. A scrutiny of the methods we actually use to determine the purpose of a magical rite reveals that what we take to be the purpose of the rite is the purpose as stated by a native informant. The native performs one rite and says that it has a definite, practical purpose. He performs another rite and says that it is performed as a matter of custom. If we call the first rite magic and the second religion, we are basing our distinction on a difference between the verbal statements a native makes about the rites. For some purposes the distinction may be a useful one, but one of the truisms of the social sciences is that we shall do well to look at the statements men make about what they do with extreme care before we take the statements at their face value. Or, to use Radcliffe-Brown's own words:

The reasons given by the members of a community for the customs they observe are important data for the anthropologist. But it is to fall into grievous error to suppose that they give a valid explanation of the custom.[6]

Without doubt there are many factors involved in the performance of magic, but the least number which must be taken into consideration are apparently the following. A sentiment which we call anxiety arises when men feel certain desires and do not possess the techniques which make them sure of satisfying the desires. This sentiment of anxiety then manifests itself in ritual behavior. We may recall to mind here Pareto's third class of residues—the need of expressing sentiments by external acts. The situation is familiar in American folklore: a man and his wife are held up in a taxi in New York traffic and in danger of missing their liner to Europe. There is nothing that either one of them can do that would be of any use, but the wife screams to her husband: "But do something, can't you?" Furthermore, the action taken under such circumstances, however useless it may be, does do something to relieve the anxiety. In the usual phrase, it "works it off."

---

[3] The word "anxiety" is used here in its ordinary common-sense meaning. This use is not to be confused with the psychoanalytic one, though of course the two are related.

[4] *Science, Religion and Reality*, p. 32.

[5] *Ibid.*, p. 38.

[6] *Taboo*, p. 25.

A better statement, from the point of view of psychology, is the following:

From clinical, physiological, and psychological data, it has been shown that throwing into conflict powerful excitations toward and against motor reaction regularly results in disorganization of behavior, subjective distress, and persistent drive toward relief. This syndrome has been called variously "affect," "tension," "anxiety," and "neurosis." . . . The drive toward relief tends to set into operation implicit or explicit forms of behavior, the principal characteristic of which is their abbreviated or condensed or symbolic character and their relative indifference and impermeability (because of the necessity of attaining relief as quickly as possible) to the ordinary checks, delays, and inhibitions imposed by objective reality; thus they are objectively non-adaptive, but are subjectively adaptive to the extent that the relief aimed at is actually effected.[7]

In magic in a primitive society there is a further factor which must be taken into consideration. The primitives feel anxiety and perform ritual actions which have some effect in relieving the anxiety, but they also produce a statement. They say that magical action does in fact produce a "definite, practical result." This statement is to be taken simply as a rationalization, similar in character to other rationalizations. If the rationalization is to be used as a means of distinguishing magic from religion, it should at least be recognized for what it is.

The writer doubts whether the distinction between magic and religion, as formulated by Malinowski, is a useful one. In an effort to get away from the rationalizations, magic might be defined as the ritual which is closely associated with practical activities: hunting, fishing, husbandry. Then religion would be the ritual which is not associated with practical activities, in the sense that, for instance, the Mass of the Catholic Church is not so associated. But could a distinction be made in many societies between magic and religion as so defined? Anthropologists will be aware that in many primitive societies native informants say of the most fundamental and sacred rituals, i.e., those ordinarily called religious, that if they are not performed the food supply will fail. Are these rituals closely associated with practical activities? The food supply is certainly a practical concern. Once more we are involved in the native rational-

izations. In a sense these rituals are both magical and religious.

Nevertheless, Malinowski's general theory of magic seems sound, and it may be well to cite one of his statements as a summary:

We have seen that all the instincts and emotions, all practical activities, lead man into impasses where gaps in his knowledge and the limitations of his early power of observation and reason betray him at a crucial moment. The human organism reacts to this in spontaneous outbursts, in which rudimentary modes of behavior and rudimentary beliefs in their efficiency are engendered. Magic fixes upon these beliefs and rudimentary rites and standardizes them into permanent traditional forms.[8]

One word of explanation is needed here. The present paper is concerned with ritual so far as it arises out of the sentiment we call anxiety. But there is no implication that other sentiments besides anxiety do not give rise to ritual behavior.

There are other and more important criticisms which Radcliffe-Brown makes of Malinowski's theory of ritual. He wisely bases them upon a consideration of an actual case, the ritual of birth in the Andaman Islands. In order to follow his discussion, his material should first be cited:

In the Andaman Islands when a woman is expecting a baby a name is given to it while it is still in the womb. From that time until some weeks after the baby is born nobody is allowed to use the personal name of either the father or the mother; they can be referred to only by teknonymy, i.e., in terms of their relation to the child. During this period both the parents are required to abstain from eating certain foods which they may freely eat at other times.[9]

To be sure, this is an example of negative ritual—avoidance of behavior which under other circumstances might be proper—rather than of positive ritual, but the same problems arise in either case.

Radcliffe-Brown admits that Malinowski's theory might seem to be applicable as an interpretation of this body of ritual. For a woman, childbirth is always a dangerous process, in which tragedy may suddenly appear for inexplicable reasons. It is dangerous today; it was supremely dangerous under primitive conditions. Under these circumstances, the woman may feel great anxiety, and the husband is naturally interested in the fate of his wife. But the husband and the wife perform certain rites and say that they

[7] R. R. Willoughby, "Magic and Cognate Phenomena: An Hypothesis," in C. Murchison (ed.), *Handbook of Social Psychology*, p. 471.

[8] *Science, Religion and Reality*, p. 82.
[9] *Taboo*, p. 33.

are efficacious in warding off the dangers of childbirth. Therefore their fears are, to a certain extent, lulled.

Without explicitly rejecting Malinowski's interpretation, Radcliffe-Brown offers an alternative. He writes:

The alternative hypothesis which I am presenting for consideration is as follows. In a given community it is appropriate that an expectant father should feel concern or at least make an appearance of doing so. Some suitable symbolic expression of his concern is found in terms of the general ritual or symbolic idiom of the society, and it is felt generally that a man in that situation ought to carry out the symbolic or ritual actions or abstentions.[10]

Radcliffe-Brown presents this interpretation as an alternative to Malinowski's. The point to be made here is that the question is not one of either/or. The hypothesis is not an alternative but a supplement: both hypotheses must be taken into consideration.

In fact the problem which is raised is the ancient one of the individual and his society. Malinowski is looking at the individual, Radcliffe-Brown at society. Malinowski is saying that the individual tends to feel anxiety on certain occasions; Radcliffe-Brown is saying that society expects the individual to feel anxiety on certain occasions. But there is every reason to believe that both statements are true. They are not mutually exclusive. Indeed the writer has difficulty in believing that it should have ever come about that "in a given community it is appropriate that an expectant father should feel concern" if individual fathers had not in fact showed such concern. Of course, once the tradition had been established, variations in two directions would naturally be produced. There would be, on the one hand, fathers who felt no concern but thought that the expedient thing to do was to put on a show of concern, and on the other hand, fathers who felt concern but did not express it in the manner appropriate in the given society. But on the whole these persons would be few. The average citizen would feel concern at the birth of his child but also would express his concern in the traditional manner. The custom of the society would provide the appropriate channel of his sentiments. In short, a theory adequate to the facts would combine the hypotheses of Malinowski and Radcliffe-Brown.

A statement made by Malinowski in another connection is appropriately quoted here:

The tendency represented largely by the sociological school of Durkheim, and clearly expressed in Professor Radcliffe-Brown's approach to primitive law and other phenomena, the tendency to ignore completely the individual and to eliminate the biological element from the functional analysis of culture, must in my opinion be overcome. It is really the only point of theoretical dissension between Professor Radcliffe-Brown and myself, and the only respect in which the Durkheimian conception of primitive society has to be supplemented in order to be really serviceable in field work, in theoretical studies, and in the practical application of sociology.[11]

Radcliffe-Brown makes a second and more important objection in applying Malinowski's theory to the ·ritual of childbirth in the Andamans. While a woman is expecting a child, and for some weeks after the birth of the child, both parents are required to abstain from eating certain foods which they may properly eat under ordinary circumstances, these foods apparently being dugong, pork, and turtle meat. Furthermore,

If the Andaman Islanders are asked what would happen if the father or mother broke this taboo, the usual answer is that he or she would be ill, though one or two of my informants thought it might perhaps also affect the child. This is simply one instance of a standard formula which applies to a number of ritual prohibitions.[12]

On the basis of this observation, Radcliffe-Brown goes on to make the following attack on Malinowski's anxiety theory:

I think that for certain rites it would be easy to maintain with equal plausibility an exactly contrary theory, namely, that if it were not for the existence of the rite and the beliefs associated with it the individual would feel no anxiety, and that the psychological effect of the rite is to create in him a sense of insecurity or danger. It seems very unlikely that an Andaman Islander would think that it is dangerous to eat dugong or pork or turtle meat if it were not for the existence of a specific body of ritual the ostensible purpose of which is to protect him from those dangers. Many hundreds of similar instances could be mentioned from all over the world.[13]

This attack on Malinowski's theory appears at first glance to be devastating. But let us examine it a little more closely. Put in simpler

[10] *Ibid.*, p. 41

[11] I. Hogbin, *Law and Order in Polynesia*, xxxviii. The introduction is by Malinowski.
[12] *Taboo*, p. 35.
[13] *Ibid.*, p. 39.

language, what Radcliffe-Brown is saying is that the Andaman mother and father do not apparently feel anxiety at the fact of approaching childbirth. They feel anxiety only when the ritual of childbirth is not properly performed. There is no doubt that similar observations could be made of backward peoples all over the world. It is true that their techniques do not allow them to control completely the natural forces on which their lives depend. Nevertheless when they have done their practical work as well as they know how and have performed the proper rituals, they display little overt anxiety. If anxiety is present, it remains latent. They are, as we say, fatalists. What Thomas and Znaniecki have observed of the Polish peasant seems to be true of most primitive peoples. They write:

The fact is that when the peasant has been working steadily, and has fulfilled the religious and magical ceremonies which tradition requires, he "leaves the rest to God," and waits for the ultimate results to come; the question of more or less skill and efficiency of work has very little importance.[14]

When the primitive or the peasant has done his practical work as well as he knows how, and has "fulfilled the religious and magical ceremonies which tradition requires," he displays little overt anxiety. But he does feel anxiety if the ceremonies have not been properly performed. In fact he generalizes beyond this point and feels that unless all the moralities of his society are observed, nature will not yield her fruits. Incest or murder in the camp will lead to a failure of the crops just as surely as will a breach of ritual. In the shape of famine, pestilence, or war, God will visit their sins upon the people. Accordingly when, in a village of medieval Europe, the peasants, led by the parish priest, went in procession about the boundaries of the village in the Rogation Days in order to bless the growing crops, they offered up prayers at the same time for the forgiveness of sins. This association of ideas is characteristic: nature and morality are mutually dependent.

As a matter of fact, the above observations are implicit in Malinowski's theory, and he was undoubtedly aware of them. He points to the initial anxiety situation, but he also states that ritual dispels the anxiety, at least in part, and gives men confidence. He implies, then, that anxiety remains latent so long as

ritual is properly performed. Radcliffe-Brown's criticism does not demolish Malinowski's theory but takes the necessary further step. Once again, it is not an alternative but a supplement. Using the ritual of childbirth in the Andamans as an example, he asks what happens, or rather what would happen, if the ritual is not performed. And he shows that this occasion is the one in which the natives feel anxiety. The anxiety has, so to speak, been displaced from the original situation. But even granted that it has been displaced, Malinowski's general theory is confirmed by the existence of a secondary ritual which has the function of dispelling the secondary anxiety which arises from a breach of ritual and tradition. We call this the ritual of purification, of expiation.

In his description of the Australian Murngin, W. L. Warner sums up admirably what the writer has been trying to say. He writes:

The Murngin in their logic of controlling nature assume that there is a direct connection between social units and different aspects of nature, and that the control of nature lies in the proper control and treatment of social organization. Properly to control the social organization, the rituals must also be held which rid society of its uncleanliness. The society is disciplined by threat of what will happen to nature, the provider, if the members of the group misbehave.[15]

In summary, it appears from the discussion of the theories of Malinowski and Radcliffe-Brown that at least seven elements must be taken into consideration in any study of the rituals we are accustomed to call magic. Of course, there are other elements which are not considered here. The seven are the following:

1. *Primary anxiety.* Whenever a man desires the accomplishment of certain results and does not possess the techniques which will make him certain to secure these results, he feels a sentiment which we call anxiety.

2. *Primary ritual.* Under these circumstances, he tends to perform actions which have no practical result and which we call ritual. But he is not simply an individual. He is a member of a society with definite traditions, and among other things society determines the form of the ritual and expects him to perform the ritual on the appropriate occasions. There is, however, evidence from our own society that when ritual tradition is weak, men will invent ritual when they feel anxiety.

[14] W. I. Thomas and F. Znaniecki, *The Polish Peasant in Europe and America,* I, 174.

[15] W. L. Warner, *A Black Civilization,* p. 410.

3. *Secondary anxiety.* When a man has followed the technical procedures at his command and performed the traditional rituals, his primary anxiety remains latent. We say that the rites give him confidence. Under these circumstances, he will feel anxiety only when the rites themselves are not properly performed. In fact this attitude becomes generalized, and anxiety is felt whenever any one of the traditions of society is not observed. This anxiety may be called secondary or displaced anxiety.

4. *Secondary ritual.* This is the ritual of purification and expiation which has the function of dispelling secondary anxiety. Its form and performance, like those of primary ritual, may or may not be socially determined.

5. *Rationalization.* This element includes the statements which are associated with ritual. They may be very simple: such statements as that the performance of a certain magic does ensure the catching of fish, or that if an Andaman mother and father do not observe the food taboos they will be sick. The statements may be very elaborate. Such are the statements which accompany the fundamental rituals of any society: the equivalents of the Mass of the Catholic Church.

6. *Symbolization.* Since the form of ritual action is not determined by the nature of a practical result to be accomplished, it can be determined by other factors. We say that it is symbolic, and each society has its own vocabulary of symbols. Some of the symbol-ism is relatively simple: for example, the symbolism of sympathies and antipathies. Some is complicated. In particular, certain of the rituals of a society, and those the most important, make symbolic reference to the fundamental myths of the society. The ceremonies of the Murngin make reference to the fundamental myths of that society just as surely as the Mass makes reference to Christ's sacrifice on Calvary.

7. *Function.* Ritual actions do not produce a practical result on the external world—that is one reason why we call them ritual. But to make this statement is not to say that ritual has no function. Its function is not related to the world external to the society but to the internal constitution of the society. It gives the members of the society confidence; it dispels their anxieties; it disciplines the social organization. But the functions of ritual have been discussed elsewhere, and in any case they raise questions which are beyond the scope of the present paper.

Finally, a study of the theories of Malinowski and Radcliffe-Brown illustrates a common feature of scientific controversies: two distinguished persons talking past one another rather than trying to find a common ground for discussion, presenting their theories as alternatives when in fact they are complements. Such a study suggests also that the theory necessary for an adequate description of any phenomenon is often more complicated than the theories of the phenomenon which exist at any given time.

Talcott Parsons

RELIGIOUS PERSPECTIVES IN SOCIOLOGY AND SOCIAL PSYCHOLOGY

Among the works of recent American sociologists, those of Talcott Parsons have been of the most general significance in defining the role and function of religion in human society. Parsons' classic paper on this subject is "The Theoretical Development of the Sociology of Religion," in which he synthesizes the theories of Durkheim, Pareto, Weber, and Malinowski. Since this earlier paper is readily available in his *Essays in Sociological Theory* (1949), a briefer and less available essay has been selected for inclusion in this volume.

Adapted from Talcott Parsons, "Sociology and Social Psychology," in Hoxie N. Fairchild (ed.), *Religious Perspectives in College Teaching* (New York: Ronald Press, 1952), pp. 286–305. Copyright 1952, The Ronald Press Company. Used with permission.

In addition to setting forth a definition of religion as a universal feature of human society, Parsons (following leads suggested by Malinowski) also provides a cogent discussion of the two main types of frustration in the human situation that provide focal points for the development of religious patterns. One of these types is due to the fact that men are "hit" by events which they cannot either foresee and prepare for or control, such as the occurrence of premature death. The second type is present where there is a strong emotional investment in the success of human endeavor, where energy and skill count for much, but where unknown or uncontrollable factors often intervene to upset the balance between effort and success, such as in the exposure of agriculture to uncontrollable weather.

These frustrations of established expectations pose "problems of meaning," in the sense that Max Weber wrote much about; that is, we can explain how an automobile accident caused a premature death, but we cannot explain why it had to happen to a particular person at a particular time; we can explain how it is that "the wicked flourish like a green bay tree," but not why it has to come out this way in societies. Hence the significance of religion in human life is that it is made up of those aspects of the life situation to which men cannot remain indifferent, which they cannot in the long run evade, but which they cannot control or adjust to through the ordinary techniques and attitudes of practical utilitarian life.

The present essay is written from the point of view of the social scientist, not that of the representative of any religious denomination.

Sociology we will define as the science interested in the institutional structure of social systems, and the motivational processes in human beings which are involved in the maintenance and change of institutions. Social psychology is an interstitial science between psychology and sociology, much like biochemistry in the natural sciences. It is concerned with the study of motivational processes of behavior and the structure of personalities, in the context of their relevance to social systems and their problems, notably their institutional structure.

A religion we will define as a set of beliefs, practices and institutions which men have evolved in various societies, so far as they can be understood, as responses to those aspects of their life and situation which are believed not in the empirical-instrumental sense to be rationally understandable and/or controllable, and to which they attach a significance which includes some kind of reference to the relevant actions and events to man's conception of the existence of a "supernatural" order which is conceived and felt to have a fundamental bearing on man's position in the universe and the values which give meaning to his fate as an individual and his relations to his fellows.

Defined in this way, a religion or religious system will include at a minimum: (1) a more or less integrated set of beliefs concerning entities which are "supernatural," sacred, or, as Durkheim said, "set apart" from the ordinary objects and events of utilitarian or instrumental significance of human affairs and interests on his relation to which the meaning of man's life is fundamentally dependent; (2) a system of symbols, objects, acts, persons, empirical and non-empirical, which have the quality of sacredness and in relation to which men express the emotional states relevant to the religious sphere, in short, a system of expressive symbols; (3) a set of more or less definitely prescribed activities which are interpreted as important and often obligatory in the light of the beliefs involved, but which from the point of view of the instrumental interests of daily life are "useless" in that they do not "accomplish anything." These activities will usually be prescribed for different types of occasions, forbidden on others and may be differentiated for different statuses in the social group; (4) to some degree a sense that "we" who share common beliefs of this character, and participate in what is felt to be an integrated system of such activities, constitute a "collectivity"—a group which by virtue of that fact is bound together in what Durkheim called a "moral community"; finally, (5) a sense that man's relation to the supernatural world is in some way intimately connected with his moral values, with the nature of the goals he is called upon to live for and the rules of conduct he is expected to comply with. The sharing of these common moral values as well as more specifically "religious" beliefs and practices will be constitutive of the moral community spoken of above.

In addition to these five minimum features of what the sociologist would call a religion or religious system, certain others may be expected to appear in different types of religious systems. These are all aspects of the differentiation and corresponding modes of organization of the social relationship systems which religious beliefs and practices involve. The most important aspect of differentiation is the differentiation of the roles of individuals and of classes of them relative to those of others participating in the same religious system. There are in turn two main aspects of this differentiation. The first is the differentiation of types of individuals and groups relative to their relations to the sacred and supernatural sphere independent of functions on behalf of the religious collectivity, while the second is differentiation of roles with such specialized functions. In the first direction we find such types as the individual ascetic or monastic order. In the second falls the minister or priest who functions on behalf of his congregation. The prophet can be regarded in both contexts, as having established a *new* relation to the supernatural and as the leader of a *movement* to implement its implications in the life of society.

Closely related to the differentiation of roles is the development of the character of the religious collectivity itself. There are several important aspects of this but two may be singled out for mention here. One is the mode of integration—or lack of it—of the religious collectivity itself with the rest of the group structure of the society. Thus it may be an aspect of a single overall collective organization as in the case of the most nonliterate societies, or there may be a distinctive religious grouping as with the Christian church or denominational organization. The other aspect is that of the internal organization of the religious collectivity above all the ways and extent of the development of formal organization of explicit canons formally interpreted and enforced, and the like.

The analysis of the conditions determining the specific type of belief or symbol system, of activities or moral roles, of differentiation of roles, of modes of collectivity organization, constitutes one main aspect of the sociology of religion in a more detailed sense. The other main aspect concerns the ways in which differences of religious systems in these respects are interdependent with other aspects of the social systems of which they are a part. Unfortunately limitations of space preclude entering into the fascinating analysis of these problems here. The reader should, however, keep in mind that solid grounding of many of the empirical generalizations stated in later sections of this essay would require carrying through the relevant analysis on this level in full detail. It is only space limitation which makes this impossible.

MOTIVATION OF RELIGIOUS BELIEF AND BEHAVIOR

With the above sketch of some of the principal components of religious systems on the social level in mind we may now turn to some aspects of the "social psychology" of religion, of the characteristic of man as an "actor" in a situation, and of that situation, which helps us to understand his need for and relations to religious institutions. We will develop this theme in two sections; in the present one we will attempt to sketch some of the main sources of the motivation to religious belief and behavior, and in that following to indicate some of the complicated interrelations between religious and secular motivations on this level.

Man is distinguished from the other animals, from the point of view of the social scientist, above all by the fact that he is a creator and bearer of culture. He creates and lives by systems of symbols and of artifacts; he not only modifies his environment but his orientation to it is generalized in terms of systems of symbolic meaning; he communicates with his fellow men through language and other symbols; he perpetuates and develops his knowledge, and he expresses his feelings, not directly and crudely, but in elaborately symbolic form.

A "culture" is not and cannot be just a discrete collection of disconnected artifacts and symbols, but to a greater or lesser degree must constitute a *system*. It must, that is, have coherence as a set of orientations which tie together the many particular aspects of men's experience and needs. Above all it has three types of functions. In the cognitive aspects, as a system of beliefs, it attempts to answer man's questions about himself and the world he lives in, and we all know that we cannot consciously hold contradictory beliefs without strain. Second, it provides "forms" or expressive symbols for expressing and communicating his feelings, forms which conform to standards of "taste." Finally, and from the sociological point of view perhaps most important, it provides standards for evaluation above all the moral standards which regulate man's conduct, particularly in his relation with his fellows. It can be proved quite definitely that once the step from regulation by "instinct" to the plastic dependence on learned patterns of behavior has been taken by man as organism, a society of men cannot subsist without what sociologists call the institutionalization of a relatively consistent system of patterns of culture, above all of moral values.

The role of culture in human life implies that men must be concerned, in a sense somewhat different from the animals, with the *meaning* of their experience, that is, not merely with whether a given experience gratifies a wish or fills a need or contrariwise involves pain or deprivation, but also with the *fit* between the *expectations* of experience which have been defined for him in his culture, and the actuality which he himself experiences.

There is in every system of human action, in every society, a smooth, "normal" pattern of everyday functioning, of ways in which people go "about their business" without particular strain, where the means available to them are adequate to attain the goals they have been taught to strive for, and where the all-important other people fulfill their expectations. But if all human life were like that, religion would certainly not have the significance that it does. We would be much more likely to think of the "problems" of life as mainly of a practical "utilitarian" kind, to be solved by good "horse sense."

There are certain fundamental respects in which this is an inadequate picture of the human life situation. In whatever kind of society *some* human expectations, in the fulfillment of which people have acquired a deep emotional investment, are doomed to frustration. These frustrations are of two main types. One of them consists in the fact that men are "hit" by events which they either cannot foresee and prepare for, or control, or both; to which, however, they must make major adjustments, sometimes practical but always emotional. The type case of this kind of frustration is the occurrence of premature death. Certainly the fact that though we all know we have to die almost no man knows when he will die is one of the cardinal facts

of the human situation. But not only for the person facing death himself, if he has time to think about it, but quite clearly for the survivors, there is a major problem of adjustment, for the simple reason that the human individual as an object of emotional attachment is of such fundamental importance. Even the loss of a "beloved enemy" can, we know, be very upsetting. Though religious orientations to death, which are universal and fundamental to religion, contain many shadings of belief about the "life after death," the fundamental feature of this orientation is not "wishful thinking." As one historian of religion has put it, "No major religion has ever claimed to be able to 'beat death.'" The dead are dead, and cannot be brought back to life; but the living must still adjust themselves to that fact. From the point of view of the social scientist, what they believe and do in this situation has significance as a set of "mechanisms" which in some ways facilitate this adjustment. From the secular social point of view to hold funeral ceremonies does not "accomplish anything," the functions of such ceremonies are "latent," but they may none the less be highly important.

In general it is extremely conspicuous that ceremonialism not only concerns the directly bereaved, but directly symbolizes the belongingness of the deceased and of the bereaved in larger social groupings. On the one hand these larger groups which are not so directly affected give their "support" to the bereaved, but on the other they set a "tone" for the occasion which in general says, "the traditional values of the society must be upheld." Death must be only a temporary interruption, the important thing on one level is to "get over it" and to go on living. Though it is by no means obvious, there are many features of funeral ceremonies which are closely similar to those of psychotherapy.

There are other types of uncontrollable events besides death which have what in certain respects is a similar bearing on human interests, natural catastrophes being one of them. Furthermore it should be noted that not only frustration in the usual sense, but unexpected and therefore "unearned" good fortune may also have an upsetting effect and require processes of adjustment. Perhaps our own Thanksgiving fits in that category. The Pilgrim Fathers may well have felt that they were extremely "lucky," or as they said, favored by God, to have survived their first terrible year in the wilderness at all.

A second type of frustrating experience is connected with what has come to be called in a special sense "uncertainty." By this is meant the very common type of situation where there is a strong emotional investment in the success of certain human endeavors, where energy and skill undoubtedly count for much, but where unknown and/or uncontrollable factors may and often do intervene to upset any "reasonable" balance between action and success. The exposure of agriculture the world over, with few exceptions, to the vagaries of uncontrollable and unpredictable weather, is one of the most important examples. No matter how industrious and capable a farmer may be, his crops may be ruined by drought or flood. The field of health is another classic example, and there are a variety of others. The unpredictable character of human conduct in many fields, from love to war, is also prominent.

In all these situations rational techniques must of course loom large; no farmer ever grew good crops by magic alone. But these are the classic situations in which what anthropologists call "magic" flourishes. Whatever the distinction made. magic is always continuous with religion, it always involves some relation to the strains occasioned by uncertainty, and to human emotional adjustment to such situations. Magical beliefs and practices constitute, from the point of view of social psychology, mechanisms of adjustment to these situations of strain. They give an opportunity to "act out" some of the psychological products of that strain, thus to "place the blame" for the frustration—most conspicuous in the cases of belief in witchcraft. They give people the sense of "doing something about it" in areas where their rational techniques are powerless or untrustworthy. Above all they act as a tonic to self-confidence; they are a protection against allowing the risk of failure to lead to a fatalistic discouragement, the attitude that since success cannot be assured, it is no use trying at all. At the same time, magic may act as a stereotyping agency in situations where empirical knowledge and technique are applicable, and thus block technological advance—this in spite of the fact which Malinowski makes so clear, that magic cannot take the place of rational technique. The Trobriand Islander does not believe that he can make up for failing to cultivate his garden properly by more or better magic; it is a supplement, not a substitute.

The frustrations of established expectations of which we have been speaking pose "problems of meaning" in a double sense. On the one hand, man, being a culture-bearing animal, does not merely "take it" when things go as he does not expect. He has to give these things a meaning, in the first instance emotionally, so that his adjustments to such experiences can become integrated in the *system* of experience, which means among other things that his reactions are coordinated and organized with those of his fellows; he can communicate his feelings and receive adequate responses to his expressions of them.

But beyond this, as we have noted at the beginning of this section, the culture in which a social group lives constitutes a more or less integrated system. As such it must have a certain level of consistency; it must "cover" the principal ranges of men's experience in such a way that all of them to some degree "make sense," together as a whole.

Besides the direct problem of emotional adjustment to the frustration of particular experiences, the "generalization" which is involved in the integration of a cultural system brings up two further particularly crucial "problem" areas. The culture links the experience and expectations of any particular individual or subgroup with those of others in a society. There is not only the question of why must this happen *to me*, or to those close to me, but why must it happen at all to anyone? Above all, since men universally seek gratification of their wishes and needs there is the generalized problem of suffering, of why men must endure deprivation and pain and so unequally and haphazardly, or, indeed, at all, and, since all societies must live by moral standards, there is equally the problem of "evil," of why men violate the moral standards of their society and why the "economy" of rewards and punishments fails, as it *always* does to some extent, to balance out. Good fortune and suffering must always, to cultural man, be endowed with meaning. They cannot, except in limiting cases, be accepted as something that "just happens." Similarly it is impossible to live by moral standards and yet be wholly indifferent either to the extent of conformity with them or to the fate of conformists and violators respectively. It is necessarily disconcerting that to some degree "the good die young while the wicked flourish as the green bay tree."

The sociologist is in a position to state that some significant degree of discrepancy between expectations in both these respects and the actual state of affairs in a society is inevitable, though it varies greatly in degree and in incidence. Both expectations of gratification and moral standards vary from society to society, but this fundamental fact of discrepancy seems to be a constant, grounded in the nature of human personality, society, and culture and their relations to each other.

This complex of circumstances constitutes from a certain sociological point of view the primary focus of the differential significance of religion in human life. It is made up of aspects of the life situation to which men, being what they are, cannot remain emotionally indifferent, and which at the same time in the long run they cannot evade. But adequate adjustment on either the emotional or the cognitive level to these situations cannot be worked out through the "ordinary" techniques and attitudes of practical utilitarian life. The content and incidence of the problems vary, but their presence is a constant. Almost another way of putting the essential point is to say that tragedy is of the essence of the human situation.

Clyde Kluckhohn

MYTHS AND RITUALS: A GENERAL THEORY

The question of the functional relationship of myths to rituals is one that has concerned students of comparative religion for over a century. Are rituals developed as enactments of myths? Or are myths developed to justify rituals? This latter point of view is vigorously held to by such scholars as Lord Raglan (*The Hero*, 1936) and Stanley Edgar Hyman ("The Ritual View of Myth and the Mythic," 1955) but opposed by Bascom ("The Myth-Ritual Theory," 1957) and others.

In this illuminating paper Kluckhohn discusses the theoretical issues involved, and then shows that there is no necessary primacy of myth over ritual, or vice versa. In some cases, myths were composed to justify rituals. But, in general, there is a tendency for the two to be intricately interrelated and to have important functional connections with the social and psychological life of a particular people. Kluckhohn then tests these generalities by a review of the Navaho Indian case in which he shows in detail the interconnections between myth and ritual and the functions of both in Navaho society.

The identification of a "type anxiety" (that of concern for health) and the function of the ceremonial system (which in Navaho society is almost entirely composed of curing ceremonies) in dealing with this anxiety at both the societal and individual level brings the discussion into sharp focus and shows clearly how myths and rituals can be systematically studied as cultural products.

Reprinted with minor abridgements by permission of the publishers from Clyde Kluckhohn, "Myths and Rituals: A General Theory," *Harvard Theological Review*, XXXV (January, 1942), 45–79. Cambridge, Mass.: Harvard University Press, 1942. The author kindly undertook some minor reworking of the text and deleted most of the footnotes.

I

Nineteenth-century students strongly tended to study mythology apart from associated rituals (and indeed apart from the life of the people generally). Myths were held to be symbolic descriptions of phenomena of nature. One prominent school, in fact, tried to find an astral basis for all mythic tales. Others, among whom Andrew Lang was prominent, saw in the myth a kind of primitive scientific theory. Mythology answered the insistent human HOW? and WHY? How and why was the world made? How and why were living creatures brought into being? Why, if there was life, must there be death? To early psychoanalysts such as Abraham and Rank myths were "group fantasies," wish fulfillments for a society strictly analogous to the dream and daydream of individuals. Mythology for these psychoanalysts was also a symbolic structure par excellence, but the symbolism which required interpretation was primarily a sex symbolism which was postulated as universal and all-pervasive. Reik recognized a connection between rite and myth, and he, with Freud, verbally agreed to Robertson Smith's proposition that mythology was mainly a description of ritual. To the psychoanalysts, however, mythology was essentially (so far as what they did with it is concerned) societal phantasy material which reflected impulse repression. (Many psychoanalysts today consider myths simply "a form of collective daydreaming." I have heard a prominent psychoanalyst say "Creation myths are for culture what early memories (true or fictitious) are to the individual.") There was no attempt to discover the practical function of mythology in the daily behaviors of the members of a society nor to demonstrate specific interactions of mythology and ceremonials. The interest was in supposedly panhuman symbolic meanings, not in the relation of a given myth or part of a myth to particular cultural forms or specific social situations.

To some extent the answer to the whole question of the relationship between myth and ceremony depends, of course, upon how wide or how restricted a sense one gives to "mythology." In ordinary usage the Oedipus tale is a "myth," but only some Freudians believe that this is merely the description of a ritual! The famous stories of the Republic are certainly called "μῦθος," and while a few scholars believe that Plato in *some* cases had reference to the Orphic and/or Eleusinian mysteries there is certainly not a shred of evidence that all of Plato's immortal "myths" are "descriptions of rituals." To be sure, one may justifiably narrow the problem by saying that in a technical sense these are "legends," and by insisting that "myths" be rigorously distinguished from "legends," "fairy tales," and "folk tales." If, however, one agrees that "myth" has Durkheim's connotation of the "sacred" as opposed to

the "profane" the line is still sometimes hard to draw in concrete cases. What of "creation myths"? In some cases (as at Zuni) these are indeed recited during ritual performances (with variations for various ceremonies). In other cases, even though they may be recited in a "ritual" attitude, they do not enter into any ceremonial. Nevertheless, they definitely retain the flavor of "the sacred." Moreover, there are (as again at Zuni) exoteric and esoteric forms of the same myth. Among the Navaho many of the older men who are not ceremonial practitioners know that part of a myth which tells of the exploits of the hero or heroes but not the portion which prescribes the ritual details of the chant. Granting that there are sometimes both secular and sacred versions of the same tale and that other difficulties obtrude themselves in particular cases, it still seems possible to use the connotation of the sacred as that which differentiates "myth" from the rest of folklore.

But defining "myth" strictly as "sacred tale" does not carry with it by implication a warrant for considering mythology purely as a description of correlative rituals. Generally speaking, we do seem to find rich ritualism and a rich mythology together. But there are cases (like the Toda) where an extensive ceremonialism does not appear to have its equally extensive mythological counterpart and instances (like classical Greece) where a ramified mythology appears to have existed more or less independent of a comparatively meager rite system. For example, in spite of the many myths relating to Ares the rituals connected with Ares seem to have been few in number and highly localized in time and space. The early Romans, on the other hand, seemed to get along very well without mythology. The poverty of the ritual which accompanies the extremely complex mythology of the Mohave is well known. Kroeber indeed says, "Public ceremonies or rituals as they occur among almost all native Americans cannot be said to be practiced by the Mohave." The Bushmen likewise had many myths and very little ritual. On the other hand, one can point to examples like the Central Eskimo, where every detail of the Sedna myth has its ritual analogue in confessional, other rites, or hunting taboos, or, for contrast, to the American Indian tribes (especially some Californian ones) where the creation myth is never enacted in ceremonial form. In different sectors of one culture, the Papago, all of these possibilities are represented. Some myths are never ceremonially enacted. Some ceremonies emphasize content foreign to the myth. Other ceremonies consisting only of songs have some vague place in the mythological world; between these and the myths "there is a certain tenuous connection which may be a rationalization made for the sake of unity."

The anthropology of the past generation has tended to recoil sharply from any sort of generalized interpretation. Obsessed with the complexity of the historical experience of all peoples, anthropologists have (perhaps overmuch) eschewed the inference of regularities of psychological reaction which would transcend the facts of diffusion and of contacts of groups. Emphasis has been laid upon the distribution of myths and upon the mythological patterning which prevailed in different cultures and culture areas. Study of these distributions has led to a generalization of another order which is the converse of the hypothesis of most nineteenth-century classical scholars that a ritual was an enactment of a myth. In the words of Boas: "The uniformity of many such rituals over large areas and the diversity of mythological explanations show clearly that the ritual itself is the stimulus for the origin of the myth. . . . The ritual existed, and the tale originated from the desire to account for it."

While this suggestion of the primacy of ritual over the myth is probably a valid statistical induction and a proper statement of the modal tendency of our evidence, it is, it seems to me, as objectionably a simple unitary explanation (if pressed too far) as the generally rejected nineteenth-century views. Thus we find Hocart recently asking: "If there are myths that give rise to ritual where do these myths come from?" A number of instances will shortly be presented in which the evidence is unequivocal that myths did give rise to ritual. May I only remark here that—if we view the matter objectively—the Christian Mass, as interpreted by Christians, is a clear illustration of a ritual based upon a sacred story. Surely, in any case, Hocart's question can be answered very simply: from a dream or a waking fantasy or a personal habit system of some individual in the society. The basic psychological mechanisms involved would seem not dissimilar to those whereby individuals in our own (and other) cultures construct private rituals or carry out private divination— e.g., counting and guessing before the clock strikes, trying to get to a given point (a traffic light, for instance) before something else happens. As DuBois has suggested, "the explanation may be that personal rituals have been taken over and socialized by the group." These "personal rituals" could have their genesis in idiosyncratic habit formations (similar to those of obsessional neurotics in our culture) or in dreams or reveries. Mrs. Seligman has convincingly suggested that spontaneous personal dissociation is a frequent mechanism for rite innovations. The literature is replete with instances of persons "dreaming" that supernaturals summoned them, conducted them on travels or adventures, and finally admonished them thereafter to carry out certain rites (often symbolically repetitive of the adventures).

Moreover, there are a number of well-documented actual cases where historical persons, in the memory of other historical persons, actually instituted new rituals. The ritual innovations of the American Indian Ghost Dance cult and other nativistic cults of the New World provide striking illustration. In these cases the dreams or fantasies— told by the innovators before the ceremonial was ever actualized in deeds—became an important part of traditionally accepted rite-myths. Lincoln has presented plausible evidence that dreams are the source of "new" rituals. Morgan, on the basis of Navaho material, says:

. . . delusions and dreams . . . are so vivid and carry such conviction that any attempt to reason about them afterwards on the basis of conscious sense impressions is unavailing. Such experiences deeply condition the individual, sometimes so deeply that if the experience is at variance with a tribal or neighborhood belief, the individual will retain his own variation. There can be no doubt that this is a very significant means of modifying a culture.

Van Gennep asserts that persons went to dream in the sanctuary at Epidaurus as a source for new rites in the cult of Asclepius. To obtain ceremony through dream is, of course, itself a pattern, a proper traditional way of obtaining a ceremony or power. I do not know of any cases of a society where dreaming is generally in disrepute, as at Zuni, and where ceremony has yet demonstrably originated through dream. But where dreaming is accepted as revelation it must not be assumed that the content (or even, entirely, the structure) of a new myth and its derived ceremony will be altogether determined by pre-existent cultural forms. As Lowie has remarked, "That they themselves (dreams) in part reflect the regnant folklore offers no ultimate explanation." Anthropologists must be wary of what Korzybski calls "self-reflexive systems"—here, specifically, the covert premise that "culture alone determines culture."

The structure of new cultural forms (whether myths or rituals) will undoubtedly be conditioned by the pre-existent cultural matrix. But the rise of new cultural forms will amost always be determined by factors external to that culture: pressure from other societies, biological events such as epidemics, or changes in the physical environment. Barber has recently shown how the Ghost Dance and the Peyote Cult represent alternative responses of various American Indian tribes to the deprivation resultant upon the encroachment of whites. The Ghost Dance was an adaptive response under the earlier external conditions, but under later conditions the Peyote Cult was the more adaptive response, and the Ghost Dance suffered what the stimulus-response psychologists would call "extinction through non-reward." At any rate, the Ghost Dance became extinct in some tribes; in others it has perhaps suffered only partial extinction.

There are always individuals in every society who have their private rituals; there are always individuals who dream and who have compensatory fantasies. In the normal course of things these are simply deviant behaviors which are ridiculed or ignored by most members of the society. Perhaps indeed one should not speak of them as "deviant"— they are "deviant" only as carried to extremes by a relatively small number of individuals, for everyone probably has some private rituals and compensatory fantasies. When, however, changed conditions happen to make a particular type of obsessive behavior or a special sort of fantasy generally congenial, the private ritual is then socialized by the group, the fantasy of the individual becomes the myth of his society. Indeed there is evidence that when pressures are peculiarly strong and peculiarly general, a considerable number of different individuals may almost simultaneously develop substantially identical fantasies which then become widely current.

Whether belief (myth) or behavior (ritual) changes first will depend, again, both upon cultural tradition and upon external circumstances. Taking a very broad view of the matter, it does seem that behavioral patterns more frequently alter first. In a rapidly changing culture such as our own many ideal patterns are as much as a generation behind the corresponding behavioral patterns. There is evidence that certain ideal patterns (for example, those defining the status of women) are slowly being altered to harmonize with, to act as rationalizations for, the behavioral actualities. On the other hand, the case of Nazi Germany is an excellent illustration of the ideal patterns ("the myth") being provided from above almost whole cloth and of the state, through various organizations, exerting all its force to make the behavioral patterns conform to the standards of conduct laid down in the Nazi mythology.

Some cultures and subcultures are relatively indifferent to belief, others to behavior. The dominant practice of the Christian Church, throughout long periods of its history, was to give an emphasis to belief which is most unusual as seen from a cross-cultural perspective. In general, the crucial test as to whether or not one was a Christian was the willingness to avow belief in certain dogmas. The term "believer" was almost synonymous with "Christian." It is very possibly because of this cultural screen that until this century most European scholars selected the myth as primary.

II

To a considerable degree, the whole question of the primacy of ceremonial or mythology is as meaningless as all questions of "the hen or the egg" form. What is really important, as Malinowski has so brilliantly shown, is the intricate interdependence of myth (which is one form of ideology) with ritual and many other forms of behavior. He examines myths not as curiosa taken out of their total context but as living, vitally important elements in the day-to-day lives of his Trobrianders, interwoven with every other abstracted type of activity. From this point of view one sees the fallacy of all unilateral explanations. One also sees the aspect of truth in all (or nearly all) of them. There are features which seem to be explanatory of natural phenomena. There are features which reveal the peculiar forms of wish fulfillments characteristic of the culture in question (including the expression of the culturally disallowed but unconsciously wanted). There *are* myths which are intimately related to rituals, which may be descriptive of them, but there are myths which stand apart. If these others are descriptive of rituals at all, they are, as Durkheim (followed by Radcliffe-Brown and others) suggested, descriptions of rituals of the social organization. That is, they are symbolic representations of the dominant configurations of the particular culture. Myths, then, may express not only the latent content of rituals but of other culturally organized behaviors. Malinowski is surely in error when he writes "...myth...is not symbolic...." Durkheim and Mauss have pointed out how various nonliterate groups (notably the Zuni and certain tribes of southeastern Australia) embrace nature within the schema of their social organization through myths which classify natural phenomena precisely according to the principles that prevail in the social organization.

Boas, with his usual caution, is skeptical of all attempts to find a systematic interpretation of mythology. But, while we can agree with him when he writes "...mythological narratives and mythological concepts should not be equalized; for social, psychological, and historical conditions affect both in different ways," the need for scrupulous inquiry into historical and other determinants must not be perverted to justify a repudiation of all attempts to deal with the symbolic processes of the all-important covert culture. At all events, the factual record is perfectly straightforward in one respect: neither myth nor ritual can be postulated as "primary."

This is the important point in our discussion at this juncture, and it is unfortunate that Hooke and his associates in their otherwise very illuminating contributions to the study of the relations between myth and ritual in the Near East have emphasized only one aspect of the system of interdependences which Malinowski and Radcliffe-Brown have shown to exist. When Hooke points out that myths are constantly used to justify rituals this observation is quite congruent with the observed facts in many cultures. Indeed all of these data may be used toward a still wider induction: man, as a symbol-using animal, appears to feel the need not only to act but almost equally to give verbal or other symbolic "reasons" for his acts.

Hooke rightly speaks of "the vital significance of the myth as something that works," but when he continues "and that dies apart from its ritual" he seems to imply that myths cannot exist apart from rituals and this, as has been shown, is contrary to documented cases. No, the central theorem has been expressed much more adequately by Radcliffe-Brown: "In the case of both ritual and myth the sentiments expressed are those that are essential to the existence of the society." This theorem can be regarded as having been well established in a general way, but we still lack detailed observations on change in myths as correlated with changes in ritual and changes in a cultural generally. Navaho material gives certain hints that when a culture as a whole changes rapidly its myths are also substantially and quickly altered.

In sum, the facts do not permit any universal generalizations as to ritual being the "cause" of myth or vice versa. Their relationship is rather that of intricate mutual interdependence, differently structured in different cultures and probably at different times in the same culture. As Benedict has pointed out, there is great variation in the extent to which mythology conditions the religious complex—"the small role of myth in Africa and its much greater importance in religion in parts of North America." Both myth and ritual satisfy the needs of a society and the relative place of one or the other will depend upon the particular needs (conscious and unconscious) of the individuals in a particular society at a particular time. This principle covers the observed data, which show that rituals are borrowed without their myths, and myths without any accompanying ritual. A ritual may be reinforced by a myth (or vice versa) in the donor culture, but satisfy the carriers of the recipient culture simply as a form of activity (or be rationalized by a quite different myth which better meets their emotional needs). In short, the only uniformity which can be posited is that there is a strong tendency for some sort of interrelationship between myth and ceremony and that this is dependent upon what appears, so far as present information goes, to be an invariant function of both myth and ritual: the gratification (most often in the negative form of anxiety reduction) of a large proportion of the individuals in a society.

If Malinowski and Radcliffe-Brown (and their followers) turned the searchlight of their interpretations as illuminatingly upon specific human animals and their impulses as upon cultural and social abstractions, it might be possible to take their work as providing a fairly complete and adequate general theory of myth and ritual. With Malinowski's notion of myth as "an active force" which is intimately related to almost every other aspect of a culture we can only agree. When he writes: "Myth is a constant by-product of living faith which is in need of miracles; of sociological status, which demands precedent; of moral rule which requires sanction," we can only applaud. To the French sociologists, to Radcliffe-Brown, and to Warner we are indebted for the clear formulation of the symbolic principle. Those realms of behavior and of experience which man finds beyond rational and technological control he feels are capable of manipulation through symbols. Both myth and ritual are symbolical procedures and are most closely tied together by this, as well as by other, facts. The myth is a system of word symbols, whereas ritual is a system of object and act symbols. Both are symbolic processes for dealing with the same type of situation in the same affective mode.

But the French sociologists, Radcliffe-Brown, and—to a lesser extent—Malinowski are so interested in formulating the relations between conceptual elements that they tend to lose sight of the concrete human organisms. The "functionalists" do usually start with a description of some particular ritualistic behaviors. Not only, however, do the historical origins of this particular behavioral complex fail to interest them. Equally, the motivations and rewards which persons feel are lost sight of in the preoccupation with the contributions which the rituals make to the social system. Thus a sense of the specific detail is lost and we are soon talking about myth in general and ritual in general. From the "functionalist" point of view specific details are about as arbitrary as the phonemes of a language are with respect to "the content" of what is communicated by speech. Hence, as Dollard says, "What one sees from the cultural angle is a drama of life much like a puppet show in which 'culture' is pulling the strings from behind the scenes." The realization that we are really dealing with "animals struggling in real dilemmas" is lacking.

From this angle, some recent psychoanalytic interpretations of myth and ritual seem preferable. We may regard as unconvincing Roheim's attempts to treat myths as historical documents which link human phylogenetic and ontogenetic development, as we may justly feel that many psychoanalytic discussions of the latent content of mythology are extravagant and undisciplined. Casey's summary of the psychoanalytic view of religion, "... ritual is a sublimated compulsion; dogma and myth are sublimated obsessions," may well strike us as an oversimplified, overneat generalization, but at least our attention is drawn to the connection between cultural forms and impulse-motivated organisms. And Kardiner's relatively sober and controlled treatment does "point at individuals, at bodies, and at a rich and turbulent biological life"—even though that life is admittedly conditioned by social heredity: social organization, culturally defined symbolic systems, and the like.

In a later section of this paper, we shall return to the problem of how myths and rituals reinforce the behavior of individuals. But first let us test the generalities which have been propounded thus far by concrete data from a single culture, the Navaho.

III

The Navaho certainly have sacred tales which, as yet at all events, are not used to justify associated rituals. A striking case, and one where the tale has a clear function as expressing a sentiment "essential to the existence of the society," is known from different parts of the Navaho country. The tales differ in detail but all have these structural elements in common: one of "the Holy People" visits one or more Navahos to warn them of an impending catastrophe (a flood or the like) which will destroy the whites—but believing Navahos will be saved if they retire to the top of a mountain or some other sanctuary. It is surely not without meaning that these tales became current at about the time that the Navahos were first feeling intensive and sustained pressure (they were not just prisoners of war as in the Fort Sumner epoch) from the agents of our culture. Father Berard Haile has recently published evidence that Navaho ceremonials may originate in dreams or visions rather than being invariably *post hoc* justifications for existent ritual practices. A practitioner called "son of the late Black Goat" instituted a new ceremonial "which he had learned in a dream while sleeping in a cave." Various informants assured Father Berard that chant-way legends originated in the "visions" of individuals. We have, then, Navaho data for (a) the existence of myths without associated rituals, and (b) the origin of both legends and rituals in dreams or visions.

It is true that all ceremonial practice among the Navaho is, in cultural theory, justified by an accompanying myth. One may say with Dr. Parsons on the Pueblos: "Whatever the original relationship between myth and ceremony, once made, the myth supports the ceremony or ceremonial office and may suggest ritual increments." One must in the same breath, however, call attention to the fact that myth also supports accepted ways of secular behavior. As Dr. Hill has pointed out, "Women are required to sit with their legs under them and to one side, men with their legs crossed in front of them, because it is said that in the beginning Changing Woman and the Monster Slayer sat in these positions." Let this one example suffice for the many which could easily be given. The general point is that in both sacred and secular spheres myths give some fixity to the ideal patterns of cultures where this is not attained by the printed word. The existence of rituals has a similar effect. Although I cannot agree with Wissler that "the primary function" of rituals is "to perpetuate exact knowledge and to secure precision in their application," there can be no doubt that both myths and rituals are important agencies in the transmission of a culture and that they act as brakes upon the speed of culture change.

Returning to the connections between myth and rite among the Navaho, one cannot do better than begin by quoting some sentences from Washington Matthews: "In some cases a Navajo rite has only one myth pertaining to it. In other cases it has many myths. The relation of the myth to the ceremony is variable. Sometimes it explains nearly everything in the ceremony and gives an account of all the important acts from beginning to end, in the order in which they occur; at other times it describes the work in a less systematic manner. . . . Some of the myths seem to tell only of the way in which rites, already established with other tribes, were introduced among the Navajos. . . . The rite-myth never explains all of the symbolism of the rite, although it may account for all the important acts. A primitive and underlying symbolism which probably existed previous to the establishment of the rite, remains unexplained by the myth, as though its existence were taken as a matter of course, and required no explanation."

To these observations one may add the fact that knowledge of the myth is in no way prerequisite to the carrying out of a chant. Knowledge does give the singer or curer prestige and ability to expect higher fees, and disparaging remarks are often heard to the effect "Oh, he doesn't know the story," or "He doesn't know the story very well yet." And yet treatment by a practitioner ignorant of the myth is regarded as efficacious. Navahos are often a little cynical about the variation in the myths. If someone observes that one singer did not carry out a procedure exactly as did another (of perhaps greater repute) it will often be said "Well, he says *his* story is different." Different forms of a rite-myth tend to prevail in different areas of the Navaho country and in different localities. Here the significance of the "personality" of various singers may sometimes be detected in the rise of variations. The transvestite "Left-handed" who died a few years ago enjoyed a tremendous reputation as a singer. There is some evidence that he restructuralized a number of myths as he told them to his apprentices in a way tended to make the hermaphrodite *be ʔgočidi* a kind of supreme Navaho deity—a position which he perhaps never held in the general tradition up to that point. I have heard other Navaho singers say that sand paintings and other ceremonial acts and procedures were slightly revised to accord with this tenet. If this be true, we have here another clear instance of myth-before-ritual.

Instances of the reverse sort are also well documented. From a number of informants accounts have been independently obtained of the creation (less than a hundred years ago) of a new rite: Enemy Monster Blessing Way. All the information agreed that the ritual procedures had been devised by one man who collated parts of two previously existent ceremonials and added a few bits from his own fancy. And three informants independently volunteered the observation "He didn't have any story. But after a while he and his son and another fellow made one up." This is corroborated by the fact that none of Father Berard's numerous versions of the Blessing Way myth mentions an Enemy Monster form.

Besides these notes on the relations between myth and rite I should like to record my impression of another function of myth—one which ranges from simple entertainment to "intellectual edification." Myth among the Navaho not only acts as a justification, a rationale for ritual behavior and as a moral reinforcement for other customary behaviors. It also plays a role not dissimilar to that of literature (especially sacred literature) in many literate cultures. Navahos have a keen expectation of the long recitals of myths (or portions of them) around the fire on winter nights.[1] Myths have all the charm of the familiar. Their very familiarity increases their efficacy, for, in a certain broad and loose sense, the function of both myths and rituals is "the discharge of the emotion of individuals in socially accepted channels." And Hocart acutely observes: "Emotion is assisted by the repetition of words that have acquired a strong emotional coloring, and this coloring again is intensified by repetition." Myths are expective, repetitive dramatizations—their role is similar to that of books in cultures which have few books. They have the (to us) scarcely understandable meaningfulness which the tragedies had for the Greek populace. As Matthew Arnold said of these, "their significance appeared inexhaustible."

IV

The inadequacy of any simplistic statement of the relationship between myth and ritual has been established. It has likewise been maintained that the most adequate generalization will not be cast in terms of the primacy of one or the other of these cultural forms but rather in terms of the general tendency for the two to be interdependent. This generalization has been arrived at through induction from abstractions at the cultural level. That is, as we have sampled the evidence from various cultures we have found cases where myths have justified rituals and have

appeared to be "after the fact" of ritual; we have also seen cases where new myths have given rise to new rituals. In other words, the primary conclusion which may be drawn from the data is that myths and rituals tend to be very intimately associated and to influence each other. What is the explanation of the observed connection?

The explanation is to be found in the circumstance that myth and ritual satisfy a group of identical or closely related needs of individuals. Thus far we have alluded only occasionally and often obliquely to myths and rituals as cultural forms defining individual behaviors which are adaptive or adjustive responses. We have seen how myths and rituals are adaptive from the point of view of the society in that they promote social solidarity, enhance the integration of the society by providing a formalized statement of its ultimate value-attitudes, and afford a means for the transmission of much of the culture with little loss of content—thus protecting cultural continuity and stabilizing the society. But how are myth and ritual rewarding enough in the daily lives of individuals so that individuals are instigated to preserve them, so that myth and ritual continue to prevail at the expense of more rational responses?

A systematic examination of this question, mainly again in terms of Navaho material, will help us to understand the prevailing interdependence of myth and ritual which has been documented. This sketch of a general theory of myth and ritual as providing a cultural storehouse of adjustive responses for individuals is to be regarded as tentative from the writer's point of view. I do not claim that the theory is proven—even in the context of Navaho culture. I do suggest that it provides a series of working hypotheses which can be tested by specifically pointed field procedures.

We can profitably begin by referring to the function of myth as fulfilling the expectancy of the familiar. Both myth and ritual here provide cultural solutions to problems which all human beings face. Burke has remarked, "Human beings build their cultures, nervously loquacious, upon the edge of an abyss." In the face of want and death and destruction all humans have a fundamental insecurity. To some extent, all culture is a gigantic effort to mask this, to give the future the simulacrum of safety by making activity repetitive, expective—"to make the

[1] Why may the myths be recited only in winter? In Navaho feeling today this prohibition is linked in a wider configuration of forbidden activities. There is also, as usual, an historical and distributional problem, for this same prohibition is apparently widely distributed in North America. For example, it is found among the Berens River Salteaux and among the Iroquois. But I wonder if in a certain "deeper" sense this prohibition is not founded upon the circumstance that only winter affords the leisure for telling myths, that telling them in summer would be unfitting because it would interfere with work activities?

future predictable by making it conform to the past." From one angle our own scientific mythology is clearly related to that motivation, as is the obsessive, the compulsive tendency which lurks in all organized thought.

When questioned as to why a particular ceremonial activity is carried out in a particular way, Navaho singers will most often say "because the *diɣin diné*—the Holy People —did it that way in the first place." The *ultima ratio* of nonliterates strongly tends to be "that is what our fathers said it was." An Eskimo said to Rasmussen: "We Eskimos do not concern ourselves with solving all riddles. We repeat the old stories in the way they were told to us and with the words we ourselves remember." The Eskimo saying "we keep the old rules in order that we may live untroubled" is well known.

. . .

Goldstein, a neurologist, recognizes a neurological basis for the persistence of such habit systems: "The organism tends to function in the accustomed manner, as long as an at least moderately effective performance can be achieved in this way."

Nevertheless, certain objections to the position as thus far developed must be anticipated and met. It must be allowed at once that the proposition "man dreads both spontaneity and change" must be qualified. More precisely put, we may say "most men, most of the time, dread both spontaneity and change in most of their activities." This formulation allows for the observed fact that most of us *occasionally* get irked with the routines of our lives or that there are certain sectors of our behavior where we fairly consistently show spontaneity. But a careful examination of the totality of behavior of any individual who is not confined in an institution or who has not withdrawn almost completely from participation in the society will show that the larger proportion of the behavior of even the greatest iconoclasts is habitual. This must be so, for by very definition a socialized organism is an organism which behaves mainly in a predictable manner. . . .

Existence in an organized society would be unthinkable unless most people, most of the time, behaved in an expectable manner. Rituals constitute "tender spots" for all human beings, people can count upon the repetitive nature of the phenomena. For example, in Zuni society (where rituals are highly calendrical) a man whose wife has left him or whose crops have been ruined by a torrential downpour can yet look forward to the Shalako ceremonial as something which is fixed and immutable. Similarly, the personal sorrow of the devout Christian is in some measure mitigated by anticipation of the great feasts of Christmas and Easter. Perhaps the even turn of the week with its Sunday services and mid-week prayer meetings gave a dependable regularity which the Christian clung to even more in disaster and sorrow. For some individuals daily prayer and the confessional gave the needed sense of security. Myths, likewise, give men "something to hold to." The Christian can better face the seemingly capricious reverses of his plans when he hears the joyous words "lift up your hearts." Rituals and myths supply, then, fixed points in a world of bewildering change and disappointment.

If almost all behavior has something of the habitual about it, how is it that myths and rituals tend to represent the maximum of fixity? Because they deal with those sectors of experience which do not seem amenable to rational control and hence where human beings can least tolerate insecurity. That very insistence upon the minutiae of ritual performance, upon preserving the myth to the very letter, which is characteristic of religious behavior must be regarded as a "reaction formation" (in the Freudian sense) which compensates for the actual intransigence of those events which religion tries to control.

To anticipate another objection: do these "sanctified habit systems" show such extraordinary persistence simply because they are repeated so often and so scrupulously? Do myths and rituals constitute repetitive behavior par excellence not merely as reaction formations but because the habits are practiced so insistently? Perhaps myths and rituals perdure in accord with Allport's "principle of functional autonomy"—as interpreted by some writers? No, performances must be rewarded in the day-to-day lives of participating individuals. Sheer repetition in and of itself has never assured the persistence of any habit. If this were not so, no myths and rituals would ever have become extinct except when a whole society died out. It is necessary for us to recognize the somewhat special conditions of drive and of reward which apply to myths and rituals.

It is easy to understand why organisms eat. It is easy to understand why a defenseless man will run to escape a charging tiger. The physiological bases of the activities represented by myths and rituals are less obvious. A recent statement by a stimulus-response psychologist gives us the clue: "The position here taken is that human beings (and also other living organisms to varying degrees) can be motivated either by organic pressures (needs) that are currently felt *or* by the mere anticipation of such pressures, and that those habits tend to be acquired and perpetuated (reinforced) which effect a reduction in either of these two types of motivation." That is, myths and rituals are reinforced because they reduce the anticipation of disaster. No living person has died—but he has seen others die. The terrible things which we have seen happen to others may not yet have plagued us, but our experience teaches us that these are at least potential threats to our own health or happiness.

If a Navaho gets a bad case of snow blindness and recovers after being sung over, his disposition to go to a singer in the event of a recurrence will be strongly reinforced. And, by the principle of generalization, he is likely to go even if the ailment is quite different. Likewise, the reinforcement will be reciprocal—the singer's confidence in his powers will also be reinforced. Finally there will be some reinforcement for spectators and for all who hear of the recovery. That the ritual treatment rather than more rational preventatives or cures tends to be followed on future occasions can be understood in terms of the principle of the gradient of reinforcement. Delayed rewards are less effective than immediate rewards. In terms of the conceptual picture of experience with which the surrogates of his culture have furnished him, the patient *expects* to be relieved. Therefore, the very onset of the chant produces some lessening of emotional tension—in technical terms, some reduction of anxiety. If the Navaho is treated by a white physician, the "cure" is more gradual and is dependent upon the purely physico-chemical effects of the treatment. If the native wears snow goggles or practices some other form of prevention recommended by a white, the connection between the behavior and the reward (no soreness of the eyes) is so diffuse and so separated in time that reinforcement is relatively weak. Even in those cases where no improvement (other than "psychological") is effected, the realization or at any rate the final acceptance that no help was obtained comes so much later than the immediate sense of benefit that the extinction effects are relatively slight.

Navaho myths and rituals provide a cultural storehouse of adjustive[2] responses for individuals. Nor are these limited to the more obvious functions of providing individuals with the possibility of enhancing personal prestige through display of memory, histrionic ability, etc. Of the ten "mechanisms of defense" which Anna Freud suggests that the ego has available, their myths and rituals afford the Navaho with institutionalized means of employing at least four. Reaction formation has already been discussed. Myths supply abundant materials for introjection and likewise (in the form of witchcraft myths) suggest an easy and culturally acceptable method of projection of hostile impulses. Finally, rituals provide ways of sublimation of aggression and other socially disapproved tendencies, in part, simply through giving people something to *do*.

All of these "mechanisms of ego defense" will come into context only if we answer the question, "adjustive with respect to what?" The existence of motivation, of "anxiety," in Navaho individuals must be accounted for by a number of different factors. In the first place—as in every society—there are those components of "anxiety," those "threats" which may be understood in terms of the "reality principle" of psychoanalysis: life *is* hard—an unseasonable temperature, a vagary of the rainfall does bring hunger or actual starvation; people *are* organically ill. In the second place, there are various forms of "neurotic" anxiety. In our own society it is probably sexual, although this may be true only of those segments of our society who are able to purchase economic and physical

[2] It is not possible to say "adaptive" here because there are not infrequent occasions on which ceremonial treatment aggravates the condition or actually brings about death (which would probably not have supervened under a more rational treatment or even if the patient had simply been allowed to rest). From the point of view of the society, however, the rituals are with little doubt adaptive. Careful samples in two areas and more impressionistic data from the Navaho country generally indicate that the frequency of ceremonials has very materially increased concomitantly with the increase of white pressure in recent years. It is tempting to regard this as an adaptive response similar to that of the Ghost Dance and Peyote Cult on the part of other American Indian tribes

security. In most Plains Indians sexual anxiety, so far as we can tell from the available documents, was insignificant. There the basic anxiety was for life itself and for a certain quality of that life (which I cannot attempt to characterize in a few words).

Among the Navaho the "type anxiety" is certainly that for health. Almost all Navaho ceremonials (essentially every ceremonial still carried out today) are curing ceremonials. And this apparently has a realistic basis. A prominent officer of the Indian Medical Service stated that it was his impression that morbidity among the Navaho is about three times that found in average white communities. In a period of four months' field work among the Navaho, Drs. A. and D. Leighton found in their running field notes a total of 707 Navaho references to "threats" which they classified under six headings. Of these, sixty per cent referred to bodily welfare, and are broken down by the Leightons as follows:

Disease is responsible for sixty-seven per cent, accidents for seventeen per cent, and the rest are attributed to wars and fights. Of the diseases described, eighty-one per cent were evidently organic, like smallpox, broken legs, colds, and sore throats; sixteen per cent left us in doubt as to whether they were organic or functional; and three per cent were apparently functional, with symptoms suggesting depression, hysteria, etc. Of all the diseases, forty per cent were incapacitating, forty-three per cent were not, and seventeen per cent were not sufficiently specified in our notes to judge. From these figures it can easily be seen that lack of health is a very important concern of these Navahos, and that almost half of the instances of disease that they mentioned interfered with life activities ["Some Types of Uneasiness," p. 203].

While I am inclined to believe that the character of this sample was somewhat influenced by the fact that the Leightons were white physicians—to whom organic illnesses, primarily, would be reported—there is no doubt that these data confirm the reality of the health "threat." In terms of clothing and shelter which are inadequate (from our point of view at least), of hygiene and diet which similarly fail to conform to our health standards, it is not altogether surprising that the Navaho need to be preoccupied with their health. It is unequivocally true in my experience that a greater proportion of my Navaho friends are found ill when I call upon them than of my white friends.

The Navaho and Pueblo Indians live in essentially the same physical environment. Pueblo rituals are concerned predominantly with rain and with fertility. This contrast to the Navaho preoccupation with disease cannot (in the absence of fuller supporting facts) be laid to a lesser frequency of illness among the Pueblos, for it seems well documented that the Pueblos, living in congested towns, have been far more ravaged by endemic diseases than the Navaho. The explanation is probably to be sought in terms of the differing historical experience of the two peoples and in terms of the contrasting economic and social organizations. If one is living in relative isolation and if one is largely dependent (as were the Navaho at no terribly distant date) upon one's ability to move about hunting and collecting, ill-health presents a danger much more crucial than to the Indian who lives in a town which has a reserve supply of corn and a more specialized social organization.

That Navaho myths and rituals are focused upon health and upon curing has, then, a firm basis in the reality of the external world. But there is also a great deal of uneasiness arising from interpersonal relationships, and this undoubtedly influences the way the Navaho react to their illnesses. Then, too, one type of anxiousness always tends to modify others. Indeed, in view of what the psychoanalysts have taught us about "accidents" and of what we are learning from psychosomatic medicine about the psychogenic origin of many "organic" diseases we cannot regard the sources of disease among the Navaho as a closed question. Some disorders (especially perhaps those associated with acute anxieties) may be examples of what Caner has called "superstitious self-protection."

Where people live under constant threat from the physical environment, where small groups are geographically isolated and "emotional inbreeding" within the extended family group is at a maximum, interpersonal tensions and hostilities are inevitably intense. The prevalence of ill-health which throws additional burdens on the well and strong is in itself an additional socially disruptive force. But if the overt expression of aggressive impulses proceeds very far the whole system of "economic" co-operation breaks down and then sheer physical survival is more than precarious. Here myths and rituals constitute a series of highly adaptive responses from the point of view of the society. Recital of or reference to the myths reaffirms the solidarity of the Navaho sentiment system. In the words of a Navaho informant: "Knowing a good story will protect your home and children and property. A myth is just like a big stone foundation— it lasts a long time." Performance of rituals likewise heightens awareness of the common system of sentiments. The ceremonials also bring individuals together in a situation where quarreling is forbidden. Preparation for and carrying out of a chant demands intricately ramified co-operation, economic and otherwise, and doubtless thus reinforces the sense of mutal dependency.

Myths and rituals equally facilitate the adjustment of the individual to his society. Primarily, perhaps, they provide a means of sublimation of his antisocial tendencies. It is surely not without meaning that essentially all known chant myths take the family and some trouble within it as a point of departure.

. . .

While as a total explanation the following would be oversimple, it seems fair to say that the gist of this may be interpreted as follows: the chant myth supplies a catharsis for the traumata incident upon the socialization of the Navaho child. That brother and sister are the principal *dramatis personae* fits neatly with the central conflicts of the Navaho socialization process. This is a subject which I hope to treat in detail in a later paper.

Overt quarrels between family members are by no means infrequent, and, especially when drinking has been going on, physical blows are often exchanged. Abundant data indicate that Navahos have a sense of shame which is fairly persistent and that this is closely connected with the socially disapproved hostile impulses which they have experienced toward relatives. It is also clear that their mistrust of others (including those in their own extended family group) is in part based upon a fear of retaliation (and this fear of retaliation is soundly based upon experience in actual life as well as, possibly, upon "unconscious guilt"). Certain passages in the myths indicate that the Navaho have a somewhat conscious realization that the ceremonials act as a cure, not only for physical illness, but also for antisocial tendencies. The following extract from the myth of the Mountain Top Way Chant will serve as an example: "The ceremony cured Dsiliyi Neyani of all his strange feelings and notions. The lodge of his people no longer smelled unpleasant to him."

Thus "the working gods" of the Navaho are their sanctified repetitive ways of behavior. If these are offended by violation of the culture's system of scruples, the ceremonials exist as institutionalized means of restoring the individual to full rapport with the universe: nature and his own society. Indeed "restore" is the best English translation of the Navaho word which the Navaho constantly use to express what the ceremonial does for the "patient." The associated myths reinforce the patient's belief that the ceremonial will both truly cure him of his illness and also "change" him so that he will be a better man in his relations with his family and his neighbors. An English-speaking Navaho who had just returned from jail where he had been put for beating his wife and molesting his stepdaughter said to me: "I am sure going to behave from now on. I am going to be changed—just like somebody who has been sung over."

Since a certain minimum of social efficiency is by derivation a biological necessity for the Navaho, not all of the hostility and uneasiness engendered by the rigors of the physical environment, geographical isolation, and the burdens imposed by illness is expressed or even gets into consciousness. There is a great deal of repression and this leads, on the one hand, to projection phenomena (especially in the form of fantasies that others are practicing witchcraft against one) and, on the other hand, the strong feelings of shame at the conscious level are matched by powerful feelings of guilt at the unconscious level. Because a person feels guilty by reason of his unconscious hostilities towards members of his family (and friends and neighbors generally), some individuals develop chronic anxieties. Such persons feel continually uncomfortable. They say they "feel sick all over" without specifying organic ailments other than very vaguely. They feel so "ill" that they must have ceremonials to cure them. The diagnostician and other practitioners, taking myths as their authority, will refer the cause of the illness to the patient's having seen animals struck by lightning, to a past failure to observe ritual requirements, or to some similar violation of a cultural scruple. But isn't this perhaps basically a substitution of symbols acceptable to consciousness, a displacement of guilt feelings?

It is my observation that Navahos other than those who exhibit chronic or acute anxieties tend characteristically to show a high level of anxiety. It would be a mistake, however, to attribute all of this anxiety to intra-familial tensions, although it is my impression that this is the outstanding pressure. Secondary drives resultant upon culture change and upon white pressure are also of undoubted importance. And it is likewise true, as Mr. Homans has pointed out, that the existence of these ritual injunctions and prohibitions (and of the concomitant myths and other beliefs) gives rise to still another variety of anxiety. In other words, the conceptual picture of the world which Navaho culture sets forth makes for a high threshold of anxiety in that it defines all manner of situations as fraught with peril, and individuals are instigated to anticipate danger on every hand.

But the culture, of course, prescribes not only the supernatural dangers but also the supernatural means of meeting these dangers or of alleviating their effects. Myths and rituals jointly provide systematic protection against supernatural dangers, the threats of ill-health and of the physical environment, antisocial tensions, and the pressures of a more powerful society. In the absence of a codified law and of an authoritarian "chief" or other father substitute, it is only through the myth-ritual system that Navahos can make a socially supported, unified response to all of these disintegrating threats. The all-pervasive configurations of words symbols (myths) and of act symbols (rituals) preserve the cohesion of the society and sustain the individual, protecting him from intolerable conflict. As Hoagland has remarked:

Religion appears to me to be a culmination of this basic tendency of organisms to react in a configurational way to situations. We must resolve conflicts and disturbing puzzles by closing some sort of a configuration, and the religious urge appears to be a primitive tendency, possessing biological survival value, to unify our environment so that we can cope with it.

V

The Navaho are only one case. The specific adaptive and adjustive responses performed by myth and ritual will be differently phrased in different societies according to the historical experience of these societies (including the specific opportunities they have had for borrowing from other cultures), in accord with prevalent configurations of other aspects of the culture, and with reference to pressures exerted by other societies and by the physical and biological environment. But the general nature of the adaptive and adjustive responses performed by myth and ritual appears very much the same in all human groups. Hence, although the relative importance of myth and of ritual does vary greatly, the two tend universally to be associated.

For myth and ritual have a common psychological basis. Ritual is an obsessive repetitive activity—often a symbolic dramatization of the fundamental "needs" of the society, whether "economic," "biological," "social," or "sexual." Mythology is the rationalization of these same needs, whether they are all expressed in overt ceremonial or not. Someone has said "every culture has a type conflict and a type solution." Ceremonials tend to portray a symbolic resolvement of the conflicts which external environment, historical experience, and selective distribution of personality types have caused to be characteristic in the society. Because different conflict situations characterize different societies, the "needs" which are typical in one society may be the "needs" of only deviant individuals in another society. And the institutionalized gratifications (of which rituals and myths are prominent examples) of culturally recognized needs vary greatly from society to society. "Culturally recognized needs" is, of course, an analytical abstraction. Concretely, "needs" arise and exist only in specific individuals. This we must never forget, but it is equally important that myths and rituals, though surviving as functioning aspects of a coherent culture only so long as they meet the "needs" of a number of concrete individuals, are, in one sense, "supra-individual." They are usually composite creations; they normally embody the accretions of many generations, the modifications (through borrowing from other cultures or by intra-cultural changes) which the varying needs of the group as a whole and of innovating individuals in the group have imposed. In short, both myths and rituals are cultural products, part of the social heredity of a society.

3
SYMBOLISM

Introduction

Man is a cultural being, which in essence means that he is a symbol-using animal. Indeed, his capacity to symbolize has often been given as a criterion placing him apart from the beasts. Language may be the most important kind of symbolization, but it is not the only one. It has been said that religion may be viewed as a vast symbolic system, as indeed it may, and it is to this possibility that the present chapter addresses itself.

Reduced to its barest essentials, a symbol may be defined as something which stands for or represents something else. Symbols take many forms and have many functions, from the numbers that stand for quantities of goods in the keeping of accounts to the actions in dreams that serve to disguise the repressed wishes of the individual subconscious. The class of symbols that should be termed "religious" would be delineated differently by different scholars. Few anthropologists attempt to make explicit the criteria they use to identify a religious symbol or even to enumerate the kinds of symbols they would include in that category. In practice, the anthropology of religion normally concerns itself with symbols of nonempirical cultural knowledge, notably cosmologies, and the symbols used in ritual (see Chapter 6), two classes which, of course, overlap considerably. Anthropologists do not restrict their inquiry into ritual symbols to the ritual context, however, for it is precisely the extension of these symbols and the

beliefs and principles they represent into the most mundane activities that creates the remarkable consistency of many non-Western cultures.

Recent studies have revealed some of the common properties of religious symbols. One such property is the pervasiveness, the apparent relevance to life and the cosmos in general. Another important feature is that, unlike symbols in science and mathematics, which are intended to be unambiguous, religious symbols may have many referents at once, even some that are not strictly compatible. This is the quality called "multivocality" by Victor Turner, who has demonstrated it vividly with the ritual symbols of the Ndembu. This charges even the simplest ceremonies with multiple levels of meaning, with referents from cosmology to social relations.

Perhaps the most important characteristic of religious symbols is that they have both intellectual and emotional significance to the people who hold them—they are both understood and believed in. Symbols seem to aid comprehension of the conceptions they represent and also to attract and guide the application of value and commitment to those conceptions.

Symbols promote understanding in several ways. They can translate the abstract to concrete, formless to formed, complex to simple, or unknown to familiar, and they often do several of these at once. They express what is mysterious in terms of what is already understood. The translation may have several stages, so that one may detect a series of more and more concrete representations between an abstract conception and a material ritual symbol. For example, the qualities *good* and *bad* may be represented by the general ordering principle of *right* versus *left* as well as embodied in the actual right and left hands of a shaman in a séance.

In a sense, then, symbols aid understanding by providing models to guide the processes of comprehension through imperfectly perceived territory. As Clifford Geertz points out in the final article of this chapter, religious symbols are both models *of* and models *for* "reality." Models *of* reality express the culturally defined conceptions of the way the world is actually organized, while models *for* reality represent the way it should be organized insofar as man can influence it. The latter set ideal goals for behavior; they are connected with the norms of a society. Thus, if people can be motivated to believe in their religious symbols, they not only adopt the culture's mode of understanding reality but also embrace a standard of proper social behavior.

The emotional commitment to religious symbols, which gives them their power to influence thought and action, seems to derive partly from the idiosyncratic experiences of individuals and societies and partly from universal features of human psychology. The article by Eric Wolf in this chapter shows how the historical experiences and social conditions of a people can make certain symbols especially meaningful and compelling for them. At the same time, properties of the symbol may evoke emotions through primitive associations between sensory experience and the subconscious, a possibility explored especially by psychoanalysts. Few symbols of any complexity can truly be said to be universal in significance or meaning, but there does seem to be a dimension of psychological appropriateness that restricts the theoretically infinite range of possible associations between signs and meanings. The predominance of right over left and the prominence of the colors red, white, and black around the world are examples of the skewing of probability by apparently universal principles. Whether these are explained by reference to bodily processes, as by Turner, childhood experiences, as in Freudian interpretations, or Jungian universal archetypes,

some universal as well as conventional and culturally defined meanings seem almost certainly to contribute to the emotional load of religious symbols. (See Leach's "Magical Hair," 1958, for a discussion of this problem.) Not only do meanings and contexts vary in the complex analysis of symbolism, but interpretations equally may alter according to theoretical preoccupation. For example, much attention has been focused on the symbolism of subincision among the Australians. Bruno Bettelheim, in *Symbolic Wounds* (1954), has suggested that the operation is the symbolic carving of a vulva on a male penis, thus indicating that *both* sexes experience envy of the opposite's sexuality, rather than the one-sided penis envy reported for females. Years later, another theory was put forth by Philip Singer and Daniel E. DeSole, in an article entitled "The Australian Subincision Ceremony Reconsidered: Vaginal Envy or Kangaroo Bifid Penis Envy" (1967), and was followed by a communication by J. E. Cawte (1968) which endorsed the observation that the subincised penis was a symbolic representation of the naturally split kangaroo penis. The bifid penis allows for greater size and prolonged coitus, two sexual values highly prized in cultures where the fertility rite and symbol is of utmost importance. Finally, Mary Douglas mentions in *Purity and Danger* (1966) that the subincision ceremony could symbolize the carving of the two moieties of the tribe on the part of the body which helps to generate its members. This controversy illustrates the many meanings which can be read into the nature of symbolism—furthermore, all interpretations may indeed be correct, depending on one's theoretical concerns. It is necessary to agree with J. E. Cawte, who is concerned "to show that we have long passed a point at which anyone, least of all those of us interested in psychoanalysis, should expect to find a simplistic theory" (p. 963).

Ritual seems to be the most important arena in which emotion becomes attached to symbols and, through them, to their referents. The emotions derived from the sources mentioned above, aroused by the ceremony and under a general pressure for social conformity, are shaped and channeled by the ritual symbols. In this way, individuals become committed to both the models *for* reality, the social norms, and the models *of* reality, the culture's world view.

This chapter is intended to serve only as a general introduction to the nature of religious symbolism; more specific symbolic problems are treated in subsequent chapters, especially those on symbolic classification, myth, and ritual. The articles are arranged to show, first, the ways symbols represent the most basic aspects of the world—time and space—and then the ways in which symbols become infused with emotion. Students interested in pursuing the subject of symbolism in general might consult, among others, Ogden and Richards' *The Meaning of Meaning* (1923, etc.) or Whitehead's *Symbolism* (1927).

Edmund R. Leach

TWO ESSAYS CONCERNING THE SYMBOLIC REPRESENTATION OF TIME

It is a truism that time, especially in its calendrical aspects, has been endowed by men everywhere with sacred meaning. A look at a Roman Catholic calendar gives testimony to the persistence of the ancient connection that has been made between sacred rituals and the yearly round, based in large measure on the ever-recurring change of seasons, in animal and plant life, and in celestial phenomena, these serving as a simple kind of measurement. Social and religious life are regulated by and come to center around "natural" calendars, the moon being overwhelmingly important in the simpler societies, and traces of the lunar month can be found even today in almost all calendrical systems.

In his analysis of the symbolization of time, Leach has restated some of the standard notions of time and given them novel interpretations. His first essay, "Cronus and Chronos," opens with the suggestion that we tend to think of time both in terms of repetition and of irreversibility, especially the latter, and that much of the religion is concerned with trying to deny the reality of death by equating the second of these two concepts with the first. Some primitives, however, do not experience time in either of these two ways but perceive it as a sequence of oscillations between opposite poles. The rest of the essay is devoted toward demonstrating that this third concept involves a third entity, to wit, the thing that does the oscillating, and that an animistic concept of this sort is bound up with a belief in reincarnation, justified by a mythology, an example of which is provided from classical Greece.

In his second essay, "Time and False Noses," Leach's indebtedness to the Durkheimian school of sociology is again apparent, as it was in the first, where the influence of Lévi-Strauss was specifically acknowledged. Leach gives his solution to the question of why men throughout the world mark their calendars by festivals, at which time they indulge either in formality, masquerade, or role reversal. He sees these three involved, respectively, with three phases of sacred time: *separation*, with its rites of sacralization; a marginal state of *suspended animation*, when ordinary time stops; and *aggregation*, with its rites of desacralization. He attempts to structure the three practices of formality, masquerade, and role reversal in terms of opposites, placing the first and third in opposition to the second.

Reprinted from Edmund R. Leach, *Rethinking Anthropology* (London: The Athlone Press, University of London, 1961), pp. 124–136, by permission of the author and The Athlone Press.

INTRODUCTORY NOTE

These two short essays originally appeared in the Toronto University publication *Explorations*. The amendments which have been made to the text of "Cronus and Chronos" are largely due to the very helpful suggestions of Mr. M. I. Finley of Jesus College, Cambridge.

I. CRONUS AND CHRONOS

My starting point in this essay is simply *time* as a word in the English language. It is a word which we use in a wide variety of contexts and it has a considerable number of synonyms, yet is oddly difficult to translate. In an English–French dictionary *time* has one of the longest entries in the book; time is *temps*, and *fois*, and *heure*, and *age*, and *siècle*, and *saison* and lots more besides, and none of these are simple equivalents; *temps* perhaps is closest to English *time*, but *beau temps* is not a "lovely time"!

Outside of Europe this sort of ambiguity is even more marked. For example, the language of the Kachin people of North Burma seems to contain no single word which corresponds at all closely to English *time*; instead there are numerous partial equivalents. For example, in the following expressions the Kachin equivalent of the word *time* would differ in every case:

The *time* by the clock is	*ahkying*
A long *time*	*na*
A short *time*	*tawng*
The present *time*	*ten*
Spring *time*	*ta*
The *time* has come	*hkra*
In the *time* of Queen Victoria	*lakhtak, aprat*
At any *time* of life	*asak*

and that certainly does not exhaust the list. I do not think a Kachin would regard these words as in any way synonyms for one another.

This sort of thing suggests an interesting problem which is quite distinct from the purely philosophical issue as to what is the *nature* of Time. This is: How do we come to have such a verbal category as *time* at all? How does it link up with our everyday experiences?

Of course in our own case, equipped as we are with clocks and radios and astronomical observatories, time is a given factor in our social situation; it is an essential part of our lives which we take for granted. But suppose we had no clocks and no scientific astronomy, how then should we think about time? What obvious attributes would time then seem to possess?

Perhaps it is impossible to answer such a very hypothetical question, and yet, clocks apart, it seems to me that our modern English notion of time embraces at least two different kinds of experience which are logically distinct and even contradictory.

Firstly, there is the notion of repetition. Whenever we think about measuring time we concern ourselves with some kind of metronome; it may be the ticking of a clock or a pulse beat or the recurrence of days or moons or annual seasons, but always there is something which repeats.

Secondly, there is the notion of non-repetition. We are aware that all living things are born, grow old and die, and that this is an irreversible process.

I am inclined to think that all other aspects of time, duration for example or historical sequence, are fairly simple derivatives from these two basic experiences:

(a) that certain phenomena of nature repeat themselves,
(b) that life change is irreversible.

Now our modern sophisticated view tends to throw the emphasis on the second of these aspects of time. "Time," says Whitehead, "is sheer succession of epochal durations": it goes on and on. All the same we need to recognize that this irreversibility of time is psychologically very unpleasant. Indeed, throughout the world, religious dogmas are largely concerned with denying the final "truth" of this common sense experience.

Religions of course vary greatly in the manner by which they purport to repudiate the "reality" of death; one of the commonest devices is simply to assert that death and birth are the same thing—that birth follows death, just as death follows birth. This seems to amount to denying the second aspect of time by equating it with the first.

I would go further. It seems to me that if it were not for religion we should not attempt to embrace the two aspects of time under one category at all. Repetitive and non-repetitive events are not, after all, logically the same. We treat them both as aspects of "one thing," *time*, not because it is rational to do so, but because of religious prejudice. The idea of Time, like the idea of God, is one of those categories which we find necessary because we are social animals rather than because of anything empirical in our objective experience of the world.

Or put it this way. In our conventional way of thinking, every interval of time is marked by repetition; it has a beginning and an end which are "the same thing"—the tick of a clock, sunrise, the new moon, New Year's day . . . but every interval of time is only a section of some larger interval of time which likewise begins and ends in repetition . . . so, if we think in this way, we must end by supposing that "Time itself" (whatever that is) must repeat itself. Empirically this seems to be the case. People *do* tend to think of time as something which ultimately repeats itself; this applies equally to Australian aborigines, Ancient Greeks, and modern mathematical astronomers. My view is that we think this way not because there is no other possible way of thinking, but because we have a psychological (and hence religious) repugnance to contemplating either the idea of death or the idea of the end of the universe.

I believe this argument may serve to throw some light upon the representation of time in primitive ritual and mythology. We ourselves, in thinking about time, are far too closely tied to the formulations of the astronomers; if we do not refer to time as if it were a coordinate straight line stretching from an infinite past to an infinite future, we describe it as a circle or cycle. These are purely geometrical metaphors, yet there is nothing intrinsically geometrical about time as we actually experience it. Only mathematicians are ordinarily inclined to think of repetition as an aspect of motion in a circle. In a primitive, unsophisticated community the metaphors of repetition are likely to be of a much more homely nature: vomiting, for example, or the oscillations of a weaver's shuttle, or the sequence of agricultural activities, or even the ritual exchanges of a series of interlinked marriages. When we describe such sequences as "cyclic" we innocently introduce a geometrical notation which may well be entirely absent in the thinking of the people concerned.

Indeed in some primitive societies it would seem that the time process is not experienced as a "succession of epochal durations" at all; there is no sense of going on and on in the same direction, or round and round the same wheel. On the contrary, time is experienced as something discontinuous, a repetition of repeated reversal, a sequence of oscillations between polar opposites: night and day, winter and summer, drought and flood, age and youth, life and death. In such a scheme the past has no "depth" to it, all past is equally past; it is simply the opposite of now.

It is religion, not common sense, that persuades men to include such various oppositions under a single category such as *time*. Night and day, life and death are logically similar pairs only in the sense that they are both pairs of contraries. It is religion that identifies them, tricking us into thinking of death as the night time of life and so persuading us that non-repetitive events are really repetitive.

The notion that the time process is an oscillation between opposites—between day and night or between life and death—implies the existence of a third entity—the "thing" that oscillates, the "I" that is at one moment in the daylight and another in the dark, the "soul" that is at one moment in the living body and at another in the tomb. In this version of animistic thinking the body and the grave are simply alternative temporary residences for the life-essence, the soul. Plato, in the *Phaedo*, actually uses this metaphor explicitly: he refers to the human body as the *tomb* of the soul (psyche). In death the soul goes from this world to the underworld; in birth it comes back from the underworld to this world.

This is of course a very common idea both in primitive and less primitive religious thinking. The point that I want to stress is that this type of animism involves a particular conception of the nature of time and, because of this, the mythology which justifies a belief in reincarnation is also, from another angle, a mythological representation of "time" itself. In the rest of this essay I shall attempt to illustrate this argument by reference to familiar material from classical Greece.

At first sight it may appear that I am arguing in a circle. I started by asking what sort of concrete real experience lies at the back of our abstract notion of time. All I seem to have done so far is to switch from the oscillations of abstract time to the oscillations of a still more abstract concept, soul. Surely that is worse than ever. For us, perhaps, yes. We can "see" time on a clock; we cannot see people's souls; for us, souls are more abstract than time. But for the Greeks, who had no clocks, time was a total abstraction, whereas the soul was thought of as a material substance consisting of the marrow of the spine and the head, and forming a sort of concentrated essence of male semen. At death, when the body was placed in the tomb this marrow coagulated into a live snake. In Greek ancestor cults the marked emphasis on snake worship was not a residue of totemism: it was simply that the hero-ancestor in his chthonic form was thought to be an actual snake. So for the Greeks, of the pre-Socratic period anyway, the oscillation of the soul between life and death was quite materially conceived—the soul was either material bone-marrow (in the living body) or it was a material snake (in the tomb).

If then, as I have suggested, the Greeks conceived the oscillations of time by analogy with the oscillations of the soul, they were using a concrete metaphor. Basically it is the metaphor of sexual coitus, of the ebb and flow of the sexual essence between sky and earth (with the rain as semen), between this world and the underworld (with marrow-fat and vegetable seeds as semen), between man and woman. In short, it is the sexual act itself which provides the primary image of time. In the act of copulation the male imparts a bit of his life-soul to the female; in giving birth she yields it forth again. Coitus is here seen as a kind of dying for the male; giving birth as a kind of dying for the female. Odd though this symbolism may appear, it is entirely in accord with the findings of psycho-analysts who have approached the matter from quite a different point of view.

All this I suggest throws light upon one of the most puzzling characters in classical Greek mythology, that of Cronus, father of Zeus. [Aristotle] (de Mundo Ch. 7) declared that Cronus (Kronos) was a symbolical representation of Chronos, Eternal Time—and it is apparently this association which has provided our venerable Father Time with his scythe. Etymologically, however, there is no close connection between kronos and chronos, and it seems unlikely that [Aristotle] should have made a bad pun the basis for a major issue of theology, though this seems to be the explanation generally put forward. Whatever may have been the history of the Cronus cult—and of that we know nothing—the fact that at one period Cronus was regarded as a symbol for Time must surely imply that there was something about the mythological character of Cronus which seemed appropriate to that of a personified Time. Yet it is difficult for us to understand this. To us Cronus appears an entirely disreputable character with no obvious temporal affinities.

Let me summarize briefly the stories which relate to him:

1. Cronus, King of the Titans, was the son of Uranus (sky) and Ge (earth). As the children of Uranus were born, Uranus pushed them back again into the body of Ge. Ge to escape this prolonged pregnancy armed Cronus with a sickle with which he castrated his father. The blood from the bleeding phallus fell into the sea and from the foam was born Aphrodite (universal fecundity).

2. Cronus begat children by his sister Rhea. As they were born he swallowed them. When the youngest, Zeus, was born, Rhea deceived Cronus by giving him a (phallic) stone wrapped in a cloth instead of the new-born infant. Cronus swallowed the stone instead of the child. Zeus thus grew up. When Zeus was adult, Cronus vomited up his swallowed children, namely: Hades, Poseidon, Hestia, Hera, Demeter, and also the stone phallus, which last became a cult object at Delphi. Zeus now rebelled against King Cronus and overthrew him; according to one version he castrated him. Placed in restraint, Cronus became nevertheless the beneficient ruler of the Elysian Fields, home of the blessed dead.

3. There had been men when King Cronus ruled but no women; Pandora, the first woman, was created on Zeus' instructions. The age of Cronus was a golden age of bliss and plenty, when the fields yielded harvests without being tilled. Since there were no women, there was no strife! Our present age, the age of Zeus, will one day come to an end, and the reign of Cronus will then be resumed. In that moment men will cease to grow older: they will grow younger. Time will repeat itself in reverse: men will be born from their graves. Women will once more cease to be necessary, and strife will disappear from the world.

4. About the rituals of Cronus we know little. In Athens the most important was the festival known as Kronia. This occurred at harvest time in the first month of the year and seems to have been a sort of New Year celebration. It resembled in some ways the Roman saturnalia (Greek Cronus and Roman Saturn were later considered identical). Its chief feature seems to have been a ritual reversal of roles—masters waiting on slaves and so on.

What is there in all this that makes Cronus an appropriate symbol for Time? The third story certainly contains a theme about time, but how does it relate to the first two stories? Clearly the time that is involved is not time as we ordinarily tend to think of it—an endless continuum from past to future. Cronus's time is an oscillation, a time that flows back and forth, that is born and swallowed and vomited up, an oscillation from father to mother, mother to father and back again.

Some aspects of the story fit well enough with the views of Frazer and Jane Harrison about Corn Spirits and Year Spirits (*eniautos daimon*). Cronus, as the divine reaper, cuts the "seed" from the "stalk" so that Mother Earth yields up her harvest. Moreover, since harvest is logically the end of a sequence of time, it is understandable enough that, given the notion of time as oscillation, the change over from year's end to year's beginning should be symbolized by a reversal of social roles—at the end point of any kind of oscillation everything goes into reverse. Even so the interpretation in terms of vegetation magic and nature symbolism does not get us very far. Frazer and Jane Harrison count their Corn Spirits and Year Spirits by the dozen and even if Cronus does belong to the general family this does not explain why Cronus rather than any of the others should have been specifically identified as a symbol of Time personified.

My own explanation is of a more structural kind. Fränkel has shown that early Greek ideas about time underwent considerable development. In Homer *chronos* refers to periods of empty time and is distinguished from periods of activity which are thought of as days (*ephemeros*). By the time of Pindar this verbal distinction had disappeared, but a tendency to think of time as an "alternation between contraries" active and inactive, good and bad, persisted. It is explicit in Archilochus (seventh century B.C.). In the classical period this idea underwent further development so that in the language of philosophy, time was an oscillation of vitality between two contrasted poles. The argument in Plato's *Phaedo* makes this particularly clear. Given this premise, it follows logically that the "beginning of time" occurred at that instant when, out of an initial unity, was created not only polar opposition but also the sexual vitality that oscillates between one and the other—not only God and the Virgin but the Holy Spirit as well.

Most commentators on the Cronus myth have noted simply that Cronus separates Sky from Earth, but in the ideology I have been discussing the creation of time involves more than that. Not only must male be distinguished from female but one must postulate a third element, mobile and vital, which oscillates between the two. It seems clear that the Greeks thought of this third element in explicit concrete form as male semen. Rain is the semen of Zeus; fire the semen of Hephaestos; the offerings to the dead (*panspermia*) were baskets of seeds mixed up with phallic emblems; Hermes the messenger of the gods, who takes the soul to Hades and brings back souls from the dead, is himself simply a phallus and a head and nothing more.

This last symbolic element is one which is found to recur in many mythological systems. The logic of it seems clear. In crude pictorial representation, it is the presence or absence of a phallus which distinguishes male from female, so, if time is represented as a sequence of role reversals, castration stories linked up with the notion of a phallus trickster who switches from side to side of the dichotomy "make sense." If Kerenyi and Jung are to be believed there are psychological explanations for the fact that the "messenger of the gods" should be part clown, part fraud, part isolated phallus, but here I am concerned only with a question of symbolic logic. If time be thought of as alternation, then myths about sex reversals are representations of time.

Given this set of metaphors Cronus's myth *does* make him "the creator of time." He separates sky from earth but he separates off at the same time the male vital principle which, falling to the sea reverses itself and becomes the female principle of fecundity. The shocking part of the first story, which at first seems an unnecessary gloss, contains, as one might have expected, the really crucial theme. So also in the second story the swallowing and vomiting activities of Cronus serve to create three separate categories— Zeus, the polar opposites of Zeus, and a material phallus. It is no accident that Zeus's twice born siblings are the five deities named, for each is the "contrary" of Zeus in one of his recognized major aspects: the three females are the three aspects of womanhood, Hestia the maiden, Hera the wife, Demeter the mother; they are the opposites of Zeus in his roles as divine youth (*kouros*), divine husband, divine father and divine son (Dionysus). Hades, lord of the underworld and the dead, is the opposite of Zeus, lord of the bright day and the living; Poseidon, earth shaker, god of the sea (salt water), is the opposite of Zeus, sky shaker (thunderer), god of rain and dew.

The theme of the child which is swallowed (in whole or part) by its father and thereby given second birth, crops up in other parts of Greek mythology—e.g. in the case of Athena and of Dionysus. What is peculiar to the

Cronus story is that it serves to establish a mythological image of interrelated contraries, a theme which recurs repeatedly in mature Greek philosophy. The following comes from Cary's translation of the *Phaedo*:

"We have then," said Socrates, "sufficiently determined this—that all things are thus produced, contraries from contraries?"

"Certainly."

"What next? Is there also something of this kind in them, for instance, between all two contraries a mutual twofold production, from one to the other, and from the other back again . . . ?"

For men who thought in these terms, "the beginning" would be the creation of contraries, that is to say the creation of male and female not as brother and sister but as husband and wife. My thesis then is that the philosophy of the *Phaedo* is already implicit in the gory details of the myth of Cronus. The myth is a creation myth, not a story of the beginning of the world, but a story of the beginning of time, of the beginning of becoming.

Although the climate may seem unfamiliar, this theme is not without relevance for certain topics of anthropological discussion. There is for instance Radcliffe-Brown's doctrine concerning the identification of alternating generations, whereby grandfather and grandson tend to exhibit "solidarity" in opposition to the intervening father. Or there is the stress which Lévi-Strauss has placed upon marriage as a symbol of alliance between otherwise opposed groups. Such arguments when reduced to their most abstract algebraic form may be represented by a diagram such as this:

$$A.1 \rightarrow B.1$$
$$A.2 \rightarrow B.2$$

In Radcliffe-Brown's argument the As and the Bs, that are opposed yet linked, are the alternating generations of a lineage; in Lévi-Strauss's, the As and the Bs are the males of contending kin groups allied by the interchange of women.

My thesis has been that the Greeks tended to conceptualize the time process as a zig-zag of this same type. They associated Cronus with the idea of time because, in a structural sense, his myth represents a separation of A from B and a creation of the initial arrow $A \rightarrow B$, the beginning of life which is also the beginning of death. It is also nicely relevant that Heraclitus should have defined "a generation" as a period of thirty years, this being calculated "as the interval between the procreation of a son by his father and the procreation of a son's son by the son," the interval, that is $A.1 \rightarrow B.1 \rightarrow A.2$.

I don't want to suggest that all primitive peoples necessarily think about time in this way, but certainly some do. The Kachins whom I mentioned earlier have a word *majan*, which, literally, ought to mean "woman affair." They use it in three main contexts to mean (*a*) warfare, (*b*) a love-song, and (*c*) the weft threads of a loom. This seems to us an odd concatenation yet I fancy the Greeks would have understood it very well. Penelope sits at her loom, the shuttle goes back and forth, back and forth, love and war, love and war; and what does she weave? You can guess without looking up your *Odyssey*—a *shroud* of course, the time of Everyman. 'Tis love that makes the world go round; but women are the root of all evil. (The Greek Ares god of war was paramour of Aphrodite goddess of love.)

II. TIME AND FALSE NOSES

Briefly my puzzle is this. All over the world men mark out their calendars by means of festivals. We ourselves start each week with a Sunday and each year with a fancy dress party. Comparable divisions in other calendars are marked by comparable behaviours. The varieties of behaviour involved are rather limited yet curiously contradictory. People dress up in uniform, or in funny clothes; they eat special food, or they fast; they behave in a solemn restrained manner, or they indulge in license.

Rites de passage, which mark the individual's social development—rituals of birth, puberty, marriage, death—are often similar. Here too we find special dress (smart uniform or farcical make-believe), special food (feast or fast), special behaviour (sobriety or license). Now why?

Why should we demarcate time in this way? Why should it seem appropriate to wear top hats at funerals, and false noses on birthdays and New Year's Eve?

Frazer explained such behaviours by treating them as survivals of primitive magic.

Frazer may be right, but he is inadequate. It is not good enough to explain a world-wide phenomenon in terms of particular, localized, archaic beliefs.

The oddest thing about time is surely that we have such a concept at all. We experience time, but not with our senses. We don't see it, or touch it, or smell it, or taste it, or hear it. How then? In three ways:

Firstly we recognize repetition. Drops of water falling from the roof; they are not all the same drop, but different. Yet to recognize them as being different we must first distinguish, and hence define, time-intervals. Time-intervals, durations, always begin and end with "the same thing," a pulse beat, a clock strike, New Year's Day.

Secondly we recognize aging, entropy. All living things are born, grow old and die. Aging is the irreversible fate of us all. But aging and interval are surely two quite different kinds of experience? I think we lump these two experiences together and describe them both by one name, time, because we would like to believe that in some mystical way birth and death are really the same thing.

Our third experience of time concerns the rate at which time passes. This is tricky. There is good evidence that the biological individual ages at a pace that is ever slowing down in relation to the sequence of stellar time. The feeling that most of us have that the first ten years of childhood "lasted much longer" than the hectic decade 40–50 is no illusion. Biological processes, such as wound healing, operate much faster (in terms of stellar time) during childhood than in old age. But since our sensations are geared to our biological processes rather than to the stars, time's chariot appears to proceed at ever increasing speed. This irregular flow of biological time is not merely a phenomenon of personal intuition; it is observable in the organic world all around us. Plant growth is much faster at the beginning than at the end of the life cycle; the ripening of the grain and the sprouting of the sown grain proceed at quite different rates of development.

Such facts show us that the regularity of time is not an intrinsic part of nature; it is a man made notion which we have projected into our environment for our own particular purposes. Most primitive peoples can have no feeling that the stars in their courses provide a fixed chronometer by which to measure all the affairs of life. On the contrary it is the year's round itself, the annual sequence of economic activities, which provides the measure of time. In such a system, since biological time is erratic, the stars may appear distinctly temperamental. The logic of astrology is not one of extreme fatalism, but rather that you can never be quite sure what the stars are going to get up to next.

But if there is nothing in the principle of the thing, or in the nature of our experience, to suggest that time must necessarily flow past at constant speed, we are not required to think of time as a constant flow at all. Why shouldn't time slow down and stop occasionally, or even go into reverse?

I agree that in a strictly scientific sense it is silly to pretend that death and birth are the same thing, yet without question many religious dogmas purport to maintain precisely that. Moreover, the make-believe that birth follows death is not confined to beliefs about the hereafter, it comes out also in the pattern of religious ritual itself. It appears not only in *rites de passage* (where the symbolism is often quite obvious) but also in a high proportion of sacrificial rites of a sacramental character. The generalizations first propounded by Hubert and Mauss and Van Gennep have an extraordinarily widespread validity; the rite as a whole falls into sections, a symbolic death, a period of ritual seclusion, a symbolic rebirth.

Now *rites de passage*, which are concerned with demarcating the stages in the human life cycle, must clearly be linked with some kind of representation or conceptualization of time. But the only picture of time that could make this death–birth identification logically plausible is a pendulum type concept. All sorts of pictorial metaphors have been produced for representing time. They range from Heraclitus's river to Pythagoras's harmonic spheres. You can think of time as going on and on, or you can think of it as going round and round. All I am saying is that in fact quite a lot of people think of it as going back and forth.

With a pendulum view of time, the sequence of things is discontinuous; time is a succession of alternations and full stops. Intervals are distinguished, not as the sequential markings on a tape measure, but as repeated opposites, tick-tock tick-tock. And surely our most elementary experiences of time flow are precisely of this kind: day-night day-night; hot-cold hot-cold; wet-dry wet-dry? Despite the word *pendulum*, this kind of metaphor is

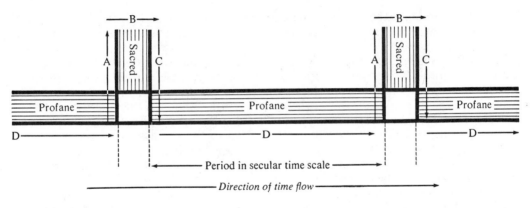

FIGURE 1

not sophisticated; the essence of the matter is not the pendulum but the alternation. I would maintain that the notion that time is a "discontinuity of repeated contrasts" is probably the most elementary and primitive of all ways of regarding time.

All this is orthodox Durkheimian sociology. For people who do not possess calendars of the Nautical Almanac type, the year's progress is marked by a succession of festivals. Each festival represents, for the true Durkheimian, a temporary shift from the Normal-Profane order of existence into the Abnormal-Sacred order and back again. The total flow of time then has a pattern which might be represented by such a diagram as the one shown in Figure 1.

Such a flow of time is man made. It is ordered in this way by the Societies (the "moral persons" to use Durkheimian terminology) which participate in the festal rites. The rites themselves, especially sacrificial rites, are techniques for changing the status of the moral person from profane to sacred, or from sacred to profane. Viewed in this Durkheimian way, the total sequence embraces four distinct phases or "states of the moral person."

Phase A. The rite of sacralization, or separation. The moral person is transferred from the Secular-Profane world to the Sacred world; he "dies."

Phase B. The marginal state. The moral person is in a sacred condition, a kind of suspended animation. Ordinary social time has stopped.

Phase C. The rite of desacralization, or aggregation. The moral person is brought back from the Sacred to the Profane world; he is "reborn," secular time starts anew.

Phase D. This is the phase of normal secular life, the interval between successive festivals.

So much for Durkheim, but where do the funny hats come in? Well, let me draw your attention to three features in the foregoing theoretical argument.

Firstly let me emphasize that, among the various functions which the holding of festivals may fulfil, one very important function is the ordering of time. The interval between two successive festivals of the same type is a "period," usually a named period, e.g. "week," "year." Without the festivals, such periods would not exist, and all order would go out of social life. We talk of measuring time, as if time were a concrete thing waiting to be measured; but in fact we *create time* by creating intervals in social life. Until we have done this there is no time to be measured.

Secondly, don't forget that, just as secular periods begin and end in festivals, so also the festivals themselves have their ends and their beginnings. If we are to appreciate how neatly festivity serves to order time, we must consider the system as a whole, not just individual festivals. Notice for example how the 40 days between Carnival (Shrove Tuesday) and Easter is balanced off by the 40 days between Easter and Ascension, or how New Year's Eve falls precisely midway between Christmas Eve and Twelfth Night. Historians may tell you that such balanced intervals as these are pure accidents, but is history really so ingenious?

And thirdly there is the matter of false noses, or to be more academic, role reversal. If we accept the Durkheimian analysis of the structure of ritual which I have outlined above, then it follows that the rituals of Phase A and the rituals of Phase C ought, in some sense, to be the reverse of one another.

Similarly, according to the diagram, Phase B ought somehow to be the logical opposite to Phase D. But Phase D, remember, is merely ordinary secular life. In that case a logically appropriate ritual behaviour for Phase B would be to play normal life back to front.

Now if we look at the general types of behaviour that we actually encounter on ritual occasions we may readily distinguish three seemingly contradictory species. On the one hand there are behaviours in which formality is increased; men adopt formal uniform, differences of status are precisely demarcated by dress and etiquette, moral rules are rigorously and ostentatiously obeyed. An English Sunday, the church ceremony at an English wedding, the Coronation Procession, University Degree taking ceremonials are examples of the sort of thing I mean.

In direct contrast we find celebrations of the Fancy Dress Party type, masquerades, revels. Here the individual, instead of emphasizing his social personality and his official status, seeks to disguise it. The world goes in a mask, the formal rules of orthodox life are forgotten.

And finally, in a few relatively rare instances, we find an extreme form of revelry in which the participants play-act at being precisely the opposite to what they really are; men act as women, women as men, Kings as beggars, servants as masters, acolytes as Bishops. In such situations of true orgy, normal social life is played in reverse, with all manner of sins such as incest, adultery, transvestitism, sacrilege, and lèse-majesté treated as the natural order of the day.

Let us call these three types of ritual behaviour (1) formality, (2) masquerade, (3) role reversal. Although they are conceptually distinct as species of behaviour, they are in practice closely associated. A rite which starts with formality (e.g. a wedding) is likely to end in masquerade; a rite which starts with masquerade (e.g. New Year's Eve; Carnival) is likely to end in formality. In these puritanical days explicit role reversal is not common in our own society but it is common enough in the ethnographic literature and in accounts of Mediaeval Europe. You will find such behaviours associated with funerals, or with *rites de passage* (symbolic funerals) or with the year's end (e.g., in Europe: Saturnalia and the Feast of Fools).

My thesis is then that *formality* and *masquerade*, taken together, form a pair of contrasted opposites and correspond, in terms of my diagram, to the contrast between Phase A and Phase C. *Role reversal* on the other hand corresponds to Phase B. It is symbolic of a complete transfer from the secular to the sacred; normal time has stopped, sacred time is played in reverse, death is converted into birth. This Good King Wenceslas symbolism is something which has a world wide distribution because it makes logical sense independently of any particular folklorish traditions or any particular magical beliefs.

Clark E. Cunningham

ORDER IN
THE ATONI HOUSE

In this article Cunningham masterfully unfolds the principles of house construction, living arrangements, and decoration to serve as reference points for the understanding of Atoni symbolic categorization. Ostensibly, the Atoni house is merely a home, but this home embodies the dyadic symbolism and notions of unity and diversity pervasive through the classification of all Atoni social, religious, and political activity. "... The Atoni house is a model of the cosmos. However, it is more than simply analogous to the universe; it is integrated within

Reprinted with slight abridgement from *Bijdragen tot de Taal-, Land- en Volkenkunde*, Deel 120, le Aflevering (1964), 34–68, by permission of the author and Koninklijk Instituut voor Taal-, Land- en Volkenkunde, Leiden, The Netherlands.

it." For Cunningham, most important are the principles of classification which can apply objectively to any aspect of the society, rather than the particular aspect which is chosen. But the house as a cultural universal extends its symbolic references "beyond the social order: space and time, man and animals, man and plants, and man and supernatural are conceived to be ordered by principles related to those expressed in the house, and symbols involving all of these occur in the house." The comparative study of house order, particularly in societies where house-building follows patterns established by generations of tradition, may prove highly significant in revealing the basic preoccupations of symbolic classification in thought systems throughout the world.

The house may be an effective means to communicate ideas from generation to generation in a preliterate society. Ritual is a similar—though perhaps less effective—means. The Atoni of Indonesian Timor do not build houses intending to express abstract notions. They build homes. However, they do so in a way taught and managed by elders, according to rules regarded as a vital part of their heritage, and houses follow patterns, not individual whim.

As I studied Atoni houses, I was told how parts, sections and appurtenances are made and used. Villagers are equally explicit, however, concerning another aspect of the house, the order in which things are placed and used. When they are asked why a particular order is necessary, one simple answer predominates: "*Atoran es ia*." (This is the *atoran*, the order or arrangement.)

In this paper I consider what this just-so question of "order" involves. I believe that order in building expresses ideas symbolically, and the house depicts them vividly for every individual from birth to death. Furthermore, order concerns not just discrete ideas or symbols, but a system; and the system expresses both principles of classification and a value for classification *per se*, the definition of unity and difference.

The Atoni of Indonesian Timor number a quarter of a million, speak a Malayo-Polynesian language, and have named patrilineal descent groups. They grow maize and rice by shifting cultivation on mountainous terrain, and they keep cattle, water buffalo, pigs, and chickens. Few villages have easy access to a road and an exchange, rather than a market, economy is the rule. Atoni share many elements of a common culture, though there are variations over the ten princedoms. Atoni princes are among the few "native rulers" still recognized within the Indonesian republic, and the princedom is the maximal native political unit and the limit of society for most people. Christianity, Dutch and later Indonesian administrations, and education came less intensively to the Atoni than to some nearby peoples and began only in the second decade of this century. Most Atoni still live by their traditions in a village environment, though these outside forces are becoming more influential following Indonesian independence.

The house (*ume*) is the residential, economic, and ritual unit at the base of Atoni society. It is inhabited ideally, and in the majority of cases, by an elementary family, the members of which eat and sleep there, and guests are entertained in the house. There are no communal houses for lineages or hamlets. A woman usually works at her house when, for example, weaving or pounding grain, and food is prepared for consumption there. Grain from the fields of a household is smoked on racks over the hearth and stored in the attic. There are no communal granaries for local lineages or hamlets, and there is a minimum of economic cooperation between households. There is, however, obligatory participation in life-cycle activities and ritual for agnates, affines, and hamletmates, and a general value on aid within the hamlet in time of need.

The house is a ritual centre for prayer, sacrifice and feasts. Ritual of the life-cycle (birth, marriage, house-building, and death) is conducted normally at the house of those immediately involved, and sacred heirlooms are kept there. Houses (with their *sacra*) should endure; heirs should maintain them and eventually inhabit them. Prayers may be directed from the house to the Divinity (*Uis Neno*), the Powers (*pah meni*), the ancestors (*nitu*), and to special tutelary spirits. Sorcery may be initiated from the house and victims are often (in my experience) affected there, and diviners (*mnane*) normally work at the houses of clients. Agricultural ritual begins and ends at the house.

In the following discussion I consider only the type of house found in the princedom of

Amarasi where I stayed longest. Space does not allow analysis of two different types found in other areas. Suffice it to say here that common structural principles and common symbols underlie these variations, and these are my concern. Also limited space forbids my discussing house-building ritual, though I appreciate its relevance.

THE AMARASI HOUSE

Atoni say that the door should be oriented southward, the direction they call *ne'u* (right). North is *ali'* (left); east, *neonsaen* (sunrise); west, *neontes* (sunset). The word *neno* (*neon* in metathesis) may mean sun, sky, or day, the reference here being sun. It is forbidden to orient the door directly east-west, say informants, "because that is the way of the sun" or "because the sun must not enter the house." In fact, houses are oriented variously, though rarely (in my experience) directly east-west; yet the front (or door) direction is called *ne'u* (right *or* south). Within the house, orientation is established as a person faces the door from the inside—just as Atoni compass directions are fixed facing "sunrise" —and again *ne'u* and *ali'* (right *and* left) sides of the house are determined.

The metaphor *ne'u ma li'* (right and left *or* south and north) is a common Atoni one for "good and evil." East ("sunrise") is the direction where prayers are made to the Divinity, *Uis Neno* (Lord of the Sun, Sky, or Day), a Divinity who, though not otiose, is little concerned with moral issues. East is considered to be the direction of origin where the "ancient hill, ancient hamlet" (*fatu mnasi, kuan mnasi*) of each lineage is located, but the "way of the deceased" (*ran nitu*) upon death is toward the west or the sea. Noble lines all have myths of origin and migration from the east which are recited at their festivals; however, there are tales told surreptitiously in nearly every princedom that the ruling line actually came from some other direction and usurped power and then authority. In colour symbolism, east is associated with white; south with red; west with black; north with yellow. The native cloth worn by men is red and white (the colours of south and east); the traditional woman's cloth is black (the colour of west). Yellow is not used as a main colour in cloths, but the colour is associated with sorcerers (*araut*) who may be termed *mat molo* (yellow eye). Rulers are associated with white; warriors with red, and village headmen with

black in their costumes. In their totality, rulers may be termed *uis mnatu, uis muni* (gold lord, silver lord) in opposition to all commoners who are termed *to' muti, to' metan* (white commoners, black commoners).

The Amarasi house consists of the following elements, sections, and appurtenances. (The numbers in parentheses refer to figures. The figure number precedes the colon; the reference in that figure follows it.)

nanan (inside *or* centre):
inner section (2:a)

Ume nanan (house inside *or* house centre) may refer to the "inner section" or to the whole area under the roof, depending upon contexts which I discuss later. *Nanan* may mean "inside" opposed to outside; the "inner" part opposed to the outer part of an area; or the "centre" part opposed to the periphery within a circle. (However, *nanan* does not mean "centre point" which is *mat*, eye, or *usan*, navel.)

The *nanan*, or inner section, is reserved for agnates of the householder, while the *ume nanan*, house centre—the whole area under the roof—is for agnates, affines, and guests. Guests should not enter the inner section through the door (2:b), though they may enter freely the outer section (*si'u*) through the unclosed entrance (2:c). Guests are not entertained in the inner section, though wife-giving affines may be received there on occasion. A wife has free access to the inner section of her husband's house (or the house of his parents) only after her initiation to his descent group ritual. Affines or guests may not sleep in the inner section, but a married daughter may do so if she returns alone to visit her parents. If her husband comes too, they sleep together on a platform in the outer section. Unmarried sons and daughters sleep in the inner section, but a boy on reaching his late teens may sleep in the outer section. All of the householders normally eat in the inner section when there are no guests. The mood is relaxed and the door is closed, and it is considered impolite to interrupt a family meal.

si'u (elbow): outer section (2:d)

This section, also covered by the roof and ceiling, is used to receive guests and for work by householders. It may be open (as in Figures 1 and 2) or enclosed by walls, an option of the householder. There are one or more fixed "platforms" (*harak*) in the outer

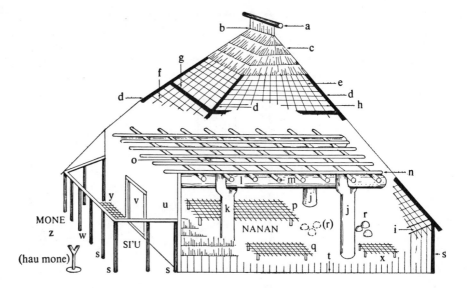

Key:

a	fuf manas	"sun cranium"	n	nesa'	rafter
b	fuf ai	"fire cranium"	o	toi	"entrance" (attic)
c	hun	"grass" (thatch roof)	p	harak ko'u	"great platform"
d	suaf bidjaekase	"horse spar"	q	harak tupa'	"sleeping platform"
e	suaf benaf	"benaf spar"	r	tunaf	"hearth"
f	suaf susuf	"susuf spar"	s	ni manu	"chicken post"
g	aka'nunu	"pillow"	t	haef	"foot"
h	tak pani	"cross-spar"	u	piku	"wall"
i	tnat oe	"hold water" cross-spars	v	eno	"door"
j	ni ainaf	"mother post"	w	toi	"entrance" (outer section)
k	ni ainaf (nakan)	"mother post" ("head")	x	harak manba'at	"agreement platform" (serving platform)
l	atbat	beam	y	harak	"platform"
m	kranit	cross-beam	z	mone	"outside; male" (yard).

FIGURE 1

section where guests sleep, eat or sit. (2:t) When guests come, the men eat in this section and are served by young people or women; the women eat in the inner section where the food is prepared. (A man of some social importance may eat here regularly. He is served by his wife or children who crouch in the doorway while he eats and talk with him.) The right side of the outer section is used first for receiving guests, and there is often only one fixed platform, at this side. If there are many guests, persons of higher rank sit at the right and their food is served there. During the day, women may use the outer section for work such as weaving, spinning, basketmaking, or pounding corn and rice. More often though, since light is poor under the roof's shade, they work in the yard which is termed *mone*, a word meaning both "outside" and "male." This yard (1:z or 2:e),

normally bounded by stones and sometimes by a fence, is often slightly elevated and paths should not cross it

harak ko'u (great platform)   (2:f)

This is the principal and largest "platform" (*harak*) in the house, on the inner section. Though I use the pale word "platform," a *harak* may serve as a bed, bench, couch, table, or rack. The form is always the same, but the use varies as may the appellation. The "great platform" is always on the right side within the inner section. Tools, household possessions, and pounded corn and rice are kept here, usually stored in baskets. Babies may sleep here, but children and youths should not. They sleep on mats on the floor by the hearth. Informants stipulate that neither women nor affines may sleep on the "great platform."

Top view

"left"

"sunset" ← → "sunrise"

"right"

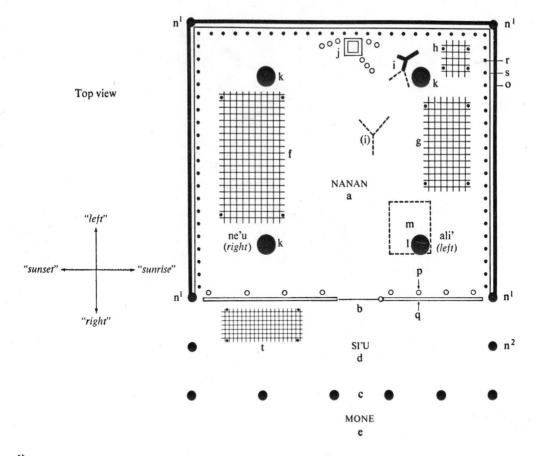

FIGURE 2

Key:

a	nanan	"inside; centre" (inner section)
b	eno	"door"
c	toi	"entrance"
d	si'u	"elbow" (outer section)
e	mone	"outside; male" (yard)
f	harak ko'u	"great platform"
g	harak tupa'	"sleeping platform"
h	harak manba'at	"agreement platform" (serving platform)
i	tunaf	"hearth"
(i)	tunaf	"hearth" (alternate place)
j	nai oe teke	"fixed water jar"
k	ni ainaf	"mother post"
l	ni ainaf (nakan)	"mother post" ("head")
m	toi	"entrance" (attic)
n¹	ni manu	"chicken post" (corner)
n²	ni manu	"chicken post"
o	haef	"foot"
p	haef mese	"first foot"
q	piku	"wall"
r	rusi	inner wall post
s	rupit	wall slat
t	harak	"platform"

harak tupa' (sleeping platform) (2:g)

This platform, smaller and lower than the other, is always on the left side of the inner section. The elder male and female of the household sleep here, and a partition of split-bamboo may enclose this bed to give privacy for their sleep and personal possessions. Parents should not sleep on mats on the ground, consistent with all other daily and ceremonial usages in which a place on a platform signifies superior status.

harak manba'at (agreement platform): serving platform (2:h)

This platform, smaller than the others, is near the hearth on the left side, and it holds cooking utensils and dishes. Food, after cooking, is placed here, it being improper to serve directly from a pot on the hearth. Here also women may be placed when they give birth. A fire then burns under them during confinement and they are bathed in hot water from this fire which is tended by the husband.

The word *manba'at* is a substantive from the verb *manba'an* (to agree, arrange, or put in order). I return later to consider this name.

The use of three platforms, as described above, is common in Amarasi, but not essential. Quite often there are only two, in the places of what are here described as the "great platform" (2:f) and the "sleeping platform" (2:g), and the two then bear these names. The rules that I mentioned concerning their use remain the same. The former is used for storing household goods, food, and tools, and as a seat for men and elders of the household or wife-giving affines on occasion. The latter is reserved as a bed for the elder couple, and a woman gives birth here. The "sleeping platform" may also be used for serving food, especially when there are guests, or else a flat stone may be placed by the hearth for this purpose. Thus the "agreement platform" is assimilated in function to the "sleeping platform."

tunaf (hearth) (2:i)

The hearth fire should be kept lit all the time by women, except during their confinement when the husband is responsible. The hearth ideally consists of three stones, two at the back and one at the front. The back two should point toward the posts called *ni manu* (chicken post) (2:n1) at the rear of the house, and the front one toward the door, "so that the heat may go out," say informants. The hearth may also consist of five stones, two at the front and two at the back, all pointing toward corner "chicken posts," and one at the centre pointing toward the door. The hearth may be at the centre of the inner section, or to the back, but not forward; it may be on the centre-line of the house or to the left, but not to the right.

nai oe teke (fixed water jar) (2:j)

An earthenware jar must stand at the back of the inner section by the wall. It is normally opposite the door, though informants say it may be left of centre. (Like the hearth, it may not be to the right.) The jar is set with ceremony when the house is consecrated, and it must not be moved. (It is filled from a water carrier with smaller jars or cups which usually stand beside it.) If a new house is built (e.g. after a fire), the jar must be moved with ceremony to the new house.

According to informants, the door, water jar, hearth, and the two platforms are the main points of *atoran*, order, in the house.

Their positions are invariable—or variable within the fixed limits I mentioned—and known to nearly all people. Items of European furniture, like tables, chairs, and wardrobes, are rarely found in the inner section, though some people have them in the outer section which is otherwise bare except for a platform or two. (If these items are found in the inner section, they do not upset the "order" described.) These elements, I believe, are not the only ordered ones; nearly all aspects of the house express *atoran*. However, it is significant that Atoni view these points as fundamental—the door, water jar, hearth, and the two platforms—and I shall discuss this fact later.

ni ainaf (mother post) (2:k)

Four "mother posts" of equal size support the rafters and the ceiling (which is also the attic floor). The so-called "head" (*nakaf*) is the "mother post" at the front and left (2:1). The entrance to the attic is by this post, as is a ladder, and when villagers are asked why this post is called the "head," they say, "because it is by the hatch to the attic." This "head mother post," which plays a part in ritual, has a flat stone altar at its base and sacred objects of the ancestors may hang from it. It is forbidden to put a nail in this post or to hang tools or other daily objects from it, and none of the "mother posts" are decorated by carving.

ni manu (chicken post) (2:n1, n2)

Twelve "chicken posts" help support the roof at its outer extremity. Four of these, each at a corner of the house (2:n1), touch the four main roof spars which are termed "horse spars" (*suaf bidjaekase*) (1:d). The remaining "chicken posts" (2:n2) surround the outer section, and these may be decorated with carved designs or pictures.

haef (foot) (2:o)

The "feet" are the peripheral wall posts, slightly smaller than the "chicken posts," on which the roof spars (*suaf*) rest. These "feet" enclose the inner section; also the four ribs on each side of the partition (2:p) are called "feet," or more completely, *haef mese* (first foot). I was told that there should be 120 "feet" to 12 "chicken posts." This proportion, if not exact numbers, seemed to be maintained in most Amarasi houses. Many people did not know this fact, which I was told by elders, but counting generally verified it. It is appropriate, in terms of other fixed numbers for house parts and for the general importance of numbers in Atoni ritual, that some proportion is established and that the totals are multiples of four, the numerical expression of unity for Atoni.

These tightly-packed "feet" form a low wall about 3 or 4 feet high, but they are not conceived as the unit which our term "wall" implies (and which Atoni would term *piku*). On the inside, and parallel to these "feet," is a row of smaller posts called *rusi* (2:r), and between these rows are slats called *rupit* (2:s). (I do not know any other meanings for these words.) This form—two concentric rows of posts with horizontal slats between—is the same as the fence which surrounds Atoni swiddens, corrals, and hamlets, and rulers and warriors are likened, in ritual speeches, to these posts of a fence which surrounds and protects. As I show later, this fence form is repeated in the roof which is also round.

piku (wall *or* partition) and *eno* (door) (2:q and 2:b)

A partition separates the inner and outer sections, but it is of no structural significance in supporting the ceiling or roof. A heavy wooden door (*eno*), either solid or of fitted slabs, is found at the centre of the partition. The hinges must be fixed so that the door swings onto the left side of the house, i.e. toward the "sleeping platform," thus favouring entrance to the right. The doorway is quadrangular, with separate pieces for the lintel, jambs, and threshold. The lintel, termed *eben*, may be straight or arched, ideally the latter, say informants, but usually the former. The name is related to *ebe*, the term for the moon-shaped silver comb worn by women (which may also be termed *funan*, moon). The jambs are both called *su'tai* which means "to support," usually in the moral sense "to be responsible for." (*Su'* alone means "to carry on the head.") The threshold is termed *teri*, the verb "to step on" used as a substantive.

atbat, kranit, and *nesa'*: the ceiling beams and rafters

Each of the four "mother posts" has a curved fork at the top, and they support two large beams termed *atbat* (1:l) which must run parallel to the centre-line of the house. Lying above and across them are beams called *kranit* (1:m) which are each the same length

and which number 8, 12, 16, or 24, depending upon house size. The rafters, *nesa'* (1:n), lie above and across these, parallel to the *atbat*, and usually number the same as the *kranit*. These rafters project over part of the outer section and their front ends may be decorated. The *atbat* and *kranit* beams are located over the inner section and are not decorated. A ceiling, usually split bamboo, rests on the rafters and also forms the attic floor. The attic (*po'af*) is reserved for storing unpounded maize and rice, and for an altar stone used in agricultural ritual. Entrance to the attic is forbidden to anyone who is not an agnate of the householder. The elder male and female in the household usually manage it, sometimes with the help of a son, but daughters rarely go there. Atoni say that the presence of another person in the attic "makes the soul of the rice and maize flee."

hun (grass): the roof (1:c)

The roof, called simply "grass" after its thatch, is conical in appearance and extends almost to the ground. Seen from the outside, the Atoni house appears to be one great roof, and has been described as bee-hive shaped by more than one observer. The roof, like the walls, is rounded, and Atoni refer to their houses as *ume bubu'* (round house) in contrast to those of Rotenese or townsmen. From the inside, however, the substructure of the roof is rectangular. It consists of four main corner spars called "horse spars" (*suaf bidjaekase*) (3:d), which meet the "chicken posts," and slightly smaller spars (*suaf*) all around. The latter are divided in two groups: *suaf susuf*, front and back (3:g1, g2), and *suaf benaf*, right and left sides (3:f1, f2). These two groups are subdivided into *susun pin* (lower *susuf*) and *susun faof* (upper *susuf*), *benan mat* (centre-point *benaf*) and *benan koitne* (outside *benaf*). The *benaf*, which are placed first, should have a somewhat greater diameter than the *susuf*. I return later to the meaning of these two words.

All of the roof spars converge along the top between two horizontal beams, the *susuf* spars forming a cross between them. These beams are termed *fuf manas* (sun cranium) and *fuf ai* (fire cranium) (3:a, b). The former is larger and above, and its ends show after the summit thatch decoration is tied. These beams are tied at the middle by a rope termed *mausak* (a type of liana), though the rope need not be made of *mausak* (3:c). One old specialist on the Amarasi house told me,

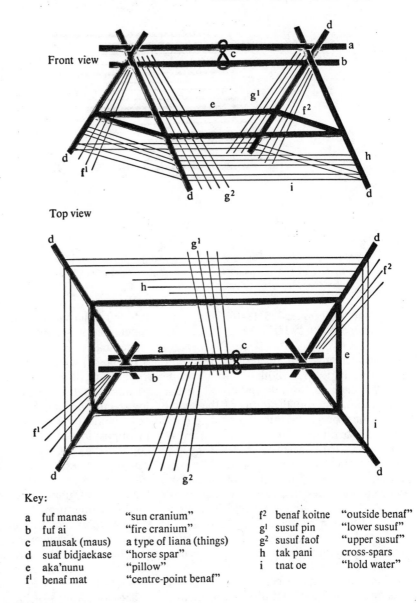

Front view

Top view

Key:

a	fuf manas	"sun cranium"	f²	benaf koitne	"outside benaf"
b	fuf ai	"fire cranium"	g¹	susuf pin	"lower susuf"
c	mausak (maus)	a type of liana (things)	g²	susuf faof	"upper susuf"
d	suaf bidjaekase	"horse spar"	h	tak pani	cross-spars
e	aka'nunu	"pillow"	i	tnat oe	"hold water"
f¹	benaf mat	"centre-point benaf"			

FIGURE 3

"These two beams guard the sun (*manas*) and guard the fire." When *manas* is used for "sun," it refers specifically to the "heat of the sun."

At the lower (or outer) periphery of the roof are two parallel and tied cross-spars which also encase the roof spars (*suaf*) and which encircle the roof. These are together termed *tnat oe* (hold water) (3:i). Higher up, at the middle of the roof, are one or more larger cross-spars termed *aka'nunu* (pillow) (3:e), and up and down the roof are smaller cross-spars termed *tak pani* (3:h) to which bundles of thatch are tied. The reader will note that the spars running between the "sun cranium" and "fire cranium," the "pillows" and the *tak pani*, and the "hold water" cross-spars reproduce a fence form (Figure 4), to which I return later.

Having given ethnographic detail, I now consider the structure of the Amarasi house and its symbolism in greater depth.

THE DIVISION OF SPACE

A striking aspect of Atoni house structure is the cross pattern. The use of the number four, expressing unity, and regularly intersecting lines characterize this pattern which consists of the following elements:

(1) the four points of the Atoni compass (5:1–4)
(2) the four corner "chicken posts" (5:5–8)
(3) the four emphasized points of *atoran*, order: water jar, sleeping platform, door, and great platform (5:9–12)

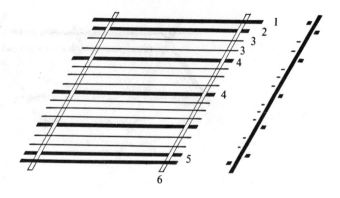

Key.

1	fuf manas	4	aka'nunu
2	fuf ai	5	tnat oe
3	tak pani	6	suaf

FIGURE 4

(4) the four "mother posts" (5:13–16)
(5) the central hearth (5:17)

These elements can be represented, and linked, in two ways, both of which continually recur in Atoni symbolism, ritual usages, and conceptualizations of the social and political order: (a) intersecting, and concentrically arranged, crosses in the form + and ×, and (b) concentric circles. Figure 5 illustrates these patterns, each circle representing a step nearer the centre of the house. Figure 6 illustrates the way in which the + and × alternate with each circle. The regularity in this pattern might be fortuitous, but the facts I have given argue the contrary, I believe. If anything, these figures represent a model of the house.

A second striking aspect of Atoni house structure is the continual division of wholes into halves, and the intersection of these divisions with units which are halves of greater wholes. The complete house under the roof, the *ume nanan* or "house centre," is divided in two parts in opposition to the yard termed *mone* (male; outside), and both in turn are on an elevated area in opposition to a further "outside" (*kotin*). The first division within the house creates right and left sides of the inner and outer sections; the second divides the house back and front into inner and outer sections. The inner section is divided, by the arrangement of its fixed elements and their symbolic associations, into "male" and "female" (or "right" and "left") halves in opposition to the bare outer section. (When guests come to the outer section, however, they may be ordered right

and left in terms of seniority.) The inner and outer sections (*nanan* and *si'u*) form partitioned halves in opposition to the undivided attic (*po'af*) which covers both.

This type of division is conceived by Atoni to apply to the cosmos. Earth (*pah pinan*: lower land *or* land base) is divided into the "dry land" (*pah meto*) and the "sea" (*tasi*) in opposition to the "sky" (*neno*) which is conceived as a dome over them. (The Atoni call themselves *Atoin Pah Meto*, People of the Dry Land. Their origin is believed to have been originally from the sky; they have myths of migration over land, but not over the sea with which they eschew contact.) The sea, in turn, is conceived to be in two parts, the "female sea" (*tasi feto*) and the "male sea" (*tasi mone*). The former part is the inner circle of sea near the coast and bays, appropriate to other associations of "inner" and "female"; the latter part is the distant circle of sea. Both parts stand opposed to the "dry land." In all of these oppositions—dry land and sea to sky, male sea and female sea to dry land, right and left sides of the "house centre" to the yard, right and left sides of the inner section to the outer section, and inner and outer sections of the house to the attic—a conceptually subordinate pair is opposed to a superordinate unit.

In one sense, therefore, the Atoni house is a model of the cosmos. However, it is more than simply analogous to the universe; it is integrated within it. Prayers are made to the Divinity from the *hau mone* (male tree *or* outside tree) set in the yard, facing sunrise. Thus the Atoni compass is ordered as I described earlier, with south = right, north

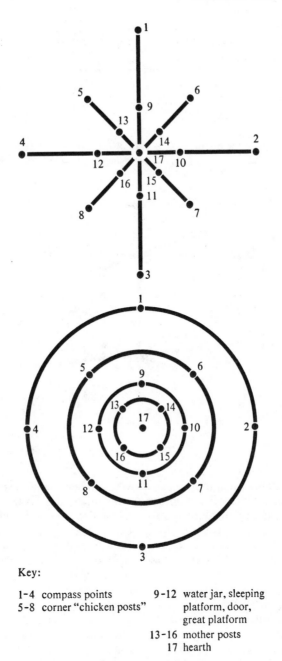

Key:

1-4 compass points
5-8 corner "chicken posts"

9-12 water jar, sleeping
       platform, door,
       great platform
13-16 mother posts
   17 hearth

FIGURE 5

= left. The house must not face east-west, say informants, "because that is the way of the sun" or "because the sun must not enter the house." These reasons, or better, symbolic statements express one fact: the house is set in opposition to the sun, sky, or day (all *neno* in Atoni). It is segregated from all three, windowless and dark, and even in daytime its light and heat are generated by the perpetual fire. The door orientation symbolically blocks the "sun's way" (*ran neno*). The pervasive interior division, right and left, is then made facing the door. The next division, back and front, is made by a line parallel to the sun's way, the partition. After that, the next beams, the *atbat*, are perpendicular to this "way," the *kranit* parallel, and so forth up to the two summit beams, the "fire cranium" and the "sun cranium."

The naming of the two summit beams is opposite: it concerns an opposition of "heats," one of the hearth fire (*ai*) and the other of the sun (*manas*). The two "heats" are symbolically opposed, or separated, by

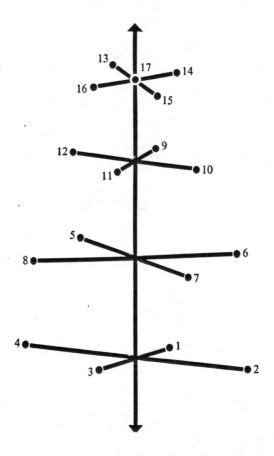

FIGURE 6

these beams, just as door orientation blocks the way of the sun. The reader will remember that one reason for orienting the door southward was "because the sun must not enter the house" and that the hearth stones are oriented toward the back and the door "so that the heat may go out." The opposition of the house to the sky is illustrated further in the naming of the two linked cross-spars at the roof edge, the *tnat oe* (hold water). These cross-spars do not literally "hold water"; they are not gutters. Rain water, for which most prayers to the Divinity are made, is symbolically kept from touching the ground by the house, the epitome of segregation of sky and earth. The tying of thatch, and its trimming along these spars, are the final steps in house-building. The trimming (*atref*: to cut) is a ritual act done by a representative of the wife-giving affines, and is said to make the house "cool" (*mainikin*), again an aspect of opposition to the sun's heat. Appropriately, it is considered physically dangerous for men to work on a house during the rain.

Atoni believe that all human activity should take place on "dry land." They avoid the sea

which is believed to be inhabited by monsters, crocodiles, and large snakes, and the "way of the deceased" (*ran nitu*) is by the sea. The dome-shaped sky is under the authority of the Divinity (*Uis Neno*: Lord of the Sky), who in ritual may be referred to as "*Uis Neno' aobet, abenit, aneot*" (*Uis Neno*, the dome-shaped, the protecting, the overshadowing) (Middelkoop 1960:14). (Princes on earth are termed *uis pah*, lord of the land, and are said to be *naneom, namaf*, "the shadowing ones, the shading ones.") I have noted that the attic is proscribed for ritual reasons and access is allowed only to certain persons. Atoni conceive the Divinity also to be isolated from man, and approachable only through prayer and sacrifice at designated places (normally marked by a stone and a post), but not otiose. Divinity is concerned with rain, sun, and fertility of the land, and with the formation of the human being, both as creator and preserver, originally and in any birth. It is not fortuitous, or merely practical, I believe, that the attic of a house is devoted only to rice and maize, produce of the fields; that a ritual stone is kept there;

and that entrance is restricted in a ritual idiom. Dome-shaped as it is, it represents *neno* and all that it implies.

Given this point, it is understandable why in some Atoni areas the roof thatch is termed *unu*. This word may be used for "eldest" (e.g. *tataf unuf*: eldest older brother); in Taebenu, the "head mother post" is termed *ni unuf*; and a cognate, *un-unu*, is invariably used by Atoni for the "distant past." This distant past refers to the time, in myth *cum* history, when an original order was fixed (e.g. when political authorities became established; when a place was founded; when certain clans first settled an area; when men obtained certain plants or animals). It is this period when rules or customs were established by ancestors which guide behaviour at the present, the ancestor spirits (*nitu*) guarding their perpetuation by sanctions on the living. Appropriately, when an individual tells things which are said by others to have occurred later, therefore not an ultimate precedent, they are said to have occurred *tnana'*, i.e. in the "inner" (or middle) past, an inferior recent time.

The association of the roof with a superordinate and supernatural sphere is further reflected in the naming of the "hold water" (*tnat oe*) cross-spars at the roof edge (3:i). The word *tnat* is an abbreviation of *atnatas*, "to hold in giving or receiving," in the ceremonial context when a gift is made to a social superordinate, e.g. tribute, bridewealth, or food to a host at a feast. (The gift is held with both hands at head level in giving and receiving.)

The idea of a gift, or ritual tie, introduces another important point in Atoni house symbolism, the link between opposed areas and the stress on mediation. In a house the posts termed *ni* link the lower section with the attic, and the "head mother post" is the main place of ritual according to informants "because it is by the entrance to the attic." Forked posts, in the *ni* form and with a flat stone (*fatu*) or a ring of stones (*baki*) at the base, are used by Atoni in all prayer and sacrifice, i.e. in communication with the supernatural. (Where such posts are used outside the house, they are termed *hau*, wood *or* tree, an example being the *hau mone* in the yard.)

The notion of a link between opposed spheres is best illustrated in the rope termed *mausak* or *maus* for short, which ties together the "sun cranium" and "fire cranium" beams at the roof summit (3:c). This rope is not essential structurally; however, it serves an important symbolic function, and I have already noted the significant symbolism in the naming of the two beams. *Maus* has two meanings in Atoni; "a type of liana" and "things." In ceremony, *maus* may be used to refer to tribute, bridewealth, or an inheritance, all of which are "things" which unite in political, affinal, or descent contexts. Descent group ritual is termed *nono*, also a type of liana. Binding together, symbolized by a liana, is appropriate to the house, but the idea applies in many other contexts, since the keynote of opposition is complementarity not utter separation. The association of gift, "things," a liana, and a binding in this term *maus*—with its use at the important summit of the house—represents a vivid Atoni expression of "total prestations," as Mauss (1954:3) termed them.

RIGHT AND LEFT, MALE AND FEMALE

I would now like to consider further the dyadic categories symbolized by "right-left" (*ne'u-ali'*) and "male-female" (*mone-feto*), in relation to house structure and the social order.

Inside the Atoni house there is a constant association of male activities and symbols with the right side generally, the outer section, the right side of the inner section, and the attic; female activities and symbols with the inner section and, particularly, the left side of the inner section. These two sets of associations are constants in Atoni symbolism, expressing superordination and subordination respectively, and space here allows mention of only a few examples.

The door, as I said, is oriented "right" (*ne'u*) (or south) and men predominate in the outer section (*si'u*). They receive male guests there, and the men eat there while women remain in the inner section. Boys may move to sleep there in their late teens, but girls may not. This pattern is analogous to that of the traditional Atoni princedom where a ritual lord called the *atupas* (sleeping one) remained at the centre of the princedom in a palace area called *ba'af* (root). Though the ritual lord was always a man, he was called *feto* (female). As one informant said, "The ritual lord, the sleeping one, was female. He only knew how to sleep and eat." The rest of the princedom was divided in four "great quarters" (*suku naek*), each assigned to a cardinal point and each headed by a secular lord termed *monef-atonif* (male-man). The secular lords were responsible for warfare, tribute to the ritual lord, adjudication and public order generally, and they had warrior chiefs who guarded the gate and the way of the princedom, controlling the movement of persons and tribute. The four secular lords were ordered by seniority in a pattern analogous to the colour symbolism mentioned earlier, i.e. from east clockwise to north.

In wartime, men went outside the hamlets while women remained behind with a ritual officiant to play drums and gongs and conduct ritual. In wars of the princedom as a whole, the symbolically "female" ritual lord remained at the centre to conduct ceremonies. It should be noted that the secular lords (the "male-men") are on the periphery but within the circle of the princedom. Similarly, the area for males in a house—the *si'u*, or outer section—is on the outside but within the circle of the "chicken posts" and under the roof. In neither case are the males "outside" (*kotin*) which is another sphere entirely and conceptually subordinate.

Within the inner section, there is a division right and left which is perpendicular to the *si'u-nanan* division. The door swings toward the left, thus favouring entrance to the "right," a procedure consistent with the symbolism of the *si'u* section and which honours a guest with superordinate (i.e. "right" or "male") status. The right side of the inner section contains the "great platform" where males, elders, and wife-giving affines are seated, all of whom have superordinate status. The main provisions and tools of the household are also kept here, including the pounded corn and rice for meals. Thus the right side of the inner section, like the attic, is devoted to food supplies for which men are primarily responsible; the left side is devoted to their preparation, for which women are responsible. (In both collection and preparation of food in certain contexts, both sexes may play a part. When they do, either their activities or the items handled are classified as appropriately "male" or "female." For example, in the fields women may weed or gather crops by hand, but men must handle the knife; at ritual meals, women cook rice with chicken broth while men cook beef, buffalo, or pork at separate hearths.)

On the left side of the inner section are the hearth, water jar, and "sleeping platform." These elements are permanent aspects of *atoran*, order, stressed by informants. Within the Atoni princedom, the ritual lord called *atupas* (sleeping one), who was considered "female" and who occupied the "inside" or "centre" (*nanan*) position in a palace area called the "root," is a symbolic correlate of the woman and her position in the house, on whose side (the left) is located the hearth and "sleeping platform." Informants said of the ritual lord, "He only knows how to sleep and eat," and these are the two secular activities of the left side or back of any Atoni house.

This complementary symbolism—of which "right" and "left," "male" and "female" are symbolic expressions—is clearly exemplified in the naming of the roof spars and the house posts. The uppermost roof beam, the "sun cranium," is opposed to the "fire cranium" below it; furthermore, it is opposed to the "hold water" cross-spars at the outer extremity of the roof. Here, in symbolic terms, "fire" and "water" stand together, below, in opposition to "sun," as the hearth and water jar stand together permanently in the left and back side of the inner section, and fire is more central than water in both cases.

The roof spars share this opposition. I mentioned earlier that the roof spars, the *susuf-benaf*, are divided respectively as "upper susuf" and "lower *susuf*," "centre-point *benaf*" and "outside *benaf*," the former in each case being slightly larger. The terms *benaf* and *susuf* are related, I believe, to *benas*, the machet which only men may use, and *susu*, milk, which women both handle and provide. This interpretation is consistent with the symbolic pattern in the betel-nut basket (*oko*) which women make and carry: the upper part is called *suin* and the lower part *aina*. The former word is *suni* (in common Atoni metathesis), the head-hunting sword carried by men; the latter word, "mother."

The main roof spars, the "horse spars," rest on the "chicken posts." Though neither horses or chickens play a large part in Atoni ritual, they are associated with males and females respectively in several contexts. Only men tend horses (though both sexes may ride), and warriors were formerly trained to manage them and to hunt and fight from them. (Also, a horse accompanies the corpse of a prince to the grave and subsequently is given to the chief representative of the wife-giving affines.) Women care for chickens and prepare the chicken broth served with rice at feasts. This symbolic use of large "horses" over small "chickens" is appropriate to the general superordinate characterization of the roof and attic over the lower part of the house. The general use of tree symbols for rulers also is relevant. The princes are said to be *naneom, namaf*, the shadowing ones, the shading ones. The four secular lords ("male-men") are likened to four types of trees— *nunu, neke, nisum, rete*—and the ritual lord (whose palace area is the "root") to the *usapi*.

The posts which surround the inner section, which are smaller, shorter, and more numerous than the four main posts, are opposed to them in the same dyadic idiom. In Amarasi, the "mother post": "chicken post":: a large female animal: small animal. In another area, Taebenu, the posts are termed *ni inaf* (mother post) and *ni ana* (child post), the two terms being applicable to animals or humans. Since the main posts are characterized in a "female" idiom, the outer posts are characterized in a similar, but lesser, idiom.

An identical pattern is found in the opposition of the main posts and roof to the jambs and lintel of the doorway, each representing a supported dome or arch. (In house types of other Atoni areas, there are often only two main roof spars, rather than four as here, thus stressing the arch idiom in the roof more clearly.) These two structures are opposed as inside-outside, greater-lesser, male-female, and sun-moon in their size and symbols. I have already discussed "male" associations of the roof, a dome-shaped symbol of the "sky" or "sun," *neno*. The lintel (*eben*) is related in naming and arch form to the woman's comb (*ebe*) which is made of silver and shaped like a half-moon. This same type of opposition was found by Middelkoop applied to two ritual posts (*hau mone*) in one village: they were termed "tall Divinity" and "short Divinity," and villagers said they were like the sun and the moon or, alternatively, the moon and morning star (1960: 23). The opposition of gold and silver, sun and moon, is common for Atoni, and may be used also for the ritual lord and the secular lords respectively in contexts where the superordination of the former is expressed. It would be inconsistent within Atoni symbolism to give either the outer posts of the house or the door jambs and lintel an equal size to the main posts and beams or a symbolically "male" characterization.

INSIDE AND OUTSIDE

In Atoni, *nanan* may mean either "inner" or "centre." In both meanings, "female"

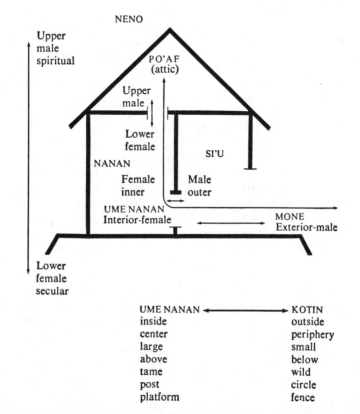

FIGURE 7

symbolism is used in the house; but in different contexts the question of superordination or subordination may vary. I have shown how inner and outer parts of the house or the princedom are opposed with "female" and "male" symbols and subordinate and superordinate characterization respectively. However, I have noted also the concentric pattern in which the larger and higher elements are found at the centre of the house, the smaller on the periphery, and I have said that the further into the house one moves, the greater the rights and obligations. This apparent inconsistency can be understood, I believe, by viewing other Atoni social categorizations and the contexts in which superordination is expressed.

Agnates of a householder have full rights in the house which is believed to be guarded by ancestor spirits (*nitu*) and which contains sacred objects used in the descent group ritual termed *nono*. The household and lineage form a community of worship, and the descent group may be referred to as *nono*. This word refers to a type of liana, the symbol implying that ritual practices encircle (or perhaps ensnare) the members of a descent group as a liana does a tree. Descent group membership is referred to as *su' nono* (carry the descent group ritual on the head), with the implication that it is both a shelter and a burden. Birth ritual is said to *ansae nono* (elevate the *nono*), and an equivalent ritual is held for a newly-married wife so that she may enter the inner section of her husband's parent's house and the couple may have a house consecrated for themselves.

All Atoni have continuing obligations toward their father's lineage, the *nono mnuke* (young *nono*), and their mother's lineage, the *nono mnasi* (old *nono*), and a boy should marry a girl from the latter. Marriage with a cross-cousin, whom a boy calls *fe ranan* (wife way), is termed *matsau ume nanan* (marriage within the house), the affinal alliance of the lineages of a mother and father having placed the groups within a house. The wife-giving affines are superordinate in daily and ceremonial affairs, which their *nono* designation as "old" denotes. Their representative, usually the mother's brother, is termed *atoni-amaf* (man-father), both terms expressing superordination and their conjunction emphasizing it. The house thus balances symbolically the interests of agnation and affinity.

Though the norm and idiom of Atoni descent is patrilineal, in fact many people gain their lineage affiliation through their mother. They are then said to *su' nono mnasi* (carry the old *nono* on the head). In doing so, however, they hold subordinate status in the lineage, their position having the qualities of a wife-taking affine *vis-à-vis* their "agnates" in that lineage. Thus most lineages have a so-called "male house" (*uem mone*) and "female house" (*uem feto*), i.e. people who gain membership through the father or the mother.

Any local lineage is considered the centre of the social world and, as I said, its members have greater rights at the centre of the house. In expressing this lineage-centric view, Atoni refer to either the lineage or household group as the *uem tuan* (house master) and to its affines as "male child" (*an mone*) and "female child" (*an feto*), the former wife-givers and the latter wife-takers. The use of "male" and "female" here indicates both the child whose marriage formed the affinal tie and the symbolic character of the wife-givers as superordinate, wife-takers subordinate. When affines are invited to any feast by the "house masters," they are termed collectively the *ranan* (way), i.e. the way to affinal alliance. The reference to affines as either "child" or "way" indicates their subordination to the "house masters." At a feast, all other guests —either affines of affines or other people—are termed collectively *kotin* (outside), i.e. outside affinity or agnation.

Respect, however, must be shown to all guests at a feast, and they are seated in special places. The wife-givers are seated in the *si'u* section and served by the householders. If the wife-takers are received there too, they are seated on the left, the wife-givers on the right. Sometimes, at small gatherings, wife-takers are received in the inner section and seated on the "great platform" at the right. The wife-takers are then seated in the outer section. All other guests, those called *kotin* (outside), are seated at temporary platforms outside the house. Thus the agnates of the household and their affines are seated inside under the roof, and it is their marriages which are said to be "marriage within the house."

This seating pattern expresses covertly the superiority, unity, and closeness of those nearer the "house centre." However, respect to guests is mandatory, and the hosts must strive to reverse the symbolic primacy of the "house centre" by stressing the *nanan* as subordinate "inner" opposed to outer rather than superordinate "centre" opposed to periphery. The hosts must abase themselves, remain at the left or in bowed positions, and serve others. They claim that their food and gifts are inadequate in quantity and quality, and the guests may assent and claim more, though all know that the hosts are exhausting themselves to provide their best. The claims about the poor food are particularly important in this reversal since feeding is pre-eminently an obligation of a superior to an inferior. Finally, the wife-givers may not be called "male child" on these occasions; they must be called *atoni-amaf* (man-father). The symbolic characterization of the "great platform," outer section, and yard as "male" ensures that this reversal will be complete.

This leads to the next related point. Despite the subordinate connotations of the "inner" section (expressed in "female" or "left" symbols), this area is the ritual centre. The "head mother post" is located on the inner left. Given the connotations of "left" and "female," this would seem to associate the ritual (or supernatural) with a subordinate sphere. The same would appear true in the princedom where the ritual lord has the same associations. Within the princedom, the four secular lords, "male-men," in the outer area (which might be called the *si'u* of the princedom), are predominant in daily affairs. They even have the authority to beat the ritual lord and his guardians if they leave the palace area without permission of the secular lords and an escort. The association of ritual or supernatural concerns with a subordinate sphere is not, however, the case; spiritual matters are considered superior to secular ones. When spiritual matters are at hand, the idea of *nanan* as "centre" is expressed, and the symbolically "female" becomes pivotal in the relation of Man to Divinity.

The presence of the "head mother post" on the left illustrates this fact within the house. As "head" it is foremost; it is the route to the attic which has symbolic superordination and it is the route to the supernatural, being the place for prayer and certain sacred heirlooms. This post may not be otherwise adorned or decorated. Only the "chicken posts" and the front ends of the *nesa'* rafters in the outer section are decorated. Thus, the nearer the "centre," the greater the purity, a symbolic pattern identical to that in great Indian monuments of Southeast Asia such as the Borobudur. There elaborate design is found at the outer and lower parts, blankness at the centre and upper parts, an architectural

expression of the story of the Buddha's life—from riotousness to liberation. It is the left side of the house which is the way to the supernatural for Atoni men who would pray to Divinity or their agnatic ancestors. The same was true for the secular lords, the "male-men," in a princedom who would pray for fertility or rain for their land and crops. They had to do so through the ritual lord, the symbolically female "sleeping one" at the centre of the territory.

This symbolically pivotal position of females, or the "female" category, is not limited among Atoni to ritual. The mother (*ainaf*) or sister (*fetof*), like the wife (*fe*), in a household or lineage is socially pivotal as mediator to the two types of affines, the so-called "way." As "mother," she is mediator to her natal patrilineage which stands superordinate to that of her husband and from which her son should obtain his wife. Furthermore, it is this wife-giving group—appropriate to their superordination—which is responsible for major ritual elements in the life-cycle of their wife-takers. Without this service, the placenta cannot be cut from a new-born child and removed from the house; a bride and rights to her offspring cannot be secured to perpetuate the lineage; the roof cannot be placed on a house, its making and ritual "cooling" being the duty of the wife-givers; and the soul of the deceased cannot be sent on its way in death-ritual to join its ancestors.

Given the points and symbols I have sketched, it is not surprising that the bride-wealth given to the wife-givers consists of live animals (*muit*) and paddy (*ane*) or pounded rice (*mnes*), while the counterprestation from the wife-givers consists of cooked meat (*sisi*), cooked rice (*maka'*), and woven cloth (*tais*). The former items within the house are associated with the "great platform" and attic, the la er with the left side of the inner section and woman's hand. The former are raw, the latter cooked; the former derive directly from the fertility of the land (Divinity's concern), the latter are worked by human hands; the former are alive when given, the latter dead. These associations in the prestations are made explicitly by Atoni, and the symbolic character of the gift always suits the status of the group to which it is given. Thus the link between Man and Divinity (or ancestors) through the symbolically "female" side of the house, and the type of gift given—live animal sacrifice and the sprinkling of pounded rice (*mnes*) during prayer—is analogous to the link between a lineage and its wife-giving affines through the mediation of the woman received in marriage. As mediator at feasts, she must be referred to by her natal clan name (though she has been initiated to her husband's *nono* ritual) and she must go out to escort her natal agnates as they arrive.

In referring to females as pivotal, I am translating the Atoni idea expressed in the continual association of the *nanan*, or centre, of the house and the princedom with female elements and symbols. In secular concerns, females are jurally subordinate, as the *nanan-si'u* usages or the secular organization of the princedom illustrate. Like a ritual lord, a woman in a household may be ordered about or beaten by men, her husband and brothers. In ritual, however, the reverse is true. In war dances, the main Atoni dance, women stand still and beat drums and gongs while men circulate and brandish swords, imitating the flying of a cockatoo, the head of which decorates the sword handle. The dance is called *foti*, fly. Furthermore, Atoni consider women to be more fixed generally than men, more trustworthy and more stable in personality. Women control the purse-strings, and children in a home (particularly a broken home) gravitate toward the mother. Children commonly follow a divorced mother, in time if not immediately, even though the children remain agnates of their *genitor* or *pater*, and the completion of a stage in bridewealth transfers jural rights over a child from the mother's patrilineage to the father's. When Atoni children are sick or troubled, they moan "mother, mother, mother" incessantly, whereas the common expression "*am honi!*" (my genitor) is used when people are startled. Conversely, the swear word "*ainaf tinen!*" (mother's genitals) is the height of abuse and causes a violent reaction.

This pivotal position of females is illustrated in the naming of the *harak manba'at* (agreement platform) (2:h) which is used by women to serve guests at the common meal concluding every ritual. *Manba'an* means "to agree; to put things in order by mutual agreement; the give and take needed in agreement on division of labor when some common activity such as a feast is planned." It is appropriate, given the Atoni view of the female position, that women are associated with such an activity in the naming of this platform which is for women's use in the

house. Correlatively, women are forbidden the knife, and formerly they remained in the village to conduct ceremonial dancing and cooking for the feast to welcome back the warriors. (I have mentioned the importance of tying in ritual, with cutting its opposite.) Middelkoop (1960: 23) mentions that "the ritual cooking is called dancing" (*anbilu am nasbo*)" (1960: 23), i.e. circle dancing, and the one type of song and dance which does not express unity, the *ne si'u* (elbow quatrain) —a reproach against people in a hamlet who have misbehaved, in which they are metaphorically "elbowed out"—is linked in name with the outer section of the house where men predominate.

Having discussed dyadic symbolism and the pivotal position of the "centre," I wish to mention two other usages which recur in Atoni ritual and conceptualizations of their social and political order, the door (*eno*) and the way (*ranan*). Related to this is the issue of the cross.

The traditional Atoni princedom has four "door-ways" (*eno-ranan*) at the outer periphery and also between the outer and inner circles (the "great quarter" of the secular lords and the "root" area of the ritual lord respectively). At both points officials from assigned lineages are said to guard the doorway, and passage is attended by elaborate protocol (cf. the amusing description by Forbes 1885: 442). The officials who guard the outer gates are warriors termed *meo naek*; those who guard the gates between the ritual lord's centre and each "great quarter" are termed *atoni mnasi*, *bife mnasi* (old man, old woman). In the warrior costume, animal and plant symbols are rife, and these warriors are called *meo naek* (great cat). The other gate guardians, the "old man, old woman," are the only officials whose title combines a male and female term. Thus the two types of gate guardians are symbolically either therianthropic or hermaphroditic, appropriate to their positions between opposed areas, the former between the circle of the princedom and the wilds, the latter between conceptually "male" and "female" areas.

In Atoni usage, an "open door" denotes peace and good relations; a "closed door," enmity. Marriage is initiated by gifts said to "open the door." As long as the door is open, gifts are exchanged between the prospective parents-in-law and a couple may conduct courtship. This culminates in marriage, after which the groom serves for a time in the house of his bride before they remove to his own area and their own house. A break in marriage negotiations is said to "close the door"; gifts no longer move and the door of the girl's house is literally closed to the boy. Any continuation of the affair must be done *kotin* (outside), i.e. in the forest or orchards.

Alliance (affinal or political), the movement of gifts, and mutual visits are inseparable, as are the reception of guests in a house, their seating at designated places, and the passing of betel-nut. "Closing the door" in any social or political situation denotes disruption, epitomized in the Atoni word *lasi* (enmity; legal dispute; fight; conflict). Death, the great divide, is termed either *lasi nitu* (enmity of the ancestors) or *lasi neno* (enmity of the sky), the two supernatural spheres. Avoidance of *lasi*, enmity, and the maintenance of a "way" are vital concerns for Atoni in all contexts. The reader will remember the earlier point about the *tnat oe* (hold water) cross-spars (3:i), the word *atnatas* meaning "to hold in giving or receiving, when a gift is given to a social superordinate." This term *atnatas* is also used for spars at each end of a rack on which coffins are carried; the rack (with its four assigned carriers at each corner, two wife-giving affines in front and two agnates behind) is like a platform (*harak*). The leading of the corpse to the grave by the wife-givers is a prestation from the living to the supernatural which serves to heal this "enmity of the sky" or "enmity of the ancestors." The deceased is still considered to be "alive" (*ahoni*), appropriate to the other prestations to a superordinate. He is considered "dead" (*mates*) only after a ritual following burial.

At its broadest level, "order" (*atoran*) in the Atoni house expresses two simple, but pervasive, concerns—unity and difference—and their continual interpretation. The house structure is a model of these concerns. The central structure, the "mother posts" and the web of beams they support, is identical to a platform, as is the roof substructure, and the names for parts of a platform recur in its various uses. This platform structure contrasts with the fence form of the outer wall and roof. The repetition of these two forms—the only two the Atoni use in building—expresses, I believe, the two concerns which underlie any system of classification, unity and difference. The platform is invariably used to express status difference, whether in

seating elders over younger people, nobles over commoners, rulers over headmen, guests over hosts, or rice and meat over corn. The fence form, on the other hand, encircles spheres which possess some kind of unity and which Atoni call *ain* (tame or domesticated) in contrast to those outside called *fui* (wild). It is thus, for example, that civil wars within a princedom are with a *mus ain* (tame enemy); wars with another princedom are with a *mus fui* (wild enemy). The wall and roof, in the fence form, mark the unity of a house and the social groups it comprises, and the house, viewed from the outside, is an almost solid circle and dome with no windows and one small entrance. From within, however, the house is a constant web of intersecting sections and beams, all symbolized as complementary, appropriate to the Atoni view of any structured social or political grouping in which the premise of inequality is pervasive.

The patterns of concentricity and intersection in the "order" of the house continually concern what spheres, or groupings, are to be included or excluded. The circle (or quadrangle) and the cross are ubiquitous symbols in Atoni material culture, I believe, as expressions of these basic concerns, and decoration (like house-building) follows repeated patterns. It is not without reason that these patterns mainly decorate cloths, door frames, outer house posts, betel and lime containers, and baskets and mats used on ceremonial occasions, all of which are used in gifts, or the point of meeting, between groups. Similarly, the figures representing men and animals are normally composites of quadrangles or circles and crosses. It is significant, perhaps, that often one cannot tell whether a pattern of crosses or a pattern of quadrangles is intended; the two fuse in expressing unity and opposition, or unity and difference.

These points explain, I believe, why the resolution of conflict in Atoni society demands an oath made by drawing a cross in the ground and eating a bit of earth from the point of intersection. The cross marks the transgression; the point of intersection, the resolution. (Many people say that the ceremony should be done at a crossroads, but this is not strictly maintained.) Whether settling disputes over land, possessions, adultery, contract-breaking, or fights, this form of resolution is the same, and transcendental justice is believed to support the oath.

The reader will remember that the *susuf* spars (3:g) of the roof—with a symbolically "female" association—form a cross at the summit between the two "cranium" beams, this cross marking a point of segregation between the heats of the sun and hearth (or sky and earth). The *mausak* rope then links the segregated spheres. I believe (though no Atoni said so) that this usage is related to that of cross patterns in tattoos which old Atoni women have on their hands and faces. The usual explanation of these tattoos is that they are used to trade for fire in the afterworld, though the just-so character of this explanation is such that Atoni cannot elaborate on it and many find it incomprehensible or ridiculous though they repeat it. I noted earlier the association of women with fire in the house and the symbolic importance of segregating "heats"; again, in regard to the tattoos, the role of women is pivotal in approaching the afterlife, and the item they trade for fire in the transition to death bears cross symbols.

At ceremonies, it is always the young people who must serve, just as in the past it was a young person who took food out to the hut in the fields where head-taking warriors were secluded from women and the village before a purificatory ceremony allowed them to re-enter. Atoni say that a young person was selected, "because they did not yet know the difference between good and bad": that is, they were not yet polarized in a society where social relationships and loyalties depend upon membership in one group and alliance or opposition toward others. To use the Atoni expression, "they did not yet know right and left." The most common tale of origin for Atoni noble lines vividly illustrates this idiom. The following tale concerns the ritual lord of Insana, but it is told for many other princely lines:

The ritual lord came alone to Maubesi and was impressed by the fine coconut and areca palms already planted there. He had a very handsome face; but when he came, his face and the rest of his body were blackened with charcoal. He visited a spring and saw a child of the ruling line, Afenpah, fetching water. He asked for a drink, but the child would not give the ruler's water to such an ugly man. Taking a leaf, he washed away the charcoal, revealing his handsomeness. The child then ran home, telling what had happened and describing the handsome face; he said that the man was the true ane-pena tuan (paddy-corn master). When the people heard this, they came to see the man and acknowledged him as their ritual

lord. He then established himself with his secular lords at Maubesi.

Again, the child is the mediator in the discovery, and the idiom of the tale is transition. Two aspects of "order" in the inner left side of the house, fire and water, are first associated with the man who is blackened by charcoal at the spring. His transformation involves the elimination of these associations, his handsome face marking him as the proper "head," and he can then be acknowledged "master" and delivered the tribute of the fields. The young, in these contexts, are like the symbolically therianthropic or hermaphroditic gate guardians of the princedom; they mediate and hence combine (or, correlatively, are free of) the associations of the sides they mediate.

In conclusion, I would like to repeat that the house—with its constituent parts, divisions, form, symbols, and prescriptions concerning order, arrangements, and the behaviour of those included and excluded—may be like a mechanical model of the cosmos as conceived by a people. The Atoni are explicitly concerned with "order" as expressed in the house, and so much in their social and political order is related in form and naming to it. However, the references extend beyond the social order: space and time, man and animals, man and plants, and man and supernatural are conceived to be ordered by principles related to those expressed in the house, and symbols involving all of these occur in the house.

Hertz said that "dualism marks the entire thought of primitive men" (1960: 96). In so saying, he was delimiting a principle of classification. His formulation may appear one-sided in the context of the Atoni house, stressing expressions of difference over those of unity, but he was on the right track. In using the house to consider ideas of order in Atoni society, I do not mean to imply that the house need necessarily be a basic reference, even for Atoni. The principles of categorization, not their expression, are important. However, as I said, the house is one of the best modes available to a preliterate society to encapsulate ideas, given the absence of literature and the sporadic occurrence and varying degree of individual participation in ritual, and it exemplifies, I believe, what Mauss meant by "total social phenomena" (1954: 1). In addition, the house illustrates more than particular principles of classification; it illustrates the value of classification *per se*.

A comparative sociology of the house might begin with this question of unity and difference and its expression in architectural forms, with particular attention to the relation between the symbolic and social order (cf. Needham 1958). The house form, expressing these concerns and exhibiting over the world so many common aspects of structure, is certainly an example of a cultural universal, to which anthropologists have been urged to attend. I hope that this discussion contributes to the effort, and also places the houses of the remote Atoni within such great and ancient traditions as Hindu-Buddhist architecture and ancient Asian, Near Eastern, and Central and South American cities.

Gary H. Gossen

TEMPORAL AND SPATIAL EQUIVALENTS IN CHAMULA RITUAL SYMBOLISM

In this paper, prepared especially for this volume, the author describes some of the cosmological referents for the religious symbolism of a modern Maya community. In Chamula, the Ancient Maya sun and moon deities and other supernaturals appear to have merged in a meaningful way with the Christian pantheon which the Dominican missionaries introduced after the Spanish Conquest. The paper illustrates that internal consistency and meaning in religious symbolism do not necessarily atrophy in cases of culture contact and syncretism. (See, for example, the similarity between the modern Chamulas' belief system and that of the Ancient Maya [León-Portilla, 1968, and Thompson, 1970].) Chamulas believe that the sun-Christ not only delimits the spatial boundaries of their universe, but also maintains the critical temporal cycles which regulate their agricultural activity and ritual life. Hence, most of the fundamental discriminations in Chamula ritual symbolism—right/left, up/down, counterclockwise/clockwise—emphasize the primacy of the sun and all that he represents. The paper also illustrates the usefulness of Victor Turner's concept of multivocality (multiple symbolic referents) in describing and attempting to make intelligible the complexity of belief systems which are not our own.

Printed with the author's permission.

The Jews saw that it was written
That Our Father would give heat
When he ascended to the sky.
But he did not go directly to the sky.
First he went to the underworld for two days,
And for two days the Jews were sad.
On the third day Our Father returned.
And the Jews cried,
For Our Father had begun his ascent to the sky.
On the third day, the Jews gathered together
  awaiting their fate.
Then they felt it!
There was a bit of heat from Our Father.
Slowly the heat on the land increased.
By ten o'clock the Jews were very ill.

By the time Our Father reached the center of the sky
The Jews had perished.

—A fragment of an account of the creation, as dictated by Salvador López Sethol, age 24, a ritual assistant to the First Alcalde of Barrio San Juan, Chamula

I. INTRODUCTION

My purpose in this paper is to discuss some fundamental discriminations which appear in Chamula ritual symbolism. I shall attempt to demonstrate that some of the implicit rules which govern Chamula ritual action and symbolism seem to derive ultimately from a time-space principle whose primary cosmological referent is the sun deity, *htotik*. It will be evident from the fragment of myth text cited above that the sun and Christ are one and the same in the syncretistic belief system of the Chamulas. Furthermore, as the text fragment indicates, the sun-Christ deity was responsible for delimiting the major temporal and spatial cycles by means of his death and subsequent ascent into the sky, thus defeating the forces of chaos, cold, and evil. The sun is therefore the initial and primary symbol of ethical, spatial, and temporal order in the Chamula universe. He represents the most distant and most sacred extreme in a continuum of social categories which begins at the ceremonial center of Chamula, the "navel of the earth," in Chamula terminology, and the center of the moral universe.

Chamula is a Tzotzil-speaking municipio of approximately 40,000 modern Maya Indians which lies at the top of the Central Chiapas Highlands of southern Mexico. All Chamulas engage to a greater or lesser extent in subsistence maize, squash, and bean agriculture. Nearly all Chamula families also keep a few sheep for wool for their own clothing and for a small surplus which is sold to Indians in nearby municipios. They supplement their income by engaging in economic specializations such as pottery or furniture manufacture or in employment as day laborers in the Ladino trade center of San Cristóbal or on maize fields or coffee plantations in the lowlands. Chamulas live virilocally in dispersed hamlets which belong to one or more of the three barrios of the municipio. The barrios are ranked in order of ritual importance: first, Barrio San Juan, which is generally east of the ceremonial center; second, Barrio San Pedro, which is generally north of the ceremonial center; finally, Barrio San Sebastián, which lies to the west and south of the ceremonial center. The three barrios converge on the ceremonial center, which has virtually no permanent population. The center serves as the symbolic focus of nearly all public ritual and administrative activity. Rental houses there provide homes for the political and religious officials while they serve their terms in office, ranging from one to three years. Chamulas are governed by a political organization which is partly traditional (Ayuntamiento Regional, consisting of sixty-three positions, or cargos) and partly pre-scribed by Mexican law (Ayuntamiento Constitucional, consisting of twelve positions, including that of the chief magistrate, the Presidente). A religious organization consisting of sixty-one positions supervises ceremonial activities and cults to the saints and the sun and moon dieties; it also coordinates its activities with those of the political organization. Political and religious authority at the local hamlet level lies in the hands of past cargo-holders, heads of segments of patrilineages, and shamans. (See Pozas, 1959 and 1962, and Gossen, 1970, for more ethnographic background.)

Chamula is among the most conservative and self-conscious of the Indian communities of Highland Chiapas, and has apparently been a discrete cultural entity since before the time of the Spanish conquest and Dominican missionization. At present it permits no Spanish-speaking Mexicans to live permanently or to hold property within its boundaries except for one family, that of the Mexican secretary who helps the Chamulas in their dealings with the state and national governments. The Ladino (Mexican) schoolteachers, the Ladino priest, and the Instituto Nacional Indigenista doctor are permitted to stay overnight on a semi-regular basis, but all other persons must get specific permission from municipal authorities to spend the night in the municipio. Chamula is also one of the largest and most rapidly growing communities in the highlands and the population explosion is forcing people to use whatever means they can find to acquire additional land outside the municipio boundaries. They take maximum advantage of agrarian reform laws and are relocating in large and small groups throughout the state of Chiapas. These relocated groups, however, do not generally become acculturated nor do they cease to speak Tzotzil, for they generally move in units large enough to maintain a microcosm of "normal" Chamula life. Their ties to their home municipio remain very strong and they continue to regard it as "the navel of the earth," the center of the moral universe.

II. THE CHAMULA UNIVERSE

Chamulas believe that the earth is an inclined island which is higher in the east than in the west. This belief is supported by Chamula experience in the outside world. Men go frequently to the south and west to the nearby lowlands of the Grijalva River Valley to work on rented maize fields and to the Pacific slope to work on coffee plantations. This tropical lowland area is relatively close to their cool highland home, but its elevation is spectacularly lower than that of Chamula. In other words, the drop-off to the south and west is dramatic; to the north and east there is no immediate drop-off, only a continuation of small highland valleys and basins. Significantly, Tzontevitz Mountain, the highest in the Central Chiapas Highlands and the most sacred of all mountains to Chamulas, lies both to the east of Chamula ceremonial center and within Barrio San Juan, which is the highest ranking of the three barrios. Chamulas have few economic reasons to travel extensively to the north and east beyond their own boundary. This is not the case with the lowland south and west, which are relatively well known to most Chamula men. Economic activity, travel, social oganization, and topography, therefore, support and reflect the prevailing belief that the island-earth is generally high in the east and low in the west. This is suggested by the Tzotzil words which are sometimes used to designate these directions: *ta ʔak'ol* ("above" or "up") means east; *ta ʔolon* ("below" or "down") means west.[1]

Chamulas believe that the earth is laced with caves and tunnels which eventually reach the edges of the earth. These limestone caves and passages are also believed to provide channels for the drainage of the highlands. Chamulas also believe that the earthlords, who live in the mountain caves, provide all forms of precipitation, including accompanying clouds, lightning, and thunder. These beliefs are supported by the fact that the Central Chiapas Highlands are in fact a karst-type limestone area in which internal drainage is extremely important. Only earthlords, snakes (which are the familiars and alternate forms of the earthlords), and demons inhabit the internal cave networks of the earth. Hence, all are associated with dampness, darkness, and lowness.

The earth is the middle of three major horizontal layers of the Chamula universe. The sky and the underworld make up the remainder. Three layers, which informants draw as concentric domes, make up the sky. The first and smallest of these domes is the only level of the sky which is visible to most human beings. This first level, however, is only a reflection of what is happening at the upper two levels. The moon (who is conceptually equivalent to the Virgin Mary, *hme ʔtik* or "Our Mother") and minor constellations travel in the second level. The sun (who is conceptually equivalent to Christ, *htotik* or "Our Father"), Saint Jerome, the guardian of animal souls, and major (bright) constellations reside and travel in the third level. The heat and brilliance of the sun's head are so great that they penetrate the two inferior layers of the sky. Thus, it is only the reflection of the sun's face and head which we perceive on earth.

The underworld is the dwelling place of the dead and is characterized by inversions of many kinds. When it is dark on earth, it is light in the underworld, for the sun travels that part of his circular path around the earth at that time. Conversely, night in the underworld occurs during the daytime on earth. There is no proper food in the underworld. The dead eat charred food and flies in place of normal food. The dead must also refrain from sexual intercourse. With these exceptions, life in the underworld is much like life on earth. People do not suffer there. Those who have murdered or committed suicide are exceptions. These are burned by the sun as he travels his circuit there during the night on earth. The underworld is also the point from which the universe is supported. Opinions vary on the nature of this support, but most Chamulas think that (1) a single earthbearer carries the universe on his back, or that (2) four earthbearers

---

[1] It is important to clarify that, although the tropical lowlands actually lie mostly south and slightly west of Chamula, the whole lowland area is conceptually united by the qualities of lowness and association with the setting sun. Thus, Chamulas will frequently say that they are going west (*ta ʔolon*, "down" or "below") to the coffee plantations. This is not an error in their directional sense, but simply an expression of certain conceptual equivalences in their cosmology. Furthermore, many of the traditional travel routes which Chamulas have used to reach the lowlands in the past (and continue to use in the present) take them first to the west and then back to the south and east to reach their destinations. One of these routes takes them down the Ixtapa Valley of Zinacantan. The orientation of this valley is close to "true east/up–west/down." Furthermore, this valley appears, archaeologically and historically, to have been a principal channel for trade and other forms of contact (including the Spanish Conquest) between the lowlands and the Central Highlands (see Vogt, 1969: 1–31, and Wasserstrom, 1970: 1–22). It should also be noted that names and subjective evaluation of the directions are not exactly the same in all of the Tzotzil-speaking communities of the highlands. Compare, for example, the case of Zinacantan, which shares a long boundary with Chamula (Vogt, 1969: 298, 422, 442, 602).

support the universe at the intercardinal points.

The whole cosmological system is bound and held together by the circular paths of the sun and the moon, who are the principal deities in the Chamula pantheon. Each day they pass by the eastern and western edges of the earth on their trips to the sky and underworld. It is not surprising that these deities effectively represent most of the fundamental assumptions which Chamulas make about order, for they mark temporal and spatial categories which are critical for the maintenance of life as Chamulas know it. In the remainder of this paper, I shall explore some of the components of the ideal order which Chamulas represent by means of ritual symbolism.

III. SOME FUNDAMENTAL DISCRIMINATIONS
THE SUN AS THE FIRST PRINCIPLE OF ORDER

A primary and irreducible symbol of Chamula thinking and symbolism is the sun, "Our Father," *htotik*. At once in the concept of the sun, most units of lineal, cyclical, and generational time are implied, as well as the spatial limits and subdivisions of the universe, vertical and horizontal. Most of the other deities (earthlords are important exceptions) and all men are related lineally or spiritually to the sun-creator, who is the son of the moon. Day and night, the yearly agricultural and religious cycles, the seasons, the divisions of the day, most plants and animals, the stars and the constellations, all are the work of the creator, *htotik*, the lifeforce itself. Only the demons, monkeys, and Jews are logically prior to and hostile to the coming of order. These forces killed the sun and forced him to ascend into the heavens, thus providing heat, light, life, and order (see text fragment which precedes Section I). Hence, the Tzotzil words for "day" (*k'ak'al*) and "fiesta" (*k'in*), which provide fundamental time references for Chamulas, are directly related to the words for "fire" (*k'ok'*) and "hot" (*k'išin*), respectively. It is also relevant that one of the several names for the sun-creator is *htotik k'ak'al* or "Our Father Heat (Day)."

The fundamental spatial divisions of the universe, the cardinal directions, are also derived from the relative positions of the sun on his east-west path across the heavens:

East: *lok'eb k'ak'al*, "emergent heat (or day)"

West: *maleb k'ak'al*, "waning heat (or day)"

North: *šokon vinahel ta baƈ'i k'ob*, "the edge of heaven on the right hand"

South: *šokon vinahel ta ƈ'et k'ob*, "the edge of heaven on the left hand"

The principal temporal divisions of each day are also described in terms of the relative position of the sun on his path across the heavens. For example, "in the afternoon" is generally expressed in Tzotzil as *ta mal k'ak'al*, "in the waning heat (or day)." "In the mid-morning" is expressed as *štoy ša k'ak'al*, "the heat (day) is rising now." Temporal divisions of the year are expressed most frequently in terms of the fiesta cycle. One is able to specify almost any day in the year by referring to stages of, or day before or after, one of the more than thirty religious fiestas which are celebrated annually in Chamula. In referring to a certain day in relation to the fiesta cycle, one says, for example, "*sk'an to ʔošib k'ak'al ta k'in san huan* ("It is three days until the fiesta of San Juan"). This is usually understood as I have translated it, yet the relationship and similarity of words (*k'ok'*, "fire," and *k'ak'al*, "heat" or "day"; *k'in*, "fiesta," and *k'išin*, "hot") in the concepts noted above is such that is is possible to understand this as: "three daily cycles of heat before a major (religious) cycle of heat." These are but a few examples which suggest that the sun and his life-giving heat determine the basic categories of temporal and spatial order.

THE SUN AND THE PRIMACY OF THE RIGHT HAND

Chamula cosmological symbolism has as its primary orientation the point of view of the sun as he emerges on the eastern horizon each day, facing his universe, north on his right hand, south on his left hand (see Figure 1, which is a Chamula's drawing of this fundamental cosmological moment). This orientation helps to explain the derivation of the descriptive terms for north ("the edge of heaven on the right hand") and south ("the edge of heaven on the left hand"). Furthermore, the adjective "right," *baƈ'i*, is positively evaluated in innumerable words and idioms in Tzotzil. By extension, it means "actual," "very," "true," or "the most representative," as in "Tzotzil" (*baƈ'i k'op*), which may be translated literally as "the true language"; or "right hand," (*baƈ'i k'ob*),

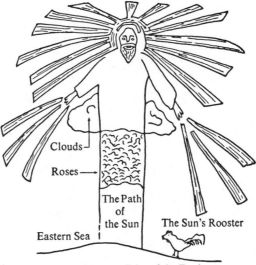

Clouds
Roses
The Path of the Sun
Eastern Sea
The Sun's Rooster
Edge of the Earth

FIGURE 1

The sun-Christ emerging from the Eastern horízon, *original drawing by Marian López Calixto.*

which may also be read as the "real hand" or "true hand." North is on the right hand of the sun-creator as he traverses the sky. This orientation appears to be related to the belief that north is a direction of good omen and virtue. Chamulas often express this as *mas lek sk'an yo ʔnton ta baȼ'i k'ob li htotike,* or "Our Father's heart prefers the right hand way." This fundamental orientation may also contribute to an understanding of Chamula ritual treatment of space. It is first of all necessary to understand that religious cargo-holders themselves have an aspect of deity in that they share with the sun and the saints (the sun's kinsmen) the responsibility and the burden of maintaining the social order. While imparting a sacred aspect to themselves through exemplary behavior and constant use of sacred symbols and objects such as strong rum liquor, incense, candles, fireworks, and cigarettes, most of which have actual or metaphoric qualities of heat, they metaphorically follow the sun's pattern of motion by moving to their own right through any ritual space which lies before them. This helps to explain the overwhelming tendency of almost all Chamula ritual motion to follow a counterclockwise pattern. This direction is the horizontal equivalent of the sun's daily vertical path across the heavens from east to west. One can derive this transformation according to Chamula premises by pretending to face the universe from the eastern horizon, as the sun does each morning, and "turning" the vertical solar orbit to the right so that it lies flat on

the earth. I should emphasize that no Chamula ever stated the derivation as simply as I have stated it here. However, informants consistently said that east is the sun's position at *šlok' htotik* ("the sun appears" or "dawn"); north is the horizontal equivalent to the sun's vertical position at *ʔolol k'ak'al* ("half heat," "half-day," or "noon"); west is *šbat htotik* ("the sun departs" or "sundown"); and south is the horizontal equivalent to the sun's vertical position at *ʔolol ʔak'obal* ("half-night" or "midnight"). This horizontal transformation allows cargo officials to "move as the sun moves," thereby restating symbolically both the temporal and spatial cycles for which the sun is responsible. This makes the beginning of any ritual (counterclockwise) circuit "conceptual east." North in this system becomes the horizontal equivalent of the point of "maximum heat" of the sun at noon at the zenith of his orbit; west and south also follow the solar circuit. This helps to explain why the cardinal direction north shares with the east the sign of good omen and positive orientation; west and south are generally negative in the cosmological system. I attempt to summarize some of this information in Figure 2.

The positive symbolic value of the north ıs also intelligible in that Chamulas are quite conscious of the fact that the apparent position of the rising sun shifts northward on the eastern horizon during the increasingly longer days between the vernal equinox and the summer solstice. This period is also associated with the first rains of the wet

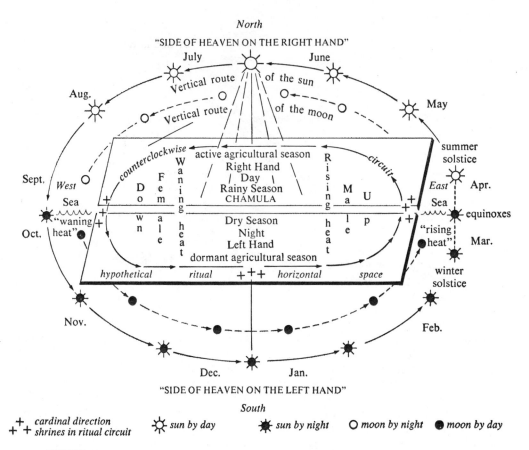

FIGURE 2

Some category relationships in Chamula cosmology, showing particularly the spatial equivalence of vertical solar and counterclockwise ritual circuits.

season (in early May) and with the beginning of the annual growing cycle for highland crops. South, on the other hand, is associated with night and the underworld in the daily cycle. South is also associated with the time of shortening days, the autumnal equinox to the winter solstice, which marks the end of the growing season and the beginning of killing frosts and death in the annual solar cycle. This helps to explain why the south is negatively regarded in some respects, for it represents both night and frost, dry weather and the nonproductive agricultural season. West represents incipient death in the life cycle, twilight in the daily cycle, as well as the period between the summer solstice and the autumnal equinox. It is significant that the intercardinal direction southeast is the first point in the spatio-temporal symbolic scheme which represents an "upswing" or emergence of the sun from the negative nadir (south) of

the system. This may be important in explaining why the southeast is frequently an alternate to the east as the initial position in ritual circuits and positions or ritual personnel (see Figure 2).

Ritual circuits, therefore, carry a great deal more information than they appear to at first glance. They proceed counterclockwise because that direction is the logical horizontal equivalent of the annual solar cycle and the daily solar cycle. Even though circumstances may not allow all individual circuits to begin in the actual east or southeast, the principles of the right hand and counterclockwise motion appear to serve as ritual surrogates for the eastern solar orientation and the solar cycle. Any initial ritual location can thus become "conceptual east." In this way men are better able to base their ritual orientation on the first principle of life itself, which is the sun.

THE PRIMACY OF "UP"

The primacy of the sun as giver of order implies still another symbolic discrimination: primacy of "up" over "down." Cosmologically, increasing height and goodness are associated with the rising sun; decreasing height and threat, with the setting sun. It will be recalled from the discussion above (Section II) that the eastern part of the earth is believed to be tilted upward (*ta ʔak'ol*) and the western part downward (*ta ʔolon*). Living in what they believe to be the highest place on the earth, they as a group are at a point closer to the sun when at its zenith of potency and heat (at noon) than any other Indian or Ladino community with which they are acquainted. Furthermore, Tzontevitz, the sacred mountain which lies in the highest-ranking of the three barrios, is also the home of their patron saint San Juan. In addition, as I mentioned above, Tzontevitz Mountain happens in fact to be the highest peak in the Central Highlands. Chamulas therefore enjoy an especially close relationship with the sun in a physical and metaphorical sense. This position also places the predominantly Indian Highlands in a more desirable (i.e., closer) relationship with the sun that the predominantly Ladino Lowlands. This factor is not unrelated to the Chamula view of social distance, in which the highlands are generally considered to be less dangerous and less asocial than the lowlands.

In the ritual setting, the primacy of "up" is expressed metaphorically in the positions of saints in relation to human beings. They ride and sit habitually on litters and platforms which raise them above the level of men. Cargo-holders who serve them achieve thereby elevation of goodness, virtue, and prestige. For Alféreces (religious cargo-holders who are in charge of saints' objects, particularly their banners and clothing), this ritual height is expressed by special pole and branch towers, fifteen feet high, which are constructed at their homes at the time when they leave office. A representative of the Alférez sits in the tower and thus symbolizes the new heights of the desirable which the outgoing official has achieved in his year in office. In so doing, he has helped the sun to maintain order and thus partakes of the sun's good, rising aspect.

Related to the good, rising aspect of ritual cycles is the importance of head over feet. Heads and faces of images of saints receive a great amount of attention in ritual action and symbolism, the reason being that the head is the source of their heat and power. An example of this is the cult to the sacred flagpole tips which the Pasión sponsors at the "Fiesta of Games" in February. The tips symbolize the head and halo of the sun and, by extension, the whole concept of the sun. It appears to be significant that this fiesta, which is the major annual cult to the sun deity, occurs in February, a time of drought, frost, and agricultural dormancy, but *also* the time of the beginning upswing of the solar cycle from its nadir in the symbolic system (see symbolic associations in Figure 2).

THE PRIMACY OF HEAT

The primacy of heat over cold in Chamula symbolism has been apparent in several of the above discussions. The importance of heat is ever present in Chamula life, from daily household activity to ritual settings. The daily round of Chamula domestic life centers on the hearth, which lies near the center of the dirt floor of nearly all Chamula houses. The working day usually begins and ends around the fire, men and boys sitting and eating to the right of the hearth (from the point of view of one who faces the interior from the front door), women and girls to the left of the hearth (see Figure 3). Furthermore, men in this patrifocal society always sit on tiny chairs, thus raising them above the cold, feminine ground, and wear sandals, which separate them from the ground and complement their masculine heat. Women, on the other hand, customarily sit on the ground, which is symbolically cold, and always go barefooted, which, symbolically, does not separate them, but rather gives them direct contact with the cold, feminine earth. Coldness, femininity, and lowness are logically prior to heat, masculinity, and height. This follows from the mythological account of the coming of order. The male sun was borne from the womb of the female moon and was then killed by the forces of evil and darkness (the demons and the Jews). This in turn allowed him to arise into the sky as the life-giving source of order (see the myth fragment which precedes Section I).

The very words for time and space are related to heat, for the sun symbolizes the source of earthly heat as he does nearly all other aspects of cosmological order. Days, fiesta intervals, seasons, and years are all measured by increasing and decreasing cycles of heat. The opposite of order is symbolized by the cold darkness in which the demons,

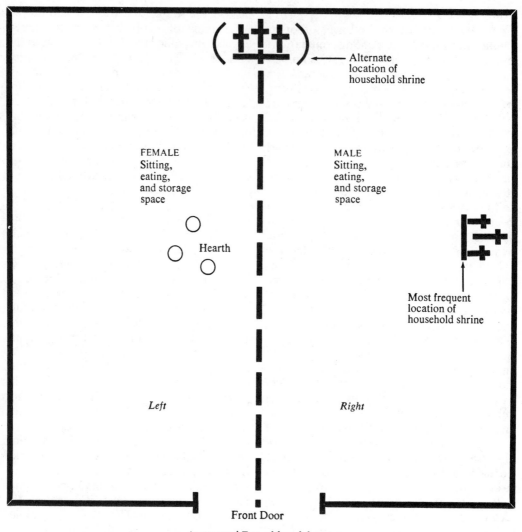

FIGURE 3

Space in a Chamula house.

Jews, and monkeys lived before the forced ascension of the sun into the sky. The life cycle is also conceived as a cycle of increasing heat from a cold beginning. A baby has a dangerously cold aspect. This is reflected in the term *maš* ("monkey"), which refers to an unbaptized child. A child acquires steadily increasing heat with baptism and sexual maturity. The heat of the life cycle reaches a fairly high level with social maturity, which is expressed by marriage and reproduction. The acquisition of heat may be carried further through a cargo or shamanistic career. Life and death are also elementary expressions of the hot-cold syndrome of Chamula values. Life crisis rituals and cargo initiations include symbols of both life (hot and integrative) and death (cold and disjunctive). Hot and cold are also fundamental categories in the bewildering complexity of Chamula theory of illness. In nearly all of these domains (with the exception of illness, in which a hot-cold disequilibrium is frequently a cause), increasing heat expresses the divine and order-giving will of the sun himself.

Most ritual substances also have the quality of heat, actual and metaphoric. Tobacco, rum, incense, candles, and fireworks generate or emit heat. Furthermore, the raw materials for them are believed to be of lowland, tropical origin—which is certainly true for the most part. Resin for incense, beef tallow and wax for candles, the ingredients for gunpowder, sugarcane for rum, and tobacco for cigarettes do in fact come from, or at least through, the lowlands. This tropical origin is interesting because it illustrates a paradox in Chamula thinking about the world. Although the highlands are closer than the lowlands to the sun in a vertical sense, the climate of the highlands is actually much colder than that of the lowlands. It may be that the ambiguous quality of the lowlands (physically hot yet socially distant) makes them a logical source for some sacred symbols and substances. This symbolic ambiguity may be complemented by the fact that Chamulas are economically dependent on the lowlands in many ways.

THE PRIMACY OF LIGHT

It follows from *htotik*'s primordial force in Chamula symbolism that light also represents the desirable and the good. This has precedent in the cosmogonic moment when the sun ascended into the sky, creating the categories of temporal and spatial order. Light and heat were the first manifestations of the new order. Light has many other aspects—among them, heat and ability to penetrate. These are qualities which cargo-holders and shamans share with the deities; all are known to have penetrating, all-seeing vision. It is also significant in a consideration of the meaning of light to note that Chamula men and boys customarily wear white wool tunics; women and girls generally wear brown and black wool skirts and blouses. The days and the seasons have greater and lesser proportions of light to darkness and generally are imbued with positive significance according to increasing proportion of light. The logical inverse of this principle is expressed in the Fiesta for the Dead (All Saints' Day, November 1, the beginning of the cold, dry season), in which a meal is prepared and served to the dead in the middle of the night and in a season of decreasing proportion of light to darkness each day. Similarly, funerals involve, among other things, nocturnal ritual sequences, the consumption of charred maize kernels (not cooked before charring) and black tortillas (made with a bluish-black variety of maize).

Another important light-dark syndrome occurs at Christmas, just after the winter solstice, when the sun begins to renew its strength. The climax ritual of the birth of Christ (which is also, of course, the birth of the sun) consists in Chamula of a midnight torchlight procession (December 24) around the church atrium. In this ritual an image of the Virgen del Rosario is carried around the atrium, preceded by the image of the Christ child. The female image is carried by widowed women who wear white shawls; the Christ child is carried by the male *sacristán* and his assistants. This is the only time in the ritual year (except for the immediately preceding *posadas*) in which a *single* female religious figure is carried around the atrium in procession. It is also the only time in the ritual year in which an equal number of male (one) and female (one) images participate in the procession. Usually there are more male images than female images in these processions. Furthermore, it is the only time in the ritual year in which the saints' procession occurs at night, precisely at midnight; the other processions occur slightly before noon or just at noon. These reversals in the Christmas ritual make cosmological sense because they occur at a time of the year when the nights are longest, when frost has already killed most plant life, and when the sun has just been ritually reborn. The forces of light will prevail as the sun grows up and the days increase in length in proportion to night. These gradually lengthening days will bring heat and a new growing season for the sun's body, which is maize, the most basic and most sacred of all Chamula foods.

THE PRIMACY OF MALENESS

The sun gave mankind maize from his body. This is reflected in a ritual term, *šohobal*, which is frequently used to refer to maize foods. It means "radiance" or "halo of the sun." According to Chamula mythology, maize (which is "hot" in the hot-cold scheme of food evaluation) came from a piece of the sun's groin (but not his penis) and included a part of his pubic hair, which is the silk of the ear of maize. The moon only gave potatoes (her breast milk) and beans (her necklace). The contrast is great, for maize is *the* staple; potatoes and beans are less important items in the diet. That relationship is analogous to that of the male principle to the female principle in this patrifocal society. Maleness receives ritual primacy; the female principle complements it. In the beginning, the moon bore the sun as her child, but very soon afterwards he asserted his authority over his mother in innumerable ways. Among other

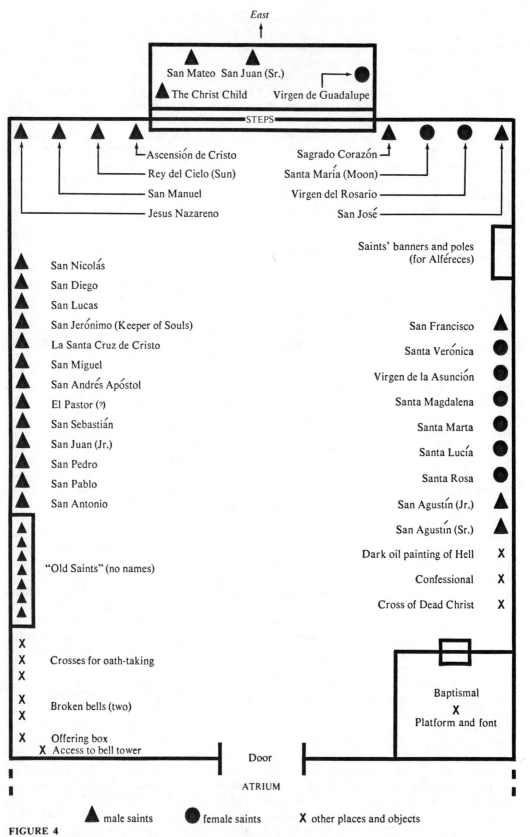

FIGURE 4
Chamula church interior.

tricks, the sun blinded his mother with hot water while they were taking a sweat bath together. This explains the moon's lesser radiance and her tendency (according to Chamula belief) to follow behind the sun in the sky at a point in her circular path (second level of the sky) which is nearly always just opposite his position in his path (third level). Furthermore, the moon has the responsibility of leaving a breakfast of maize gruel for the sun each morning at the eastern horizon. In sum, she has a relationship to her son like that which prevails between the female principle and the male principle in Chamula life: one of submission within a larger sphere of economic interdependence.

The primacy of maleness is also expressed symbolically in nearly all ritual proceedings, for women have no official cargo positions. They do have some special ritual tasks, but these do not count in the cargo system. All wives of cargo-holders receive the title of their husbands, prefixed by *me?* ("mother"), suggesting a ritual relationship of male and female like that which prevails between the sun and the moon. The primacy of maleness has other expressions. In general, right, counterclockwise motion is associated with male saints; left, clockwise motion is associated with female saints. This contrast is expressed also in the distribution of sitting and working space within Chamula houses (see Figure 3). As noted above, the space to the right of the front door of a house interior (from the point of view of one looking in the front door) is male sitting and eating space. The space to the left of the front door is female sitting, eating and working space. This pattern prevails in nearly all Chamula homes which I have seen and applies only to the times of day in which both sexes are present, particularly at mealtimes. At other times during the day, women customarily work throughout the house interior. The pattern does not seem to apply to sleeping positions in the household.

In a very similar manner, the male/right–female/left rule applies to the permanent positions of all female saints and all major male saints in the Chamula church (see Figure 4). The female saints reside on the left side (south) of the church, from the point of view of the patron saint San Juan, who stands above the altar in the center of the east end of the church. While there are no female saints on the "male (north) side," there are a few unimportant male saints on the "female (south) side." I believe that it is also significant that an oil painting of Hell (a very dark one which has never been cleaned), the cross of the dead Christ, and the baptistry are all found in the "most negative," "female" part of the church, the southwestern corner. These objects are negative within the symbolic scheme. The opposite (northeastern) corner of the church is the "most positive," "most masculine" part of the church. This corner lies to the patron saint's immediate right. It is here that the major male saints and images of Christ (the sun) line the north and east walls. These ideal positions may be seen as microcosmic representations of the categories of Chamula cosmology and cosmogony. North was on the sun's right hand when he rose into the heavens in the east, just as the north is on San Juan's and Christ's right hand in the Chamula church. What more logical place could there be for the male images? When processions take place at the climax of some major fiestas in honor of male saints, the male saints march out of the church and around the atrium to the right (counterclockwise). Female saints, on the other hand, march out to the left (clockwise) around the atrium, meet at the half-way point (the west entrance to the atrium) and bow to each of the male saints in sequence. The female saints then reverse their direction of motion and line up behind the last male saint. They march around the last 180 degrees of the circuit behind the male saints, but this time in counterclockwise direction, which is associated with the male principle. The female saints thus "capitulate" symbolically to the male principle and follow the male saints as the moon follows the sun and Chamula women follow their husbands (see Figure 5). At minor fiestas in honor of male saints and at major fiestas in honor of female saints, the two sexes do not march in opposite directions. The female saints simply follow the male saints all around the atrium in the male, counterclockwise direction.

Temporally, there appear to be yet other ways in which maleness asserts its primacy. The fiesta cycle, for example, does not honor a single major female saint during the half-year between the winter and summer solstices, a time which is under the influence of increasing atmospheric heat and increasing length of days in proportion to night. This is the time of the two most important fiestas in the annual cycle: Carnaval, in honor of the sun, in February; and the fiesta of San Juan,

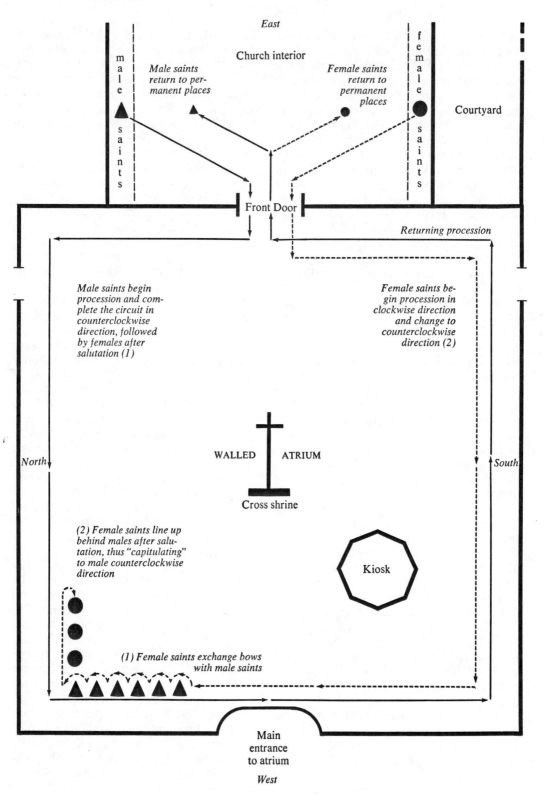

FIGURE 5
Pattern of male and female saints' motion in a procession.

from June 21 to 24. In the latter half of the year, four major female saints are honored by fiestas (Santa Rosa and La Virgen de la Asunción, both in August; La Virgen del Rosario, in October; and La Virgen de Guadalupe in December), but these are not as important or as well attended as those which occur in the "male" half of the year.

This distribution of major female saints in the annual fiesta cycle parallels certain aspects of the female principle in each day. One-half day (from midnight to noon, a time of the sun's rising heat from the depth of the underworld to the zenith of the heavens) is believed to be the time of the sun's influence over the female principle, thus causing women to behave properly and morally during these hours. On the other hand, from noon to midnight (the time of waning heat), women are believed to be more prone to commit adultery and do evil in general, for they are under the influence of the *pukuh* (demon) at that time. This belief has mythical precedent in the fact that it was the *pukuh* (not the sun) who originally taught the first woman (not the first man) to have sexual intercourse. Hence, Chamulas believe that men, like the sun, have had to assume the major ritual responsibility for guaranteeing moral order and stability.

THE PRIMACY OF THE SENIOR PRINCIPLE
Another symbolic pattern seems to follow from the aspects of sun-primacy which have already been discussed. This is the primacy of "senior" over "junior" in the classificatory system. The sun is the senior (*bankilal*) kinsman of all of the other saints (except the Virgin and San José, who are "prior" to the sun and are sometimes difficult for Chamulas to classify). The *bankilal-ʔi¢'inal* (senior-junior) relationship is used in evaluating many domains, from sibling terminology in the kinship system to aspects of animal soul companions, relative rank of cargo-holders, and ranking of topographical features. It is a many-valued system in which relative age, size, distance, strength, wealth, or one of many other criteria may be applied to the ranking of a closed domain of objects or individuals. Vogt has discussed this principle at length as it exists in nearby Zinacantan (1969: 238–245). Here I should only like to point out that the "senior" primacy over "junior" has a background of time-space associations which contributes to its strength as a ritual principle.

"Senior" is first of all prior to "junior" in the rather fuzzy genealogy of the deities. "Senior" aspects of domains therefore have priority over "junior" aspects of domains in ritual expressions of the social order. Spatially interpreted, this means that "senior" personnel, from their own point of view, usually stand or sit to the right of "junior" personnel. Female counterparts (usually wives) of these officials stand still further to the left, from their own point of view, or behind the male cargo officials. Whether or not they are formally placed by ritual position, individuals receive drinks and other ritual sacraments in equal portions according to the principle of more "senior" first, more "junior" last. The male principle, seniority, and higher-ranking cargo positions take precedence over the female principle, youth, and lower-ranking cargo positions. Any ritual group, then, can be ranked according to the primacy of the "senior" principle. (See Rosaldo, 1968, also reprinted in this volume, for a discussion of this ritual principle as it occurs in nearby Zinacantan.)

To confuse matters, the most "senior" official hardly ever moves in the front position of a group which is traversing a ritual circuit. In fact, he usually brings up the rear of the group. This positioning is not a paradox if one remembers that cargo-holders share certain attributes of deities, particularly of the sun himself, as they traverse ritual circuits in a counterclockwise direction. Assuming "conceptual east" as the point of orientation and beginning for a ritual circuit (discussed above), it follows that the member of the party who has greatest "heat," which is a fundamental attribute of the sun symbol of the east, should remain closest to the source of that "heat." It is a simple spatial rule of "like remains close to like." And it places the most "senior" official at the end of a procession nearly every time. While this pattern seems to prevail almost without exception in groups of male cargo-holders, it is nevertheless intriguing that females customarily follow men in daily life and in ritual processions as well. Since men in this patrifocal society outrank women for most purposes, one might assume, according to the pattern of "senior-last," that women would *precede* men. The opposite is in fact the case. It seems plausible that the female principle is *both logically prior to patrifocal order* (for the female moon gave birth to the male sun) *and* subordinate *(junior) to patrifocal order* (for the precocious sun blinded his mother and began to give her orders shortly after his birth). I believe that this dual attribute of the female principle may be expressed in the ritual sequence which is described in Figure 5, in which female saints begin moving to their own left (clockwise) and then line up behind the male saints, joining them to complete a counterclockwise (male) circuit.

The pattern in which most "senior" (*bankilal*) remains closest to "conceptual east" is shown in Figure 6 (Part A). Figure 6 also shows how the "senior-east" association

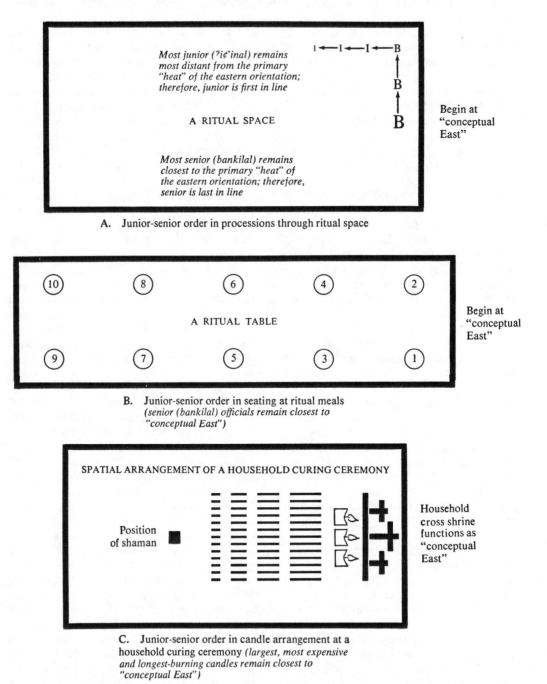

A. Junior-senior order in processions through ritual space

B. Junior-senior order in seating at ritual meals
    (senior (bankilal) officials remain closest to "conceptual East")

C. Junior-senior order in candle arrangement at a household curing ceremony *(largest, most expensive and longest-burning candles remain closest to "conceptual East")*

FIGURE 6
A relationship of some expressions of the junior-senior principle to orientation of "conceptual East."

makes intelligible such diverse spatial patterns as seating order at ritual meals (Part B) and distribution of candles at shamanistic curing rituals (Part C). In the case of the ritual table, the most senior-ranking members of the group sit closest to "conceptual east" in the cosmological microcosm and the most junior members sit closest to "conceptual west." Similarly, the cross-shrine in shamanistic rituals appears to serve as "conceptual east." The many required sizes of candles are always arranged (except in case of witchcraft rituals) so that the most "senior" candles (white, largest, longest-burning, and most expensive) are lined up closest to "conceptual east" and the most "junior" ones toward "conceptual west." I use the term "conceptual" because it is sometimes not physically possible to begin sequences or to place shrines in the position of true east. However, time-space symbolic equivalents, which appear to be assumed knowledge of most Chamulas, can make almost any situation ritually effective if the correct relationships are maintained.

IV. MICROCOSM AND REDUNDANCY

Those symbols which are most effective imply a great deal at once. The sun, the giver and maintainer of order, is such a symbol in Chamula thought. No Chamula ritual passes without innumerable references to patterns whose precedent is found in the cosmogonic moment of the sun's ascent into the heavens. All that accompanied that event is now fixed in Chamula custom and belief, for that moment provided the necessary spatial and temporal categories for an orderly social existence. The ritual task is to state what is essential about all of this in the most economical form possible. Relatively few words and actions must encapsulate what really matters; hence, the importance of sun symbolism and its multivocality, to borrow Victor Turner's useful term (1967:50). For example, a microcosmic action such as the movement of personnel through ritual space takes its meaning from the great universe, the macrocosm of the sun. The primacy of the right hand and masculinity, the cycles of heat in the day and the year, the point of view of the eastern horizon, the counterclockwise motion —all join to recreate the past in the present and to draw in the limits of the great universe to manageable size within the sacred precincts of the Ceremonial Center. The procession of religious images around the atrium of the church at the climax of each major fiesta recreates the cosmogonic moment of the coming of the first light, the first heat, the first maize—the coming of order itself. Moreover, the procession occurs at noon, when the sun is at the zenith of the heavens, giving maximum heat. The event states not a part, but all of this at once.

Eric Wolf

THE VIRGIN OF GUADALUPE: A MEXICAN NATIONAL SYMBOL

There hardly exists a better example of a highly evocative national symbol and a clearer illustration of the relations of microcosm to macrocosm than that of the Virgin of Guadalupe of Mexico. Like her famous Polish counterpart, the Black Madonna of Czenstochowa, she embodies abstract principles and precepts of the nation to which she belongs. The complexity and heterogeneity of Mexico are reconciled in Guadalupe in a special way that no other symbol can rival. Political overtones are blended with individual and societal aspirations, particularly for the Indian, for it was to an Indian that the Virgin revealed herself in 1531. Eric Wolf provides us with a masterful analysis of Guadalupe in this article.

Reprinted with slight abridgements from the *Journal of American Folklore*, LXXI (1958), 34–39, by permission of the author and The American Folklore Society, Inc.

Occasionally, we encounter a symbol which seems to enshrine the major hopes and aspirations of an entire society. Such a master symbol is represented by the Virgin of Guadalupe, Mexico's patron saint. During the Mexican War of Independence against Spain, her image preceded the insurgents into battle. Emiliano Zapata and his agrarian rebels fought under her emblem in the Great Revolution of 1910. Today, her image adorns house fronts and interiors, churches and home altars, bull rings and gambling dens, taxis and buses, restaurants and houses of ill repute. She is celebrated in popular song and verse. Her shrine at Tepeyac, immediately north of Mexico City, is visited each year by hundreds of thousands of pilgrims, ranging from the inhabitants of far-off Indian villages to the members of socialist trade union locals. "Nothing to be seen in Canada or Europe," says F. S. C. Northrop, "equals it in the volume or the vitality of its moving quality or in the depth of its spirit of religious devotion."

In this paper, I should like to discuss this Mexican master symbol, and the ideology which surrounds it. In making use of the term "master symbol," I do not wish to imply that belief in the symbol is common to all Mexicans. We are not dealing here with an element of a putative national character, defined as a common denominator of all Mexican nationals. It is no longer legitimate to assume "that any member of the [national] group will exhibit certain regularities of behavior which are common in high degree among the other members of the society." Nations, like other complex societies, must however, "possess cultural forms or mechanisms which groups involved in the same overall web of relationships can use in their formal and informal dealings with each other." Such forms develop historically, hand in hand with other processes which lead to the formation of nations, and social groups which are caught up in these processes must become "acculturated" to their usage. Only where such forms exist, can communication and coördinated behavior be established among the constituent groups of such a society. They provide the cultural idiom of behavior and ideal representations through which different groups of the same society can pursue and manipulate their different fates within a coordinated framework. This paper, then, deals with one such cultural form, operating on the symbolic level. The study of this symbol seems particularly rewarding, since it is not restricted to one set of social ties, but refers to a very wide range of social relationships.

The image of Guadalupe and her shrine at Tepeyac are surrounded by an origin myth. According to this myth, the Virgin Mary appeared to Juan Diego, a Christianized Indian of commoner status, and addressed him in Nahuatl. The encounter took place on the Hill of Tepeyac in the year 1531, ten years after the Spanish Conquest of Tenochtitlan. The Virgin commanded Juan Diego to seek out the archbishop of Mexico and to inform him of her desire to see a church built in her honor on Tepeyac Hill. After Juan Diego was twice unsuccessful in his efforts to carry out her order, the Virgin wrought a miracle. She bade Juan Diego pick roses in a sterile spot where normally only desert plants could grow, gathered the roses into the Indian's cloak, and told him to present cloak and roses to the incredulous archbishop. When Juan Diego unfolded his cloak before the bishop, the image of the Virgin was miraculously stamped upon it. The bishop acknowledged the miracle, and ordered a shrine built where Mary had appeared to her humble servant.

The shrine, rebuilt several times in centuries to follow, is today a basilica, the third highest kind of church in Western Christendom. Above the central altar hangs Juan Diego's cloak with the miraculous image. It shows a young woman without child, her head lowered demurely in her shawl. She wears an open crown and flowing gown, and stands upon a half moon symbolizing the Immaculate Conception.

The shrine of Guadalupe was, however, not the first religious structure built on Tepeyac; nor was Guadalupe the first female supernatural associated with the hill. In pre-Hispanic times, Tepeyac had housed a temple to the earth and fertility goddess Tonantzin, Our Lady Mother, who—like Guadalupe—was associated with the moon. Temple, like basilica, was the center of large scale pilgrimages. That the veneration accorded Guadalupe drew inspiration from the earlier worship of Tonantzin is attested by several Spanish friars. F. Bernardino de Sahagún, writing fifty years after the Conquest says: "Now that the Church of Our Lady of Guadalupe has been built there, they call her Tonantzin too.... The term refers ... to that ancient Tonantzin and this state of affairs should be remedied, because the proper name of the Mother of God is not Tonantzin, but Dios and Nantzin. It seems to be a satanic device to mask idolatry . . . and they come from far away to visit that Tonantzin, as much as before; a devotion which is also suspect because there are many churches of Our Lady everywhere and they do not go to them; and they come from faraway lands to this Tonantzin as of old." F. Martín de León write in a similar vein: "On the hill where Our Lady of Guadalupe is they adored the idol of a goddess they called Tonantzin, which means Our Mother, and this is also the name they give Our Lady and they always say they are going to Tonantzin or they are celebrating Tonantzin and many of them understand this in the old way and not in the modern way. . . ." The syncretism was still alive in the seventeenth century. F. Jacinto de la Serna, in discussing the pilgrimages to Guadalupe at Tepeyac, noted: ". . . it is the purpose of the wicked to [worship] the goddess and not the Most Holy Virgin, or both together."

Increasingly popular during the sixteenth century, the Guadalupe cult gathered emotional impetus during the seventeenth. During this century appear the first known pictorial representations of Guadalupe, apart from the miraculous original; the first poems are written in her honor; and the first sermons announce the transcendental implications of her supernatural appearance in Mexico and among Mexicans. Historians have long tended to neglect the seventeenth century which seemed "a kind of Dark Age in Mexico." Yet "this quiet time was of the utmost importance in the development of Mexican Society." During this century, the institution of the hacienda comes to dominate Mexican life. During this century, also, "New Spain is ceasing to be 'new' and to be 'Spain.'" These new experiences require a new cultural idiom, and in the Guadalupe cult, the component segments of Mexican colonial society encountered cultural forms in which they could express their parallel interests and longings.

The primary purpose of this paper is not, however, to trace the history of the Guadalupe symbol. It is concerned rather with its functional aspects, its roots and reference to the major social relationships of Mexican society.

The first set of relationships which I would like to single out for consideration are the ties of kinship, and the emotions generated in the play of relationships within families. I want to suggest that some of the meanings of the Virgin symbol in general, and of the Guadalupe symbol in particular, derive from these emotions. I say "some meanings" and I use the term "derive" rather than "originate," because the form and function of the family in any given society are themselves determined by other social factors: technology, economy, residence, political power. The family is but one relay in the circuit within which symbols are generated in complex societies. Also, I used the plural "families" rather than "family," because there are demonstrably more than one kind of family in Mexico. I shall simplify the available information on Mexican family life, and discuss the material in terms of two major types of families. The first kind of family is congruent with the closed and static life of the Indian village. It may be called the Indian family. In this kind of family, the husband is ideally dominant, but in reality labor and authority are shared equally among both marriage partners. Exploitation of one sex by the other is atypical; sexual feats do not add to a person's status in the eyes of others. Physical punishment and authoritarian treatment of children are rare. The second kind of family is congruent with the much more open, mobile, manipulative life in communities which are actively geared to the life of the nation, a life in which power relationships between individuals and groups are of great moment. This kind of family may be called the Mexican family. Here, the father's authority is unquestioned on both the real and the ideal plane. Double sex standards prevail, and male sexuality is charged with a desire to exercise domination. Children are ruled with a heavy hand; physical punishment is frequent.

The Indian family pattern is consistent with the behavior towards Guadalupe noted by John Bushnell in the Matlazinca speaking community of San Juan Atzingo in the Valley of Toluca. There, the image of the Virgin is addressed in passionate terms as a source of warmth and love, and the *pulque* or century plant beer drunk on ceremonial occasions is identified with her milk. Bushnell postulates that here Guadalupe is identified with the mother as a source of early satisfactions, never again experienced after separation from the mother and emergence into social adulthood. As such, Guadalupe embodies a longing to return to the pristine state in which hunger and unsatisfactory social relations are minimized. The second family pattern is also consistent with a symbolic identification of Virgin and mother, yet this time within a context of adult male dominance and sexual assertion, discharged against submissive females and children. In this second context, the Guadalupe symbol is charged with the energy of rebellion against the father. Her image is the embodiment of hope in a victorious outcome of the struggle between generations.

This struggle leads to a further extension of the symbolism. Successful rebellion against power figures is equated with the promise of life; defeat with the promise of death. As John A. Mackay has suggested, there thus takes place a further symbolic identification of the Virgin with life; of defeat and death with the crucified Christ. In Mexican artistic tradition, as in Hispanic artistic tradition in general, Christ is never depicted as an adult man, but always either as a helpless child, or more often as a figure beaten, tortured, defeated and killed. In this symbolic equation we are touching upon some of the roots both of the passionate affirmation of faith in the Virgin, and of the fascination with death which characterizes Baroque Christianity in general, and Mexican Catholicism in particular. Guadalupe stands for life, for hope, for health; Christ on the cross, for despair and for death.

Supernatural mother and natural mother are thus equated symbolically, as are earthly and other worldly hopes and desires. These hopes center on the provision of food and emotional warmth in the first case, in the successful waging of the Oedipal struggle in the other.

Family relations are, however, only one element in the formation of the Guadalupe symbol. Their analysis does little to explain Guadalupe as such. They merely illuminate the female and maternal attributes of the more widespread Virgin symbol. Guadalupe is important to Mexicans not only because she is a supernatural mother, but also because she embodies their major political and religious aspirations.

To the Indian groups, the symbol is more than an embodiment of life and hope; it restores to them the hopes of salvation. We must not forget that the Spanish Conquest signified not only military defeat, but the defeat also of the old gods and the decline of the old ritual. The apparition of Guadalupe to an Indian commoner thus represents on one level the return of Tonantzin. As Tannenbaum has well said, "The Church ... gave the Indian an opportunity not merely to save his life, but also to save his faith in his own gods." On another level, the myth of the apparition served as a symbolic testimony that the Indian, as much as the Spaniard, was capable of being saved, capable of receiving Christianity. This must be understood against the background of the bitter theological and political argument which followed the Conquest and divided churchmen, officials, and conquerors into those who held that the Indian was incapable of conversion, thus inhuman, and therefore a fit subject of political and economic exploitation; and those who held that the Indian was human, capable of conversion and that this exploitation had to be tempered by the demands of the Catholic faith and of orderly civil processes of government. The myth of Guadalupe thus validates the Indian's right to legal defense, orderly government, to citizenship; to supernatural salvation, but also to salvation from random oppression.

But if Guadalupe guaranteed a rightful place to the Indians in the new social system of New Spain, the myth also held appeal to the large group of disinherited who arose in New Spain as illegitimate offspring of Spanish fathers and Indian mothers, or through impoverishment, acculturation or loss of status within the Indian or Spanish group. For such people, there was for a long time no proper place in the social order. Their very right to exist was questioned in their inability to command the full rights of citizenship and legal protection. Where Spaniard and Indian stood squarely within the law, they inhabited the interstices and margins of constituted society. These groups acquired influence and wealth in the seventeenth and eighteenh centuries, but were yet barred from social recognition and power by the prevailing economic, social and political order. To them, the Guadalupe myth came to represent not merely the guarantee of their assured place in heaven, but the guarantee of their place in society here and now. On the political plane, the wish for a return to a paradise of early satisfactions of food and warmth, a life without defeat, sickness or death, give rise to a political wish for a

Mexican paradise, in which the illegitimate sons would possess the country, and the irresponsible Spanish overlords, who never acknowledged the social responsibilities of their paternity, would be driven from the land.

In the writings of seventeenth century ecclesiastics, Guadalupe becomes the harbinger of this new order. In the book by Miguel Sánchez, published in 1648, the Spanish Conquest of New Spain is justified solely on the ground that it allowed the Virgin to become manifest in her chosen country, and to found in Mexico a new paradise. Just as Israel had been chosen to produce Christ, so Mexico had been chosen to produce Guadalupe. Sánchez equates her with the apocalyptic woman of the Revelation of John (12:1), "arrayed with the sun, and the moon under her feet, and upon her head a crown of twelve stars" who is to realize the prophecy of Deuteronomy 8:7–10 and lead the Mexicans into the Promised Land. Colonial Mexico thus becomes the desert of Sinai; Independent Mexico the land of milk and honey. F. Francisco de Florencia, writing in 1688, coined the slogan which made Mexico not merely another chosen nation, but the Chosen Nation: *non fecit taliter omni nationi*, words which still adorn the portals of the basilica, and shine forth in electric light bulbs at night. And on the eve of Mexican independence, Servando Teresa de Mier elaborates still further the Guadalupan myth by claiming that Mexico had been converted to Christianity long before the Spanish Conquest. The apostle Saint Thomas had brought the image of Guadalupe-Tonantzin to the New World as a symbol of his mission, just as Saint James had converted Spain with the image of the Virgin of the Pillar. The Spanish Conquest was therefore historically unnecessary, and should be erased from the annals of history. In this perspective, the Mexican War of Independence marks the final realization of the apocalyptic promise. The banner of Guadalupe leads the insurgents; and their cause is referred to as "her law." In this ultimate extension of the symbol, the promise of life held out by the supernatural mother has become the promise of an independent Mexico, liberated from the irrational authority of the Spanish father-oppressors and restored to the Chosen Nation whose election had been manifest in the apparition of the Virgin on Tepeyac. The land of the supernatural mother is finally possessed by her rightful heirs. The symbolic circuit is closed. Mother; food, hope, health, life; supernatural salvation and salvation from oppression; Chosen People and national independence—all find expression in a single master symbol.

The Guadalupe symbol thus links together family, politics and religion; colonial past and independent present; Indian and Mexican. It reflects the salient social relationships of Mexican life, and embodies the emotions which they generate. It provides a cultural idiom through which the tenor and emotions of these relationships can be expressed. It is, ultimately, a way of talking about Mexico: a "collective representation" of Mexican society.

Victor W. Turner

PLANES OF CLASSIFICATION IN A RITUAL OF LIFE AND DEATH

The following excerpt from Victor Turner's *The Ritual Process* is an especially fine example of a method of symbolic analysis originally developed by Turner to explain the rituals of the Ndembu of Zambia but which have had considerable impact on the study of ritual symbolism in general. The method has both theoretical and practical aspects; the analytical divisions of symbolic meaning that he defines are tied up to the processes used to obtain the information in the field. He distinguishes three levels or fields of meaning: exegetical, operational, and positional. Exegetical meaning consists of the explanations received from the actors, both laymen and ritual specialists, which, for the Ndembu, cluster around the (sometimes fictitious) etymology of the name of the symbolic object or act and its observable properties, mainly shape and substantial attributes for material symbols. Operational meaning equates the meaning of a symbol with its use, how and by whom it is obtained, set up, and manipulated in the rite. Finally, positional meaning is that meaning a symbol derives from relations with other symbols in a symbolic system, either a given ceremony or the total set of ritual symbols of the society.

Turner's analyses convincingly demonstrate, for the Ndembu at least, the property of "multivocality" (multiple reference) in symbols and show how this allows the unification of disparate meanings in major, "dominant" symbols. Turner considers the total meaning of a dominant symbol to have two poles: ideological and sensory. The former refers to components of the moral and social orders and the latter to natural and physiological phenomena and processes. The former expresses social norms while the latter arouses feelings and desires. A major function of ritual, Turner says, is to channel emotion into the norms of society, to make the obligatory desirable.

ISOMA

My main aim in this chapter is to explore the semantics of ritual symbols in *Isoma*, a ritual of the Ndembu, and to construct from the observational and exegetical data a model of the semantic structure of this symbolism. The first step in such a task is to pay close attention to the way the Ndembu explain their own symbols. My procedure will be to begin with particulars and move to generalization, letting the reader into my confidence at every step along this road. I am now going to look closely at a kind of ritual which I observed on three occasions and for which I have a considerable quantity of exegetical material. I must crave the reader's indulgence for the fact that I shall have to mention a number of Ndembu vernacular terms, for an important part of the Ndembu explanation of symbols rests upon folk etymologizing. The meaning of a given symbol is often, though by no means invariably, derived by Ndembu from the name assigned to it, the sense of which is traced from some primary word, or etymon, often a verb. Scholars have shown that in other Bantu societies this is often a process of fictitious etymologizing, dependent on similarity of sound rather than upon derivation from a commom source. Nevertheless, for the people themselves it constitutes part of the "explanation" of a ritual symbol; and we are here trying to discover "the Ndembu inside view," how the Ndembu themselves felt and thought about their own ritual.

REASONS FOR PERFORMING *ISOMA*

The *Isoma* (or *Tubwiza*) ritual belongs to a class (*muchidi*) of rituals, recognized as such by Ndembu, known as "women's rituals" or "rituals of procreation," which itself is a subclass of "rituals of the ancestral spirits or 'shades'"—a term I borrow from Monica Wilson. The Ndembu word for "ritual" is *chidika*, which also means "a special engagement" or an "obligation." This is connected with the idea that one is under an obligation to venerate the ancestral shades, for, as Ndembu say, "are they not the ones who have begotten or borne you?" The rituals I am speaking of are in fact performed because persons or corporate groups have failed to meet this obligation. Either for his own default or as representative of a group of kin, a person is believed to have been "caught," as Ndembu say, by a shade and afflicted with a misfortune thought to be appropriate to his sex or social role. The misfortune appropriate to women consists in some kind of interference with the victim's reproductive capacity. Ideally, a woman who is living at peace with her fellows and is mindful of her deceased kin should be married and a mother of "live and lovely children" (to translate an Ndembu expression). But a woman who is either quarrelsome herself or a member of a group riven with quarrels, and who has simultaneously "forgotten her [deceased mother or mother's mother or some other senior deceased matrilineal kinswoman's] shade in her liver [or, as we would say, 'heart']," is in peril of having her procreative power (*Lusemu*) "tied-up" (*ku-kasila*) by the offended shade.

The Ndembu, who practice matrilineal descent combined with virilocal marriage, live in small, mobile villages. The effect of this arrangement is that women, through whom children derive their primary lineage and residential affiliation, spend much of their reproductive cycle in the villages of their husbands and not of their matrilineal kin. There is no rule, as there is, for example, among the matrilineal Trobriand Islanders, that the sons of women living in this form of marriage should go to reside in the villages of their mother's brothers and other matrikin on reaching adolescence. One consequence of this is that every fruitful marriage becomes an arena of covert struggle between a woman's husband and her brothers and mother's brothers over the residential affiliation of her children. Since there is also a close bond between a woman and her children, this usually means that after a short or long period a woman will follow her children to her village of matrilineal affiliation. My figures on Ndembu divorce indicate that the tribal ratios are the highest among all the matrilineal societies in Central Africa for which reliable quantitative data exist—and all have high divorce rates. Since women return to their matrikin on divorce—and *a fortiori* to their children resident among those kin—in a very real sense village continuity, through women, depends upon marital discontinuity. But, while a woman is residing with her husband with her young children, and thus fulfilling the valid norm that a woman should please him, she is not fulfilling an equally valid norm that she should contribute children to the contemporaneous membership of her matrilineal village.

Interestingly, it is the shades of direct matrilineal kinswomen—own mothers or own mothers' mothers—that are held to afflict women with reproductive disorders, resulting in temporary barrenness. Most of these victims are residing with their husbands when divination decrees that they have been caught with infertility by their matrilineal shades. They have been caught, so Ndembu regularly say, because they have "forgotten" those shades who are not only their direct ascendants but also the immediate progenetrices of their matrikin—who form the core membership of villages different from those of their husbands. The curative rites, including *Isoma*, have as one social function that of "causing them to remember" these shades, who are structural nodes of a locally residing matrilineage. The condition of barrenness these shades bring about is considered to be a temporary one, to be removed by performance of the appropriate rites. Once a woman remembers the afflicting shade, and thus her primary allegiance to matrikin, the interdiction on her fertility will cease; she can go on living with her husband but with a sharpened awareness of where her and her children's ultimate loyalties lie. The crisis brought on by this contradiction between norms is resolved by rituals rich in symbolism and pregnant with meaning.

PROCESSUAL FORM

Isoma shares with the other women's cults a common diachronic profile or processual form. In each a woman suffers from gynecological disorders; then either her husband or a matrikinsman seeks out a diviner, who denominates the precise mode of affliction in which the shade, as Ndembu say, has "come out of the grave to catch her." Dependent upon that mode, the husband or kinsman employs a doctor (*chimbuki*), who "knows the medicines" and the correct ritual procedures for appeasing the afflicting shade to act as master of ceremonies for the coming performance. This doctor then summons other doctors to help him. These are either women who have undergone exposure to the same kind of ritual and have thus gained entry into the curative cult, or men closely linked by matrilineal kinship or affinity to a previous patient. The patients (*ayeji*) may be regarded as "candidates" for membership of the cult, the doctors as its "adepts." The afflicting shades (*akishi*) are believed to have been former adepts. Cult membership thus transects village and lineage membership and brings into temporary operation what may be termed "a community of suffering"—or, rather, of "former sufferers" from the same type of affliction as now besets the candidate patient. Membership of a cult such as *Isoma* cuts across even tribal boundaries, for members of the culturally and linguistically related Luvale, Chokwe, and Luchazi tribes are entitled to attend Ndembu *Isoma* rites as adepts, and as such to perform ritual tasks. The "senior" (*mukulumpi*) or "great" (*weneni*) adept is usually a man, even for such women's cults as *Isoma*; as in most matrilineal societies, while social placement is through women, authority is in the hands of men.

Women's cults have the tripartite diachronic structure made familiar to us by the work of van Gennep. The first phase, called *Ilembi*, separates the candidate from the profane world; the second, called *Kunkunka* (literally, "in the grass hut"), partially secludes her from secular life; while the third, called *Ku-tumbuka*, is a festive dance, celebrating the removal of the shade's interdiction and the candidate's return to normal life. In *Isoma* this is signalized by the candidate's bearing a child and raising it to the toddling stage.

INDIGENOUS EXEGESIS OF SYMBOLS

So much for the broad social and cultural setting of *Isoma*. If we now desire to penetrate the inner structure of ideas contained in this ritual, we have to understand how the Ndembu themselves interpret its symbols. My method is perforce the reverse of that of those numerous scholars who begin by eliciting the cosmology, which is often expressed in terms of mythological cycles, and *then* explain specific rituals as exemplifying or expressing the "structural models" they find in the myths. But the Ndembu have a paucity of myths and cosmological or cosmogonic narratives. It is therefore *necessary* to begin at the other end, with the basic building-blocks, the "molecules," of ritual. These I shall call "symbols," and for the moment I shall eschew involvement in the long debate on the difference between such concepts as symbol, sign, and signal. Since the preliminary approach is from the "inside" perspective, let us rather first inquire into the *Ndembu* usage.

In an *Ndembu* ritual context, almost every article used, every gesture employed, every song or prayer, every unit of space and time, by convention stands for something other than itself. It is more than it seems, and often a good deal more. The Ndembu are aware of the expressive or symbolic function of ritual elements. A ritual element or unit is called *chijikijilu*. Literally, this word signifies a "landmark" or "blaze." Its etymon is *ku-jikijila*, "to blaze a trail"—by slashing a mark on a tree with an axe or breaking one of its branches. This term is drawn originally from the technical vocabulary of hunting, a vocation heavily invested with ritual beliefs and practices. *Chijikijilu* also means a "beacon," a conspicuous feature of the landscape, such as an ant hill, which distinguishes one man's gardens or one chief's realm from another's. Thus, it has two main significations: (1) as a *hunter's blaze* it represents an element of connection between known and unknown territory, for it is by a chain of such elements that a hunter finds his way back from the unfamiliar bush to the familiar village; (2) as both *blaze* and *beacon* it conveys the notion of the structured and ordered as against the unstructured and chaotic. Its ritual use is already metaphorical: it connects the known world of sensorily perceptible phenomena with the unknown and invisible realm of the shades. It makes intelligible what is mysterious, and also dangerous. A *chijikijilu* has, further, both a known and an unknown component. Up to a point it can be explained, and there are principles of explanation available to Ndembu. It has a name (*ijina*) and it has an appearance (*chimwekeshu*), and both of these are utilized as the starting points of exegesis (*chakulumbwishu*).

THE NAME "*ISOMA*"

At the very outset, the name *Isoma* itself has symbolic value. My informants derive it from *ku-somoka*, "to slip out of place or fastening." This designation has multiple reference. In the first place, it refers to the specific condition the rites are intended to dispel. A woman who is "caught in *Isoma*" is very frequently a woman who has had a series of miscarriages or abortions. The unborn child is thought to "slip out" before its time has come to be born. In the second place, *kusomoka* means "to leave one's group," perhaps also with the implication of prematurity. This theme seems to be related to the notion of "forgetting" one's matrilineal attachments. In discussing the meaning of the word *Isoma*, several informants mentioned the term *lufwisha* as indicative of the patient's condition. *Lufwisha* is an abstract noun derived from *ku-fwisha*, itself derived from *ku-fwa*, "to die." *Ku-fwisha* has both a generic sense and a specific one. Generically, it means "to lose relatives by death," specifically "to lose children." The noun *lufwisha* means both "to give birth to a dead child" and the "constant dying of children." One informant told me: "If seven children die one after the other, it is *lufwisha*." *Isoma* is thus a manifestation of a shade that causes a woman to bear a dead child or brings death on a series of infants.

THE MASK "*MVWENG'I*"

The shade that has emerged in *Isoma* manifests itself in other ways, too. It is thought to appear in the patient's dreams dressed like one of the masked beings in the boys' circumcision rites (*Mukanda*). These masked beings, known as *makishi* (singular *ikishi*), are believed by women to be shades of ancient ancestors. The one known as *Mvweng'i* wears a bark kilt (*nkambi*), like the novices during their seclusion after circumcision, and a costume consisting of many strings made from bark cloth. He carries a hunting bell (*mpwambu*) used by hunters to keep in touch with one another in the deep bush or to summon their dogs. He is known as "grandfather" (*nkaka*), appears after the boys circumcision wounds are healed, and is greatly feared by women. If a woman touches *Mvweng'i*, it is thought that she will have miscarriages. A song traditionally sung when this *ikishi* first appears near the lodge where the novices are secluded in the bush runs as follows:

Kako nkaka eyo nkaka eyo eyo nkaka yetu nenzi, eyo eyo, nkaka yetu, mwanta;
"Grandfather, O Grandfather, our grandfather has come, our grandfather, the chief";

mbwemboye mbwemboye yawume-e
"the glans penis, the glans is dry,

mwang'u watulemba mbwemboye yawumi.
a scattering of *tulemba* spirits, the glans is dry."

The song represents for Ndembu a concentration of masculine power, for *nkaka* also signifies "an owner of slaves," and a "chief" owns many slaves. The dryness of the glans is a symbol of the attainment of an auspicious masculine adult status, one of the aims of the *Mukunda* circumcision rites, for the glans of an uncircumcised boy is regarded as wet and filthy, hence inauspicious, beneath the prepuce. *Tulemba* spirits, propitiated and exorcised in another type of ritual, cause infants to sicken and pine. *Mvweng'i* drives them from the boys. The strings of his costume are believed to "tie up" (*ku-kasila*) female fertility. In brief, he is a symbol of mature masculinity in its pure expression— and his hunting attributes further support this—and as such is dangerous to women in their most feminine role, that of mother. Now, it is in the guise of *Mvweng'i* that the shade appears to the victim. But here there is some ambiguity of exegesis. Some informants say that the shade is identified with *Mvweng'i*, others that shade (*mukishi*) and masker (*ikishi*) operate in conjunction. The latter say that the shade rouses *Mvweng'i* and enlists his aid in afflicting the victim.

It is interesting to note that the shade is always the spirit of a deceased *female* relative, while *Mvweng'i* is almost maleness personified. This motif of linking reproductive disorder to the identification of a female with a type of masculinity is found elsewhere in Ndembu ritual. I have mentioned it in connection with rites to cure menstrual difficulties in *The Forest of Symbols* (1967): "Why then is the woman patient identified with male bloodspillers? The [social] field context of these symbolic objects and items of behavior suggests that the Ndembu feel that the woman, in wasting her menstrual blood and in failing to bear children, is actively renouncing her expected role as a mature married female. She is behaving like a male killer [i.e., a hunter or homicide], not like a female nourisher" (p. 42. For a fuller analysis of the *Nkula* curative rites, see Turner, 1968, pp. 54–87). The situation in *Isoma* is not dissimilar. It should be noticed that in these cults, the victim is in various episodes and symbolisms often identified with the shade that afflicts her: she is being persecuted, one might say with fair legitimacy, by a part or aspect of herself, projected onto the shade. Thus a cured victim in *Isoma* will become, in Ndembu thought, herself an afflicting shade after death, and as such will be identified with or closely conjoined to the masculine power *Mvweng'i*.

But it would, I think, be erroneous to see in the *Isoma* beliefs merely an expression of the "masculine protest." This unconscious attitude may well be more prominent in the *Nkula* rites than in *Isoma*. The structural tension between matrilineal descent and virilocal marriage seems to dominate the ritual idiom of *Isoma*. It is because the woman has come too closely in touch with the "man's side" in her marriage that her dead matrikin have impaired her fertility. The right relation that should exist between descent and affinity has been upset; the marriage has come to outweigh the matrilineage. The woman has been scorched by the dangerous fires of male sacredness. I use this metaphor because Ndembu themselves do: if women see the flames of the boys' seclusion lodge when it is burned down after the circumcision ritual, it is believed that they will be striped as with flames, or, like the zebra (*ng'ala*), with leprosy, or, alternatively, will run mad or become simpletons.

AIMS OF *ISOMA*

Thus the implicit aims of *Isoma* include: restoration of the right relation between matriliny and marriage; reconstruction of the conjugal relations between wife and husband; and making the woman, and hence the marriage and lineage, fruitful. The explicit aim of the rites, as Ndembu explain it, is to remove the effects of what they call a *chisaku*. Broadly, *chisaku* denotes "misfortune or illness due to the displeasure of ancestral shades or a breach of taboo." More specifically, it also denotes a curse spoken by a living person to arouse a shade and may include medicines concocted to harm an enemy. In the case of *Isoma*, the *chisaku* is of a particular kind. It is believed that a matrilineal relative of the victim has gone to the source (*kasulu*) of a stream in the vicinity of the village of her matrikin and there spoken a curse (*kumushing'ana*) against her. The effect of this curse has been "to awaken" (*ku-tonisha*) a shade who was once a member of the *Isoma* cult. As one informant said (and I translate literally): "At *Isoma* they behead a red cock. This stands for the *chisaku* or misfortune through which people die, it must go away (*chisaku chafwang'a antu, chifumi*). The *chisaku* is death, which must not happen to the woman patient; it is sickness (*musong'u*), which must not come to her; it is suffering (*ku-kabakana*), and this suffering is from the grudge (*chitela*) of a witch (*muloji*). A person who curses another with death has a *chisaku*. The *chisaku* is spoken at the source of a river. If someone passes there and steps on it (*ku-dyata*) or crosses over it (*ku-badyika*), bad luck (*malwa*) or lack of success (*ku-halwa*) will go with her wherever she goes. She has gotten it at that place, the stream source, and she must be treated (*ku-uka*) there. The shade of *Isoma* has come out as the result of that curse, and comes like *Mvweng'i*."

As the reader can see, there is in all this a strong overtone of witchcraft. Unlike other women's rites, *Isoma* is not performed merely to propitiate a single shade; it is also aimed at exorcising malign mystical influences emanating from the living as well as the dead. There is here a grisly alliance of witch, shade, and the *Ikishi Mvweng'i* to be dealt with. The rites involve symbolic reference to all these agencies. It is significant that a matrilineal relative should be regarded as the precipitating cause of the affliction, the arouser of these two grades of ancestral beings, remote and near, *Mvweng'i* and the female shade. It is also significant that the rites are performed, whenever possible, near a village inhabited by the victim's *matrilineal* kin. Furthermore, she is partially secluded at that village for a considerable time afterward, and her husband must reside with her uxorilocally during that period. There seems to be some ambiguity in my informants' accounts about the interpretation of the precipitating curse. It is felt to smack of witchcraft and hence to be "bad," but, at the same time, to be partially justified by the victim's neglect of her matrilineal ties past and present. The rites are partially to effect a reconciliation between the visible and invisible parties concerned, though they contain episodes of exorcism as well.

PREPARATION OF SACRED SITE

So much for the social settings and the major beliefs underlying *Isoma*. Now let us turn to the rites themselves, and consider the interpretations of symbols in order of their occurrence. These will expand our picture of the belief structure, for Ndembu, who, as I said, have remarkably few myths, compensate for this by a wealth of item-by-item exegesis. There are no short cuts, through myth and cosmology, to the structure—in Lévi-Strauss's sense—of Ndembu religion. One has to proceed atomistically and piecemeal from "blaze" to "blaze," "beacon" to "beacon," if one is properly to follow the indigenous mode of thinking. It is only when the symbolic path from the unknown to the known is completed that we can look back and comprehend its final form.

As with all Ndembu rites, the pattern of procedure in each specific case is set by the diviner originally consulted about the patient's affliction. He is the one who establishes that the woman has lost a succession of children by miscarriage or death in infancy—misfortunes summarized in the term *lufwisha*. It is he who decrees that the rites must begin at the hole or burrow, either of a giant rat (*chituba*) or of an ant-bear (*mfuji*). Why does he make this rather odd prescription? Ndembu explain it as follows: Both these animals stop up their burrows after excavating them. Each is a symbol (*chijikijilu*) for the *Isoma* shade-manifestation which has hidden away the woman's fertility (*lusemu*). The doctor adepts must open the blocked entrance of the burrow, and thus symbolically give her back her fertility, and also enable her to raise her children well. The diviner decides which of these species has hidden the fertility in the particular case. The burrow must be near the source of the stream where the curse was uttered. The utterance of a curse is usually accompanied by the burial of "medicines," often pressed (*ku-panda*) into a small antelope's horn. From my knowledge of other Ndembu rites, I strongly suspect that these are hidden near the river source. The animal's burrow provides the reference point of orientation for the spatial structure of the sacred site. The rites I am discussing here are "the rites of separation," known as *ku-lembeka* or *ilembi*, a term Ndembu connect materially with ways of using medicines or medicine containers prominent in some kinds of women's cults, and etymologically with *ku-lemba*, "to supplicate, beg forgiveness, or be penitent." The notion of propitiation is prominent in them, for the doctors are partly pleading on the patient's behalf with the shades and other preter-human entities to give her back her mother-hood.

In all *ilembi* rites one of the first steps is for the doctor adepts, led by the senior adept or "master of ceremonies," to go into the bush to collect the medicines they will treat the patient with later. This episode is known as *ku-lang'ula* or *ku-hukula yitumbu*. In *Isoma*, before this step is taken the patient's husband, if she has one currently, constructs for her use during the subsequent seclusion period a small round grass hut, just outside the ring of a dozen or so huts that constitutes an Ndembu village. Such a hut (*nkunka*) is also made for girls undergoing seclusion after their puberty rites, and the *Isoma* hut is explicitly compared with this. The patient is like a novice. Just as a puberty novice is "grown" into a woman, according to Ndembu thinking, so the *Isoma* candidate is to be regrown into a fertile woman. What has been undone by the curse has to be done all over again, although not in precisely the same way, for life crises are irreversible. There is analogy but not replication.

A red cock, supplied by the husband, and a white pullet, supplied by the patient's matri-kin, are then collected by the adepts, who proceed to the particular stream source where divination previously indicated that the curse was laid. They then examine the ground carefully for signs of a giant rat's or ant-bear's burrow. When they find it, the senior adept addresses the animal as follows: "Giant rat (ant-bear), if you are the one who kills children, now give the woman back her fertility, may she raise children well." Here the animal seems to represent the whole "troika" of afflicting agencies—witch, shade, and *ikishi*. The next task is to tie hanks of grass into two knots, one above the filled-in entrance to the burrow, the other about four feet away above the tunnel made by the animal. The clods beneath these are removed by hoe, and the senior adept and his major male assistant begin to dig deep holes there, known as *makela* (singular, *ikela*), a term reserved for holes serving a magico-religious purpose. Next, two fires are kindled at a distance of about ten feet from the holes and nearer the second than the first. One fire is said to be "on the right-hand side," (i.e., looking from the animal's burrow to the new hole) and is reserved for the use of the male adepts; the other, "on the left-hand side," is for the women. The senior adept then puts down a piece of broken calabash near the burrow-entrance hole, and female adepts, led by the patient's mother if she is an adept, put in it some portions of edible roots from their gardens, including cassava rhizomes and sweet potato tubers. In ritual idiom these represent "the body" (*mujimba*) of the patient. It is significant that they are supplied by women, notably by women of the patient's matrilineage.

After the senior adept and his principal male assistant have inaugurated the digging, they hand over their hoes to other male adepts, who continue to excavate the holes until they are about four to six feet deep. The burrow entrance is known as "the hole of the giant rat" (or "ant-bear"), the other as "the new hole." The animal is known as the "witch" (*muloji*), and the burrow entrance is said to be "hot" (*-tata*). The other hole is called *ku-fomwisha* or *ku-fomona*, verbal nouns that signify respectively "cooling down" and "domesticating." When they have reached the appropriate depth, the adepts commence to dig toward one another until they meet about halfway, having completed a tunnel (*ikela dakuhanuka*). This has to be wide enough for one person to pass through. Other adepts break or bend the branches of trees in a wide ring around the whole scene of ritual activity, to create a sacred space that rapidly achieves structure. To ring something around is a persistent theme of Ndembu ritual; it is usually accompanied by the process of making a clearing (*mukombela*) by hoe. In this way a small realm of order is created in the formless milieu of the bush. The ring is known as *chipang'u*, a term that is also used for the fence around a chief's dwelling and his medicine hut.

COLLECTION OF MEDICINES

While the junior adepts prepare the sacred site, the senior adept and his principal assistant go to the adjacent bush to find medicines. These are collected from different species of trees, each of which has a symbolic value derived from the attributes and purposes of *Isoma*. In most Ndembu rituals there is considerable consistency in the sets of medicines used in different performances of the same kind of ritual, but in the *Isoma* rites I attended there was wide variation from performance to performance. The first tree from which portions are taken for medicine (*yitumbu*) is always known as the *ishikenu*, and it is here that invocation is made, either to the afflicting shade or to the species itself, whose power (*ng'ovu*) is said to be "awakened" (*ku-tona*) by the words addressed to it. At one performance I attended, the senior adept went to a *kapwipu* tree (*Swartzia madagascariensis*), which is used because its wood is hard. Hardness represents the health and strength (*wukolu*) desired for the patient. The senior adept cleared the base of the tree of weeds with his ritual hoe, then put the pieces of edible tubers representing the patient's body on the cleared space (*mukombela*) and spoke as follows: "When this woman was pregnant before, her lips, eyes, palms and the soles of her feet turned yellow [a sign of anemia]. Now she is pregnant again. This time make her strong, so that she may bear a living child, and may it grow strong." The doctor then cut bark chips from another tree of the same species with his medicine ax, and put them in his piece of broken calabash. After that he proceeded to cut bark chips from sixteen further species of trees.

It would take too long to discuss the meaning of each of these here, suffice it to say that many Ndembu can attach not merely a single significance but in some cases (such as *musoli*, *msueng'u*, and *mukombukombu*) many connotations to a single species. Some of these species are used in many different kinds of rituals and in herbalist practice (where, however, different types of associational link-ages are utilized from those employed in ritual, depending more on taste and smell than on natural properties and etymology). Some (e.g., *kapwipu*, *mubang'a*) are used because they have tough (hence "strengthening") wood, others (e.g., *mucha*, *musafwa*, *mufung'u*, *museng'u*, *musoli*, and *mubulu*) because they are fruit-bearing trees, representing the ritual intention of making the patient fruitful once more; but all share the ritually important property that bark string cannot be taken from them, for this would "tie up" the fertility of the patient. In this sense, they may all be said to be counter-*Mvweng'i* medicines, for, as the reader will recall, his costume is largely made up of bark strings, deadly to women's procreation.

I cannot refrain, however, from mentioning in more detail a smaller set of *Isoma* medicines, from another performance, for the native interpretation of these throws light on many of the ritual's underlying ideas. Here the doctors went first to a *chikang'anjamba* or *chikoli* tree (*Strychnos spinosa*). This they described as the *mukulumpi*, "senior" or "elder," of the medicine. After invoking its powers, they took a portion of one of its roots and some leaves. *Chikang'anjamba* means "the elephant fails" (to uproot it), on account of its tenacity and toughness. Its alternative name, *chikoli*, they derived from *ku-kola*, "to be strong, healthy, or firm," a designation that accords with its extreme toughness and durability. This same tree provides medicine for the circumcision rites, where it is thought to confer on the novices exceptional virility. In *Isoma*, its use stresses the connection between these rites and *Mukanda*, the circumcision rites, while it is also a specific against the infirmity—and in many cases the anemia—of the patient. A comparison of the dominant medicines of these two performances shows that the same principle or idea can be expressed in different symbols. The dominant medicine of the first performance, *kapwipu*, is also a strong tree, and one from which is often taken the forked branch that forms the central element of shrines set up to the shades of hunters, considered to be "tough and virile men." Such shrine trees, peeled of bark, are exceptionally resistant to the action of termites and other insects. Decoctions of *kapwipu* leaves and bark are also used as aphrodisiacs.

The second medicine collected in this performance represents another theme of Ndembu ritual—that of representing the patient's inauspicious condition. This is the *mulendi* tree. It has a very slippery surface, from which climbers are prone to slip (*ku-selumuka*) and come to grief. In the same way the patient's children have tended to "slip out" prematurely. But the "glossiness" (*ku-senena*) of this tree also has therapeutic value, and this side of its meaning is prominent in other rites and treatments, for its use makes the "disease" (*musong'u*) slip away from the patient. It is, indeed, not uncommon for Ndembu symbols, at all levels of symbolism, to express simultaneously an auspicious and an inauspicious condition. For example, the name *Isoma* itself, meaning "to slip out," represents both the patients' undesirable state and the ritual to cure it.

Here we come across another ritual principle, expressed in the Ndembu term *ku-solola*, "to make appear, or reveal." What is made sensorily perceptible, in the form of a symbol (*chijikilu*), is thereby made accessible to the purposive action of society, operating through its religious specialists. It is the "hidden" (*chamusweka*) that is "dangerous" or "noxious" (*chafwana*). Thus, to name an inauspicious condition is halfway to removing that condition; to embody the invisible action of witches or shades in a visible or tangible symbol is a big step toward remedying it. This is not so very far removed from the practice of the modern psychoanalyst. When something is grasped by the mind, made capable of being thought about, it can be dealt with, mastered. Interestingly enough, the principle of revelation itself is embodied in an Ndembu medicine-symbol used in *Isoma*. This is the *musoli* tree (whose name is derived by informants from *ku-solola*), from which leaves and bark chips are also taken. It is widely used in Ndembu ritual, and its name is linked with its natural properties. It produces many small fruits, which fall to the ground and lure out of hiding various species of edible animals, which can be killed by the hunter. It literally "makes them appear." In hunting cults, its employment as medicine is intended to produce animals to the view (*ku-solola anyama*) of the hitherto unlucky hunter; in women's cults, it is used "to make children appear" (*ku-solola anyana*) to an unfruitful woman. As in so many cases, there is in the semantics of this symbol a union of ecology and intellect that results in the materialization of an idea.

To return to the medicine-collecting: the doctors next collect roots and leaves from a *chikwata* tree (*Zizyphus mucronata*), a species in whose thereapeutic meaning etymology once more combines with its natural characteristics. *Chikwata* has "strong thorns," which "catch" (*ku-kwata*) or arrest the passer-by. It is thus said both to represent "strength" and, by its thorns, to "pierce disease." I could, if time permitted, expatiate upon the ritual theme of "catching" or "snatching," which is expressed in many symbols. It pervades the idiom of hunting symbolism, as might be expected, but is also exemplified in the phrase "to catch a child" (*ku-kwala mwana*), which means "to give birth." But I will pass on to the next medicine species from which portions are taken, *musong'asong'a* (*Ximenia caffra*), again a hardwood tree, making thus for health and strength, but also derived by folk etymology from *ku-song'a*, "to come to fruit or develop fruit," a term that is metaphorically applied to giving birth to children, as in *ku-song'a anyana*. The *muhotuhotu* tree (*Canthium venosum*) is used for medicine "because of its name." Ndembu derive this from *ku-hotomoka*, "to fall suddenly," like a branch or fruit. The inauspicious condition, it is hoped, will suddenly cease by its application. Next, medicine is taken from the *mutunda* tree, whose derivation is from *ku-tunda*, which means "to be higher than those around it." In *Isoma* it stands for the good growth of an embryo in the womb and the child's continued exuberant growth thereafter. *Mupapala* (*Anthocleista species*) is the name of the next medicine species, and once more we have a representation of the patient's inauspicious condition. Ndembu derive its name from *kupapang'ila*, which means "to wander about in confusion" without knowing where one is. One informant put it in this way: "A woman goes this way and that without children. She must not do this any more. That is why we cut *mupapala* medicine." Behind this idea, and behind the idea of "slipping out," is the notion that it is good and appropriate when things adhere to their proper place and when people do what is appropriate for them to do in their stage of life and status in society.

In another performance of *Isoma*, the principal medicine or "dominant symbol" was not a particular species of tree but any kind of tree whose roots were thoroughly exposed to view. Such a tree is called *wuvumbu*, derived from the verb *ku-vumbuka*, meaning "to be unearthed" and "to emerge from hiding," for example, like a hunted animal. Thus, one informant adumbrated its meaning as follows: "We use *wuvumbu* tree to bring everything to the surface. In just the same way everything in *Isoma* must be clear" (-*lumbuluka*). Another variant upon the theme of "revelation."

HOT AND COOL MEDICINES: APERTURES OF DEATH AND LIFE

Sometimes a portion of wood is taken from a decayed, fallen tree. This, once more, represents the patient's *musong'u*, or diseased, afflicted condition. Equipped with this array of strengthening fecundatory, revelatory, clarifying, health-giving, affixing medicines, some of which in addition represent the manner of the patient's affliction, the adepts return to the sacred site where treatment will be given. They now complete the arrange-

ments that give that consecrated space its visible structure. The medicine leaves and bark fragments are pounded by a female adept in a consecrated meal-mortar. Then they are soaked in water and the liquid medicine is divided into two portions. One is put into a large, thick piece of bark (*ifunvu*) or into a potsherd (*chizanda*), and is then heated on a fire that is kindled just outside the hole dug through the entrance to the giant rat's or ant-bear's burrow. The other is poured cold into an *izawu*, a term that refers to either a clay pot or a medicine trough, or into a broken calabash, and this is placed by the "new hole." According to one informant, the holes stand for "graves (*tulung'a*) and for procreative power (*lusemu*)" —in other words, for tomb and womb. The same informant continued: "The *ikela* (hole) of heat is the *ikela* of death. The cool *ikela* is life. The *ikela* of the giant rat is the *ikela* of the misfortune or grudge (*chisaku*). The

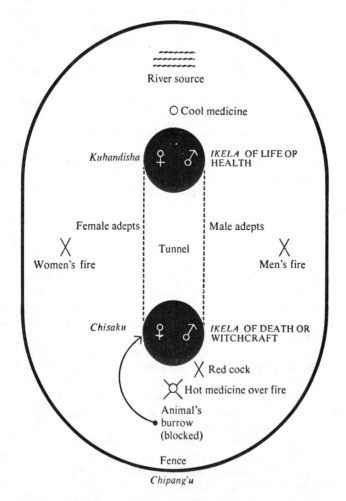

Schematic Representation of the Spatial Symbolism of the *Isoma* Ritual

new *ikela* is the *ikela* of making well (*kuhandisha*) or curing. An *ikela* is located at or near the source of a stream; this represents *lusemu*, the ability to produce offspring. The new *ikela* should blow away from the patient (*muyeji*); in this way the bad things must leave her. The circle of broken trees is a *chipang'u*. [This is a multivocal term that stands for (1) an enclosure; (2) a ritual enclosure; (3) a fenced courtyard around a chief's dwelling and medicine hut; (4) a ring around the moon.] The woman with *lufwisha* [i.e., who has lost three or four children by stillbirth or infant mortality] must go into the hole of life and pass through the tunnel to the hole of death. The big doctor sprinkles her with cold medicine, while his assistant sprinkles her with hot medicine."

We are now beginning to see the development of a whole series of classifications, symbolized in spatial orientations and in different kinds of objects. They are for the most part arranged in a set of what Lévi-Strauss might well call "binary discriminations." But, before we analyze the pattern, a few more variables have to be fed into the system. At performances I observed, the patient's husband entered the "cool" *ikela* with her, standing on the "right-hand side" nearer the men's fire, while she stood on the left. Then, after having been splashed with cool and hot medicine, she entered the connecting tunnel first, while he followed her. As a variant the senior adept (or "big doctor") swept both wife and husband with cool and hot medicine. This his assistant took over for a while and did likewise.

WHITE AND RED FOWLS

When the patient first enters the cool *ikela*, she is given the young white pullet to hold; during the rites she clasps it against her left breast, where a child is held. Both husband and wife, incidentally, are naked except for narrow waist-cloths. This is said to represent the fact that they are at once like infants and corpses. The adepts, in contrast, are clothed. The mature red cock is laid, trussed up by the feet, on the right of the hot *ikela*, in fact on the men's side, ready to be sacrified by beheading at the end of the rites. Its blood and feathers are poured into the hot *ikela* as the final act of the rites, as the antithesis of the reception of the white pullet by the woman patient, which begins the rites. The white chicken is said to stand for *ku-koleka*, "good luck or strength," and *ku-tooka*, "whiteness,

purity, or auspiciousness." But the red cock, as we have seen, represents the *chisaku*, or mystical misfortune, the "suffering" of the woman. The white pullet, according to one informant, also stands for *lusemu*, procreative capacity. "That is why it is given to the woman," he said, "for she is the one who becomes pregnant and gives birth to children. A man is just a man and he can't be pregnant. But a man gives power to women to have children who can be seen, who are visible. The red cock stands for the man, perhaps the grudge is there" [i.e., against him]. "If the woman still has no children after the rites, the grudge would be with the woman" [i.e., would not be connected with her marital situation, but would have arisen in other sets of relations]. Finally, it is probably of significance, although unstated, that the red cock remains trussed up and unmoving through the rites, while the white hen accompanies the woman as she moves through the tunnel from "life" to "death" and back to "life" again. In other Ndembu ritual contexts, movement represents life and stillness death: the cock is consecrated for slaughter.

THE CURATIVE PROCESS

The rites in the *makela* follow a processual pattern. The first phase consists of a passage from the cool to the hot *ikela*, the woman leading and the man following. At the hot *ikela* the doctors mingle their splashings of medicine with exhortations to any witches or curse-layers to remove their inimical influences. Next the marital pair, in the same order, return to the cool *ikela*, where they are again splashed with medicine. Then they cross once more to the hot *ikela*. There follows a temporary lull, during which the husband is escorted out of the *ikela* to fetch a small cloth to wipe the medicine from the faces of the couple and the body of the pullet. He returns to the cool *ikela*, and after further medication, there is a prolonged interval, during which beer is brought and drunk by the attenders and the husband. The patient, herself, is forbidden to drink any. After beer, beginning again in the cool *ikela*, the splashing is resumed. This time around, the husband leads the way to the hot *ikela*. They return to the cool *ikela* in the same order. After splashing, there is another interval for beer. Then the sequence cool-hot-cool follows, the wife leading. Finally, there is a like sequence at the end of which the red cock is beheaded and its blood poured into the hot *ikela.* Then the couple are swept once more with both types of medicine and cold water is poured over them. In all, the couple are splashed twenty times, thirteen of them in the cool *ikela,* seven in the hot, a ratio of nearly two to one.

While splashing goes on, the male adepts on the right and the female adepts on the left sing songs from the great life-crisis and initiation rites of the Ndembu: from *Mukanda,* boys' circumcision; *Mung'ong'i,* the rites of a funerary initiation; *Kayong'u,* initiation into divining; *Nkula,* a traditional women's cult; and *Wuyang'a,* initiation into hunters' cults. Periodically, they sing the *Isoma* song "*mwanami yaya punjila,*" accompanied by a swaying dance called *kupunjila,* which represents the dancing style of the *Mvweng'i ikishi* and, further, mimes the contractions of an abortive labor.

CLASSIFICATORY STRUCTURE: TRIADS

There is enough data to attempt to analyze the structure of the rites so far. First, there are three sets of triads. There is the invisible triad—witch, shade, and *Mvweng'i*—to which is opposed the visible triad—doctor, patient, and patient's husband. In the first triad, the witch is the mediator between the dead and the living in a hostile and lethal connection; in the second, the doctor is the mediator between the living and the dead in a conciliatory and life-giving connection. In the first, the shade is female and the *ikishi* male, while the witch may be of either sex; in the second, the patient is female and her husband male. The doctor mediates between the sexes, in that he treats both. The Ndembu doctor, in fact, has many attributes that are regarded as feminine in Ndembu culture; he can pound medicine in a meal mortar, a task normally undertaken by women; and he handles women and talks to them about private

matters in a way that would be impermissible to men in secular roles. One term for "doctor," *chimbanda,* is said by Ndembu themselves to be connected with the term *mumbanda,* standing for "woman."

In both triads there are close bonds of relationship between two of the partners. In the first, the shade and the witch are believed to be matrilineal kin; in the second, the husband and the wife are linked by affinity. The first pair afflicts the second pair with misfortune. The third partner, *Mvweng'i,* represents the mode of that misfortune, and the other third partner, the doctor, the mode of its removal.

The third triad is represented by the 2:1 ratio between the cold and hot ablutions, which further may be held to symbolize the ultimate victory of life over death. Herein is contained a dialectic that passes from life through death to renewed life. Perhaps, at the level of "deep structure," one might even connect the movement of the patient in the tunnel with her actual movement through marriage from village to village, matrikin to spouse's kin, and back again on the death or divorce of that spouse.

CLASSIFICATORY STRUCTURE: DYADS

The other structural features of the rites may be arrayed in terms of criss-crossing binary oppositions. In the first place, there is the major opposition between the ritual site and the wild bush, which is roughly similar to that made by Eliade between "cosmos" and "chaos." The other oppositions are best arranged in three sets in columnar form, as shown at the bottom of this page.

These sets of pairs of opposed values lie along different planes in ritual space. The first set is *longitudinal* and is spatially polarized by the "*ikela* of life" and the "*ikela* of

LONGITUDINAL	LATITUDINAL	ALTITUDINAL
Burrow/new hole	Left-hand fire/ right-hand fire	Below surface/above surface
Grave/fertility	Women/men	Candidates/adepts
Death/life	Patient/patient's husband	Animals/humans
Mystical misfortune/ curing	Cultivated roots/bush medicines	Naked/clothed
Hot medicine/cool medicine	White pullet/red cock	Medicine roots/ medicine leaves
Fire/absence of fire		Shades/living
Blood/water		White pullet/red cock
Red cock/white pullet		

death." The second set is *latitudinal* and is spatially bounded by the male fire on the right and the female fire on the left. The third set is *altitudinal* and is spatially bounded by the surface of the ground and the floor of the combined *makela* and connecting tunnel. These oppositions are made by the Ndembu themselves in exegesis, in practice, or in both. In terms of spatial orientation the main oppositions are: animal-made hole/man-made hole; left/right; below/above. These correspond respectively to the paired values: death/life; female/male; candidates/adepts. But, since these sets of values transect one another, they should not be regarded as equivalent.

In *Isoma*, the Ndembu are not saying, in the nonverbal language of ritual symbols, that death and femininity, and life and masculinity, are equivalent; nor are they saying that candidates are in a feminine role in relation to adepts (though they are certainly in a passive role). Equivalences may be sought *within* each set (or column), not *between* them. Thus, the animal's blocked lair-entrance is regarded as similar to the filled-in graves of people, to death, which blocks up life; to the mystical misfortune that results in the deaths of infants; to "heat," which is a euphemism for witchcraft and for grudges that "burn"; the red cock, whose color stands for "the blood of witchcraft" (*mashi awuloji*) in *Isoma* (Ndembu witchcraft is necrophagous, and in anti-witchcraft rites, red stands for the blood exposed in such feasts [see Turner, 1967, p. 70]); and to "blood" as a general symbol for aggression, danger, and, in some contexts, ritual impurity. The new hole, made in the direction of the river source, symbolizing the spring of fertility, is regarded, on the other hand, as having affinities with fertility, life, curative procedures, coolness or coldness—a synonym for freedom from the attacks of witches or shades and hence for "health" (*wukolu*); with the absence of "fire"—in this context a symbol for the wasting and dangerous power of witchcraft; with the white pullet—which in this ritual represents and even embodies the patient's fertility and by its color symbolizes (as I have shown elsewhere—e.g., 1967, pp. 69–70) such desirable qualities as "goodness, health, strength, purity, good fortune, fertility, food, etc."; and finally with water, which has much the same range of senses as "whiteness," though in terms of process rather than state.

These positive and negative qualities are suprasexual in their attribution, and I believe that it would be a mistake to equate them too narrowly with sexual differences. The latter are more closely linked with the left-hand/right-hand opposition. In this set, it can hardly be said that the patient, her white pullet, and the cultivated roots supplied by the women have the inauspicious connotations allocated to the grave/death/heat symbolism of the first set. I mention this because other writers, such as Herz, Needham, Rigby, and Beidelman, admittedly in regard to other cultures, have tended to list as members of the same set such pairs as left/right, female/male, inauspicious/auspicious, impure/pure, etc., thus regarding the linkage between femininity and inauspiciousness as a frequent —indeed, almost a universal-human—item of classification. Nor should the below/above dichotomy be correlated, in Ndembu culture, with the sex division. The set of terms arrayed under these heads is once more sex-free, since, for example, the patients below and the doctors above contain members of both sexes.

SITUATION AND CLASSIFICATION

In other types of ritual contexts other classifications apply. Thus, in male circumcision rites, females and female attributes may be regarded as inauspicious and polluting, but the situation is reversed in girls' puberty rites. What is really needed, for the Ndembu and, indeed, for any other culture, is a typology of culturally recognized and stereotyped situations, in which the symbols utilized are classified according to the goal structure of the specific situation. There is no single hierarchy of classifications that may be regarded as pervading all types of situations. Rather, there are different planes of classification which transect one another, and of which the constituent binary pairs (or triadic rubrics) are only temporarily connected: e.g., in one situation the distinction red/white may be homologous with male/female, in another with female/male, and in yet another with meat/flour without sexual connotation.

PLANES OF CLASSIFICATION

Indeed, single symbols may represent the points of interconnection between separate planes of classification. It will have been noted that the opposition red cock/white pullet in *Isoma* appears in all three columns. In the life/death plane, the white pullet equals life and fertility as against the red cock, which equals death and witchcraft; in the right/left plane, the cock is masculine and the pullet feminine; and in the above/below plane, the cock is above, since it is to be used as "medicine" (*yitumbu*), poured down from above, while the pullet is below, since it is closely linked, as child to mother, with the patient who is being medicated. This leads me to the problem of the "polysemy" or multi-vocality of many symbols, the fact that they possess many significations simultaneously. One reason for this may be found in their "nodal" function with reference to inter-secting sets of classifications. The binary-opposition red cock/white hen is significant in at least three sets of classifications in *Isoma*. If one is looking atomistically at each of these symbols, in isolation from one another and from the other symbols in the symbolic field (in terms of indigenous exegesis or symbol context), its multivocality is its most striking feature. If, on the other hand, one is looking at them holistically in terms of the classifica-tions that structure the semantics of the whole rite in which they occur, then each of the senses allocated to them appears as the exemplification of a single principle. In binary opposition on each plane each symbol becomes univocal.

COGNITION AND EXISTENCE IN RITUAL SYMBOLISM

I conclude this chapter by relating its findings to the standpoint of Lévi-Strauss in *The Savage Mind*. Lévi-Strauss is quite correct in stressing that *la pensée sauvage* contains properties such as homologies, oppositions, correlations, and transformations which are also characteristic of sophisticated thinking. In the case of the Ndembu, however, the symbols they use indicate that such properties are wrapped up in a material integument shaped by their life experience. Opposition does not appear as such but as the con-frontation of sensorily perceptible objects, such as a hen and a cock of different ages and colors, in varying spatial relationships and as

undergoing different fates. Although Lévi-Strauss devotes some attention to the role of ritual and mythical symbols as instigators of feeling and desire, he does not develop this line of thought as fully as he does his work on symbols as factors in cognition. (I have considered this elsewhere at some length—for instance, 1967, pp. 28–30, 54–55.) The symbols and their relations as found in *Isoma* are not only a set of cognitive classifications for ordering the Ndembu universe. They are also, and perhaps as importantly, a set of evocative devices for rousing, channeling, and domesticating powerful emotions, such as hate, fear, affection, and grief. They are also informed with purposiveness and have a "conative" aspect. In brief, the whole person, not just the Ndembu "mind," is existentially involved in the life or death issues with which *Isoma* is concerned.

Finally, *Isoma* is not "grotesque" in the sense that its symbolism is ludicrous or incongruous. Every symbolic item is related to some empirical item of experience, as the indigenous interpretations of the vegetable medicines clearly reveal. From the standpoint of twentieth-century science, we may find it strange that Ndembu feel that by bringing certain objects into a ring of consecrated space they bring with these the powers and virtues they seem empirically to possess, and that by manipulating them in prescribed ways they can arrange and concentrate these powers, rather like laser beams, to destroy malignant forces. But, given the limited knowledge of natural causation transmitted in Ndembu culture, who can doubt that under favorable circumstances the use of these medicines may produce considerable psychological benefit? The symbolic expres-sion of group concern for an unfortunate individual's welfare, coupled with the mobil-ization of a battery of "good" things for her benefit, and the conjunction of the indivi-dual's fate with symbols of cosmic processes of life and death—do these really add up for us to something merely "unintelligible"?

Clifford Geertz

RELIGION AS A CULTURAL SYSTEM

Man, says Clifford Geertz in this splendidly written interpretation of religion as a symbolic system, is confronted with the constant impingement upon him of certain chaotic forces that give him a sense of analytic, emotional, and moral impotence. The first involves *ignorance*—bafflement in the face of his limited analytic ability to explain anomalous events; the second involves *pain*—making suffering sufferable when he can no longer endure; and the third involves *injustice*—coping with a sense of ethical paradox when he reaches the limits of his moral insight. The affirmation of these forces, as well as the denial that they are characteristic of the world in general, is made in terms of religious symbolism.

For Geertz, a symbol means any object, act, event, quality, or relation that serves as a vehicle for a conception, the conception being the symbol's meaning. Cultural patterns are of course symbolic systems, religious symbols being those that induce and define dispositions in man. Geertz's aim is to demonstrate that sacred symbols deal with bafflement, pain, and moral paradox by synthesizing a people's ethos and their world view. The ethos of the group is rendered intellectually more reasonable by religious belief and practice. If man's denial of chaos comes to be believed in it is because of the special perspective of religion, which goes outside the realities of daily life to wider realities that complete them in a context of faith. Ritual is a powerful means for providing the conviction that religious concepts are truthful and that religious directives are sound, and the latter effective because they induce moods and motivations. They help make the group's ethos intellectually reasonable.

This article, which must be read in its unabridged form for substantiation of many of the author's premises, is at once both an interpretation of the role of symbolism and an appreciation of the importance of religion in transcending the chaos that threatens man.

Reprinted in greatly abridged form from Michael Banton (ed.), *Anthropological Approaches to the Study of Religion* ("Association of Social Anthropologists Monographs," No. 3 [London: Tavistock Publications, 1965]), by permission of the Association of Social Anthropologists, the publisher, and the author. This monograph is distributed in the United States by Barnes & Noble, Inc., New York.

Any attempt to speak without speaking any particular language is not more hopeless than the attempt to have a religion that shall be no religion in particular. . . . Thus every living and healthy religion has a marked idiosyncrasy; its power consists in its special and surprising message and in the bias which that revelation gives to life. The vistas it opens and the mysteries it propounds are another world to live in; and another world to live in—whether we expect ever to pass wholly over into it or not—is what we mean by having a religion.

—Santayana: *Reason in Religion* (1906)

As we are to deal with meaning, let us begin with a paradigm: *viz.*, that sacred symbols function to synthesize a people's ethos—the tone, character and quality of their life, its moral and aesthetic style and mood—and their world-view—the picture they have of the way things in sheer actuality are, their most comprehensive ideas of order. In religious belief and practice a group's ethos is rendered intellectually reasonable by being shown to represent a way of life ideally adapted to the actual state of affairs the world-view describes, while the world-view is rendered emotionally convincing by being presented as an image of an actual state of affairs peculiarly well-arranged to accommodate such a way of life. This confrontation and mutual confirmation has two fundamental effects. On the one hand, it objectivises moral and aesthetic preferences by depicting them as the imposed conditions of life implicit in a world with a particular structure, as mere common sense given the unalterable shape of reality. On the other, it supports these received beliefs about the world's body by invoking deeply felt moral and aesthetic sentiments as experiential evidence for their truth. Religious symbols formulate a basic congruence between a particular style of life and a specific (if, most often, implicit) metaphysic, and in so doing sustain each with the borrowed authority of the other.

Phrasing aside, this much may perhaps be granted. The notion that religion tunes human actions to an envisaged cosmic order and projects images of cosmic order onto the plane of human experience is hardly novel. But it is hardly investigated either, so that we have very little idea of how, in empirical terms, this particular miracle is accomplished. We just know that it is done, annually, weekly, daily, for some people almost hourly; and we have an enormous ethnographic literature to demonstrate it. But the theoretical framework which would enable us to provide an analytic account of it, an account of the sort we can provide for lineage segmentation, political succession, labor exchange or the socialization of the child, does not exist.

Let us, therefore, reduce our paradigm to a definition, for although it is notorious that definitions establish nothing in themselves they do, if they are carefully enough constructed, provide a useful orientation, or reorientation, of thought, such that an extended unpacking of them can be an effective way of developing and controlling a novel line of inquiry. They have the useful virtue of explicitness: they commit themselves in a way discursive prose, which, in this field especially, is always liable to substitute rhetoric for argument, does not. Without ado, then, a *religion* is: (1) a system of symbols which acts to (2) establish powerful, pervasive and long-lasting moods and motivations in men by (3) formulating conceptions of a general order of existence and (4) clothing these conceptions with such an aura of factuality that (5) the moods and motivations seem uniquely realistic.

I. ... A SYSTEM OF SYMBOLS WHICH ACTS TO ...

Such a tremendous weight is being put on the term "symbol" here that our first move must be to decide with some precision what we are going to mean by it. This is no easy task, for, rather like "culture," "symbol" has been used to refer to a great variety of things, often a number of them at the same time. In some hands it is used for anything which signifies something else to someone: dark clouds are the symbolic precursors of an oncoming rain. In others it is used only for explictly conventional signs of one sort or another: a red flag is a symbol of danger, a white of surrender. In others, it is confined to something which expresses in an oblique and figurative manner that which cannot be stated in a direct and literal one, so that there are symbols in poetry but not in science, and symbolic logic is misnamed. In yet others, however, it is used for any object, act, event, quality or relation which serves as a vehicle for a conception—the conception is the symbol's "meaning"—and that is the approach I shall follow here. The number "6," written, imagined, laid out as a row of stones, or even punched into the program tapes of a computer is a symbol. But so also is the Cross, talked about, visualized, shaped worriedly in air or fondly fingered at the neck, the expanse of painted canvas called "Guernica" or the bit of painted stone called a churinga, the word "reality," or even the morpheme "-ing." They are all symbols, or at least symbolic elements, because they are tangible formulations or notions, abstractions from experience fixed in perceptible forms, concrete embodiments of ideas, attitudes, judgments, longings or beliefs. To undertake the study of cultural activity— activity in which symbolism forms the positive content—is thus not to abandon social analysis for a Platonic cave of shadows, to enter into a mentalistic world of introspective psychology or, worse, speculative philosophy and wander there forever in a haze of "Cognitions," "Affections," "Conations" and other elusive entities. Cultural acts, the construction, apprehension and utilization of symbolic forms, are social events like any other; they are as public as marriage and as observable as agriculture.

They are not, however, exactly the same thing; or, more precisely, the symbolic dimension of social events is, like the psychological, itself theoretically abstractable from those events as empirical totalities. There is still, to paraphrase a remark of Kenneth Burke's, a difference between building a house and drawing up a plan for building a house, and reading a poem about having children by marriage is not quite the same thing as having children by marriage. Even though the building of the house may proceed under the guidance of the plan or— a less likely occurrence—the having of children may be motivated by a reading of the poem, there is something to be said for not confusing our traffic with symbols with our traffic with objects or human beings, for these latter are not in themselves symbols, however often they may function as such. No matter how deeply interfused the cultural, the social and the psychological may be in the everyday life of houses, farms, poems and marriages, it is useful to distinguish them in analysis, and, so doing, to isolate the generic traits of each against the normalized backgrounds of the other two.

So far as culture patterns, i.e., systems or complexes of symbols, are concerned, the generic trait which is of first importance for us here is that they are extrinsic sources of information. By "extrinsic," I mean only that—unlike genes, for example—they lie outside the boundaries of the individual organism as such in that intersubjective world of common understandings into which all human individuals are born, pursue their separate careers, and leave persisting behind them after they die. By "sources of information," I mean only that—like genes—they provide a blueprint or template in terms of which processes external to themselves can be given a definite form. As the order of bases in a strand of DNA forms a coded program, a set of instructions or a recipe, for the synthesization of the structurally complex proteins which shape organic functioning, so culture patterns provide such programs for the institution of the social and psychological processes which shape public behavior. Though the sort of information and the mode of its transmission are vastly different in the two cases, this comparison of gene and symbol is more than a strained analogy of the familiar "social heredity" sort. It is actually a substantial relationship, for it is precisely the fact that genetically programmed processes are so highly generalized in men, as compared with lower animals, that culturally programmed ones are so important, only because human behavior is so loosely determined by intrinsic sources of information that extrinsic sources are so vital. To build a dam a beaver needs only an appropriate site and the proper materials—his mode of procedure is shaped by his physiology. But man, whose genes are silent on the building trades, needs also a conception of what it is to build a dam, a conception he can get only from some symbolic source—a blueprint, a textbook or a string of speech by someone who already knows how dams are built, or, of course, from manipulating graphic or linguistic elements in such a way as to attain for himself a conception of what dams are and how they are built.

This point is sometimes put in the form of an argument that cultural patterns are "models," that they are sets of symbols whose relations to one another "model" relations among entities, processes or what-have-you in physical, organic, social or psychological systems by "paralleling," "imitating" or "simulating" them. The term "model" has, however, two senses—an "of" sense and a "for" sense—and though these are but aspects of the same basic concept they are very much worth distinguishing for analytic purposes. In the first, what is stressed is the manipulation of symbol structures so as to bring them, more or less closely, into parallel with the preestablished non-symbolic system, as when we grasp how dams work by developing a theory of hydraulics or constructing a flow chart. The theory or chart models physical relationships in such a way—i.e., by expressing their structure in synoptic form—as to render them apprehensible: it is a model *of* "reality." In the second, what is stressed is the manipulation of the non-symbolic systems in terms of the relationships expressed in the symbolic, as when we construct a dam according to the specifications implied in an hydraulic theory or the conclusions drawn from a flow chart. Here, the theory is a model under whose guidance physical relationships are organized: it is a model *for* "reality." For psychological and social systems, and for cultural models that we would not ordinarily refer to as "theories," but rather as "doctrines," "melodies" or "rites," the case is in no way different. Unlike genes, and other non-symbolic information sources, which are only models *for*, not models *of*, culture patterns have an intrinsic double aspect: they give meaning, i.e., objective conceptual form, to social and psychological reality both by shaping themselves to it and by shaping it to themselves.

It is, in fact, this double aspect which sets true symbols off from other sorts of significative forms. Models *for* are found, as the gene example suggests, through the whole order of nature, for wherever there is a communication of pattern such programs are, in simple logic, required. Among animals, imprint learning is perhaps the most striking example, because what such learning involves is the automatic presentation of an appropriate sequence of behavior by a model animal in the presence of a learning animal which serves, equally automatically, to call out and stabilize a certain set of responses genetically built into the learning animal. The communicative dance of two bees, one of which has found nectar and the other of which seeks it, is another, somewhat different more complexly coded, example. Craik has even suggested that the thin trickle of water which first finds its way down from a mountain spring to the sea and smoothes a little channel for the greater volume of water which follows after it plays a sort of model *for* function. But models *of*—linguistic, graphic, mechanical, natural, etc., processes which function not to provide sources of information in terms of which other processes can be patterned, but to represent those patterned processes as such, to express their structure in an alternative medium—are much rarer and may perhaps be confined, among living animals, to man. The perception of the structural congruence between one set of processes, activities, relations, entities, etc., and another set for which it acts as a program, so that the program can be taken as a representation, or conception—a symbol—of the programmed, is the essence of human thought. The inter-transposability of models *for* and models *of*, of which symbolic formulation makes possible, is the distinctive characteristic of our mentality.

2. ... TO ESTABLISH POWERFUL, PERVASIVE AND LONG-LASTING MOODS AND MOTIVATIONS IN MEN BY ...

So far as religious symbols and symbol systems are concerned this inter-transposability is clear. The endurance, courage, independence, perseverance and passionate willfulness in which the vision quest practices the Plains Indian are the same flamboyant virtues by which he attempts to live: while achieving a sense of revelation he stabilizes a sense of direction. The consciousness of defaulted obligation, secreted guilt and, when a confession is obtained, public shame in which [a] Manus' seance rehearses him are the same sentiments that underlie the sort of duty ethic by which his property-conscious society is maintained: the gaining of an absolution involves the forging of a conscience. And the same self-discipline which rewards a Javanese mystic staring fixedly into the flame of a lamp with what he takes to be an intimation of divinity drills him in that rigorous control of emotional expression which is necessary to a man who would follow a quietistic style of life. Whether one sees the conception of a per-

sonal guardian spirit, a family tutelary or an immanent God as synoptic formulations of the character of reality or as templates for producing reality with such a character seems largely arbitrary, a matter of which aspect, the model *of* or model *for*, one wants for the moment to bring into focus. The concrete symbols involved—one or another mythological figure materializing in the wilderness, the skull of the deceased household head hanging censoriously in the rafters, or a disembodied "voice in the stillness" soundlessly chanting enigmatic classical poetry—point in either direction. They both express the world's climate and shape it.

They shape it by inducing in the worshipper a certain distinctive set of dispositions which lend a chronic character to the flow of his activity and the quality of his experience. A disposition describes not an activity or an occurrence but a probability of an activity being performed or an occurrence occurring under certain circumstances: "When a cow is said to be a ruminant, or a man is said to be a cigarette smoker, it is not being said that the cow is ruminating now or that the man is smoking a cigarette now. To be a ruminant is to tend to ruminate from time to time, and to be a cigarette-smoker is to be in the habit of smoking cigarettes." Similarly, to be pious is not to be performing something we would call an act of piety, but to be liable to perform such acts. So, too, with the Plains Indian's bravura, the Manus' compunctiousness or the Javanese's quietism which, in their contexts, form the substance of piety. The virtue of this sort of view of what are usually called "mental traits" or, if the Cartesianism is unavowed, "psychological forces" (both unobjectionable enough terms in themselves) is that it gets them out of any dim and inaccessible realm of private sensation into that same well-lit world of observables in which reside the brittleness of glass, the inflammability of paper and, to return to the metaphor, the dampness of England.

So far as religious activities are concerned (and learning a myth by heart is as much a religious activity as detaching one's finger at the knuckle), two somewhat different sorts of dispositions are induced by them: moods and motivations.

The major difference between moods and motivations is that where the latter are, so to speak, vectorial qualities, the former are merely scalar. Motives have a directional cast, they describe a certain overall course, gravitate toward certain, usually temporary, consummations. But moods vary only as to intensity: they go nowhere. They spring from certain circumstances but they are responsive to no ends. Like fogs, they just settle and lift; like scents, suffuse and evaporate. When present they are totalistic: if one is sad everything and everybody seems dreary; if one is gay, everything and everybody seems splendid. Thus, though a man can be vain, brave, willful and independent at the same time, he can't very well be playful and listless, or exultant and melancholy at the same time. Further, where motives persist for more or less extended periods of time, moods merely recur with greater or lesser frequency, coming and going for what are often quite unfathomable reasons. But perhaps the most important difference, so far as we are concerned, between moods and motivations is that motivations are "made meaningful" with reference to the ends toward which they are conceived to conduce, while moods are "made meaningful" with reference to the conditions from which they are conceived to spring. We interpret motives in terms of their consummations, but we interpret moods in terms of their sources. We say that a person is industrious because he wishes to succeed, we say that a person is worried because he is conscious of the hanging threat of nuclear holocaust. And this is no less the case when the interpretations invoked are ultimate. Charity becomes Christian charity when it is enclosed in a conception of God's purposes; optimism is Christian optimism when it is grounded in a particular conception of God's nature. The assiduity of the Navaho finds its rationale in a belief that, as "reality" operates mechanically, it is coercible; their chronic fearfulness finds its rationale in a conviction that, however "reality" operates, it is both enormously powerful and terribly dangerous.

3. ... BY FORMULATING CONCEPTIONS OF A GENERAL ORDER OF EXISTENCE AND ...

That the symbols or symbol systems which induce and define dispositions we set off as religious and those which place those dispositions in a cosmic framework are the same symbols ought to occasion no surprise. For what else do we mean by saying that a particular mood of awe is religious and not secular except that it springs from entertaining a conception of all-pervading vitality like mana and not from a visit to the Grand Canyon? Or that a particular case of asceticism is an example of a religious motivation except that it is directed toward the achievement of an unconditioned end like nirvana and not a conditioned one like weight-reduction? If sacred symbols did not, at one and the same time, induce dispositions in human beings and formulate, however obliquely, inarticulately or unsystematically, general ideas of order, then the empirical differentia of religious activity or religious experience would not exist. A man can indeed be said to be "religious" about golf, but not merely if he pursues it with passion and plays it on Sundays: he must also see it as symbolic of some transcendent truths. And the pubescent boy gazing soulfully into the eyes of the pubescent girl in a William Steig cartoon and murmuring, "there is something about you, Ethel, which gives me a sort of religious feeling," is, like most adolescents, confused. What any particular religion affirms about the fundamental nature of reality may be obscure, shallow or, all too often, perverse, but it must, if it is not to consist of the mere collection of received practices and conventional sentiments we usually refer to as moralism, affirm something. If one were to essay a minimal definition of religion today it would perhaps not be Tylor's famous "belief in spiritual beings," to which Goody, wearied of theoretical subtleties, has lately urged us to return, but rather what Salvador de Madariaga has called "the relatively modest dogma that God is not mad."

Usually, of course, religions affirm very much more than this: we believe, as James remarked, all that we can and would believe everything if we only could. The thing we seem least able to tolerate is a threat to our powers of conception, a suggestion that our ability to create, grasp and use symbols may fail us, for were this to happen we would be more helpless, as I have already pointed out, than the beavers. The extreme generality, diffuseness and variability of man's innate (i.e., genetically programmed) response capacities means that without the assistance of cultural patterns he would be functionally incomplete, not merely a talented ape who had, like some under-privileged child, unfortunately been prevented from realizing his full potentialities, but a kind of formless monster with neither sense of direction nor power of self-control, a chaos of spasmodic impulses and vague emotions. Man depends upon symbols and symbol systems with a dependence so great as to be decisive for his creatural viability and, as a result, his sensitivity to even the remotest indication that they may prove unable to cope with one or another aspect of experience raises within him the gravest sort of anxiety.

There are at least three points where chaos—a tumult of events which lack not just interpretations but *interpretability*—threatens to break in upon man: at the limits of his analytic capacities, at the limits of his powers of endurance, and at the limits of his moral insight. Bafflement, suffering and a sense of intractable ethical paradox are all, if they become intense enough or are sustained long enough, radical challenges to the proposition that life is comprehensible and that we can, by taking thought, orient ourselves effectively within it—challenges with which any religion, however "primitive," which hopes to persist must attempt somehow to cope.

Of the three issues, it is the first which has been least investigated by modern social anthropologists (though Evans-Pritchard's classic discussion of why granaries fall on some Azande and not on others, is a notable exception). Even to consider people's religious beliefs as attempts to bring anomalous events or experiences—death, dreams, mental fugues, volcanic eruptions or marital infidelity—within the circle of the at least potentially inexplicable seems to smack of Tyloreanism or worse. But is does appear to be a fact that at least some men—in all probability, most men—are unable to leave unclarified problems of analysis merely unclarified, just to look at the stranger features of the world's landscape in dumb astonishment or bland apathy without trying to develop, however fantastic, inconsistent or simple-minded, some notions as to how such features might be reconciled with the more ordinary deliverances of experience. Any chronic failure of one's explanatory apparatus, the complex of received culture patterns (common sense, science, philosophical speculation, myth) one has for mapping the empirical world, to explain things which cry out for explanation, tends to lead to a deep disquiet—a tendency rather more widespread and a disquiet rather deeper than we have sometimes supposed since the pseudoscience view of religious belief was, quite rightfully, deposed. After all, even that high priest of heroic atheism, Lord Russell, once remarked that although the problem of the existence of God has never bothered him, the ambiguity of certain mathematical axioms had threatened to unhinge his mind. And Einstein's profound dissatisfaction with quantum mechanics was based on a—surely religious—inability to believe that, as he put it, God plays dice with the universe.

But this quest for lucidity and the rush of metaphysical anxiety that occurs when empirical phenomena threaten to remain intransigently opaque is found on much humbler intellectual levels. Certainly, I was struck in my own work, much more than I had at all expected to be by the degree to which my more animistically inclined informants behaved like true Tyloreans. They seemed to be constantly using their beliefs to "explain" phenomena: or, more accurately, to convince themselves that the phenomena were explainable within the accepted scheme of things, for they commonly had only a minimal attachment to the particular soul possession, emotional disequilibrium, taboo infringement or bewitchment hypothesis they advanced and were all too ready to abandon it for some other, in the same genre, which struck them as more plausible given the facts of the case. What they were *not* ready to do was abandon it for no other hypothesis at all; to leave events to themselves.

The second experiential challenge in whose face the meaningfulness of a particular pattern of life threatens to dissolve into a chaos of thingless names and nameless things—the problem of suffering—has been rather more investigated, or at least described, mainly because of the great amount of attention given in works on tribal religion to what are perhaps its two main loci: illness and mourning. Yet for all the fascinated interest in the emotional aura which surrounds these extreme situations, there has been, with a few exceptions such as Lienhardt's recent discussion of Dinka divining, little conceptual advance over the sort of crude confidence type theory set forth by Malinowski: viz., that religion helps one to endure "situations of emotional stress" by "open [ing] up escapes from such situations and such impasses as offer no empirical way out except by ritual and belief into the domain of the supernatural." The inadequacy of this "theology of optimism," as Nadel rather drily called it, is, of course, radical. Over its career religion has probably disturbed men as much as it has cheered them; forced them into a head-on, unblinking confrontation of the fact that they are born to trouble as often as it has enabled them to avoid such a confrontation by projecting them into a sort of infantile fairy-tale world where—Malinowski again—"hope cannot fail nor desire deceive." With the possible exception of Christian Science, there are few if any religious traditions, "great" or "little," in which the proposition that life hurts is not strenuously affirmed and in some it is virtually glorified.

As a religious problem, the problem of suffering is, paradoxically, not how to avoid suffering but how to suffer, how to make of physical pain, personal loss, wordly defeat or the helpless contemplation of others' agony something bearable, supportable—something, as we say, sufferable.

The problem of suffering passes easily into the problem of evil, for if suffering is severe enough it usually, though not always, seems morally undeserved as well, at least to the sufferer. But they are not, however, exactly the same thing—a fact I think Weber, too influenced by the biases of a monotheistic tradition in which, as the various aspects of human experience must be conceived to proceed from a single, voluntaristic source, man's pain reflects directly on God's goodness, did not fully recognize in his generalization of the dilemmas of Christian theodicy Eastward. For where the problem of suffering is concerned with threats to our ability to put our "undisciplined squads of emotion" into some sort of soldierly order, the problem of evil is concerned with threats to our ability to make sound moral judgments. What is involved in the problem of evil is not the adequacy of our symbolic resources to govern our affective life, but the adequacy of those resources to provide a workable set of ethical criteria, normative guides to govern our action. The vexation here is the gap between things as they are and as they ought to be if our conceptions of right and wrong make sense, the gap between what we deem various individuals deserve and what we see that they get—a phenomenon summed up in that profound quatrain:

The rain falls on the just
And on the unjust fella;
But mainly upon the just,
Because the unjust has the just's umbrella.

Or if this seems too flippant an expression of an issue that, in somewhat different form, animates the Book of Job and the Baghavad Gita, the following classical Javanese poem, known, sung, and repeatedly quoted in Java by virtually everyone over the age of six, puts the point—the discrepancy between moral prescriptions and material rewards, the seeming inconsistency of "is" and "ought"—rather more elegantly ·

We have lived to see a time without order
In which everyone is confused in his mind.
One cannot bear to join in the madness,
But if he does not do so
He will not share in the spoils,
And will starve as a result.
Yes, God; wrong is wrong:
Happy are those who forget,
Happier yet those who remember and have
*   deep insight.*

The problem of evil, or perhaps one should say the problem *about* evil, is in essence the same sort of problem of or about bafflement and the problem of or about suffering. The strange opacity of certain empirical events, the dumb senselessness of intense or inexorable pain, and the enigmatic unaccountability of gross iniquity all raise the uncomfortable suspicion that perhaps the world, and hence man's life in the world, has no genuine order at all—no empirical regularity, no emotional form, no moral coherence. And the religious response to this suspicion is in each case the same: the formulation, by means of symbols, of an image of such a genuine order of the world which will account for, and even celebrate, the perceived ambiguities, puzzles and paradoxes in human experience. The effort is not to deny the undeniable—that there are unexplained events, that life hurts or that rain falls upon the just—but to deny that there are inexplicable events, that life is unendurable and that justice is a mirage. The principles which constitute the moral order may indeed often elude men in the same way as fully satisfactory explanations of anomalous events or effective forms for the expression of feeling often elude them. What is important, to a religious man at least, is that this elusiveness be accounted for, that it be not the result of the fact that there are no such principles, explanations or forms, that life is absurd and the attempt to make moral, intellectual or emotional sense out of experience is bootless.

The Problem of Meaning in each of its intergrading aspects (how these aspects in fact intergrade in each particular case, what sort of interplay there is between the sense of analytic, emotional and moral impotence, seems to me one of the outstanding, and except for Weber untouched, problems for comparative research in this whole field) is a matter of affirming, or at least recognizing, the inescapability of ignorance, pain and injustice on the human plane while simultaneously denying that these irrationalities are characteristic of the world as a whole. And it is in terms of religious symbolism, a symbolism relating man's sphere of existence to a wider sphere within which it is conceived to rest, that both the affirmation and the denial are made.

4. ... AND CLOTHING THOSE CONCEPTIONS WITH SUCH AN AURA OF FACTUALITY THAT ...

There arises here, however, a profounder question: how is it that this denial comes to be believed? how is it that the religious man moves from a troubled perception of experienced disorder to a more or less settled conviction of fundamental order? just what does "belief" mean in a religious context? Of all the problems surrounding attempts to conduct anthropological analysis of religion this is the one that has perhaps been most troublesome and therefore the most often avoided, usually by relegating it to psychology, that raffish outcast discipline to which social anthropologists are forever consigning phenomena they are unable to deal with within the framework of a denatured Durkheimianism. But the problem will not go away, it is not "merely" psychological (nothing social is), and no anthropological theory of religion which fails to attack it is worthy of the name. We have been trying to stage Hamlet without the Prince quite long enough.

It seems to me that it is best to begin any approach to this issue with frank recognition that religious belief involves not a Baconian induction from everyday experience—for then we should all be agnostics—but rather a prior acceptance of authority which transforms that experience. The existence of bafflement, pain and moral paradox—of The Problem of Meaning—is one of the things that drive men toward belief in gods, devils, spirits, totemic principles or the spiritual efficacy of cannibalism (an enfolding sense of beauty or a dazzling perception of power are others), but it is not the basis upon which those beliefs

rest, but rather their most important field of application.

In tribal religions authority lies in the persuasive power of traditional imagery; in mystical ones in the apodictic force of supersensible experience; in charismatic ones in the hypnotic attraction of an extraordinary personality. But the priority of the acceptance of an authoritative criterion in religious matters over the revelation which is conceived to flow from that acceptance is not less complete than in scriptural or hieratic ones. The basic axiom underlying what we may perhaps call "the religious perspective" is everywhere the same: he who would know must first believe.

But to speak of "the religious perspective" is, by implication, to speak of one perspective among others. A perspective is a mode of seeing, in that extended sense of "see" in which it means "discern," "apprehend," "understand" or "grasp." It is a particular way of looking at life, a particular manner of construing the world, as when we speak of an historical perspective, a scientific perspective, an aesthetic perspective, a common-sense perspective, or even the bizarre perspective embodied in dreams and in hallucinations. The question then comes down to, first, what is "the religious perspective" generically considered, as differentiated from other perspectives; and second, how do men come to adopt it.

If we place the religious perspective against the background of three of the other major perspectives in terms of which men construe the world—the common-sensical, the scientific and the aesthetic—its special character emerges more sharply. What distinguishes common-sense as a mode of "seeing" is, as Schutz (1962) has pointed out, a simple acceptance of the world, its objects and its processes as being just what they seem to be—what is sometimes called naive realism —and the pragmatic motive, the wish to act upon that world so as to bend it to one's practical purposes, to master it, or so far as that proves impossible, to adjust to it. The world of everyday life, itself, of course, a cultural product, for it is framed in terms of the symbolic conceptions of "stubborn fact" handed down from generation to generation, is the established scene and given object of our actions. Like Mt. Everest it is just there and the thing to do with it, if one feels the need to do anything with it at all, is to climb it. In the scientific perspective it is precisely this givenness which disappears (Schutz, 1962). Deliberate doubt and systematic inquiry, the suspension of the pragmatic motive in favor of disinterested observation, the attempt to analyze the world in terms of formal concepts whose relationship to the informal conceptions of commonsense become increasingly problematic—there are the hallmarks of the attempt to grasp the world scientifically. And as for the aesthetic perspective, which under the rubric of "the aesthetic attitude" has been perhaps most exquisitely examined, it involves a different sort of suspension of naive realism and practical interest, in that instead of questioning the credentials of everyday experience that experience is merely ignored in favor of an eager dwelling upon appearances, an engrossment in surfaces, an absorption in things, as we say, "in themselves": "The function of artistic illusion is not 'make-believe' ... but the very opposite, disengagement from belief—the contemplation of sensory qualities without their usual meanings of 'here's that chair,' 'That's my telephone' ... etc. The knowledge that what is before us has no practical significance in the world is what enables us to give attention to its appearance as such" (Langer, 1953, p. 49). And like the common-sensical and the scientific (or the historical, the philosophical and the autistic), this perspective, this "way of seeing" is not the product of some mysterious Cartesian chemistry, but is induced, mediated, and in fact created by means of symbols. It is the artist's skill which can produce those curious quasi-objects—poems, dramas, sculptures, symphonies—which, dissociating themselves from the solid world of common-sense, take on the special sort of eloquence only sheer appearances can achieve.

The religious perspective differs from the common-sensical in that, as already pointed out, it moves beyond the realities of everyday life to wider ones which correct and complete them, and its defining concern is not action upon those wider realities but acceptance of them, faith in them. It differs from the scientific perspective in that it questions the realities of everyday life not out of an institutionalized scepticism which dissolves the world's givenness into a swirl of probabilistic hypotheses, but in terms of what it takes to be wider, non-hypothetical truths. Rather than detachment, its watchword is commitment; rather than analysis, encoun-

ter. And it differs from art in that instead of effecting a disengagement from the whole question of factuality, deliberately manufacturing an air of semblance and illusion, it deepens the concern with fact and seeks to create an aura of utter actuality. It is this sense of the "really real" upon which the religious perspective rests and which the symbolic activities of religion as a cultural system are devoted to producing, intensifying, and, so far as possible, rendering inviolable by the discordant revelations of secular experience. It is, again, the imbuing of a certain specific complex of symbols—of the metaphysic they formulate and the style of life they recommend—with a persuasive authority which, from an analytic point of view is the essence of religious action.

Which brings us, at length, to ritual. For it is in ritual—i.e., consecrated behavior—that this conviction that religious conceptions are veridical and that religious directives are sound is somehow generated. It is in some sort of ceremonial form—even if that form be hardly more than the recitation of a myth, the consultation of an oracle, or the decoration of a grave—that the moods and motivations which sacred symbols induce in men and the general conceptions of the order of existence which they formulate for men meet and reinforce one another. In a ritual, the world as lived and the world as imagined, fused under the agency of a single set of symbolic forms, turn out to be the same world, producing thus that idiosyncratic transformation in one's sense of reality to which Santayana refers in my epigraph. Whatever role divine intervention may or may not play in the creation of faith—and it is not the business of the scientist to pronounce upon such matters one way or the other—it is, primarily at least, out of the context of concrete acts of religious observance that religious conviction emerges on the human plane.

However, though any religious ritual, no matter how apparently automatic or conventional (if it is truly automatic or merely conventional it is not religious), involves this symbolic fusion of ethos and worldview, it is mainly certain more elaborate and usually more public ones, ones in which a broad range of moods and motivations on the one hand and of metaphysical conceptions on the other are caught up, which shape the spiritual consciousness of a people. Employing a useful term introduced by

Singer (1955) we may call these full-blown ceremonies "cultural performances" and note that they represent not only the point at which the dispositional and conceptual aspects of religious life converge for the believer, but also the point at which the interaction between them can be most readily examined by the detached observer.

Of course, all cultural performances are not religious performances, and the line between those that are, and artistic, or even political ones is often not so easy to draw in practice, for, like social forms, symbolic forms can serve multiple purposes. But the point is that, paraphrasing slightly, Indians —"and perhaps all peoples"—seem to think of their religion "as encapsulated in these discrete performances which they [can] exhibit to visitors and to themselves" (Singer, 1955). The mode of exhibition is however radically different for the two sorts of witnesses, a fact seemingly overlooked by those who would argue that "religion is a form of human art." Where for "visitors" religious performances can, in the nature of the case, only be presentations of a particular religious perspective, and thus aesthetically appreciated or scientifically dissected, for participants they are in addition enactments, materializations, realizations of it—not only models *of* what they believe, but also models *for* the believing of it. In these plastic dramas men attain their faith as they portray it.

5. ... THAT THE MOODS AND MOTIVATIONS SEEM UNIQUELY REALISTIC.

But no one, not even a saint, lives in the world religious symbols formulate all of the time, and the majority of men live in it only at moments. The everyday world of common-sense objects and practical acts is, as Schutz says, the paramount reality in human experience—paramount in the sense that it is the world in which we are most solidly rooted, whose inherent actuality we can hardly question (however much we may question certain portions of it), and from whose pressures and requirements we can least escape. A man, even large groups of men, may be aesthetically insensitive, religiously unconcerned and unequipped to pursue formal scientific analysis, but he cannot be completely lacking in common-sense and survive. The dispositions which religious rituals induce thus have their most important impact—from a human point of view—

outside the boundaries of the ritual itself as they reflect back to color the individual's conception of the established world of bare fact. The peculiar tone that marks the Plains vision quest, the Manus confession or the Javanese mystical exercise pervades areas of the life of these peoples far beyond the immediately religious, impressing upon them a distinctive style in the sense both of a dominant mood and a characteristic movement. Religion is sociologically interesting not because, as vulgar positivism would have it, it described the social order (which, insofar as it does, it does not only very obliquely but very imcompletely), but because, like environment, political power, wealth, jural obligation, personal affection, and a sense of beauty, it shapes it.

The movement back and forth between the religious perspective and the common-sense perspective is actually one of the more obvious empirical occurrences on the social scene, though, again, one of the most neglected by social anthropologists, virtually all of whom have seen it happen countless times. Religious belief has usually been presented as an homogeneous characteristic of an individual, like his place of residence, his occupational role, his kinship position, and so on. But religious belief in the midst of ritual, where it engulfs the total person, transporting him, so far as he is concerned, into another mode of existence, and religious belief as the pale, remembered reflection of that experience in the midst of everyday life are not precisely the same thing, and the failure to realize this has led to some confusion, most especially in connection with the so-called "primitive mentality" problem. Much of the difficulty between Lévy-Bruhl and Malinowski on the nature of "native thought," for example, arises from a lack of full recognition of this distinction; for where the French philosopher was concerned with the view of reality savages adopted when taking a specifically religious perspective, the Polish-English ethnographer was concerned with that which they adopted when taking a strictly common-sense one. Both perhaps vaguely sensed that they were not talking about exactly the same thing, but where they went astray was in failing to give a specific accounting of the way in which these two forms of "thought"—or as I would rather say, these two modes of symbolic formulation—interacted, so that where Lévy-Bruhl's savages tended to live, despite his postludial disclaimers, in a world composed entirely of mystical encounters, Malinowski's tended to live, despite his stress on the functional importance of a religion, in a world composed entirely of practical actions. They became reductionists (an idealist is as much of a reductionist as a materialist) in spite of themselves because they failed to see man as moving more or less easily, and very frequently, between radically contrasting ways of looking at the world, ways which are not continuous with one another but separated by cultural gaps across which Kierkegaardian leaps must be made in both directions.

For an anthropologist, the importance of religion lies in its capacity to serve, for an individual or for a group, as a source of general, yet distinctive conceptions of the world, the self and the relations between them on the one hand—its model *of* aspect— and of rooted, no less distinctive "mental" dispositions—its model *for* aspect—on the other. From these cultural functions flow, in turn, its social and psychological ones.

Religious concepts spread beyond their specifically metaphysical contexts to provide a framework of general ideas in terms of which a wide range of experience—intellectual, emotional, moral—can be given meaningful form. The Christian sees the Nazi movement against the background of The Fall which, though it does not, in a casual sense, explain it, places it in a moral, a cognitive, even an effective sense. A Zande sees the collapse of a granary upon a friend or relative against the background of a concrete and rather special notion of witchcraft and thus avoids the philosphical dilemmas as well as the psychological stress of indeterminism. A Javanese finds in the borrowed and reworked concept of *rasa* ("sense-taste-feeling-meaning") a means by which to "see" choreographic, gustatory, emotional and political phenomena in a new light. A synopsis of cosmic order, a set of religious beliefs is also a gloss upon the mundane world of social relationships and psychological events. It renders them graspable.

But more than gloss, such beliefs are also a template. They do not merely interpret social and psychological processes in cosmic terms—in which case they would be philosophical, not religious—but they shape them. In the doctrine of original sin is embedded also a recommended attitude toward life, a recurring mood and a persisting set of motivations. The Zande learns from witchcraft conceptions not just to understand apparent "accidents" as not accidents at all, but to react to these spurious accidents with hatred for the agent who caused them and to proceed against him with appropriate resolution. Rasa, in addition to being a concept of truth, beauty and goodness, is also a preferred mode of experiencing, a kind of affectless detachment, a variety of bland aloofness, an unshakeable calm. The moods and motivations a religious orientation produces cast a derivative, lunar light over the solid features of a people's secular life.

The tracing of the social and psychological role of religion is thus not so much a matter of finding correlations between specific ritual acts and specific secular social ties—though these correlations do, of course, exist and are very worth continued investigation, especially if we can contrive something novel to say about them. More, it is a matter of understanding how it is that men's notions, however implicit, of the "really real" and the dispositions these notions induce in them, color their sense of the reasonable, the practical, the humane and the moral. How far it does so (for in many societies religion's effects seem quite circumscribed, in others completely pervasive); how deeply it does so (for some men, and groups of men, seem to wear their religion lightly so far as the secular world goes, while others seem to apply their faith to each occasion, no matter how trivial); and how effectively it does so (for the width of the gap between what religion recommends and what people actually do is most variable cross-culturally) —all these are crucial issues in the comparative sociology and psychology of religion. Even the degree to which religious systems themselves are developed seems to vary extremely widely, and not merely on a simple evolutionary basis. In one society, the level of elaboration of symbolic formulations of ultimate actuality may reach extraordinary degrees of complexity and systematic articulation; in another, no less developed socially, such formulations may remain primitive in the true sense, hardly more than congeries of fragmentary by-beliefs and isolated images, of sacred reflexes and spiritual pictographs. One need only think of the Australians and the Bushmen, the Toradja and the Alorese, the Hopi and the Apache, the Hindus and the Romans, or even the Italians and the Poles, to see that degree of religious articulateness is not a constant even as between societies of similar complexity.

The anthropological study of religion is therefore a two stage operation: first, an analysis of the system of meanings embodied in the symbols which make up the religion proper, and, second, the relating of these systems to social structural and psychological processes. My dissatisfaction with so much of contemporary social anthropological work in religion is not that it concerns itself with the second stage, but that it neglects the first, and in so doing takes for granted what most needs to be elucidated. To discuss the role of ancestor worship in regulating political succession, of sacrificial feasts in defining kinship obligations, of spirit worship in scheduling agricultural practices, of divination in reinforcing social control or of initiation rites in propelling personality maturation are in no sense unimportant endeavors, and I am not recommending they be abandoned for the kind of jejune cabalism into which symbolic analysis of exotic faiths can so easily fall. But to attempt them with but the most general, common-sense view of what ancestor worship, animal sacrifice, spirit worship, divination or initiation rites are as religious patterns seems to me not particularly promising. Only when we have a theoretical analysis of symbolic action comparable in sophistication to that we now have for social and psychological action, will we be able to cope effectively with those aspects of social and psychological life in which religion (or art, or science, or ideology) plays a determinant role.

4
SYMBOLIC CLASSIFICATION

Introduction

Anthropologists engaged in field work in exotic cultures are continually confronted with phenomena labeled "different" which they see as the "same"; and, correspondingly, they are confused by attributions of sameness to things they want to call different: "cows" are called "people" and "men" are called "birds." Frequently, they discover that "uncles" are called "fathers" and "cousins" are called "wives."

Such observations could be multiplied almost endlessly and matched only by the variety of theories put forth by social thinkers to account for the vagaries of the human mind. But exotic notions lose their strangeness when it becomes clear that somewhere to some people they make sense. Just as a language becomes intelligible when we learn its grammar, a culture appears reasonable when we discover its codes. One task of the anthropologist is to discover the logic or "grammar" of a system of beliefs, to account for what is ordered, intelligible, and acceptable within a native code.

The investigation of native categories and their relationships derives from a theoretical position formulated by Durkheim and Mauss in their classic book, *Primitive Classification* (1963), and from the anthropological linguists Edward Sapir (1931), Benjamin Whorf (Carroll, 1956), and others. Durkheim and Mauss perceived the origins of classificatory or logical thought in the totemic equivalence of social groups with natural species of animals and plants; they discovered in the prescriptive marriage systems of the Australian aborigines striking homologies between social structure and beliefs and concluded that man's notion of order in the universe is modeled on social order among men. Sapir and Whorf looked to vocabulary and grammar for models for cultural and social styles. While their formulations proved not to be adequate, they became the focus for important later work. Rather than asking if aborigines believed in God, the followers of Sapir and Whorf set out to examine native concepts in their own terms. They directed attention toward the discovery and description of native order and definitions. What, they asked in a given culture, were the objects, associations, and distinctions properly attached to a set of symbols or names; what assumptions did an observer have to make to translate or represent them accurately in his own speech? While it may seem obvious that anthropological description should be true to what the "native himself believes," the difficulty of breaking through the observer's own linguistic categories and expectations will always be great. Some of the best monographs in primitive religion have been devoted largely to a detailed exposition of one or two key symbols in native thought; Evans-Pritchard's classic, *Nuer Religion* (1956), is largely an exploration of Nuer notions of Spirit, *Kwoth*; and, with different approaches, the "structural" descriptions by

Dumont, Frake, and Vogt in this chapter attempt to define native categories by describing the linguistic and social contexts to which they relate.

These studies share the conviction that symbols do not exist in isolation, as names or labels merely. Symbols represent native categories; they include some things and not others, and there are rules which govern their proper understanding and use. Lest their associations appear arbitrary, the anthropologist is forced to consider them in relation to one another. Only in considering *systems* of classification, the relations between categories, can he begin to understand systems strange to his own. Nothing in the anthropologist's experience might, for instance, lead him to associate "left" and "female," but when he learns that in a certain African society the opposition of right and left is readily associated with the series male/female, white/red, bone/blood, and so on, the association seems to make sense. It appears, not that "left" is *like* "female," but that right and left, and male and female, are equally different pairs. As Hertz (1960) and recent scholars like Needham and Beidelman have suggested, right/left seems to be a paradigm of a certain form of relation; the principle of *opposition* orders the set.

Similarly, the French structuralist, Lévi-Strauss (1962) stresses the power of binary oppositions in ordering cultural symbols. He points out that there are two ways of relating unlike domains. The first, homology, often corresponds to folk theory: men of the bear clan are said to be bearlike, a white plant cures eyes that are pink. But, he warns, accounts like these do not explain. As an alternative, he proposes a model of oppositions similar to that described above: as the bear is *unlike* the raven, so bear clan and raven clan are unrelated men. This position, that the categories of our perceptions are not —as "folk" theorists have it—absolute, but the product of a series of binary distinctions, derives from "distinctive feature" phonological theory developed by Jakobson (1956) and other linguists. By this theory, all meaning is relational: no single sound is really "p," but we distinguish "p" from "b" by the presence or absence of a feature called "voice." With Lévi-Strauss and other structuralists, cultural categories, by analogy, are treated as the products of binary relations. Dumont, for example, points out that castes in India exist only in opposition to other castes, in his article in this chapter. But while distinctive feature theory yields elegant accounts of phonemes it remains, for anthropologists, more a metaphor than a technique. Few anthropologists would question Lévi-Strauss's insight, but few have dared ask if it is more than just that. Leach, in his article on "animal avoidance," a critical application of structuralist method, points out that Lévi-Strauss's binary model is overhasty in abolishing analogic and qualitative modes of thought.

Lévi-Strauss stresses binary classification as a mechanical function of nature and of the human mind. Other studies have indicated equally simple classificatory principles at the basis of a symbolic system. Both Vogt and Rosaldo argue in this volume that a simple model for formal relations orders extremely complex ritual interaction. Douglas provides the necessary link. Binary distinctions are only one aspect of man's need for order, his abhorrence for what is dirty, anomalous, or out of place. When rules are violated, when the system itself is unclear, Douglas suggests, we fear "pollution"; when rules, distinctions, are stressed, we feel holy and clean.

Douglas's treatment of classification turns Durkheim on his head. In her view, the need for logic comes first, and because of it man manages to keep his society neat. Only a need for order could explain the American's horror at men who wear skirts, or man's universal fear of incest. In a similar vein, Needham, in his introduction to Durkheim and Mauss (1963), points out that men often employ inverted and incestuous symbolism to represent the world at Creation and after Death: if order is human, chaos characterizes the margins of human life. The insights of Douglas, and with her, Leach, and many others have opened an exciting direction of inquiry which relates formal semantic description to structural insight and places a new and highly concrete demand on the anthropologist's ability to look inward to discover a "grammar" with universal sense.

Claude Lévi-Strauss

THE BEAR
AND THE BARBER

While Lévi-Strauss ostensibly addresses himself in this article to similarities between totemic groups and castes, he is really using them to express a methodological approach wherein he tries to reduce the variables of society to certain basic means for the solution of human problems. As in his provocative book on kinship and marriage, *The Elementary Structures of Kinship* (1969), which has exerted a profound influence on current social anthropology, his goal is to demonstrate that symmetry and exchange pervade human relations. He feels in the present instance that he has found a common language to express the structural relationship between totemic groups and castes, these two systems being ways that societies have evolved for allowing their members to express affiliation with the group into which they were born. But if exchange is to be possible between groups, social diversification must be established. In societies where there is no division of labor or specialization, as among the Australians, the only possible objective model that can be used by groups to define themselves is a natural rather than cultural one, namely, the diversity of natural species. This makes it possible for exogamous groups to exchange women between themselves even though women are biologically similar. In complex societies, nature is not taken as the model for diversification; instead, cultural products and services are used, these being true social species. But women cannot be exchanged outside their castes because they are not acknowledged to be similar from one occupational group to another. Australian totemic groups and Indian castes both specialize in "controlling" something necessary to the well-being of the whole group. Both are "exopractical" in that one produces women for marriage and the other produces goods and services. Both are "endopractical" in that each is kept closely self-contained—the Australian tribes through their preferred type of matrimonial exchange, the Indian castes by virtue of their rule of endogamy.

These ideas are admittedly involved and controversial, with insufficient testing on a wide scale, but at the same time they open the way to new insights regarding the nature of symbolic classification.

Reprinted from the *Journal of the Royal Anthropological Institute*, XCIII (1963), 1–11, by permission of the author and the Royal Anthropological Institute of Great Britain and Ireland.

Human societies have evolved a number of means for allowing their members to express affiliation with the group into which they were born. Among these we shall single out two strongly contrasted ones. In one case, a given individual will make such a statement as "I am a bear," in the other case he will make such a statement as "I am a barber." One case exemplifies the so-called "totemic" groups, the other the caste system. My purpose is to examine the nature of the structural relationship—if there be one—between the two.

The words "bear" and "barber" were not chosen at random. Barbers cut and shave other people's hair, while—at least among the Chippewa Indians—people born in the Bear clan were reputed to have long, thick hair and never to grow bald. This doubly inverted relation—presence or absence of a given trait on the one hand, in respect to self or other on the other hand—plus perhaps an opposition between nature and culture (since the kind of hair one grows is a natural trait, while to remove it is a cultural custom), this threefold relation then is endowed, as I shall try to show, with an inner meaning since it symbolizes so to speak the structure of the scheme I am about to develop.

As a preliminary, I should like to caution the reader with regard to my use of the word "totemism."

Although I shall use it freely in the course of my talk, I fully endorse the general trend that has prevailed for a good many years among anthropologists to consider that there is no real institution which corresponds to the term "totemism" and that totemistic theories proceed from an arbitrary carving out of the objective facts. Nevertheless, it would be too easy simply to discard all past and present speculations concerning what is generally referred to as "totemism." If so many scholars whom we all admire have been, as it were, fascinated by the idea of "totemism," it is probably because, at a deeper level than the one they have been mistakenly considering, phenomena arbitrarily put together to make up a pseudo-institution are endowed with some inner meaning which makes them worthy of interest. This I believe was first discovered by Radcliffe-Brown, whose position in respect to "totemism" started by being a purely negative one in his early paper, "The Sociological Theory of Totemism" (1929), but who twenty-two years later in his Huxley Memorial Lecture entitled "The Comparative Method in Social Anthropology," without reverting in the least to a conception of "totemism" as an actual institution, succeeded nevertheless in unravelling the importance of the use of animal and plant names to characterize the relationship between the segments of human society. But this process led Radcliffe-Brown to modify considerably his earlier conception of this relationship.

In 1929, he believed that primitive people attached an intrinsic importance to animals for the reason that, as food, they were supposed to arouse man's spontaneous interest; whereas, in 1951 it was his theory that both animals and plants were to be regarded as mere figures of speech—symbols as it were. Thus, while in 1929, Radcliffe-Brown believed that interest was conferred upon animals and plants because they were "eatable," in 1951 he saw clearly that the real reason for this interest lay in the fact that they are, if I may use the word, "thinkable." It is interesting to note that each one of these two successive theories is in one way more abstract and in another way more concrete than the other. The first theory is more abstract since all animals which can be consumed are merged into a vague category characterized by the one single aspect that has been abstracted: that of constituting merely animal food. From this point of view, animals that can be eaten are all regarded as similar, while men who partake of this common food are also held to be similar. Thus the link between the distinction of biological species and the segments of society is not perceived, though this first theory is also more concrete, since it only envisages the point of view of practical utility and physio-logical need. In its turn the second theory is more abstract, since it relies far less on the animals themselves than on the discovery that these animals or plants, or rather their properties, can be put to use as symbols to express contrasts and oppositions. Nevertheless, it is more concrete, because we are now asked in each special case to look for a definite reason which can account for the selection of a given animal and not of any other. So the choice made by one culture among the whole gamut of animals and plants which are empirically present becomes a means to express differences between men.

If Radcliffe-Brown's second theory is valid, as I believe it to be, we must admit that behind what was erroneously called "totemism" lie three very precise ideas. First, the idea of a culturally discrete set, that is, a segmentary society; second, the idea of a naturally discrete set, that is, the awareness of the empirical discontinuity of the biological species and third, the idea that there is some kind of homology between the above two systems of differences. Therefore totemic ideas appear to provide a code enabling man to express isomorphic properties between nature and culture. Obviously, there exists here some kind of similarity with linguistics, since language is also a code which, through oppositions between differences, permits us to convey meanings and since in the case of language as well as in that of "totemism," the complete series of empirical media provided in one case by vocal articulation, and in the other by the entire wealth of the biological world, cannot be called upon, but rather (and this is true in both cases) only a few elements which each language or each culture selects in order that they can be organized in strongly and unequivocally contrasting pairs. Such being the answer, we may be in a position to solve the problem raised by Boas in his paper "Mythology and Folk-tales of the North American Indians," where he says, "the essential problem regarding the ultimate origin of mythologies remains—why human tales are preferably attached to animals, celestial bodies and other personified phenomena of nature." The answer lies, so it seems, not, as the functionalist school assumes, in the utilitarian properties of biological species as mankind conceives them, but rather in their logical properties, that is, their ability to serve as symbols expressing contrasts and oppositions. This was demonstrated for a limited area by Dr. Freeman in his recent paper "Iban Augury," in which he shows how the Ibans by selecting a few species of birds out of a very large set provided by their forest environment, and by selecting for each species a very small number of significant properties, have been able to use these differential elements by opposing them and also combining them so as to convey different messages.

Having cleared up these general problems, I shall now enter into my subject proper. When going over the work of early investigators in Australia, I was struck by the fact that approximately between 1830 and 1850, these authors, although they knew that Australian sections and sub-sections were probably connected with the laws of intermarriage, nevertheless believed them to differ in rank; and to describe them, they frequently used the word "caste." This, I think, should not be neglected. In the first place, because there may have been something more "caste-like" in these divisions than what was subsequently found among interior, mostly desert, people and because it seems obvious that even from a superficial point of view there is something similar between Australian tribes and caste societies; each segment performs a special task which benefits the community as a whole and which is complementary to functions that devolve upon other segments. This appears clearly among the Australian tribes described by Spencer & Gillen in which moieties or clans are bound together by a rule of reciprocity. The Kaitish and the Unmatjera, who are northern neighbours of the Aranda, know of rules that require an individual who gathers wild seeds in a territory belonging to a totemic group named after those seeds, to obtain permission from its head before consuming them; according to these rules, each totemic group is obliged to provide others with plants or animals whose "production" it allegedly controls. Thus the totemic food prohibition appears to be in such a case merely a negative way of expressing a positive obligation towards the others. This is clearly shown in a few well documented examples presented by Spencer & Gillen. The lone hunter belonging to the Emu clan cannot touch the bird, but in company he can and must kill it so as to present it as food to hunters belonging to other clans, and conversely the hunter belonging to the Water clan is permitted to drink alone, but when in company he can drink only if

the water is presented to him by members of the opposite moiety. Among the Warramunga too each totemic group is held responsible for the natural species consumed by other groups. The Warramunga and the Walpari have secondary prohibitions against consuming the maternal totem but these are lifted when food is obtained from the opposite moiety. Generally speaking, and for each totem, there is a threefold distinction between those groups who never consume it because it is their own totem, those that may consume it when obtained from the opposite moiety (in case it should be the maternal totem), and those that can consume it in all circumstances, because it is not their totem. The same is true for the sacred well which women may never approach, while uninitiated men, though they may approach them, may not drink from them, while still other groups of uninitiated men may both approach the wells and drink of the water, providing it is offered them by men belonging to the group that is allowed to drink freely.

Notwithstanding these similarities between totemic groups and castes, it is clear that the line which I have followed so far is too general to be convincing. It is well known that castes and totemic groups are widely different and opposed institutional systems, that one is linked with the highest cultures and the other with the lowest cultures with which anthropologists are acquainted. In a traditional way, totemism is linked to exogamy in its strictest forms, which in a game of free association, ninety-nine out of a hundred anthropologists would probably associate the word "caste" with the word "endogamy."

Thus the distinctive character of the extreme cases is clear, but would these appear as extreme if we could dispose of intermediary forms? In earlier writings I have tried to show that exchange in human society is a universal means of ensuring the interlocking of its constitutive parts and that this exchange can operate at different levels among which the more important are food, goods and services, and women. Two cases should be distinguished, however. Sometimes the three forms (or two of them) are called upon, so to speak, to cumulate their effects and to complement each other, either positively or negatively. In the second case, one form only is retained because it supplements the others. A good positive example of the first case is provided by those Australian groups where exchange of women and food prohibitions (which, as we have seen, can be equally well expressed as an obligatory exchange of foods), reinforce each other, and we find a negative example of the same phenomenon in some parts of Melanesia and in peasant Europe of the past, where endogamy or exogamy unwillingly practised seems to be connected with what we may call "endo-agriculture," that is, an extreme unwillingness to exchange seeds. Turning now to the second case, we may perhaps be permitted to consider the type of structure to be found in the so-called Crow-Omaha kinship systems as being in diametrical opposition to the Aranda systems in so far as, in the former, everything not forbidden is allowed, while in the latter the exact opposite is true: everything not allowed is forbidden. Now if this be granted, it is rather remarkable that in an African group such as the Nandi of Kenya, whose kinship system has been classified rightly or wrongly by Radcliffe-Brown as Omaha, there should be an extraordinary development of clan prohibitions bearing upon food and costume, and accompanied by individual marriage prohibitions based, not on clan affiliation, but on peculiar events pertaining to the individual history of each prospective groom and bride, which means that, in such a case, the structural arrangement of the alliance network—if any—would result from statistical fluctuations, exactly as happens with rules of marriage of the Crow-Omaha type. Let us consider a final example: that of the Baganda such as described by Roscoe. We are told that the Baganda had about forty clans, each possessing two totems, the first one being subject to food prohibition "so as to make it available to others in greater quantity," which is a modest counterpart of the Australian belief that, by refraining from consuming its totem, each clan acquires the power to multiply it. As in Australia too, each clan was linked to a territory which, in the case of the Baganda, was usually a sacred hill. In addition, each clan had a great many privileges, obligations, and prohibitions as, for instance, eligibility to kingship and other dignities, providing kingly wives, making and caring for regalia, providing other clans with certain kinds of food, and also special occupations. The Mushroom clan, for instance, was said to be sole maker of bark cloth and all the blacksmiths were supposed to come from the clan of the Tailless Cow. In such cases, we may well ask ourselves whether we are dealing with totemic clans, occupational castes, or with an intermediary form pertaining to both these types. Let us tackle this problem through application of our axiomatic principle.

We have seen that the so-called totemic concept amounts to a belief in an homology *not* between social groups and natural species, but between differences existing, on the one hand within the social system, and on the other within the natural system. Two systems of differences are conceived as isomorphic, although one is situated in nature, and the other in culture.

Let us now suppose that in addition to an homology of relationships, we have an homology of terms, and going one step further, that the homology of relationships shifts and becomes an homology between terms. The result will no longer be that Clan 1 can be held to differ from Clan 2 as for instance, Eagle differs from Bear, but that Clan 1 is in itself like Eagle and Clan 2 in itself like Bear. The system of differences will continue to exist, but, first, it will be conceived in reference to nature instead of to culture, and second, exogamy will inevitably break down because it implies that while woman are sociologically conceived of as being different, they are naturally (though unconsciously) conceived of as similar, or else they could not be exchanged.

It so happens that this theoretical transformation may be exemplified by concrete examples. In volume 5 of the Haddon-Rivers Expedition to Torres Straits (p. 184) we find that at Mabuiag, for instance, "A definite physical and psychological resemblance was postulated for the human and animal members of the clan. There can be little doubt that this sentiment reacted on the clansmen and constrained them to live up to the traditional character of their respective clans." Thus the Cassowary, Crocodile, Snake, and Shark clans were reputed to love fighting, while the Shovel-nosed Skate, Ray and Sucker-Fish clans were said to be peaceable. Intermediate between the fierce and the gentle clans was the Dog clan, which was thought to be sometimes pugnacious and sometimes pacific, just like real dogs. The men of the Crocodile clan were said to be very strong and ruthless, while the men of the Cassowary clan were reputed for their long legs and their ability to run fast, like real cassowaries. Similar observations have been made in North America among Eastern

Indians such as the Delaware, the Menomini, and the Chippewa. Among the latter, people of the Fish clan were reputed to be long lived, frequently to grow bald or to have thin hair, and all bald people were assumed to come from this clan. People of the Bear clan had long, thick, coarse hair that never turned white; they were said to be bellicose and quick to anger. People of the Crane clan had loud, ringing voices. Orators were always supposed to come from this clan.

From a theoretical point of view, we may now appraise the implications of these two opposite conceptions. In the first hypothesis, society on the one hand, nature on the other, will each retain its systematic integrity. Social segments will be referred to social segments; each natural species will be referred to other natural species. In the second hypothesis, instead of two "horizontal" systems situated at different levels, we shall have a plurality of "vertical" systems, considerably impoverished in fact, since instead of *two systems* each consisting of *numerous elements* we shall have *numerous systems* each consisting of *two elements*, heterogeneous (one natural, one cultural) instead of homogeneous (entirely natural or entirely cultural). Should this interpretation prove to be true, it should be possible, first to translate or re-code a "totemic" system into a caste system and conversely, and also to give concrete examples of societies which have actually done so. This is what I intend to exemplify now.

Tribes of the Muskogi linguistic group in the South-Eastern United States such as, for instance, the Chickasaw and the Creek, did have clans and moieties the first of which were perhaps exogamous and the second endogamous. In any case moieties were noted for overt manifestations of exclusivism that bordered on hostility. Ritual was jealously guarded by each moiety and members of another moiety who had witnessed a ceremony, even inadvertently, were put to death (an attitude recalling that held by the Aranda in relation to their cult groups). What is even more important, moieties were said to differ by their respective ways of life and their disposition of mind; one was said to be warlike and to prefer open country, the other one to be peaceable and to live in the woods. They may also have been hierarchized, as is suggested by some of the names under which they were known, one moiety being called "their-hickory-choppings," meaning that they had substantial lodges, while the other

moiety was called "their worn-out place," meaning that it consisted of inferior people living mostly under trees and in the woods. These differences were both more complex and more marked between clans, lineages, and hamlets. When informants were called upon to describe these secondary units, they used as a kind of leit-motiv, practically always the same words. "These people had ways of their own . . . they were very peculiar . . . different from all others . . . they had their own customs." These peculiarities were said to belong to different types: environment, economic activities, costume, food preferences, talents and tastes.

For instance, people of the Raccoon clan fed mostly on fish and wild fruits. Those of the Panther clan lived in mountains, avoided water, which they greatly feared, and fed on game. People of the Wild-Cat clan slept in the daytime, hunted by night since they were gifted with an especially keen sight, and were not interested in women. Those of the Bird clan woke up before daylight: "they were like real birds in that they would not bother anybody . . . the people of this clan have different sorts of minds, just as there are different species of birds . . . they had many wives . . . they did not work at all, but had an easy time going through life and went anywhere they wanted to . . . they had many offspring, as birds have."

People of the Red-Fox clan lived only in the woods, made a living by stealing from other people . . . doing whatever they liked. The "Wandering Iska" or "No-Home Iska" were a shiftless people "who did not want to own anything . . . they did not do anything for themselves . . . they were healthy looking, strong, for they did not do anything to run themselves down . . . they moved very slowly . . . they thought they were going to live forever . . . they did not care how they dressed or appeared . . . sometimes they wore dirty dresses . . . they were beggars and lazy."

The same kind of differences are emphasized between hamlets, for instance the Bending-Post-Oak-House Group lived in the wood, they were not very energetic, they loved to dance. They were prone to anxiety, had no foresight, were early risers, and made many mistakes, while people of the High-Corncrib House Group were not much esteemed by others but thought a great deal of themselves: "They were industrious, raised large crops, did not hunt much, bartered corn for venison. They were very wise, people of one mind, truthful, and they knew a great deal about the weather."

All these statements, which I have borrowed from Swanton, cannot be taken literally. They refer to a period when the traditional culture had already broken down and were obtained from old informants. They clearly belong to folk ethnology since, theoretically, it would be impossible for a human society to mimic nature to such an extent without running the risk of breaking down into several distinct groups hostile to one another. However, the testimony collected by Swanton is so rich, so concordant even when it comes from different tribes, that it must contain if not the literal truth at least the expression of a conceptual model which must have existed in the minds of the natives.

Allowing for these restrictive considerations, these statements have a threefold importance. In the first place, they describe what appears to have been a kind of caste system. In the second place, castes and their mutual relationships are being coded, so to speak, according to a natural model, after the diversity of natural species, as happens with totemic groups; and in the third place, from an historical point of view, these Muskogi tribes constituted a kind of link between the "true" totemic societies of the Plains and the only "true" caste-societies which are known to have existed in North America, such as the Natchez. Thus, I have established so far that in two parts of the world traditionally conceived as "totemistic," Australia's so-called "totemic" groups can be interpreted as occupational groups, while in America, social segments which can actually function as castes, were conceived after a "totemic" model.

Let us now shift to India, also a classical land, though of castes rather than totemic groups. Here, instead of castes being conceived after a natural model, vestiges of totemic groups tend to be conceived after a cultural model. But before exemplifying this point let me remind the reader that I am using the word "totemic" in such a way as to be able to leave entirely aside the question of whether or not there are actual vestiges of totemism in India. From my present point of view, the problem is irrelevant since, when I make loose usage of the term totemism, I never refer to a past or present institution but to a classificatory device whereby discrete elements of the external world are associated with the discrete elements of the social world.

Bearing this in mind, we may be struck by the fact that whereas so-called "totemic" names in Bengal are mostly of animal or vegetable origin, further south an increasing proportion of names borrowed from manufactured objects is to be found. For instance the Devanga who are a caste of weavers in Madras, use very few plant names for their clans and almost no animal names, but rather names such as buttermilk, cattle-pen, money, dam, houses, collyrium, knife, scissors, boat, clay lamp, female cloth, clothes, ropes for hanging pots, old plough, monastery, cart, funeral pyre, tile, etc., and the Kuruba of Mysore, who have sixty-seven exogamous clans, with few plant and animal names, designate them by names such as, among others, drum, booth, cart, cup, woollen thread, bangle, gold, pick-axe, hut, gold ring, bell-metal, coloured border of a cloth, stick, blanket, measure, metal toe-ring, moustache, loom, bamboo tube, lace, ring, etc.

These manufactured objects are not only used as clan names, but they also receive attention, and serve to express obligations and prohibitions as in totemic systems. It is true that the use of manufactured objects as totemic names is well known elsewhere in the world, particularly in Northern Australia and in some parts of Africa, very good examples having been recently (1961) presented for the Dinka by Dr. Lienhardt in his book *Divinity and Experience*. However, this never happens to such an extent as in India. Thus it seems that while in America castes confusedly conceived have been contaminated by totemic classifications, in India, where products or symbols of occupational activities are clearly differentiated as such and can be put to use in order to express differences between social groups, vestiges or remnants of totemic groups have come to make use of a symbolism that is technological and occupational in origin.

This appears less surprising when one attempts to express Australian institutions (the first ones which we have envisaged) differently, and in a more direct way, in the language of the caste system. What we have done thus far was to compare Australian totemic groups one to another from the standpoint of their specialization in control of a given animal or vegetable species, while occupational castes "control" the technical activities necessary to the well-being of the whole group.

There are nevertheless two differences. In the first place, a potter caste makes pots, a laundryman caste does actual laundry work, and barbers do shave. The performances of Australian totemic groups, however, are unreal, imaginary, and even though the participants believe in their reality, we shall see later that this characteristic makes a great deal of difference. In the second place, the connexion between the sorcerer and the natural species that he claims to control is not of the same type as the link between the craftsman and his product. Only in mythical times did the animals or plants actually originate from the ancestor's body. Nowadays, kangaroos produce kangaroos and man can only help them to do so.

But the similarity is much stronger if we adopt a different point of view. An Australian section or sub-section actually produces its women for the benefit of the other sections, much as an occupational caste produces goods and services which the other castes cannot produce and must seek from this caste alone. Thus, it would be inaccurate to define totemic groups and caste systems as being simply one exogamous and another endogamous. These are not real properties existing as such, but superficial and indirect consequences of a similarity which should be recognized at a deeper level. In the first place, both castes and totemic groups are "exo-practical": castes in relation to goods and services, totemic groups in relation to marriage. In the second place, both remain to some extent "endo-practical": castes by virtue of the rule of endogamy and Australian groups as regards their preferred type of matrimonial exchange, which being mostly of the "restricted" type, keeps each tribe closely self-contained and, as it were, wrapped up in itself. It would seem that allowing for the above restrictive considerations, we have now reached a satisfactory formulation, in a common language, of the relationship between totemic groups and castes. Thus we might say that in the first case—totemic groups—women, that is, biological individuals or natural products, are begotten naturally by other biological individuals, while in the second case—castes—manufactured objects or services rendered through the medium of manufactured objects are fabricated culturally through technical agents. The principle of differentiation stems in the one case from nature and in the other from culture.

However, this kind of parallelism would be purely formal and without any concrete basis, for occupational castes are truly different from one another as regards culture, and also complementary. The same cannot be said, as regards nature, of exogamic groups which specialize, so to speak, in the production of women belonging to different "species." Occupational activities are true social species; they are objectively distinct. Women, on the other hand, even when they are born in different sections of sub-sections, belong nevertheless to one and the same natural species.

Social logic appears at this point to be caught in a dialectical trap. The assumed parallelism between natural products (actually, women) and social products is wholly imaginary. This explains why exogamous groups are so often inclined to define themselves as totemic groups, for over and above exogamy they need an objective model to express their social diversity. In societies where division of labour and occupational specialization do not exist, the only possible objective model has to be sought in the natural diversity of biological species; for there are only two objectively given models of concrete diversity: one on the level of nature, made up by the taxonomic system of natural species, the other on the level of culture, made up by the social system of trades and occupations.

The rules of exogamy establish an ambiguous system which lies somewhere in between: as regards nature, women are all alike, and only as regards culture may they be claimed to be different.

If the first point of view prevails, that is, when men borrow from nature their conceptual model of diversification, they must unconsciously abide also by a natural model of womankind. Exogamous groups make the overt claim that women are culturally different and, consequently, may be exchanged. But actually, they can only be exchanged because, at a deeper level, they are known to be similar. This provides an explanation to what I have said earlier and permits, so to speak, one to deduce exogamy from more general principles.

Conversely, when the overt conceptual model is cultural, as in the caste system, women are acknowledged to be similar only within the limits of their respective social groups and this being projected on to the natural plane, their exchange between groups consequently becomes impossible.

In other words, both the caste system and the so-called totemic systems postulate isomorphism between natural and cultural differences. The validation of this postulate involves in each case a symmetrical and inverted relationship. Castes are defined after a cultural model and must define their matrimonial exchange after a natural model. Totemic groups pattern matrimonial exchange after a cultural mode, and they themselves must be defined after a natural model. Women, homogeneous as regards nature, are claimed to be heterogeneous as regards culture, and conversely, natural species, although heterogeneous as regards nature, are claimed to be homogeneous as regards culture, since from the standpoint of culture, they share common properties in so far as man is believed to possess the power to control and to multiply them.

In totemic systems, men exchange culturally the women who procreate them naturally, and they claim to procreate culturally the animal and vegetable species which they exchange naturally: in the form of foodstuffs which are interchangeable, since any biological individual is able to dispense with one and to subsist on the others. A true parallelism can therefore be said to exist between the two formulas, and it is possible to code one into the terms of the other. Indeed, this parallelism is more complex than we believed it to be at the beginning. It can be expressed in the following tortuous way: castes naturalize fallaciously a true culture while totemic groups culturalize truly a false nature. "False" in two respects: first, from a natural point of view, women belong to one and the same natural species; and second, as a natural species, men do not have the power to increase and control other natural species.

However, this symmetry can never be rigorous; soon enough it reaches its limits. During their procreative period, women are naturally equivalent; anatomical structure and physiological function are, grossly speaking, identical in all female individuals. On the other hands, foods are not so easily replaceable. Speaking of the Karuba of Mysore, Thurston quotes the Arisana gotram which bears the name of turmeric. But since it is not easy to go without turmeric it has adopted as its food-prohibition *korra* seeds which can be more easily dispensed with. And in his book already referred to, Dr. Lienhardt states something similar about

clans whose divinity is the giraffe. This is an all-important food, and instead of prohibiting it, these clans content themselves with avoiding to shed its blood. The same limitation exists with occupational castes. They too have to remain to some extent endo-functional, in order to render themselves the services they give to others. Otherwise who is going to shave the barber?

By way of conclusion I should like to emphasize four points. First, totemism which has been formalized in what may be called the "language of primitiveness" can equally well be formalized in the "language of castes" which were thought to be the very opposite of primitiveness.

Secondly, in its social undertakings, mankind keeps manoeuvering within narrow limits. Social types are not isolated creations, wholly independent of each other, and each one an original entity, but rather the result of an endless play of combination and recombination, forever seeking to solve the same problems by manipulating the same fundamental elements. This game always consists in a give-and-take, and what is given or taken must always belong either to the realm of nature (natural products) or to the realm of culture (goods and services), the exchange of women being the only formula that makes it possible to overcome this duality. Thus exchange of women not only ensures a horizontal mediation between groups of men, it also ensures a mediation, which we might call vertical, between nature and culture.

Thirdly, as we have seen, the tremendous differences existing between totemic groups and caste systems, in spite of their logical inverted similarity, may be ascribed to the fact that castes are right and totemic systems are wrong, when they believe that they provide real services to their fellow groups. This should convince us that the "truth-value" is an unavoidable dimension of structural method. No common analysis of religion can be given by a believer and a non-believer, and from this point of view, the type of approach known as "religious phenomenology" should be dismissed.

Lastly, by analysing a specific example, I have attempted to validate a methodological approach which I have been trying to follow in France and which Dr. Leach is following in England. According to this approach societies are not made up of the flotsam and jetsam of history, but of variables; thus widely different institutions can be reduced to transformations of the same basic figure, and the whole of human history may be looked upon merely as a set of attempts to organize differently the same means, but always to answer the same questions.

Louis Dumont

A STRUCTURAL DEFINITION OF A FOLK DEITY OF TAMIL NAD: AIYANAR, THE LORD

In this article Louis Dumont confronts one of the perennial and fundamental problems in the interpretation of non-Western religions—how to understand contradictions in belief systems. The fact that many religions allow apparent contradiction has led such writers as Lévy-Bruhl to regard this as a basic feature of primitive thought. Yet what is contradiction from one point of view, Dumont points out, may be consistent from another.

Dumont's work on Indian religions and particularly on the ideology behind the Hindu caste system has led him to the belief that relations, not identities, are the constants of Indian thought. In the caste system the principle of purity versus impurity defines the positions of the subcastes relative to each other but not in relation to an absolute standard. Unlike the European notions of good and bad, purity and impurity have no absolute qualities or values to be, in themselves, desired or rejected. Being mutually defining, they are necessary conceptually to each other, and this is reflected in the social field as the interdependence of the castes, high castes requiring the services of low (to perform polluting tasks) as much as the reverse.

The Hindu pantheon is notoriously resistant to analysis in Western terms. The identities of even the most important deities are multifaceted and apparently changeable from one situation to another, so that, for example, Shiva may appear in male and female forms in the same story. Dumont contends that while the attributes of gods may change, the relations among them will not. If two gods are opposites in some features, they will remain opposite though the features may change. The god Aiyanar is defined within a complex system of relations, and for the system to remain logically consistent the particular qualities of Aiyanar must change from one ceremony to another. The contradictions in Indian thought, according to Dumont, preserve the integrity of the system of relations at the expense of constancy of its component parts. For another interpretation of closely similar religious symbols in Ceylon, see Edmund Leach's article "Pulleyar and the Lord Buddha" in Chapter 5.

Reprinted from Louis Dumont, *Religion, Politics and History in India*, Collected Papers in Indian Sociology. Paris–The Hague: Mouton, 1970, Section 2, which contains more detailed bibliographical and other information the interested reader may consult. The data derived from field work are published in the monograph *Une Sous-caste de l'Inde du Sud* (Paris–The Hague: Mouton, 1957).

For the European observer, the God Aiyanar (*aiyaNār*) presents a problem. His ill-defined personality seems to contradict the prominent position he enjoys in Tamil villages. It is not that nothing is known of him, but there seems to be so little consistency among his characteristics that his nature cannot be grasped. In order to solve this problem and, without making an arbitrary assumption, to define the incoherent picture which emerges from the literature, I propose in this paper to study the god less in himself than in the relations he maintains in the village pantheon. I shall draw upon data collected at first hand in some localities of Madura District (Kokkulam, in Tirumangalam taluk) and Ramnad District (Kamuthi, Mudukkulattur taluk). Although the method is generally applicable, and the basic relations involved prevail very widely, the conclusions do not bear automatically for other areas. The neighboring Tinnevelly District would probably require some adaptation. As to the deities of Kerala or Mysore who are sometimes considered as homologous to Aiyanar, they are left out altogether.

THE PROBLEM

Three main authors have studied the god in detail at first hand or discussed him at length. The description of Ziegenbalg, a Danish missionary in Tranquebar (Tanjore District) belongs to the first half of the eighteenth century. It was used later by Oppert, Professor of Sanskrit at Madras, who completed it with a sanskrit mantras, but added arbitrary speculations of his own. Finally, Bishop Whitehead, in a little book containing some excellent descriptions of village cults, discussed the god from a theoretical point of view in connection with the districts of Tanjore and Trichinopoly. A brief summary of these three authors will reveal the problem.

We are told that the god has his temple in almost all the villages (which is true), and that he is their principal and sole male divinity (which seems less true, but allowance has perhaps to be made for regional differences). But who is this universally found god, and whence comes his preeminence? To these questions our authors give two different answers. Oppert is quite arbitrary: for him the god is autochthonous or Dravidian, an eater of blood offerings, chief among the demons, a masculine counterpart of the Mother Goddess as represented by the village goddesses. Whitehead takes an opposite view: for him, Aiyanar is a Brahmanic god, or a strongly brahmanized one, to whom such sacrifices are not offered and who is opposed in this matter to the village goddesses, whom alone he considers to be Dravidian. Thus the cult of Aiyanar in the Tamil country would be an index of greater brahmanization, as compared to the Telugu country. Such divergent opinions may be due in part to insufficient observation or to local variations, which are possible, as we shall see. But they result first of all from hasty interpretations rooted in the idea, which has done so much harm, that Indian culture is merely a juxtaposition of Aryan and so-called Dravidian or other elements. In order to avoid this pitfall, we shall attempt to get a more reliable view of the data by insisting upon the god's double relation, on the one hand, with the "demons" and with the goddesses on the other.

If Aiyanar's essence is doubtful, what in fact are his main characteristics? In oral tradition, he was born from Shiva who was seduced by the feminine form Vishnu had assumed in order to free him from a threatening Asura. Oppert gives a good version of the episode though the commentary is of poorer quality: there is no justification for speaking of "incest" (in popular tradition and elsewhere, Vishnu and Shiva are brothers-in-law), nor for supposing that the Brahmans invented this "disgusting" story in order to degrade Aiyanar. We shall find that it has quite another function.

Aiyanar may be represented either as a warrior, on foot or riding a white elephant or a horse, or as seated between his two wives, carrying a sceptre or whip and wearing a meditation band. The Seven Mothers (or Seven Virgins) are sometimes mentioned as present in his temple. Outside are found horses usually in terracotta. These are offered to the god and his suite for his mainly nocturnal rounds. The escort is composed either of the god's generals or vassals, or of demons. The troop riding in midair in the night recalls the well-known theme of the Wild Hunt, but here it is a matter of watching the village land, of which Aiyanar is first of all the guardian. The god also has occasionally to do with the rain, and in any case his temple is usually situated on the bank of the reservoir in which rainwater is gathered for irrigation purposes. There may be a daily cult, and there is a yearly festival, when blood sacrifice is offered, either to the god himself or to his attendants.

Most of the authors take Aiyanar to be "the king of the demons." One *District Gazetteer* gives a much better formula of Aiyanar's relation with the demons: "He is their master although he is not one of them."

AIYANAR AND THE VILLAGE GODDESS

If the association of Aiyanar and the Village Goddess does not appear in the preceding summary, this is because it appears only in their local functions: the goddess is also concerned with the protection or prosperity of the village. To make this clear, we should first of all remove the misunderstandings arising from the use of such terms as "village god," "mother goddess" or "mother goddess of the village." The term "village god" is ambiguous because it can have the broader meaning of the gods who have their temples in the village (which has a social implication, opposing as it does the popular gods to the official gods of the Brahmanic temples), or more strictly it can signify the gods of the local community. There is a difference between the two, for in the village gods and temples are found which interest only a part of the inhabitants. There are lineage temples in a village with one and the same caste, and there are temples belonging to one or the other caste in a multicaste village. The question deciding the issue is: "Who participates in the collection which covers the expenses of the festival?" If each household in the village takes part, strangers excluded, then and only then are we dealing with a village cult in the strict sociological sense. In general, the female deities which our authors call "village goddesses" are of this nature: there is one, or several of them, in each village, in whose cult the whole community collaborates and from whom it derives benefit. But if, going a step further, we are told to regard these goddesses as identical with the village like eponymous goddesses, or if we are invited to qualify them, in what appears to be an analogous manner, as "mother goddesses," then we should be on our guard. In reading Whitehead's work, which for the greater part is devoted to them, we might get the impression that each of these goddesses is necessarily peculiar to one village. On the contrary, in each region they are relatively few in number, each one generally honoured in several places and some of them from one end of the country to the other. Moreover their essential function is the protection of the village against epidemics, and one of the most widely spread is *māriyammaN* or *māriyammei*, the smallpox goddess. A linguistic fact has played a part in the identification of these goddesses as "mothers." Their name is generally a compound the second part of which, as in the preceding example, is very like *ammā(ḷ)*, which in kinship terminology designates, among others, the mother. But *ammā(ḷ)* in its widest sense refers also, in the language of politeness, to all women and girls. For instance, this is the case with divinized virgins (*kaNNi*). Rather than translate *māriammaN* as "Death-Mother," we shall call her Smallpox Lady. While it is true that the village places itself under the protection of such a Lady, it does not follow that it honours her as a (or its) Mother.

It is advisable to interpret Aiyanar in the same manner. Certainly *aiyaN*, *aiya(r)* (Sanskrit *ārya*) is "father," but it is also an equivalent of "Sir" and, as we shall see, is a name for the Brahmans. If *aiyaNār* is opposed to *ammaN* (locally also *aiyēN-ammaN*) it is as the Lord or Master to the Lady and not exactly as the father to the mother (locally *aiya-amma*). This is confirmed by observation: there is no question here of these deities being coupled together as husband and wife, as is so frequently the case. Their temples are distinct and one deity is not represented in the other's temple: Aiyanar's wives are altogether different. If the two deities are complementary in sex and name, this is in connection with their relation to the village, with the role they both play in its prosperity. Even their priests are different. While the goddess' priest is usually a *paṇḍāram* (garland-maker), a vegetarian, a sort of imitation of a Brahman, the priest of Aiyanar is generally the potter who makes images and horses, a meat-eater and the authentic priest of meat-eaters (Madura and Ramnad Districts).

A concrete example will show how Aiyanar and the Goddess are actually brought together in ritual. In Kokkulam and in the neighbouring localities the festival of *vaḍakku vāsal selli ammaN*, the Lady of the North Gate, is celebrated in the month of *puraṭṭāsi* (September–October) in rough synchronism with the great Hindu festival of the Goddess (*navarāttri*, the Nine "Nights"). The ceremonies are spread over several days and the cult of Aiyanar takes place on the day after that of the Lady. The one removes the disease (that is the reason for the orientation of her temple towards the north, and her name), the other with his temple on the banks of the tank seems to be concerned with the prosperity of the fields. It is difficult in these localities to get at a more precise value or function; the date of the cult of Aiyanar is probably different in those places where he acts explicitly as rain-maker.

Two facts that I think are new allow us to insist upon Aiyanar in his male aspect, identical in that with Shiva, as is indicated in the myth of his birth. Like his father he is identified with the linga on one side and with the bull on the other.

At Kokkulam I collected a version of the Aiyanar birth story which on the whole is close to that reported by Oppert. The story is very widespread. In this account, Shiva's semen is, with the cooperation of the Black God, deposited on the bank of the reservoir to protect it. There, it assumes the form of the linga. If the latter has disappeared in our time this is said to be because the cult it requires is too complicated. But it still exists and one could find it if one were to dig in the earth beneath the present anthropomorphic image of the god. This idea is also found elsewhere.

The bull is well known as Shiva's vehicle, honoured as Nandi in Shivaite temples. The villagers identify the two; thus in Kokkulam (in the settlement called Tengalapatti) a bull, attached to a lineage temple and exclusively used for stud services, lives practically at liberty and on occasion charges the carts on the road; the villagers referring to these bursts of temper smilingly call their author *sivaN*. One kind of bull race, witnessed in a neighbouring village, is known from the literature. It is a rather profane and sportive occasion, similar to the "courses à la cocarde" of Provence. But apart from this *jalli-kaṭṭu*, I found, under the name of *erudu kaṭṭu* (tying the bull), a different sort of race. In Kokkulam as well as in Kamuthi, where I observed one, the race is dedicated to Aiyanar and takes place near his temple the day after the erection of the terracotta horses. A huge rope made by the Untouchables is tied at one end round the bull's neck, while the other end is allowed to trail far behind him so that it hampers his movements. The young men try to master the bull by seizing the rope. In this manner, one after the other and in hierarchical order, the bulls of the local notables are brought into the game. At the end the rope is left looped up in a tree near the temple. In both associations, with the linga and with the bull, Aiyanar appears as a doublet of Shiva. However, we can note one difference: just as the linga is said to be buried, the sexual aspect of Aiyanar is latent and applied rather than affirmed and celebrated, just as the couple the god forms with the Goddess exists only in relation to the village.

That a couple should appear in this way, on a functional level says much in favour of the reality and depth of the notion.[1] Still,

when confronted with explicit couples, like Shiva and his consort, in Hinduism, some writers have been at pains to "explain" them as a sort of accidental reunion of two deities of opposite sex. If, on the contrary, one admits that the couple is itself a religious entity, then one can take an overall view of some tribal religions and well-known Hindu figures, as well as of our Tamil village deities. Among the Maria Gonds of Bastar the male god of the clan is associated in each village with a different goddess, the mother of the village, so that there is a couple of gods in each village, the male element being the same in all villages of the same clan (Grigson). In orthodox Hinduism the same Shiva has different wives in different towns, as Kamakshi in Conjeeveram, Minakshi in Madura. (It is true that the god changes his name in each place, but he is everywhere the same while his wife on the other hand is conceived of each time as a distinct incarnation of Parvati.) Half-way between these two cases, in our Tamil villages, we can observe the local functions divided between a god and a goddess. Aiyanar is the same everywhere (although he can always be distinguished by a different name). The goddess is neither different in each village, nor is she everywhere the same. She is not the goddess of the village except in a functional sense. Beneath the difference in personalities and functions, the couple is present from one end of the chain to the other, and the diversity in the forms which the couple assumes only bears witness to the reality of the category, whether overt or implied.

AIYANAR ASSOCIATED WITH THE "BLACK GOD"

This second association is still more important than the first. In order to understand it, we shall temporarily leave Aiyanar and sum up the structure of the lineage pantheons. The descriptions of the lineage temples belonging to the Pramalai Kallar in Kokkulam will be our source. These people, or rather some specialists among them, have more definite ideas on the subject than others, and one can verify the principles they express in many less theologically minded groups.

---

[1] The division of labour between our two gods is much like that between father and mother in the conjugal family, and more generally like the pattern of leadership in small groups according to Bales' experiments: a leader No. 1 being in charge of the relation of the group with the environment while a leader No. 2 deals with the

group itself (in our case, means of livelihood for Aiyanar, health, and collective health in particular, for the goddess); see Talcott Parsons, R. F. Bales and E. S. Shils, *Working Papers in the Theory of Action* (Glencoe, Ill., 1953).

It is in the lineage temples, where the priests are Kallar, that the pantheon is most numerous and best articulated. These temples comprise at least twenty-one gods, all present at the time of the annual cult at least, whether or not they are otherwise identifiable by representations or even plain stones. These gods are classed into two categories: the pure (suttam) gods who do not eat meat, and the meat-eating gods who are impure (asuttam) for this reason. This opposition bears some relation to a distinction often made in the literature between gods of Brahmanic origin and inspiration, borrowed from the large official temples, and local and popular gods, often called "demons" by the authors. But such formulas are not rigorous; we must stick to the only clear distinction applied by the worshippers themselves, which bears on diet. It has a social implication which will be emphasized later.

The opposition between vegetarian and meat-eating gods is very strongly marked; it is expressed in a real dichotomy in space, in the priesthood and in the cult implements. The temple is turned to the East and the chapel sheltering the principal god is situated almost on the East–West axis; the vegetarian gods are to the North (Brahmanism, as they say, came from the North), and the meat-eating gods to the South. Next, in view of the two different kinds of food to be served, it is best to have two kitchens, two priests (a "great" priest and a "little" priest, otherwise serious complications are to be expected), and also two sets of implements as well as two boxes to keep them in and shelter the divine in its latent form in the interval between two festivals. The opposition is marked also in legends such as that in which with extreme violence the main local god opposes the attempt of a Brahmanic trinity to establish itself in his neighbourhood, but is finally forced to give in. More dramatic perhaps is the legend which depicts the confusion of a man in whom are incarnate at the same time a vegetarian and a meat-eating god—both, however, present in an entirely regular and even necessary manner—until an arbitrator ascribes to them respectively the right and the left sides of the man's body. We might take this as a symbol of the necessity of the co-existence of the two opposing principles: the body of the possessed man is divided like the temple itself, the divine is a whole constituted precisely by this fundamental opposition.

This structure of the divine needs to be considered in relation to the social order. It is clear that the relation between the vegetarian and the meat-eating deities is of the same order as that between vegetarian and meat-eating men. The criterion of diet is one of the main criteria in the hierarchical ordering of castes in South India. The two kinds of gods of which the temple is composed are in relation of superior caste (the Brahman caste, for example) to inferior caste (that of the meat-eating devotees in our case). Moreover, the distinction is a particular form of the opposition of purity and impurity, the principle of the caste system. Finally, the temple reflects the society in a simplified form, it symbolizes it. This is probably the reason for what might at first sight appear a strange syncretism, but is in fact much more.

Hence, important consequences follow. Not only are pure and impure gods as closely interdependent as pure and impure castes, but we can also say something about the degree and nature of the belief bearing on the two kinds of gods and on the rites addressed to them. The people are meat-eaters, and in their lineage temples, where they themselves officiate, the essential rite is blood-sacrifice. There is no doubt that they identify themselves only with the impure gods who occupy a position in the pantheon homologous to their position in society. These, it would seem, are their gods, and they believe in them more, and more immediately. Why therefore are they not content with them, and why in addition do they install pure gods that, by their own confession, they serve badly and frequently annoy? Gods of whom it cannot be said that they feel them as intrinsically more powerful? One might speak here of imitation or, following Hocart, of "snobbery." It is true that among those groups the cult of the pure gods shows the mark of pharisaism, that belief in them is relatively conventional and that in the last analysis the pure god is not present in the temple by virtue of his intrinsic superiority, but as the god of the superior castes. It would appear as if the caste joins to its own gods those of the castes that dominate it. Here we have to substitute a psychology of imitation and addition for a psychology of conversion.

This again is not enough, for the inferior meat-eating gods themselves only exist at this stage by the sanction or guarantee of the superior gods. Only the presence of the latter maintains the reality of the former.

The same legend which praises the omnipotence of a Black God and widens its domain beyond all measure, also recognizes that he was originally the servant of a great Brahmanic god. As regards the nature of this Black God, the village theologian engages in a complicated but revealing discussion. On the one hand, the Black God is identical with one of those evil demons, pēy, who have only an ephemeral existence and are not the object of any cult; on the other, he rules by virtue of a sort of proxy of the great (vegetarian) gods, and one is even told that he takes on his black, demonic appearance only in order to deceive the demons whom he fights. (This is clearly the position of the castes of intermediary status: they have no being, they do not exist for themselves but are opposed in turn to the Brahmans like nonbeing to being and to the Untouchables as being to non-being, solidary in the first place with all those who are below them and in the second with all who are above.) One can see that the illogicality of a dichotomy in the divine does not entirely escape the indigenous mind, which sees it as a contradiction between affectivity (identification with the Black God) and speculation (the pure god is supreme). This contradiction reflects the social position of the meat-eater: he must not only recognize the superiority of the vegetarian but even admit that he derives his own reality from him.

This is important from a theoretical point of view: we can say that in a very particular way a characteristic does not exist here except in its relation to its opposite. In the caste society, nothing is true by nature and everything by situation, there are no essences but only relations. To say caste is to say structure. This is the origin of the familiar impossibility of universal judgements in India: as long as one considers particular objects—instead of relations—no consistency, no principle can be found.

We are now able to return to Aiyanar. The opposition described is met with again, under an exemplary form, in the relation of Aiyanar as a pure, vegetarian god, to a meat-eating god locally called the Black God, *kaRuppu-sāmi* or *kaRuppaN*. In fact, these names can be seen as referring to categories rather than to individual gods: each concrete Aiyanar or Karuppu has his own particular name. This pair constitutes the simplest and most concentrated illustration of the divine as we have defined it. This is clearly expressed in the Karuppu temples, where most often the

central shrine is double, one part sheltering Karuppu and the other Aiyanar. In this context Aiyanar appears as condensing Brahmanism in his person; in him Shivaism and Vishnuism are not distinguished but, on the contrary, blended as they were at his birth. If he is a duplicate of Shiva, it is an enlarged duplicate, for it transcends the distinction of the two great gods of Hinduism. Also, in the story of his birth the interdependence of castes is very pronounced: the two great gods are embarrassed by the semen of one of them, and "just as important people sometimes have need of a sweeper," in the same way they call for Karuppan and extricate themselves from the affair with his assistance.

Aiyanar and Karuppan are as master and servant, and while being opposed they participate the one in the other. Thus, at the time of the festival when terracotta horses are offered, at least a pair must be given: one for Aiyanar, to whose nature alone the gift is befitting, as we shall see presently, but another also for Karuppan who accompanies him (this corresponds to the legitimation of the lower gods already mentioned). Conversely, the blood-sacrifice which is properly offered only to Karuppan can, if it is offered in Aiyanar's temple, appear to apply to him also. Here is the contradiction which we promised to solve at the outset. There are in fact two ways of seeing the main god of a temple. He can be regarded either in himself or as embracing all the deities which surround him, vegetarian and meat-eating deities together. In the first case, a curtain is drawn before Aiyanar at the time of blood-sacrifice to isolate him from it; in the second case, it would seem to the observer, and indeed ordinary villagers themselves might say, that the sacrifice is offered to him. More generally, we can suppose that the pantheon tends to become homogeneous, the superior gods adopting the characteristics of the lower and vice versa. Thus, in the village the great gods become incarnate like the others in a possessed dancer. This tendency is held in check only in circumstances where the distinction is felt to be pertinent, as is the case here for the distinction in diet.

Aiyanar, then, commands the inferior gods, not because he is one of them, but precisely because he is different from them—such is hierarchy in the caste society. But at this point again interesting complications arise. If, in the theory of caste, the first rank belongs to the Brahman, we can say that in actual fact the hierarchy is bicephalous, except that the second head, the king, is not recognized when confronted with the first. Aiyar is the commonest name for the Brahman, and Aiyanar as his name indicates is above all a Brahman; he is a vegetarian, he sometimes wears the sacred thread and more often the meditation band, and no doubt in the first place it is as such that he rules over the inferior gods. But the royal component is also present. He is, we were told, "the king of the demons," he holds a sceptre (or perhaps a whip), he has for his mount a white elephant or a horse (this is definitely a royal feature in South India), he is a warrior, and his suite, sometimes said to be composed of "demons" —i.e., in our language inferior gods, is also represented as a body of feudatory horsemen (*pāḷeiyakkārar*, "poligar"). Also, as we shall see, he has two wives. To sum up, we can say that what characterizes Aiyanar is the union of these two series of features; in him the Brahman and the warrior king are blended. He is the Lord *par excellence*, first by his sacerdotal purity, but also by his temporal power.

CONCLUSION

The double association of the god, with the goddess on the one hand and with Karuppan on the other, is reflected in the calendar in some places as for instance in Kokkulam. The cult of Aiyanar occurs twice a year. While in the September festival it follows that of the Goddess, in May–June, on the contrary, Aiyanar is associated with the Black God, and the festival in its full development comprises, on the first day, the erection of the clay horses mainly in the temple of the Black God, on the second day, the bull race in front of Aiyanar's temple. (Actually this entails great expense and does not take place each year.) This clear expression of Aiyanar's double association is not general; it is due here to the circumstances that the temples in Kokkulam have a dual value, as local temples (September) and as lineage temples, or more precisely as temples common to the seven local lineages (May).

It may well be imagined that the two fundamental oppositions which have helped us to define the nature of the god play in a variety of ways. In fact, one may wonder whether the whole of South Indian society, at least according to the idea which the people themselves have of it, is not constructed on these two principles. In the present case it may be that their combination is also responsible for the fact that Aiyanar has two wives. This cannot be positively demonstrated, but it would be accordance with a frequent pattern. According to Ziegenbalg, only one of Aiyanar's two consorts bears the Shivaite mark on her brow. The triad would then combine the sexual couple with the lack of sectarian differentiation of the god which has been noted above. But this kind of triad is also found in the case of other gods. It is permissible to see in it a condensed picture of polygamy as consecrated by custom. In this case one of the two wives is normally of her husband's rank, the other of inferior rank, this combination being a royal, rather than a Brahmanic trait. The hypothesis seems verified when we learn that one of the wives has a clear complexion (high caste) and the other a dark complexion, as for Murugan-Subrahmanya between *deyvayāNei* (Skrt. *devasenā*) and *vaḷḷi*, for Vishnu between Lakshmi and Bhumidevi (in agreement with the royal aspect of Vishnu). More remotely one thinks of Krishna and Rukmini on the one hand, of Krishna and Radha on the other. Only, in the case of Aiyanar, we know nothing of the wives but their names, nothing, in particular, about their complexion.

To sum up, Aiyanar is the Lord: the Lord as complement of the Lady, the Lord as high caste god ruling low caste gods. High caste he is on two counts: as a "pure" god transcending sectarian limitations, and as a king ruling his subordinates. He concentrates in himself the religion and the state at the level of the village, while at the same time keeping the value of a god attached to a particular place.

Mary Douglas

POLLUTION

Mary Douglas begins with a classic anthropological problem: The "primitive" world seems to abound with objects that are at once worshipped and feared, sacred, yet defiling and surrounded with taboo. The near universal occurrence of pollution beliefs which symbolically demarcate the sacred, must, she suggests, be seen as a special case of classification, a human and cultural activity *par excellence*. Pointing out that even in our own society dirt is simply "matter out of place," Douglas asserts that notions of pollution and taboo are no more than rules which protect men and societies from ambiguity and dissonance; they create and preserve boundaries by which a moral and social order may exist. Thus, for example, a society or social group—say, a caste—that is deeply concerned about its integrity, its boundaries, is likely to symbolize that concern in beliefs about the margins of the human body: hair and nail clippings, feces, and so on, are likely to be ritually tabooed. In another society, crimes, like incest, which deny the reality of social categories of, say, marriageable and nonmarriageable kin, are sanctioned, not by political authority, but by pollution beliefs and the fear of supernatural reprisals. In every case, order is asserted in the ritualized avoidance of ambiguity and indiscretion; man creates the holy by putting it in its place.

One of the great puzzles in comparative studies of religion has been the reconciliation of the concept of pollution, or defilement, with that of holiness. In the last half of the nineteenth century, Robertson Smith asserted that the religion of primitive peoples developed out of the relation between a community and its gods, who were seen as just and benevolent. Dependent on a sociological approach to religion, Robertson Smith continued always to draw a line between religious behavior, concerned with ethics and gods, and nonreligious, magical behavior. He used the term *taboo* to describe nonreligious rules of conduct, especially those concerned with pollution, in order to distinguish them from the rules of holiness protecting sanctuaries, priests, and everything pertaining to gods. The latter behavior he held to be intelligible and praiseworthy and the former to be primitive, savage, and irrational—"magical superstition based on mere terror."

He clearly felt that magic and superstition were not worth a scholar's attention. But Sir James Frazer, who dedicated *The Golden Bough* to Robertson Smith, tried to classify and understand the nature of magical thinking. He formulated the two principles of sympathetic magic: action by contagion and action by likeness. Frazer followed Robertson Smith in assuming that magic was more primitive than religion, and he worked out an evolutionary scheme in which primitive man's earliest thinking was oriented to mechanical ideas of contagion. Magic gradually gave way to another cosmology, the idea of a universe dominated by supernatural beings similar to man but greatly superior to him. Magic thus came to be accepted as a word for ritual which is not enacted within a cult of divine beings. But obviously there is an overlap between nonreligious ideas of contagion and rules of holiness. Robertson Smith accounted for this by making the distinction between holiness and uncleanness a criterion of the advanced religions:

The person under taboo is not regarded as holy, for he is separated from approach to the sanctuary as well as from contact with men, but his act or condition is somehow associated with supernatural dangers, arising, according to the common savage explanation, from the presence of formidable spirits which are shunned like an infectious disease. In most savage societies no sharp line seems to be drawn between the two kinds of taboo . . . and even in more advanced nations the notions of holiness and uncleanness often touch . . . [to] distinguish between the holy and the unclean, marks a real advance above savagery. ([1889] 1927, *p.* 153)

Frazer echoes the notion that confusion between uncleanness and holiness marks primitive thinking. In a long passage in which he considers the Syrian attitude to pigs, he concludes: "Some said this was because the pigs were unclean; others said it was because the pigs were sacred. This . . . points to a hazy state of religious thought in which the ideas of sanctity and uncleanness are not yet sharply distinguished, both being blent in a sort of vaporous solution to which we give the name of taboo" ([1890] 1955, vol. 2, part 5, p. 23).

The work of several modern-day students of comparative religion derives not directly from Frazer but from the earlier work of Durkheim, whose debt to Robertson Smith is obvious in many ways. On the one hand, Durkheim was content to ignore aspects of defilement which are not part of a religious cult. He developed the notion that magical injunctions are the consequence of primitive man's attempt to explain the nature of the universe. Durkheim suggested that experimentation with magical injunctions, having thus arisen, has given way to medical science. But on the other hand, Durkheim tried to show that the contagiousness of the sacred is an inherent, necessary, and peculiar part of its character.

His idea of the sacred as the expression of society's awareness of itself draws heavily on Robertson Smith's thesis that man's relation to the gods, his religious behavior, is an aspect of prescribed social behavior. It followed, for Durkheim, that religious ideas are different from other ideas. They are not referable to any ultimate material reality, since religious shrines and emblems are only themselves representations of abstract ideas. Religious experience is an experience of a coercive moral force. Consequently, religious ideas are volatile and fluid; they float in the mind, unattached, and are always likely to shift, or to merge into other contexts at the risk of losing their essential character: there is always the danger that the sacred will invade the profane and the profane invade the sacred. The sacred must be continually protected from the profane by interdictions. Thus, relations with the sacred are always expressed through rituals of separation and demarcation and are reinforced with beliefs in the danger of crossing forbidden boundaries.

If contemporary thinkers were not already well prepared to accept the idea that "religious" restrictions were utterly different from primitive superstitions about contagion, this circular distinction between two kinds of contagion could hardly have gone unchallenged. How can it be argued that contagiousness is the peculiar characteristic of ideas about the sacred when another kind of contagiousness has been bracketed away by definition as irrelevant?

This criticism of Durkheim's treatment of sacred contagion is implicit in Lévy-Bruhl's massive work on primitive mentality (1922). Lévy-Bruhl documented a special kind of outlook on the universe, one in which the power to act and to be acted upon regardless of restrictions of space and time is widely attributed to symbolical representations of persons and animals. He himself explained the belief in such remote contagion by the dominance of the idea of the supernatural in the primitive view of the world. And since he would expect "supernatural" to be equated with Durkheim's "sacred," he seems to have seen no conflict between his and the master's views.

We cannot accept Durkheim's argument that there are two kinds of contagion, one the origin of primitive hygiene and the other intrinsic to ideas about the sacred, because it is circular. If we approach the problem of contagion in Lévy-Bruhl's terms, then the scope of the answer is broadened: there is not simply a residual area of magical behavior that remains to be explained after primitive religious behavior has been understood but rather a whole mentality, a view of how the universe is constituted. This view of the universe differs essentially from that of civilized man in that sympathetic magic provides the key to its control. Lévy-Bruhl is open to criticism; his statement of the problem is oversimple. He bluntly contrasts primitive mentality with scientific thought, not fully appreciating what a rare and specialized activity scientific thinking is and in what well-defined and isolated conditions it takes place. His use of the word "prelogical" in his first formulation of primitive thinking was unfortunate, and he later discarded it. But although his work seems to be discredited at present, the general problem still stands. There is a whole class of cultures, call them what you will, in which great attention is paid to symbolic demarcation and separation of the sacred and the profane and in which dangerous consequences are expected to follow from neglect of the rituals of separation. In these cultures lustrations, fumigations, and purifications of various kinds are applied to avert the dangerous effect of breach of the rules, and symbolic actions based on likeness to real causes are used as instruments for creating positive effects.

THE CULTURAL DEFINITION

If we are not to follow Robertson Smith in treating the rules of uncleanness as irrational and beyond analysis, we need to clear away some of the barriers which divide up this whole field of inquiry. While the initial problem is posed by the difference between "our" kind of thinking and "theirs," it is a mistake to treat "us" the moderns and "them" the ancients as utterly different. We can only approach primitive mentality through introspection and understanding of our own mentality. The distinction between religious behavior and secular behavior also tends to be misleadingly rigid. To solve the puzzle of sacred contagion we can start with more familiar ideas about secular contagion and defilement. In English-speaking cultures, the key word is the ancient, primitive, and still current "dirt." Lord Chesterfield defined dirt as matter out of place. This implies only two conditions, a set of ordered relations and a contravention of that order. Thus the idea of dirt implies a structure of ideas. For us dirt is a kind of compendium category for all events which blur, smudge, contradict, or otherwise confuse accepted classifications. The underlying feeling is that a system of values which is habitually expressed in a given arrangement of things has been violated.

This definition of defilement avoids some historical peculiarities of Western civilization. For example, it says nothing about the relation between dirt and hygiene. We know that the discovery of pathogenic organisms is recent, but the idea of dirt antedates the idea of pathogenicity. It is therefore more likely to have universal application. If we treat all pollution behavior as the reaction to any event likely to confuse or contradict cherished classifications, we can bring two new approaches to bear on the problem: the work of psychologists on perception and of anthropologists on the structural analysis of culture.

Perception is a process in which the perceiver actively interprets and, in the course of his interpreting, adapts and even supplements his sensory experiences. Hebb has shown that in the process of perception, the perceiver imposes patterns of organization on the masses of sensory stimuli in the environment (1949; 1958). The imposed pattern organizes sequences into units—fills in missing events which would be necessary to justify the recognition of familiar units. The perceiver learns to adjust his response to allow for modification of stimuli according to changes in lighting, angle of regard, distance, and so forth. In this way the learner develops a scheme or structure of assumptions in the light of which new experiences are interpreted. Learning takes place when new experience lends itself to assimilation in the existing structure of assumption or when the scheme of past assumptions is modified in order to accommodate what is unfamiliar. In the normal process of interpretation, the existing scheme of assumptions tends to be protected from challenge, for the learner recognizes and absorbs cues which harmonize with past experience and usually ignores cues which are discordant. Thus, those assumptions which have worked well before are reinforced. Because the selection and treatment of new experiences validates the principles which have been learned, the structure of established assumptions can be applied quickly and automatically to current problems of interpretation. In animals this stabilizing, selective tendency serves the biological function of survival. In men the same tendency appears to govern learning. If every new experience laid all past interpretations open to doubt, no scheme of established assumptions could be developed and no learning could take place.

This approach may be extended to the learning of cultural phenomena. Language, for example, learned and spoken by individuals, is a social phenomenon produced by continuous interaction between individuals. The regular discriminations which constitute linguistic structure are the spontaneous outcome of continual control, exercised on an individual attempting to communicate with others. Expressions which are ambiguous or which deviate from the norm are less effective in communication, and speakers experience a direct feedback encouraging conformity. Language has more loosely and more strictly patterned domains in which ambiguity has either more or less serious repercussions on effective communication. Thus there are certain domains in which ambiguity can be better tolerated than in others (Osgood & Sebeok, 1954, p. 129).

Similar pressures affect the discrimination of cultural themes. During the process of enculturation the individual is engaged in ordering newly received experiences and bringing them into conformity with those already absorbed. He is also interacting with other members of his community and striving to reduce dissonance between his structure of assumptions and theirs (Festinger, 1957). Frenkel-Brunswik's research among school-children who had been variously exposed to racial prejudice illustrate the effects of ambiguity on learning at this level. The children listened to stories which they were afterwards asked to recall. In the stories the good and bad roles were not consistently allocated to white and Negro characters. When there was dissonance between their established pattern of assumptions about racial values and the actual stories they heard, an ambiguous effect was received. They were unable to recall the stories accurately. There are implications here for the extent to which a culture (in the sense of a consistent structure of themes, postulates, and evaluations) can tolerate ambiguity. It is now common to approach cultural behavior as if it were susceptible to structural analysis on lines similar to those used in linguistics (Lévi-Strauss, 1958; Leach, 1961). For a culture to have any recognizable character, a process of discrimination and evaluation must have taken place very similar to the process of language development—with an important difference. For language the conditions requiring clear verbal communication provide the main control on the pattern which emerges, but for the wider culture in which any language is set, communication with others is not the only or principal function. The culture affords a hierarchy of goals and values which the community can apply as a general guide to action in a wide variety of contexts. Cultural interaction, like linguistic interaction, involves the individual in communication with others. But it also helps the individual to reflect upon and order his own experience.

The general processes by which language structure changes and resists change have their analogues at the higher level of cultural structure. The response to ambiguity is generally to encourage clearer discrimination of differences. As in language, there are different degrees of tolerance of ambiguity. Linguistic intolerance is expressed by avoidance of ambiguous utterances and by pressure to use well-discriminated forms where differences are important to interpretation and appropriate responses. Cultural intolerance of ambiguity is expressed by avoidance, by discrimination, and by pressure to conform.

THE FUNCTIONS OF POLLUTION BELIEFS

To return to pollution behavior, we have already seen that the idea of dirt implies system. Dirt avoidance is a process of tidying up, ensuring that the order in external physical events conforms to the structure of ideas. Pollution rules can thus be seen as an extension of the perceptual process: insofar as they impose order on experience, they support clarification of forms and thus reduce dissonance.

Much attention has been paid to the sanctions by which pollution rules are enforced (see Steiner, 1956, p. 22). Sometimes the breach is punished by political decree, sometimes by attack on the transgressor, and sometimes by grave or trivial sanctions; the sanction used reflects several aspects of the matter. We can assume that the community, insofar as it shares a common culture, is collectively interested in pressing for conformity to its norms. In some areas of organization the community is capable of punishing deviants directly, but in others this is not practicable. This may happen, for example, if political organization is not sufficiently developed or if it is developed in such a way as to make certain offenses inaccessible to police action. Homicide is a type of offense which is variously treated according to the relationship between killer and victim. If the offender is himself a member of the victim's group and if this is the group which is normally entrusted with protection of its members' interests, it may be held contradictory and impossible for the group to inflict punishment. Then the sanction is likely to be couched in terms of a misfortune that falls upon the offender without human intervention. This kind of homicide is treated as a pollution.

We would expect to find that the pollution beliefs of a culture are related to its moral values, since these form part of the structure of ideas for which pollution behavior is a protective device. But we would not expect to find any close correspondence between the gravity with which offenses are judged and the danger of pollution connected with them. Some moral failings are likely to be met with prompt and unpleasant social consequences. These self-punishing offenses are less likely to be sanctioned by pollution beliefs than by other moral rules. Pollution beliefs not only reinforce the cultural and social structure, but they can actively reduce ambiguity in the moral sphere. For example, if two moral standards are applied to adultery, so that it is condemned in women and tolerated in men, there will inevitably be some ambiguity in the moral judgment since adultery involves a man and a woman. A pollution belief can reduce the ambiguity. If the man is treated as dangerously contagious, his adulterous condition, while not in itself condemned, endangers the outraged husband or the children; moral support can be mustered against him. Alternatively, if attention is focused on the pollution aspect of the case, a rite of purification can mitigate the force of the moral condemnation.

This approach to pollution allows further applications of Durkheimian analysis. If we follow him in assuming that symbolism and ritual, whether strictly religious or not, express society's awareness of its own configuration and necessities, and if we assume that pollution rules indicate the areas of greater systematization of ideas, then we have an additional instrument of sociological analysis. Durkheim held that the dangerous powers imputed to the gods are, in actual fact, powers vested in the social structure for defending itself, as a structure, against the deviant behavior of its members. His approach is strengthened by including all pollution rules and not merely those which form part of the religious cult. Indeed, deriving pollution behavior from processes similar to perception comes close to Durkheim's intention of understanding society by developing a social theory of knowledge.

Pollution rules in essence prohibit physical contact. They tend to be applied to products or functions of human physiology; thus they regulate contact with blood, excreta, vomit, hair clippings, nail clippings, cooked food, and so on. But the anthropologist notes that the incidence of beliefs in physiological pollution varies from place to place. In some communities menstrual pollution is gravely feared and in others not at all; in some, pollution by contact with the dead is feared, in others pollution of food or blood. Since our common human condition does not give rise to a common pattern of pollution observances, the differences become interesting as an index of different cultural patterning. It seems that physiological pollutions become important as symbolic expressions of other

undesirable contacts which would have repercussions on the structure of social or cosmological ideas. In some societies the social definition of the sexes is more important than in others. In some societies social units are more rigorously defined than in others. Then we find that physical contact between sexes or between social units is restricted even at second or third remove. Not only may social intercourse be restricted, but sitting on the same chair, sharing the same latrine, or using the same cooking utensils, spoons, or combs may be prohibited and negatively sanctioned by pollution beliefs. By such avoidances social definitions are clarified and maintained. Color bars and caste barriers are enforced by these means. As to the ordered relation of social units and the total structure of social life, this must depend on the clear definition of roles and allegiances. We would therefore expect to find pollution concepts guarding threatened disturbances of the social order. On this, nearly everything has been said by van Gennep. His metaphor of society as a kind of house divided into rooms and corridors, the compartments carefully isolated and the passages between them protected by ceremonial, shows insight into the social aspects of pollution. So also does his insistence on the relative character of the sacred:

Sacredness as an attribute is not absolute; it is brought into play by the nature of particular situations. . . . Thus the "magic circles" pivot, shifting as a person moves from one place in society to another. The categories and concepts which embody them operate in such a way that whoever passes through the various positions of a lifetime one day sees the sacred where before he has seen the profane, or vice versa. Such changes of condition do not occur without disturbing the life of society and the individual, and it is the function of rites of passage to reduce their harmful effects. (Gennep [1909] 1960, pp. 12–13)

Van Gennep saw that rites of transition treat all marginal or ill-defined social states as dangerous. His treatment of margins is fully compatible with the sociological approach to pollution. But Van Gennep's ideas must be vastly expanded. Not only marginal social states, but all margins, the edges of all boundaries which are used in ordering the social experience, are treated as dangerous and polluting.

Rites of passage are not purificatory but are prophylactic. They do not redefine and restore a lost former status or purify from the effect of contamination, but they define entrance to a new status. In this way the permanence and value of the classifications embracing all sections of society are emphasized.

When we come to consider cosmological pollution, we are again faced with the problem unresolved by Lévy-Bruhl. Cosmological pollution is to the Westerner the most elusive, yet the most interesting case. Our own culture has largely given up the attempt to unify, to interpenetrate, and to cross-interpret the various fields of knowledge it encompasses. Or rather, the task has been taken over by natural science. A major part of pollution behavior therefore lies outside the realm of our own experience: this is the violent reaction of condemnation provoked by anything which seems to defy the apparently implicit categories of the universe. Our culture trains us to believe that anomalies are only due to a temporarily inadequate formulation of general natural laws. We have to approach this kind of pollution behavior at second hand.

The obvious source of information on the place of cosmic abnormality in the mind of the primitive is again Lévy-Bruhl. Earthquakes, typhoons, eclipses, and monstrous births defy the order of the universe. If something is thought to be frightening because it is abnormal or anomalous, this implies a conception of normality or at least of categories into which the monstrous portent does not fit. The more surprising that anomaly is taken to be, the clearer the evidence that the categories which it contradicts are deeply valued.

At this point we can take up again the question of how the culture of civilization differs from that which Lévy-Bruhl called primitive. Recalling that dirt implies system and that pollution beliefs indicate the areas of greatest systematization, we can assume that the answer must be along the same lines. The different elements in the primitive world view are closely integrated; the categories of social structure embrace the universe in a single, symbolic whole. In any primitive culture the urge to unify experience to create order and wholeness has been effectively at work. In "scientific culture" the apparent movement is the other way. We are led by our scientists to specialization and compartmentalism of spheres of knowledge. We suffer the continual breakup of established ideas. Lévy-Bruhl, looking to define the distinction between the scientific and the primitive outlook, would have been well served if he had followed Kant's famous passage on his own Copernican revolution. Here Kant describes each great advance in thought as a stage in the process of freeing "mind" from the shackles of its own subjective tendencies. In scientific work the thinker tries to be aware of the provisional and artificial character of the categories of thought which he uses. He is ready to reform or reject his concepts in the interests of making a more accurate statement.

Any culture which allows its guiding concepts to be continually under review is immune from cosmological pollutions. To the extent that we have no established world view, our ways of thinking are different from those of people living in primitive cultures. For the latter, by long and spontaneous evolution, have adapted their patterns of assumption from one context to another until the whole of experience is embraced. But such a comprehensive structure of ideas is precarious to the extent that it is an arbitrary selection from the range of possible structures in the same environment. Other ways of dividing up and evaluating reality are conceivable. Hence, pollution beliefs protect the most vulnerable domains, where ambiguity would most weaken the fragile structure.

EMOTIONAL ASPECTS OF POLLUTION BEHAVIOR

Pollution beliefs are often discussed in terms of the emotions which they are thought to express. But there is no justification for assuming that terror, or even mild anxiety, inspires them any more than it inspires the housewife's daily tidying up. For pollution beliefs are cultural phenomena. They are institutions that can keep their forms only by bringing pressure to bear on deviant individuals. There is no reason to suppose that the individual in a primitive culture experiences fear, still less unreasoning terror, if his actions threaten to modify the form of the culture he shares. His position is exactly comparable to a speaker whose own linguistic deviations cause him to produce responses which vary with his success in communicating. The dangers and punishments attached to pollution act simply as means of enforcing conformity.

As to the question of the rational or irrational character of rules of uncleanness, Robertson Smith is shown to have been partly right. Pollution beliefs certainly derive from rational activity, from the process of classifying and ordering experience. They are, however, not produced by strictly rational or even conscious processes but rather as a spontaneous by-product of these processes.

Mary Douglas

THE ABOMINATIONS OF LEVITICUS

The subtle and suggestive implications of Mary Douglas's theoretical approach, first advanced in her book *Purity and Danger* (1966), have led to reconsiderations of so-called magical attitudes in all parts of the world. Douglas provides an excellent application of her ideas in her consideration of Jewish dietary laws, most specifically the taboo against eating pork. She argues that the prohibited "abominations of Leviticus" are animals which appear anomalous in the classification of natural things handed down by God in Genesis. By avoiding what in nature challenges God's order, men confirm that order. Through a dietary observance, God is made holy—separate and whole.

Reprinted in abridged form from Mary Douglas, *Purity and Danger* (1966), pp. 41–58, by permission of the author, Routledge & Kegan Paul Ltd. (London), and Frederick A. Praeger, Inc. (New York).

Defilement is never an isolated event. It cannot occur except in view of a systematic orderings of ideas. Hence any piecemeal interpretation of the pollution rules of another culture is bound to fail. For the only way in which pollution ideas make sense is in reference to a total structure of thought whose key-stone, boundaries, margins and internal lines are held in relation by rituals of separation.

To illustrate this I take a hoary old puzzle from biblical scholarship, the abominations of Leviticus, and particularly the dietary rules. Why should the camel, the hare and the rock badger be unclean? Why should some locusts, but not all, be unclean? Why should the frog be clean and the mouse and the hippopotamus unclean? What have chameleons, moles and crocodiles got in common that they should be listed together? [To help follow the argument the reader is referred to Deuteronomy XIV and Leviticus XI using the text of the New Revised Standard Translation.]

. . .

All the interpretations given so far fall into one of two groups: either the rules are meaningless, arbitrary because their intent is disciplinary and not doctrinal, or they are allegories of virtues and vices. Adopting the view that religious prescriptions are largely devoid of symbolism, Maimonides said:

The Law that sacrifices should be brought is evidently of great use . . . but we cannot say why one offering should be a lamb whilst another is a ram, and why a fixed number of these should be brought. Those who trouble themselves to find a cause for any of these detailed rules are in my eyes devoid of sense. . . .

. . .

Any interpretations will fail which take the Do-nots of the Old Testament in piecemeal fashion. The only sound approach is to forget hygiene, aesthetics, morals and instinctive revulsion, even to forget the Canaanites and the Zoroastrian Magi, and start with the texts. Since each of the injunctions is prefaced by the command to be holy, so they must be explained by that command. There must be contrariness between holiness and abomination which will make over-all sense of all the particular restrictions.

Holiness is the attribute of Godhead. Its root means "set apart." What else does it mean? We should start any cosmological enquiry by seeking the principles of power and danger. In the Old Testament we find blessing as the source of all good things, and the withdrawal of blessing as the source of all dangers. The blessing of God makes the land possible for men to live in.

God's work through the blessing is essentially to create order, through which men's affairs prosper. Fertility of women, livestock and fields is promised as a result of the blessing and this is to be obtained by keeping covenant with God and observing all His precepts and ceremonies (Deut. XXVIII, 1–14). Where the blessing is withdrawn and the power of the curse unleashed, there is barrenness, pestilence, confusion. For Moses said:

But if you will not obey the voice of the Lord your God or be careful to do all his commandments and his statutes which I command you to this day, then all these curses shall come upon you and overtake you....
(Deut. XXVIII, 15–24)

From this it is clear that the positive and negative precepts are held to be efficacious and not merely expressive: observing them draws down prosperity, infringing them brings danger. We are thus entitled to treat them in the same way as we treat primitive ritual avoidances whose breach unleashes danger to men. The precepts and ceremonies alike are focussed on the idea of the holiness of God which men must create in their own lives. So this is a universe in which men prosper by conforming to holiness and perish when they deviate from it. If there were no other clues we should be able to find out the Hebrew idea of the holy by examining the precepts by which men conform to it. It is evidently not goodness in the sense of an all-embracing humane kindness. Justice and moral goodness may well illustrate holiness and form part of it, but holiness embraces other ideas as well.

Granted that its root means separateness, the next idea that emerges is of the Holy as wholeness and completeness. Much of Leviticus is taken up with stating the physical perfection that is required of things presented in the temple and of persons approaching it. The animals offered in sacrifice must be without blemish, women must be purified after childbirth, lepers should be separated and ritually cleansed before being allowed to approach it once they are cured. All bodily discharges are defiling and disqualify from approach to the temple. Priests may only come into contact with death when their own close kin die. But the high priest must never have contact with death.

He must be perfect as a man, if he is to be a priest.

This much reiterated idea of physical completeness is also worked out in the social sphere and particularly in the warriors' camp. The culture of the Israelites was brought to the pitch of greatest intensity when they prayed and when they fought. The army could not win without the blessing and to keep the blessing in the camp they had to be specially holy. So the camp was to be preserved from defilement like the Temple. Here again all bodily discharges disqualified a man from entering the camp as they would disqualify a worshipper from approaching the altar. A warrior who had had an issue of the body in the night should keep outside the camp all day and only return after sunset, having washed. Natural functions producing bodily waste were to be performed outside the camp (Deut. XXIII, 10–15). In short the idea of holiness was given an external, physical expression in the wholeness of the body seen as a perfect container.

. . .

Other precepts develop the idea of wholeness in another direction. The metaphors of the physical body and of the new undertaking relate to the perfection and completeness of the individual and his work. Other precepts extend holiness to species and categories. Hybrids and other confusions are abominated.

LEV. XVIII
23. *And you shall not lie with any beast and defile yourself with it, neither shall any woman give herself to a beast to lie with it: it is perversion,*

The word "perversion" is a significant mistranslation of the rare Hebrew word *tebhel*, which has as its meaning mixing or confusion. The same theme is taken up in Leviticus XIX, 19.

You shall keep my statutes. You shall not let your cattle breed with a different kind; you shall not sow your field with two kinds of seed; nor shall there come upon you a garment of cloth made of two kinds of stuff.

All these injunctions are prefaced by the general command:

Be holy, for I am holy.

We can conclude that holiness is exemplified by completeness. Holiness requires that individuals shall conform to the class to which they belong. And holiness requires that different classes of things shall not be confused.

Another set of precepts refines on this last point. Holiness means keeping distinct the categories of creation. It therefore involves correct definition, discrimination and order. Under this head all the rules of sexual morality exemplify the holy. Incest and adultery (Lev. XVIII, 6–20) are against holiness, in the s mple sense of right order. Morality does not conflict with holiness, but holiness is more a matter of separating that which should be separated than of protecting the rights of husbands and brothers.

Then follows in Chapter XIX another list of actions which are contrary to holiness. Developing the idea of holine s as order, not confusion, this list upholds rectitude and straight-dealing as holy, and contradiction and double-dealing as against h liness. Theft, lying, false witness, cheating in veights and measures, all kinds of dissembling such as speaking ill of the deaf (and presumably smiling to their face), hating your brother in your heart (while presumably speaking kindly to him), these are clearly contradictions between what seems and what is. This chapter also says much about generosity and love, but these are positive commands, while I am concerned with negative rules.

We have now laid a good basis for approaching the laws about clean and unclean meats. To be holy is to be whole, to be one; holiness is unity, integrity, perfection of the individual and of the kind. The dietary rules merely develop the metaphor of holiness on the same lines.

First we should start with livestock, the herds of cattle, camels, sheep and goats which were the livelihood of the Israelites. These animals were clean inasmuch as contact with them did not require purification before approaching the Temple. Livestock, like the inhabited land, received the blessing of God. Both land and livestock were fertile by the blessing, both were drawn into the divine order. The farmer's duty was to preserve the blessing. For one thing, he had to preserve the order of creation. So no hybrids, as we have seen, either in the fields or in the herds or in the clothes made from wool or flax. To some extent men covenanted with their land and cattle in the same way as God covenanted with them. Men respected the first born of their cattle, obliged them to keep the Sabbath. Cattle were literally domesticated as slaves. They had to be brought into the social order in order to enjoy the blessing. The difference between cattle and the wild beasts is that the wild beasts have no covenant to protect them. It is possible that the Israelites were like other pastoralists who do not relish wild game. The Nuer of the South Sudan, for instance, apply a sanction of disapproval of a man who lives by hunting. To be driven to eating wild meat is the sign of a poor herdsman. So it would be probably wrong to think of the Israelites as longing for forbidden meats and finding the restrictions irksome. Driver is surely right in taking the rules as an *a posteriori* generalisation of their habits. Cloven hoofed, cud chewing ungulates are the model of the proper kind of food for a pastoralist. If they must eat wild game, they can eat wild game that shares these distinctive characters and is tnerefore of the same general species. This is a kind of casuistry which permits scope for hunting antelope and wild goats and wild sheep. Everything would be quite straightforward were it not that the legal mind has seen fit to give ruling on some borderline cases. Some animals seem to be ruminant, such as the hare and the hyrax (or rock badger), whose constant grinding of their teeth was held to be cud-chewing. But they are definitely not cloven-hoofed and so are excluded by name. Similarly for animals which are cloven-hoofed but are not ruminant, the pig and the camel. Note that this failure to conform to the two necessary criteria for defining cattle is the only reason given in the Old Testament for avoiding the pig; nothing whatever is said about its dirty scavenging habits. As the pig does not yield milk, hide nor wool, there is no other reason for keeping it except for its flesh. And if the Israelites did not keep pig they would not be familiar with its habits. I suggest that originally the sole reason for its being counted as unclean is its failure as a wild boar to get into the antelope class, and that in this it is on the same footing as the camel and the hyrax, exactly as is stated in the book.

After these borderline cases have been dismissed, the law goes on to deal with creatures according to how they live in the three elements, the water, the air and the earth. The principles here applied are rather different from those covering the camel, the pig, the hare and the hyrax. For the latter are excepted from clean food in having one but not both of the defining characters of livestock. Birds I can say nothing about, because, as I have said, they are named and not described and the translation of the name is open to doubt. But in general the underlying principle of cleanness in animals is that they shall conform fully to their class. Those species are unclean which are imperfect members of their class, or whose class itself confounds the general scheme of the world.

To grasp this scheme we need to go back to Genesis and the creation. Here a three-fold classification unfolds, divided between the earth, the waters and the firmament. Leviticus takes up this scheme and allots to each element its proper kind of animal life. In the firmament two-legged fowls fly with wings. In the water scaly fish swim with fins. On the earth four-legged animals hop, jump or walk. Any class of creatures which is not equipped for the right kind of locomotion in its element is contrary to holiness. Contact with it disqualifies a person from approaching the Temple. Thus anything in the water which has not fins and scales is unclean (XI, 10–12). Nothing is said about predatory habits or of scavenging. The only sure test for cleanness in a fish is its scales and its propulsion by means of fins.

Four-footed creatures which fly (XI, 20–26) are unclean. Any creature which has two legs and two hands and which goes on all fours like a quadruped is unclean (XI, 27). Then follows (v. 29) a much disputed list. On some translations, it would appear to consist precisely of creatures endowed with hands instead of front feet, which perversely use their hands for walking: the weasel, the mouse, the crocodile, the shrew, various kinds of lizards, the chameleon and mole (Danby, 1933), whose forefeet are uncannily hand-like. This feature of this list is lost in the New Revised Standard Translation which used the word "paws" instead of hands.

The last kind of unclean animal is that which creeps, crawls or swarms upon the earth. This form of movement is explicitly contrary to holiness (Lev. XI, 41–44). Driver and White use "swarming" to translate the Hebrew *shérec*, which is applied to both those which teem in the waters and those which swarm on the ground. Whether we call it teeming, trailing, creeping, crawling or swarming, it is an indeterminate form of movement. Since the main animal categories are defined by their typical movement, "swarming" which is not a mode of propulsion proper to any particular element, cuts across the basic classification. Swarming

things are neither fish, flesh nor fowl. Eels and worms inhabit water, though not as fish; reptiles go on dry land, though not as quadrupeds; some insects fly, though not as birds. There is no order in them. Recall what the Prophecy of Habacuc says about this form of life:

For thou makest men like the fish of the sea, like crawling things that have no ruler. (I, v.14)

The prototype and model of the swarming things is the worm. As fish belong in the sea so worms belong in the realm of the grave, with death and chaos.

The case of the locusts is interesting and consistent. The test of whether it is a clean and therefore edible kind is how it moves on the earth. If it crawls it is unclean. If it hops it is clean (XI, v. 21). In the Mishnah it is noted that a frog is not listed with creeping things and conveys no uncleanness (Danby, p. 722). I suggest that the frog's hop accounts for it not being listed. If penguins lived in the Near East I would expect them to be ruled unclean as wingless birds. If the list of unclean birds could be retranslated from this point of view, it might well turn out that they are anomalous because they swim and dive as well as they fly, or in some other way they are not fully bird-like.

Surely now it would be difficult to maintain that "Be ye Holy" means no more than "Be ye separate." Moses wanted the children of Israel to keep the commands of God constantly before their minds:

DEUT. XI
18. *You shall therefore lay up these words of mine in your heart and in your soul; and you shall bind them as a sign upon your hand, and they shall be as frontlets between your eyes.*
19. *And you shall teach them to your children, talking of them when you are sitting in your house, and when you are walking by the way, and when you lie down and when you rise.*
20. *And you shall write them upon the doorposts of your house and upon your gates.*

If the proposed interpretation of the forbidden animals is correct, the dietary laws would have been like signs which at every turn inspired meditation on the oneness, purity and completeness of God. By rules of avoidance holiness was given a physical expression in every encounter with the animal kingdom and at every meal. Observance of the dietary rules would thus have been a meaningful part of the great liturgical act of recognition and worship which culminated in the sacrifice in the Temple.

Edmund R. Leach

ANTHROPOLOGICAL ASPECTS OF LANGUAGE: ANIMAL CATEGORIES AND VERBAL ABUSE

Nature is, by nature, undifferentiated and unclassified. It is man who, in his social behavior and his language, distinguishes fish from fowl, man from god. In this ingenious article, Edmund Leach expands Mary Douglas's hypothesis that human classificatory systems depend not only on our matching names and things, but in avoiding or tabooing those things which fall on the boundaries between categories or names. Thus, Leach argues, we eat fish, birds, and beasts—inhabitants of water, air, and land—but avoid reptiles which live on land and sea, or insects, which move between land and air. Eating prohibitions enforce a simplified, disjunctive classification of natural things. Further, he suggests, the reason we refuse to consider dogs edible is that, in our society, dogs are too much like men. By avoiding dog meat, we enforce a cultural rule which forbids men to eat men. And, in our horror at the accusation "you're a bitch"—but not, "you're a polar bear"—we provide further evidence to the notion that ambivalent entities have a potency which may be manipulated (and worshiped) as well as feared. The argument introduces an additional complexity, however, in taking into account the fact that neither the tabooed nor the sacred is of a piece. If dogs are inedible, pigs are edible if castrated, deer edible (in season), and lions and tigers are not eaten at all: these degrees of taboo, or sacredness, correspond to the relative distance of animals from a postulated SELF. These same degrees are paralleled in the social classification of unmarriageable close kin, "kissing cousins," marriageable neighbors, and unmarriageable strangers. Sex and eating are symbolically associated in many cultures; here Leach is suggesting that, rather than simple binary oppositions, complex systems of social classification provide a model for both dietary and sexual taboos.

Reprinted from *New Directions in the Study of Language* by Eric H. Lenneberg (1964, pp. 23–63) by permission of the M.I.T. Press, Cambridge, Massachusetts. Copyright © 1964 by The Massachusetts Institute of Technology.

The central theme of my essay is the classical anthropological topic of "taboo." This theme, in this guise, does not form part of the conventional field of discourse of experimental psychologists; yet the argument that I shall present has its psychological equivalents. When psychologists debate about the mechanism of "forgetting" they often introduce the concept of "interference," the idea that there is a tendency to repress concepts that have some kind of semantic overlap (Postman, 1961). The thesis which I present depends upon a converse hypothesis, namely, that we can only arrive at semantically distinct verbal concepts if we repress the boundary percepts that lie between them.

To discuss the anthropological aspect of language within the confines of space allotted to me here is like writing a history of England in thirty lines. I propose to tackle a specific theme, not a general one. For the anthropologist, language is a part of culture, not a thing in itself. Most of the anthropologist's problems are concerned with human communication. Language is one means of communication, but customary acts of behavior are also a means of communication, and the anthropologist feels that he can, and should, keep both modes of communication in view at the same time.

LANGUAGE AND TABOO

This is a symposium about language but my theme is one of nonlanguage. Instead of discussing things that are said and done, I want to talk about things that are not said and done. My theme is that of taboo, expression which is inhibited.

Anthropological and psychological literature alike are crammed with descriptions and learned explanations of apparently irrational prohibitions and inhibitions. Such "taboo" may be either behavioral or linguistic, and it deserves note that the protective sanctions are very much the same in either case. If at this moment I were really anxious to get arrested by the police, I might strip naked or launch into a string of violent obscenities: either procedure would be equally effective.

Linguistic taboos and behavioral taboos are not only sanctioned in the same way, they are very much muddled up: sex behavior and sex words, for example. But this association of deed and word is not so simple as might appear. The relationship is not necessarily causal. It is not the case that certain kinds of behavior are taboo and that, therefore, the language relating to such behavior becomes taboo. Sometimes words may be taboo in themselves for linguistic (phonemic) reasons, and the causal link, if any, is then reversed; a behavioral taboo comes to reflect a prior verbal taboo. In this paper I shall only touch upon the fringe of this complex subject.

A familiar type of purely linguistic taboo is the pun. A pun occurs when we make a joke by confusing two apparently different meanings of the same phonemic pattern. The pun seems funny or shocking because it challenges a taboo which ordinarily forbids us to recognize that the sound pattern is ambiguous. In many cases such verbal taboos have social as well as linguistic aspects. In English, though not I think in American, the word *queen* has a homonym *quean*. The words are phonetically indistinguishable (KWĪN). Queen is the consort of King or even a female sovereign in her own right; quean which formerly meant a prostitute now usually denotes a homosexual male. In the non-human world we have queen bees and brood queen cats, both indicating a splendid fertility, but a quean is a barren cow. Although these two words pretend to be different, indeed opposites, they really denote the same idea. A queen is a female of abnormal status in a positive virtuous sense; a quean is a person of depraved character or uncertain sex, a female of abnormal status in a negative sinful sense. Yet their common abnormality turns both into "supernatural" beings; so also, in metaphysics, the contraries God and the Devil are both supernatural beings. In this case, then, the taboo which allows us to separate the two ambiguous concepts, so that we can talk of queens without thinking of queans, and vice versa, is simultaneously both linguistic *and* social.

We should note that the taboo operates so as to distinguish two identical phonemic patterns; it does not operate so as to suppress the pattern altogether. We are not inhibited from saying KWĪN. Yet the very similar phonemic pattern produced by shifting the dental N to bilabial M and shortening the medial vowel (KWĬM) is one of the most unprintable obscenities in the English language. Some American informants have assured me that this word has been so thoroughly suppressed that it has not crossed the Atlantic at all, but this does not seem entirely correct as there is dictionary evidence to the contrary.[1] It is hard to talk about the unsayable but I hope I have made my initial point. Taboo is simultaneously both behavioral and linguistic, both social and psychological. As an anthropologist, I am particularly concerned with the social aspects of taboo. Analytical psychologists of various schools are particularly concerned with the individual taboos which center in the oral, anal, and genital functions. Experimental psychologists may concern themselves with essentially the same kind of phenomenon when they examine the process of forgetting, or various kinds of muscular inhibition. But all these varieties of repression are so meshed into the web of language that discussion of any one of three frames, anthropological, psychological, or linguistic, must inevitably lead on to some consideration of the other two.

ANIMAL CATEGORIES AND VERBAL OBSCENITIES

In the rest of this paper I shall have relatively little to say about language in a direct sense, but this is because of the nature of my problem. I shall be discussing the connection between animal categories and verbal obscenities. Plainly it is much easier to talk about the animals than about the obscenities! The latter will mostly be just off stage.

[1] The Oxford English Dictionary says nothing of the obscenity but records *Quim* as a "late Scottish variant" of the now wholly obsolete *Queme* = "pleasant." Partridge (1949) prints the word in full (whereas he balks at f*ck and c*nt). His gloss is "the female pudend" and he gives *queme* as a variant. Funk and Wagnalls, and Webster, latest editions, both ignore the term, but H. Wentworth and S. B. Flexner (1961) give: *quim* n. 1 = queen; 2 (taboo) = the vagina. That this phonemic pattern is, in fact penumbral to the more permissible *queen* is thus established.

The American dictionaries indicate that the range of meanings of *queen* (*quean*) are the same as in England, but the distinction of spelling is not firmly maintained.

But the hearer (and the reader) should keep his wits about him. Just as queen is dangerously close to the unsayable, so also there are certain very familiar animals which are, as it were, only saved by a phoneme from sacrilege or worse. In seventeenth century English witchcraft trials it was very commonly asserted that the Devil appeared in the form of a Dog—that is, God backwards. In England we still employ this same metathesis when we refer to a clergyman's collar as a "dog collar" instead of a "God collar." So also it needs only a slight vowel shift in *fox* to produce the obscene *fux*. No doubt there is a sense in which such facts as these can be deemed linguistic accidents, but they are accidents which have a functional utility in the way we use our language. As I shall show presently, there are good sociological reasons why the English categories *dog* and *fox*, like the English category *queen* (*quean*), should evoke taboo associations in their phonemic vicinity.

As an anthropologist I do not profess to understand the psychological aspects of the taboo phenomenon. I do not understand what happens when a word or a phrase or a detail of behavior is subject to repression. But I can observe what happens. In particular I can observe that when verbal taboos are broken the result is a specific social phenomenon which affects both the actor and his hearers in a specific describable way. I need not elaborate. This phenomenon is what we mean by obscenity. Broadly speaking, the language of obscenity falls into three categories: (1) dirty words—usually referring to sex and excretion; (2) blasphemy and profanity; (3) animal abuse—in which a human being is equated with an animal of another species.

These categories are not in practice sharply distinguished. Thus the word "bloody," which is now a kind of all-purpose mildly obscene adjective, is felt by some to be associated with menstrual blood and is thus a "dirty" word, but it seems to be historically derived from profanity—"By our Lady." On the other hand, the simple expletive "damn!" —now presumed to be short for "damnation!"—and thus a profanity—was formerly "goddam" (God's animal mother) an expression combining blasphemy with animal abuse. These broad categories of obscenity seem to occur in most languages.

The dirty words present no problem. Psychologists have adequate and persuasive

explanations of why the central focus or the crudest obscenity should ordinarily lie in sex and excretion. The language of profanity and blasphemy also presents no problem. Any theory about the sacredness of supernatural beings is likely to imply a concept of sacrilege which in turn explains the emotions aroused by profanity and blasphemy. But animal abuse seems much less easily accounted for. Why should expressions like "you son of a bitch" or "you swine" carry the connotations that they do, when "you son of a kangaroo" or "you polar bear" have no meaning whatever?

I write as an anthropologist, and for an anthropologist this theme of animal abuse has a very basic interest. When an animal name is used in this way as an imprecation, it indicates that the name itself is credited with potency. It clearly signifies that the animal category is in some way taboo and sacred. Thus, for an anthropologist, animal abuse is part of a wide field of study which includes animal sacrifice and totemism.

RELATION OF EDIBILITY AND SOCIAL VALUATION OF ANIMALS

In his ethnographic studies the anthropologist observes that, in any particular cultural situation, some animals are the focus of ritual attitudes whereas others are not; moreover, the intensity of the ritual involvement of individual species varies greatly. It is never at all obvious why this should be so, but one fact that is commonly relevant and always needs to be taken into consideration is the edibility of the species in question.

One hypothesis which underlies the rest of this paper is that animal abuse is in some way linked with what Radcliffe-Brown called the ritual value of the animal category concerned. I further assume that this ritual value is linked in some as yet undetermined way with taboos and rules concerning the killing and eating of these and other animals. For the purposes of illustration, I shall confine my attention to categories of the English language. I postulate, however, that the principles which I adduce are very general, though not necessarily universal. In illustration of this, I discuss as an appendix to my main argument the application of my thesis to categories of the Kachin language spoken by certain highland groups in northeast Burma.

Taboo is not a genuine English word, but a category imported from Polynesia. Its meaning is not precisely defined in conventional

English usage. Anthropologists commonly use it to refer to prohibitions which are explicit and which are supported by feelings of sin and supernatural sanction at a conscious level; incest regulations provide a typical example; the rules recorded in Leviticus XI, verses 4–47, which prohibited the Israelites from eating a wide variety of "unclean beasts," are another. In this paper, however, I shall use the concept of food taboo in a more general sense, so that it covers all classes of food prohibition, explicit and implicit, conscious and unconscious.

CULTURAL AND LINGUISTIC DETERMINATION OF FOOD VALUES

The physical environment of any human society contains a vast range of materials which are both edible and nourishing, but, in most cases, only a small part of this edible environment will actually be classified as potential food. Such classification is a matter of language and culture, not of nature. It is a classification that is of great practical importance, and it is felt to be so. *Our* classification is not only correct, it is morally right and a mark of our superiority. The fact that frogs' legs are a gourmet's delicacy in France but not food at all in England provokes the English to refer to Frenchmen as Frogs with implications of withering contempt.

As a consequence of such cultural discriminations, the edible part of the environment usually falls into three main categories:

1. Edible substances that are recognized as food and consumed as part of the normal diet.
2. Edible substances that are recognized as possible food, but that are prohibited or else allowed to be eaten only under special (ritual) conditions. These are substances which are *consciously tabooed.*
3. Edible substances that by culture and language are not recognized as food at all. The substances are *unconsciously tabooed.*

Now in the ordinary way when anthropologists discuss food taboos they are thinking only of my second category; they have in mind such examples as the Jewish prohibitions against pork, the Brahmin prohibition against beef, the Christian attitude to sacramental bread and wine. But my third category of edible substances that are not classed as food deserves equal attention. The nature of the taboo in the two cases is quite distinct. The Jewish prohibition against pork is a ritual matter and explicit. It says, in effect, "pork is a food, but Jews must not eat it." The Englishman's objection to eating dog is quite as strong but rests on a different premise. It depends on a categorical assumption: "dog is not food."

In actual fact, of course, dogs are perfectly edible, and in some parts of the world they are bred for eating. For that matter human beings are edible, though to an Englishman the very thought is disgusting. I think most Englishmen would find the idea of eating dog equally disgusting and in a similar way I believe that this latter disgust is largely a matter of verbal categories. There are contexts in colloquial English in which man and dog may be thought of as beings of the same kind. Man and dog are "companions"; the dog is "the friend of man." On the other hand man and food are antithetical categories. Man is not food, so dog cannot be food either.

Of course our linguistic categories are not always tidy and logical, but the marginal cases, which at first appear as exceptions to some general rule, are often especially interesting. For example, the French eat horse. In England, although horsemeat may be fed to dogs, it is officially classed as unfit for human consumption. Horsemeat may not be sold in the same shop that handles ordinary butchers' meat, and in London where, despite English prejudice, there are low foreigners who actually eat the stuff, they must buy it in a shop labeled *charcuterie* and not *butcher!* This I suggest is quite consistent with the very special attitude which Englishmen adopt toward both dogs and horses. Both are sacred supernatural creatures surrounded by feelings that are ambiguously those of awe and horror. This kind of attitude is comparable to a less familiar but much more improbable statutory rule which lays down that Swan and Sturgeon may only be eaten by members of the Royal Family, except once a year when Swan may be eaten by the members of St. John's College, Cambridge! As the Editor of *The New Yorker* is fond of telling us, "There will always be an England!"

Plainly all such rules, prejudices, and conventions are of social origin; yet the social taboos have their linguistic counterparts and, as I shall presently show, these accidents of etymological history fit together in a quite surprising way. Certainly in its linguistic aspects horse looks innocent enough, but so do dog and fox. However, in most English colloquial, horse is 'orse or 'oss and in this form it shares with its companion *ass* an uncomfortable approximation to the human posterior.[2]

The problem then is this. The English treat certain animals as taboo—sacred. This sacredness is manifested in various ways, partly behavioral, as when we are forbidden to eat flesh of the animal concerned, partly linguistic, as when a phonemic pattern penumbral to that of the animal category itself is found to be a focus of obscenity, profanity, etc. Can we get any insight into why certain creatures should be treated this way?

TABOO AND THE DISTINCTIVENESS OF NAMABLE CATEGORIES

Before I proceed further, let me give you an outline of a general theory of taboo which I find particularly satisfactory in my work as an anthropologist. It is a theory which seems to me to fit in well with the psychological and linguistic facts. In the form in which I present it here, it is a "Leach theory" but it has several obvious derivations, especially Radcliffe-Brown's discussions of ritual value, Mary Douglas's thinking (still largely unpublished) on anomalous animals, and Lévi-Strauss's version of the Hegelian–Marxist dialectic in which the sacred elements of myth are shown to be factors that mediate contradictories.

I postulate that the physical and social environment of a young child is perceived as a continuum. It does not contain any intrinsically separate "things." The child, in due course, is taught to impose upon this environment a kind of discriminating grid which serves to distinguish the world as being composed of a large number of separate things, each labeled with a name. This world is a representation of our language categories, not vice versa. Because my mother tongue is English, it seems self evident that *bushes* and *trees* are different kinds of things. I would not think this unless I had been taught that it was the case.

Now if each individual has to learn to construct his own environment in this way,

it is crucially important that the basic discriminations should be clear-cut and unambiguous. There must be absolutely no doubt about the difference between *me* and *it*, or between *we* and *they*. But how can such certainty of discrimination be achieved if our normal perception displays only a continuum? A diagram may help. Our uninhibited (untrained) perception recognizes a continuum (Figure 1).

FIGURE 1

The line is a schematic representation of continuity in nature. There are no gaps in the physical world.

We are taught that the world consists of "things" distinguished by names; therefore we have to train our perception to recognize a discontinuous environment (Figure 2).

FIGURE 2

Schematic representation of what is named. Many aspects of the physical world remain unnamed in natural languages.

We achieve this second kind of trained perception by means of a simultaneous use of language and taboo. Language gives us the names to distinguish the things; taboo inhibits the recognition of those parts of the continuum which separate the things (Figure 3).

The same kind of argument may also be represented by a simplified Venn diagram employing two circles only. Let there be a circle p representing a particular verbal category. Let this be intersected by another circle $\sim p$ representing the "environment" of p, from which it is desired to distinguish p. If by a fiction we impose a taboo upon any consideration of the overlap area that is common to both circles, then we shall be able to persuade ourselves that p and $\sim p$ are wholly distinct, and the logic of binary

---

[2] English and American taboos are different. The English spell the animal *ass* and the buttocks *arse* but, according to Partridge (1949), *arse* was considered almost unprintable between 1700 and 1930 (though it appears in the O.E.D.). Webster's Third Edition spells both words as *ass*, noting that *arse* is a more polite variant of the latter word, which also has the obscene meaning, sexual intercourse. Funk and Wagnalls (1952) distinguish *ass* (animal) and *arse* (buttocks) and do not cross reference. Wentworth and Flexner (1961) give only *ass* but give three taboo meanings, the rectum, the buttocks, and the vagina.

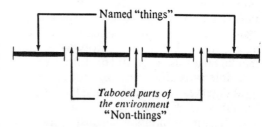

FIGURE 3

The relationship of tabooed objects to the world of names.

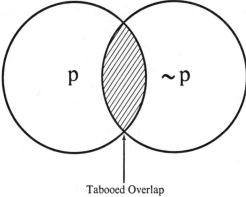

Tabooed Overlap
"both p and ~ p"

FIGURE 4
The relationship between ambiguity and taboo.

discrimination will be satisfied (Figure 4).

Language then does more than provide us with a classification of things; it actually molds our environment; it places each individual at the center of a social space which is ordered in a logical and reassuring way.

In this paper I shall be specially concerned with verbal category sets which discriminate areas of social space in terms of "distance from Ego (self)." For example, consider the three sets (a), (b), (c).

(a) Self · · Sister · · Cousin · · Neighbor · · Stranger
(b) Self · · House · · Farm · · Field · · Far (Remote)
(c) Self · · Pet · · Livestock · · "Game" · · Wild Animal

For each of these three sets, the words, thus arranged, indicate categories that are progressively more remote from Self, but I believe that there is more to it than that. I hope to be able to show that, if we denote these word sets as

(a) A1 B1 C1 D1 E1
(b) A2 B2 C2 D2 E2
(c) A3 B3 C3 D3 E3

then the relational statement A1:B1:C1:D1:E1 is the same as the relational statement A2:B2:C2:D2:E2 or the relational statement A3:B3:C3:D3:E3. In other words, the way we employ the words in set (c), a set of animals, allows us to make statements about the human relationships which belong to set (a).

But I am going too fast. Let us go back to my theory of taboo. If we operate in the way I have suggested, so that we are only able to perceive the environment as composed of separate things by suppressing our recognition of the nonthings which fill the interstices, then of course what is suppressed becomes

especially interesting. Quite apart from the fact that all scientific enquiry is devoted to "discovering" those parts of the environment that lie on the borders of what is "already known," we have the phenomenon, which is variously described by anthropologists and psychologists, in which whatever is taboo is a focus not only of special interest but also of anxiety. Whatever is taboo is sacred, valuable, important, powerful, dangerous, untouchable, filthy, unmentionable.

I can illustrate my point by mentioning diametrically contrasted areas where this approach to taboo fits in well with the observable facts. First, the exudations of the human body are universally the objects of intense taboo—in particular, feces, urine, semen, menstrual blood, hair clippings, nail parings, body dirt, spittle, mother's milk.[3] This fits the theory. Such substances are ambiguous in the most fundamental way. The child's first and continuing problem is to determine the initial boundary. "What am I, as against the world?" "Where is the edge of me?" In this fundamental sense, feces, urine, semen, and so forth, are both me and not me. So strong is the resulting taboo that, even as an adult addressing an adult audience, I cannot refer to these substances by the monosyllabic words which I used as a child but must mention them only in Latin. But let us be clear, it is not simply that these substances are felt to be dirty—they are powerful; throughout the world it is precisely such substances that are the prime ingredients of magical "medicines."

At the opposite extreme, consider the case of the sanctity of supernatural beings. Religious belief is everywhere tied in with the discrimination between living and dead. Logically, *life* is simply the binary antithesis of *death*; the two concepts are the opposite sides of the same penny; we cannot have either without the other. But religion always tries to separate the two. To do this it creates a hypothetical "other world" which is the antithesis of "this world." In this world life and death are inseparable; in the other world they are separate. This world is inhabited by imperfect mortal men; the other world is inhabited by immortal nonmen (gods). The category god is thus constructed as the binary

---

[3] An interesting and seemingly unique partial exception to this catalogue is "tears." Tears can acquire sacredness, in that the tears of Saints have been turned into relics and tears are proper at sacred situations, e.g., funerals, but tears are not, I think, felt to be dirty or contaminating after the manner of other exudations.

antithesis of man. But this is inconvenient. A remote god in another world may be logically sensible, but it is emotionally unsatisfying. To be useful, gods must be near at hand, so religion sets about reconstructing a continuum between this world and the other world. But note how it is done. The gap between the two logically distinct categories, this world/other world, is filled in with tabooed ambiguity. The gap is bridged by supernatural beings of a highly ambiguous kind—incarnate deities, virgin mothers, supernatural monsters which are half man/half beast. These marginal, ambiguous creatures are specifically credited with the power of mediating between gods and men. They are the object of the most intense taboos, more sacred than the gods themselves. In an objective sense, as distinct from theoretical theology, it is the Virgin Mary, human mother of God, who is the principal object of devotion in the Catholic church.

So here again it is the ambiguous categories that attract the maximum interest and the most intense feelings of taboo. The general theory is that taboo applies to categories which are anomalous with respect to clear-cut category oppositions. If A and B are two verbal categories, such that B is defined as "what A is not" and vice versa, and there is a third category C which mediates this distinction, in that C shares attributes of both A and B, then C will be taboo.

But now let us return to a consideration of English animal categories and food taboos.

ANIMAL AND FOOD NAMES IN ENGLISH

How do we speakers of English classify animals, and how is this classification related to the matters of killing and eating and verbal abuse?

The basic discrimination seems to rest in three words:

Fish creatures that live in water. A very elastic category, it includes even crustacea—"shell fish."

Birds two-legged creatures with wings which lay eggs. (They do not necessarily fly, e.g., penguins, ostriches.)

Beasts four-legged mammals living on land.

Consider Table 1. All creatures that are edible are fish or birds or beasts. There is a large residue of creatures, rated as either *reptiles* or *insects*, but the whole of this ambiguous residue is rated as not food. All reptiles and insects seem to be thought of as

evil enemies of mankind and liable to the most ruthless extermination. Only the bee is an exception here, and significantly the bee is often credited with quite superhuman powers of intelligence and organization. The hostile taboo is applied most strongly to creatures that are most anomalous in respect of the major categories, e.g., snakes—land animals with no legs which lay eggs.

The fact that birds and beasts are warm-blooded and that they engage in sexual intercourse in a "normal" way makes them to some extent akin to man. This is shown by the fact that the concept of *cruelty* is applicable to birds and beasts but not to fish. The slaughter of farm animals for food must be carried out by "humane" methods;[4] in England we even have humane rat traps! But it is quite proper to kill a lobster by dropping it alive into boiling water. Where religious food taboos apply, they affect only the warm-blooded, near human, meat of birds and beasts; hence Catholics may eat fish on Fridays. In England the only common fish subject to killing and eating restrictions is the salmon. This is an anomalous fish in at least two respects; it is red-blooded and it is simultaneously both a sea fish and a fresh water fish. But the mammalian *beasts* are much closer to man than the egg-laying *birds*. The Society for the Prevention of Cruelty to Animals, the Anti-Vivisection Society, Our Dumb Friends League and such organizations devote most of their attention to four-footed creatures, and as time is short I shall do the same.

STRUCTURE OF FOOD AND KINSHIP TERMINOLOGIES

Anthropologists have noted again and again that there is a universal tendency to make ritual and verbal associations between eating and sexual intercourse. It is thus a plausible hypothesis that the way in which animals are categorized with regard to edibility will have some correspondence to the way in which human beings are categorized with regard to sex relations.

Upon this matter the anthropologists have assembled a vast amount of comparative data. The following generalization is certainly not a universal, but it has a very wide general validity. From the point of view of any male SELF, the young women of his social world will fall into four major classes:

[4] The word *humane* has become distinguished from *human* only since the 17th century.

TABLE 1. ENGLISH LANGUAGE DISCRIMINATIONS OF LIVING CREATURES

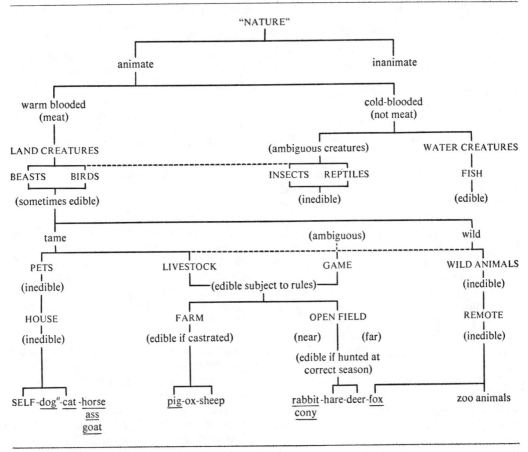

ª The species underlined on the bottom line are those which appear to be specially loaded with taboo values, as indicated by their use in obscenity and abuse or by metaphysical associations or by the intrusion of euphemism.

1. Those who are very close—"true sisters," always a strongly incestuous category.
2. Those who are kin but not very close—"first cousins" in English society, "clan sisters" in many types of systems having unilineal descent and a segmentary lineage organization. As a rule, marriage with this category is either prohibited or strongly disapproved, but premarital sex relations may be tolerated or even expected.
3. Neighbors (friends) who are not kin, potential affines. This is the category from which SELF will ordinarily expect to obtain a wife. This category contains also potential enemies, friendship and enmity being alternating aspects of the same structural relationship.
4. Distant strangers—who are known to exist but with whom no social relations of any kind are possible.

Now the English put most of their animals into four very comparable categories:

1. Those who are very close—"pets," always strongly inedible.
2. Those who are tame but not very close—"farm animals," mostly edible but only if immature or castrated. We seldom eat a sexually intact, mature farm beast.[5]
3. Field animals, "game"—a category toward which we alternate friendship and hostility. Game animals live under human protection but they are not tame. They are edible in sexually intact form, but are killed only at set seasons of the year in accordance with set hunting rituals.
4. Remote wild animals—not subject to human control, inedible.

[5] Two reasons are usually offered for castrating farm animals. The first, which is valid, is that the castrated animal is more amenable to handling. The second, which I am assured is scientifically invalid, is that a castrated animal produces more succulent meat in a shorter time.

Thus presented, there appears to be a set of equivalents

incest prohibition	inedible
marriage prohibition coupled with premarital sex relations	castration coupled with edibility
marriage alliance, friend/enemy ambiguity	edible in sexually intact form; alternating friendship/hostility
no sex relations with remote strangers	remote wild animals are inedible

That this correspondence between the categories of sexual accessibility and the categories of edibility is rather more than just an accident is shown by a further accident of a linguistic kind. The archaic legal expression for game was beasts of venery. The term venery had the alternative meanings, hunting and sexual indulgence.

A similar accident yields the phonemic resemblance between *venery* and *venerate* which is reminiscent of that between *quean* and *queen*. Sex and authority are both sources of taboo (respect) but in contrary senses.

A fifth major category of English animals which cuts across the others, and is significantly taboo-loaded, is vermin. The dictionary definition of this word is comprehensively ambiguous:

mammals and birds injurious to game, crops, etc.; foxes, weasels, rats, mice, moles, owls, noxious insects, fleas, bugs, lice, parasitic worms, vile persons.

Vermin may also be described as *pests* (i.e., plagues). Although vermin and pests are intrinsically inedible, rabbits and pigeons, which are pests when they attack crops, may also be classed as game and then become edible. The same two species also become edible when kept under restraint as farm animals. I shall have more to say about rabbits presently.

Before we go further, let me review the latest part of my argument in rather different form. The thesis is that we make binary distinctions and then mediate the distinction by creating an ambiguous (and taboo-loaded) intermediate category. Thus:

p	both *p* and ~*p*	~*p*
man (not animal)	"man-animal" ("pets")	not man (animal)
TAME (friendly)	GAME (friendly/hostile)	WILD (hostile)

We have already given some indication that ritual value (taboo) attaches in a marked way to the intermediate categories *pets* and *game*, and I shall have more to say about this, but we shall find that even more intense taboo attitudes are revealed when we come to consider creatures which would only fit into the interstices of the above tabulation, e.g., goats, pigs, and horses which are not quite pets, rabbits which are not quite game, and foxes which are wild but treated like game in some respects (see bottom of Table 1).

In Table 2 are listed the more familiar names of the more familiar English animals. These name sets possess certain linguistic characteristics.

Nearly all the house pets, farm, and field (game) animals have monosyllabic names: dog, cat, bull, cow, ox, and so on, whereas among the more remote wild beasts monosyllables are rare. The vocabulary is most elaborated in the farm category and most attenuated in the inedible house-pet and wild-beast categories.

Thus farm animals have separate terms for (1) an intact male, (2) an intact female, (3) a suckling, (4) an immature female, (5) a castrated male (e.g., bull, cow, calf, heifer, bullock, with local variants). This is not surprising in view of the technical requirements of farming, but it seems odd that the pet vocabulary should be so restricted. Thus dog has only: dog, bitch, pup, and of these bitch is largely taboo and seldom used; cat has only: cat, kitten.

If sex discrimination must be made among pets, one can say "bitch" and "tom cat." This implies that a dog is otherwise presumed male and a cat female. Indeed cat and dog are paired terms, and seem to serve as a paradigm for quarreling husband and wife.

Among the field animals all males are *bucks* and all females *does*. Among the wild animals, in a small number of species we distinguish the young as *cubs*. In a smaller number we distinguish the female as a variant of the male: tiger—tigress; lion—lioness; but most are sexless. Fox is a very special case, exceptional in all respects. It is a monosyllable, the male is a *dog*, the female a *vixen*, the young a *cub*. Elephants and some other "zoo animals" are distinguished as bulls, cows, and calves, a direct borrowing from the farm-animal set.

A curious usage suggests that we are ashamed of killing any animal of substantial size. When dead, bullock becomes *beef*, pig

TABLE 2. ENGLISH SUBCATEGORIES OF FAMILIAR ANIMALS

	Female	Male	Infant	Young Male[a]	Young Female[a]	Castrated Male	Baby Language	Carcass Meat
Dog	Bitch		Puppy				Bow wow	
Hound			Whelp				Doggy	
Cat		(Tom)	Kitten				Pussy	
Goat	(Nanny)	(Billy)	Kid				?	(Mutton
Pig	Sow	Boar	Piglet	Hogget[b]	Gilt	Hog[c] Porker	Piggy	Pork, bacon, ham
							Ee-yaw	
Ass								
Horse[d]	Mare	Stallion	Foal	Colt	Filly	Gelding	Gee-gee	
Cow (ox)[e]	Cow	Bull	Calf		Heifer	Steer Bullock	Moo-cow	Veal; beef[f]
Sheep	Ewe	Ram	Lamb	Teg			Baa-lamb	Mutton
Fowl	Hen	Cock	Chick	Cockerel	Pullet	Capon	?	Chicken
Duck	Duck	Drake	Duckling				Quack-quack	
Goose	Goose	Gander	Gosling					
Pigeon			Squab					
Rabbit	Doe	Buck					Bunny	
Hare	Doe	Buck	Leveret					
Deer	Doe	Buck						Venison
	Hind	Stag[g]						
Swan			Cygnet					
Fox	Vixen	Dog	Cub[h]					

[a] *Other sex distinctions:*
Most birds other than duck and goose may be distinguished as cocks and hens.
The whale, walrus, elephant, moose, and certain other large animals are distinguished as bulls and cows
Lion and tiger are presumed male since they have feminine forms lioness, tigress.
The female of certain other species is marked by prefixing the pronoun "she"; thus, she-bear.
[b] *Hogget*—a boar in its second year. The term may also apply to a young horse (colt) or to a young sheep (teg).
[c] *Hog*—may also refer to pigs in general as also *swine*.
[d] Note also *pony*, a small horse suitable for children.
[e] *Ox (Oxen)*—properly the term for the species in general, but now archaic and where used at all refers to a castrated male. The common species term is now *cow (cows)* or *cattle*. Cattle is in origin the same as capital = "live stock." The archaic plural of *cow* is *kine* (cf. *kin*).
[f] *Beef*—in singular = dead meat, but *beeves* plural refers to live animals = bullocks.
[g] *Hart*—an old stag with sur-royal antlers.
[h] *Cub (whelp)*—includes young of many wild animals: tiger, bear, otter, etc.

becomes *pork*, sheep becomes *mutton*, calf becomes *veal*, and deer becomes *venison*. But smaller animals stay as they are: lamb, hare, and rabbit, and all birds are the same alive or dead. Goats are "nearly pets" and correspondingly (for the English) goat meat is nearly inedible. An English housewife would be outraged if she thought that her mutton was goat!

ANIMAL ABUSE AND EATING HABITS

Most of the monosyllables denoting familiar animals may be stretched to describe the qualities of human beings. Such usage is often abusive but not always so. Bitch, cat, pig, swine, ass, goat, cur (dog) are insults; but lamb, duck, and cock are friendly, even affectionate. Close animals may also serve

as near obscene euphemisms for unmentionable parts of the human anatomy. Thus cock = penis, pussy = female pubic hair, and, in America, ass = arse.

The principle that the close, familiar animals are denoted by monosyllables is so general that the few exceptions invite special attention. The use of phonetically complex terms for "close" animals seems always to be the result of a euphemistic replacement of a tabooed word. Thus *donkey* has replaced *ass*, and *rabbit* has replaced *coney*. This last term now survives only in the fur trade where it is pronounced to rhyme with Tony, but its etymological derivation is from Latin *cuniculus*, and the 18th century rabbit was a cunny, awkwardly close to *cunt*, which only became printable in English with the licensed publication of *Lady Chatterley's Lover*. It is interesting that while the adult cunny has switched to the innocuous rabbit, baby language has retained bunny. I gather that in contemporary New York a Bunny Club has at least a superficial resemblance to a London eighteenth century Cunny House.[6]

Some animals seem to carry an unfair load of abuse. Admittedly the pig is a general scavenger but so, by nature, is the dog and it is hardly rational that we should label the first "filthy" while making a household pet of the second. I suspect that we feel a rather special guilt about our pigs. After all, sheep provide wool, cows provide milk, chickens provide eggs, but we rear pigs for the sole purpose of killing and eating them, and this is rather a shameful thing, a shame which quickly attaches to the pig itself. Besides which, under English rural conditions, the pig in his backyard pigsty was, until very recently, much more nearly a member of the household than any of the other edible animals. Pigs, like dogs, were fed from the leftovers of their human masters' kitchens. To kill and eat such a commensal associate is sacrilege indeed!

In striking contrast to the monosyllabic names of the close animals, we find that at the other end of the scale there is a large class of truly wild animals, most of which the ordinary individual sees only in a zoo. Such creatures are not classed as potential food at all. To distinguish these strangers as lying outside our English social system, we have given them very long semi-Latin names —elephant, hippopotamus, rhinoceros, and so forth. This is not due to any scholastic perversity; these words have been a part of the vernacular for a thousand years or so.

The intermediate category of fully sexed, tame-wild, field animals which we may hunt for food, but only in accordance with set rules at special seasons of the year, is in England now much reduced in scope. It now comprises certain birds (e.g., grouse, pheasant, partridge), hares, and, in some places, deer. As indicated already, rabbits and pigeons are both marginal to this category. Since all these

creatures are protected for part of the year in order that they may be killed in the other, the collective name *game* is most appropriate. Social anthropologists have coined the expression *joking relationship* for a somewhat analogous state of affairs which is frequently institutionalized between affinally related groups among human beings.

Just as the obscene rabbit, which is ambiguously game or vermin, occupies an intermediate status between the farm and field categories (Table 1), the fox occupies the borderline between edible field and inedible wild animals. In England the hunting and killing of foxes is a barbarous ritual surrounded by extraordinary and fantastic taboos. The intensity of feeling aroused by these performances almost baffles the imagination. All attempts to interfere with such customs on the grounds of "cruelty" have failed miserably. Some aspects of fox-hunting are linguistic and thus directly relevant to my theme. We find, for example, as commonly occurs in other societies in analogous contexts, that the sacredness of the situation is marked by language inversions, the use of special terms for familiar objects, and so on.

Thus foxes are hunted by packs of dogs and, at the conclusion of the ritual killing, the fox has its head and tail cut off, which are then preserved as trophies, but none of this may be said in plain language. It is the fox itself that can be spoken of as a *dog*, the dogs are described as *hounds*, the head of the fox is a *mask*, its tail a *brush*, and so on. It is considered highly improper to use any other words for these things.

Otters, stags, and hares are also sometimes hunted in a comparable ritual manner, and here again the hunting dogs change their identity, becoming either hounds or beagles. All of which reinforces my original hypothesis that the category *dog*, in English, is something very special indeed.

The implication of all this is that if we arrange the familiar animals in a series according to their social distance from the human SELF (Table 1, bottom) then we can see that the occurrence of taboo (ritual value), as indicated by different types and intensities of killing and eating restrictions, verbal abuse, metaphysical associations, ritual performance, the intrusion of euphemism, etc., is not just randomly distributed. The varieties of taboo are located at intervals across the chart in such a way as to break up the continuum into sections. Taboo serves to

---

[6] In general, birds fall outside the scope of this paper, but while considering the ambiguities introduced by the accidents of linguistic homonyms we may note that all edible birds are *fowl* (i.e., foul = filthy); that *pigeon* has replaced *dove*, perhaps because of the association of the latter with the Holy Ghost; and that the word *squabble* (a noisy quarrel, particularly between married couples) is derived from *squab*, a young pigeon.

separate the SELF from the world, and then the world itself is divided into zones of social distance corresponding here to the words farm, field, and remote.

I believe that this kind of analysis is more than just an intellectual game; it can help us to understand a wide variety of our non-rational behavior. For example, anyone familiar with the literature will readily perceive that English witchcraft beliefs depended upon a confusion of precisely the categories to which I have here drawn attention. Witches were credited with a power to assume animal form and with possessing spirit familiars. The familiar might take the form of any animal but was most likely to appear as a dog, a cat, or a toad. Some familiars had no counterpart in natural history; one was described as having "paws like a bear but in bulk not fully as big as a coney." The ambiguity of such creatures was taken as evidence of their supernatural qualities. As Hopkins, the celebrated seventeenth century witchfinder, remarked, "No mortal alone could have invented them."

But my purpose has been to pose questions rather than to offer explanations. The particular diagrams which I have presented may not be the most useful ones, but at least I have established that the English language classification of familiar animals is by no means a simple matter; it is not just a list of names, but a complex pattern of identifications subtly discriminated not only in kind but in psychological tone. Our linguistic treatment of these categories reflects taboo or ritual value, but these are simply portmanteau terms which cover a complex of feeling and attitude, a sense perhaps that aggression, as manifested either in sex or in killing, is somehow a disturbance of the natural order of things, a kind of necessary impiety.

A NON-EUROPEAN EXAMPLE

If this kind of analysis were applicable only to the categories of the English language it would amount to no more than a parlor game. Scientifically speaking, the analysis is interesting only in so far as it opens up the possibility that other languages analyzed according to similar procedures might yield comparable patterns. A demonstration on these lines is not easy: one needs to know a language very well indeed before one can play a game of this kind. Nevertheless it is worth trying.

Kachin is a Tibeto-Burman language spoken by hill tribesmen in Northeast Burma. Since it is grammatically and syntactically wholly unlike any Indo-European language it should provide a good test case. At one time I spoke the language fluently though I cannot do so now. I have a firsthand anthropological understanding of Kachin customary behaviors.

Kachin is essentially a monosyllabic language in which discrimination is achieved by varying the "prefixes" of words rather than by tonal variation, though, as in other Tibeto-Burman languages, tones play their part. It follows that homonyms are very common in this language, and the art of punning and *double entente* is a highly developed cultural feature. A special form of lovers' poetry (*nchyun ga*) depends on this fact. A single brief example will suffice as illustration:

Jan du	gawng lawng	sharat a lo
At sunset	the clapper of the cattle bell	swings back and forth.
Mai bawt	gawng nu	sharat a lo[7]
The (buffalo's)	short tail and the base of the bell	are wagged.

Nothing could be more superficially "innocent" than this romantic image of dusk and cattle bells. But the poem takes on a very different appearance once it is realized that *jan du* (the sun sets) also means "the girl comes (has an orgasm)" while *mai bawt* (the short tail) is a common euphemism for the human penis. The rest of the Freudian images can easily be worked out by the reader!

On the other hand, it cannot be said that the Kachin is at all "foulmouthed." Precisely because of his cultivated expertness at *double entente*, he can almost always appear to be scrupulously polite. But verbal obscenities do exist, including what I have called animal abuse; the latter are mainly concentrated around the dog (*gwi*).

Kachins are a primitive people living in steep mountained forest country. Their diet consists mainly of rice and vegetables, but they keep cattle, pigs, and fowls. There are very few edible creatures which they will not eat, though they draw the line at dogs and rats and human beings. The domesticated animals are killed only in the context of a sacrificial ritual. The meat of such sacrifices is

---

[7] All Kachin linguistic usages cited here except the obscene connotation of *jan du* can be verified from O. Hanson (1906).

eaten by members of the attendant congregation, and sacrifices are frequent. Despite this frequency, the occasion of a sacrifice is a sacred occasion (na) and there is a sense in which all domestic animals are sacred.

Until very recently the Kachins had an institution of slavery. It is an indication of their attitude to animals rather than of their attitude to slaves that a slave was classed as a yam, a category which includes all domesticated animals. It is also relevant that the word ni meaning near also means tame.

The linguistic correlates of all this are not simple. In general, everything that has a place in ritual occasions falls into the wide category WU (U) meaning pollution. This has sundry subcategories:

(a) birds
(b) various species of bamboo
(c) creatures classed as nga—mainly fish and cattle
(d) creatures classed as wa—mainly human beings and pigs.

Ignoring the human beings and the bamboo, this is a category of polluted foods, i.e., foods which may properly be eaten only in the context of sacrifice. It contrasts with ordinary clean food and meat (shat, shan). Other creatures such as dog (gwi) and rat (yu) may sometimes be offered in sacrifice, but these would not be eaten except as part of some special magical performance. I have arranged these and other terms (Table 3) on a scale of social distance comparable to that shown for English language categories in Table 1. The parallels are very striking. Let us consider the items in this table reading from left

to right, that is to say, from very close to very far.

The closest creatures are the dog and the rat. Both are inedible and heavily loaded with taboo. To call a man a dog is an obscenity; yu (rat) also means witchcraft. In some contexts it may also mean affinal relative on the wife's or mother's side. For a variety of structural reasons which I have described in other publications, a Kachin's feelings toward these mayu ni are ordinarily highly ambivalent. My wife's mother, a strongly incestuous category, is ni, which we have already seen also means very near, and tame.

The domesticated creatures that are edible if sacrificed have been considered already. These "farm" creatures are much more closely identified with the self than the corresponding English categories. They are as human as slaves; they all live in the same house as their owners. The term wa (pig) also means man, father, tooth. It is veritably a part of "me"!

In the English schema I suggested that field (game) animals have the same structural position, in terms of social distance, as the category of potential wives. In the Kachin case the category of animals comparable to English game are the forest animals hunted for meat. They live in the forest (nam). Now the Kachin have a prescriptive rule of marriage which requires a man to marry a girl of a certain category; this category is also nam. But in other respects the Kachin case is the inverse of the English situation. An Englishman has free choice in obtaining a wife, but he must go further afield than a

TABLE 3. KACHIN CATEGORIES OF FAMILIAR ANIMALS
(for comparison with bottom three lines of Table 1)

	HOUSE (inedible)	FARM (edible if sacrificed)	FOREST (edible, no rules)		REMOTE (inedible)
			(near)	(far)	
	SELF-dog-rat	pig-cattle	small deer—	large deer	elephant-tiger
		wu			
	gwi yu	wa nga	hkyi tsu	shan shat	gwi raw
Alternative English meanings of Kachin animal names in line above	(witch)		(feces) (ghost)	(meat) (food)	(monster)

first cousin; on the other hand he hunts his game according to precise rules. In contrast the Kachin has his category of possible wives defined in advance and, as first preference, should choose a particular first cousin (the mother's brother's daughter). But he is subject to no rules when he hunts in the forest.

The creatures of the forest which are thus obtained for meat by hunting are mainly deer of various sizes. The smaller ones are found close to the village. Like the English rabbit these are regarded as vermin as well as game, since they raid the rice fields. The larger deer are found in the deep forest. There are in all four categories of deer: *hkyi* and *tsu* are both small species living close in, *shan* and *shat* are large creatures living far out. All these words have homonym meanings: *hkyi*: feces, filth; *tsu*: a disembodied human spirit, ghost; *shan*: ordinary (clean) meat food; *shat*: ordinary (clean) food of any kind.

Thus the pattern is quite consistent. The more remote animals are the more edible, and the homonym meanings of the associated words become less taboo loaded as the social distance is increased.

However, the over-all situation is not quite so simple. Monkeys of many kinds abound. They are sometimes eaten, occasionally tamed as pets, and their blood is credited with magical aphrodisiac qualities. They seem to be thought of as wild animals rather abnormally close to man, like the little deer *tsu*. A monkey is *woi*, a term which also means grandmother. The status of squirrels is very similar. The squirrel figures prominently in Kachin mythology, since it was the death of a squirrel that led man to become mortal. Squirrels are hunted and eaten, but again the attitude is ambiguous. Squirrels are *mai* (tails), but *mai* as we have already seen means a human penis.

Moreover, as remoteness is increased, we finally reach, as in English, a category of unknown and therefore inedible creatures, and the pattern is then reversed. There are two great beasts of the forest which the ordinary Kachin knows about but seldom sees. The first is the elephant, called *magwi* but also *gwi*. Since *gwi* is a dog this may seem odd, but the usage is very similar to that by which the English call the male fox a dog. The other is the tiger (*sharaw, raw*) which stands as the prototype for all fabulous monsters. *Numraw*, literally woman tiger, is a creature which figures prominently in Kachin

mythology; she (?) has many attributes of the Sphinx in the Oedipus story, an all-devouring horror of uncertain sex, half man, half beast.[8]

This over-all pattern, as displayed in Table 3, is certainly not identical to that found in English, but it is clearly very much the same kind of pattern, and the resemblances seem too close to be the product of either mere accident, as that phrase would ordinarily be understood, or the obsessional prejudices of myself as investigator. I suggest that the correspondences are at least sufficient to justify further comparative studies. On the other hand, I readily agree that it is easy to be over-persuaded by such evidence, especially when dealing with a language such as Kachin where the incidence of homonyms is very high.

In writing of English I suggested that there was a correspondence between the sequence of sex relationships: sister (incest); cousin (premarital relations possible, no marriage); neighbor (marriage possible); stranger (marriage impossible); and the sequence of "edibility relationships" displayed in Table 1. How far does this apply for Kachin? How does one make the comparison? The difficulty is that Kachin has a kinship system quite different from that of English. True sisters are a strongly incestuous category, but remote classificatory clan sisters are persons with whom liaisons are possible but marriage is not. Elder sister is *na* and younger sister is *nau*. The homonyms are *na*, a sacred holiday, an occasion on which a ritual sacrifice is made; *nau*, a sacred dance occurring on *na* occasions to the accompaniment of sacrifice. This of course fits very nicely with my thesis, for Table 3 can now be translated into human as opposed to animal relationships (in Table 4).

Perhaps all this is too good to be true, but I think that it deserves further investigation.

Those who wish to take my argument seriously might well consider its relevance to C. Lévi-Strauss's most remarkable book *La pensée sauvage* (1962). Though fascinated by that work I have also felt that some dimension to the argument is missing. We need to

[8] This greatly simplifies a very complex mythological category. The *numraw* (also *maraw*) are "luck" deities, vaguely comparable to the furies (erinyes) of Greek mythology. The *numraw* are not always female nor always of one kind. *Baren numraw* lives in the water and seems to be thought of as some kind of alligator, *wa numraw* is presumably a wild boar, and so on.

TABLE 4. KACHIN CATEGORIES OF HUMAN RELATIONSHIPS

	Incest	No Marriage Illicit Relations	Marriage	Remote Nonrelative
SELF	NI	NA/NAU	NAM	RAW
	mother-in-law	"sister"	marriageable cross-cousin	
	near	sacred occasion	forest	forest fire
	(inedible)	(edible if sacrificed)	(edible)	(inedible)

[a] There are two relevant homonyms of *raw* = tiger. *Raw* as a verb means cease to be related; it applies in particular when two affinally related groups cease to recognize their relationship. *Raw* also means forest fire. It is thus the dangerous aspect of the forest, where *nam* is friendly.

consider not merely that things in the world can be classified as sacred and not sacred, but also as more sacred and less sacred. So also in social classifications it is not sufficient to have a discrimination me/it, we/they; we also need a graduated scale close/far, more like me/less like me. If this essay is found to have a permanent value it will be because it represents an expansion of Lévi-Strauss's thesis in the direction I have indicated.

Charles O. Frake

A STRUCTURAL DESCRIPTION OF SUBANUN "RELIGIOUS BEHAVIOR"

The new field of "ethnoscience" has a number of active and creative young anthropologists who promise much in the way of developing more precise methods for eliciting and ordering ethnographic facts in terms of contrasts that are inherent in the data. In the judgment of the editors, the attempt to analyze data in terms of native categories is *not* novel. Anthropologists have long been attempting to do just such types of field studies. But what *is* novel are the methods that are being developed to the point where there should no longer be debate about ethnographic fact. In the past there has been controversy wherever there has been a "revisit" of a tribe; there continues to be controversy in the contemporary literature about tribes who have become extinct or so acculturated that it is impossible for a new field worker to return to the field and check results. With full control of the native language and with methods of procedure that lead to sharply focused research, we are reaching the point where the data elicited and ordered by one field ethnographer can be replicated by another without distortion and without argument.

One of the leading proponents of this type of approach is Charles O. Frake, whose earlier paper "The Diagnosis of Disease Among the Subanun of Mindanao" (1961) has already become a classic, and whose more recent paper reprinted here attempts for the first time to apply his methods to complex religious behavior.

The recent collection of articles in Tyler, *Cognitive Anthropology* (1969), provides an overview of this movement in ethnography.

Reprinted from *Explorations in Cultural Anthropology: Essays in Honor of George Peter Murdock*, edited by Ward H. Goodenough (New York: McGraw-Hill Book Co., 1964), pp. 111–129. Copyright © 1964, McGraw-Hill Book Company. Used by permission.

The purpose of this paper is not to present anything approaching a complete description of Subanun "religion" but rather to raise the question of what kind of statement would constitute an adequate ethnographic description of an aspect of a culture. This is not, I think, a trivial question to ask. A theory of how to describe cultural behavior implies a theory of culture. Ethnography, the science of cultural description, can potentially fill a role as critical to our general theoretical understanding of the nature of culture as has modern descriptive linguistics toward our understanding of the nature of language.

A description of a culture, an *ethnography*, is produced from an *ethnographic record* of the events of a society within a given period of time, the "events of a society" including, of course, informants' responses to the ethnographer, his queries, tests, and apparatus. *Ethnographic technique*, ignored in this paper, is the task of devising means for producing an adequately ample record of events. *Ethnographic methodology* is the task of devising operations for producing an ethnography from an ethnographic record. *Ethnographic theory* is the task of devising criteria for evaluating ethnographies. These three aspects of the ethnographic task are interdependent. The adequacy of the record and the validity of the methodology cannot be determined unless the data are subjected to analysis and the results tested against the criteria of the theory during the course of field investigation. The production of an ethnography should imply a task more challenging than "writing up one's notes."

When an ethnographer first enters a strange society, each encountered event is new, unanticipated, improbable, and, hence, highly informative in the communication-theory sense. As he learns the culture of the society, more and more of what happens becomes familiar and anticipatable. The ethnographer can plan his own activities on the basis of these anticipations. The more he learns of a culture, the more his anticipations match those of his informants. Similarly for a person born in a society, as he learns his culture, the events of his life become more probable, becoming parts of familiar *scenes* which he and his fellows plan for, stage, and play their roles in. To describe a culture, then, is not to recount the events of a society but to specify what one must know to make those events maximally probable. The problem is not to state what someone did but to specify the conditions under which it is culturally appropriate to anticipate that he, or persons occupying his role, will render an equivalent performance. This conception of a cultural description implies that an ethnography should be a theory of cultural behavior in a particular society, the adequacy of which is to be evaluated by the ability of a stranger to the culture (who may be ethnographer) to use the ethnography's statements as instructions for appropriately anticipating the scenes of the society. I say "appropriately anticipate" rather than "predict" because a failure of an ethnographic statement to predict correctly does not necessarily imply descriptive inadequacy as long as the members of the described society are as surprised by the failure as is the ethnographer. The test of descriptive adequacy must always refer to informants' interpretations of events, not simply to the occurrence of events.

With this criterion of descriptive adequacy in mind the formulation of an ethnographic statement would seem to include at least the following tasks:

1. Discovering the major categories of events or *scenes* of the culture.
2. Defining scenes so that observed interactions, acts, objects, and places can be assigned to their proper scenes as roles, routines, paraphernalia, and settings.
3. Stating the distribution of scenes with respect to one another, that is, providing instructions for anticipating or planning for scenes.

These three methodological problems will be discussed with reference to a portion of the Subanun record, a record which is inadequate at several points because much of this analysis was completed only after I had left the field.

The Subanum are a pagan people practicing swidden agriculture in the mountainous interior of Zamboanga Peninsula on the island of Mindanao in the Philippines. The data of this paper pertain only to the Eastern Subanun of the Gulu Disakan and Lipay regions northeast of Sindangan Bay in the interior of Zamboanga del Norte Province, studied in the field in 1953–1954 and 1957–1958. In terms of segmentation and stratification, Subanun society displays remarkable simplicity. Each nuclear family is the focus of a partially unique and variable network of social ties with kin and neighbors which constitutes, for that family, the "total society."

This maximal, nondiscrete sphere of social relationships has no corporate organization and is not segmented into lineages, age-sets, secret societies, territorial districts, political factions, or the like. Despite this simplicity of their social structure, the Subanun carry on constant and elaborate interfamily social activities—litigation, offerings, feasts—all well lubricated with ample quantities of rice wine. Warfare is lacking.

THE IDENTIFICATION OF "RELIGIOUS BEHAVIOR"

One of the most frequent and regularly recurrent events in the Subanun record is eating. Most, *but not all*, Subanun events which we should consider instances of "eating" as a category of activity fall into an easily distinguishable Subanun scene, a 'meal.' To qualify as a 'meal' a scene must include at least one actor, the 'eater,' and a 'cooked starchy-staple food.' A meal characteristically marks a clear interruption of other activity, requiring the performers to squat before a setting of food on the floor or ground; it is scheduled at least once daily; it requires prior planning and preparation; and, although one actor is sufficient, it is generally staged as a social performance.

In the typical recorded meal, those participating in the role "joint eaters" belong to a single nuclear family, the side dish is a nonmeat food, the staple may be a root crop or a cereal, and no 'rice wine' (*gasi*) is served. These are *ordinary meals*. If one of the features of an ordinary meal changes, the others change as well. Meals with multifamily joint eaters, meat side dish, cereal staple, and 'rice wine' are *festive meals* or, simply, *feasts*.

Festive meals occur at irregular intervals and must be occasioned: i.e., there must be a legitimizing event which serves as a reason for the feast. It is always appropriate to ask in Subanun, "What is the reason for this feast?" To ask, "What is the reason for this meal?" would sound somewhat odd in uncontrived contexts. Festive meals substitute for ordinary ones. A meal is scheduled at least once daily. If there is a legitimizing occasion and the necessary components are procurable, a festive meal is staged; otherwise an ordinary meal is staged. A central part of Subanun planning involves anticipating festive occasions so that the necessary components for staging a feast be procurable whenever a legitimizing event occurs. The occurrence of one of the components, as an event, can itself be a reason for a feast, requiring the mustering of the other essential components. If a wild pig (meat-side-dish component) is caught in a trap, its consumption requires a feast. If guests congregate (multifamily-performance component), they must be feasted. The festive meal itself occurs in a context of a wide range of other activities: competitive drinking, displays of verbal art, singing, dancing. All activities occurring from the arrival to the departure of participants in a feast together constitute a *festivity*.

During some festivities occur episodes which themselves seem to be feasts, but of a rather special sort. The festive provisions are set up on distinctive paraphernalia and the 'eaters,' though sometimes audible, are not visible to the ethnographer nor, by report, to the ordinary Subanun. Feasts of this sort whereby 'mortals' feed the various categories of 'nonvisible' or 'supernatural' inhabitants of the Subanun universe, the Subanun call *kanu*, here glossed as 'offerings.' During the course of a festivity, one to several offerings may be performed. A festivity during which offerings occur is a *ceremony*. A ceremony may be *simple* or *complex* depending on whether one or more than one offering is held. This contrast between simple and complex ceremonies is not matched by a lexical distinction in Subanun, but is necessary in order to describe the denota of names for types of offerings and ceremonies. Ceremonies are named for one constituent offering. Thus *beklug* denotes a particular kind of offering or a ceremony in which the *beklug* offering is one of many constituents. If a Subanun offering name is given as "instructions to perform," one must know from context whether the referent is an offering or a ceremony and, if a ceremony, whether it is simple or complex. The term *kanu* may likewise, depending on context, refer to an offering or to a ceremony.

A ceremony, then, is one kind of festivity. Other kinds are 'litigation,' 'labor-recruiting feasts,' 'game-sharing feasts,' 'meat-division feasts,' and 'hospitality feasts.' Several kinds of festivities may be jointly held. If for some reason it is necessary to provide a feast, it is often economic to discharge as many festive functions as possible during its course. Thus a legal case and an offering may occur during a festivity originally staged as a hospitality feast.

To the naïve observer an offering may seem like a minor episode in a festive event. But when one considers how offerings and ceremonies vary in paraphernalia, social participation, routines, planning, and programming, and when one considers the range of events which are relevant to staging ceremonies, it becomes clear that the behavioral complex centering on offerings penetrates deeply into many crucial areas of Subanun life. The programming and staging of ceremonies forms a major segment of Subanun cultural activity comparable in scope and content to the traditional ethnographic category of "religion." The comparability suggests (but does not require) the term *religious behavior* as a label for this activity, and it suggests *Subanun religion* as a label for what is described by an ethnographic statement which accounts for this behavior. But the only criterion of whether a particular act is an instance of *religious behavior* is its relevance to the programming and performing of 'offerings.' The ethnographic (in contrast to the ethnological) issue is not whether instances of *religious behavior* so defined conform to any particular cross-cultural notion of "what religion is," but whether they do in fact comprise a meaningful descriptive category of Subanun cultural activity and, if so, how is this category to be described.

THE PERFORMANCE OF AN 'OFFERING'

The first step in describing Subanun *religious behavior* is to describe the performance of offerings themselves in terms of discovered categories of constituent locales, objects, performers, and acts. Only a brief outline of the constituent structure of offerings as performances can be presented here.

SETTINGS

There are no special buildings, rooms, or outdoor areas reserved for staging offerings. Offerings may be held inside nuclear family residences, in house yards, in fields, in forests, or on stream banks, the specific locale depending on the type of offering as well as on sociological, ecological, and meteorological conditions.

PROVISIONS

A festive meal must be provided for both mortal and supernatural participants. A feast for supernaturals requires special components: the staple must be of rice, eggs are added to the required meat side dish, the proffered wine (or fermented mash) must be of rice and be ritually prepared, the proffered betel quids must be prepared with domesticated betel-pepper leaf and areca palm nuts (mortals often use substitute ingredients). Some categories of supernaturals take their food raw, others in a a cooked state. These provisions are first offered to the invited supernaturals on an altar, then removed and consumed, generally as part of a larger feast, by humans. (The supernaturals conveniently consume only the 'intangible essence,' *seŋaw*, of food and drink.) The kind and quantity of provisions within these constituent categories varies with type of offering, with the kind of event occasioning the offering, with the whims of individual supernaturals, and with particular bargains struck beforehand between mortal host and supernatural guest. From an economic standpoint the side dish, requiring sacrifice of valuable livestock, is the most significant feature of an offering. The market value of pigs and chickens slaughtered for the offering and accompanying feast provides a direct index of the occasion's importance.

PARAPHERNALIA

Humans settle for a banana leaf on the floor, but the supernaturals demand elaborate devices from which to partake of their meals. The Subanun construct at least thirty types of altars, varying in number of platforms, method of construction, materials employed, means of support or suspension, decoration, and size. Sometimes the type of altar is determined by the deity being propitiated. Thus the 'raw-food-eating gods' (*kemuŋluq*) always eat from a platformless *seleŋsaŋan*, but a personal 'guardian god' (*tipun*) generally prefers a *bibalay* altar, the defining attributes of which are rectangular shape, no sides, stick floor, and parallel legs. More often the type of altar or altars is specific to a particular kind of offering or ritual occasion, and a variety of supernaturals will in turn eat from it during the ceremony. Some more elaborate offerings require special equipment other than altars: various kinds of barriers to inhibit the movements of malevolent supernaturals, folded cloths to capture lost souls, miniature wooden replicas of weapons, model rafts and canoes, decorative and rustling leaves. With few exceptions all of this equipment is constructed anew (usually in a rather slipshod fashion) for each offering and then discarded. Since human drinking and feasting cannot proceed until the offering is completed, the few Subanun who are prone to spend time lavishing care on the construction of ritual paraphernalia become the butt of criticism from their more secular-minded fellows. Every offering also requires a resonant porcelain bowl (struck rhythmically to announce the occasion to the supernatural guests) and incense (the fumes of which augment the aroma of the offerings as a lure).

PARTICIPANTS

The participants in an offering all belong to the category of 'persons' (*getaw*), those 'living things' (*tubuqan*) with whom one can establish communicatory relations. A dichotomous dimension of reported conscious visibility divides 'persons' into two subcategories with fundamentally distinct roles in offerings. 'Persons' reported to be consciously visible to the ordinary Subanun are 'mortals' (*kilawan*). 'Persons' whom the ordinary Subanun are reportedly unable to see consciously are 'supernaturals' (*kanaq kilawan*). Only the exceptional perceptual powers of certain prominent 'mediums' can reportedly record a conscious visual image of the 'supernaturals.' Others may 'see' a supernatural without being aware of it—a possible cause of illness if the unconscious image is particularly terrifying. The non-empirical nature of Subanun 'supernaturals' refers only to the visual sense; these beings are (reportedly) able to make an impression on one's auditory and tactile senses.

The English word 'supernatural' thus serves as a *label* for the Subanun category of 'persons' reportedly not consciously visible to the ordinary Subanun. There are, of course, in the verbally revealed Subanun universe many creatures ('persons' and 'non-persons') which the ethnographer feels confident he will never see and which many informants admit they have never seen (but only because they have never encountered them, except perhaps in the dark). Some of these "natural" (i.e., visible) but rarely encountered phenomena play an important role in Subanun life, but they do not appear at offerings and hence are not relevant to the present discussion. Only by attending to Subanun criteria can we assign the bow-and-arrow-wound-inflicting *menubuq* pygmies to the category 'supernatural' and the body-

dismembering *meŋayaw* marauders to the category 'mortal.' Neither class appears to the ethnographer to have any empirically substantiable members in the Subanun habitat at the present time, though they both may once have had. Yet to discuss both categories together as aspects of Subanun *religion* because they are both "supernatural" according to the ethnographer's notions would seriously distort the structure of Subanun culture.

At the most general level of terminological contrast the Subanun classify 'supernaturals' as 'souls' (*gimuud*), 'spirits' (*mitubuq*), 'demons' (*getau-telunan*), and 'gods' (*diwata*) (cf. Table 1). Two semantic dimensions suffice to define these four categories in terms of necessary and sufficient contrasts in verbal descriptions:

1. Inherent connection with mortals
   1.1 Inherently connected with a living mortal
   1.2 Once inherently connected with a mortal now dead but still remembered by at least one living mortal
   1.3 Not inherently connected to a living or remembered mortal
2. Habitat connection with mortals
   2.1 Regularly residing with mortals in 'this world' (*glumbaŋ*)
   2.2 Not regularly residing in 'this world'

Using the numbering of the outline above, the four categories are definable as follows:

'Souls'	: 1.1
'Spirits'	: 1.2
'Demons'	: 1.3 2.1
'Gods'	: 1.3 2.2

'Souls' play a role in offerings through attempts to use offerings to recapture, for the sake of their owners' health, lost souls lured away by fragrant blossoms, attractive supernaturals, and the offerings of sorcerers. ('Souls,' a kind of 'supernatural,' must be distinguished from *gina* 'life stuff,' associated with consciousness, cognition, and emotion but not a 'person' who attends offerings.)

After death the soul survives to become a 'spirit,' a bodiless soul who wanders about 'this world' until sent on a tour of sacred places and other worlds by a series of offerings performed on his behalf by his survivors. Becoming eventually forgotten in the sky world, he then acquires the necessary attributes of a 'god' (cf. definition above). It is the spirits of the recent dead—close kin whom he remembers personally and toward

TABLE 1. CATEGORIES OF PARTICIPANTS IN SUBANUN 'OFFERINGS'

'Persons'		*Getaw:*
[a]1.	'supernaturals'	*kanaq kilawan*
1.1.	'souls'	*gimuud*
1.2.	'spirits'	*mitubuq*
1.3.	'demons'	*getau-telunan*
1.3.1.	'ogres'	*menemad*
1.3.2.	'goblins'	*memenwa*
1.3.3.	'pygmies'	*menubuq*
1.4.	'gods'	*diwata*
1.4.1.	'sky gods'	*getau-laŋit*
1.4.2.	'raw-food-eating gods'	*kemuŋluq, meŋilaw*
1.4.2.1.	'sunset gods'	*getau-sindepan*
1.4.2.2.	'sea gods'	*getau-dagat*
1.4.2.3.	'ocean gods'	*getau-land*
1.4.3.	'sunrise gods'	*getau-sebaŋan, tumiag*
1.4.4.	'underworld gods'	*getau-bayaq*
2	'mortals'	*kilawan*
[a]2.1.	'functionaries'	*sug mikanu dun*
2.1.1.	nonprofessional functionaries	
2.1.2.	'professional functionaries'	*belian*
2.1.2.1.	'invocators'	*bataq belian*
2.1.2.2.	'mediums'	*gulaŋ belian*
2.1.2.2.1.	'shamans'	*guleligan*
2.1.2.2.2.	'interviewers'	*meninduay*
2.2.	'assistants'	*gimpaŋ*
[a]2.3.	'beneficiaries'	*sug pikanuan dun*
2.4.	'audience'	*sug suminaup dun*

[a] Marks categories which must be represented at any offering.

whom he still has ritual obligations—that concern a Subanun. When he dies, others will remember him, and those he remembered will be forgotten. Ties between spirits and mortals are reformulated in successive generations rather than continuing through time as an ancestor cult—just as the corporate social groups of Subanun society, the nuclear families, do not survive through successive generations as descent groups but are constantly dissolving and reforming.

Remembered spirits are important to the Subanun because they are the closest friends a mortal has among the supernaturals. They willingly attend seances for sentimental reunions with their loved ones (though even they demand an offering of food and drink). At seances they typically act as intermediaries between mortals and less friendly supernaturals, often filling a role not unlike that of a legal authority in arbitrating a dispute between plaintiff (the offended supernatural) and defendant (the mortal offender and victim of the plaintiff's wrath). Spirits respond to emotional appeal "for oldtimes' sake" and consequently tend to be less greedy in their demands than other supernaturals. They can be troublesome, however,

if their mortal kin shirk their ritual obligations. Also they may become so afflicted with the prevalent Subanun sentiment of 'loneliness' (*bugaq*) that they desire to transform a mortal loved one to spirit status, a transformation few mortals are willing to undergo, no matter how fond they were of the departed. Several informants have voiced a suspicion, founded on their remembrance of the deceased, that the spirit in such cases is not always as sentimental as he pretends; he has merely discovered a neat wedge for extorting food and drink from his survivors.

'Demons,' while not usually so viciously malevolent as the 'raw-food-eating gods,' are dangerous because they live so close at hand. Any chance encounter with them is likely to result in illness, and the disturbance of many of their habitats caused by swidden activities requires regular propitiation.

Of greatest importance among the 'gods' are the various types of 'raw-food eaters' (see Table 1) who periodically ascend the streams of Subanun country to inflict severe illness and epidemics and through their 'pets,' the rats and locusts, cause agricultural disasters. Their annual 'new year's' propitiation at strategic river confluences provides a common ritual interest for all settlements whose drainages converge upon a single convenient blocking place.

Other 'gods,' especially the 'sky gods,' are generally much less malevolent if not actually friendly. Perversely, they do not participate nearly so regularly in human affairs, although some exert important control over rice growth. During the course of an illness-studded life, most adult male Subanun acquire a personal 'guardian supernatural' (*tipun*), frequently a 'sky god,' who must receive annual propitiation at harvest time for the sake of the health of the man's family and rice.

'Gods' and 'demons' come in large numbers of varieties distinguished by habitat specifications, appearances, malevolence, diet, altar preferences, natural phenomena under their provenience, and so on. The verbal expositions of this pantheon vary greatly from informant to informant and from region to region. To present any one of these systems in all of its detail as "the Subanun pantheon" would do violence to cultural reality. The striking feature of Subanun theology is that, at any but the most general levels (see Table 1), it is not a consistent body of cherished lore at the tip of everyone's tongue. Beyond the generalizations given here, Subanun 'supernaturals' are, with some exceptions, diffuse in their functions. Almost any supernatural can cause almost any ailment or interfere in almost any activity. Consequently an elaborate and precise taxonomy of supernaturals correlated with their functional roles need not be shared by all participants in the performance of an offering. Individuals and groups can differ considerably in their theological speculations with little consequence for the practical conduct of *religious behavior*.

Direct observation and Subanun descriptions of role performances both make it clear that a 'mortal' participant in an offering occupies at least one of the following roles: 'functionary,' 'assistant,' 'beneficiary,' or 'audience' (see Table 1).

The 'functionary' has the task of extending the invitation to the supernatural guest, once the offering has been prepared. He invokes the supernaturals by incantation, bowl striking, and incense burning. The functionary, furthermore, assumes the responsibility of supervising all proceedings connected with the offering to ensure their proper performance. Every adult male household head has frequent occasion to serve as functionary for simple household ceremonies. Women rarely assume this role in fact, except during one type of agricultural offering, but are not proscribed from it by custom. A person must always act as his own functionary in offerings to his personal 'guardian god' (*tipun*).

The complexity of Subanun religious techniques, however, demands specialized knowledge of functionaries for all but the simplest offerings. A 'professional functionary' (*belian*) is an acknowledged specialist in religious techniques who regularly acts as a functionary for offerings involving beneficiaries outside his own household. If a 'professional functionary' has one or more supernatural 'familiars' (*bilaq*) and can thereby conduct seances, he is a 'medium' (*gulaŋ belian*, or simply *belian* if context makes the level of contrast clear); otherwise he is an 'invocator' (*bataq belian*, literally, "a little bit of a professional functionary"). There are two kinds of 'mediums': 'shamans' (*guleligan*), who are 'possessed' (*tenaqan*) by their familiars, and 'interviewers' (*meninduay*) who carry on conversations with the supernatural guests as the latter partake of the offering.

Of the special statuses which a Subanun can achieve, that of 'medium' is the most formalized in method of recruitment and in social acknowledgment. It can never, however, replace a Subanun's full-time occupational role of farming. There are two routes, open to any adult man or woman, for becoming a medium: by 'training' (*pigubasan*) and by 'revelation' (*gemaw*). All mediums of my acquaintance selected the former route, involuntarily, when the supernaturals imposed the role upon them as the price of recovery from an illness. In this manner the gods recruit new members to the profession which is so essential to their well-being. A person so selected assists a qualified medium and acts as an 'invocator' until the gods inform him that he is ready to assume a medium's role himself. A medium of the other type (*gemaw*) allegedly receives his training direct from the gods and needs no apprenticeship.

The Subanun expects a good medium to exhibit certain peculiarities of 'habitual behavior' (*kebetaŋ*). His personality should emphasize to a fault the Subanun virtues of a quiet, passive, rather phlegmatic approach to interpersonal relationships with the consequence that he becomes, by Subanun evaluation, somewhat impractical in daily affairs.

These traits of the personality type called *melemen* are the polar opposites of the forceful aggressiveness (*gembeluq*) required of a legal authority. Hence the same person cannot easily occupy both the role of mediator with the supernaturals and the role of mediating among human disputants. Furthermore, by Subanun standards, the personality expected of a medium is more commendable, if less entertaining, than that of the extroverted legal authority.

Almost every settlement has someone who can assume the role of 'invocator' for certain ceremonies, but, in the area of my fieldwork, over half of the settlements lacked resident mediums. Mediums must therefore extend their services beyond their own settlements on a community-wide or even a region-wide basis, depending on their reputation. The travel required takes sufficient time from the medium's agricultural and technological tasks at home to counterbalance what material rewards his profession brings —a problem paralleling that of prominent legal authorities. Probably the most important material reward for mediums is the opportunity they have to attend a large number of feasts and drinking parties without any obligation to reciprocate. In addition, when called upon to perform special ceremonies for the cure of illness, they collect a small fee. They receive no fee for communal ceremonies in which they themselves are beneficiaries.

The other roles assumed by participants at an offering are functions of the particular social context; they are not permanent attributes of a person's status in the society at large. 'Assistants' are any persons who, under the functionary's supervision, prepare and set up the food and material equipment for the offering. They are recruited for the occasion from apprentice mediums, personnel of the beneficiary's household, the beneficiary himself, or simply from people "who like to do that sort of thing." The 'beneficiary' is the person or persons for whose benefit the offering is being given. The beneficiary may be one person, a household, a settlement, or even an entire region, depending on the purpose of the offering. The responsibility of providing a locale for the ceremony, of securing the necessary provisions, and of recruiting assistants falls to the beneficiaries. Any person or family intending to assume the role of beneficiary must make a contribution to the offering.

The 'audience' comprises all persons who are present because of the offering but who have no special role in its actual performance. It may include uninvited people who "happened to drop by" (in unexpressed anticipation of a feast), but it is largely composed of people with a special interest in the beneficiary. Major ceremonies of illness and death provide the only formalized occasions which bring large numbers of a person's dispersed kindred together as participants in a single event. Scheduled agricultural and prophylactic ceremonies, on the other hand, recruit audience and group beneficiaries along lines of local group affiliation. Except during seances, the majority of the audience and even beneficiaries, when these are in large number, generally show very little interest in the proceedings of the offering proper; that is the task of the functionary and his assistants. A Subanun offering is a technique for accomplishing a practical purpose. It is not an obvious source of inspiration or a forceful expression of ultimate values to an awe-stricken congregation. There are, of course, sources of inspiration and forceful expressions of values in Subanun life, but they are more likely to be communicated during secular gatherings around rice-wine jars after the offering is completed. Seances, however, rival legal disputes as foci of lively interest: they provide all persons present with an opportunity to interrogate, beg, cajole, bargain, and debate with the supernaturals themselves.

ROUTINES

To complete a description of the constituent structure of offerings there should be an analysis of the actions or routines followed in the performance. Such a description, however, would require a much more detailed discussion of offerings in all their varieties than is possible here. Consequently I merely list below the categories under which such a description of routines would be organized:

1. Preliminary staging talk
2. Assembly of participants
3. Preparing of provisions and paraphernalia
4. Setting up of offering
5. Invocation
6. Seance, if any
7. Removing provisions

(Routines 4–7 repeated for each offering of the ceremony)

8. Festivities (routines of festive eating, drinking, singing, etc.)
9. Dispersal of participants
10. Postperformance critique

THE DISTRIBUTION OF 'CEREMONIES'

If we assume that the foregoing description adequately accounts for the identification and performance of offerings within ceremonial contexts, the problem remains of formulating a statement which accounts for the scheduling of ceremonies in relation to other scenes of the culture. A distributional analysis seeks to answer the question: what does the occurrence of a given event imply to the knower of the culture about the occurrences of other possible events in the system? A statement of the distribution of ceremonies will specify what features of a Subanun's experience are relevant to the staging of a religious performance of a given kind at a given time.

Formulating a statement of the distribution of religious scenes requires examination of the ethnographic record for observed reported events which, by the criteria already formulated, are instances (or "tokens") of this scene. Next we list the other scenes regularly occurring before and after religious scenes. To judge the extent to which the occurrence of one scene implies another, the record of observed sequences must be checked against the record of informant's statements about anticipated sequences and of their interpretations of actual sequences in terms of these anticipations. This list of scenes provides a distributions *frame* for the set of events labeled 'religious scenes' or 'ceremonies.' The diagram A| |B, where A is the set of scenes regularly anticipated before ceremonies and B the set regularly anticipated after ceremonies, represents the frame. Such a distributional frame specifies the necessary conditions for anticipating the occurrence of a ceremony. Note that these conditions depend not only on the actual occurrence of an anticipated event, but also on plans made for producing or coping with future events. The model of distributional structure is a two-sided, before-and-after frame, such as that required in linguistic description, and not a Markov chain in which the probability of an event is a sole function of the outcome of the preceding event. In acting as well as in speaking persons have an image of the pattern to be completed and make plans accordingly.

Description of a frame requires a statement of: (1) the probability of the events that comprise the frame, (2) the alternative scenes, other than ceremonies, that can be anticipated to occur in the same frame, (3) the alternative kinds of ceremonies that can be anticipated to occur given the occurrence of *a* ceremony.

The significance of ceremonies in Subanun life relates strikingly to the probability of events which, in terms of legitimate cultural expectations, imply ceremonies. Among the most probable events of Subanun life are those that make up the scenes of the annual agricultural cycle: swidden slashing, felling, burning, planting, protecting, and harvesting. The annual staging of each of these scenes in this order by each family is an essential feature of the Subanun ecological adaptation. These scenes and their constituents provide a frame for scheduling about nine annual complex ceremonies, the exact number varying locally. Each of these ceremonies is of a specific named kind with prescribed settings, kinds of provisions, paraphernalia, routines, and social participation. These ceremonies are *scheduled ceremonies*. Their distribution has the following characteristics:

1. The scenes of the distributive frames are highly probable.
2. Each frame calls for a specified kind of ceremony.
3. There are no anticipatable alternatives to any of these ceremonies.

Thus the annual occurrence of a given kind of scheduled ceremony is highly probable, and learning that a given scheduled ceremony has indeed occurred is not very informative (it is not 'news') to the person who knows the culture. The occurrence of a scheduled ceremony is, in effect, a structural marker of the anticipatable sequence of scenes in Subanun culture. It signals that events are unfolding as scheduled. [Compare the linguistic frames marked in the following English utterance: "I want | |go| |Hawaii." The person who knows English can legitimately anticipate only one form, *to*, in the first slot; whereas in the second slot a number of alternatives can be anticipated: *to, through, by, near, away from*, etc. The actual occurrence of a given form in the second slot is less probable and much more informative about the nonlinguistic world than the occurrence of a form in the first slot which can inform us only whether or not the utterance is correctly constructed.]

To the Subanun, the occurrence of a scheduled ceremony not only signals the expected unfolding of events, but it is also necessary if future anticipations of probable events are to be fulfilled. The failure of one of the scenes of the agricultural cycle to occur as anticipated is a sign of a major *crisis*—an unanticipatable occurrence with far-reaching consequences for future anticipations. If harvesting does not follow swidden planting and protecting then a crisis—drought, locusts, crop disease, human sickness—has occurred. The anticipated structural sequence of scenes has been broken. Correspondingly, to the Subanun, the failure properly to stage the correct ceremony on schedule can only lead to crisis. Unanticipated crises are caused by the supernaturals when *their* anticipations of regular feasts are not met. The explicit rationale for performing scheduled offerings is to prevent the occurrence of crises, to ensure the proper unfolding of events.

The performance of scheduled ceremonies is necessary to prevent crises, but, as is obvious to any Subanun, it is by no means sufficient to do so. Serious crises do occur. The distributive frames of many ceremonies are composed of unscheduled events that disrupt the ordinary routine of activities. Since their scheduling in relation to other scenes cannot, with great probability, be planned in advance, ceremonies occupying such frames are *unscheduled ceremonies*. Their distribution has the following characteristics:

1. The events which comprise the distributive frame are relatively improbable in the sense that other events could more legitimately have been expected at that time instead.
2. In a given frame there are often alternative courses of action to staging a religious scene.
3. Given the staging of a religious scene, a variety of types of ceremonies can occur in many of these frames.

Thus, knowing Subanun culture, one cannot predict when the conditions for an unscheduled ceremony will occur, and given the occurrence of such conditions, one cannot directly predict if a ceremony or an alternative scene will be staged, and given the staging of a ceremony, one cannot directly predict what kind of ceremony will be held. In a typical unscheduled situation there are a number of alternative courses of action—a range of doubt over what to anticipate. When a particular course of action is selected from these alternatives, the decision is highly informative—it is news—even to one who knows the culture.

The occurrence of illness exemplifies an unscheduled frame. Oversimplifying somewhat (by ignoring disease stages and states of 'relapse' and 'recuperation'), the anticipated outcomes of an illness are continued sickness, cure, or death, giving the frame:

$$\text{sickness} \mid \text{diagnosis} \mid \begin{array}{l}\text{continued sickness}\\\text{cure}\\\text{death}\end{array}$$

All English terms comprising the frame are labels for categories of events as identified by the Subanun. The alternatives anticipatable are:

1. No formal therapy
2. 'Medication' (one or more of about eight hundred alternatives)
3. 'Religious' therapy
   3.1 Consulting the supernaturals
   3.2 'Ritual contract'
   3.3 Performance of a 'contracted offering' 3.3.1–61 +. (List of alternative types of offerings)

The initial choice is made in relation to the anticipatable outcome, or prognosis, predicated by diagnosis, and subsequent choices are made in relation to the results of previous choices (Frake, 1961). 'Medication' (*kebuluŋan*), relying on the special power inherent in certain, generally botanical, substances, comprises a set of techniques conceptually distinct both from reliance on 'skills' (*kependayan*) and from appeals to the supernaturals through offerings. These three contrasting techniques are applicable to a wide range of endeavors apart from illness: agriculture, technology, social control, lovemaking, etc.

Because of the greater expense and more elaborate planning required, religious therapy for illness is resorted to only if medication fails or its failure is immediately obvious from prognosis. If religious therapy does occur, it is informative of the seriousness of the case. The particular kind of ceremony required, if any, cannot be determined from diagnosis, but only by consulting the supernaturals through divination or seance.

Once a patient has learned he must perform a specific kind of ceremony and has ritually acknowledged his intention to do so, he has acquired a *binalaq*, a term appropriately glossed as 'ritual debt,' for a Subanun's procrastination and legalistic evasion with *binalaq* obligations closely parallels his handling of ordinary 'debts' (*gutaŋ*) with his fellow mortals. The 'ritual acknowledgment' (*penebiin*) of a *binalaq*, which generally follows considerable haggling with the supernaturals, can be labeled 'ritual contract.' It is sound policy to contract to pay one's ritual debt *after* one is cured. In this way one is assured that the supernaturals will abide by their side of the agreement. The Subanun knows that even the most generous offering does not always cure his afflictions, and that, if he pays his ritual debts while he is sick, the supernaturals may keep him sick in the hope of extorting more and more from him.

But in this contest between mortal and supernatural, the former shows no more conscientiousness in fulfilling his obligations than the latter. Once he is cured, the Subanun patient becomes very reluctant to expend his resources on the supernaturals. Yet most Subanun have had enough experience with relapses of sickness to be somewhat wary of neglecting their ritual obligations without making an effort to do it legitimately by obtaining an extension of the contract through assiduous divination or through pleading with the supernaturals during a seance. Obtaining an extension often means an increase in the offering as interest, but despite past experience, the Subanun frequently hopes that with enough extensions his supernatural creditors will eventually forget about the debt and not inflict illness on him again in an effort to recover it. These hopes are generally in vain. The supernaturals hound their debtors with the same diligence as mortal creditors. Sooner or later, the Subanun who has neglected a ritual debt becomes ill. Then he remembers his outstanding obligations, which are likely to be numerous, and, if indications from seances and divination are affirmative, he may actually perform the contracted offering. But he may also acquire a new obligation pertinent to his new illness and penalizing him for the long delay in paying the debt for the old. With the new obligation, depending on the course of the illness, he may go through the same delaying tactics until he is once again afflicted. Because of these tactics of debt evasion, in many a crisis ceremony of disease the beneficiary is indeed sick but not with the illness that originally incurred the obligation to perform *that* ceremony. (There are, of course, many complexities and deviations from this simplified description that cannot be dealt with here.)

SUMMARY

In contrasting religious scenes with alternative and complementary kinds of cultural activity, it becomes clear that the entire behavior complex of which 'offerings' are the ultimate constituents serves the Subanun essentially as a technique, a way of getting things done. To build a house, to grow crops, to cure disease, or to make love, a Subanun may rely on his own 'skills' (*kepandayan*), resort to the 'medicinal' properties of certain substances (*kebuluŋan*), or call upon the supernaturals for assistance (*kanu*). Religion, generally the most expensive and complex of these techniques, belongs especially to the context of crises or potential crises—unanticipatable events with severe consequences and uncertain outcomes. The regular performance of scheduled ceremonies is designed to prevent crises. Unscheduled ceremonies are staged to cope with crises and put events back on their proper course.

The rationale for *religion* (i.e., 'offering'-focused behavior) as a technique lies in the belief that one can accomplish an end by inducing others to act in his behalf. This principle, valid enough in social relationships, the Subanun extend by peopling the universe with unseen beings who have the power to inflict and thereby cure illness. These beings, the 'supernaturals,' are terminologically a species of 'persons' (*getaw*), and they can be influenced by methods resembling those proved effective in social relationships among mortals: offering food and drink, verbal appeals, attention to paraphernalia. A unique network of relationships, canalized by ritual obligations incurred through illness and the threat of illness, links each Subanun with the supernatural inhabitants of the universe, just as his network of social ties is patterned by secular obligations. The supernaturals sanction their demands with their power over health, whereas one's mortal fellows generally employ subtler sanctions of public opinion. In both cases the sanctions prove effective: social relationships are maintained, the supernaturals are fed, and the Subanun patient, if not cured, is perhaps consoled.

These characterizations of Subanun *religion* are summaries of the distributional properties of a structural segment of Subanun cultural activity with respect to contrasting and complementary activities. They are not,

in intention at any rate, simply intuitive impressions of "the meaning of religion in Subanun life" unrelatable to operations performed on ethnographic data. As an adequate ethnographic statement the present paper is deficient in detail and rigor. It merely suggests some of the methodological features of such a statement.

Evon Z. Vogt

STRUCTURAL AND CONCEPTUAL REPLICATION IN ZINACANTAN CULTURE

Utilizing a combination of systematic sequences of behavior, performed repeatedly in rituals observed over a series of years, and of concepts that are expressed explicitly in the Tzotzil language spoken in the Highland Chiapas community of Zinacantan (see Vogt, 1969) in Southern Mexico, this article provides methodological suggestions for the description and interpretation of certain symbolic classifications in Zinacanteco culture. The rules of behavior for a ritual meal are specified and it is shown how they apply to all structural levels in the society from the small domestic family groups up to the tribal affairs in the ceremonial center. Similarly, the Tzotzil concept of "embracing" is traced through several domains of Zinacanteco life, including socialization within the family, as well as baptismal, wedding, and curing ceremonies, and how it is extended symbolically to the activities of the ancestral gods that are believed to reside inside the mountains. These "replications" of important rules of behavior and key Tzotzil concepts in various domains appear to form an amazingly consistent network of symbols, or "code" of the type that Lévi-Strauss describes in his article "The Bear and the Barber" (1963). For a more recent interpretive paper on Zinacantan, the reader should consult E. Vogt and C. Vogt, "Lévi-Strauss Among the Maya" (1970).

Reprinted from *American Anthropologist*, LXVII (1965), 342–353, by permission of the author and the American Anthropological Association.

I. INTRODUCTION

In this essay I propose to examine an organizational principle of Zinacantan culture which I have chosen to call "replication." After seven seasons (1957–1963) of field work in Zinacantan, I believe I am beginning to understand something of the patterns of the culture. One of its patterned aspects that now strikes me forcibly is the systematic manner in which certain ritual behaviors are replicated at various structural levels in the society, and certain concepts, expressed quite explicitly in Tzotzil, are replicated in various domains of the culture. It is as if the Zinacantecos have constructed a model for ritual behavior and for conceptualization of the natural and cultural world which func-

tions like a kind of computer that prints out rules for appropriate behavior at each organizational level of the society and for the appropriate conceptualizing of phenomena in the different domains of the culture.

In my thinking about this principle of "replication" I have been influenced by Evans-Pritchard's description of the concept of *cieng* ("home") among the Nuer, by Kluckhohn's treatment of "patterns" and "configurations," by Lévi-Strauss' ideas about "models" and "codes" for the analysis of social structure and culture, and by Leach's paper on "Rethinking Anthropology," but more especially by what the Zinacantecos have been striving to communicate to me over the past seven years. I have also come to agree strongly with those of my colleagues who propose that a description of cultural behavior is attained by a formulation of what one must know in order to respond in a culturally appropriate manner in a given socio-ecological context. If the ethnographer working in Zinacantan can come to understand the model and the rules that are printed out, then he will have mastered the codes that are necessary to know in order to behave appropriately in the myriad of settings and contexts he confronts in Zinacanteco society. Although I am still some distance from understanding and being able to describe all facets of the model with precision, I offer this description and analysis of the principle of replication as a step in the direction I am following in a monograph now in preparation on Zinacantan.

II. THE MUNICIPIO OF ZINACANTAN

The Highland Maya of Chiapas comprise a nucleus of some 175,000 conservative Indians living in municipio units distributed around the Ladino town of San Cristobal Las Casas. Each municipio speaks a distinct dialect of Tzotzil or Tzeltal, possesses distinctive styles of dress, and has local customs that differ in varying degrees from neighboring municipios. Zinacantan with a 1960 population of 7600 Indians is located just to the west of San Cristobal Las Casas. I have elsewhere described the settlement pattern as typically Maya with ceremonial center and outlying hamlets, or "parajes" as these are called in Chiapas. About 800 Zinacantecos live in the densely settled valley in which the ceremonial center is located; the other 6800 live in the eleven outlying parajes. The ceremonial center contains the Catholic churches, the "cabildo," and a plaza where markets are held during important fiestas. In and around this ceremonial center are located a series of sacred mountains and waterholes which figure importantly in the religious life.

The most important structural feature of the ceremonial center is a religious hierarchy with 55 cargo positions attached to the cult of the saints and the temples. This hierarchy consists of a ranked series of four levels in a ceremonial ladder. To pass through this ceremonial ladder a man must serve a year at each level, and during the time he holds the cargo he must move into the ceremonial center and engage in a complex annual round of ceremonies. The ceremonies are ex-

pensive, costing him as much as 14,000 Mexican pesos for some cargoes, and time-consuming. But while he fills the role, he enjoys special prestige and wears special costumes for ritual occasions. At the end of the year he turns the office over to the next incumbent, and moves back to his paraje to become a corn-farmer again. Some years must elapse before he can work himself out of debt and accumulate enough wealth to ask for a cargo position at the next higher level. The process continues until he passes through the ladder and becomes an honored "pasado."

In addition, there are some 100 to 150 *h ʔiloletik* in Zinacantan. These *h ʔiloletik* are the "curanderos" or shamans in the system. Most of them are men, but some are women, and some are as young as 15 years of age. To become a *h ʔilol*, one dreams three times that one's *ch'ulel* ("inner soul") has been called before the council of the ancestral gods inside the most important sacred mountain and taught how to perform ceremonies. The ceremonies performed by the *h ʔiloletik* include eight types of curing ceremonies, semi-annual ceremonies (held in May and October) for waterhole groups and lineage groups in the parajes, new house ceremonies, rain-making ceremonies in the fields, and three annual ceremonies for the "New Year," the "Middle of the Year" and the "End of the Year." A remarkable feature of the *h ʔiloletik* is the degree to which they are formally organized. For example, they are all in rank order from one to 100 or 150, the rank order depending upon number of years that have elapsed since the practitioner made his debut as a *h ʔilol*.

The subsistence system that supports this complex ceremonial organization is based upon crops of maize, beans, and squash grown in milpas located in the Highlands, but more importantly on lands in Tierra Caliente along the north side of the Rio Grijalva. The diet is supplemented by chickens, eaten especially on ritual occasions, and by beef, especially when cattle are purchased and butchered by cargo-holders for important fiestas in the ceremonial center. Small herds of sheep are owned by Zinacanteco women, with the wool providing materials for many items of clothing woven on the backstrap loom.

III. STRUCTURAL REPLICATION

Just as the settlement pattern of Zinacantan appears to take the form of an aggregate of aggregates ranging from the domestic family house up to the ceremonial center, so also the social structure and ceremonial organization appears to manifest an orderly replication of increasing structural scale.

The social structure of the outlying hamlets is based upon the following residential units: the patrilocal extended family occupying a house compound; the *sna* composed of one or more localized patrilineages; the waterhole groups composed of two or more *snas*; and the paraje.

The house compounds, or "sitios" as they are called in Chiapas, are often enclosed by some type of pole or brush fence and contain one or more dwelling houses, a granary for the storage of maize, a sweat house, and, in the center, a patio cross that serves ritually as a house shrine for the family unit that shares a single corn supply.

The house compounds are grouped into larger units which I call *snas*. The term *sna* means literally "the house of," and it is the term the Zinacantecos themselves use to refer to these residential units that are typically composed of one or more localized patrilineages in which genealogical connections can be traced. The *sna* takes its name from the lineages. In cases where the unit contains only one lineage, there is no problem. The unit is simply called, for example, *sna ʔakovetik*, or the "houses of the wasp nests." In the case of larger *snas* containing two or more lineages, the unit takes its name from the predominant lineage. Thus *sna ʔok'iletik* "the houses of the coyotes," contains the coyote lineage, but also contains two smaller lineages that have settled next to the coyotes and intermarried with them.

The *snas* are in turn grouped into waterhole groups each with distinctive names that are used by the Indians to describe where a persons lives within a paraje. The waterholes are highly sacred, and there are myths about each of them describing the circumstances under which the ancestors found the waterhole and how it acquired its distinctive name. Each waterhole group is composed of two to seven *snas*, the size depending basically upon the amount of water available in the waterhole for household water and for watering sheep and other livestock, such as horses and mules.

There is finally the paraje unit which is composed of one or more waterhole groups. Some small parajes, such as *Elamvo ʔ*, are composed of a single waterhole group; but all of the large parajes, such as *Paste ʔ*, *Nachih*, or *Navenchauk*, are subdivided into two or more waterhole groups.

Just as there exists a social order of ascending scale from the patrilocal extended family in its house compound, through the *sna*, the waterhole group, and up to the paraje, so there is also a ceremonial order of ascending scale that exactly parallels and expresses the social order both in terms of ritual paraphernalia and in terms of ceremonies of increasing size and complexity. Each of the social structural units I have described is symbolized by shrines composed of crosses that are conceptualized by the Zinacantecos as "doorways," or in other words, as means of communication with the *totilme ʔiletik* (the ancestral deities living in the mountains) and with *yahval balamil* (the earth god).

Within the context of the patrilocal extended family living in its house compound there are a series of ceremonies that involve basically the members of the family and never require the services of more than one *h ʔilol*. Typical examples are curing ceremonies for individual members of the family and new house dedication ceremonies.

For each *sna* there are *k'in krus* ceremonies performed in May and in October that involve the services of all of the *h ʔiloletik* who live in the *sna* and the participation of all of the families in the *sna*. This ceremony appears to be a symbolic way of expressing the rights of the members of the *sna* in the lands they now occupy which have been inherited from their patrilineal ancestors.

For each waterhole group there are also *k'in krus* ceremonies performed semi-annually, typically preceding by a few days in May and in October the *k'in krus* rituals of the *snas*. Again, all of the *h ʔiloletik* living in the waterhole group assemble to perform and the participation of all of the families living in the waterhole group is expected. What this ceremony appears to express by its ritual forms are the rights which the members of the waterhole group have to use water from a common waterhole and the obligation they have to care for the waterhole properly.

Finally, the paraje unit is ritually expressed by two annual ceremonies performed by all of the *h ʔiloletik* living in the paraje. These ceremonies are called *ʔach' habil* ("New Year") and *slaheb habil* ("End of Year"), and their function seems to be to symbolize the unity of the paraje and its relationship to the tribal *totilme ʔiletik* in the ceremonial center.

THE RITUAL MEAL: AN ILLUSTRATION OF STRUCTURAL REPLICATION

I now focus upon one aspect of ritual behavior which appears to exemplify in its details the printing out of rules from the general model for appropriate behavioral sequences at various levels in the system, and hence to provide a clear illustration of structural replication.

Ordinary meals in Zinacanteco homes are served on the ground in pottery or gourd bowls. The men sit on small chairs and eat the tortillas and beans from the containers; the women eat later sitting on the ground near the fire. But whenever there is a ritual occasion, there is a *ve ʔel ta mesha* ("meal on a table") which follows carefully prescribed etiquette. The important rules are these:

Rule 1: The meal must be served on a wooden rectangular table. Every Zinacanteco house contains one or more of these small wooden tables. Most of them range in size from approximately 30 × 45 cm. to 60 × 90 cm. and are approximately 45 cm. high. Some are constructed by the Zinacantecos; more commonly they are purchased from the neighboring Chamulas who specialize in the making of small wooden tables and chairs which they sell in the market in San Cristobal Las Casas.

Rule 2: The table must always be oriented with the long axis running East–West. The Zinacantecos have no words in their Tzotzil language with which to distinguish North and South by our compass reckoning, but they do express the East to West axis by speaking of *lok'eb k'ak'al* ("rising or coming up sun") and *maleb k'ak'al* ("setting or disappearing sun").

Rule 3: The table must be covered with a pink and white striped cloth, called mantresh. The women weave this cloth on backstrap looms from cotton thread. The same cloth is used to carry candles from San Cristobal for the ritual.

Rule 4: A bottle of posh ("aguardiente") must be placed in the center of the East end of the table. This action designates the East end of the table as the "head" of the table.

Rule 5: The commensalists must sit in small wooden chairs (also made by Chamulas) at the table in strict rank order. The

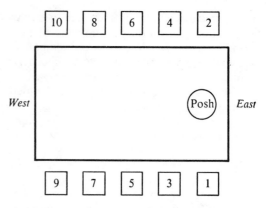

FIGURE 1

most common rank order is expressed in [Figure 1].

Rule 6: The meal consists of posh, maize tortillas, chicken cooked in broth with chile, coffee, and kashlan vah (small round loaves of bread made by Ladinos of wheat flour). Pork or dried fish may be substituted if the family has been unable to afford a chicken, but such substitution is always noted and it is clear that chicken is ideally *the* dish to serve.

Rule 7: The eating of the meal must follow a strictly prescribed sequence which consists of eleven basic steps.

(1) A young man designated as *hp'is vo ʔ* ("drink pourer" or "measurer") serves a round of *posh* using the same shot glass and serving in rank order. The senior man present receives his shot glass of *posh* and engages in appropriate "toasting" and "bowing and releasing" behavior. Briefly, the "toasting" behavior consists of his raising his glass and saying *kich'ban*, followed by a kin term or name, to each person at the table in rank order and receiving the response of *ʔich'o*. The "toasting" is accompanied by the "bowing and releasing"—that is, each of the more junior persons bows his head toward this senior man and is released by the senior man touching the back of his right hand to the forehead of the junior person. The senior man then drinks the shot of *posh* in one gulp, grimaces to show how strong the liquor is, spits a few drops on the floor, and returns the glass of the *hp'is vo ʔ* who proceeds to serve the next man in rank order and the sequence is repeated until the round is complete.

(2) The *mantresh* is either rolled up to the "head" of the table or both sides are rolled to the middle, and a gourd bowl of warm water is placed on the table for wash-

ing hands. The senior man washes his hands and is followed by the others in rank order.

(3) A gourd bowl of water is passed for rinsing out the mouth. The senior man rinses his mouth, spits out the water, and is followed by the others in rank order. The *mantresh* is rolled out again to cover the table.

(4) The chicken in the broth is then served in individual pottery bowls and a stack of tortillas in a gourd container are placed on the table by one of the younger men who receives them from the women cooks. The senior man takes a tortilla, tears off a small piece and dips it into his broth, and eats it. The others follow his lead.

(5) The senior man picks up his bowl and begins to drink the chicken broth. The others follow.

(6) The senior man takes a piece of chicken, places it in a tortilla, and eats it. The others follow. All of the commensalists finish eating at approximately the same time, and they must either eat all of the food served them, or wrap the leftover chicken up in a tortilla and take it home with them.

(7) The *hp'is vo?* serves a second round of *posh*. The sequence of behavior is the same as on the first round.

(8) Each commensalist is then served an individual cup of coffee (sweetened with "panela") with a piece of *kashlan vah* on top. The senior man begins to drink the coffee and eat the bread; the others follow.

(9) The *mantresh* is then removed from the table, and the hand rinsing sequence is repeated, initiated by the senior man.

(10) The mouth washing sequence is repeated, initiated by the senior man.

(11) The *hp'is vo?* serves a third round of *posh*. The same sequence of behavior is followed as on the first and second rounds; and the meal is formally over.

The rules of behavior I have described apply to the *ve?el ta mesha* at all levels in the social system. In the small domestic ceremonies, e.g., at curing or new house dedication ceremonies, a very small table is used and as few as four or five people will eat at the table. The *h?ilol* sits in position 1 and is followed by other men, and then women, in rank order.

In the *k'in krus* ceremonies for the *sna* the table will be larger, and more people will sit at the table. The senior members of the lineage are seated in the most senior position, then followed by the *h?iloletik* in rank order,

and finally by the more junior ritual assistants.

For *k'in krus* for a waterhole group, the scale increases. As many as eight to ten *h?iloletik* have to be seated at the table, along with the ritual assistants, and often two or more tables have to be placed together to provide a larger surface for the meal. For the "New Year" and "End of Year" ceremonies for an entire paraje, the scale becomes still larger and as many as fifteen to twenty *h?iloletik* plus assistants are involved.

The maximum scale is reached at the Fiesta of San Sebastian in January when the entire religious hierarchy of 55 cargo-holders plus the *presidente* and his assistants, sit down to eat at an enormous table and are served not just pieces of chicken, but a whole chicken per person!

But whether the *ve?el ta mesha* involves only one family in a small domestic ritual with a handful of people sitting at a ridiculously tiny table, or, at the other end of the scale, involves the entire religious hierarchy seated in full regalia at the enormous table and consuming entire chickens, the rules of behavior are precisely the same. What is done in the small thatched house of individual families is replicated in ever increasing scale for the lineage, for the waterhole group, for the paraje, and for the whole municipio in the ceremonial center.

The same type of analysis can be made for many other aspects of ritual life in Zinacantan. For example, in ritual processions there are also a set of basic rules—the marching order is always junior man in front and senior man in the rear, the movement of the procession from one sacred place to the next is always counterclockwise and the circuit always brings them back to the house where the procession was initiated, etc. Again, these behavioral sequences are followed whether the procession involves three or four people in a small domestic ceremony, or at the other end of the scale, the procession involves the entire religious hierarchy of cargo-holders performing rituals in the ceremonial center.

These ritual patterns have important symbolic connections with the Zinacanteco view of the world and the relation of their social system to it. The most important *totilme?il-etik* (ancestral deities) are believed to live in the East, and it is no accident that the principal sacred mountain (see below) lies to the

East of the ceremonial center. During a *ve ?el ta mesha* these ancestral deities are believed to appear and to partake of the food and *posh* that is served their living descendants. The living descendants are arranged in rank order at the table in such a way that the eldest (and hence ones closest to becoming deceased ancestors) are seated closest to the East end of the table, next to the *totilme ?iletik*. The more junior members, with more time still to live, are seated further away. Why the marching order in processions follows the rank order from junior man in front to senior man in the rear is still a mystery to me. Nor can I yet explain why processions move around circuits counterclockwise, except to point out that this appears to be an ancient and quite general Maya pattern.

IV. CONCEPTUAL REPLICATION

I now turn to what I have chosen to call conceptual replication. By this I mean that the world of the Zinacantecos is segmented conceptually in systematic ways that are replicated in different domains of Zinacanteco culture.

"EMBRACING": AN ILLUSTRATION OF CONCEPTUAL REPLICATION

Again, for purposes of explanation, I shall focus upon one Zinacanteco concept which appears to exemplify in its details the printing out of beliefs from the general model for appropriate conceptualizing of phenomena in various domains.

There is a word stem in Tzotzil, *-pet*, which means "to embrace" or "to caress." Thus, for example *hpetom* means "embracer" or "caresser." The concept of "embracing" occurs in at least the following domains of Zinacanteco life: the socialization process in the family, the baptismal ceremonies, the wedding ceremonies, the curing ceremonies, and the activities of ancestral gods inside the mountains.

Within the Zinacanteco family it is believed that one of the most important duties of the father and the mother called *tot* and *me'*, is to "embrace" a child and care for it well so that it does not lose its *ch'ulel* ("inner soul") composed of 13 parts. For if the child loses one or more parts of its *ch'ulel*, it will become ill, and may die.

At the baptismal ceremony a child always has a godfather and a godmother, called *ch'ultot* and *ch'ulme?*, or literally "divine father" and "divine mother." Their principal duties during the baptismal ceremony are to "embrace" their godchild while this important ritual is taking place. And perhaps the most important function of the ceremony from the Zinacantecos' point of view is to fix more permanently in the body the child's *ch'ulel* so that it will not be lost so easily.

At a wedding ceremony a ritual specialist called *hpetom* ("embracer") is in charge of introducing the bride into her new home— i.e. the groom's father's house in this system of patrilocal residence. In performing these ritual functions he is believed to "embrace" or "caress" the bride and groom, or in other words, to create a new relationship that will last, one in which the bride will come to like and not run home to her parents' house. In performing this duty he goes through a number of ritual sequences, such as taking the bride and groom into the house, removing their wedding clothes, giving the new couple lectures on how they should behave in their new marriage, instructing the bride's mother-in-law on how she should take care of her new daughter-in-law, and then leading the bride's relatives into the house and introducing them to the groom's parents.

During curing ceremonies a patient who is believed to have lost parts of his *ch'ulel* calls the *h?ilol* ("curer") *tot*. The ritual *tot* in this case is believed to "embrace" the patient in the process of helping him recover the lost parts of his *ch'ulel*.

High above Zinacantan center stands an extinct volcano, rising up to 9000 feet, called *bankilal muk'ta vits* ("older brother great mountain"). Inside the mountain, according to the Zinacantecos, are a series of corrals: one full of jaguars, another full of coyotes, another full of ocelots, and still another full of smaller animals such as squirrels, raccoons, and anteaters. These animals are the *chanuletik* of the Zinacantecos, and the total number adds up to 7600, the same as the population, for each Zinacanteco has a *chanul* as an animal spirit companion—a kind of wild animal alter ego, so to speak. The life of a Zinacanteco is intimately bound to his *chanul* in that anything that happens to the *chanul* automatically happens to him.

Ordinarily, the ancestral gods, called *totilme ?iletik* (literally "fathers-mothers"), live in their houses inside the mountain and take good care of the *chanuletik*. They have their *mayoletik* ("assistants") feed and water them, and they "embrace" them. In other words, we have here the supernatural father and mother "embracing" the alter ego children, if you will.

However, if a Zinacanteco does something wrong, then the *totilme ?iletik* stop "embracing" his *chanul*; in fact, he may be let out of his corral and left to wander loose and uncared for in the forest. In this event, he may be shot at or otherwise injured, and, if so, his human companion will suffer the same fate.

In a very dramatic symbolic way the connection between the real world of people and the supernatural world of *totilme ?iletik* and *chanuletik* is made clear in one ritual sequence in the largest and most complex curing ceremony. Toward the end of the ceremony the patient is placed in a platform bed surrounded with pine boughs, just as the corral of his *chanul* inside the mountain is surrounded by pine trees. As the patient passes through the gateway of his decorated platform bed, called a "corral," in this ceremony, he is like a *chanul* being rounded up and herded through the gate into the supernatural corral inside the "older brother great mountain." In this instance, what is done inside the mountain is replicated in the curing ceremony, and in both domains a *tot* is "embracing" and caring for a patient or his alter ego in the spiritual world.

In a word, in the socialization process within the family, in the ritual life of the baptismal, wedding, and curing ceremonies, and in the supernatural world inside the mountain "fathers" and "mothers" are "embracing" their children. What is conceptualized in one of these domains appears to be replicated in the others, and the result is an amazingly consistent network of symbols that forms a "code" of the type that Lévi-Strauss (1963) writes about in his recent article.

The same kind of analysis can be made for many other concepts in Zinacantan culture. I will mention two by way of example. Another important word stem in Tzotzil is *-il*, which means "to see." Thus, for example *h ?ilol* means "seer." In the Zinacanteco view of the world, there was an ancient mythological time in the past when all Zinacantecos could "see" into the mountains where the ancestral gods are now living. Now, however, only *h ?iloletik* possess this special ability to "see" the gods and communicate directly with them. It follows that *h ?iloletik* are critically important links between ordinary Zinacantecos and the gods for any important ceremony that requires communication and exchange of goods and services with these ancestral gods. Similarly, it is significant that the large complex curing ceremony (described above) is called *muk'ta ?ilel* ("the big seeing") to describe the process by which a patient goes on a pilgrimage to the sacred mountains and "sees" the gods with the aid of the *h ?ilol*.

Another crucial concept in Zinacanteco culture is the contrast between *bankilal* and *?its'inal*. Literally, these terms mean "older brother" and "younger brother," and they are expressed in Zinacanteco kinship terminology. But they are replicated in so many domains of Zinacanteco culture that they lead us to conclude that something much more generic is involved. Indeed, they appear as a way of classifying phenomena in almost any domain in the universe one can mention: there are older and younger brother mountains, crosses, *h ?iloletik*, drums, waterholes, cargo-holders in the religious hierarchy, etc. They are even applied to the Christ figure, for we have discovered that the Nativity scene in the Christmas ceremonies contains Joseph and Mary and then not one, but *two* small Christ children lying in the manger—*bankilal* and *?its'inal*!

They certainly appear to serve as symbols expressing some basic contrasts and oppositions in Zinacanteco life (Lévi-Strauss 1963: 2), and one hypothesis I am working on is that they give general expression to the contrasts and oppositions found in the principle of age-ranking. If this proves to be correct, *bankilal* and *?its'inal* are symbolically expressing both the fact (and probably also the stress) found in not only "older" versus "younger" but also "more powerful" versus "less powerful," "more prestigeful" versus "less prestigeful," etc.

I suggest that these data have implications not only for our understanding of the integration of contemporary Zinacanteco culture, but also for the study of one of the probable processes of Maya cultural development over time. One can imagine how Maya ritual behavior and belief might have developed in complexity by gradual elaboration of the basic elements of domestic ceremonies that were originally performed by small household and hamlet units and were replicated on an increasing scale as the population expanded and the size of the social units increased to encompass the magnificent ceremonial centers with their large sustaining areas containing thousands of households and dozens of small hamlets.

Peter Rigby

SOME GOGO RITUALS OF "PURIFICATION": AN ESSAY ON SOCIAL AND MORAL CATEGORIES

In Gogo society an inauspicious occurrence, like the birth of twins, is a sign that the world is in a bad state and that the male ritual leaders have failed. Women then dress as men and act like warriors to effect a ritual cure. Their violent, transvestite dances, in Peter Rigby's analysis, are seen to be a reversal of normal female domesticity and a parody of the male's violent role. When women act like men, he claims, the ritual state of society is "turned around," the inauspicious banished and a "good" state regained. Transvestism is readily understood as a manipulation of socially opposed categories—women act like supermen, "domestic" becomes "wild"—to achieve a mystical end.

This original consideration of a transvestite ritual follows Durkheim in treating social categories—in this case, "male" and "female"—as the basis for the classification and manipulation of ritual time. At the same time, Rigby's concern for the symbolic structure of the ritual leads him to reject at least one kind of sociological reduction. He refuses to follow Max Gluckman (1954) who analyzed a similar rite as a "ritual of rebellion," a mock battle in which women could vent their frustration with their isolated and inferior social role. While such explanation has some value, Rigby rightly points out that it cannot account for the full complexity of the ritual symbolism, the particular form of role reversal, and other aspects of these Gogo rituals of "purification."

Reprinted in abridged form from E. R. Leach (ed.), *Dialectic in Practical Religion* (Cambridge, England: Cambridge University Press, 1968), pp. 153–178, by permission of the author and the publishers.

The purpose of this paper is an attempt to analyse and explain certain Gogo rituals and religious concepts involving role reversal as a central component. I try to utilize a combination of various analytical ideas put forward recently by several social anthropologists in papers on the sociological analysis of ritual and ritual symbolism (e.g., Lévi-Strauss, 1958; Turner, 1961, 1962*a*, 1962*b*, 1964; Horton, 1960, 1962, 1964; Leach, 1961*a*; and so on). . . .

I

The Gogo are a Bantu-speaking people who inhabit the dry central region of Tanzania, comprising all of the Dodoma Area and parts of Manyoni and Mpwapwa (Mhamvwa) Areas. Gogo numbered some 300,000 persons in the 1957 census.

They have strong cultural and economic attachments to pastoralism and livestock, particularly cattle. Many Gogo have large herds and most values are expressed in terms of cattle. But they subsist basically upon the rather precarious cultivation of sorghum and bulrush-millet crops.

Gogo are divided into about eighty-five patrilineal clans (*mbeyu*, lit. "seeds"). There is a high residential mobility of homestead groups, owing to periodic drought, the exigencies of pastoralism, and witchcraft and sorcery accusations. Land of any category, whether used for cultivation, grazing, or residence, is not inherited. Clan members are therefore dispersed over large parts of the Gogo area. Clans are not corporate and are non-exogamous. But each clan is associated with one or more small ritual areas of "countries" (*yisi*) through the possession of the rainstones (*mabwe gemvula* or "*zimvula*") and the stool (*igoda*) upon which they are kept, which establishes the ritual precedence and authority of the clan within a defined area.

. . .

Gogo cosmological, religious and, in some contexts, social categories may be arranged in two series of opposing but complementary symbolic classifications (Rigby, 1966). In relation to the units with which we are here concerned, the homestead is associated with men, agnatic descent, livestock (the cattle-byre), and a physical independence implied by its residential mobility as a domestic unit together with its livestock. However, within the homestead, centred as it is about the homestead-head, his herd, and concepts of patrilineal descent, each married woman has her own "house" (*nyumba*). She occupies her own set of two rooms, an inner (*kugati*) and an outer (*ikumbo*). In the inner room are all her household effects (*viya*), her grain stores (*madong'a*), her bed (*wulili*), and her hearth (*mafigwa*). Each wife has her own fields, and all the crops cultivated in them are under her control, for the exclusive use of herself, her children (her "house"), and her share in supporting her husband and his guests if he is a polygynist. The husband also allocates parts of his herd (*itewa lyakwe*) to each wife, who uses the milk and other products from her "own" animals only. Upon the death of the husband/homestead-head, only her sons will inherit that part of the herd allocated to her house, and their increase.

Hence each "house" of the homestead group is economically independent of the others, but the homestead-head retains control over the deployment, use, and welfare of the livestock during his lifetime. It is in the context of agricultural subsistence that each married woman is more completely independent, and of course this in turn depends upon the fertility of her fields and the rainfall.

Thus the limited series of oppositions which come into play in this context is as follows:

WOMEN	MEN
matrilateral kin and affines	agnatic kin
crop fertility and rain	livestock health, fertility, and inheritance
influence of ritual leader over fields (land)	human health and fertility
ritual independence of "house" units, but linked to "area"	ritual unity of homestead, independent of area in which it is located

These series have a critical significance for the role women play in Gogo rituals of "purification."

II

Gogo religious concepts imply that the "ritual state" of any area of space may be affected by a variety of agents. The "spirits of the dead" (*milungu*) of the clan with ritual precedence in any area are frequently approached in the ceremonies to ensure fertility and rain. But the spirits of the dead of all persons who died after attaining social maturity are thought to reside in their gravestones (*vitenjelo*), which are their "homesteads" (*kaya*). Gravestones always mark the homesteads of past generations, for the bodies of all persons who did not die of "contagious" (*lona*) diseases or other unusual causes are buried in the cattle-byre in the middle of the homestead.

. . .

Thus in some senses the spirits of the dead are associated with the *areas* in which their gravestones lie. This is particularly so for the spirits of the clan with ritual leadership in the area; at least the spirits of those who have been ritual leaders, and their close kin. But the association of *milungu* with area is not a rigid one, and *milungu* are thought to "be around" and retain their interest in their descendants (in all lines), wherever they may be. Hence it is possible to hold a beer propitiation (*uwujumbi wemisambwa*) to the *milungu* in the front room of the appropriate house of any homestead, wherever the gravestones are.

. . .

But apart from such actions directed explicitly (however vaguely) towards the spirits and designed to ensure the safety of both individual and area, there are many rites which only indirectly refer to the *milungu*. They thus have little to do with the ritual leader's influence. All the Gogo rituals involving role reversal which I analyse here are of this latter type. They are all concerned with the "ritual state" (*mbeho*) of an area of space, and hence the concept *mbeho* needs further elaboration.

In some contexts, the word *mbeho* simply means "wind" or "cold." But even at this basic "sensory" level it has implications for certain religious notions. For during the protracted dry season (seven months or more) the wind blows almost continuously from the east. When the rains come it veers to the northwest. Influence over the "wind" is essential in rainmaking. When *mbeho* denotes "ritual state," however, it can imply either a good, auspicious state (*mbeho swanu*) or a bad one (*ibeho*, or *mbeho mbi*). For example, before initiation ceremonies can be opened (*kugwisa sona*) in a ritual area, the elders and the ritual leader must await the correct physical and ritual conditions (*mbeho swanu*).

The propitious ritual state of any area of space may be upset by actions and events other than offending the spirits of the dead. A variety of other mishaps, misbehaviour, and "unnatural" occurrences might affect it. A "bad" ritual state is symbolized in experiential terms as a strong, violent wind (*ibeho*, lit.). An elder, when discussing the rituals designed to alleviate this state, illustrated it thus:

Truly, a bad ritual state is not productive (. . . libeho mbeka sililelaga, that is, causes destruction and infertility).

He held his stick upright and said:

You see this stick, it is standing up straight? A strong "wind" has not blown it (ilibeho silyaputa). *Perhaps it was protected* (yali yiciwizwe) *by another large plant or tree* (as crops are protected by medicines), *and so it is straight and strong. But if the "wind" were to blow it* (tilting the stick over), *perhaps it would be flattened thus* (as crops are by storms and uncontrolled elements, brought about by a bad ritual state).

Hence, in the present discussion of "purification" rituals, whatever events necessitate them in particular circumstances, the "control" and manipulation of the ritual state (*mbeho*) of an area of space, and the prevention of the destructive forces of a bad ritual state (*libeho*), are the central issues in Gogo thought.

III

All Gogo rituals concerned with the restoration or maintenance of a desirable ritual state in an area of space involve the active participation of women, primarily married women (*wacekulu*). In these contexts, the normative role assigned to men is a passive one, and they are "beaten" by the women if they get in the way. They do, however, often make scathing remarks about the conduct of the women involved in the ritual activities, and risk retaliation if the women are within earshot.

For a set period of time, a certain number of married women, acting in concert, dress like men and ceremonially carry out male tasks performed in "normal" circumstances exclusively by men, or even "prohibited" (*mwiko*) to women. Apart from donning beaded belts (*ndalamai*), smearing on red

ochre (*nghusi*), carrying spears (*migoha*), sticks, and knives (*vipe*, weapons), all normally confined to men, the women sing "lewd" songs and behave in a generally aggressive manner. A major element in all the rituals is dancing (*kuvina*), and the women are said to "dance away" (*kuvinira*) the ritual contamination. In fact, the dancing is the primary "curative" aspect of the ritual, and no other "medicines" (*miti*) are used. In certain cases the dabbing on of soot (*masizi*) is also a preventative measure.

The scale and scope of a particular ritual is determined by the nature of the event which precipitates it. The precipitating events may be classed in two categories: (*a*) those concerned with childbirth and the early development of children, and (*b*) those concerned with the health and fertility of the livestock, particularly cattle. We have seen that, in Gogo theory, these matters should be under the *ritual* control of men. In the case of livestock, it is the man's (the homestead-head's) sole responsibility to ensure their physical and ritual welfare, and to provide fertility medicines (*nghome yang'ombe*) to maintain productivity.

The ritual conditions for success in childbirth and the early development of children are also the responsibility of men. When a girl has her first baby she should be (and usually is) at her natal homestead, and her father or other guardian will kill a goat "to compensate her for the pain and danger" (*kumudesa*) of childbirth. Strong meat broths (*muhuzi*) are made for her from the meat, fat, and bones, to help her regain strength. Traditionally, the skin of this animal became the "carrying skin" (*sambo*) for the child when the mother carried it on her back (*kupapila umwana*). Today the father must also supply a cloth for this purpose. For all children after the first, it is the husband's duty to provide these objects for his wife. He must also obtain from a diviner the small beads or wooden objects (*mhiji*) which are tied over the baby's forehead to ensure closure of the fontanelle suture; and various other objects and medicines. As the children mature, however, his "wife's brothers" (the children's "mother's brothers") will take an increasing interest in their ritual welfare (Rigby, 1964: 322–5).

Why then should women be the only *active* agents in rituals which concern abnormalities in these matters, and behaving like "men" at that? The answer to this question lies upon two levels. The first is that in Gogo theory women are implicated through *mbeho*, which is endangered by unusual events concerning the health and fertility (reproduction) of humans and domestic animals. "Bad" *mbeho* endangers the crops, which are associated with women, "land," areas of space. The second is that, when these events occur and *mbeho* becomes *ibeho* (dangerous ritual state), actions and events must be reversed to restore the "normal" again. Why this is so, and how it relates to Gogo structural and moral categories, is our central problem.

IV

I begin with a description of unusual events concerning childbirth and the upbringing of children, for they involve the less elaborate and inclusive rituals. An appreciation of Gogo ideas about them is necessary before the role of women in the more complex rituals may be fully understood. . . .

Unusual childbirth and early development may be classified under several categories in Gogo thought, and there are some local variations in the classifications and appropriate actions recommended. In southern Ugogo, a breech delivery (*mwana mono akulongoza iciwino*, or *migulu*) is classed as *wufuli*. In this area, little or no public ritual may be involved in this event. Some people believe that such children should not be caught in a rainstorm, lest they and others with them be struck by lightning, *imuli* (cf. Beidelman, 1963:54–5). An *wufuli* child may be struck even inside a building, and those with him should smear soot (*masizi*) from the cooking-pots on him to prevent any mishap. No other rituals are involved and the parents of such children are not required to undergo any ceremony. There is, however, a mild feeling of concern with possible ritual danger (*ibeho*).

In central Ugogo, a breech delivery is classed as *nghalamanje*, which also includes children who cut their upper teeth first and twins. And, in central Ugogo at least, *nghalamanje* demands a ritual of purification lest *ibeho* result and the crops be destroyed. Such children suffer no personal disabilities, although they constitute a "danger" to their fellows and the area in which they live if this is not averted by ritual action. It is the *event* of their unusual birth or development that precipitates the danger and this must be rectified by ritual.

On the birth of twins (*wana wematundu* or *imetundu*), only three or four married women, the midwives, neighbours in the homestead cluster, or kin need be involved in the ritual. They dress up in men's garb (*masweko gacilumelume*), take spears, and dance away the ritual danger (which is not great in such a case) to the west. They need not even go to the western boundary of the ritual area to "throw it away" (*kutaga* or *kukupa*) as they do in more serious cases. They may take it only two or three hundred yards west of the homestead, and then return. In such a case it is primarily the homestead cluster which is implicated.

If there is a miscarriage, however, or the twins are still-born, or die soon after birth, a much more serious situation results. Married women of the whole neighbourhood, or even the ritual area, are involved, and the *ibeho* must be taken to the extreme western boundary of the ritual area before it is thrown away, preferably into a pool or swamp.

Although I observed several of the rituals related with cattle disease (*cahola*) described in the following section, I did not witness one for the prevention of *ibeho* brought about by the birth of twins (*nghalamanje*). But I did get several descriptions of these *nghalamanje* rituals from various informants, all of which tallied pretty closely with each other, and, with certain differences, with my own observations for the cattle ceremonies. I present one informant's version here:

The people who bring ibeho *into the country are women who give birth to twins. Even if they bear them during the dry season* (ibahu) *and do not "dance it [the danger] away"* (wekale siwavinire), *when the rains come they will be the rains of ritual danger* (mvula yabeho). *So the married women do the* ibeho *dance* (wuvina webeho), *for they say, "When the rain comes, it will destroy the grain* (yomala uwuhemba) *and will destroy the [fertility] medicines* (miti)."

When they go out to dance the ibeho *dance, the women don cloths, "caps"* (nghofila), *and they take spears, knives, and umbrellas* (minvuli). *They then search out perhaps a woman who bears children who always die* (mono katagaga iwana), *and they dab* (kutona) *spots of soot on her, and ochre, ashes, and white clay upon themselves and her. They go dance with her, and they say, "Nhembo zabaka iwana malongo" ["the elephants have smeared the 'children' with wet clay"].*

When women go to dance the proper ibeho *dance, many of them gather together, some coming from the east, some from the south, some from the north, and some from the west. They agree to meet at the* homestead of one of their number at the appropriate time.

When they meet, they move off in a group, towards the west, giving the alarm call (kucenga lwanji), and singing abusive songs (membo gamaligo) like:

Cisumbili cibeneka,
The little homestead building-pole is broken,

Citombele hasi![1]
So that we must have intercourse upon the ground!

And so they go off, singing, until they reach a water-pan or swamp (ilamba) to the west, where they "throw down" (kikupa) the ibeho . . . When they have thrown away the ibeho and bathed, they cannot sing such a song again; it is forbidden (mwiko). They may perhaps go to the ritual leader (mutemi), taking him a "good cloud" (livunde liswanu, i.e., good rains, and all their consequences). They have thrown away that bad rain of the ibeho.

So they go to the mutemi's homestead and assemble there in the cattle-byre. The mother of the ritual leader (or his senior wife if the former is dead) emerges and comes over to spray them with water, "cooling" them (. . . yakuwapoza). She says, propitiating for them:

Lipole livunde,
Let the cloud be cool,

Yeza tonya mholo,
So that it will rain gently,

Ninga libeho likatale!
But let the ritual danger pass!

Libeho likatale,
Let the ibeho pass,

Sililelaga.
For it is not fertile.

Then the women disperse, and that one [who caused the ibeho] will bear again, properly [not twins, if they were alive; or living twins if the nghalamanje was a result of a miscarriage].

The ritual is thought not only to help "cure" the person who caused the ibeho, but to have a good effect upon all childbirth in the area and to prevent the occurrence of unusual events.

It should be noted that in the nghalamanje purification ritual, the women take the necessary action automatically after the event, and do not have to consult divination first. This is unusual, in that almost all other ritual action in Gogo society is preceded by

[1] Such songs are always difficult to interpret exactly, and opinions vary. One informant suggested, "They sing like this because the homestead has fallen (kaya yagwa; due to the nghalamanje birth), so people have intercourse (wakwigonya) upon the ground—a very bad thing." It appears certain that cisumbili (lit. small, upright, building-pole) refers also to "penis." Reference to the male sexual organs by women in these rituals is recurrent; unheard-of behaviour in a "normal" context. Kutomba is also a crude word for the sexual act.

divination. Here the event of nghalamanje or wulfuli is the indicator, rather like an omen (ndeje) or serious portent of danger (ipoto) (cf. Beidelman, 1963). The ritual leader need not be consulted beforehand, although he is informed of the ritual when it has been completed. All these are indicators of the "abnormal" or "unusual" character of the role reversal rituals themselves. Also emphasized is the fact that it is the mother or senior wife of the ritual leader who "cools" the women of their "hot/dangerous" state resulting from the rite, even though they have bathed themselves after throwing away the ibeho.

V

The most common reason for role reversal purification rituals, and one which also involves the concept of mbeho, is the incidence of a cattle disease called masaho. When the cattle are stricken by this disease, it is immediately apparent to the observer, and again no prior divination is required before countermeasures can be taken. The first symptoms of masaho are the absence of the correct amount of cream in the milk, its thinness, and the fact that it goes bad almost immediately it is in the milking gourds (nhoma). The men and boys then begin watching the cattle themselves. Further symptoms become apparent when the animals begin to walk slowly and stiffly (zikusenzegula), dragging their hooves, and they become rapidly thinner. Another sign is that the bulls do not mount the cows when they should. The men are then convinced that the cattle are sick, and that ritual action is necessary. For in spite of their own constant efforts to protect the herd, they have been affected by masaho. They then go to the women and say, "The cattle are stricken; go and herd cahola" (Mubite mukadime cahola, zing'ombe zeza tamwa).

Cahola is thus the ritual "cure" (uwuganga) for the disease masaho. For Gogo the cure in cahola does not involve the use of medicines per se (miti); they say simply that the men ask the women to "dance for the cattle" (kuvinira zing'ombe), just as in the nghalamanje ritual they dance away the ibeho. The women may also be said to be "giving the alarm call for the cattle" (wakucenjera zing'-ombe). The linked notions are of violent action by women masquerading as men, and war. But although the women are primarily concerned in this case with effecting a "cure" for the livestock, the concept of *mbeho* is also incorporated in the ritual action, for they are at the same time ridding the country (*yisi*) of diseases:

Women simply herd *the cattle; there are no medicines involved* (. . . musina miti). *They dance for the cattle. But they do this to "cool" (kupoza) the cattle and the country* (nesi), *so that diseases may be removed from it* (. . . ziwuce ndigana).

I saw several *kudima cahola* rituals and the account I present here is based primarily upon my observations. Further information from informants who described the formal aspects of the ceremony is added. I therefore do not follow a particular ritual but give a generalized description of its main elements.

It is the men who go to the women and ask them to perform the ritual when they realize that *masaho* has affected the livestock. This is the first indication of their explicit consent in the passive role they are to play during the ceremony. Married women with children (*wadala*), who are still active, usually take the leading part, although unmarried girls may join in. They may come only from the homesteads whose herds are apparently affected, but during the course of the ritual other herds may be involved (see later), and in fact the whole ritual area is concerned if the situation appears to be serious.

As with other role reversal rituals, the women dress up as men, putting on men's dancing bells (*ncinda*, tied on below the knee), knives, and beaded belts. They also take spears, sticks, and machetes, and tie on their clothes (*myenda*) in male fashion, knotted over the right shoulder, leaving the left shoulder bare.

The evening before the ritual begins, the women begin giving the alarm call (*kucenga lwanji*) at occasional intervals. This is "to inform each other" of the ritual on the morrow (*kwilalika*, from *kulalika*, "to invite") so that all who wish to participate may be prepared.

Early the following morning, the women, attired as men, drive out the cattle of the affected homesteads to pastures in the bush. They do this noisily, giving the alarm call and singing:

Cahola, cahola,
Cahola, cahola,

Leka ng'ombe zidime!
Let the cattle graze!

The men of the affected homesteads remain at home, idling or attending to other tasks;

the older and less active women and young girls are also there.

The women, now called *wanyacahola* ("those with the *cahola*"), herd the cattle in the bush all day, as the men normally do. If they come across a youth grazing another herd in the bush, they "attack" him with switches (*mikotya*) and drive him away. Then, giving the alarm call and singing triumphantly, they add his herd to their own (*wakutowerera zose*) and drive them on. They are "raiding" the cattle (*kutanga zing'ombe*, "to take livestock by force"), and the emphasis is again upon their "warlike" behaviour. Cattle-raiding was the main occasion for warlike aggression in Gogo society, and when the women carry out these symbolic raids, they sing:

Wazelelo, mulawile hai?
Young men, where do you come from?

And the refrain is taken up:

Cilawile kutanga imagombe,
We come from raiding the big cattle,

Catanga ho, go Mutaturu!
Oh how we raided, those [the cattle] of the Taturu.

The youth who may have had his herd snatched away by the women passively returns home and joins the men waiting for the return of the herds. He tells them, "Those with *cahola* have raided [them]" (*Watanga wanyacahola*).

The first day of the ritual is called *muwango*. This is derived from *kuwanga*, which denotes the activities of the first day of *any* rituals that may be spread over several days. On the second day the same actions are repeated, and it is called *mwiyajiko*, from *kwiyajika* ("to perform the second day of any ritual," *kwituma yakejete*). These terms are used for no activities other than ritual ones.

On each day, when the women drive the cattle back to the homesteads in the evening, they do so with stylized aggressive behaviour. With their herding switches they attack the men and youths standing about, scornful of the inability of the women to herd properly. The *wanyacahola* also make feints at the men with their sticks and knives, and sing:

Mahumha gaza,
The terrible Masai have come,

Manya Cisongo, hoyo ho,
The awful Kisongo Masai, hoyo ho,

Mahumha gaza!
The Masai have come!

The women visit in turn each of the home-steads involved (including those from which they have "stolen" the herds), separating out the cattle (*wakukoma zing'ombe*) them-selves and returning them to their home byres. They are met at each homestead by the old women and girls; it is forbidden (*mwiko*) for the men to meet them or to help in returning the livestock to their byres. The women also close the byre gates (*kudinda madeha*), very much a man's job. If it is wrongly done and the gate-poles are not firmly in place, the herd is left seriously open to attack by hyenas and other animals during the night. The men cannot do it because the *cahola* women have "snatched" the function from them (*wawa-boka*).

At each homestead, the *wanyacahola* are given a meal of sorghum or millet porridge (*uwugali*), milk, and a relish made with oil or fat (*mboga yamafuta*, considered specially delicious and therefore unusual). This meal is prepared for them by the older women, and is left for them *outside* the homesteads, to the west of them, and they eat it there. In some cases they may even eat it near or on the rubbish midden (*cugulu*), which is situated to the west of each homestead (cf. Rigby, 1966). But more generally they have their brief meals simply outside the gate, in the cleared area near each homestead (*mulazo*) or in the "bush" (*mbago*) (Rigby, 1964: 176, 190–1; Cory, 1951: ch. VIn.). Although meat at sacrifices may be eaten outside the home-stead at the gravestones of the spirits of the dead, the staple meal (*uwugali*) is always provided by a married woman for her hus-band and children in the *inner* room (*kugati*) of her own house (*nyumba*). Even guests and strangers must be invited into the *nyumba* of a woman who has cooked them a meal.

On the first day of *cahola*, the women disperse to their own homesteads after the meal. On the second and final day, however, they return the cattle, finish their "meals," then dance, singing, to the western boundary where they "throw down" (*kukupa*) the disease (*ibeho*) into a swamp, as in the *nghalamanje* rites described in the previous section. After this, they may or may not in-form the ritual leader and go through the "cooling" ritual, depending upon the serious-ness of the epidemic.

Throughout the ritual the women actively involved are thought of *as a group* (*wanya-cahola*) with particular, identifiable qualities;

that is, the overemphasized stereotypes of aggressive male sexuality and behaviour. When the ritual is over, the *wanyacahola* are said to "disperse" (*kwiyagala*) in order to return to "normal" life and form.

During the two days and nights of the ritual, the women are strictly forbidden (*mwiko*) from sleeping with men; that is, until they have "completed the second day of ritual action" (*sunga weyajice*). As soon as the men take up their herding sticks again, on the third morning, the prohibition lapses and the women can sleep with their husbands again. Apart from the aggressive, "male" behaviour and the singing of rude songs, the only other prohibition upon women which is explicitly *suspended* during the *cahola* ritual is that prohibiting menstruating women from touching their husband's (or any man's) weapons (*vipe*). Contrary to the position obtaining amongst most other cattle-keeping peoples in east, central, and southern Africa, Gogo women are not prohibited from close contact with cattle in normal circumstances. Women frequently herd livestock when no one else is available, although this is not normatively correct. Only they milk the cattle in the mornings and evenings; cir-cumcized youths and men do so only if no woman is available. Woman are allowed to move freely into and through the cattle-byres (*mabululu*, *magagala*), even during men-strual periods. But in normal circumstances, a menstruating woman must not touch her husband's weapons or tools; if she does, they will be "spoiled" (*zikuvila*). My evidence in-dicates that this prohibition is suspended during *cahola*, and a menstruating woman may thus take part in the ritual, carrying her husband's or another man's weapons. This would emphasize even further the complete-ness of the symbolic role reversal which takes place, for how could a "man" be prohibited from touching weapons? But there may be considerable local variation in this.

VI

A remarkable similarity of outline in ritual action and symbolism is evident in the Gogo *cahola* and *nghalamanje* rituals and the Zulu *Nomkubulwana* ceremonies. It is equally clear that explanation in terms of conflict and rituals of rebellion is inadequate for an understanding in sufficient depth of the details of symbolic action and symbols in the Gogo rituals.

. .

VII

But if we abandon a purely functional approach and a theory of conflict, what alternative explanation may we offer for the Gogo *nghalamanje* and *cahola* rituals (and, by implication, perhaps the Zulu *Nomkubulwana* ceremonies as well) which takes sufficient account of the relevant structural processes of each society? And furthermore, what depth of detail in symbolism and meaning may be explained, which is not explained by Gluckman's theory?

We have seen that an interpretation in terms of rebellion accounts for few of the symbolic actions and meanings of the *Nomkubulwana* ceremonies; they are all reduced to the same functional common denominator. It may explain the "aggressive," "warlike" behaviour of the women in terms of "conflict"; but it does not explain such features as their obscene behaviour, their dancing, or the fact that they take something "bad" from the country and "throw it away" (not mentioned by Gluckman in his analysis). Surely, if we are to explain these rituals satisfactorily, such details must be accounted for on more than a descriptive level. And, clearly, they cannot be explained by rebellion.

Again, an essential feature of the Gogo *cahola* ritual (the most extended of the reversal rituals) is that the women must eat their symbolic meal in the "bush," away from "normal" humanity and outside the homestead where all meals are normally eaten. How is this related to conflict and rebellion? And we find that exactly the same symbolic action occurs in the Zulu *Nomkubulwana* ritual but remains unaccounted for:

Towards midday, our herding girls brought home the cattle from the veld; but no sooner had the cows been milked than back they went with them again to graze, the reason for the hurry being that they were not allowed that day to eat at home. But they circumvented the tabu by taking back with them calabashes of the Nomdede [ritual] beer and dishes of more substantial fare; upon which, on a selected spot, the assembled girls ate, drank and made merry. But here again no male, old or young, dared approach the girls while thus out on the veld. As the sun was setting, the girls brought the cattle home, doffed their male attire and resumed their own ubendle *girdles (Bryant 1949:661).*

We may therefore legitimately conclude that the richness of symbolic meaning and behaviour evident in the Gogo *cahola* and *nghalamanje* rituals cannot be explained by a functional theory of ritual rebellion, and much of it remains unaccounted for in the Zulu ceremonies. The cohesive functions for social groups that rituals may have are important; but this is undoubtedly a very limited aspect of them, and leads eventually to an explanatory dead end.

In fact, it is not necessary to postulate equilibrium and social cohesion as the functional roots of social structures when attempting to find structural explanation for role reversal rituals. Instead, we must attempt to establish a relationship between the categories of meaning on all levels, exegetical, operational, and positional, expressed in ritual, and the structural categories (the categories of persons and their interrelationships) relevant to the rituals. In order to do this, the structural principles underlying the symbolic and social orders must be isolated. Their structural interrelationship may then be established.

The question arises: why should the structure of symbolic meaning in ritual and the structure of social categories be in any way connected in any society? Religious ideas and the myths which underlie them (and hence the symbolic meanings of ritual actions and their associated concepts) are, at least in part, attempts to *explain* the "order" or "disorder" of natural objects and events and man's place in them. They are aspects of cosmological systems (Horton, 1964: 96). Such explanations must necessarily be in terms of abstractions; of what may be termed "theoretical models." Models are, however, based upon analogies, and the prototypes of models are usually taken from the more ordered objects, processes, or events in everyday life (Horton, 1964:98). In small-scale societies such as those of the Gogo and the Zulu,

people's activities in society present the most markedly ordered and regular area of their experience, whereas their biological and inanimate environment is by and large less tidily predictable. Hence it is chiefly to human activities and relationships that such communities turn for the sources of their most important explanatory models (Horton, 1964: 99; cf. Leach 1961a: 133).

Hence we ". . . often see the prototypes of African religious models in the social life of the peoples who have evolved them" (Horton, 1964: 98). Lévi-Strauss also tells us in his brilliant analysis of myth (1958: ch. XI) that ". . . social life validates cosmology by its similarity of structure. Hence cosmology is true."

I have demonstrated in considerable detail elsewhere (Rigby, 1966), and have outlined briefly in an earlier section of this paper, that Gogo symbolic values constitute a system of dual and complementary categories. This is true not only of the complementary opposition of cosmological concepts and values such as: east-south-up-"good" as opposed to west-north-down-"bad," but also of social and physical categories and the relations between them, such as: male-right/female-left. In the Ego-oriented network of kin relationship categories, those related through the female ("mother") are given opposed but complementary characteristics to those related through the male ("father"). I have outlined the relevant associations above.

But "time," or the process of events both natural and social, is also subject to classification under complementary dualistic notions. As a process of events, "time" may imply either "good" or "bad" (ritual) states. I have indicated that Gogo perceive ritual states as being of two opposing kinds. A good or auspicious ritual state (mbeho swanu) is signified by a series of good or auspicious events. This state, however, can be upset (or "inverted") by inauspicious events, such as those connected with childbirth in the case of nghalamanje or wulfuli, or masaho cattle disease in the case of cahola. These produce bad ritual states (ibeho).

When this occurs, "time," in a sense, is "reversed" (Leach, 1961a: 133). That Gogo think of good and bad ritual states as the complete obverse of one another and as alternations in "time" is illustrated by the following. Of a year which is characterized by disasters such as droughts, crop pests and so on, and marked by bad omens (ndeje mbi) or events which are auguries of greater disaster (miyogo, mapoto, malubolubo, minozo), Gogo say "Myaka yipituce" (lit. "the years have turned about"). Thus:

A friend of mine, Malenga ala Nghuli, had fallen from a baobab tree while collecting honey, and severely damaged his spine. While on our way to help him to hospital, one of my companions said, "A, the work of honey-collecting is hard indeed!" Another replied, "But don't they do it all the time? [This accident] . . . is just one of the signs of a bad year [i.e. in the "normal" course of events, people collect honey without accident]. The years have indeed turned about (myaka yipituce)!"

Thus time between good and bad ritual states (implied by a series of good or bad events) is thought of by Gogo as an alterna-

tion (cf. Leach 1961a: 130). The fact that these "alternations" do not occur at regular seasonal or other intervals like the Nomkubulwana rituals does not affect the interpretation. There is a good deal of evidence to show that similar rituals occurred[*] at odd intervals amongst other Bantu-speaking peoples, usually when crops were affected by pests, or diseases attacked humans or domestic animals.

It remains to demonstrate the connexion between this alternation (however irregular) in "time" or ritual states and the role reversals involved in nghalamanje and cahola rituals. This may be effected only by establishing the operational and positional meanings of the symbols and symbolic actions of the rituals, in terms of the general series of dual symbolic classifications obtaining in Gogo social and value categories.

I have shown that men, as a social category, are expected in Gogo society to provide for the control of the safety, health, and fertility of the human and animal populations in their homesteads. Women, on the other hand, are concerned with the medicines obtained from the ritual leader and used to ensure good crops and protect them from damage and pestilence. Thus, when unusual or unnatural events occur in the reproductive processes or general health and productivity of humans or animals (which covers both nghalamanje and cahola) in spite of the men's constant efforts, "time" is reversed and a bad ritual state (ibeho ibi) is created. The complementary opposition between the sexes as social categories now provides the "model" for the manipulation of ritual symbols to attain a desired end. That end is a "re-reversal" of time and a return to the previous ritual state and events (mbeho swanu). In order to bring this about, this reversal of time and thus a return to the previous state, a ritual involving role reversal presents itself as the model for symbolic action.

It is the women who carry out the active part of the ritual. They invade the sphere of men, where the latter have failed. But they can do so only "as men." Their role reversal is a "caricature" of the stereotypes of masculinity and male activities in Gogo society. This caricature has elements both of "exaggerated role" and satirical intent. As women, their reversal is complete; they are more "male" than the men. The men passively condone this, even ask the women to perform it in the case of cahola. The ritual inversion of the "model" provided by the social categories of men and women, with their associations of opposed and complementary characteristics, is a ritual manipulation of "time" and ritual state. And the link between them can only be isolated in terms of the positional meaning of the symbols and symbolic actions in the rituals, in relation to the total system of dual symbolic categories which permeates Gogo social and moral values.

I noted earlier that limited exegetical meaning can be obtained for the Gogo *nghalamanje* and *cahola* rituals, in spite of rich exegesis in other ritual activities. Some exegetical meaning can, of course, be seen from the songs. But once the positional meaning of role reversal and its associated symbolic actions has been established, as I have now done for the Gogo rituals, the operational meanings of various detailed symbolic actions immediately become clearer. The "obscene" behaviour of the women is seen to be primarily manifested in songs referring to the male sexual organ, the phallus. The aggressive behaviour in "attacking" the men emphasizes the role of men in war and cattle theft, and is again a caricature of the male stereotype. The women in *cahola* takes cattle by force and call themselves "Masai," which clearly lends force to this interpretation. So, too, does the noisy dancing by the women, wearing men's leg-bells (*ncinda*). The insistence that it is the "dancing" (*wuvina*) that is the curative power, *uwuganga*, is also explained. But a further element is involved here.

During the course of the ritual, the "male women" are "sacred" (cf. Leach, 1961a: 133–4); they are in the transitional state of *marge* (Van Gennep, 1908). Although they are caricaturing the stereotypes of masculinity, in themselves the women are beyond the pale of normal society. They represent the ritual symbols being manipulated for a desired end. This is expressed in their references to themselves as "enemies," outsiders who kill and steal cattle, but most strongly in their symbolic meals "in the bush." They cannot eat in the homestead as "normal" people do, and they cannot have sexual intercourse with "men." But the association of women with the "bush" (*mbago*), "wild-

ness," and the "undomesticated" during the rituals is quite consistent with the general series of dual symbolic classifications. Its positional meaning is seen immediately when we realize that, in general classification, women are associated with the "domesticated," "cultivated" parts of fields; men with the wild, the bush, and the tasks of bringing it into common use and domestication (Rigby, 1966). It is thus a further symbolic expression of the women's temporary "maleness."

Having returned "time" and the ritual state to the normal end of the alternation by "throwing away" the *ibeho*, they themselves go through a minor rite of aggregation (in the more extensive rituals) by "washing" and "being cooled" (*kupozwa*) by the ritual leader's mother or senior wife.

The final act of "throwing away" the *ibeho* over the western boundary (*mimbi yomwezi*) of the area involved is also directly linked with the general series of symbolic oppositions. Its symbolic meaning therefore lies primarily in the positional and operational contexts. The west is associated with death, darkness, sorcery, and evil spirits. It is the way in which the wind (*mbeho*) blows. You cannot "throw" sickness or contamination away to the east, for the wind will blow it back in again.

VIII

An investigation of the structural principles underlying the total range of symbolic meanings in Gogo *nghalamanje* and *cahola* rituals enables us to relate them to the structure of Gogo social categories on the relevant level of complementary opposition between the sexes. Interpretation and explanation of rituals involving role reversal are attained in terms of the structure of Gogo social and moral categories, by exposing the symbolic meanings expressed in the rituals on all three levels, positional, operational, and exegetical. This is aided by a consideration of the rituals in their manipulative aspects. Such an approach avoids the imposition of teleological and functional assumptions upon the data. It also prevents neglect, as important elements in explanation and understanding, of the details of ritual action and symbolic meaning which distinguish one ritual from another.

5
MYTH

Introduction

In many respects the study of myth may be seen as a microcosm of the development of anthropology. Nearly all of the theoretical and methodological trends which have been current at one time or another in the past century in Europe and in America have had something to say about myth. Some ideas on the nature of myth belong very much to their time and have ceased to provoke much more than a smile or a sigh of wonderment. An example is the celebrated debate which raged at the turn of the twentieth century between the German philologist F. Max Müller and the Scottish anthropologist Andrew Lang. Müller contended that modern Indo-European myth was a "disease of language," a fragmentary and degenerate survival of phrases and words from an ancient Indo-European solar cult. Lang, influenced by the work of Sir James Frazer (author of *The Golden Bough*), countered this diffusionist fantasy with the evolutionary notion that primitive peoples everywhere had similar beliefs, tales, and customs, and that these survived in classic Greek and Roman myths and in modern European folklore. Lang spent decades in mustering evidence from the corners of the earth to refute Müller's naïve notions. Ironically, Lang's own assumptions about universal evolutionary stages of development from barbarism to civilization (with concomitant change in kind and function of myth) shared some of Müller's rather simplistic ideas concerning cultural process and

origins. This debate, now something of a curiosity in the history of folklore studies and anthropology, is well reported in Richard Dorson's paper "The Eclipse of Solar Mythology" (1955).

Other anthropological works about myth have fared better with time and more comprehensive ethnographic data than those of the solar mythologists, diffusionists, and evolutionists. In fact, some have endured so well that their basic tenets have become a part of what we "assume" about the nature of belief systems in nonliterate societies. Such a perennial classic is Bronislaw Malinowski's *Myth in Primitive Psychology* (1926), in which he disposed once and for all of the notion that myth was a trivial cultural decoration. He suggested, on the basis of extensive field work in the Trobriand Islands, that myth was an integral part of social life, that it provided a "charter for belief," a sacred underpinning and legitimizer for all that people do and think. Although he has been rightly criticized for the static nature of his concept of "myth as charter" (Leach, 1954, and Firth, 1961), students of oral tradition in general and of myth in particular owe him a considerable debt.

Malinowski also has a respected place in the development of the anthropological tradition of field work, a way of gathering primary data which places emphasis on intensive observation of and participation in the daily lives of those whom the anthropologist is studying. With regard to myth studies, the obvious advantage of this method over the use of libraries and archives is that it enables the observer to rely on firsthand performances of narratives in their proper cultural contexts. Slightly before the time of Malinowski's major field work, Franz Boas, in America, and A. R. Radcliffe-Brown, in England, were also responsible for doing and encouraging others to do field collections and holistic interpretations of oral traditional material. All have been influential in the development of anthropological thinking about mythology. Good discussions and bibliographies on the history of anthropological treatment of myth can be found in Cohen (1969), Dundes (1963 and 1965), and Georges (1968).

Definitions of myth have been debated since primitive religion became a topic of scholarly attention. The term "myth" at best serves as a unifying concept which enables anthropologists to talk about etiological narratives and other forms which, for the society involved, make up a body of "assumed knowledge" about the universe, the natural and supernatural worlds, and man's place in the totality. At worst, the term "myth" is a weak one, for it implies a uniform, sacred explanatory power for etiological narratives everywhere. The disadvantages inherent in this assumption are obvious. For example, secular narratives which are classed as *märchen* in European taxonomies frequently enter the oral traditions of societies which have experienced contact with the West as narratives which have some sacred significance. What is a secular tale for one society often becomes a sacred myth for another, and vice versa. Furthermore, most societies have their *own* taxonomies of verbal behavior. Such taxonomies often reveal that even within a single society all genres of etiological narrative do not have equal sacred value or explanatory power. The term "myth," therefore, should be used advisedly as a convenient general label for an enormous diversity of narrative styles, contents, forms, and functions.

This chapter presents several anthropological approaches to myths from Western and non-Western societies. All of the writers share the point of view that significant statements about myth should be context-conscious. That is to say that myth texts stand alone only feebly. Myths and other narratives, as well as analysis of them, must be accompanied by considerable ethnographic background if they are to become intelligible for one who does not know them as a part of his own cultural experience. (See Bascom, 1953, and Dundes, 1963, for clear statements of this point of view.) Myth may be profitably analyzed from several context-conscious perspectives. Several of these approaches are represented in this chapter.

William Lessa's paper "Discoverer-of-the-Sun" is both a critique and an example of a method which seeks in myth a reflection of cultural content which might otherwise escape the attention of the anthropologist. W. E. H. Stanner, in his paper "The Dreaming," also approaches myth as a source of native projective information. He is concerned with the Australian aborigines' cosmological and philosophical concept of "dream time," which serves as the temporal backdrop of their myths. Unlike Franz Boas, an important precursor of this tradition of myth interpretation (see his *Kwakiutl Culture as Reflected in Mythology*, 1935), Lessa and Stanner have been careful *not* to assume a one-to-one relationship between myth on the one hand and cognitive or social reality on the other. They demonstrate in their respective papers that the relationship is far more subtle and elusive than that.

Whereas the culture-reflector method generally treats myth as a reservoir of information about the cultural whole, the psychoanalytic methods of myth analysis—based on the work of Sigmund Freud, Géza Róheim, Carl Jung, and others—usually approach myth as an expressive phenomenon whose primary referents are the individual and his unconscious conflicts with societal constraints on the one hand and his biological, animal nature on the other. The method generally assumes certain symbolic representations of these conflicts to be universal. In an interesting paper included in this chapter, Professor Dundes explores the psychoanalytic implications of a widely encountered myth motif, that of the creation of the earth from dirt or mud brought from the bottom of the primeval waters. Bibliographies of other good studies in this vein may be found in Fischer (1963) and Kiell (1963).

The second part of this chapter is devoted to a new tradition of myth analysis, which approaches the phenomena of myth as ideal statements about social categories and their interrelationships. In other words, myths are treated not as simple culture reflectors or as universal unconscious projections of individual conflicts, but, rather, as cultural codes or logical models by means of which the human mind can order experience, especially contradictions in experience. This general orientation to myth analysis has received increasing attention recently largely because of the influence of Claude Lévi-Strauss. Among his many contributions to the study of myth have been *La Pensée sauvage* (1962) and his ambitious *Mythologiques* series on the New World (1964, 1966, and 1968), the latter of which has impressed many as the major piece of myth scholarship of our time. A relatively early formulation (1955) of his method of analysis is reprinted in this chapter. Lévi-Strauss's brilliant contributions to the study of myth have been wide-ranging. Among them, he has focused our attention on the logic of myths. This perspective requires that primary attention be given to myth form (structure); myth content for him is a complementary consideration. Related to his interest in logical homologies (structure) in various texts and other expressive domains is his insistence that *all* versions of myths are "correct" versions. In focusing our attention upon "binary oppositions"—nature/culture, high/low, sky/earth, raw/cooked, and so on—and the role of myths in mediating these oppositions, and upon the ways in which myths are like a "science of the concrete"—instead of the *p* and *q* of mathematical thinking, we have jaguars and wild pigs related to each other in formal logic—Lévi-Strauss has added a dimension to the study of myths that anthropologists can ill afford to ignore in spite of the methodological pitfalls facing the analyst who chooses to work with the concepts. Perhaps most important of all has been Lévi-Strauss's rekindling of anthropological interest in myth studies. Useful summaries, applications, and critiques of his treatment of myth may be found in Hayes and Hayes (1970) and Leach (1967; 1970).

Although they have generally been sympathetic with Lévi-Strauss's objectives in the study of myth, British social anthropologists have provided some of the more incisive criticisms of his methods and conclusions, which often appear to be intuitively derived and difficult to verify (see Cohen, 1969; Hayes and Hayes, 1970; and Leach, 1967). Two good examples of more empirically based social anthropological approaches to myth are included in this chapter. In his paper "Pulleyar and the Lord Buddha," Edmund Leach demonstrates with rich concrete data that myth provides multiple ideal models for belief and behavior rather than the simple static charters which have been sought by many anthropologists since Malinowski's time. Leach also demonstrates the effectiveness of mediating symbols in myth for making belief systems logically operative. Also in the empirical tradition, R. G. Willis's paper on the Fipa of Africa represents an explicit challenge to Lévi-Strauss's methods. Willis suggests that the analysis of mythological thought need not eschew concrete ethnographic data and *can* be accommodated within the normal parameters of social anthropological investigation. (See John Middleton's collection *Myth and Cosmos*, 1967, for other examples of analysis in this tradition.) An example of how Lévi-Strauss's concepts can similarly be applied to ritual may be found in E. Vogt and C. Vogt's article "Lévi-Strauss Among the Maya" (1970).

The methods of analysis included in this chapter may often appear to contradict one another. That, however, need not be the case. The diversity of approaches represented here illustrates that meaning in myth, like the symbols of which myth is often composed, may become clearer by analyzing it on many different levels and from many different points of view.

William A. Lessa

"DISCOVERER-OF-THE-SUN"

In this paper, which considers a text from the "heroic period" of Micronesian mythology, the author calls attention to the pitfalls that may await the student of religion and folklore if he assumes that a myth will reflect an exact image of the culture which produces it. Myths, like other social facts, do not speak for themselves. They require interpretation in light of information which they do not themselves supply. Frequently the information which they do supply is fragmentary and not at all a true mirror of a culture's life style, for myths incorporate elements of culture selectively. The author demonstrates here that *even* when historical circumstances, supporting ethnographic data, and supplementary material from other myths are known, we still may find ourselves with a text which defies easy interpretation. "Discoverer-of-the-Sun" is such a text. Lessa attempts to assess the potential for interpretation candidly and honestly. As such, the paper amounts to a critique of the "culture-reflector school" of literal interpretation of myth. Though abridged from its original form, this paper should provide sufficient textual and ethnographic information to enable the reader to attempt analyses from several other points of view. Related comparative and ethnographic material on Ulithi, a Micronesian atoll in the Caroline group, may be found in some of the author's own publications (see Lessa, 1956, 1961, 1962; Lessa and Spiegelman, 1954).

Reprinted in abridged form from the *Journal of American Folklore*, LXXIX (1966), 3–51, by permission of the author and The American Folklore Society, Inc.

Almost anyone except the actual collector of a non-Western folktale—and sometimes even he—has experienced boredom and frustration in trying to comprehend its content or warm up to its style. The collector himself may develop an appreciation of the tale only after he has studied it carefully and related it to its cultural milieu. The native listener need not be looked upon with incredulity if he reacts with anxiety, sadness, or mirth upon hearing what may seem to the uninitiated to be an insipid and confusing narrative, for the raconteur galvanizes his hearer's cultural reflexes with verbal and visual stimuli well known to all from generations of storytelling. The outsider understandably needs an exegesis by someone in a position to analyze the tale, and it is gratifying that at long last anthropologists have aroused themselves sufficiently to reduce some of the skepticism and disinterest experienced by folklorists whose principal interests may lie elsewhere. It is my modest hope that my analysis of a certain body of folktales, principally through the study of one story, will contribute toward the lifting of the pall.

"Discoverer-of-the-Sun" is a narrative I collected on Ulithi Atoll, where I have pursued ethnological research on four separate occasions beginning two years after the end of World War II. . . . Before dealing with Ulithian oral tradition as such, and more particularly with this specific tale, it seems appropriate to look into the culture from which it emanates.

I

Ulithi is a seagirt land consisting of many islands arranged around a central lagoon of great expanse. The atoll is located in the Carolinian archipelago in the doldrum belt of the western Pacific, where typhoons often incubate. It lies ten degrees north of the equator. The people are Micronesians, having close affinities with the natives of such places as Yap, Truk, and Ponape, as well as (to a lesser extent) Palau, the Marianas, the Marshalls, and the Gilberts. They practice a simple agriculture and do much fishing. Pigs and chickens are raised to supplement the basic foods, which consist mostly of coconut and taro. The coralline nature of the soil restricts the food supply, but in addition the land surface is tiny so that the population has usually averaged only about five hundred persons, who live in small villages bordering the lagoon.

Material possessions are meager but well adapted to the environment. The people live in elongated, hexagonal-shaped huts whose interiors are divided by partitions into compartments. They make use of the true loom, with which they weave garments out of banana and hibiscus-bark fibers. Perhaps their chief pride is in their extraordinarily fast outrigger sailing canoes, in which they criss-cross the lagoon for local transportation or set out for more distant islands for visits, trade, and other business.

The division of labor is relatively simple, with men doing the more arduous and dangerous tasks and women for the most part working in the garden plots and the home. The specialists are all men and carry on their skills part time, particularly in canoe building, house building, navigation, divination, and magic. Money is not used and goods circulate primarily through gift and ceremonial exchanges. People perform services for friends and relatives, keeping close account of their work so that they can call on their obligees when occasion demands. A good deal of labor is carried on cooperatively and communally.

The people do not live exclusively in either nuclear or extended family groups, but they have a strong sense of kinship solidarity and obligations. Marriage is monogamous, even though in theory polygyny is permissible. The prevailing rule of residence is not clear-cut but may be described as essentially patri-local, with frequent and regular domiciliation with the wife's family for the chief purpose of working the garden plots of her group.

Matrilineal lineages constitute a strong organizing principle of social relations, entering into the ownership of land, canoes, and other property, and the regulation of work, marriage, and religion. A man cannot change his lineage affiliation, even though he may be adopted by someone in another lineage, a very common practice. . . .

The natives are permissive in matters of sex, with premarital relations common and extra-marital relations not unusual for married individuals. Divorce is simple and especially resorted to when the couple is still young and childless. Various tabus surround sex and reproduction, placing limits on the activities of new parents, specialists in magic, and others. During their menstrual period women are particularly subject to proscriptions and must live apart in special huts provided for them near the shore. Abortion and infanticide are unknown; children are greatly desired, and are treated with kindness and tolerance.

Political organization has a twofold character. Internally, there is a system of district chiefs in which a so-called king is dominant. Each of the villages of the atoll has a council of male elders which decides its everyday problems and directs its communal activities. Externally, there is a highly complex linkage with Yap, which maintains a suzerainty over Ulithi, as well as over a string of other islands extending hundreds of miles to the east. Ulithi is considered to be low caste with reference to Yap, but it in turn has a superior status over the other islands of the Yapese domain.

Social control is effected through the usual channels of gossip, ridicule, and "enlightened self-interest," with kinsmen playing a strong role in keeping the individual in line. Sanctions for the punishment of delicts are fairly diffuse and in any event are administered on a private basis with virtually no intervention by the king or territorial chiefs.

Before the pagan religion began to crumble, it was a mixture of ancestor worship, animism, and polytheism, with belief in a dualistic afterworld located in Lang, the Sky. The keeper of the lineage ancestral shrines was the closest approach to a priest that the society provided for. Other specialists in the supernatural were essentially magicians who concerned themselves with the typical anxieties of their clients, particularly illness and the hazards of wind and sea. Sorcery provided an outlet for aggression without becoming too disruptive and was especially attributed to the natives of Yap, who punished their Ulithian underlings for failure to show proper deference or to send sufficient tribute.

The first possible contacts that Ulithi had with the Western world may have occurred in 1526, when Diogo da Rocha was in the vicinity, or later, in 1543, when it may have been discovered by Ruy López de Villalobos. The first undisputed visit to the atoll was made in 1712 by the Spaniard Bernardo de Egui y Zabalaga. Father Antonio Cantova set up a small Catholic mission there in 1731 but he was soon assassinated and the outside world shunned Ulithi for almost a century. After that there were occasional visits by European explorers and traders. In 1899 the Spaniards transferred the Caroline Islands to the Germans, so that from then until 1914, when the Japanese took over the German possessions in Micronesia, there was a period of moderate outside control and influence over the islands. The Japanese were interested in exploiting the atoll for copra but did little to affect the native way of life. When in 1944 the Americans took over the islands, they set in motion a process of acculturation that at first was moderately slow but has now begun to accelerate.

The culture as described above is essentially what it was just before World War II. The pagan religion had already been largely supplanted by Christianity. Nowadays the society is becoming particularly altered in the economic sphere, moving toward a cash economy.

II

After this excursion into the cultural and historical background of the atoll we may return to its folklore. This material is a conglomerate with indisputable affinities not only with the rest of Micronesia but with Polynesia, Melanesia, and Malaysia as well. It shows a wide range in type and content, dealing with gods and mortals, lovers and lunatics, ogres and children, animals and fish. It does not especially serve to support magical ritual, though sometimes it indeed acts as a "charter" for certain procedures. Occasionally it explains origins without being unduly etiological. Sometimes but not often it purports to be a chronicle of actual events outside the mythological realm. Many of the tales are lamentably truncated; others are fairly full. The people do not appear to classify the narratives. Informally they are said to deal with the *musuwe*, or times bygone. Often, specific ones are called *fiung*, a label I find difficult to define but which does not apply to purportedly historical events. Others are called *kaptal*, or story, again hard to interpret consistently.

. . . Ulithian storytellers are monologists of a sort, much of their presentation being given in the form of a dialogue in which actors in the story are imitated by varying the voice. They do not constitute a special class, although I am willing to believe that in the past some of them may have been members of an elite group for the preservation and handing down of the more sacred of the narratives.

The narrator of "Discoverer-of-the-Sun" is Taiethau, a young man of twenty-nine who was one of my chief informants, being surpassed quantitatively only by another and much older man who had helped me in collecting both my first group of stories and my second as well. Taiethau is generally conceded to be one of the more indolent members of the community but is endowed with a flair for entertaining. He was the only Ulithian I ever encountered who had a driving desire to learn and recount as many tales as he possibly could. His manner of presentation was easily the most animated and perhaps the most skilled, and one could see that he was endowed with a vivid imagination. How much he may have superimposed his own embellishments I cannot say, although I am convinced that his materials bear the stamp of age and authenticity.

He first heard "Discoverer-of-the-Sun" when he was about thirteen years of age from an old man on Ulithi named Iungal. He heard it many times thereafter from many old men, but the parts of the narrative varied with the teller. Taiethau does not know whether his present version is as he first heard it or is a synthesis of several versions. . . .

The text of the tale "Discoverer-of-the-Sun" that follows herewith is freely translated.

DISCOVERER-OF-THE-SUN

There were two sisters. The older sister married a man from earth. The younger sister one day went out to collect some *iuth* flowers for a head wreath, and a man from Lang came down and saw her. They agreed to get married—she said "Yes." So the man from Lang told her to wait for him until he should come and get her. But he used to come down and see her and she became pregnant. He went to Lang waiting until she would have a baby. When it had grown a little the man wanted to take the baby up to Lang and take its mother too, but the older sister knew this and asked the young sister if she would not leave her child with her saying she would take care of it in memory of her. So she [the younger sister] left her child and went to Lang with her husband.

The older sister had told her sister a lie. She never took care of the baby but gave it bad food and did not let the baby sleep beside her; she put the baby in her small firewood shed. The baby became thin and she always hit the child. When she took her own child for a bath in the sea, the child of the younger sister followed them to the beach. There was an orange tree near their house and the woman took a fruit from the tree and she took off the skin and gave her own child the orange and the other child the skin. After the child had eaten the orange, she took her child to the sea and gave it a bath and told her sister's child to go and take a bath himself. They came back from taking a bath and the boy went to his shed and stayed there.

The next morning the woman took her child to the beach and gave it a bath, and the husband came from cutting *hachi* and saw the boy in the shed. He did not know what had been happening to the boy —that his wife was not taking care of him. He told the boy to come and drink *hachi*, and the boy came out and drank all the *hachi* in the coconut shell. After he had drunk the *hachi*, the woman and her child came from the beach and looked in the coconut shell and saw there was no *hachi* in it. She asked the boy and he said that he had drunk all the *hachi* by himself. She took a sprouting coconut and hit the boy with it in his shed, and hit him so hard he could not get up. She told the boy, "Why did you do this? Didn't you know that your mother left you here and went to Lang and has never come back?" The boy heard for the first time that he had a real mother somewhere. When he had had trouble there he had thought that it was with his real mother.

He lay down and stayed in his house and watched the woman. When she was not looking he went out from his shed and crawled to the place where his mother used to go and collect *iuth* flowers. He came to the *iuth* tree and climbed it and went to Lang. He reached there and came to the menstrual house and walked near there, and there were lots of children playing around the house. His mother had had many children after she had gone to Lang. The women who were in the menstrual house looked at him and they said, "Let us run away from the house, there is a *ialus* coming near us!" His hair was very long and his body was all dirty. His mother was there with a newly born child and she heard what the women said, so she came out of the house and looked for the boy. When she looked at the boy she knew that it was her own child. She ran to the boy and called him and she told the women not to run out of the house, because this was her first child. The mother of the child had married an important man from Lang. The women came and took him and gave him a bath and cut his hair and he became a handsome boy. His mother asked the boy what had happened to make him come up to Lang from earth, and he told her what had happened to him—that her sister had not taken care of him and that is why he left earth and went to Lang. She told him that it was better for him not to go back but to stay with her because her husband was his real father and he should stay with them there. They took care of him and fed him for three days.

Iolofath came the third day for recreation around the houses in the village. He happened to look in the menstrual house and saw a lot of children in and around the house, and he asked the people in the village where the children came from and who was their father and mother. The people told Iolofath that the children belonged to that man from Lang and his wife. Iolofath went to the menstrual house to see if she would give him a child to adopt. She gave him the boy who came from earth. Iolofath asked his mother the child's name and she told him that they had no name for the boy. "We just call him Seugau, or Baby Boy." So Iolofath took him and called him just Seugau.

When they reached home his wife asked him where he got the boy, and Iolofath told her to be quiet and go ahead and make food for him because they were lucky to get this boy that he had adopted from somebody. She made food ready and fed some of it to the boy. When they were through eating they went to sleep.

The next morning Iolofath made *bwongbwong* over him, and when he was finished with the spell he threw him over the house. When the child fell to the other side of the house he grew bigger than he had been before. Iolofath performed the spell again and threw the boy over the house, and he got a little bigger again. He did this to him many times and he became a youth. Iolofath told him that from then on he must go and take a bath every morning in the sea. The youth did what Iolofath had told him.

After a year Iolofath told him that he should change his place for taking his bath, and to go and take a bath where he [Iolofath] used to take a bath. The boy asked him where the place was, and Iolofath told him it was at the end of the island. He told him he must also change the time for taking his bath, and that from now on he must take his bath early, before sunrise.

The lad was anxious to take the bath the next day. That night they slept and the next morning the boy got up early and was walking outside the house and saw a spirit standing outside there. His name was Limichikh [Smart, Wise, or Intelligent]. He seized the boy and swallowed him, but after a few minutes he took him out of his mouth. The boy became a *limichikh*, too. The *ialus* told the boy to go ahead and do what his father had told him. All the while that the spirit was doing this and talking to the boy, Iolofath knew everything that was going on.

The boy went to the end of the island and scraped some coconut meat and rubbed himself with it for the oil. While he was doing this he looked at some sand bars and saw a spirit come from the sand bars. The spirit came to the boy and asked him who he was and why he had come here, for people were not allowed to bathe here. "If you are a strong man you will see what I will do to you." He took some spears made from coconut trunks—the spears are called *kei*. The boy answered, "I am ready for a fight. If you want to fight I am ready." The boy did not feel any fear of him. The *ialus* took a spear and threw it at the boy and hit him in the abdomen. The boy fell down dead and the spirit came and took the spear out of him and made him alive again. He told the boy that he should not come here again because he was a weak man, and only strong and able men could come here. He did this to try to make the youth angry—to feel bad. He told the boy that now he knew that the boy wanted to learn what he knew, so he gave the boy some of the spears and took some himself. He taught him how to throw spears and fight, and the boy learned very fast, because he was a *limichikh*. After practicing these things he knew everything about fighting. All this happened before the sun came up. The spirit was in a hurry because he had to get back before sunrise. He asked the boy his name, and the boy told him his name was Seugau. The *ialus* laughed at him and asked him why, since he was a big man, they called him Seugau. "You are not a baby. I will make a new name for you." He gave him the name Thilefial, or Discoverer-of-the-Sun. He told him to remember his name and not forget it, and to tell his father. He also told him that now he was going to leave him, and that the next morning he should come to see him at the same time so they could have some fun there.

The boy went home and when he was close to his house he forgot the name the spirit had given him. He did not tell his father what had happened. Iolofath waited and waited for him to tell him, because he knew. Iolofath asked him, "Did something happen to you when you were there?" Then he told Iolofath that he had met a spirit there and he had given him a name, but he had forgotten it. Iolofath told him that the next morning early he should go and ask the spirit what name he had given him because he knew that he would give the best of names.

The next morning the boy woke up early and went to the end of the island on the sand and started to make some coconut oil to bathe himself, and he saw the spirit coming. The spirit told the boy, "Are you ready?" and he answered, "Yes," and the spirit took some spears and threw them at the boy and the boy dodged them. When the *ialus* was through throwing all the spears he had not succeeded in hitting the boy. The boy said, "All right. Are you ready? It is now my time to throw the spears back to you." He threw the spears at the spirit but he did not strike him. When he was through, the spirit was tired from jumping around because the boy was more skillful in throwing the spears. The spirit took the spears and brought them to him, and they sat down and took a rest. The spirit asked him, "Did you tell your father your name?" and he answered, "I did not, because I forgot it." The spirit said that he should go back home now and while he was going he should keep calling out his name over and over again so that he would not forget it. The spirit told him that now he was going to leave him because soon the sun would come up. He said to him, "I am the sun. Walk back to your house and if you forget your name turn around and look at the sun. Then you will know that your name is Thilefial, because you are the man who discovered the sun."

The boy walked along, and whenever he forgot his name he would turn around and look at the sun and remember his name. Then he went on again, and every time he forgot his name he would turn around and remember. He reached his house and his father Iolofath was waiting for him. He shouted, "My name is Thilefial!" His father told him that from now on he could go and take a bath any place he wanted, because the reason he had told him to go there was that he had to learn things.

One day he got up early in the morning and went to that place and took a bath there. This was just before the sun came up. He looked and saw some islands. He had a *khurukhur* stick. He took it and pointed it to the islands, and the sea became firm. He walked on it to one of the islands. There were some people on the island. He took a coconut leaf and whisked it over his hair to dry it. Some women saw him and wondered who this handsome man could be, and if one could become his wife. They went and told the people on the island that there was a handsome man on the island. The men became jealous hearing about him. The men said, "Let us kill him."

There was a man on the island who was the best warrior there. He was a deputy for Iolofath, and his name was Rasim. Another man, Solal, who lived under the earth, was another deputy for Iolofath, like Rasim. Rasim and the people decided to kill the man. Rasim told the people to go ahead and kill him themselves, that he could not go with them because he was the best warrior and could not stoop to do the deed himself.

They took many spears and went to the youth. They threw them but he dodged them all, jumping farther and farther back. When the last spear came at him he was at the tip of the island, and he caught it and threw it at the men. He picked up one spear after another and kept throwing them until he came to the place where they had started. Some of the men died, and some were wounded, and the rest ran back to the village. They told the people that they could not kill him. A man with yaws all over his body was staying in the *metalefal*. He told the men they had better not try to kill him because no one could come on the island except the son of Iolofath. The men answered by telling him to be quiet, because they knew that Iolofath's wife had never been pregnant. Rasim told the men he would go with them and they would try again.

They started fighting against him and the youth did the same as before, jumping back from the spears so they would not strike him. He took the last spear, and as Rasim came in front of the men, he threw it at him. Rasim was frightened and ran away. The men went back to the village and Rasim told the men they must trick the youth to kill him. The man who had yaws all over him told them, "You had better stop fighting him, because we know that only the son of Iolofath can come here."

They did not listen to the man and tried again. They fought him and he kept jumping back and back until he reached the end of the beach. While they were fighting, Rasim hid behind a coconut trunk. When the youth caught the last spear he hurled it at the men, and they ran away, some having been killed. When he got near Rasim, he did not see him, and as he walked past the tree Rasim threw a spear at his back. He fell down dead and Rasim and the men took him and buried him.

Three days after they had buried him, Iolofath, who knew what had been happening, came to the island looking for him. The old man with yaws said, "Now we are in trouble, because if Iolofath comes what are we going to tell him?" The men were very angry at him and told him to stop saying that or else they would kill him, because they knew that Iolofath's wife had never been pregnant and they had no son. Iolofath came and sat in front of the *metalefal*. The people did not talk to him [they knew who he was]. He sat until noontime and then he talked to them. He told them, "I have a man who came to my island before and he fought against people on my island and I tried to kill him but could not. And he ran away. I have come here to ask you if you have seen that man or not." Rasim smiled and said, "Do not worry, *tamol*. The man you are worrying about we have already killed." Iolofath told the men they should show him the place where they had buried him, and they showed him the spot. He told them to dig up the man and put him in a basket, but the youth had started to rot. Iolofath took the basket and put it on a pole and put him on his back. He told the people, "This is my son." He took his son and went back to his island.

The men went to the *metalefal* and the old man with yaws told them, "Now you see what I had told you—not to kill the man and you did it." The men answered him, "We did not know that he was the son of a chief. Iolofath is not angry with us because he knows we did not know."

Iolofath reached home and took his son into his house and wrapped him in a mat. He told a man named Machokhochokh to go and bring back breath to his son. The man asked him where he should go and find breath. Iolofath told him to go down to Solal. Machokhochokh went down to Solal. He told him what Iolofath had told him. Solal told him, "You have come here now but I do not have anything to give you to eat. Go and take that sprouting coconut to eat." Machokhochokh took the coconut but did not have a husking stick, and he asked Solal what he should do with the coconut. Solal told him to go to the swordfish and use its mouth to husk the coconut. When he was through taking off the husk he asked Solal, "What should I use to open the coconut shell?" He told him, "Go and break it on that turtle's back." The man ate the coconut meat and when he was finished he asked Solal where he should go to put the shells. Solal told him to put the two pieces together and place them in an Alocasia plant, and he told him to climb a certain coconut tree and hold his breath as he climbed. The coconut tree was very high, and he told him that when he reached the top and had climbed the *ubwoth*, or growing leaves, he should look to see which way the *ubwoth* pointed and to jump in that direction. "When you fall down to the ground, take the coconut shell and go back with it to Iolofath. The youth's breath is in the shell." He did what he was told and climbed the tree and jumped in the direction in which the *ubwoth* pointed. When he fell and reached the bottom he took the shell and it [the breath] back to Iolofath.

As he was returning, Iolofath's son's body began gradually to be restored. He grew better and better. When he reached Iolofath's house the body was as it had been before. He was alive again. The son got up from the mat and when he looked around him he saw some maggots around him on his body, and he asked his father why he had put him in the midst of all the maggots. His father told him they had put him there because he was not a strong man and then went and told him what had happened to him on the island. His son felt bad about this and wanted to go to the island sometime to fight again, but he did not tell his father how he felt.

One day early in the morning he went to the tip of the island and he took a bath there and did what he had done before—he took his stick and pointed it to the island, and the water became firm. He went to the island and took a coconut leaf and brushed his hair. The women said, "The handsome man has come back again!" The men had a meeting and said they should kill him again. The man with yaws said, "Why do you want to kill him? You know that Iolofath told us it was his son. Why should you want to kill him again?" The men paid no attention to him. They wanted to fight the youth. They fought and Iolofath knew that they were fighting. He turned himself into the fruit of a Barringtonia and floated on the sea to the shore of the island and watched the men and his son fighting. They could not beat him, and Rasim hid behind a coconut tree as he had done before. While he was hiding, Iolofath turned himself back into a man and stood up on the beach. He said to Rasim, "Do not hide! Come out and fight with me! The boy is too young for you. You and I are about the same age and skill." Rasim came out but he did not try to fight. He gave in, but Iolofath did not forgive him. Iolofath took a spear. He told Rasim that now he would throw it at him. "Even if you run away or turn your back to me my spear will strike you in the abdomen [just below the ensiform process]. He threw the spear at that place and Rasim died. Iolofath then told his son, "Go ahead and do what you want. If you wish to kill all the people on the island, that will be all right. Do what you want because the men on the island are of the same age and skill as you. Except for the man with yaws."

The son went to the village and killed everyone in the village except the old man in the men's club-house. He went to see him and told him that from now on he was the chief of the island and that if anyone came to live there he was their chief. The youth then went back to his own island. He already knew that Iolofath had adopted him and he told him he was going to visit his real mother and father. He went to visit them and he lived there for about half a month. While he was living with them he recalled what had happened to him when he was a little boy, and he went down to earth and killed his mother's sister.

Then he returned to Iolofath and lived with him.

III

The content of this story is less recondite than that of most Ulithian narratives, yet for the uninitiated it poses many questions that can be answered only with a substantial amount of exposition.

I have reduced native words to a minimum in order to spare discomfort to the reader but a few of them seemed sufficiently appropriate to be retained.

The *iuth* is a shrub or small tree known to botanists as *Guettarda speciosa* and is used not only to make leis but for medicines, amulets, lumber, and firewood as well. *Hachi* is palm toddy, and to "cut *hachi*" is the native's way of saying in English that one is cutting the stalk which normally bears the inflorescence of the tree so that the sap will bleed more readily into the waiting cup tied below it. A *ialus* is any kind of a spirit, evil or benevolent, trivial or lofty, terrestrial or celestial. *Bwongbwong* is white magic, distinguished from black magic or sorcery. The *khurukhur* stick which Thilefial uses to cause the sea to become firm is literally "orange wood," although not actually made of this substance, being made instead of any of a number of woods, such as *hangi* (*Pemphis acidula*) or *iar* (*Premna integrifolia*). Normally it is a walking staff with a slight bulge in the middle and a flare at each end. Occasionally it is used in dances. But in this story it takes on the character of a magical wand. It appears in other tales, and always has a magical meaning. It is mentioned in songs called *hachuchu*, which are sung by an audience when a medium is being possessed, it being said that the singing will not only induce a spirit to enter the medium but will keep him content during possession. A *tamol* is a chief. Literally, the word means "my father," and is a kin term of basic importance, being applied both to one's real and classificatory fathers. A *metalefal* is a large house for men, being used for meetings, lounging, idling, and sleeping. Each village has one, and it occupies a central place in the settlement. *Ubwoth* is the whitish growing leaf of the coconut palm before it begins to unfold. It has usefulness in decorating the body as well as in imparting a certain magical potency to anything or anyone to which its leaflets are tied.

We may now deal briefly with the locale of the hero's adventures. Lang is of course the Sky or the Sky World, the abode of the celestial deities, particularly the three great ones—Ialulep, his son Lugeilang, and the latter's son Iolofath. At the same time it is the home of all the dead. Those souls who come to it for admittance are interrogated, and the good are sent to that part of Lang which is reserved for them. The landscape, the mode of life, and the social relations of this portion are much the same as on earth. Bad souls are condemned to either Gum Well, in which they wallow endlessly, attacked by animals, or to Garbage Pit, filled with a horrible stench. Lang has various levels, but it is never clear to Ulithians how each differs from the other, though the lower levels seem to be essentially stages that must be traversed before reaching the top. Thirteen of the stories in my Ulithian

collection either wholly or partially involve Lang as a locale, although in a few of them there is no action there; instead, characters leave the Sky World and have their experiences on earth.

There is two-way traffic between Lang and earth, and the passage is traversed by both deities and mortals. The occasional mating of a god with a human is not rare; we have seen one sample of it in our story.

Cosmic pillars by means of which men ascend to or descend from the sky are found widespread in the mythology of the world, and in Ulithi there are some references to it. In "Discoverer-of-the-Sun" the young hero climbs a *iuth* tree to reach his mother in Lang. Asked to comment on the nature of an unspecified tree called Sur Lang, or Pillar of the Sky, which in another myth a hero named Haluwai climbs, an elderly informant who had not, however, narrated the myth offered the opinion that in reality the pillar is made of stone, rising upwards out of a distant place in the sea. The divergence of opinion may reflect the varying provenances of myths, for the narrator of this particular story expressed his belief that the tale came from Yap. On the other hand, in another tale from Ulithi, again of probable Yapese source, which tells how disk money came to Yap, we find that some men use a bamboo to climb to the Sky World. Perhaps the exact nature of the pillar is unimportant, and in any event the pillar itself seems of no special consequence in Carolinian mythology. If the truth be told, the hero is more apt to make his ascent on a cloud of smoke, a method especially associated with Olofat.

Who is Iolofath? Only his name and his ability to transform himself into the fruit of the Barringtonia betray him as Iolofath or Olofat, the trickster of the Caroline Islands. How changed is the wild youth of yesterday who walked alone in an unfriendly world and strove so hard to be recognized! Now he is married and staid, filled with paternal affection and responsibility.

Other Ulithian tales have chronicled his early life. In "Iolofath and Lugeilang" we learn of his birth. His father was the great celestial god, Lugeilang, who had a mortal mistress named Thilpelap. Lugeilang's wife in the sky learned of his love affair and tried to explore the matter by descending to earth, but each time she was thwarted by the magic of a dance gesture performed by Thilpelap's mother, Octopus. Nature eventually took its customary course and Thilpelap became pregnant. Her celestial lover wanted to hasten to her side but was prevented from doing so because he was obligated to help in the building of the House of the Gods. Filled with solicitude he dispatched a messenger instead, instructing the girl to make an object of coconut and hibiscus fibers intertwined with a coconut leaflet. This she was to twist in a lock of her hair, and when the moment of delivery drew near she was to give the thing a pull, causing the baby to be born from her head. He also instructed her to name the infant Iolofath. When the time came she did as she was bidden. The boy was already somewhat mature when he issued forth, and to say the least he was precocious. For reasons never disclosed but apparently not connected with any rejection of his child, Lugeilang did not want the boy to go up to the Sky World to visit him. However, the irrepressible lad discovered who his father was and where he lived. His mother had dutifully done her best to keep him in ignorance and when he learned the truth she was unable to dissuade him from his single-minded determination to ascend to the Sky World. He made his way up on a cloud of smoke. In each of the several levels of the Carolinian otherworld the boy had adventures, always encountering hostile children who would not play with him. At the first level, in retaliation, he caused a scorpion fish with which the children were playing to develop spines that pricked their fingers. Their angry parents beat him. At the next level he caused a shark to bite some boys who had scorned him. Again he was beaten. At the third level he caused a sting ray to develop a stinger and jab some boys who had hit him. Their parents too smote him. When the young Iolofath finally reached the fourth and highest level he again was repulsed, this time by some men who were digging a posthole for the House of the Gods. No one knew that he was the son of the god, Lugeilang; they were antagonistic merely because he was a stranger. Filled with deceit, they had the lad go down into a posthole, into which they then rammed a great post. The lad escaped all injury by having already constructed a small pocket off to the side of the hole, and in order to throw his would-be murderers off the track he spewed up some green and red substances he had secreted in his mouth. Thinking these were his viscera the men left the scene, confident they had rid themselves of the brash young stranger. Iolofath enlisted the aid of some termites to eat a hole upward through the post, enabling him to climb up out of his intended grave. A yellow ant, following his bidding, brought him a small morsel of coconut meat, which he caused magically to grow into a full-sized coconut. The ant fetched him a piece of taro, and the lad magically brought it to full bulk. Finally, he had the ant fetch him a grain of sand. He caused this to grow to the size of a rock. He bashed the coconut against the rock and cried out "Soro!"—the word used by inferiors when they crawl before a chief. The workmen below were startled, and after discovering he was the son of the god they in turn became frightened. The boy sat at the side of his father. After the great house was completed, preparations were made for a feast. The workmen caught turtles for the event, but Iolofath stealthily stole all the meat from them and stuffed it into a small crustacean he had caught. The men discovered their loss. Iolofath invited them to kill his little crustacean, and when they did all the turtle meat spilled out. Iolofath was assigned the chore of delivering the meat to the people. He went from house to house. When eventually he arrived at the home of Halfbeak, he found him away but his wife was there. He made love to her. Caught in *flagrante delicto*, he was killed by Halfbeak. Lugeilang conducted a search for his son and eventually found him when he noticed that a plant was trembling in the ground. He found the lad underneath and upbraided him—for not having beat Halfbeak. Then he restored him to life. After that he seized a branch and struck Halfbeak, breaking off his upper jaw and leaving only the lower jaw. Then he and Iolofath returned to the House of the Gods.

The meanness of the youthful Iolofath is brought out in a sequel to the above. I have given the story the title, "Iolofath and Khiou." The trickster did not know that he had a half brother living in the third level of the Sky World named Khiou, who was treated solicitously by his people and not permitted to exert himself. He had suspected he might have a brother when he noticed that some men from the third level always came at night with fish for his father. He demanded to know if he had a brother, but his father always laughed off the suggestion. But one day Iolofath turned himself into a lizard and discovered the unpalatable truth. He was so jealously enraged at discovering he had a sibling that the following night he descended to the third level and cut off Khiou's head, which he proceeded to place in the House of the Gods, where his father slept. In the morning the old man discovered his favored son's head and was horrified. He surmised that the guilt lay with Iolofath, and when he angrily denounced him the young man denied that he knew that he had killed a brother. After all, had not his father adamantly refused to admit he had another son? Lugeilang brought his son back to life. One day Khiou and Iolofath started to swim to a nearby island for recreation. Khiou caused a strong current to come up, endangering Iolofath, who struggled in vain. At the last moment Khiou caused the current to ease up, letting his half brother know by this action that he could outpower him if he wanted.

These two myths of the cycle bear enough testimony to Iolofath's youthful personality to reveal him as an earthling who strove mightily to take his place alongside his celestial father in the Sky World. He was rebuffed at every turn by haughty children and callous men, and even his father seemed to be less than cheered by his presence. He was bold and aggressive. He was cunning. And he was unscrupulous; he thought nothing of seducing another person's wife.

. . .

It is by now obvious that the Iolofath of "Discoverer-of-the-Sun" has undergone a reformation. He is married but childless, so he eagerly adopts Baby Boy and impresses on his wife how lucky they are. He solicitously feeds the tot and performs magic to cause him to grow up rapidly. He secretly arranges for the boy to be made a *limichikh*. When the young man is killed by Rasim, he does not go into a blind rage or wreak vengeance on his murderers. He methodically sets about having the breath of life brought to Thilefial. Here then is a man who commands others and controls himself. Only when his foster son is again killed by the formidable Rasim does he hurl a spear at the warrior and bring about his death. When he then invites the young man to go ahead and do away with all the men of the island who had harassed him, he is not shrill or sadistic. He is merely suggesting an act of justifiable vengeance. He points out that the boy's adversaries are of the same age and skill as he, although, to be sure, we know that Thilefial has had special traits bestowed on him. He thoughtfully lets him visit his true parents on earth and then upon his return has the boy live with him.

Iolofath's metamorphosis, fortunately, need not be left as tenuous as this, for we have other folkloristic records from Ulithi attesting to his adult personality. In the last of a trilogy centering about him there is a tale I have called "The Handsome Spouses," in which the central plot revolves around a young man who has stupidly alienated his beautiful wife. At one time he becomes so violent that Iolofath is summoned to pacify him. Imagine the young trickster ever being called on for that! Iolofath contrives to bring the separated spouses together by an elaborate plot in which he has them meet at a dance competition. There, through the judicious use of some special oil and turmeric he had earlier stolen from the house of a woman, he magically causes the lovely estranged wife to fall in love with her desperate husband. Altruistic deeds of this sort would have been utterly incongruous for the younger Iolofath. However, the trickster never loses his capacity to transform himself into a bird or coconut leaf, and he remains capable of much cleverness, but he acts out of a sense of responsibility rather than mischievousness or deceit. He has put the erratic ways of youth behind him.

. . .

It is proper to ask if Iolofath's change of personality is not actual but merely the result of the transference of his name from one character to another. This question is proper because it is not unusual in folklore for names to be juggled about with little regard for the characters who bear them. I concede that this is a possibility.

Another possibility has already been suggested: Iolofath has merely grown older and secure. He is now accepted and need not struggle for the recognition he feels due him on account of his semidivinity.

Most likely, the answer to the difference between the one personality and the other is a combination of these two possibilities. There is enough in the literature to indicate that the new Iolofath retains some trickster traits and cleverness. At the same time, the new man conceivably could exist entirely independently of the old, to whom he owes very little in the way of personal traits. The thread of connection is there, but it is thin and weak. The transition is probably the result of an effort to retain the use and prestige of an already established mythical personage. Name dropping need not be any more alien to a primitive people than to a more sophisticated one.

There is an unmistakable resemblance between Iolofath and such other Oceanic tricksters as the Polynesian Maui, the Gilbertese Nareau, and the Melanesian Qat, Ambat, and Tagaro. In fact, some genetic connection is easily implied. Almost all of them are high born, experience a strange birth, manifest developmental precocity, and are parties to strong sibling rivalry. And of course all of them have universal trickster traits. The one important attribute lacking in our Ulithian hero is that he is not the originator of culture traits nor the benefactor of mankind; he is not a culture hero. Maui fished up islands, slowed the sun in its course so women had more time for their work, wrested fire from the fire god, introduced cooked food, and even tried to conquer Death. Other Oceanic tricksters too have in some way aided humanity. It is true that in some Caroline islands Iolofath succeeds in giving fire to mankind and decrees that man shall be immortal, but credit for these deeds is given in utterly inadequate fashion, as if their authenticity were not beyond debate. The strange thing is that in Micronesia the Polynesian Maui is in fact depicted by two heroes, for in addition to the tricksterism of Iolofath we have the benefactory deeds of another personage, whose name is Motikitik. Obviously, Motikitik is the same as Maui-tikitiki, as he is often known in Polynesia. But Motikitik, while he fishes up an island and goes down beneath the surface of the earth, where he finds food, is a colorless conformist who knows no deceit, guile, malevolence, or adulterousness. He is fair-minded and sensible, and shows strong loyalty toward his dear dead mother, whom his two brothers have scorned. Even though he is confronted with the jealousy of his siblings, he cannot be aroused to retaliate. No, it is Iolofath and not Motikitik who shares Maui's colorful temperament.

Who is Discoverer-of-the-Sun's adversary, Rasim? He is a relatively obscure character whose name appears every so often in Carolinian tales. In general he is powerful and combative, but he is not a consistent character, suggesting that the name transference associated with Iolofath may be more extreme here.

I first learned of Rasim in an Oedipal tale from Ulithi which I have called "Sikhalol and His Mother." Rasim is a chief who discovers an abandoned baby in his fish trap and raises him as his own. He performs magic to make the boy grow rapidly. One day the lad is playing with his canoe when a woman, his mother,

sees him and becomes so smitten by his comeliness that she seduces him. Her husband finally suspects that her protracted lingering at the menustrual house can only be for illicit reasons and sets out to discover who is her lover. The lad is the last one to be subjected to an identity test, consisting of the matching of fingernail scratches on the wife's face with the fingers of her lover. Rasim, who has already revealed to the boy that he has been dallying with his own mother, now prepares him in the art of self-defense. When the real father confronts the boy with the evidence of his guilt— the scratches made by his own hand—the lad resists and slays him. We do not in truth learn much about Rasim in this tale, but it is obvious that he knows something about combat.

The Rasim of "Discoverer-of-the-Sun" is less kindly than this, but even more the knowledgeable warrior. He must have had some virtues to become a deputy for Iolofath. We are not completely sure of his motivation in wishing to harm the young Thilefial. Mention is made of the men's jealousy of the youth, but what spurs Rasim to take a hand himself in the effort to murder him is the boy's skill in overcoming the men's attack, killing some and putting the others to rout. Rasim may have been additionally incensed at the audacity of a stranger in becoming Iolofath's son. It is notable that despite his own talent for fighting, Rasim finds that escape is the better part of valor. It is only when he has had a chance to recoup that he decides on the use of guile instead of a frontal assault. He kills Thilefial from behind, and then smugly assures the boy's adoptive father that he no longer has to worry about the young stranger. Later, when Thilefial comes back to life and again engages the men of the village, Rasim gets set to repeat his previous tactic, signifying a rebellion of a sort against his superior, Iolofath, who he now knows is indeed the "father" of the youth. The demigod finds it necessary to step in and take a direct hand, throwing a well-placed spear into his body. Thus, it appears that Rasim was too stubborn to compromise with reality. It was more important for him to follow his combative instincts than to yield to his master's will.

Of course the Rasim of the patricidal tale of Sikhalol is a mortal, whereas the Rasim of our immediate story is a being in the Sky World, although the difference between these two realms, it must be conceded, is often vague. One way to explain the use of a common name for two such disparate characters is that in the course of narration a character may have his traits and milieu considerably altered. Another way is to assume that an already known name has been transferred from one character to another one.

. . .

Who is Solal? On Ulithi he is considered to be the god of the underworld and therefore the opposite number of Ialulep, the highest deity of the Sky World. But he seems to lack the authority of his counterpart. Indeed he is usually thought of as a benevolent sea spirit who has become the patron of fish magicians. Details concerning him are scanty, and there is little to go by in assembling a personality portrait. Solal is known throughout the west central Carolines. Generally he is said to be half fish and half human, neither male nor female, and to have created heaven and earth by rolling a grain of sand from one hand to another. He is recognized as the god of the underworld. Sometimes he is said to control the supply of fish. The literature gives few details of his personality or life history. Certainly in "Discoverer-of-the-Sun" Solal is cooperative in giving breath to Machokhochokh to take back for the resuscitation of the hero, and in addition he gives indication of being conversant with the skills of his position.

The marvelous and miraculous are commonly encountered in Ulithian folklore. A hero ascends to the upper world on smoke, another hero can hold his breath and travel great distances under water, and still another hero descends to a world beneath the sea. There are people who sprout twigs from their bodies from having hidden so long in the woods, and porpoises which by removing their tails become transformed into girls. A spirit causes a woman to see him in a vision and demands that she give him her yellow skirt, while another spirit swallows a girl by inhaling her through his mouth.

It is in this climate of fantasy that much of the plot of "Discoverer-of-the-Sun" unfolds itself. A man from Lang descends to earth, an earth woman ascends to Lang with him. Later, their child also ascends to the Sky World. By a device known to folklorists as "recognition by the force of nature," his mother immediately and magically recognizes him (just as in another myth Lugeilang recognizes the adolescent Iolofath, his son). The hero grows rapidly through treatment by magic applied by his adoptive father. A spirit swallows

Thilefial, who then emerges transformed into a *limichikh*. Another spirit kills him and restores him to life. Thilefial twice causes the sea to become firm enough for him to walk upon. Iolofath brings him back to life after he again has been killed, sending Machokhochokh down to the nether regions to fetch his life breath. Iolofath turns himself into a fruit. Anything can happen in a world of miracles, and it is noteworthy that none of these things happen in the several tales in my collection that are narrated as historically true.

The performance of magic has strong and ample representation elsewhere in Ulithian folklore. By means of an Open Sesame formula a hero causes the sea to open up, permitting him to descend to the underworld. Blowing on a shell trumpet, a spirit brings into play an irresistible countergravitational force that pulls a man on Yap upwards to the sky, even though he tries to cling to firmly rooted objects. Our trickster, Iolofath, after he had escaped from the posthole where some men tried to kill him, recited an incantation while performing a bouncing gesture with his palm to cause a bit of coconut to become a full-sized nut, and a morsel of an aroid to become a full root. Again, three women from Lang sing a song and dance a dance to cause an aroid to become a girl. Two parents teach their son a song which allows him to make his toy canoe go fast. A spirit recites some magical words and a tree that has been felled by a youth to make a canoe becomes whole again.

The source of the magical power is not always clear and it is necessary to invoke a very broad definition of the term if one is to include the numerous instances in which supernatural power is tapped through some inner capacity rather than a ritual. Iolofath's ability to transform himself at will into a child or a bird falls into this category. So does the power that some characters have to make food or drink inexhaustible simply by willing it. Another example is that of a man who constructs a wooden bird that flies off with him inside.

The magic in "Discoverer-of-the-Sun" partakes of both the orthodox type involving ritual and the looser type involving inner capacity. When the hero is thrown over a house to make him grow, a ritual comes into play. Probably the transformation of the youth into a *limichikh* by swallowing involves contact magic, although further details would be desirable. The source of power when

Thilefial firms the sea is not clear, especially since he uses a kind of a "wand" to help him. Is the power in him, in the wand, in the gesture, or in a combination of all three? All those baths he takes are not explained, but the implication is clear that they have something to do with his conversion into a superman. I have been unable to fathom the magic behind the spear thrown at Rasim by Iolofath. It is a spear that hits the warrior in the abdomen when he is in flight, so we presume it was able to take a reverse course through the air.

Physical aggression, including battles, murders, and cannibalism, constitute a noticeable ingredient of Ulithian folklore, occurring in greater and lesser degrees of importance in almost three fourths of the tales in my collection. . . . True, goriness and horror are not much elaborated upon but it is inescapably obvious that some concession to aggression is considered an important part of storytelling. While most of the violence is between persons, in some instances it is between a human and an animal or spirit, occurring frequently, as one might suppose, in tales involving ogres. . . . One might have cause to wonder if Ulithians are themselves a violent people. The answer is not simple. Certainly today they are most gentle, and one could with justice assert either that the tales are not entirely of their own creation, or even that, original or borrowed, they are a kind of outlet for repressions. Psychologists may be able to fathom these puzzles according to their own favorite theories, but I deem it advisable that we drop the matter here.

Deception, trickery, and prevarication are amply represented in Ulithian folklore, although only weakly so in "Discoverer-of-the-Sun," as when the older sister tells the younger one that she will take care of her child, when Rasim hides behind a tree to kill the hero, and when Iolofath pretends while searching for the youth that he does not know the men have killed him.

. . .

Craftiness is one of Iolofath's traits as a trickster and there is no better instance of it than the ruse he employs to escape death when some men ram a post into the hole they have asked him to dig. Less distinguished heroes are also capable of cleverness. To save himself from a pursuing ogre a man uses the ruse of releasing rats to divert the ogre's attention. The same Atalanta trick is used by a girl pursued by a cannibalistic spirit. She casts behind her some head hair, pubic hair, and spittle from the kindly mother of the spirit. An old standby, "Wait till I get fat," is used by two captive men not only to gain time but to hoodwink an ogre into giving them fat birds to eat while he is left with the lean ones.

. . .

Humor is obviously an important ingredient of Ulithian folklore. Sometimes it is grim, sometimes subtle, and often blatant. It cannot always be detected in a cold text narrated without an audience of natives. The narrator who does not use his voice and body to express himself and arouse response may be incapable of imparting a sense of the comic to the interviewer. Yet even the relatively lifeless accounts appearing in writing are often patently sprinkled with the laughable, and by adding to them the fuller contexts that I was able to perceive, I feel that I have been able to extract a good deal more than appears on the surface.

In this respect "Discoverer-of-the-Sun" does not help us much, for it is almost devoid of humor. The *ialus* laughs when he learns that the hero is called Baby Boy, so perhaps this is an instance that needs to be recorded. The hero's inability to remember his new name has laughable overtones. Machokhochokh's use of a swordfish to husk a coconut is amusing. Little else is. But abundant illustrations are provided by other tales in my repertoire. However, I wish to defer consideration of them until we consider matters of folkloristic style, for I am more interested in the devices of humor than in its content.

Up to this point I have considered the content of Ulithian folklore without much deliberate reference to the question of cultural reflection, and it is to this old anthropological problem that we may now address ourselves. It should be obvious to even the most casual reader that there is not much to be learned about the cultural and social life of Ulithians from the one story under consideration. It tells us a little bit about the Sky World, certain deities, magic, the belief in spirits, chieftainship, adoption, palm toddy, council houses, menstrual houses, spears, mats, and taro and coconut used as food. The uninformed person, however, would have no way of knowing the importance of these things in the culture, nor would he without further information know much about their characteristics. Nothing is left but to concede that any inquiry into cultural reflection demands access to a wider collection of tales, so the question then becomes one of the adequacy of a given body of folklore in supplying an "ethnography" of a people who may or may not already have been studied by the ethnographer. Sixty-six is certainly not a large number of tales to go by but it is all that I have and all that I could obtain, although I concede that greater persistence would likely have turned up some more.

The human organism of course does not fall under the rubric of "cultural reflection," but it is tempting to reconstruct the appearance of a Ulithian individual from the folklore. "Discoverer-of-the-Sun" is of no help. Neither are the other tales. If one were completely gullible, which no one of course is, the inhabitants of both the earthly world and the celestial one would be variously constituted of many-headed monsters, beings ranging in stature from one span to ten, men with stars on their heads, men limping on one leg, men possessed of enormous weight, and so on. These are the unusual beings, and it is taken for granted that a listener knows what an ordinary human being looks like. Still, we have no way of knowing from the stories anything about a Ulithian's hair form, hair color, skin color, eye color, nose shape, cephalic index, and all the other anthropomorphic details so cherished not only by the physical anthropologist but by the nonspecialist as well.

"Discoverer-of-the-Sun" tells us that yaws is present, and this is substantiated in many other tales, where the disease is used to describe people who are usually in pitiful or repulsive situations. But no other ailments—elephantiasis, ringworm, influenza, asthma, poliomyelitis—to name a few of many recognized and described by the natives—are given notice. One could be misled into thinking that the Ulithians are immune to illness, which they certainly are not, even though they impress one as being unusually healthy. Health simply does not have dramatic expression in their story plots.

Let us digress further by considering the habitat, which because of what man does to it has some cultural implications. Would a person knowing nothing about Ulithi be able to tell from the folklore the nature of the environment?

"Discoverer-of-the-Sun" lets one know that the land is insular and lies in the tropics. It mentions coconuts and a few other species of plants but omits mention of over one

hundred other kinds of species and varieties that have some economic usefulness. It says nothing of fish, birds, or other animals. It tells us nothing about rainfall, which is abundant, or storms, which are devastating enough to constitute a central concern in the lives of the people. We have no way of knowing if the topography is flat or hilly. It is too much to ask of one tale, however, that it give such details. If the whole repertoire is examined it ought to be possible to derive a fairly extensive notion of the natural environment, and so in all fairness we turn to them for the answer to our question.

The clue that Ulithi is insular, made up of many islands surrounding a central lagoon, and has an encircling reef broken here and there by channels, is brought out in some of the narratives. Sand and coral are often mentioned. Economically useful trees of seventeen kinds are given notice. Although the list of trees is far from complete it at least has the virtue of including those that are the most vital economically. Orange trees are mentioned in a tale or two but always in a non-Ulithian locale, though I think that they, like lemon trees, are capable of growing on the atoll. The principal cultigens and cultivars receive mention. Although reference is made to bamboo and yams, one must bear in mind that these are not referred to as growing on Ulithi, as indeed they do not, for they cannot be cultivated successfully there. Three bushes or shrubs growing wild are named.

Surprisingly there is only one reference to domesticated food animals in all sixty-six tales. To be sure, the only such animals are the pig and the chicken, and each may be a relatively recent introduction, even though known for some time elsewhere on the high islands of Micronesia. The chicken is mentioned only once in the tales, and the pig never. Just a few years ago two carabao were brought to Ulithi, but for obvious reasons they have not been incorporated into the stories, although they could have been mentioned in connection with Yap, where they have been much longer. Dogs are never once referred to. In an explanatory ending to a tale which has widespread occurrence in Malaysia and may have an ultimate source in ancient India, mention is made of a cat. Cats are few in Ulithi and are not well thought of. Birds are mentioned in proportionately greater abundance than are any other faunal species, for despite their general paucity they enter as actors into many tales. None however appear in "Discovere.-

of-the-Sun." Fifteen kinds of fish are named. Although this may seem to be a large number, one should bear in mind that Ulithians can readily identify between two and three hundred species and varieties of fish. Sea mammals that gain attention are the whale, porpoise, and dugong. Various other animals are named, some of them only incidentally but others as important characters in the narratives.

I have been tempted by the thought that Ulithian narrators are prone to specify the particular nature of a tree or plant—or animal species, for that matter—because of the connotative value it may have. In magic, romantic songs, and folktales repeated reference is made to this plant or that, or to one fish or another. However, on serious consideration of this possibility I cannot stand by my hypothesis. For one thing, on Ulithi nearly everything in the universe can at one time or another be the object of folkloristic attention, whether it is a millipede, octopus, frigate bird, or blue coral. Or it may be a coconut tree, spider lily, taro, or pandanus. No consistent symbolism is attributed to any of these, except for a rare few such as the *iar* tree (*Premna integrifolia*), which is often associated with lovers, and *ubwoth* or young coconut leaves, which are associated with things religious or magical. One is forced to conclude that probably the frequency of specificity is an aspect of the great concreteness manifested by Ulithians.

Exploitative activities, barely hinted at in "Discoverer-of-the-Sun," are given much more attention elsewhere but always superficially. Horticulture is occasionally referred to directly but is more often implied. While fishing is mentioned time and again, it is not treated in a manner that sheds much light on how it is done. . . . The hunting of birds, now abandoned on the atoll, is the object of attention in more than one tale, and we are told that it is effected through snaring.

Economic exchange is only dimly revealed in Ulithian folklore. In real life it is mostly effected on a personal basis involving either relatives or friends, although not infrequently it is accomplished as part of the sharing of foods and other goods that have been acquired through common effort. Some customs pertaining to gift exchange are alluded to in the tales, as in "The Poor Lizard Girl," but for the most part they are omitted. Notably slighted are first-fruit rites, ostensibly for the benefit of the king but in effect involving a redistribution of foods to the whole community. Other distributive mechanisms, such as the feasts given on certain occasions by women to men, and by men to women, are not mentioned. Trade between Ulithi and Yap, as well as such other islands as Fais, Woleai, Sorol, Ifaluk, and Lamotrek, is not mentioned except indirectly in a tale or two involving the sending of tribute to Yap.

We would learn nothing of native technology if we had to rely on the single tale, "Discoverer-of-the-Sun," except for such meager details as the use of a sharply pointed object (in this instance, a swordfish's mouth!) to husk a coconut and the shredding of coconut preparatory to extracting oil from it. Elsewhere, however, we find out more, but not much more. . . . Technology does not seem to impart excitement or interest to a Ulithian folktale.

Items of material culture are moderately well covered. Some of them have already been mentioned, such as fish traps, fish hooks, men's houses, menstrual houses, and canoes. Beverages, cordage, clothing, ornaments, food vessels, weapons, earth ovens, and firemaking implements draw passing attention but the list is not long. The two special types of houses mentioned above, and the canoes, are given so much attention that it seems useful to look into them in more detail.

The *metalefal*, a combination of meeting house, clubhouse, and dormitory for unmarried men and visitors, is referred to in more than a fifth of the tales. It is always the nucleus of activity in any village, so this is not unexpected. Often, however, in the folktales the *metalefal* is put to some strange use, such as allowing women to stay there with their husbands. Dances occasionally are depicted as taking place in such houses, which is not at all unreasonable, but I never heard of their occurrence in real life.

The menstrual houses or menstruation are frequently referred to. No emphasis is placed on the tabus surrounding either the place or the condition. We are able to learn that children are born in these houses, and that while male adults are excluded, boys are not. An Oepidal tale has a youth make love incestuously to his mother in such a place, but no reference is made to the improbability that such trespass could be permitted, let alone that the couple would carry on their affair even after mutually discovering their identities.

No adequate portrayal of the Ulithian community and community life is provided in the folklore, possibly because of the inherent nature of the folktale with its unreal spatial qualities. We know the people live in villages, which contain men's houses, menstrual houses, cook houses, ordinary dwellings, and firewood sheds. We assume that the *metalefal* is located geographically in the middle. But we have no way of knowing that the menstrual houses in the atoll are always built at right angles to other houses, and therefore parallel to the shore, near which they are located. We feel that there must be a good deal of community activity and responsibility arising out of territoriality rather than kinship but there is no way of documenting the cooperative obligations necessary to maintain the village. The size of the village is never revealed, although one gains the impression it is fairly small, which would reflect existing conditions. We know that dances often take place in the village. But we do not know what economic activities occur. We do not know that the village is divided, as it always is, into plots and other kinds of subdivisions. Most likely these matters are so taken for granted by narrators that it seems superfluous to include them. Although once in a while specific places are named, it is perhaps considered best to give a timeless and spaceless character to the settings.

Kinship and the family are given moderately adequate attention in the tales, but only a person already familiar with their forms and functions could make much sense out of the references that are made. "Discoverer-of-the-Sun" of course is fairly silent on these matters, but not entirely so. Other tales, however, are necessary to round out even a simple picture. They tell us that marriage is essentially monogamous, families are both nuclear and extended, divorce easy, adoption common, descent matrilineal, and residence usually patrilocal.

Kin terms are greatly obscured through translation but the native rendition of such terms in the original narration covers all the ones that are employed in daily use: *tomai* for father, *silei* for mother, *bwisi* for sibling of ego's sex, *mwangai* for sibling of the opposite sex to ego, *lai* for child, *ri* for spouse, and *ochemai* for sibling-in-law of ego's sex. All these terms have extensions, and by studying them in the original language one could detect their classificatory character. However, it would not be possible except in a general way to know the extent to which they refer to one's own or one's father's lineage. One would be hard put to identify them as conforming to the Crow system of terminology, but the experienced anthropologist might make a close reconstruction, not only by analyzing the terms but by the unilineal descent groups that sometimes receive mention. The frequent application of some kinship terms to nonrelatives is often reflected in stories, although this might be confusing to the unalerted novice. The collective term *ieramatai* is sometimes used, and it designates all relatives—maternal and paternal, consanguineal and affinal—serving to remind us that bilaterality is not a neglected principle of kinship structure and function. The rights and obligations that kinsmen possess are not, however, adequately revealed in the folklore, and one gets only a confused picture of brother-sister avoidance, joking relationships, funeral obligations, and economic exchange.

In adopting Baby Boy, Iolofath is acting in accordance with a widespread practice in Ulithi and the rest of the Carolines. Field research indicates that in 1949 the number of people who had been formally adopted in the atoll was forty-five per cent. An adoption must take place while the mother of the child is still pregnant, so Iolofath's adopting of the boy after his birth is not strictly proper; nevertheless, this kind of adoption, which of course is the type one usually encounters throughout the world, is found even on Ulithi, but the formal term, *fam*, does not apply. My informants, pressed on this matter, held their ground in insisting that a prepartal adoption was the only "legal" kind. The motivations for adoption are not at all clear, and it is useless to try to get informants to analyze their reasons, which anyhow are complex enough to defy definitive pronouncements. In any event, people seek adoptions rather than have them thrust on them, and it is not incongruent for Iolofath to tell his wife to be quiet and go ahead and make food for their boy because they were lucky to get him. The storyteller is here really expressing a human rather than a divine reaction. It seems a little sad, incidentally, that the god should be in the position of having to ask for a child to adopt; but that only goes to show how changed he has become.

.   .   .

The freedom with which Ulithians view sex is not reflected in "Discoverer-of-the-Sun" but has ample expression elsewhere. In one tale a young man sleeps night after night with five sisters. In another, a great god comes down from Lang and causes his mortal mistress to become pregnant. It is not unusual in the folklore for married men and women to have extramarital lovers.

But also given attention are some sexual forms that are in reality emphatically forbidden in Ulithian society. In real life incest is looked upon with horror; not, however, in folklore. Two brothers, as we have already noted, trick a gullible sister into becoming their mistress. Two fond but vain parents promote the incestuous marriage of their unusually attractive son and daughter on the grounds that no suitably handsome mates are available to them. A mother and son delight in their incest and then marry one another. These things happen with impunity in the lore. Rape does not occur on Ulithi, yet it is mentioned in a tale, purportedly historical, involving trouble between Ponape and Kusaie, the rapists being nephews of the ravished woman's dead husband. They choose this means of angering her new husband, who through sorcery has brought about her previous husband's death.

Ulithians resort to euphemisms when discussing sex and elimination in mixed company. In many cases they must use complete circumlocutions. Thus, one does not use the word *haloloi*, to urinate; instead one says *suchol*, "to stand water." One does not say *leweth*, anus, but *metal tagorom*, "end of the back." There are scores of avoided words, sometimes without any euphemism. Many words are avoided also in the company of elders and sometimes when religious specialists are present. Yet many of the tales I collected use words that are subject to tabu, even though they were told by a parent to a child of different sex. For example, "The Feces Girl" was learned by Taiethau from an adult woman when he was still in his teens, and I am sure that she could not have used a euphemism for *piakh*, or excrement, when she related it, for the comic effect would thus have been destroyed. I regret that I have not looked into this matter explicitly in order to see, when stories of erotic or obscene nature are told in mixed company, whether euphemisms are used and certain words altogether circumvented. My feeling is that in these instances the barriers are let down.

Greater stratification than actually exists on Ulithi is portrayed in various ways. The reason for the stronger depiction of class differences as well as status differences is probably twofold. A good number of the stories have a provenance in which stratification is marked, as in Yap, Ponape, and Kusaie. In addition, dominance of the political system by foreign countries has diminished the power of traditional kings and chiefs. In the tale "Haluwai" mention is made of low-caste Yapese known as *res fach*, but otherwise no reference is made to this important and complex social differentiation, which has direct and important linkages with Ulithi even today.

It is possible to make inferences about the political system. Obviously, there are chiefs, with one chief apparently acting as a paramount who has strong authority. Iolofath, for instance, is one of the latter in "Discoverer-of-the-Sun," and has deputies who obey his wishes. He is a god, however, and not altogether characteristic, except to the extent that the Carolinian pantheon is an invention of actual human beings and therefore reflects conditions on earth. But there are many kinds of chiefs in Ulithi whose specific traits are not revealed through folklore. For instance, the political authority of lineage chiefs receives no expression, nor does the authority of district chiefs. But the *malkaweiach*, or council elders, and their *metalefal*, or meeting place, gain adequate attention throughout. Within the atoll the system of authority and the chain of command is stratified but receives no reflection in the folklore. There are definite rules of succession for the various kinds of chiefs, yet we get a distorted picture of the manner in which people become chiefs. Often they are designated, whether male or female, to be village heads as a reward for services such as killing off ogres or repelling an enemy. Most likely such accession is possible, but in modern times it violates the strictly hereditary character of chiefly succession.

The complex tributary and religious relationship of Ulithi to Yap gains some attention in the folklore (collected as well by others on both Yap and Ulithi), being explicitly expressed in "Why Ulithians Take Offerings to Yap," a fragmentary account.

If one is to be guided by the implications of Iolofath's revenge for the murder of his adoptive son, justice is private and informal. Admittedly, one might argue that Iolofath, being the superordinate person of the community, would be the logical person to punish the chief conspirator, Rasim, but this argument dissolves if one bears in mind that the father is not acting as the surrogate of the society. He has not been selected to carry out justice. His act is private and highly personal, and of course exerted in his role as kinsman. Law in the true sense, implying code, procedure, and court, is absent.

. . .

Ingroup conflict receives only faint expression in "Discoverer-of-the-Sun," taking the form of a woman's neglect of her absent sister's child and a community's resentment against a stranger mostly because he is a stranger. Neither of these two instances truly expresses a condition of internal strife but they may nevertheless be examined for typicality.

The mistreatment of a child is not consonant with actual practice, for in Ulithi children are treated permissively and kindly, in evidence whereof I hasten to make mention that in all my time on the atoll I saw a child struck only twice. I am not naïve enough to think that I saw everything, but the whole atmosphere is one in which a child could never be subjected to much abuse. Yet the oral literature of Ulithi does make mention of other instances of child neglect or chastisement. A poignant example is one recorded in my tale, "The Selfish Mother," in which a widow with ten children greedily forbids them to touch the fruit of a tree outside their house. Hungry, the first child, a girl, eats a fruit, and her mother beats her to death. The same thing happens with all the other children except the two youngest, a girl of five and her brother of three. The little girl is very protective and tries to see that the boy does not endanger himself by eating any of the fruit. But he does, while she is asleep. They flee and eventually grow up in the midst of much food. One day they return to visit their mother, who is old and weak from having nothing to eat but her fruit. They give her food but refuse to live with her, promising, however, to keep her supplied. She is at long last filled with remorse for her foul deeds.

. . .

I conclude that in reality Ulithians are always preoccupied with the welfare of young children, and that stories depicting their mistreatment have the function of holding up such dastardliness to disapprobation by society. Certainly the overwhelming bulk of the tales depict nothing but fondness and consideration for youngsters, an attitude frequently remarked upon by Oceanic ethnographers working with real people.

Strangers in Ulithian folklore are almost invariably suspect and greeted with commensurate action, usually violence. Our hero, Thilefial, finds this all too true. Likewise, in a myth concerning his younger days, Iolofath is scorned and beaten at every level of the Sky World which he visits, although he was admittedly brash enough to compound the provocation caused by his foreignness. . . . In actual life today a stranger arriving alone on Ulithi or even in a group would be the object of compassion, if he arrived shipwrecked. Should a stranger arrive on a ship he would be treated courteously as a guest. In precontact days the situation of course would have been different. An example of a hostile expedition of strangers is given in "Mogmog's Battle with the Eastern Warriors," where the visitors make their hostility immediately evident by not observing the amenities.

The causes of quarrels in Ulithian folktales approximate those in actual life. Men quarrel over women, women quarrel over men. Boys fight over playthings. A woman becomes angered because she is given the flippers of a turtle to eat instead of the better portions. A young girl petulantly leaves her parents because she avers they do not treat her right. A young man (Iolofath) tries to kill his half brother out of sheer jealousy over the affections of their father. Two men dispute over land—one of the most common sources of ingroup conflict on the atoll, but inadequately reflected in the tales. In a tragic story a poor family is given a bad share of coconuts following a typhoon, and after the mother has taught her son magically to procure carapaces from afar she refuses to let the rest of the community in on their secret.

No warfare appears in "Discoverer-of-the-Sun," unless one chooses to think of the hero's single-handed fight against his numerous enemies as an expression of warfare. But frequent depiction of war occurs in other tales, some of whose titles give us a glimpse into the matter: "An Attack on a Ship at Ulithi," "The Fight between Kusaie and Ponape," "Mogmog's Battle with the Eastern Warriors," and "Mogmog's Defeat by Losiep." The weapons employed, especially the spear and sling, are faithfully depicted, and the tactics of battle, to judge from ethnohistorical accounts which I have extensively examined for the Carolines, are as portrayed.

The training of the hero in the art of fighting is consistent with Carolinian practice. I have some brief field information on the subject, particularly with regard to close-fighting, known on Ulithi as *bwang*. The term is also used to express attack against one's opponent, whereas defense is referred to as *pelet*. Training may be given by a relative or a friend, who receives gifts for his services. . . . There are fifteen named positions in attacks with a combination staff-spear and five in an attack with a knife. I mention these details because until 1960 I did not know that Ulithians had a formal training in fighting (only a few men on the atoll knew anything about it). Therefore, when the *ialus* in the story teaches Thilefial how to fight we can take it for granted that it was not a vague unsystematic kind of instruction. Similarly, in another tale when Rasim teaches his adopted boy to protect himself against his real father we can assume that something like *bwang* was used. . . .

Myths being the sacred tales that they are, it comes as no surprise that more is reflected in Ulithian folklore about religion than almost any other facet of their way of life. We learn something about ancestor worship, the names and attributes of the gods, the nature of magic and divination, the kinds of religious personnel, the origins of tabus, and all the many beliefs and practices that are embodied in narrative form. "Discoverer-of-the-Sun," as we have had occasion to see, tells us something about Lang and the beings who live there. Much more informative in this respect, however, are such myths as "Iolofath and Lugeilang," "Iolofath and Khiou," "Iolofath and the Handsome Spouses," and "'Palulop' and His Family." All these are supplemented in one way or another by a whole series of minor stories dealing with spirits, ogres, cultural origins, and adventures that mortals have in the Sky World.

To some extent the tales give the mythological basis for ritual. "How Men Were Taught Fish Magic" explains the lengthy procedures to be followed by the fish-magician in his annual effort to assure an abundance of fish for the people of the atoll. Other stories are only slightly less a ritual fountainhead than this, as in a narrative explaining how divination with knots in palm leaves came to Ulithi; another explaining why certain religious offerings must be sent to Yap, where the people of Gagil district keep the magical fishhook by which the island of Fais was raised up out of the sea; and still another

explaining the practice of trap fishermen of sending two fish to a spirit named Libwong-ongo on the island of Potangeras.

Tabus are occasionally given expression, sometimes reflecting sacred prohibitions still extant in Ulithian culture, as in a myth listing the fish that may not be eaten by a godling named Furabwai because, apparently, these are reserved for his brother, Ialulwe, the patron of navigators. . . . Sometimes, however, the tabus do not reflect specific interdicts practiced on the atoll, as when a mother in a myth says it is tabu for her son Motikitik to follow her when she sets out each day for the world beneath the sea. Punishments for the breaking of tabus are not always forthcoming, and it is startling to find that in one tale a brother and a sister at first hesitatingly and then enthusiastically commit incest, ending by living as man and wife without disapprobation on the part of their parents. In a jocular vignette two brothers trick their sister into becoming their paramour. In an Oedipal tale a youth who has killed his father goes on to live with his mother, to whom he has been making love right along; presumably they live happily ever after.

In "Discoverer-of-the-Sun" no mention is made of tabus, but an actual interdict is broken when Iolofath goes to the menstrual house in search of a child to adopt. On Ulithi in real life males, except small children, are forbidden to trespass on the grounds bordering the hut where women go at the time of their periods or parturitions. An exception is made only under dire circumstances, as when a typhoon threatens the safety of the women and they must be evacuated to a safer spot. Iolofath may have been excluded from the tabu because of his special nature, but somehow this does not seem to be the reason. It is a pity that our story is not better illustrative of tabus, but enough has been said to indicate that they do find ample expression in the wider body of narrative.

. . .

IV

The intention of this study has been to stress that the outsider must be provided with exegetic assistance to gain as much as a minimal understanding of a tale from a culture even as simple as that of Ulithi. Most stories transferred out of their native setting and recorded on paper obviously lose much of their charm and virility when stripped, not only of their narrator's use of gesture and intonation, but, more seriously still, of their cultural meaning as well. "Discoverer-of-the-Sun," the sample selected for analysis, is more lucid than most Ulithian tales, and yet demands as much from an audience as it gives to it. As a yarn it has elements which almost anyone can respond to with interest; but when a reader lacks adequate comprehension of the many little understandings needed to transform the skeleton of its plot into a live and vibrant story, his appreciation is greatly reduced.

In considering the extent to which culture is reflected in "Discoverer-of-the-Sun" and other Ulithian narratives, it is at once obvious that some aspects are more favored than others, many being given no attention at all. It is fortunately possible, owing to the availability of an ethnographic study of the atoll, to contrast folkloristic content with cultural reality. Whatever may be the merits of other bodies of folklore, it cannot be said that Ulithian tales are an adequate source on which to rely for a reconstruction of the native culture. They omit or slight many of the important details of ordinary life, at the same time incorporating practices that are either alien or obviously in the realm of fantasy. Nor can they be regarded, except for a few tentative accounts, as reliable records of historical events. Speaking of folktales in general, it is always puzzling to know why certain real happenings, documented by written records, fail to gain inclusion into a corpus of folklore, and it will perhaps never become clear why Ulithians fail to include in their stories historical episodes of dramatic and severe impact, such as the massacre of Father Cantova's missionary party in 1731. If major episodes disappear without leaving a trace in contemporary tales, there is even less reason to believe that the trivial ones will have been preserved, at least in recognizable form.

Part of the dilemma of both historicity and cultural reflection is indubitably linked with the problem of provenance. Many, perhaps most, Ulithian tales are from sources elsewhere in the Carolinian archipelago and beyond. Of course, diffusion characterizes folklore anywhere, yet we know that in the transference there is sufficient recasting and adjustment of the details so as to fashion the tales in the direction of local values and forms. Another source of difficulty lies in the probability that the body of Ulithian tales which has here been considered represents only a diminished corpus of the original, either because of deterioration of the folklore tradition or failure to collect all that is actually extant. Notwithstanding this possible lack of completeness, it is likely that there is something inherent in all bodies of folktales which renders them inadequate—even though useful —as sources of cultural content.

. . .

W. E. H. Stanner
THE DREAMING

The Australian concept of the Dreaming, a kind of epoch in which the mythical ancestors of the aborigines lived but which is not thought of as a time that is past in the ordinary sense of the word, has long fascinated anthropologists and psychologists. The myths of the dream time are the basis for the elaborate ritual of the Australians, seen particularly in the increase and initiation ceremonies. The highly sacred churingas of the aborigines are symbols of the heroes of the eternal dream time, as it has been called, and serve to transfer life and power from them to men. The myths of this state or time are connected at least psychically with dream-life, sharing many of its characteristics, and this has led such psychoanalysts as Róheim to interpret the Dreaming as representing a phase of totemism preceding the contrition that was felt following the bloody prehistoric parricide

Reprinted from W. E. H. Stanner, "The Dreaming," in T. A. G. Hungerford (ed.), *Australian Signpost* (Melbourne: F. W. Cheshire, 1956), pp. 51–65, by permission of the author and F. W. Cheshire Pty., Ltd.

hypothesized by Freud. Róheim believes that the myths of the Dreaming depict the various phases of the ontogenetic and phylogenetic Oedipus complex. Other interpretations have of course been made, but there is agreement that the Dreaming is no ordinary kind of past, not even the usual mythical past of other peoples. It has a strange quality that few investigators have truly understood, and we owe a great debt of gratitude to Stanner for his exquisite clarification of its true nature. He gives us a feeling of the remarkable beauty to be found in this focal point of Australian culture, and leaves us wondering anew that it could ever be asserted that here we have an "Old Stone Age" people representing the crudest level of human achievement. Those who wish to pursue further the interpretations of the religion may consult not only the monograph *On Aboriginal Religion* (1963), referred to in the introduction to this chapter, but also the author's recent "Religion, Totemism, and Symbolism" (1965).

I

The blackfellow's outlook on the universe and man is shaped by a remarkable conception, which Spencer and Gillen immortalized as "the dream time" or *alcheringa* of the Arunta or Aranda tribe. Some anthropologists have called it "The Eternal Dream Time." I prefer to call it what the blacks call it in English— "The Dreaming," or just "Dreaming."

A central meaning of The Dreaming is that of a sacred, heroic time long long ago when man and nature came to be as they are; but neither "time" nor "history" as we understand them is involved in this meaning. I have never been able to discover any aboriginal word for *time* as an abstract concept. And the sense of "history" is wholly alien here. We shall not understand The Dreaming fully except as a complex of meanings. A blackfellow may call his totem, or the place from which his spirit came, his Dreaming. He may also explain the existence of a custom, or a law of life, as causally due to The Dreaming.

A concept so impalpable and subtle naturally suffers badly by translation into our dry and abstract language. The black sense this difficulty. I can recall one intelligent old man who said to me, with a cadence almost as though he had been speaking verse:

White man got no dreaming,
Him go 'nother way.
White man, him go different,
Him got road belong himself.

In their own dialects, they use terms like *alcheringa*, *mipuramibirina*, *boaradja*—often almost untranslatable, or meaning literally something like "men of old." It is as difficult to be sure of the objective effects of the idea on their lives as of its subjective implications for them.

Although, as I have said, The Dreaming conjures up the notion of a sacred, heroic time of the indefinitely remote past, such a time is also, in a sense, still part of the present. One cannot "fix" The Dreaming *in* time: it was, and is, everywhen. We should be very wrong to try to read into it the idea of a Golden Age, or a Garden of Eden, though it was an Age of Heroes, when the ancestors did marvelous things that men can no longer do. The blacks are not at all insensitive to Mary Webb's "wistfulness that is the past," but they do not, in aversion from present or future, look back on it with yearning and nostalgia. Yet it has for them an unchallengeably sacred authority.

Clearly, The Dreaming is many things in one. Among them, a kind of narrative of things that once happened; a kind of charter of things that still happen; and a kind of *logos* or principle of order transcending everything significant for aboriginal man. If I am correct in saying so, it is much more complex philosophically than we have so far realized. I greatly hope that artists and men of letters who (it seems increasingly) find inspiration in aboriginal Australia will use all their gifts of empathy, but avoid banal projection and subjectivism, if they seek to borrow the notion.

Why the blackfellow thinks of "dreaming" as the nearest equivalent in English is a puzzle. It may be because it is by *the act* of dreaming, as reality and symbol, that the aboriginal mind makes contact—thinks it makes contact—with whatever mystery it is that connects The Dreaming and the Here-and-Now.

II

How shall one deal with so subtle a conception? One has two options: educe its subjective logic and rationale from the "elements" which the blackfellow stumblingly offers in trying to give an explanation; or relate, as best one may, to things familiar in our own intellectual history, the objective figure it traces on their social life. There are dangers in both courses.

The first is a matter, so to speak, of learning to "think black," not imposing Western categories of understanding, but seeking to conceive of things as the blackfellow himself does.

In our modern understanding, we tend to see "mind" and "body," "body" and "spirit," "spirit" and "personality," "personality" and "name" as in some sense separate, even opposed, entities though we manage to connect them up in some fashion into the unity or oneness of "person" or "individual." The blackfellow does not seem to think this way. The distinctiveness we give to "mind," "spirit," and "body," and our contrast of "body" versus "spirit" are not there, and the whole notion of "the person" is enlarged. To a blackfellow, a man's name, spirit, and shadow are "him" in a sense which to us may seem passing strange. One should not ask a blackfellow: "What is your name?" To do so embarrasses and shames him. The name is like an intimate part of the body, with which another person does not take liberties. The blacks do not mind talking about a dead person in an oblique way but, for a long time, they are extremely reluctant even to breathe his name. In the same way, to threaten a man's shadow is to threaten him. Nor may one treat lightly the physical place from which his spirit came. By extension, his totem, which is also associated with that place, and with his spirit, should not be lightly treated.

In such a context one has not succeeded in "thinking black" until one's mind can, without intellectual struggle, enfold into some kind of oneness the notions of body, spirit, ghost, shadow, name, spirit-site, and totem. To say so may seem a contradiction, or suggest a paradox, for the blackfellow can and does, on some occasions, conceptually isolate the "elements" of the "unity" most distinctly. But his abstractions do not put him at war with himself. The separable elements I have mentioned are all present in the metaphysical heart of the idea of "person," but the overruling mood is one of belief, not of inquiry or dissent. So long as the belief in The Dreaming lasts, there can be no "momentary flash of Athenian questioning" to grow into a great movement of skeptical unbelief which destroys the given unities.

There are many other such "onenesses" which I believe I could substantiate. A blackfellow may "see" as "a unity" two persons, such as two siblings or a grandparent and grandchild; or a living man and something inanimate, as when he tells you that, say, the woolly-butt tree, his totem, is his wife's brother. (This is not quite as strange as it may seem. Even modern psychologists tend to include part of "environment" in a "definition" of "person" or "personality.") There is also some kind of unity between waking-life and dream-life: the means by which, in aboriginal understanding, a man fathers a child, is not by sexual intercourse, but by the act of dreaming about a spirit-child. His own spirit, during a dream, "finds" a child and directs it to his wife, who then conceives. Physical congress between a man and a woman is contingent, not a necessary prerequisite. Through the medium of dream-contact with a spirit an artist is inspired to produce a new song. It is by dreaming that a man divines the intention of someone to kill him by sorcery, or of relatives to visit him. And, as I have suggested, it is by the act of dreaming, in some way difficult for a European to grasp because of the force of our analytic abstractions, that a blackfellow conceives himself to make touch with whatever it is that is continuous between The Dreaming and the Here-and-Now.

The truth of it seems to be that man, society, and nature and past, present, and future are at one together within a unitary system of such a kind that its ontology cannot illumine minds too much under the influence of humanism, rationalism, and science. One cannot easily, in the mobility of modern life and thought, grasp the vast intuitions of stability and permanence, and of life and man, at the heart of aboriginal ontology.

It is fatally easy for Europeans, encountering such things for the first time, to go on to suppose that "mysticism" of this kind rules *all* aboriginal thought. It is not so. "Logical" thought and "rational" conduct are about as widely present in aboriginal life as they are on the simpler levels of European life. Once one understands three things—the primary intuitions which the blackfellow has formed about the nature of the universe and man, those things in both which he thinks interesting and significant, and the conceptual system from within which he reasons about them—then the suppositions about prelogicality, illogicality, and nonrationality can be seen to be merely absurd. And if one wishes to see a really brilliant demonstration of deductive thought, one has only to see a blackfellow tracking a wounded kangaroo, and persuade him to say why he interprets given signs in a certain way.

The second means of dealing with the notion of The Dreaming is, as I said, to try to relate it to things familiar in our own intellectual history. From this viewpoint, it is a cosmogony, an account of the begetting of the universe, a story about creation. It is also a cosmology, an account or theory of how what was created became an orderly system. To be more precise, how the universe became a moral system.

If one analyzes the hundreds of tales about The Dreaming, one can see within them three elements. The first concerns the great *marvels* —how all the fire and water in the world were stolen and recaptured; how men made a mistake over sorcery and now have to die from it; how the hills, rivers, and water holes were made; how the sun, moon, and stars were set upon their courses; and many other dramas of this kind. The second element tells how certain things were *instituted* for the first time —how animals and men diverged from a joint stock that was neither one nor the other; how the black-nosed kangaroo got his black nose and the porcupine his quills; how such social divisions as tribes, clans, and language groups were set up; how spirit-children were first placed in the water holes, the winds, and the leaves of trees. A third element, if I am not mistaken, allows one to suppose that many of the main institutions of present-day life were *already ruling* in The Dreaming, e.g., marriage, exogamy, sister-exchange, and initiation, as well as many of the well-known breaches of custom. The men of The Dreaming committed adultery, betrayed and killed each other, were greedy, stole, and committed the very wrongs committed by those now alive.

Now, if one disregards the imagery in which the verbal literature of The Dreaming is cast, one may perhaps come to three conclusions.

The tales are a kind of commentary, or statement, on what is thought to be permanent and ordained at the very basis of the world and life. They are a way of stating the principle which animates things. I would call them a poetic key to Reality. The aborigine does not ask himself the philosophical types of questions: What is "real"? How many "kinds" of "reality" are there? What are the "properties" of "reality"? How are the properties "interconnected"? This is the idiom of Western intellectual discourse and the fruit of a certain social history. His tales are, however, a kind of answer to such questions so far as they have been asked at all. They may not be a "definition," but they are a "key" to reality, a key to the singleness and the plurality of things set up once-for-all when, in The Dreaming, the universe became man's universe. The active philosophy of aboriginal life transforms this "key," which is expressed in the idiom of poetry, drama, and symbolism, into a principle that The Dreaming determines not only what life *is* but also *what it can be*. Life, so to speak, is a one-possibility thing, and what this is, is the "meaning" of The Dreaming.

The tales are also a collation of *what is validly known* about such ordained permanencies. The blacks cite The Dreaming as a charter of absolute validity in answer to all questions of *why* and *how*. In this sense, the tales can be regarded as being, perhaps not a definition, but a "key" of Truth.

They also state, by their constant recitation of what was done rightly and wrongly in The Dreaming, the ways in which good men should, and bad men will, act now. In this sense, they are a "key" or guide to the norms of conduct, and a prediction of how men will err.

One may thus say that, after a fashion—a cryptic, symbolic, and poetic fashion—the tales are "a philosophy" in the garb of a verbal literature. The European has a philosophic literature which expresses a largely deductive understanding of reality, truth, goodness, and beauty. The blackfellow has a mythology, a ritual, and an art which express an intuitive, visionary, and poetic understanding of the same ultimates. In following out The Dreaming, the blackfellow "lives" this philosophy. It is an implicit philosophy, but nevertheless a real one. Whereas we hold (and may live) a philosophy of abstract propositions, attained by someone standing professionally outside "Life" and treating it as an object of contemplation and inquiry. The blackfellow holds his philosophy in mythology, attained as the social product of an indefinitely ancient past, and proceeds to live it out "in" life, in part through a ritual and an expressive art, and in part through nonsacred social customs.

European minds are made uneasy by the facts that the stories are, quite plainly, preposterous; are often a mass of internal contradictions; are encrusted by superstitious fancies about magic, sorcery, hobgoblins, and superhuman heroes; and lack the kind of theme and structure—in other words, the "story" element—for which we look. Many of us cannot help feeling that such things can only be the products of absurdly ignorant credulity and a lower order of mentality. This is to fall victim to a facile fallacy. Our own intellectual history is not an absolute standard by which to judge others. The worst imperialisms are those of preconception.

Custom is the reality, beliefs but the shadows which custom makes on the wall. Since the tales, in any case, are not really "explanatory" in purpose or function, they naturally lack logic, system, and completeness. It is simply pointless to look for such things within them. But we are not entitled to suppose that, because the tales are fantastical, the social life producing them is itself fantastical. The shape of reality is always distorted in the shadows it throws. One finds much logic, system, and rationality in the blacks' actual scheme of life.

These tales are neither simply illustrative nor simply explanatory; they are fanciful and poetic in content because they are based on visionary and intuitive insights into mysteries; and, if we are ever to understand them, we must always take them in their complex context. If, then, they make more sense to the poet, the artist, and the philosopher than to the clinicians of human life, let us reflect on the withering effect on sensibility of our pervasive rationalism, rather than depreciate the gifts which produced the aboriginal imaginings. And in no case should we expect the tales, *prima facie*, to be even interesting if studied out of context. Aboriginal mythology is quite unlike the Scandinavian, Indian, or Polynesian mythologies.

III

In my own understanding, The Dreaming is a proof that the blackfellow shares with us two abilities which have largely made human history what it is.

The first of these we might call "the metaphysical gift." I mean ability to transcend oneself, to make acts of imagination so that one can stand "outside" or "away from" oneself, and turn the universe, oneself, and one's fellows into objects of contemplation. The second ability is a "drive" to try to "make sense" out of human experience and to find some "principle" in the whole human situation. This "drive" is, in some way, built into the constitution of the human mind. No one who has real knowledge of aboriginal life can

have any doubt that they possess, and use, both abilities very much as we do. They differ from us only in the directions in which they turn their gifts, the idiom in which they express them, and the principles of intellectual control.

The blacks have no gods, just or unjust, to adjudicate the world. Not even by straining can one see in such culture heroes as Baiame and Darumulum the true hint of a Yahveh, jealous, omniscient, and omnipotent. The ethical insights are dim and somewhat coarse in texture. One can find in them little trace, say, of the inverted pride, the self-scrutiny, and the consciousness of favor and destiny which characterized the early Jews. A glimpse, but no truly poignant sense, of moral dualism; no notion of grace or redemption; no whisper of inner peace and reconcilement; no problems of worldly life to be solved only by a consummation of history; no heaven of reward or hell of punishment. The blackfellow's afterlife is but a shadowy replica of worldly life, so none flee to inner sanctuary to escape the world. There are no prophets, saints, or *illuminati*. There is a concept of goodness, but it lacks true scruple. Men can become ritually unclean, but may be cleansed by a simple mechanism. There is a moral law but, as in the beginning, men are both good and bad, and no one is racked by the knowledge. I imagine there could never have been an aboriginal Ezekiel, any more than there could have been a Job. The two sets of insights cannot easily be compared, but it is plain that their underlying moods are wholly unlike, and their store of meaningfulness very uneven. In the one there seem an almost endless possibility of growth, and a mood of censoriousness and pessimism. In the other, a kind of standstill, and a mood which is neither tragic nor optimistic. The aborigines are not shamed or inspired by a religious thesis of what men might become by faith and grace. Their metaphysic assents, without brooding or challenge, to what men evidently have to be because the terms of life are cast. Yet they have a kind of religiosity cryptically displayed in their magical awareness of nature, in their complex totemism, ritual, and art, and perhaps too even in their intricately ordered life.

They are, of course, nomads—hunters and foragers who grow nothing, build nothing, and stay nowhere long. They make almost no physical mark on the environment. Even in areas which are still inhabited, it takes a knowledgeable eye to detect their recent presence. Within a matter of weeks, the roughly cleared campsites may be erased by sun, rain, and wind. After a year or two there may be nothing to suggest that the country was ever inhabited. Until one stumbles on a few old flint tools, a stone quarry, a shell midden, a rock painting, or something of the kind, one may think the land had never known the touch of man.

They neither dominate their environment nor seek to change it. "Children of nature" they are not, nor are they nature's "masters." One can only say they are "at one" with nature. The whole ecological principle of their life might be summed up in the Baconian aphorism—*natura non vincitur nisi parendo*: "Nature is not to be commanded except by obeying." Naturally, one finds metaphysical and social reflections of the fact.

They move about, carrying their scant possessions, in small bands of anything from ten to sixty persons. Each band belongs to a given locality. A number of bands—anything from three or four up to twelve or fifteen, depending on the fertility of the area—make up a "tribe." A tribe is usually a language or dialect group which thinks of itself as having a certain unity of common speech and shared customs. The tribes range in size from a few hundred to a few thousand souls.

One rarely sees a tribe as a formed entity. It comes together and lives as a unit only for a great occasion—a feast, a corroboree, a hunt, an initiation, or a formal duel. After a few days—at the most, weeks—it breaks up again into smaller bands or sections of bands: most commonly into a group of brothers, with their wives, children, and grandchildren and perhaps a few close relatives. These parties rove about their family locality, or, by agreement, the territories of immediate neighbors. They do not wander aimlessly, but to a purpose, and in tune with the seasonal food supply. One can almost plot a year of their life in terms of movement towards the places where honey, yams, grass seeds, eggs, or some other food staple, is in bearing and ready for eating.

The uncomplex visible routine, and the simple segmentation, are very deceptive. It took well over half a century for Europeans to realize that behind the outward show was an inward structure of surprising complexity. It was a century before any real understanding of this structure developed.

In one tribe with which I am familiar, a very representative tribe, there are about 100 "invisible" divisions which have to be analyzed before one can claim even a serviceable understanding of the tribe's organization. The structure is much more complex than that of an Australian village of the same size. The complexity is in the most striking contrast with the comparative simplicity which rules in the two other departments of aboriginal life—the material culture, on the one hand, and the ideational or metaphysical culture on the other. We have, I think, to try to account for this contrast in some way.

Their creative "drive" to make sense and order out of things has, for some reason, concentrated on the social rather than on the metaphysical or the material side. Consequently, there has been an unusually rich development of what the anthropologist calls "social structure," the network of enduring relations recognized between people. This very intricate system is an intellectual and social achievement of a high order. It is not, like an instinctual response, a phenomenon of "nature"; it is not, like art or ritual, a complex type of behavior passionately added to "nature," in keeping with metaphysical insight but without rational and intelligible purposes which can be clearly stated; it has to be compared, I think, with such a secular achievement as, say, parliamentary government in a European society. It is truly positive knowledge.

One may see within it three things: given customs, "of which the memory of man runneth not to the contrary"; a vast body of cumulative knowledge about the effects of these customs on a society in given circumstances; and the use of the power of abstract reason to rationalize the resultant relations into a system.

But it is something much more: It has become *the source of the dominant mode of aboriginal thinking*. The blacks use it to give a bony structure to parts of the world outlook suggested by intuitive speculation. I mean by this that they have taken some of its fundamental principles and relations and have applied them to very much wider sets of phenomena. This tends to happen if any type of system of thought becomes truly dominant. It is, broadly, what Europeans did with "religion" and "science" as systems: extended their principles and categories to fields far beyond the contexts in which the systems grew.

Thus, the blacks have taken the male-female social principle and have extended it to the nonhuman world. In one tribe I have studied, all women, without exception, call particular birds or trees by the same kinship terms which they apply to actual relatives. In the same way, all men without exception use comparable terms for a different set of trees or birds. From this results what the anthropologist calls "sex totemism." The use of other principles results in other types of totemism. An understanding of this simple fact removes much of the social, if not the ritual, mystery of totemism. Again, the principle of relatedness itself, relatedness between known people by known descent through known marriages, is extended over the whole face of human society. The same terms of kinship which are used for close agnatic and affinal relatives are used for every other person an aborigine meets in the course of his life: strangers, friends, enemies, and known kin may all be called by the same terms as one uses for brother, father, mother's sister, father's mother's brother, and so on. This is what an anthropologist means when he says "aboriginal society is a society of kinship."

It might even be argued that the blacks have done much the same thing with "time." Time as a continuum is a concept only hazily present in the aboriginal mind. What might be called *social* time is, in a sense, "bent" into cycles or circles. The most controlled understanding of it is by reckoning in terms of generation-classes, which are arranged into named and recurring cycles. As far as the blackfellow thinks about time at all, his interest lies in the cycles rather than in the continuum, and each cycle is in essence a principle for dealing with social interrelatedness.

IV

Out of all this may come for some an understanding of the blackfellow very different from that which has passed into the ignorance and vulgarity of popular opinion.

One may see that, like all men, he is a metaphysician in being able to transcend himself. With the metaphysic goes a mood and spirit, which I can only call a mood and spirit of "assent": neither despair nor resignation, optimism nor pessimism, quietism nor indifference. The mood, and the outlook beneath it, make him hopelessly out of place in a world in which the Renaissance has triumphed only to be perverted, and in which the products of secular humanism, rationalism, and science challenge their own hopes, indeed, their beginnings

Much association with the blackfellow makes me feel I may not be far wrong in saying that, unlike us, he seems to see "life" as a one-possibility thing. This may be why he seems to have almost no sense of tragedy. If "tragedy is a looking at fate for a lesson in deportment on life's scaffold," the aborigine seems to me to have read the lesson and to have written it into the very conception of how men should live, or else to have stopped short of the insight that there are gods either just or unjust. Nor have I found in him much self-pity. These sentiments can develop only if life presents real alternatives, or if it denies an alternative that one feels should be there. A philosophy of assent fits only a life of unvarying constancy. I do not at all say that pain, sorrow, and sadness have no place in aboriginal life, for I have seen them all too widely. All I mean is that the blacks seem to have gone beyond, or not quite attained, the human *quarrel* with such things. Their rituals of sorrow, their fortitude in pain, and their undemonstrative sadness seem to imply a reconciliation with the terms of life such that "peace is the understanding of tragedy and at the same time its preservation," or else that they have not sensed life as baffled by either fate or wisdom.

Like all men, he is also a philosopher in being able to use his power of abstract reason. His genius, his métier, and—in some sense—his fate, is that because of endowment and circumstance this power has channeled itself mainly into one activity, "making sense" out of the social relations among men living together. His intricate social organization is an impressive essay on the economy of conflict, tension, and experiment in a life situation at the absolute pole of our own.

Like all men, too, he pays the price of his insights and solutions. We look to a continuous unfolding of life, and to a blissful attainment of the better things for which, we say, man has an infinite capacity. For some time, nothing has seemed of less consequence to us than the maintenance of continuity. The cost, in instability and inequity, is proving very heavy. Aboriginal life has endured feeling that continuity, not man, is the measure of all. The cost, in the world of power and change, is extinction. What defeats the blackfellow in the modern world, fundamentally, is his transcendentalism. So much of his life and thought are concerned with The Dreaming that it stultifies his ability to develop. This is not a new thing in human history. A good analogy is with the process in Chinese poetry by which, according to Arthur Waley, its talent for classical allusion became a vice which finally destroyed it altogether.

A "philosophy of life," that is, a system of mental attitudes towards the conduct of life, may or may not be consistent with an actual way of life. Whether it is or is not will depend on how big a gap there is, if any, between what life *is* and what men think life *ought to be*. If Ideal and Real drift too far away from one another (as they did at the end of the Middle Ages, and seem increasingly to do in this century) men face some difficult options. They have to change their way of life, or their philosophy, or both, or live unhappily somewhere in between. We are familiar enough with the "war of the philosophies" and the tensions of modern life which express them. Problems of this kind had no place, I would say, in traditional aboriginal life. It knew nothing, and could not, I think, have known anything of the Christian's straining for inner perfection; of "moral man and immoral society"; of the dilemma of liberty and authority; of intellectual uncertainty, class warfare, and discontent with one's lot in life— all of which, in some sense, are problems of the gap between Ideal and Real.

The aborigines may have been in Australia for as long as 10,000 years. No one at present can do more than guess whence or how they came, and there is little more than presumptive evidence on which to base a guess. The span of time, immense though it may have been, matters less than the fact that, so far as one can tell, they have been almost completely isolated. Since their arrival, no foreign stimulus has touched them, except on the fringes of the northern and northwestern coasts. To these two facts we must add two others. The physical environment has, evidently, not undergone any marked general change, although there has been a slow desiccation of parts of the center into desert, and some limited coastline changes. The fourth fact is that their tools and material crafts seem to have been very unprogressive.

If we put these four facts together—an immensely long span of time, spent in more or less complete isolation, in a fairly constant environment, with an unprogressive material culture, we may perhaps see why sameness, absence of change, fixed routine, regularity, call it what you will, is a main dimension of their thought and life. Let us sum up this aspect as leading to a metaphysical emphasis on abidingness. They place a very special value on things remaining unchangingly themselves, on keeping life to a routine which is known and trusted. Absence of change, which means certainty of expectation, seems to them a good thing in itself. One may say, their Ideal and Real come very close together. The value given to continuity is so high that they are not simply a people "without a history": they are a people who have been able, in some sense, to "defeat" history, to become ahistorical in mood, outlook, and life. This is why, among them, the philosophy of assent, the glove, fits the hand of actual custom almost to perfection, and the forms of social life, the art, the ritual, and much else take on a wonderful symmetry.

Their tools and crafts, meager—pitiably meager—though they are, have nonetheless been good enough to let them win the battle for survival, and to win it comfortably at that. With no pottery, no knowledge of metals, no wheel, no domestication of animals, no agriculture, they have still been able not only to live and people the entire continent, but even in a sense to prosper, to win a surplus of goods and develop leisure-time occupations. The evidences of the surplus of yield over animal need are to be seen in the spider web of trade routes criss-crossing the continent, on which a large volume of nonutilitarian articles circulated, themselves largely the products of leisure. The true leisure-time activities—social entertaining, great ceremonial gatherings, even much of the ritual and artistic life—impressed observers even from the beginning. The notion of aboriginal life as always preoccupied with the risk of starvation, as always a hair's breadth from disaster, is as great a caricature as Hobbes' notion of savage life as "poor, nasty, brutish, and short." The best corrective of any such notion is to spend a few nights in an aboriginal camp, and experience directly the unique joy in life which can be attained by a people of few wants, an otherworldly cast of mind, and a simple scheme of life which so shapes a day that it ends with communal singing and dancing in the firelight.

The more one sees of aboriginal life the stronger the impression that its mode, its ethos, and its principle are variations on a single theme—continuity, constancy, balance, symmetry, regularity, system, or some such quality as these words convey.

One of the most striking things is that there are no great conflicts over power, no great contests for place and office. This single fact explains much else, because it rules out so much that would be destructive of stability. The idea of a formal chief, or a leader with authority over the persons of others in a large number of fields of life—say, for example, as with a Polynesian or African chief—just does not seem to make sense to a blackfellow. Nor does even the modified Melanesian notion— that of a man becoming some sort of a leader because he accumulates a great deal of garden wealth and so gains prestige. There are leaders in the sense of men of unusual skill, initiative, and force, and they are given much respect; they may even attract something like a following; but one finds no trace of formal or institutionalized chieftainship. So there are no offices to stimulate ambition, intrigue, or the use of force; to be envied or fought over; or to be lost or won. Power—a real thing in every society—is diffused mainly through one sex, the man, but in such a way that it is not to be won, or lost, in concentrations, by craft, struggle, or coup. It is very much a male-dominated society. The older men dominate the younger, the men dominate the women. Not that the women are chattels—Dr. Phyllis Kaberry in her interesting book *Aboriginal Woman* disposed of that Just-So story very effectively—but there is a great deal of discrimination against them. The mythology justifies this by tales telling how men had to take power from women by force in The Dreaming. The psychology (perhaps the truth) of it is as obvious as it is amusing. If women were not kept under, they would take over!

At all events, the struggle for power occurred once-for-all. Power, authority, influence, age, status, knowledge, all run together and, in some sense, are the same kind of thing. The men of power, authority, and influence are old men—at least, mature men; the greater the secret knowledge and authority the higher the status; and the initiations are so arranged (by the old men) that the young men do not acquire full knowledge, and so attain status and authority, until they too are well advanced in years. One can thus see why the great term of respect is "old man"—*maluka*, as in *We of the Never-Never*. The system is self-protective and self-renewing. The real point of it all is that the checks and balances seem nearly perfect, and no one really seems to want the kind of satisfaction that might come from a position of domination. At the same time, there is a serpent in Eden. The narrow self-interest of men exploits The Dreaming.

Power over things? Every canon of good citizenship and common sense is against it, though there are, of course, clear property arrangements. But what could be more useless than a store of food that will not keep, or a heavy pile of spears that have to be carried everywhere? Especially, in a society in which the primary virtues are generosity and fair dealing. Nearly every social affair involving goods—food in the family, payments in marriage, intertribal exchange—is heavily influenced by equalitarian notions; a notion of reciprocity as a moral obligation; a notion of generously equivalent return; and a surprisingly clear notion of fair dealing, or making things "level" as the blackfellow calls it in English.

There is a tilt of the system towards the interests of the men, but given this tilt, everything else seems as if carefully calculated to keep it in place. The blacks do not fight over the land. There are no wars or invasions to seize territory. They do not enslave each other. There is no master-servant relation. There is no class division. There is no property or income inequality. The result is a homeostasis, far-reaching and stable.

I do not wish to create an impression of a social life without egotism, without vitality, without cross-purposes, without conflict. Indeed, there is plenty of all, as there is of malice, enmity, bad faith, and violence, running along the lines of sex-inequality and age-inequality. But this essential humanity exists, and runs its course, within a system whose first principle is the preservation of balance. And, arching over it all, is the *logos* of The Dreaming. How we shall state this when we fully understand it I do not know, but I should think we are more likely to ennoble it than not. Equilibrium ennobled is "abidingness." Piccarda's answer in the third canto of the *Paradiso* gives the implicit theme and logic of The Dreaming: *e la sua volontate è nostra pace*, "His will is our peace." But the gleam that lighted Judah did not reach the Australian wilderness, and the blacks follow The Dreaming only because their fathers did.

Alan Dundes

EARTH-DIVER: CREATION OF
THE MYTHOPOEIC MALE

In this interesting paper, Alan Dundes presents a psychoanalytic interpretation
of a myth motif which has strikingly wide distribution in both the Old World and
the New World. Following one of the basic assumptions of the psychoanalytic
tradition—that people everywhere share unconscious biological attributes and
urges which come into conflict with social constraints—he attempts to relate the
widespread occurrence of the male earth-diver motif to the (theoretically) universal presence of unconscious male pregnancy envy and desire to give anal birth.
In other words, since he is deprived of truly giving birth, the mythopoeic male
unconsciously "asserts himself" in creating the earth itself from what is often mud
or fecal material from the primeval waters. Dundes uses orthodox Freudian
theory together with his own impressive control of world folk literature to build
a case in favor of this interpretation of the motif. He is aware of the speculative
and controversial nature of his problem and he presents his material with a
scholarly moderation which has not always characterized psychological interpretations of myth.

This paper and other temperate psychoanalytic writings will perhaps be of
increasing interest in relation to some of the recent anthropological treatments of
religious symbolism, particularly those of Victor Turner (see his *Forest of Symbols*,
1967). The differences between the theoretical and methodological approaches
are considerable and perhaps irreconcilable, yet it is possible that culture-specific
formulations about the nature of religious symbolism may find some common
ground with universal psychological prototypes. For example, male/female–
right/left–up/down discriminations, which occur widely in religious symbolism,
appear to refer to something quite fundamental in human nature.

The reader may wish to consult the bibliographies listed in Dundes (1965),
Kiell (1963), and Fischer (1963) for further reading on psychoanalytic studies of
myth and folklore. Géza Róheim's *The Gates of the Dream* (1952) and Sigmund
Freud and D. E. Oppenheim's *Dreams in Folklore* (1958) will also provide
interesting (and orthodox) reading on the topics of myth, dreams, and psycho-
analysis.

Reprinted from *American Anthropologist*, LXIV (1962), 1032–1051, by permission of the
author and the American Anthropological Association.

Few anthropologists are satisfied with the
present state of scholarship with respect to
primitive mythology. While not everyone
shares Lévi-Strauss's extreme pessimistic o-
pinion that from a theoretical point of view
the study of myth is "very much the same as
it was fifty years ago, namely a picture of
chaos" (1958:50), still there is general agreement that much remains to be done in elucidating the processes of the formation, transmission, and functioning of myth in culture.

One possible explanation for the failure of
anthropologists to make any notable advances
in myth studies is the rigid adherence to two
fundamental principles: a literal reading of
myth and a study of myth in monocultural
context. The insistence of most anthropologists upon the literal as opposed to the symbolic interpretation, in terms of cultural relativism as opposed to transcultural universal-
ism, is in part a continuation of the reaction

against 19th century thought in which universal symbolism in myth was often argued and
in part a direct result of the influence of two
dominant figures in the history of anthropology, Boas and Malinowski. Both these pioneers favored studying one culture at a time in
depth and both contended that myth was
essentially nonsymbolic. Boas often spoke of
mythology reflecting culture, implying something of a one-to-one relationship. With this
view, purely descriptive ethnographic data
could be easily culled from the mythological
material of a particular culture. Malinowski
argued along similar lines: "Studied alive,
myth, as we shall see, is not symbolic, but a
direct expression of its subject matter" (1954:
101). Certainly, there is much validity in the
notion of mythology as a cultural reflector, as
the well documented researches of Boas and
Malinowski demonstrate. However, as in the
case of most all-or-nothing approaches, it

does not account for all the data. Later students in the Boas tradition, for example, noted that a comparison between the usual descriptive ethnography and the ethnographical picture obtained from mythology revealed numerous discrepancies. Ruth Benedict (1935) in her important *Introduction to Zuni Mythology* spoke of the tendency to idealize and compensate in folklore. More recently, Katherine Spencer has contrasted the correspondences and discrepancies between the ethnographical and mythological accounts. She also suggests that the occurrence of folkloristic material which contradicts the ethnographic data "may be better explained in psychological than in historical terms" (1947:130). However, anthropologists have tended to mistrust psychological terms, and consequently the pendulum has not yet begun to swing away from the literal to the symbolic reading of myth. Yet it is precisely the insights afforded by advances in human psychology which open up vast vistas for the student of myth. When anthropologists learn that to study the products of the human mind (e.g., myths) one must know something of the mechanics of the human mind, they may well push the pendulum towards not only the symbolic interpretation of myth but also towards the discovery of universals in myth.

Freud himself was very excited at the possibility of applying psychology to mythology. In a letter to D. E. Oppenheim in 1909, he said, "I have long been haunted by the idea that our studies on the content of the neuroses might be destined to solve the riddle of the formation of myths . . ." (Freud and Oppenheim, 1958:13). However, though Freud was pleased at the work of his disciples, Karl Abraham and Otto Rank, in this area, he realized that he and his students were amateurs in mythology. In the same letter to Oppenheim he commented: "We are lacking in academic training and familiarity with the material." Unfortunately, those not lacking in these respects had little interest in psychoanalytic theory. To give just one example out of many, Lewis Spence in his preface to *An Introduction to Mythology* stated: "The theories of Freud and his followers as to religion and the origin of myth have not been considered, since, in the writer's opinion, they are scarcely to be taken seriously." What was this theory which was not to be taken seriously? Freud wrote the following: "As a matter of fact, I believe that a large portion of the

mythological conception of the world which reaches far into the most modern religions, is *nothing but psychology projected to the outer world*. The dim perception (the endopsychic perception, as it were) of psychic factors and relations of the unconscious was taken as a model in the construction of a *transcendental reality*, which is destined to be changed again by science into *psychology of the unconscious*" (1938:164). It is this insight perhaps more than any other that is of value to the anthropologist interested in primitive myth.

There is, however, an important theoretical difficulty with respect to the psychoanalytic interpretation of myth. This difficulty stems from the fact that there are basically two ways in which psychoanalytic theory may be applied. A myth may be analyzed *with* a knowledge of a particular myth-maker, or a myth may be analyzed *without* such knowledge. There is some doubt as to whether the two methods are equally valid and, more specifically, whether the second is as valid as the first. The question is, to employ an analogy, can a dream be analyzed without a knowledge of the specific dreamer who dreamed it? In an anthropological context, the question is: can a myth be interpreted without a knowledge of the culture which produced it? Of course, it is obvious that any psychoanalyst would prefer to analyze the dreamer or myth-maker in order to interpret more accurately a dream or myth. Similarly, those anthropologists who are inclined to employ psychoanalysis in interpreting myths prefer to relate the manifest and latent content of myths to specific cultural contexts. However, this raises another important question. Do myths reflect the present, the past, or both? There are some anthropologists who conceive of myths almost exclusively in terms of the present. While tacitly recognizing that traditional myths are of considerable antiquity, such anthropologists, nevertheless, proceed to analyze a present-day culture in terms of its myths. Kardiner's theory of folklore, for instance, reveals this bias. Speaking of the myths of women in Marquesan folklore, Kardiner observes, "These myths are the products of the fantasy of some individual, communicated and probably changed many times before we get them. The uniformity of the stories points to some common experience of all individuals in this culture, not remembered from the remote past, but currently experienced." According to Kardiner, then, myths are responses to current realities (1939: 417,

214). Roheim summarizes Kardiner's position before taking issue with it. "According to Kardiner, myths and folklore always reflect the unconscious conflicts of the present generation as they are formed by the pressure brought to bear on them by existing social conditions. In sharp contrast to Freud, Reik, and myself, a myth represents not the dim past but the present" (1940:540).

The evidence available from folklore scholarship suggests that there is remarkable stability in oral narratives. Myths and tales re-collected from the same culture show considerable similarity in structural pattern and detail despite the fact that the myths and tales are from different informants who are perhaps separated by many generations. Excluding consideration of modern myths (for the myth-making process is an ongoing one), one can see that cosmogonic myths, to take one example, have not changed materially for hundreds of years. In view of this, it is clearly not necessarily valid to analyze a *present-day* culture in terms of that culture's traditional cosmogonic myths, which in all likelihood date from the prehistoric *past*. An example of the disregard of the time element occurs in an interesting HRAF-inspired cross-cultural attempt to relate child-training practices to folk tale content. Although the tales were gathered at various times between 1890 and 1940, it was assumed that "a folk tale represents a kind of summation of the common thought patterns of a number of individuals . . ." (McClelland and Friedman, 1952:245). Apparently common thought patterns are supposed to be quite stable and not subject to cultural change during a 50 year period. Thus just one version of a widely diffused North American Indian tale type like the Eye Juggler is deemed sufficient to "diagnose the modal motivations" of the members of a culture. Nevertheless, Kardiner's theoretical perspective is not entirely without merit. Changes in myth do occur and a careful examination of a number of variants of a particular myth may show that these changes tend to cluster around certain points in time or space. Even if such changes are comparatively minor in contrast to the over-all structural stability of a myth, they may well serve as meaningful signals of definite cultural changes. Thus, Martha Wolfenstein's comparison of English and American versions of Jack and the Beanstalk (1955) showed a number of interesting differences in detail, although the basic plot remained the same. She suggested that the more phallic

details in the American versions were in accord with other cultural differences between England and America. Whether or not one agrees with Wolfenstein's conclusions, one can appreciate the soundness of her method. The same myth or folk tale can be profitably compared using versions from two or more separate cultures, and the differences in detail may well illustrate significant differences in culture. One thinks of Nadel's (1937) adaptation of Bartlett's experiment in giving an artificial folk tale to two neighboring tribes in Africa and his discovery that the variations fell along clear-cut cultural lines, rather than along individualistic lines. However, the basic theoretical problem remains unresolved. Can the myth as a whole be analyzed meaningfully? Margaret Mead in commenting briefly on Wolfenstein's study begs the entire question. She states: "What is important here is that Jack and the Beanstalk, when it was first made up, might have had a precise and beautiful correspondence to the theme of a given culture at a given time. It then traveled and took on all sorts of forms, which you study and correlate with the contemporary cultural usage" (Tax, 1953:282). The unfortunate truth is that rarely is the anthropologist in a position to know when and where a myth is "first made up." Consequently, the precise and beautiful correspondence is virtually unattainable or rather unreconstructible. The situation is further complicated by the fact that many, indeed, the majority of myths are found widely distributed throughout the world. The historical record, alas, only goes back so far. In other words, it is, practically speaking, impossible to ascertain the place and date of the first appearance(s) of a given myth. For this reason, anthropologists like Mead despair of finding any correspondence between over-all myth structure and culture. Unfortunately, some naïve scholars manifest a profound ignorance of the nature of folklore by their insistent attempts to analyze a specific culture by analyzing myths which are found in a great many cultures. For example, the subject of a recent doctoral dissertation was an analysis of 19th century German culture on the basis of an analysis of the content of various Grimm tales (Mann, 1958). Although the analyses of the tales were ingenious and psychologically sound, the fact that the Grimm tales are by no means limited to the confines of Germany, and furthermore are undoubtedly much older than the 19th century, completely vitiates the theoretical premise

underlying the thesis. Assuming the validity of the analyses of the tales, these analyses
would presumably be equally valid wherever
the tales appeared in the same form. Barnouw
(1955) commits exactly the same error when
he analyzes Chippewa personality on the
basis of a Chippewa "origin legend" which, in
fact, contains many standard North American
Indian tale types (Wycoco). It is clearly a
fallacy to analyze an international tale or
widely diffused myth *as if* it belonged to only
one culture. Only if a myth is known to be
unique, that is, peculiar to a given culture, is
this kind of analysis warranted. It is, however,
perfectly good procedure to analyze the
differences which occur as a myth enters
another culture. Certainly, one can gain considerable insight into the mechanics of
acculturation by studying a Zuni version of a
European cumulative tale or a native's re-
telling of the story of Beowulf. Kardiner is at
his best when he shows how a cultural element
is adapted to fit the basic personality structure
of the borrowing culture. His account of the
Comanche's alteration of the Sun Dance from
a masochistic and self-destructive ritual to a
demonstration of feats of strength is very convincing (1945:93).

The question is now raised: if it is theoretically only permissible to analyze the differen-
tiae of widely diffused myths or the entire
structure of myths peculiar to a particular
culture, does this mean that the entire structure of widely diffused myths (which are often
the most interesting) cannot be meaningfully
analyzed? This is, in essence, the question of
whether a dream can be analyzed without
knowledge of the dreamer. One answer may
be that to the extent that there are human
universals, such myths may be analyzed.
From this vantage point, while it may be a
fallacy to analyze a world-wide myth as if it
belonged to only one culture, it is not a fallacy
to analyze the myth as if it belonged to all
cultures in which it appears. This does not
preclude the possibility that one myth found
in many cultures may have as many meanings
as there are cultural contexts (Boas, 1910b:
383). Nevertheless, the hypothesis of a limited
number of organic human universals suggests
some sort of similar, if not identical, meaning.
It should not be necessary to observe that, to
the extent that anthropologists are scientists,
they need not fear anathematic reductionism
and the discovery of empirically observable
universals. The formula $e = mc^2$ is nonetheless valid for its being reductionistic.

A prime example of an anthropologist interested in universals is Kluckhohn. In his
paper "Universal Categories of Culture,"
Kluckhohn contends that "The inescapable
fact of cultural relativism does not justify the
conclusion that cultures are in all respects
utterly disparate monads and hence strictly
noncomparable entities" and "Valid cross-
cultural comparison could best proceed from
the invariant points of reference supplied by
the biological, psychological, and socio-
situational 'givens' of human life" (1953: 520,
521). Of even more interest is Kluckhohn's
conviction that these "givens" are manifested
in myth. In "Recurrent Themes in Myths and
Mythmaking," he discusses "certain features
of mythology that are apparently universal or
that have such wide distribution in space and
time that their generality may be presumed to
result from recurrent reactions of the human
psyche to situations and stimuli of the same
general order" (1959:268). Kluckhohn's recurrent themes appear somewhat similar to
Freud's typical dreams. Although Freud
specifically warned against codifying symbolic translations of dream content and,
although he did clearly state his belief that the
same dream content could conceal a different
meaning in the case of different persons or
contexts, he did consider that there are such
things as typical dreams, "dreams which
almost every one has dreamed in the same
manner, and of which we are accustomed to
assume that they have the same significance
in the case of every dreamer" (1938:292, 39).
While there are not many anthropologists
who would support the view that recurrent
myths have similar meaning irrespective of
specific cultural context, that does not mean
that the view is false. For those who deny
universal meanings, it might be mentioned
that the reasons why a particular myth has
widespread distribution have yet to be given.
The most ardent diffusionist, as opposed to
an advocate of polygenesis or convergence,
can do little more than show how a myth
spreads. The how rarely includes the why. In
order to show the plausibility of a symbolic
and universal approach to myth, a concrete
example will be analyzed in some detail.

One of the most fascinating myths in North
American Indian mythology is that of the
earth-diver. Anna Birgitta Rooth in her study
of approximately 300 North American Indian
creation myths found that, of her eight
different types, earth-diver had the widest
distribution. Earl W. Count who has studied

the myth for a number of years considers the notion of a diver fetching material for making dry land "easily among the most widespread single concepts held by man" (1952:55). Earth-diver has recently been studied quite extensively by the folklorist Elli Kaija Köngas (1960) who has skillfully surveyed the mass of previous pertinent scholarship. The myth as summarized by Erminie Wheeler-Voegelin is:

In North American Indian myths of the origin of the world, the culture hero has a succession of animals dive into the primeval waters, or flood of waters, to secure bits of mud or sand from which the earth is to be formed. Various animals, birds, and aquatic creatures are sent down into the waters that cover the earth. One after another animal fails; the last one succeeds, however, and floats to the surface half dead, with a little sand or dirt in his claws. Sometimes it is Muskrat, sometimes Beaver, Hell-diver, Crawfish, Mink who succeeds, after various other animals have failed, in bringing up the tiny bit of mud which is then put on the surface of the water and magically expands to become the world of the present time (1949: 334).

Among the interesting features of this myth is the creation from mud or dirt. It is especially curious in view of the widespread myth of the creation of man from a similar substance (Frazer, 1935:4–15). Another striking characteristic is the magical expansion of the bit of mud. Moreover, how did the idea of creating the earth from a particle of dirt small enough to be contained beneath a claw or fingernail develop, and what is there in this cosmogonic myth that has caused it to thrive so in a variety of cultures, not only in aboriginal North America but in the rest of the world as well?

Freud's suggestion that mythology is psychology projected upon the external world does not at a first glance seem applicable in the case of the earth-diver myth. The Freudian hypothesis is more obvious in other American Indian cosmogonic conceptions, such as the culture hero's Oedipal separation of Father Sky and Mother Earth (Róheim, 1921:163) or the emergence myth, which appears to be man's projection of the phenomenon of human birth. This notion of the origin of the emergence myth was clearly stated as early as 1902 by Washington Matthews with apparently no help from psychoanalysis. At that time Matthews proposed the idea that the emergence myth was basically a "myth of gestation and of birth." A more recent study of the emergence myth by Wheeler-Voegelin and Moore makes a similar suggestion en passant, but no supporting details are given

(1957: 73–74). Róheim, however, had previously extended Matthews' thesis by suggesting that primitive man's conception of the world originated in the pre-natal perception of space in the womb (1921:163). In any event, no matter how close the emergence of man from a hole in Mother Earth might appear to be to actual human birth, it does not appear to help in determining the psychological prototype for the earth-diver myth. Is there really any "endo-psychic" perception which could have served as the model for the construction of a cosmogonic creation from mud?

The hypothesis here proposed depends upon two key assumptions. The two assumptions (and they are admittedly only assumptions) are: (1) the existence of a cloacal theory of birth; and (2) the existence of pregnancy envy on the part of males. With regard to the first assumption, it was Freud himself who included the cloacal theory as one of the common sexual theories of children. The theory, in essence, states that since the child is ignorant of the vagina and is rarely permitted to watch childbirth, he assumes that the lump in the pregnant woman's abdomen leaves her body in the only way he can imagine material leaving the body, namely via the anus. In Freud's words: "Children are all united from the outset in the belief that the birth of a child takes place by the bowel; that is to say, that the baby is produced like a piece of faeces" (1953: 328). The second assumption concerns man's envy of woman's child-bearing role. Whether it is called "parturition envy" (Boehm) or "pregnancy envy" (Fromm), the basic idea is that men would like to be able to produce or create valuable material from within their bodies as women do. Incidentally, it is this second assumption which is the basis of Bruno Bettelheim's explanation of puberty initiation rites and the custom of couvade. His thesis is that puberty rites consist of a rebirth ritual of a special kind to the effect that the initiate is born anew *from males*. The denial of women's part in giving birth is evidenced by the banning of women from the ceremonies. Couvade is similarly explained as the male's desire to imitate female behavior in childbirth. A number of psychoanalysts have suggested that man's desire for mental and artistic creativity stems in part from the wish to conceive or produce on a par with women (Jones, 1957: 40; Fromm, 1951: 233; Huckel, 1953: 44). What is even more significant from the point of view of mythology is the large number of clinical cases in which men seek to have babies in the form of feces, or cases in which men imagine themselves excreting the world. Felix Boehm makes a rather sweeping generalization when he says: "In all analyses of men we meet with phantasies of anal birth, and we know how common it is for men to treat their faeces as a child" (1930:455; see also Silberer, 1925:393). However, there is a good deal of clinical evidence supporting the existence of this phantasy. Stekel (1959:45), for example, mentions a child who called the feces "Baby." The possible relevance of this notion to the myth of the origin of man occurred to Abraham (1948:320), Jung (1916:214), and Rank (1922:54). Jung's comment is: "The first people were made from excrement, potter's earth and clay." (Cf. Schwarzbaum, 1960:48.) In fact, Jung rather ingeniously suggests that the idea of anal birth is the basis of the motif of creating by "throwing behind oneself" as in the case of Deucalion and Pyrrha. Nevertheless, neither Abraham, Jung, nor Rank emphasized the fact that anal birth is especially employed by men. It is true that little girls also have this phantasy, but presumably the need for the phantasy disappears upon the giving of birth to a child. (There may well be some connection between this phantasy and the widespread occurrence of geophagy among pregnant women [Elwin, 1949: 292, n. 1].)

Both of the assumptions' underlying the hypothesis attempting to explain the earth-diver myth are found in Genesis. As Fromm points out (1951:234), the woman's creative role is denied. It is man who creates and, in fact, it is man who gives birth to woman. Eve is created from substance taken from the body of Adam. Moreover, if one were inclined to see the Noah story as a gestation myth, it would be noteworthy that it is the man who builds the womb-ark. It would also be interesting that the flood waters abate only after a period roughly corresponding to the length of human pregnancy. Incidentally, it is quite likely that the Noah story is a modified earth-diver myth. The male figure sends a raven once and a dove twice to brave the primordial waters seeking traces of earth. (Cf. Schwarzbaum, 1960:52, n. 15a.) In one apocryphal account, the raven disobeys instructions by stopping to feast on a dead man, and in another he is punished by having his feathers change color from white to black (Ginzberg, 1925:39, 164). Both of these incidents are found in American Indian earth-diver myths

(Rooth, 1957:498). In any case, one can see that there are male myths of creation in Genesis, although Fromm does not describe them all. Just as Abraham, Jung, and Rank had anal birth without pregnancy envy, Fromm has pregnancy envy without anal birth. He neglects to mention that man was created from dust. One is tempted to speculate as to whether male creation myths might be in any way correlated with highly patriarchal social organization.

Of especial pertinence to the present thesis is the clinical data on phantasies of excreting the universe. Lombroso, for example, describes two artists, each of whom had the delusion that they were lords of the world which they had excreted from their bodies. One of them painted a full-length picture of himself, naked, among women, ejecting worlds (1895:201). In this phantasy world, the artist flaunting his anal creativity depicts himself as superior to the women who surround him. Both Freud and Stekel have reported cases in which men fancied defecating upon the world, and Abraham cites a dream of a patient in which the patient dreamed he expelled the universe out of his anus (Freud, 1949b:407; Stekel, 1959:44; Abraham, 1948:320). Of course, the important question for the present study is whether or not such phantasies ever occur in mythical form. Undoubtedly, the majority of anthropologists would be somewhat loath to interpret the earth-diver myth as an anal birth fantasy on the basis of a few clinical examples drawn exclusively from Western civilization. However, the dearth of mythological data results partly from the traditional prudery of some ethnographers and many folklorists. Few myths dealing with excretory processes find their way into print. Nevertheless, there are several examples, primarily of the creation of man from excrement. John G. Bourke (1891: 266) cites an Australian myth of such a creation of man. In India, the elephant-headed god Ganesh is derived from the excrement of his mother (Berkeley-Hill, 1921:330). In modern India, the indefatigable Elwin has collected quite a few myths in which the earth is excreted: For instance, a Lanjhia Saora version describes how Bhimo defecates on Rama's head. The feces is thrown into the water which immediately dries up and the earth is formed (1949: 44). In a Gadaba myth, Larang the great Dano devoured the world, but Mahaprabhu "caught hold of him and squeezed him so hard that he excreted the earth he had devoured. . . . From the earth that Larang excreted, the world was formed again" (1949:37). In other versions, a worm excretes the earth, or the world is formed from the excreta of ants (1949:47; 1954:9). An example closer to continental North America is reported by Bogoras. In this Chukchee creation myth, Raven's wife tells Raven to go and try to create the earth, but Raven protests that he cannot. Raven's wife then announces that she will try to create a "spleen-companion" and goes to sleep. Raven "looks at his wife. Her abdomen has enlarged. In her sleep she creates without effort. He is frightened, and turns his face away." After Raven's wife gives birth to twins, Raven says, "There, you have created men! Now I shall go and try to create the earth." Then "Raven flies and defecates. Every piece of excrement falls upon water, grows quickly, and becomes land." In this fashion, Raven succeeds in creating the whole earth (Bogoras, 1913:152). Here there can be no doubt of the connection between pregnancy envy and anal creation. Unfortunately, there are few examples which are as clear as the Chukchee account. One of the only excremental creation myths reported in North America proper was collected by Boas. He relates (1895:159) a Kwakiutl tale of Mink making a youth from his excrement. However, the paucity of American Indian versions does not necessarily reflect the non-existence of the myth in North America. The combination of puritanical publishing standards in the United States with similar collecting standards may well explain in part the lack of data. In this connection it is noteworthy that whereas the earlier German translation of Boas' Kwakiutl version refers specifically to excrement, the later English translation speaks of a musk-bag (1910a: 159). Most probably ethnographers and editors alike share Andrew Lang's sentiments when he alludes to a myth of the Encounter Bay people, "which might have been attributed by Dean Swift to the Yahoos, so foul an origin does it allot to mankind" (1899:166). Despite the lack of a great number of actual excremental myths, the existence of any at all would appear to lend support to the hypothesis that men do think of creativity in anal terms, and further that this conception is projected into mythical cosmogonic terms.

There is, of course, another possible reason for the lack of overtly excremental creation myths and this is the process of sublimation. Ferenczi in his essay "The Ontogenesis of the Interest in Money" (1956) has given the most explicit account of this process as he traces the weaning of the child's interest from its feces through a whole graduated series of socially sanctioned substitutes ranging from moist mud, sand, clay, and stones to gold or money. Anthropologists will object that Ferenczi's ontogenetic pattern is at best only applicable to Viennese type culture. But, to the extent that any culture has toilet training (and this includes any culture in which the child is not permitted to play indiscriminately with his feces), there is some degree of sublimation. As a matter of fact, so-called anal personality characteristics have been noted among the Yurok (Posinsky), Mohave (Devereux), and Chippewa (Barnouw, Hallowell). Devereux (1951:412) specifically comments upon the use of mud as a fecal substitute among the Mohave. Moreover, it may well be that the widespread practices of smearing the body with paint or daubing it with clay in preparation for aggressive activities have some anal basis. As for the gold-feces equation, anthropologists have yet to explain the curious linguistic fact that in Nahuatl the word for gold is *teocuitlatl*, which is a compound of *teotl*, "god," and *cuitlatl*, "excrement." Gold is thus "excrement of the gods" or "divine excrement" (Saville, 1920:118). This extraordinary confirmation of Freudian symbolism which was pointed out by Reik as early as 1915 has had apparently little impact upon anthropologists blindly committed to cultural relativism. (See also Róheim, 1923:387. However, for an example of money/feces symbolism in the dream of a Salteaux Indian, see Hallowell, 1938.) While the gold-feces symbolism is hardly likely in cultures where gold was unknown, there is reason for assuming that some sort of sublimation does occur in most cultures. (For American Indian instances of "jewels from excrements" see Thompson, 1929:329, n. 190a. In this connection, it might be pointed out that in Oceanic versions of the creation of earth from an object thrown on the primeval waters, as found in Lessa's recent comprehensive study [1961], the items thrown include, in addition to sand, such materials as rice chaff, betel nut husks, and ashes, which would appear to be waste products.) If this is so, then it may be seen that a portion of Ferenczi's account of the evolutionary course of anal sublimation is of no mean importance to the analysis of the earth-diver myth. Ferenczi states: "Even the interest for the specific odour of excrement does not cease at once, but is only displaced on to other odours that in any way resemble this. The children continue to show a liking for the smell of sticky materials with a characteristic odour, especially the strongly smelling degenerated produce of cast off epidermis cells which collects between the toes, nasal secretion, ear-wax, and the dirt of the nails, while many children do not content themselves with the moulding and sniffing of these substances, but also take them into the mouth" (1956:273). Anyone who is familiar with American Indian creation myths will immediately think of examples of the creation of man from the rubbings of skin (Thompson, 1955: Motif A 1263.3), birth from mucus from the nose (Motif T 541.8.3), etc. The empirical fact is that these myths do exist! With respect to the earth-diver myth, the common detail of the successful diver's returning with a little dirt under his fingernail is entirely in accord with Ferenczi's analysis. The fecal nature of the particle is also suggested by its magical expansion. One could imagine that as one defecates one is thereby creating an ever-increasing amount of earth. (Incidentally, the notion of creating land masses through defecation has the corollary idea of creating bodies of water such as oceans through micturition [Motif A 923.1]. For example, in the previously mentioned Chukchee myth, Raven, after producing the earth, began to pass water. A drop became a lake, while a jet formed a river.)

The present hypothesis may also serve to elucidate the reasons why Christian dualism is so frequently found in Eurasian earth-diver versions. Earl Count considers the question of the dualistic nature of earth-diver as one of the main problems connected with the study of the myth (1952:56). Count is not willing to commit himself as to whether the earth-diver is older than a possible dualistic overlay, but Köngas agrees with earlier scholars that the dualism is a later development (Count, 1952: 61; Köngas, 1960:168). The dualism usually takes the form of a contest between God and the devil. As might be expected from the tradition of philosophical dualism, the devil is associated with the body, while God is concerned with the spiritual element. Thus it is the devil who dives for the literally lowly dirt and returns with some under his nails. An interesting incident in view of Ferenczi's account of anal sublimation is the devil's attempt to save a bit of earth by putting it in his mouth. However, when God expands the earth, the stolen bit also expands, forcing the devil to spit it out, whereupon mountains or rocks are formed (Köngas, 1960:160–161). In this connection, another dualistic creation myth is quite informative. God is unable to stop the earth from growing and sends the bee to spy on the devil to find a way to accomplish this. When the bee buzzes, in leaving the devil to report back to God, the devil exclaims, "Let him eat your excrement, whoever sent you!" God did this and the earth stopped growing (Dragomanov, 1961:3). Since the eating of excrement prevented the further growth of the earth, one can see the fecal nature of the substance forming the earth. In still another dualistic creation myth, there is even an attempt made to explain why feces exists at all in man. In this narrative, God creates a pure body for man but has to leave it briefly in order to obtain a soul. In God's absence, the devil defiles the body. God, upon returning, has no alternative but to turn his creation inside out, which is the reason why man has impurities in his intestines (Campbell, 1956:294). These few examples should be sufficient to show that the dualism is primarily a matter of separating the dross of matter from the essence of spirit. The devil is clearly identified with matter and in particular with defecation. In a phrase, it is the devil who does the dirty work. Thus Köngas is quite right in seeing a psycho-physical dualism, that is, the concept of the soul as being separable from the body, as the basis for the Christian traditional dualism. However, she errs in assuming that both the creator and his "doppelgänger" are spiritual or concerned with the spiritual (1960:169). Dualism includes one material entity and, specifically in earth-diver dualism, one element deals with dirt while the other creates beauty and valuable substance from the dirt.

It should be noted that earth-diver has been previously studied from a psychoanalytic perspective. Géza Róheim, the first psychoanalytic anthropologist, made a great number of studies of the folklore and mythology of primitive peoples. In his earlier writings, Róheim tended to follow along the lines suggested by Freud, Abraham, and Rank in seeing folk tales as analogous to dreams (1922:182), but later, after he discovered, for example, that the Aranda word altjira meant both dream and folk tale (1941:267), he began to speculate as to a more genetic relationship between dream and folk tale or myth. In a posthumously published paper, "Fairy

Tale and Dream" (1953a), this new theory of mythology and the folk tale is explained. "To put this theory briefly: It seems that dreams and myths are not merely similar but that a large part of mythology is actually derived from dreams. In other words, we can not only apply the standard technique of dream interpretation in analyzing a fairy tale but can actually think of tales and myths as having arisen from a dream, which a person dreamed and then told to others, who retold it again, perhaps elaborated in accord with their own dreams" (1953a:394; for a sample of Róheim's exegesis of what he terms a dream-derived folk tale, see 1953b). The obvious criticism of this theory has been made by E. K. Schwartz in noting that "one can accept the same psychoanalytic approach and techniques for the understanding of the fairy tale and the dream, without having to accept the hypothesis that the fairy tale is nothing else but an elaboration of a dream" (1956: 747–748). Thus Schwartz, although he lists 12 characteristics of fairy tales which he also finds in dreams, including such features as condensation, displacement, symbolism, etc., does conclude that it is not necessary to assume that fairy tales are dreams. Róheim, in *The Gates of the Dream*, a brilliant if somewhat erratic full-length treatment of primitive myth and dream, had already addressed himself to this very criticism. He phrases the criticism rhetorically: "Then why assume the dream stage, since the unconscious would contain the same elements, even without dreams?" His answer is that the dream theory would explain not only the identity in content but also the striking similarity in structure and plot sequence (1951:348). Actually, the fundamental criticism is not completely explained away. There is no reason why both dream and myth cannot be derived from the human mind without making the myth only indirectly derived via the dream.

Róheim's theory comes to the fore in his analysis of earth-diver. In fact, he even states that the earth-diver myth is "a striking illustration of the dream origin of mythology" (1951:423). Róheim has assumed the existence of what he calls a basic dream in which the dreamer falls into something, such as a lake or a hole. According to Róheim, this dream is characterized by a "double vector" movement consisting both of a regression to the womb and the idea of the body as penis entering the vagina. In interpreting the earth-diver as an example of this basic dream, Róheim considers the diving into the primeval waters of the womb as an erection. Of considerable theoretical interest is Róheim's apparent postulation of a monogenetic origin of earth-diver: "*The core of the myth is a dream actually dreamed once upon a time by one person*. Told and retold it became a myth . . ." (1951: 428). Actually, Róheim's over-all theory of the dream origin of myth is not at all necessarily a matter of monogenesis. In fact, he states that it is hardly likely as a general rule that an original dream was dreamed by one person in a definite locality, from which the story spread by migration. Rather, "many have dreamed such dreams, they shaped the narrative form in many centers, became traditional, then merged and influenced each other in the course of history" (1951:348).

The validity of Róheim's interpretation of earth-diver depends a great deal on, first of all, his theory of the dream origin of myth and, secondly, the specific nature of his so-called basic dream. One could say, without going so far as to deny categorically Róheim's theoretical contentions, that neither the dream origin of myth nor the existence of the "basic dream" is necessary for an understanding of the latent content of the earth-diver myth. Curiously enough, Róheim himself anticipates in part the present hypothesis in the course of making some additional comments on earth-diver. In discussing the characteristic trait of the gradual growth of the earth, Róheim cites an Onondaga version in which he points out the parallelism between a pregnant woman and the growing earth. From the point of view of the present hypothesis, the parallelism is quite logically attributable to the male creator's desire to achieve something like female procreativity. Thus the substance produced from his body, his baby so to speak, must gradually increase in size, just as the process of female creativity entails a gradually increasing expansion. (Here again, the observation of the apparently magically expanding belly of a pregnant woman is clearly a human universal.) Róheim goes on to mention what he considers to be a parallel myth, namely that of "the egg-born earth or cloacal creation." As will be shown later, Róheim is quite correct in drawing attention to the egg myth. Then following his discussion of the Eurasian dualistic version in which the devil tries to keep a piece of swelling earth in his mouth, Róheim makes the following analysis: "If we substitute the rectum for the mouth the myth makes sense as an awakening dream conditioned by excremental pressure" (1951: 429). In other words, Róheim does recognize the excremental aspects of earth-diver and in accordance with his theory of the dream origin of myth, he considers the myth as initially a dream caused by the purely organic stimulus of the need to defecate. Róheim also follows Rank (1912, 1922:89) in interpreting deluge myths as transformations of vesical dreams (1951:439–465). Certainly, one could make a good case for the idea that some folk tales and myths are based upon excremental pressures, perhaps originally occurring during sleep. In European folklore, there are numerous examples, as Freud and Oppenheim have amply demonstrated, of folk tales which relate how individuals attempt to mark buried treasure only to awake to find they have defecated on themselves or on their sleeping partners. It is quite possible that there is a similar basis for the Winnebago story reported by Radin (1956:26–27) in which Trickster, after eating a laxative bulb, begins to defecate endlessly. In order to escape the rising level of excrement, Trickster climbs a tree, but he is forced to go higher and higher until he finally falls down right into the rising tide. Another version of this Trickster adventure is found in Barnouw's account of a Chippewa cycle (1955:82). The idea of the movement being impossible to stop once it has started is also suggested in the previously cited Eurasian account of God's inability to stop the earth's growth. That God must eat excrement to stop the movement is thematically similar to another Trickster version in which Trickster's own excrement, rising with flood waters, comes perilously close to his mouth and nose. However, the fact that there may be "excremental pressure myths" with or without a dream origin does not mean that excremental pressure is the sole underlying motivation of such a myth as earth-diver. To call earth-diver simply a dream-like myth resulting from a call of nature without reference to the notions of male pregnancy envy and anal birth theory is vastly to oversimplify the psychological etiology of the myth. Róheim, by the way, never does reconcile the rather phallic interpretation of his basic dream with the excremental awakening dream interpretation of earth-diver. A multi-causal hypothesis is, of course, perfectly possible, but Róheim's two interpretations seem rather to conflict. In any event, Róheim sees creation myths as prime examples of his dream-myth thesis. He says, "It seems very probable that

creation myths, wherever they exist, are ultimately based on dreams" (1951:430).

The idea of anal creation myths spurred by male pregnancy envy is not tied to the dream origin of myth. That is not to say that the dream theory is not entirely possible but only to affirm the independence of the two hypotheses. In order to document further the psychological explanation of earth-diver, several other creation myths will be very briefly discussed. As already mentioned, Róheim drew attention to the cosmic egg myths. There is clinical evidence suggesting that men who have pregnancy phantasies often evince a special interest in the activities of hens, particularly with regard to their laying of eggs (Eisler, 1921:260, 285). The hens appear to defecate the eggs. Freud's famous "Little Hans" in addition to formulating a "lumf" baby theory also imagined that he laid an egg (1949b:227–228). Lombroso (1895:182) mentions a demented pseudo-artist who painted himself as excreting eggs which symbolized worlds. Ferenczi, moreover, specifically comments upon what he calls the "symbolic identity of the egg with faeces and child." He suggests that excessive fondness for eggs "approximates much more closely to primitive coprophilia than does the more abstract love of money" (1950:328). Certainly the egg-creation myth is common enough throughout the world (Lukas, 1894), despite its absence in North America. It is noteworthy that there are creations of men from eggs (Motifs T 542 or A 1222) and creation of the world from a cosmic egg (Motif A 641). As in the case of feces (or mud, clay, or dirt), the cloacal creation is capable of producing either men or worlds or both.

Another anal creation myth which does occur in aboriginal North America has the spider as creator. The Spider myth, which is one of Rooth's eight creation myth types found in North America, is reported primarily in California and the Southwest. The spider as creator is also found in Asia and Africa. Empirical observation of spiders would quite easily give rise to the notion of the spider as a self-sufficient creator who appeared to excrete his own world, and a beautiful and artistic world at that. Although psychoanalysts have generally tended to interpret the spider as a mother symbol (Abraham, 1948:326–332; cf. Spider Woman in the Southwest), Freud noted at least one instance in folklore where the thread spun by a spider was a symbol for evacuated feces. In a Prussian-Silesian tale, a peasant wishing to return to earth from heaven is turned into a spider by Peter. As a spider, the peasant spins a long thread by which he descends, but he is horrified to discover as he arrives just over his home that he could spin no more. He squeezes and squeezes to make the thread longer and then suddenly wakes up from his dream to discover that "something very human had happened to him while he slept" (Freud and Oppenheim 1958:45). The spider as the perfect symbol of male artistic creativity is described in a poem by Whitman entitled "The Spider." In the poem, the spider is compared to the soul of the poet as it stands detached and alone in "measureless oceans of space" launching forth filament out of itself (Wilbur and Muensterberger 1951:405). Without going into primitive Spider creation myths in great detail, it should suffice to note that, as in other types of male myths of creation, the creator is able to create without any reference to women. Whether a male creator spins material, molds clay, lays an egg, fabricates from mucus or epidermal tissue, or dives for fecal mud, the psychological motivation is much the same.

Other cosmogonic depictions of anal birth have been barely touched upon. As Ernest Jones has shown in some detail (1951:266–357), some of the other aspects of defecation such as the sound (creation by thunder or the spoken word), or the passage of air (creation by wind or breath), are also of considerable importance in the study of mythology. With respect to the latter characteristic, there is the obvious Vedic example of Pragapati who created mankind by means of "downward breathings" from the "back part" cited by Jones (1951:279). One account of Pragapati's creation of the earth relates the passing of air with the earth-diver story. "Prajapati first becomes a wind and stirs up the primeval ocean; he sees the earth in the depths of the ocean; he turns himself into a boar and draws the earth up" (Dragomanov, 1961:28). Another ancient male anal wind myth is found in the Babylonian account of Marduk. Marduk conquers Tiamat by the following means: "The evil wind which followed him, he loosed it in her face. . . . He drove in the evil wind so that she could not close her lips. The terrible winds filled her belly" (Guirand, 1959:51). Marduk then pierces Tiamat's belly and kills her. The passage of wind by the male Marduk leads to the destruction of the female Tiamat. Marduk rips open the rival creator,

the belly of woman, which had given birth to the world. There is also the Biblical instance of the divine (af)flatus moving on the face of the waters. Köngas (1960:169) made a very astute intuitive observation when she suggested that there was a basic similarity between the spirit of God moving upon the primeval water and the earth-diver myth. The common denominator is the male myth of creation whereby the male creator uses various aspects of the only means available, namely the creative power of the anus.

Undoubtedly anthropologists will be sceptical of any presentation in which evidence is marshalled à la Frazer and where the only criteria for the evidence appears to be the gristworthyness for the mill. Nevertheless, what is important is the possibility of a theory of universal symbolism which can be verified by empirical observation in the field in decades to come. Kluckhohn, despite a deep-seated mistrust of pan-human symbolism, confesses that his own field work as well as that of his collaborators has forced him to the conclusion that "Freud and other psychoanalysts have depicted with astonishing correctness many central themes in motivational life which are universal. The styles of expression of these themes and much of the manifest content are culturally determined but the underlying psychological drama transcends cultural difference" (Wilbur and Muensterberger, 1951:120). Kluckhohn bases his assumptions on the notion of a limited number of human "givens," such as human anatomy and physiology. While it is true that thoughts about the "givens" are not "given" in the same sense, it may be that their arising is inevitable. In other words, man is not born with the idea of pregnancy envy. It is acquired through experience, that is, through the mediation of culture. But if certain experiences are universal, such as the observation of female pregnancy, then there may be said to be secondary or derived "givens," using the term in an admittedly idiosyncratic sense. This is very important for the study of myth. It has already been pointed out that from a cultural relativistic perspective, the only portion of mythology which can be profitably studied is limited to those myths which are peculiar to a particular culture or those differences in the details of a widely diffused myth. Similarly, the literal approach can glean only so much ethnographic data from reflector myths. Without the assumption of symbolism and universals in myth, a vast amount of mythology remains of little use to the anthropologist. It should also be noted that there is, in theory, no conflict between accepting the idea of universals and advocating cultural relativism. It is not an "either/or" proposition. Some myths may be universal and others not. It is the all-or-nothing approach which appears to be erroneous. The same is true for the polygenesis-diffusion controversy; they also are by no means mutually exclusive. In the same way, there is no inconsistency in the statement that myths can either reflect or refract culture. (The phrase was suggested by A. K. Ramanujan.) Lévi-Strauss (1958:51) criticizes psychoanalytic interpretations of myth because, as he puts it, if there's an evil grandmother in the myths, "it will be claimed that in such a society grandmothers are actually evil and that mythology reflects the social structure and the social relations; but should the actual data be conflicting, it would be readily claimed that the purpose of mythology is to provide an outlet for repressed feelings. Whatever the situation may be, a clever dialectic will always find a way to pretend that a meaning has been unravelled." Although Lévi-Strauss may be justified insofar as he is attacking the "Have you stopped beating your wife?" antics of some psychoanalysts, there is not necessarily any inconsistency stemming from data showing that in culture A evil grandmothers in fact are also found in myth, while in culture B conscious norms of pleasant grandmothers disguise unconscious hatred for "evil" grandmothers, a situation which may be expressed in myth. In other words, myths can and usually do contain both conscious and unconscious cultural materials. To the extent that conscious and unconscious motivation may vary or be contradictory, so likewise can myth differ from or contradict ethnographic data. There is no safe monolithic theory of myth except that of judicious eclecticism as championed by E. B. Tylor. Mythology must be studied in cultural context in order to determine which individual mythological elements reflect and which refract the culture. But, more than this, the cultural relative approach must not preclude the recognition and identification of transcultural similarities and potential universals. As Kluckhohn said, ". . . the anthropologist for two generations has been obsessed with the differences between peoples, neglecting the equally real similarities—upon which the 'universal culture pattern' as well as the psychological uniformities are clearly built (Wilbur and Muensterberger, 1951:121)." The theoretical implications for practical field work of seeking psychological uniformities are implicit. Ethnographers must remove the traditional blinders and must be willing to collect *all* pertinent material even if it borders on what is obscene by the ethnographer's ethnocentric standards. The ideal ethnographer must not be afraid of diving deep and coming up with a little dirt; for, as the myth relates, such a particle may prove immensely valuable and may expand so as to form an entirely new world for the students of man.

Claude Lévi-Strauss

THE STRUCTURAL STUDY OF MYTH

The eminent French anthropologist Claude Lévi-Strauss has been providing the anthropological world with a most stimulating and provocative series of articles and books in the past decade, several of them dealing with the analysis of myths, rituals, and native categories of thought. In our judgment, his key paper on myth is "The Structural Study of Myth," which was first published in the *Journal of American Folklore* in 1955 but was revised by the author for his *Anthropologie structurale* (1958) and then translated into English for *Structural Anthropology* (1963).

Reprinted from the *Journal of American Folklore*, LXVII (1955), 428–444, by permission of the author and The American Folklore Society, Inc.

In this article Lévi-Strauss makes the suggestion that our sociological and psychological interpretations of mythology have up to this point been far too facile. As he expresses it:

> If a given mythology confers prominence to a certain character, let us say an evil grandmother, it will be claimed that in such a society grandmothers are actually evil and that mythology reflects the social structure and the social relations; but should the actual data be conflicting, it would be readily claimed that the purpose of mythology is to provide an outlet for repressed feelings. Whatever the situation may be, a clever dialectic will always find a way to pretend that a meaning has been unravelled.

He therefore suggests that the basic function of myth is to furnish a culture with a "logical" model by means of which the human mind can evade unwelcome contradictions, and he proceeds to apply this theory to the Oedipus myth and to the Zuni emergence myth.

As the student who attempts to put this provocative theory to a test will soon discover, there are a number of exceedingly difficult operational problems, of which we will mention only a few. Lévi-Strauss suggests that the analysis proceed by dividing the myth into "the shortest possible sentences, and writing each sentence on an index card bearing a number corresponding to the unfolding of the story." The problem here is that if the analyst is operating in the native language (say Zuni), how does he decide on what are "the shortest possible sentences?" Lévi-Strauss then goes on to propose that the cards be arranged into columns, so that ultimately the myth reads like an orchestra score. There is a question as to whether two or more analysts, working independently, will end up with the same cards in the same columns. Finally, we may ask precisely how an analyst moves from short sentences on index cards to the quite general themes presented in, for example, the four columns devoted to the Oedipus myth.

But having presented these operational difficulties, we are left with the conviction that there is a novel, and we hope ultimately testable, theory in this notion of Lévi-Strauss about mythology. We present his article in order that new students can profit by the insights and proceed to cope with the methodological problems.

1.0. Despite some recent attempts to renew them, it would seem that during the past twenty years anthropology has more and more turned away from studies in the field of religion. At the same time, and precisely because professional anthropologists' interest has withdrawn from primitive religion, all kinds of amateurs who claim to belong to other disciplines have seized this opportunity to move in, thereby turning into their private playground what we had left as a wasteland. Thus, the prospects for the scientific study of religion have been undermined in two ways.

1.1. The explanation for that situation lies to some extent in the fact that the anthropological study of religion was started by men like Tylor, Frazer, and Durkheim who were psychologically oriented, although not in a position to keep up with the progress of psychological research and theory. Therefore, their interpretations soon became vitiated by the outmoded psychological approach which they used as their backing. Although they were undoubtedly right in giving their attention to intellectual processes, the way they handled them remained so coarse as to discredit them altogether. This is much to be regretted since, as Hocart so profoundly noticed in his introduction to a posthumous book recently published, psychological interpretations were withdrawn from the intellectual field only to be introduced again in the field of affectivity, thus adding to "the inherent defects of the psychological school . . . the mistake of deriving clear-cut ideas . . . from vague emotions." Instead of trying to enlarge the framework of our logic to include processes which, whatever their apparent differences, belong to the same kind of intellectual operations, a naïve attempt was made to reduce them to inarticulate emotional drives which resulted only in withering our studies.

1.2. Of all the chapters of religious anthropology probably none has tarried to the same extent as studies in the field of mythology. From a theoretical point of view the situation remains very much the same as it was fifty years ago, namely, a picture of chaos. Myths are still widely interpreted in conflicting ways: collective dreams, the outcome of a kind of esthetic play, the foundation of ritual. . . . Mythological figures are considered as personified abstractions, divinized heroes or decayed gods. Whatever the hypothesis, the choice amounts to reducing mythology either to an idle play or to a coarse kind of speculation.

1.3. In order to understand what a myth really is, are we compelled to choose between platitude and sophism? Some claim that human societies merely express, through their mythology, fundamental feelings common to the whole of mankind, such as love, hate, revenge; or that they try to provide some kind of explanations for phenomena which they cannot understand otherwise: astronomical, meteorological, and the like. But why should these societies do it in such elaborate and devious ways, since all of them are also acquainted with positive explanations? On the other hand, psychoanalysts and many anthropologists have shifted the problems to be explained away from the natural or cosmological towards the sociological and psychological fields. But then the interpretation becomes too easy: if a given mythology confers prominence to a certain character, let us say an evil grandmother, it will be claimed that in such a society grandmothers are actually evil and that mythology reflects the social structure and the social relations; but should the actual data be conflicting, it would be readily claimed that the purpose of mythology is to provide an outlet for repressed feelings. Whatever the situation may be, a clever dialectic will always find a way to pretend that a meaning has been unraveled.

2.0. Mythology confronts the student with a situation which at first sight could be looked upon as contradictory. On the one hand, it would seem that in the course of a myth anything is likely to happen. There is no logic, no continuity. Any characteristic can be attributed to any subject; every conceivable relation can be met. With myth, everything becomes possible. But on the other hand, this apparent arbitrariness is belied by the astounding similarity between myths collected in widely different regions. Therefore the problem: if the content of a myth is contingent, how are we going to explain that throughout the world myths do resemble one another so much?

2.1. It is precisely this awareness of a basic antinomy pertaining to the nature of myth that may lead us towards its solution. For the contradiction which we face is very similar to that which in earlier times brought considerable worry to the first philosophers concerned with linguistic problems; linguistics could only begin to evolve as a science after this contradiction had been overcome. Ancient philosophers were reasoning about language the way we are about mythology. On the one hand, they did notice that in a given language certain sequences of sounds were associated with definite meanings, and they earnestly aimed at discovering a reason for the linkage between those sounds and that meaning. Their attempt, however, was thwarted from the very beginning by the fact that the same sounds were equally present in other languages though the meaning they conveyed was entirely different. The contradiction was surmounted only by the discovery that it is the combination of sounds, not the sounds in themselves, which provides the significant data.

2.2. Now, it is easy to see that some of the more recent interpretations of mythological thought originated from the same kind of misconception under which those early linguists were laboring. Let us consider, for instance, Jung's idea that a given mythological pattern—the so-called archetype—possesses a certain signification. This is comparable to the long supported error that a sound may possess a certain affinity with a meaning: for instance, the "liquid" semivowels with water, the open vowels with things that are big, large, loud, or heavy, etc., a kind of theory which still has its supporters. Whatever emendations the original formulation may now call for, everybody will agree that the Saussurean principle of the arbitrary character of the linguistic signs was a prerequisite for the acceding of linguistics to the scientific level.

2.3. To invite the mythologist to compare his precarious situation with that of the linguist in the prescientific stage is not enough. As a matter of fact we may thus be led only from one difficulty to another. There is a very good reason why myth cannot simply be treated as language if its specific problems are to be solved; myth *is* language: to be known, myth has to be told; it is a part of human speech. In order to preserve its specificity we should thus put ourselves in a position to show that it is both the same thing as language, and also something different from it. Here, too, the past experience of linguists may help us. For language itself can be analyzed into things which are at the same time similar and different. This is precisely what is expressed in Saussure's distinction between *langue* and *parole*, one being the structural side of language, the other the statistical aspect of it, *langue* belonging to a revertible time, whereas *parole* is non-revertible. If those two levels already exist in language, then a third one can conceivably be isolated.

2.4. We have just distinguished *langue* and *parole* by the different time referents which they use. Keeping this in mind, we may notice that myth uses a third referent which combines the properties of the first two. On the one hand, a myth always refers to events alleged to have taken place in time: before the world was created, or during its first stages—anyway, long ago. But what gives the myth an operative value is that the specific pattern described is everlasting; it explains the present and the past as well as the future. This can be made clear through a comparison between myth and what appears to have largely replaced it in modern societies, namely, politics. When the historian refers to the French Revolution it is always as a sequence of past happenings, a non-revertible series of events the remote consequences of which may still be felt at present. But to the French politician, as well as to his followers, the French Revolution is both a sequence belonging to the past —as to the historian—and an everlasting pattern which can be detected in the present French social structure and which provides a clue for its interpretation, a lead from which to infer the future developments. See, for instance, Michelet who was a politically-minded historian. He describes the French Revolution thus: "This day . . . everything was possible. . . . Future became present . . . that is, no more time, a glimpse of eternity." It is that double structure, altogether historical and anhistorical, which explains that myth, while pertaining to the realm of the *parole* and calling for an explanation as such, as well as to that of the *langue* in which it is expressed, can also be an absolute object on a third level which, though it remains linguistic by nature, is nevertheless distinct from the other two.

2.5. A remark can be introduced at this point which will help to show the singularity of myth among other linguistic phenomena. Myth is the part of language where the formula *traduttore, traditore* reaches its lowest truth-value. From that point of view it should be put in the whole gamut of linguistic expressions at the end opposite to that of poetry, in spite of all the claims which have been made to prove the contrary. Poetry is a kind of speech which cannot be translated except at the cost of serious distortions; whereas the mythical value of the myth remains preserved, even through the worst translation. Whatever our ignorance of the language and the culture of the people where it originated, a myth is still felt as a myth by any reader throughout the world. Its substance does not lie in its style, its original music, or its syntax, but in the *story* which it tells. It is language, functioning on an especially high level where meaning succeeds practically at "taking off" from the linguistic ground on which it keeps on rolling.

2.6. To sum up the discussion at this point, we have so far made the following claims: 1. If there is a meaning to be found in mythology, this cannot reside in the isolated elements which enter into the composition of a myth, but only in the way those elements are combined. 2. Although myth belongs to the same category as language, being, as a matter of fact, only part of it, language in myth unveils specific properties. 3. Those properties are only to be found *above* the ordinary linguistic level; that is, they exhibit more complex features beside those which are to be found in any kind of linguistic expression.

3.0. If the above three points are granted, at least as a working hypothesis, two consequences will follow: 1. Myth, like the rest of language, is made up of constituent units. 2. These constituent units presuppose the constituent units present in language when analyzed on other levels, namely, phonemes, morphemes, and semantemes, but they, nevertheless, differ from the latter in the same way as they themselves differ from morphemes, and these from phonemes; they belong to a higher order, a more complex one. For this reason, we will call them *gross constituent units.*

3.1. How shall we proceed in order to identify and isolate these gross constituent units? We know that they cannot be found among phonemes, morphemes, or semantemes, but only on a higher level; otherwise myth would become confused with any other kind of speech. Therefore, we should look for them on the sentence level. The only method we can suggest at this stage is to proceed tentatively, by trial and error, using as a check the principles which serve as a basis for any kind of structural analysis: economy of explanation; unity of solution; and ability to reconstruct the whole from a fragment, as well as further stages from previous ones.

3.2. The technique which has been applied so far by this writer consists in analyzing each myth individually, breaking down its story into the shortest possible sentences, and writing each such sentence on an index card bearing a number corresponding to the unfolding of the story.

3.3. Practically each card will thus show that a certain function is, at a given time, predicated to a given subject. Or, to put it otherwise, each gross constituent unit will consist in a relation.

3.4. However, the above definition remains highly unsatisfactory for two different reasons. In the first place, it is well known to structural linguists that constituent units on all levels are made up of relations and the true difference between our gross units and the others stays unexplained; moreover, we still find ourselves in the realm of a non-revertible time since the numbers of the cards correspond to the unfolding of the informant's speech. Thus, the specific character of mythological time, which as we have seen is both revertible and non-revertible, synchronic and diachronic, remains unaccounted for. Therefrom comes a new hypothesis which constitutes the very core of our argument: the true constituent units of a myth are not the isolated relations but *bundles of such relations* and it is only as bundles that these relations can be put to use and combined so as to produce a meaning. Relations pertaining to the same bundle may appear diachronically at remote intervals, but when we have succeeded in grouping them together, we have reorganized our myth according to a time referent of a new nature corresponding to the prerequisite of the initial hypothesis, namely, a two-dimensional time referent which is simultaneously diachronic and synchronic and which accordingly integrates the characteristics of the *langue* on one hand, and those of the *parole* on the other. To put it in even more linguistic terms, it is as though a phoneme were always made up of all its variants.

4.0. Two comparisons may help to explain what we have in mind.

4.1. Let us first suppose that archaeologists of the future coming from another planet would one day, when all human life had disappeared from the earth, excavate one of our libraries. Even if they were at first ignorant of our writing, they might succeed in deciphering it—an undertaking which would require, at some early stage, the discovery that the alphabet, as we are in the habit of printing it,

should be read from left to right and from top to bottom. However, they would soon find out that a whole category of books did not fit the usual pattern: these would be the orchestra scores on the shelves of the music division. But after trying, without success, to decipher staffs one after the other, from the upper down to the lower, they would probably notice that the same patterns of notes recurred at intervals, either in full or in part, or that some patterns were strongly reminiscent of earlier ones. Hence the hypothesis: what if patterns showing affinity, instead of being considered in succession, were to be treated as one complex pattern and read globally? By getting at what we call *harmony*, they would then find out that an orchestra score, in order to become meaningful, has to be read diachronically along one axis—that is, page after page, and from left to right—and also synchronically along the other axis, all the notes which are written vertically making up one gross constituent unit, i.e. one bundle of relations.

4.2. The other comparison is somewhat different. Let us take an observer ignorant of our playing cards, sitting for a long time with a fortune-teller. He would know something of the visitors: sex, age, look, social situation, etc. in the same way as we know something of the different cultures whose myths we try to study. He would also listen to the séances and keep them recorded so as to be able to go over them and make comparisons—as we do when we listen to myth telling and record it. Mathematicians to whom I have put the problem agree that if the man is bright and if the material available to him is sufficient, he may be able to reconstruct the nature of the deck of cards being used, that is: fifty-two or thirty-two cards according to case, made up of four homologous series consisting of the same units (the individual cards) with only one varying feature, the suit.

4.3. The time has come to give a concrete example of the method we propose. We will use the Oedipus myth which has the advantage of being well-known to everybody and for which no preliminary explanation is therefore needed. By doing so, I am well aware that the Oedipus myth has only reached us under late forms and through literary transfigurations concerned more with esthetic and moral preoccupations than with religious or ritual ones, whatever these may have been. But as will be shown later, this apparently unsatisfactory situation will strengthen our demonstration rather than weaken it.

4.4. The myth will be treated as would be an orchestra score perversely presented as a unilinear series and where our task is to re-establish the correct disposition. As if, for instance, we were confronted with a sequence of the type: 1,2,4,7,8,2,3,4,6,8,1,4,5,7,8,1,2,5, 7,3,4,5,6,8 . . . , the assignment being to put all the 1's together, all the 2's, the 3's, etc.; the result is a chart:

1	2		4			7	8
	2	3	4		6		8
1			4	5		7	8
1	2			5		7	
		3	4	5			
					6		8

4.5. We will attempt to perform the same kind of operation on the Oedipus myth, trying out several dispositions until we find one which is in harmony with the principles enumerated under 3.1. Let us suppose, for the sake of argument, that the best arrangement is the [one shown below] (although it might certainly be improved by the help of a specialist in Greek mythology).

4.6. Thus, we find ourselves confronted with four vertical columns each of which include several relations belonging to the same bundle. Were we to *tell* the myth, we would disregard the columns and read the rows from left to right and from top to bottom. But if we want to *understand* the myth, then we will have to disregard one half of the diachronic dimension (top to bottom) and read from left to right, column after column, each one being considered as a unit.

4.7. All the relations belonging to the same column exhibit one common feature which it is our task to unravel. For instance, all the events grouped in the first column on the left have something to do with blood relations which are over-emphasized, i.e. are subject to a more intimate treatment than they should be. Let us say, then, that the first column has as its common feature the *overrating of blood relations.* It is obvious that the second column expresses the same thing, but inverted: *underrating of blood relations.* The third column refers to monsters being slain. As to the fourth, a word of clarification is needed. The remarkable connotation of the surnames in Oedipus' father-line has often been noticed. However, linguists usually disregard it, since to them the only way to define the meaning of a term is to investigate all the contexts in which it appears, and personal names, precisely because they are used as such, are not accompanied by any context. With the method we propose to follow the objection disappears since the myth itself provides its own context. The meaningful fact is no longer to be looked for in the eventual sense of each name, but in the fact that all the names have a common feature: i.e. that they may eventually mean something and that all these hypothetical meanings (which may well remain hypothetical) exhibit a common feature, namely they refer to *difficulties to walk and to behave straight.*

Kadmos seeks his sister Europa ravished by Zeus			
		Kadmos kills the dragon	
	The Spartoi kill each other		
			Labdacos (Laios' father) = *lame* (?)
	Oedipus kills his father Laios		
			Laios (Oedipus' father) = *left-sided* (?)
		Oedipus kills the Sphinx	
Oedipus marries his mother Jocasta	Eteocles kills his brother Polynices		
			Oedipus = *swollen foot* (?)
Antigone buries her brother Polynices despite prohibition			

4.8. What is then the relationship between the two columns on the right? Column three refers to monsters. The dragon is a chthonian being which has to be killed in order that mankind be born from the earth; the Sphinx is a monster unwilling to permit men to live. The last unit reproduces the first one which has to do with the *autochthonous origin* of mankind. Since the monsters are overcome by men, we may thus say that the common feature of the third column is *the denial of the autochthonous origin of man.*

4.9. This immediately helps us to understand the meaning of the fourth column. In mythology it is a universal character of men born from the earth that at the moment they emerge from the depth, they either cannot walk or do it clumsily. This is the case of the chthonian beings in the mythology of the Pueblo: Masauwu, who leads the emergence, and the chthonian Shumaikoli are lame ("bleeding-foot," "sore-foot"). The same happens to the Koskimo of the Kwakiutl after they have been swallowed by the chthonian monster, Tsiakish: when they returned to the surface of the earth "they limped forward or tripped sideways." Then the common feature of the fourth column is: *the persistence of the autochthonous origin of man.* It follows that column four is to column three as column one is to column two. The inability to connect two kinds of relationships is overcome (or rather replaced) by the positive statement that contradictory relationships are identical inasmuch as they are both self-contradictory in a similar way. Although this is still a provisional formulation of the structure of mythical thought, it is sufficient at this stage.

4.10. Turning back to the Oedipus myth, we may now see what it means. The myth has to do with the inability, for a culture which holds the belief that mankind is autochthonous (see, for instance, Pausanias, VIII, xxix, 4: vegetals provide a *model* for humans), to find a satisfactory transition between this theory and the knowledge that human beings are actually born from the union of man and woman. Although the problem obviously cannot be solved, the Oedipus myth provides a kind of logical tool which, to phrase it coarsely, replaces the original problem: born from one or born from two? born from different or born from same? By a correlation of this type, the overrating of blood relations is to the underrating of blood relations as the attempt to escape autochthony is to the im-

possibility to succeed in it. Although experience contradicts theory, social life verifies the cosmology by its similarity of structure. Hence cosmology is true.

4.11.0. Two remarks should be made at this stage.

4.11.1. In order to interpret the myth, we were able to leave aside a point which has until now worried the specialists, namely, that in the earlier (Homeric) versions of the Oedipus myth, some basic elements are lacking, such as Jocasta killing herself and Oedipus piercing his own eyes. These events do not alter the substance of the myth although they can easily be integrated, the first one as a new case of auto-destruction (column three) while the second is another case of crippledness (column four). At the same time there is something significant in these additions since the shift from foot to head is to be correlated with the shift from: autochthonous origin negated to: self-destruction.

4.11.2. Thus, our method eliminates a problem which has been so far one of the main obstacles to the progress of mythological studies, namely, the quest for the *true* version, or the *earlier* one. On the contrary, we define the myth as consisting of all its versions; to put it otherwise: a myth remains the same as long as it is felt as such. A striking example is offered by the fact that our interpretation may take into account, and is certainly applicable to, the Freudian use of the Oedipus myth. Although the Freudian problem has ceased to be that of autochthony *versus* bisexual reproduction, it is still the problem of understanding how *one* can be born from *two*: how is it that we do not have only one procreator, but a mother plus a father? Therefore, not only Sophocles, but Freud himself, should be included among the recorded versions of the Oedipus myth on a par with earlier or seemingly more "authentic" versions.

5.0. An important consequence follows. If a myth is made up of all its variants, structural analysis should take all of them into account. Thus, after analyzing all the known variants of the Theban version, we should treat the others in the same way: first, the tales about Labdacos' collateral line including Agavé, Pentheus, and Jocasta herself; the Theban variant about Lycos with Amphion and Zetos as the city founders; more remote variants concerning Dionysos (Oedipus' matrilateral cousin), and Athenian legends where Cecrops takes the place of Kadmos, etc. For each of them a similar chart should be drawn, and then compared and reorganized according to the findings: Cecrops killing the serpent with the parallel episode of Kadmos; abandonment of Dionysos with abandonment of Oedipus; "Swollen Foot" with Dionysos *loxias*, i.e. walking obliquely; Europa's quest with Antiope's; the foundation of Thebes by the Spartoi or by the brothers Amphion and Zetos; Zeus kidnapping Europa and Antiope and the same with Semele; the Theban Oedipus and the Argian Perseus, etc. We will then have several two-dimensional charts, each dealing with a variant, to be organized in a three-dimensional order so that three different readings become possible: left to right, top to bottom, front to back. All of these charts cannot be expected to be identical; but experience shows that any difference to be observed may be correlated with other differences, so that a logical treatment of the whole will allow simplifications, the final outcome being the structural law of the myth. [See Figure 1.]

5.1. One may object at this point that the task is impossible to perform since we can only work with known versions. Is it not possible that a new version might alter the picture? This is true enough if only one or two versions are available, but the objection becomes theoretical as soon as a reasonably large number has been recorded (a number which experience will progressively tell, at least as an approximation). Let us make this point clear by a comparison. If the furniture of a room and the way it is arranged in the room were known to us only through its reflection in two mirrors placed on opposite walls, we would theoretically dispose of an almost infinite number of mirror-images which would provide us with a complete

FIGURE 1

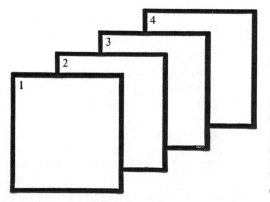

knowledge. However, should the two mirrors be obliquely set, the number of mirror-images would become very small; nevertheless, four or five such images would very likely give us, if not complete information, at least a sufficient coverage so that we would feel sure that no large piece of furniture is missing in our description.

5.2. On the other hand, it cannot be too strongly emphasized that all available variants should be taken into account. If Freudian comments on the Oedipus complex are a part of the Oedipus myth, then questions such as whether Cushing's version of the Zuni origin myth should be retained or discarded become irrelevant. There is no one true version of which all the others are but copies or distortions. Every version belongs to the myth.

5.3. Finally it can be understood why works on general mythology have given discouraging results. This comes from two reasons. First, comparative mythologists have picked up preferred versions instead of using them all. Second, we have seen that the structural analysis of *one* variant of *one* myth belonging to *one* tribe (in some cases, even *one* village) already requires two dimensions. When we use several variants of the same myth for the same tribe or village, the frame of reference becomes three-dimensional and as soon as we try to enlarge the comparison, the number of dimensions required increases to such an extent that it appears quite impossible to handle them intuitively. The confusions and platitudes which are the outcome of comparative mythology can be explained by the fact that multi-dimensional frames of reference cannot be ignored, or naïvely replaced by two- or three-dimensional ones. Indeed, progress in comparative mythology depends largely on the cooperation of mathematicians who would undertake to express in symbols multi-dimensional relations which cannot be handled otherwise.

6.0. In order to check this theory, an attempt was made in 1953–54 towards an exhaustive analysis of all the known versions of the Zuni origin and emergence myth: Cushing, 1883 and 1896; Stevenson, 1904; Parsons, 1923; Bunzel, 1932; Benedict, 1934. Furthermore, a preliminary attempt was made at a comparison of the results with similar myths in other Pueblo tribes, Western and Eastern. Finally, a test was undertaken with Plains mythology. In all cases, it was found that the theory was sound, and light was thrown, not only on North American mythology, but also on a previously unnoticed kind of logical operation, or one known only so far in a wholly different context. The bulk of material which needs to be handled almost at the beginning of the work makes it impossible to enter into details, and we will have to limit ourselves here to a few illustrations.

6.1. An over-simplified chart of the Zuni emergence myth would read as [shown at the bottom of this page].

6.2. As may be seen from a global inspection of the chart, the basic problem consists in discovering a mediation between life and death. For the Pueblo, the problem is expecially difficult since they understand the origin of human life on the model of vegetal life (emergence from the earth). They share that belief with the ancient Greeks, and it is not without reason that we chose the Oedipus myth as our first example. But in the American case, the highest form of vegetal life is to be found in agriculture which is periodical in nature, i.e. which consists in an alternation between life and death. If this is disregarded, the contradiction surges at another place: agriculture provides food, therefore life; but hunting provides food and is similar to warfare which means death. Hence there are three different ways of handling the problem. In the

Cushing version, the difficulty revolves around an opposition between activities yielding an immediate result (collecting wild food) and activities yielding a delayed result—death has to become integrated so that agriculture can exist. Parsons' version goes from hunting to agriculture, while Stevenson's version operates the other way around. It can be shown that all the differences between these versions can be rigorously correlated with these basic structures. [See the top of page 298.]

Since fiber strings (vegetal) are always superior to sinew strings (animal) and since (to a lesser extent) the gods' alliance is preferable to their antagonism, it follows that in Cushing's version, men begin to be doubly underprivileged (hostile gods, sinew string); in Stevenson, doubly privileged (friendly gods, fiber string); while Parsons' version confronts us with an intermediary situation (friendly gods, but sinew strings since men begin by being hunters). Hence:

	CUSHING	PARSONS	STEVENSON
gods/men	−	+	+
fiber/sinew	−	−	+

6.3. Bunzel's version is from a structural point of view of the same type as Cushing's.

INCREASE			DEATH
mechanical growth of vegetals (used as ladders)	emergence led by Beloved Twins	sibling incest	gods kill children
food value of wild plants	migration led by the two Newekwe		magical contest with people of the dew (collecting wild food *versus* cultivation)
		sibling sacrificed (to gain victory)	
food value of cultivated plants		sibling adopted (in exchange for corn)	
periodical character of agricultural work			war against Kyanakwe (gardeners *versus* hunters)
hunting	war led by two war-gods		
			salvation of the tribe (center of the world found)
warfare		sibling sacrificed (to avoid flood)	
DEATH			PERMANENCY

	CUSHING	PARSONS	
Gods } Kyanakwe }	allied, use fiber strings on their bows (gardeners)	Kyanakwe alone, use fiber string	Gods } Men } allied, use fiber string
Men	VICTORIOUS OVER alone, use sinew (hunters) (until men shift to fiber)	VICTORIOUS OVER Gods } Men } allied, use sinew string	VICTORIOUS OVER Kyanakwe alone, use sinew string

However, it differs from both Cushing's and Stevenson's inasmuch as the latter two explain the emergence as a result of man's need to evade his pitiful condition, while Bunzel's version makes it the consequence of a call from the higher powers—hence the inverted sequences of the means resorted to for the emergence: in both Cushing and Stevenson, they go from plants to animals; in Bunzel, from mammals to insects and from insects to plants.

6.4. Among the Western Pueblo the logical approach always remains the same; the starting point and the point of arrival are the simplest ones and ambiguity is met with halfway. [See Figure 2.]

The fact that contradiction appears in the middle of the dialectical process has as its result the production of a double series of dioscuric pairs the purpose of which is to operate a mediation between conflicting terms [as shown at the top of page 299], which consists in combinatory variants of the same function (hence the war attribute of the clowns which has given rise to so many queries).

6.5. Some Central and Eastern Pueblos proceed the other way around. They begin by stating the identity of hunting and cultivation (first corn obtained by Game-Father sowing deer-dewclaws), and they try to derive both life and death from that central notion. Then, instead of extreme terms being simple and intermediary ones duplicated as among the Western groups, the extreme terms become duplicated (i.e., the two sisters of the Eastern Pueblo) while a simple mediating term comes to the foreground (for instance, the Poshaiyanne of the Zia), but endowed with equivocal attributes. Hence the attributes of this "messiah" can be deduced from the place it occupies in the time sequence: good when at the beginning (Zuni, Cushing), equivocal in the middle (Central Pueblo), bad at the end (Zia), except in Bunzel where the sequence is reversed as has been shown.

6.6. By using systematically this kind of structural analysis it becomes possible to organize all the known variants of a myth as a series forming a kind of permutation group, the two variants placed at the far-ends being in a symmetrical, though inverted, relationship to each other.

7.0. Our method not only has the advantage of bringing some kind of order to what was previously chaos; it also enables

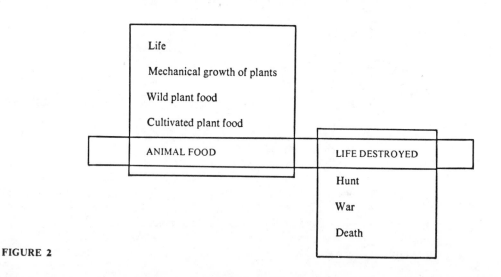

Life

Mechanical growth of plants

Wild plant food

Cultivated plant food

ANIMAL FOOD

LIFE DESTROYED

Hunt

War

Death

FIGURE 2

1. 2 divine messengers	2 ceremonial clowns		2 war-gods
2. homogeneous pair: dioscurs (2 brothers)	siblings (brother and sister)	couple (husband and wife)	heterogeneous pair: grandmother/ grandchild

us to perceive some basic logical processes which are at the root of mythical thought. Three main processes should be distinguished.

7.1.0. The trickster of American mythology has remained so far a problematic figure. Why is it that throughout North America his part is assigned practically everywhere to either coyote or raven? If we keep in mind that mythical thought always works from the awareness of oppositions towards their progressive mediation, the reason for those choices becomes clearer. We need only to assume that two opposite terms with no intermediary always tend to be replaced by two equivalent terms which allow a third one as a mediator; then one of the polar terms and the mediator become replaced by a new triad and so on. Thus we have:

INITIAL PAIR	FIRST TRIAD	SECOND TRIAD
Life		
	Agriculture	
		Herbivorous animals
		Carrion-eating animals (raven; coyote)
	Hunt	
		Prey animals
	War	
Death		

With the unformulated argument: carrion-eating animals are like prey animals (they eat animal food), but they are also like food-plant producers (they do not kill what they eat). Or, to put it otherwise, Pueblo style: ravens are to gardens as prey animals are to herbivorous ones. But it is also clear that herbivorous animals may be called first to act as mediators on the assumption that they are like collectors and gatherers (vegetal-food eaters) while they can be used as animal food though not themselves hunters. Thus we may have mediators of the first order, of the second order, and so on, where each term gives birth to the next by a double process of opposition and correlation.

7.1.1. This kind of process can be followed in the mythology of the Plains where we may order the data according to the sequence:

Unsuccessful mediator between earth and sky (Star husband's wife)

Heterogeneous pair of mediators (grandmother/grandchild)

Semi-homogeneous pair of mediators (Lodge-Boy and Thrown-away)

While among the Pueblo we have:

Successful mediator between earth and sky (Poshaiyanki)

Semi-homogeneous pair of mediators (Uyuyewi and Matsailema)

Homogeneous pair of mediators (the Ahaiyuta)

7.1.2. On the other hand, correlations may appear on a transversal axis (this is true even on the linguistic level; see the manifold connotation of the root *pose* in Tewa according to Parsons: coyote, mist, scalp, etc.). Coyote is intermediary between herbivorous and carnivorous in the same way as mist between sky and earth; scalp between war and hunt (scalp is war-crop); corn smut between wild plants and cultivated plants; garments between "nature" and "culture"; refuse between village and outside; ashes between roof and hearth (chimney). This string of mediators, if one may call them so, not only throws light on whole pieces of North American mythology—why the Dew-God may be at the same time the Game-Master and the giver of raiments and be personified as an "Ash-Boy"; or why the scalps are mist producing; or why the Game-Mother is associated with corn smut; etc.—but it also probably corresponds to a universal way of organizing daily experience. See, for instance, the French for vegetal smut, *nielle*, from Latin *nebula*; the luck-bringing power attributed to refuse (old shoe) and ashes (kissing chimney-sweepers); and compare the American Ash-Boy cycle with the Indo-European Cinderella: both phallic figures (mediator between male and female); master of the dew and of the game; owners of fine raiments; and social bridges (low class marrying into high class); though impossible to interpret through recent diffusion as has been sometimes contended since Ash-Boy and Cinderella are symmetrical but inverted in every detail (while the borrowed Cinderella tale in America—Zuni Turkey-Girl—is parallel to the prototype) [as shown at the bottom of this page].

7.2.0. Thus, the mediating function of the trickster explains that since its position is halfway between two polar terms he must retain something of that duality, namely an ambiguous and equivocal character. But the trickster figure is not the only conceivable form of mediation; some myths seem to devote themselves to the task of exhausting all the possible solutions to the problem of bridging the gap between *two* and *one*. For instance, a comparison between all the variants of the Zuni emergence myth provides us with a series of mediating devices, each of which creates the next one by a process of opposition and correlation:

$$\text{messiah} > \text{dioscurs} > \text{trickster} > \frac{\text{bisexual}}{\text{being}} >$$

$$\frac{\text{sibling}}{\text{pair}} > \frac{\text{married}}{\text{couple}} > \frac{\text{grandmother-}}{\text{grandchild}} >$$

$$\frac{4 \text{ terms}}{\text{group}} > \text{triad}$$

In Cushing's version, this dialectic is accompanied by a change from the space dimension (mediating between sky and earth) to the time dimension (mediating between summer and winter, i.e., between birth and death). But while the shift is being made from space to time, the final solution (triad) re-introduces space, since a triad consists in a dioscur pair *plus* a messiah simultaneously present; and while the point of departure was ostensibly formulated in terms of a space referent (sky and earth) this was nevertheless implicitly conceived in terms of a time referent (first the messiah calls; *then* the dioscurs descend). Therefore the logic of myth confronts us with a double, reciprocal exchange of functions to which we shall return shortly (7.3.).

7.2.1. Not only can we account for the ambiguous character of the trickster, but we may also understand another property of mythical figures the world over, namely, that

the same god may be endowed with contradictory attributes; for instance, he may be *good* and *bad* at the same time. If we compare the variants of the Hopi myth of the origin of Shalako, we may order them so that the following structure becomes apparent:

$$(\text{Masauwu}: x) \simeq (\text{Muyingwu}: \text{Masauwu}) \simeq$$
$$(\text{Shalako}: \text{Muyingwu}) \simeq (y: \text{Masauwu})$$

where x and y represent arbitrary values corresponding to the fact that in the two "extreme" variants the god Masauwu, while appearing alone instead of associated with another god, as in variant two, or being absent, as in three, still retains intrinsically a relative value. In variant one, Masauwu (alone) is depicted as helpful to mankind (though not as helpful as he could be), and in version four, harmful to mankind (though not as harmful as he could be); whereas in two, Muyingwu is relatively more helpful than Masauwu, and in three, Shalako more helpful than Muyingwu. We find an identical series when ordering the Keresan variants:

$$(\text{Poshaiyanki}: x) \simeq (\text{Lea}:\text{Poshaiyanki}) \simeq$$
$$(\text{Poshaiyanki}: \text{Tiamoni}) \simeq (y: \text{Poshaiyanki})$$

7.2.2. This logical framework is particularly interesting since sociologists are already acquainted with it on two other levels: first, with the problem of the pecking order among hens; and second, it also corresponds to what this writer has called *general exchange* in the field of kinship. By recognizing it also on the level of mythical thought, we may find ourselves in a better position to appraise its basic importance in sociological studies and to give it a more inclusive theoretical interpretation.

7.3.0. Finally, when we have succeeded in organizing a whole series of variants in a kind of permutation group, we are in a position to formulate the law of that group. Although it is not possible at the present stage to come closer than an approximate formulation which will certainly need to be made more accurate in the future, it seems that every myth (considered as the collection of all its

	EUROPE	AMERICA
Sex	female	male
Family Status	double family	no family
Appearance	pretty girl	ugly boy
Sentimental status	nobody likes her	in hopeless love with girl
Transformation	luxuriously clothed with super-	stripped of ugliness with super-
	natural help	natural help

variants) corresponds to a formula of the following type:

$$^fx(a): ^fy(b) \simeq {^fx(b)}: {^fa - I(y)}$$

where, two terms being given as well as two functions of these terms, it is stated that a relation of equivalence still exists between two situations when terms and relations are inverted, under two conditions: 1. that one term be replaced by its contrary; 2. that an inversion be made between the *function* and the *term* value of two elements.

7.3.1. This formula becomes highly significant when we recall that Freud considered that *two traumas* (and not one as it is so commonly said) are necessary in order to give birth to this individual myth in which a neurosis consists. By trying to apply the formula to the analysis of those traumatisms (and assuming that they correspond to conditions 1. and 2. respectively) we should not only be able to improve it, but would find ourselves in the much desired position of developing side by side the sociological and the psychological aspects of the theory; we may also take it to the laboratory and subject it to experimental verification.

8.0. At this point it seems unfortunate that, with the limited means at the disposal of French anthropological research, no further advance can be made. It should be emphasized that the task of analyzing mythological literature, which is extremely bulky, and of breaking it down into its constituent units, requires team work and secretarial help. A variant of average length needs several hundred cards to be properly analyzed. To discover a suitable pattern of rows and columns for those cards, special devices are needed, consisting of vertical boards about two meters long and one and one-half meters high, where cards can be pigeon-holed and moved at will; in order to build up three-dimensional models enabling one to compare the variants, several such boards are necessary, and this in turn requires a spacious workshop, a kind of commodity particularly unavailable in Western Europe nowadays. Furthermore, as soon as the frame of reference becomes multi-dimensional (which occurs at an early stage, as has been shown in 5.3.) the board-system has to be replaced by perforated cards which in turn require I.B.M. equipment, etc. Since there is little hope that such facilities will become available in France in the near future, it is much desired that some American group, better equipped than we are here in Paris, will

be induced by this paper to start a project of its own in structural mythology.

8.1.0. Three final remarks may serve as conclusion.

8.1.1. First, the question has often been raised why myths, and more generally oral literature, are so much addicted to duplication, triplication or quadruplication of the same sequence. If our hypotheses are accepted, the answer is obvious: repetition has as its function to make the structure of the myth apparent. For we have seen that the synchro-diachronical structure of the myth permits us to organize it into diachronical sequences (the rows in our tables) which should be read synchronically (the columns). Thus, a myth exhibits a "slated" structure which seeps to the surface, if one may say so, through the repetition process.

8.1.2. However, the slates are not absolutely identical to each other. And since the purpose of myth is to provide a logical model capable of overcoming a contradiction (an impossible achievement if, as it happens, the contradiction is real), a theoretically infinite number of slates will be generated, each one slightly different from the others. Thus, myth grows spiral-wise until the intellectual impulse which has originated it is exhausted. Its growth is a continuous process whereas its structure remains discontinuous. If this is the case we should consider that it closely corresponds, in the realm of the spoken word, to the kind of being a crystal is in the realm of physical matter. This analogy may help us understand better the relationship of myth on one hand to both *langue* and *parole* on the other.

8.1.3. Prevalent attempts to explain alleged differences between the so-called "primitive" mind and scientific thought have resorted to qualitative differences between the working processes of the mind in both cases while assuming that the objects to which they were applying themselves remained very much the same. If our interpretation is correct, we are led toward a completely different view, namely, that the kind of logic which is used by mythical thought is as rigorous as that of modern science, and that the difference lies not in the quality of the intellectual process, but in the nature of the things to which it is applied. This is well in agreement with the situation known to prevail in the field of technology: what makes a steel ax superior to a stone one is not that the first one is better made than the second. They are equally well made, but steel is a different thing than stone. In the same way we may be able to show that the same logical processes are put to use in myth as in science, and that man has always been thinking equally well; the improvement lies, not in an alleged progress of man's conscience, but in the discovery of new things to which it may apply its unchangeable abilities.

Edmund R. Leach

PULLEYAR AND THE LORD BUDDHA: AN ASPECT OF RELIGIOUS SYNCRETISM IN CEYLON

Edmund Leach, in this stimulating paper, presents a structural analysis of sacred personaes and trickster figures in Ceylonese mythology. Combining concrete ethnographic data with some insights from Lévi-Straussian structural analysis and Freudian psychoanalysis, Leach explores the function of mediating figures—those who share various attributes of two logically opposed domains—in the syncretistic belief system of modern Ceylon. He emphasizes the effectiveness of the "totality of symbols" in resolving the seemingly universal problems of preservation of life and preparation for death. Leach is also able to show that relatively simple logical principles underlie the most seemingly complex religions. Observing man's need for a mediating figure between Man and the Infinite (which Leach discusses for Buddhism, Hinduism, and Christianity), one should remember that the mediating figures may be not only deities, but also priests and shamans. For example, the shaman is often a being who is as asexual in his or her practice as the Ganesha figure (described in this paper) or Christ. It is often through this betwixt-and-between attribute that shamans and other religious officials are able to mediate between Earth and the Other World or between Man and God. It is not surprising that precedent for such logically intermediary beings frequently occurs in mythology.

In relation to this paper, the reader may wish to consult Leach's monograph on Ceylon (Leach, 1961) and H. R. Zimmer's excellent works on Indian symbolism (Zimmer, 1946, 1951, 1955).

Reprinted in abridged form from *Psychoanalysis and the Psychoanalytic Review*, XLIX (1962), 80–102, by permission of the author and the National Psychological Association for Psychoanalysis, Inc.

Let me start by explaining my title. Pulleyar is the Sinhalese version of the Tamil word *Pillaiyar* (Pillear). In Tamil, but not in Sinhalese, this word means "the son" and is the name given to Ganesha, the elephant headed Hindu deity who is rated the son of Shiva and Parvati. In the Hindu system Shiva (God) has many aspects. Because he is a potent warrior his emblems include the *lingam* (phallus), trident and spear; because he is an ascetic monk they include a rosary and a begging bowl.

The philosophic dialectic which makes such contradictions sensible is not easily understood; in village Hinduism the various aspects of Shiva are distributed among secondary deities who are thought of as members of his family. His consort Parvati, like Aphrodite, represents sexual love; his sons Skanda and Aiyanar are warriors, and his third son Ganesha is, after a fashion, an ascetic. But Ganesha's qualities are ambiguous and it is with this ambiguity that this essay is largely concerned.

If Parvati be equated with Aphrodite, then Ganesha is the equivalent of Hermes, "breaker of the way and guide of the soul." He is the doorkeeper of heaven, a trickster whose friendly help can clear all obstructions but whose enmity can cause disaster. Now one of Ganesha's special characteristics is that he has a broken tusk which he carries around in his hand, and in the context of heavenly tricksters such symbolism is familiar. The American Indian Winnebago Trickster "takes his phallus off and carries it around in a box," "the phallus is Trickster's double and alter ego." In Ancient Greece, Hermes' most characteristic representation was as an erect phallus, yet his sexuality was equivocal. Contrasted with his twin sister Aphrodite he stood as Shiva stands to Parvati, but Hermes' union with Aphrodite produced the sexually ambiguous Hermaphroditos. Moreover, although Hermes started his career as a bearded adult, he ended as a graceful, though athletic, adolescent. Even the ecstatic Dionysus is sexually ambiguous; "he is never represented as a noticeably phallic deity; he is shown either clothed in a long robe, or in some other effeminate form. The carrying around of a phallus, its erection and unveiling, played some part in his cult; . . . even though separated from him, it was something peculiarly his own." Ganesha is one of this crew.

It is part of my thesis that Ganesha's broken tusk is a phallic emblem and that its detachability denotes a certain ambivalence about Ganesha's sexual nature. There are contexts in which the *lingam*-phallus, which is properly an emblem of Shiva, may serve as a manifestation of any one of Shiva's sons, Ganesha included. In such a context Ganesha may be virile and potent. But there are other contexts where Ganesha seems to be an effeminate eunuch.

This ambivalence is not haphazard. Ganesha does not exist by himself but in association with other members of Shiva's family. The sexual qualities which are attributed to Ganesha depend upon context and, generally speaking, are the opposite of those attributed to his father (Shiva) or to one or other of his two brothers Skanda and Aiyanar. As Shiva varies so also Ganesha varies, but in the inverse direction.

Now, although Ganesha is a Hindu deity he also receives worship from Sinhalese-speaking Buddhists and this is particularly the case in the district of Nuvarakalaviya in Northern Ceylon which lies just to the south of a zone inhabited by Tamil-speaking Hindus. In the cult of the Nuvarakalaviya Buddhists, Ganesha is known by the name Pulleyar, and is thought of as the elephant lord of the forest.

Aiyanar his elder brother is revered as guardian of the village reservoir and of the village itself. There is no cult of Shiva and no mother goddess, but instead a reverence for the Lord Buddha.

For Hindus, Ganesha and his mother and brothers are simply appendages and aspects of Shiva, the Great God (Mahadeva), who is virile; but among the Sinhalese of Nuvarakalaviya, Pulleyar and his brother Aiyanar are without specific parents. Instead they are the feudal dependants of the Lord Buddha, and the Lord Buddha is the supreme ascetic. So we can investigate a relatively simple question; what happens to Shiva's son Ganesha when he is transferred to a Buddhist context as a servant of the Lord Buddha?

(To avoid ambiguity, I shall hereafter use *Pulleyar* to refer to the special form of the elephant headed deity that is worshipped by the Sinhalese Buddhists of Nuvarakalaviya and I shall use *Ganesha* to refer to all other forms whether Ceylonese or Indian, Hindu or Buddhist.)

By posing this question I face attack from two sides. First, there are those who would argue that my problem is a specialized topic for professional Indologists. In a sense this is true, but it is a problem which relates to a much more general issue: How far do religious ideologies really differ?

Psychoanalysts are familiar with the notion that the characteristics which Christians attribute to the separate persons of the Trinity and of the Holy Family are projections from attitudes and ideas developed in the context of ordinary family life, but this style of analogy has not been pursued far outside the confines of Christian and Jewish eschatology and the mythology of Ancient Greece. One of the themes in this paper is that the facts to which I shall draw attention have their strict parallels in much more familiar materials from European cultural contexts.

Second, I face the criticism of the Indologists themselves. Most anthropologists who write about the religious behaviors of Village India are at pains to emphasize the complexity and fluidity of all that they observe (for example, Marriott). No one can deny that the facts are complicated. But so also are the facts which a patient presents to his psychoanalyst. The analyst operates with the assumption that, despite the apparent complexity of the data, the patient is really returning again and again to a few very simple and fundamental issues. I claim that the complicated facts of Indian religion are likewise reducible to an elementary structural pattern. The special circumstances of Northern Ceylon make feasible a demonstration of this underlying simplicity.

Although it is palpable that from the historical point of view religious behaviors of the Sinhalese represent a mixture of traits, the villagers do not feel that they are members of several different religious systems at the same time. In the course of any ordinary year the villagers participate in a great variety of religious ceremonies and among these ceremonies they make category distinctions. The Buddha is worshipped in the Buddha-temple (*Vihare*); Pulleyar is worshipped at an open shrine called *Kovil*; the other *devata* are worshipped in the "God-house" (*Devale*), and apart from these there are a great variety of magical-exorcism rites which may take place almost anywhere. But the *Devale* is an annex of the *Vihare* and the *Kovil* is just across the road, at the gate to the *Vihare* compound; at the major annual two-day celebration of the *devata*, called *Mutti Mangalaya*, the proceedings are opened and closed by a prayer from the Buddhist monk. From the villagers' point of view the whole set of ceremonies forms a single system.

This kind of syncretism is linked with the fact that sectarianism in Asia is nearly always much less specific than it is in Christendom. An individual in South India is the follower of a particular deity—he is not a member of a sectarian church. It is perfectly proper for a follower of Shiva to attend ceremonials organized by the followers of Vishnu or some other major deity. In each case he will merely reinterpret what is going on in the light of his own theological doctrine. Followers of Vishnu say that the Buddha was a manifestation of Vishnu. On that account all Buddhist rites are also Vishnuite rites. At Kataragama in South Ceylon there has been held annually, since remote antiquity, a fourteen-day festival primarily in honor of the god Kataragama (Skanda) and his consort, Valli Amma. Vast numbers of pilgrims assemble for the occasion. Those who attend include Hindus, Buddhists, Moslems, Christians. All act devoutly. None appear to think that they are participating in heathen rites.

This Asian attitude, that contrasted religious dogmas are complementary rather than antagonistic, is very relevant to my theme. Many of the theological propositions

implicit in the stories which I shall presently relate appear flatly contradictory; they are not felt to be so in their original cultural context. The contradictions merely reflect the thesis that divinity must necessarily have many aspects. Christianity says "there are three Persons of the Trinity but only one God"; Hinduism says that the cosmos embraces many different deities whose functions are complementary.

In sophisticated Hinduism, Brahma, Vishnu and Shiva represent the three prime principles of Creation, Preservation and Destruction. This classification may be elaborated by crediting each male deity with a separate species of divine force (*sakti*) to which female sex is attributed, and then each *sakti* may be given a separate personality and thought of as the wife of her male counterpart. Thus Sarasvati is the *sakti*-wife of Brahma, Lakshmi the *sakti*-wife of Vishnu, and Uma the *sakti*-wife of Shiva. And then, carrying category distinctions yet further, the attributes of Uma may be distributed between three different goddesses—Parvati as sexuality, Durga as strength, and Kali as destructiveness. (See Diagram, Section A top left. Page 305.) Contrariwise, as we have already seen, the complexities of Shiva's masculine attributes may be made more readily acceptable by distributing them among his sons.

This highly elaborate theogony seems to contrast sharply with the orthodox Christian view that one and the same God gives us life, preserves us in sickness and in health, and finally brings us to death. It is small help to a "rationally" oriented European to be told that the gods and goddesses of Hinduism may not only be subdivided indefinitely, both by function and by name, but may also on occasion be merged. Followers of Shiva do not deny the existence of a multiplicity of other deities but they commonly assert that Shiva is, in himself, Creator, Preserver and Destroyer.

Yet this too needs to be understood. Even in Village Hinduism where the multiplicity of deities is a matter of homeliness rather than logical distinction the different members of the pantheon are not fully distinct from one another. Shiva's attributes are distributed among the various members of his family, but they still all remain aspects of Shiva himself. In this way any Hindu deity can assume almost any role. We need to pay attention to the roles rather than to the gods who fill them. Different aspects of deity are given emphasis

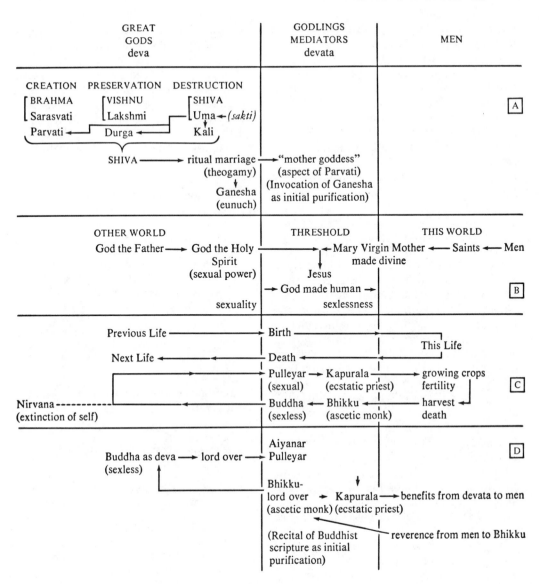

in different kinds of context and it is to the association between aspect and context that I would draw attention.

One aspect of divinity, which I label *deva*, is that of first cause, the original source of supernatural power. The purpose of all religious activity is to obtain benefit from this ultimate sacred source but, as a rule, direct approach to the *deva* is felt to be too dangerous. In defense against this danger, religions have created a great variety of secondary gods, goddesses, godlings, saints, prophets, mediums, who are thought to exercise supernatural power by derivation from the original source and who can, on that account, act as intermediaries between man and God. These secondary deities I label *devata*.

One version of this distinction is that which is made in European Catholicism between the worship of God and the worship of a local Saint. Quantitatively the local Saint receives far more attention than God himself but the two cults are not really distinct. The power of the Saint originates in God and the Saint is appealed to as mediator rather than as supernatural authority. So also, in the Hindu context, the localized deities (*devata*) receive more ritual attention than the Great Gods (*deva*). But, in the last analysis, the *devata* are only potent because they are manifestations or aspects of the *deva*. In South India the most common form of *devata* is a "mother goddess." Hundreds of such localized "mother goddesses" are distinguished by name and rite. Such divinities always turn out to be the spouse, and hence the *sakti*, of one of the better known deities from the Hindu pantheon. I have already mentioned one such case from Ceylon. Valli Amma is a localized "mother goddess," but she is held to be the wife of Skanda-Kataragama, who in turn is the son of Shiva. In my terminology, Shiva is a *deva*; Skanda and Valli Amma are both *devata*.

In the Christian Catholic system, God the Father is absolute deity, remote and all powerful; God the Holy Spirit is the creative essence of God the Father—his sexual power which served to make pregnant the Virgin Mary; God the Son is God become human and therefore more accessible; and finally the Virgin is a human who has been granted by special dispensation a semi-divine status. (See Diagram, Section B.) Jesus, God the Son, and Mary, his Mother, both belong in different degrees, to an intermediate mediating category of deity, whose potency is derived rather than original. In the terminology which I am employing here both are *devata* rather than *deva*. A Catholic Saint is likewise a "divinity" of the mediating *devata* class, but even closer to the human end of the spectrum.

If we compare the lower part of Section A of my diagram (p. 305) with the (Catholic) Christian pattern displayed in Section B, the structural similarity of the two systems of ideas will be obvious. The only difference is the slight variation of role given to the theme of sexuality.

In Section A, Shiva and his *sakti*, as mother goddess, are both emphatically sexual in an active sense. They are distinguished only as male versus female. In contrast, Ganesha, God the Son, is, as I shall show presently, sexually passive.

In Section B, God the Holy Spirit is the active male force of God the Father, but Jesus, God the Son, and Mary the "Mother Goddess" are both ascetic and sexless. It is a point of doctrine that Mary remains a virgin despite her motherhood; Jesus is not specified as a eunuch, but he does not engage in sex relations and his close resemblance to the eunuch deity Attis has frequently been noted. There is a long tradition in Christian iconography that the genitals of the Christ figure should be of childish proportions or non-existent. A notable early example is the huge mosaic figure of a naked Christ in the roof of the apse of the Monastery at Daphne (Greece) which has no genitals at all.

The parallelism to which my diagram draws attention indicates that whereas Christ is a secondary but sexually inert manifestation of a sexually potent God the Father, Ganesha should be a secondary but sexually inert manifestation of a sexually potent Shiva. It is therefore to the physical and sexual characteristics of Ganesha that we must now turn our attention. The most obvious features of his cult are:

(a) That he is the most widely revered of all Hindu deities, especially in South India.
(b) That his figure shows an obese, effeminate, male, with an elephant's head, and a long flaccid trunk. He has only one tusk but carries the other in his hand. He rides a rat.
(c) His magical names confirm this appearance. They refer to his "twisted trunk," "single tusk," "fawn colored eyes," "elephant face," "pot belly," "moon-like brow." He is "double bodied," "lord of demons," "rider of rats."
(d) He is a Janus trickster, facing both ways. He "causes and removes obstacles," he "withdraws and bestows success," he "ignores and fulfills desires."

Ganesha is seldom treated as a major deity and it is rare to find a major temple of which Ganesha is the principal occupant. But shrines to Ganesha are very numerous. Wilkins quotes Sonnerat, a 19th century authority on Coramandel as follows:

The Indians would not on any account build a house without having placed on the ground an image of this deity which they sprinkle with oil and adorn every day with flowers. They set up his image in all their temples, in the streets and in the high roads and in the open plains at the foot of some tree so that persons of all ranks may invoke him before they undertake any business and travellers worship him before they proceed on any journey.

Myth makes Ganesha into a "clever baby," a clumsy fellow but a trickster who gets his way by ingenuity rather than strength. Since he is the doorkeeper of Shiva's harem we might postulate, even without the details given below, that Ganesha must be either a eunuch or in some other way sexually inadequate. As guardian of the threshold, he is treated as guardian of entrances in general. It is on this account that he is addressed at the beginning of enterprises of all sorts—journeys, constructions, hunts, business adventures, the writing of books. On this last account he is thought of as a God of Wisdom and his *sakti* wives are Siddhi (knowledge) and Buddha (understanding). His portly figure is sometimes attributed to gluttony. Martin suggests that he is intended to resemble a *buniah*, a successful village money lender. Others say that his elephant head and his rodent steed show that he can overcome and penetrate all obstacles. The psychoanalytically inclined might take a more drastic view. In myth, Ganesha's elephant head, like his tusk, is detachable and its monstrous form strongly resembles that of the Greek Priapos. Ganesha was born of Parvati. Priapos was born of Aphrodite, "a child so monstrous with a huge tongue and a mighty belly, a creature excessively phallic, and indeed phallic to the rear ... that she cast him from her ..." Indeed Ganesha's head is strikingly like the obscene little Greek pottery figurine which was the subject of one of Freud's observations. And as to the incongruous rat—well yes, a rat can penetrate even the smallest openings, like Rumpelstiltskin in the fairy tale.

The mythological tales which surround Ganesha's personality are mostly concerned with how he got his elephant's head and how he broke his tusk. A thinly masked theme of castration, mother-love, and sexual frustration pervades all these stories. I give below a selection of these. I also include a few associated myths in which Ganesha himself does not appear.

A. 1—Shiva left home to go hunting. He took all his servants with him. Parvati wished to take a bath, but there was no one to guard the door so she made a guardian out of the dirt from her own body. Shiva, returning, was furious that he was prevented from entering his own house and struck off the head of the guardian, Ganesha. Parvati in turn was furious and ordered her husband to restore Ganesha to life. Shiva could not find the head so replaced it with the head of an elephant which was the first animal that his servants happened to see when they went out into the forest. Thereafter Ganesha became the favorite son of Parvati and Shiva and is above all the guardian of entrances.

A. 2—Ganesha was born from Shiva's head while Shiva was gazing upon the beauty of his *sakti* Uma. This Ganesha was a youth of outstanding beauty endowed with the qualities of Shiva himself. Uma in jealousy put a curse of ugliness upon him so that he acquired an elephant's head and a pot belly.

A. 3—Maha Ishvara (Shiva) is God. Uma his wife lives in his turban because from the turban it is very easy to have sexual intercourse. One day Uma saw a man of great beauty. She had sex relations with the man. When Maha shvara heard of this he was angry and gazed on the man with his third eye. The man was reduced to ashes. Uma craved Maha Ishvara's pardon and begged him to recreate the man. The man was recreated but he was without genitals.

A. 4—One day Uma wanted to go visiting so she made a man to look after the house. When Maha Ishvara came the man would not let him in.

A. 5—Ganesha was the offspring of Shiva and Kali. When Kali first looked at her child its head was burnt to ashes. Shiva sent servants to bring in the head of the first animal they found asleep with its face to the North. This proved to be an elephant. Shiva fixed the elephant head to the child's decapitated body.

B. 1—Vishnu, at Shiva's request, manifested himself as a female, (Mohini). Shiva, enraptured at the sight, had an ejaculation. He caught the divine sperm in his hand. This turned into a *lingam* which was the godling Aiyanar. Mohini changed back into Vishnu.

B. 2—Parasurama (Rama with the Axe) was a manifestation of Vishnu and a devotee of Shiva to whom Shiva gave his magic axe. Parasurama was fifth son of Jamed Agni and his wife, Renuka. Renuka observed an act of copulation and the purity of her mind was sullied with sexual thoughts. Jamed Agni, indignant at his wife's fall from grace, ordered his sons to kill her. The elder sons refused but Parasurama obeyed. For this act of filial piety he was rewarded with invulnerability and a single wish. He wished that his mother be restored to life, forgetful of the past and with a pure mind.

B. 3—Parasurama paid a visit to his lord and master Shiva. The gate was barred by Ganesha. Parasurama and Ganesha fought. Parasurama threw his axe. Ganesha recognized his own father's axe and bowed before it, catching it on his tusk which was immediately severed.

B. 4—The union of Shiva and Parvati was sterile. Vishnu in pity manifested himself as an infant and became their son. The gods assembled to admire this child of outstanding beauty. Sani (Saturn) had neglected the caresses of his wife and he had cursed him, saying that the first child he looked at would be burnt to ashes. Sani attended the gathering of the gods but warned Parvati of the consequences. Parvati resigned herself to fate. Sani looked at the child which was immediately destroyed. At Brahma's behest Parvati was allowed to recreate the child in the deformed Ganesha shape.

C. 1—There was a beautiful mango (*amba*) in the garden. Ganesha and his brother Kataragama (Skanda) both wanted the mango. They were told by their mother to race around a salt sea. Kataragama set off around the sea but Ganesha ran around a salt dish in the kitchen. Ganesha won the mango but Kataragama hit him and broke off his tusk. (The mango, in Ceylon, is an explicit vagina symbol and is one of the main emblems of the mother goddess Pattini. In India, Amba is one of the names of Shiva's *sakti*, more particularly of Durga. It is also the name of one of the semi-divine heroines in the Mahabharata.)

C. 2—Skanda was courting a Vedda Princess (Valli Amma). Ganesha offered to assist. Skanda turned Ganesha into an elephant headed monster who frightened Valli who ran for help to Skanda. Skanda lost the magic formula so Ganesha forever retains his monstrous form.

C. 3—Ganesha and his brother Karttikeya (Skanda) were both courting the same two girls, Siddhi and Buddhi. It was agreed that the brother who could first circumnavigate the world should win the girls. Skanda made the journey, but Ganesha stayed at home and "proved by his logical talents and his aptness for quotation" that he had already completed the journey. Ganesha won the girls who are described as his *sakti*. (This is a North Indian story.)

C. 4—In South India and Ceylon it is said that Ganesha has no wife but that he is sought after by many girls. He refuses them all because he is looking for someone as beautiful as his own mother, Parvati. (Reported by an Indian graduate student, Chicago, 1961.)

D.　—Shiva was too kind and granted remission of sins and final bliss to all who worshiped at his shrine at Somnath. The Gods complained. Parvati created Ganesha so that "he should create obstacles to men and by deluding them will deprive them of all wish to visit Somnath so that they shall fall into Hell." (This story from Western India stresses the "ascetic" aspect of Shiva. I include it here because it displays Ganesha very plainly as a "trickster" who frustrates man's efforts to unite himself with God.)

The "original" versions of most of these stories appear in the Brahma Vaivarta Purana.

In this set of myths a number of familiar Oedipal elements are clearly present but they share another feature to which I would draw attention. In these stories the contrasts of male versus female and of sexuality versus asexuality are employed as binary pairs in such a way as to "mediate a contradiction" in the manner which has been demonstrated for other materials by Lévi-Strauss. This logic of contradiction and mediation can be more readily appreciated if we reduce the stories to a skeletal form as shown below. We shall then see that A 1–5, B 1–4, and C 1–4 form three sets in each of which the paired variables male-female, sexual-asexual, father-son, mother-son, husband-wife, brother-brother are combined and recombined in such a way as to leave the final impression that Ganesha's deformity somehow eliminates the jealousy and hostility implicit in his creation. The stories summarize as follows:

A. 1—Male sexuality (Shiva) is opposed to female sexuality (Parvati). Parvati creates a secondary complete male who separates Shiva and Parvati. Shiva destroys the secondary male and is reunited with Parvati. Ganesha is recreated deformed and unites Shiva and Parvati.

A. 2—Male sexuality (Shiva) is opposed to female sexuality (Uma). Shiva creates a secondary male who separates Shiva and Uma. Parvati reduces the secondary male to a deformity and is reunited with Shiva.

A. 3—Shiva and his *sakti* Uma are united in Shiva's head. A secondary male appears and separates Uma from Shiva. Shiva destroys the secondary male and then recreates him devoid of genitals.

A. 4—Parvati creates a secondary male who replaces Shiva as householder. Shiva reasserts his rights by destroying the secondary male and recreating him as a deformity.

A. 5—The union of Shiva and his *sakti*, Kali, creates a secondary male. Kali destroys the secondary male. Shiva recreates him as a deformity.

B. 1—Male *deva* (Shiva) stands opposed to male *deva* (Vishnu). The association is sterile. Vishnu is replaced by his female equivalent Mohini. The association of Shiva and Mohini produces a new male, a duplicate of Shiva. Mohini then reverts to her male form Vishnu.

B. 2—Male (Shiva) stands opposed to male (Vishnu). Vishnu changes into a youth, Rama, armed with Shiva's axe. Rama, at his father's behest, slays his own mother and restores her to virgin purity.

B. 3—Rama tries to unite with Shiva but is frustrated by a secondary male, Ganesha, who is son of Shiva. Rama "castrates" Ganesha with Shiva's axe and is united with Shiva.

B. 4—Shiva (male) is opposed to Parvati (female). Shiva (male age) is opposed to Vishnu (male youth). Vishnu becomes the son of Shiva and Parvati. This son is destroyed because of the neglect of a husband (Saturn) for his wife's caresses. The deformed Ganesha is created to replace the Vishnu-son.

C. 1—Two brothers (Skanda and Ganesha) are rivals for their mother's love. Skanda fails to achieve his objective through a display of virility. Ganesha achieves his ends by cunning but suffers mutilation at the hands of his rival.

C. 2—A virile brother (Skanda) and a cunning brother (Ganesha) cooperate to gain a woman for Skanda. Ganesha suffers mutilation at the hands of his virile brother.

C. 3—Two brothers are rivals for the love of women. The cunning brother (Ganesha) defeats the virile brother (Skanda).

C. 4—Love for his mother makes Ganesha impotent—(but precisely on that account Ganesha is the most sought-after of mediating deities).

The themes throughout seem quite consistent. The male principle and the female principle stand opposed; a third principle (Ganesha), a kind of impersonalized sexuality, stands in the middle and serves both to unite and to separate. The combination male-plus-female is fertile but if the outcome is a secondary complete male, then jealousy will separate what was united. The alternative male-plus-male is sterile, and the two males will be jealous over the possession of women. The myth offers a "resolution" of the paradox. If male unites with female to produce a sterile offspring then the latter will serve as a mediation between the sexes instead of a source of hostility. The "man in the middle" must be either no sex at all or both sexes in alternation. As I have indicated, the Greek parallels are very close.

But all this refers to the prototype figure Ganesha. What becomes of Ganesha when he is transferred, in the guise of Pulleyar, to the inappropriate surroundings of Buddhist Sinhalese culture in Northern Ceylon?

First, I must make it clear that in the Nuvarakalaviya village we are discussing, Pulleyar is not thought of as the son of Shiva at all. In a vague way it is no doubt well known that Pulleyar is "the same as" the Tamil Pillaiyar and that Pillaiyar is the same as Ganesha but, so far as my Sinhalese villagers were concerned, Pulleyar was really a god in his own right. He is the elephant Lord of the Forest. He is a sort of independent baron among the deities, which is appropriate, since in the old days Nuvarakalaviya was the territory of an independent human baron who paid scant respect to his theoretical overlord, the Sinhalese king. When my villagers made a shrine to Pulleyar he was represented by a *lingam* shaped stone on which was painted an elephant's head.

In this representation, Pulleyar had both his tusks intact. There may be some doubt about whether the orthodox Ganesha is a eunuch, but there is no doubt at all that the Nuvarakalaviya Pulleyar is in very full possession of his sexual powers.

But let me return to my earlier point. We need to look at the Sinhalese situation not as a mixture of Hindu and Buddhist elements but as a system in its own right, which is different from, but comparable to, the South Indian system. In the South Indian conception Shiva and Ganesha are associated as father and son; the father representing potency, the son representing mediation. Ganesha is a gatekeeper like St. Peter rather than a God in his own right. In the Sinhalese conception Shiva is absent but Buddha and Pulleyar are associated. What then is this association between Buddha and Pulleyar, and how does it compare with the Shiva-Ganesha, father-son, relationship of the Indian structure?

We need to remember that from an historical point of view Buddhism originally developed as a reformist sect within the body of Hinduism and that South Indian Saivite Hinduism is the result of a counter-reformation away from Buddhism. Modern Hinduism and Modern Theravada Buddhism share a great deal of common ideology. For example, the notion that death is ordinarily followed by rebirth and the supplementary notion that it is desirable to escape from this endless cycle of rebirths by achieving Nirvana —that is, by the extinction of individuality— both occur in both systems of belief.

In orthodox Buddhist theology, the Buddha was a supremely enlightened human being whose wisdom gives his sayings the authority of a messenger of God. But the Buddha himself is not a god; and Buddhist orthodoxy regards the very notion of god as an unnecessary illusion.

The philosophic subtleties of this Hindu and Buddhist concept of illusion (*maya*) need not detain us. My point is that, because the orthodox Buddha is an enlightened human being and not a deity, he is, properly speaking, a mediator between Man and the Infinite and not a source of divine power. In terms of my diagrammatic schema he should be placed in the middle column along with the Virgin Mary, Jesus Christ and Ganesha, Lord of Entrances.

From this point of view it is quite appropriate that the Buddha, who mediates between death and the next life should have a counterpart who mediates between the previous life and birth. And it is appropriate that just as the cult of the Buddha lays stress on the ascetic, the sexless, the repudiation of emotion, the cult of his counterpart should be concerned with sex and fertility. One aspect of the relation between Pulleyar and the Lord Buddha is then that Pulleyar is a *devata* of birth, while the Buddha is a *devata* of death. (Diagram, Section C.)

But that is only part of the story. The orthodox theological view that the Buddha is an example of enlightenment and not a god is far too difficult for the ordinary imagination of the ordinary Sinhalese villager. In village practice, as distinct from orthodox theory, the Buddha is unquestionably the supreme God. His images are objects which are potent of themselves and must be venerated at all times, not simply on special ritual occasions. The Buddha represents authority, not mediation. In these circumstances the role of mediator, that is of a secondary deity who can "fix things," which in orthodox theory should belong to the Buddha, is filled by a variety of godlings of the type I have labelled *devata*. In Nuvarakalaviya the chief of these are Pulleyar and his elder brother Aiyanar (Diagram, Section D). Buddhist rituals and *devata* rituals are meshed in together roughly as follows:

BUDDHIST RITUALS

The calendar is specified by Buddhist rites. Each quarter day of the moon (*poya*) should be the occasion for Buddhist devotions as with the Christian Sunday. This is a matter to which the younger members of the community pay scant attention. Buddha's birthday (*Wesak*) is New Years Day. This determines the date of sowing for the Yala cultivation season and hence fixes the whole agricultural calendar. The ritual restrictions of *Vas* (the Buddhist Lent) end with a ceremony called *Katina Pinkama* at which the local Buddhist priest is presented with a new robe. This comes at the end of harvest and part of the ritual plays on the theme that harvested grain is "dead" seed which must be buried to be born again.

Apart from these calendar festivals the great majority of Buddhist rituals belongs to a category covered by the word *pirit*, which denotes a form of magical exorcism and purification. It is believed that the recital of the Buddhist scriptures in proper form is itself sufficient to drive away evil influences. *Pirit* type ceremonies are particularly prominent in the weeks following a death, but they may also be held in connection with an illness, a

wedding, the building of a new house, the dedication of a new temple, the ceremony when a baby takes its first solid food and so on. In short, *pirit* is a purificatory threshold ceremony. The occasions on which the recital of Buddhist scriptures are used in this magical way are very much the same as those on which it would be appropriate, in South India, to invoke the threshold deity Ganesha.

The *pirit* type rituals of mortuary ceremonial are of special importance. These resemble both in form and function the Hindu rite of obsequies known as *sraddha*. In *sraddha* the heirs of the deceased provide food for kinsmen and Brahman priests; in mortuary *pirit* the heirs provide food for kinsmen and Buddhist monks.

It is an inescapable fact that Village Buddhism concentrates a tremendous weight of attention upon the phenomenon of death. It is a cult which exploits the belief that comfort in the next life will depend upon moral virtue in this one and it is therefore a cult which directs its appeal to the elderly. Young and vigorous people have little use for Buddhist ritual; it is only when men and women begin to feel that they must prepare for death that they start to carry out the eight ritual duties which are theoretically prescribed for all.

There is nothing in the least ambiguous about this interest in morbidity. The main shrine of a Buddhist temple—the *dagoba*—is a tomb raised over the relics of some deceased Buddha or Buddhist saint. These relics are spoken of as *dhattu*, seeds, and the idea is that although they are but dead bones placed in the ground they will in due course sprout again and give forth life. Within the temple itself the figures of the Buddha are passive in contemplation; the Buddha is shown seated and motionless or else asleep. Outside the temple within the temple courtyard there is a Bo tree, a sacred fig, the characteristic of which is that it is immortal. In short, a Buddhist temple is a place where the worshiper goes to sit quietly and contemplate on the fact that death is but a welcome rest and that life itself is endless.

It is because this death-focused Lord Buddha is so remote from day-to-day personal affairs that the villagers feel themselves free to transfer their devout attentions to the local *devata*. Despite their obvious Hindu affiliations, worship of the *devata* is not treated as sacrilegious by the Buddhist monks. The monks simply say that the *devata* are the servants of the Lord Buddha and so long as the villagers are ready to admit this, the monks will not interfere.

DEVATA RITUALS

Whereas, in this area, the principal annual Buddhist festivals, *Wesak* and *Katina Pinkama*, synchronize with the beginning of a Yala cultivation period and the end of a Yala harvest, the principal *devata* festivals, *Mutti Mangalaya* and *New Rice*, are timed for the period when the rice is green and in ear and for the beginning of harvest respectively. They relate to living crops rather than to dead seed. But apart from these occasions, Pulleyar, as distinct from the other *devata*, receives a great deal of special attention. It is Pulleyar who makes women and cattle pregnant, who assures bountiful crops, who gives success in hunting, who heals sick children. And it is especially Pulleyar who may be consulted through the vehicle of a medium priest (*kapurala*) concerning the outcome of village quarrels, lawsuits and so on. I observed that private ceremonials took place at the Pulleyar *kovil* every few days, whereas the rituals at the Buddha *vihare* and at the *devale* of the other *devata* were reserved for formal occasions.

The symbols of Pulleyar were *lingam*-shaped phallic objects which in India would be more appropriate to Shiva than to Ganesha. Except when mediumistic trance seances were involved, the actual rites of Pulleyar were broadly similar to those made at Buddhist shrines. Buddhist devotees offered flowers and to a lesser extent vegetable foods. Pulleyar devotees offered food rather than flowers. But here we may note a contrast. Contact with the Buddha shrine gives the offerings the pollution of death and feces so they are later thrown away. Contact with the Pulleyar shrine makes the food magically beneficial to humans and it is usually consumed by children.

In some situations contact with Pulleyar is achieved directly, for when the *kapurala* priest goes into a trance he is thought to speak with the voice of Pulleyar himself. Here the contrast between Buddha and Pulleyar is exact. The priests of the Buddha are yellow-robed monks who from an early age live a life cut off from the ordinary world. Their whole training is concentrated on the avoidance of emotion; they achieve enlightenment by detachment from the tribulations of the ordinary world. They are, as it were, men who, among the living, are already half dead. They are revered as the dead are revered; they are admired but not loved.

In contrast, the typical priest of Pulleyar (or Aiyanar) is a medium who has learned how to go into ecstatic trances. Where the Buddhist priest wears his head shaved and moves always at a sedate steady pace, the Pulleyar priest wears his hair in long pigtails and achieves a state of ecstasy by violent dancing. The Buddhist priest bridges the gap between this world and the next by moving himself half way into the next world. The medium priest of Pulleyar bridges the same gap by bringing the deity himself into this world. The Pulleyar priest, a human being, becomes incarnate of his deity and manifests his power visibly for the congregation to see.

To summarize, these details are consistent with a binary antithesis: Pulleyar is what Buddha is not:

On the one hand we have the Buddha cult— the concern of the elderly, asceticism, contemplation of death, absence of emotion, polluted food offerings.

On the other hand we have the Pulleyar cult —the concern of the young, ecstasy, preoccupation with fertility and sex, food offerings fit for children.

But we should notice also how the qualities of this Nuvarakalaviya Pulleyar differ from those of his historical prototype Ganesha. Ganesha is seemingly a eunuch in contrast to his virile father Shiva. Nuvarakalaviya Pulleyar is sexually potent in contrast to the ascetic Buddha.

At the same time, although the Pulleyar cult and the Buddha cult stand opposed as ecstasy and asceticism are opposed, they are also integrated as part of one system. The monks insist that Pulleyar is a servant of the Lord Buddha; the force of this was brought home to me when I learned that the local *Kapurala*, the medium priest of Pulleyar, worked as a personal servant for the local Buddhist monk (*Bhikku*). (Diagram, Section D.)

Let us compare this structure with that of the Christian Holy Family and the Saivite Holy Family, remembering that, in the Nuvarakalaviya situation, there is no mother goddess—no equivalent of either Parvati or of the Virgin Mary; the role contrast is based simply upon the sexuality or asexuality of males. In Christianity, sexuality is kept in the background and described as Holy Spirit, the potency of God the Father; Mary, the

Mother, remains a virgin; Jesus is a sexless, effeminate figure. In South Indian Saivite Hinduism, sexuality is a central theme and is the main attribute of God the Father, and also of Parvati, the Goddess Mother; Ganesha, the son, is again an effeminate figure—a castrated male.

In Nuvarakalaviya, Buddha is treated as God but retains his characteristic of the supreme ascetic, sexless and devoid of emotion; there is no mother goddess; Pulleyar, the son, becomes the essence of sexuality. Whereas Ganesha has only one tusk but carries the other in his hand, Pulleyar has both tusks intact; he is moreover the source of fertility in women, in crops and among animals.

As between Christianity and the Sinhalese situation the contrast seems complete: God the Father is sexual—Jesus is sexless; Buddha is sexless—Pulleyar is sexual.

Yet again in certain other respects the Christian and the Sinhalese patterns are similar. In both cases it is God the son who is the friend of the children and in both cases God the son is only a secondary divinity, a mediator between the other world and this. Furthermore, Pulleyar (Ganesha) is, like Jesus Christ, the slain "Son of God" who has been restored to life.

In these two patterns, the European Christian and the North Sinhalese Buddhist, the same set of ideas appear, though arranged in a different fashion. We have various contrasts, the contrast between the authority of virility and the authority of age. The contrast between the mystery of creative life and the horror of destructive death. The common need for some deity who is a divinity in something less than a complete sense so that he or she can bridge the gap between the other world and this world, and again the common element of filiation, of parenthood and sonship, as a symbol for the representation of this bridge.

But as between Christianity and Sinhalese Buddhism the different and contradictory aspects of deity are differently distributed between the symbolic figures of the trinity. Arbitrary power which, for the Christian, is an attribute of God the Father, appears in the Sinhalese story as an aspect of "God the Son," the unpredictable elephant lord of the forest. But the passive ascetism of the suffering Christ is here an aspect of Buddha, supreme lord, who replaces Shiva, the God and Father of the Hindu trinity.

I would draw particular attention to the fact that the most typical devotional act in Buddhism is to sit in quiet contemplation within the *Vihare* precincts and ponder on the close approach of death, while the most characteristic ritual activity in the Pulleyar-*devata* cult is to invoke the presence of Pulleyar himself in the person of a trance-bound medium.

These are complementary aspects of a single idea and I suggest that the passive and active elements in divine worship are always complementary in this way, for always the active ecstatic element involves the notion that God comes down to earth, while the passive ascetic behavior implies that man reaches up to heaven. I think too that these two complementary types of religious behavior are nearly always found in close association.

On one hand, supernatural power seems to be located in the other world of the dead, so that we can reach that power only through the practice of asceticism and the appeal to ascetic, sexless, mediating divinities. On the other hand, supernatural power seems to be located here in this world and is manifested in the mystery of creative fertility. This latter kind of potency implies the existence of deities who are close at hand, sexually vigorous, ecstatic. The theologians may devise their elaborate theoretical systems and (in terms of theology) the Lord Buddha may be far removed from any Hindu god, but Buddhism alone is not a practical religion. Ordinary human beings cannot sustain at all times a totally ascetic view of the relation between man and God. In practice (as opposed to theory) every religious system is made up of complementary behaviors. Holidays are mixed with holy days, feasts are mixed with fasts. Indeed these pairs of words are one and the same.

I think I may be able to pull this together by going back to the beginning. The ordinary members of a religious congregation are not greatly concerned with the subtleties of theology. What matters is that their total religious ideology should seem to them consistent. In the religions of the West consistency is provided by the Book which incorporates the whole body of sacred dogma. In the East consistency is provided by the totality of symbols The theology is not consistent. One of the major functions of religion is to provide man with reassurance in the face of threatened danger. In active life he needs to be assured that life will go on, that sickness and threatened dangers will not succeed. But in old age Man needs to be reconciled with his inevitable fate; the fearfulness of death must be eliminated. It is perfectly logical that these two concerns of religious activity —the maintenance of life and the reconciliation with death—should be separated out and emphasized as separate sets of ritual.

So I come back to my title and my original question. Is this usefully considered a situation of syncretism at all? Are we concerned here with a merging of different religious ideas or is it just one particular manifestation of a complex of ideas which appears in a great variety of religious systems and even within the sacred precincts of the psychoanalyst's consulting room?

R. G. Willis

THE HEAD AND THE LOINS: LÉVI-STRAUSS AND BEYOND

R. G. Willis's paper, on a myth of a Bantu people of Africa, is both an excellent piece of analysis and a pertinent critique of Lévi-Strauss's methods for deriving binary discriminations in mythical thought. One of the most justifiable and frequently voiced criticisms of Lévi-Strauss's work is that the binary oppositions or discriminations which he claims to be the fundamental logical categories of mythical thought are in fact extremely difficult to verify or replicate with concrete ethnographic data. Some have suggested that this "intuitive flaw" makes his conceptual formulations extremely vulnerable to common, "grass-roots" ethnographic facts (Maybury-Lewis and others in Hayes and Hayes, 1970, and Leach, 1967). Willis contends that binary discriminations in Fipa myth do have empirical referents in Fipa social life, and that without these concrete social facts, a Lévi-Straussian structural analysis of Fipa mythology might amount to no more than a "passionless structure of remote and mathematical beauty." Far from rejecting Lévi-Strauss's concepts, Willis uses and enriches them with ethnographic and affective data from Fipa social life. His paper may serve, therefore, as an object lesson to many who are stimulated and fascinated by the French professor's formulations, but who nevertheless remain skeptical of them. Willis has demonstrated that constructive skepticism of Lévi-Strauss and solid ethnographic data go very well together.

Reprinted from *Man*, II (1967), 519–534, by permission of the author and the Royal Anthropological Institute of Great Britain and Ireland.

This article examines, in a central African context, the relation between myth and social organization. This is a question which has been raised implicitly but acutely by the recent work of Lévi-Strauss (1964). The development of the analytical exposition of Amerindian mythology in *Le cru et le cuit* strongly suggests that the structural solidity for the analyst of mythological thought varies inversely with its distance from ethnographical reality: the more remote its connexion with observable social facts, the more substantial it can be shown to be, and vice versa. By contrast, this article attempts to show how the analysis of mythological thought, which is intrinsically paradoxical and elusive, *can* be accommodated within the normal parameters of social anthropological investigation. The subject is a myth collected among the Fipa of south-west Tanzania.

MYTH AND MYTH-MAKERS
The Fipa are a Bantu people fairly distantly related linguistically to the Bemba. They inhabit a high, rolling and largely treeless plateau near the south end of Lake Tanganyika, which forms the western boundary of their country; another lake, Rukwa, marks

the easterly limit of Fipa territory. The people live in compact village settlements and numbered 86,462 at the last census in 1957. In the middle of the Fipa plateau there is a mountain called Itweelele which is the centre of a small kingdom (or chiefdom) about four miles in diameter called Milansi; this tiny kingdom is supposed to be the oldest and original source of authority in Ufipa (the name given to the land of the Fipa). Traditionally Ufipa was further divided into two kingdoms ruled by rival but related dynasties called Twa; these two kingdoms, Nkansi and Lyangalile, are supposed to have been one in the earliest days. The origin of Twa power and its relation to the aboriginal kingdom of Milansi form the subject of the myth to be considered.

The story appears several times in early writings of the colonial period about the Fipa —an indication of its central importance as an embodiment of the Fipa sense of their own identity. I collected a number of different versions of this key myth, some of the variations in which corresponded to the differing, and sometimes opposed, political interests of focal groups in Fipa society (Willis, 1964); all versions, however, possessed the same common structure, which is typified in the following (translated) text which I collected in 1964 from an illiterate old man:

There were once three sisters who came from a far country in search of somewhere to settle. They reached Ufipa from the east and went round the western part of the country. After walking for a long time they at length reached a hillock and they said to themselves, "Let us rest here." One of the women sat down on a rock, another on the ground and a third was holding a red fruit called isuku. *The one who was holding the fruit* isuku *became known as the Child of Isuku, the one who was sitting on the ground was called Earth-Person and the one who sat on the rock as the Child of the Stone.*

Meanwhile the king of Milansi said one day to his wife: "Something is going to happen to us before long. If certain strange people come here be sure not to give them my royal stool, even if they say, 'Give it to us.' If you do they will take away our kingdom."

Soon afterwards he went into the wilderness to hunt, spending the night out there. The three women meanwhile had arrived at the place called Kanda, where even today you can see their footprints. Not long afterwards they arrived at Itweelele mountain, the home of the king of the Fipa. There they were met by the queen, his wife, and they said to her, "Give us stools so that we may sit down."

The queen took out one stool and the leader of the three women passed it on to her younger sister; she then produced another and the leader passed it on to

her elder sister, saying, "I don't want that one but the king's own stool: bring it to me."

The queen refused. Then the strange woman entered the hut herself and finally overbore the queen so that she was obliged to surrender the royal stool. Taking it, the stranger said, "This country is mine: may the people live long." Then the three sisters sat down.

Meanwhile the king, where he was in the wilderness, heard a buzzing noise in his ears and knew it meant that the long-awaited strangers had arrived. Straight away he returned to the royal village, and when he reached it he met the three sisters. They greeted one another with all courtesy, then the king went inside his hut with his wife.

"O wife, what did I tell you?" he said. "Did I not warn you against giving my royal stool to the strangers? Now they have taken the kingdom from us."

Next morning the three regal sisters said to the king, "Let us go to the top of the mountain, so that you may show us the limits of your domain." Now it happened that the king had allowed his under-arm hair to grow very long, and, when they reached the summit, he felt ashamed of exhibiting it to the three women. So he kept his arm low, and said, "My country ends just there."

"Why, his country extends only as far as the mountain!" the three women said, and their leader stood erect and pointed, saying, "My rule extends from Lake Tanganyika in the west to Lake Rukwa in the east; and from Unyamwanga in the south to Lyamfipa [an escarpment at the northern end of the Fipa plateau] in the north!"

So it was that the rule of the Twa began in Ufipa; and the king of Milansi remained as priest of Itweelele, the sacred mountain.

This is a moving and a tragic tale. Considered purely as a story, as entertainment (which is why Fipa like to tell and hear it) it is effective for much the same reasons that *Hamlet* and *Cinderella* are effective as stories: because its form is psychologically arresting and satisfying. In the Fipa myth an initial situation of conflict is brought to a climax (and note how artfully the tension is prolonged and heightened during the episode with the stools); the inevitable moment of triumph and tragedy occurs when the strange and majestic woman asserts her claim to sovereignty over the country of Fipa, in a way that (as we know already) must compel acceptance by the established king: she performs the symbolic act of sitting on the royal stool of Milansi.

So the Twaci (the feminine form of Twa) have conquered. What happens now? Here the story surprises us with an unexpected "twist": the king returns, sees and knows he has lost, in spite of all his efforts to avoid such a consummation—and he accepts his fate with calm and dignity, royally in fact. In his defeat, the king establishes his *moral superiority* over the aggressive intruders, a superiority which is given formal recognition later in the Twa acceptance of the permanent rule of the king and his line over Milansi and the sacred mountain of Itweelele, and his perpetual priesthood. This surprising development recreates, on another and higher plane, the initial situation of opposition and tension between Milansi and Twa.

The final episode, the ascent of the mountain and the demarcation of the two, territorially unequal, kingdoms of Milansi and the Twa, introduces a new affective element into the story—that of comedy: like us, Fipa find the incident of the under-arm hair amusing. In this episode too, the king gives further evidence of his social self-control: his sense of shame (*insoni*) over his inappropriate growth of hair leads him to sacrifice a claim he might still have made to a wider territorial sovereignty, for the story implies that Milansi's domain originally embraced the whole country. The final irony is that the king himself, by his own action, effectively cedes the land of Fipa to the strangers, at the same time as he, seemingly, makes a claim to the central core of his old kingdom—a claim which is almost contemptuously granted by the Twaci women, interested as they are in real power.

In thus summarizing and interpreting the story, we have encountered its most obvious structural characteristic, one which it shares with most, if not all, members of the genus "story": an initial situation, in which two basic elements or factors are brought into relation, unfolds, as it were in spiral form, through successive stages of crisis, partial resolution, renewed crisis, and final reformulation. The concluding resolution contains latent ambiguities (Did the king really mean to give away the country or does it still belong to him? Did the Twaci recognition of Milansi's authority over the sacred mountain mean that the Twa think of the king of Milansi as their superior? Or is Milansi really Twa territory and the king there as a political dependant? etc.) which gives the effect of continuing the dialectical "spiral" indefinitely, and accounts for the story's "timeless" quality.

Obviously too, the existence of contradictions which the narrative appears to resolve but succeeds only in transforming into new and latent contradictions, relates to the func-

tion of the story as what Malinowski (1948: 120) called a "sociological charter"—a retrospective justification and validation for an existing and rather complex social order, in which there is inherent and fundamental inner conflict.

This article is principally concerned to reveal and analyze the configuration of opposed, complementary and associated ideas and values which Fipa see as contained in the basic situation of the sovereignty myth: the relation of Milansi and Twa. Through what I call its "conceptual-affective structure," itself formed from the basic "bricks" of mythological thought—sets of binary discriminations—the myth, I shall argue, both reflects and maintains the formal similarity of two apparently disparate dimensions of Fipa society: sovereignty and descent.

To begin with, let us return to the manifest subject of the myth, the kingdoms of Milansi and the Twa. These two foci of Fipa concepts and values are linked in a relation of complementary opposition which inheres in the fact that they represent two qualitatively different and incommensurate kinds of sovereignty (ritual and political, respectively); that nevertheless they are interdependent (the Twa derive their legitimacy, their right to rule, from Milansi; Milansi in turn depends upon Twa power, on the ability of the Twa administrative-military apparatus to maintain Ufipa as a political entity); and that both terms, Milansi and Twa, have attributes implying superiority *and* inferiority vis-à-vis the other: Milansi is the ritual superior of the Twa, but its political and territorial inferior; Milansi is the senior kingdom, but strength, in the form of organized coercive force, is all on the side of the Twa.

The more important concepts associated with the Milansi-Twa relation, and their differential value-loading, are summarized in the following diagram, in which a double-headed arrow represents a relation of complementary opposition and "plus" and "minus" signs represent relative values:

MILANSI   TWA

Ritual authority $(+)\leftrightarrow$ Ritual dependency $(-)$
Political dependency $(-)\leftrightarrow$ Political supremacy $(+)$
Seniority $(+)\leftrightarrow$ Juniority $(-)$
Lack of power $(-)\leftrightarrow$ Possession of power $(+)$

More abstractly, the opposition and combination of differentially-valued concepts in the Milansi-Twa relation could be represented as follows:

$$\left\{ \begin{matrix} + \leftrightarrow - \\ - \leftrightarrow + \end{matrix} \right\}$$

These conceptual oppositions are entirely explicit in the minds of all Fipa who concern themselves with such matters. Thus the reigning king of Nkansi, the northern and larger of the two Twa "states," said to me of the king of Milansi, "He is our priest." At the same time he objected to my referring to the latter personage by the title "*Mweene,*" implying political sovereignty, and said he should be called *i Waku Milansi,* "the one of Milansi," on the model of titles given to subordinate administrators in the Twa kingdoms. For his part, the present king of Milansi, Catakwa Mauto, told me that the whole of Ufipa was "his" country, and the Twa ultimately derived their authority from him.

DESCENT: "HEAD" AND "LOINS"

If we now turn from the Fipa conceptual scheme of sovereignty to another social dimension, that of descent, we encounter a further system of ideas. It will be argued that there is a formal similarity amounting to structural congruence between this idea-system and that associated with sovereignty.

Fipa conceptualize descent, experienced as a complex of consanguineal, marital and affinal relations, in terms of two composite symbols: "head" (*unntwe*) and "loins" (*unnsana*). At the most abstract level, "head" stands for the organizing and controlling function or aspect of the most inclusive Fipa descent group or category, the *uluko*, with its elected chief, the *umweenekasi,* and its network of reciprocal rights and duties binding members together; the symbol "head" evokes the *uluko* as a formal and continuing entity. The symbol "loins," at a similarly abstract level, evokes for Fipa the *uluko* in its regenerative and developmental capacities and functions: the descent group as a changing entity, in reciprocal relationship, through exchange of women and bridewealth, with the world outside it.

Less abstractly, "head" is associated with masculinity or maleness, patrilineality, paternity, intellect and authority and "loins" with femininity or femaleness, matrilineality, maternity, sexuality and reproduction. In terms of social categories, and consistently with these abstract associations, "head"

denotes patrilateral relatives and "loins" denotes matrilateral relatives; these are ego-centred categories.

At the most concrete level, the two symbols refer, as the English terms used to translate them imply, to distinct and separate regions or parts of the human body. The literal meaning of *unntwe* is "head," in the physiological sense; but although I translate *unnsana* as "loins," this is not an exact equivalent. Physiologically *unnsana* refers to the lower abdomen and lower back in both men and women; it adjoins, though it does not include, the genital regions in both sexes. Even so the word *unnsana* has marked sexual associations for Fipa, probably because complete control of the muscles of this region is considered a prerequisite of erotic maturity; it is the object of a style of ventral dancing called *imiteete,* which is taught to pubescent girls and which boys imitate, to facilitate such control.

"Head" and "loins" then are foci for sets of ideas from markedly different areas and levels of experience within the world of Fipa descent: they are what Turner calls "dominant symbols" (1964: 35, 50).

But not only do these two symbols separately focus and englobe clusters of ideas, but these ideas are themselves polarized in oppositional pairs analogously to the relation of complementary opposition between the "dominant" or "key" symbols, "head" and "loins." Some of these concepts have already been mentioned. They include, for example, "maleness" ("head"), which is opposed to "femaleness" ("loins"), "intellect" ("head") opposed to "sexuality" ("loins") and "authority" ("head") opposed to "reproduction" ("loins"); from the latter opposition (authority versus reproduction) is derived that between "seniority" ("head") and "juniority" ("loins"). To the first terms in all these pairs Fipa give a relatively higher value, so that this cluster of concepts can be represented in the following way:

"HEAD" $\leftrightarrow$ "LOINS"
$$(+) \left\{ \begin{matrix} \text{maleness} \leftrightarrow \text{femaleness} \\ \text{intellect} \leftrightarrow \text{sexuality} \\ \text{authority} \leftrightarrow \text{reproduction} \\ \text{seniority} \leftrightarrow \text{juniority} \end{matrix} \right\} (-)$$

But this is far from being the whole story. In another cluster of polarized concepts associated respectively with "head" and "loins" the relative value-loading is reversed. For, as Fipa see it, "weight," "numbers," "strength" and "fellowship" are associated with *unnsana*, "loins"; and "lightness," "few-ness," "weakness" and "constraint" are the corresponding attributes of *unntwe*, "head." A well known Fipa proverb says, "The loins are heavy, the head is light" (*Uk' unnsana kwanwama, uk'unntwe kwapepela*): it is the women who come into the descent group, the *unnsana* side, Fipa says, who make the *uluko* strong. Another proverb contrasts the "meat" associated with "loins" with its entire lack on the "head" side: in the huts of his mother and her siblings a man can expect food and friendship while the father and his siblings are supposed to be far less forthcoming. To the father's sister (*imaangu seenje*) is attributed a power of lethal cursing over her brother's children.

We thus have a further cluster of conceptual pairs associated with the dominant symbols "head" and "loins" and which is relatively valued in the opposite sense from the first cluster:

"HEAD" ↔ "LOINS"

$$(-)\begin{cases} \text{lightness} \leftrightarrow \text{heaviness} \\ \text{fewness} \leftrightarrow \text{numbers} \\ \text{weakness} \leftrightarrow \text{strength} \\ \text{constraint} \leftrightarrow \text{fellowship} \end{cases}(+)$$

The complementary opposition of the dominant symbols "head" and "loins" is thus characterized by a contrary valuation of some of the most important pairs of subordinate and associated concepts. From our consideration of the meaning for Fipa of the descent-based symbolism of "head" and "loins" there thus emerges a picture of a conceptual-affective structure which could be most abstractly represented as follows:

$$\begin{cases} + \leftrightarrow - \\ - \leftrightarrow + \end{cases}$$

This is the same representation as that derived from our analysis of the manifest meaning of the sovereignty myth.

EXPLICIT AND IMPLICIT PATTERNS

Empiricist critics of structural analysis in anthropology often raise the question—frequently with justice, no doubt—of how far the "pattern" elicited in any particular case reflects the thinking of the people being analyzed; coupled with this question there is usually the implication that the "structure" supposedly revealed is, to a greater or lesser extent, a creation of the analyst, who has arbitrarily imposed an order of his own on the ethnographical material. This accusation

lurks behind the charge of "formalism" frequently levelled against Lévi-Strauss (cf. Yalman, 1967). In dealing with the Fipa material I have sought, on purely methodological grounds, to avoid this pitfall for the unwary structuralist: as far as the main argument is concerned, I have confined myself to sets of complementary oppositions which are perfectly explicit in Fipa thinking. Having made what I hope can be accepted as a *prima facie* case for the existence of a structural congruence between the idea-systems associated respectively with sovereignty and with descent, I feel the more justified in going on to strengthen that case with evidence from less clearly formulated areas of Fipa thought.

In dealing with this material, a regularity of another kind emerges: a conceptual opposition that is implicit in one dimension—sovereignty or descent—is always explicit in the other, as in the following examples.

1. Male(ness)—female(ness). This complementary opposition is explicit in the descent context. A Fipa who is asked for his descent name "on the head side" (*uk'unntwe*) will reply with a name he inherits from his father and which is transmitted patrilineally; asked for his name "on the loins side" (*uk'unnsana*), he will mention one of another category of names which he inherits from his mother. But the same opposition is also implicit at the level of sovereignty: the dynasty of Milansi was founded by a *man*, while the Twa trace their origin to a *woman*. The intrinsic maleness of Milansi may be seen in the fact that all the rulers recorded in oral tradition and including the present incumbent have been men, whereas women, as well as men, have at various times ruled in the two Twa kingdoms of Nkansi and Lyangalile.

2. Up—down. This relation is explicit, as a fact of geography, in the political dimension. Milansi, the royal village of the kingdom of the same name, is and always has been—according to tradition—situated on the slopes of Itweelele, the sacred mountain. The royal villages of the Twa, on the other hand, have always been situated at one point or another on the Fipa plateau—never on a mountain. That is to say, Milansi is recognized by Fipa as being "up" or "high," in relation to the centres of Twa power, which are "down" or "low." An analogous relation is implicit in Fipa conceptualization of the principles of descent and derives from the physiological model of the two symbolic terms, "head" and "loins": in the human body, in its normal

erect posture, "head" is "up" or "high" and "loins" are "down" or "low."

3. Fixed—moving. Here again the oppositional relation is explicit between Milansi and the Twa. The royal village of Milansi is and always has been geographically fixed; but the location of Twa royal villages, up to the colonial period, was frequently changing— Twa rulers sometimes changed the site of their capitals several times during the course of a single reign. Again an analogous relation is implicit in the context of descent and inheres in the fact that Fipa marriage is predominantly virilocal: it is men, the "head" side in descent terms, who stay put, while women, the "loins" side, move.

MYTHS AND "MYTHICAL THINKING"

Although Lévi-Strauss has so much to tell us about myths, he does not explicitly define the concept "myth." Instead, he seems to proffer an implied "operational" definition, which would take some such form as: "myths are linguistic phenomena characterized by a multi-dimensional structure of binary oppositions; separate myths can be shown by analysis to form transformation groups in which constituent elements and oppositions in different myths are reciprocally complementary." It is also characteristic of myth and "mythical thinking," according to Lévi-Strauss, that the number of structural dimensions in any myth, and the number of myths in a transformation group, are in principle unlimited: in this way myths produced by societies widely separated in space (and presumably also, in time) can be shown to be related, and to illuminate one another.

On these terms, and without committing ourselves at this stage on the "logical status" (Yalman, 1967: 86) of Lévi-Strauss's analytical framework, the thinking of the Fipa would appear to conform well enough to the Lévi-Straussian formalization of the "mythical." The two idea-systems considered in this article, the first derived from analysis of the sovereignty myth, and the second from analysis of Fipa notions about descent, can be shown, by following standard Lévi-Straussian procedure, to form a single "transformation group."

To begin with, certain elements—oppositional pairs—in these two systems are common to both: e.g., seniority versus juniority; and up versus down. Other pairs in the two idea-systems, Milansi-Twa and "head"-"loins" appear on analysis to be analogues of

one another and therefore capable of reciprocal transformation, thus:

SYSTEM 1	SYSTEM 2
Milansi	"head"
ritual authority ⟷	authority—intellect
territorial inferiority ⇆	"lightness"
weakness ⟷	"fewness"

SYSTEM 1	SYSTEM 2
Twa	"loins"
political power (= proliferation of offices ⟷	sexuality—reproduction
territorial superiority ⇆	"heaviness"
strength ⟷	"numbers"

Moreover, if we now return to our point of departure, the Fipa sovereignty myth, it can be seen to be rich in clues and references to an underlying system of binary discriminations in the best Lévi-Straussian tradition. Thus the version given here associates a fruit called *isuku* with one of the Twaci women, who is called Mwaana Kasuku (*isuku* and *Kasuku* are derived from the Fipa word for "redness," *ukasuke*). Ethnographical evidence shows that the colours red and white are symbolically significant for Fipa. The Twa rulers of the country were traditionally buried in a red ox-skin; and red, being associated with blood, was a symbol of war and violence: men painted red marks on their faces before going into battle. Red is therefore particularly appropriate as the colour of the Twaci women (in some versions of the myth they are themselves said to have been of reddish hue), the bringers of change and war to the originally simple and peaceful land of the Fipa.

The colour white, on the other hand, is symbolic of spiritual power for Fipa and hence appropriate to Milansi, the ritual capital of Ufipa. In another sense white is appropriate to Milansi as the guardian of peace, as opposed to the turbulent Twa. In the sphere of descent, spiritual authority is also attributed to the *umweenekasi*, the head of the *uluko*, whose duty it is to mediate with the ancestral spirits on behalf of his group.

Returning to the myth again, another of the Twaci women is called Earth-Person (*Unnsi*); this association of Twa with the earth naturally suggests to anyone acquainted with the Lévi-Straussian idiom that Milansi might, by way of opposition, be associated with the sky: and sure enough, Fipa tradition says that Milansi "fell with the earth" from the sky at the beginning of time (Willis, 1964)—and the same is said of the first king of Milansi, Ntatakwa. In similar vein, the name of the third Twaci woman, "Child of the Stone," could be seen as belonging to the same oppositional group, with "stone" as metonymous for "earth."

Perhaps enough has now been said to indicate that Fipa notions about sovereignty and descent belong to a wider cosmological pattern of dualistic classification and opposition which is *the same kind of pattern* as that which Lévi-Strauss has sought to reveal elsewhere in the "primitive" world. This kind of "mythical" thinking, as Lévi-Strauss has said (1964: *passim*), has the characteristic of appearing to the analyst as "unending": always revealing new dimensions, new series of oppositions. Such thought, in this case among the Fipa, admits of no exhaustive or conclusive exposition; but this same characteristic, once recognized, points to the existence within the basic oppositional forms of Fipa thought of more abstruse cognitive potentialities than we have yet indicated. Thus I would argue that in the opposed concepts of Milansi and Twa, "head" and "loins," there are contained, partly latent and partly explicit, notions of complementary duality akin to those which have exercised the minds of philosophers and theologians through the ages: such as the ideas of "being and becoming," "transcendent and contingent" and "continuity and change." The name "Milansi," briefly translated, means "the eternal village"—an implied contrast with the transitory settlements of the Twa. A similar opposition of ideas of continuity and fixity, on the one hand, and of movement and change on the other, is associated with the opposed symbols "head" and "loins." In their most basic thought categories Fipa thus unite in complementary opposition the ideas of society as a continuing entity, and therefore in some sense unchanging, and as the subject of historical mutation.

The time has now come however to leave these rarified and irremediably hypothetical heights and consider more closely the nature of mythological thought and, within the Fipa context, the central question of its relation to more substantial aspects of the social order.

THOUGHT IN AURAL CULTURES

It seems to me that in his analysis of the structure of mythological thought Lévi-Strauss has formalized the experience of every fieldworker who has gained some intimacy with the thought-forms of a pre-literate society. In what McLuhan calls "aural" (or sometimes "oral") cultures thought is integral, it entertains contradictions (which can be resolved only by conversion into other contradictions, as in *La geste d'Asdiwal*), it has no centre and no boundaries (Stearn, 1967: 52). The apparent "centre" of Lévi-Strauss's exposition of Amerindian mythology in *Le cru et le cuit*— the "myth of reference"—has been arbitrarily chosen, as the author admits, for the purpose of the argument (Lévi-Strauss, 1964: 10). The subsequent arrangement of the material is in a sense no less arbitrary, based as it is on the working-out of an elaborate analogy with the structure of music. But this unexpected approach, in which a few basic themes in the repertoire of Amerindian mythology are repetitively explored and developed, is palpably in harmony with the spirit of mythological thinking: it works. The book is itself fashioned in the shape of a gigantic myth—as Lévi-Strauss says, "in spiral form" ("*en spirale*") (1964: 12).

Some part of the as-yet-unassimilated significance of this experiment in controlled *participation mystique*, I would suggest, derives from the fact that every myth is an allegory of the field experience, just as the inner life of the fieldworker is necessarily mythical. For an "observer"—the word is itself indicative of cultural bias—from a "visual" culture to immerse himself in what McLuhan calls an integral, "ear" culture is to suffer a profound disorientation. He enters a world of apparent contradictions which are resolvable, it seems, only and always in an inappropriate context, at another "level": the "resolution" is thus always provisional, always dissolving into other contradictions, which are equivocally resolved in similar manner. Yet from the first the contradictions are *felt*, rather than *seen*, to form a pattern which is regular even, or rather especially, in its very discontinuities. This is why Lévi-Strauss has chosen music, which is structure apprehended through the ear instead of the eye, to represent the spirit of mythological thought.

It is not surprising that the edifice Lévi-Strauss has constructed in *Le cru et le cuit* escapes the empirical constraints which he initially seeks to place upon it, emphasizing "... la position centrale de nos mythes, et leur adhérence aux contours essentials de l'organisation sociale et politique" (1964: 63). But just as, for the fieldworker, a true rendering of indigenous thought involves

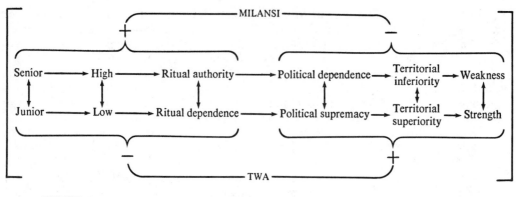

FIGURE 1
Conceptual-affective systems of
sovereignty and descent.

abandoning the neat categories of social compartmentalization he had brought with him, so in mythical analysis, "chaque matrice de significations renvoie à une autre matrice, chaque mythe à d'autres mythes" (1964: 346). And the brilliant work of synthesis represented by *Le cru et le cuit* is achieved at the cost of jettisoning sociological correlates in favour of "the human spirit" (*l'esprit*) as the ultimate point of reference: "... l'unique réponse que suggère ce livre est que les mythes signifient l'esprit, qui les élabore au moyen du monde dont il fait lui-même partie. Ainsi peuvent être simultanément engendrés, les mythes eux-mêmes par l'esprit qui les cause, et par les mythes, une image du monde déjà inscrite dans l'architecture de l'esprit" (1964: 346).

This is not a position which suggests possibilities of practical and theoretical advance—at least in social anthropology. It opens an enormous gulf between social thought—the collective representations of a vast culture area—and social action, the institutions to which these thought-forms must in some way correspond. The question that arises is: can mythological thought, which is endlessly dualistic, elaborate the more complex conceptual structures appropriate to systems of social relations?

One way in which this *might* be done is suggested by an earlier work of Lévi-Strauss, his *La geste d'Asdiwal* (1958), in which the myth goes through successive oppositional transformations at various levels—geographical, economic, sociological and cosmological. All these oppositions are, according to Lévi-Strauss's interpretation of the Asdiwal myth, reflections of a basic social contradiction inherent in the custom of matrilateral cross-cousin marriage among the Tsimshian

Indians. This theory, which has been subjected to some criticism, is essentially speculative and unverifiable. As a solution to the problem of the relation between mythological thought and social organization it is unsatisfactory. The Fipa example, on the other hand, points to a way in which dualistic ideas can be combined so as to form, as it were, a higher order of conceptual organization which will be appropriate to the complexity of its social referents.

If we now return to the Fipa sovereignty myth, we see that its manifest meaning relates to a system of ideas and values which, though of considerable complexity, is contained within the complementary opposition of two "key" terms, "Milansi" and "Twa." We have also drawn attention to the existence of another system of ideas and values in the universe of descent, derived from and contained within the complementary opposition of the dominant symbols "head" and "loins"; and we have argued that there is a structural congruence between these two conceptual-affective systems. If this latter point is conceded, the sovereignty myth becomes not merely a "charter," in Malinowski's sense, for the relation between the kingdoms of Milansi and the Twa, but is also, at another level, an allegory of the world of descent, as Fipa experience it. The myth has meaning at different cognitive levels in two apparently unrelated dimensions of Fipa society. The first meaning (concerning the relation between ritual and political sovereignty) is overt and manifest; the second meaning, in terms of descent, is latent; both meanings, it must be presumed, contribute to the significance for Fipa of the sovereignty myth.

The interpretation of the Fipa sovereignty myth put forward in this paper does not

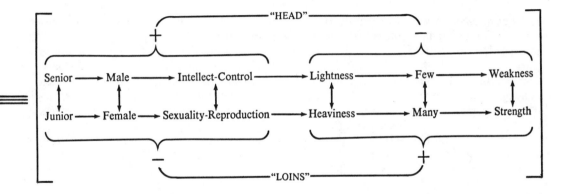

preclude its analysis in terms of a system of binary discriminations in the standard Lévi-Straussian manner; indeed the assumption, already made explicit, is that the myth is basically structured in accordance with such a system. But the central significance of the myth for Fipa, it is argued, is its embodiment, at different cognitive levels, of what I have called "conceptual-affective" structures which directly reflect social organization. In these structures clusters of ideas, which are opposed on the model of englobing "key" oppositions, are themselves divided into opposed sub-clusters or sub-sets—vertically, as it were—by a contrary value-loading. Figure 1, as shown above attempts to convey some of the complexity of this conceptual-affective system. In it a single arrow ($\rightarrow$) represents the operation of logical or empirical (or logico-empirical) transformation; a double arrow ($\leftrightarrow$) represents the complementary opposition of two concepts; a plus or a minus sign indicates the relative value given to the concepts enclosed within the round brackets; square brackets enclose the two idea-systems; and the sign $\equiv$ indicates structural congruence between them.

The actual situation is a good deal more complex than this. The diagram shows only a few of the more important, and entirely explicit, oppositional concepts associated with the two pairs of key ideas; a more comprehensive representation would have to indicate the theoretically infinite number of oppositional pairs which *could* be derived from the key oppositions and, in doing so, it would also be desirable to indicate another variable quantity—the relative explicitness or otherwise of all these ideas in Fipa thinking. The diagram may be incomplete in another way, since other idea-systems may exist,

structurally congruent with those related to sovereignty and descent, in other dimensions of Fipa society: this article describes two which I have been able to isolate and analyze.

The approach to mythical analysis attempted in this article is in a sense opposite to that exemplified in Lévi-Strauss's recent work (1964). Where Lévi-Strauss *begins* "at the most concrete level ... in the heart of a population" (1964: 9) and ends amidst "the architecture of the spirit" (346), this approach begins with the myth, veiled as it is in primal music and mystery, and works towards the socially concrete, in terms of identifiable institutions and systems of relations.

Further reflection suggests that these two approaches, and others too, may all be necessary, or at least desirable: the demonstration that myth, and myths, can be understood in terms of a system of binary discriminations does not exhaust the possibilities of structural analysis, as Burridge has pointed out (1967). For if, on the one hand, the implication of the Lévi-Straussian procedure and precedent is that the full meaning of, for example, the Fipa myth can emerge only when it is examined in the course of an analysis ranging over the whole corpus of Bantu mythology, on the other hand the method results in and operates through an intractable paradox. The synoptic approach exemplified in *Le cru et le cuit*, in which Lévi-Strauss has taken the entire mythical heritage of the Amerindians for his province, achieves astonishing coherence and complexity—but at the price of severing virtually all links with the solid ground of ethnography. In following so faithfully the spirit of mythological thought, Lévi-Strauss has been obliged, in the manner of that thought itself, to elude the straightforward categories of everyday tribal life for the elliptical linkages of *participation mystique* (Lévy-Bruhl). It has been Lévi-Strauss's achievement to discover a rigorous logical pattern, a paradoxically abstract "science of the concrete," behind these seemingly random juxtapositions.

The object of the more recent work of Lévi-Strauss, it seems to me, has not been to elaborate any kind of empirically verifiable "map" of mythological thought, but to demonstrate, through sympathetic and uninhibited participation in *la pensée sauvage*, the vastness and richness of the territory yet to be explored by social anthropology. Reading *Le cru et le cuit*, in particular, is like inhabiting the mind of some super-ethnographer as he undergoes a field experience ranging through seemingly limitless expanses of time and space.

These portentous "field notes" are a notable challenge to the assumptions of particularistic and relativistic empiricism. But they will remain theoretically barren unless translated, like all such information, into the common language of social anthropology. What is needed to complement the synoptic labours of Lévi-Strauss and to begin the complex task of incorporating the immense new territory he has prospected into the body of our discipline, is not less structuralism but more—at the "grass-roots" level of ethnography. In this article I have tried to indicate, in the context of my own fieldwork, how such an approach could be made. Structuralist and obviously "Lévi-Straussian" in inspiration, it is also empirically-oriented, since it relates to "concrete" social institutions.

SUMMARY

In conclusion, the following assumptions and hypotheses seem to arise from or be suggested by, the arguments in this article.

1. Thought in pre-literate or "aural" cultures is characterized by what Lévy-Bruhl called *participation mystique*, Lévi-Strauss has described in terms of an "unending" series of conceptual oppositions, resolutions and transformations, and McLuhan has most recently called "a total field of simultaneous relations, without centre or margin" (Stearn, 1967:52).

2. "Myths" and "mythological thinking" are, *at a certain level of analysis* (which has become almost synonymous with the name of Lévi-Strauss) alike insofar as they are composed of formally similar systems of opposi-

tions and "participations" (or "binary discriminations").

3. But, according to the evidence adduced in this article, "myths" are also *particular* in that they relate, through what I have called their conceptual-affective structure, or structures, to one or more organisational aspects of the society that produced them. This conclusion, or hypothesis, if found to be generally true by comparison with other societies, would have at least one significant consequence: it would restrict the anthropological use of the term "myth," which in the work of Lévi-Strauss seems indistinguishable from the wider category of "story," to oral forms exhibiting the necessary structural characteristics.

4. Conceptual-affective systems, or structures, in the sense the term has been used here, are aspects of social institutions and systems of relations. They are made out of the basic mythological "bricks" of oppositions and participations and their relatively greater complexity is explained by the presence of an affective, "value" component which results in cross-cutting internal oppositions of clusters of concepts within the total system. In a "myth" all the major constituent elements of such structures (value-loaded ideas) are directly or symbolically embodied.

It is precisely the affective element in mythological thought, on which Lévy-Bruhl particularly insisted (1949: 167–9), that evaporates during the course of an overall analysis of *Le cru et le cuit* dimensions, leaving a passionless structure of remote and mathematical beauty: the "music" takes on form, but loses its emotional content, which can be derived only from communication with human beings—the "field" situation.

5. Analysis of the Fipa material has suggested that a single myth can include, and relate to, more than one conceptual-affective structure—because these structures, though aspects of institutions and systems of relations which are "disparate" to conventional analysis, are in fact, like the numberless versions of the myth itself, formally congruent. The evidence presented here suggests that the central Fipa myth is a "sociological charter" of a depth and comprehensiveness which might well have surprised Malinowski, and that the language of the charter is a sort of ultra–Lévi-Straussian one.

6
RITUAL

Introduction

In its broadest sense ritual may include all behavior from "How are you?" and the etiquette of daily greetings to the solemnities of the High Mass, from magical spells uttered in a Trobriand garden to the studied dignity of the Zuni Shalako ceremony. Leach, who uses the term "ritual" in its broadest sense, emphasizes that the distinction between what people say and what they do should not be confused with that between myth and ritual (see Kluckhohn, Chapter 2). Speech (prayers, spells, chants) comprises an integral part of ritual behavior, as much so as gesture and the manipulation of objects. Ritual is not the dumb, silent cousin of myth. Turner, while underlining the importance of speech in his detailed consideration of prayer and native exegesis, would restrict the term ritual to the classes of behavior which accompany social transitions and use ceremony to denote behaviors which serve to confirm a particular social status. Whether they use ritual in a wide or narrow sense, most writers would agree that ritual (in Turner's sense) shows continuities with ceremony and everyday etiquette and, for some purposes, it may be useful to call all these kinds of behavior ritual (in Leach's sense).

Religious ritual, for Durkheim and his followers (see Chapter 1), is a set of practices through which the participants relate to the sacred. Sacred and profane activities are seen as antithetical, profane activities typically being economic and subsistence routines. Within the broad category of religious rites,

Titiev (see Chapter 8), for instance, would distinguish between calendrical and critical rites, depending on whether a ritual is regular or occasional in its performance. Curing and magic (see Chapters 7 and 8) are critical rites and Zinacantecan cargo ritual is calendrical. Firth's treatment of the economic factors involved in sacrifice takes as its point of departure the earlier writings of Tylor, Frazer, Robertson Smith, and Hubert and Mauss as to the nature of sacrifice. To oversimplify, Tylor saw the sacrificial gift as an attempt to minimize the hostility of the deity; Frazer interpreted the offering as an effort to rejuvenate the supernatural being for whom it was intended; Robertson Smith viewed the sacrificial meal as a communion of the participants with one another and with the deity. Hubert and Mauss followed Robertson Smith's notion that religious action is a means by which a society achieves a heightened awareness of its own reality, but they also defined, in general terms, some of the formal properties of sacrifice as ritual action. Their interpretation of the offering as a mediator between men and gods has been elaborated upon by Evans-Pritchard, Lienhardt, Middleton, and Lévi-Strauss.

Those rituals which mark social transition, be it territorial (the treatment of the guest, the visitor), succession to office or part of the life cycle (birth, initiation, marriage, death), comprise a general class, termed rites of passage in Arnold van Gennep's classic work on their shared characteristics. Ndembu initiation and the Crow vision quest fall into this general class which may be further subdivided into rites of separation, transition, and incorporation. Each phase of the rite of passage has its typical symbolic expressions: separation may be marked by haircutting and cutting or severing in general; incorporation is indicated by tying a knot, putting on a belt, a ring, a bracelet, or a veil. Turner directs himself to characteristic expressions of transition, or liminality, an area slighted in van Gennep's treatment.

It is worth noting that the Freudian theory which would equate the behavior of obsessional neurotics in our culture with that of performers of religious rites in all cultures (see Kluckhohn, Chapter 2) is not relevant to the writings in this chapter. Teeth filing, for instance, might be a rite of separation for van Gennep and his followers, while, for the Freudian, it would represent symbolic castration related to Oedipal anxieties. In Freud's paper on "Obsessive Acts and Religious Practices" (1948–1950), the private rite, performed in isolation, e.g., meticulously laying one's clothes by the bedstool in a particular order, with its strictly followed compulsions and prohibitions, its impelling sense of guilt, is equated with religious rites. The primary difference between the two is that neuroses are bound to sexual drives and motives, and their repression, and religious rites derive from the supression of egoistic, anti-social impulses. Thus sacred license, a culminating moment in a rite of passage and, for van Gennep, a rite of incorporation, would be seen by the Freudian in relation to the supression and denial of egoistic desires associated with religious belief and practice. In part because of the cavalier equation by some students of psychoanalysis of symptomatic behavior (involuntary acts, resulting directly from inner drives and conflicts) and symbolic action (voluntary acts, which may, or may not, correspond to inner psychological dispositions and needs)—ritual tears may be wiped away by a smile and a "hello," only to be resumed again—explanation of ritual in terms of fundamental psychological needs and motives is no longer in vogue. The writings in this chapter typify the current trend in that they direct themselves less to functional problems (see Chapter 2) than to problems of symbolic classification (see Chapter 4) and explicating the internal logic of the ritual itself. The problem is not so much what ritual does for people as what it says to them, how it is intelligible to the participants.

Raymond Firth

OFFERING AND SACRIFICE: PROBLEMS OF ORGANIZATION

Firth approaches the problem of sacrifice by looking behind the rite, which he considers in the final analysis to be a personal act—a giving of the self or a part of the self—to discover the influence and importance that a people's ideas about control of economic resources have on their concepts of sacrifice. He addresses himself to the organization of the rite, particularly the mobilizing of material objects and human beings and the way in which the solution to such problems as the determination of the time, the selection of the animal, and the drain on resources influence the central ideology, the style, and the frequency of sacrifice itself. He does not argue, however, that concepts of sacrifice can be reduced to economic rationality and prudent calculation, for sacrifice is fundamentally a symbolic act of critical significance for a human personality and has important social components.

Reprinted from the *Journal of the Royal Anthropological Institute*, XCIII (1963), 12–24, by permission of the author and the Royal Anthropological Institute of Great Britain and Ireland.

Offering in some form appears to occur in nearly all religious systems. The custom of making religious offering is part of a vast series of actions involving conceptions of transfer of good or service from one person to another person, or to a putative entity, without direct and immediate counter-transfer of any visible equivalent. An offering is a species of gift. This means: (*a*) that the thing given is *personal* to the giver, his own property, or something over which he has rights of alienation; (*b*) that the thing transferred must have some *value* for the person who hands it over; and, (*c*) that it is transferred with some degree of *voluntary initiative*—it is not given by compulsion nor does it occur as a technical part of a series of actions dictated by some generally planned end. What distinguishes an offering from a gift—though the two terms are often used synonymously—is that an offering implies an asymmetrical *status relationship*, an inferiority on the part of the person making the offering and superiority on the part of the recipient. A gift may also involve a status relationship if not between equals, but this relationship tends to be created by the act of giving and receiving, not acknowledged or partially resolved by such act. (A subject in a kingdom may make an offering to his Sovereign, but the Sovereign does not make an offering to the subject; he makes a gift.) The effect of gift and offering may be directly opposite in social terms. A gift may put the recipient in a state of social inferiority and may indeed emphasize that inferiority. An offering emphasizes that it is the giver who is inferior and that the recipient is in a state of social superiority. *De facto*, the manner of transfer, the words and actions employed, may determine which terminology is most appropriately used in classification.

The concept of offering may carry other qualities. Linked with the notion of status difference is that of *uncertainty*—decision as to the acceptability of the transfer of value may be thought to rest with the person designated as recipient, who may refuse it. So also with a gift, but this concept carries with it a more positive idea of handing-over as a *fait accompli*. Another quality often attached especially to an offering is the suggestion of an *emotional element*. A gift may be emotionally neutral; an offering carries with it the notion of some outgoing sentiment of respect.

This brief semantic discussion is only in a very general sense, since neither gift nor offering are precise terms. I do not want to overdrive their meaning, especially since in common usage they shade into each other. But for analytical purposes it is useful to draw attention to such elements which frequently, though not necessarily always, occur implicitly in the usage of these terms, since they enter into an understanding of much religious practice and belief.

A religious offering or oblation embodies these ideas more definitely. Status difference, volitional aspect of acceptance, emotional attitudes of offerer—all are recognizable, and often present to a marked degree. They are correlated with the special notion of the recipient being an extra-human, supernormal being.

The concept of sacrifice includes a further element. As Gusdorf has pointed out, gift is a first approximation to sacrifice. Sacrifice is a species of offering or oblation, but implies a relation between what is offered and the *availability of resources*. Offering indicates an allocation or transfer of resources, but implies nothing about the degree or quality of allocation in relation to the total resources at the command of the giver. "Sacrifice" implies that the degree or quality is significant—that the resources are limited, that there are alternative uses for them, and that there is some abstention from an alternative use in making the offering. The sacrifice is giving up something at a cost. This is indicated in dictionary equivalents—that sacrifice means "the loss entailed by devotion to some other interest," or "the destruction or surrender of something valued or desired for the sake of something having a higher or more pressing claim."

The notion that a sacrifice is involved in the diversion of some valued object from one end to another which is regarded as more pressing, raises the question of alternative response or equivalents to be expected according to the end served. When a gift is made from one person to another, later reciprocity in the form of counter-gift or counter-service is common. If there is no such reciprocity, presumably the giver regards himself as compensated by the satisfaction arising from the knowledge of the effects of the gift or by the moral virtue attaching to the act of giving itself. Such vicarious action is characteristic of most forms of sacrifice. When in the religious sphere offering or sacrifice is made, no direct counter-gift of a material kind is normally expected, although ensuing material benefits—in the form of fertility of crops or health of persons maintained or restored—are frequently regarded as its outcome. But even where no such material benefit is thought to arise, religious offering and sacrifice have other compensatory functions. These may be generalized as benefits arising from belief in the establishment of appropriate relations between the offerer or sacrificer and some spirit entity or extra-human power. Commonly, too, the performance of sacrifice in particular is regarded as inducing or marking a change in the spiritual constitution of the sacrificer, renewing or intensifying his moral qualities. But sometimes the concept of sacrifice involves the ideal of a dual loss, to the victim as well as to the sacrificer. The issue is then not always clear from the moral point of view, as when Agamemnon sacrificed Iphigenia to his political loyalties and ambitions.

In a religious sense sacrifice is one of the most critical acts. In its Western etymology it is akin to the notion of consecration, of removal from secular to sacred sphere. It has been called "a peculiarly religious term" and to many people it expresses more than almost any other concept the heart of a religious system.

In the religious field various meanings have been given to the term. But the most common is that sacrifice is a voluntary act whereby, through the slaughter of an animal, an offering of food or other substance is made to a spiritual being. Sacrifice then ordinarily implies immolation, a living victim, e.g., the *zebah*, animal-offering or "bloody oblation" of the Hebrews. At the same time most anthropologists would probably be prepared to agree with Robertson Smith and with Hubert and Mauss that the notion of sacrifice can properly include even a vegetal offering, provided that some portion of it is destroyed with intent in the act. The element, if not of destruction, at least of transformation or transmutation of what is sacrificed is basic to the concept. It is related to what Hubert and Mauss and others have referred to as the aspect of abnegation, the denial of something to the self, which does seem to be involved in every sacrificial action. In the doctrines of many religions a concept of legitimacy is also strong; a sacrifice is valid only when offered by an authorized officiant or minister.

The theme of sacrifice in religion has provided copious literature, from William Outram and John Davison through Robertson Smith and Alfred Loisy to H. C. Trumbull, E. O. James, and R. K. Yerkes, and it has received special attention in recent Africanist anthropology. There has been a spate of theories to account for the origins of sacrifice and to describe its functions. The gift theory, the homage theory, the abnegation theory, are all in Tylor's writings, with the idea of development of one from another. The communion theory and the piacular theory of Robertson Smith have stimulated many later writers. The rejuvenation theory and the cathartic theory of Sir James Frazer, the intermediary theory of Hubert and Mauss, the symbolic parricide theory of Freud and Money-Kyrle, help to round out the interpretations. As Evans-Pritchard has shown, elements of many of these may be discerned in the sacrificial system of any one community.

The treatment of sacrifice in recent general anthropological studies of religion has been very uneven, though Goode (1951) has some significant observations. Apparent lack of interest in sacrifice as a feature of primitive religions may be partly because the view has been taken, as by Hocart or Howells, that sacrifices are special forms of ritual and not of first significance in general religious development. Recent ethnographic accounts, however, as by Evans-Pritchard, Middleton, and G. Lienhardt, have brought out in a most penetrating way the religious meaning of sacrifice, its relation to concepts of divinity and of human personality, its symbolic force, and its sociological significance.

But considering that sacrifice normally involves the use of material resources, often important ones, how much reference is there in the older or in the more recent literature to the means of mobilizing these resources, to the social problems posed by the procurement of sacrifices and to the implications of the solutions for the ideology of sacrifice itself?

When is the decision to make a sacrifice made? Which animal shall be sacrificed? These are unorthodox but relevant questions.

In studies of sacrifice, preoccupation has been with the concrete ritual procedures and with the underlying beliefs; the organization of the sacrifice has been neglected. From Robertson Smith, Lord Almoner's Professor of Arabic in the University of Cambridge or from Royden Keith Yerkes, a professional theologian, this is natural enough. But it is surprising to find how this aspect of the subject has been largely passed over by social anthropologists. Recent studies of African peoples, embodying several hundred references to sacrifices, give a good deal of interesting data on who provides the sacrifice and who attends it, together with occasional information about types and numbers of beasts furnished. But when one asks, what do the sacrifices represent in terms of proportionate loss to the people who make them? there is no adequate answer obtainable. These frontal problems, the drain upon the owner's resources which the sacrifice represents, the calculations involved in deciding what particular animals are to be sacrificed and when, and the relation of the sacrificial activities to other economic activities, are hardly ever studied. This is the more notable because, in theory at least, the necessity for such calculations may have some bearing upon the central ideology of the sacrificial act.

Briefly put, the problem may be expressed in this way. When people are said to make sacrifices, does this mean simply that they kill animals ritually? What is the relation of what they sacrifice to what they possess? What loss do they suffer? How can they afford this loss? What social movements do they go through in order to be able to make sacrifices? In case of illness, for example, do they make sacrifices even when they cannot "afford" them? How do they manage in such event? If they can afford sacrifices, what is the relation of religious dictate to personal initiative? Has this anything to do with the frequency and style of the sacrifices they do make?

Of course even bare information about numbers of available stock allows us to make some inferences. Evans-Pritchard gives some data about the average number of livestock in a Nuer byre in the early 1930s and Middleton gives data about livestock and about the number of sacrifices performed during a period of about a year in a Lugbara compound. But though Lienhardt has given a most impressive account of the significance of cattle to the Dinka, he seems to have taken their economic importance for granted, and one can therefore not find any details of the number of livestock at the command of a family or larger social group and the relation of those sacrifices to the group resources. (The Dinka dislike numbering their herds, but did this debar the anthropologist from counting? See Lienhardt, 1961, p. 22.) We are told that the Dinka prefer in theory to sacrifice strong beasts (as a reflection of their own prowess) but "must often make the best of what they think they can afford" (Lienhardt, 1961, p. 293). But what *do* they think they can afford? And if they must compromise, how do they explain it to themselves?

If one wished to be challenging, one might put forward as a hypothesis that, in default of information to the contrary, the frequency, amount, and quality of sacrifices in a given community are determined primarily not by the type of social structure, nor by the specifically religious ideology, nor by the chance events demanding resolution, but by the availability of material resources of the domestic animal population. (I use the term "domestic" because, as Robertson Smith has shown by implication, the sacrifice of wild animals which can be regarded as the free gift of nature is rarely allowable or efficient. The sacrifice must be something of the operator's own or his community's. The offering must be detached from himself.)

That sacrifices are the result not of ritual actions but of economic actions has some plausibility if one considers the utilization of the meat for food. Among many peoples, e.g., Dinka, Nuer, and Lugbara, livestock (or at least cattle), it is stated, should not be killed primarily for meat, but kept for sacrifice. But if cattle are very plentiful, then there need be no real problem in securing meat. Provided that the occasion can be found for a sacrifice —and it is usually simple—enough cattle could be sacrificed to provide a frequent meat supply. On the other hand, where cattle are not plentiful, sacrifices simply cannot be very frequent. But the number of them in a stated period, and their spacing, may reflect the relation between cattle supply and meat demand as well as the intensity of ritual obligations. The relation between sacrifice and ritual slaughter is also at times close. Sacrifice is presumably a killing which is not in the immediate food interest of the slaughterer, but of some more general obligation. But if each beast that is killed must, according to the dictates of the religion, be slaughtered according to a set ritual form, the line between killing for meat according to rules laid down by God, announcing the killing to God, and offering the slain beast to God must be very tenuous. As a reverse proposition to the local statement one might put it that implicitly cattle are killed for meat and only explicitly or nominally offered for sacrifice.

But in the crude form that sacrifice is a reflex of economic resources the hypothesis cannot of course be sustained. We remember at once that in many religious systems there are specific obligations to perform a sacrifice, irrespective of the economic situation. There may be a requirement for a regular annual or other periodic sacrifice: the Pawnee "Morning Star" sacrifice; the "year-minding" of the Beduin for their deceased male kin and ancestors; the Ketsá and other rituals of the Kede to secure the welfare of the people on the Niger River; or the sacrifices of the Tallensi at sowing and harvest. There are also the irregular but recurrent human contingencies to deal with: the sacrifice at the installation of a new chief as among the Ashanti; to rectify a homicide, as among the Tallensi and Nuer; to cure illness or avert accident as among the Swazi and Nuer; or after it as with the Lugbara; to expiate incest as among the Ashanti and Dinka, or to expiate fighting at some very sacred rites, as among the Owele Ibo. There are also the sacrifices to avert disasters of nature, as when the Lovedu try to secure rain. In all such cases the regular religious need, to establish communication with the god or with the spirit world, or in whatever other terms the sacrifice be defined, would seem to be pressing and primary. "Afford it or not," the attitude might seem to be, "we must offer up our cow, our goat, our chicken." There may be also implicit reasons of sociological pressure. A sacrifice may be necessary to seal a man's assumption of office; a sacrifice may be needed as a symbol of the restoration of threatened social relations between kin. Here too sanctions for a sacrifice may be so strong that postponement of it is inconceivable.

Yet this merely pushes the problem a stage further back. If indeed there are some types of sacrifice which are obligatory and immediate, brooking no omission or delay, then how are they effected? Some organizational devices in the economic sphere must come into play in order that the ritual need may be satisfied. If the would-be sacrificer has the resources at hand, how has he managed this: has he ample for all his wants, or has he had to practise prudent husbandry by careful anticipation, or has he just had luck? How will he fare afterwards if a further unanticipated sacrifice is necessary? How well can he sustain a "run on the sacrifice-bank" if a series of misfortunes demanding the attention of gods and ancestors should strike him and his family? If he has not the resources at hand, to what shifts is he put to mobilize them? Does he forego sacrifice and risk the anger of the unseen world? Does he resort to makeshift devices or substitutes, and if he does, what is their validity for him and his belief in the views of his ancestors and gods? In particular, what additional social relations are entailed thereby, and with

whom? Does he contract credit obligations, mortgaging his future income against his present demand? Does the system ever break down? If something has to go, some sacrifice to be omitted, which one? Some indication of the nature of the problem is given by the case of the Lugbara father reported by Middleton who, when his son was sick, waited and did not sacrifice a goat, having it in mind presumably that his son was not *very* sick. Here may be a test of the relative importance of values. In modern conditions of social change and of conflict between traditional and Western values, competing demands may well make these organizational issues of high significance.

In the ethnographic record, relatively thin in this matter as it is, there are enough examples of the prudent handling of resources to show that sacrifice does seem to be a matter of some economic calculation as well as ritual obligation. Goode notes that the religious goal of establishing one's ancestral dead by worship and sacrifice causes a decrease in immediate consumption and may necessitate prior saving. What he terms the "economic burden on the distributive system of the collectivity" should not be ignored. It is fairly common in the literature to state that sacrifices are performed in proportion to the issue at stake. This involves the concept that the less important the issue the less valuable the object sacrificed. But it leaves untouched another side of the question—granted that the issue was of major importance, how then were resources handled, and in particular were they so organized as to reduce as far as possible the economic loss? Evans-Pritchard has reported that normally (in the early '30's) the Nuer killed stock only for ritual purposes, not for food. Yet according to him they got thereby (apart from the odd cattle which died) enough meat to satisfy their craving. But the balance would seem to have been not altogether easy, and care to have been exercised lest the stock be unduly depleted. The "proper" Nuer sacrifice was an ox. But on minor occasions or "more usually" (including piacular sacrifices to God, who did not require larger beasts) sheep or goats were sacrificed by the Nuer rather than oxen because they were of less value. Again, a barren cow was sacrificed rather than a fertile one, which was immolated only in mortuary rites. Then again a cucumber might be presented instead of an ox, a point which I discuss again later. Moreover, the Nuer held that some men, in their desire for meat, sacrificed "without due cause." Yet there is inconsistency here, since on their own showing there were always spirits and ghosts to whom sacrifice would be appropriate and such sacrifices were often said to be long overdue.

The implication from all this is that the occasions for sacrifice have a strong economic control. Evans-Pritchard does mention the relevance of the smallness of their herds and says that "doubtless their high value is an important consideration." But he implies that religious intention, tradition, and convention are the prime factors involved in sacrifice, and that the requirements of the spirit are relevant rather than the prudent calculations of men. Yet the significance of the latter is reinforced when one remembers that Evans-Pritchard estimated the average stock at the time he worked with the Nuer to be only about ten head of cattle and five goats and sheep to a byre, the related personnel being about eight people. Cows probably composed about two-thirds of the cattle, which were fairly evenly distributed. Therefore, allowing for natural increase, these figures would seem to imply that, if the livestock average was to be maintained, not much more than one or two sacrifices a month per byre could occur. This does not seem to have allowed a very heavy meat diet, though the system of meat distribution presumably meant that the people of the byre shared in the flesh from other animals sacrificed elsewhere.

The general conclusion that frequency and quality of sacrifice are affected by economic position is supported by further evidence. In the general summary list of factors which Fortes gives as responsible for the selection of animals among the Tallensi, he mentions: importance of the shrine; importance of the occasion; and status of the suppliant or his group. He does not include reference to the *resources* of the person or group as being in any way significant. Yet he does note in a few cases a direct relation between the size of the sacrifice and the wealth of the person making it. He also gives examples of the postponement of sacrifice on apparently economic grounds. Likewise Nadel who, in general, does not deal with this aspect of the subject, notes that the Muslim Nupe sacrifice of a fattened ram at the 'Id festival takes place "in every household that can afford it." He also gives a little information about the relative infrequency of Nupe sacrifice to ancestors which suggest that these, at least, occur so rarely as to present a small economic problem. That sacrifices are related to command of resources by the Ibo is made very clear by Meek. He records the view that stumbling or being bitten by a snake is interpreted by Ibo as possibly due to a man's personal genius being annoyed at the sacrifice of a chicken when the man could easily have afforded a goat (which indicates some prudent calculation somewhere). He notes also the ingenious mechanism whereby a diviner, it is alleged, thinking that a patient will die, prescribes as a sacrifice to save him one that is far beyond the means of the kinsman who consults him. In addition, he gives examples of the sharing of the expense of a sacrifice, as by dividing equally the cost of the sacrificial animal among the segments of relevant kinsfolk or, for public sacrifices, deciding at a general meeting the manner of earning the necessary funds.

Incidentally, the fact noted by Hubert and Mauss and others that the species, sex, colour, and other markings of the sacrificial animal are often laid down by traditional rule, divination or other ritual procedures has an organizational implication that is usually overlooked, the problem of finding one which will conform to specification. That this is not a purely academic question is indicated by instances given by Kuper and by Krige, showing the delay and difficulties that can result from such a ritual specification. Only where livestock are particularly abundant, as appears to be the case among the Dinka, can such prescriptions not be particularly onerous. Such economic control can be applied directly in two obvious ways, by spacing out at wider intervals the sacrifices it is deemed necessary to make, or by selecting among the possible recipients of sacrifices only those gods and ancestors deemed to be of primary importance. Social anthropologists have stressed the importance of the operation of selective mechanisms in the record of genealogies. It could be that considerations of such an economic kind have played some part in the reduction of spirit entities in communities which offer animals as sacrifice, and thereby have affected the structural character of the genealogical record.

But apart from its possible effect on the frequency of sacrifices, economic controls may affect their quality. R. K. Yerkes, who was not directly concerned with this problem, nevertheless stressed that for the ancient religions of the Near East sacrifices were always as large as possible, and that the larger they were the more joyful the occasion, and contrasted this with the "unworthy modern view" that a sacrifice is a loss and a misfortune, and that the outgo should be minimal. Robertson Smith, too, seems to have frowned on the notion that a sacrifice might be a matter of prudent calculation. He rejected, probably with justice, the allegation that the sacrifice of very young animals at the annual piacular rites of the ancient Semites was getting rid of a sacred obligation at the very cheapest rate. But in another context he said that "the introduction of ideas of property into the relation between men and their gods seems to have been one of the most fatal aberrations in the development of ancient religions," which looks as if he had had some inkling of an economic problem and was antipathetic to it. An anthropologist might surmise that this property idea was not an aberration but was in fact basic in the relationship.

Some writers not concerned with the more abstract aspects of the theory of sacrifice have seen the situation empirically and more clearly. C. M. Doughty, living among the Beduin in the nineteenth century, pointed out that sacrifices were performed according to ability, and gave examples. A suckling camel calf was killed, he noted, despite protestations that it was a female and that a sheep or goat should be slain instead. In reply to these arguments the answer was very sensibly, "she refuses the teat and we have determined to kill her." He noted again that Beduin did not use a cow camel as a sacrifice to the dead because the households were so indigent, and it was impossible to cut off this "womb of the stock." In its place the Beduin bought, for three or four sheep or goats, a decrepit old camel that had lost its front teeth and was past bearing, and released it from work for several months to fatten it up. Thus the Beduin got meat as well as the credit for the religious act.

But variation in the quality of the sacrifice and use of low-grade animals on occasion is not just a matter of economic organization. It involves an interpretation of the ideology of the sacrifice.

A procedure of collective sacrifice involves concepts both of economy and of religious ideology. The collectivity of a sacrifice is commonly regarded as a symbol of group unity—the members of a descent group or a neighbourhood, by sharing in the common ritual act, give overt expression to social bonds which are significant for them, and strengthen the value of the sacrifice for an individual particularly concerned. But a collective sacrifice often means not only a common presentation of a victim, but also a lightening of the economic burden upon each participant. Collective sacrifices may be of various types. In one the sacrifice specifically represents an offering not by an individual who is the foremost participant but by the lineage or other group he represents. In another type no descent group as such may be involved, but some members of the community may in free association pool their contributions. Such a sacrifice is that of a bull or cow offered by Kelantan Malays in celebration of the annual pilgrimage in Mecca. The animal is usually bought by subscription from several people, the price always being made up in seven shares. Over a period of years, by accumulation of shares so contributed, a person may acquire as it were a complete sacrificial animal for himself and so secure the appropriate merit. Such collective acts of immolation of an animal may not necessarily reduce the number of sacrifices performed in a community, but they spread both the cost and the benefits. They also usually allow people with few resources to take advantage of the relative wealth of others, so that the ideology of charity may be subjoined to that of sacrifice. Again, the emphasis upon the ritual unity of the sacrificing group may be a virtue which is closely allied to necessity.

Another way of meeting the problem of resources in sacrifice which raises important questions of meaning is the use of permissible substitutes or surrogates. Robertson Smith mentioned this subject briefly, though he did not examine it. He regarded such substitution, as that of a sheep for a stag in a certain Roman rite if a stag could not be procured, as an evasion. (He called it bluntly a fraud.) Only in passing did he admit that otherwise the ceremony might fall through. More sophisticated discussion of this whole question is given by modern social anthropologists. Evans-Pritchard's argument takes the form that ultimately the sacrifice of an ox by the Nuer is a surrogate for the sacrifice of a man, and that man and ox are symbolic equivalents. For the Nuer, oxen are the appropriate sacrifice *par excellence*. If there were enough oxen a man might always sacrifice an ox; but there are not enough. Hence, a Nuer will sacrifice a lesser number of livestock or even in some circumstances will bisect a wild cucumber in sacrificial manner. Such a wild cucumber is a symbolic equivalent to an ox. For the Nuer, a cucumber is equivalent to an ox in respect to God who they think accepts it in the place of an ox. Ideologically the position here is very interesting. When a cucumber is so used as a "sacrificial victim" the Nuer speak of it as *yang*, "cow" i.e., normally an ox. Sometimes they appear to regard it as only a temporary substitute, an anticipatory offering in terms of an ox to be sacrificed later on. At other times they appear to regard it as a final substitute. It is spoken of as an ox and, for ritual purposes, an ox it is. The conception of a wild cucumber as an acceptable substitute for an ox involves an attribution to the cucumber of a quality not proper to it in any material sense.

A significant point to an anthropologist, though whether the Nuer clearly perceive it is not brought out, is that a wild cucumber is a most *economical* way of meeting one's *ritual* obligations. In order that what seems to be an expenditure of minimal resources shall be ritually valid, the Nuer have had to enlarge their sacrificial ideology and attribute to the cucumber an arbitrary religious quality. It is not clear from the evidence just how much trouble a person has to take in order to secure a cucumber for sacrifice, but the inference is that it is not too difficult to find one. It may be suspected that this readiness of the Nuer to compromise in the sacrificial field, and to clothe cucumbers with the attributes of oxen for ritual purposes, is to some degree a reflex of their economic position—in particular their scarcity of oxen—perhaps by reference to their neighbours the Dinka. That in a somewhat analogous situation such a solution does not find favour is seen by the views of the Lugbara, who were incredulous when told of the Nuer practice, and obviously were not prepared to cheat the spirits by such worthless surrogates. The complexity of Nuer thought on this surrogate is indicated by the statement that the Nuer say that a man must make invocation "in truth," and if the sacrifice is to be effective what is said must be true. How they square this with calling a cucumber an ox is not apparent. The Dinka, who also split sacred cucumbers, use them specifically as temporary substitutes for animal victims and as an earnest of intention to provide such a victim when possible.

An interesting variant of this principle of substitution is the Swazi practice of the *licabi*. This is a particularly fine beast which every family priest dedicates to his ancestors. If a sacrifice is to be made the *licabi* animal is driven into the byre with the other cattle and the real victim is shepherded near it to acquire something of its ritual qualities, "so that by proxy the best goes to the dead." But the *licabi* itself serves the role many times; it is not killed until it becomes too old to serve as the display animal. By this practice clearly the proxy which is actually slain can be an inferior animal, thus conserving family resources.

The ideology of symbolic equivalents of things which may be offered in sacrifice may therefore be directly correlated with the problem of allocation of scarce resources. In the last resort the greatest surrogate of all is the sacrifice of the mind and heart, the abnegation of individual judgement and desire in favour of devotion to more general moral ends. Such a substitution is in line with very general trends of ethical and religious interpretation, and the material sacrifices are often regarded as one early developmental phase in a long line of substitutions. One ancient Rabbi is said to have held that the Mosaic laws appertaining to animal sacrifices were primarily designed for the generation of the desert; that burnt offerings were but time-conditioned ways of doing honour to God; that at a later time the sacrifices of righteousness would have precedence over offerings upon the altar. This view is clearly compatible with our modern attitudes towards human personality, but one need not overlook entirely that removal of the notion of sacrifice from the material to the immaterial plane does away with an awkward problem of organization. Readers of Max Weber and of R. H. Tawney do not need to be reminded how an ethical view can emerge side by side with a convenient economic doctrine.

If the elasticity of a surrogate is not possible, then other alternatives may be found. One method is to borrow for a sacrifice. But as Wagner has shown for the Logoli and Evans-Pritchard for the Nuer, this may lead to social difficulties for the borrower. In other words, though obligation is translated from the ritual to the social sphere the economic problem is apt to remain.

Again, the material of a sacrifice can be treated in either of two main ways: by complete destruction or by reservation. In destruction, if solid it can be consumed by fire, by water, or by exposure; if liquid it can be poured away. In reservation, it can be offered to god or spirit and then withdrawn for the consumption of the worshippers. Empirically, this latter seems to be by far the most usual course. Interest in the meat or other ingredients, as much ethnographic evidence shows, may be at least as important an element in attendance at the occasion as interest in the religious aspect of the sacrifice itself. While the sharing of sacrificial food may be a significant ritual act, it is very frequently nothing more than ordinary commensality.

The legitimization of such an economic rebate has very important implications for the practice and the theory of sacrifice. On the one hand it allows the sacrifice to be performed with much greater frequency than would certainly be the case if the sacrificial material was always destroyed. On the other hand it necessitates special beliefs about the manner in which the gods or spirits take their fill. Either they must be satisfied with the killing and display of the sacrificed object, or they must be satisfied to consume its least valuable portions, or to absorb some immaterial aspect or equivalent of it. In other words, the practice of reservation of the sacrificial material for the human participants almost inevitably demands some theory of essences, representations or symbols. Such, for example is the theory of the Tikopia, who regard all their offerings as having an immaterial, invisible counterpart. They describe the immaterial counterpart in some detail, linking it with analogous spirit counterparts in man, and give it various names according to circumstances. This whole set of notions is part of an integral system of ideas about the meaning of ritual behaviour. When food offerings are set out it is this counterpart, invisible to men, that is thought to be taken away by the gods and spirits, and presumably consumed by them. The Tikopia describe in terms of such spirit action the wilting of fresh vegetable plants such as taro, set up on a grave as an offering to the spirit of the dead. But they are relatively uninterested in the process by which this abstraction of immaterial counterpart is believed to be done. They describe it as being "after the manner of spirits" and leave the subject there.

The point I wish to make here is this. From our Western angle of approach, like Robertson Smith, we probably regard the notion that it is the essence and not the substance of a sacrifice that is consumed by the god or spirit as a more refined idea than the crass belief that the god or spirit actually eats the material bread or meat or drinks the material beer. It may be so. But it is not only more refined; it is also more economical. The point was made essentially by Tylor many years ago. "Through the history of sacrifice it has occurred to many nations that cost may be economized without impairing efficiency. The result is seen in ingenious devices to lighten the burden on the worshipper by substituting something less valuable than what he ought to offer, or pretends to."

I think that one is entitled to say then that even at the heart of primitive religious ideology in such a basically important phenomenon as sacrifice, notions of rationality and prudent calculation enter. In other words, the concepts of sacrifice held by any people must be understood in relation to their notions about control of resources. I want to stress that it is not my argument that concepts of sacrifice can simply be reduced to rational, economic terms. Sacrifice is essentially a symbolic act of grave significance to human personality, and normally has important social components. But my basic point of view here is that, to understand the operations of a religious system even in such a highly symbolic rite as sacrifice, we must consider the implications of organization in men, material and timing of procedures. Much of the effect of these organizational concomitants is seen only in the magnitude and the style of the rites, but their quality, their content and their ideology can also be affected.

I conclude as follows: sacrifice is ultimately a personal act, a giving of the self or a part of the self. The self is represented or symbolized by various types of material object. Such a material object must have social significance or value, or the implication will be that the self is trivial or worthless. Part of the theory of sacrifice then is the giving of a valued object involving some immediate personal loss. In this giving of a valued object there are elements of rational calculation, or organization, of matching material loss against command of material resources, as well as against immaterial or spiritual gain. This element of rational calculation may condition the value or the quality of the object offered. It may also condition the mode of offering, for example by withdrawal of material once offered with the explanation that its essence has been taken. But rational calculation may also condition the ideology of the sacrifice, which may be elaborated in explanation of the particular operation of the offering. Into this field of ideas comes the notion of the surrogate, of a ram instead of a human being, of a cucumber instead of an ox. These are physical substitutes, but they are often offered instead of a man not only as a physical substitute but also as a moral substitute. This notion interpreted conventionally is that it is not the thing itself but the spirit of the gift that is important. It is the act of giving rather than the gift that matters, that is, the expenditure of time and energy is significant, and beyond this the expenditure of thought and of emotion. But sacrifice as a moral act is a conception at a different level from sacrifice as a material loss.

All this implies that the value of the thing offered is attributed to it only conventionally by virtue of its being selected for offering. This is distinct from the value of the thing in ordinary economic transactions. Granting this, nevertheless one function of such beliefs is that they may allow the retention of objects of economic value. One may serve God without losing touch with Mammon. In the last resort, then, sacrifice in primitive religions is the action of giving up something to which has been allotted an arbitrary or specially circumscribed attribution of value. Communal objects of the highest economic value are regarded as most appropriate for sacrifice. But the use of them represents an equation of decision, the result of the effects of a number of variables in respect of the value put on the self and on its various properties in a specific social milieu. Sacrifice is a critical act for a human personality, but it is an act performed in terms laid down by the evaluations of the society.

Edmund R. Leach

RITUALIZATION IN MAN IN RELATION TO CONCEPTUAL AND SOCIAL DEVELOPMENT

Ritual is often viewed as a nonrational means (however efficacious for the actors) to achieve culturally defined ends; its symbols are characterized as condensed, containing multiple meanings, and, as action, it is elaborate, drawn out, highly repetitive human behavior. Leach suggests a novel way to view the protracted repetitiveness of ritual behavior; phrasing the problem in terms of communication theory, he asks, why the redundancy? Why does ritual seem to say the same thing—repeat the same message, in so many ways, through different channels? The information embodied in ritual action and speech pertains to the local habitat and social life of a particular culture. The often noted economy and condensation of ritual symbols are considered highly efficient means of information storage and transmission—one way in which members of a culture encode and communicate relevant cultural knowledge through the generations. In Leach's view, then, ritual in nonliterate societies has affinities, not with irrational, prelogical, or mystical thought, but with modern mathematics and the information storage of computers.

Reprinted from *Philosophical Transactions of the Royal Society of London*, 1966, Series B, No. 772, Vol. 251, pp. 403–408, by permission of the author and the Royal Society.

It has become plain that the various contributors to this Symposium use the key term *ritual* in quite different ways. The ethologists are consistent with one another; Professor Hinde's definition will serve for all: "ritualization refers to the evolutionary changes which the signal movements of lower vertebrates have undergone in adaptation to their function in communication." Such a definition has no relevance for the work of social anthropologists. Unfortunately, although *ritual* is a concept which is very prominent in anthropological discourse, there is no consensus as to its precise meaning. This is the case even for the anthropologist contributors to this Symposium; for example, I myself use the term in a different way from Professor Fortes whose paper immediately follows my own. Even so certain major differences between the positions of the ethologist and the social anthropologist need to be noted. For the ethologist, ritual is adaptive repetitive behaviour which is characteristic of a whole species; for the anthropologist, ritual is occasional behaviour by particular members of a single culture. This contrast is very radical. Professor Erikson has suggested, by implication, that we may bridge the gap by referring to "culture groups" as "pseudo-species." This kind of analogy may be convenient in certain very special kinds of circumstance, but it is an exceedingly dangerous kind of analogy. It is in fact precisely this analogy which provides the basis for racial prejudice wherever we encounter it. It cannot be too strongly emphasized that ritual, in the anthropologist's sense, is in no way whatsoever a genetic endowment of the species.

Anthropologists are in the main concerned with forms of behaviour which are not genetically determined. Three types of such behaviour may be distinguished:

(1) Behaviour which is directed towards specific ends and which, *judged by our standards of verification*, produces observable results in a strictly mechanical way . . . we can call this "rational technical" behaviour.

(2) Behaviour which forms part of a signalling system and which serves to "communicate information" not because of any mechanical link between means and ends but because of the existence of a culturally defined communication code . . . we can call this "communicative" behaviour.

(3) Behaviour which is potent in itself in terms of the cultural conventions of the actors but *not* potent in a rational-technical sense, as specified in (1), or alternatively behaviour which is directed towards evoking the potency of occult powers even though it is not presumed to be potent in itself . . . we can call this "magical" behaviour.

These distinctions commonly apply to aspects of individual acts rather than actions considered as wholes, but crude examples are: (1) cutting down a tree, (2) an Englishman shaking hands, (3) an Englishman swearing an oath.

The orthodox convention in anthropology, to which Professor Fortes still adheres, is to reserve the term *ritual* for behaviours of class (3) only and to call behaviours of class (2) by some other term, e.g. etiquette, ceremonial. For complex reasons which cannot be developed here I myself hold that the distinction between behaviours of class (2) and behaviours of class (3) is either illusory or trivial so that I make the term *ritual* embrace both categories.

Although swearing an oath can be a brief and simple action which all anthropologists would rate as ritual, a "typical" ritual, as conceived by most anthropologists, would be a performance of a much more prolonged and complex kind . . . e.g., the whole sequence of operations surrounding the disposal of the dead. It is characteristic of such complex ritual sequences that they have a "structure" which is in a crude sense analogous to a prose passage in that the sequence as a whole is self-segmented into elements of decreasing scale. Where, in a prose passage, we can distinguish successively paragraphs, sentences, phrases, words, syllables, phonemes, so in a complex ritual we can distinguish sub-sequences and ritual elements of different "levels." Professor Turner's paper provides some illustrations of this point. Professor Turner's paper also demonstrates the enormous complexity of the problems which face the anthropologist who seeks to interpret or decode the "messages" embodied in a ritual sequence. One feature, however, is very plain and virtually universal. A ritual sequence when performed "in full" tends to be very repetitive; whatever the message may be that is supposed to be conveyed, the redundancy factor is very high.

Here it is worth reflecting on a general point of communication theory. If a sender seeks to transmit a message to a distant receiver against a background of noise, ambiguity is reduced if the same message is repeated over and over again by different channels and in different forms. For example, suppose that on a windy day I want to say something to a companion standing on a hill some distance away. If I want to make sure that my message has been understood I will not only repeat it several times over in different forms, but I will add visual signals to my verbal utterances. In so far as human rituals are "information bearing procedures" they are message systems of this redundant, interference loaded, type.

From an ethologist's point of view an example of ritualized adaptation in *Homo sapiens* is the capacity for speech, but the evolutionary developments which resulted in this capacity took place a very long time ago and the findings of contemporary anthropology have absolutely no bearing on the matter. Nevertheless, the relation between speech and ritual (in the anthropologist's sense) deserves close attention. When anthropologists talk about ritual they are usually thinking, primarily, of behaviours of a non-verbal kind, so it is worth reminding my anthropologist colleagues that (as I use the term) speech itself is a form of ritual; non-verbal ritual is simply a signal system of a different, less specialized, kind. To non-anthropologist readers I would simply say that the focus of interest in this paper is the relation between ritual as a communication system and ordinary speech as a communication system.

Professor Lorenz told us that the ethologists have two prime questions to ask about any ritual sequence. The philo-genetic question "How come?" and the functional question "What for?" The enormous complexity of the ritual sequences which anthropologists have to study make any guesses of the "How come?" type more or less absurd. Functional explanations of the "What for?" kind may look more plausible. A very general, very plausible, functional proposition is that an isolated human society must be so organized and so adapted to its environment that it can survive. For the sake of simplicity let us then confine our attention to ultra-primitive human societies as they existed in their erstwhile self-sufficient economic condition.

One common characteristic of such primitive peoples is that they are illiterate. Another is that each particular primitive society seems to be very well adapted to the environmental conditions in which it exists. Thus the Eskimos, the Australian Aborigines, and the Kalahari Bushmen all manage to live quite comfortably in conditions in which an ordinary white man would find himself incapable of sustaining life at all. This is possible because these people are somehow capable of transmitting from generation to generation an extremely elaborate body of information about the local topography, and its contents and how it may best be utilized. How is this achieved in the absence of any written documents or of any kind of formal schooling? In brief, my answer is that the performance of ritual serves to perpetuate knowledge which is essential for the survival of the performers. But this is altogether too slick. I need to explain how.

The first point to understand is an important difference between the kind of verbal classifications which we employ and those found in primitive society.

We act as if we believed that all the things in the world belonged to "natural kinds"—I am not concerned here with the truth or falsity of this proposition but only with the fact that in our ordinary life we tend to assume that we can ask of any object whatsoever: "What is it?" and that there is a unique particular correct answer to that question. In primitive society, on the other hand, it is broadly true that only things which are in some sense useful or significant to the speaker have names. With this limitation it is still possible for the classification of the things in the world to be enormously complex, but in general the vocabulary of primitive peoples is not cluttered up with concepts which are wholly irrelevant to the user—as is invariably the case with written languages.

Put in a different way one may say that when man attaches a particular category word to a class of objects he *creates* that class of objects. If an object has no name it is not recognized as an object and in a social sense "it does not exist." Thus the world of primitive man's experience contains fewer kinds of things than the world of our experience; but the fewer things all have names and they are all of social significance.

It is characteristic of many ritual and mythical sequences in primitive society that the actors claim to be recapitulating the creation of the world and that this act of creation is mythologized as a list of names attached to persons, places, animals and things. The world is created by the process of classification and the repetition of the classification of itself perpetuates the knowledge which it incorporates.

The next point I would emphasize is that although the languages of primitive non-literate peoples contain relatively few concepts which are purely abstract, this does not mean that primitive man is incapable of apprehending abstract notions. To take a case in point which is of cardinal importance to anthropologists the words Nature and Culture are both high-level abstractions. The social anthropologist sees his task as being specifically concerned with what is cultural rather than natural. I think it goes almost without saying that concepts such as Nature and Culture do not occur in primitive languages, yet primitive people must still be aware of the distinction Nature/Culture, for a concern with the distinction between Man and non-Man must always have a central place in any system of human knowledge. But how? I only have time to provide a single illustration. Professor Lévi-Strauss has recently drawn attention to a group of South American Indian myths which constantly hark back to a contrast between raw meat and cooked meat on the one hand (that is a human —i.e. *cultural*—mode of transformation) and a contrast between fresh vegetables and putrid vegetables on the other (that is a non-human —i.e. *natural*—mode of transformation). Raw meat, cooked meat, fresh vegetables, putrid vegetables are all explicit concrete things, but placed in a pattern these few categories can serve to express the highly abstract idea of the contrast between cultural process and natural process. Furthermore, this patterning can be expressed *either* in *words* (*raw, cooked, fresh, putrid*) and displayed in a myth, *or* alternatively it can be expressed in *things* with the ritual manipulation of appropriate objects. *In such ways as this the patterning of ritual procedures can serve as a complex store of information.*

We ourselves ordinarily store our information by patterned arrangements of a small number of simple signs marked on paper or punched cards or computer tape. Primitive peoples use the objects which they employ in ritual in analogous ways—the message is not conveyed by the objects as such but by their patterned arrangement and segmental order. [Here again Professor Turner's paper provides some exemplification of what I mean.]

Non-literate peoples have every incentive to economize in their use of information storing messages. Since all knowledge must be incorporated in the stories and rituals which are familiar to the living generation, it is of immense advantage if the same verbal categories (with their corresponding objects) can be used for multiple purposes.

Broadly speaking the information which must be stored and transmitted from generation to generation is of two kinds: (1) information about Nature: that is about the topography, the climate, usable and dangerous plants, animals, inanimate things and so on; (2) information about Society: the relations of men to other men, the nature of social groups, the rules and constraints which make social life possible. These broad categories of "information about Nature" and "information about Society" belong to separate fields, and no great ambiguity is likely to be introduced if we express both kinds of information in the same kind of language. Australian totemism which has fascinated but baffled several generations of anthropologists seems to be a phenomenon of this kind. Australian aborigines classify the categories of human society by means of the same words which

they use to classify the categories of Nature so that a group of human beings, a verbal concept, and a class of natural objects may all be thought of as representations of the same entity. It is only because we use words in a different way that we find this strange. For example, it makes sense in English to say: "A kangaroo is a different species of mammal from a wallaby." It also makes sense to say: "A Londoner is a different kind of man from a Parisian." But in English it does *not* make sense to economize with concepts and say: "A kangaroo–Londoner is a different species-kind of mammal–man from a wallaby–Parisian." But it is only because of our linguistic conventions that this last sentence does not make sense—it is in no way ambiguous. The peculiarity of Australian totemic myths and rituals is that they constantly make condensed statements of precisely this kind. Since modern computers do the same thing I cannot really feel that our own normal mode of expression can properly be said to be the more highly developed; it merely takes up more verbal space.

A rather similar point is that in primitive society it is hardly possible to make any clear-cut distinction between information which is expressed in verbal form and information which is expressed in non-verbal action.

A generation ago Jane Harrison, Malinowski and others made a clear distinction between myth on the one hand and ritual on the other, and argued that ritual was the dramatization of myth, while myth was a recapitulation of the drama, but this seems to me too simple. "Ritual" as one observes it in primitive communities is a complex of words and actions. There are doubtless some purposes for which it is useful to distinguish, within this complex, actions which are ritual, words which are spells, and words which are myth. But it is not the case that the words are one thing and the rite another. The uttering of the words is itself a ritual.

Educated peoples in our society have such a mastery of grammatically ordered speech that they can put *all* forms of information into words—and most of us tend to imagine that this is a normal capacity. But I think that Dr. Bernstein will bear me out if I say that it is not. For ordinary non-literate people there are many kinds of information which are never verbalized but *only* expressed in action. Verbal utterance then consists of chunks of conventionalized and often wholly non-grammatical "noise behaviour." *In its proper context* the totality of the behaviour—words plus action—conveys meaning, but the meaning is conveyed because of what we know already about the context; if you record the performance on a tape and play it back, you will often find that what was said, taken by itself, was virtually gibberish.

This is true even of "ordinary conversation" among intimates but it is much more true of ritual sequences. In any ritual performance some of the actors are likely to be novices but the majority will have participated in the "same kind" of ritual many times before; indeed the stability of the form of the ritual through time is dependent on the fact that it is familiar to most of the actors. But while the familiarity of the actors makes it possible to reproduce past performances with little variation this same familiarity allows the combination of words and actions to be drastically condensed without final loss of communication value . . . precisely as happens in the conversation of intimates.

One implication of this is that attempts to interpret the "meaning" of ritual by anthropological intuition must be viewed with great scepticism. This kind of interpretation has been very common in the past and we have had some examples put forward even in this Symposium. I would assert quite categorically that no interpretation of ritual sequences in man is possible unless the interpreter has a really detailed knowledge of the cultural matrix which provides the context for the rite under discussion. The gap between Sir James Frazer and Professor Turner is very wide and it seems to me that Sir Maurice Bowra has not fully appreciated this fact.

The distinction between condensed, action-supported, ritual utterance and fully grammatical ordered utterance does not lie between primitive man and modern man but between the thought of non-literate, partially verbalized man, and that of fully literate, fully verbalized man. Both types occur in our own society. In the latter mode concepts are apprehended as *words* which exist as distinct abstract entities capable of manipulation by themselves irrespective of any particular referent; in the former mode concepts lie in the relations between things, and between persons, and between persons and things, so that words are a kind of amalgam linking up things and persons. In this mode of thought the name of a thing or of an action is not separable from that to which it refers, and things and persons which belong to the same verbal category are thereby fused together in a manner which to us seems "mystical" or "non-logical." I do not rate this as *primitive* thinking but rather as *economical* thinking. In primitive society the whole of knowledge has to be encapsulated into a memorizable set of formalized actions and associated phrases: in such circumstances the use of a separate word for every imaginable category (which is the normal objective of literate people) would be a thoroughly wasteful procedure.

These really are the main points I want to make in this brief paper:

(1) In ritual, the verbal part and the behavioural part are not separable.

(2) As compared with written or writable speech the "language" of ritual is enormously condensed; a great variety of alternative meanings being implicit in the same category sets. This is also an attribute of mathematics. Primitive thought is transformational in the sense that mathematics is transformational.

(3) We tend to think this odd because of our own speech habits, but in fact our writable speech contains a vast amount of redundancy. This redundancy is valuable when, as is normally the case with us, we wish to convey information at a distance by means of speech alone without reference to context. In contrast the more condensed message forms which are characteristic of ritual action are generally appropriate to all forms of communication in which speaker and listener are in face to face relations and share a common body of knowledge about the context of the situation. In these restricted circumstances, which are normal in primitive society, the condensed and multi-faceted concepts to which I have been referring do not lead to ambiguity. In any event in ritual sequences the ambiguity latent in the symbolic condensation tends to be eliminated again by the device of thematic repetition and variation. This corresponds to the communication engineer's technique of overcoming noisy interference by the use of multiple redundancy.

Victor W. Turner

BETWIXT AND BETWEEN: THE LIMINAL PERIOD IN *RITES DE PASSAGE*

In his seminal essay *The Rites of Passage*, Arnold van Gennep characterized a class of rituals with three successive and distinct moments in ritual time: separation, margin, and aggregation. Working within Van Gennep's framework, Turner concentrates on the properties of the hitherto neglected, and supposedly amorphous, period in rites of passage, the marginal or liminal period. Initiation rites have particularly well-marked liminal periods, where neophytes typically are removed, secluded, darkened, hidden, without rank or insignia; in terms of social structure, neophytes are invisible. In effect, the initiate is "betwixt and between," neither here nor there, no longer a child and not yet an adult. During this period of transition between states symbolic themes characteristically concern death and decomposition, or gestation and parturition, referring to the culturally defined person the initiate has been and will become. Because of the economy of symbolic reference, the opposed states—the having been and the becoming—may be represented by a single object, act, or phrase. Turner's originality lies in uncovering the potential richness and cultural significance of what all too often is dismissed as a residual category, an interstructural phase which does not bear much study.

Reprinted from Victor W. Turner, "Betwixt and Between: The Liminal Period in *Rites de Passage*," *The Proceedings of the American Ethnological Society* (1964), Symposium on New Approaches to the Study of Religion, pp. 4–20, by permission of the author and the University of Washington Press.

In this paper, I wish to consider some of the sociocultural properties of the "liminal period" in that class of rituals which Arnold van Gennep has definitively characterized as *"rites de passage."* If our basic model of society is that of a "structure of positions," we must regard the period of margin or "liminality" as an interstructural situation. I shall consider, notably in the case of initiation rites, some of the main features of instruction among the simpler societies. I shall also take note of certain symbolic themes that concretely express indigenous concepts about the nature of "interstructural" human beings.

Rites de passage are found in all societies but tend to reach their maximal expression in small-scale, relatively stable and cyclical societies, where change is bound up with biological and meteorological rhythms and recurrences rather than with technological innovations. Such rites indicate and constitute transitions between states. By "state" I mean here "a relatively fixed or stable condition" and would include in its meaning such social constancies as legal status, profession, office or calling, rank or degree. I hold it to designate also the condition of a person as determined by his culturally recognized degree of maturation as when one speaks of "the married or single state" or the "state of infancy."

The term "state" may also be applied to ecological conditions, or to the physical, mental or emotional condition in which a person or group may be found at a particular time. A man may thus be in a state of good or bad health; a society in a state of war or peace or a state of famine or of plenty. State, in short, is a more inclusive concept than status or office and refers to any type of stable or recurrent condition that is culturally recognized. One may, I suppose, also talk about "a state of transition," since J. S. Mill has, after all, written of "a state of progressive movement," but I prefer to regard transition as a process, a becoming, and in the case of *rites de passage* even a transformation—here an apt analogy would be water in process of being heated to boiling point, or a pupa changing from grub to moth. In any case, a transition has different cultural properties from those of a state, as I hope to show presently.

Van Gennep himself defined *"rites de passage"* as "rites which accompany every change of place, state, social position and age." To point up the contrast between "state" and "transition," I employ "state" to include all his other terms. Van Gennep has shown that all rites of transition are marked by three phases: separation, margin (or *limen*), and aggregation. The first phase of separation comprises symbolic behavior signifying the detachment of the individual or group either from an earlier fixed point in the social structure or a set of cultural conditions (a "state"); during the intervening liminal period, the state of the ritual subject (the "passenger") is ambiguous; he passes through a realm that has few or none of the attributes of the past or coming state; in the third phase the passage is consummated. The ritual subject, individual or corporate, is in a stable state once more and, by virtue of this, has rights and obligations of a clearly defined and "structural" type, and is expected to behave in accordance with certain customary norms and ethical standards. The most prominent type of *rites de passage* tends to accompany what Lloyd Warner (1959, 303) has called "the movement of a man through his lifetime, from a fixed placental placement within his mother's womb to his death and ultimate fixed point of his tombstone and final containment in his grave as a dead organism —punctuated by a number of critical moments of transition which all societies ritualize and publicly mark with suitable observances to impress the significance of the individual and the group on living members of the community. These are the important times of birth, puberty, marriage, and death." However, as Van Gennep, Henri Junod, and others have shown, *rites de passage* are not confined to culturally defined life-crises but may accompany any change from one state to another, as when a whole tribe goes to war, or when it attests to the passage from scarcity to plenty by performing a first-fruits or a harvest festival. *Rites de passage*, too, are not restricted, sociologically speaking, to movements between ascribed statuses. They also concern entry into a new achieved status, whether this be a political office or membership of an exclusive club or secret society. They may admit persons into membership of a religious group where such a group does not include the whole society, or qualify them for the official duties of the cult, sometimes in a graded series of rites.

Since the main problem of this study is the nature and characteristics of transition in relatively stable societies, I shall focus attention on *rites de passage* that tend to have well-developed liminal periods. On the whole, initiation rites, whether into social maturity or cult membership, best exemplify transition, since they have well-marked and protracted marginal or liminal phases. I shall pay only brief heed here to rites of separation and aggregation, since these are more closely implicated in social structure than rites of liminality. Liminality during initiation is, therefore, the primary datum of this study, though I will draw on other aspects of passage ritual where the argument demands this. I may state here, partly as an aside, that I consider the term "ritual" to be more fittingly applied to forms of religious behavior associated with social transitions, while the term "ceremony" has a closer bearing on religious behavior associated with social states, where politico-legal institutions also have greater importance. Ritual is transformative, ceremony confirmatory.

The subject of passage ritual is, in the liminal period, structurally, if not physically, "invisible." As members of society, most of us see only what we expect to see, and what we expect to see is what we are conditioned to see when we have learned the definitions and classifications of our culture. A society's secular definitions do not allow for the existence of a not-boy-not-man, which is what a novice in a male puberty rite is (if he can be said to be anything). A set of essentially religious definitions co-exist with these which do set out to define the structurally indefinable "transitional-being." The transitional-being or "liminal *persona*" is defined by a name and by a set of symbols. The same name is very frequently employed to designate those who are being initiated into very different states of life. For example, among the Ndembu of Zambia the name *mwadi* may mean various things: it may stand for "a boy novice in circumcision rites," or "a chief-designate undergoing his installation rites," or, yet again, "the first or ritual wife" who has important ritual duties in the domestic family. Our own terms "initiate" and "neophyte" have a similar breadth of reference. It would seem from this that emphasis tends to be laid on the transition itself, rather than on the particular states between which it is taking place.

The symbolism attached to and surrounding the liminal *persona* is complex and bizarre. Much of it is modeled on human biological processes, which are conceived to be what Lévi-Strauss might call "isomorphic" with structural and cultural processes. They give an outward and visible form to an inward and conceptual process. The structural "invisibility" of liminal *personae* has a twofold character. They are at once no longer classified and not yet classified. In so far as they are no longer classified, the symbols that represent them are, in many societies, drawn from the biology of death, decomposition, catabolism, and other physical processes that have a negative tinge, such as menstruation (frequently regarded as the absence or loss of a fetus). Thus, in some boys' initiations, newly circumcised boys are explicitly likened to menstruating women. In so far as a neophyte is structurally "dead," he or she may be treated, for a long or short period, as a corpse is customarily treated in his or her society. (See Stobaeus' quotation, probably from a lost work of Plutarch, "initiation and death correspond word for word and thing for thing." [James, 1961, 132.]) The neophyte may be buried, forced to lie motionless in the posture and direction of customary burial, may be stained black, or may be forced to live for a while in the company of masked and monstrous mummers representing, *inter alia*, the dead, or worse still, the un-dead. The metaphor of dissolution is often applied to neophytes; they are allowed to go filthy and identified with the earth, the generalized matter into which every specific individual is rendered down. Particular form here becomes general matter; often their very names are taken from them and each is called solely by the generic term for "neophyte" or "initiand." (This useful neologism is employed by many modern anthropologists.)

The other aspect, that they are not yet classified, is often expressed in symbols modeled on processes of gestation and parturition. The neophytes are likened to or treated as embryos, newborn infants, or sucklings by symbolic means which vary from culture to culture. I shall return to this theme presently.

The essential feature of these symbolizations is that the neophytes are neither living nor dead from one aspect, and both living and dead from another. Their condition is one of ambiguity and paradox, a confusion of all the customary categories. Jakob Boehme, the German mystic whose obscure writings gave Hegel his celebrated dialectical "triad," liked to say that "In Yea and Nay all things consist." Liminality may perhaps be regarded as the Nay to all positive structural assertions, but as in some sense the source of them all, and, more than that, as a realm of pure possibility whence novel configurations of ideas and relations may arise. I will not pursue this point here but, after all, Plato, a speculative philosopher, if there ever was one, did acknowledge his philosophical debt to the teachings of the Eleusinian and Orphic initiations

of Attica. We have no way of knowing whether primitive initiations merely conserved lore. Perhaps they also generated new thought and new custom.

Dr. Mary Douglas, of University College, London, has recently advanced (in a magnificent book *Purity and Danger* [1966]) the very interesting and illuminating view that the concept of pollution "is a reaction to protect cherished principles and categories from contradiction." She holds that, in effect, what is unclear and contradictory (from the perspective of social definition) tends to be regarded as (ritually) unclean. The unclear is the unclean: e.g., she examines the prohibitions on eating certain animals and crustaceans in Leviticus in the light of this hypothesis (these being creatures that cannot be unambiguously classified in terms of traditional criteria). From this standpoint, one would expect to find that transitional beings are particularly polluting, since they are neither one thing nor another; or may be both; or neither here nor there; or may even be nowhere (in terms of any recognized cultural topography), and are at the very least "betwixt and between" all the recognized fixed points in space-time of structural classification. In fact, in confirmation of Dr. Douglas's hypothesis, liminal *personae* nearly always and everywhere are regarded as polluting to those who have never been, so to speak, "inoculated" against them, through having been themselves initiated into the same state. I think that we may perhaps usefully discriminate here between the statics and dynamics of pollution situations. In other words, we may have to distinguish between pollution notions which concern states that have been ambiguously or contradictorily defined, and those which derive from ritualized transitions between states. In the first case, we are dealing with what has been defectively defined or ordered, in the second with what cannot be defined in static terms. We are not dealing with structural contradictions when we discuss liminality, but with the essentially unstructured (which is at once destructured and prestructured) and often the people themselves see this in terms of bringing neophytes into close connection with deity or with superhuman power, with what is, in fact, often regarded as the unbounded, the infinite, the limitless. Since neophytes are not only structurally "invisible" (though physically visible) and ritually polluting, they are very commonly secluded, partially or completely, from the realm of culturally defined and ordered states and statuses. Often the indigenous term for the liminal period is, as among Ndembu, the locative form of a noun meaning "seclusion site" (*kunkunka, kung'ula*). The neophytes are sometimes said to "be in another place." They have physical but not social "reality," hence they have to be hidden, since it is a paradox, a scandal, to see what ought not to be there! Where they are not removed to a sacred place of concealment they are often disguised, in masks or grotesque costumes or striped with white, red, or black clay, and the like.

In societies dominantly structured by kinship institutions, sex distinctions have great structural importance. Patrilineal and matrilineal moieties and clans, rules of exogamy, and the like, rest and are built up on these distinctions. It is consistent with this to find that in liminal situations (in kinship-dominated societies) neophytes are sometimes treated or symbolically represented as being neither male nor female. Alternatively, they may be symbolically assigned characteristics of both sexes, irrespective of their biological sex. (Bruno Bettelheim [1954] has collected much illustrative material on this point from initiation rites.) They are symbolically either sexless or bisexual and may be regarded as a kind of human *prima materia*—as undifferentiated raw material. It was perhaps from the rites of the Hellenic mystery religions that Plato derived his notion expressed in his *Symposium* that the first humans were androgynes. If the liminal period is seen as an interstructural phase in social dynamics, the symbolism both of androgyny and sexlessness immediately becomes intelligible in sociological terms without the need to import psychological (and especially depth-psychological) explanations. Since sex distinctions are important components of structural status, in a structureless realm they do not apply.

A further structurally negative characteristic of transitional beings is that they *have* nothing. They have no status, property, insignia, secular clothing, rank, kinship position, nothing to demarcate them structurally from their fellows. Their condition is indeed the very prototype of sacred poverty. Rights over property, goods, and services inhere in positions in the politico-jural structure. Since they do not occupy such positions, neophytes exercise no such rights. In the words of King Lear they represent "naked unaccommodated man."

I have no time to analyze other symbolic themes that express these attributes of "structural invisibility," ambiguity and neutrality. I want now to draw attention to certain positive aspects of liminality. Already we have noted how certain liminal processes are regarded as analogous to those of gestation, parturition, and suckling. Undoing, dissolution, decomposition are accompanied by processes of growth, transformation, and the reformulation of old elements in new patterns. It is interesting to note how, by the principle of the economy (or parsimony) of symbolic reference, logically antithetical processes of death and growth may be represented by the same tokens, for example, by huts and tunnels that are at once tombs and wombs, by lunar symbolism (for the same moon waxes and wanes), by snake symbolism (for the snake appears to die, but only to shed its old skin and appear in a new one), by bear symbolism (for the bear "dies" in autumn and is "reborn" in spring), by nakedness (which is at once the mark of a newborn infant and a corpse prepared for burial), and by innumerable other symbolic formations and actions. This coincidence of opposite processes and notions in a single representation characterizes the peculiar unity of the liminal: that which is neither this nor that, and yet is both.

I have spoken of the interstructural character of the liminal. However, between neophytes and their instructors (where these exist), and in connecting neophytes with one another, there exists a set of relations that compose a "social structure" of highly specific type. It is a structure of a very simple kind: between instructors and neophytes there is often complete authority and complete submission; among neophytes there is often complete equality. Between incumbents of positions in secular politico-jural systems there exist intricate and situationally shifting networks of rights and duties proportioned to their rank, status, and corporate affiliation. There are many different kinds of privileges and obligations, many degrees of superordination and subordination. In the liminal period such distinctions and gradations tend to be eliminated. Nevertheless, it must be understood that the authority of the elders over the neophytes is not based on legal sanctions; it is in a sense the personification of the self-evident authority of tradition. The authority of the elders is absolute, because it represents the absolute, the axiomatic values of society in which are expressed the "common good" and the common interest. The essence of the complete obedience of the neophytes is to submit to the elders but only in so far as they are in charge, so to speak, of the common good and represent in their persons the total community. That the authority in question is really quintessential tradition emerges clearly in societies where initiations are not collective but individual and where there are no instructors or *gurus*. For example, Omaha boys, like other North American Indians, go alone into the wilderness to fast and pray (Hocart, 1952, 160). This solitude is liminal between boyhood and manhood. If they dream that they receive a woman's burden-strap, they feel compelled to dress and live henceforth in every way as women. Such men are known as *mixuga*. The authority of such a dream in such a situation is absolute. Alice Cummingham Fletcher tells of one Omaha who had been forced in this way to live as a woman, but whose natural inclinations led him to rear a family and to go on the warpath. Here the *mixuga* was not an invert but a man bound by the authority of tribal beliefs and values. Among many Plains Indians, boys on their lonely Vision Quest inflicted ordeals and tests on themselves that amounted to tortures. These again were not basically self-tortures inflicted by a masochistic temperament but due to obedience to the authority of tradition in the liminal situation —a type of situation in which there is no room for secular compromise, evasion, manipulation, casuistry, and maneuver in the field of custom, rule, and norm. Here again a cultural explanation seems preferable to a psychological one. A normal man acts abnormally because he is obedient to tribal tradition, not out of disobedience to it. He does not evade but fulfills his duties as a citizen.

If complete obedience characterizes the relationship of neophyte to elder, complete equality usually characterizes the relationship of neophyte to neophyte, where the rites are collective. This comradeship must be distinguished from brotherhood or sibling relationship, since in the latter there is always the inequality of older and younger, which often achieves linguistic representation and may be maintained by legal sanctions. The liminal group is a community or comity of comrades and not a structure of hierarchically arrayed positions. This comradeship transcends distinctions of rank, age, kinship position, and, in some kinds of cultic group, even of sex.

Much of the behavior recorded by ethnographers in seclusion situations falls under the principle: "Each for all, and all for each." Among the Ndembu of Zambia, for example, all food brought for novices in circumcision seclusion by their mothers is shared out equally among them. No special favors are bestowed on the sons of chiefs or headmen. Any food acquired by novices in the bush is taken by the elders and apportioned among the group. Deep friendships between novices are encouraged, and they sleep around lodge fires in clusters of four or five particular comrades. However, all are supposed to be linked by special ties which persist after the rites are over, even into old age. This friendship, known as *wubwambu* (from a term meaning "breast") or *wulunda*, enables a man to claim privileges of hospitality of a far-reaching kind. I have no need here to dwell on the lifelong ties that are held to bind in close friendship those initiated into the same age-set in East African Nilo-Hamitic and Bantu societies, into the same fraternity or sorority on an American campus, or into the same class in a Naval or Military Academy in Western Europe.

This comradeship, with its familiarity, ease and, I would add, mutual outspokenness, is once more the product of interstructural liminality, with its scarcity of jurally sanctioned relationships and its emphasis on axiomatic values expressive of the common weal. People can "be themselves," it is frequently said, when they are not acting institutionalized roles. Roles, too, carry responsibilities and in the liminal situation the main burden of responsibility is borne by the elders, leaving the neophytes free to develop interpersonal relationships as they will. They confront one another, as it were, integrally and not in compartmentalized fashion as actors of roles.

The passivity of neophytes to their instructors, their malleability, which is increased by submission to ordeal, their reduction to a uniform condition, are signs of the process whereby they are ground down to be fashioned anew and endowed with additional powers to cope with their new station in life. Dr. Richards, in her superb study of Bemba girls' puberty rites, *Chisungu*, has told us that Bemba speak of "growing a girl" when they mean initiating her (1956, 121). This term "to grow" well expresses how many peoples think of transition rites. We are inclined, as sociologists, to reify our abstractions (it is indeed a device which helps us to understand many kinds of social interconnection) and to talk about persons "moving through structural positions in a hierarchical frame" and the like. Not so the Bemba and the Shilluk of the Sudan who see the status or condition embodied or incarnate, if you like, *in* the person. To "grow" a girl into a woman is to effect an ontological transformation; it is not merely to convey an unchanging substance from one position to another by a quasi-mechanical force. Howitt saw Kuringals in Australia and I have seen Ndembu in Africa drive away grown-up men before a circumcision ceremony because they had not been initiated. Among Ndembu, men were also chased off because they had only been circumcised at the Mission Hospital and had not undergone the full bush seclusion according to the orthodox Ndembu rite. These biologically mature men had not been "made men" by the proper ritual procedures. It is the ritual and the esoteric teaching which grows girls and makes men. It is the ritual, too, which among Shilluk makes a prince into a king, or, among Luvale, a cultivator into a hunter. The arcane knowledge or *"gnosis"* obtained in the liminal period is felt to change the inmost nature of the neophyte, impressing him, as a seal impresses wax, with the characteristics of his new state. It is not a mere acquisition of knowledge, but a change in being. His apparent passivity is revealed as an absorption of powers which will become active after his social status has been redefined in the aggregation rites.

The structural simplicity of the liminal situation in many initiations is offset by its cultural complexity. I can touch on only one aspect of this vast subject matter here and raise three problems in connection with it. This aspect is the vital one of the communication of the *sacra*, the heart of the liminal matter.

Jane Harrison has shown that in the Greek Eleusinian and Orphic mysteries this communication of the *sacra* has three main components (1903, 144–160). By and large, this threefold classification holds good for initiation rites all over the world. *Sacra* may be communicated as: (1) exhibitions, "what is shown"; (2) actions, "what is done"; and (3) instructions, "what is said."

"Exhibitions" would include evocatory instruments or sacred articles, such as relics of deities, heroes or ancestors, aboriginal *churingas*, sacred drums or other musical instruments, the contents of Amerindian medicine bundles, and the fan, cist and tympanum of Greek and Near Eastern mystery cults. In the Lesser Eleusinian Mysteries of Athens, *sacra* consisted of a bone, top, ball, tambourine, apples, mirror, fan, and woolly fleece. Other *sacra* include masks, images, figurines, and effigies; the pottery emblems (*mbusa*) of the Bemba would belong to this class. In some kinds of initiation, as for example the initiation into the shaman-diviner's profession among the Saora of Middle India, described by Verrier Elwin (1955), pictures and icons representing the journeys of the dead or the adventures of supernatural beings may be shown to the initiands. A striking feature of such sacred articles is often their formal simplicity. It is their interpretation which is complex, not their outward form.

Among the "instructions" received by neophytes may be reckoned such matters as the revelation of the real, but secularly secret, names of the deities or spirits believed to preside over the rites—a very frequent procedure in African cultic or secret associations (Turner, 1962a, 36). They are also taught the main outlines of the theogony, cosmogony, and mythical history of their societies or cults, usually with reference to the *sacra* exhibited. Great importance is attached to keeping secret the nature of the *sacra*, the formulas chanted and instructions given about them. These constitute the crux of liminality, for while instruction is also given in ethical and social obligations, in law and in kinship rules, and in technology to fit neophytes for the duties of future office, no interdiction is placed on knowledge thus imparted since it tends to be current among uninitiated persons also.

I want to take up three problems in considering the communication of *sacra*. The first concerns their frequent disproportion, the second their monstrousness, and the third their mystery.

When one examines the masks, costumes, figurines, and such displayed in initiation situations, one is often struck, as I have been when observing Ndembu masks in circumcision and funerary rites, by the way in which certain natural and cultural features are represented as disproportionately large or small. A head, nose, or phallus, a hoe, bow, or meal mortar are represented as huge or tiny by comparison with other features of their context which retain their normal size. (For a good example of this, see "The Man Without Arms" in *Chisungu* [Richards, 1956, 211], a figurine of a lazy man with an enormous penis but no arms.) Sometimes things retain their customary shapes but are portrayed in unusual colors. What is the point of this exaggeration amounting sometimes to caricature? It seems to me that to enlarge or diminish or discolor in this way is a primordial mode of abstraction. The outstandingly exaggerated feature is made into an object of reflection. Usually it is not a univocal symbol that is thus represented but a multivocal one, a semantic molecule with many components. One example is the Bemba pottery emblem *Coshi wa ng'oma*, "The Nursing Mother," described by Audrey Richards in *Chisungu*. This is a clay figurine, nine inches high, of an exaggeratedly pregnant mother shown carrying four babies at the same time, one at her breast and three at her back. To this figurine is attached a riddling song:

My mother deceived me!
Coshi wa ng'oma!
So you have deceived me;
I have become pregnant again.

Bemba women interpreted this to Richards as follows:

Coshi wa ng'oma was a midwife of legendary fame and is merely addressed in this song. The girl complains because her mother told her to wean her first child too soon so that it died; or alternatively told her that she would take the first child if her daughter had a second one. But she was tricking her and now the girl has two babies to look after. The moral stressed is the duty of refusing intercourse with the husband before the baby is weaned, i.e., at the second or third year. This is a common Bemba practice (1956, 209–210).

In the figurine the exaggerated features are the number of children carried at once by the woman and her enormously distended belly. Coupled with the song, it encourages the novice to ponder upon two relationships vital to her, those with her mother and her husband. Unless the novice observes the Bemba weaning custom, her mother's desire for grandchildren to increase her matrilineage and her husband's desire for renewed sexual intercourse will between them actually destroy and not increase her offspring. Underlying this is the deeper moral that to abide by tribal custom and not to sin against it either by excess or defect is to live satisfactorily. Even to please those one loves may be to invite calamity, if such compliance defies the immemorial wisdom of the elders embodied in the *mbusa*. This wisdom is vouched for by the mythical and archetypal midwife *Coshi wa ng'oma*.

If the exaggeration of single features is not irrational but thought-provoking, the same may also be said about the representation of monsters. Earlier writers—such as J. A. McCulloch (1913) in his article on "Monsters" in *Hastings Encyclopaedia of Religion and Ethics*—are inclined to regard bizarre and monstrous masks and figures, such as frequently appear in the liminal period of initiations, as the product of "hallucinations, night-terrors and dreams." McCulloch goes on to argue that "as man drew little distinction (in primitive society) between himself and animals, as he thought that transformation from one to the other was possible, so he easily ran human and animal together. This in part accounts for animal-headed gods or animal-gods with human heads." My own view is the opposite one: that monsters are manufactured precisely to teach neophytes to distinguish clearly between the different factors of reality, as it is conceived in their culture. Here, I think, William James's so-called "law of dissociation" may help us to clarify the problem of monsters. It may be stated as follows: when *a* and *b* occurred together as parts of the same total object, without being discriminated, the occurrence of one of these, *a*, in a new combination *ax*, favors the discrimination of *a*, *b*, and *x* from one another. As James himself put it, "What is associated now with one thing and now with another, tends to become dissociated from either, and to grow into an object of abstract contemplation by the mind. One might call this the law of dissociation by varying concomitants" (1918, 506).

From this standpoint, much of the grotesqueness and monstrosity of liminal *sacra* may be seen to be aimed not so much at terrorizing or bemusing neophytes into submission or out of their wits as at making them vividly and rapidly aware of what may be called the "factors" of their culture. I have myself seen Ndembu and Luvale masks that combine features of both sexes, have both animal and human attributes, and unite in a single representation human characteristics with those of the natural landscape. One *ikishi* mask is partly human and partly represents a grassy plain. Elements are withdrawn from their usual settings and combined with one another in a totally unique configuration, the monster or dragon. Monsters startle neophytes into thinking about objects, persons, relationships, and features of their environment they have hitherto taken for granted.

In discussing the structural aspect of liminality, I mentioned how neophytes are withdrawn from their structural positions and consequently from the values, norms, sentiments, and techniques associated with those positions. They are also divested of their previous habits of thought, feeling, and action. During the liminal period, neophytes are alternately forced and encouraged to think about their society, their cosmos, and the powers that generate and sustain them. Liminality may be partly described as a stage of reflection. In it those ideas, sentiments, and facts that had been hitherto for the neophytes bound up in configurations and accepted unthinkingly are, as it were, resolved into their constituents. These constituents are isolated and made into objects of reflection for the neophytes by such processes as componental exaggeration and dissociation by varying concomitants. The communication of *sacra* and other forms of esoteric instruction really involves three processes, though these should not be regarded as in series but as in parallel. The first is the reduction of culture into recognized components or factors; the second is their recombination in fantastic or monstrous patterns and shapes; and the third is their recombination in ways that make sense with regard to the new state and status that the neophytes will enter.

The second process, monster- or fantasy-making, focuses attention on the components of the masks and effigies, which are so radically ill-assorted that they stand out and can be thought about. The monstrosity of the configuration throws its elements into relief. Put a man's head on a lion's body and you think about the human head in the abstract. Perhaps it becomes for you, as a member of a given culture and with the appropriate guidance, an emblem of chieftainship; or it may be explained as representing the soul as against the body; or intellect as contrasted with brute force, or innumerable other things. There could be less encouragement to reflect on heads and headship if that same head were firmly ensconced on its familiar, its all too familiar, human body. The man-lion monster also encourages the observer to think about lions, their habits, qualities, metaphorical properties, religious significance, and so on. More important than these, the relation between man and lion, empirical and metaphorical, may be speculated upon, and new ideas developed on this topic. Liminality here breaks, as it were, the cake of custom and

enfranchises speculation. That is why I earlier mentioned Plato's self-confessed debt to the Greek mysteries. Liminality is the realm of primitive hypothesis, where there is a certain freedom to juggle with the factors of existence. As in the works of Rabelais, there is a promiscuous intermingling and juxtaposing of the categories of event, experience, and knowledge, with a pedagogic intention.

But this liberty has fairly narrow limits. The neophytes return to secular society with more alert faculties perhaps and enhanced knowledge of how things work, but they have to become once more subject to custom and law. Like the Bemba girl I mentioned earlier, they are shown that ways of acting and thinking alternative to those laid down by the deities or ancestors are ultimately unworkable and may have disastrous consequences.

Moreover, in initiation, there are usually held to be certain axiomatic principles of construction, and certain basic building blocks that make up the cosmos and into whose nature no neophyte may inquire. Certain *sacra*, usually exhibited in the most arcane episodes of the liminal period, represent or may be interpreted in terms of these axiomatic principles and primordial constituents. Perhaps we may call these *sacerrima*, "most sacred things." Sometimes they are interpreted by a myth about the world-making activities of supernatural beings "at the beginning of things." Myths may be completely absent, however, as in the case of the Ndembu "mystery of the three rivers" (which I have described, pp. 61–65). This mystery (*mpang'u*) is exhibited at circumcision and funerary cult association rites. Three trenches are dug in a consecrated site and filled respectively with white, red, and black water. These "rivers" are said to "flow from Nzambi," the High God. The instructors tell the neophytes, partly in riddling songs and partly in direct terms, what each river signifies. Each "river" is a multivocal symbol with a fan of referents ranging from life values, ethical ideas, and social norms, to grossly physiological processes and phenomena. They seem to be regarded as powers which, in varying combination, underlie or even constitute what Ndembu conceive to be reality. In no other context is the interpretation of whiteness, redness, and blackness so full; and nowhere else is such a close analogy drawn, even identity made, between these rivers and bodily fluids and emissions: whiteness = semen, milk; redness = menstrual blood, the blood of birth, blood shed by a weapon, etc.; blackness = feces, certain products of bodily decay, etc. This use of an aspect of human physiology as a model for social, cosmic, and religious ideas and processes is a variant of a widely distributed initiation theme: that the human body is a microcosm of the universe. The body may be pictured as androgynous, as male or female, or in terms of one or other of its developmental stages, as child, mature adult, and elder. On the other hand, as in the Ndembu case, certain of its properties may be abstracted. Whatever the mode of representation, the body is regarded as a sort of symbolic template for the communication of *gnosis*, mystical knowledge about the nature of things and how they came to be what they are. The cosmos may in some cases be regarded as a vast human body; in other belief systems, visible parts of the body may be taken to portray invisible faculties such as reason, passion, wisdom and so on; in others again, the different parts of the social order are arrayed in terms of a human anatomical paradigm.

Whatever the precise mode of explaining reality by the body's attributes, *sacra* which illustrates this are always regarded as absolutely sacrosanct, as ultimate mysteries. We are here in the realm of what Warner (1959, 3–4) would call "nonrational or nonlogical symbols" which

arise out of the basic individual and cultural assumptions, more often unconscious than not, from which most social action springs. They supply the solid core of mental and emotional life of each individual and group. This does not mean that they are irrational or maladaptive, or that man cannot often think in a reasonable way about them, but rather that they do not have their source in his rational processes. When they come into play, such factors as data, evidence, proof, and the facts and procedures of rational thought in action are apt to be secondary or unimportant.

The central cluster of nonlogical *sacra* is then the symbolic template of the whole system of beliefs and values in a given culture, its archetypal paradigm and ultimate measure. Neophytes shown these are often told that they are in the presence of forms established from the beginning of things. (See Cicero's comment [De Leg. II. 14] on the Eleusinian Mysteries: "They are rightly called initiations [beginnings] because we have thus learned the first principles of life.") I have used the metaphor of a seal or stamp in connection with the ontological character ascribed in many initiations to arcane knowledge.

The term "archetype" denotes in Greek a master stamp or impress, and these *sacra*, presented with a numinous simplicity, stamp into the neophytes the basic assumptions of their culture. The neophytes are told also that they are being filled with mystical power by what they see and what they are told about it. According to the purpose of the initiation, this power confers on them capacities to undertake successfully the tasks of their new office, in this world or the next.

Thus, the communication of *sacra* both teaches the neophytes how to think with some degree of abstraction about their cultural milieu and gives them ultimate standards of reference. At the same time, it is believed to change their nature, transform them from one kind of human being into another. It intimately unites man and office. But for a variable while, there was an uncommitted man, an individual rather than a social *persona*, in a sacred community of individuals.

It is not only in the liminal period of initiations that the nakedness and vulnerability of the ritual subject receive symbolic stress. Let me quote from Hilda Kuper's description of the seclusion of the Swazi chief during the great *Incwala* ceremony (1961, 197–225). The *Incwala* is a national First-Fruits ritual, performed in the height of summer when the early crops ripen. The regiments of the Swazi nation assemble at the capital to celebrate its rites, "whereby the nation receives strength for the new year." The *Incwala* is at the same time "a play of kingship." The king's well-being is identified with that of the nation. Both require periodic ritual strengthening. Lunar symbolism is prominent in the rites, as we shall see, and the king, personifying the nation, during his seclusion represents the moon in transition between phases, neither waning nor waxing. Dr. Kuper, Professor Gluckman (1954), and Professor Wilson (1961) have discussed the structural aspects of the *Incwala* which are clearly present in its rites of separation and aggregation. What we are about to examine are the interstructural aspects.

During his night and day of seclusion, the king, painted black, remains, says Dr. Kuper, "painted in blackness" and "in darkness"; he is unapproachable, dangerous to himself and others. He must cohabit that night with his first ritual wife (in a kind of "mystical marriage"—this ritual wife is, as it were, consecrated for such liminal situations).

The entire population is also temporarily in a state of taboo and seclusion. Ordinary activities and behavior are suspended; sexual intercourse is prohibited, no one may sleep late the following morning, and when they get up they are not allowed to touch each other, to wash the body, to sit on mats, to poke anything into the ground, or even to scratch their hair. The children are scolded if they play and make merry. The sound of songs that has stirred the capital for nearly a month is abruptly stilled; it is the day of bacisa (cause to hide). The king remains secluded; . . . all day he sits naked on a lion skin in the ritual hut of the harem or in the sacred enclosure in the royal cattle byre. Men of his inner circle see that he breaks none of the taboos . . . on this day the identification of the people with the king is very marked. The spies (who see to it that the people respect the taboos) do not say, "You are sleeping late" or "You are scratching," but "You cause the king to sleep," "You scratch him (the king)"; etc. (Kuper, 1947, 219–220).

Other symbolic acts are performed which exemplify the "darkness" and "waxing and waning moon" themes, for example, the slaughtering of a black ox, the painting of the queen mother with a black mixture—she is compared again to a half-moon, while the king is a full moon, and both are in eclipse until the paint is washed off finally with doctored water, and the ritual subject "comes once again into lightness and normality."

In this short passage we have an embarrassment of symbolic riches. I will mention only a few themes that bear on the argument of this paper. Let us look at the king's position first. He is symbolically invisible, "black," a moon between phases. He is also under obedience to traditional rules, and "men of his inner circle" see that he keeps them. He is also "naked," divested of the trappings of his office. He remains apart from the scenes of his political action in a sanctuary or ritual hut. He is also, it would seem, identified with the earth which the people are forbidden to stab, lest the king be affected. He is "hidden." The king, in short, has been divested of all the outward attributes, the "accidents," of his kingship and is reduced to its substance, the "earth" and "darkness" from which the normal, structured order of the Swazi kingdom will be regenerated "in lightness."

In this betwixt-and-between period, in this fruitful darkness, king and people are closely identified. There is a mystical solidarity between them, which contrasts sharply with the hierarchical rank-dominated structure of ordinary Swazi life. It is only in darkness, silence, celibacy, in the absence of merriment and movement that the king and people can thus be one. For every normal action is involved in the rights and obligations of a structure that defines status and establishes social distance between men. Only in their Trappist sabbath of transition may the Swazi regenerate the social tissues torn by conflicts arising from distinctions of status and discrepant structural norms.

I end this study with an invitation to investigators of ritual to focus their attention on the phenomena and processes of mid-transition. It is these, I hold, that paradoxically expose the basic building blocks of culture just when we pass out of and before we re-enter the structural realm. In *sacerrima* and their interpretations we have categories of data that may usefully be handled by the new sophisticated techniques of cross-cultural comparison.

Robin Horton

RITUAL MAN IN AFRICA

Horton begins with a critique of Gluckman, who reduces ritual to social relations, and Turner, who sees religion as a universal and nonreducible human aspiration. While granting that much of African ritual involves communion with supernatural beings, and hence is not reducible to nonreligious terms, Horton emphasizes the concern of African religions with puzzling observations in the natural and social realms. Such speculations are seen as analogous with the construction of models or theories in Western science; they are attempts to explain and influence

Reprinted in abridged form from *Africa*, XXXIV (1964), 85–104, by permission of the author and the International African Institute.

the commonplace workings of nature and society. Scientific models, after all, are constructed by partial analogy with known and observable phenomena in the world of the scientist; the scientist's model is an attempt to explain the flux, the seeming disorder, of the natural world with reference to parsimonious underlying mechanisms. Just as it may not make sense to ask the scientist what color a proton is, so African cosmologies may remain silent as to the appearance of a deity, whether he is tall or short, thin or fat. The issue here is what should be considered an appropriate translation label for religious beliefs and practices. Horton would submit that the language of religion and science—often viewed as antithetical spheres of Western discourse—both are necessary in rendering African religious systems intelligible.

This paper starts with a critique of two recent essays on African religion—Professor Max Gluckman's essay "Les Rites de Passage," and Dr. V. W. Turner's *Chihamba: the White Spirit.* Though the first is a generalized interpretation of African rituals, and the second a close study of one rite in a particular culture, the two make an interesting comparison. First of all, they are inspired by strongly contrasted theoretical premises. Secondly, one represents a well-established approach to the study of ritual, while the other includes a powerful objection to this approach. Thirdly, the two essays exhibit a polarity of attitude which I suspect has a wider currency both in Social Anthropology and in Comparative Religion. In what follows, I shall argue that the polarization of thought suggested by these two essays is basically unhelpful to the study of African religions; and I shall go on and suggest an approach which seems to me a fruitful middle way into the subject.

Gluckman's essay takes as its point of departure an appraisal of van Gennep's work on *rites de passage*—i.e., those rituals which in pre-industrial societies accompany major changes of role and status. Gluckman praises van Gennep for his analysis of the mechanism of such rites, and for his exposition of the way in which they help to make role changes easier for all those involved. But, he says, van Gennep gives no adequate explanation of why *rites de passage* are so common in "tribal societies," and so rare in modern industrial states. Van Gennep simply begs the question by saying that, to the semi-civilized mind, no act is entirely free from the sacred. According to Gluckman, it would in fact have been impossible for him to have provided an explanation: for he lacked the consistent vision of social relations essential to such a task. Gluckman sets out to make up for the deficiency which he sees in his predecessor's work. He contrasts his own approach, which sees rituals primarily "in terms of social structure," with the older approach of van Gennep, Tylor, and Frazer, who are said to have treated rituals "as the fruits of mental processes and ideas." . . .

In modern industrial society, as Gluckman points out, people tend to play their various roles with different partners in different places; and these circumstances obviate the need for any additional devices designed to prevent confusion of roles. In "tribal society," on the other hand, people tend to play several different roles with the same partners in the same setting: hence there is a need for role-segregating devices of which ritual, together with other types of ceremonial, is one.

. . .

How successful is Gluckman's attempt to tackle the problems left unsolved by van Gennep? On the one hand, his characterization of the differences in role-organization between tribal and industrial societies seems definitely illuminating. So too does his thesis that a concern for harmonious social life in tribal societies must give rise to a host of role-segregating and role-defining devices which are unnecessary in industrial society. On the other hand, though ritual can be pressed into the service of role-definition and role-segregation, there is surely more to it than this. Most African ritual is directed to entities that are inaccessible to normal observation, and are in addition personal beings. To many people these properties present the central problem of Comparative Religion. Why, in tribal societies especially, should there be constant resort to entities *of this kind* in every conceivable human predicament? And why, coming back to Gluckman, should it be entities *of this kind* that are invoked on so many occasions when there is a transition or affirmation of important roles? If one grants that all human populations spend a certain amount of ingenuity on securing harmony in their social life, it follows that difficulties in maintaining harmony, which Gluckman shows to be inherent in the role-organization of "tribal societies," will evoke a multitude of counteractive responses. But there is nothing to show that the elaboration of ritual is the only effective kind of response, or indeed that the required counteractive functions could not be discharged by a whole assortment of activities and institutions other than ritual. In fact, there is nothing in the essence of ritual which makes it a particularly obvious solution to the problem of maintaining harmony in tribal societies: for sectional and individual rites abound in African communities, and they are concerned as much with disruption as with harmony. Finally, why should it be entities with the characteristic properties of "the mystical" that are invoked as a link between fluctuations of the social order and fluctuations of nature? Why should not people just assume a direct and unmediated link between the one and the other—as when a man believes that walking under a ladder is likely to be followed by misfortune? For the anthropologist who asks questions of this kind, Gluckman's essay is likely to bring no stilling of curiosity.

Some indication of why Gluckman does not attempt to answer questions of this sort comes from the introductory paragraphs of his essay. Here, as we have seen, he not only contrasts the nineteenth-century view of rituals as "the fruits of mental processes and ideas" with the modern view which sees them "in terms of social relations." He goes on to assert that modern minds are bored by the nineteenth-century approach. What this seems to mean is that while Van Gennep, Tylor, Frazer, and other nineteenth-century writers treated religious beliefs as serious attempts to account for the world and its workings, those of their modern successors who follow Gluckman are unable to see such beliefs as having any serious intellectual content, and so tend to treat them as nothing more than a sort of all-purpose social glue. Again, while the nineteenth-century writers felt that the invisibility, personality, and other equally curious properties attributed to mystical beings posed fascinating problems that demanded answers, their modern successors find little of interest in any aspect of religion other than its postulated capacity to keep society running smoothly.

But why this curious change of emphasis which, in sweeping so many unsolved problems out of sight, seems more of a sideways movement than one of intellectual progress? The change cannot be simply ascribed to changes in personal religious conviction; for as far as I know all the writings involved reflect an agnostic outlook. What seems more important is that whereas the earlier writers were living in an environment dominated by religious believers, the modern agnostic is often the product of a milieu in which such believers are rather marginal beings. Hence, while the earlier writers found no difficulty in conceiving of people who really did look out on the world through religious spectacles, their successors find this a difficult feat of imagination. Again, for the earlier writers religion was a dangerous force whose every characteristic had to be charted and accounted for—even if only as an intelligence operation prior to a campaign. In the social milieu of modern agnosticism, however, religion has largely ceased to be regarded as effective. Hence attentive concern has given way to incurious apathy. But agnostic pronouncements on religion have evoked a number of recent reactions from Christian colleagues; and it is here that we move from Gluckman to Turner.

The setting of Turner's essay is the Ndembu culture of Central Africa—a culture whose population consists of shifting cultivators and hunters living in small villages organized about nuclei of matrilateral kin. The villages are unstable, being prone to conflicts and fission arising from land shortage, disputes between husbands and wives' brothers, struggles for headmanship, etc. Turner has described these communities and their cycles of conflict in his previous book *Schism and Continuity in an African Society.* . . .

When we come to *Chihamba* fresh from a reading of *Schism and Continuity*, we are in for a surprise. For this is not just a detailed study of one of the rituals presented in outline in the former book: it is a work informed by a very different theoretical approach.

. . .

In *Chihamba*, Turner is much more interested in the meaningful content of the ritual performance than in its unintended integrative functions. And this interest has led him to give us one of the most detailed and best-documented descriptions of a piece of ritual to appear in anthropological literature.

When a man or woman has been afflicted in the mode of *Chihamba*, this means that a female ancestor, in alliance with the male nature-spirit *Kavula*, is the cause of the trouble. The superficial intention of the ritual which ensues is to extricate afflicted people from their dangerous relationship with *Kavula* and the ancestress, and to establish a more beneficial bond with them.

The highlights of the *Chihamba* ritual are as follows. First, the afflicted victims are summoned to a hut where a hidden male adept, impersonating *Kavula*, asks them why they have sought him out, reviles them, and gives them special ritual names. On the next day, adepts clear a ritual enclosure in the bush, and there bury a bundle of symbolic objects. In so doing they are at once burying misfortune and installing *Kavula*. Later, they set up in the enclosure an image of *Kavula* made from a wooden framework covered by a white blanket and capped by an inverted wooden mortar.

While these preparations are going on, other adepts start to chase the candidates for submission to the ritual back and forth between the enclosure and the house of the senior victim of affliction. Songs sung at this time imply that the candidates have become slaves of *Kavula*, and to emphasize this they are made to carry heavy slave-yokes. With each chasing the candidates are brought closer and closer to the sacred enclosure until, at sundown, they are brought up one by one to make humble obeisance before the image of *Kavula*. Then, immediately afterwards, they are made to strike the image on the head with sacred rattles. The image shakes and finally keels over. *Kavula* is declared dead and all the participants return to the village.

The next day, candidates are taken out to a species of tree called *Ikamba da Chihamba*. A senior female adept bares the white tap-root of this tree, which is said to represent *Kavula*. Then a senior male adept cuts off a branch of the root; and this, together with other symbolic vegetable objects, is taken back to the village. Here again, this episode is said to be a "wounding" of *Kavula*. On the way back to the village the adepts stop to draw a white clay image of *Kavula* on the ground. They cover this with a medicine basket, and make a double arch at its foot with a split sapling. The candidates are made to crawl up to the image and greet it as they greeted the forest image on the previous day. Then they too are ceremonially "killed" by having a knife passed over their shoulders.

Back in the village the final important step is the setting-up, for each of those who have submitted to the ritual, of a personal shrine to the *Chihamba* spirits. These will henceforth be a source of benefit to their former victims. The setting-up of shrines begins with that of the senior female candidate. To make the latter's shrine, a bundle of twigs cut from trees symbolic of the *Chihamba* spirits is thrust into a hole, tamped with stream mud and libated with beer. A pot is placed near the bundle, and the blood of a cock poured into it. Finally, a piece of the *Ikamba da Chihamba* root is placed near by. Later, the shrines of the other candidates are set up in a similar manner. Four weeks afterwards the participants in *Chihamba* are released from their ritual taboos, and all is finished.

Through much of this ritual sequence, events are carried forward by the performance of elaborate symbolic actions and the manipulation of innumerable symbolic objects, the latter being largely drawn from the trees and plants of the surrounding forest. Turner has some interesting things to say about the structure of this luxuriant symbolism. Its chief features are: (*a*) that elementary symbols tend to be organized and used in complexes; (*b*) that each elementary symbol tends to have a large "fan" of diverse potential meanings; and (*c*) that different selections from this fan of meanings are mobilized when a given symbol features in different complexes. Hence, though a given symbol has a restricted overt significance in any given context of use, it carries with it a vast penumbra of dimly apprehended latent meanings. It is these latent meanings, Turner suggests, which make people react with fear and awe to some of the more commonly recurring symbols, and which lead them to think of such symbols as charged with a mysterious power. Although much that Turner says on this score is sufficiently interesting to merit pages of discussion, he himself soon passes on from the structure of Ndembu symbolism to its actual content; and, in order to stick to the theme of this paper, we must follow him.

Turner admits that a good deal of the symbolism and organization of the *Chihamba* ritual reflects more general features of Ndembu social life. Thus the death and rebirth both of *Kavula* and of the candidates is one example of a common idiom for the expression of radical changes of status—used here to signify and indeed to bring about a crucial change in the relations between men and the spirits. Much the same could be said of the complementary action of the male *Kavula* and the female ancestress, and of the complementary position in the ritual of senior male adepts and senior female candidates: for this theme of male–female complementarity clearly echoes the basic principle of Ndembu social organization, which is that male authority is dependent on descent through the female line.

But, says Turner, there is much more in the *Chihamba* ritual which we cannot begin to understand if we insist that it is a mere reflection of Ndembu social structure. This is especially true of the spirit *Kavula*, of his personality, and of the symbols associated with him. If we go carefully through the attributes assigned to *Kavula*, we shall find that he sums up in his being almost all the major forces which Ndembu see operating in their world. Thus he is associated with gerontocratic authority, with the unity of the whole of Ndembuland, with the fertility of crops and people, with rainfall and the elements, and with hunting. At the same time, he is associated with disease and death, and with the destructive powers of lightning. But *Kavula* is not just the sum of all these forces: he is something beyond them and more than them. And it is to emphasize this that the *Chihamba* ritual lays such stress on paradox. Thus, by presenting *Kavula* first as one in the forest image, and then as many in the personal shrines made at the end of the ritual, Ndembu show that he transcends the opposition between the one and the many. Again, by commanding candidates to strike down *Kavula* after they have given him the obeisance due to a chief, they show that he transcends the opposition between authority and subordination. And by presenting him in renewed life after he has been killed, they not only show by means of allegory his ultimate elusiveness from conceptual control. In fact, one might regard the whole of the *Chihamba* ritual as a lesson that *Kavula* is at once identifiable with most of the major forces in the Ndembu world, and at the same time transcends them all.

What, then, is *Kavula*? This question can only be answered, Turner feels, in terms of the traditional Thomist distinction between particular existing things and the pure existence which is the ground and support of all of them. *Kavula* is the Ndembu representation of this pure existence, or, as Turner puts it following Étienne Gilson, this "pure-act-of-being." Because it is in the nature of language to be concerned with particular existing things, a literal conceptualization of pure-act-of-being is im-

possible; and this is why *Kavula* can only be defined with the aid of symbol and paradox. This too is why the *Chihamba* ritual appears as a concentration of white symbols: for whiteness represents both that which is whole or total and that which is devoid of particular attributes. On this interpretation, the *Chihamba* ritual must be seen as an attempt both to say obliquely what cannot be said directly about pure-act-of-being, and to express dependence on this primal entity. These ends, says Turner, cannot be treated as the product of some specific kind of social organization. For they are not merely the ends of Ndembu worshippers: they are the ends of "ritual man" the world over.

To help convince the reader that *Chihamba* is "the local expression of a universal-human problem," Turner traces its close parallels with two better-known representations of pure-act-of-being—that found in the New Testament story of Christ's Death and Resurrection, and that found in Herman Melville's saga of the doomed quest for the great white whale Moby Dick. Although he clearly feels that the Christian representation carries with it certain unique claims to truth and value, he nevertheless sees basic similarities between the representations of *Kavula*, Christ, and the white whale. Thus in all three there is the feeling of the impossibility of direct statement, and the development of symbol and allegory to "grasp the ungraspable." There is the predominance of white symbols, aimed at representing that which is at once the ground of all things and the transcender of all things. There is the great development of paradox, and especially of the theme of the striking-down which yet does not annihilate—an allegory of that which by its very nature can never be finally pinned down by human thought.

Anthropologists in the tradition of Frazer and Durkheim, says Turner, would prefer not to recognize these constants of the religious situation. They would rather explain away religious phenomena or reduce them to non-religious terms. For, like Melville's Captain Ahab, they seek to destroy that belief in a deity which wounds and menaces their self-sufficiency. But only if they become humble in the face of religious experience, like the harpooneer Queequeg, can they ever discover anything worth while about "ritual man."

Any reader of Turner's essay will be struck by a deep feeling for the importance of religious ritual in human intellectual and emotional life—a feeling notably absent from too many current analyses. Readers of my own persuasion will also be refreshed by the message that different areas of human social behaviour need to be explained in terms of different motives—a welcome change from the kind of anthropological interpretation that apparently assumes no human motives other than the quest for social harmony, the quest for power, and the quest for food. Having said this, however, I must confess uneasiness about the particular framework of interpretation that Turner favours.

First of all, it is clear from Turner's essay that the Ndembu already have in *Nzambi* a supreme being who, even though he does not feature prominently in their ritual, certainly occupies a significant place in their thought. Now if *Kavula* really is an attempt to represent pure-act-of-being, the primal entity that underlies and supports all things in man's world, why do Ndembu not identify him with *Nzambi* or at least treat him as the latter's special manifestation? The nearest Turner gets to showing that they do either of these is with an informant who says that "*Kavula* is more like *Nzambi* than an ancestor spirit." But judging from the context of this statement it seems specifically designed to emphasize the non-ancestral nature of *Kavula*, and would probably have been applicable to other non-ancestral spirits (*Chihamba*, p. 22). It is rather as if the Thomist philosophers, having worked out their theory of pure-act-of-being, were to claim that the latter's representation was to be found neither in God nor in Jesus Christ, but in the most important of the archangels. One would certainly want some explanation of what would seem to be a deliberate obscurantism on their part.

It is even a little doubtful whether *Kavula* really does sum up in his person all the major social and natural forces which Ndembu see operating in their world, and whether he transcends all the salient oppositions and contrasts in this world. We have already noted that, in the *Chihamba* ritual, *Kavula* acts as the husband of an afflicting ancestress. And there is more than a hint that this ancestress embodies a set of forces which are distinct from and complementary to those summed up in the person of *Kavula*. Thus at one point she is said to be associated with narrow and localized matrilineage loyalties, while *Kavula* is associated with the unity of all Ndembu or even of all Lunda. Again, she is said to be associated with matrilineal descent, while *Kavula* is associated with male authority over

women (*Chihamba*, pp. 77–78). Instead of transcending all salient oppositions and contrasts, then, *Kavula* appears to be on one side of at least some of them.

Perhaps one could only give a conclusive verdict on Turner's interpretation if all the various connotations of *Kavula* were plotted alongside those of the various other categories of non-ancestral and ancestral spirit. Since Turner says that the present essay is merely a progress report, to be followed by a full-scale book on Ndembu religion, one hopes that he may eventually lay out his material in this way, and so enable us to make a more definite assessment.

At once more important and more controversial than Turner's application of Thomist concepts to the translation of Ndembu ideas is his advocacy of such concepts as the appropriate translation instruments for religious ideas generally. This emerges in the last chapter of *Chihamba*, where, so far as I can grasp his rich and complex analysis, he seems to be asserting the following propositions:

1. The difficulty of grasping the nature of pure existence (or pure-act-of-being in Turner's terminology) as distinct from particular existing things and their properties is "indissociable from the very structure of language and conceptualization." That is, it is a human universal. (See *Chihamba*, p. 82, para 2.)

2. We can define "Ritual Man" as one who has a sense of dependence on pure existence or pure-act-of-being, and as one who, in all ages and places, is passionately engaged in trying to overcome the inherent difficulty of expressing this sense of dependence. (See p. 84, para. 1; and p. 87, para. 2.)

3. The concept of "Ritual Man," defined in these terms, might be made central to the comparative study of religion. This is implied by the analogy with the concept of "Economic Man" as used in economics, and with that of "The Reasonable Man" as used in law. (See p. 84, para. 1.)

Turner also appears to be asserting a less specific thesis, which is entailed by the foregoing, but could also be asserted independently. This thesis can be summarized in the following propositions:

4. All the behaviour and belief we call religious, from one end of the world to the other, is a product of the same essential human aspiration. Though some people may deny having such an aspiration because it involves a sense of dependence on a supreme

being which is wounding to self-sufficiency, it is in fact universal. (P. 84, para. 1; p. 92, end of para. 1.)

5. The essential aspiration of religion cannot be explained in terms of any other human aspirations nor can it be reduced to any other such aspirations. (P. 86, para. 2.)

6. This follows from (4). For the European anthropologist, acceptance of religious insights couched in the idiom of his own culture is the key to understanding of religions generally. Rejection of such insights makes this wider understanding impossible. (P. 84, para. 1; p. 92, end of para. 1.)

Now there is nothing prima facie wrong with this set of propositions. True, they appear to be closely connected with the author's own religious beliefs; but this need not necessarily be a defect. A first step in the analysis of an alien religious system must always be the search for an area of discourse in one's own language which can appropriately serve as a translation instrument. And in so far as he is thoroughly at home in the religious discourse of his own culture, the Christian would seem to be at an advantage over the agnostic in this matter. The reasonableness of this argument receives support from the defects of most of the religious analyses carried out by agnostic anthropologists. Since their errors and their omissions are often so patently related to their personal hostility or apathy to things religious, the remedy seems straightforward enough: the Christian must make full use of his own religious discourse in translating the religious ideas of alien cultures.

Reasonable as they seem, however, the propositions which Turner appears to be asserting in the last chapter of *Chihamba* must stand or fall by their applicability to the raw data of religious belief and behaviour throughout the world. And here, of course, we shall be particularly interested in their applicability to African data.

Before confronting Turner's narrower thesis with the data, it might be as well to remind ourselves of the essentials of the Thomist position from which this thesis starts out. According to Thomist premises, everything in the world around us has certain definitive properties (its essence) and, in addition, the property of existence. Since the essences of things can be thought of apart from their existence, they are said to be contingent. Existence in itself, however, is logically prior to the other properties; hence pure being is the necessary ground and support of all the other

attributes of all the particular things in the world. Not only this: pure being is identical with its own essence; and since its essence cannot be thought of apart from its existence, it is self-necessitating. It is this pure being, necessary ground of all things and sufficient reason for its own existence, that Thomists identify with the Absolute, the First Cause, the Godhead, etc. But having established the necessity of pure being, one can make no further direct statements about it: for language, by its very nature, is concerned only with the distinguishing properties of individual things (essences). Thus it is that in order to delineate pure being one is driven into the obliqueness of symbol and allegory.

Now Turner implies that this conception of pure being, of its relation to the world, and of the difficulties of making direct statements about it, is forced upon all men by the very structure of their thought and language (*Chihamba*, p. 82, para. 2). But this cannot be true. For the whole complex of problems and preoccupations sketched here is indissociable from the particular meaning which Thomists attach to the word "exists." Since they treat this as a predicate which in some respects is on the same level as "is-hard," "is-green," "is-alive," and so on, it is possible for them to have meaningful discussions about an entity which has the sole attribute of existence—i.e., pure being. But there is another conceptual framework, just as widely current in modern Western culture, in which "exists" has quite a different meaning. Within this framework, to say that "*X* has properties *Y and* exists" is merely to say that "the statement '*X* has properties *Y*' is true." Here, no sense can be attached to statements about pure existence; and the problems and preoccupations associated with this concept just do not arise. Although this latter conceptual framework is commonly associated with logical positivism, it is also one in which many Protestant thinkers are at home; and correspondingly, their thought about God's relation to the world tends to follow very different lines from that of the Thomists. Since by no means even all Christian thinkers acknowledge the usefulness and relevance of the Thomist conceptual framework, it would appear to be a poor candidate for the translation of religious ideas on a world-wide basis.

When we come to the study of African traditional religions, the picture seems equally unpromising. In so far as nearly all known African traditional religions feature a supreme being who is the creator and sustainer of all that is, one could perhaps say that such religions take account of something vaguely akin to the Thomist pure-act-of-being. But where we have nothing that evidently corresponds to the crucial Thomist distinctions between existence and essence, and between self-necessitating and contingent entities, the kinship would seem to be vague indeed. More important still, it would be a distortion to say that African religion was in any way centred on the struggle to adumbrate in symbols what could not be directly said about this primal entity, or that such a struggle "engaged the passionate attention of ritual man" throughout the continent. Indeed, though African thought-systems are very variable in this respect, the predominant atmosphere in many of them is one of apathy about the supreme being. Often, he is acknowledged to be the ultimate sustainer of everything in the world; but at the same time people say little about him either directly or in symbolism. Their thought and energy is focused mainly on the lesser spirits who, though they are the creation of the supreme being, are directly associated with most of the happenings in people's immediate environment. These lesser spirits are just as real to their worshippers as the supreme being; and relations with them are surely as much a part of religion as relations with this being.

What of the wider thesis implicit in the last chapter of *Chihamba*—the thesis that the same essential human aspiration is at the root of religious activity in all ages and in all places; that this aspiration is not to be explained by or reduced to any others; and that acknowledgement of this aspiration in one's own life gives one the only real key to understanding religions of other cultures very different from one's own?

. . .

Perhaps the best way to set about testing the usefulness of Turner's wider thesis is to start out with a sketch of contemporary Christian preoccupations that might be acceptable to most branches of the faith. For the sake of argument, let us adopt the following. Christians are centrally preoccupied with a supreme being whose reality transcends the space-time order. Knowledge of this being and of His perfect love and goodness gives life a depth, fullness, and richness which non-believers confined to the space-time plane can never suspect. It is as if life had one less

dimension for the non-believer; and this is why he is often compared to a blind man. Much as modern Christianity has to say about the joys of living in the light of God's love and goodness, however, it shows little interest in furnishing a detailed interpretation of connections between phenomena in the space-time world. Efforts to give it such an interest, like that of Teilhard de Chardin, are not even greatly approved of by the Churches. Indeed, one could say that the Churches take the detailed working of the space-time world with no further explanatory comment than the statement that whatever happens in this realm is ultimately ordained by God.

If we take this sketch of Christian preoccupations into the field of African traditional religions, two great questions arise. First, does our sketch in any way tally with a sketch one might make of the central preoccupations of African religions? Secondly, can familiarity with Christian preoccupations and acceptance of their validity give us some special key to the understanding of African religions?

As with Turner's narrower Thomist thesis, the answers once again seem rather negative. First of all, there is the frequent apathy about the supreme being, and the concentration of intellectual and emotional energies on the figures of the lesser spirits. Again, though there is a good deal in African traditional religions which suggests the central Christian experience of intense personal communion with a loving God, such communion seems more often associated with the lesser spirits than with the supreme being. Finally and most strikingly, the primary intention of much African religious thought seems to be just that mapping of connections between space-time phenomena which modern Christian thought feels is beyond its proper domain. Though, by the standards of the more advanced contemporary sciences, these religions seldom provide valid explanations or make completely successful predictions, there is a very real sense in which they are just as concerned with explanation and prediction as the sciences are. In this respect, they are as close to the latter as they are to modern Christianity.

So far as a confrontation of modern Christianity with traditional African religions is concerned, then, it looks as though the essential aspiration of the one is often the marginal aspiration of the other, and vice versa. This being so, Christian discourse can be a translation instrument of only limited use where African religions are concerned; and familiarity with it cannot promise any general key to understanding which is not available to the agnostic.

Again, this confrontation throws doubt on the proposition that religious aspirations are not to be explained in terms of any others or reduced to them. As I have said, many African traditional religions, with their passionate interest in the explanation and prediction of space-time events, are as close to the sciences as they are to modern Christianity. Hence I venture to suggest that, over much of Africa, Ritual Man is not really a distinctive being, but is rather a sub-species of Theory-building Man.

This last suggestion leads directly to the constructive part of my argument. Professor Gluckman's programme for interpreting African ritual depends on the assumption of a dominant concern for the harmonious and smooth running of social life. Turner's reaction to this sort of programme depends on the assumption of a dominant concern with "saying the unsayable" about the ultimate ground of all particular forms of existence. I prefer to be thoroughly old-fashioned and go back to the sort of assumption that guided Tylor, Frazer, and Van Gennep—that the really significant aspiration behind a great deal of African religious thought is the most obvious one; i.e. the attempt to explain and influence the working of one's everyday world by discovering the constant principles that underlie the apparent chaos and flux of sensory experience. In so far as we make this aspiration central to our analysis, we shall find ourselves searching for translation instruments not so much in the realm of Christian discourse as in that of the sciences and their theoretical concepts.

All this may sound at first like some dreadful humanist commando raid—designed to snatch Africa from the hands of the Thomists only to deliver it into the ranks of the scientists. It is, of course, nothing of the sort; for, as the reader will see, the analysis that follows takes full account of the crucial things that divide the pre-scientific thought-systems of Africa from the thought of the sciences. Nevertheless, as I shortly hope to show, an exploration of the common patterns of reasoning that underlie these crucial differences could be a valuable preliminary to the interpretation of African religious thought.

Now one very common way of trying to explain a set of observed phenomena is in terms of a scheme of underlying processes or events. To provide the basis of a satisfying explanation this scheme must be such as to display the diversity and complexity of observed phenomena as the product of an underlying unity, simplicity, and regularity. Thus an important part of modern chemical thought is the body of theory which explains the vast diversity of recorded substances as a product of the combination and recombination of a limited number of elements according to a few relatively simple rules. Given certain assumptions about regularities of events in the theoretical scheme, and certain identifications of these events with observed phenomena, it becomes possible to deduce the occurrence of the latter as necessary. And when such deduction is applied to future occurrences, we have prediction. Thus the theory of chemical elements and their combination can be used either to show the necessity of the occurrence of certain substances already observed, or to predict the future occurrence of substances not yet observed.

When they are used in the sciences, such explanatory and predictive schemes are known as "theoretical models." And the commonly approved criteria for accepting or rejecting such models are what we call "the Rules of Scientific Method." By and large, these criteria are simply an inventory of the conditions which make for maximum efficiency in fulfilling the aims of explanation and prediction. The African religious systems which contain the counterparts of these theoretical models are, as we have said, sustained by the same basic aims of explanation and prediction. They differ from the thought-systems of science most notably in the absence of any guiding body of explicit acceptance/rejection criteria that would ensure the efficiency with which they pursue their aims.

In devoting itself almost exclusively to exploring the rules for acceptance and rejection of theoretical models, modern philosophical analysis has concentrated on that aspect of Western scientific thought which most distinguishes it from the thought-systems of Africa. In more recent years, however, the philosophers have begun to turn their attention to another aspect in which the resemblances are probably more significant than the differences. Here I am thinking of the actual generation of theoretical models—the process whereby an area of puzzling observations provokes speculation as to a possible underlying mechanism, and gives birth to the tentative explanatory scheme which "scientific logic" then goes to work on.

Perhaps the only thing we know for certain about this process is that most theoretical models are drawn from phenomena already observed in the visible and tangible world. The investigator is impressed by an analogy between the puzzling observations he wants to explain and the structure of certain phenomena whose behaviour has already been well explored. Because of this analogy, he postulates a scheme of events with structure akin to that of the prototype phenomena, and equates this scheme with the reality "behind" the observations that puzzle him. Such well-known models are those involving the molecule, the planetary atom, the electric current, and the light wave all have fairly obvious prototypes in the world of everyday phenomena. Similarly, we can often see the prototypes of African religious models in the social life of the peoples who have evolved them.

What is not so well established is why a particular set of phenomena is drawn upon as the prototype of an explanatory model in a particular situation. As Stephen Toulmin has remarked, there is no possible step of inductive or deductive inference which can lead unambiguously from a given set of puzzling observations to a given theoretical model. And as for the perception of structural analogy which is the basis of the model-making process, this too would seem to permit a considerable range of choice in any given observational situation. Indeed, Toulmin's appraisal has led him to state that in the thought of science, as well as in that of pre-science, model-making probably owes as much to the wider thought-patterns and fashions of the age as it does to the nature of the observations to be explained.

This brings us to the point at which we can reintroduce one of the central questions that we raised in connection with Gluckman's essay. What cultural variables are responsible for the fact that Western scientific thought tends to choose things rather than people as the basis of its explanatory models, while African thought-systems by and large tend to make the opposite choice?

Though I do not think we are yet in a position to give a fully satisfactory answer to this question, we can perhaps get a clue to some of the factors involved by going back to what the philosophers of science define as the essential feature of an explanatory model. According to them, the logic of explanation demands first and foremost that the underlying events postulated by any theoretical model should be connected in an orderly and regular fashion: for explanation *is* the demonstration of order underlying apparent chaos and of regularity underlying apparent haphazardness. Hence, to qualify as a suitable prototype for a model, a set of phenomena needs not only to be thoroughly familiar, but also to be manifestly orderly and regular in its behaviour.

Now in technologically backward communities which have a relatively simple social organization and are not in a state of rapid and self-conscious change, people's activities in society present the most markedly ordered and regular area of their experience, whereas their biological and inanimate environment is by and large less tidily predictable. Hence it is chiefly to human activities and relationships that such communities turn for the sources of their most important explanatory models. It is probably fair to say that much of traditional African society typifies this pattern.

. . .

Again, take what, for the want of a better word, one may call the "incompleteness" of the African gods. Between different African religions, and even between different sectors of the same religion, there is a good deal of variation in the number of dimensions of human life which are incorporated into the figures of the various gods. Nearly always, however, some dimensions are missing. What these are varies from case to case. Perhaps one only notices that they are missing if one has the naivety to ask all the questions about a god that one would ask about a man. Does he beget children? How many has he? What kind of a house does he live in? Is he handsome? How tall is he? Is he kind to his wives? One has only to go a little way along this road before getting the sort of blank stare which indicates that one has been asking entirely meaningless questions. Probably one will be told curtly: "We are talking about the spirits; not about men."

That there is nothing in this situation peculiar to African gods becomes apparent if one asks the same sort of questions about the theoretical entities of the sciences. What is the temperature of a hydrogen molecule? What is the colour of a proton? However appropriate such questions would have been if asked of the prototype phenomena from which these entities were drawn, they are certainly quite out of order if asked of the entities themselves. The reason is directly connected with the explanatory function of theoretical entities. Earlier, we noted that the creation of a new theoretical model takes place when an investigator traces an analogy between the structure of certain puzzling observations and that of certain phenomena whose regularities of behaviour he is already familiar with. He draws on these phenomena as the basis of a model which he equates with the reality underlying his initial observations. But the structural analogy between the observations and the prototype phenomena seldom involves more than a limited aspect of the latter. And it is only this limited aspect that is taken over and incorporated into the model. The rest is left behind: for, from the point of view of explanatory function, it is just so much dross. Thus the atomic physicist Rutherford, in forming his revolutionary planetary model of the atom, left behind such features as the colour and temperature of the planets as irrelevant to his explanatory task. In just the same way, when he fashions the gods from people, the African thinker leaves behind as irrelevant many features of human activity and physical appearance.

Another feature of African traditional thought which now becomes less puzzling is the often-remarked tendency towards definition of the various units of society in "mystical" or religious terms. Thus the Kalabari village is defined as that group of people which has its own *amatemeso*—the personal force that guides the thread of its history. The autonomous Ibo political unit is the largest group of communities sharing a common cult of *ala*—spirit of the earth. The Ashanti state is that unit which is guided and held together by the souls of the royal ancestors. And so on. Such definitions, again, are a logical consequence of the explanatory role of religious ideas. For theoretical models inevitably dictate the ways in which the data they explain are classified and hence described. Things apparently diverse at the level of observation may be manifestations of a single process in the model, and will be classified accordingly; while things which show superficial similarities at the level of observation may be manifestation of diverse aspects of the model, and

classification, again, will proceed accordingly. Hence the sheerest description may contain implicit references to the model. A chemist, asked to give a thorough description of some substance in his laboratory, can hardly avoid mentioning such characteristics as molecular weight and formula, which refer implicitly to a massive body of chemical theory. In the same way, an African villager, who is trying to describe what his community is, can hardly avoid implicit reference to religious concepts. In so far as one can only start to understand social relations through familiarity with the terms in which those involved think about them, it is probably true to say that he who wishes to understand many African societies must first understand their religions.

We can now reconsider some of the questions raised by Professor Gluckman. First: why is ritual, in the sense of approach to mystical powers, such a frequent accompaniment of *rites de passage* in which an individual is taken from one role to another? The answer seems clear in the light of what has been said in the last few paragraphs. These changes of role usually involve incorporation into a new group or a new set of relationships; and, as we have seen, a corporate group is apt to be defined in terms of the personal beings who are "behind" the co-ordinated activities of its members. It is these beings who keep the group flourishing, or weaken it in response to breaches of group norms. Because membership of the group implies having one's life partially controlled by such beings, becoming a member logically involves a process of being put under their control.

The second question which interests Gluckman is: why, in so many African rituals where the members of a corporate group approach a mystical power, do those concerned participate in a manner which lays exaggerated emphasis on the patterns of behaviour proper among each other in the wider context of social life? Here again, I think, the answer follows clearly from what has already been said about African religious ideas. In most African societies, the strength and welfare of corporate groups is seen as intimately bound up with their members' close observance of their moral norms. Consequently with this, the spirits that underpin the various corporate groups of a society nearly always support the moral norms of such groups; and their strengthening action is conditional upon observance of these norms. When a group assembles to approach its guiding spirit, it is therefore appropriate that its members, in their behaviour to one another during the ritual, should demonstrate their readiness to observe group norms.

The sketch of an approach to African traditional religions I have given in the last few paragraphs is brief, impressionistic, and highly tentative. Yet I think it indicates a line of inquiry more fruitful than that favoured by Gluckman. For it seems capable of explaining the salient morphological features of African religious beliefs *as well as* the relation of these beliefs to the social organization. Again, I hope my sketch has shown clearly enough that Turner's answer to the agnostic anthropologist is by no means the only permissible one and that one might even be able to go further in the interpretation of his Ndembu material in the terms sketched above than in his own Thomist terms. Thus one can look at the beliefs about *Kavula* and the ancestress as means of bringing intellectual order into a variety of everyday experience: more specifically, that they constitute the basis of a theoretical model which enables one to place such diverse oppositions as masculinity/ femininity, pan-Lunda loyalties/matrilineage loyalties, authority/descent (and possibly others such as settlement area/forest), as instances of the operation of a single pair of underlying forces related to one another as contrasting complementaries. This would make *Kavula* very different from a representation of pure-act-of-being; but it would avoid some of the crucial difficulties of Turner's interpretation.

I am not, of course, trying to say that the approach I have suggested here is the only way towards an understanding of African religions; nor am I saying that it must exclude the sort of insight which modern Christians are equipped to provide. Indeed, as I noted earlier, there is a good deal in African traditional religions which recalls the Christian experience of communion with a loving God —even though in the African context such communion seems to be associated more with the lesser spirits than with the supreme being. Involving as it does intense personal relationships with beings beyond the human social order, the communion aspect of African religion tends to take people outside the daily round of visible and tangible experience. In this sense it moves thought in the opposite direction from the explanatory aspect, which starts in the realm of unobservable beings, and brings these to bear on visible and tangible things. Formally opposed though they are, these two aspects of religion are found intermingled in many African cultures. Nor is the tension between these two opposites always an unfruitful one: for in the shamans, prophets, and mystics of traditional religion, we see people who both pass out of the sphere of visible and tangible things in their communion, and also return from time to time with explanatory schemes which make new sense of the visible and tangible world.

This intermingling of explanation and communion seems to have been typical of Christianity down through medieval times. But after the revolution of thought in seventeenth-century Europe there was a steady differentiation, science progressively taking over the explanatory aspect, and religion becoming more and more a matter of communion. Opposites once fruitfully mingled became clearly distinguished and even set against one another. So much so that today a rare feat of imagination is required of the man who would both commit himself wholeheartedly to the ideals of Western science and at the same time remain fully committed to the Christian faith.

Hence, if it is true that the primary problem of the social anthropologist is one of finding the areas of discourse in his own language whose logic comes nearest that of the alien discourse he wishes to analyse, the would-be student of African religions is faced with a heavy task. For he must bring together in his own single mind areas of discourse which modern Western culture tends to make the preserve of different categories of people.

Renato I. Rosaldo, Jr.
METAPHORS OF HIERARCHY IN A MAYAN RITUAL

Working within the framework provided by van Gennep, Hubert and Mauss, and Leach, who have characterized the formal properties of ritual action, Rosaldo examines a calendrical ritual, honoring an important local saint, performed in a highland Maya community of Chiapas, Mexico. Just as the subject of much modern poetry is poetry itself, so this ritual performed by members of the Zinacantecan civil-religious hierarchy concerns hierarchy itself. A formal analysis, something on the order of a grammar of ritual action, takes as its units the various representations of hierarchy—sitting in rows, walking in lines, serving drinks in a fixed order—which are shown to be combined in ways consistent with classic theories of ritual. While the various representations of hierarchy are continuous with obligatory and widespread acts in hamlet life denoting the recognition of a difference in age, in the ritual context they stand for differences in wealth. Though the tokens—bowing or whatever—of rank order remain the same, the contradictions between these two hierarchies (age and wealth) are problematic for the performers and may contribute to the power and sacred quality of the ritual itself.

Reprinted in abridged form from *American Anthropologist*, LXX (1968), 524–536, by permission of the author and the American Anthropological Association.

This is a study of a ritual performed by members of the religious cargo system in Zinacantan, a Tzotzil township of some 7000 in the highlands of Chiapas, Mexico. Zinacantecos are milpa farmers who live in a ceremonial center and a number of scattered hamlets. When a man decides to fulfill his religious obligations he leaves home and moves into the ceremonial center for a year. There he becomes a full-time ritual performer. "At the present time virtually all Zinacanteco adult males participate in the cargo system" (Cancian, 1965: 126).

There are four levels to the religious hierarchy; to perform as a second level official a man must perform in a first level position, to reach the fourth level he must go through the first three. It is expensive to be a religious official, so those who take another cargo position, on the next level, return to their hamlets and wait for some years, hoeing corn and saving money. Within each level of the cargo system religious officials are ranked one above the other in a single lineal hierarchy. This hierarchy is not so much a chain of command as a set of honorific positions. In their own hamlets men know one another by name; in the ceremonial center officials who perform together call one another by their titles—*martomorei* rather than Jose—and they "often do not know each other's full names" (Cancian, 1965: 34). The official rank order—seen in drinking order, processions, and seating arrangements—roughly corresponds to the cost and prestige of each cargo position (Cancian, 1965: 80–96).

My paper concerns the expressions of hierarchy in the weekly ceremonies performed by four of the cargo officials in the chapel of Our Lord of Esquipulas, one of the more important saints in the ceremonial center. The officials are ranked as follows:

1. *martomorei bankilal*
2. *martomorei ?ič'inal*
3. *mexon bankilal*
4. *mexon ?ič'inal*

Both *martomoreietik* spend about the same for their cargos—much more than the two *mexonetik*—and prestige correlates with the traditional rank order of the four officials who attend Our Lord of Esquipulas. It is the conventional way in which members of the religious hierarchy act out their own rank order that shall comprise my analysis.

In their descriptions of ritual for Esquipulas, informants narrate in painstaking detail the various kinds of obligatory behavior that indicate relative rank: cargo-holders bow to one another, walk in lines, sit in rows, drink in a fixed order, and so on. . . .

My thesis is that these Zinacantecan representations of social status, in and of themselves, comprise an articulate mode of ritual action. For the official these gestures are clear, coherent, and systematic; rules for such behavior do not require verbal rationalization —like rules of grammar, they are recognized when they are violated. Bowing and other related acts are at once expressions of hierarchical social order and of ritual order. Gestures derived from the ritual of daily affairs, they underlie and shape the cargo rite.

CARGO RITUAL

Ritual for Esquipulas is extremely scheduled. Every Sunday of the year at least two cargo officials, a martomorei and a mexon, perform the same ceremony in honor of Our Lord of Esquipulas: they uncover the medallions of the saint, *xlok' ʔual*. On alternate Saturdays they also change the flowers on the arch above the household and chapel altars, *balte ʔ*. The martomorei bankilal keeps Esquipulas' medallions four weeks, then gives them to martomorei *ʔiȼ'inal*—his lesser counterpart, equal in all but prestige—and the medallions go back and forth throughout the year. During some major "fiestas" the officials have additional duties; they may participate in a swearing-in ceremony or a large ritual meal, but the weekend ceremony is performed as ever. At planting time and harvest time the ceremonies remain the same; they do not vary with the natural cycle. In short, it is hard to imagine a ritual more regular in its performance, one more free from unpredictable contingencies. Such rites "are always social or communal in character" (Titiev, 1960: 294). Cargo ritual is decidedly social in content as well; it repeatedly represents a hierarchical order of society.

My language may call to mind the "effervescent" collective representations of a Durkheimian societal rite (1915). But not all scheduled rituals are the same; cargo ceremony appears private and esoteric, with none of the thrill and excitement of a crowd. Durkheim's ideal type aptly characterizes a major "fiesta," taken as a whole, but not that part of it performed by the cargo-holder. Ruth Bunzel, speaking of Chichicastenango, brings out this contrast in a passage that could well have referred to Zinacantan:

To me, an outsider, seeing the fiesta as an expression of the social life of a great village, the unwonted concentration of people, the mounting excitement, the changing temper of the ceremonies and of the crowd, the dramatic contrasts, the abandoned drunkenness of Manuel and the austere sobriety of Juan were the significant facts, and the prayers and explanations that Juan related to me with such meticulous care, were just another long speech in the cofradias. In the cumulative excitement of a big fiesta the inner sacred core, what the prayers characterized as "the heart and soul"

of the ceremony, gets drowned in an uproar of drum and bells and marimbas and fireworks [1952: 252].

Cargo ritual is removed from the intense activity of the "fiesta" it sometimes accompanies; its audience is limited, at most, to two ritual advisors, three musicians, and a handful of helpers, the officials' close kinsmen and neighbors.

These rites lack dramatic quality. They appear to be elaborate, protracted, redundant communiqués about hierarchy and rank; over and over they emphasize and maximize order among men. They contrast sharply with curing ceremonies in which the shaman, a man with a calling, prays in deep resonant tones, reminiscent of medieval plain-song. The curer preserves and creates the customs; at many points in the ceremony he is consulted —should the chicken be boiled with herbs? What kind of herbs? How many of each herb? This charismatic figure directs parts of his ceremony; he does more than follow a programmed set of actions. Cargo-holders, on the other hand, perform the same ceremony every weekend of the year, just as, they say, it was performed in the past. They preserve the ancient custom.

Their song, dance, incense, high-backed sandals, all suggest that these men indeed are an incarnation of customs seen in the codices or the *Popol-Vuh*. But a cargo-holder's lifelong occupation is corn farming; he takes on his role as an official when he is an adult, with no previous formal training. Formal instruction for ritual performance begins in the ceremonial center, where old men and musicians, experienced in the cargo ritual, serve as advisors, guiding the officials through their first month or so of service. But they cannot teach everything. Consider that the biweekly ceremonies are long and complex, and that over their twenty-four hour period the cargoholder becomes drunk to the point of passing out. How does a drunken man learn, perhaps find meaningful, at least perform, such a set of actions?

Cargo ritual is not autonomous; it exists at once as a system in its own right and as part of a more general system of social action. The corn farmer immediately recognizes most of his ritual duties because he already has become familiar with them in the social and ceremonial contexts of his own hamlet. The code of such ritual is shaped primarily by other social convention, by hamlet ceremonies, and by that aspect of social behavior that symbolizes relative social status. The main subject of ritual performed by members of the religious hierarchy is hierarchy itself, expressed in the conventional code of Zinacantan.

CARGO RITUAL AND SOCIAL CONVENTION

I will illustrate some of the ways in which social conventions relate to, and make intelligible, the ritual performed for Our Lord of Esquipulas. These conventional modes of behavior are considered arbitrary cultural products, as much so as the acoustic shape of words. Clearly some acts—bowing to express respect, for instance—are widespread enough to call for a psychological explanation, but that is another story. My present purpose is to describe vocabulary and usage of Zinacanteco ritual language.

Zinacantecan rituals are not closed systems; they mutually influence and shape one another. Cargo rites, though recognizably the same from one year to the next, are flexible, and permit various degrees of innovation. It is above all in their ideology that they are static; innovation quickly becomes normative —the great transformation of twenty-three years ago is now the rule, the ancient custom. In 1944, for unknown reasons, the cargo-holders elaborated on their weekly ceremonies, and began not only to take out, but also to count, the medallions of Our Lord of Esquipulas. This change is a case of borrowing from another sector of ritual life.

The count, which shares many features of the shaman's divination, now occupies a central place in this ritual. Before beginning the count, or any action he calls "work," the official loosens the kerchief on his head, as does the shaman. The martomorei counts the medallions—Mexican and Guatemalan coins from one to thirty pesos in value—while the mexon records the count with grains of corn, one per peso. The outcome is uncertain; the number of grains more than the value of the coins indicates the fortune of the official—the more the better. Similarly, in divination "the number of floating grains indicates the number of lost parts of the *ch'ulel*" (Vogt, 1965a: 45). The official, for an important part of his ceremony, adopts the sacred conventions of the shaman and makes them his own.

At the same time, this ritual reflects and reinforces patterns of hamlet life; much of the ritual action is a condensed elaborate version of daily social intercourse in Zinacantan, in particular of the various ways in which in-

dividuals signal their recognition of difference in age. In drinking, the eldest male is served first, then the next oldest, and so on; in cargo ritual it is the highest ranking official who drinks first. When two men meet on the path and stop to talk, the younger bows to the older. The cargo-holder elaborates on this action and, at many points in the ceremony, bows repeatedly to a higher ranking man, while speaking to him formally, in couplets.

Cargo-holders, in one salient case, invert the expression of rank order seen in daily conduct. On the narrow paths of Zinacantan the eldest male walks ahead; the rest follow in order of relative age. In cargo processions it is the low ranking man who walks first. It seems reasonable to interpret this action in relation to the etiquette of daily affairs: when there is a "formal greeting situation"—when, for example, a man comes to ask a woman's hand in marriage—the youngest male leads the procession to the door of the house. Here, the Zinacanteco puts his worst foot forward. In their processions officials do not simply walk from one place to another; they stop to pray a number of times: at the cross by the door of the house, before crosses on the path —often "considered as a doorway to the abode of the gods" (Early, 1965: 63). As in daily life, they invert their order to say they are greeting, presenting themselves to, the gods.

In any particular year few people witness cargo rites, yet most would find the elements or ritual acts of these ceremonies familiar. I found I could read prayers, which vary in content from one cargo-holder to another, to several young men, who had neither held cargoes, nor seen the ritual for Esquipulas, and they would recognize the speakers and situation. These rites, private in their performance, are written in a public language.

THE RITUAL

Now I shall describe a part of the ceremony held in honor of Our Lord of Esquipulas, with a view to showing how the language of social conventions is used in ritual. A complete narrative of these rites is impossible in my limited space (for other material on this ritual see Cancian [1965: 52–55] and Early [1965: 110–113; 1966: 337–354]). What follows, then, is an account of the first two or three hours of the bi-weekly ritual: the flower-change ceremony (balte?) at the house of the martomorei

Women are present in the household, but do not enter into this description; they do not participate in ranking, except when the officials enter and leave the house and speak with the eldest woman. As the cargo-holder faces the sacred altar, on the east side of the house, the women are seated on the floor to his left, in no particular order. They pass food from left to right, from the hearth to the men who sit on chairs, arranged and ranked on the right-hand side. A woman with a named role keeps the supply of sugar cane liquor and gives it to the boys who in turn serve it to the men. As Hertz (1960) would expect, women sit on the ground, on the left, in disorder; they comprise the counterpart of masculine metaphors of hierarchy.

The martomorei (*Mr*), seated before his household altar, turns to his mexon (*M*) and says in formal couplet speech:

Let us speak together
Let us speak to the musicians.
We shall change the flowers
we shall change the leaves
of the sacred seat
of the sacred place
of the flowery face
of the flowery countenance
of Lord Esquipulas my father
of Lord Esquipulas my owner.
We are here on sacred Saturday
we are here on sacred Sunday.
We have united
we have come together
to spend
to pass
the sacred Saturday
the sacred Sunday
of Lord Esquipulas my father
of Lord Esquipulas my owner.

While speaking—as if to rehearse the lines they will say to the musicians and to the saint —they repeatedly perform the conventional everyday greeting gesture of bowing and releasing. *M*, lower in rank, bows to *Mr*, who touches him on the forehead with the back of his hand.

Then *M* gets up, followed by *Mr*, and goes to speak with the musicians, first the violinist (*Mu₁*), then the harpist (*Mu₂*), finally the guitarist (*Mu₃*), as diagramed in Figure 1. Cargo-holder and musician speak almost simultaneously, saying the same thing: they are going to change the flowers and leaves for Our Lord of Esquipulas. They too bow and release repeatedly, the younger man this time bowing to the older.

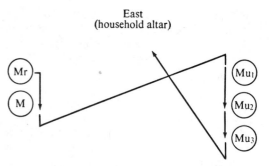

East
(household altar)

FIGURE 1

Cargo-holders greeting the musicians and praying before the household altar at the beginning of the flower-change ceremony in the house of Mr.

Now the cargo-holders go before the household altar and kneel to pray. They touch the altar with the back of their right hand and bow to touch it with their foreheads, while they pray to God, Jesus Christ, My Lord Esquipulas; they shall change his flowers and leaves.

Each group of men begins its task; musicians sing and play, cargo-holders change the flowers. *Mr* and *M* take off their woolen cloaks, loosen the kerchiefs tied around their heads, then proceed to remove the ferns, geraniums, and pine boughs from the flowered arch of the household altar. As the cargo-holders finish, the musicians sing a verse which all recognize as a signal to drink. Two little boys, one for *Mr*, the other for *M*, take their liter bottles and shot glasses and begin to serve all present in this order: *Mr*, *M*, *Mu₁*, *Mu₂*, *Mu₃*, helpers (by sex, men first, and age, oldest first). After drinking, the officials continue their work and put new flowers on the arch above the household altar. When the new flowers are in place, everybody drinks again, and in the same order.

The old dry flowers and boughs, lying on a reed mat before the altar, still have to be thrown out. *Mr* and *M* slip two one-fifth liter bottles of liquor beneath the dried flowers, and take the reed mat with its trash into the cornfield. When they throw out the dead leaves, one of the men discovers a bottle and suggests they drink it. But if the liquor has been bewitched, it means instant death to he who drinks, they say. Not wanting to die alone, they drink a little and set aside the rest for the musicians. They return to the house, *M* again preceding *Mr*, and approach the musicians to speak and drink with them. *M* asks *Mu₁* to drink a little with him: he says he found a bottle in the trash. The bottle may, or may not, be good, who knows? But since the officials drank from it, the musicians should as well. The musicians are not certain they should trust what the cargo-holders say, they reply. It would be best if M drank first before their eyes. This joke is as much a part of the biweekly ceremony as changing the flowers itself.

The flower change at the house of the martomorei ends in the opposite way that it began. Everyone drinks from shot glasses, in the same order as before. Then the cargo-holders light candles and incense, and kneel before the altar to pray: God, Jesus Christ, Our Lord Esquipulas; they have changed his flowers and leaves. They rise and, M before Mr, go speak to the musicians (order: Mu_1, Mu_2, Mu_3), saying, as they bow and release again and again, that they have changed the flowers and leaves of Our Lord of Esquipulas. They have finished and begin to dance before going to change the flowers in the chapel.

After changing the flowers in the chapel they dance once again. Cargo-holders and musicians then return to the house of the martomorei where they eat and rest for a short while. The first ceremony has ended, the flowers and leaves have been changed. About two A.M. on Sunday the officials rise to take out the medallions of Our Lord of Esquipulas; this initiates the second ceremony, called xlok' ʔual. While in the house of the marto-morei, they count the medallions, dance, and eat. Then they move on to the chapel to place the medallions on the saint, dance, eat, and dance again, until mid-afternoon when they return for the last time to the house of the martomorei. This completes the weekend ritual for Esquipulas.

A FORMAL ANALYSIS

Even my descriptive account does not include all the facts about the ceremony; the analysis that follows is more selective, yet comprehensive. It isolates certain observable and salient features of this ritual, that is, the extreme and repetitious way in which cargo officials order and rank themselves, then subsumes every instance of a wide range of seemingly diverse phenomena—all defined as "ranking"—under a simple model. Ranking includes the following kinds of action: a cargo-holder bows to some people and, by touching their foreheads, releases those who bow to him; he sits, with his fellow officials, in neat single file rows; they all march in a

straight line; drinks are served in a fixed order, one man first, another second, and so on. Every instance of programmed ranking by participants in the rite may be represented by a concise formal notation. Here I derive relative rank from seating and procession orders; I encode only those acts where exchange, verbal or material, takes place. This notation refers to a series of overt ritual acts which informants consistently emphasize in their descriptions of the ceremonies.

I shall consider the order in which people are served drinks an expression of, or metaphor for, hierarchy. When people drink from the shot glasses, the liquor is served first to the highest in rank, then on down to the lowest. Let an arrow, running from left to right, denote this rank order as follows: →. "Prayer" is more difficult to represent because it may occur in either of two ways: (1) in the chapel there is free variation in rank orientation, the high man kneels on either side of the altar, and (2) in his home the martomorei ranks highest and kneels on the north side of his altar. These two metaphors for hierarchy occur in different places; they are in complementary distribution and may be seen as variants of the same message about ranking. My notation corresponds to what takes place in the chapel: but an arrow running in two directions—with heads on either end—represents both cases of "prayer": ↔.

I encode the elaborate bowing and releasing between cargo-holders and musicians as shown in Figure 2. The upper arrow, running from right to left, denotes that the officials invert their rank order prior to, and while, speaking with the musicians; the lower arrow indicates that the musicians are spoken to in rank order, highest to lowest (Mu_1, Mu_2, Mu_3). The two arrows are the same in length and represent a sequence of gestures rather

Descriptive Diagram
East
(household altar)

Formal Notation

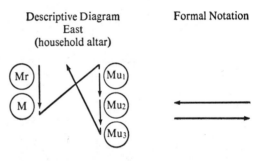

FIGURE 2

Descriptive and formal notation for bowing and releasing between cargo-holders and musicians.

than relative number of actors; in the chapel four, not two, cargo-holders invert their order to speak with the musicians, yet the notation remains the same.

The same notation ($\leftrightarrows$) also refers to the drinking and joking between cargo-holders and musicians after the old flowers are thrown out; here the men drink from bottles, not shot glasses, in this order: M, Mr, Mu_1, Mu_2, Mu_3. Again officials invert their order; musicians do not. On this level of analysis, the basic structural units or elements are messages or metaphors of rank order and hierarchy rather than concrete actions. It is not these elements themselves, but the relations among them which shall comprise my analysis.

I

A formal account of the flower change at the house of the martomorei eliminates the drama, but it reveals a high degree of structure in the ritual, something not apparent in a conventional description. Figure 3—like the method Lévi-Strauss (1963a) proposes for diagraming the structural study of myth—reads, from left to right and top to bottom, as the temporal sequence of metaphors in the ceremony, and vertically, as repetitions of the same metaphor. This represents the following sequence: cargo-holders invert their order and speak with the musicians ($\leftrightarrows$), then they pray ($\leftrightarrow$). Everyone, from highest to lowest is served a shot of liquor ($\rightarrow$); they drink again ($\rightarrow$). The officials have just thrown out the dry flowers and come drink and joke with the musicians ($\leftrightarrows$). All present drink for the third time ($\rightarrow$); officials then pray ($\leftrightarrow$), and speak with the musicians ($\leftrightarrows$). This pattern recurs over and over during the ritual for Our Lord of Esquipulas.

The same diagram describes, for example, the flower change at the chapel. The equivalence of these two portions of the ritual is not

Dancing

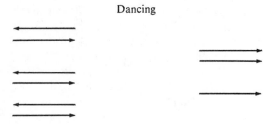

FIGURE 4

A formal description of dancing at the house of the martomorei and in the chapel.

obvious from observation: in the chapel the two cargo-holders join the other martomorei and mexon to redecorate five, rather than one, flowered arches; this flower change takes longer to perform than the first, but the number and sequence of messages about rank remain constant. Two ceremonies, then, appear to be distinct, but formally—seen as a sequence of metaphors for hierarchy—they are the same.

After the flower changes in the house and chapel, the officials dance and sing with the musicians, who are seated playing their instruments. Ritual dancing differs from the flower change only in that it omits one of the messages about rank, "prayer" ($\leftrightarrow$) [see Figure 4]. Zinacantecos call the flower change "work" (*abtel*); dancing is relaxation—the cargo-holders "rest the heart of the gods" (*ta hkux yo ʔon kahvaltik*). While the two portions of the ritual formally resemble one another, it is appropriate that the flower change contain more messages about rank. Formal elaboration and something like "sacredness" go together.

Flower change and dance, in the house and chapel, plus two periods of eating constitute the entire six hour (Saturday, usually 6–12 P.M.) flower change ceremony, the balte ʔ (Table 1). Like what has preceded, the two segments glossed as "eat" share certain formal properties (Vogt, 1965b: 345–349); in the first case people eat coffee and bread, served on the ground, and in the second instances they have beef with broth and "tortillas," wash their mouths, then eat coffee and bread. Whether they are served on the ground or at the table varies, depending on what the musicians want. The relationship between the two "eats" is homologous with that between "change flowers" and "dance"; in both cases, structurally similar units differ in that an element of one is lacking in the other.

Flower Change

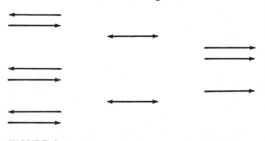

FIGURE 3

A formal description of the flower change at the house of the martomorei.

TABLE 1. SUMMARY DESCRIPTION
OF THE COMPLETE BALTE ʔ

balte ʔ	
at house *Mr*	eat (coffee and bread) change flowers dance
at chapel	change flowers dance
at house *Mr*	eat (meal)

TABLE 2. SUMMARY DESCRIPTION
OF THE FIRST SEVEN
SEGMENTS OF THE XLOK'
ʔUAL

xlok' ʔual	
at house *Mr*	eat (coffee and bread) count medallions dance eat (meal)
at chapel	place medallions on saint dance eat (egg, coffee, bread)

Ritual time in the balte ʔ, then, is an ordered alternation between greater and lesser units of the same order. "Cyclical," "repetitive," or other familiar Western terms do not describe this alternation as aptly as do the Tzotzil relational concepts bankilal and ʔicʼinal, which appear in Zinacantan "as a way of classifying phenomena in almost any domain in the universe" (Vogt, 1965b: 351). These concepts, represented in the kin terminology, are confined in most Zinacantecan hamlets to male siblings (J. F. Collier, personal communication): hbankil refers to a man's older brother; ki¢ʼin refers to a younger. Cargo-holders go one step further and use these as terms of address. The two martomoreietik call the mexonetik—men who spend much less on their cargoes than they—mexon and are addressed in turn as htot martomorei, following the rule for terms of address across generations (male or female speaker); but the martomoreietik, who share title and cost of cargo, call one another hbankil and ki¢ʼin, "More and less, two of a kind": the relation of bankilal and ʔi¢ʼinal obtains between the martomoreietik, brothers, and, I suggest, segments of the ritual for Esquipulas. The same principle structures ritual time and social space during the cargo performance. It is order among men—metaphors of hierarchy—that shapes each segment of the balte ʔ, and it seems reasonable that the relations of these segments and certain human relations structurally coincide.

The same alternations obtain in taking out the medallions of the saint, xlok' ʔual, the ceremony that follows the balte ʔ after a break for sleep. The first seven segments of the xlok' ʔual—lasting from about 2 A.M. to 10 A.M. on Sunday—formally resemble the balteʔ; as shown in Table 2. "Count medallions" and "place medallions on saint" occupy the same structural position as "flower change" in the balte ʔ. Yet xlok' ʔual differs with its additional "eat"; here, the second "eat" is a meal that must be served on a table; the third takes

place outside the chapel. That xlok' ʔual is the same as, and more than, the balte ʔ is consistent with other indications of its relative importance. This ceremony is the defining feature of ritual for Esquipulas; as opposed to the semiweekly flower change, it is performed whenever the cargo-holders participate in a "fiesta" and every Sunday of the year.

After the third "eat," from about ten to two on Sunday, the crystalline structure of the ritual becomes less and less apparent. During certain segments of the rite, people drink twice instead of three times. Informants, even in ideal simulations, note that such performance is at once odd and occurs every week· the *mayol*, they explain, wants to go home, and acts drunk, puts on his hat, refuses to dance. Or the musicians get hungry. Furthermore, dance follows dance, and each segment is protracted, with fewer metaphors of hierarchy per unit time, by the clock. It is no accident that this ritual becomes less structured, more continuous; this is the way with other Zinacanteco ritual practices. An otherwise different rite, curing, begins at the patient's house with a similar degree of structure, with much bowing, releasing, and passing of the shot glass. As the ceremony proceeds and the shaman and his party walk and pray before crosses on various sacred mountains, these messages about rank are more widely spaced. The long curing trek has affinities with the repetitious two-step, the rhythm of the cargo-holders' drawn out ritual dance late on Sunday morning.

II

My thesis has been that the alternation of segments—alike in kind, greater and lesser in degree—marks the flow of time in the weekend ritual. The principle that underlies the sequence of segments is bankilal and ʔi¢ʼinal; when the ritual begins, this pattern is compact and salient, becoming less clearly marked as the ceremony proceeds. This rhythm, I think, is analogous to the way a Zinacanteco conceives of the relation between an older and younger brother, or two religious officials with the same title, or, for that matter, a number of other aspects of his world. What matters is that ritual time is cut up into pieces that are basically the same, yet a little different. I would not insist on the interpretation that these alternations somehow grow out of, or mirror, the social relations of males, same generation, with close ties (either family or title), but I suspect that this is the case, and all these relations are formally equivalent.

While the rite as a whole is seen as a rhythmic alternation, the nature and structure of metaphors for hierarchy within each segment remain to be seen. I shall now consider the rules by which messages about rank are combined in "flower change," "count the medallions," "take out the medallions," "dance," and other phases of the ritual. Two principles govern the occurrence of metaphors in all segments: (1) entrance and exit of each phase are marked by metaphors that are counterparts, either the same or the opposite, and (2) intervening ritual action is marked by three repetitions of drink from the shot glass ($\rightarrow$). I add a rule: each segment of the ritual tends toward symmetry, except for messages that vary from segment to segment and are contingent on the ritual action itself.

To illustrate the operation of these principles, in Figure 5 I show the flower change and the count of medallions in the house of the martomorei. The notation remains the same.

The count has a novel metaphor ($\leftrightarrow$), which represents the fact that all present come forward (order: musicians, male helpers, female helpers, officials) to pray before the medallions. I bracket the second occurrence of this metaphor because it was performed in 1964, but not in 1965 and 1966.

Two of the above metaphors are motivated by aspects of the ritual action: (1) $\leftrightarrows$ occurs in the middle of the flower change because the officials have thrown away the dried flowers and must greet the musicians on reentering the house, and (2) $\leftrightarrow$ occurs because people must pray when the saint's medallions are taken out of their chest. These messages, contingent or motivated, are not predictable in a schema valid across segments; they are high in information, pointing up the distinction of one segment from another. The presence of an elaborate metaphor ($\leftrightarrow$) seems to correlate with variation in "sacredness" across two segments that occupy the same structural position in the ritual. In both "flower change" and "count" the cargo-holder loosens his kerchief, as does the shaman; but during the count the official seems to imitate the sacred divination—the count tells his fortune. Consistent with a heightening of "sacred" behavior is the appearance of a novel and complex metaphor: all participants pray ($\leftrightarrow$).

Aside from such motivated messages, the middle section of each segment is marked by three repetitions of drink ($\rightarrow$); this seems to be a particularly rich metaphor. When drink is served people are in various positions, corresponding to their social or ritual status; women to the north and men to the south; musicians seated along the south wall, in a row; martomorei on the north side of the altar (its right hand), mexon on the south, and so on. But, as the young boy pours drinks, he includes everybody in a single hierarchy—all present are served, one before the other. While rank is absolute, groups are united. At the same time that drink ranks men, it signifies complete equality; each person receives the same kind and amount of liquor. The participants are joined in an inclusive hierarchy, with equal portions for all. The unifying message of drink differs radically from the discontinuous metonymy Lévi-Strauss (1963b) and Leach (1964) discuss, where one category of men might receive fruit wine and another sugar cane liquor. In cargo ritual, as with many religious ceremonies, the differences among men appear to have been overcome (Lienhardt, 1966: 148). Drink, the central and critical portion of every segment, is another expression of the oft-repeated words of formal couplet speech: "We have united; we have all come together."

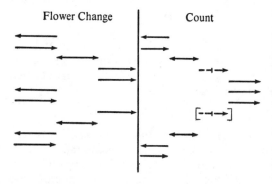

Flower Change   Count

FIGURE 5

A formal description of flower change and count in the house of the martomorei.

All segments have "drink" as their center; they also have well-characterized limits. In considering entrance and exit I include all acts of bowing and releasing, accompanied by speech in couplet form. Three kinds of behavior mark entrance and exit: (1) couplet speech with the musicians, (2) prayers that immediately follow, and echo, speech to the musicians: the officials kneel, bow, release—they greet the gods as men—and repeat the phrases they have just spoken, and (3) on occasion, just following the prayer, speech with elderly women, in the same manner. Couplet speech is easily recognized: the two lines are identical, differing only in their terminal words. In general, the second terminal word is phonetically longer than the first, and often, the less common, more elegant, or archaic. Thus in

c'ul senior ʔeskipula htot
c'ul senior ʔeskipula kahval

htot has one syllable and *kahval* two, and kahval means "my lord," and is elegant, while htot is simply "my father." It is significant that when the officials reenter the house after throwing out the dried flowers they bow, release, and joke with the musicians, but they do not speak in couplets. The point here is that coming into the house, even with bowing and releasing, does not equal entrance to a "sacred" phase of the ritual: "sacred" phases have clearly marked boundaries.

Leach, in an attempt to refine classic theories of ritual, predicts that entrance and exit of "sacred" segments—like "flower change" and "count" will be "contrasted opposites" (1961: 136), i.e., entrance $\leftrightarrows \leftrightarrow$ and exit $\leftrightarrow \leftrightarrows$. He fails, however, to predict the many other phases of the ritual that end as they begin, such as the dancing. To account for my data I must return to the more general and accurate formulations of Hubert and Mauss (1964: 46, 48) and van Gennep (1960:24): rites of entrance and exit are "counterparts," either the same or the reverse. My material, though, does make some refinement possible; I can specify the difference between the segments that end and begin in the same way and those that are opposites. By now it should be no surprise that inversion occurs only in the phases termed "work," where the official loosens his kerchief as a shaman. The cargo-holder seems to signal his creation of a "sacred phase" by finishing in the opposite way that he began.

CARGO-HOLDERS, MUSICIANS, AND HELPERS

A description of cargo ceremonies in terms of rank creates something on the order of a grammar of ritual action. Formal relations are both intelligible and prescribed; this is not a trivial grammar, for three reasons: (1) structure is revealed in the ritual, (2) rank is ever-present and obligatory in Zinacantecan social life, and (3) elaboration of metaphors for hierarchy corresponds to increased "sacredness" in ritual action.

I will now relate the principles of ranking to patterned modes of behavior in the ritual for Esquipulas. My purpose is to discover some reasons for the institutionalized joking between cargo-holders and musicians, and for the more spontaneous disputes that often arise among the officials themselves. What follows suggests that hierarchy is a matter of deep concern for the participants, and that it poses a moral dilemma, which is part of the ritual's meaning and its power.

The three categories of individuals who participate in the weekend ritual are defined over and over in messages about rank. I list them in Table 3. The principles of ranking differ for each of the groups as does the way in which they are recruited for service.

The helpers are friends and relatives of the official who selects them, and they are ranked, as in daily life, by age. For the cargo-holders "a universalistic criterion, economic resources, determines eligibility" (Cancian, 1964: 342), and it is their titled office that determines position in the hierarchy. Musicians, on the other hand, are chosen for their ability to play an instrument and through personal acquaintance and recommendation. In ranking, officials speak to musicians in accord with the instrument they play, first violin, then harp, last guitar, but the younger of the two men bows. The musician's status is mixed, at once acquired and ascribed.

TABLE 3. CARGO-HOLDERS, MUSICIANS, AND HELPERS, WHO PARTICIPATE IN THE RITUAL FOR ESQUIPULAS

I Cargo-Holders *hpas ʔabteletik*	II Musicians *hvabahobetik*	III Helpers *hcomiletik*
1. *martomorei bankilal*	1. *hvob violin*	1. eldest male
2. *martomorei ʔiɔ'inal*	2. *hvob ʔarpa*	2. ...
3. *mexon bankilal*	3. *hvob kitara*	3. youngest male
4. *mexon ʔiɔ'inal*		

Musicians and officials cooperate to perform a ritual, but their relationship is ambiguous. Musicians instruct the newly initiated cargo-holder in his duties. As one informant explained, they are like shamans: public servants possessing special ritual knowledge, they are paid for their services in food and drink. Cancian describes the relation between the two kinds of groups in this manner:

In Zinacantan today, quite different kinds of prestige accrue to individuals who provide the two kinds of service, that of the cargo-holder and that of the ritual specialist. The ritual specialists are respected for their knowledge and their services to the saints and the community, but in the last analysis it is the people who supply the money, the cargo-holders, who receive the lion's share of the prestige. The prestige given the cargo-holders is rather finely graded according to how much they have spent [1964: 341].

In effect, musicians are food-drink receivers, the cargo-holders food-drink givers; they depend on one another. The structural relation between musicians and officials has the "conjunctive and disjunctive components" that Radcliffe-Brown associates with the joking relation (1952: 95).

It is appropriate that joking between these two groups occurs, for the most part, when officials are giving—a drink from their bottles or a ritual meal. Giving during the meal is mediated by young men who serve; here, joking centers around sex and other themes. But, when the officials give most overtly, when they hand the musicians a bottle of liquor, jokes focus explicitly on status relations. During the flower change there is the programmed joke about trust and mistrust between the two groups of men. At other times, as the official offers the bottle, the musician grasps hand and bottle, saying the cargo-holder does not really want to give. Or the musician releases his opposite with his left hand instead of right. In one sequence the cargo-holder speaks to the musician as if he were asking his future father-in-law for his daughter's hand. The joking relation between the two categories of men is structurally analogous to that between affines in other areas of the world; they laugh about what divides and unites them.

Joking here is programmed and defined by a conflict in roles—a formal opposition with a formal solution. Another set of conflicts—more spontaneous and overt—obtains among the cargo-holders themselves. Their arbitrary ranking may subordinate older to younger,

and peer to peer. In 1966 martomorei ?i¢'inal was older than bankilal, and sensitive to this difference. He changed the normal seating arrangement for ritual meals as shown in Figure 6. In past years older officials have taken the positions assigned by their titles; other Zinacantecos find it hard to believe that a man would not take his given place. Rank order is not a matter of indifference.

Disputes related to ritual performance cannot be predicted; these most explicit statements of conflict often become public court cases. In 1965, for instance, martomorei bankilal was very drunk when it came time to count the saint's medallions; he came out 110 short. ?i¢'inal, who usually wound up 30 to 50 ahead, wondered aloud, "How can a man count so badly?" He was promptly hit by the son of bankilal. This incident was discussed before members of the civil hierarchy, with emphasis on the embarrassing count. In the end, amends were made, as might be expected, with a number of rounds of drink. Such squabbles arise for a number of reasons—personalities of the actors, difficulties in getting along with strangers, and so on—but their primary reference is inherent in ranking itself.

The rank order among officials for Esquipulas roughly corresponds to a hierarchy based on relative wealth and prestige in the community. A man does not ordinarily have the opportunity to display and flaunt his wealth; witchcraft threatens the show-off. In cargo ritual the bowing and releasing behavior —in daily life, a metaphor expressing respect for age—is, in effect, a recognition of economic superiority. A metaphor for ascribed status (age) is translated into one for acquired status (wealth). Not only does the cargo system reflect and confer prestige within the community, but also, in its ritual, it gives men a culturally appropriate way to act out a

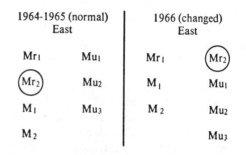

FIGURE 6

Normal and changed seating arrangements for officials at the ritual meal.

social order based on acquired status, an order forbidden in hamlet life.

Metaphors of hierarchy in cargo ritual are those of daily life; Leach correctly says that ritual denotes "*aspects* of almost any kind of action" (1964: 13). It also is true, as has been seen, that ritual and daily life may be two different kinds of action. Leach fails to see that these two sectors of social life may be at once continuous and discontinuous (1954: 10–14); here it makes more sense to speak of "both-and" than "either-or." "Both-and" because helpers are ranked, as in daily life, by age, and cargo-holders by wealth. Messages about rank in Zinacantan are not like ink-blots that each person, or category of person, reads in his own way; the meaning of a bow is never questioned. A single message, in ritual and in daily life, unambiguously denotes two principles of ranking, acquired status and ascribed.

If the ways Zinacantecos denote relative social status are the "model schema of the social structure in which they live" (Leach, 1961b:299), there remains a profound difference between everyday affairs and ritual action. This is the difference between a rank order where anyone, by simply growing older, reaches the top, and a hierarchy closed at the top to the man who lacks the economic means to ascend. The former is one hypothetical model of a just society, with equal distribution of commodities (portions of drink) and equal opportunity to rise; the latter is more open to question. Adult males live in both worlds, they must acknowledge the existence of both hierarchies. To the extent that this dilemma is felt by the participants, the contradictions between these two systems must give the relation among the cargo-holders its problematic, and its "sacred," quality.

Pobert H. Lowie

THE VISION QUEST AMONG THE NORTH AMERICAN INDIANS

The vision quest among the Indians and Eskimo of North America was a ritualistic means of acquiring supernatural power through personal contact with the supernatural. But there have been many misunderstandings regarding the quest. As Ruth Fulton Benedict has demonstrated in her authoritative monograph, "The Concept of the Guardian Spirit in North America" (1923), the vision experience was not at all always associated with acquiring a guardian spirit. It was used in California by shamans wishing to effect a cure; among the Montagnais and Mistassini to promote success in a hunt; among the Plains Indians for mourning, warpaths, revenge, curing disease, calling the bison, naming a child, acquiring a design, entering a secret society, and so on; power or commands were received directly rather than by acquiring a guardian spirit. Nor was the vision quest, as Hutton Webster supposed, synonymous with the puberty rite; it was not a rite of passage except in certain areas. True, the two often went together, but frequently the vision cycle led only to supernatural power and the puberty rite qualified only for membership in the tribe. The two concepts were remarkably distinct in California. Another mistake is to regard the vision quest as something sought by all young men of the tribe. Some Indians reserved the quest only for shamans seeking a tutelary spirit to be used to punish trespassers on family hunting grounds and to fight with rival shamans in supernatural contests. Often the attempt to induce a vision failed and the individual might resort to acquiring a share in someone else's

Reprinted with permission of McGraw-Hill Book Co., Inc., from *Indians of the Plains*, pp. 157–161, by Robert H. Lowie, published for the American Museum of Natural History by McGraw-Hill Book Co., Inc. Copyright 1954 by the American Museum of Natural History.

vision through purchase. It should be remembered, too, that visions were not always sought; west of the Rockies they ordinarily came involuntarily. Benedict has reminded us that guardian spirits could be acquired by means other than a vision. She insists that the vision and not the guardian spirit was the unifying religious fact of North America.

The hallucinatory side of the vision quest is of interest because it supports the hypothesis that religious ritual often affords an opportunity for self-transcendence, either through consciousness-changing drugs, purgatives, self-torture, or fasting. It leads to what is usually referred to as the "religious thrill," which many theorists regard as the source of religion. But while the experience is an individual and solitary one, it is culturally patterned both in the methods for inducing the vision and in the contents which are revealed. It is a socially created ritual, and not one whose genesis is to be sought in the unique experience of the individual.

The account of the vision quest that follows comes from Lowie's considerable field experience with American Indians, especially the Crow. The reader wishing to go beyond the descriptive type of account should consult the article by Benedict mentioned earlier.

Most North American Indians attached great importance to visions, and in the Plains these took precedence in the religious life. However, the spirits did not always appear to their prospective protégé, but might merely become audible to him, issuing instructions and promising definite benefits. In Siberia and parts of western North America supernatural visitants were not sought; in fact, often the spirit compelled a native to accept his guardianship much against the future protégé's wishes. By way of contrast, Woodland and Plains Indians deliberately went out to a lonely spot in order to obtain a revelation. Some Crow individuals received favors unsought when in a predicament. Occasionally it even happened that a spirit came under ordinary circumstances from a pure desire to befriend the mortal. However, the normal procedure was to go into solitude, fast and thirst for four days, and supplicate the spirits to take pity on the sufferer. A Crow usually cut off a finger joint of his left hand or in some other way mortified his flesh by way of arousing supernatural pity.

Certain tribal differences are noteworthy with respect to the vision quest. In the Woodlands, Ojibwa and Winnebago parents regularly instructed boys, possibly not over seven years of age, to fast in order to obtain the blessing of a spirit, and on the Plains the Hidatsa elders likewise prompted their children to seek a revelation at an early age. But no such admonition was customary among the Crow. There a lad grew up, constantly hearing that all success in life was derived from visions; hence, being eager for horses and for social recognition, an adolescent would go out to fast, praying for rich booty, for a chance to strike a coup, or for some other

benefit. A mature man or woman would seek a vision whenever a special cause arose—if his children were sick, if he had lost his property, if he longed to revenge the killing of a close relative, and so on. Again, the Arapaho seem to have sought a vision only as adults.

We naturally wonder what really happened on such quests. There is no doubt that the vast majority of informants firmly believed in the reality of the experiences they described. In order to explain this phenomenon psychologically, several factors have to be considered. First of all, the god seeker was usually under a strong emotional impulse—either yearning to shine before his fellows or desiring relief from want or disease or the grief over an unavenged kinsman. By seclusion in a lonely spot, by his fast, by self-mutilation, he naturally intensified his emotional state. What is more, the myths told by his people and the accounts of the supernatural experiences of contemporary tribesmen had left an imprint on his mind and helped to shape the sense impressions that came to him. His longings at the time blended with the visionary pattern of his tribe and with the sounds or sights actually experienced under highly abnormal conditions so as to inspire an interpretation of things seen and heard. Individual peculiarities likewise entered: an Indian of a predominantly auditory type might imagine a whole series of distinguishable sounds—the call of a bird, the rustling of leaves, the neighing of a horse, the speech of an alien tribe, and what not. If his was a decidedly visual type, he would see specific details, as when a would-be raider caught sight of a mount he was to steal—say, a bay horse with docked tail, heavy mane, and a zigzag line painted down its legs. A man who subsequently arranged his sensations for his own enlightenment or to give a clear statement to an audience was in the position of ourselves when trying to give a coherent account of a dream. Without trying to deceive or to invent, he would unconsciously bridge over obscure points, filling in the gaps, adapting his memories of the experience to one of the tribal vision patterns familiar to him from listening to earlier accounts.

A good example of such a pattern is the following. Several Crow informants independently tell how on their lonely vigil they saw a spirit or several spirits riding along, how the rocks and trees in the neighborhood turned into enemies who attacked the horsemen, but were unable to inflict any harm. The symbolical meaning of these apparitions is that the spirits are making the visionary invulnerable. This is, of course, a generally prized blessing, but several persons could not independently conceive the identical image of spiritual riders shot at by transformed bits of the landscape, especially when the very same motif appears also in traditional stories apart from the narration of the teller's personal experiences. Evidently the image, however it may have originated, became part of tribal folklore and was readily worked into the report of their revelations by persons who particularly craved invulnerability. Again, it was certainly a part of the tribal pattern that most Crow Indians obtained their spiritual blessing on the fourth night of their seclusion, four being the mystic number within the area.

The supernatural beings who befriend man vary enormously in character. Animals were very frequent visitants of Plains Indians; buffalo, elk, bears, eagles (sometimes conceived as birds producing thunder by flapping their wings), and sparrow hawks constantly figure in the narratives, but also quite lowly beasts such as dogs or rabbits. A Pawnee legend even describes the invocation of mosquitoes, and according to Cree tradition a mosquito gave one tribesman the gift of chieftaincy. Curious contradictions do not seem to have been recognized as such by the Indians. In a Crow story a rabbit pursued by a hawk promises to give supernatural power to an Indian if he will shield him from the bird of prey. Correspondingly, a Pawnee boy gets supernatural aid from mice who are unable to extricate themselves from a relatively simple difficulty. That is, though animals are possessed of supernatural powers, they may be

dependent on mortals for specific services, for which they reward them. Celestial patrons are also frequent, stars figuring prominently among the Pawnee. Fanciful creatures of more or less human shape likewise appear in visions, e.g., a dwarf with a very powerful musculature. Sometimes the patron comes in human guise but in disappearing assumes his true shape or otherwise gives a clue to his identity.

The Crow interpreted the relationship between patron and protégé as that of a father and his child, and accounts of visions often explicitly quote the spirit as pronouncing the formula of adoption: "I will have you for my child." In any case the spirit normally taught the Crow a sacred song, instructed him just how he must dress in battle or if a man was to become a doctor what medicines or curing devices he must use, and frequently imposed certain taboos as to diet or behavior. Any infraction of the rules was liable to precipitate a loss of the guardian's protection or even a dire calamity. Often the visionary not only wore some token of his vision or painted it on, say, his shield cover, but also on the strength of successive visions assembled the ingredients to build up a "medicine bundle," i.e., a wrapper containing a set of sacred objects indicated by the spirit. A Pawnee bundle contained as a minimum one pipe, tobacco, paints, certain birds, and corn—all assembled in a container of buffalo hide that was hung from the wall of the lodge. The opening of a bundle and the treatment of its contents were accompanied by definite rites. As already stated, it is often difficult to tell whether the native consistently considered such objects sacred in their own right, in other words, made them fetishes wholly independent of any personal spirit, or whether they become sacred only as gifts of the spirit; very likely the attitude of a person varied at different times.

If because of visions, one individual worshiped above all a supernatural buffalo, another an eagle, and a third the morning star, the question arises how these several beings ranked in relation to one another. With the Comanche and the Crow this problem arose only when there was a clash of interests between tribesmen, each man falling back on the protection of his own guardian and the issue showing whose patron was the stronger. In the absence of a coherent system of the universe, the religious consciousness assigned priority to individual visitants. Thus, an

Indian once told the author that a feather he cherished as memento of his vision of a bird was the greatest thing in the world. At the opposite extreme stood the Pawnee, who had brought their beliefs into a logical system, venerating a Supreme Being named Tirawa, a sky-dwelling creator who rules the universe, his commands being executed by lesser deities. Utterances by Dakota medicine men suggest a similar fondness for metaphysical speculation and integration. A question that remains unanswered is whether the average Pawnee or Dakota individual in his daily life was actually guided by priestly generalizations or whether in practice, without overtly rejecting them, he followed the Crow pattern.

Though all persons coveted a revelation, not all were able to obtain one. Those who did not succeed naturally did not wish to be thereby doomed to failure throughout life. The Crow and some other tribes resolved the dilemma by permitting a successful visionary to sell part of his power to less fortunate tribesmen, adopting them as his supernatural patron had adopted *him*, making for each of his disciples a replica of his sacred paraphernalia, teaching him the sacred songs, and warning against breach of any taboo associated with his medicine.

Edmund Wilson

THE ZUNI
SHALAKO CEREMONY

One of the most important Southwestern Indian ceremonials is the Zuni Shalako, which is the high point in the annual Zuni ceremonial calendar. Since the ceremony takes place in late November or early December in Zuni Pueblo, located in an isolated region of western New Mexico, relatively few Americans have seen this colorful and dramatic affair. When one of our foremost writers and literary critics, Edmund Wilson, visited Zuni and attended the Shalako in the autumn of 1947, we were provided with this absorbing and perceptive account, which first appeared as an article in the *New Yorker* and was later published in his book, *Red, Black, Blond and Olive* (1956).

The account is an accurate ethnographic description of the main features of the Shalako, but more important, it provides in its interpretations an understanding of the meaning and significance of a rite of intensification for an American Indian culture. As Wilson expresses it, "It seems as if the dancer by his pounding were really generating energy for the Zunis; by his discipline, strengthening their fortitude; by his endurance, guaranteeing their permanence." Watching the dance, the people receive strength and revitalization. The dance is the climactic event of the year and sets the moral standard. As Wilson observes, the whole social structure of the Zuni revolves around the ceremony, and by keeping the dances up throughout the night "they know that their honor and stamina, their favor with the gods, are unimpaired."

An interesting treatment of the Shalako by a French scholar, Jean Cazeneuve, *Les Dieux dansant à Cibola* (1957), is the first full-scale account of the ceremony.

Reprinted in abridged form from Edmund Wilson, *Red, Black, Blond and Olive* (New York: Oxford University Press, 1956), pp. 3–4, 9–12, 23–31, and 33–42, by permission of the author.

Ever since reading, some years ago, a book called *Dancing Gods*, by Miss Erna Fergusson, which describes the ceremonials of the Pueblo Indians in New Mexico and Arizona, I had had an ambition to attend what seemed from her account the most spectacular of them: the Zuni festival called Shalako. But this takes place under what are, for an Easterner, rather inconvenient conditions: in midwinter, at a date which varies and which may be set only a few days in advance; and at a place, in northwestern New Mexico, which is off the tourist route and not very easily accessible. When I did finally get a chance to visit the Shalako festival, I discovered certain other difficulties.

The little pueblo of Zuni is one of the Indian communities that have survived, since the arrival of the whites, most successfully as a social organism. Its strength and cohesion it seems mainly to owe to the extraordinary tribal religion: a complicated system of priest-hoods, fraternities, and clans which not only performs the usual functions of religions but also supplies it with a medical service, a judiciary machinery, and year-long entertain-ment. This cult includes the whole community, distributing and rotating offices, and organiz-ing it so tightly that it is completely self-contained, in a way that perhaps no white community is, and equipped to resist the pressures that have disintegrated other Indian groups. The ceremonies are partly in the nature of the enactment of a national myth, and they present a sort of sacred drama whose cycle runs through the entire year. The legends show a good deal of imagination and the impersonations a good deal of art, and the cast is so enormous that a very considerable proportion of the little town of twenty-six hundred has, at one time or another, a chance to play some role. With this, the Zuni religion imposes an effective discipline, involving periods of continence and fasting, and insist-ing on truthfulness—"speaking with one tongue"—and on civility and gentleness in personal relations. The Zunis as a group are extremely self-controlled, industrious, and self-reliant.

. . .

Coming down into the village proper—among one-story adobe houses and the bee-hive-shaped outdoor ovens that are both the same purplish pink as the bare grassless earth they are made of—is a descent into a foreign country. The air is full of piñon smoke that has a smell as rich and fragrant as roast chest-nuts. The dogs come out everywhere to bark at you—half-wild and rather horrid mongrels: some look like degenerate huskies, others as if they were crossed with coyotes. I saw one family of half-grown pups in which every one was different. I was reminded for a moment by the earth and the smell, the women wearing gay shawls and carrying baskets or jars on their heads, of the towns in southern Europe.

But this is something remote from Europe, at once newer and older: a piece of prehistoric America that has absorbed some of the cus-toms of the United States.

There are great preparations in evidence: everywhere men chopping wood and women baking loaves in the ovens; outside the houses hang sheepskins, fresh from the dozens of sheep that will be barbecued or stewed for the feasts. Against the monotonous background, the blankets are bright green or red. The people have an Eskimo Mongoloid look: stout, compact, and not very tall, with round black eyes that shine. Some of the men have frank friendly faces, but all look as if they had been cut out of some very hard substance, and they are in general reserved and solemn, talk-ing little among themselves and not even glancing at visitors. The women have bulky swathed bodies on feet and legs made enor-mous by a kind of wound puttees, and their wrapped and wadded bodies go along on legs that seem spindling. There are many small primitive corrals, mere rows of rough stakes, with sheep, burros, cattle, and horses. Here and there is a domesticated wild turkey or an eagle in a wooden cage, both kept to furnish feathers for costumes. Beyond rises Corn Mountain, which belongs to the Zunis and to which they belong, now transformed by the setting sun: the upper part of the mesa is for a moment vividly reddened, and its markings and outlines become distinct, then suddenly it is all left in shadow. On the other side of the sky, the clouds are a dull brickish red that corresponds with the color of the mesa and harmonizes with that of the soil. The little Zuni River shines palely as twilight falls.

The town is no longer the anthill (the Zunis themselves called it the Middle Anthill of the World) that the travelers of the eighteen-eighties found and that the Taos pueblo still is—with the houses piled up in terraces and scaled by outside ladders. There is a nucleus of these old buildings left that encloses the little plaza, but the Zunis have prospered so much that they have built themselves capa-cious houses, which now cover a relatively large area. They seem to put them wherever they like, at various distances from and angles to one another, and there is scarcely in the whole pueblo anything that can be called a street. The typical Zuni house has only a single story and not more than three or four rooms. These rooms are hung with shawls and blankets, and one of the more preten-tious houses is decorated with maps. I saw none that showed any signs of squalor—though the Zunis' ideas about bedding are not so nice as ours—and none that did not smell clean. In spite of the generally high standard of living, there are different degrees of wealth, and the families I visited were pretty well off. Yet, even with their chairs and beds, these houses, to a non-Indian, seem rather bare, because they are still the dwellings of people who have for millennia been used to sitting and sleeping on the ground and have not yet had the time to acquire the sense of furniture. The pieces are set around without system, often at great distances from one another, just as the conversations that take place when a white visitor calls are full of immense silences that are the product not of embarrassment but of the natural taciturnity of the Indian. There are two or three houses with a second floor, but this is merely "conspicuous waste," as the owners do not live in the upper part but use it, if at all, to store corn. Lately, the Zunis have shifted from round to square beams, because the women have found that the latter are easier to dust—a motivation of a kind which, as a visiting anthropologist says, could hardly be guessed in the ruins of the past by a student of archaeology.

Some of these houses have curious features that are the result of their having been built to receive the Shalako gods, or Shalakos. There are six of these gods, and tradition demands that each of them be received in a house especially built for the purpose. There have also in the past been two houses to entertain other groups of divinities. Now, the building of these eight houses and the banquets, on a medieval scale, with which the gods are welcomed have in some cases ruined for the whole of the year the families that have undertaken them. So the Zunis sometimes cheat on the expense and merely replaster old houses or build on a new room or two or entertain two Shalakos in one house. Even so, this means that every year there are several new houses, equipped for the requirements of the Shalako dance. They must have each a long room, which sometimes runs to sixty feet, and a ceiling at least twelve feet high to accommodate the enormous masks. Each must also have a row of windows that opens on the Shalako room from another large chamber next to it and from which certain special groups have the privilege of watching the performance, as if from theater boxes. These windows, which have regular sashes and panes, with little paper stickers on them to advertise the company that makes them, are one of the queerest examples of the mixture in Zuni of the old and the new. When the celebration is over, and a family comes to live in the house, the windows become a nuisance and are usually walled up.

.   .

I started for the first night of the Shalako festival (December 16 this year), with a small party of other visitors, at about four in the afternoon. All cars going down the hill were stopped by the police and searched for liquor. This, I was later told, failed almost completely in its purpose, since the Zunis by way of their grapevine would send the word back to Gallup for their bootleggers to come in around the hills.

We arrived at the pueblo just in time for the advent of the Council of the Gods, a group in which the Shalakos are not included. A fording place of mud and stones had been built across the Zuni River, and the gods, coming down from a stone formation known as the White Rocks, made their entrance over it into the town. The young Fire God comes first—a boy in his early teens, his nude body painted black and spotted with red, yellow, white and blue, wearing a black spotted mask, like a helmet that covers the whole of his head, and carrying a smoldering brand. We missed his arrival, however, and did not see him till later The main procession, which was now approaching, produced an uncanny impression. First comes the high god of the festival, Sayatasha, the Rain God of the North; and behind him his deputy, Hututu, the Rain God of the South. Sayatasha, in his mask, has what looks from a distance like a blank black-and-white pierrot face, between a black-banged wig and a black-and-white striped ruff, and he is dressed in a white gown. He stalks pompously in a long slow stride, accompanied by a short sharp rattle, made by shaking a cluster of deer scapulae every time he puts down his foot. It is the rhythm of authority and dignity which is reserved for him alone and—like the music for Wotan in the *Ring*—accompanies him all through the ceremonies. As he comes closer, we make out his accoutrements. A long flat horn, in place of an ear, sticks out from the right side of his mask, like an up-curved turquoise pennon; it has a heavy black fringe on its underside and a white feather dangling at the end. This horn presages long life for the Zuni people; and the left eye, a long black streak prolonged through an outstanding wooden ear, also heavily fringed, invokes a special long life for the "people of one heart." The right eye, not extended beyond the face, is intended to threaten short life to those who practice witchcraft. Sayatasha has a bow and arrows, and "prayer plumes"— that is, sticks with feathers attached that are supposed to give wings to the prayers. His follower Hututu is much the same, except that he has two ears and no horn, and that his eyes are set in a single black stripe which stretches across his mask, and from the tip of one ear to that of the other. Each is followed by a Yamuhakto, or Wood Carrier, who comes to pray for the trees, so that the people may have firewood and beams for their houses. The masks of the Yamuhakto are turquoise and bell-glass-shaped, with expressionless holes for the eyes and mouth, and each of these masks is surmounted with an untrimmed black wig, a tuft of yellow macaw feathers, and a kind of long green wand, from which hang down toward the shoulders long tassels of many-colored yarns. The Yamuhakto are wearing white buckskin skirts, and the naked upper parts of their bodies are painted a kind of purple and festooned with great garlands of beads. They carry deer antlers and bunches of feathers. All four of these principal divinities are wearing enormous round collars— shaped like life preservers and striped black-on-white like peppermints—that extend far beyond their faces and conceal the joint made by the mask. The two whippers, the Salimopiya, come last, carrying yucca switches. Both have bell-glass-shaped masks, noses like long pipes, eyeholes that are connected like spectacles, yellow topknots of feathers that stick out behind like weather vanes, and huge ruffs of black raven feathers. Both are nude except for a loincloth and wear spruce wreaths on wrists and ankles; but they are decorated in different ways: one, the Warrior of the Zenith, has a mask that is checkered in bright squares of color, with much yellow and red, which represents a spectrum of the midday sun, and red sunbursts where the ears would be. The other, the Warrior of the Nadir, is wearing a black mask with blue eyes and a blue snout.

All these figures proceed at a rhythm that is set by Sayatasha's rattle, but involves at least three different gaits. Hututu paces at a shorter stride than Sayatasha, and the Salimopiyas move with a quicker, a running step. All the time one hears a soft lively whistling that resembles the calling of birds. One cannot tell which of the figures is making these sounds, because one cannot see their faces; and, arising from no visible human source, scanning no human chant, yet filling the quiet air, the song seems the genuine voice of deities that are part of Nature. So they pass, while the people wait in silence, across the little dwindled river, where a dead dog lies on the bank and old tin cans and paper boxes have been caught here and there on the mud flats; they march up between the rude corrals, in one of which a big sow is grunting.

The Council now blesses the village, proceeding to six different points, where small holes have been dug in the ground. The people come out of the houses and sprinkle the divinities with sacred meal, and the Council, at every excavation, plants prayer plumes and sprinkles meal and performs some solemn maneuvers. Sayatasha and Hututu, each with his Yamuhakto, make two units that parade back and forth, while the Salimopiya mark time, never slackening their running pace but turning around in one spot. The climax of the ceremony comes when Sayatasha and Hututu walk up to one another and stop. Sayatasha cries, "Hu-u-u," and his vis-à-vis answers "Hu-tu-tu. Hu-tu-tu." The livelier calls, one decides, must be made by the Salimopiya, since they seem to match the brisker tempo. It is evident that all these calls have been imitated directly from bird-cries—one remembers the expertness at this of Fenimore Cooper's Indians—bird-cries, perhaps, heard at dusk or at night and attributed to elemental beings. Though owls, with the Indians, have a bad reputation, being usually connected with witchcraft, Hututu is obviously an owl. I assumed at first that the voices were whistles in the snouts of the Salimopiyas, but learned that they were produced by the throat and lips. I was told of a conversation in English in which one Zuni had said to another, "Gee, you make that noise good!" At one year's Shalako, Miss Bunzel says, the Salimopiyas were severely criticized for not being sufficiently handsome, for not showing sufficient animation, and for not giving loud enough calls. Yet the whistling is never shrill, it is always under perfect control; and the confrontation of Sayatasha and Hututu is performed with an unearthly impressiveness. At last, with much ceremonial, they enter the house prepared for them—it has a cozy, brand-new, suburban look. Though we whites have been behaving with discretion, the

Indians are afraid we may go too close and warn us to keep our distance.

In the meantime, the six Shalakos, the guests of honor, have been sitting out in front of a cabin, in which the actors put on their costumes, in a field back of one of the trading posts. These creatures are gigantic birds, the messengers of the rain gods, which, erect, stand ten or twelve feet tall. They have cylindrical turquoise faces with protruding eyes that roll up and down, long wooden beaks that snap, and upcurving tapering turquoise horns on either side of their heads. They wear big ruffs of raven feathers, black-banged wigs and towering fan-shaped crests of black-and-white eagle tail-feathers. But their entrance into the village is arranged to take place just at the moment when twilight is falling, and one can now see them only dimly as, proceeding in single file and escorted by men in black blankets, they make their way to the river and, with a rhythmic jingle of bells fastened around their ankles, come slowly across the ford. The dark is blotting them out at the moment they arrive on the hither side; they squat in a row of six on the road by which the Council came. Now, with night, it grows very cold. The visitors hang around for a time—there is a group of young men and women, anthropological students from the University of New Mexico —afraid to ask the Zunis what is going to happen next or when it is going to happen. We lean on the egg-shaped ovens, and one of the girls gets a present of a loaf of white Zuni bread, made from sour dough, which she breaks up and offers around: it is still warm and tastes delicious. But the last orange-yellow light has faded out of the sky to our left, and still the birds do not move. The Zunis have gone indoors, and the whites drift away, too. Only the Indian Agent and I remain.

An hour and a half pass. We walk up and down to unfreeze our feet. The Shalakos utter from time to time a single reiterated bird-note, which sounds as if it came, not from close at hand, but from the other side of the river; and at intervals they clack their beaks—which we can hear with remarkable distinctness—not at random, but one at a time, like counting-off in the Army. At one point, while they are making this sound, the bell in one of the churches, with a strange irrelevance, begins to ring. The men, wrapped in black blankets, go back and forth silently with flashlights, which are never allowed to play on the birds. They are only revealed now and then for a second by the swerve of an occasional Zuni

car. An airplane passes above us, winking green and red. The Indians begin to emerge and line up along the road; we assume that the show is starting, but we still have a long time to wait. At last, with other blanket-swathed figures, a group of twelve men arrives, jingling bells on their ankles; surprisingly, they seem costumed like characters in a production of *Romeo and Juliet*. These are the Shalako impersonators. (The birds, during the interval of waiting, have apparently been worked by "managers," who accompany and supervise them.) For each bird there are two dancers, who will alternate through the night. These twelve dancers, appointed a year ago, have been in training for their work ever since. Their roles, which bring much prestige, are exacting and responsible ones. Besides learning the difficult dances and memorizing endless speeches, they have had to build the Shalako houses. Though they begin by impersonating the gods, these latter, the night of the festival, will actually enter into them, and the men, with their masks, become sacred objects. If anyone touches a Shalako, or if the Shalako stumbles or falls—as it seems one of them did last year—the dancer is supposed to be struck dead by the god. A mistake on the part of the impersonator means either that someone has seen his mask while it was still in the dressing room and has not been whipped for impiety or that he himself has been making love to somebody else's wife and is unworthy to play the role. When a disaster of this kind occurs, the crowd must at once go away: the Salimopiya drive them off with whips. The dancer, of course, does not actually die, but his family go into mourning and behave as if he had. And though the Shalako actor must pull the cords that control the beak and the eyes, he is never—on pain of instant death—allowed to look up toward the top of the mask to watch the mystery in operation. Nobody except the manager may understand the Shalako's mechanics. These, then, were the dancers whom we now heard returning from six different points of the pueblo. We counted the jingling groups till the sixth had disappeared in the shadow where the birds were sitting.

Then suddenly, at some signal, a chorus of voices was raised. The Shalakos were on their feet. They came up from the road to the river and filed past us with their escort and choir; and the effect of this was thrilling and lovely in a way that it would be hard to imagine. The great birds, not rigidly erect but bent forward with the dignity of their kingly crests and their beardlike feathery ruffs, as if they were intent on their errand and knew each its destination, did not, in the frosty night, the pale moonlight, and the window lamplight, appear in the least comic, as they had in the pictures that one had seen; they hardly seemed even grotesque. And the welcoming hymns that accompanied them, in a harmony one did not understand but with the voices intertangled and singing against one another, had a beauty one could not have expected—not wild but both solemn and joyful—not entirely unlike our own anthems. Each of the Shalako birds is brought to the house prepared for it, and when it has come, it kneels down in front of the door, while prayer meal is sprinkled before it. The warm yellow light from inside gives comfort and life in the winter dark. The chants of reception are sung, and the bird, curt and proud in acceptance, snaps its beak in response to the welcome. Then the Shalako goes into the house and takes its seat before a turquoise altar. The impersonator comes out from inside, while a blanket is held up to screen him, and he and his alternate make offerings of seeds. Then they take seats beside the host, who hands them a cigarette, which he and they pass back and forth as they smoke it. The host addresses as "Father!" that one of the impersonators who is supposed to speak for the Shalako, and the latter replies, "Son!" They exchange other terms of relationship; then the host asks it, "How have you prayed for us? If you will tell us that, we shall be very glad to know it."

"I have come," says the Shalako, "from the sacred lake, and I have come by all the springs." He enumerates all the springs that the Zunis in their wanderings passed, when they were looking for a site for their town. "I have come to see my people. For many years I have heard of my people living here at Itiwana (the Middle), and for long I have wanted to come. I want them to be happy, and I have been praying for them; and especially I want the women to be fortunate with their babies. I bring my people all kinds of seeds, all the different kinds of corn, and all the different kinds of fruit and wild green things. I have been praying for my people to have long life; and whoever has an evil heart should stand up in the daylight. I have been praying that my people may have all different kinds of seeds and that their rooms may be full of corn of all colors and beans of all colors and pumpkins and water gourds, and that

they may have plenty of fresh water, so that they may look well and be healthy because of the pumpkins and the beans and the corn. I want to see them healthy.... Yes, I have worked hard and prayed for all my people. I do not want any of the roots to rot. I do not want anyone to sicken and die, but I want everyone to stand firmly on his feet all year. This is how I have prayed for you."

. . .

The dances do not begin till midnight, for the ceremonies connected with the reception of the gods are affairs of tremendous length. The speech made by Sayatasha alone—which the actor has had to learn by heart—takes him six hours to deliver. I did not try to visit the house where this god was being entertained. The old lady from California who was suspected of sinister designs, had walked in and sat down in front, and immediately been asked to leave. The Agent himself with his wife had been moved on from there by an officious visiting Navaho. The whole atmosphere was quietly hostile. Elsewhere a discourteous visitor was invited "kindly" to remove his hat; and another, who was standing at the door, was ordered not to come in by a boy of about twelve, who fixed him with a hateful eye. When the visitor tried to explain that his intention had been merely to look on from there, the boy grimly told him, "Don't look!" I did not, therefore, go into the house, but simply peered through the misted windows—where some of the Indians had also gathered—casually walking away and then walking up again. One cannot in the least blame the Zunis for wanting to keep strangers out of these ceremonies, for they are services of the most solemn kind, comparable in dignity and devotion to any that I have ever seen.

Besides the six houses prepared for the reception and the dances of the Shalakos, there are supposed to be one for the Council of the Gods and one for another group, called the Koyemshi, or Old Dance Men; but just as two pairs of Shalakos had doubled up this year, so the Koyemshi and the Council have combined. As I gazed in through the panes at these latter, the Council were beyond my vision, but I got a good view of the Koyemshi. These are a group of ten clown-priests, familiarly known as the Mudheads, who play roles of the first importance, being threaded in and out of ceremonies which continue through the whole year. When the Zunis, according to their legend, were wandering in search of a home, they sent out a brother and sister on a prospecting expedition. But the boy raped the girl in her sleep, and she gave birth to a brood of nine idiots. These are the Mudheads, who stand as a warning of the danger of incestuous unions. Largely naked and painted pink, they wear masks that are pink and bald and knobbed with enormous warts, and have imbecile round pop-eyes, gaping mouths like tadpoles or frogs, and fleshy topknots or catfish antennae. Each of these masks differs slightly from the others, and the roles of the Mudheads differ. One tries to repeat sacred rituals and always breaks down into gibberish; one is a coward, who hides under ladders and hangs back behind the rest; another is called the Bat and is supposed to be blind, so that he is always stumbling about and bumping into things; another believes himself invisible and hides his head like an ostrich; another can only laugh; another is glum, etc. When they are in character and wearing their masks, they pass in and out of the houses, performing all sorts of antics or—in infantile simpleton voices that seem to whimper and wheedle, to bubble and ooze from their masks—entertaining the spectators with ribald jokes that often probe into their private affairs. When the festival was announced by them eight days before, it was in such terms as these: "In eight days my people come. You must look around for nice girls and stay with them. . . . I come to tell you that in eight days everyone will be happy and have a good time. Men should trade wives." But they, too, are sacred beings, venerated as well as loved. During the year of their impersonation, the actors in the mythical dramas partly lose their own identities and become for the people of the pueblo the personages they represent. In the case of Sayatasha, the actor even loses his own name and is known by the name of the god. The affection and reverence felt for the mythical role that a man is playing is said sometimes to contrast sharply with the opinion his neighbors have had of him.

It is strange now to see these ten men (the incestuous Father makes the tenth), their masks pushed up on the tops of their heads, here dedicating themselves with prayer, after days of retreat and fasting, to the impish and ridiculous parts it is their duty to resume at midnight. Some of them are rather old, and have arms of skin-and-bone and aquiline Dantesque profiles. The audience sits on one side of the room, with a space between it and the celebrants. The Koyemshi, by themselves in a row, sit against the opposite wall; the man of the house sits facing them, flanked with five men of his own clan, the Dogwood, and four men of the Frog clan, his wife's, each drawn up so close to his vis-à-vis that their knees are almost touching. Long cigarettes made of reeds have been lighted from burning coals and are being passed back and forth between the Mudhead and the man who is receiving him, each taking six whiffs and waving the cigarette in the direction of the six Zuni points of the compass—North, South, East, West, Up, and Down. The Father recites a long speech like that of Sayatasha, while the others answer, "*Athlu*" (Amen). Says the Father of the Koyemshi to his hosts, "I leave my children with you for five days. They will dance in your houses; they will then go to the home of the gods in the East. . . . Give us food that we may eat, and next year we will bring you all kinds of seeds." They have little packets of seeds concealed under their black neckclothes, and the knobs on their heads are filled with seeds.

The young people came and went, looking in for a time through the windows or lingering on the porch. This part of the evening's ceremonies did not interest them much. A boy who had been in the war greeted two other boys with a "*Come sta, signori?*" and they showed off with Italian conversation. A boy and a girl had a moment of necking as they sat on the rail of the porch. He enveloped her plump round figure, dressed in poinsettia red, with a wing of his black blanket-cloak, and for a moment they rubbed their cheeks. Then he carried her off as she softly laughed, still with his cloak about her.

The monotonous chanting of the ritual went on without pause for hours: an unvarying repetition of six beats that ended in a kind of short wail.

The first Shalako house I visited, when, later, the dancing began, made upon me a tremendous impression. The rooms where the dances are held are dazzling with electric light and blazing with decorations. The walls are completely covered with brilliant blankets and shawls, pale buckskins, and queer blue or green hangings, made by the Navahos, on which square-headed elongated figures represent the Navaho gods. At one end of the room is a turquoise altar, ornamented with eagle feathers. A group of fetishistic animals, carved from stone, is set out in a row before it. In the audience, most of the men, having discarded their modern clothes, are wrapped in their best black blankets, and the women wear over their heads their best green or red or flowered shawls, and sometimes a kind of black apron, made of silk with fancy designs.

Against this background and before this audience, a Shalako and his alternate are dancing, balancing one another in a bizarre moving composition that seems to fill and charge the whole room. The unmasked dancer here is putting on such an extraordinary performance that he distracts attention from the bird. His costume has a suggestion of the Renaissance that may have been derived from the Spaniards. He wears a tight-fitting white buckskin cap with a curtain that hangs down behind, like the headwear of Giotto's Dante, and a fillet of red ribbon with silver bells. His black shirt is trimmed at the shoulders and sleeves with ribbons of many colors; his black kilts are embroidered in blue and circled with embroidered sashes. His knees are painted red, and the lower part of his legs is yellow, and he has tassels of blue yarn tied below the knees. With his brown bare feet he treads up and down—at a rate, as one observer has calculated, of about four times as many steps a minute as a marathon runner takes—in a quick, sharp, unflagging rhythm. This rhythm is also marked with a pointed yucca wand held before him in the right hand at an unwavering phallic angle. His eyelids are dropped, his eyes seem closed; the firm line of his mouth is drawn down—as if, in dedicating himself to his role, he has achieved a solemn sublimation and is shut off from the rest of the world. His whole demeanor is perfectly disciplined as he slowly moves thus back and forth from one end of the room to the other. And the Shalako, towering above him, actually seems lighter than he and dancing to an easier rhythm, as it turns in place or marks time or—astonishing in its swiftness and grace—swoops the length of the floor in a birdlike flight, never butting into the wall or ceiling and never so much as brushing the spectators, who sit close on either side.

These spectators rarely move, they are receptive, quiet, and calm; and the white visitor, too, becomes rapt. He, too, feels the thrill and the awe at the elemental power summoned. It seems as if the dancer by his pounding were really generating energy for the Zunis; by his discipline, strengthening their fortitude; by his endurance, guaranteeing their permanence. These people who sit here in silence, without ever applauding or commenting, are sustained and invigorated by watching this. It makes the high point of their year, at which the moral standard is set. If the Zunis can still perform the Shalako dances, keeping it up all night, with one or other of the performers always dancing and sometimes both dancing at once, they know that their honor and their stamina, their favor with the gods, are unimpaired. The whole complicated society of Zuni in some sense depends on this dance. Our ideas of energy and power have tended to become, in the modern world, identified with the natural forces—electricity, combustion, etc.—which we manipulate mechanically for our benefit, and it is startling to see human energy invoked and adored as a force that is at once conceived as a loan from the nonhuman natural forces and as a rival pitted against them; or rather, to put it in terms that are closer to the Zuni point of view, to see all the life of the animal world and the power of the natural elements made continuous with human vitality and endowed with semihuman form.

Here, too, one finds theater and worship before they have become dissociated, and the spectacle suggests comparisons in the fields of both religion and art. In the theatrical connection, it seems curious at first to be reminded of the Russian Ballet, but the reason soon becomes quite plain. It must have been true that Dyaghilev brought into the conventional ballet, with its formal routines and patterns, something that was genuinely primitive. He had really opened the way for an infusion of old Russia—by giving new life to the music of Rimsky and Borodin, who had already returned to folk material; through the Mongolian wildness of Nizhinsky; through the barbaric splendors of Bakst; through the atavistic stridencies and iterative beat of the Stravinsky of Le Sacre du Printemps. The kind of thing one sees in the Shalako dance must be something like the kind of thing that was revived by the Russian Ballet—not brought to the point of refinement to which Dyaghilev was able to carry it, but, in its color and variety and style, in the thoroughness of the training involved and the scrupulous care for detail, a great deal more accomplished and calculated than one could easily conceive without seeing it. In the other, the religious, connection, one comes quite to understand the student of comparative religions quoted by Erna Fergusson, who said that it was "no wonder missionaries have had no luck in converting these people to Christianity. It will never be done. The essential mental rhythm of the two races is too far apart. You could imagine reducing that Shalako figure two feet or even four; you could not possibly turn it into Christ on the Cross." The difficulty, one sees, would be to induce the flourishing Zunis—who have maintained their community for centuries, as sound and as tough as a nut, by a religion that is also a festive art—to interest themselves in a religion that has its origin in poverty and anguish. The Zunis, moreover, have no sense of sin; they do not feel that they need to be pardoned. What the Shalako bird brings is not pardon, but good cheer and fecundity. It is formidable; the children hide from it the day it comes into town, and if anybody falls asleep, it leans over and wakes him by snapping its beak. But the great bird loves the people, and the people love the bird. They build a house for it and spread it a feast, and it dances before them all night to show them its satisfaction.

In each of the other two Shalako houses, two Shalakos were dancing together, occasionally assisted by Mudheads. At one place, where I looked through a window, I saw people holding a blanket while the Shalako sat down in a corner; and the alternate changed places with the weary man who had just been performing his role. In the house of Sayatasha, the Council of the Gods, with their masks off, were performing stately evolutions, accompanied by the adolescent Fire God, who—slim and handsome in his speckled nudity—danced with the dropped eyelids and resolute lips of the Shalako impersonator. But the great success of the evening was a Shalako who danced alone. It was marvelous what this dancer could do, as he balanced his huge bird-body. He would slowly pavane across the floor; he would pirouette and teeter; he would glide in one flight the whole length of the room as smoothly as a bird alighting. The masks are constructed like crinolines; there are hoops sewn inside a long cylinder that diminishes toward the top; and the whole thing hangs from a slender pole attached to the dancer's belt. So the movements are never stiff. The Shalakos, ungainly though they may seem at first when one watches them from afar by daylight, are created in the dance as live beings; and this one was animated from top to toe, vibrating as if with excitement—gleaming with its turquoise face, flashing its white embroidered skirt, while its foxskins flapped like wings at the shoulders. The dance conveyed both delicacy and ecstasy, and the music—produced by a small group of men who sat, as if in a huddle, facing one another, as they chanted, beat a drum and shook rattles—exercised a peculiar enchantment. There are many different songs for the dances, and they vary in mood and pace; but each consists of a single theme repeated over and over, with a rest after so many bars and occasional changes in tempo, which momentarily relieve the dancer. In this case, the recurrent lapses—during which the Shalako, poised for flight, marked time and snapped his beak at the end of his room-long runway—would be followed by brisk pickings-up, when the bird would skim across the floor; and this reprise always had about it an element of the miraculous, of the miracle of the inexhaustible energy, leaping up after every subsidence with the same self-assertive joy. Carried along by the rhythm yourself, alternately let down and lulled, then awakened and stimulated, in a sequence that never faltered, you were held by a kind of spell. The great blue-and-white creature irresistibly took on for you, too, an extra-human personality, became a thing you could not help watching, a principle of bounding and soaring life that you could not help venerating. A white woman who had once seen the dance told me that it had given her a shudder and thrill, in her chair at the end of the room, to feel the eaglelike bird swooping down on her. And I found that it was only with effort that I, too, could withstand its hypnotic effect. I had finally to take myself in hand in order to turn my attention and to direct myself out of the house. For something in me began to fight the Shalako, to reject and repulse its influence just at the moment when it was most compelling. One did not want to rejoin the Zunis in their primitive Nature cult; and it was hardly worth while for a Protestant to have stripped off the mummeries of Rome in order to fall a victim to an agile young man in a ten-foot mask.

Yet the effect of it lingered and haunted me even after I was back in my guest-house. Kept wakeful as I was with coffee, the monotonously repetitive music, the indefatigable glowing bird that had dominated the crowded room, drawn toward it all upward-turned eyes, suspended in a trance all wills, stayed with me and continued to trouble me. I was glad to find a letter in my room which recalled me to my own urban world and which annoyed me, when I read it, so much that I was distracted from the vision of the Shalako.

7
SHAMANISM

Introduction

In the comparative analysis of religious organization one of the useful analytical distinctions has been the contrast between the "shaman" and the "priest." These two polar types of ceremonial practitioners are found in all parts of the world, and the difference between their religious roles provides a significant index of contrasts between different types of religious systems.

A "shaman" is a ceremonial practitioner whose powers come from direct contact with the supernatural, by divine stroke, rather than from inheritance or memorized ritual; a "priest" is a ceremonial practitioner who often inherits his position and who learns a body of codified and standardized ritual knowledge from older priests and later transmits it to successors. Shamanism is more usually found in the loosely structured food-gathering cultures, where the more common ceremonial is a curing rite performed for one or more patients within the context of an extended family group. The ceremonial takes place on a noncalendrical basis, usually when a person falls ill and needs the ritual. The priest, and especially the organization of priests into elaborate sets of priesthoods, is characteristically found in tightly structured and relatively elaborate food-producing— usually agricultural—societies, where the more common ceremonial is a public rite performed for the benefit of a whole village or community. The ceremony typically takes place on a calendrical basis at the proper time within the annual ceremonial calendar. Many societies, of course, have both shamans and priests, as, for example, in Navaho society where the hand-tremblers who diagnose illness are technically shamans, in the sense that they derive their power directly from a supernatural source, while the singers who perform the curing ceremonies are technically priests, in the sense that they have learned standardized ritual by apprenticing themselves to an older singer. But our evidence suggests that the presence of these singers has been a relatively recent development in Navaho history, a pattern which the Navahos borrowed from contact with the Southwestern Pueblos. Earlier in their history all Navaho ceremonial practitioners were probably of the shamanistic type. Among the neighboring Apache tribes the practitioners are still more shamanistic in type, as indicated in the Opler article in Chapter 9.

Another way of looking at the difference between shamans and priests is in terms of communication between supernaturals and men. Shamans are essentially mediums, for they are the mouthpieces of spirit beings. Priests are intermediaries between people and the spirits to whom they wish to address themselves. This is what Evans-Pritchard has in mind when, writing about the priests and prophets (shamans) of the Nuer of the Sudan, he says: "Whereas in the priest man speaks to God, in the prophet . . . God speaks to man."

The outstanding area for the study of shamanism has been Siberia—in fact, the very word comes from the Tungus word "shaman"—and northern and western North America. The selections from Bogoras and Rasmussen provide excellent descriptive accounts of shamanistic performances among the Chukchee and Eskimo. But the phenomenon is by no means restricted to this area, as will be apparent in the other articles in this chapter.

In this third edition of the *Reader* we have chosen to focus upon the "shaman" rather than the "priest" as a ceremonial practitioner. The behavior of priests and the organization of priesthoods are touched upon in many selections, especially in the pieces by Edmund Wilson, Ruth Bunzel, John Middleton, Renato Rosaldo, and others. But it appears to us that there are perhaps more intriguing problems still unsolved in the questions of recruitment, roles, performances, and defining characteristics of the shamans of the world. Our selections begin with the classic descriptions of shamanistic performances provided by Bogoras and Rasmussen. We then offer a provocative theoretical article by Rodney Needham on the possible relationship between percussion and transition in shamanistic and other types of rituals in the world. The selection from Duane Metzger and Gerald Williams provides an excellent methodological example of how the precise procedures of "ethnographic semantics" can be applied to a study of shamans. The final selection by Richard A. Shweder is a pioneering attempt to utilize experimental procedures to show how the cognitive capacities of shamans are definitively different from those of nonshamans in the Maya Indian society of Zinacantan in Southern Mexico.

Waldemar Bogoras

SHAMANISTIC PERFORMANCE IN THE INNER ROOM

The anthropological literature reveals few phenomena more interesting, and none more dramatic, than the shamanistic performance. In the following selection Bogoras calls upon his intimate knowledge of the nomadic, reindeer-herding Chukchee of Siberia to provide a description of the shaman in action. He reveals the consummate artistry of the shaman without becoming so enamored of the shaman's skill as to be unable to view his performance objectively. The Chukchee shaman employs superb verbal and manual skills—ventriloquism, singing, beating the omnipresent drum, sleight of hand—to capture his audience in a semi-trance state.

Although Bogoras discusses the procedural techniques of the shaman and at times tends to portray him as a ventriloquist and conjurer, it must be remembered that the Chukchee do not visit a shaman with a critical analysis of his technique in mind. They cannot suspect him of fraud or wither him with ruthless logic, for if he is a fraud then so are they, and if he is open to logical criticism then so are they, since they both share the same logical premises. It should be clear then that the Chukchee cannot afford the luxury of skepticism, for they need the shaman and his wonderful powers. When the shaman becomes hysterical in his spirit possession, the audience knows this as a sign that they will soon hear the voices of powerful spirits able to divine their vital problems. When the shaman transports himself to the spirit world to divine or cure, the audience does not look for tricks; they anxiously and respectfully await answers.

Reprinted from Waldemar Bogoras, *The Chukchee*, Vol. VII of Franz Boas (ed.), *The Jesup North Pacific Expedition* ("Memoirs of the American Museum of Natural History," Vol. XI, Parts 2 and 3 [Leiden: E. J. Brill, 1904–1909]), pp. 433–441, by permission of the American Museum of Natural History.

The typical shamanistic performance is carried out in the following manner. After the evening meal is finished and the kettles and trays are removed to the outer tent, all the people who wish to be present at the séance enter the inner room, which is carefully closed for the night. Among the Reindeer Chukchee, the inner room is especially small, and its narrow space causes much inconvenience to the audience, which is packed together in a tight and most uncomfortable manner. The Maritime Chukchee have more room, and may listen to the voices of the spirits with more ease and freedom. The shaman sits on the "master's place," near the back wall; and even in the most limited sleeping-room, some free space must be left around him. The drum is carefully looked over, its head tightened, and, if it is much shrunken, it is moistened with urine and hung up for a short time over the lamp to dry. The shaman sometimes occupies more than an hour in this process, before he is satisfied with the drum. To have more freedom in his movements, the shaman usually takes off his fur shirt, and remains quite naked down to the waist. He often removes also his shoes and stockings, which of course gives free play to his feet and toes.

In olden times, shamans used no stimulants; but at present they often smoke a pipeful of strong tobacco without admixture of wood, which certainly works like a strong narcotic. This habit is copied from the Tungus shamans, who make great use of unmixed tobacco as a powerful stimulant.

At last the light is put out and the shaman begins to operate. He beats the drum and sings his introductory tunes, at first in a low voice; then gradually his voice increases in volume, and soon it fills the small closed-up room with its violent clamor. The narrow walls resound in all directions.

Moreover, the shaman uses his drum for modifying his voice, now placing it directly before his mouth, now turning it at an oblique angle, and all the time beating it violently. After a few minutes, all this noise begins to work strangely on the listeners, who are crouching down, squeezed together in a most uncomfortable position. They begin to lose the power to locate the source of the sounds; and, almost without any effort of imagination, the song and the drum seem to shift from corner to corner, or even to move about without having any definite place at all.

The shaman's songs have no words. Their music is mostly simple, and consists of one short phrase repeated again and again. After repeating it many times, the shaman breaks off, and utters a series of long-drawn, hysterical sighs, which sound something like "Ah, ya, ka, ya, ka, ya, ka!" After that, he comes back to his songs. For this he draws his breath as deep as possible in order to have more air in his lungs, and to make the first note the longest.

Some of the tunes, however, are more varied, and are not devoid of a certain grace. Not a few are improvised by the shaman on the spot; others are repeated from séance to séance. Each shaman has several songs of his own, which are well known to the people; so that if anybody uses one of them, for instance at a ceremonial, the listeners recognize it immediately, and say that such and such a man is using the particular song of such and such a shaman.

There is no definite order for the succession of the songs, and the shaman changes them at will, sometimes even returning to the first one after a considerable interval has elapsed. This introductory singing lasts from a quarter of an hour to half an hour or more, after which the ke'let make their first appearance.

The shaman sings all alone, and the auditors take no part in the performance. From time to time, however, some one of the listeners will cry out, "Hık, hık!" or "Hıč, hıč!" (interjection of wonder) or "Qai'vo" ("of course") or "Emño'lık" ("certainly")—all of which are meant to express the full approbation by those present of the doings of the shaman. The Chukchee have a special word for these exclamations, "o'cıtkǝk" ("to give answering calls"). Without an očıtkǝ'lın (participle), a Chukchee shaman considers himself unable to perform his calling in a proper way; therefore novices, while trying to learn the shamanistic practices, usually induce brother or a sister to respond, thus encouraging the zeal of the performer. Some shamans also require those people who claim their advice or treatment to give them answering calls during the particular part of the performance which refers to their affairs. The storytellers of the Chukchee also usually claim the assistance of their listeners, who must call out the same exclamations.

Among the Asiatic Eskimo, the wife and other members of the family form a kind of chorus, which from time to time catches up the tune and sings with the shaman. Among the Russianized Yukaghir of the lower Kolyma the wife is also the assistant of her shaman husband, and during the performance she gives him encouraging answers, and he addresses her as his "supporting staff."

In most cases the ke'let begin by entering the body of the shaman. This is marked with some change in his manner of beating the drum, which becomes faster and more violent; but the chief mark is a series of new sounds, supposed to be peculiar to the ke'let. The shaman shakes his head violently, producing with his lips a peculiar chattering noise, not unlike a man who is shivering with cold. He shouts hysterically, and in a changed voice utters strange, prolonged shrieks, such as "O to, to, to, to," or "I pi, pi, pi, pi"—all of which are supposed to characterize the voice of the ke'let. He often imitates the cries of various animals and birds which are supposed to be his particular assistants. If the shaman is only a "single-bodied" one—that is, has no ventriloquistic power—the ke'let will proceed to sing and beat the drum by means of his body. The only difference will be in the timbre of the voice, which will sound harsh and unnatural, as becomes supernatural beings.

With other shamans the ke'let appear all at once as the "separate voices." They manifest themselves with sounds and shrieks of the same harsh and unnatural character, and these are located outside the body of the shaman. After that a varied exhibition begins, in which the performance of the shaman far transcends anything attainable by a person of ordinary powers.

The Chukchee ventriloquists display great skill, and could with credit to themselves carry on a contest with the best artists of the kind of civilized countries. The "separate voices" of their calling come from all sides of the room, changing their place to the complete illusion of their listeners. Some voices are at first faint, as if coming from afar; as they gradually approach, they increase in volume, and at last they rush into the room, pass through it and out, decreasing, and dying away in the remote distance. Other voices come from above, pass through the room and seem to go underground, where they are heard as if from the depths of the earth. Tricks of this kind are played also with the voices of animals and birds, and even with the howling of the tempest, producing a most weird effect.

I heard a voice which professed to be an echo. It repeated faithfully all sounds and cries which we chose to produce in its presence, including phrases in English or Russian.

The foreign words were, of course, slightly mispronounced, still the reproduction proved the "spirit" to be possessed of a fine ear, catching quickly the sounds of an unknown language. The only way in which the "spirit" could imitate the clapping of our hands (another test to which we put him) was by clacking his tongue, which caused much mirth even among the native listeners. I heard also the "spirits" of a grasshopper, horsefly, and mosquito, who imitated exceedingly well the sounds produced by the real insects.

In proof of his accuracy as to the location of the sounds, the shaman Qora'wge, previously spoken of, made one of his "spirits" shout, talk, and whisper directly into my ear, and the illusion was so perfect that involuntarily I put my hand to my ear to catch the "spirit." After that he made the "spirit" enter the ground under me and talk right in between my legs, etc. All the time that he is conversing with the "separate voices," the shaman beats his drum without interruption in order to prove that his force and attention are otherwise occupied.

I tried to make a phonographic record of the "separate voices" of the "spirits." For this purpose I induced the shaman Scratching-Woman to give a séance in my own house, overcoming his reluctance with a few extra presents. The performance, of course, had to be carried out in utter darkness: and I arranged my machine so as to be able to work it without any light. Scratching-Woman sat in the farthest corner of the spacious room, at a distance of twenty feet from me. When the light was put out, the "spirits," after some "bashful" hesitation, entered, in compliance with the demand of the shaman, and even began to talk into the funnel of the graphophone. The records show a very marked difference between the voice of the shaman himself, which sounds from afar, and the voices of the "spirits," who seemed to be talking directly into the funnel.

All the while, Scratching-Woman was beating the drum incessantly to show that he was in his usual place, and occupied with his usual function, that of beating the drum without interruption. He brought some of the entering "spirits" to my special notice. One was a fawn of a wild reindeer, found by him in the wilderness beside the carcass of its mother, which had been killed by a wolf. The fawn, when he found it, was trying to suck the carcass. The strange sight had evidently struck Scratching-Woman, and he took the fawn for one of his assisting ke'let. The "spirit" manifested his presence by characteristic short snorts, peculiar to the fawn when calling for its mother. Another "spirit" entered with a dismal howl. This was the wolf who killed the reindeer dam.

Scratching-Woman explained that when he desired to wreak his vengeance on some one of his foes, he transformed himself into this wolf, taking care beforehand to turn the other party into a reindeer. Then, of course, he was quite certain of victory. The idea that shamans, in case of need, not only may send their "spirits" to a destined place, but also may turn themselves into any of their "spirits," and carry out their intentions, appears in many tales.

For instance, in the tale of the Shaman with Warts (Kuku'lpin), this shaman, during a shamanistic contest asks his adversary, "Which ke'lE are you going to employ?" The other answers, "The small black hawk." —"And you?"—"The great diver." Then they turn into these birds, and the contest begins.

Those episodes of the tales in which men in distress have recourse to their animal amulets —either reviving them and bidding them fight their enemies, or transforming themselves into their living likenesses—are evidently quite analogous.

Still another of the ke'let introduced by Scratching-Woman was a raven who cawed lustily. The shaman used him when working with magic medicine, because the raven could devour all germs of sickness and disease. Still another was a little mouse, who could travel very fast underground, and was employed on errands requiring haste.

There followed the leather bucket, which forms a part of a "bonebreaking set," and is used as a receptacle for pounded bones. Once when Scratching-Woman was hunting wild reindeer, he succeeded in wounding a strong buck in the right foreleg, but still he could not overtake it. Then he called for the Skin Bucket, bade it overtake the buck and entrap its head. After that the reindeer was easily caught.

After having entered the room and produced a few sounds, by way of making his presence known, the "spirit" usually offers to "try his breath," that is, he beats the drum for a while, singing a tune in the special harsh voice peculiar to the "spirits." This, however, lasts only a short time, after which the "spirit" declares that his breath is ebbing away. Then he either begins to talk, or straightway takes his departure with characteristic quivering

sounds somewhat similar to the buzzing of a fly. These sounds are called by the Chukchee "gibbering" (moomga'tɪrgɪn), and are always associated with the "spirits." The same name is applied to the chattering alluded to before.

Often the shaman declares to the "spirit" first entering, that the sound of his drum is bad, or even that the cover of it is broken, and this is corroborated by a few dull strokes. The "spirit" must then mend the drum by breathing upon it, which he does accordingly. This treatment is resorted to especially in cases of magic medicine. After the drum is mended, the shaman explains to the patient that it is a good sign. He says also, that, if the "spirit" were not able to mend the drum, it would forebode a bad turn in the disease.

I must again repeat that the animal "spirits" produce their own characteristic sounds. The walrus and the bear roar, the reindeer snorts, the wolf howls, the fox bays, the raven caws. The last three, however, are able to talk but use a particular timbre of voice, and intersperse among their words, from time to time, their peculiar cries.

In most cases the ventriloquistic performance soon takes on a dramatic character. A number of "spirits" appear in succession. They talk to the shaman and to one another, pick quarrels, abuse and denounce one another. It is superfluous to add that only one voice may talk at a time, so that even the most lively dialogue consists of a series of interpolations following each other in succession. The talk of the "spirits" is often carried on in strange, quite unintelligible words, such as "papire kuri muri," etc. To make it understood, the shaman has to call for an interpreter, who from that time on takes part in all conversations, and also explains to the auditors the words of the other "spirits." Thus the shaman is supposed to be unable to understand the language of the "separate spirits."

The same idea obtains among other neighboring tribes. The most curious case of all is that of the shamans of the Russians and the Russianized natives of the Kolyma and the Anadyr, who know no other language than the Russian. The "spirits," however, even when speaking through the mouth of the shaman, employ only the usual unintelligible gibberish mixed with some distorted and mispronounced phrases in the Koryak, Yakut, and Yukaghir languages. After a while the shaman calls for an interpreter, and at last, after some controversy, the spirits send for one who can speak Russian and who translates the orders of the "spirits."

The Chukchee shamans have no special language of their own, with the exception of a few words and expressions. Thus the drum is called "a′′twet" ("canoe"), which is an additional proof of the preponderance of maritime pursuits in the former life of the people. The idea of shamanistic ecstasy is expressed by the word "an·ña′arkın" ("he sinks"), which refers to the belief that the shaman, during the period of ecstasy, is able to visit other worlds, and especially that underground.

Among the northwestern branch of the Koryak, the "spirits" are said to use a special mode of pronunciation, similar to that used by the southeastern Koryak and the Chukchee. A few words are also said to be peculiar to them. Among the Asiatic Eskimo the "spirits" are said to have a special language. Many words of it were given to me by the shamans, and most of them are analogous to the "spirit" language known to various Eskimo tribes of America, both in Alaska and on the Atlantic side.

Tricks of various kinds break up the monotony of the performance, which may last for several hours. The "spirits" will scratch from the outside at the walls of the sleeping-room, running around it in all directions, so that the clattering of their feet is quite audible. In contrast to this, the motion of the ke′let inside of the room produces but slight noise. The rustling of their flight is similar to the buzzing of a mosquito, and the rattling of their tiny feet as they run over the surface of the drum is hardly perceptible.

Often, however, a mischievous "spirit" suddenly tugs at the skin spread in the center of the room with such force that things lying on it fly about in all directions. Therefore the housemates of the shaman usually take the precaution to remove kettles and dishes from the room. Sometimes an invisible hand seizes the whole sleeping-room by its top, and shakes it with wonderful strength, or even lifts it up high, letting in for a moment the twilight from the outer tent. This, of course, is possible only with the movable tent of the Reindeer people, where the sleeping-room is fastened none too firmly. Other invisible hands toss about lumps of snow, spill cold water and urine, and even throw blocks of wood, or stones, at the imminent risk of hurting some of the listeners.

All these things happened several times in my presence. The "spirits" would ask me,

through the shamans, whether I really felt afraid; and, when I did not give a satisfactory answer, the "spirits" would try to increase my respect for them by such material manifestations. I must mention that the audience is strictly forbidden to make any attempts whatever to touch the "spirits." These latter highly resent any intrusion of this kind, and retaliate either on the shaman, whom they may kill on the spot, or on the trespassing listener, who runs the risk of having his head broken, or even a knife thrust through his ribs in the dark. I received warnings of this kind at almost every shamanistic performance. In some cases the shaman would lay a bare knife within his own reach as an additional warning against any infringement.

The size of the sleeping-room is so small that it is really wonderful how a shaman can keep up the illusion even under cover of the dark and with the protection of his resentful "spirits." Many times I sat so near the performer that I could almost touch him with my outstretched hand, and the warning against too great inquisitiveness on my part was of course quite necessary.

All these tricks strangely resemble the doings of modern spiritualists, and without doubt they cannot be carried out without the help of human assistants.

The second part of the shamanistic performance is of a magical character. To give a clearer idea of it, I will describe a few instances.

The shaman Tilu′wgi, of whom I shall speak again, after some preliminary intercourse with the "spirits," called a peculiar ke′lE of his, who said she was an old maid, living alone in her house, and she expressed apprehension lest we should laugh at her talk with the peculiar feminine pronunciation. After that, however, she proceeded to give the magic instructions and explanations.

She told one of those present, Enmu′wgi by name, who had recently been vanquished in a wrestling-match, that his defeat was caused by the use of malignant incantations by his adversary, and she advised him to take the matter into his own hands.

This female "spirit" reproached one of my fellow travelers, a great hunter, with illtreating those "walking afoot," which is the usual periphrasis for the bears. When he tried to defend himself, the female "spirit" reminded him of a hunting expedition, in which he took part about two months before, which was directed against a bear sleeping in its den.

From the old Chukchee point of view, this certainly was a rather dangerous pursuit. In the end the "spirit" said that the man in question, because of his offenses against those "walking afoot," was in danger of losing his powers of endurance in walking. To his question as to the means of warding off the danger, the female "spirit" said that he must procure for himself the skin of the nose of a newly killed bear, and perform a thanksgiving ceremonial over it. That, probably, would appease those "walking afoot."

Afterward she told another listener that she saw that in the last autumn he had killed a wild reindeer buck. Though this happened far away from his herd, he should have made a sacrifice to the buck, which he omitted to do; therefore the following winter he was visited by bad luck, in that the wolves attacked his herd, and killed nine fat bucks. To check the recurrence of such a misfortune, it is necessary to take a small crotch of willow cut on the place of the attack by wolves, and perform over it the required ceremonial.

Galmu'urgin, the soothsaying shaman already spoken of, who gave a prescription at the very beginning of the séance predicted in my presence to the master of the tent that the next fall many reindeer would come to his house. "One buck will stop on the right side of the entrance, and pluck at the grass, attracted by a certain doe of dark-gray hair. This attraction must be strengthened with a special incantation. The reindeer buck, while standing there, must be killed with a bow, and the arrow to be used must have a flat rhomboid point. This will secure the successful killing of all the other wild reindeer."

After that the shaman recollected himself for a while, and addressed the brother of the master, who, with one companion, lived in a separate camp. This companion was married to one of his relatives. The shaman said that, before the fall, they would part company, nor would they look at each other with clear eyes; and, by the way, his prediction was fulfilled much earlier than the time designated.

To still another of the listeners he said that he feared lest the "bad things" might conceive a desire to approach his house. By this he meant the "spirits of disease." In order to thwart their intentions, the man was told to go through some special preventive ceremonies during the celebration of the cere-

monial of the antlers, which was then at hand. The ceremonies consisted in drawing several lines across the snow near the tent, and putting some small stones before the entrance. These were supposed to transform themselves into a large river, and high, inaccessible cliffs, on the route of the "bad beings."

In this way the usual shamanistic performance is carried on in the inner room, and with the light put out.

In other cases the shaman actually "sinks"; that is, after some most violent singing, and beating of the drum, he falls into a kind of trance, during which his body lies on the ground unconscious, while his soul visits "spirits" in their own world, and asks them for advice. Chukchee folklore is full of episodes referring to such shamanistic trances; but in real life they happen very rarely, especially in modern times, when shamans are so much less skillful than of old. Even the word "an·ña'arkɪn" ("to sink"), from the explanation of modern shamans, has reference simply to the immersion of the performer into the depths of shamanistic ecstasy without its literal fulfillment.

In folk stories the shamans sink into the other worlds chiefly for the purpose of finding one of the missing souls of a patient who claims their power for his treatment. In important cases, even at the present day, the shamans, when treating a well-to-do patient, will at least pretend to have sunk into the required unconsciousness. On one or two occasions I had an opportunity of witnessing such a state, but the whole performance was of a rather poor kind.

It began, as usual, in the dark; but when the shaman suddenly broke off beating the drum, the lamp was again lighted and the face of the shaman immediately covered with a piece of cloth. The mistress of the house, who was the wife of the shaman, took up the drum and began to beat it with light, slow strokes. This lasted the entire time that the shaman lay under the cloth, or about a quarter of an hour. Then he suddenly awoke, and, removing the cloth from his face, sat up in his place, took the drum from his wife, beat it for a while, and sang a few tunes as in the beginning. After that he began to give the patient magical advice regarding his illness, which, however, was nothing else than an elaborate incantation in dramatized form.

Knud Rasmussen

A SHAMAN'S JOURNEY
TO THE SEA SPIRIT

Shamans ordinarily deal with spirits by acting as their mouthpieces while in a state of possession; this article illustrates a less usual procedure in which the shaman's soul dissociates itself from his body and travels to the spirit world.

In this moving account, Knud Rasmussen, one of the great authorities on the Eskimo, describes one of the principal rituals of an Eskimo shaman—to make a journey to the bottom of the sea to propitiate the Spirit of the Sea (often called "Sedna" or "Sea Goddess" in other monographs on the Eskimo). The Eskimos believe that this goddess controls the sea mammals, whence come the most important food, fuel, and skins for clothing, and sends nearly all the worst misfortunes to the Eskimo people. These misfortunes are due to misdeeds and offenses committed by men and they gather in dirt and impurity over the body of the goddess. It is necessary for the shaman to go through a dangerous ordeal to reach the sea goddess at the bottom of the sea. He must then stroke her hair and report the difficulties of his people. The goddess replies that breaches of taboos have caused her to send the misfortunes. Whereupon the shaman returns for the mass confession from all the people who have committed misdeeds. Presumably when all sins are confessed, the sea goddess releases the game, returns lost souls, cures illnesses, and generally makes the world right with the Eskimos again.

Reprinted in abridged form from Knud Rasmussen, *Report of the Fifth Thule Expedition, 1921–1924*, Vol. VII, No. 1, *Intellectual Culture of the Iglulik Eskimos* (Copenhagen: Gyldendalske Boghandel, Nordisk Forlag, 1929), pp. 123–129, by permission of Rudolf Sand.

The girl who was thrown into the sea by her own father and had her finger joints so cruelly cut off as she clung in terror to the side of the boat has in a strange fashion made herself the stern goddess of fate among the Eskimos. From her comes all the most indispensable of human food, the flesh of sea beasts; from her comes the blubber that warms the cold snow huts and gives light in the lamps when the long arctic night broods over the land. From her come also the skins of the great seal which are likewise indispensable for clothes and boot soles, if the hunters are to be able to move over the frozen sea all seasons of the year. But while Takánakapsâluk gives mankind all these good things, created out of her own finger joints, it is she also who sends nearly all the misfortunes which are regarded by the dwellers on earth as the worst and direst. In her anger at men's failing to live as they should, she calls up storms that prevent the men from hunting, or she keeps the animals they seek hidden away in a pool she has at the bottom of the sea, or she will steal away the souls of human beings and send sickness among the people. It is not strange, therefore, that it is regarded as one of a shaman's greatest feats to visit her where she lives at the bottom of the sea, and so tame and conciliate her that human beings can live once more untroubled on earth.

When a shaman wishes to visit Takána-kapsâluk, he sits on the inner part of the sleeping place behind a curtain, and must wear nothing but his kamiks and mittens. A shaman about to make this journey is said to be ᴎak·a·ɜɔq: one who drops down to the bottom of the sea. This remarkable expression is due perhaps in some degree to the fact that no one can rightly explain how the journey is made. Some assert that it is only his soul or his spirit which makes the journey; others declare that it is the shaman himself who actually, in the flesh, drops down into the underworld.

The journey may be undertaken at the instance of a single individual, who pays the shaman for his trouble, either because there is sickness in his household which appears incurable, or because he has been particularly unsuccessful in his hunting. But it may also be made on behalf of a whole village threatened by famine and death owing to scarcity of game. As soon as such occasion arises, all the adult members of the community assemble in the house from which the shaman is to start, and when he has taken up his position—if it is winter, and in a snow hut, on the bare snow;

if in summer, on the bare ground—the men and women present must loosen all tight fastenings in their clothes, the lacings of their footgear, the waistbands of their breeches, and then sit down and remain still with closed eyes, all lamps being put out, or allowed to burn only with so faint a flame that it is practically dark inside the house.

The shaman sits for a while in silence, breathing deeply, and then, after some time has elapsed, he begins to call upon his helping spirits, repeating over and over again: "The way is made ready for me; the way opens before me!"

Whereat all present must answer in chorus: "Let it be so!"

And when the helping spirits have arrived, the earth opens under the shaman, but often only to close up again; he has to struggle for a long time with hidden forces, ere he can cry at last:

"Now the way is open."

And then all present must answer: "Let the way be open before him; let there be way for him."

And now one hears, at first under the sleeping place: "Halala—he—he—he, halala—he —he—he!" and afterwards under the passage, below the ground, the same cry: "Halele— he!" And the sound can be distinctly heard to recede farther and farther until it is lost altogether. Then all know that he is on his way to the ruler of the sea beasts.

Meanwhile, the members of the household pass the time by singing songs in chorus, and here it may happen that the clothes which the shaman has discarded come alive and fly about round the house, above the heads of the singers, who are sitting with closed eyes. And one may hear deep sighs and the breathing of persons long since dead; these are the souls of the shaman's namesakes, who have come to help. But as soon as one calls them by name, the sighs cease, and all is silent in the house until another dead person begins to sigh.

In the darkened house one hears only sighing and groaning from the dead who lived many generations earlier. This sighing and puffing sounds as if the spirits were down under water, in the sea, as marine animals, and in between all the noises one hears the blowing and splashing of creatures coming up to breathe. There is one song especially which must be constantly repeated; it is only to be sung by the oldest members of the tribe, and is as follows:

We reach out our hands
to help you up;
We are without food,
we are without game.
From the hollow by the entrance
you shall open,
you shall bore your way up.
We are without food,
and we lay ourselves down
holding out hands
to help you up!

An ordinary shaman will, even though skillful, encounter many dangers in his flight down to the bottom of the sea; the most dreaded are three large rolling stones which he meets as soon as he has reached the sea floor. There is no way round; he has to pass between them, and take great care not to be crushed by these stones, which churn about, hardly leaving room for a human being to pass. Once he has passed beyond them, he comes to a broad, trodden path, the shaman's path; he follows a coastline resembling that which he knows from on earth, and entering a bay finds himself on a great plain, and here lies the house of Takánakapsâluk, built of stone, with a short passageway, just like the houses of the tunit. Outside the house one can hear the animals puffing and blowing, but he does not see them; in the passage leading to the house lies Takánakapsâluk's dog stretched across the passage taking up all the room; it lies there gnawing at a bone and snarling. It is dangerous to all who fear it, and only the courageous shaman can pass by it, stepping straight over it as it lies; the dog then knows that the bold visitor is a great shaman, and does him no harm.

These difficulties and dangers attend the journey of an ordinary shaman. But for the very greatest, a way opens right from the house whence they invoke their helping spirits; a road down through the earth, if they are in a tent on shore, or down through the sea, if it is in a snow hut on the sea ice, and by this route the shaman is led down without encountering any obstacle. He almost glides as if falling through a tube so fitted to his body that he can check his progress by pressing against the sides, and need not actually fall down with a rush. This tube is kept open for him by all the souls of his namesakes, until he returns on his way back to earth.

Should a great shelter wall be built outside the house of Takánakapsâluk, it means that she is very angry and implacable in her feelings towards mankind, but the shaman must fling himself upon the wall, kick it down and level it to the ground. There are some who declare that her house has no roof, and is open at the top, so that she can better watch, from her place by the lamp, the doings of mankind. All the different kinds of game: seal, bearded seal, walrus, and whale are collected in a great pool on the right of her lamp, and there they lie puffing and blowing. When the shaman enters the house, he at once sees Takánakapsâluk, who, as a sign of anger, is sitting with her back to the lamp and with her back to all the animals in the pool. Her hair hangs down loose all over one side of her face, a tangled, untidy mass hiding her eyes, so that she cannot see. It is the misdeeds and offenses committed by men which gather in dirt and impurity over her body. All the foul emanations from the sins of mankind nearly suffocate her. As the shaman moves towards her, Isarrataitsoq, her father, tries to grasp hold of him. He thinks it is a dead person come to expiate offenses before passing on to the Land of The Dead, but the shaman must then at once cry out: "I am flesh and blood" and then he will not be hurt. And he must grasp Takánakapsâluk by one shoulder and turn her face towards the lamp and towards the animals, and stroke her hair, the hair she has been unable to comb out herself, because she has no fingers; and he must smooth it and comb it, and as soon as she is calmer, he must say:

"Those up above can no longer help the seals up by grasping their foreflippers."

Then Takánakapsâluk answers in the spirit language: "The secret miscarriages of the women and breaches of taboo in eating boiled meat bar the way for the animals."

The shaman must now use all his efforts to appease her anger, and at last, when she is in a kindlier mood, she takes the animals one by one and drops them on the floor, and then it is as if a whirlpool arose in the passage, the water pours out from the pool and the animals disappear in the sea. This means rich hunting and abundance for mankind.

It is then time for the shaman to return to his fellows up above, who are waiting for him. They can hear him coming a long way off; the rush of his passage through the tube kept open for him by the spirits comes nearer and nearer, and with a mighty "Plu—a—he—he" he shoots up into his place behind the curtain: "Plu-plu," like some creature of the sea, shooting up from the deep to take breath under the pressure of mighty lungs.

Then there is silence for a moment. No one may break this silence until the shaman says: "I have something to say."

Then all present answer: "Let us hear, let us hear."

And the shaman goes on, in the solemn spirit language: "Words will arise."

And then all in the house must confess any breaches of taboo they have committed.

"It is my fault, perhaps," they cry, all at once, women and men together, in fear of famine and starvation, and all begin telling of the wrong things they have done. All the names of those in the house are mentioned, and all must confess, and thus much comes to light which no one had ever dreamed of; everyone learns his neighbors' secrets. But despite all the sin confessed, the shaman may go on talking as one who is unhappy at having made a mistake, and again and again break out into such expressions as this:

"I seek my grounds in things which have not happened; I speak as one who knows nothing."

There are still secrets barring the way for full solution of the trouble, and so the women in the house begin to go through all the names, one after another; nearly all women's names; for it was always their breaches of taboo which were most dangerous. Now and again when a name is mentioned, the shaman exclaims in relief:

"Taina, taina!"

It may happen that the woman in question is not present, and in such a case, she is sent for. Often it would be quite young girls or young wives, and when they came in crying and miserable, it was always a sign that they were good women, good penitent women. And as soon as they showed themselves, shamefaced and weeping, the shaman would break out again into his cries of self-reproach:

"I seek, and I strike where nothing is to be found! I seek, and I strike where nothing is to be found! If there is anything, you must say so!"

And the woman who has been led in, and whom the shaman has marked out as one who has broken her taboo, now confesses:

"I had a miscarriage, but I said nothing, because I was afraid, and because it took place in a house where there were many."

She thus admits that she has had a miscarriage, but did not venture to say so at the time because of the consequences involved, affecting her numerous housemates; for the rules provide that as soon as a woman has had a miscarriage in a house, all those living in the same house, men and women alike, must throw away all the house contains of qituptɔq: soft things, i.e., all the skins on the sleeping place, all the clothes, in a word all soft skins, thus including also ilupɛrɔq: the sealskin covering used to line the whole interior of a snow hut as used among the Iglulingmiut. This was so serious a matter for the household that women sometimes dared not report a miscarriage; moreover, in the case of quite young girls who had not yet given birth to any child, a miscarriage might accompany their menstruation without their knowing, and only when the shaman in such a case as this, pointed out the girl as the origin of the trouble and the cause of Takánakapsâluk's anger, would she call to mind that there had once been, in her menstruation skin (the piece of thick-haired caribou skin which women place in their underbreeches during menstruation) something that looked like "thick blood." She had not thought at the time that it was anything particular, and had therefore said nothing about it, but now that she is pointed out by the shaman, it recurs to her mind. Thus at last the cause of Takánakapsâluk's anger is explained, and all are filled with joy at having escaped disaster. They are now assured that there will be abundance of game on the following day. And in the end, there may be almost a feeling of thankfulness towards the delinquent. This then was what took place when shamans went down and propitiated the great Spirit of the Sea.

Rodney Needham

PERCUSSION AND TRANSITION

Although the hypothesis advanced by Needham—that there is a connection in human life between percussion and transition—has broader implications than the more specialized study of the phenomenon of shamanism, the postulated relationship occurs very frequently and was first noted by Needham in shamanistic performances. Hence, we have included his article in this chapter to call attention to his novel hypothesis and to stimulate further research into this phenomenon that occurs not only in shamanistic rituals but in many other types of transition rituals in both tribal and modern societies. We suggest that percussive sound not be labeled as "noise" since in terms of communications theory, "noise" consists of sounds that interfere with the meaningful messages being transmitted, or are "nonmessages." And, clearly, if Needham is correct, the percussive sounds are transmitting meaningful messages about a transition in social life. Apart from this small matter of terminology, we find the article both cogent and stimulating and the hypothesis very promising for further exploration. We suggest for further exploration the reading of William C. Sturtevant's comment entitled "Categories, Percussion and Physiology" (1968), which especially calls attention to Andrew Neher's paper "A Physiological Explanation of Unusual Behavior in Ceremonies Involving Drums" (1962) and discusses the psychological states produced by rhythmical drumming.

Reprinted from *Man*, II (1967), 606–614, by permission of the author and the Royal Anthropological Institute of Great Britain and Ireland.

La faculté de sentir est la première faculté de l'âme.
—Laromiguière (1826, 1, 86)

This article indicates a problem which seems to relate to matters of fundamental importance in social anthropology. The present observations are tentative, and I am not in a position to construct a formal argument. Moreover, I have deliberately cited as few authorities as possible, partly for the reason that the relevant literature is so immense that I can neither list it all nor pretend to know what is best in it, and partly because the intended force of this article is that I think everybody will recognize at once what phenomena and institutions it is about and will not need any direction to pertinent facts. What I hope for especially in publishing these uncertain remarks is that colleagues will help to frame the appropriate conceptual terms for coming to grips with the large and universal matters that are at issue. Alternatively, perhaps it can be shown that there is no problem after all, or that there is a problem but that it has been badly defined. It may even be that this has all been worked out before, but I suspect that in such a case I am not the only one to be ignorant of the fact.

The problem initially presented itself in this form: why is noise that is produced by striking or shaking so widely used in order to communicate with the other world?

This formulation changed as my reflections on the question shaped themselves, and the scope of the enquiry became far wider, but let me begin with the particular puzzle which first caught my attention and which others may also find as intriguing. The starting point is the common report, encountered again and again in the ethnographical literature, that a shaman beats a drum in order to establish contact with the spirits. It is so well described, and has been so thoroughly recognized as a characteristic feature of a shaman's activities, that the question seems not to have been asked (so far, at least, as I can discover) just why he beats a drum, and why this banging noise is essential if he is to communicate with spiritual powers.

My own first recourse was to turn to Wilken's famous study of shamanism in Indonesia, and to see whether he had anything to say about the matter. He does not, it turns out, isolate this specific problem, but he does help to place the question in a wider context. He points out, namely, that a drum is beaten, not only at a shamanic séance, but also on other occasions in order to call the spirits (Wilken, 1887: 479 n. 156), i.e., that drumbeating, though indeed characteristic of the shaman, is not peculiar to his office but is a widely recognized means of making contact with the spiritual world. The obvious comment, however, is that a shaman does not always beat a drum, and that neither do other people always do so when they want to communicate with the other world. But as Eliade says in discussing shamanic ritual, "there is always some instrument that, in one way or another, is able to establish

contact with the 'world of the spirits'" (1964: 179), and this in itself is surely a very curious fact.

What are these instruments? Here is a list: drum, gong, bell, cymbal, tambourine, xylophone, metallophone, rattle, rasp, stamping tube, sticks (struck against each other), sticks on stretched mats, resounding rocks, clashing anklets. No doubt this catalogue is very incomplete, but it is already impressively extensive and varied. I am not saying, of course, that these instruments are used only in order to contact the spirits, or that no other instruments are used for this purpose; but they are all, to even a casual recollection, employed in order to communicate with the other world—and they are all *percussive*. With this defining term, yet other means can be isolated, which strictly speaking are noninstrumental, of doing the same thing, for example, clapping, striking the palm against various surfaces of the body, or simply stamping the feet or drumming with the heels. All over the world it is found that percussion, by any means whatever that will produce it, permits or accompanies communication with the other world.

But is "percussion" really the defining feature? It is not the most general, for the first characteristic of these instruments and procedures is simply that they generate noise. This is an interesting fact, for it is certainly not necessary that noise of any kind shall attract or greet spirits; smoke, gestures, dances, or objects such as masks or images can all do as much, and they are of course actually employed together with noise. This definition will not serve, however, for there are innumerable methods of producing noise in addition to those which we are considering. The second most general feature is that the methods in question make rhythmic noise; rhythm has already attracted sociological attention (Bücher, 1899), and it is certainly a cultural phenomenon of great importance, but it is clearly not specific enough to answer to our purpose. Melody, on the other hand, is far too specific and is obviously inappropriate as a criterion; some of our noise-makers produce distinct notes and are capable of elaborating melodies or of generating other tonal effects, but others (e.g., rattles, sticks, clapping) cannot do so. This brief survey of types of noise-production is very elementary, and a long way from being exhaustive, but it is enough to confirm the first indication that the defining feature is indeed percussion.

How, next, is one to make sense of this association between percussion and the spiritual world? This is a difficult question to approach in the first place because this range of noise-makers does not (so far as I know) correspond to a standard musicological category; percussion instruments are of course commonly distinguished, but not the total range of percussive devices and procedures under consideration, since not all of these are instruments. In the second place, even familiar percussion instruments may not be grouped together in description or analysis, but they may be divided up according to material of manufacture, construction, quality of sound, origin, and so forth. For example, to take an old but eminently useful authority, the *Encyclopaedia of Religion and Ethics* devotes one article to "Drums and Cymbals" (Crawley, 1912), another to "Gongs and Bells" (Wheeler, 1913), and appends to the latter a semi-independent article on "American Bells" (Chamberlain, 1913). These are in fact most interesting and valuable surveys, well worth recommending today, but together they cover only four of the fourteen types of noise-maker in my provisional classification, and the fragmentary treatment of them introduces a gratuitous source of difficulty in grappling with the problem. The real difficulty, however, is presented by the problem itself, in that if the relationship in question has not been isolated before (or even if it is not commonly recognized) one then lacks the support and the stimulation, in the form of analytical terms and ideas, which the discipline otherwise normally provides. I readily admit that I do not know (although I have tried hard enough to find out) what previous work may have been done in this connection, but I feel fairly sure that the relationship between percussion and communication with the other world is not an everyday preoccupation among social anthropologists.

There is, however, one work which is of special interest, namely the paper "The origin of bell and drum" by Maria Dworakowska (1938). It touches on part of my present problem, and it is methodologically instructive too. Dworakowska begins with the blunt declaration: "The bell is usually considered to be exclusively a musical or signalling instrument although this is quite erroneous" (1938: 1). (This sentence has a promising ring which reminds one that it is really Hocart or the late Lord Raglan who might best have dealt with the present problem.) She states that the bell plays a role similar to that of the drum among many peoples, and contends that there is a "genetic union" between the two instruments. To this assimilation she adds the gong, "a form which is as closely allied to the bell as to the drum." Her first intention is to construct an evolutionary series, the first member of which would be the drum and the last the bell of western Europe. This is a conventional kind of ethnological aim, and intrinsically a most interesting one; but where Dworakowska engages the special attention of the social anthropologist is in her explicit rejection of museum criteria in favour of a sociological concentration on "a striking similarity between the bell and the drum as regards the role which they play in everyday life, in magic and in religion" (1938: 9). I need not recapitulate the details in her exposition of the facts, nor her consideration of other approaches to the instruments, but will take up directly the hypothesis which she advances. Her argument is that the drum is a "continuation of the coffin-log" (22–23), which may or may not be historically sound, but what is more immediately relevant is that Dworakowska argues centrally that "there is a close connection between the drum and the dead" (20–22), so that the genetic series of drum, gong, bell and cognate instruments are all characteristically part of the cult of the dead.

I have outlined this argument not only because it may not be well known, but also because of the value in Dworakowska's procedure. She deliberately ignores the materials, methods of manufacture, forms and mechanisms of the instruments in order to concentrate on their social meaning; she examines these particular instruments because of their recognized prominence in cultures all around the world; and she makes a connexion, even if not a wholly satisfactory one, between certain types of percussion instruments and the dead. Her argument is also negatively instructive, in that it does not deal with, and cannot explain, the use of so many other means of producing percussive sound; it neglects, by its essentially developmental cast, the constant factors which may be operative throughout any historical changes; and it is framed in terms which are unduly circumstantial (a certain original instrument, a certain initial religious institution) and are insufficiently general or abstract.

Dworakowska's paper, then, is an encouraging and useful example, but it is not fundamental enough. A far more promising approach, in this respect, is that of Crawley, who writes: "The music of the drum is more closely connected with the foundations of aurally generated emotion than that of any other instrument. It is complete enough in itself to cover the whole range of human feeling" (1912:91). This is the right approach, I think, because it is psychological. Now it has been well enough shown, of course, that "en aucun cas la sociologie ne saurait emprunter purement et simplement à la psychologie telle ou telle de ses propositions, pour l'appliquer telle quelle aux faits sociaux" (Durkheim [1901] 1967: XIX), but the more nearly a cultural phenomenon approaches the universal the more necessary it becomes to seek the grounds of it in the general psychic characters of mankind. In the present case, the remarkably wide distribution of percussive noise-makers, employed in communication with the other world, indicates that an historical or sociological interpretation would be quite inappropriate. It is this circumstance that makes the problem especially difficult for the social anthropologist, for whereas the discipline provides notions and techniques which serve relatively well in explaining social institutions or the structure of collective representations, it provides as yet no way of understanding the elementary forms of experience. Psychology, on the other hand, has on the whole turned away from such concerns, and for obvious scientific reasons has concentrated increasingly on more limited and manipulable phenomena. Psycho-analytical work is likely in principle to be more enlightening, and that of Jung in particular is highly suggestive, but studies in this field have so far not expanded their compass to match the worldwide evidence which the anthropologist takes for granted and which must be addressed if an integral understanding of humanity is ever to be achieved.

But if Crawley's psychological (and even neurological) orientation is right, his specific proposition about the drum is not so satisfactory. We all know something of the effects of the drum because we have felt them, but is it possible, to begin with, to put the proposition to empirical test? There is no readily apparent means, at any rate, of doing so with the proposition as it stands, and to a rigidly positivistic view this would rob it of any decisive value. It might then be maintained that Crawley's assertions, whatever their immediate appeal, are merely subjective and metaphorical. This criticism raises a general issue of epistemological or heuristic principle; it calls into question not only Crawley's proposition but also others of the kind which might be equally plausible and seem on other grounds to be appropriate to the type of problem. My own response to this form of objection would be that by rigidly confining oneself to empirically testable propositions one will never get very far in understanding man and his works. There are methodological justifications of this position, not to speak of other considerations of a philosophical kind, but since the issue is basically one of intellectual temper rather than resoluble argument there is little point in offering a defence here. For the present, it will suffice to concede that the position is defensible, and that Crawley's (and similar) views need not be rejected simply because it may not be possible to test them objectively.

A related criticism is that the very terms of the proposition are difficult to define: closeness of connexion, in this regard, is an extremely obscure idea; "aurally generated emotion" is not a precise description; and it is not at all clear how the music of the drum might be "complete," and in such a way that it might cover "the whole range," whatever this may comprise, of human feeling. But as Kant himself writes, "If we could not undertake anything with a concept until we had defined it, all philosophizing would be in a bad way" (1787: 759 n). Let me emphasize again, also, that the issue is not the suitability of the particular words that Crawley chooses to employ, nor the degree of his expository skill, nor the exactness of his observation. The difficulties of expression and interpretation encountered in his proposition about the drum are typical, it seems to me, of the generality of attempts to describe elemental feelings, and one cannot expect to begin with clear definitions of the problem. It is not so much the particular terms that cause the trouble, but the inherent difficulty in translating the phenomena into any terms at all.

But how, in this case, is one to make sense of the bangs, thumps, taps, rattles, and other reverberations which indisputably have such a wide social importance, and the individual effects of which are known? One expedient is to adopt the premise that everybody knows the subject, and that there is therefore no need to strive for a precise formulation—just as one does not bother, after all, to demonstrate the importance of sex, or to define erotic sensations. This, of course, is a position which should be adopted only when others are obviously unnecessary or have appeared unfeasible, which cannot yet be claimed in this case; but there seem nevertheless to be some grounds for adopting it. One might even suggest, indeed, that it is an unavoidable position, at some stage of the enquiry, and one that is peculiarly appropriate to the phenomena themselves. In the matter of dealing with the universal psychic appeal of a certain kind of noise, presumably the question of exact discrimination by the distinctive categories of any single culture should not be decisive. This is not the sphere of rational discourse and inference, even, but that of feeling. Admittedly, society itself defines and organizes feelings, and conditions its members to respond to certain sounds rather than to others—in one society the effect will be produced by the drum, in another by the gong, and in another by clapping—but practically everywhere it is found that percussion is resorted to in order to communicate with the other world, and it is the non-cultural affective appeal of percussion which I have to try to relate to the concept of spiritual existence.

Essentially, Crawley seems to be right: drums do have the kind of effect which he attempts impressionistically to describe, and so do other percussion instruments. Gongs also have such an effect, especially perhaps the deeper ones, and similarly with bells. The effect in question is not so patent in the case of some other items in the list above, such as rattles and sticks, but all these noise-makers tend to produce a comparable affective impact. This impact is produced, let me repeat, not simply by rhythm or melody or a certain note or period of resonance, but by percussion. There is no need to go intensively into the literature on the neurological grounds of this kind of effect: apart from the common experience of percussive musical instruments, the internal quaking produced by thunder, and the similar effects of gunfire or other explosive noises which vibrate the environment are well-known. (The word "percussion" comes from the Latin *quatere*, to strike, shake.) There is no doubt that sound-waves have neural and organic effects on human beings, irrespective of the cultural formation of the latter. The reverberations produced by musical instruments thus have not only aesthetic but also bodily effects. These effects may be more or less consciously undergone, but they are in any case unavoidable. The sounds

mark off points on a scale of intensity the effects of which range from an agonizing disruption of the organism down to subliminal thrills or other bodily responses which contribute to the conscious affective appreciation of the sounds. Prominent among such sounds are those produced by percussion, which may well be said to involve "the foundations of aurally generated emotion."

From the point of view of culture history, also, it may be important that percussive sounds are the easiest to make, and the most obviously possible: they do not depend upon special materials, techniques, or ideas, but can readily be made with the human body alone or by its abrupt contact with any hard or resonant part of the environment. In two senses, therefore, it may be concluded that percussion is a primary and elemental phenomenon.

So far, then, I have generalized one term ("noise produced by striking or shaking") in the matter under investigation, and I have placed the shaman's drum in a far wider context of percussive phenomena and their physiological effects. But this leaves a corresponding term ("communication with the other world") which then seems much too explicit and ideational to account for so general a relation.

How am I to generalize this second term? Wilken (1887) has pointed out that drums are used not only to establish contact with spirits, but also to repel them, but this is still a form of communication with the other world. What other situations and institutionalized forms of behaviour are marked by percussion? Once the question is put in this way, it is seen that percussive devices are used in a very large number of situations other than that of contacting spirits. Dworakowska has indeed indicated the importance of bells and drums in the normal course of social life, in healing, prophylaxis, hunting, warfare, funerals, etc. (1938: 9–12); and one has only to review ethnographical literature to appreciate that percussion is typical of a remarkably wide range of other situations such as birth, initiation, marriage, accession to office, sacrifice, lunar rites, calendrical feasts, declaration of war, the return of head-hunters, the reception of strangers, the inauguration of a house or a communal building, market days, sowing, harvest, fishing expeditions, epidemics, eclipses, and so on. Often the instruments are identified with the events, and are themselves the material symbols of them; their players may be not just normal participants but indispensable officiants at the rites and ceremonies which are distinguished by the sounds.

What is it that these events have in common? Obviously that they are *rites de passage*. In other words, the class of noise-makers is associated with the formal passage from one status or condition to another. Once again, though, I am not saying that such rites cannot be accomplished without percussive noise-makers, or that only such devices are used to mark them, but simply that there is a constant and immediately recognizable association between the type of sound and the type of rite. What I am proposing, namely, is that there is a significant connexion between percussion and transition.

This, I suggest, is the definitive relation, and the nature of the connexion is the real problem. There is certainly no intrinsic relationship between the phenomena, yet the association is too firm for the answer to be sought in the contingent particulars of cultural tradition. An obvious and conventional resort is to look at other usual means of marking the transition from one category to another. One such expedient is the use of a special vocabulary (van Gennep, 1909: 241; [1960: 169]; cf. 1908), which might even be thought formally comparable, to some slight extent, in that it involves the production of distinctive sounds. Another means is the assumption of special clothes, ornaments, or masks—or alternatively the divestiture of all such external distinctions; and yet another is to change location, so that the passage from one social or mystical status to another is symbolized, as van Gennep shows, by a territorial passage. But these comparisons are not helpful, for a number of reasons; firstly, these institutions are individually less general and more variable than the feature of percussion; secondly, they themselves are severally and typically accompanied by percussive sounds; and, thirdly, they are simply alternative means of marking transition, so that they merely pose the same fundamental problem but in more complex forms. Moreover, they actually lead away from the specific question, in that they demand an analysis of transition rites as such. But the necessary feature of transition will equally inescapably be marked in some way or other (i.e., not only by a tripartite ritual), and the question posed here is why precisely percussion should be so prominently and so very widely employed as a specially suitable kind

of marker. The answer is not going to be arrived at, I suspect, by this kind of comparison, for the things compared in this case belong to different orders. On the one hand the institutions (beating of drums, etc.) have been defined reductionally by physical criteria (sound-waves, neural responses) which have no social content, whereas on the other hand institutions (sacrifice, etc.) which are equally social have merely been classed together sociologically in a way which retains their social and contingent nature. These considerations give all the more reason to revert to "transition" as the second term in the relation.

This offers a formally satisfactory definition of the problem, but in the end it only shows all the more clearly how profound and seemingly intractable a problem it is. What I am dealing with is the conjunction of two primal, elementary, and fundamental features: (1) the affective impact of percussion, (2) the logical structure of category-change. According to common notions, these components pertain to two quite disparate modes of apprehension: emotion and reason. Yet empirically there seems to be a significant connexion between them. This connexion cannot be derived exclusively from one or the other mode, i.e., either affectively or else logically, since by definition neither contains or implies the distinctive and irreducible features of the other. Nor is there, it would appear, anything in the social context of transition which might account externally for the connexion between these conventionally disjoined features. It would be easy enough to say that we should ignore common notions, or even a philosophically established opposition between feeling and thought, and instead consider directly the association that is postulated; but to do so would still leave an evident contrast between percussion and transition, and it is this ineluctable disparity, however defined, which frames the problem.

It seems, therefore, that one is committed to an anthropological kind of "depth analysis," in a synoptic attempt to transcend conventional academic distinctions and to account for human phenomena, psychic and social, in their integrity. Turner (1966) and more especially Beidelman (1964; 1966a; 1966b) have provided valuable exploratory examples of this sort of investigation, and much of my own work on classification (e.g., Needham, in press) has been directed by the same concern. So far, I think it will be agreed, this kind of research has served, at a theoretical level (as distinct from ethnographical interpretation) only to delineate the problems involved, not to solve them. This at least is the position in which I find myself at this point in the face of this new problem. But I do not find such a conclusion especially dismaying, for whereas social anthropology (like philosophy) has had considerable success in discerning and formulating problems, it is very much a matter of opinion whether it can be said ever to have solved any of them. In the present instance I shall be gratified if it is only thought that these problematical comments have contributed in any way to a clearer conception of the primary factors of human experience, and particularly of the basic importance of feeling in coming to terms with phenomenal reality.

Whether or not it is agreed that there is a real problem here, or that my own rather baffled observations are at all cogent, at least there is a methodological precept which it may prove useful for the ethnographer and the theoretical social anthropologist to keep in mind, namely to pay special attention to percussion. For the rest, I conclude simply and mnemonically by restating the problem in the form of the unduly forthright and apparently unlikely hypothesis:

There is a connexion between percussion and transition.

Notes.—This paper was originally given, in its present form, as a lecture at the University of Oxford in April, 1967. Certain further facts have since come to my notice and should be noted here.

1. The question why a shaman beats a drum has in fact been adverted to by van der Leeuw. Without posing this specific question, or considering the issue in any detail, he very briefly states that drumming and dancing induce a state of ecstasy in the shaman (1933, ch. 26. 2).

This possibility has been gone into more fully by Francis Huxley, in a fascinating paper which was published while the present article was in press. Writing about voodoo in Haiti, he reports that: "It is the drummers who largely provoke dissociation; they are skilful in reading the signs, and by quickening, altering, or breaking their rhythm they can usually force the crisis on those [dancers] who are ready for it" (1967: 286). Sometimes the dancer collapses before he has been possessed by the commanding presence of the god; he is put on his feet by the audience, who send him out on to the dance floor again "till the buffets of sound have their full effect" (286).

The effect in question is said to be produced through disturbances of the inner ear, an organ which modulates postural attitude, muscle tonus, breathing rhythms, heartbeat, blood pressure, feelings of nausea and certain eye reflexes. Huxley convincingly proposes that "the apparatus of drumming, dancing, and singing" can not only affect the inner ear, but is actually "aimed at it in an effort to dissociate the waking consciousness from its organization in the body" (287).

From what I have shown above, however, it is unfortunately plain that even a radical explanation of this kind, though very apt (as Crawley would have agreed) in the case of certain instruments, does not answer to the range of phenomena and related considerations to which the shaman's drum is merely an introduction. (It may be remarked, incidentally, that the vocational mark of a voodoo priest or priestess is a rattle (294).)

2. Professor Maurice Freedman has independently furnished a splendid complement to the argument of the present article, both supporting the hypothesis and extending the range of relevant phenomena, in his observations on Chinese marriage ritual.

When the bride leaves her home and is separated from her family she is in "a phase of transition" from which she will emerge only in her bridal chamber at the end of her journey. During this phase she may be "possessed," according to one authority (Johann Frick), by the God of Happiness (Freedman 1967: 16). "The special character of the transition is marked by another feature: as the procession moves off, as it arrives, and sporadically along the route, firecrackers are let off" (17).

Freedman comments upon the little intellectual curiosity which has been excited by firecrackers, and he then proposes his own provisional interpretation. Crackers are part of a series of noise-producers which stretches from salt in the fire at one end to the cannon at the other. "Noise is used as a marker. It punctuates approaches to and separations from spirits and certain formal approaches to and separations from humans" (17). In these contexts neither the fear of evil spirits nor the expression of joy—which are motives expressed by Chinese themselves—need be relevant: "The marker [i.e., noise] is . . . neutral."

Freedman goes on to consider further connexions of noise with symbols such as fire, light, and colour, and to suggest certain ideological components of setting off firecrackers; but it is his relational discernment of a connexion between *explosions* and transition which makes such a remarkable contribution to the line of enquiry taken up here. I did indeed make a reference above to the effects of gunfire "and other explosive noises," but I had missed the fact that such sounds (percussive in the extreme) are also symbolically relevant. Yet in our own culture, after all, solemn entrances and exits are most prominently marked by explosions: a head of state is greeted with a twenty-one gun salute, and rifle volleys are fired at the graveside of a dead soldier. Marriage rites are relevant, too, for at a European wedding there is a traditional parallel to the Chinese firecrackers: pans—more recently replaced by tin cans—are tied behind the wedding carriage, where they bang, resound and clash like mad.

Now this last is a crucial fact which shows a more fundamental correspondence with firecrackers, and with cordite salutations, namely that in these cases there is no rhythm. The jangling cacophony of the pans is quite random, and the furious rattle of Chinese fireworks (numbers of which are set off at once, moreover, so that they produce bursts of overlapping reports) is equally non-rhythmical. The same is true of European transition-marking by means of firearms, for in both of the ceremonies instanced the interval between the shots is too long to compose any rhythm. What counts, therefore (and I am grateful to Freedman for having led me to see this new proof), is not rhythm, and certainly not melody, but nothing other than percussion.

The arresting convergence and mutual implications of the papers by Crawley, Dworakowska, Huxley and Freedman (on topics as initially disparate as drums and cymbals, bell and drum, voodoo, and Chinese marriage rites), together with my own tentative conspectus, seem to show at least that there really is something in the hypothesis. But this in turn only shows again that there is a real problem.

Duane Metzger and Gerald Williams

TENEJAPA MEDICINE I: THE CURER

The ethnographer Metzger and the linguist Williams have collaboratively formulated a set of very precise procedures for ethnographic description and analysis that have been important in the last decade in the development of what has been variously called "ethnoscience," "ethnographic semantics," or "cognitive anthropology" (see the excellent collection of articles in Tyler, *Cognitive Anthropology*, 1969). In this article they have applied these procedures to the shamans, or "curers," that perform in the Highland Chiapas community of Tenejapa in southern Mexico. Their procedures involve the establishment and employment of specifiable eliciting frames, formulated in the informants' language and in terms that are meaningful to the informants. The use of these frames enables the ethnographer to produce cultural descriptions which mirror the discriminations made by the informants rather than discriminations that would be made by the observers utilizing categories drawn from our culture.

Reprinted from the *Southwestern Journal of Anthropology*, XIX (1963), 216–234, by permission of the authors and the *Southwestern Journal of Anthropology*.

The treatment of serious illness in Tenejapa—a Tzeltal-speaking community in the Chiapas highlands—is primarily the province of the /hpošil/, "curer." We propose to examine the role of the curer, placing particular emphasis on the characteristics and performances which not only define the role but which also, in their internal variation, are the basis for evaluation of curers and selection of one curer rather than another.

The procedures employed in the collection of the data and in the descriptive analysis of it are in part revealed in the body of the paper where eliciting frames and typical responses have been shown. The establishment and employment of specifiable eliciting frames, formulated in the informants' language and in terms "entertainable" by informants, constrains their response in some great degree to a focus or foci which are in turn defined in the informants' terms, rather than by the categories of the investigator. In this sense the description stems from the material itself. The structure and limits of the description bear a significant relation to structure and limits of the informants' "knowledge."

1. /HPOŠIL/, THE CURER

1.1. THE ROLE OF THE CURER

Working with seven Tenejapa informants from six *parajes*, we were able to compile a list of some three hundred curers known to them. The approximate population of all Tenejapa *parajes* being about 10,000 (1960 Census) and calculating a population of curers of two or three times the size of the list obtained, since our informants' acquaintance did not extend over the whole of the *municipio*, it appears that the ratio of curers to total population is somewhere between one to ten and one to twenty-five. This ratio indicates something of the importance of the performances engaged in by curers and of the situations which call up these performances. It may be observed as well that the variety and frequency of illness are equally of a large order and that, though we have not attempted any sort of statistical confirmation, the subject of illness figures with great frequency in conversation.

Virtually anything that upsets the Tenejapaneco's equanimity is a potential source of illness, while the maintenance of the health of the members of the family is a major drain upon available resources. It is the curer whose role is central to these concerns and who exercises major control over the disposition of these resources. Also, it appears, at least in some instances, it is the curer who decides whether an illness may be treated or not, and thus, at least indirectly, has some power of decision over the life or death of the patient. An illustration of two of these points is the curer's recommendation in instances of apparent imminent death to refrain from great expenditure in a hopeless attempt at a cure. The curer who fails to show such concern for the welfare of the patient's family is accused of avarice and failure to fulfill his obligation to /ya školta te muk' b'ik'it/, "watch over the people." Derogation of this duty leads to punishment in the form of illness.

Being known as a curer confers a status which overrides other status achieved, such as that of great age. It is usual for a respected elder to address even young curers as /tatik pošil/, /tatik/ being the most respectful, reverential term of address available, and, in general, curers are so addressed rather than by name.

1.2. ATTRIBUTES OF CURERS— CRITERIAL AND ENTAILED

Curers may be of any age (including children) or sex (though male curers are more numerous than female). No formal training is provided for those who fill the role.

The primary distinguishing characteristic of curers is their ability to "pulse" (/ya sna ʔik lek ʔa ʔy k'ab'al/, "They know well how to 'feel of the hand.'"). /ʔa ʔy k'ab'al/ or /pik k'ab'al/ or /¢ahtae k'ab'al/, which refers to the process of pulsing, and thereby sensing, the movement of the blood of the patient, allows the identification of the illness, its etiology, cure, etc. This skill comes to the curer only as a "gift of God," usually discovered in himself by the curer (even while still a child). It is said that by praying to God in the church and burning candles, it is possible to obtain the necessary power to cure for the asking and without danger. Informants, though reporting this to be the case, cannot name any person who has become a curer in this way. More generally, persons attempting to acquire without the gift the knowledge of pulsing that characterizes curers run the danger of being punished by a visitation of illness.

In contrast to pulsing, a second performance characteristic of curers is not limited to them but is shared by non-curers of high status. This is the "true prayer," /b'a¢'il č'ab'/, which is an integral part of the public performances of the civil and religious officials as well as of heads of families, whose perceived function is to /sk'anel kušlehal/, "ask for the life (of the *pueblo* or household)." Public prayer, occurring at conventionally appropriate times, anticipates a potentially great number of dangers to the community and its individual members; within the context of curing, the focus of prayer is upon the life of an individual in relation to a single specific danger to that life.

While any non-curer who is skilled in praying (/ya sna ʔ lek č'ab'/, "he knows how to pray well") may attempt, and sometimes succeed at, curing, the curer's ability to pulse makes his use of prayer more surely effective. Since there are many varieties of /b'a¢'il č'ab'/, differentiated by the god to whom addressed and specific to the disease, the ability to identify the disease (by pulsing) and the knowledge, which is essentially restricted to curers, of the association between specific diseases and gods is crucial. The would-be curer, like anyone else in the community, can learn these associations by closely observing curers at work when there is illness in his household. However, he must be circumspect in his learning. Attempts at acquiring such knowledge are generally punished by illness /ya stikun tal te hč'ultatik/ ~ /te ryos/, "sent by God," because /ya htohb'e ryos tame ya hk'an ya hnop pošile/, "God punishes me if I want to learn to cure."

Like prayer, skill in the use of medicinal plants, which is characteristic of curers, is shared in a general sense by non-curers but becomes unique in the hands of curers because of its association with their other attributes. Medicinal plants are known by all adults in Tenejapa, and association of specific plant remedies with common illnesses is well-known. The curer's use of these plants is special in that, first he alone can surely identify the illness. Then, once the illness is identified, knowledge of the specific herbal remedy for the illness is more or less restricted (as in the case of prayer) to the curer. Finally, /tuhtael/, the preparation and administration of the remedy, involves prayer and spitting into the mixture, both of which invest the medicine with the curer's power.

Other curing skills are exclusive to curers but not common to all of them. Among these are blood-letting, and the curing of various specific types of diseases. Still other curing skills are neither common to all curers nor exclusive to them. These coincide with a set of infirmities which are not /čamel/, "illness(es)": /ti ʔb'en čan/, "snake bite," /k'asem sb'akel/, "broken bones" /k'ahk'et/, "burns," /b'eȼ'em/, "sprains," and /mahel/, "bruises."

Another somewhat peripheral phenomenon sometimes associated with curers is the /sánto/ or /hč'ultatik/, the "talking saint." These generally are in boxes in the house of their owner and may not be seen, though the more reliable are audible, sometimes "speaking" in a high-pitched whining noise, sometimes in recognizable words. The most highly regarded instance reported is that of one which can be heard speaking from inside the house while the listeners remain outside. The primary function of the saint is divinatory and ranges beyond divining the causes of illness and the identification of witches to the finding of lost objects.

The man who owns a saint is the /yahwal hč'ultatik/ or /b'ankilal mučáču yuʔun hč'ultatik), "dueño del santo," and need not be a curer at all. The curer who has a saint, /ʔay hč'ultatik ta sna/, "there's a saint in his house," may employ his saint as a substitute for his own pulsing, but more generally uses it to confirm pulsing. The saint, then, is a supplement or substitute for more traditional (and generally more respected) modes of obtaining information; it has no apparent function in other segments of the cure.

1.3. CLASSES OF CURERS

Having established the attributes of /hpošil/ we asked the question /hay ten hpošiletik ʔay ta b'alamilal/, "How many kinds of curers are there in the world?" One reply was /ʔay ča ʔten/, "There are two kinds," specified as /b'ankilal hpošil/, "(literally, older brother curer) master curer" and /ʔihȼ'inal hpošil/, "(literally younger sibling curer) junior curer."

1.31. By knowledge. In respect to knowledge, these two classes contrast on several interrelated dimensions. One of these dimensions is the types of knowledge attributed to them. The ability to treat specific illnesses distinguishes all /b'ankilal hpošil/ and some /ʔihȼ'inal hpošil/ from all others. For example, /spisil b'ankilal hpošiletik ya snaʔik te *hulawe*/, "All master curers know how to let blood (specifically from the head)," but /ʔay ʔolil ʔihȼ'inal hpošiletik ma sna ʔik te *hulawe*/, "There are some junior curers who do not know how to let blood."

The presentation of the names of other illnesses or modes of treatment elicited further differentiated statements of the same kind in which the following were some of the items substitutable for /hulaw/ in the statements above:

1. /ya sna ʔik lek č'ab'/
   "they know how to pray well"
2. /ya sna ʔik tuhtawaneh/
   "they know how to prepare and bless medicine"
3. (ya sna ʔik čonaw/ or /ya sna ʔik suhtesel čonel/
   "they know how to send an illness back (to the hostile person who caused it)"
4. /ya sna ʔik poštawan yu ʔun me ʔtik tatik/
   "they know the cure for /me ʔtik tatik/"
5. /ya sna ʔik špoštael ʔak'b'il čamel/
   "they know the cure for illness caused by witchcraft"

This knowledge, while characteristic of /b'ankilal hpošil/, may be possessed as well by individual /ʔihȼ'inal hpošil/, but the latter as a class cannot be said to be characterized by the knowledge. It will be noted that at least some abilities are clearly matters of degree (see 1 above), while in other cases the master curer and junior curer are distinguishable by the types of illness they are competent to cure; thus, of a junior curer who pretends to cure a /tulan čamel/, "a strong illness" such as /me ʔtik tatik/, it is said /ya špoštawan ha ʔte ma lom s ʔuȼub' yu ʔun te mač'a ya špoštae/, "he cures (treats), but the person treated does not recover well." There are attributed to the /ʔihȼ'inal hpošil/, who knows the limits of his ability, such statements as /ha ʔin čamel ʔa ʔwu ʔuni ma šhu ʔ ku ʔun lek špoštael melel lom tulan čamel ʔa ʔtaohi/, "This illness of yours, I cannot cure, because (you have) met with a very strong illness" or /ha ʔlek leaiktal te mač'a ya sna ʔ lek špoštael te tulan čamele/, "Better summon someone who knows well the cures of serious illnesses."

A general statement of the difference may be seen in the following regarding the /ʔihȼ'inal hpošil/: /ma ʔma spisil ʔak'b'il ta yok ta sk'ab' yu ʔun hč'ultatik/, "Not all is given into his hands by God"—while of the /b'ankilal hpošil/ it is said, /spisil ʔak'b'il ta yok ta sk'ab'/, "All is given into his hands."

It will be noted that among the abilities characteristic of /b'ankilal hpošil/ is that of curing /ʔak'b'il čamel/, "given illness," i.e., illness attributed to an act of will of a /h ʔak' čamel/, "giver of illness." The classes /h ʔak' čamel/ and /hpošil/ intersect in some of the same persons. However, not all /h ʔak' čamel/ are /hpošil/, and while all /b'ankilal hpošil/ may be able to cure such illness, not all master curers can induce illness. Those who are so able are said to /ča ʔten ya sna ʔ/, "he knows two kinds (classes)." A master curer never induces illness in this way in his role as curer, and the cure for /ʔak'b'il čamel/ does not include counter-measures of the same kind.

"Sending the illness back," /suhtesel čonel/, another ability characteristic of the master curer, is concerned not with /ʔak'b'il čamel/, but /čamel yu ʔun čonel/, "illness induced through ritual 'sale' (of the victim)." This illness is attributed to a /hčonawal/, who implements his ill will by cutting candles into small pieces and praying over them as they burn. The master curer performs the same ritual as an integral part of the cure for /čamel yu ʔun čonel/. Thus, while not all /hčonawal/ are /hpošil/, all /b'ankilal hpošil/ are /hčonawal/; moreover, the latter, unlike the role of /h ʔak' čamel/, is entailed in the master curer's role.

One type of specialized knowledge which is characteristic of /b'ankilal hpošil/ is not common to all of them. The ability to handle /čamel yu ʔun ʔalahel/, "childbirth," is more or less restricted to women; while there are a few men who share this ability, they are reportedly little used because women are "embarrassed" to be attended by men in childbirth. The knowledge of such curers is not restricted to the problem of childbirth; they are general practitioners as well. The

curing skills mentioned earlier as neither exclusive to curers nor shared by all of them—e.g., bone-setting—do not distinguish between /b'ankilal/ and /ʔihȼ'inal/ curers, for many master curers lack some or all of these skills.

1.32. By performance. The knowledge attributed to the master curer which distinguishes him from the junior curer is manifest in his performances in the curing setting. The /b'ankilal/-/ʔihȼ'inal/ contrast, previously defined in general terms of reputation, is carried out on another level in the performances which contribute to—and which at the same time reflect—that reputation.

Within the performances of the curer and others involved in the cure there may be distinguished 1) pulsing: /ʔa ʔy k'ab'al/-/ȼahtae k'ab'al/, and 2) prayer saying: /č'ab'atael/.

Previous to performances differentiating curers from other visitors who are not curers, the usual formulae of greeting are exchanged by the visiting curer and the family of the /čamel/, "sick person."

1.32.1. Differentiation of the curer's reception begins with the request of the family that he "pulse" the patient: Head of the family: /ma ʔyuk š ʔob'ol b'ahat ša ʔȼahtab'en sk'ab'in hčamel ku ʔuni/, "Would you not do me the favor of feeling for him his hand?"

Pulsing generally consists indeed of taking the pulse of both wrists for lengths of time ranging from five minutes to a half-hour per wrist. *In extremis*, the pulse at the wrist being too weak to "hear," pulsing may be done inside the elbow joint or inside the upper arm. This stage in the cure and its constituent performances are much more than diagnostic, leading not only to the identification of the illness, but to a variety of other information regarding the illness as well.

Among the information extracted by the master curer from his pulsing are the following:

/ya yal šč'ič'el te hčamel te b'i čamelil ya šti ʔwan ya ya ʔye/
"The blood of the patient says what illness it is he is suffering"

/te b'i čamelil ya štaot te hčamele/
". . . what illness has seized him, the patient"

/te b'anti ya štaot te hčamele/
". . . where it seized him, the patient"

/te b'a č'ab'atael ya sk'ane/
". . . which prayer is required"

/ta me ʔay čuhkem šč'ulele/
". . . if his soul has been captured"

/ta me ʔay skape/
". . . if there is a combination (of illnesses)"

/ta me ʔay ščohe/
". . . if there is envy (involved)"

/ta me ʔay sme ʔ šwiše/
". . . if the soul is not well guarded (by the old woman who is responsible for it)"

Thus, virtually everything concerning a disease, from its provenience, etiology, to specific medicines and locations in which specific prayers must be said, is available to the curer through pulsing. The curer can also point the finger of guilt at the person whose misbehavior has resulted in the illness, even to parents and ancestors:

/ya sna ʔbʼe lek ya ʔyel ščʼičʼel te hčamel te bʼi smul skola ʔal hahčemtal yu ʔun te hmam hme ʔčuntike/
"The blood of the patient knows well what sins of parents (or ancestors)"

During the course of the pulsing, the curer may carry on conversation with the family, the subject of conversation being unlimited, and the occasion not necessarily excluding jokes and laughter. If, during this conversation, the curer makes obvious attempts to elicit from the patient or the attending family the information which is properly forthcoming from pulsing, it is likely to be said that he is /ihɕʼinal/ and not /bʼankilal/.

/te me ya sna ʔ ya ʔyel kʼabʼale ma ya shohkʼo/
" 'If he knew how to pulse, he would not ask questions,' he said"

In such a situation, the family may deliberately withhold information:

Curer: /bʼitʼil ʔa ʔ lihk te ščamel te ʔanɕe/
"How did the illness of the woman begin?"
or
/bʼanti ʔa ʔ sɕakat te čamele/
"Where did the illness grasp you?"

Family: /hič naš ʔa ʔ ɕakot/
"It just grasped."

Curer: /ma ʔyuk bʼa tʼušah/
"Couldn't it be she has fallen?"

Family: /ma ʔyuk/
"No."

In contrast, the /bʼankilal hpošil/ displays his lack of concern by engaging in small talk, gossip, and jokes. Silence, or any other apparent sign of concern on the part of the curer (e.g., trembling of the hand while pulsing, /ya šnihk/, "(his hand) trembles") is negatively evaluated.

Duration of the pulsing constitutes another potential point on which differentiation between /bʼankilal/ and /ʔihɕʼinal hpošil/ is based. Thus a short pulsing (followed by a clear, unhesitating explication) is characteristic of the master curer, while a long pulsing (and hesitation in explaining the results) indicates skill of a lesser order.

Family: /bʼi yael te skʼabʼe/
"What says his hand?"

Curer: /ma škil mama ya yal ʔa ʔ ka ʔy te skʼabʼe/
"I don't know. His hand does not speak, I feel."

The pulsing completed, the curer is expected to explain what he has learned. The master curer's explication of the circumstances antecedent to the disease generally conforms to what the family and patient know of them, while the junior curer's may not.

An instance of a highly evaluated set of performances by a curer will be seen in this example: The curer, a woman in this case, was called to a "gravely" ill patient. Without asking questions, and after a brief pulsing, she indicated that the patient was suffering illness as a punishment for complaining of the rigors and inconveniences of the *cargo*, "public office," he had recently assumed. The /ryos/ of his cargo was punishing the cargo-holder for remarks which he admitted to having made, the remarks being known as well to the family.

Further, the contrast between master and junior curers extends to the curer's statements with respect to the severity of the disease and the possibility of curing it. Accuracy of such estimation, as evidenced in subsequent developments and in the costs involved in the cure, is characteristic of the master curer. Informants report that /ʔihɕʼinal hpošil/ are prone to underestimate the severity of disease, while the confidence of the /bʼankilal hpošil/ does not deter him from staking his reputation on an extended and expensive cure. The /bʼankilal hpošil/ admits the gravity of the illness and characteristically undertakes the cure with due humility: /skʼan ryos ya š ʔuɕubʼ/, "With the help of God he will recover."

The conclusion of the pulsing is the point of selection between alternative courses in the cure, depending upon the identification of the disease, perceived cause of the disease, etc. The curer may rest while preparations are made for whatever course is to be followed in the subsequent segment, and he will generally be fed.

1.32.2. The succeeding segment of the curing sequence consists of the components directed toward the curing itself. The constituent components depend upon the results of the preceding segment. Among possible components are the preparation and administration of medicine or other physical attempts at curing, the burning of incense and candles, the saying of prayers to appropriate gods (the prayers being said in specific places depending on the illness and its provenience), and possibly a ceremonial meal. Among these potential components, there are relations of mutual exclusion, of sequential order, of co-occurrence, the description of which will constitute a subsequent account of Tenejapa Tzeltal curing practices.

We will confine ourselves here to an outline of the general sequence of performances which constitute this segment.

Encompassing the variability arising from different results of pulsing and the variability arising from apparent changes as the cure proceeds, the three highest order sequential components appear to be as follows: (1) /b'aȼ'il č'ab'/, "prayer," (2) /tuhtael/, "preparation and administration of blessed medicine" and (3) /hulaw/, "bloodletting." The time span of a single sequence (there is always the possibility of the iteration of the sequence) can be as long as four days. If the pulsing segment indicated that /b'aȼ'il č'ab'/ is appropriate, it will be anterior to other co-occurring components, if any. The /b'aȼ'il č'ab'/ itself is divided into four or six parts (practice appears to vary from one *paraje* to another), the parts being distributed in sequence on succeeding mornings and evenings, the first occurring in the evening. Special routines, however, may be accorded severe illness, or certain specific illnesses such as /me ?tik tatik/, and the requisite number of prayers may be said in sequence without interruption. Severity may also dictate simultaneity of several segments, requiring the participation of a person other than the curer. This person, the /hč'ab'owil/, "prayer sayer," is not a curer, but one who can recite the appropriate prayer as determined by the curer. A prayer cycle, once begun, must be carried to its conclusion by the person reciting it without his engaging in any other curing component; thus, in order for other components to be simultaneous with the prayer, the latter must be said by another person (the /hč'ab'owil/) while the other component is carried out by the curer. Prayer, in this sense, is the only component which may be delegated.

Two of the above sequential components, /tuhtael/ and /b'aȼ'il č'ab'/, are both regarded as /č'ab'/, a superordinate category which contrasts directly with /hulaw/, "bloodletting." Within /b'aȼ'il č'ab' ' are a variety of disease-specific prayers, each of which intersects, as shown in Table 1, with settings appropriate to their performance. /tuhtael/

TABLE 1. THE STRUCTURE OF THE PRAYER (/c'ab'/)

In Setting:	tuhtael		b'aȼ'il čab'[a]					
	č'ulelal	kušlehal	me ?el wišil	skap sk'ab'	me ?tik tatik	k'ašim b'ehtael	čonel	šiwel
ta yut na, "in the house"								
1. ta kurus "before the cross"	X	X	X					
2. ta ti ?k'al "before the fire"								X
3. ta b'ayuk naš "anywhere"	X				X			
ta ?amak' "before the house"	X				X	X		
ta kurus ta ?anhel "at a (wayside) cross"							X	

[a] The names of prayers shown here in Table 1 are renderings, by and large, of homonymous names of diseases to which the prayers are specific. Glossing these names would be at best only vaguely suggestive, and at worst very much misleading. Were this paper part of an already completed description of Tzeltal medicine, these would be cross-referenced to sections in which criterial attributes of /čamel/, "diseases," as a class would be laid out together with the defining dimensions in terms of which members of the class contrast and are differentiated. Only one of these is shown here, i.e., location of the saying of the appropriate prayers, since it relates to one aspect of curers' performances.

may be applied to the preparation and application of a variety of disease-specific medicines, but the location of their preparation is indifferently before or within the house.

Table 2 shows a simple case (an illness requiring six prayers) in which the curer is performing all components, thus displaying the linear ordering of components most clearly.

The components stand in a transitive relation; at the close of any component, depending upon the state of the patient, the next numbered component may succeed. After the accomplishment of component 2, /tuhtael/, or 3, /hulaw/, the cycle may be reiterated by returning to component 1, /b'aȼ'il č'ab'/, except that /hulaw/ is invariably succeeded by another instance of /tuhtael/ at the same curing session. The time intervening between the major components may be compressed or it may be expanded such that components succeed each other on succeeding days.

At the beginning of component 2, /tuhtael/, the curer and assembled company may begin drinking, a performance which is mutually exclusive with component 1, /b'aȼ'il č'ab'/. The preparation and administration of medicine generally involves the use of /poš/, "*aguardiente* (in this case, distilled cane alcohol)," together with the saying of prayers (but not /b'aȼ'il č'ab'/) over the medicine.

If /hulaw/, component 3, is to be carried out, a fragment of broken glass is secured with which the necessary wounds will be made. There would seem to be two types of appropriate /hulaw/, one involving small incisions in the skin on the sides of the head and in the scalp, the other, incisions in other parts of the body. In the former case, the blood is collected on leaves and removed from the house, the disease being removed from the body along with or in the blood. In the latter case, in addition to blood, some other substance may be removed by the curer and eaten by him to prevent contagion (/ton č'i'č'/, literally "blood stones," in the case of the disease of the same name).

If the cure is to be continued, the repetition of the cycle will be limited to /b'aȼ'il č'ab'/, given that the cure is continued by the same curer. Where a different curer is called in, however, the complete cycle may be begun again.

The components of the curing segment proper also show variation in terms of which evaluation of the curer may be made. In prayer, whether the /b'aȼ'il č'ab'/ or that of /tuhtael/, the performance of the /b'ankilal hpošil/ shows variety, that of the /ʔihȼ'inal/ repetitiveness; and the repertory of the /b'ankilal/ allows him to continue longer, with consequent greater effectiveness.

In the preparation and administration of medicines the /ʔihȼ'inal hpošil/ may always rely on the same medicine; /ma lom sna ʔb'e sb'a spisil pošiletike/, "He doesn't know all the kinds of medicines." To the /b'ankilal/ there is attributed, at least, the knowledge of "all classes (of medicine)," /ya sna ʔb'e sb'a spisil stukel/.

The physical manipulations of /hulaw/, "blood letting," make clear the curer's confidence or lack thereof, in that the incisions made should be regular and the hand steady, while the trembling hand of the incompetent leads to ragged incisions.

Upon termination of the curing segments, the curer is offered a gift of 10–30 ears of corn. The amount of corn varies neither with his status nor with the success of the cure (although he may decline it if the patient has died), but with the wealth of the patient's family. Daily consumption of corn is estimated at five ears per person per day.

1.32.3. Throughout the curing sequence, then, there are opportunities to evaluate—or to re-evaluate—the curer in terms of the /b'ankilal/-/ʔihȼ'inal/ contrast. (In the course of the cure, a curer who has claimed a master's knowledge and skill may betray his junior status by injudicious eliciting of information, trembling hands, etc.; or, even in the absence of these signs of lesser status, he may incorrectly predict the course of the illness, e.g.,

TABLE 2. CYCLING OF COMPONENTS OF THE CURE PROPER

Time	Day 1	Day 2	Day 3	Day 4	± Day 5
/sakub'el k'inal/ "becomes light the day"		b'aȼ'il č'ab'	b'aȼ'il č'ab'	b'aȼ'il č'ab'	tuhtael
/č'ul ʔahk'ub'al/ "(holy) night"	b'aȼ'il č'ab'	b'aȼ'il č'ab'	b'aȼ'il č'ab'		±(hulaw + tuhtael)

the patient may fail to recover or die in contradiction of a favorable prognosis.) An informant's evaluation of a curer is primarily based on the personal observations which he or his close associates have made of that curer. The relative lack of consensus in such evaluations by our informants suggests that these experiences vary greatly and that the classes of /b'ankilal hpošil/ and /ʔihȼ'inal hpošil/ are, in general, not to be regarded as groups with fixed memberships. Where multiple judgments were obtained as to the ability of various curers, there was disagreement between the informants in two-thirds of the cases. However, in the remaining third of the cases, where there was agreement, the overwhelming majority of curers were evaluated as /b'ankilal/, a fact which suggests that there may be a certain amount of consensus at the highly skilled end of the scale. The apparent lack of consensus below this level makes the selection of a curer problematic and involves the trial-and-error employment of /ʔihȼ'inal hpošil/ (labelled after the fact), as well as masters. In any case, there is a floor, as it were, underlying any evaluation, a level below which the definition of a person as a curer will not permit evaluation to go. Thus, an obviously poor curer can still, despite negatively evaluated performances, produce reactions of fear in the family of the patient by a prediction of death. Informants confirm that, in the position of patient, they find themselves vacillating between belief and disbelief of such predictions.

2. THE CURER VIS-A-VIS THE PATIENT-HOUSEHOLD

2.1. CONDITIONS APPROPRIATE TO THE SUMMONING OF THE CURER

The curer is not summoned in every instance in which a person defines himself as /ʔayon ta čamel/ or /čamelon/, "I am sick," or is defined as such by others, /ʔay ta čamel/, "he/she is sick." The criteria which appear to operate in distinguishing between occasions appropriate and inappropriate to calling the curer generally involve the contrast between 1) /muk'ul čamel/, "great illness," /ʔip čamel/, "powerful illness," /tulan čamel/, "hard illness," versus 2) /solel k'ašlel čamel/, "illness which passes," /č'uhč'ul čamel/, "a little illness."

In reply to the question, /b'it'il ya šb'aht taluk te hpošile/, "When do you call the curer?" there emerges the following family of responses:

/ha ʔ hič ya šb'a yič' tal ʔik'el hpošil/
"One is going to call a curer,"

A. /te me ʔay muk'ul čamele/
"if there is a great illness"

/te me ʔay ʔip čamele/
"if there is a great illness"

/te me ʔay tulan čamele/
"if there is a strong illness"

We take this one level further by asking, /b'inti ʔut'il ʔay te ʔip čamele/, "How is (what is) a powerful illness?" and eliciting the response:

/ha ʔ ʔip čamel ta me ʔay ma sk'an šhelaw ta ʔora te čamele/
"It is a powerful illness if it does not (wish to) be cured in (normal) course, the illness."

Other conditions for calling the curer include:

B. /ta me ʔay b'ayel k'uš hkok k'ab'tike/
"If there is great pain in our bodies"

/ta me ʔay me šȼ'ihk' sti ʔaw te čamel ya ka ʔytike/
"If we cannot bear the pain of the illness we feel"

Other conditions require anticipation of illness, as:

C. /ha ʔ lek ta nail ya šb'aht tal ta ʔik'el te hpošile/
"It is best first to call the curer" or

/ha ʔ lek te ʔalan ya kak' hb'ahtik ta poštaele/
"It is best to send for curing beforehand"

/ta me ʔay b'i ši ʔotike/
"if we are *espantado*' or

/ya ka ʔytik ta me ʔay mač'a ya ščap hk'olaltik ta ʔak'b'il čamele/
"We feel that there is someone trying to give illness (through witchcraft)"

Sometimes the calling of a curer follows the failure of another curer to restore the patient to health. Indeed, the lay diagnosis of "powerful" illness may follow—as the definition in A suggests—from an unsuccessful attempt to cure it; along with the diagnosis goes the after-the-fact evaluation of the curer as /ʔihȼ'inal hpošil/.

2.2. OBTAINING THE SERVICES OF THE CURER

The recognition of the above conditions within the household is up to the head of the house, and the decision to obtain the services of the curer is his. If the head of the house himself is the patient, it may be his wife or one among the children of the household who will make the decision to call the curer, if the head of the house is perceived to be ill but does not act himself. In general, if the patient is perceived as ill, but in such a condition as to refuse or be unable to recognize it, the curer will be called, even against the will of the patient.

Occasionally, if the illness is defined as "powerful" but the patient is not too sick to walk, the patient may go himself to the curer's house with a keg of *chicha* (a fermented sugar cane beverage) to request and participate in the cure. Usually, however, the curer is summoned to the patient's house.

The actual performance of going to request the services falls under the general heading of /ʔabat/, "errand," a performance mutually exclusive with the performances appropriate to the senior members of the household, and particularly to those of the senior male, generally the father in the predominantly nuclear family household. A child or young adult is usually sent, though he (or she) may be reluctant or afraid if he has not done such an errand before. The informants were encouraged to supply hypothetical but appropriate instances of verbal behavior to fit this situation. We constructed the interaction by setting up the question frames used by the person requiring information, in this case the young person who is to run the errand. Thus,

Child: /meʔ b'inti mahtanalil ya kič'b'el yu ʔun ¢'in hpošile/
"Mother, what is the gift I should take for the curer?"

Parent: /haʔ ʔič'a b'el htab'uk ʔišimi/
"Take these twenty ears of corn."

The parent's response constitutes a substitution frame for the eliciting of other appropriate gifts:

/haʔ ʔič'a b'el hunuk pulatu čenek'i/
"Take this one bowl of beans." *or*

/haʔ ʔič'a b'el čeb'uk pulatu čenek'i/
"Take those two bowls of beans." *or*

/haʔ ʔič'ab'el hunuk pulatu ʔiči/
"Take this one bowl of *chiles*." *or*

/haʔ ʔič'a b'el čeb'uk pulatu ʔiči/
"Take these two bowls of *chiles*."

Child: /b'inti ya šk'o kalb'e ¢'in hpošile/
"What shall I say (on coming) to the curer?"

Parent: /haʔ ya šk'o walb'e ¢'in te ʔay hčamel ku ʔuntike/
"Arriving, tell him that we have a sick person."

Child: /b'inti ya kalb'e ¢'in ta me ʔay ma sk'an štale/
"What shall I say if he does not wish to come?"

Parent: /yaniš ʔa ʔwokol k'opta tal ta pórsa ¢'in/
"Ask him please to come under any circumstances." *or*

/te ʔay š ʔob'ol b'a štal yilotike melel ʔip hčamel ku ʔuntik ya ʔwil/
"That he do us the favor of coming to see us, because our sick person is serious(ly ill)."

The errand-boy is quite likely to find the curer is away from home, as curers of good reputation are often employed, and a single cure may require as much as four full days if travelling time to distant patients is included. Moreover, while no curer is busy curing every day, all of them carry on the usual adult occupations as well—the men in the cornfields, the women in their kitchens and courtyards. There are no full-time specialists in curing; the meager fees paid for curer's services are incommensurable with such specialization, and the time that curing subtracts from subsistence activities is so great as to cause curing to be considered a somewhat sacrificial vocation.

The response of the curer to the request and gift may be one of three: (1) he may come as requested, and at once; (2) he may protest a previous obligation, undertaking to come later; or (3) he may refuse the "gift" and thus decline to undertake the cure. The second may be interpreted as a disguised attempt to pursue some work of his own, and the third may indicate some history of conflict between curer and the family of the patient. In both types of situation, the curer places himself in jeopardy of supernatural punishment in that he is refusing what is considered an obligation contingent upon his role as curer.

2.3. THE SELECTION OF A CURER
First and foremost, the curer selected by the patient's household is generally one with whom they have had favorable first-hand experience in previous curing situations; at least initially, curers known only by hearsay are not considered. Proximity is a factor important in the initial stages and often associated with this acquaintance, except that normally the curer does not treat his own children or members of his own household. Proximity may also be crucial in emergency. Given these guiding principles, the selection of a curer takes into account the household's guess diagnosis of the illness and involves an attempt to

match the illness and the curer's skills as they have observed them. A "powerful" illness requires a known /b'ankilal hpošil/, while for a "little" illness an /ʔihȼ'inal hpošil/ may be chosen. The guesswork involved both in identifying the illness and in evaluating the curer often means that the first curer called will not be the last. However, the ideal rationalization of the selection of a curer is phrased in firm, positively evaluative terms:

/mač'a hunuk hpošilil ya šb'a kik'tik tal/
"Which curer shall we send for to come?"

/haʔ ya šba kik'tik tal te hʔaluš lopis howil ȼ'iʔe melel haʔ ya snaʔ šȼiknatesel spisil te b'i ya šti ʔwan ya kaʔytike/
"Let us summon Alonso López 'Mad Dog' because he knows how to explain all the things that we suffer."

3. CONCLUSION

In this paper, some aspects of the role of the Tenejapa Tzeltal curer have been described in terms consistent with discriminations made by the Tenejapa Tzeltal themselves; the discrimination of curers from non-curers, the evaluation of and distinction between curers, the establishment of recognized units within the curing performance (and their relation to the evaluation of the curer), the relation of evaluation to the selection of the curer, etc.

The techniques here employed seem to us to be applicable in ethnographic description generally. Whether through these or other techniques, the arrival at cultural descriptions which mirror the discriminations made by informants is a desirable end for ethnography. The present paper is, of course, only a sample; Tzeltal curers and their activities constitute a focus which if articulated with a number of other such foci will place the Tzeltal curers within a potentially ever-widening description, having as its end a Tzeltal-centered "whole-culture" description of the Tenejapa Tzeltal community.

Richard A. Shweder

ASPECTS OF COGNITION IN ZINACANTECO SHAMANS: EXPERIMENTAL RESULTS

Ever since the time that ethnographers began to observe the behavior of shamans in the various tribal cultures of the world there have been comments and speculations about the extent to which the shamans are somehow different from the nonshamans in these societies. The shamans have always been observed to occupy special roles in their social systems and to perform special rituals. But are they also psychologically different or distinct in some definable ways? The early ethnographers like Bogoras (1904–1909), Paul Radin (1937), and others suggested that the behavior of shamans displayed "neurotic," or even "psychotic," symptoms. But a more common observation, as more data were collected, was to the effect that while *some* shamans might be "half crazy," more of them in any given society displayed no such symptoms. This brief but pioneering article by Shweder opens up a whole new area for exploration as he reports on his experimental results to the effect that the Zinacanteco shamans possess certain cognitive capacities that clearly distinguish them from nonshamans in this society. The extent to which these findings may be true in other societies remains to be investigated, but we suggest that Shweder has pointed up a new way in which we may come to understand the distinctive characteristics of shamans. The paper was prepared especially for this volume.

Printed with permission of the author.

THE COGNITIVE ROLE OF SHAMANS IN ZINACANTAN

Among the Zinacanteco Indians of Chiapas, Mexico, the shaman's role is interpretive and constructive. The h?ilol (meaning "one who sees" or "seer") is a part-time specialist who diagnoses illness by means of divine revelation and by means of pulsing the blood of the infirmed, and who administers remedies, performs new-house ceremonies, lineage and year renewal ceremonies, rain-making ceremonies, and agricultural rituals, and tries to ritually avert epidemics (Silver, 1966: 42, 268; Vogt, 1969: 416–420). But it is as curer that his repertoire of cognitive skills is most apparent.[1]

The healthy Zinacanteco shares his imminent soul (c'ulel) with a wild animal (canul). Under normal circumstances the animal counterpart is held in custody in a mythical corral by the ancestral gods and the supernatural equivalent of the native police force (Silver, 1966: 19). A man's vulnerability is increased, and the conditions which are sufficient for the genesis of illness, distress, anxiety, and fear are created when the canul is free of its bondage. Freedom is the result of escape or abandonment by displeased gods. The freedom is a negative one. In its natural state of wildness the canul is endangered by all the contingencies of untamed and undomesticated nature. Illness results from such uncontrolled and uncontrollable encounters.

The native belief conceives of the supernatural, and especially the ancestral gods, as a sort of "superego," a control which imposes order upon the disordered and chaotic wild. The sick individual is like a man with high dependency needs alone in the jungle, forced to fend for himself, yet incapable of adaptation to his surroundings, and wishing only to understand why he is condemned to such jeopardy and what he must do to escape from his unsought and unwanted freedom.

The curer's role in this situation is to bring the canul back to the corral (Silver, 1966: 43) and convince the ancestral gods to tend to the canul properly, feed him, and contain him.

There are other themes in the native belief, but from my perspective the shaman emerges as an agent of ancestral control and order who tames the wild by placing it into a cultural framework, the corral, where ancestral authority supports customary behavior, and the integrity of the individual person is unmaligned and protected.

From the native point of view the shaman has extraordinary cognitive capacities.[2] The shaman is recruited when he realizes his innate calling in a dream or vision and is thereby selected by the ancestral gods as one capable of "seeing" into the supernatural.

Diagnosis is not related to biological information, but to information concerning divine, supernatural intent. Diagnosis can be variable from patient to patient even when they have similar objective symptoms, and the shaman is free to creatively determine the appropriate explanation of the illness in the light of what he knows of the individual, the family, and the circumstances surrounding the illness. The shaman, of course, may take none of this information into consideration.

The cure is a propitiation, a show of respect to the gods, an attempt to convince them to place things back in order, to not leave anyone abandoned in the wilds. The shaman is indispensable because only he is capable of supernatural revelation into the significance and cure of the illness. The shaman is the individual who in the face of those contingencies of the environment which threaten the Zinacanteco with ill health, anxiety, distress, and fear interprets the uninterpretable and leads the way to security and health.

THE SAMPLE

In the summer of 1967 I designed an experiment the aim of which was to distinguish the cognitive style of Zinacanteco shamans from non-shamans. There are approximately 8000 Zinacantecos, of whom 118 were male shamans in 1966 (Silver, 1966: 24). Thirty-three of these 118 male shamans were selected for testing. They were matched with thirty-three non-shaman males on the basis of three criteria: age, socioeconomic status, and degree of acculturation.

Since Zinacantecos do not convey to the anthropologist much confidence in their knowledge of their exact age, I considered it wise to age-match on the basis of three age categories: ages 22–30, 31–49, and 50 years

[1] The research was conducted in the summer of 1967 under the auspices of Professor Evon Z. Vogt's Harvard Chiapas Project. I thank him warmly for his patience and invaluable assistance. I wish to thank George Collier, Robert Hahn, José (Cep) Hernández, Klaus Koch, and Evon Z. Vogt for helpful suggestions on an earlier report of this data, and Candy, my wife, for reordering the data. The research was supported by a grant from NIMH-02100.

[2] I use cognitive to include perceptual processes.

and over. This division of the age continuum corresponds roughly to the triadic distinction made in Zinacantan between a man who has reached the appropriate age for marriage (*vinik xa*), a man who has reached the halfway point en route to becoming a respected elder (*o ?lol vinik*), literally "half man," and old man (*baz'i mol xa*) (Fred Whelan: personal communication, summer 1967).

Socioeconomic status matching was based on subjective ratings and reduced to three categories: rich, middle, poor. In some cases up to three native informants who knew a particular subject were asked to rate him in terms of wealth as rich, middle, or poor. If two of the three concurred, the rating was accepted. In no case did all three informants produce different ratings. A pool of five informants made it possible to always have available three informants who knew all of my 66 subjects. A similar subjective rating was compiled in 1967 by Frank Cancian for household heads in the village of ?Apas. Cancian had two informants rate subjects on three quantitative scales: 1–10, 1–8, 1–3. Wherever possible I used this data as a further confirmation of, or arbitrator between, the judgments of two informants.

Finally, subjects were matched by the degree of their acculturation. Since Zinacantecos speak a preconquest Mayan tongue called Tzotzil, the handiest (perhaps best) indicator of acculturation was the ability to speak Spanish.

EXPERIMENTAL DESIGN

Subjects were presented with and forced to confront concrete examples of chaos, i.e., diffuse, unstructured stimuli. The experimental design consisted of six *series* of photographs of objects familiar to Zinacantecos. Each series developed through twelve stages from a complete blur to perfectly defined focus. The six series (twelve photos each) were as follows: Evon Z. Vogt with a horse, a market scene, a close-up shot of a foot in a ritual sandal, San Lorenzo, a close-up shot of an ear, and a turkey. The seventy-two photos were arranged into twelve rounds. Each round presented all six scenes in the first degree of focus (a full blur). With each subsequent round there was a gradual development from blur to focus. The last round presented all six scenes in full focus.

Subjects were given the following instructions: "Look carefully and for as long as you like at each photograph I show you. With each photograph if you are sure you know what the photograph is of, tell me. If you are not sure, say 'I don't know.'"

For three of the six series three alternative responses were presented to the subject. For example, with the turkey series the following additional instructions were given: "With this photograph there are three possibilities as to what the photograph is of. It is either a man with a ball, flowers, or a turkey. If you are sure you know what it is tell me. If you are not sure say 'I don't know.'"

All instructions were administered in the native tongue by means of a tape recorder; the design presented to the subject by a Tzotzil informant.

The main independent variable was the difference between shamans and non-shamans matched for age, socioeconomic status, and degree of acculturation. The main dependent variables were the subject's willingness to say "I don't know" to stimuli which were undefinable, and below the threshold of recognition, and the formal patterns to be found in the responses given throughout the experiment.

The point in each series at which the object of the series was recognizable was determined by independent experiments with native informants. These norms of objective recognition set the cutoff point in the photograph design before which a refusal to say "I don't know" was taken to indicate an imposition of form by the subject on diffuse and unorganized stimuli.

RESULTS[3]

Shamans are significantly different from non-shamans in three aspects of cognitive style. The significance of the differences is determined by the application to the data of Student's T test between matched groups. First, shamans avoid bafflement more than non-shamans. They are imposers of form on diffuse sense data. Second, shamans are more productive in their responses; they are more generative of different responses. Third, shamans seem to have available to themselves their own constructive categories and remain relatively insensitive to the alternative categories provided by the experimenter. Below I list the experimental evidence for each of these three distinctive cognitive capacities of shamans, and the statistical level of significance of the evidence.

---

[3] These results have been cited by Vogt (1969: 476).

1. HIGH AVOIDANCE OF BAFFLEMENT—IMPOSERS OF FORM ON UNSTRUCTURED SENSE DATA

In response to the photographic series where no alternative responses were given to the subject, shamans say "I don't know" less than non-shamans (.006) and classify the photos in the series at an earlier point in the sequence (.04). The dramatic nature of the shaman's refusal to say "I don't know" is revealed by comparing the number of shamans and non-shamans who say "I don't know" five or less times over the entire design. If the norms on objective visual recognition are used as a standard, a subject ought to say "I don't know" fifty-nine times during the experiment. In fifty-nine of the seventy-two photos in the whole design it is simply impossible to determine the true nature of the series.

Twenty-three of thirty three shamans respond with "I don't know" less than five times. Only eight of the thirty-three non-shamans follow the same pattern.

There is a larger increase in the number of "I don't know" responses given by non-shamans when confronting a series where no alternatives are supplied as opposed to a series where alternative responses are provided (.03). Non-shamans also delay the point in the sequence at which they are willing to classify the stimuli (.04).

These results indicate the shaman's capacity to be an *imposer* of form. He refuses to be baffled by stimuli which are diffuse and lacking in significance. It is crucial to note that the difference between the two groups in the number of "I don't know" responses is directional but *not* significant (.10) for the series where alternative responses were presented by the experimenter. In other words, when alternatives and choices of meaning are apparent there is a reduced need to utilize the special array of cognitive capacities possessed by the shaman. In response to a series with readily available alternative responses non-shamans behave in a very "shaman-like" manner. They also stop saying "I don't know." They have a form (the alternatives) with which to order the chaos set before their eyes. They, so to speak, do not need a shaman. It is in situations where significance is not clear, and alternative responses lacking that the shaman's abilities are at a premium.

The same function of the shaman as imposer of form in situations where alternative responses are not forthcoming is revealed by the point of earliest classification in the two groups. When moving from a series with provided alternatives to a series with no alternatives provided the shamans continue to impose form early in the sequence, while non-shamans switch to an "I don't know" response mode and remain baffled.

2. HIGH GENERATIVE CAPACITY—MORE PRODUCTIVE

The number of *different* categories suggested by shamans to classify photos over a fixed number of identifications per series is higher both for series with, and without, alternatives provided by the experimenter (.005 and .001). The shaman either has a richer repertoire of categories with which to classify incoming stimuli or uses his available repertoire more creatively.

3. AVAILABILITY OF OWN CONSTRUCTIVE CATEGORIES—"INNER-DIRECTEDNESS" OF RESPONSES

In those series where alternative responses were provided by the experimenter, shamans more often gave responses which were *not* included in the presented choices (.03). If we add to this consideration the fact that shamans are generally unwilling to say "I don't know" when confronted with chaotic stimulation the shaman appears to be cognitively "inner-directed," utilizing his internal classificatory powers to dominate external disorder.

It is my belief that these aspects of the cognitive style of the shaman, the avoidance of bafflement and the imposition of form, the productivity of response patterns, and the self-centeredness of classification are functions of personality and somewhat enduring across situations. The test situation was not a role context. The shamans were not recruited to perform rituals. In the case of avoidance of bafflement, it seems justified to call it a "need" to avoid bafflement. The instructions demanded "I don't know" responses. Unless the shaman, standing as he was before a diffuse and unidentifiable stimulus, found these instructions frustrating his need for certainty he could easily have said "I don't know," as so many non-shamans chose to do.

In closing this section on test results I should note that with only one exception there were no differences between the two groups in the final degree of accuracy of responses. The close-up shot of an ear was the exception. For some reason shamans had considerable difficulty in making a correct identification of the ear, even in full focus!

ROLE EXPERIENCE AND
PREEXISTING PERSONALITY

Once it has been ascertained that shamans have some distinctive cognitive capacities it might be asked whether these capacities have developed with experience in performing the role, or whether they are part of the array of personality features which exist before a man becomes a shaman, and which help filter him into the role. Considerable data of a more refined and extensive nature than I have been able to collect would be needed to resolve this issue with any rigor. I can only suggest a way to formulate the problem so as to be able to test it, and exhibit the results of the test on my more crude data.

If role experience is sufficient to account for such distinctive cognitive capacities of shamans as the need to impose form, productivity of response pattern, and "inner-directedness" of classification, then we should expect an increase in the magnitude of these variables in the responses of shamans as their experience in the role increases. If we could rank all thirty-three shamans in terms of some measure of role experience, and then rank them again in terms of the magnitude of the three distinctive cognitive variables in their response patterns, we should expect a significant correlation between the two rankings.

A number of measures of role experience suggest themselves: the number of years a man has been a shaman, the number of ceremonies he has performed, the frequency with which he performs ceremonies.

But difficulties arise when considering the ranking of shamans by their scores on variables distinctive of their cognitive style. Ideally we would like *one* measure which would indicate the extent to which a given shaman reflects in his test scores the cognition distinctive of shamans. However, we have three distinctive capacities. We do not know how to weigh and combine each of these three features into one measure. I treated all three features as equal in weight and simply added them together. This is bound to be wrong and is one reason this discussion is only suggestive.

The thirty-three shamans were ranked on all three distinctive cognitive capacities. Each ranking of thirty-three scores was divided into eight ranks. Each shaman was given a mean rank over the three rankings and partitioned again into one of eight ranks. This final rank was an ordering based on the equal weighting of the three distinctive capacities.

The final ranking was correlated with a ranking of the shamans into eight ranks or divisions on the basis of a number of measures of role experience. The number of years as shaman lent the strongest support to the role experience hypothesis but fell short of statistical significance (.14; Kendall's Rank Order Correlation Coefficient was used). The result, however, is certainly directional.

The hypothesis that cognitive capacities such as avoidance of bafflement and imposition of form on unstructured stimuli, productivity of response, and "inner-directedness" of classification are aspects of the personality which existed before the role of shaman was assumed suggests a different, although not exclusive, test of the data. Of those *non-shamans* whose cognitive styles are quantitatively the same as those of a prototypical shaman, a significant number should be in the younger half of the non-shaman sample.

The median age for non-shamans in my sample is forty years. It happens that after this age a man becoming a shaman is somewhat suspected of insincerity (Silver, 1966: 46). I noted the age of every non-shaman with "shaman-like" responses. If preexisting personality is a factor in selection for the role, we can assume that "shaman-like" personalities will have been selected for the role by the age of forty, decreasing the "shaman-like" personalities in the non-shaman sample who are over forty. The preexisting personality hypothesis also proved nonsignificant but directional ($X^2 = 1.88$, .18 significance level).

This second suggestion is even more tentative than the first. It can easily be argued that to have a "shaman-like" cognitive style is not necessarily to become a shaman. But both the role experience and the preexisting personality hypotheses test out in the right direction, and the data is limited. Perhaps a predisposing personality interacts with experience in the role, as a proper combination of sufficient data might indicate.[4]

---

[4] It is also possible that my evidence provides indirect support for the view that the process of becoming a shaman involves a sudden and radical reorganization "of values, attitudes and beliefs which 'make sense' of a hitherto confusing and anxiety-provoking world" (Wallace, 1961: 192). In such a case we do not expect statistical support for either the role-experience or preexisting personality hypotheses. The shaman's cognitive style would not have existed previous to the conversion experience, and would be a "fait accompli" soon after it.

CONCLUSION

Zinacanteco Indians believe that their shamans have distinctive cognitive capacities. An experiment indicated that indeed they do. Their special qualities include a need to avoid bafflement and impose form on unstructured stimuli, a highly productive and generative response pattern, and an "inner-directed" or self-centered style of classification.

8

MAGIC, WITCHCRAFT, AND DIVINATION

Introduction

The three concepts of magic, witchcraft, and divination are more than heuristic labels; they are real in that they represent actual classes of actions and beliefs intimately related to the human problem of control in known cultures. All men strive to control their social and physical environments and to determine, or at least to have prior knowledge of, their own lives. Through manipulation, explanation, and prediction the operations of magic, witchcraft, and divination work toward this vital human end.

Magic consists of a variety of ritual methods whereby events can be automatically influenced by supernatural means. While magic and religion have many mutual resemblances —both are supernatural, beyond the realm of experience, and dominated by symbolism and ritual—they are basically quite different. Religion is supplicative; by ritual it conciliates personal powers in order to request their favors. Magic is manipulative; it acts ritually upon impersonal powers in order automatically to make use of them. Magic is a formula or set of formulas. It is not a force as is mana. Magic is analogous to science in its use, but its premises—its theoretical bases— are supernatural and antithetical to science.

While magic is overwhelmingly private and individual in nature, there are many instances of magic being conducted publicly as an attempt to benefit a whole society. Private magic may be either malevolent (black) or well-intentioned (white); it may be designed to destroy a rival or to cure an ailing child. Public magic is always directed toward the welfare of the group which performs it, but it may be calculated to bring evil to other groups or tribes. The term "sorcerer" refers to a practitioner of black magic, while "medicine man" usually refers to a man who performs primarily white magic and cures through natural means, dealing only secondarily in black magic. The "law of sympathy," so basic to magic, will be thoroughly discussed by Sir James Frazer in the first article of this section.

The magical formula usually consists of a spoken and acted ritual, often called a "spell," and of material objects, often called "medicine." A "fetish" is an object or a bundle of objects, such as the famous Plains Indian medicine bundle, which has magical properties. While a fetish is sometimes thought to contain a spirit, it is used magically and is not, as is frequently claimed, worshiped. Neither should the term be used in the psychiatric sense of an inanimate object compulsively used in attaining sexual gratification.

When magic fails, as it often must, there are several explanations that serve to perpetuate belief in the particular formula: the ritual is said to have been incorrectly performed; the magician may have violated a taboo and thus have lost his power to perform the ritual, or there may have been strong counter-magic. When people want to believe, they will believe.

Although magic often has an emotional origin, the performance of magic is routine, and while the ritual may appear to be dramatic, it is almost always nonemotional. This is especially so if, as often happens, a client takes his complaint to a magical specialist who has no emotional involvement with the problem.

Magic gives the individual confidence in the face of fear and provides an outlet for hostility. Magic explains misfortune and failure and reveals the cause of illness. Magic assigns a human cause to terrifying events, and in so doing converts these events into a human rather than an extrahuman context. Socially, magic may act to drain off tensions which might otherwise result in physical combat and death. Unfortunately, magic creates problems as well. People die from fear of sorcery or fall ill from putatively magical attacks, and whole societies may live in constant fear of black magic. Whether magic is functionally more useful than it is harmful no one can positively say. However, magic is believed to have existed as early as the Upper Paleolithic in Europe, and it is known and practiced by all societies; this is strong positive evidence for its functional utility.

Witchcraft is the exercise of evil through an immanent power. Witchcraft, unlike sorcery, is derived from within, and cannot be learned. A witch's power to do evil may lie dormant and not be used or it may be increased by practice, but it is nearly always inherited. Whereas magic may be either malevolent or beneficent, witchcraft is invariably evil. A witch frequently has an animal form such as a cat, a werewolf, or a bat. Witches can project evil over great distances without moving, or they may transport themselves at great speeds in order to do some needed mischief. The evil eye and evil tongue are variants of witchcraft; some people can cause terrible harm simply by looking or speaking, often without evil intent. Witchcraft, like magic and divination, is undoubtedly worldwide, and its antiquity is great.

Witchcraft is far more than a grisly aberration of the human spirit; despite its macabre elements, it has positive functional value. All societies have the problem of providing an outlet for aggressions engendered by the conflicts, antagonisms, and frustrations of social living. Witches exist as convenient scapegoats for such aggressions. All societies also spawn individuals who in some degree do not find satisfactions within their culture, and a person of this sort may find an acceptable self-identity by considering himself to be a witch. Witchcraft may serve to regulate sex antagonisms (in some cultures, such as the Nupe of West Africa, witches are always women) or to provide a means of demanding cultural conformity by furnishing a criminal act or state of which deviants may be accused. Like magic, witchcraft may also explain unhappiness, disease, and bad luck. Similarly, witchcraft has its dysfunctional aspects. Witches do real harm, cause real fears, and promote dangerous conflicts. As with magic, it is difficult to construct a balance sheet which can indicate the relative value of these practices within any sociocultural system. For further information on these points the reader may consult Clyde Kluckhohn, *Navaho Witchcraft* (1944), and John Middleton and Edward Winter (eds.), *Witchcraft and Sorcery in East Africa* (1963). A recent paperback by Lucy Mair on *Witchcraft* (1969) provides a useful summary of our anthropological knowledge of the phenomena.

Divination, the art or practice of foreseeing future events or discovering hidden knowledge through supernatural means, is a cultural universal. From the Kaingang of South America, who seek answers in the volume of their belching, to the Hollywood movie star who daily consults a horoscope, divination assumes infinite forms and intensities. There are two general types of divination, inspirational and noninspirational. In the former, answers are revealed through a change in the psychology or emotional state of the individual. Shamanism, crystal gazing, and shell hearing are some inspirational forms of divination. Noninspirational divination may be either fortuitous, such as finding meanings in black cats, hairpins, sneezing, and countless other omens, or deliberate, by means of astrology, scapulimancy, chiromancy, ordeals, and the like. For a penetrating study of divination in a tribal context the reader is referred to Victor W. Turner, *Ndembu Divination: Its Symbolism and Techniques* (1961).

All men, as we know them, eagerly seek to know the unknowable and to control the uncontrollable. Divination allows man to control chance and to know the future. Divination permits the man who is immobilized by a difficult decision to make a choice, and to make it with confidence. Or have you never flipped a coin? Man is an animal doubly cursed; he knows that there is a future, and he fears that he cannot control it. That divination lessens these curses is attested to by the flourishing vigor of many forms of divinatory art in modern Western European culture, despite all the efforts of religion and science to brand such practices as sinful or ignorant.

Magic, witchcraft, and divination all aid man in some respects and trouble him in others. The articles that follow will do much to clarify the nature and function of these phenomena.

James G. Frazer

SYMPATHETIC MAGIC

Although Sir James G. Frazer was not an outstanding theorist, he was adept at compiling and classifying fact, had some feeling for problem, and stimulated a whole generation of ethnologists to take an interest in the theoretical questions involved in the subject of magic. His classic work, *The Golden Bough*, is one of the best known of all ethnological publications. Many a layman who has never heard of or read other anthropological books has at least perused this one, usually in its abridged, one-volume form.

The portion of this vast work that is reprinted here presents Frazer's well-known distinction between "imitative" and "contagious" magic. This classification, while it assuredly does not encompass the whole range of magical phenomena, does cover the greatest portion. Frazer shows that the common factor in these two kinds of magic is the sympathetic principle: things act on each other at a distance through a "secret sympathy." As long as Frazer restricted himself to classificatory interests of this sort, he remained unchallenged. But when he turned to either historical or analytic problems, he enjoyed less immunity. For example, his argument that magic is older than religion because it is psychologically simpler than the concept of spirit agents and because it is more uniform than religious cults does not stand up against criticism. As Marett and Goldenweiser have demonstrated, Frazer's separation of magic from religion has some merit, but it goes too far, because it overlooks the vast areas in which the alleged differences actually overlap and because it tends to obscure the common supernatural basis for each. Frazer's view that magic is comparable to science because both involve mental operations that are alike breaks down because, as Malinowski has insisted, the magical practitioner himself makes a distinction between things that lie in the empirical realm and those that lie in the supernatural.

The following article contains a great many illustrative examples of the nature of magic. The functions of magic are not explicitly considered, but many of them may be recognized in Frazer's descriptions of diverse magical practices. It is cautioned that the author's closing dictum that magic has been ". . . the mother of freedom and truth," can be true only in a most allegorical sense.

Reprinted in abridged form from James George Frazer, *The Golden Bough: A Study in Magic and Religion* (12 vols.; 3d ed., rev. and enl.; London: Macmillan & Co., Ltd., 1911–1915), I, 52–219, by permission of Trinity College, Cambridge, Macmillan & Co., Ltd., and St. Martin's Press, Inc.

1 THE PRINCIPLES OF MAGIC

If we analyze the principles of thought on which magic is based, they will probably be found to resolve themselves into two: first, that like produces like, or that an effect resembles its cause; and, second, that things which have once been in contact with each other continue to act on each other at a distance after the physical contact has been severed. The former principle may be called the "Law of Similarity," the latter the "Law of Contact or Contagion." From the first of these principles, namely the Law of Similarity, the magician infers that he can produce any effect he desires merely by imitating it: from the second he infers that whatever he does to a material object will affect equally the person with whom the object was once in contact, whether it formed part of his body or not. Charms based on the Law of Similarity may be called "Homeopathic or Imitative Magic." Charms based on the Law of Contact or Contagion may be called "Contagious Magic." To denote the first of these branches of magic the term Homeopathic is perhaps preferable, for the alternative term Imitative or Mimetic suggests, if it does not imply, a conscious agent who imitates, thereby limiting the scope of magic too narrowly. For the same principles which the magician applies in the practice of his art are implicitly believed by him to regulate the operations of inanimate nature; in other words, he tacitly assumes that the Laws of Similarity and Contact are of universal application and are not limited to human actions. In short, magic is a spurious system of natural law as well as a fallacious guide of conduct; it is a false science as well as an abortive art. Regarded as a system of natural law, that is, as a statement of the rules which determine the sequence of events throughout the world, it may be called "Theoretical Magic": regarded as a set of precepts which human beings observe in order to compass their ends, it may be called "Practical Magic." At the same time it is to be borne in mind that the primitive magician knows magic only on its practical side; he never analyzes the mental processes on which his practice is based, never reflects on the abstract principles involved in his actions. With him, as with the vast majority of men, logic is implicit, not explicit; he reasons, just as he digests his food, in complete ignorance of the intellectual and physiological processes which are essential to the one operation and to the other. In short, to him magic is always an art, never a science; the very idea of science is lacking in his undeveloped mind. It is for the philosophic student to trace the train of thought which underlies the magician's practice; to draw out the few simple threads of which the tangled skein is composed; to disengage the abstract principles from their concrete applications; in short, to discern the spurious science behind the bastard art.

If my analysis of the magician's logic is correct, its two great principles turn out to be merely two different misapplications of the association of ideas. Homeopathic magic is founded on the association of ideas by similarity: contagious magic is founded on the association of ideas by contiguity. Homeopathic magic commits the mistake of assuming that things which resemble each other are the same: contagious magic commits the mistake of assuming that things which have once been in contact with each other are always in contact. But in practice the two branches are often combined; or, to be more exact, while homeopathic or imitative magic may be practiced by itself, contagious magic will generally be found to involve an application of the homeopathic or imitative principle. Thus generally stated the two things may be a little difficult to grasp, but they will readily become intelligible when they are illustrated by particular examples. Both trains of thought are in fact extremely simple and elementary. It could hardly be otherwise, since they are familiar in the concrete, though certainly not in the abstract, to the crude intelligence not only of the savage, but of ignorant and dull-witted people everywhere. Both branches of magic, the homeopathic and the contagious, may conveniently be comprehended under the general name of "Sympathetic Magic," since both assume that things act on each other at a distance through a secret sympathy, the impulse being transmitted from one to the other by means of what we may conceive as a kind of invisible ether, not unlike that which is postulated by modern science for a precisely similar purpose, namely, to explain how things can physically affect each other through a space which appears to be empty.

It may be convenient to tabulate as follows the branches of magic according to the laws of thought which underlie them:

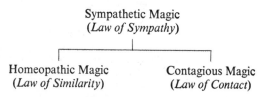

Sympathetic Magic
(*Law of Sympathy*)

Homeopathic Magic   Contagious Magic
(*Law of Similarity*)   (*Law of Contact*)

I will now illustrate these two great branches of sympathetic magic by examples, beginning with homeopathic magic.

2. HOMEOPATHIC OR IMITATIVE MAGIC

Perhaps the most familiar application of the principle that like produces like is the attempt which has been made by many peoples in many ages to injure or destroy an enemy by injuring or destroying an image of him, in the belief that just as the image suffers, so does the man, and that when it perishes he must die. A few instances out of many may be given to prove at once the wide diffusion of the practice over the world and its remarkable persistence through the ages. For thousands of years ago it was known to the sorcerers of ancient India, Babylon, and Egypt, as well as of Greece and Rome, and at this day it is still resorted to by cunning and malignant savages in Australia, Africa, and Scotland. Thus the North American Indians, we are told, believe that by drawing the figure of a person in sand, ashes, or clay, or by considering any object as his body, and then pricking it with a sharp stick or doing it any other injury, they inflict a corresponding injury on the person represented. So when a Cora Indian of Mexico wishes to kill a man, he makes a figure of him out of burnt clay, strips of cloth, and so forth, and then, muttering incantations, runs thorns through the head or stomach of the figure to make his victim suffer correspondingly.

If homeopathic or imitative magic, working by means of images, has commonly been practiced for the spiteful purpose of putting obnoxious people out of the world, it has also, though far more rarely, been employed with the benevolent intention of helping others into it. In other words, it has been used to facilitate childbirth and to procure offspring for barren women. Thus among the Eskimos of Bering Strait a barren woman desirous of having a son will consult a shaman, who commonly makes, or causes her husband to make, a small doll-like image over which he performs certain secret rites, and the woman is directed to sleep with it under her pillow. In Anno, a district of West Africa, women may often be seen carrying wooden dolls strapped, like babies, on their backs as a cure for sterility. In the seventh month of a woman's pregnancy common people in Java observe a ceremony which is plainly designed to facilitate the real birth by mimicking it. Husband and wife repair to a well or to the bank of a neighboring river. The upper part of the woman's body is bare, but young banana leaves are fastened under her arms, a small opening, or rather fold, being left in the leaves in front. Through this opening or fold in the leaves on his wife's body the husband lets fall from above a weaver's shuttle. An old woman receives the shuttle as it falls, takes it up in her arms and dandles it as if it were a baby, saying, "Oh, what a dear little child! Oh, what a beautiful little child!" Then the husband lets an egg slip through the fold, and when it lies on the ground as an emblem of the afterbirth,

he takes his sword and cuts through the banana leaf at the place of the fold, obviously as if he were severing the navel-string.

The same principle of make-believe, so dear to children, has led other peoples to employ a simulation of birth as a form of adoption, and even as a mode of restoring a supposed dead person to life. If you pretend to give birth to a boy, or even to a great bearded man who has not a drop of your blood in his veins, then, in the eyes of primitive law and philosophy, that boy or man is really your son to all intents and purposes. Thus Diodorus tells us that when Zeus persuaded his jealous wife Hera to adopt Hercules, the goddess got into bed, and clasping the burly hero to her bosom, pushed him through her robes and let him fall to the ground in imitation of a real birth; and the historian adds that in his own day the same mode of adopting children was practiced by the barbarians. At the present time it is said to be still in use in Bulgaria and among the Bosnian Turks. A woman will take a boy whom she intends to adopt and push or pull him through her clothes; ever afterwards he is regarded as her very son, and inherits the whole property of his adoptive parents. In ancient Greece any man who had been supposed erroneously to be dead, and for whom in his absence funeral rites had been performed, was treated as dead to society till he had gone through the form of being born again. He was passed through a woman's lap, then washed, dressed in swaddling clothes, and put out to nurse. Not until this ceremony had been punctually performed might he mix freely with living folk.

Another beneficent use of homeopathic magic is to heal or prevent sickness. In ancient Greece, when a man died of dropsy, his children were made to sit with their feet in water until the body was burned. This was supposed to prevent the disease from attacking them. In Germany yellow turnips, gold coins, gold rings, saffron, and other yellow things are still esteemed remedies for jaundice, just as a stick of red sealing wax carried on the person cures the red eruption popularly known as St. Anthony's fire, or the bloodstone with its red spots allays bleeding. Another cure prescribed in Germany for St. Anthony's fire is to rub the patient with ashes from a house that has been burned down; for it is easy to see that as the fire died out in that house, so St. Anthony's fire will die out in that man.

One of the great merits of homeopathic magic is that it enables the cure to be performed on the person of the doctor instead of on that of his victim, who is thus relieved of all trouble and inconvenience, while he sees his medical man writhe in anguish before him. For example, the peasants of Perche, in France, labor under the impression that a prolonged fit of vomiting is brought about by the patient's stomach becoming unhooked, as they call it, and so falling down. Accordingly, a practitioner is called in to restore the organ to its proper place. After hearing the symptoms he at once throws himself into the most horrible contortions, for the purpose of unhooking his own stomach. Having succeeded in the effort, he next hooks it up again in another series of contortions and grimaces, while the patient experiences a corresponding relief. Fee five cents. In like manner a Dyak medicine man, who has been fetched in a case of illness, will lie down and pretend to be dead. He is accordingly treated like a corpse, is bound up in mats, taken out of the house, and deposited on the ground. After about an hour the other medicine men loose the pretended dead man and bring him to life; and as he recovers, the sick person is supposed to recover too.

Further, homeopathic and in general sympathetic magic plays a great part in the measures taken by the rude hunter or fishermen to secure an abundant supply of food. On the principle that like produces like, many things are done by him and his friends in deliberate imitation of the result which he seeks to attain; and, on the other hand, many things are scrupulously avoided because they bear some more or less fanciful resemblance to others which would really be disastrous.

Nowhere is the theory of sympathetic magic more systematically carried into practice for the maintenance of the food supply than in the barren region of Central Australia. Here the tribes are divided into a number of totem clans, each of which is charged with the duty of propagating and multiplying their totem for the good of the community by means of magical ceremonies and incantations. The great majority of the totems are edible animals and plants, and the general result supposed to be accomplished by these ceremonies or *intichiuma*, as the Arunta call them, is that of supplying the tribe with food and other necessaries. Often the rites consist of an imitation of the effect which the people desire to produce; in other words, their magic is of the homeopathic or imitative sort. Thus among the Arunta the men of the witchetty-grub totem perform a series of elaborate ceremonies for multiplying the grub which the other members of the tribe use as food. One of the ceremonies is a pantomime representing the fully developed insect in the act of emerging from the chrysalis.

The Indians of British Columbia live largely upon the fish which abound in their seas and rivers. If the fish do not come in due season, and the Indians are hungry, a Nootka wizard will make an image of a swimming fish and put it into the water in the direction from which the fish usually appear. This ceremony, accompanied by a prayer to the fish to come, will cause them to arrive at once. The islanders of Torres Straits use models of dugong and turtles to charm dugong and turtle to their destruction. The Toradjas of Central Celebes believe that things of the same sort attract each other by means of their indwelling spirits or vital ether. Hence they hang up the jawbones of deer and wild pigs in their houses, in order that the spirits which animate these bones may draw the living creatures of the same kind into the path of the hunter. In the island of Nias, when a wild pig has fallen into the pit prepared for it, the animal is taken out and its back is rubbed with nine fallen leaves, in the belief that this will make nine more wild pigs fall into the pit, just as the nine leaves fell from the tree.

The western tribes of British New Guinea employ a charm to aid the hunter in spearing dugong or turtle. A small beetle, which haunts coconut trees, is placed in the hole of the spear haft into which the spearhead fits. This is supposed to make the spearhead stick fast in the dugong or turtle, just as the beetle sticks fast to a man's skin when it bites him. When a Cambodian hunter has set his nets and taken nothing, he strips himself naked, goes some way off, then strolls up to the net as if he did not see it, lets himself be caught in it, and cries, "Hello! what's this? I'm afraid I'm caught." After that the net is sure to catch game. A Malay who has baited a trap for crocodiles, and is awaiting results, is careful in eating his curry always to begin by swallowing three lumps of rice successively; for this helps the bait to slide more easily down the crocodile's throat. He is equally scrupulous not to take any bones out of his curry; for, if he did, it seems clear that the sharp-pointed stick on which the bait is skewered would similarly work itself loose, and the crocodile would get off with the bait.

Hence in these circumstances it is prudent for the hunter, before he begins his meal, to get somebody else to take the bones out of his curry, otherwise he may at any moment have to choose between swallowing a bone and losing the crocodile.

This last rule is an instance of the things which the hunter abstains from doing lest, on the principle that like produces like, they should spoil his luck. For it is to be observed that the system of sympathetic magic is not merely composed of positive precepts; it comprises a very large number of negative precepts, that is, prohibitions. It tells you not merely what to do, but also what to leave undone. The positive precepts are charms: the negative precepts are taboos. In fact the whole doctrine of taboos, or at all events a large part of it, would seem to be only a special application of sympathetic magic, with its two great laws of similarity and contact. Though these laws are certainly not formulated in so many words nor even conceived in the abstract by the savage, they are nevertheless implicitly believed by him to regulate the course of nature quite independently of human will. He thinks that if he acts in a certain way, certain consequences will inevitably follow in virtue of one or the other of these laws; and if the consequences of a particular act appear to him likely to prove disagreeable or dangerous, he is naturally careful not to act in that way lest he should incur them. In other words, he abstains from doing that which, in accordance with his mistaken notions of cause and effect, he falsely believes would injure him; in short, he subjects himself to a taboo. Thus taboo is so far a negative application of practical magic. Positive magic or sorcery says, "Do this in order that so and so may happen." Negative magic or taboo says, "Do not do this, lest so and so should happen." The aim of positive magic or sorcery is to produce a desired event; the aim of negative magic or taboo is to avoid an undesirable one. But both consequences, the desirable and the undesirable, are supposed to be brought about in accordance with the laws of similarity and contact. And just as the desired consequence is not really effected by the observance of a magical ceremony, so the dreaded consequence does not really result from the violation of a taboo. If the supposed evil necessarily followed a breach of taboo, the taboo would not be a taboo but a precept of morality or common sense. It is not a taboo to say, "Do not put your hand in the Fire"; it is a rule of common sense, because the forbidden action entails a real, not an imaginary, evil. In short, those negative precepts which we call taboo are just as vain and futile as those positive precepts which we call sorcery. The two things are merely opposite sides or poles of one great disastrous fallacy, a mistaken conception of the association of ideas. Of that fallacy, sorcery is the positive and taboo the negative pole. If we give the general name of magic to the whole erroneous system, both theoretical and practical, then taboo may be defined as the negative side of practical magic. To put this in tabular form:

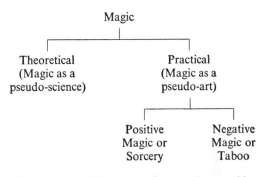

I have made these remarks on taboo and its relations to magic because I am about to give some instances of taboos observed by hunters, fishermen, and others, and I wished to show that they fall under the head of Sympathetic Magic, being only particular applications of that general theory. Among the Eskimos of Baffin Land boys are forbidden to play cat's cradle, because if they did so their fingers might in later life become entangled in the harpoon-line. Here the taboo is obviously an application of the law of similarity, which is the basis of homeopathic magic; as the child's fingers are entangled by the string in playing cat's cradle, so they will be entangled by the harpoon-line when he is a man and hunts whales. Again, among the Huzuls of the Carpathian Mountains, the wife of a hunter may not spin while her husband is eating, or the game will turn and wind like the spindle, and the hunter will be unable to hit it. Here again the taboo is clearly derived from the law of similarity. So, too, in most parts of ancient Italy women were forbidden by law to spin on the highroads as they walked, or even to carry their spindles openly, because any such action was believed to injure the crops. Probably the notion was that the twirling of the spindle would twirl the cornstalks and prevent them from growing straight. So, too, among the Ainos of Saghalien a pregnant woman may not spin nor twist ropes for two months before her delivery, because they think that if she did so the child's guts might be entangled like the thread. For a like reason in Bilaspore, a district of India, when the chief men of a village meet in council no one present should twirl a spindle; for they think that if such a thing were to happen, the discussion, like the spindle, would move in a circle and never be wound up. In the East Indian Islands of Saparoea, Haroekoe, and Noessalaut, any one who comes to the house of a hunter must walk straight in; he may not loiter at the door, for were he to do so, the game would in like manner stop in front of the hunter's snares and then turn back, instead of being caught in the trap. For a similar reason it is a rule with the Toradjas of Central Celebes that no one may stand or loiter on the ladder of a house where there is a pregnant woman, for such delay would retard the birth of the child; and in various parts of Sumatra the woman herself in these circumstances is forbidden to stand at the door or on the top rung of the house-ladder under pain of suffering hard labor for her imprudence in neglecting so elementary a precaution.

Among the taboos observed by savages none perhaps are more numerous or important than the prohibitions to eat certain foods, and of such prohibitions many are demonstrably derived from the law of similarity and are accordingly examples of negative magic. Just as the savage eats many animals or plants in order to acquire certain desirable qualities with which he believes them to be endowed, so he avoids eating many other animals and plants lest he should acquire certain undesirable qualities with which he believes them to be infected. In eating the former he practices positive magic; in abstaining from the latter he practices negative magic.

The reader may have observed that in some of the foregoing examples of taboos the magical influence is supposed to operate at considerable distances; thus among the Blackfeet Indians the wives and children of an eagle hunter are forbidden to use an awl during his absence, lest the eagles should scratch the distant husband and father; and again no male animal may be killed in the house of a Malagasy soldier while he is away at the wars, lest the killing of the animal should entail the killing of the man. This belief in the sympathic influence exerted on each other by persons or things at a distance is of the essence of magic. Whatever doubts science may entertain as to the possibility of action at a distance, magic has none; faith in telepathy is one of its first principles. A modern advocate of the influence of mind upon mind at a distance would have no difficulty in convincing a savage; the savage believed in it long ago, and what is more, he acted on his belief with a logical consistency such as his civilized brother in the faith has not yet, so far as I am aware, exhibited in his conduct. For the savage is convinced not only that magical ceremonies affect persons and things afar off, but that the simplest acts of daily life may do so too. Hence on important occasions the behavior of friends and relations at a distance is often regulated by a more or less elaborate code of rules, the neglect of which by the one set of persons would, it is supposed, entail misfortune or even death on the absent ones. In particular when a party of men are out hunting or fighting, their kinsfolk at home are often expected to do certain things or to abstain from doing certain others, for the sake of ensuring the safety and success of the distant hunters or warriors. I will now give some instances of this magical telepathy both in its positive and in its negative aspect.

In Laos when an elephant hunter is starting for the chase, he warns his wife not to cut her hair or oil her body in his absence; for if she cut her hair the elephant would burst the toils, if she oiled herself it would slip through them. When a Dyak village has turned out to hunt wild pigs in the jungle, the people who stay at home may not touch oil or water with their hands during the absence of their friends; for if they did so, the hunters would all be "butter-fingered" and the prey would slip through their hands. While a Gilyak hunter is pursuing the game in the forest, his children at home are forbidden to make drawings on wood or on sand; for they fear that if the children did so, the paths in the forest would become as perplexed as the lines in the drawings, so that the hunter might lose his way and never return. A Russian political prisoner once taught some Gilyak children to read and write; but their parents forbade them to write when any of their fathers was away from home; for it seemed to them that writing was a peculiarly complicated form of drawing, and they stood aghast at the idea of the danger to which such a drawing would expose the hunters out in the wild woods.

Many of the indigenous tribes of Sarawak are firmly persuaded that were the wives to commit adultery while their husbands are searching for camphor in the jungle, the camphor obtained by the men would evaporate. Husbands can discover, by certain knots in the tree, when their wives are unfaithful; and it is said that in former days many women were killed by jealous husbands on no better evidence than that of these knots. Further, the wives dare not touch a comb while their husbands are away collecting the camphor; for if they did so, the interstices between the fibers of the tree, instead of being filled with the precious crystals, would be empty like the spaces between the teeth of a comb. In the Kei Islands, to the southwest of New Guinea, as soon as a vessel that is about to sail for a distant port has been launched, the part of the beach on which it lay is covered as speedily as possible with palm branches, and becomes sacred. No one may thenceforth cross that spot till the ship comes home. To cross it sooner would cause the vessel to perish. Moreover, all the time that the voyage lasts three or four young girls, specially chosen for the duty, are supposed to remain in sympathetic connection with the mariners and to contribute by their behavior to the safety of and success of the voyage.

Where beliefs like these prevail as to the sympathetic connection between friends at a distance, we need not wonder that above everything else, war, with its stern yet stirring appeal to some of the deepest and tenderest of human emotions, should quicken in the anxious relations left behind a desire to turn the sympathetic bond to the utmost account for the benefit of the dear ones who may at any moment be fighting and dying far away. Hence, to secure an end so natural and laudable, friends at home are apt to resort to devices which will strike us as pathetic or ludicrous, according as we consider their object or the means adopted to effect it. Thus in some districts of Borneo, when a Dyak is out headhunting, his wife or, if he is unmarried, his sister must wear a sword day and night in order that he may always be thinking of his weapons; and she may not sleep during the day nor go to bed before two in the morning, lest her husband or brother should thereby be surprised in his sleep by an enemy. Among the Sea Dyaks of Banting in Sarawak the women strictly observe an elaborate code of rules while the men are away fighting. Some of the rules are negative and some are positive, but all alike are based on the principles of magical homeopathy and telepathy. Amongst them are the following. The women must wake very early in the morning and open the windows as soon as it is light; otherwise their absent husbands will oversleep themselves. The women may not oil their hair, or the men will slip. The women may neither sleep nor doze by day, or the men will be drowsy on the march. The women must cook and scatter popcorn on the veranda every morning; so will the men be agile in their movements. The rooms must be kept very tidy, all boxes being placed near the walls; for if any one were to stumble over them, the absent husbands would fall and be at the mercy of the foe. At every meal a little rice must be left in the pot and put aside; so will the men far away always have something to eat and need never go hungry. On no account may the women sit at the loom till their legs grow cramped, otherwise their husbands will likewise be stiff in their joints and unable to rise up quickly or to run away from the foe. So in order to keep their husbands' joints supple the women often vary their labors at the loom by walking up and down the veranda. Further, they may not cover up their faces, or the men would not be able to find their way through the tall grass or jungle. Again, the women may not sew with a needle, or the men will tread on the sharp spikes set by the enemy in the path. Should a wife prove unfaithful while her husband is away, he will lose his life in the enemy's country.

Among the Thompson Indians of British Columbia, when the men were on the warpath, the women performed dances at frequent intervals. These dances were believed to ensure the success of the expedition. The dancers flourished their knives, threw long, sharp-pointed sticks forward, or drew sticks with hooked ends repeatedly backward and forward. Throwing the sticks forward was symbolic of piercing or warding off the enemy, and drawing them back was symbolic of drawing their own men from danger. The hook at the end of the stick was particularly well adapted to serve the purpose of a life-saving apparatus. The women always pointed their weapons towards the enemy's country. They painted their faces red and sang as they danced, and they prayed to the weapons to preserve their husbands and help them to kill many foes. Some had eagledown stuck on the points of their sticks. When the dance was over, these weapons were hidden. If a woman whose husband was at the war thought she saw hair or a piece of scalp on the weapon when she took it out, she knew that her husband had killed an enemy. But if she saw a stain of blood on it, she knew he was wounded or dead. When the men of the Yuki tribe of Indians in California were away fighting, the women at home did not sleep; they danced continually in a circle, chanting and waving leafy wands. For they said that if they danced all the time, their husbands would not grow tired. When a band of Carib Indians of the Orinoco had gone on the warpath, their friends left in the village used to calculate as nearly as they could the exact moment when the absent warriors would be advancing to attack the enemy. Then they took two lads, laid them down on a bench, and inflicted a most severe scouring on their bare backs. This the youths submitted to without a murmur, supported in their sufferings by the firm conviction, in which they had been bred from childhood, that on the constancy and fortitude with which they bore the cruel ordeal depended the valor and success of their comrades in the battle.

Among the many beneficent uses to which a mistaken ingenuity has applied the principle of homeopathic or imitative magic, is that of causing trees and plants to bear fruit in due season. In Thüringen the man who sows flax carries the seed in a long bag which reaches from shoulders to his knees, and he walks with long strides, so that the bag sways to and fro on his back. It is believed that this will cause the flax to wave in the wind. In the interior of Sumatra rice is sown by women who, in sowing, let their hair hang loose down their back, in order that the rice may grow luxuriantly and have long stalks. Similarly, in ancient Mexico a festival was held in honor of the goddess of maize, or "the long-haired mother," as she was called. It began at the time "when the plant had attained its full growth, and fibers shooting forth from the top of the green ear indicated that the grain was fully formed. During this festival the women wore their long hair unbound, shaking and tossing it in the dances which were the chief features in the ceremonial, in order that the tassel of the maize might grow in like profusion, that the grain might be correspondingly large and flat, and that the people might have abundance."

The notion that a person can influence a plant homeopathically by his act or condition comes out clearly in a remark made by a Malay woman. Being asked why she stripped the upper part of her body naked in reaping the rice, she explained that she did it to make the rice-husks thinner, as she was tired of pounding thick-husked rice. Clearly, she thought that the less clothing she wore the less husk there would be on the rice. The magic virtue of a pregnant woman to communicate fertility is known to Bavarian and Austrian peasants, who think that if you give the first fruit of a tree to a woman with child to eat, the trees will bring forth abundantly next year. On the other hand, the Baganda believe that a barren wife infects her husband's garden with her own sterility and prevents the trees from bearing fruit; hence a childless woman is generally divorced.

Thus on the theory of homeopathic magic a person can influence vegetation either for good or for evil according to the good or the bad character of his acts or states: for example, a fruitful woman makes plants fruitful, a barren woman makes them barren. Hence this belief in the noxious and infectious nature of certain personal qualities or accidents has given rise to a number of prohibitions or rules of avoidance: people abstain from doing certain things lest they should homeopathically infect the fruits of the earth with their own undesirable state or condition. All such customs of abstention or rules of avoidance are examples of negative magic or taboo.

In the foregoing cases a person is supposed to influence vegetation homeopathically. He infects trees or plants with qualities or accidents, good or bad, resembling and derived from his own. But on the principle of homeopathic magic the influence is mutual: the plant can infect the man just as much as the man can infect the plant. In magic, as I believe in physics, action and reaction are equal and opposite. The Cherokee Indians are adept in practical botany of the homeopathic sort. Thus wiry roots of the catgut plant or devil's shoestring (*Tephrosia*) are so tough that they can almost stop a plowshare in the furrow. Hence Cherokee women wash their hands with a decoction of the roots to make the hair strong, and Cherokee ballplayers wash themselves with it to toughen their muscles. It is a Galelareese belief that if you eat a fruit which has fallen to the ground, you will yourself contract a disposition to stumble and fall; and that if you partake of something which has been forgotten (such as a sweet potato left in the pot or a banana in the fire), you will become forgetful. The Galelareese are also of the opinion that if a woman were to consume two bananas growing from a single head she would give birth to twins. The Guarani Indians of South America thought that woman would become a mother of twins if she ate a double grain of millet. Near Charlotte Waters, in Central Australia, there is a tree which sprang up to mark the spot where a blind man died. It is called the Blind Tree by the natives, who think that if it were cut down all the people of the neighborhood would become blind. A man who wishes to deprive his enemy of sight need only go to the tree by himself and rub it, muttering his wish and exhorting the magic virtue to go forth and do its baleful work. In this last example the infectious quality, though it emanates directly from a tree, is derived originally from a man —namely, the blind man—who was buried at the place where the tree grew. Similarly, the Central Australians believe that a certain group of stones at Undiara are the petrified boils of an old man who long ago plucked them from his body and left them there; hence any man who wishes to infect his enemy with boils will go to these stones and throw miniature spears at them, taking care that the points of the spears strike the stones. Then the spears are picked up, and thrown one by one in the direction of the person whom it is intended to injure. The spears carry with them the magic virtue from the stones, and the result is an eruption of painful boils on the body of the victim. Sometimes a whole group of people can be afflicted in this way by a skillful magician.

These examples introduce us to a fruitful branch of homeopathic magic, namely to that department of it which works by means of the dead; for just as the dead can neither see nor hear nor speak, so you may on homeopathic principles render people blind, deaf, and dumb by the use of dead men's bones or anything else that is tainted by the infection of death. Thus among the Galelareese, when a young man goes a-wooing at night, he takes a little earth from a grave and strews it on the roof of his sweetheart's house just above the place where her parents sleep. This, he fancies, will prevent them from waking while he converses with his beloved, since the earth from the grave will make them sleep as sound as the dead. Burglars in all ages and many lands have been patrons of this species of magic, which is very useful to them in the exercise of their profession. Thus a South Slavonian housebreaker sometimes begins operations by throwing a dead man's bone over the house, saying, with pungent sarcasm, "As this bone may waken, so may these people waken"; after that not a soul in the house can keep his or her eyes open. Similarly, in Java the burglar takes earth from a grave and sprinkles it round the house which he intends to rob; this throws the inmates into a deep sleep. In Europe similar properties were ascribed to the Hand of Glory, which was the dried and pickled hand of a man who had been hanged. If a candle made of the fat of a malefactor who had also died on the gallows was lighted and placed in the Hand of Glory as in a candlestick, it rendered motionless all persons to whom it was presented; they could not stir a finger any more than if they were dead. An ancient Greek robber or burglar thought he could silence and put to flight the fiercest watchdogs by carrying with him a brand plucked from a funeral pyre. Again, Servian and Bulgarian women who chafe at the restraints of domestic life will take the copper coins from the eyes of a corpse, wash them in wine or water, and give the liquid to their husbands to drink. After swallowing it, the husbands will be as blind to his wife's peccadilloes as the dead man was on whose eyes the coins were laid.

Again, animals are often conceived to possess qualities or properties which might be useful to man, and homeopathic or imitative magic seeks to communicate these properties to human beings in various ways. Thus some Bechuanas wear a ferret as a charm, because, being very tenacious of life, it will make them difficult to kill. Others wear a certain insect, mutilated, but living, for a similar purpose. Yet other Bechuana warriors wear the hair of a hornless ox among their own hair, and the skin of a frog on their mantle, because a frog is slippery, and the ox, having no horns, is hard to catch; so the man who is provided with these charms believes that he will be as hard to hold as the ox and the frog. One of the ancient books of India prescribes that when a sacrifice is offered for victory, the earth out of which the altar is to be made should be taken from a place where a boar has been wallowing, since the strength of the boar will be in that earth. When you are playing the one-stringed lute, and your fingers are stiff, the thing to do is to catch some long-legged field spiders and roast them, and then rub your fingers with the ashes; that will make your fingers as lithe and nimble as the spiders' legs—at least so think the Galelareese. Among the western tribes of

British New Guinea, a man who has killed a snake will burn it and smear his legs with the ashes when he goes into the forest; for no snake will bite him for some days afterwards. If a South Slavonian has a mind to pilfer and steal at market, he has nothing to do but to burn a blind cat, and then throw a pinch of its ashes over the person with whom he is haggling; after that he can take what he likes from the booth, and the owner will not be a bit the wiser, having become as blind as the deceased cat with whose ashes he has been sprinkled. The thief may even ask boldly "Did I pay for it?" and the deluded huckster will reply, "Why certainly."

On the principle of homeopathic magic, inanimate things, as well as plants and animals, may diffuse blessing or bane around them, according to their own intrinsic nature and the skill of the wizard to tap or dam, as the case may be, the stream of weal or woe. In Samarkand women give a baby sugar candy to suck and put glue in the palm of its hand, in order that when the child grows up his words may be sweet and precious things may stick to his hands as if they were glued. The Greeks thought that a garment made from a fleece of a sheep that had been torn by a wolf would hurt the wearer, setting up an itch or irritation in his skin. They were also of the opinion that if a stone which had been bitten by a dog were dropped in wine, it would make all who drank of that wine to fall out among themselves. Among the Arabs of Moab a childless woman often borrows the robe of a woman who has had many children, hoping with the robe to acquire the fruitfulness of its owner. The Caffres of Sofala, in East Africa, had a great dread of being struck with anything hollow, such as a reed or a straw, and greatly preferred being thrashed with a good thick cudgel or an iron bar, even though it hurt very much. For they thought that if a man were beaten with anything hollow, his inside would waste away till he died.

In Madagascar a mode of counteracting the levity of fortune is to bury a stone at the foot of the heavy house-post. The common custom of swearing upon a stone may be based partly on a belief that the strength and stability of the stone lend confirmation to an oath. Thus the old Danish historian Saxo Grammaticus tells us that "the ancients, when they were to choose a king, were wont to stand on stones planted in the ground, and to proclaim their votes, in order to foreshadow from the steadfastness of the stones that the deed would be

lasting." But while a general magical efficacy may be supposed to reside in all stones by reason of their common properties of weight and solidity, special magical virtues are attributed to particular stones, or kinds of stone, in accordance with their individual or specific qualities of shape and color. The Indians of Peru employed certain stones for the increase of maize, others for the increase of potatoes, and others again for the increase of cattle. The stones used to make maize grow were fashioned in the likeness of cobs of maize, and the stones destined to multiply cattle had the shape of sheep. The ancients set great store on the magical qualities of precious stones; indeed it has been maintained, with great show of reason, that such stones were used as amulets long before they were worn as mere ornaments. Thus the Greeks gave the name of tree-agate to a stone which exhibits treelike markings, and they thought that if two of these gems were tied to the horns or neck of oxen at the plow, the crop would be sure to be plentiful. Again, they recognized a milkstone which produced an abundant supply of milk in women if only they drank it dissolved in honey-mead. Milkstones are used for the same purpose by Greek women in Crete and Melos at the present day; in Albania nursing mothers wear the stones in order to ensure an abundant flow of milk. Again, the Greeks believed in a stone which cured snake bites, and hence was named the snakestone; to test its efficacy you had only to grind the stone to powder and sprinkle the powder on the wound. The wine-colored amethyst received its name, which means "not drunken," because it was supposed to keep the wearer of it sober; and two brothers who desired to live at unity were advised to carry magnets about with them, which, by drawing the twain together, would clearly prevent them from falling out.

Dwellers by the sea cannot fail to be impressed by the sight of its ceaseless ebb and flow, and are apt, on the principles of that rude philosophy of sympathy and resemblance which here engages our attention, to trace a subtle relation, a secret harmony, between its tides and the life of man, of animals, and of plants. In the flowing tide they see not merely a symbol but a cause of exuberance, of prosperity, and of life, while in the ebbing tide they discern a real agent as well as a melancholy emblem of failure, of weakness, and of death. The Breton peasant fancies that clover sown when the tide is coming in will grow well, but that if the plant be sown at low water or when the tide is going out, it will never reach maturity, and that the cows which feed on it will burst. His wife believes that the best butter is made when the tide has just turned and is beginning to flow, that milk which foams in the churn will go on foaming till the hour of high water is past, and that water drawn from the well or milk extracted from the cow while the tide is rising will boil up in the pot or saucepan and overflow into the fire. According to some of the ancients, the skins of seals, even after they had been parted from their bodies, remained in secret sympathy with the sea, and were observed to ruffle when the tide was on the ebb. Another ancient belief, attributed to Aristotle, was that no creature can die except at ebb tide. In Portugal, all along the coast of Wales, and on some parts of the coast of Brittany, a belief is said to prevail that people are born when the tide comes in, and die when it goes out. Dickens attests the existence of the same superstition in England. "People can't die, along the coast," said Mr. Peggotty, "except when the tide's pretty nigh out. They can't be born, unless it's pretty nigh in—not properly born till flood."

Another application of the maxim that like produces like is seen in the Chinese belief that the fortunes of a town are deeply affected by its shape, and that they must vary according to the character of the thing which that shape most nearly resembles. Thus it is related that long ago the town of Tsuen-cheu-fu, the outlines of which are like those of a carp, frequently fell a prey to the depredations of the neighboring city of Yung-chun, which is shaped like a fishing net, until the inhabitants of the former town conceived the plan of erecting two tall pagodas in their midst. These pagodas, which still tower above the city of Tsuen-cheu-fu, have ever since exercised the happiest influence over its destiny by intercepting the imaginary net before it could descend and entangle in its meshes the imaginary carp.

Sometimes homeopathic or imitative magic is called in to annul an evil omen by accomplishing it in mimicry. The effect is to circumvent destiny by substituting a mock calamity for a real one. In Madagascar this mode of cheating the fates is reduced to a regular system. Here every mans' fortune is determined by the day or hour of his birth, and if that happens to be an unlucky one his fate is sealed, unless the mischief can be extracted, as the phrase goes, by means of a substitute. The ways of extracting the mischief are various. For example, if a man is born on the first day of the second month (February), his house will be burnt down when he comes of age. To take time by the forelock and avoid this catastrophe, the friends of the infant will set up a shed in a field or in a cattle fold and burn it. If the ceremony is to be really effective, the child and his mother should be placed in the shed and only plucked, like brands, from the burning hut before it is too late. Once more, if fortune has frowned on a man at his birth and penury has marked him for her own, he can easily erase the mark in question by purchasing a couple of cheap pearls, price three halfpence, and burying them. For who but the rich of this world can thus afford to fling pearls away?

3. CONTAGIOUS MAGIC

Thus far we have been considering chiefly that branch of sympathetic magic which may be called homeopathic or imitative. Its leading principle, as we have seen, is that like produces like, or, in other words, that an effect resembles its cause. The other great branch of sympathetic magic, which I have called Contagious Magic, proceeds upon the notion that things which have once been conjoined must remain ever afterwards, even when quite dissevered from each other, in such a sympathetic relation that whatever is done to the one must similarly affect the other. Thus the logical basis of Contagious Magic, like that of Homeopathic Magic, is a mistaken association of ideas; its physical basis, if we may speak of such a thing, like the physical basis of Homeopathic Magic, is a material medium of some sort which, like the ether of modern physics, is assumed to unite distant objects and to convey impressions from one to the other. The most familiar example of Contagious Magic is the magical sympathy which is supposed to exist between a man and any severed portion of his person, as his hair or nails; so that whoever gets possession of human hair or nails may work his will, at any distance, upon the person from whom they were cut. This superstition is world-wide; instances of it in regard to hair and nails will be noticed later on in this work. I will now illustrate the principles of Contagious Magic by examples, beginning with its application to various parts of the human body.

The Basutos are careful to conceal their extracted teeth, lest these should fall into the hands of certain mythical beings called *baloi*, who haunt graves, and who could harm the owner of the tooth by working magic on it. In Sussex some fifty years ago a maidservant remonstrated strongly against the throwing away of children's cast teeth, affirming that should they be found and gnawed by any animal, the child's new tooth would be, for all the world, like the teeth of the animal that had bitten the old one. In proof of this sne named old Master Simmons, who had a very large pig's tooth in his upper jaw, a personal defect that he always averred was caused by his mother, who threw away one of his cast teeth by accident into the hog's trough. A similar belief has led to practices intended, on the principles of homeopathic magic, to replace old teeth by new and better ones. Thus in many parts of the world it is customary to put extracted teeth in some place where they will be found by a mouse or a rat, in the hope that, through the sympathy which continues to subsist between them and their former owner his other teeth may acquire the same firmness and excellence as the teeth of these rodents.

Other parts which are commonly believed to remain in a sympathetic union with the body, after the physical connection has been severed, are the navel-string and the afterbirth, including the placenta. So intimate indeed, is the union conceived to be, that the fortunes of the individual for good or evil throughout life are often supposed to be bound up with one or other of these portions of his person, so that if his navel-string or afterbirth is preserved and properly treated he will be prosperous; whereas if it be injured or lost, he will suffer accordingly. Certain tribes of Western Australia believe that a man swims well or ill, according as his mother at his birth threw the navel-string into water or not. In Ponape, one of the Caroline Islands, the navel-string is placed in a shell and then disposed of in such a way as shall best adapt the child for the career which the parents have chosen for him. Thus if they wish to make him a good climber, they will hang the navel-string on a tree. Among the Cherokees the navel-string of a girl is buried under a corn mortar, in order that the girl may grow up to be a good baker; but the navel-string of a boy is hung up on a tree in the woods, in order that he may be a hunter.

Even in Europe many people still believe that a person's destiny is more or less bound up with that of his navel-string or afterbirth. Thus in Rhenish Bavaria the navel-string is kept for a while wrapt up in a piece of old linen, and then cut or pricked to pieces according as the child is a boy or a girl, in order that he or she may grow up to be a skillful workman or a good seamstress. In Berlin the midwife commonly delivers the dried navel-string to the father with a strict injunction to preserve it carefully, for as long as it is kept the child will live and thrive and be free from sickness. In Beauce and Perche the people are careful to throw the navel-string neither into water nor into fire, believing that if that were done the child would be drowned or burned.

A curious application of the doctrine of contagious magic is the relation commonly believed to exist between a wounded man and the agent of the wound, so that whatever is subsequently done by or to the agent must correspondingly affect the patient either for good or evil. Thus Pliny tells us that if you have wounded a man and are sorry for it, you have only to spit on the hand that gave the wound, and the pain of the sufferer will be instantly alleviated. In Melanesia, if a man's friends get possession of the arrow which wounded him, they keep it in a damp place or in cool leaves, for then the inflammation will be trifling and will soon subside. Meantime the enemy who shot the arrow is hard at work to aggravate the wound by all the means in his power. For this purpose he and his friends drink hot and burning juices and chew irritating leaves, for this will clearly inflame and irritate the wound. Further, they keep the bow near the fire to make the wound which it has inflicted hot; and for the same reason they put the arrowhead, if it has been recovered, into the fire. Moreover, they are careful to keep the bowstring taut and to twang it occasionally, for this will cause the wounded man to suffer from tension of the nerves and spasms of tetanus. Similarly when a Kwakiutl Indian of British Columbia had bitten a piece out of an enemy's arm he used to drink hot water afterwards for the purpose of thereby inflaming the wound in his foe's body. If a horse wounds its foot by treading on a nail, a Suffolk groom will invariably preserve the nail, clean it, and grease it every day, to prevent the foot from festering. A few years ago a veterinary surgeon was sent for to attend a horse which had ripped its side open on the hinge of a farm gatepost. On arriving at the farm he found that nothing had been done to the wounded horse, but that a man was busy trying to pry the hinge out of the gatepost in order that it might be greased and put away, which, in the opinion of the Cambridge wise-acres, would conduce to the recovery of the animal. Similarly, Essex rustics opine that, if a man has been stabbed with a knife, it is essential to his recovery that the knife should be greased and laid across the bed on which the sufferer is lying. So in Bavaria you are directed to anoint a linen rag with grease and tie it on the edge of the axe that cut you, taking care to keep the sharp edge upwards. As the grease on the axe dries, your wound heals.

The sympathetic connection supposed to exist between a man and the weapon which has wounded him is probably founded on the notion that the blood on the weapon continues to feel with the blood in his body. For a like reason the Papuans of Tumleo, an island off German New Guinea, are careful to throw into the sea the bloody bandages with which their wounds have been dressed, for they fear that if these rags fell into the hands of an enemy he might injure them magically thereby. Once when a man with a wound in his mouth, which bled constantly, came to the missionaries to be treated, his faithful wife took great pains to collect all the blood and cast it into the sea. Strained and unnatural as this idea may seem to us, it is perhaps less so than the belief that magic sympathy is maintained between a person and his clothes, so that whatever is done to the clothes will be felt by the man himself even though he may be far away at the time. In Tanna, one of the New Hebrides, a man who had a grudge at another and desired his death would try to get possession of a cloth which had touched the sweat of his enemy's body. If he succeeded, he rubbed the cloth carefully over with the leaves and twigs of a certain tree, rolled and bound cloth, twigs, and leaves into a long sausage-shaped bundle, and burned it slowly in the fire. As the bundle was consumed, the victim fell ill, and when it was reduced to ashes, he died. In this last form of enchantment, however, the magical sympathy may be supposed to exist not so much between the man and the cloth as between the man and the sweat which issued from his body. But in other cases of the same sort it seems that the garment by itself is enough to give the sorcerer a hold upon his victim. In Prussia they say that if you cannot catch a thief, the next best thing you can do is to get hold of a garment which he may have shed in his flight; for if you beat it soundly, the thief will fall sick. This belief is firmly rooted in the popular mind. Some eighty or ninety years ago, in the neighborhood of Berend, a man was detected trying to steal honey, and fled, leaving his coat behind him. When he heard that the enraged owner of the honey was mauling his lost coat, he was so alarmed that he took to his bed and died.

Again magic may be wrought on a man sympathetically, not only through his clothes and severed parts of himself, but also through the impressions left by his body in sand or earth. In particular, it is a world-wide superstition that by injuring footprints you injure the feet that made them. Thus the natives of southeastern Australia think that they can lame a man by placing sharp pieces of quartz, glass, bone, or charcoal in his footprints. In North Africa the magic of the footprints is sometimes used for more amiable purposes. A woman who wishes to attach her husband or lover to herself will take earth from the print of his right foot, tie it up with some of his hairs in a packet, and wear the packet next to her skin.

Similar practices prevail in various parts of Europe. Thus in Mecklenburg it is thought that if you drive a nail into a man's footprint he will fall lame; sometimes it is required that the nail should be taken from a coffin. A like mode of injuring an enemy is resorted to in some parts of France. It is said that there was an old woman who used to frequent Stow in Suffolk, and she was a witch. If, while she walked, anyone went after her and stuck a nail or a knife into her footprint in the dust, the dame could not stir a step till it was withdrawn. An old Danish mode of concluding a treaty was based on the same idea of the sympathetic connection between a man and his footprints; the covenanting parties sprinkled each other's footprints with their own blood, thus giving a pledge of fidelity. In ancient Greece superstitions of the same sort seem to have been current, for it was thought that if a horse stepped on the track of a wolf he was seized with numbness; and a maxim ascribed to Pythagoras forbade people to pierce a man's footprints with a nail or a knife.

The same superstition is turned to account by hunters in many parts of the world for the purpose of running down the game. Thus a German huntsman will stick a nail taken from a coffin into the fresh spoor of the quarry, believing that this will hinder the animal from escaping. The aborigines of Victoria put hot embers in the tracks of the animals they were pursuing. Hottentot hunters throw into the air a handful of sand taken from the footprints of the game, believing that this will bring the animal down. Thompson Indians used to lay charms on the tracks of wounded deer; after that they deemed it superfluous to pursue the animal any further that day, for being thus charmed it could not travel far and would soon die.

But though the footprint is the most obvious it is not the only impression made by the body through which magic may be wrought on a man. The aborigines of southeastern Australia believe that a man may be injured by burying sharp fragments of quartz, glass, and so forth in the mark made by his reclining body; the magical virtue of these sharp things enters his body and causes those acute pains which the ignorant European puts down as rheumatism. We can now understand why it was a maxim with the Pythagoreans that in rising from bed you should smooth away the impression left by your body on the bedclothes. The rule was simply an old precaution against magic, forming part of a whole code of superstitious maxims which antiquity fathered on Pythagoras, though doubtless they were familiar to the barbarous forefathers of the Greeks long before the time of that philosopher.

4. THE MAGICIAN'S PROGRESS

We have now concluded our examination of the general principles of sympathetic magic. The examples by which I have illustrated them have been drawn for the most part from what may be called private magic, that is, from magical rites and incantations practiced for the benefit or the injury of individuals. But in savage society there is commonly to be found in addition what we may call public magic, that is, sorcery practiced for the benefit of the whole community. Wherever ceremonies of this sort are observed for the common good, it is obvious that the magician ceases to be merely a private practitioner and becomes to some extent a public functionary. The development of such a class of functionaries is of great importance for the political as well as the religious evolution of society. For when the welfare of the tribe is supposed to depend on the performance of these magical rites, the magician rises into a position of much influence and repute, and may readily acquire the rank and authority of a chief or king. The profession accordingly draws into its ranks some of the ablest and most ambitious men of the tribe, because it holds out to them a prospect of honor, wealth, and power such as hardly any other career could offer. The acuter minds perceive how easy it is to dupe their weaker brother and to play on his superstition for their own advantage. Not that the sorcerer is always a knave and imposter; he is often sincerely convinced that he really possesses those wonderful powers which the credulity of his fellows ascribes to him. But the more sagacious he is, the more likely he is to see through the fallacies which impose on duller wits. Thus the ablest members of the profession must tend to be more or less conscious deceivers; and it is just these man who in virtue of their superior ability will generally come to the top and win for themselves positions of the highest dignity and the most commanding authority. The pitfalls which beset the path of the professional sorcerer are many, and as a rule only the man of coolest head and sharpest wit will be able to steer his way through them safely. For it must always be remembered that every single profession and claim put forward by the magician as such is false; not one of them can be maintained without deception, conscious or unconscious. Accordingly the sorcerer who sincerely believes in his own extravagant pretensions is in far greater peril and is much more likely to be cut short in his career than the deliberate impostor. The honest wizard always expects that his charms and incantations will produce their supposed effect; and when they fail, not only really, as they always do, but conspicuously and disastrously, as they often do, he is taken aback: he is not, like his knavish colleague, ready with a plausible excuse to account for the failure, and before he can find one he may be knocked on the head by his disappointed and angry employers.

The general result is that at this stage of social evolution the supreme power tends to fall into the hands of men of the keenest intelligence and the most unscrupulous character. If we could balance the harm they do by their knavery against the benefits they confer by their superior sagacity, it might well be found that the good greatly outweighed the evil. For more mischief has probably been wrought in the world by honest fools in high places than by intelligent rascals. Once your shrewd rogue has attained the height of his ambition, and has no longer any selfish end to further, he may, and often does, turn his talent, his experience, his resources, to the service of the public. Many men who have been least scrupulous in the acquisition of power have been most beneficent in the use of it, whether the power they aimed at and won was that of wealth, political authority, or what not. In the field of politics the wily intriguer, the ruthless victor, may end by being a wise and magnanimous ruler, blessed in his lifetime, lamented at his death, admired and applauded by posterity. Such men, to take two of the most conspicuous instances, were Julius Caesar and Augustus. But once a fool always a fool, and the greater the power in his hands the more disastrous is likely to be the use he makes of it. The heaviest calamity in English history, the breach with America, might never have occurred if George the Third had not been an honest dullard.

Thus, so far as the public profession of magic affected the constitution of savage society, it tended to place the control of affairs in the hands of the ablest man: it shifted the balance of power from the many to the one: it substituted a monarchy for a democracy, or rather for an oligarchy of old men; for in general the savage community is ruled not by the whole body of adult males, but by a council of elders. The change, by whatever causes produced, and whatever the character of the early rulers, was on the whole very beneficial. For the rise of monarchy appears to be an essential condition of the emergence of mankind from savagery. No human being is so hidebound by custom and tradition as your democratic savage; in no state of society consequently is progress so slow and difficult. The old notion that the savage is the freest of mankind is the reverse of the truth. He is a slave, not indeed to a visible master, but to the past, to the spirits of his dead forefathers, who haunt his steps from birth to death, and rule him with a rod of iron. What they did is the pattern of right, the unwritten law to which he yields a blind, unquestioning obedience. The least possible scope is thus afforded to superior talent to change old customs for the better. The ablest man is dragged down by the weakest and dullest, who necessarily sets the standard, since he cannot rise, while the other can fall. The surface of such a society presents a uniform dead level, so far as it is humanly possible to reduce the natural inequalities, the immeasurable real differences of inborn capacity and temper, to a false superficial appearance of equality. From this low and stagnant condition of affairs, which demagogues and dreamers in later times have lauded as the ideal state, the Golden Age, of humanity, everything that helps to raise society by opening a career to talent and proportioning the degrees of authority to men's natural abilities, deserves to be welcomed by all who have the real good of their fellows at heart. Once these elevating influences have begun to operate—and they cannot be forever suppressed—the progress of civilization becomes comparatively rapid. The rise of one man to supreme power enables him to carry through changes in a single lifetime which previously many generations might not have sufficed to effect; and if, as will often happen, he is a man of intellect and energy above the common, he will readily avail himself of the opportunity. Even the whims and caprices of a tyrant may be of service in breaking the chain of custom which lies so heavy on the savage. And as soon as the tribe ceases to be swayed by the timid and divided counsels of the elders, and yields to the direction of a single strong and resolute mind, it becomes formidable to its neighbors and enters on a career of aggrandizement, which at an early stage of history is often highly favorable to social, industrial, and intellectual progress. For extending its sway, partly by force of arms, partly by the voluntary submission of weaker tribes, the community soon acquires wealth and slaves, both of which, by relieving some classes from the perpetual struggle for a bare subsistence, afford them an opportunity of devoting themselves to that disinterested pursuit of knowledge which is the noblest and most powerful instrument to ameliorate the lot of man.

Intellectual progress, which reveals itself in the growth of art and science and the spread of more liberal views, cannot be dissociated from industrial or economic progress, and that in its turn receives an immense impulse from conquest and empire. It is no mere accident that the most vehement outbursts of activity of the human mind have followed close on the heels of victory, and that the great conquering races of the world have commonly done most to advance and spread civilization thus healing in peace the wounds they inflicted in war. The Babylonians, the Greeks the Romans, the Arabs are our witnesses in the past: we may yet live to see a similar outburst in Japan. Nor, to remount the stream of history to its sources, is it an accident that all the first great strides towards civilization have been made under despotic and theocratic governments, like those of Egypt, Babylon, and Peru, where the supreme ruler claimed and received the servile allegiance of his subjects in the double character of a king and a god. It is hardly too much to say that at this early epoch despotism is the best friend of humanity and, paradoxical as it may sound, of liberty. For after all there is more liberty in the best sense—liberty to think our own thoughts and to fashion our own destinies—under the most absolute despotism, the most grinding tyranny, than under the apparent freedom of savage life, where the individual's lot is cast from the cradle to the grave in the iron mold of hereditary custom.

So far, therefore, as the public profession of magic has been one of the roads by which the ablest men have passed to supreme power, it has contributed to emancipate mankind from the thralldom of tradition and to elevate them into a larger, freer life, with a broader outlook on the world. This is no small service rendered to humanity. And when we remember further that in another direction magic has paved the way for science, we are forced to admit that if the black art has done much evil, it has also been the source of much good; that if it is the child of error, it has yet been the mother of freedom and truth.

Mischa Titiev

A FRESH APPROACH TO THE PROBLEM OF MAGIC AND RELIGION

There has recently been an intensified interest in defining religion, particularly as it relates to magic. The following article, by Mischa Titiev, is a modest effort to clear the atmosphere without departing from what is essentially a Frazerian position. It may be contrasted with two articles by Murray and Rosalie Wax, "The Magical World View" (1962) and "The Notion of Magic" (1963), which severely attack any effort to sustain the more traditional views of magic as expressed by not only Frazer himself but also Tylor, Durkheim, and others. The Waxes' articles provide a useful review of the controversy in its historical and intellectual aspects. Less polemic efforts at grappling with the definitional problems on a broad basis have been made by Horton (1960) and Goody (1961).

Titiev's proposal to distinguish between calendrical and critical rituals has a familiar ring, although his use of the distinction is novel. Chapple and Coon, in their *Principles of Anthropology*, had earlier made a distinction between rites of intensification and rites of passage, the first usually being cyclical and recurrent, the latter nonrecurrent, but their aim was to explore these rituals in terms of the restoration of disturbed equilibrium. What Titiev has done is to show that many of the traits adhering to calendrical rituals are those we usually regard as religious, whereas many of those associated with critical rites are customarily considered to be magical. Yet he does not press the use of these criteria beyond reason, recognizing, as do indeed even those who favor the Frazerian type of dichotomy, that there simply is no hard and fast rule.

Reprinted with omission of a figure from the *Southwestern Journal of Anthropology*, XVI (1960), 292–298, by permission of the author and the *Southwestern Journal of Anthropology*.

About seventy years ago the great scholar of primitive religion, Sir James G. Frazer, found it advisable to divide all phenomena involving the supernatural into the two categories of magic and religion. Almost at once large numbers of social scientists found Frazer's dichotomy useful and began to emphasize the criteria which, in their opinion, separated the one category from the other. In the course of time it became customary to stress four factors, although others were sometimes invoked. The four attributes that came to be most often cited run somewhat as follows.

1. Magic *compels* the world of the supernatural to do its bidding. It fails to get results only if errors of procedure or text have been

made, or if stronger counter-magic has been brought to bear. Religion, on the other hand, say the supporters of Frazer's dichotomy, never guarantees results. Its use is limited to *supplication*, and its practitioners never resort to manipulation or coercion.

2. Magic, according to Durkheim and his followers, has no "church." That is to say, magical rites may be public or private but, unlike those that are religious, they do not have to have a large body of celebrants; they do not need to be held in public before a congregation of worshippers; and they may have no social or communal aspects whatsoever.

3. Magical utterances have a tendency to degenerate into spells or formulas, some of which have little or no meaning even to those who say them. It is implied that religious pronouncements are usually meaningful in terms of a society's customary language.

4. Practitioners of magic, even in primitive societies, are often set apart in one fashion or another from socially recognized priests. With occasional exceptions it is only acknowledged priests who go through a period of formal training and who then qualify to perform communal or publicly sanctioned religious exercises, leaving shamans and others to deal in magic.

Although most writers on the subject have continued to accept Frazer's distinction, somewhat apathetically, it must be confessed, others have held the criteria to be unsatisfactory because they cannot be precisely determined and because they so frequently overlap. Indeed, some contemporary anthropologists have found the customary divisions between magic and religion to be so vague and indeterminate that they have refused to recognize the traditional dichotomy and now prefer to treat both sets of practices as one. Indicative of this attitude is Dr. Hsu's statement, written only a few years ago, that "whichever criterion we employ, we are led to the conclusion that magic and religion, instead of being treated as mutually exclusive entities, must be grouped together as magico-religion or magico-religious phenomena. This is a position increasingly endorsed by anthropologists." Nevertheless, even if we grant that modern critics have many points in their favor, there are a number of anthropologists who still believe that a distinction needs to be made between what they feel are two essentially different kinds of human behavior, each of which makes an appeal to the supernatural world for help, guidance, or comfort.

As a fresh start toward a workable dichotomy, it may be well to distinguish two kinds of activities on a new basis, one that rests on a criterion that is precise, but has not been traditionally utilized by former analysts. In all primitive societies one set of practices involving the supernatural always takes place recurrently, and may, accordingly, be termed CALENDRICAL; while the other set, which is celebrated only intermittently, and then only when an emergency or crisis seems to have arisen, may be called CRITICAL.

Because of their very nature calendrical rituals can always be scheduled and announced long in advance of their occurrence. This gives the people of a community ample time to develop a shared sense of anticipation, and an opportunity to get ready for a big event. On the other hand, it must be realized that if a celebration is to be performed at a definite time of season in the future, it cannot possibly take into account the immediate desires for supernatural assistance or comfort of the whole society or of any of its parts. To cite one instance, the gigantic figure of Shalako appears in Zuni each December, regardless of the frame of mind of any particular inhabitants of the village.

One can find calendrical rites even in Christianity. Christmas is an example. Throughout the Western world it is celebrated annually on the twenty-fifth day of December, regardless of the wants or needs, on that particular day, of individual Christians or of any congregation of Christians.

As a rule, calendrical performances are entrusted to officially-sanctioned priests, rather than to other persons who may deal with the supernatural; and since ceremonies based on a calendar cannot possibly be geared to anyone's immediate desires, they can be interpreted only as having value for an entire society. In this sense, especially, calendrical observances may be said always to have a "church," and to correspond, on the whole, more nearly to established concepts of religion than to those of magic.

Moreover, since they are always social or communal in character, calendrical rites invariably tend to disappear when a society loses its distinctiveness or radically alters its old ways of life. Thus, when the Hopi Indians of Oraibi began to show greater interest in White than in native culture, the pueblo's calendrical observances were among the first cultural items to suffer disintegration.

In a similar vein, long before the establishment of Israel, the Jews were of particular interest to social scientists partly because they managed to give the impression of being a single society, even though it was patently obvious that they were not, inasmuch as they were scattered among many, many nations. What, then, gave observers the impression that the Jews constituted *a society*? Above all else, it was the fact that regardless of their places of residence the Jewish people steadfastly continued to observe such traditional calendrical (social) ceremonies as Passover and Yom Kippur. It is noteworthy in this context that whenever Jews become assimilated into any originally alien society, they stop observing their ancient calendrical rituals.

Quite different in nearly every respect are those practices, also based on a belief in the supernatural, that we have termed critical. They are, let us recall, customarily designed to meet the pressing needs of a given moment. For this reason they can never be held only because a particular time has arrived, nor can they be announced, scheduled, or prepared for far in advance. In some cases critical ceremonies may be performed by priests, but in a large number of instances they are conducted by other personages.

Unlike calendrical observances which are *invariably* communal or broadly social, critical rituals may be designed to benefit either a whole society, a relatively small group, or even a single individual. It should be obvious that every now and then a critical rite may be held to counteract a public emergency, as when a prolonged drought affects all the farmers in a given community, or when an entire nation prays for peace. However, crises on this scale are comparatively rare. For the most part critical ceremonies are staged only when a private or personal emergency has arisen, as might be the case if something important has been stolen or mislaid, or if a child has fallen gravely ill, or in the event that an individual has entered on a new social position that disturbs his former dealings with the members of his society. In such cases critical rituals are designed to benefit only those who have asked, and sometimes paid, for them. A reexamination of the rich material from Africa, as well as from other regions, pertaining to the services rendered by seers, diviners, fortune-tellers, medicine-men, and so forth, shows that their approach to the supernatural is far more often on behalf of persons who have a problem than it is for the sake of whole societies or communities. These instances show that critical observances do not inevitably need to have a "church." Since, at the same time, they do not necessarily have to be performed by socially sanctioned priests, they tend in a number of ways to correspond quite closely to traditional concepts of magic.

It should be noted further that whereas calendrical rites ordinarily disappear when a society diminishes in power or loses its identity, critical rites may persist long after an entire society has collapsed, and in a new social setting may form the basis for a large number of the carry-overs that students of religion generally call superstitions.

Since the distinction here made cannot be maintained without the existence of some form of a calendar, it is essential to show that even the most primitive and non-literate of people may have a simple way of keeping track of the year's progress. In the northern hemisphere, whose varied religions are far better known to anthropologists than are those of the people who live south of the equator, the easiest method involves no more than noting, from exactly the same spot each day, where the sun seems to rise. When this is done regularly the sun apparently travels from north to south between June 21 and December 21, and from south to north during the remaining six months. Whenever the eastern horizon happens to be irregular it appears as if the sun comes up now from a mountain peak, now from a bit of forest, now from an open stretch, and so on. In this way the coincidence of a sunrise with a particular landmark may serve as a seasonal checkpoint, and as an indication of the time when a given calendrical rite ought to be announced or performed. The terminal or turning points in the sun's annual course mark the solstices. In many communities of the northern hemisphere, even if the June solstice is unnoticed, it is customary to hold important calendrical rituals on or about December 21.

The main reason for this difference of attitude and behavior seems to stem from the fact that whenever it reaches either of its solstice points the sun at first makes so little daily progress in the opposite direction that it appears to rise in the same spot or, in a manner of speaking, to hesitate or to stand still for three or four days. When this "hesitation" takes place on June 21, there is little to fear, for vegetation is usually plentiful, crops are growing, and the weather is balmy. But it is quite another matter when the sun pauses at its southern terminal and appears reluctant to move northward, in the direction of spring and summer. Such a threatened stoppage would, indeed, be a calamity. It might result in perpetual winter, no fodder for animals, and no crops for man. That is why strenuous efforts are sometimes made to get the sun to turn from its southern to its northern path; and that is also why winter solstice observances so commonly take the form of new-fire rites, or else include a number of symbols expressive of man's desire for increased light and heat.

Never should it be thought that calendrical ceremonies, because they may disregard the needs of the moment, are only of secondary importance. Far from it! Analysis of their intent reveals that they are designed primarily to strengthen the bonds of cohesion that hold together all of a society's members or else to aid the individuals who form a social unit to adjust to one another and to their external environment.

Our dichotomy should not be interpreted as a device for classifying every conceivable aspect of primitive religion. For instance, it does not apply smoothly to all the manifestations of the famed rites of passage. It is true that three of van Gennep's stages—birth, marriage, and death—are critical, because they are concerned primarily with individuals and cannot be precisely determined in advance; whereas the fourth—puberty or tribal initiation—is often calendrically observed. Yet, all of the rites of passage drastically change a person's social relationships, and, therefore, all of them may be classed, as they usually are, as critical.

For many anthropologists in the United States, especially, the old distinction between magic and religion has lost much of its pristine vitality and freshness. Unless we are prepared to lump all supernatural phenomena into a single category, we need a fresh basis for classification and analysis. That is what the proposed difference between calendrical and critical rites is meant to provide. The likelihood is strong that every social unit's system of supernatural practices contains both calendrical and critical elements. In partnership, these may be seen to function as vital parts of every primitive society's nonempirical method for trying to gain desired ends.

Walter B. Cannon
"VOODOO" DEATH

The phenomenon of death caused by witchcraft and sorcery or due to taboo violation is common and widespread. Such deaths are frequent in aboriginal Australia, Polynesia, South America, and Africa. Similar phenomena are occasionally reported from almost every corner of the world.

Both early observers and modern investigators have accepted such deaths as being due to fear; that is, there is ample evidence that no poison or physical agent is necessary to bring about the demise of the victim. Where belief in sorcery, witchcraft, or supernatural sanctions is firmly held, fear alone can kill. While competent investigators had not doubted the actuality of "voodoo" death, it remained for Cannon to establish the physiological mechanisms by which fear, such as can be engendered by sorcery, can kill a human being. For this purpose, Cannon was able to draw upon his classic studies of the physiological changes due to hunger, rage, fear, and pain (see his classic *The Wisdom of the Body*, 1932).

In this article the author demonstrates that through fear the body is stimulated to meet an emergency. Through the sympathetic nervous system, muscles are prepared for action by the production of large amounts of adrenalin and sugar and by the contraction of certain blood vessels. When the emergency is not met by action, or is prolonged, a state of shock may result. The blood pressure is

Reprinted in abridged form from *American Anthropologist*, XLIV (1942), 169–181, by permission of the American Anthropological Association.

reduced, the heart deteriorates, and blood plasma escapes into the tissues. Lack of food and water compound this deleterious physiological state. A continuation of this condition may lead to death within a very few days.

Although this article deals with witchcraft, fear, and death in primitive societies, its implications are far-reaching. The psychogenic ailments of modern "civilized" man defy understanding, but we know that fear through suggestion and autosuggestion afflicts the modern hypochondriac and ulcer patient much as it does the Australian who is bewitched or "sung."

In records of anthropologists and others who have lived with primitive people in widely scattered parts of the world is the testimony that when subjected to spells or sorcery or the use of "black magic" men may be brought to death. Among the natives of South America and Africa, Australia, New Zealand, and the islands of the Pacific, as well as among the Negroes of nearby Haiti, "voodoo" death has been reported by apparently competent observers. The phenomenon is so extraordinary and so foreign to the experience of civilized people that it seems incredible; certainly if it is authentic it deserves careful consideration.

A question which naturally arises is whether those who have testified to the reality of voodoo death have exercised good critical judgment. Although the sorcerer or medicine man or chief may tacitly possess or may assume the ability to kill by bone-pointing or by another form of black magic, may he not preserve his reputation for supernatural power by the use of poison? Especially when death has been reported to have occurred after the taking of food may not the fatal result be due to action of poisonous substances not commonly known except to priests and wizards? Obviously, the possible use of poisons must be excluded before voodoo death can be accepted as an actual consequence of sorcery or witchcraft. Also it is essential to rule out instances of bold claims of supernatural power when in fact death resulted from natural causes; this precaution is particularly important because of the common belief among aborigines that illness is due to malevolence. I have endeavored to learn definitely whether poisoning and spurious claims can quite certainly be excluded from instances of death, attributed to magic power, by addressing inquiries to medically trained observers.

Dr. S. M. Lambert of the Western Pacific Service of the Rockefeller Foundation wrote to me concerning the experience of Dr. P. S. Clarke with Kanakas working on the sugar plantations of North Queensland. One day a Kanaka came to his hospital and told him he would die in a few days because a spell had been put upon him and nothing could be done to counteract it. The man had been known by Dr. Clarke for some time. He was given a very thorough examination, including an examination of the stool and the urine. All was found normal, but as he lay in bed he gradually grew weaker. Dr. Clarke called upon the foreman of the Kanakas to come to the hospital to give the man assurance, but on reaching the foot of the bed, the foreman leaned over, looked at the patient, and then turned to Dr. Clarke saying, "Yes, doctor, close up him he die" (i.e., he is nearly dead). The next day, at 11 o'clock in the morning, he ceased to live. A post-mortem examination revealed nothing that could in any way account for the fatal outcome.

Another observer with medical training, Dr. W. E. Roth, who served for three years as government surgeon among the primitive people of north central Queensland, has also given pertinent testimony. "So rooted sometimes is this belief on the part of the patient," Roth wrote, "that some enemy has 'pointed' the bone at him, that he will actually lie down to die, and succeed in the attempt, even at the expense of refusing food and succor within his reach: I have myself witnessed three or four such cases."

Dr. J. B. Cleland, Professor of Pathology at the University of Adelaide, has written to me that he has no doubt that from time to time the natives of the Australian bush do die as a result of a bone being pointed at them, and that such death may not be associated with any of the ordinary lethal injuries. In an article which included a section on death from malignant psychic influences, Dr. Cleland mentions a fine, robust tribesman in Central Australia who was injured in the fleshy part of the thigh by a spear that had been enchanted. The man slowly pined away and died, without any surgical complication which could be detected. Dr. Cleland cites a number of physicians who have referred to the fatal effects of bone-pointing and other terrifying acts. In his letter to me he wrote, "Poisoning is, I think, entirely ruled out in such cases among our Australian natives. There are very few poisonous plants available and I doubt whether it has ever entered the mind of the central Australian natives that such might be used on human beings."

Dr. Herbert Basedow, in his book, *The Australian Aboriginal*, has presented a vivid picture of the first horrifying effect of bone-pointing on the ignorant, superstitious, and credulous natives, and the later more calm acceptance of their mortal fate:

The man who discovers that he is being boned by any enemy is, indeed, a pitiable sight. He stands aghast, with his eyes staring at the treacherous pointer, and with his hands lifted as though to ward off the lethal medium, which he imagines is pouring into his body. His cheeks blanch and his eyes become glassy and the expression of his face becomes horribly distorted. . . . He attempts to shriek but usually the sound chokes in his throat, and all that one might see is froth at his mouth. His body begins to tremble and the muscles twist involuntarily. He sways backwards and falls to the ground, and after a short time appears to be in a swoon; but soon after he writhes as if in mortal agony, and, covering his face with his hands, begins to moan. After a while he becomes very composed and crawls to his wurley. From this time onwards he sickens and frets, refusing to eat and keeping aloof from the daily affairs of the tribe. Unless help is forthcoming in the shape of a countercharm administered by the hands of the Nangarri, or medicine man, his death is only a matter of comparatively short time. If the coming of the medicine man is opportune he might be saved.

The Nangarri, when persuaded to exercise his powers, goes through an elaborate ceremony and finally steps toward the awe-stricken relatives, holding in his fingers a small article —a stick, a bone, a pebble, or a talon— which, he avows, he has taken from the "boned" man and which was the cause of the affliction. And now, since it is removed, the victim has nothing to fear. The effect, Dr. Basedow declares, is astounding. The victim, until that moment far on the road to death, raises his head and gazes in wonderment at the object held by the medicine man. He even lifts himself into a sitting position and calls for water to drink. The crisis is passed, and the recovery is speedy and complete. Without the Nangarri's intervention the boned fellow, according to Dr. Basedow, would certainly have fretted himself to death. The implicit faith which a native cherishes in the magical powers of his tribal magician is said to result in cures which exceed anything recorded by the faith-healing disciples of more cultured communities.

Perhaps the most complete account of the influence of the tribal taboo on the fate of a person subjected to its terrific potency has come from W. L. Warner, who worked among primitive aborigines in the Northern Territory of Australia. There are two definite movements of the social group, he declares, in the process by which black magic becomes effective on the victim of sorcery. In the first movement the community contracts; all people who stand in kinship relation with him withdraw their sustaining support. This means that all his fellows—everyone he knows—completely change their attitudes toward him and place him in a new category. He is now viewed as one who is more nearly in the realm of the sacred and taboo than in the world of the ordinary where the community finds itself. The organization of his social life has collapsed, and, no longer a member of a group, he is alone and isolated. The doomed man is in a situation from which the only escape is by death. During the death-illness which ensues, the group acts with all the outreachings and complexities of its organization and with countless stimuli to suggest death positively to the victim, who is in a highly suggestible state. In addition to the social pressure upon him the victim himself, as a rule, not only makes no effort to live and to stay a part of his group but actually, through the multiple suggestions which he receives, co-operates in the withdrawal from it. He becomes what the attitude of his fellow tribesmen wills him to be. Thus he assists in committing a kind of suicide.

Before death takes place, the second movement of the community occurs, which is a return to the victim in order to subject him to the fateful ritual of mourning. The purpose of the community now, as a social unit with its ceremonial leader, who is a person of very near kin to the victim, is at last to cut him off entirely from the ordinary world and ultimately to place him in his proper position in the sacred totemic world of the dead. The victim, on his part, reciprocates this feeling. The effect of the double movement in the society, first away from the victim and then back, with all the compulsive force of one of its most powerful rituals, is obviously drastic.

The social environment as a support to morale is probably much more important and impressive among primitive people, because of their profound ignorance and insecurity in a haunted world, than among educated people living in civilized and well-protected communities. Dr. S. D. Porteus, physician and psychologist, has studied savage life extensively in the Pacific islands and in Africa; he writes:

Music and dance are primitive man's chief defenses against loneliness. By these he reminds himself that in his wilderness there are other minds seconding his own . . . in the dance he sees himself multiplied in his fellows, his action mirrored in theirs. There are in his life very few other occasions in which he can take part in concerted action and find partners. . . . The native aboriginal is above all fear-ridden. Devils haunt to seize the unwary; their malevolent magic shadows his waking moments; he believes that medicine men know how to make themselves invisible so that they may cut out his kidney fat, then sew him up and rub his tongue with a magic stone to induce forgetfulness, and thereafter he is a living corpse, devoted to death. . . . So desperate is this fear that if a man imagines that he has been subjected to the bone-pointing magic of the enemy he will straight away lie down and die.

Testimony similar to the foregoing, from Brazil, Africa, New Zealand, and Australia, was found in reports from the Hawaiian Islands, British Guiana, and Haiti. What attitude is justified in the presence of this accumulation of evidence? In a letter from Professor Lévy-Bruhl, the French ethnologist long interested in aboriginal tribes and their customs, he remarked that answers which he had received from inquiries could be summed up as follows. The ethnologists, basing their judgment on a large number of reports, quite independent of one another and gathered from groups in all parts of the world, admit that there are instances indicating that the belief that one has been subjected to sorcery, and in consequence is inevitably condemned to death, does actually result in death in the course of time. On the contrary, physiologists and physicians—men who have had no acquaintance with ethnological conditions—are inclined to consider the phenomenon as impossible and raise doubts regarding clear and definite testimony.

Before denying that voodoo death is within the realm of possibility, let us consider the general features of the specimen reports mentioned in foregoing paragraphs. First, there is the elemental fact that the phenomenon is characteristically noted among aborigines—among human beings so primitive, so superstitious, so ignorant that they are bewildered strangers in a hostile world. Instead of knowledge they have a fertile and unrestricted imagination which fills their environment with all manner of evil spirits capable of affecting their lives disastrously. As Dr. Porteus pointed out, only by engaging in communal activities are they able to develop sufficient *esprit de corps* to render themselves resistant to the mysterious and malicious influences which can vitiate their lives. Associated with these circumstances is the fixed assurance that because of certain conditions, such as being subject to bone-pointing or other magic, or failing to observe sacred tribal regulations, death is sure to supervene. This is a belief so firmly held by all members of the tribe that the individual not only has that conviction himself but is obsessed by the knowledge that all his fellows likewise hold it. Thereby he becomes a pariah, wholly deprived of the confidence and social support of the tribe. In his isolation the malicious spirits which he believes are all about him and capable of irresistibly and calamitously maltreating him, exert supremely their evil power. Amid this mysterious mark of grim and ominous fatality what has been called "the gravest known extremity of fear," that of an immediate threat of death, fills the terrified victim with powerless misery.

In his terror he refuses both food and drink, a fact which many observers have noted and which, as we shall see later, is highly significant for a possible understanding of the slow onset of weakness. The victim "pines away"; his strength runs out like water, to paraphrase words already quoted from one graphic account; and in the course of a day or two he succumbs.

The question which now arises is whether an ominous and persistent state of fear can end the life of a man. Fear, as is well known, is one of the most deeply rooted and dominant of the emotions. Often, only with difficulty can it be eradicated. Associated with it are profound physiological disturbances, widespread throughout the organism. There is evidence that some of these disturbances, if they are lasting, can work harmfully. In order to elucidate that evidence I must first indicate that great fear and great rage have similar effects in the body. Each of these powerful emotions is associated with ingrained instincts—the instinct to attack, if rage is present; the instinct to run away or escape, if fear is present. Throughout the long history of human beings and lower animals these two emotions and their related instincts have served effectively in the struggle for existence.

When they are roused they bring into action an elemental division of the nervous system, the so-called "sympathetic" or sympathico-adrenal division, which exercises a control over internal organs, and also over the blood vessels. As a rule the sympathetic division acts to maintain a relatively constant state in the flowing blood and lymph, i.e., the "internal environment" of our living parts. It acts thus in strenuous muscular effort; for example, liberating sugar from the liver, accelerating the heart, contracting certain blood vessels, discharging adrenaline, and dilating the bronchioles. All these changes render the animal more efficient in physical struggle, for they supply essential conditions for continuous action of laboring muscles. Since they occur in association with the strong emotions, rage and fear, they can reasonably be interpreted as preparatory for the intense struggle which the instincts to attack or to escape may involve. If these powerful emotions prevail, and the bodily forces are fully mobilized for action, and if this state of extreme perturbation continues in uncontrolled possession of the organism for a considerable period, without the occurrence of action, dire results may ensue.

When, under brief ether anesthesia, the cerebral cortex of a cat is quickly destroyed so that the animal no longer has the benefit of the organs of intelligence, there is a remarkable display of the activities of lower, primary centers of behavior, those of emotional expression. This decorticate condition is similar to that produced in man when consciousness is abolished by the use of nitrous oxide; he is then decorticated by chemical means. Commonly the emotional expression of joy is released (nitrous oxide is usually known as "laughing gas"), but it may be that of sorrow (it might as well be called "weeping gas"). Similarly, ether anesthesia, if light, may release the expression of rage. In the sham rage of the decorticate cat there is a supreme exhibition of intense emotional activity. The hairs stand on end, sweat exudes from the toe pads, the heart rate may rise from about 150 beats per minute to twice that number, the blood pressure is greatly elevated, and the concentration of sugar in the blood soars to five times the normal. This excessive activity of the sympathico-adrenal system rarely lasts, however, more than three or four hours. By that time, without any loss of blood or any other events to explain the outcome, the decorticate remnant of the animal, in which this acme of emotional display has prevailed, ceases to exist.

What is the cause of the demise? It is clear that the rapidly fatal result is due to a persistent excessive activity of the sympathico-adrenal system. One of my associates, Philip Bard, noted that when the signs of emotional excitement failed to appear, the decorticate preparation might continue to survive for long periods; indeed, its existence might have to be ended by the experimenter. Further evidence was obtained by another of my associates, Norman E. Freeman, who produced sham rage in animals from which the sympathetic nerves had been removed. In these circumstances the behavior was similar in all respects to the behavior described above, excepting the manifestations dependent upon sympathetic innervation. The remarkable fact appeared that animals deprived of their sympathetic nerves and exhibiting sham rage, so far as was possible, continued to exist for many hours without any sign of breakdown. Here were experiments highly pertinent to the present inquiry.

What effect on the organism is produced by a lasting and intense action of the sympathico adrenal system? In observations Bard found that a prominent and significant change which became manifest in animals displaying sham rage was a gradual fall of blood pressure toward the end of the display, from the high levels of the early stages to the low level seen in fatal wound shock. Freeman's research produced evidence that this fall of pressure was due to a reduction of the volume of circulating blood. This is the condition which during World War I was found to be the reason for the low blood pressure observed in badly wounded men—the blood volume is reduced until it becomes insufficient for the maintenance of an adequate circulation. Thereupon deterioration occurs in the heart, and also in the nerve centers which hold the blood vessels in moderate contraction. A vicious circle is then established; the low blood pressure damages the very organs which are necessary for the maintenance of an adequate circulation, and as they are damaged they are less and less able to keep the blood circulating to an effective degree. In sham rage, as in wound shock, death can be explained as due to a failure of essential organs to receive a sufficient supply of blood or, specifically, a sufficient supply of oxygen, to maintain their functions.

The gradual reduction of blood volume in sham rage can be explained by the action of the sympathico-adrenal system in causing a persistent constriction of the small arterioles in certain parts of the body. If adrenaline, which constricts the blood vessels precisely as nerve impulses constrict them, is continuously injected at a rate which produces the vasoconstriction of strong emotional states, the blood volume is reduced to the degree seen in sham rage. Freeman, Freedman, and Miller performed that experiment. They employed in some instances no more adrenaline than is secreted in response to reflex stimulation of the adrenal gland, and they found not only marked reduction of the blood plasma but also a concentration of blood corpuscles as shown by the percentage increase of hemoglobin. It should be remembered, however, that in addition to this circulating vasoconstrictor agent there are in the normal functioning of the sympathico-adrenal system the constrictor effects on blood vessels of nerve impulses and the co-operation of another circulating chemical substance besides adrenaline, viz., sympathin. These three agents, working together in times of great emotional stress, might well produce the results which Freeman and his collaborators observed when they injected adrenaline alone. In the presence of the usual blood pressure, organs of primary importance, e.g., the heart and the brain, are not subjected to constriction of their vessels, and therefore they are continuously supplied with blood. But this advantage is secured at the deprivation of peripheral structures and especially the abdominal viscera. In these less essential parts, where constriction of the arterioles occurs, the capillaries are ill-supplied with oxygen. The very thin walls of the capillaries are sensitive to oxygen-want and when they do not receive an adequate supply they become more and more permeable to the fluid part of the blood. Thereupon the plasma escapes into the perivascular spaces. A similar condition occurs in the wound shock of human beings. The escape of the plasma from the blood vessels leaves the red corpuscles more concentrated. During World War I we found that the concentration of corpuscles in skin areas might be increased as much as fifty per cent.

A condition well known as likely to be harmful to the wounded was a prolonged lack of food or water. Freeman, Morison, and Sawyer found that loss of fluid from the body, resulting in a state of dehydration, excited the sympathico-adrenal system; thus again a vicious circle may be started, the low blood volume of the dehydrated condition being intensified by further loss through capillaries which have been made increasingly permeable.

The foregoing paragraphs have revealed how a persistent and profound emotional state may induce a disastrous fall of blood pressure, ending in death. Lack of food and drink would collaborate with the damaging emotional effects to induce the fatal outcome. These are the conditions which, as we have seen, are prevalent in persons who have been reported as dying as a consequence of sorcery. They go without food or water as they, in their isolation, wait in fear for their impending death. In these circumstances they might well die from a true state of shock, in the surgical sense—a shock induced by prolonged and tense emotion.

It is pertinent to mention here that Wallace, a surgeon of large experience in World War I, testified to having seen cases of shock in which neither trauma nor any of the known accentuating facts of shock could account for the disastrous condition. Sometimes the wounds were so trivial that they could not reasonably be regarded as the cause of the shock state; sometimes the visible injuries were negligible. He cites two illustrative instances. One was a man who was buried by the explosion of a shell in a cellar; the other was blown up by a buried shell over which he had lighted a fire. In both the circumstances were favorable for terrifying experience. In both all the classic symptoms of shock were present. The condition lasted more than 48 hours, and treatment was of no avail. A post-mortem examination did not reveal any gross injury. Another remarkable case which may be cited was studied by Freeman at the Massachusetts General Hospital. A woman of 43 years underwent a complete hysterectomy because of uterine bleeding. Although her emotional instability was recognized, she appeared to stand the operation well. Special precautions were taken, however, to avoid loss of blood, and in addition she was given fluid intravenously when the operation was completed. That night she was sweating, and refused to speak. The next morning her blood pressure had fallen to near the shock level, her heart rate was 150 beats per minute, her skin was cold and clammy, and the measured blood flow through the vessels of her hand was very slight. There was no bleeding to account for her desperate condition, which was diagnosed as shock brought on by fear. When one understands the utter strangeness, to an inexperienced layman, of a hospital and its elaborate surgical ritual, and the distressing invasion of the body with knives and metal retractors, the wonder is that not more patients exhibit signs of deep anxiety. In this instance a calm and reassuring attitude on the part of the surgeon resulted in a change of attitude in the patient, with recovery of a normal state. That the attitude of the patient is of significant importance for a favorable outcome of an operation is firmly believed by the well-known American surgeon, Dr. J. M. T. Finney, for many years Professor of Surgery at the Johns Hopkins Medical School. He has publicly testified, on the basis of serious experiences, that if any person came to him for a major operation, and expressed fear of the result, he invariably refused to operate. Some other surgeon must assume the risk!

Further evidence of the possibility of fatal outcome from profound emotional strain was reported by Mira in recounting his experiences as a psychiatrist in the Spanish war of 1936–1939. In patients who suffered from what he called "malignant anxiety" he observed signs of anguish and perplexity, accompanied by a permanently rapid pulse (more than 120 beats per minute), and a very rapid respiration (about three times the normal resting rate). These conditions indicated a perturbed state deeply involving the sympathico-adrenal complex. As predisposing conditions Mira mentioned "a previous lability of the sympathetic system" and "a severe mental shock experienced in conditions of physical exhaustion due to lack of food, fatigue, sleeplessness, etc." The lack of food appears to have attended lack of water, for the urine was concentrated and extremely acid. Toward the end the anguish still remained, but inactivity changed to restlessness. No focal symptoms were observed. In fatal cases death occurred in three or four days. Post-mortem examination revealed brain hemorrhages in some cases, but, excepting an increased pressure, the cerebrospinal fluid showed a normal state. The combination of lack of food and water, anxiety, very rapid pulse and respiration, associated with a shocking experience having persistent effects, would fit well with fatal conditions reported from primitive tribes

The suggestion which I offer, therefore, is that voodoo death may be real, and that it may be explained as due to shocking emotional stress—to obvious or repressed terror A satisfactory hypothesis is one which allows observations to be made which may determine whether or not it is correct. Fortunately tests of a relatively simple type can be used to learn whether the suggestion as to the nature of voodoo death is justifiable. The pulse toward the end would be rapid and "thready." The skin would be cool and moist. A count of the red blood corpuscles, or even simpler, a determination by means of a hematocrit of the ratio of corpuscles to plasma in a small sample of blood from skin vessels would help to tell whether shock is present; for the "red count" would be high and the hematocrit also would reveal "hemoconcentration." The blood pressure would be low. The blood sugar would be increased, but the measure of it might be too difficult in the field. If in the future, however, any observer has opportunity to see an instance of voodoo death, it is to be hoped that he will conduct the simpler tests before the victim's last gasp.

E. E. Evans-Pritchard

WITCHCRAFT EXPLAINS UNFORTUNATE EVENTS

In few societies of the world does witchcraft assume a more focal interest than among the Azande, a large and complex group situated both north and south of the Sudan–Belgian Congo border. The Azande recognize witchcraft to be a psychic act, and they clearly differentiate it from sorcery, which concerns itself with spells and medicines. They believe that a person is a witch because of an inherited organ or substance called *mangu*. Mangu is oval, is located somewhere between the breastbone and the intestines, and is variously described as reddish, blackish, or hairy. A male can inherit mangu only from a male, a female only from a female. An autopsy may be performed to determine the presence or absence of mangu. Since an accusation of witchcraft may result in a stigma or a fine, or both, autopsies are sometimes carried out to clear a family name.

Witchcraft explains unfortunate events, but only if these events are unusual and inexplicable. An event which is clearly due to carelessness, sorcery, or a taboo violation would not be explained as being due to witchcraft. It is the uncommon event, the event which cannot be understood through normal causal interpretation, which is "obviously" due to witchcraft. The logic used in positing witchcraft as the cause of such strange events is impeccable. It is the basic premise, not the logic, which is at fault.

There are many plausible functions of Zande witchcraft. A man who is too successful, for example, one who finds three honeycombs in one day, is accused of witchcraft. Such accusations militate against any strong striving for success. The economic efficiency of the *kpolo* (extended family) is maintained by directing all conflicts outside the kpolo through accusations of witchcraft. A member of one's own extended family cannot be accused of witchcraft. The fact that the Azande have not engaged in feuds or raids may indicate the ability of accusations and angers against witches to absorb latent hostilities.

Most important, however, is the usefulness of witchcraft in explaining why an event occurred. Science cannot tell us what happened, beyond mentioning the laws of probability. The Azande find both comfort and an opportunity to retaliate in their explanation of why an unfortunate and unusual event took place.

Reprinted in excerpted form from E. E. Evans-Pritchard, "The Notion of Witchcraft Explains Unfortunate Events," *Witchcraft, Oracles and Magic Among the Azande* (Oxford: Clarendon Press, 1937), Part I, Chap. 4, by permission of the author and the publishers.

It is an inevitable conclusion from Zande descriptions of witchcraft that it is not an objective reality. The physiological condition which is said to be the seat of witchcraft, and which I believe to be nothing more than food passing through the small intestine, is an objective condition, but the qualities they attribute to it and the rest of their beliefs about it are mystical. Witches, as Azande conceive them, cannot exist.

The concept of witchcraft nevertheless provides them with a natural philosophy by which the relations between men and unfortunate events are explained and with a ready and stereotyped means of reacting to such events. Witchcraft beliefs also embrace a system of values which regulate human conduct.

Witchcraft is ubiquitous. It plays its part in every activity of Zande life; in agricultural, fishing, and hunting pursuits; in domestic life of homesteads as well as in communal life of district and court; it is an important theme of mental life in which it forms the background of a vast panorama of oracles and magic; its influence is plainly stamped on law and morals, etiquette and religion; it is prominent in technology and language; there is no niche or corner of Zande culture into which it does not twist itself. If blight seizes the groundnut crop it is witchcraft; if the bush is vainly scoured for game it is witchcraft; if women laboriously bail water out of a pool and are rewarded by but a few small fish it is witchcraft; if termites do not rise when their swarming is due and a cold useless night is spent in waiting for their flight it is witchcraft; if a wife is sulky and unresponsive to her husband it is witchcraft; if a prince is cold and distant with his subject it is witchcraft; if a magical rite fails to achieve its purpose it is witchcraft; if, in fact, any failure or misfortune falls upon any one at any time and in relation to any of the manifold activities of his life it may be due to witchcraft. Those acquainted either at firsthand or through reading with the life of an African people will realize that there is no end to possible misfortunes, in routine tasks and leisure hours alike, arising not only from miscalculation, incompetence, and laziness, but also from causes over which the African, with his meager scientific knowledge, has no control. The Zande attributes all these misfortunes to witchcraft unless there is strong evidence, and subsequent oracular confirmation, that sorcery or one of those evil agents which I mentioned in the preceding section has been at work, or unless they are clearly to be attributed to incompetence, breach of a taboo, or failure to observe a moral rule.

When a Zande speaks of witchcraft he does not speak of it as we speak of the weird witchcraft of our own history. Witchcraft is to him a commonplace happening and he seldom passes a day without mentioning it. Where we talk about the crops, hunting, and our neighbors' ailments the Zande introduces into these topics of conversation the subject of witchcraft. To say that witchcraft has blighted the groundnut crop, that witchcraft has scared away game, and that witchcraft has made so-and-so ill is equivalent to saying in terms of our own culture that the groundnut crop has failed owing to blight, that game is scarce this season, and that so-and-so has caught influenza. Witchcraft participates in all misfortunes and is the idiom in which Azande speak about them and in which they explain them. Witchcraft is a classification of misfortunes which while differing from each other in other respects have this single common character, their harmfulness to man.

Unless the reader appreciates that witchcraft is quite a normal factor in the life of Azande, one to which almost any and every happening may be referred, he will entirely misunderstand their behavior towards it. To us witchcraft is something which haunted and disgusted our credulous forefathers. But the Zande expects to come across witchcraft at any time of the day or night. He would be just as surprised if he were not brought into daily contact with it as we would be if confronted by its appearance. To him there is nothing miraculous about it. It is expected that a man's hunting will be injured by witches, and he has at his disposal means of dealing with them. When misfortunes occur he does not become awe-struck at the play of supernatural forces. He is not terrified at the presence of an occult enemy. He is, on the other hand, extremely annoyed. Some one, out of spite, has ruined his groundnuts or spoiled his hunting or given his wife a chill, and surely this is cause for anger! He has done no one harm, so what right has anyone to interfere in his affairs? It is an impertinence, an insult, a dirty, offensive trick! It is the aggressiveness and not the eeriness of these actions which Azande emphasize when speaking of them, and it is anger and not awe which we observe in their response to them.

Witchcraft is not less anticipated than adultery. It is so intertwined with everyday happenings that it is part of a Zande's ordinary world. There is nothing remarkable about a witch—you may be one yourself, and certainly many of your closest neighbors are witches. Nor is there anything awe-inspiring about witchcraft. We do not become psychologically transformed when we hear that someone is ill —we expect people to be ill—and it is the same with Azande. They expect people to be ill, i.e., to be bewitched, and it is not a matter for surprise or wonderment.

But is not Zande belief in witchcraft a belief in mystical causation of phenomena and events to the complete exclusion of all natural causes? The relations of mystical to common-sense thought are very complicated and raise problems that confront us on every page of this book. Here I wish to state the problem in a preliminary manner and in terms of actual situations.

I found it strange at first to live among Azande and listen to naïve explanations of misfortunes which, to our minds, have apparent causes, but after a while I learned the idiom of their thought and applied notions of witchcraft as spontaneously as themselves in situations where the concept was relevant. A boy knocked his foot against a small stump of wood in the center of a bush path, a frequent happening in Africa, and suffered pain and inconvenience in consequence. Owing to its position on his toe it was impossible to keep the cut free from dirt and it began to fester. He declared that witchcraft had made him knock his foot against the stump. I always argued with Azande and criticized their statements, and I did so on this occasion. I told the boy that he had knocked his foot against the stump of wood because he had been careless, and that witchcraft had not placed it in the path, for it had grown there naturally. He agreed that witchcraft had nothing to do with the stump of wood being in his path but added that he had kept his eyes open for stumps, as indeed every Zande does most carefully, and that if he had not been bewitched he would have seen the stump. As a conclusive argument for his view he remarked that all cuts do not take days to heal but, on the contrary, close quickly, for that is the nature of cuts. Why, then, had his sore festered and remained open if there were no witchcraft behind it? This, as I discovered before long, was to be regarded as the Zande explanation of sickness. Thus, to give a further example, I had been feeling unfit for several days, and I consulted Zande friends whether my consumption of bananas could have had anything to do with my indisposition and I was at once informed that bananas do not cause sickness, however many are eaten, unless one is bewitched. I have described at length Zande notions of disease in Part IV, so I shall record here a few examples of witchcraft being offered as an explanation for happenings other than illness.

Shortly after my arrival in Zandeland we were passing through a government settlement and noticed that a hut had been burnt to the ground on the previous night. Its owner was overcome with grief as it had contained the beer he was preparing for a mortuary feast. He told us that he had gone the previous night to examine his beer. He had lit a handful of straw and raised it above his head so that light would be cast on the pots, and in so doing he had ignited the thatch. He, and my companions also, were convinced that the disaster was caused by witchcraft.

One of my chief informants, Kisanga, was a skilled wood carver, one of the finest carvers in the whole kingdom of Gbudwe. Occasionally the bowls and stools which he carved split during the work, as one may well imagine in such a climate. Though the hardest woods be selected they sometimes split in process of carving or on completion of the utensil even if the craftsman is careful and well acquainted with the technical rules of his craft. When this happened to the bowls and stools of this particular craftsman he attributed the misfortune to witchcraft and used to harangue me about the spite and jealousy of his neighbors.

When I used to reply that I thought he was mistaken and that people were well disposed towards him he used to hold the split bowl or stool toward me as concrete evidence of his assertions. If people were not bewitching his work, how would I account for that? Likewise a potter will attribute the cracking of his pots during firing to witchcraft. An experienced potter need have no fear that his pots will crack as a result of error. He selects the proper clay, kneads it thoroughly till he has extracted all grit and pebbles, and builds it up slowly and carefully. On the night before digging out his clay he abstains from sexual intercourse. So he should have nothing to fear. Yet pots sometimes break, even when they are the handiwork of expert potters, and this can only be accounted for by witchcraft. "It is broken—there is witchcraft," says the potter simply. Many similar situations in which witchcraft is cited as an agent are instanced throughout this and following chapters.

In speaking to Azande about witchcraft and in observing their reactions to situations of misfortune it was obvious that they did not attempt to account for the existence of phenomena, or even the action of phenomena, by mystical causation alone. What they explained by witchcraft were the particular conditions in a chain of causation which related an individual to natural happenings in such a way that he sustained injury. The boy who knocked his foot against a stump of wood did not account for the stump by reference to witchcraft, nor did he suggest that whenever anybody knocks his foot against a stump it is necessarily due to witchcraft, nor yet again did he account for the cut by saying that it was caused by witchcraft, for he knew quite well that it was caused by the stump of wood. What he attributed to witchcraft was that on this particular occasion, when exercising his usual care, he struck his foot against a stump of wood, whereas on a hundred other occasions he did not do so, and that on this particular occasion the cut, which he expected to result from the knock, festered whereas he had had dozens of cuts which had not festered. Surely these peculiar conditions demand an explanation. Again, if one eats a number of bananas this does not in itself cause sickness. Why should it do so? Plenty of people eat bananas but are not sick in consequence, and I myself had often done so in the past. Therefore my indisposition could not possibly be attributed to bananas alone. If bananas alone had caused my sickness, then it was necessary to account for the fact that they had caused me sickness on this single occasion and not on dozens of previous occasions, and that they had made only me ill and not other people who were eating them. Again, every year hundreds of Azande go and inspect their beer by night and they always take with them a handful of straw in order to illuminate the hut in which it is fermenting. Why then should this particular man on this single occasion have ignited the thatch of his hut? I present the Zande's explicit line of reasoning—not my own. Again, my friend the wood carver had made scores of bowls and stools without mishap and he knew all there was to know about the selection of wood, use of tools, and conditions of carving. His bowls and stools did not split like the products of craftsmen who were unskilled in their work, so why on rare occasions should his bowls and stools split when they did not split usually and when he had exercised all his usual knowledge and care? He knew the answer well enough and so, in his opinion, did his envious, backbiting neighbors. In the same way, a potter wants to know why his pots should break on an occasion when he uses the same material and technique as on other occasions; or rather he already knows, for the reason is known in advance, as it were. If the pots break it is due to witchcraft.

We must understand, therefore, that we shall give a false account of Zande philosophy if we say that they believe witchcraft to be the sole cause of phenomena. This proposition is not contained in Zande patterns of thought, which only assert that witchcraft brings a man into relation with events in such a way that he sustains injury.

My old friend Ongosi was many years ago injured by an elephant while out hunting, and his prince, Basongoda, consulted the oracles to discover who had bewitched him. We must distinguish here between the elephant and its prowess, on the one hand, and the fact that a particular elephant injured a particular man, on the other hand. The Supreme Being, not witchcraft, created elephants and gave them tusks and a trunk and huge legs so that they are able to pierce men and fling them sky high and reduce them to pulp by kneeling on them. But whenever men and elephants come across one another in the bush these dreadful things do not happen. They are rare events. Why, then, should this particular man on this one occasion in a life crowded with similar situations in which he and his friends emerged scatheless have been gored by this particular beast? Why he and not someone else? Why on this occasion and not on other occasions? Why by this elephant and not by other elephants? It is the particular and variable conditions of an event and not the general and universal conditions that witchcraft explains. Fire is hot, but it is not hot owing to witchcraft, for that is its nature. It is a universal quality of fire to burn, but it is not a universal quality of fire to burn *you*. This may never happen; or once in a lifetime, and then only if you have been bewitched.

In Zandeland sometimes an old granary collapses. There is nothing remarkable in this. Every Zande knows that termites eat the supports in course of time and that even the hardest woods decay after years of service. Now a granary is the summerhouse of a Zande homestead and people sit beneath it in the heat of the day and chat or play the African hole game or work at some craft. Consequently it may happen that there are people sitting beneath the granary when it collapses and they are injured, for it is a heavy structure made of beams and clay and may be stored with eleusine as well. Now why should these particular people have been sitting under this particular granary at the particular moment when it collapsed? That it should collapse is easily intelligible, but why should it have collapsed at the particular moment when these particular people were sitting beneath it? Through years it might have collapsed, so why should it fall just when certain people sought its kindly shelter? We say that the granary collapsed because its supports were eaten away by termites. That is the cause that explains the collapse of the granary. We also say that people were sitting under it at the time because it was in the heat of the day and they thought that it would be a comfortable place to talk and work. This is the cause of people being under the granary at the time it collapsed. To our minds the only relationship between these two independently caused facts is their coincidence in time and space. We have no explanation of why the two chains of causation intersected at a certain time and in a certain place, for there is no interdependence between them.

Zande philosophy can supply the missing link. The Zande knows that the supports were undermined by termites and that people were sitting beneath the granary in order to escape the heat and glare of the sun. But he knows besides why these two events occurred at a precisely similar moment in time and space. It was due to the action of witchcraft. If there had been no witchcraft people would have been sitting under the granary and it would not have fallen on them, or it would have collapsed but the people would not have been sheltering under it at the time. Witchcraft explains the coincidence of these two happenings.

H. R. Trevor-Roper

THE EUROPEAN WITCH-CRAZE OF THE SIXTEENTH AND SEVENTEENTH CENTURIES

Many may think of the European persecution and execution of witches as an esoteric, barbaric craze remote from modern preoccupations. But could simple barbarism explain the prevalence of witch tortures and trials at a time of great literary and cultural excellence; their duration for two centuries; their adherence by many—not all—men, who were often the most respected scholars of their day?

The Oxford historian Hugh R. Trevor-Roper, in this comprehensive chapter, 'The European Witch-Craze of the Sixteenth and Seventeenth Centuries," breaks from traditional intellectual history, which considers the witch-craze as a breach of rationalism in the development of civilization, and explains many of the social, psychological, and intellectual forces determining the course of terror. In so doing, he presents much information and utilizes sound anthropological theory. Although he never actually uses the phrase, he discusses the "collective representations" of witchcraft in its social setting. The mythology of witches is explored in detail; the literary works affecting belief; the furious intellectual disputes ovei demons' and devils' powers and dangers; their marginality as outcast groups— often set apart religiously or economically from their neighbors; the use of witchcraft as a tool to persecute dissenters during the Reformation (by both Catholics and Protestants); not least, the powerful fear it exerted over its believers. Only when the revolution in scientific thought came about, led by Bacon and Descartes (who found demons superfluous in a world ordered by scientific, "mechanical" laws of nature) did witch persecutions as such subside.

The excerpt here is mainly the conclusion of Trevor-Roper's chapter, which summarizes his major theories and observations. Yet, to obtain the full depth and perception of the work the entire essay must be examined, for the controversy over witches and the personalities discussed reads as if it could be a vital current issue. Its immediacy is intentional, for Trevor-Roper never lets us forget that the witch-hunters change only the name of their prey from era to era.

The European witch-craze of the sixteenth and seventeenth centuries is a perplexing phenomenon: a standing warning to those who would simplify the stages of human progress. Ever since the eighteenth century we have tended to see European history, from the Renaissance onwards, as the history of progress, and that progress has seemed to be constant. There may have been local variations, local obstacles, occasional setbacks, but the general pattern is one of persistent advance. The light continually, if irregularly, gains at the expense of darkness. Renaissance, Reformation, Scientific Revolution mark the stages of our emancipation from medieval restraints. This is natural enough. When we look back through history we naturally see first those men, those ideas, that point forward to us. But when we look deeper, how much more complex the pattern seems! Neither the Renaissance nor the Reformation nor the Scientific Revolution are, in our terms, purely or necessarily progressive. Each has a Janus-face. Each is compounded both of light and of darkness. The Renaissance was a revival not only of pagan letters but of pagan mystery-religion. The Reformation was a return not only to the unforgettable century of the Apostles but also to the unedifying centuries of the Hebrew kings. The Scientific Revolution was shot through with Pythagorean mysticism and cosmological fantasy. And beneath the surface of an ever more sophisticated society what dark passions and inflammable credulities do we find, sometimes accidentally released, sometimes deliberately mobilized! The belief in witches is one such force. In the sixteenth and seventeenth centuries it was not, as the prophets of progress might suppose, a lingering ancient superstition, only waiting to dissolve. It was a new explosive force, constantly and fearfully expanding with the passage of time. In those years of apparent illumination there was at least one-quarter of the sky in which darkness was positively gaining at the expense of light.

Yes, gaining. Whatever allowance we may make for the mere multiplication of the evidence after the discovery of printing, there can be no doubt that the witch-craze grew, and grew terribly, after the Renaissance. Credulity in high places increased, its engines of expression were made more terrible, more victims were sacrificed to it. The years 1550–1600 were worse than the years 1500–1550, and the years 1600–1650 were worse still. Nor was the craze entirely separable from the intellectual and spiritual life of those years. It was forwarded by the cultivated popes of the Renaissance, by the great Protestant reformers, by the saints of the Counter-Reformation, by the scholars, lawyers and churchmen of the age of Scaliger and Lipsius, Bacon and Grotius, Bérulle and Pascal. If those two centuries were an age of light, we have to admit that, in one respect at least, the Dark Age was more civilized.

For in the Dark Age there was at least no witch-craze. There were witch-beliefs, of course—a scattered folk-lore of peasant superstitions: the casting of spells, the making of storms, converse with spirits, sympathetic magic. Such beliefs are universal, in time and

place, and in this essay I am not concerned with them. I am concerned with the organized, systematic "demonology" which the medieval Church constructed out of those beliefs and which, in the sixteenth and seventeenth centuries, acquired a terrible momentum of its own. And when we make this necessary distinction between the organized witch-craze and the miscellaneous witch-beliefs out of which it was constructed, we have to admit that the Church of the Dark Age did its best to disperse these relics of paganism which the Church of the Middle Ages would afterwards exploit.

. . .

I have suggested that the witch-craze of the sixteenth and seventeenth centuries must be seen, if its strength and duration are to be understood, both in its social and in its intellectual context. It cannot properly be seen, as the nineteenth-century liberal historians tended to see it, as a mere "delusion," detached or detachable from the social and intellectual structure of the time. Had it been so—had it been no more than an artificial intellectual construction by medieval inquisitors—it is inconceivable that it should have been prolonged for two centuries after its full formulation; that this formulation should never afterwards have been changed; that criticism should have been so limited; that no criticism should have effectively undermined it; that the greatest thinkers of the time should have refrained from openly attacking it; and that some of them, like Bodin, should even have actively supported it. To conclude this essay I shall try to summarize the interpretation I have offered.

First, the witch-craze was created out of a social situation. In its expansive period, in the thirteenth century, the "feudal" society of Christian Europe came into conflict with social groups which it could not assimilate, and whose defence of their own identity was seen, at first, as "heresy." Sometimes it really was heresy: heretical ideas, intellectual in origin, are often assumed by societies determined to assert their independence. So Manichaean ideas, carried—it seems—by Bulgarian missionaries, were embraced by the racially distinct society of Pyrenean France and "Vaudois" ideas, excogitated in the cities of Lombardy or the Rhône, were adopted in the Alpine valleys where "feudal" society could never be established. The medieval Church, as the spiritual organ of "feudal" society, declared war on these "heresies," and the friars, who waged that war, defined both orthodoxy and heresy in the process. We know that the doctrines which they ascribed both to the Albigensians and to the Vaudois are not necessarily the doctrines really professed by those "heretics," whose authentic documents have been almost entirely destroyed by their persecutors. The inquisitors ascribed to the societies which they opposed at once a more elaborate cosmology and a more debased morality than we have any reason to do. In particular, they ascribed to the Albigensians an absolute dualism between God and the Devil in Nature, and orgies of sexual promiscuity—a charge regularly made by the orthodox against esoteric dissenting societies. Both these charges would be carried forward from the first to the second stage of the struggle.

For the first stage was soon over. Orthodox "feudal" society destroyed the "Albigensian" and reduced the "Vaudois" heresies. The friars evangelized the Alpine and Pyrenean valleys. However, the social dissidence remained, and therefore a new rationalization of it seemed necessary. In those mountain areas, where pagan customs lingered and the climate bred nervous disease, the missionaries soon discovered superstitions and hallucinations out of which to fabricate a second set of heresies: heresies less intellectual, and even less edifying, than those which they had stamped out, but nevertheless akin to them. The new "heresy" of witchcraft, as discovered in the old haunts of the Cathari and the Vaudois, rested on the same dualism of God and the Devil; it was credited with the same secret assemblies, the same promiscuous sexual orgies; and it was described, often, by the same names.

This new "heresy" which the inquisitors discovered beneath the relics of the old was not devised in isolation. The Albigensians, like their Manichaean predecessors, had professed a dualism of good and evil, God and the Devil, and the Dominicans, the hammers of the Albigensians, like St. Augustine, the hammer of the Manichees, had adopted something of the dualism against which they had fought. They saw themselves as worshippers of God, their enemies as worshippers of the Devil; and as the Devil is *simia Dei*, the ape of God, they built up their diabolical system as the necessary counterpart of their divine system. The new Aristotelean cosmology stood firmly behind them both, and St.

Thomas Aquinas, the guarantor of the one, was the guarantor of the other. The two were interdependent; and they depended not only on each other, but also on a whole philosophy of the world.

The elaboration of the new heresy, as of the new orthodoxy, was the work of the medieval Catholic Church and, in particular, of its most active members, the Dominican friars. No argument can evade or circumvent this fact. The elements of the craze may be non-Christian, even pre-Christian. The practice of spells, the making of weather, the use of sympathetic magic may be universal. The concepts of a pact with the Devil, of night-riding to the sabbat, of *incubi* and *succubi*, may derive from the pagan folk-lore of the Germanic peoples. But the weaving together of these various elements into a systematic demonology which could supply a social stereotype for persecution was exclusively the work, not of Christianity, but of the Catholic Church. The Greek Orthodox Church offers no parallel. There were peasant superstitions in Greece: Thessaly was the classic home of ancient witches. There were encyclopaedic minds among the Greek Fathers: no refinement of absurdity deterred a Byzantine theologian. The same objective situation existed in the east as in the west: Manichaean dualism was the heresy of the Bogomils of Bulgaria before it became the heresy of the Albigensians of Languedoc. But even out of the ruins of Bogomilism, the Greek Orthodox Church built up no systematic demonology and launched no witch-craze. By the schism of 1054 the Slavonic countries of Europe— with the exception of Catholic Poland, the exception which proves the rule—escaped participation in one of the most disreputable episodes in Christian history.

Such, it seems, was the origin of the system. It was perfected in the course of a local struggle and it had, at first, a local application. But the intellectual construction, once complete, was, in itself, universal. It could be applied anywhere. And in the fourteenth century, that century of increasing introversion and intolerance, among the miseries of the Black Death and the Hundred Years War in France, its application was made general. The first of the Avignon popes, themselves bishops from recalcitrant Languedoc, gave a new impulse to the craze. The weapon forged for use against nonconformist societies was taken up to destroy nonconformist individuals: while the inquisitors in the

Alps and the Pyrenees continued to multiply the evidence, the warring political factions of France and Burgundy exploited it to destroy their enemies. Every spectacular episode increased the power of the myth. Like the Jew, the witch became the stereotype of the incurable nonconformist; and in the declining Middle Ages, the two were joined as scapegoats for the ills of society. The founding of the Spanish Inquisition, which empowered the "Catholic Kings" to destroy "judaism" in Spain, and the issue of the Witch Bull, which urged cities and princes to destroy witches in Germany, can be seen as two stages in one campaign.

Even so, the myth might have dissolved in the early sixteenth century. The new prosperity might have removed the need for a social scapegoat. The new ideas of the Renaissance might have destroyed its intellectual basis. We have seen that in the years 1500–1550, outside its Alpine home, the craze died down. In those years the purified Aristoteleanism of Padua corrected the extravagance of scholastic physics; the neo-Platonism of Florence offered a more universal interpretation of Nature; the new criticism of the humanists pared down medieval absurdities. All these intellectual movements might, in themselves, be ambivalent, but they might, together, have been effective. In fact they were not. In the mid-sixteenth century, the craze was revived and extended and the years from 1560 to 1630 saw the worst episodes in its long history. It seems incontestable that the cause of this revival was the intellectual regression of Reformation and Counter-Reformation, and the renewed evangelism of the rival Churches. The former gave new life to the medieval, pseudo-Aristotelean cosmology of which demonology was now an inseparable part. The latter carried into northern Europe the same pattern of forces which the Dominicans had once carried into the Alps and Pyrenees—and evoked a similar response.

The Reformation is sometimes seen as a progressive movement. No doubt it began as such: for it began in humanism. But in the years of struggle, of ideological war, humanism was soon crushed out. The great doctors of the Reformation, as of the Counter-Reformation, and their numerous clerical myrmidons, were essentially conservative: and they conserved far more of the medieval tradition than they would willingly admit. They might reject the Roman supremacy and go back, for their Church system, to the rudimentary organization of the apostolic age. They might pare away the incrustations of doctrine, the monasticism, the "mechanical devotions," the priestcraft of the "corrupted" medieval Church. But these were superficial disavowals. Beneath their "purified" Church discipline and Church doctrine, the Reformers retained the whole philosophic infrastructure of scholastic Catholicism. There was no new Protestant physics, no exclusively Protestant view of Nature. In every field of thought, Calvinism and Lutheranism, like Counter-Reformation Catholicism, marked a retreat, an obstinate defence of fixed positions. And since demonology, as developed by the Dominican inquisitors, was an extension of the pseudo-Aristotelean cosmology, it was defended no less obstinately. Luther might not quote the *Malleus*; Calvin might not own a debt to the Schoolmen; but the debt was clear, and their successors would admit it. Demonology, like the science of which it was a part, was a common inheritance which could not be denied by such conservative Reformers. It lay deeper than the superficial disputes about religious practices and the mediation of the priest.

But if the Reformation was not, intellectually, a progressive movement, it was undoubtedly an evangelical movement. Like the Dominicans of the Middle Ages the Lutheran and Calvinist clergy set out to recover for the faith—for their version of the faith—the peoples of northern Europe whom the Catholic Church had almost lost. In the first generation after Luther this evangelical movement had hardly begun. Luther's appeal was to the Christian princes, to the Christian nobility of Germany. As in the England of Henry VIII, Reform had begun as an affair of state. But by 1560 the princes, or many of them, had been won, and the immediate need was for preachers to establish religion among their people. So the second generation of Reformers, the missionaries formed in Wittenberg or Geneva, poured into the lands of hospitable princes or estates and the Word was preached not only in the ears of the great but in rural parishes in Germany and Scandinavia, France, England and Scotland.

Of course the triumph of the preachers was not always easy. Sometimes they found individual opposition; sometimes whole societies seemed obstinately to refuse their Gospel. Just as the Dominican missionaries had encountered stubborn resistance from the mountain communities of the Alps and

Pyrenees, so the Protestant missionaries found their efforts opposed by whole communities in the waste lands of the neglected, half-pagan north. The German preachers found such dissidence in Westphalia, in Mecklenburg, in Pomerania: areas, as a German physician later observed, where the peasants live miserably on thin beer, pig's meat and black bread; the more tolerant Swedish clergy found it, though they did not persecute it, in the racially distinct societies of Lapland and Finland; the Scottish Kirk found it, and persecuted it, among the Celtic Highlanders. Sometimes this opposition could be described in doctrinal terms, as "popery." The Scottish witches who set to sea in a sieve to inconvenience King James were declared to be "Papists," and Lancashire, of course, was a nest of both Papists and witches. Sometimes it was too primitive to deserve doctrinal terms, and then a new explanation had to be found. But this time there was no need to invent a new stereotype. The necessary stereotype had already been created by the earlier missionaries and strengthened by long use. The dissidents were witches.

With the Catholic reconquest a generation later, the same pattern repeats itself. The Catholic missionaries too discover obstinate resistance. They too find it social as well as individual. They too find it in particular areas: in Languedoc, in the Vosges and the Jura, in the Rhineland, the German Alps. They too describe it now as Protestant heresy, now as witchcraft. The two terms are sometimes interchangeable, or at least the frontier between them is as vague as that between Albigensians and witches in the past. The Basque witches, says de l'Ancre, have been brought up in the errors of Calvinism. Nothing has spread this pest more effectively through England, Scotland, Flanders and France, declares del Rio (echoing another Jesuit, Maldonado) than *dira Calvinismi lues*. "Witchcraft grows with heresy, heresy with witchcraft," the English Catholic Thomas Stapleton cried to the sympathetic doctors of Louvain. His argument—his very words—were afterwards repeated, with changed doctrinal labels, by Lutheran pastors in Germany. Whenever the missionaries of one Church are recovering a society from their rivals, "witchcraft" is discovered beneath the thin surface of "heresy."

Such, it seems, is the progress of the witch-craze as a social movement. But it is not only a social movement. From its social basis it also has its individual extension. It can be extended deliberately, in times of political crisis, as a political device, to destroy powerful enemies or dangerous persons. Thus it was used in France in the fourteenth and fifteenth centuries. It can also be extended blindly, in times of panic, by its own momentum. When a "great fear" takes hold of society, that society looks naturally to the stereotype of the enemy in its midst; and once the witch had become the stereotype, witchcraft would be the universal accusation. It was an accusation which was difficult to rebut in the lands where popular prejudice was aided by judicial torture: we have only to imagine the range of the Popish Plot in England in 1679 if every witness had been tortured. It is in such times of panic that we see the persecution extended from old women, the ordinary victims of village hatred, to educated judges and clergy whose crime is to have resisted the craze. Hence those terrible episodes in Trier and Bamberg and Würzburg. Hence also that despairing cry of the good senator de l'Ancre, that formerly witches were "hommes vulgaires et idiots, nourris dans les bruyères et la fougère des Landes," but nowadays witches under torture confess that they have seen at the sabbat "une infinité de gens de qualité que Satan tient voilez et à couvert pour n'estre cognus." It is a sign of such a "great fear" when the *èlite* of society are accused of being in league with its enemies.

Finally, the stereotype, once established, creates, as it were, its own folk-lore, which becomes in itself a centralizing force. If that folk-lore had not already existed, if it had not already been created by social fear out of popular superstition within an intellectually approved cosmology, then psychopathic persons would have attached their sexual hallucinations to other, perhaps more individual figures. This, after all, is what happens today. But once the folk-lore had been created and had been impressed by the clergy upon every mind, it served as a psychological as well as a social stereotype. The Devil with his nightly visits, his *succubi* and *incubi*, his solemn pact which promised new power to gratify social and personal revenge, became "subjective reality" to hysterical women in a harsh rural world or in artificial communities—in ill-regulated nunneries as at Marseilles, at Loudun, at Louviers, or in special regions like the Pays de Labourd, where (according to de l'Ancre) the fishermen's wives were left deserted for months. And because separate persons attached their illusions to the same imaginary pattern, they made that pattern real to others. By their separate confessions the science of the Schoolmen was empirically confirmed.

Thus on all sides the myth was built up and sustained. There were local differences of course, as well as differences of time; differences of jurisdiction as well as differences of procedure. A strong central government could control the craze while popular liberty often let it run wild. The centralized Inquisition in Spain or Italy, by monopolizing persecution, kept down its production, while north of the Alps the free competition of bishops, abbots and petty lords, each with his own jurisdiction, kept the furnaces at work. The neighbourhood of a great international university, like Basel or Heidelberg, had a salutary effect, while one fanatical preacher or one over-zealous magistrate in a backward province could infect the whole area. But all these differences merely affected the practice of the moment: the myth itself was universal and constant. Intellectually logical, socially necessary, experimentally proved, it had become a *datum* in European life. Rationalism could not attack it, for rationalism itself, as always, moved only within the intellectual context of the time. Scepticism, the distrust of reason, could provide no substitute. At best, the myth might be contained as in the early sixteenth century. But it did not evaporate: it remained at the bottom of society, like a stagnant pool, easily flooded, easily stirred. As long as the social and intellectual structure of which it was a part remained intact, any social fear was likely to flood it, any ideological struggle to stir it, and no piecemeal operation could effectively drain it away. Humanist critics, Paduan scientists, might seek to correct the philosophic base of the myth. Psychologists—medical men like Weyer and Ewich and Webster—might explain away its apparent empirical confirmation. Humane men, like Scot and Spee, by natural reason, might expose the absurdity and denounce the cruelty of the methods by which it was propagated. But to destroy the myth, to drain away the pool, such merely local operations no longer sufficed. The whole intellectual and social structure which contained it, and had solidified around it, had to be broken. And it had to be broken not at the bottom, in the dirty sump where the witch-beliefs had collected and been systematized, but at its centre, whence they were refreshed. In the mid-seventeenth century this was done. Then the medieval synthesis, which Reformation and Counter-Reformation had artificially prolonged, was at last broken, and through the cracked crust the filthy pool drained away. Thereafter society might persecute its dissidents as Huguenots or as Jews. It might discover a new stereotype, the "Jacobin," the "Red." But the stereotype of the witch had gone.

Evon Z. Vogt

WATER WITCHING: AN INTERPRETATION OF A RITUAL PATTERN IN A RURAL AMERICAN COMMUNITY

This article is concerned with divination in a contemporary American rural community, Homestead, New Mexico, which presents a rare opportunity for a systematic study of water witching. Water witching is a divinatory ritual; both ritual and divination are considered to be responses to emotional anxiety and cognitive frustration in a situation of uncertainty.

Because of irregularities in geological strata, ground water in the Homestead area varies considerably in depth. The area is geologically so complex that modern

Reprinted from *Scientific Monthly*, LXXV (September, 1952), 175–186, by permission of the American Association for the Advancement of Science.

geologists are unable accurately to predict where a well should best be drilled. In this uncertainty, water witching has flourished.

It was possible to approach the origin and role of the Homestead water-witching pattern from several theoretical positions. These positions are, briefly: (1) water witching is technologically valid—it finds water; (2) water witching is a superstition accepted only by the uneducated; and (3) water witching has a positive sociopsychological value for its users. These theories are empirically examined by means of comparison between Homestead and a town in the center of the area from which the Homesteaders migrated.

This study indicates that the technological utility of water witching is no better than chance—somewhat worse, in fact—and that many well-educated people subscribe to it in some degree. The evidence substantiates the third theory, that water witching does reassure people in a situation of uncertainty; it tells an individual just where and how deep a well should be dug and it is in accord with the Homesteader's value of a rational mastery over nature.

The article tends to corroborate the thesis that water witching in particular and divination in general are responses to uncertainty—to that which man is unable to know and control through rational means.

Further information on water witching as magical divination is provided in the book by Vogt and Hyman, *Water Witching U.S.A* (1959), which offers evidence that 25,000 water dowsers are currently practicing this ancient form of divination in America today and that the general conclusions of this article can be extended to the United States as a whole.

This paper will attempt an interpretation of the phenomenon of water witching as a folk-ritual pattern which has been extraordinarily persistent in rural American culture and which has not been replaced by the services of competent ground-water geologists in locating family-size wells in countless rural American communities. There is a vast literature on this water-divining pattern, but by and large the writings have centered on the problem of whether dowsing does or does not work as an empirical technique for locating underground supplies of water. The latest publication of note in this vein is the best seller by Kenneth Roberts, *Henry Gross and His Dowsing Rod*, which, as a spirited defense of the empirical validity of the dowsing technique, has renewed and publicized the age-old controversy. But, so far as this writer has been able to determine, there has been no systematic attempt to analyze the phenomenon as a folk-ritual pattern functionally equivalent to the magical practices found in the nonliterate cultures of the world.

Emanating from the writings of Pareto, Malinowski, and Weber, and continuing in the present generation of theorists—notably Parsons, Kluckhohn, and Homans—a general body of theory concerning the function of ritual in the situation of human action has emerged. Briefly stated, the essence of this theory is that when human beings are confronted with situations that are beyond empirical control and that are, therefore, anxiety-producing both in terms of emotional involvement and of a sense of cognitive frustration, they respond by developing and elaborating nonempirical ritual that has the function of relieving emotional anxiety and of making some sense of the situation on a cognitive level. Kroeber has recently questioned the universality of this relationship by pointing out that the Eskimos, who live in a far more uncertain and anxiety-producing environment than do Malinowski's Trobriand Islanders, have little ritual as compared to the Trobrianders, whereas given Malinowski's formulation one would expect more Eskimo ritual. Kroeber goes on to indicate that the arctic environment is so severe that had the Eskimos devoted much energy to the development of ritual patterns, they would long since have perished. This latter point is sound, but further analysis of Eskimo culture may reveal that, although there is little elaboration of ritual, the ritual patterns that do exist are still clustered around the greatest uncertainties of Eskimo life.

Others, notably Radcliffe-Brown, have raised the issue as to whether rituals do not create anxiety (when they are not performed or are not performed properly) rather than alleviate it. Homans has treated this problem in terms of "primary" and "secondary" rituals focused around "primary" and "secondary" types of anxiety. Primary anxiety describes the sentiment men feel when they desire the accomplishment of certain results and do not possess the techniques that make these results certain; secondary anxiety describes the sentiment resulting when the traditional rites are not performed or are performed improperly. Kluckhohn has carried the analysis further by demonstrating that ritual patterns have both a "gain" and a "cost" from the point of view of the continued functioning of a society, and that problems are created as well as solved by the presence of ritual patterns in a given culture.

Finally, I should like to advance the theory that ritual patterns which initially emerge as responses to critical areas of uncertainty in the situation of action are elaborated and reinterpreted in terms of certain selective value-orientations in a given culture.[1]

We are brought, then, to a dynamic conception of ritual which includes the following considerations: Ritual patterns develop as a response to emotional anxiety and cognitive frustration in a situation of uncertainty; but ritual patterns come to have both "functional" and "dysfunctional" aspects (both a "gain" and a "cost") for the continuing existence of a society as the patterns are elaborated and developed in terms of the selective value-orientations of a given culture.

In this paper I shall analyze the relationship of the water-witching pattern to the critical area of uncertainty in the location of underground water supplies, explore the functional and dysfunctional aspects of this pattern for the continuing survival of the community, and try to show how the pattern has become an expression of the value stress on "rational" environment control in a rural American community.

FOLK RITUAL IN RURAL AMERICA

The continuing existence of a large body of folk ritual in rural American culture is a fact of common observation by anyone who has lived in such communities and by those who have done systematic research in rural areas. For example, in *Plainville, USA*, James West wrote that "many magical practices still exist for planting crops, castrating livestock, weaning, gardening, girdling trees." Taylor reported that he had gathered 467 different signs and superstitions that are known and to some extent believed in rural communities.

Although these magical practices are found in connection with many aspects of rural culture, including the preparation of food, the curing of illness, and the weaning of babies, they are apparently concentrated in the area of farming technology and have to do mainly with weather, crops, the care of animals, and the locating of water wells. Taylor asserted that over one fourth of his 467 signs and superstitions refer to climate and weather and that the majority refer to plants and animals in addition to weather and climate.

THE WATER-WITCHING PATTERN

The phenomenon by means of which one is supposed to find underground supplies of water by the use of a divining rod is variously known as dowsing, divining, witching, and rhabdomancy. The indicator employed in water divining is called a divining rod, witching stick, dowsing rod, dipping rod, striking stick, or wand; and the practitioner may be called a diviner, dowser, witch, or finder. In current usage the word "dowsing" is more common in the literature and is used by rural people along the Eastern seaboard; "water witching" is the more common term used by rural folk who utilize the technique in the South, Middle West, and Far West.[2]

It is certain that the water-witching pattern has a respectable antiquity in Western culture and it is highly probable that the basic ideas of the technique derive ultimately from ancient divining practices that are widespread among the nonliterate cultures of the world. The "rod" is mentioned many times in the Bible in connection with miraculous performances, especially in the books of Moses. The much-quoted reference to Moses' striking the rock with his rod, thus producing water for his followers in the wilderness (Numb. XX:9–11), has been regarded by enthusiasts of water witching as a significant reference to the divining rod. Herodotus mentions the use of the divining rod by the Persians, Scythians, and Medes; and Marco Polo reports its use throughout the Orient.

But whatever significance one may attach to such references, authorities agree that the

---

[1] This theoretical point is developed in the writer's book, *Modern Homesteaders: The Life of a Twentieth-Century Frontier Community* (Cambridge: Harvard University Press, 1955).

[2] Roberts objects to the use of the term "water witch" on the ground that it perpetuates the idea of its association with witchcraft and prefers the term "dowsing." "Dowsing" comes from the Cornish word *douse* and the Middle English word *duschen*, both meaning "to strike" or "to fall." "Rhabdomancy" comes from two Greek words, *Rhabdos* ("rod") and *manteia* ("divination")

divining rod in its present form was in use in Germany by the first half of the sixteenth century. The first complete published description is contained in Agricola's *De re metallica*, published in 1556. Barrett considers that the birthplace of the modern divining rod was in the mining districts of Germany, probably in the Harz Mountains, where it was used to prospect for ore. During the reign of Queen Elizabeth (1558–1603), when German miners were imported to England to lend an impetus to the mining industry in Cornwall, they brought the *schlagruthe* ("striking rod") with them. As mining declined in Cornwall, the use of the rod was transferred to water finding. At about the same time there is mention of the use of the rod for locating water supplies in France.

Before the end of the seventeenth century the use of the divining rod had spread through Europe, everywhere arousing controversy. Its champions, among whom were some of the most learned men of the time, explained its operation on the principle of "sympathy" or "attraction and repulsion." Its adversaries, like Agricola, condemned its use as a superstitious and vain practice. Indeed, the practice even became a subject of ecclesiastical controversy when Martin Luther proclaimed in 1518 that the use of the rod violated the First Commandment, and the Jesuit Father Gaspard Schott later denounced it as an instrument controlled by the devil. From Europe the water-witching pattern spread to the New World and to such regions as Australia and New Zealand, and it is reported that as late as 1931 the government of British Columbia hired an "official" water diviner to locate wells.

Over the past four centuries the phenomenon has also been the subject of innumerable scientific (or allegedly scientific) investigations and controversies, beginning with Pierre Lebrun in 1692 and continuing off and on to the present controversy stimulated by Roberts' best-selling book. The key figures in these investigations and controversies have been such men as Sir William Barrett (professor of physics in the Royal College of Science for Ireland), Henri Mager (in France), J. W. Gregory (Glasgow University), O. E. Meinzer (U.S. Geological Survey), and more recently Solco W. Tromp (professor of geology at Fuad I University, Cairo).

The core of the water-witching pattern as it is now found in rural American culture may be characterized as follows:

Equipment. The most common item of equipment utilized is the witching stick, typically a Y-shaped green twig cut from a hazel, willow, or peach tree. The two forks vary from 14 to 18 inches in length, and the neck from 4 to 11 inches. The diameter of the stick may vary from one-eighth inch to almost an inch. Alternative types of wood used include maple, apple, dogwood, and beach twigs and, in the southwestern United States, twigs cut from piñon and juniper trees. There is even one case on record of a diviner who uses a leaf from the broad-leafed yucca plant. Less common, but widespread, are various metallic materials used for witching, including barbed wire from the nearest fence, a clock or watch spring, and especially constructed aluminum rods. Finally, some water witches use various kinds of pendulums such as small bottles of "chemicals" suspended on a string, or a key suspended by string from either a Bible or an arithmetic book.

Technique. The most common technique is to grasp the two branches of the forked twig, one in each hand, with the neck (or bottom of the Y) pointing skyward. Usually the twig is grasped with the palms of the hands up, but an alternative method is to hold the stick with the palms down. In either case, the forked twig is placed under tension in such a way that the slightest contraction of the muscles in the forearm or a slight twist of the wrists is sufficient to cause the twig to rotate toward the ground. The water witch walks over the ground in the area where a water supply is desired. When he walks over an underground supply of water, the witching stick is supposed to dip down, and a stake is then driven into the ground to mark the spot. Although most dowsers function only to locate a suitable spot to drill for a well or to dig for a spring, some also have techniques for determining the depth of the water supply. Perhaps the most common of these is to measure the distance from the place where the stick starts to dip to where it dips straight down over the water supply. Few, if any, other practitioners profess to have the sophisticated "powers" of Henry Gross that would enable them to ask questions and receive answers (by the way the rod nods) as to the quality and amount of the underground water, or to locate a water supply by "long-distance" dowsing, as Henry Gross did when he dowsed over a map of Bermuda while in New England and located water there.

Ideology. Like most ritual patterns, water witching carries with it an elaborate mythology, the core of which involves two aspects: the dowser's definition of the geological situation, summarized by the belief held by dowsers that underground water occurs in two forms: *sheet water*, which underlies a total area, and *water veins*, which may vary in magnitude from "the size of a pencil" to "underground rivers" and which run through the earth like the veins in the human body. The important thing is to locate and trace these veins, because either there may be no sheet water in a given area or it may be located at so deep a level that the only way to find suitable shallow water is "to hit a vein." The most elementary knowledge of ground-water geology is sufficient to prove that this dowsing concept bears little relation to known facts. The second aspect concerns the many and varied "explanations" and justifications advanced by dowsers for the efficacy of dowsing and the rationalization provided to account for failures. The "explanations" on record range from supernaturalistic interpretations (such as the notion that dowsers derive their mysterious power from Moses, "who was the first water witch") to supposedly scientific interpretations (such as the notion that the muscles of the water witch are affected by electromagnetic disturbances emanating from underground water supplies). Most of the ordinary and less articulate water witches in rural America provide explanations in terms of (1) a kind of magical principle by which the water in the green twig is attracted by the water in the ground, or (2) a theory —which they regard as "scientific"—that the dipping of the stick has something to do with "electricity" or "electrical currents" which run from the water through their bodies and into the stick, causing it to dip. Equally important are the rationalizations advanced to account for failures. These typically take the form of attributing the failure either to faulty equipment (e.g., "I couldn't find a straight stick that day") or to some aspect of the situation that negates the findings of the dowser (e.g., "I found I had a knife in my pocket which short-circuited the electric current," or "The vein dried up before they got around to drilling the well").

Institutionalization of role. There is considerable variation in the prestige the dowser has in a rural community, depending upon various factors. But it is clear that he occupies a special role. In the first place, the basic ability to do witching is usually believed to be a skill with which one is born and which he later discovers; it cannot be acquired by training or experience. In this respect it comprises a skill which is acquired by "divine stroke," as in the "shamanistic" tradition, rather than a body of knowledge transmitted by training in a "priestly" tradition. To be sure, it is necessary for a person to have observed (or to have heard about) the basic techniques, but it is impossible for one water witch to impart the skill to another. One is either born with it or one is not.[3] By virtue of this inborn ability, the dowser assumes a specialized role that is

[3] However, there are reputedly differences among dowsers as to the amount of skill they possess. Thus Roberts describes Henry Gross as being a highly skilled dowser. And once a dowser finds that he has the basic ability, it is possible for him to become more skilled with experience. It would be interesting to know the incidence of dowsing skill in the rural population, but no data are yet available. It is worth noting that in the community of Homestead (pop. 250) there is one dowser; and in the nearby Mormon community of Rimrock (pop. 300) there is only one. Neither community has ever been without at least one dowser. For short periods of time there have been two in each community, but never more than two at any given time.

recognized by the total community—both by the proponents and by the adversaries of dowsing.

In the second place, the water witch is almost always paid for his services, in amounts ranging from $5 to $25 (in the Southwest) for locating each well site. In this respect his position becomes a part-time occupation and some dowsers derive a substantial income from their activities. It should be pointed out that some dowsers charge a set price and collect the money in businesslike fashion; others volunteer their services and take whatever contributions are offered them. But I have not yet known a water witch who was a charlatan or who performed the operation purely for the monetary gain involved. Usually they are sincere individuals who believe thoroughly in their ability to find water. Finally, it should be noted that dowsers are usually men, although women sometimes have the witching skill. Indeed, the water diviner reported to have been employed by the government of British Columbia in 1931 was a woman.

Having described the history and general pattern of dowsing, let us turn to a more intensive treatment of water witching in terms of the concrete data from a single community —Homestead, New Mexico[4]—where the relevant historical, geological, and social facts are well known.

WATER WITCHING IN HOMESTEAD

The community of Homestead was established by families from the South Plains area of western Texas and Oklahoma who settled on homesteads in the semiarid area of western New Mexico in the early 1930's. The economy focuses around the production of pinto beans on dry-land farms, supplemented by crops of corn, winter wheat, and beef cattle. Farms now average two sections in size and are scattered as far as twenty miles from the crossroads center of the community which contains the stores, school, post office, repair shops, and other service institutions. Farming technology has shifted through the years from horse-drawn implements to mechanized equipment.

The natural environment provides an unusually hazardous setting for dry-land farming. Until the homesteaders arrived, the land had been used only for grazing purposes, and the area is still regarded as submarginal farming land by authorities in the U.S. Department of Agriculture. The soil is excellent for beans, but the necessary 90-day growing season is often cut short by late

[4] Homestead is a fictitious name, used to protect the anonymity of my informants

spring frosts or early fall frosts at this elevation (7000 feet). Heavy windstorms in the
spring add the hazard of serious wind erosion.
But the basic environmental problems are
those of inadequate and fluctuating rainfall
and the development of water resources for
livestock and household use. Annual precipitation averages 12.5–15 inches, depending
upon locality and elevation, but has varied
over the past two decades from 6 to 19 inches.

The people who established this community
defined themselves as pioneers, leaving the
"civilized" centers of Texas and Oklahoma to
seek new homes on the "frontier" west of the
Continental Divide. As pioneers, they emphasize many of the values characteristic of newly
settled American farming communities: a
stress on self-reliance and independence of the
individual, a drive to subdue and control the
natural environment, an abiding faith in the
progressive development of their community,
and a perennial optimism about the future.
With these values they confronted the semiarid environment of western New Mexico and
set about the business of developing dry-land
farms.

One of the first critical problems the homesteaders faced was the development of adequate water supplies. When they first arrived
in 1930–1931, they found it necessary to haul
water in barrels by team and wagon from a
lake three miles from the center of the community. When the lake went dry, they hauled
water from a spring seven miles distant. If a
farmer had livestock, it meant that he had to
haul water at least every other day. A few
tried drilling wells in the early years, but it was
soon discovered that, although in some places
water was struck at shallow depths (80–100
feet), in others dry holes were the only result
after drilling over 500 feet. At a cost of $1–$3
a foot for drilling a well, few homesteaders
were willing or able to take the risk.

It was in this situation that one farmer
suddenly "discovered" in 1933 that he had the
"power" to witch for water. As a young boy
in Texas he had observed witching. One day
he simply cut a forked stick from his wife's
peach tree, tried out the technique as he
remembered it, and it worked. He found two
water veins on his farm, traced them to a
point where they crossed each other, and had
a successful well drilled at this spot at a depth
of 230 feet. He rapidly achieved community-
wide reputation as a water witch and successfully witched 18 wells in the next few years.
Six wells were dowsed by a second water witch

TABLE 1

	Wells Divined	Wells Not Divined
Successful wells	24	25
Dry holes	5	7

who lived in the community for a few years,
making a total of 24 wells that were located in
this manner. During the same period, however, the original water witch dowsed five
locations where dry holes resulted after
drilling; and he often missed calculating the
depth by as much as 200–400 feet. For, in
addition to using the common technique for
locating the water vein by walking over the
ground with a forked twig and putting a stake
in the ground where the rod dipped, he
developed a special technique for determining
depth. He would hold a thin, straight stick
(5 feet in length) over the water vein, and it
would "involuntarily" nod up and down. The
number of nods indicated the depth in feet to
the water. During the same period 25 wells
were successfully drilled without benefit of
dowsing, and seven dry holes were drilled in
locations that were not dowsed (Table 1).

As time went on, the water witch killed his
wife's lone peach tree by cutting witching
sticks from it. He then made an adjustment to
the New Mexican environment by shifting to
the use of forked twigs from piñon trees. He
explains his dowsing in terms of "electricity"
and usually attributes errors to the presence
of iron (like a knife in his pocket, or an old
piece of farm machinery in the vicinity) or to
the fact that he could not find a straight stick.

There is, of course, more than a casual
relation between the early water supply
problems of homesteaders and the geology of
the Homestead area.[5] The community is
bordered on the south by a high escarpment
that exposes the upper formations underlying the area. These consist of Quaternary
basalt flows which are exposed in portions of
the eastern and northern parts, Tertiary sands
and conglomerates which underlie the western
part, and the Mesa Verde formation of Upper
Cretaceous age which underlies the above
formations at variable depths. The Mesa
Verde formation is about 1800 feet thick and
consists of alternating gray to buff sandstones,
gray clay shales, and coal.

[5] I am indebted to Tom O. Meeks for the geological
data.

During Tertiary time the shales and sandstones of the upper Mesa Verde formation were eroded, and subsequent deposition of the Tertiary sands and conglomerates filled the old channels. The existence of these buried channels and ridges, and recent erosion of the Tertiary formation, resulted in variations in the thickness of the Tertiary formation and the upper member of the Mesa Verde formation.

Ground water occurs in the Mesa Verde formation, which is the main aquifer, and in the Tertiary formation; small quantities may also be available in the recent alluvium in the valleys, especially in the north and northeast. Structural conditions are not well known, but there are indications of a number of faults and of one syncline, which also affect ground-water supplies.

Several shallow wells near the center of the community and a few wells to the west obtain water from the Tertiary formation. These wells range in depth from 225 to 260 feet, and the yield is usually small. The erosion of the Mesa Verde formation, and subsequent deposition of the Tertiary formation, have caused the base of the Tertiary sands to be an irregular surface. This accounts for the variable depth of wells and the variation in yields. Wells drilled into the old channels are likely to yield more water than others drilled on the buried ridges of the underlying Mesa Verde formation.

The majority of wells in the Homestead area, and all the wells a mile or more east of the center of the community, obtain water from the Mesa Verde formation. The yield of these wells is generally greater than those obtaining water from the Tertiary sands, but it is necessary to drill deeper. The depth varies from about 80 feet in the Tertiary sands in the western part of the area to 800 feet in the Mesa Verde formation in the eastern portion.

Thus it is readily seen that geological conditions have resulted in substantial variations in ground-water resources in different parts of the area. In some localities water is found in the Tertiary sands, usually at relatively shallow depths, but with variations running from 88 to over 300 feet. In other localities it is necessary to drill to a greater depth into the Mesa Verde formation. And the situation is further complicated by structural conditions that are not yet well known by geologists.

In the dowsing of his own well the local water witch was over the Tertiary formation,

and water in small quantities was located at 230 feet. The wells which the dowser "successfully" located were either drilled into the Tertiary formation or the farmers were willing to drill to greater depths and thus reach the Mesa Verde formation. The dry holes were cases in which the wells were either (a) located where the Tertiary sands did not exist and the farmer was unwilling to go deep enough to strike the Mesa Verde formation (two cases), or (b) located over the Tertiary formation but in places where buried channels or the presence of the syncline in the underlying Mesa Verde formation made the depth to water greater than the wells were drilled (three cases). The same geological facts account for the dry holes that resulted from drilling in locations that were not dowsed. The frequent errors in estimating depth were undoubtedly due to these same geological conditions, especially since the dowser usually named a depth that approximated, or was less than, the depth of his own well.

In addition to the water-witching pattern there are two other types of institutionalized folk ritual in Homestead: (1) the use of natural phenomena, such as the winds, clouds, or moon to predict the weather (especially the occurrence of frost) and to judge the proper time for planting crops; and (2) the use of the signs of the zodiac to know when to perform certain farming or livestock operations,[6] such as when to castrate calves "so they won't bleed to death," when to wean calves "so they won't bawl around for several days,"[7] or when to hoe weeds "so they won't come up again." Farmers who believe in and practice these three types of folk ritual are known, respectively, as "witch men," "moon men," and "sign men."

Not all the homesteaders believe in and practice these rituals. Our data indicate that opinions range from those of farmers who are wholly oriented in terms of the rational-technological methods of modern agricultural science and scoff at "those silly superstitions,"

[6] For the signs the homesteaders depend mainly upon *Dr. J. H. McLean's Almanac* (now in its 98th year of publication), which is distributed free through the local stores by the Dr. J. H. McLean Medicine Company of St. Louis.

[7] The same sign is used to judge the proper times to wean infants. Other researchers interested in the socialization process in Homestead were startled when the response to their question "When do you wean your babies?" was "I wean them when the sign is right." This would appear to be an aspect of the socialization process in rural America that has not yet been explored.

to those who believe firmly in and practice all three types of ritual—e.g., the water witch who is also full of knowledge about and belief in "signs," "planting by the moon," etc. The data further indicate that, of the three areas of ritual, the water-witching pattern is the most widespread and the most persistent in the face of formal education in the theories and methods of modern science. When the recorded instances of the practice of these rituals from our running field notes for the year's period were classified, it was found that 57 per cent of the instances were in the area of water witching, 29 per cent were in the area of the use of the almanac and the signs of the zodiac, and 14 per cent referred to the use of natural phenomena to predict and control events. It was further discovered that some of the most highly educated individuals in the community were having wells dowsed (for example, the principal of the school, who possesses an M.A. degree). Again, research revealed that opinion varied from utter skepticism on the part of some farmers who said that "the best witching stick is the end of the driller's bit" to complete faith in the ability of the dowser to locate water. The most frequent response was an attitude expressed by such statements as, "Well, I'm not sure I believe in it, but it don't cost any more," or "I'll always give it the benefit of the doubt."

Comparative data from a recent study in the Texas Panhandle, which was initiated to provide controls over certain variables in the Homestead study, are illuminating for the analysis of water witching. The Panhandle study was focused on the small community of Cotton Center (pop. 100), near the geographical center of the area that provided the families for the present population of Homestead. The kinship and intervisiting ties between the two communities are unusually close, despite the distances involved, and there is ample evidence that the cultures of the two communities are still quite similar.

Specific inquiries as to water witching and the geology and ground-water resources were made in Cotton Center. The community is located in Hale County, which is extremely flat, consisting of slightly undulating hills interspersed with many poorly drained depressions that fill with water during the rainy season. Annual rainfall averages 22 inches, or almost twice the precipitation found in Homestead. Most of the usable ground water is found in the Ogallala formation, a sandy deposit lying at or near the surface throughout the region. The ground-water table stands at a depth of about 125 feet below the surface, and good wells can be obtained at almost any point. Wells are located where water can be used to best agricultural advantage on the farms. Water witching is widely known, but it is almost never practiced. It can be classified as an unused skill in Cotton Center.

There is also evidence from this area of the Panhandle to indicate that the practice of water witching in Homestead is not due to selective migration—with the "superstitious people" moving west to New Mexico and leaving the families with a more rational-technological orientation behind. For, less than 25 miles to the southeast of Cotton Center in Floyd and Crosby counties, the ground-water situation is more variable, there is more difficulty locating wells, and water witching is currently practiced. Indeed, there are men from Cotton Center who assist their relatives in dowsing for water in these other counties.

ALTERNATIVE THEORIES OF WATER WITCHING

There are three theories to account for the persistence of water witching in rural American culture. The first may be designated as the "technological theory," which accounts for the continuing practice of water witching on the basis of the empirical validity of the technique as a reliable method for locating wells. The second theory may be designated as the "survival theory," which assumes that water witching is a folk-ritual pattern but accounts for its continued practice by defining the pattern as a "survival" from a previous, less technically oriented phase of our cultural development. The third theory may be designated as the "functional theory," which also defines water witching as a ritual pattern but emphasizes the relationship between situations of technological uncertainty in the present scene and the pattern of water witching as a ritual means of coping with situations that are beyond empirical control.

THE TECHNOLOGICAL THEORY

As indicated earlier, the controversy about water witching has centered around the problem of whether it does or does not work as a reliable empirical method for locating underground supplies of water. This theory must be examined first, because if water witching is an empirically reliable technique, it can then be regarded as part of the rational farming technology in rural American culture, and no further explanation of its continuing use is necessary.

It would be patently impossible to summarize here all the arguments pro and con on the empirical validity of water witching; our task is merely to examine the most relevant evidence. At the outset we may rule out the various "supernaturalistic" claims—as, for example, the claim that dowsers have some kind of mysterious power transmitted through the generations from Moses which enables them to find water. We may also eliminate the simple explanation of many dowsers to the effect that the water in the ground attracts and pulls the water in the freshly cut witching stick. There would appear to be no naturalistic basis for believing that water located (in some cases) as much as several hundred feet under the surface could directly affect the water in a freshly cut stick. Furthermore, as Finklestein points out, the claims of the dowsers lead one to the inevitable conclusion that if there is an empirical basis for the technique, it must be independent of the type of witching device utilized; because the same claims are made for the effectiveness of all devices.

Although we may eliminate the possibility that some kind of external physical force acts directly upon the dowsing rod, there remains the possibility that some kind of external physical force is stimulating the dowser's muscles, which then contract and cause the rod to dip. In this case the rod is merely an indicator of muscular contractions and the type of witching rod used would make no difference.

This approach to the problem has recently been explored by Tromp, who presents experimental evidence indicating that some individuals are more sensitive than others to changes in the strength and polarity of electrical fields associated with both natural and artificial objects. And the problem then becomes one of assessing the possibility that underground supplies of water may affect variations in electromagnetic fields to the extent that these changes in electrical field strength are registered in the dowser's muscles, stimulating them to contract, and thereby indicating the presence of underground water. As matters now stand, even Tromp does not appear to claim that dowsers can identify the cause of a particular change in electrical field strength (such as might result from the presence of underground water), but only that it exists. And the judgment of competent geologists is that it is impossible that changes in electromagnetic fields caused by the *specific* presence of underground water can be registered in *specific* ways in the muscular contractions of dowsers.[8]

The question may also be raised as to whether the dowser is not merely a sound practical geologist who knows the groundwater situation from experience in a given area, and that he is responding to certain surface outcroppings or other indications of underground water when his witching stick dips. In other words, perhaps the witching stick is merely an indirect way of communicating sound geological knowledge.

It is true that many dowsers respond to certain cues in the environment while they are going through the dowsing process. For example, the dowser in Homestead utilizes anthills, and piñon trees with branches that hang down unusually far, as general guides to underground water. But our evidence indicates that these are merely cues for the dowser and have no specific connection with shallow underground water. Furthermore, the dowser makes no attempt to collect information about the location and depth of other wells in the vicinity or to utilize other types of empirical data in the location of new wells.

In other areas of the world, however, there is suggestive evidence that the dowsers occasionally do possess some sound geological knowledge and that their "successes" are due to these empirical observations that are then recorded by the witching stick. But in this case it is obviously the geological observations made by the dowser (and neither the attraction of the rod by underground water nor the stimulation of the muscles of the dowser by variations in electrical fields caused by the presence of underground water) which give the technique an empirical basis.

---

[8] Personal communication from Kirtley F. Mather, April 10, 1952, as follows: "Although he [Tromp] claims that the results of his own experiments and those of other qualified scientists indicate 'that divining phenomena are not due to charlatanry and suggestion but really exist,' he also states that 'many diviners make the mistake of claiming that they are able to indicate certain hidden objects, underground ore deposits, water, etc. They fail to realize that many external influences can create the same physiological reaction, similar to readings with modern geophysical instruments, which could be the same under different external conditions.' My conclusion is that Tromp presents no valid evidence that there is any scientific basis, other than psychological, for the procedures followed by dowsers in their efforts to locate underground water supplies."

TABLE 2

	Wells Divined		Wells Not Divined	
	Number of Wells	Percentage	Number of Wells	Percentage
Bores in which supplies of serviceable water estimated at 100 gal./hr. or over were obtained	1234	70.4	1406	83.9
Bores in which supplies of serviceable water estimated at less than 100 gal./hr. were obtained	180	10.2	88	5.3
Bores in which supplies of unserviceable water were obtained	82	4.7	55	3.3
Bores—absolute failures, no water of any kind obtained	257	14.7	126	7.5
Total	1753	100.0	1675	100.0

A second approach to the problem of the empirical validity of water witching is to examine the best evidence available as to the reliability of the dowsing technique. There have been two recent relevant systematic studies. In 1939 the New South Wales Water Conservation and Irrigation Commission issued a report containing full data on wells drilled in New South Wales from 1918 to 1939. The commission drills wells and issues licences for wells drilled by private companies, so that full statistical data are available. Table 2 gives the totals from 1918 to 1939.

In 1948 P. A. Ongley, of the medical school at the University of Otago, published the results of controlled experiments performed on 58 different New Zealand water dowsers. Not a single dowser showed any reliability in any of the experiments, which consisted of the following:

1. Asking the dowser to locate an underground stream and then return to it with his eyes closed.
2. Having the dowser locate an underground stream and then later identify which pegs were on the stream and which were not—the experimenter having placed one half of a number of pegs over the underground stream designated by the dowser and the other half of the pegs off the stream.
3. Asking two or more dowsers to check one another on the location of underground water.
4. Asking the dowser to say whether a hidden bottle was full of water or empty.
5. Asking two or more dowsers to determine the depth of the water below the surface of the ground.

To these observed facts, we may add the data on dowsing from Homestead which are reported in Table 1. Although the number of wells involved is small as compared to the series from New South Wales, it is plain that the same negative results are indicated. In both instances, it does not appear to make much difference whether a well is dowsed or not; if anything, there would appear to be fewer complete failures when wells are located by methods other than dowsing, indicating that chance or common sense is a little more reliable.

Finally, I have observed two cases in Homestead in which the well driller was already drilling in a water-bearing formation when the water witch appeared with his forked twig and announced (after dowsing around the immediate area of the well rig) that the driller had best move his drill since he would never hit water in the hole he was then drilling!

It is difficult to avoid the conclusion that water witching is not an empirically reliable method for locating underground supplies of water.[9] It is plain that the witching stick dips in response to muscular contractions of the

[9] For an answer to the problem of how Henry Gross was able to locate wells in Bermuda by merely dowsing over a map, the reader is referred to Nichols' review of Kenneth Roberts' book on *Henry Gross and His Dowsing Rod*. Briefly, Nichols points out that limestone islands of the Bermuda type have little fresh water, because the limestone is so permeable that the rain water runs through it rapidly and mixes with the salt water. Most of these islands have a thin lens of fresh water floating on salt water, its thickness depending on the size of the island, the permeability of the rock, and the rainfall. The problem is not that there is no fresh water in Bermuda, but that there is not very much. What there is must be developed by a "skimming" process in which wells are dug to or just below sea level and the water is pumped at a rate that will keep its level just above that of the sea, thus preventing salt water from rising into the well. So Henry Gross did not locate "domes" of fresh water in Bermuda (where there was previously nothing but rain water trapped from the runoff of roofs); he merely located wells which reached to lenses of fresh water floating on the salt water

dowser that are due to some type of unconscious mental or psychic processes and *not* in response to the physical presence of underground water supplies. But the question remains as to why water witching continues to be practiced if it is not an empirical method for locating water. To answer this question we must turn to the other two theories.

THE SURVIVAL THEORY

A second theory that is held implicitly, and sometimes stated explicitly, by many rural sociologists, government agricultural experts, and other observers of the rural scene is the view that water witching is one of many "superstitions" that survive among the unenlightened farmers who learned them from their fathers and grandfathers. It is firmly believed by these observers that the "superstitions" will be replaced by rational-technological methods for coping with the environment as soon as there is sufficient education in the methods of modern agricultural science. Indeed, the disposition of many of these writers is to behave as if the superstitions had already been replaced by scientific methods; and despite their prevalence in rural American culture, it is rare to find an explicit treatment of the problem in rural sociology textbooks. An exception is Sims, who writes that:

The magical mind, rather than the scientific attitude, tends to prevail (in rural America). . . . This is an emotional and unreflective attitude which does not clearly perceive the steps between thoughts and actions. . . . Expressions of magical mindedness are seen in numerous superstitious beliefs and practices in regard to harvesting and planting.

Sims goes on to argue that science will eventually cause the disappearance of ritual from the rural scene, as he writes:

The impress of science is already marked and the agencies carrying it to the farmers persistent. . . . With much prestige already established for this method, there is every reason to think that fairly rapid headway will be made in the immediate future. To the degree such progress is made, the magical mindedness will disappear.

There is certainly a grain of truth in this explanation of water witching. It *is* a "superstitious" practice from the point of view of the educated observer, and the pattern has obviously been transmitted to the current generation of farmers from earlier generations. But does it persist *merely* because farmers are lacking in education and are

"magical minded"? Two observations on the basis of Homestead data may be made here. The first is that many of the most highly educated individuals in Homestead still resort to the practice when they have a well drilled. The second is the fact that although the educational level is approximately the same in the present population of Homestead as in the population of Cotton Center in the Texas Panhandle, water witching is not utilized to locate wells in Cotton Center (where the water table stands at a uniform depth), whereas the practice flourishes in Homestead (where the underground water supply is highly variable in depth). These facts strongly suggest that there is more to the phenomenon of dowsing than that it is a "superstitious survival" from an earlier phase of cultural development.

THE FUNCTIONAL THEORY

A few rural sociological writers have given some attention to this third theory in which such practices as water witching are viewed not merely as "superstitious survivals" but as ritual responses to situations of technological uncertainty in the contemporary scene. Carl Taylor, in his *Rural Sociology*, has made the following statement:

The reliance of the old-time farmer upon the almanac was proverbial, and his belief in signs, although sometimes exaggerated, is by no means extinct. . . . The point we wish to make here is not that superstitions, signs, and charms have greater influence among rural than urban people (although this is probably the case), but that farming as an enterprise is influenced by the uncertainty of weather and seasons to such an extent that specious explanations of the causes and effects of this uncertainty have become widespread among rural people.

In the elaboration and application of this functional theory to the phenomenon of water witching, we must first specify the aspects of the Homestead situation that are technologically uncertain (and hence productive of emotional and cognitive frustration) from the point of view of modern science. It is clear that a competent ground-water geologist can provide a sound general description of the geology and the water resources of the region, and that this geological knowledge indicates that ground water is available in two of the formations that underlie all or part of the region. One or the other of these aquifers can always be reached if wells are drilled deep enough. But it is equally clear that even with the most careful geological mapping, there exists a high degree of uncertainty as to the depth and amount of ground water available in any *particular* location where one may choose to drill. This factor of indeterminacy arises from the fact that surface outcroppings do not provide complete knowledge of the buried channels and ridges that resulted from erosion of the Mesa Verde formation in Tertiary times, or of the structural conditions resulting from faults. Both these geological facts result in substantial variations in the depth and quantity of ground water.

We have, then, a situation in which family-size wells on the scattered farmsteads were needed to relieve farmers of the expensive and time-consuming task of hauling water from some distance, and a situation in which there existed a zone of indeterminacy in the exact location of adequate ground-water resources. The stage was set, so to speak, for the development of a method to cope with the situation. Two things happened. On the one hand, a local farmer "discovered" that he had the power to dowse wells and began to do so throughout the community; on the other, geologists from the Soil Conservation Service began to visit the community and to make certain recommendations on the location of wells. The two alternative methods were in competition. But the geologists came to the community infrequently[10] and could only provide answers to the question of location and the depth to water in a given well in *general* terms, whereas the water witch was always available and could specify an *exact* location and an *exact* number of feet of water. These reassuring answers encouraged many homesteaders to drill wells. When good wells were obtained at near the depth named by the water witch, his praises were sung throughout the community. When a dowsed well was a failure (because it was not deep enough), there were ready-made rationalizations to account for the failure. And the most frequent stories told about dowsing involve the cases in which a farmer tried drilling without dowsing and obtained a dry hole; then he hired the water witch to locate a well on his farm and obtained good water.

In brief, there would appear to be a functional connection between technological uncertainty in locating wells in this arid environ-

ment with a complicated geological structure and the flourishing of the water-witching pattern. This conclusion is fortified by the observed fact that the area of highest anxiety in the community—the location and development of adequate water resources—is also the area of the most persistent and most utilized ritual pattern—the water-witching technique (57 per cent of the observed instances of ritual practice)—and by the fact that water witching, which is an unused skill in the ancestral region of the Texas Panhandle, was activated and has flourished in Homestead.

Thus, although a relationship can be demonstrated between technological uncertainty and ritual in the case of water witching, the pattern has been elaborated and rationalized in terms of one of the central value-orientations of Homestead. For in their relationships with the natural environment the homesteaders strongly emphasize an orientation which may be described as "rational mastery over nature"; the environment is viewed as something to be controlled and exploited for man's material comfort. And for the adherents of water witching in the community, the pattern becomes an important expression of this value stress upon "rational" environmental control. It is part of the farming process—along with clearing the land with bulldozers, plowing, planting, and cultivating the fields with power machinery—to locate a well by witching before one employs a driller. Explanations of how dowsing works are predominantly sought in terms of "electricity" and other "scientific" concepts. Rationalization for errors is provided in terms of the presence of metal objects which "short-circuit" the process, or in terms of technologically faulty equipment.

There are clearly certain functional "gains" in the practice of water witching for the development and continuing survival of a community like Homestead. The *certain* answers provided by the dowser relieve the farmers' anxiety about ground-water resources and inspire confidence to go ahead with the hard work of developing farms. The pattern also provides a cognitive orientation to the problem of why water is found (at a certain depth) on one farm and not on another —in terms of the ideas about water veins that run irregularly under the ground.

But it is equally clear that the practice of dowsing involves certain functional "costs" in this situation. Energy and resources are invested in a technique which does not pro-

---

[10] Mr. Meeks has called my attention to the fact that the Soil Conservation Service maintains only two geologists in the Southwest who give advice on locating wells; hence their visits to any given community are necessarily infrequent.

vide any better information as to the location of shallow underground water supplies than does the good judgment of individual farmers. It is also often the case that dowsed wells will be located at spots that are highly inconvenient and inefficient for the most economical operation of the farm. Some farmhouses in the community have been built in inaccessible places on the sides of hills "because that is where the water witch found the water." But the homesteaders who are adherents of dowsing believe that they are being "scientific" about locating underground water. These attitudes detract from the effort of obtaining more precise geological information which, even if it does not tell the farmer in terms of so many feet how far it is to water at a given location, is at least a more promising long-range approach to the development of water resources for the community.

SOME COMPARATIVE DATA

Homestead is located in a region inhabited by four other cultural groups: Mormon, Spanish-American, Zuni, and Navaho. The water-witching pattern is part of the cultural equipment of the Mormons and the Spanish-Americans, but it is generally absent among the Navahos and Zunis. The Mormon experience with water dowsing parallels that of Homestead. The Mormon community is located in a well-watered valley at the base of a mountain range. In this valley wells can be drilled at almost any location, and ample ground water obtained at 30–40 feet. Some of the Mormon settlers have dry-land farms and ranches in the area to the south and east in which the ground-water situation, with a high degree of variability in amount and depth, is comparable to that of Homestead. Although the Mormon community has a water witch, he has dowsed only five wells in the irrigated valley during the past forty years. On the other hand, he has been employed to witch more than fifty wells in the dry-land farming and ranching region where the ground-water situation is highly uncertain. Occasionally, the Mormon water witch is employed to dowse for the homesteaders, and the water witch from Homestead has been employed on at least three occasions to dowse for the Mormons.

Water witching is also used by the Spanish-Americans in the area. About fifty years ago there was a practicing Spanish-American dowser, but at present the Spanish-American population does not have its own dowser.

Instead, water witches from Homestead or the Mormon community dowse wells.

So far as we can determine, the water-witching pattern is unknown to the Zunis and to most Navahos, and there is no evidence that aboriginal divining techniques—such as Navaho hand-trembling—have ever been used to locate springs or wells. The only exception in the Navaho community is found in the case of three older Navahos who in the 1930's observed the techniques of the Mormon water witch. When the Navahos tried the technique themselves, the witching stick "worked" for only one of the three. This Navaho still claims to be a water witch and reports that he has (on his own initiative) dowsed three wells, two of which produced water, and one of which was a dry hole. The powers of this one Navaho water witch are not generally recognized by others in the Navaho community, and, indeed, he is usually ridiculed when he talks about dowsing. It should be noted that this dowser is the only one of the local Navahos who has become an earnest convert to Mormonism; he is now an elder in the Mormon church.

The general absence of the pattern among the Zunis and Navahos is partly a matter of history, in that it was not a part of the cultural tradition of these groups as it was in the case of the homesteaders, Mormons, and Spanish-Americans. But it is also partly a matter of geographical situation and the use made of water resources by the Indians. Before the Indian Service began to drill wells for these two tribes, the Navahos depended upon springs, natural water holes, and lakes for water; the Zunis depended upon springs, natural lakes, and the Zuni River. Although both tribes now have wells on their reservations, the problem of locating and drilling the wells is completely in the hands of Indian Service technicians.

There is one interesting case of a highly acculturated Navaho who decided to have his own well drilled. At the suggestion of the Mormon trader, he employed the Mormon water witch and paid him $25 to locate a well. The dowser designated a location with his witching stick and told the Navaho that it would be 12 feet to water. A well driller was then employed, but the only result was a dry hole 400 feet deep which cost the Navaho $1200. The Mormon trader commented, "First time I've seen the water witch miss"; the water witch explained the situation by asserting that "the vein must have dried up," since it was several months after the dowsing took place that the well was drilled. The Navaho is thoroughly disillusioned about the powers of water-diviners.

Our conclusion is that water witching is a ritual pattern which fills the gap between sound rational-technological techniques for coping with the ground-water problem and the type of control which rural American farmers feel the need to achieve. The best geological knowledge of ground-water resources that is currently available still leaves an area of uncertainty in the task of predicting the exact depth to water at a *given* location in a region with a variable ground-water table. The water-witching pattern provides a reassuring mode of response in this uncertain situation.

Thus, although water witching is to be regarded by the scientific observer as a nonempirical means for achieving empirical ends —and is functionally equivalent to the magical practices of nonliterate societies—it is generally viewed as a rational-technological procedure by its adherents in rural communities. The technique can, therefore, best be described as a type of "folk science" or "pseudo science" in the rural American cultural tradition. As a body of pseudoscientific knowledge, the water-witching pattern in our rural farming culture is the same order of phenomena as the pseudoscientific practices that cluster around situations of uncertainty in other areas of our culture; as, for example, in modern medical practice where there appears to be a pattern of "fashion change" in the use of certain drugs, an irrational "bias" in favor of active surgical intervention in doubtful cases, and a general "optimistic bias" in favor of the soundness of ideas and efficacy of procedures which bolsters self-confidence in uncertain situations.

Omar Khayyam Moore

DIVINATION— A NEW PERSPECTIVE

While divination is usually regarded as a means of overcoming ambiguity and of legitimizing a course of action, Moore's ingenious theory is that divination, by supplying a chance mechanism, directs some human activities toward randomness and may thereby serve a useful role in avoiding regularity where such regularity may be disadvantageous. He suggests in this article that scapulimancy may send Naskapi hunters off in random directions and thereby *increase* their chances of encountering the caribou herds they seek. His hypothesis needs further exploration, but it is certainly novel and merits investigation.

Reprinted from *American Anthropologist*, LIX (1957), 69–74, by permission of the author and the American Anthropological Association.

The purpose of this paper is to suggest a new interpretation of certain kinds of magical practices, especially divination. First, however, I should perhaps explain briefly the motivation for undertaking this analysis. The initial impetus came from experimental investigations of the problem-solving activities of groups. These experiments quite naturally involved the study and classification of ineffective problem-solving techniques, and it appeared that fresh insight into this whole matter might be gained through examining some "classic" cases of ineffective solutions to problems. Magic is, by definition and reputation, a notoriously ineffective method for attaining the specific ends its practitioners hope to achieve through its use. On the surface, at least, it would seem then that magical rituals are classic cases of poor solutions to problems, and for this reason should be of theoretical interest from the standpoint of research on human problem solving.

Most, if not all, scientific analyses of magic presuppose that these rituals as a matter of fact do not lead to the desired results. If the carrying out of a magical rite is followed by the hoped for state of affairs, then this is to be explained on other grounds. Scientific observers, of course, employ the criteria furnished by modern science to judge the probable efficacy of magical activities as methods for producing the ends-in-view of magicians. One of the puzzles most theories of magic seek to resolve is why human beings cling so tenaciously to magic if it does not work. Many contemporary explanations of this puzzle make use of the concept "positive latent function," that is, that even though magic fails to achieve its "manifest" ends, except by accident or coincidence, it serves its practitioners and/or their society in other critically important ways. The position developed here is compatible with the viewpoint that magical rituals may be sustained by numerous latent functions. However, it conceivably could serve as a prophylaxis against the overelaboration of these functions; in any case, it could serve as a supplementary explanation of the phenomena.

Put baldly, the thesis to be advanced here is that some practices which have been classified as magic may well be directly efficacious as techniques for attaining the ends envisaged by their practitioners. Perhaps the best way to render plausible this somewhat counterintuitive proposition is to consider in some detail an actual magical rite as it has been described by a highly competent anthropologist.

The Montagnais-Naskapi, most northerly of eastern Indian tribes, live in the forests and barren ground of the interior plateau of the Labradorian Peninsula. Speck (1935) has conducted field studies of the Naskapi and in the account that follows, primary reliance is placed upon his reports. According to Speck, "The practices of divination embody the very innermost spirit of the religion of the Labrador bands. Theirs is almost wholly a religion of divination" (p. 127). It is of interest to learn exactly how divination is carried out and what ends the Naskapi expect to achieve through it.

Animal bones and vario s other objects are used in divination. The shoulder blade of the caribou is held by them to be especially "truthful." When it is to be employed for this purpose the meat is pared away, and the bone is boiled and wiped clean; it is hung up to dry, and finally a small piece of wood is split and attached to the bone to form a handle. In the divinatory ritual the shoulder blade, thus prepared, is held over hot coals for a short time. The heat causes cracks and burnt spots to form, and these are then "read." The Naskapi have a system for interpreting the cracks and spots, and in this way they find answers to important questions. One class of questions for which shoulder-blade augury provides answers is: What direction should hunters take in locating game? This is a critical matter, for the failure of a hunt may bring privation or even death.

When a shoulder blade is used to locate game, it is held in a predetermined position with reference to the local topography, i.e., it is directionally oriented. It may be regarded as "a blank chart of the hunting territory . . ." (Speck, p. 151). Speck states (p. 151) ". . . as the burnt spots and cracks appear these indicate the directions to be followed and sought." If there is a shortage of food, the shoulder-blade oracle may be consulted as often as every three or four days and, of course, the directions that the hunts take are determined thereby.

There are certain other relevant aspects of divination that must be mentioned before turning to an analysis of the ritual. Speck explains (p. 150):

In divining with the burnt shoulder blade the procedure is first to dream. This, as we shall see, is induced by a sweat bath and by drumming or shaking a rattle. Then, when a dream of seeing or securing game comes to the hunter, the next thing to do is to find where to go and what circumstances will be encountered And since the dream is vague, and especially since it is not localized, the hunter-dreamer cannot tell where his route is to lie or what landmarks he will find. So he employs the shoulder blade. As one informant put it, the divination rite cleared up the dream. "We generally use the caribou shoulder blade for caribou hunting divination, the shoulder blade or hip bone of beaver for beaver divination, fish-jaw augury for fishing, and so on." Drumming, singing, and dreaming, next divination by scapula, then, combine as the modus operandi of the life-supporting hunt.

It is well to pause at this point to take note of certain features of these rites.

The Naskapi do not control the exact patterning of cracks and spots in the shoulder blade and, furthermore, it would not be in accord with their beliefs about divination to attempt such control; rather, they are interested in observing whatever cracks and spots appear. This means that the final decision about where to hunt, for instance, does not represent a purely personal choice. Decisions are based on the outcome of a process extrinsic to their volition—and this outcome is dependent upon the interaction of a number of relatively uncontrolled variables such as bone structure, temperature of fire, length of time bone is exposed to heat, etc.

It may be clarifying to perform a "mental experiment" in order to analyze some of the possible consequences of basing a decision on the outcome of an impersonal and relatively uncontrolled process. Imagine that the Naskapi carried out their divinatory rites as described with this exception; they did not base their decisions on the occurrence of cracks and spots in the burnt blade. They dreamed, sang, drummed, burned a shoulder blade, but ignored the cracks and spots. Under these hypothetical circumstances, decisions still would have to be made about where to hunt the game.

One question which this "mental experiment" raises is: Would the Naskapi be likely to enjoy more success in hunting if they did not permit decisions to rest upon the occurrence of cracks and spots? Would it not be sounder practice for them simply to decide where, in their best judgment, game may be found and hunt there? Of course, when the Naskapi do have information about the location of game, they tend to act upon it. Ordinarily, it is when they are uncertain and food supplies get low that they turn to their oracle for guidance.

It can be seen that divination based on the reading of cracks and spots, serves to break (or weaken) the causal nexus between final decisions about where to hunt and individual and group preferences in this matter. Without the intervention of this impersonal mechanism it seems reasonable to suppose that the outcome of past hunts would play a more important role in determining present strategy; it seems likely their selections of hunting routes would be patterned in a way related to recent successes and failures. If it may be assumed that there is some interplay between the animals they seek and the hunts they undertake, such that the hunted and the hunters act and react to the other's actions and potential actions, then there may be a marked advantage in avoiding a fixed pattern in hunting. Unwitting regularities in behavior provide a basis for anticipatory responses. For instance, animals that are "overhunted" are likely to become sensitized to human beings and hence quick to take evasive action. Because the occurrence of cracks and spots in the shoulder blade and the distribution of game are in all likelihood independent events, i.e., the former is unrelated to the outcome of past hunts, it would seem that a certain amount of irregularity would be introduced into the Naskapi hunting pattern by this mechanism.

We can indicate the point of the foregoing discussion in the following way. In the first place, the Naskapi live a precarious life; their continued existence depends on the success of their day-to-day hunting. And it is prima facie unlikely that grossly defective approaches to hunting would have survival value. Like all people, they can be victimized by their own habits; in particular, habitual success in hunting certain areas may lead to depletion of the game supply—it may lead, that is, to a success-induced failure. Under these circumstances, a device which would break up habit patterns in a more or less random fashion might be of value. The question is: To what degree, if any, does shoulder-blade augury do this?

It should be remembered that it is difficult for human beings to avoid patterning their behavior in a regular way. Without the aid of a table of random numbers or some other randomizing instrument, it is very unlikely that a human being or group would be able to make random choices even if an attempt were made to do so. The essential soundness of the last statement is recognized in scientific practice. Whenever, in the course of a scientific investigation, it is essential to avoid bias in making selections, every effort is made to eliminate the factor of personal choice. As Yule and Kendall have succinctly stated, "Experience has, in fact, shown that the human being is an extremely poor instrument for the conduct of a random selection."

Of course, it is not maintained here that the burnt shoulder blade is an unbiased randomizing device. It is likely that the bones would crack and form spots in certain ways more often than others. Regularity stemming from this source may to some degree be lessened because the Naskapi change campsites, yet in the rituals they maintain the same spatial orientation of the bones (for, as previously mentioned, the bones are oriented map-like with reference to the topography). Hence, a crack or spot appearing in the same place in the bone on a new occasion of divination at another campsite, would send them on a different route. An impersonal device of the kind used by the Naskapi might be characterized as a crude "chance-like" instrument. It seems that the use of such a device would make it more difficult to anticipate their behavior than would otherwise be the case.

It is not possible on the basis of the available evidence to determine even approximately whether shoulder-blade divination as practiced by the Naskapi actually serves to increase their hunting success, although a plausible argument has been advanced indicating that this might be the case.

If the Naskapi were the only people who engaged in scapulimancy, the question of its efficacy would perhaps not be of general theoretical interest. However, scapulimancy was widely practiced in North America and has been reported from Asia, India, and Europe. There are other divinatory rituals that also involve the use of impersonal chance-like devices in arriving at decisions, for example, the ancient Chinese divination by cracks in burnt tortoise shells. One hundred and twenty-five different figures formed by these cracks were distinguished for oracular purposes. All manner of objects and events have been used in divination. Some arrangements are perhaps not obviously chance-like, but prove to be so when analyzed, as for instance Azande divination. The basic divinatory equipment associated with the Azande "poison oracle" consists of poison, probably strychnine, and fowls. The Azande have little control over the potency of the poison they administer to the fowls since they do not make their own poison, and not all fowls have the same tolerance for this poison. The Azande ask questions of the poison oracle and base decisions on whether the fowls live or die. They have no way of knowing in advance what the outcome will be.

The heuristic analysis given here is potentially relevant to all situations in which human beings base their decisions on the outcome of chance mechanisms. It is obvious, however, that light would be shed on the actual workability of these procedures only in terms of a thorough-going investigation of the problems men face within the societal context in which these problems occur. Certainly the apparent irrelevance of such techniques is no guarantee of their inutility. On the contrary, if shoulder-blade augury, for example, has any worth as a viable part of the life-supporting hunt, then it is because it is in essence a very crude way of randomizing human behavior under conditions where avoiding fixed patterns of activity may be an advantage. The difficulty of providing an empirical test for this hypothesis points to the fact that it is an open question.

Years ago Tylor noted that "the art of divination and games of chance are so similar in principle that the very same instrument passes from one use to the other." Tylor's observation is acute. However, it would appear that the relationship in "principle" is not between divination and games of chance, but between divination and games of strategy. It is only very recently that the distinction between games of chance and games of strategy has been drawn clearly. We are indebted to von Neumann and Morgenstern for clarifying this. It is beyond the scope of this paper to discuss the theory of games of strategy, but it is worth pointing out that this theory makes evident how some classes of interactional problems can be solved optimally by means of a "mixed" or "statistical" strategy. In order to employ a statistical strategy it is necessary to have, adapt, or invent a suitable chance mechanism. Its being "suitable" is critical, for unless the chance device will generate appropriate odds for the problem at hand, then its potential advantage may be lost. It should go without saying that no one assumes that preliterate magicians are in any position to get the most out of their crude chance-like devices. Nevertheless, it is possible that through a long process of creative trial and error some societies have arrived at some approximate solutions for recurring problems.

SUMMARY

It is the object of this paper to suggest a new interpretation of some aspects of divination. It should be emphasized that this interpretation is offered as a supplement to existing theories of magic and not as a replacement. An examination of many magical practices suggests that the utility of some of these techniques needs to be reassessed. It seems safe to assume that human beings require a functional equivalent to a table of random numbers if they are to avoid unwitting regularities in their behavior which can be utilized by adversaries. Only an extremely thorough study of the detailed structure of problems will enable scientists to determine to what degree some very ancient devices are effective.

9
DEATH, GHOSTS, AND ANCESTOR WORSHIP

Introduction

Universal problems faced by all human societies are created by what Malinowski has called "the supreme and final crisis of life"—death. These problems, many-faceted to be sure, may be considered on two levels: those that face the individual and those that force adjustments on the society as a whole.

For all sane individuals eventual extinction of the organism, in the corporeal sense at least, forms an ever-present part of life expectancy; no normal human considers his own potential span to be eternal. Further, the death of a spouse or close relative disturbs an individual's social relations, often necessitating deliberate changes in family relations, economic activities, emotional exchange, and many other areas where the life pattern of the deceased formerly impinged on the lives of the survivors. Moving to a higher level of abstraction—the societal rather than the individual—the death of any member of the interacting group is likely to create points of stress which will pervade the entire social structure, particularly in small societies living in face-to-face relationships. Depending on the social importance of the deceased, the amount of disturbance felt within the system will vary. When the middle-aged but still vigorous male family head dies he leaves a vastly greater number of roles and functions unfulfilled than does, let us say, a female infant from a socially unimportant family. Yet the loss of any member from the group will have repercussions in a much wider circle than that composed of kin alone.

All cultures have techniques and methods which serve, if not to eliminate, at least to reduce problems arising out of the fact of human mortality. This they do both by reducing the individual's anxiety stemming from the contemplation of his own demise and by facilitating the orderly resumption of interpersonal relations following the death of a member of the group.

It could hardly be said that members of any culture anticipate with relish the prospect of passing from the delights of earthly existence, regardless of how few these may be; it is probably a fair generalization to say that most humans, given the option, would choose to remain among the living a while longer when the final moment of departure arrives. Myth and fiction sometimes permit an alternative but life itself never does. But though it is not possible to postulate eternal corporeal existence for members of a culture—the corpse is difficult to overlook—it is possible to extend culture-like conditions, bridging out from the known to the unknown, for the departed spirit to enjoy. Without attempting to suggest causality or primacy to either the spirit concept or that of life after death, it may be said that virtually all cultures provide both the concept of some nonmaterial aspect of life which will survive death and some beliefs regarding where and how this spirit would exist.

It might be suggested, though it is at present a better research hypothesis than a cultural law, that the individual's attitude toward death is strongly conditioned by the cultural belief regarding what becomes of that part of consciousness which survives the death crisis. Implicit belief in, and anticipation of, the survival of the cognitive being beyond the grave might do much to alleviate individual anxieties regarding termination of the material self—it merely continues to exist in another, and possibly more pleasant, form. The willingness of members of religious groups to die for causes justified by religious beliefs stands in evidence for this point. Attitudes of early Christians sacrificed for their faith, the willingness of Moslems to engage in "holy wars," and the apparent acceptance of their fates by many Aztec sacrificial victims, all attest to the overcoming of individual fears of death when promised recompense in an afterworld. This same point could be made for the Masai, the Plains Indian, and the Eskimo; death loses its sting when it is not conceived of as the complete end of the self. This cultural potential, the possibility of partially alleviating individual fears regarding death through the implicit belief in an afterlife, stands as another virtually universal feature of human existence. Referring to the belief in the survival of the human spirit after death, Frazer wrote with some petulance that "it seems probable that the great majority of our species will continue to acquiesce in a belief so flattering to human vanity and so comforting to human sorrow."

But what of the living, those who are not immediately contemplating an exit? Belief in an afterworld may assuage an individual's fears but, at the same time, it places him in more or less intimate contact with a host of nonmortal beings, either the departed members of his own group, as is the case with many simple cultures, or with the spirits of all departed human beings, as is the case with Christianity. Does the knowledge that the spirits of the dead were formerly relatives, countrymen, or fellow humans result in the enthusiastic participation of the living with the nonliving? Apparently not, except in a few cases. As Frazer has so convincingly demonstrated in a three-volume study of the subject (*The Fear of the Dead in Primitive Religion*, 1933–1936), most cultures have developed attitudes of fear and dread regarding the spirits of the deceased. Sometimes these fears are mild and noninstitutionalized,

as among the Hopi. At other times they are expressed through elaborate mechanisms which serve to pacify the ghosts or to mislead them by guile, as when the Bambwa sacrifice a goat near a shrine close to the ghost's alleged abode, or certain Australian tribes impose years of silence on widows so that the spirits of their jealous husbands will not be able to detect them. Anthropological literature is filled with fantastic examples of the efforts to which the living will go to ensure against the return of ghosts, even to the extent of supplying the dead with money for their expenses of the journey to the other world —a custom not only of the Khasis of Assam, the Burmese, the Lolos, and the Mosquito Indians, but of the ancient Greeks as well, who inserted a coin in the mouth of the corpse so that the deceased could pay Charon for ferrying him across the river Styx.

Apparently basic to the institutionalized fear of ghosts is the belief that after death, though the spirit of the individual continues to exist in the afterworld, the basic "personality" structure of the spirit undergoes a striking change—it becomes malevolent. Regardless of what the person may have been like in life, his spirit is potentially dangerous to the living. As the following articles reveal, however, this conception of spirits of the dead is not always the case. In many groups, ghosts may be only partially evil or dangerous, and in still others, they may be conceived of as ever-present members of the social group who have increased powers to influence the lives of the living, either favorably or unfavorably. When the ghosts are thought to be most concerned with members of their own kin groups, and the members of the kin groups feel that the ghosts require propitiation in order to aid their living kinsmen, ancestor worship prevails. The spirits of the dead are revered, though that reverence is possibly never free from some feelings of fear and awe. Sometimes repressive and harsh, at other times benign and beneficial, the ghosts or ancestral spirits coexist with the living, influencing and even determining the fortunes of the tribal members.

The articles in this chapter are intended to indicate something of the range of attitudes and beliefs that exist regarding death, ghosts, and ancestors, to indicate the ways in which these attitudes and practices are interrelated with other aspects of culture, and to offer some analyses of the various phenomena.

Morris E. Opler

AN INTERPRETATION
OF AMBIVALENCE OF TWO
AMERICAN INDIAN TRIBES

This article, prefaced by a Freudian proposition regarding ambivalence, contains excellent ethnographic documentation of attitudes and behaviors associated with death in Chiricahua and Mescalero Apache cultures. The ambivalent feeling that living members of the groups manifest toward the dead—mourning and grief expressed on the one hand, and dread and possibly hatred expressed on the other —is explained in purely cultural terms. Rejecting the Freudian position regarding "primordial parricides" and a consequent guilt feeling arising from this hypothetical event, Opler suggests that the apparent ambivalences may be explained through an analysis of interpersonal relations, the nature of power, and the ecological circumstances of the cultures. Fear of the dead is seen as a function of kinship and local group systems, of patterns of authority, of fear of sorcery and witchcraft, plus the basic need for interpersonal cooperation as a requisite for survival in the hostile environment.

As is true of most conclusions drawn from bodies of data partially inferred from individual psychological processes, other interpretations could be made than that presented here by Opler. Nonetheless, Opler's work stands as a well-documented, closely reasoned analysis of what is possibly a panhuman phenomenon—ambivalent feelings on the part of the living toward the deceased.

Opler has provided further data to substantiate his thesis in an article, "Further Comparative Anthropological Data Bearing on the Solution of a Psychological Problem," published in 1938.

Reprinted in abridged form from the *Journal of Social Psychology*, VII, No. 1 (February, 1936), 82–115, by permission of the author and the Journal Press.

Some time ago, in a review of *Totem and Taboo*, A. L. Kroeber referred to a number of Freud's suggestions as contributions "which every ethnologist must sooner or later take into consideration." Kroeber singled out Freud's discussion of ambivalence as particularly provocative and, in part, said of it: "Again the strange combination of mourning for the dead with the fear of them and taboos against them is certainly illumined if not explained by this theory of ambivalence."

Whether or not the ethnologist has taken this phase of Freud's writings into consideration, it remains true that few students of preliterate peoples have conducted inquiries designed to test or modify the psychoanalytic theory and conclusions upon the point.

At one time during my stay on the [Mescalero Apache] reservation, a very able and intelligent informant who wished to give me the fullest possible understanding of the culture undertook to explain native customs and beliefs for me. This Apache offered a number of native rationalizations pertaining to various rites and practices, and then bravely started to explain the peculiar belief that an Apache who possesses supernatural power and successfully practices the rite connected with it for any length of time, finally will be forced to sacrifice a close relative or permit himself to die. My informant floundered in a web of ambiguities for a few minutes and then had to confess that the whole matter was not clear to him. He could see, he said, why the power of some outsider, one who wished you ill perhaps, was to be feared; but why the power of a relative, one who could refuse you nothing in everyday life, should be a source of terror, he was unable to explain. This Apache was manifestly bewildered by the glaring inconsistency in the attitude toward kin upon which he had stumbled. On one hand he had been urged throughout his life to assist, and, in turn, to depend upon his relatives in all matters, to support them, whatever the consequences to himself, and even to avenge all wrongs inflicted upon them. Yet it was also within the traditional pattern to believe that these same people become, par excellence, a source of morbid fear for him. This contradiction or conflict in emotion and attitude towards the same person or group of people which this native sensed, we readily recognize as an expression of ambivalence.

The example cited is one of the most striking cases of contradictory attitude in respect to the same person which Apache culture affords and is the one which would, perhaps, be most noticeable to the native. But this instance by no means stands alone. The cultural forms are marked, at many points, by unmistakable evidence of such contrary emotions, and whole complexes are liberally tinged with such mixed feelings. A conspicuous affirmation of the last statement is the entire complex which has to do with death and the disposal of the dead. It will repay us to turn to this set of practices and beliefs.

One of the most impressive elements of Apache burial is the dispatch with which it must be conducted. Whenever possible burial takes place the same day on which death occurred. If this is impossible because the deceased has died in the evening, the burial always takes place the following day. The time during which the living and the dead are in contact is reduced to a minimum, a logical procedure in view of the dread sickness it is believed can be contracted from the dead, from the sight of the corpse, or from the possessions of the deceased.

As the last statement may suggest, no time is lost in disposing of the personal possessions of the dead. A certain number of his belongings are taken along by the burial party and interred with him; the rest are burned or broken into pieces at the spot where death took place. It is incumbent upon a dead Apache's relatives to dispose, in this way, of everything which had been used by him or had been in close personal contact with him. Even articles owned jointly with other members of the family, if they had been used to any extent by the deceased, had to be sacrificed. To retain any of these objects would bring back the ghost; the dead would return to claim his possessions. In any case the retention of some personal possession of a dead man would be sure to act as a reminder of him, and to think of the dead is one way of inviting the presence of the ghost and of subsequently succumbing to the serious "ghost" or "darkness sickness." In keeping with this fear of the return of the ghost to claim objects recognized by him, it is considered dangerous even to cherish presents given one by the deceased before his death.

Not only are the possessions of the dead relative destroyed or buried, but the very dwelling in which death took place is razed as well. The framework is usually burned, but even if it is not reduced to ashes, one may be sure that no Apache will enter a deserted house or use wood from it unless he is very certain that no death has occurred there. Nor does the destruction of the dwelling pave the way for a new, uncontaminated home on the old site. The family moves immediately to a new locality, one that will not be conducive to memories centering about the departed.

The effort to efface the memory of the dead relative goes much further. Those who assume the unwelcome task of dressing the corpse and burying it, burn, upon their return, all the clothes they wore while performing these duties. They also bathe their bodies in the smoke of a sage called "ghost medicine" which is thought unpleasant to ghosts and efficacious in keeping them at a distance. In fact, all members of the bereaved family are likely to "fumigate" themselves in this manner and to resort for some days to various devices which are considered useful in avoiding dreams of the dead or in warding off the visits of ghosts. Such practices consist in crossing the forehead or bed with ashes, or hanging some crossed pieces of "ghost medicine" above the head before retiring.

At the grave, just before their return, the members of the burial party take a final precautionary measure. They brush off their own bodies with green grass which they then lay at the grave in the form of a cross. The conception is that when this is done, any danger of falling victim to "ghost sickness" will be brushed away and left at the grave of the dead.

No more people than are strictly necessary to carry the possessions and prepare the grave participate in the burial. The site of the grave is not discussed thereafter; ordinarily no one would ask about the location of the grave, and no one would volunteer such information.

After the foregoing it is almost unnecessary to add that the grave is never revisited and that anyone found lingering around a grave site is suspect of witchcraft. As among so many other peoples, graves and the bones and possessions of the dead play a prominent role in ideas concerning sorcery.

To this point we have been primarily concerned with the measures taken to erase from the scene any material reminders of a dead relative and to avoid illness which may derive from actual contact with or sight of the corpse. But there are quite as many steps taken to obliterate less tangible reminders of the loss the family has suffered, and it may be instructive to turn to some of these now.

There is, first of all, a strong taboo against mentioning the name of the deceased. If it becomes necessary, for any reason, to mention his name, a phrase meaning "who used to be called" must be added.

As a result of this taboo it proved extremely difficult for me to obtain reliable genealogical material. It was considerably easier to persuade Apaches to discuss and reveal rites and ceremonies than it was to bring them to the point of talking freely of the kinship ties which had existed between them and those now dead.

The unwillingness to utter the name of the recent dead is a characteristic true of all members of these two tribes, whether they are relatives of the deceased or not. With the passage of time the taboo becomes less binding upon nonrelatives. Not so in respect to the relatives, however. For them there is no diminution of the strength of the taboo, and others, no matter what they may do elsewhere, must strictly refrain from any mention of the dead in the presence of these relatives. In fact, nothing is more insulting, provocative, and certain to precipitate conflict than to call out the name of a dead man in the presence of his relative. A surprising number of feuds between families have had such an origin or include such an episode in their histories.

Just as the calling of a dead man's name within the hearing of his relative is accounted the gravest of insults and acts of hostility, so it is considered a graceful compliment to the family of the deceased and to the memory of the dead to take elaborate precautions that the name be not called. In cases of the death of prominent men who have been named after some object or animal, that animal or object is given an alternative name or another name. Thus when a Mescalero leader named Beso (from the Spanish *peso*) died, everyone was obliged to say *dinero* instead of *peso*, especially when within earshot of members of the dead man's family.

There is another practice which utilizes similar reasoning. If an Apache called two relatives by the same kinship term, and one of these relatives dies, for a long time afterward he will refrain from using this term to the survivor. To use the term formerly addressed to the one who has died will awaken memories of him and deepest grief, it is felt.

It is interesting to note that the very existence of death cannot be allowed terminological sanction. The verb that connotes the coming of death is used only in connection with animals. Of a person the most that can be said in everyday speech is, "He is gone."

The insistence that nothing be left as it was before a death, lest it act as a reminder of the bereavement, finds expression in all departments of native life. There is the practice, for example, of never leaving the bedding as it was when in use, when camp is to be broken. If death should occur and the individual should not return to that place, the sight of his bed as last used by him would only bring sorrow to his relatives.

These attitudes are reflected in the ceremonial complex, moreover. Ceremonies usually continue through four days or nights. If a death occurs in any nearby camp after the rite has begun, when the news is brought to the officiating shaman, he terminates his work at once. The ceremonial gifts which had to be given him before he could enter upon his duties he returns to the donors. Now all is as it was before, and after the passage from one to four days the whole ceremony is repeated from the beginning.

Despite the brevity and condensation of this description of Apache customs concerning death rites, it should be reasonably clear that there is a whole set of important practices designed to suppress and obliterate all mention and memory of the dead relative. In introducing this material I have termed it an indicator of ambivalent attitudes. In the Freudian sense this would suggest that the struggle to remove the possessions, the name, even the memory of the deceased from consciousness, is nothing else than an elaborate attempt to guard against the fear of the dead which results from the unconscious hate and resentment felt for this person during his life.

It may be asked why such an interpretation, so farfetched at first thought, need be accepted. The Apaches themselves say that there is no deep-seated mystery concerning the genesis of these acts and rites. They will tell you that an Apache loves his kin—a great deal more than the white man cares for his relatives, they may add significantly. To dwell on the memory of the dead would be to emphasize the loss and deepen the grief. Therefore they engage in the practices which arouse our curiosity.

The reasoning sounds honest and logical and might be acceptable if it were not for another congeries of attitudes and practices of an altogether different flavor which exists at the time of death, side by side with those we have already noted. These last are direct and vehement expressions of grief and evidences of mourning which are in no way subdued, curbed, or repressed. When an Apache learns of a close relative's death, he tears the clothes from his back. The women wail, the men cry openly and unashamed. Close relatives cut their hair, an act which alone will mark their bereavement for at least a year. For some time they wear only such clothing as is absolutely necessary for minimum warmth, and for a generous span of time they shun the dances and festivities. Often relatives mourn thus for a long time. An old woman, whose husband has been dead many years, still can be heard bewailing her loss occasionally.

Without laboring the point or extending the discussion, enough has been said, perhaps, to indicate that contradictory practices mark the Apache rites of death; there is the tendency to publicly signify grief and attest to the loss, and an elaborately socialized machinery for banishing that grief and the objects and words which might awake it.

But to state the Freudian conception, namely, that these two sets of practices result from ambivalent emotional attitudes toward the dead; that one set derives from the affection and regard which normal human relations sponsor, and the other from unconscious dislike and fear that are no less poignant and real; to state this, merely, is not to prove it.

Indeed, it could be most reasonably argued that it is gratuitous elaboration and special pleading to conjure up fear and unconscious hate as the stimulus for the practices which serve to eradicate mention and memory of the dead. It might be insisted with as much cogency that both sets of practices can be reasonably traced to one source, the affection and regard for the dead relative. It takes no great imaginative powers to suppose that genuine love for the dead relative could expend itself through more than one channel, and that the actualizations of these emotional flows could even appear contradictory. It is intelligible that under the impact of a deeply felt loss there would be the impulse to cry out and testify to grief, and no less the realization that the future must be faced alone, that the living must somehow carry on, that memories which weaken without aiding must be laid aside.

With these two interpretations possible from the data, the inquiry is reduced bluntly to this question: Is there any concrete and conclusive evidence in Apache culture of avowed fear of the dead, and especially of dead relatives, which might give body and validity to the hypothesis that the avoidance of the dead, of their graves, their names, their possessions, and their memories is attributable to fear rather than to regard?

Fortunately the study of Apache culture affords an unequivocal answer. Fear of the dead, and fear of the dead relatives particularly, does not have to be inferred. Instead its existence is asserted and emphasized by the natives. This fear is not merely an amorphous dread which seizes individuals in varying ways and must be relieved according to personal requirements. It has become formalized into a body of beliefs and concepts, and these have been woven into the fabric of the ceremonial life.

Now Apache ceremonial life, while it has other functions, is principally concerned with the healing of the sick. The gravest illnesses are contracted, it is believed, from contact with certain animals, such as bear, snake, and the like, or from being frightened or endangered by certain natural forces, such as lightning. Each of these sicknesses has its own characteristics and symptoms, and such diseases can be cured by shamans who have supernatural power from, and therefore considerable influence over, the animal or agency which has caused the illness. But there are also some people of malevolent disposition who have likewise had supernatural experiences with these potent animals or forces of nature and who have gained a ceremony and considerable power thereby. These are the witches, who manipulate their power for evil often, and are the ultimate source of much sickness and death. The witch who "knows" Bear may cause his enemy to suffer from "bear disease." His victim's sole hope is to command the services of another who "knows" Bear, who uses such power for beneficent purposes only, and whose power is stronger than that of the witch. It is likewise possible for a person to use his ceremony for the benefit of some, yet seek to harm others. He may be a shaman at one point of his career and a witch at another. He may be both at the same time.

With this hint of background we may proceed to the expression of the fear of the dead in Apache society. The fear, in obedience to the native pattern, is expressed in terms of sickness, and the sickness, eloquently enough for our argument, is expressed in terms of fear

The particular illness attributable to persecution by the ghosts of the dead is known by three names, "ghost sickness," "owl sickness," and "darkness sickness." Ordinarily the Apache will not dare to use the words "ghost" or "owl" and will therefore give the last name only. The term "ghost sickness" is self-explanatory. The disease is also called "owl sickness" because the ghost is said to come back in the shape of an owl; owls are the ghosts of the departed. The blackest omen of which an Apache can think is the hoot of an owl around camp. The proximity of the bird, especially shortly after the death of a relative, evokes the greatest terror, and is often sufficient grounds for the requisite "ghost" or "owl ceremony." I could fill many more pages with native accounts of the dread and despair inspired by the appearance of the owl around camp or by its call. Ghosts are said to trouble people most often at night when it is dark, and most shamans who cure "ghost sickness" will not conduct their ceremony except at night. For these reasons, and also because a person afflicted with the malady is especially nervous and easily frightened at night, the name "darkness sickness" is the approved euphemism for the disease.

It is of special interest to note that the disease always strikes "from the head to the heart." All its symptoms are those of fright and include irregular beating of the heart, a choking sensation, and faintness at first seizure. As long as the illness lasts the patient suffers from excessive timidity, much trembling, weeping, and headache.

Although ghosts of nonrelatives may and do cause fear and sickness, it is far more common that the disease be the result of an encounter with the ghost of a deceased relative.

In the first place it is noteworthy that the most elaborate precautions are entered upon by the close relatives immediately after an Apache's death. Since these relatives have most contact with the corpse and the possessions of the dead, this is quite to be expected. Nevertheless, the end result and the general feeling are that the relative has more to fear from the ghost than anyone else.

Again, it is a matter of interest that most ghost ceremonies are held soon after a death in a family, and that the patient or patients are usually relatives of the deceased.

There is another impressive indication of the close nexus between relationship and fear of ghosts and owls. The hooting of the owl is accepted as speech in the Apache language which can be understood if one listens closely. The owl, according to my informants, has many unpleasant remarks to make to its uneasy hearers. It has been known to make the hair-raising statement, "I'm going to drink your blood." But more often the words of the owl have to do with its relationship to the one it is addressing. "I am your dead relative"—this is the most common sentence discerned by the tortured imagination of the Apache when the owl hoots nearby.

The owl is also prone to give ominous warnings concerning relatives. The bird is not infrequently heard reporting such melancholy news as, "All your people (relatives) are going to die." One woman, after the departure of a war party, heard this message repeated over and over by an owl, "I used to be one of your relatives." The next day the men returned without her son; he had been killed.

The owl, according to one Apache, "represents the spirit of a person" which "works by entering the body of an owl and exercises evil influence in this way." "That man is already dead and comes back. He turned to owl." "It's a ghost. It comes out of the grave, and it goes back." These are representative dicta of the natives concerning the owl.

From this equation of ghost with owl flows the belief that the ghost can appear as an owl and then transform itself at will into the semblance of the figure it bore in life. And it is possible for a shade of the dead to appear and, upon being accosted, to change into an owl and disappear.

Now to see or hear an owl is unlucky and harrowing enough, but to see the form of a ghost as you knew him in life, or, worse still, to be able to distinguish his features, is well-nigh fatal. It is the general consensus of opinion, backed by the authority of many cases, that the person who can discern the features of the ghost before him has not long to live.

Even though the evidence which has been offered is but a fraction of what could be presented, I hope that enough has been said to establish the connection between the taboos directed against the dead and fear of the dead. It should be abundantly clear, too, that the burden of both the taboos and the fear falls primarily and with unremitting force on the relatives of the deceased. But if the Apache must guard against the ill will of the dead, he must guard himself just as sedulously against the machinations of the living. Something has been said above of the duality of supernatural power as conceived of by the Apache, and of the possibility of wielding such power in the spirit of malice and revenge as well as for purposes good and holy. Granting the existence and duality of supernatural power, there is nothing obscure about the basis of fear of witches. A case will illustrate this. I was once talking to a man about charges of witchcraft which had been directed against X. The man with whom I was talking then admitted to me, "Well, I'm a little afraid of X myself." He told me how he and X had opposed each other in a dispute which nearly ended in blows. Knowing X's reputation for possessing much supernatural power, and believing him to be thoroughly unscrupulous, he wondered whether X's resentment might not spill over into supernatural channels and work some immense disaster to him. In this case there was a cause for revenge and a subsequent outgrowth of fear. In all cases of ordinary witchcraft, some reason for the murderous supernatural attack is advanced, if it is only that the witch was jealous of the sick one's good looks or envious of his promising career. When a shaman sings over a patient and determines that his client is witched, he very often describes what led the witch to such extremes. "Do you remember when you attended that dance two years ago?" he might ask. "You gave something to drink to everyone there but one woman. You did not know it, but you forgot her and she was very angry. She determined to get even for this insult. She has waited till now so no suspicion will fall upon her." The conception is that always, if one can but put a finger on it, there is some injury or insult which will account for recourse to witchcraft.

But the Apache is not only beset by fear of the supernatural power of those who have reason to hate and harm him; he must also face the possibility that the supernatural power of those who are closest and dearest to him, the supernatural power of his own relatives, may be utilized to effect his very death. The reader will remember that we began our paper with this very paradox. At that time it seemed an insoluble contradiction which puzzled my willing Apache informant as much as it puzzled us. Now we are in a position to see the concept as one more mark of the underlying fear directed toward relatives. We have already dealt with the fear of the ghosts of the dead felt by living relatives. Now we have to consider the Apache's fear of the supernatural power of his living relatives.

The fear is based on the peculiar belief which already has been introduced. It is asserted that if one who has a ceremony from a certain power, heals and prospers by means of it for many years, the time will come when his power will remind him of the benefits bestowed, of the long life that has been permitted him, of the guidance and security that have been granted. Then the power will ask payment in return for all this help, and, coming to the point, will announce that the payment must be the sacrifice of a child or close relative of the shaman. To refuse is to sign one's own death warrant; if the relative does not die, the shaman must die in his stead. Thus there is the saying, "He sacrifices his relative to prolong his own life."

I was once working in his tent with an Apache well above middle age, when I happened to glance out of the doorway and saw his father, a very old man, approaching on horseback. I innocently said, "Here comes your father. Shall I call him over?" I was not a little disturbed to hear an emphatic, "No!" uttered in a hoarse, strained whisper. Instead, I was directed in that same tense tone of voice, to stand at the door and describe the old man's movements. "Where is he now? What's he doing? Is he going away?" These were the questions thrown at me, and I answered in some bewilderment. As it happened the old man was just passing through his son's field on the way to another camp. I reported his departure and turned to demand an explanation of such unusual conduct. My friend was perspiring freely and breathing heavily. He talked readily enough about the matter. "I don't mind admitting I'm afraid of the old man," he said. "He's got all kinds of power. They say he has done a lot of good with it. Well, maybe he has done good years ago. But I haven't seen any good that he's done in the last ten years. I don't like to have him monkeying around this camp."

It is decidedly easier to establish the existence of ambivalence in Apache society, and to advance material concerning the fear of the ghosts of dead relatives and the power of living ones, than it is to account for and explain all this. One explanation has already been offered us. It is Freud's suggestion "that ambivalence, originally foreign to our emotional life, was acquired by mankind from the father complex. . . ."

There are a number of objections to such a view. In characteristic Freudian manner it would derive ambivalence from the omnipotent Oedipus complex, that hypothetical source from which so much is made to flow. Freud would have us believe that Apache ambivalence exists, not because there is anything in present Apache culture to warrant it, but because some of the younger men of a protohuman horde slew their father countless years ago. A "psyche of mass" which no psychologists have been able to understand, explain, or substantiate is supposed to have carried on and preserved the memory of the parricide for the unconscious of our Apaches. Just how this parricide can account for the fear of dead female relatives and the fear of the power of living female relatives it is difficult to imagine, and how this hypothesis can illuminate the equally strong fear of relatives other than parents has yet to be demonstrated. Divorce from reality in the interests of a threadbare theory and insistence upon tying excellent clinical data to the coattails of the unconvincing Oedipus story have done not a little to delay the benefits which should result from Freud's contributions.

I have found it more convincing, realistic, and illuminating to interpret Apache ambivalence in terms of forces and elements which actually operate in the society and whose effects are open to observation and evaluation. It will be profitable, therefore, to outline one or two aspects of Apache culture which I feel have a direct bearing upon our problem.

The Mescalero and Chiricahua Apaches were hunting and food-gathering nomads ranging over the semiarid territory which now includes northwestern Texas, southern New Mexico, southeastern Arizona, and the adjoining section of northern Old Mexico. They lived on the wild game and plant life of the region and so were constantly on the move as the fruits ripened in one locality or game seemed more abundant in another. As one would expect from this simple economy and roving life, their artifacts were few and crude. The life was arduous, and productivity was achieved only as a result of earnest effort to which all individuals had to contribute. It was the obligation of the Apache to fit himself for any situation, and, if possible, to excel his fellows in all important pursuits. From his earliest years the Apache boy was taught to develop his strength and talents and to compete with others in tests of endurance and

fortitude. Most of the games played by the children were designed to prepare them for the strenuous life of the future. At the time of puberty the boy was subjected to a prolonged ordeal of hardening and training. With this successfully passed there remained a series of four warpath expeditions which he had to attend, not as a warrior, but as an apprentice, and on these trips he was again under the severe scrutiny of the older men who looked for any signs of weakness or incompetence in the youth. Often a relative would arrange to have a distinguished hunter or warrior with much supernatural power perform a ceremony for the young man, so that he would become outstanding in those activities.

The girl, too, was urged quite as much to perfect herself in the women's tasks. In short, the Apache had infinite pride in his strength, his hunting ability, his warpath prowess, and in all the traits and aptitudes which marked him as an exceptional individual.

In the light of the meager technological advancement of the Apaches, this attitude is what might be expected. Each warrior had to know how to make his bow and arrows and to use them effectively. Everyone had to be trained and encouraged to take his place in the economy and to help win a livelihood from the barren country which constituted a large part of the Apache range. The point I wish to emphasize is the appreciation of himself as an individual of capacity and ability which every normal Apache was likely to develop. This personal independence was manifest throughout life and pervaded all types of activity.

But while it is true that each Apache had to be trained to cope with the dangers and trials which a nomadic life of hunting, raiding, and warfare imposed, it is certainly not true that he was an arrant individualist, owing obedience, cooperation, and discipline to no group. I should like, very briefly, to outline the composition of a strong unit to which the individual owed deepest loyalty, to touch upon the probable reasons for its strength, and to indicate the part it normally played in the affairs of each Apache.

It is apparent that the economy which the Apache practiced would not support a large population. From the time of earliest records to the present, the two tribes we are considering were few in numbers and there is no reason to think that their population was on the increase at the time of first white contact. Yet these two small tribes traversed and controlled a vast territory, necessary to a hunting and gathering people in a locality where soil and climate combine to limit the food supply. It was imperative, moreover, that the people be well distributed over the range; too great a number trying to subsist in a limited area would have soon exhausted the available plant and animal life. Yet some concentration of population was required, if only for defense. As far back as my informants could remember, they had always had invaders to repel. For the Mescaleros, first it was the Tonkawas, then the Comanches, later the Mexicans and the Americans. Again, a good many of the tasks which had to be discharged required the assistance of a number of men or women. A raid to obtain valuable horses is a case in point. Enough men had to participate to secure and drive away the animals quickly, and the raid was most likely to succeed when lookouts could be posted before and behind the line of march. When the women were roasting the mescal in underground ovens and preparing this important food for winter use, enough of them had to assist to perform the necessary labor.

It occasions no surprise, then, to learn that the Apaches were distributed over their range in groups whose size and composition reflected the need for a small, close-knit body of people, sufficient for the execution of the necessary tasks dictated by the simple technology, possessing means of defense and the requisite mobility.

The group which offered these valuable characteristics and which became the central unit of Apache social organization was the extended domestic family. Residence after marriage among the Apaches was matrilocal, and so the extended domestic family ordinarily included an older married couple, their married and unmarried daughters, their sons-in-law, their married daughters' children, and their unmarried sons. The individual dwellings of the several families comprising this group were scattered a short distance from one another; altogether these camps composed a cluster of related families who shared the varied fortunes of battle, feast, work, and ceremony.

It was not uncommon for two or more extended domestic families which were united by marriage to camp near one another. This larger social division I have called the local group, for its members were generally known by a name descriptive of some mountain or natural landmark near which they roamed. This local group represented the greatest con-

centration of population realized by these Apaches except during brief periods of feast or ceremony. The Apache's life, therefore, was spent largely in company with his relatives by blood and affinity.

Apache social organization is characterized by other social divisions but they are of minor importance. There are the band and the tribe. Each is demarcated from the other by a definite range and slight differences of dialect and customs. While their existence was recognized by the native, he was considerably less interested in them than is the anthropologist. The Apache was sensible of the greater uniformity of speech and culture within what we call a tribe, but the Apache tribe was so remotely concerned with the problems and activities of the individual that neither of the two peoples under discussion possessed native tribal names. For all practical purposes, the allegiance and fundamental interest of the Apache were limited to the group of relatives represented by the extended domestic family, or at least by the local group.

It would be difficult to overestimate the unity of the extended domestic family. The women, the mother and daughters, were inseparable. They acted together in the accomplishment of all tasks, whether it were food gathering, food preparation, or the cooking. The mother's home was the center of all domestic activity. All game shot by the father, unmarried sons, or sons-in-law was brought to this domestic hub. Here the daughters aided their mother with the cooking, and then each married daughter carried some of the prepared food to her own dwelling and ate with her husband and children, since the son-in-law must never see his wife's mother.

There is powerful opposition to the disruption of this nucleus of relatives. The son-in-law, as has been mentioned, is bound to his wife's family by ties of avoidance, by special forms of speech and conduct, and these carry with them obligations of continuous economic assistance and absolute respect. He must live near his parents-in-law and work for them. He is always at their command. If the young man should wish to marry a second wife (for polygomy was practiced) it would have to be a younger sister or cousin of his first wife, a member of the same relationship cluster. If his wife died, her relatives could force the widower to take a sister or female cousin of the deceased to wife. In case of domestic discord, the husband could not take easy offense and leave the camp of his parents-in-law without sufficient provocation. To do so would be to excite the enmity of a large and powerful group, and to be a marked man in its territory thereafter. So much for the structural safeguards which maintain the extended domestic family.

It will be appreciated that an organization of such strength and rigidity must exercise tremendous influence over the children which are reared in its charge. Something of the domination of this body of relatives over the affairs of the growing child has already been indicated when we were discussing that part played by relatives in the marriage choice. In all other matters of import the child is quite as dependent. If he needs a ceremony performed, it usually rests upon the bounty of his relatives to defray expenses. His instruction and training are supplied by relatives, or if outsiders are involved, the relatives pay for such services. Even as a mature person the individual can accomplish little without the aid of his relatives.

It may be wondered, perhaps, why so much space has been devoted to a discussion of Apache social groupings in a paper supposedly concerned with psychological problems. I think it is sufficient justification to point out that since the ambivalences we are attempting to comprehend are directed primarily against the members of the extended domestic family and the local group, it is plainly necessary (if we take the position that the ambivalences are stimulated by present, determinable factors) to study the common interests and also the probable causes of antagonism which these social units engender.

I am going to suggest the hypothesis that the ambivalences marked by the Apache practice of mourning for the dead and yet barring from sight or hearing anything that may arouse memories of the dead and consequent distress marked by fear, and the equally contradictory convention of avowing affection for kin and yet living in perpetual fear of their power—that these are the result of repressed and unconscious resentment and dislike of relatives which have their roots in the actual circumstances and events of Apache life.

The reader may smile at this. He may think, "Well, it is probably less fantastic to derive ambivalence from unconscious resentment against meddling relatives than it is to seek its meaning in fear of the vengeance of the sire of a primal horde, but, unfortunately, this hypothesis seems as impossible to prove as the other."

The situation may not be quite so desperate, however After all, it should be possible to determine whether there are tangible causes of antagonism between relatives in Apache culture and whether these points of friction are substantial enough to cause noticeable disruption, and thus find a way into the field notes of the ethnologist. An affirmative answer of these two inquiries would afford much more conviction to my hypothesis. Therefore I am going to subject my hypothesis to four germane questions: (1) Is there any reason, inherent in Apache society, to expect conflict of desires between an Apache and his relative or body of relatives? (2) Do such conflicts occur openly enough and frequently enough to call themselves to the attention of an observer of the culture? (3) Can such open and public conflicts as do occur be definitely correlated with the existence or strength of ambivalence? (4) Agreeing that clashes between relatives may occur because of marked divergences in personalities and aims, how shall we account for the socialization of such oppositions, and their appearances as ambivalences taboos, and customs to which all, including those who seemingly get along well with their kin, are subject?

In answer to the first question it may be said that while the strength and unity of the extended domestic family were prime necessities for the functioning of Apache culture at its technological level, and while innumerable benefits and kindnesses flowed to the individual Apache from such an arrangement, it also had its suppressive and irritating side. Merely to view the matter theoretically and apart from actual cases, it would seem inevitable that to train the youth to self-reliance and pride in personal achievement and yet leave him so completely under the control of a body of kin, would be to invite dissatisfaction and discord.

Let us now turn to our second inquiry and determine whether the undercurrent of revolt and dissatisfaction that seems theoretically possible really existed. I have abundant reason to believe that the absolutism of control over the individual by older kin or kin in a greater position of authority is compensated for by a definite tenseness in these relations which not infrequently flares up into acrimonious disputes.

The matter is not one into which it is easy to delve. The important material bearing on the point is not obtained through general questions which aim at understanding the formal outlines of the culture. Only considerable contact with the natives over a respectable length of time, and the establishment of close and friendly contacts can furnish the requisite data. An actual incident of field work will illustrate the point. During the early stages of my Mescalero research I hired an elderly informant and had no reason to complain of his services. As many others did after him, he gave me the ideal picture of Apache society. He emphasized, as will any reliable informant, the great respect and obedience which the Apache husband owes to his wife's relatives, and he enumerated the avoidances, polite forms, and usages which mark such observances. No one would have gathered from his sober and consistent discourse, that any Apache would dare slight these obligations or could live among his people if he had done so. About a year later I learned that this same informant, when a young man, had not only violated the proprieties to the extent of seeing his mother-in-law, but had come within an ace of scalping the poor lady. He had led an armed, one-man revolt against his wife's family, bottled them up together in a dwelling, and was only subdued by force in a successful attack from the rear.

Once the surface of things was scratched, it was not difficult to find comparable material which told a tale of resistance of individuals against domination by relatives of blood and affinity. Stories were obtained describing how girls fled from home rather than submit to marriage with repugnant men chosen by their relatives. A number of such unfortunates are said to have been killed by bears. I have the case of a young woman forced into a "shotgun" marriage by her father. She was so incensed that she refused to see her father any more, and she lived, in contrast to the usual Apache rule, with her husband's relatives.

One elderly informant, after I had absorbed considerable Apache decorum, rather shocked me by asserting that his mother-in-law was "no good." Upon investigation it turned out that the mother-in-law, after some family difficulties, had insulted him outrageously. Angered at something he had done, and in spite of the strict rule of avoidance, she faced him in the company of some others and freely aired her opinion of him. Another bitter antagonism between son-in-law and mother-in-law was masked behind avoidance and polite forms for some years. Then it culminated in a hand-to-hand scuffle in which the man emerged victorious but with considerable

damage to his reputation. Still another mother-in-law, after scrupulous attention to all the forms for a long time, is reported to have assisted her daughter in driving her son-in-law out of camp under a barrage of rocks.

If we are satisfied that differences between Apache kin can arise and often terminate somewhat violently, we can pass to the next question and ask whether there is any discernible correlation between the expressions of ambivalence and conflicts such as we have been describing above. To answer briefly, I believe that evidence for such a correlation exists. It is certain that when conflict between relatives occurs, the fear of the power of the relative becomes stronger and avowed. The reader will remember the informant who was thrown into such a panic at the approach of his father. It will perhaps clarify the incident to remark that at the time of this scene, these two were opposing each other upon an issue which meant much to them. The father was about to instruct the son's bitterest political foe in his personal power.

We may say that when fear of the ghosts of relatives or fear of the power of living relatives is admitted and avowed, there is a definite correlation between this fear and tangible factors which led these people to oppose and dislike each other. We also note that exceptionally tranquil and satisfactory relations between individuals who are kin diminish the likelihood of the development of such fears, at least in overt form. If these be accepted as valid generalizations a long stride has been taken toward the validation of my hypothesis, for the connection between ambivalence and experience has been made in these instances.

But, while we have accounted for such manifestations of ambivalence in terms of conflict between the respect which the Apache is taught to tender all relatives and the antagonism and dislike which he cannot help feeling towards some of them, the general problem of ambivalence in Apache society is not yet entirely clarified.

After all, most Apache youths do not attempt to scalp their mothers-in-law, and most Apache mothers-in-law do not stone their sons-in-law. . . . While I have listed a number of the more spectacular deviations from Apache canons of good conduct, the truth of the matter is that the ordinary Apache obeyed the mores of his society and behaved himself so as to precipitate little scandal. And yet every Apache, though most were not involved in any open and discernible conflicts with relatives, practiced all the taboos of the death rite and believed in the possibility of their sacrifice by relatives—elements which we have said are indicative of fear and resentment felt toward kin.

I believe we will understand the matter better if we regard the cases of admitted and overt hostility toward relatives as symptoms of a far more general psychic disorder. These are the exceptional cases where friction has been so continuous and galling that the trouble could not subside and be dismissed.

While the occasional explosions furnish valuable clews to the nature of disagreements in the society, such incidents were not the general rule. Nevertheless, I have little doubt that most Apaches at some stage of their careers found the control of their affairs by relatives somewhat at variance with their own plans and desires. There is ample evidence to show that individual marriage choices were overruled and personal inclinations rejected any time they interfered with the best interests of the larger group. But, though the individual often felt circumscribed, limited, and curbed by the decisions of his relatives, he generally subordinated his personal inclinations to their rulings. To do otherwise, to invite an open rupture, would be to cut himself off from future economic and moral assistance. No man stood more isolated and alone than one who could not depend on his kin to furnish him a haven. It goes without saying that only extreme provocation would induce an Apache to break with his relatives. What resentment he felt when his wishes were thwarted, he swallowed. . . . He bowed to the inevitable and was guided by tradition and his own best interests. He suppressed the memory of the whole incident, banished it from consciousness, and followed whither the cultural forms led.

But the repression of conscious wishes does not make them less real for unconscious mental life. The longings, which had to be denied so that the extended domestic family might flourish, lodged their protest in the unconscious. The resentment, which could not normally be expressed in everyday life if the solidarity and unity essential to the health of the society were to be maintained, emerged in the guise of a mysterious terror of the dead relatives and a puzzling dread of the power of living relatives. The disguise is ingenious. Everything is arranged to mask from consciousness the reality of the ill feeling against the relative. The ghost of the dead becomes an owl, and one can revile the owl, shoot at it, drive it away from camp with good conscience. The fact that it is your relative whom you treat in this manner is obscured by the feeling that you are thus harassing an evil bird. You fear the supernatural power of your relative, but again the grim truth is glossed over. For some unexplained reason his power forces him to act against you. In conscious thought the power is represented as malevolent and blameworthy, and the relative escapes the greater part of the censure. But these sops to the traditions and amenities which guide conscious thought are rather transparent, and, as we have seen, they yield readily to analysis when a total picture is presented.

In conclusion I would say that the material and interpretation offered are an attempt to explain aspects of Apache psychology, conscious and unconscious, from the circumstances under which actual people lived in a society that really existed. Such an approach stands in direct contrast to the general trend of "depth psychology" wherein it has been the fashion to derive psychological phenomena, and even social phenomena, from such remote events and concepts as "primal parricides" and "primordial images." If what has been written here proves suggestive and worthy of consideration, it is hoped that other and more penetrating studies of mental life from this angle will be accomplished, and that the important relationship between culture and psychology will be richly exploited.

Melford E. Spiro
GHOSTS, IFALUK, AND
TELEOLOGICAL FUNCTIONALISM

Attitudes toward the dead found among the inhabitants of the small atoll of
Ifaluk are in many ways similar to those expressed among the Apaches. Here fear
and hatred of the spirits of the dead are focused on only one type of ghost, the
malevolent *alusengau* (it should be noted that Spiro deals primarily with the
psychosocial effect of the belief in the malevolent spirits only), yet these beliefs
approximate those found in Apache culture directed toward all spirits of the dead.
Spiro raises the question, as the Ifaluks might themselves, "Would not the people
be better off if there were no *alusengau*?" He concludes that the fear and personal
anxieties that stem from the culturally created belief in malevolent ghosts, so
apparently dysfunctional, are balanced in the culture on the manifest level by the
contributions that the concept makes to the understanding of the causes of disease and pathological behavior, and on the latent level by the outlet that the
concept provides for the culturally and environmentally engendered hostility and
aggression which is unacceptable when expressed interpersonally.

Points of similarity between the conclusions presented by Opler and Spiro are
striking when their different points of departure are considered. Opler makes an
analysis on the manifest cultural level; Spiro utilizes a neo-Freudian framework.
Hatred and fear of the dead are seen by both authors as stemming, in part, from
the size and nature of the society, and from the necessity of maintaining extremely
amicable in-group relations.

Parenthetically, it should be noted that Lessa (1961) and De Beauclair (1963)
have recently established that sorcery exists on Ifaluk. Spiro (1961) feels this does
not invalidate his general thesis.

Reprinted from *American Anthropologist*, LIV (1952), 497–503, by permission of the
author and the American Anthropological Association.

Ifaluk, a small atoll in the Central Carolines
(Micronesia), is inhabited by about 250 people, whose culture, with minor exceptions,
reveals very few indications of acculturation.
The subsistence economy consists of fishing
and horticulture, the former being men's work
and the latter, women's. Politically, the
society is governed by five hereditary chiefs,
who are far from "chiefly," however, in their
external characteristics. Descent is matrilineal
and residence is matrilocal. Though clans and
lineages are important social groups, the extended family is the basic unit for both
economic and socialization functions. This
culture is particularly notable for its ethic of
nonaggression and its emphasis on helpful-
ness, sharing, and cooperation.

Ifaluk religion asserts the existence of two
kinds of supernatural beings, or *alus*: high
gods and ghosts. The former, though important, do not play as significant a role in the
daily lives of the people as the latter. Ghosts
are of two varieties—benevolent and malevolent. Benevolent ghosts (*alusisalup*) are the
immortal souls of the benevolent dead, while
malevolent ghosts (*alusengau*) are the souls of
the malevolent dead. One's character in the
next world is thus not a reward or punishment
for activity in this one, but rather a persistence
in time and space of one's mortal character.

Malevolent ghosts delight in causing evil.
They are ultimately responsible not only for
all immoral behavior, but, more importantly,
for illness which they cause by indiscriminately possessing any member of their lineage.
Benevolent ghosts attempt to help the people,
and with their assistance the shaman may
exorcise the malevolent spirits. These malevolent ghosts are the most feared and hated
objects in Ifaluk by persons of all ages and
both sexes. This fear and hatred, found on
both a conscious and unconscious level, is
attested to by abundant evidence, derived
from linguistics, overt behavior, conscious
verbal attitudes, projective tests, and dreams.
As a consequence, most Ifaluk ceremonial
life is concerned with these *alusengau*, and
much of their nonceremonial life is preoccupied with them.

We must now ask ourselves, what are
the functions of the belief in the alus in
Ifaluk? On a manifest level this belief is both

functional and dysfunctional, providing both for the individual and for the group a consistent theory of disease. In the absence of scientific medicine, this function is not to be lightly dismissed. The two areas of life over which the Ifaluk have no technological control are illness and typhoons, and the belief in alus serves to restrict the area of uncertainty. For it affords not only an explanation for illness, but also techniques for its control, minimizing the anxieties arising from intellectual bewilderment in the face of crucial life crises, and the feeling of impotence to deal with them.

Furthermore, the belief serves to explain another problem—the existence of evil and defective people. Native psychological theory has it that man is born "good" and "normal." In the absence of the concept of the alus, the people would be hard put to explain such phenomena as aggression and abnormality, for it also serves to explain these inexplicable and potentially dangerous phenomena. All abnormalities—in which the Ifaluk include violations of the ethic of nonaggression, as well as what we would label mental subnormality, neurosis, and psychosis—are termed *malebush*, and are explained by possession by an alus. The manifest functions of this belief, however, seem to be outbalanced by its obvious dysfunctions. The alus cause worry, fear, and anxiety, as well as sickness and death; and by causing the death of individuals they can, potentially, destroy the entire society. From the point of view of the people, it would be better if there were no alus.

We are thus presented with a difficult question: Why does such a manifestly dysfunctional belief continue to survive? To answer this question we must turn to other aspects of Ifaluk culture. This culture, we have observed, is characterized by a strong sanction against aggression. No display of aggression is permitted in interpersonal relationships; and in fact, no aggression is displayed at all. The people could not remember one instance of antisocial behavior, aside from the malebush, nor were any examples of it observed in the course of this investigation. To this striking fact another, equally striking, may be added: namely, that the absence of overt aggression in interpersonal relationships is found in persons who may be characterized as having a substantial amount of aggressive drive. But aggressive drives, like other imperious drives, demand expression; if they are not permitted expression they are deflected from their original goal and are either inverted or dis

placed. Some Ifaluk aggression is inverted; but that all aggression should be turned inward is impossible, assuming even the lowest possible level of psychological functioning. For if this were the case, we would have to predict the probable disintegration of personality, if not the destruction of the organism. This has not happened in Ifaluk, because the Ifaluk have a socially acceptable channel for the expression of aggression—the alus.

The alus, as already observed, are feared and hated; and this hatred is expressed in conversation, dreams, and fantasies, as well as in overt behavior patterns of public exorcism, ritual, and ceremony, whose purpose is to drive off the alus and to destroy them. Thus, though the intrinsically hated qualities of the alus are sufficient to arouse aggressive responses, the belief in their existence allows the individual to displace his other aggressions onto the alus, since all the hatred and hostility which is denied expression in interpersonal relationships can be directed against these evil ghosts. As Dollard, following Lasswell, has put it, in any instance of direct aggression, "there is always some displaced aggression accompanying it, and adding additional forces to the rational attack. Justifiable aggressive responses seem to break the way for irrational and unjustifiable hostilities. . . . The image of the incredibly hostile and amoral out-grouper is built up out of our own real antagonism plus our displaced aggression against him."

Thus antisocial aggressive drives are canalized into culturally sanctioned, aggressive culture patterns. The possibility for this is important in any society: it is particularly important for the Ifaluk because of their ethic of nonaggression, as well as of the smallness of the land mass which they inhabit. Kluckhohn, for example, points out that belief in witchcraft provides an outlet for Navaho aggression and, as such, serves a crucial function for the Navaho, despite the fact that they have other channels for aggression as well. The Navaho show aggression in interpersonal relationships by quarreling, murder, and violent physical fighting. These avenues are closed to the Ifaluk; indeed, they are inconceivable to them. Furthermore, Kluckhohn points out, the Navaho can "withdraw" from unpleasant situations, either physically or emotionally, by drinking. The Ifaluk cannot "withdraw." As Burrows has put it: "The people of Ifaluk are so few (two-hundred fifty of them); their territory so restricted (about one-half square mile of land surrounding a square mile of lagoon); and their lives all forced so much of the time into the same channels by the routine of getting a livelihood, that it would be nearly impossible for any part of them to keep aloof from the rest. So there is next to no segregation. Each individual surely has some face-to-face contact with every other." Nor can they "withdraw" by drinking, since they have no liquor that is genuinely intoxicating.

Given this situation, therefore, as concerns both the physical and cultural reality, there is no way to deal with aggression except to displace it. Hence a latent psychobiological function of the alus is to provide an outlet for Ifaluk aggressions, preventing the turning of all aggression inward, and thus precluding the collapse of Ifaluk personality. That this problem is not unique to Ifaluk, but is found with equal intensity on other tiny atolls, is revealed in Beaglehole's discussion of Puka-Puka. Here, too, we find an ethic of nonaggression in a tiny Pacific atoll, whose culture is similar to that of Ifaluk. And here, too, socially sanctioned channels exist for the expression of aggression, serving the same functions that the alus serve in Ifaluk. "Life is such," writes Beaglehole, "that no one may get away from his fellow villagers. Privacy and solitude as we know them are almost nonexistent. Day and night, month in and month out, the individual is continuously in contact with others. He cannot get away from them no matter what the provocation. Were it not for certain socially approved ways of expressing otherwise repressed emotions the society would disintegrate under the weight of its own neuroses."

But the Ifaluk must deal with their anxieties, as well as with their aggressions. The Ifaluk experience certain anxieties in childhood which establish a permanent anxiety "set" in the Ifaluk personality. This anxiety is particularly crippling, for it is "free-floating"; that is, its source is unknown or repressed, so that there is no way of coping with it. In this connection, belief in alus serves another vital latent function for the individual, since it converts a free-floating anxiety into a culturally sanctioned, real fear. That is, it provides the people with a putative source of their anxiety —the alus—at the same time that it provides them with techniques to deal with this fear by the use of time-proven techniques, in the form of ritual, incantations, and herbs, whereby the imputed source of the anxiety may be manipulated and controlled.

Thus we see that the belief in the alus has certain consequences for the psychological functioning of the Ifaluk, which, though they are unaware of them, are nonetheless vital and crucial for their functioning at an optimum level of psychological adjustment. For the Ifaluk individual, that is, the latent function of the cultural belief in alus is to protect him from psychological disorganization. Without this belief—or its *psychological equivalent*— the tensions arising within the individual as a result of his anxieties and repressed aggressions could well become unbearable.

But the belief in alus has important sociological functions, as well. If there were no alus and the people repressed their aggressions, the society, as well as individual personalities, would disintegrate. On this level, then, the consequences for the group follow from the consequences for the individual; if all individuals collapse, it follows that the group collapses. But the probabilities of the repression of all aggression in any society are very small. In all likelihood, the strength of the Ifaluk ethic of nonaggression would be weaker than the strength of the aggressive drives, because of the strength of the tensions created by the latter, so that these drives would seek overt expression. But this is exactly what could not occur in Ifaluk without leading to the disintegration of the entire society. The Ifaluk ethic of nonaggression is a necessary condition for the optimal adaptation of a society inhabiting a minute atoll. The minimal aggression permitted in other societies inhabiting large land masses does not lead to disastrous consequences; but here even this minimum cannot be permitted because of the impossibility of isolation. The physical presence of others is a constantly obtruding factor, and the existence of even a modicum of aggression could set up a "chain reaction" which could well get out of control. This fact is recognized by some of the people. Thus our interpreter told of an individual who had offended others by his unseemly conduct, who had made no attempt to rebuke him. When asked for an explanation of their behavior, it was pointed out that any action on their part would have led to strife, and since "very small this place," other people would become involved, until "by'm-by no more people this place."

Even if the expression of aggression in interpersonal relationships would not lead to the physical destruction of Ifaluk society, it would result in the dissolution of the distinctive aspect of its culture—sharing, co-operation, and kindliness toward others. Sharing and co-operation have enabled the Ifaluk to exploit their natural environment to its fullest extent with the technology at their disposal, and to live at peace with one another, in mutual trust and respect. In short, it has given them both physical and psychological security. The breakdown of the Ifaluk ethic of non-aggression, even a minimum of aggressive behavior, would destroy the positive attitudes that make cooperation and sharing possible, which would seriously reduce economic efficiency and psychological security. The disappearance of co-operation, then, would result in a precariously low level of adaptive integration.

With their belief in the alus, however, it is possible for the people to turn their aggressions from their fellows and direct them against a common enemy. The common hatred that results not only enables the people to displace most of their aggressions from the in-group to the out-group, but also serves to strengthen the bonds of group solidarity. For all the people may suffer the same fate—attack by the alus. All must defend themselves against this, and all attempt to defend others from it. The resultant solidarity is both expressed and symbolized in the medicine ceremonies, both therapeutic and prophylactic, which are occasions for convening the entire group.

Thus we again see that the belief in alus has certain latent consequences of which the people are unaware, but which are vital to the functioning of this society and the preservation of its culture. The absence of this belief, or of some other institution with the same functions, would be disastrous for Ifaluk society as we know it today.

Having assessed the belief in malevolent ghosts in terms of the total social functioning of one society, it may be instructive to compare this belief with institutions in other societies, which have the same functional importance. Sorcery and witchcraft play the same functional role among the Ojibwa and Navaho, respectively, that ghosts play in Ifaluk. But we can now perceive the supe-riority of the belief in ghosts over witchcraft and sorcery for the achievement of their common latent end—the release of aggression. For though the latter beliefs serve to deflect some aggressive drives from other members of society onto the sorcerers or witches, they also serve to instigate other aggressive drives. Since witches and sorcerers are members of one's society, and since their identity is usually obscure, one tends to become suspicious, wary in interpersonal relationships, and insecure with one's fellows. Thus though the belief in witches and sorcerers succeeds in deflecting aggressive drives and contributing to social solidarity, it also increases aggressive drives and decreases social solidarity. Belief in ghosts, however, serves the dual function of both decreasing in-group aggression and increasing group solidarity. It may not be irrelevant to observe in this connection that societies, such as Dobu, Kwoma, Ojibwa, and Navaho, which practice sorcery or witchcraft, are also characterized by individualism and insecurity, whereas Ifaluk is characterized by communalism and mutual trust.

We have observed that the belief in the alus is crucial to the psychobiological functioning of the individual and to the survival of Ifaluk society and its culture. This analysis thus enables us to understand how an apparently irrational belief continues to survive with such tenacity. As Merton points out: "Seemingly irrational social patterns" may be seen to "perform a function for the group, although this function may be quite remote from the avowed purpose of the behavior."

This interpretation of the Ifaluk malevolent ghosts is not meant to imply that no dysfunctions can be attributed to this belief. We have already indicated the important manifest dysfunctions. The latent dysfunctions are equally severe: the belief serves to drain energy from creative enterprise to that of defense against the alus; it serves to preclude investigations of alternative disease theories; it channels much economic activity into nonproductive channels; finally, though it resolves many anxieties, it creates a very serious one in its own right—the anxiety created by fear of the alus itself.

Elizabeth Colson

ANCESTRAL SPIRITS AND SOCIAL STRUCTURE AMONG THE PLATEAU TONGA

Among the Tongas, individuals are considered to have several spirits which are released at the time of death. As among the Ifaluks, some such spirits are evil, others are beneficial. The Tongas make the added distinction that each individual contributes at least one of each, and that the number and kind of spirits he contains is determined, in part, by the social position he held during life. The ease with which Colson describes the social structure of the group by listing and analyzing the types of *mizimu* points strongly to the intimate relationship that exists here, and in many other cultures, between social structure and religious beliefs.

To be noted especially here is the way in which the mizimu serve to validate the Tonga life pattern, tie together potentially divergent kin groups, and reinforce the major status changes encountered by the Tonga adult.

Reprinted in abridged form from the *International Archives of Ethnography*, XLVII Part 1 (1954), 21–68, by permission of the author and the publishers.

In this paper I am going to describe beliefs held by the Plateau Tonga about the activities of a particular type of spirits, the *mizimu*, and attempt to show how these reflect the ideal organization of Tonga social structure. The term *mizimu* (*muzimu* in the singular) is usually translated by anthropologists as "ancestral spirits," but I shall use the native term since this translation does not cover the various ways in which the Tonga use the term and I can find no adequate English equivalent.

I have already published a sketch of Tonga social organization. I need only say here in introduction that the Plateau Tonga are a Bantu-speaking people inhabiting Mazabuka District in the Southern Province of Northern Rhodesia. Their number today has been variously estimated as between 80,000 and 120,000 people. Until the British administration introduced a Native Authority system, they had no large-scale political organization of their own. The basis of their own system was twofold: an organization into a large number of small dispersed groups of matrilineal kinsmen, and an organization into local neighborhoods composed of a few villages with a common rain shrine and cult. Although the rain shrines no longer hold the allegiance of many Tonga, the local neighborhoods continue. To most Tonga they are of greater importance than the chiefdoms or the Plateau Tonga Native Author.y, which have been imposed upon the old structure. The matrilineal groups are still important units, although their functions have been curtailed

with the outlawing of self-help and the institution of courts. They have also been affected by the diminished importance of the cult of the mizimu which is an integral element in the organization of such groups.

In this paper I shall write as though all the Tonga still held to the old beliefs about the mizimu. This, of course, is not true. Missions have worked in the area since 1905. Many Tonga are Christians, of eight different sects. Others are skeptics who deny the old beliefs without accepting those introduced by the missionaries. Many claim that they have forgotten the mizimu, and that these no longer affect them in any way. There are whole villages where no one makes offerings to the mizimu or considers them in any way. On the other hand, there are many Tonga to whom the mizimu are a vital part of life. They would claim, along with the old man who heard a woman suggest that the mizimu had disappeared since people stopped believing in them: "No, the mizimu can never die. They will always be there affecting us."

THE NATURE OF THE MIZIMU

Mizimu and ghosts (*zelo*) are both thought to be the spirits of former living people, but the two are distinct. A few Tonga have told me that mizimu and ghosts are one and the same thing. Others have argued that the ghost exists only for the period between a death and the time when the kinsmen assemble for the final mourning rite and that this transforms the ghost into the muzimu. But most maintain that the two are completely different entities, and a study of their actions on different occasions is consistent with this interpretation and not with any identification of ghost and muzimu.

When a person dies, therefore, two spirits remain, one the muzimu and one the ghost. The ghost is always a newly created spirit, some saying that it originates in the dying breath. Not all people produce a new muzimu when they die, and I have never been able to get a clear statement as to how the muzimu originates. Indeed, various people have told me: "I have never been able to understand this myself, and I don't think anyone else does either." There is general agreement, however, that only those who have achieved a certain status during their lifetime give rise to a new muzimu after death, while others leave behind them only the already existing muzimu associated with them since their naming. Once created, moreover, the mizimu are not immortal like the ghosts, who are independent of the devotion of living people for their continued existence. When the living cease to remember the mizimu and no longer call upon them by name, they become nameless spirits wandering at large, who now work only for evil. "They have become like ghosts." Over these the living have no control, for in forgetting the names they have lost the means of summoning or propitiating the spirits.

Over ghosts the living have no direct control, unless they are sorcerers, and ghosts are presumed to be only evil. They may act against the living of their own volition, or they may be agents of sorcerers who have pressed them into service. A sudden dangerous or mortal illness is therefore usually attributed to ghosts. The muzimu is not actively evil in the same way. It may cause injury to the living, but this is not its primary purpose, nor is it free like the ghost to cause injury to anyone with whom it comes in contact. The muzimu is dependent upon the living for its own continued existence, and it causes injury to keep its memory alive in the living so that they may provide the offerings on which it depends. If the living refuse to listen to its demands, then it is thought to enlist the aid of the ghosts to inflict more drastic punishment. Some Tonga say that the muzimu travels always with the ghost which originated with it on a person's death and which acts as its intermediary with other ghosts.

The mizimu are thought to be concerned that they should not be forgotten, and so they send sickness and other misfortune to the living as a reminder that beer and other offerings must be provided. They are anxious that the living should maintain the customs that they practiced when they were alive, and therefore they punish departures from custom. In return they offer to the living some protection against other spirits and against sorcery. They should also assist the living to obtain the good things of life—children, good harvests, herds of cattle, and an orderly existence. These in turn permit the living to procure grain for beer, to marry wives who will brew the beer for offerings, and to perpetuate the names of the mizimu through the children whom they beget and who, to some extent, are regarded as the living representatives of the mizimu. The living propitiate the spirits to ensure for themselves the good things which they desire; the spirits assist the living to these goods so that they in turn may continue to exist. Each is dependent upon the other, and there is partnership between the living and the mizimu in achieving their common ends.

But the mizimu are not concerned with all the living, and the living are not concerned with all the mizimu. The relationships between them are a projection of those which exist between living persons organized in the kinship system. Mizimu and living members of a kinship group are parts of a single whole, and the ties between them transcend the bounds of time and space. Or rather, since the Tonga kinship system is not given a local focus, nor does an ordered genealogical framework or any scheme of historical incidents create a time scale into which the living and the mizimu can be fitted—the system exists outside time and space in a perpetual present.

INDIVIDUALS AND THEIR MIZIMU
The Tonga maintain that the mizimu which are concerned with them, and therefore with which they are concerned, are the spirits of former members of the matrilineal kinship groups of their mothers and fathers, though they also say that the spirits of the matrilineal groups of their two grandfathers may occasionally intervene in their affairs. Nevertheless, it is the affiliation with the two parental groups which is primarily stressed in relation to the mizimu, as it is throughout social life. Some of these mizimu, however, are of more importance to an individual than are others. When a Tonga speaks of his mizimu, or refers to the mizimu of someone else, he may be

using the term very broadly to include all those spirits which are concerned with him, or more narrowly to refer to particular mizimu who stand in a special relationship to him. His meaning is usually clear from the context. For analysis, however, it is necessary to distinguish the different uses of the term, and I shall therefore use the following classification in writing about the role of the mizimu in any one individual's life.

1. *Mizimu* as a general term includes all the spirits of former members of the lines of the father and mother, and may even be used still more generally for all the spirits of former members of any group with which a person feels a kinship relationship. If I write of the mizimu of a matrilineal group, however, it refers only to the spirits of former members of this group.
2. *Guardian Mizimu* are those associated with the names which each person receives soon after birth. They act as his special guardians throughout life, and from them he is thought to derive his personality.
3. *House Mizimu* are the particular spirits which an adult person installs as the guardians of his household.
4. *Inherited Mizimu* are those which are associated with a person because he has been given the name of someone recently deceased as part of the funeral rites.
5. *Own Muzimu*. This is the new muzimu which comes into existence only after a person's death. No living person has his own muzimu.

The guardian mizimu have a special significance in each person's life. They can be regarded as symbolic representations of the overwhelming importance of the paternal and maternal matrilineal groups in determining the original social status of any individual, and of their responsibility for his well-being throughout life. Names are identified with mizimu, and the giving of a name implies assumption of social responsibility for a child. A man who begets a child by an unmarried woman may obtain the right to name his child, which is then affiliated to his matrilineal group and comes under the power of its mizimu in the same fashion as any child born in wedlock. A man who begets an adulterine child by a married woman has no such right. The woman's husband is the legal father. He names the child, thus bestowing upon it a guardian muzimu, and it comes under the protection of the mizimu of his line quite as much as do children he has begotten. The names, which thus recognize the existence of the child and give it its initial place in society, are bestowed some months after birth. The

first name is given by the father or his relatives, and it is a name belonging to a former member of this line. The second is given by the mother's relatives and is the name of a former member of her line. Each name is associated with a muzimu. The Tonga say that the mizimu themselves may decide which of their living kin shall receive their names, and thus become their special charges. When a woman is in labor, the midwives call the names of various mizimu, saying, "Nangoma, come forth! Mavwali, come forth! Nankambula, come forth! Cimuka, come forth!" The child should be born when they call the appropriate name, and they then know that it is this muzimu which has chosen to give its name to the child. They may have no such indication, and may later learn the appropriate name through divination. If the child becomes ill, the diviner may attribute the illness to the desire of a particular muzimu to give its name to the child. Even if the child's name has been decided at its birth, the name may still be changed since the guardian muzimu has failed in its duty by permitting the illness, or the relatives may decide that henceforth the child shall bear both names and both mizimu will be regarded as its guardians and as concerned with its fate. In addition, it will have a name and a guardian muzimu from the other parent's side. Occasionally the name is chosen by the relatives without any form of divination. However a name is chosen, it is not identified with the child until the time of the formal naming rite.

The guardian mizimu may thus be viewed as symbols of the identification of a person with his kinship groups. But when as an adult he establishes his own independent household, he acquires a new social position. His household is one of the units in the local community, and he takes his place within the community as its head. Within the household are joined not only the interests of his own paternal and maternal matrilineal kinship groups, but also of the matrilineal groups of his wife. The importance of his new position is ritually recognized, for he now for the first time becomes capable of making offerings to the mizimu. At the same time, the new household is also given a ritual recognition, by the installation of one or more of the husband's mizimu as special guardians of the house. Significantly enough, these are rarely the husband's guardian mizimu, which stress his identification with his paternal and maternal kinship groups. These remain as his individual guardians, but henceforth his house mizimu will hold a dominant position in all that concerns him as his interests are centered in the well-being of his household.

The fact that he has achieved a position of his own is further recognized, for when he dies he himself will become a muzimu. Those who die before they set up a household leave behind them only the guardian mizimu of their names. I argue that this is because their social personality is still derived from attachment to their matrilineal groups, and their death is of concern only to these two groups. The head of a household is of importance to others besides his own paternal and maternal kinsmen, and his importance to his kinsmen is now at least partially a reflection of the position which he occupies in the community. This is given recognition by attributing to him a muzimu of his own when he dies.

At the same time, the primary affiliation of each person to his matrilineal kinsmen is stressed, for the new muzimu which he has created bears the name of his guardian muzimu from his maternal line, and it has power to affect only those of his line and their offspring. His death breaks the tie which has been created between his own matrilineal group and that of his father by their common interest in him. His father's group have no concern with his own muzimu, and it cannot affect them. Part of the funeral rite emphasizes the finality of the break with the father's line in contrast to the continuity with the maternal line. This is embodied in every funeral, whether or not a new muzimu is thought to be involved. For, although not every person becomes a muzimu, each person once named is associated with his guardian mizimu. Formerly, when a child died before it was named, there was no mourning, for no mizimu were involved. Even today, the old women will tell the mother to hush her wailing, saying that this is only a ghost (*celo*) or only a person (*muntu*), and the mourning is usually curtailed. But if a person dies after being named, someone must be chosen to inherit the muzimu (*kwanga muzimu*). This is the deceased's guardian muzimu from his maternal line in the case of one who dies before establishing a household; it is his own muzimu otherwise. The father's group come to the mourning, and they are said to take away with them the name which they gave to their child and with it the associated guardian muzimu. The name from the maternal side is perpetuated in another member of the group. The person chosen is anointed with oil at the nape of the neck, given tobacco, and as beads are placed about his neck, he is told: "Your name is now such and such." This rite is thought to continue the attachment of the now inherited muzimu to the group to which it belongs. If it is a newly created muzimu, however, a further rite is performed some months after the death, when the people gather for the final mourning. In the interim, though the muzimu has been inherited, it is thought to be wandering disconsolately in the bush. At the final rite, an offering is poured in its name, and it is told to take its place among the other mizimu of the line with the assurance that the living will not forget it while it remembers them. Henceforth it may appear in many different roles—it may be installed as the guardian of a household, its name may be given to any number of children to whom it will be thought to act as guardian, or it may only be invoked occasionally by a diviner who attributes illness to its anger at being neglected. Its importance will reflect the importance which the person attained in life. Those of little importance to their kinsmen are usually soon forgotten

THE MIZIMU AND THE MATRILINEAL GROUP

So far this analysis of the cult of the mizimu has been concerned with the way in which it reflects the identification of the individual with the kinsmen of his father and mother. In this section I shall analyze the way in which the cult reflects the relationships which exist between kinsmen within a matrilineal group. Each such group claims that it is a united body in relationship to the mizimu of its line, and indeed the members are likely to describe the common tie that binds them together as due to the fact that all of them are affected by the same mizimu.

The matrilineal group is the basic kinship unit of Tonga society. It is a group of kinsmen who claim a putative descent through females from a common ancestress, though they are not concerned to trace their descent and are frequently ignorant of their exact relationship to each other. The duties of members of the group involve the obligation of visiting each other when ill, of mourning the deaths of members of each other's families, of helping to provide bride-wealth for the males of the group, of assisting each other to pay fines and damages, of purifying the spouses of those who die, and of finding people to inherit the positions and mizimu of their dead. In case of need, they should assist each other with food and other gifts. In former days they formed a vengeance group to uphold each other's right against outsiders, and were held jointly responsible by outsiders for each other's actions. They also have certain joint rights. They should share in the bride-wealth given for the women of the group and they share the estates of their deceased members.

SUMMARY

In the foregoing paper it has been shown that various aspects of the Tonga social system are reflected in the set of beliefs they hold about the mizimu.

1. The affiliation of each individual with the two matrilineal groups of his father and his mother is reflected in the belief that a person receives at his naming a guardian muzimu from each line, which is important in determining character and actions. It is further reflected in the belief that all mizimu of either line may affect him.

2. The system of matrilineal inheritance, and the primary affiliation with the matrilineal group of the mother, is reflected in the belief that when a person dies his own muzimu is inherited by the matrilineal line, and has no power over members of the father's group.

3. The dogma that the matrilineal group is undifferentiated is reflected in the belief that any muzimu belonging to the line may affect any member of it.

4. The lack of instituted formal leadership within the group is reflected in the belief that every adult may approach the mizimu of his matrilineal line on his own behalf, and in the fact that no one person acts as priest for the rest of the group or for any division within it.

5. The local dispersion of the matrilineal group is reflected in the absence of local shrines for the propitiation of the mizimu, and in the belief that they are present wherever living members of the line live.

6. The importance of the household is reflected in the belief that only men and women who have formed their own households become mizimu in their own right when they die.

7. The dominant role of the husband as representative of the household is reflected in the domination of his mizimu over the mizimu of the wife in household ritual.

8. The necessity for integrating people into a local community composed of members of many matrilineal groups is reflected in the stress upon the importance of the paternal mizimu for whose propitiation an intermediary is necessary.

John Middleton

THE CULT OF THE DEAD: ANCESTORS AND GHOSTS

For the Lugbara the dead remain an integral and important part of the social structure, and their role is little changed from that of a living lineage elder. Their personalities do not appreciably worsen, and they are not the objects of generalized fear that they are in many societies. The only social significance of their death is that by dying they gain the power to bring sickness to rebellious kinsmen and become, thereby, the ultimate sanction for proper lineage behavior. Lineage elders may invoke certain ghosts when their authority is challenged, or ghosts may voluntarily interfere to right an injustice, but usually do so in response to the grumblings of the offended. Thus lineage elders occupy a marginal status, being aligned sometimes with the living and sometimes with the dead. It is interesting that elders are especially prone to being accused of witchcraft, of abusing their influence with the ghosts by turning it to personal ends. Witches for the Lugbara

Extracted from John Middleton, Chapter 2 of *Lugbara Religion: Ritual and Authority Among an East African People* (1960), pp. 25, 32–39, 44–46, published for the International African Institute, by permission of the author and the International African Institute.

are semisocial beings, within society but with inverted and antisocial charac
teristics. That elders should be accused of witchcraft is consistent with the
theories of Mary Douglas (see Chapter 4), who proposes that ambiguously
defined entities will be assigned extraordinary and sometimes dangerous attributes.

The close connection between living and dead fits Lugbara notions of time and
space as well as the requirements of their social system. As Middleton explains
elsewhere in his book (*Lugbara Religion*), the Lugbara see beings distant in time
and space, beyond social control, as inverted and antisocial. Instead of a gradual
transition through time from social chaos to social order, the Lugbara consider
the transformation to have been accomplished in one generation by a set of
mythical heroes. Thus, while many societies define a radical break, often an
inversion of properties, between the living and the dead, for the Lugbara this
contrast, which characteristically serves to help define the proper social order,
occurred but once for all Lugbara. This places the living and recent dead together,
both on the side of social order, and set off against the previous disorder.

Lugbara religion comprises several cults, that
of the dead being the most important. Most
sacrifices are made to the dead. This cult is
concerned mainly with relations within the
family cluster and the inner lineage. It is primarily a lineage cult, in that agnatic ancestors
are the most significant. Non-agnatic ancestors are important in some situations in which
the interests of the cluster and the lineage as
groups are not essentially involved.

The lineage includes both living and dead
members:

*Are our ancestors not people of our lineage? They are
our fathers and we are their children whom they have
begotten. Those that have died stay near us in our
homes and we feed and respect them. Does not a man
help his father when he is old?*

. . .

The "ancestors" are not physical entities.
To express their nature, and their significance
for the living in the various situations in which
they come into contact with them, Lugbara
use certain terms. These express what might
be called different aspects or qualities of the
status of ancestor, relevant in different contexts in the relationship between living and
dead. A difficulty for the observer is that the
concepts denoted by these terms are not
explicitly defined by Lugbara: definition is
possible only by analysis of the situations in
which they are significant. The most important of these concepts are those denoted by
the terms *a'bi* and *ori*. It is to ancestors in one
or other of these aspects that most sacrifices
are made.

A'bi is a term used for all the forebears of a
person through whatever lines of descent.
Lugbara know that their ancestors are many,
and no one man knows the names of more

than a limited number of the ancestors of his
clan, let alone of those related to him through
women. He knows only those who are significant to him as points of reference for the
articulation of descent groups. But all, whether known by name or not, are "ancestors."
The word *a'bi* is used also for certain living
kin, both as a term of reference and of address.
These kin are the mother's father and wife's
father, and the term is used for classificatory
kin also. It is often used, as a term of reference,
to include the father's father, but he is addressed as *baba*. This is to say, *a'bi* is used for
the forebears or progenitors of any line of
descent of *ego* or *ego's* children. I shall translate the term as "ancestor," since in the
situations described in this book this is the
most common meaning, and alternatives such
as "forebear" or "progenitor" are less adequate translations of it. The concept includes
the notion of "progenitor," but it includes
also that of a kinsman to whom is due respect,
deference and obedience. "Respect" (*ru*) is at
the centre of the attitude towards anyone
referred to as *a'bi*, whether living or dead.
They might appropriately, though cumber-
somely, be called "the respected ones."

Ancestors thus include all the dead and
living forebears of *ego's* lineage down to *ego's*
son's generation. They are both male and
female and include both those who have
begotten or borne children and also those who
have died childless.[1] The dead among them

---

[1] The verb *ti* means both to beget and to bear children.
It also is used to refer to succession to status, for example
a man's succession to the status of his brother. In Lugbara
though a childless ancestor may thus be in the line of
succession to lineage status, even though he was not a
forebear in the strict physical sense. I should add here
that Lugbara do not practise ghost marriage.

are important in ritual as the objects of sacrifice. These are thought of as forming a collectivity, in which individual ancestors are not significant *qua* individuals. They send sickness to the living, but they send it collectively, and shrines are erected for them as collectivities also.

Shrines are also erected for *ori*, and these are the more important. Ancestors are thought of as *ori* when individual shrines are placed for them by agnatic or uterine descendents; it is said that an *ori* shrine cannot be placed for a man who has no male children. An ancestor with such a shrine does not change his status from *a'bi* to *ori*: the extra status of *ori* is acquired by him while he continues, in other contexts, to be *a'bi* as well. The essence of the status of *ori* is that he is an individual ancestor, who is in personal and responsible contact with living descendents. *Orindi* (the soul) is the essence of the *ori*, and the soul is a representation of the socially responsible *persona* of a living person. Only adult men and old women are believed invariably to have souls. Ancestors as a collectivity can send sickness to the living, and are said to do so if offended by lack of respect and consideration by their descendants. But *ori* are said actually to listen to the words of their living kin, to know their thoughts and to observe their actions. It is especially the more recently dead *ori* who do this; the individual relationships between them and the living that they had while alive are continued after their deaths. *Ori* are individual ancestors in certain situations which are significant in relation to responsible kinship behaviour and authority. Lugbara use different terms for these concepts and I wish to do the same. I call *a'bi* "ancestor" and *ori* "ghost." This is at variance with common English usage, in which all the dead, or their spirits, are ghosts. In my usage all ghosts are ancestors but not all ancestors are ghosts.[2]

The ghosts are those ancestors who are remembered in genealogies, or at least the more important of these; whereas the ancestors include all the ancestors, whether their names are remembered or not. The ghosts' position in genealogies does not mean that they are remembered as individuals and their personal qualities while alive attributed to them when dead. But it means that they are given as the

apical ancestors of segments and lines of descent, and are so seen as having been "big" men. It is axiomatic that such men were responsible and conscientious: even those who have recently died are so considered, in spite of the fact that in some cases I was told that while alive they were not greatly respected. I was told that while alive a man may not be respected by his son, or at least may not be obeyed by him, because the son wishes to acquire the father's status for himself. "But this is because sons do not respect their fathers, who are 'big' men." It is also said that a man puts shrines for his dead father "because he respects him"—the contradiction is a situational one and needs no explanation for Lugbara. It follows that a ghost, who is defined by his having a shrine for himself, is a respected ancestor and so also a responsible one.

Men come into contact with the dead primarily at the rite of sacrifice. The dead affect men by sending sickness to them to express displeasure at actions considered to weaken the harmony and unity of the lineage and the local group based upon it; these are the actions considered to be sins. As a response the living make offerings to the dead at shrines set up for them. The shrine is the local focus of the relationship between living and dead members of the agnatic lineage. Today some homesteads, where the head of the household is a Christian, have no shrines. An elder said to me, speaking of such people:

These people are not real Lugbara. Have they no ancestors? Do they not respect them? Do they not even respect their fathers while they are alive? What will happen to their children if they do not respect their fathers?

And another elder, a Catholic, said:

I do not "cut" at the shrines of my lineage. But when my people "cut," I sit near, since it is my work to "cut" meat. Some say these things are of Satan, but that is not true. They are good, the things of our ancestors.

The values that are at the centre of social life, those of kinship and the lineage, are sustained in the cult of the dead.

I have said that the ghosts are the more important in Lugbara ritual. Sacrifices to them are more frequent than others and are of living animals, whereas those to ancestors and other agents are usually of grain or dried meat; their shrines are placed in the centre of the homestead, and Lugbara talk of the ghosts

[2] I could call *a'bi* "ancestors" and *ori* "ancestor spirits," since *orindi* might be translated "spirit" as well as "soul." But I think it better to keep the word spirit to refer to manifestations of divinity.

more often than they do of ancestors when discussing ritual. The relationship between the living and the ghosts is a latent one; it is made actual or immediately significant for the living, in two ways. They are known as *ole ro*, to which I refer as the process of ghost invocation, and *ori ka*, to which I refer as that as ghostly vengeance. Literally *ole ro* is to "bring sickness (because of) indignation," the bringing of sickness referring to the action on the part of a living person who invokes his ghosts to bring sickness to one of his kin or dependents whose behaviour he wishes to control. *Ori ka* is "the ghost brings sickness" on its own account, without prior invocation; it may be said that the "ghost shrine brings sickness" (*orijo ka*). Sickness comes from the ghosts, in their shrines under the granaries, through the operation of these processes. In the case of ghost invocation the sickness is caused by someone invoking his ghosts. The ritual guardian of the sick person consults the oracles to discover the identity of the agent concerned and the cause of his anger, and the oracles also state whether sacrifice is to be made and of what it should consist. The sacrificial object for ghosts is usually an animal; it is consecrated and dedicated to them, with a promise to sacrifice if the patient should recover from his sickness. If he does not recover, then the oracle was mistaken and there is no point in making the sacrifice. If he does recover the sacrifice is made at the shrines, the meat shared among the members of a congregation, the patient anointed and blessed, and the matter is regarded as closed.

The typical situation of ghost invocation was given to me on many occasions in words such as

Ghost invocation is like this: a man cries to the ghosts that his son is bad, and they hear his words and send sickness to strike that son.

This, the father invoking his ghosts against his child, is always the example given. I was told that in face of an insult or offence by a dependent a man makes no open move; he should stay silent.

Then this man goes home. He sits and thinks: "if I complain at the shrines, the ghosts will do that son of mine much harm." So he sits and thinks, but he does not say words at the shrines. But the ghosts, his father and his father's father, see him sitting and see his heart is heavy and that he wails. They think among themselves and bring sickness to that son. To say words with the mouth at the shrines is bad. If a man, or an elder says words thus, his child will surely die. If he does not say words the child becomes sick and

learns to obey his father, but he will not die. If he does die people will grumble and blame his father. Then the father would think later: "I did badly to ask the ghosts to bring trouble to my son" and he must give two bulls to the child's mother's brother, because those people there are angry because he harmed their sister's child. These are the cattle called avuta (*corpse things*).

A man invokes the ghosts against a kinsman whom he considers to have committed a sin, and he "thinks these words in his heart" in his hut at night while he lies thinking about the matter or sitting near the granaries in the daytime. He thinks about it quite deliberately; if he merely muses idly while elsewhere or discusses it with friends over beer, this is said not to be ghost invocation. It may lead to "bad luck" (*drilonzi*), "striking" the offender, but that is another matter. Because invocation is thought and not said aloud, I do not use the word "curse" for it. A curse is a deliberate utterance of words against an offender, and especially it includes the words "you will see" or "we shall see."

For an elder to invoke is part of his expected role. He conceals his action until sickness seizes the offender, and when oracles point out his part in the affair will acknowledge it. Indeed, it is usually he who puts the case to the oracles and so actually suggests himself as responsible, although Lugbara do not see the importance of this aspect of oracles. Certain actions are expected to lead to the process being set in motion. After a long quarrel between Abaloo, an unruly and conceited young man who had become a government headman and had shamed his seniors by lording it over them as the chief's local representative, and his dead father's brother, Ozua, a man of considerable importance and prestige, I was told:

Now Abaloo has shamed his "father" on many occasions. Now Ozua has gone to the ghost shrines to cry to the ghosts and to Abaloo's father, his brother. But sickness has not yet taken that child. So Ozua has not yet told people because at first you hide those words.

The assumption was made that after such a quarrel it is incumbent for the senior kinsman to invoke his ghosts, although there is no way of knowing whether he really does so consciously. Since the process in fact comes into being only after an oracular diagnosis of the sickness that occurs some time after the action that is said to have led to invocation, a specific case of invocation cannot be discussed before then. I have asked men who were in the position of Ozua whether they intended to invoke the ghosts, and have been told "perhaps; it is good that I should do so," but since a man does not know whether he has succeeded in invoking the ghosts over a specific offence until the sickness appears and the oracles point to him as responsible, it is clear that some such answer is the only one possible. A man later remembers that he had been thinking about the offence and concludes that he had invoked the ghosts, but he cannot know at the time of his anger whether or not he has succeeded in doing so. If later the oracles point to him, then he can in all honesty admit to having invoked the ghosts by the mere fact of his having been angry in his homestead. Since invocation is done by "thinking" and not by "saying the words by mouth," there is no contradiction. In many cases of which I know a man had both threatened the offender and has also mentioned this to a close kinsman. The latter later remembers this and the name of the man concerned is among those first put to the oracles and may easily be accepted by them. However, I remember two or three cases in which the oracles pointed out men who were clearly taken aback at the diagnosis and who argued, saying that the oracles had lied—always an accepted possibility. They were not willing to admit that they had put their feelings into action. As I show later, and as the statement quoted on page 490 shows also, there is considerable ambivalence in the position of a man who invokes the ghosts against his own son.

Lugbara do not say what is the actual power of invocation, nor how it develops in a man, except that his father should be dead. Details of this sort are not directly relevant to the process of which ghost invocation is a link. Although even a child may have the power, if his father is dead, it is mainly old men who exercise it. It is akin to the power of witchcraft in that the older a man is the more likely he is to have it; and indeed . . . an old man who invokes too often will easily be considered to be a witch. A man of great personality is likely to invoke and to be heard by the ghosts. It is the man whose status is such that insult to him is seriously disruptive to the family-cluster who is thought to need to do so. It is clear that such a belief needs no elaboration: it is the situation that defines the invoker, as it is the situation that defines a witch, rather than any intrinsic characteristics.

The motive for a man's invoking the ghosts is the sentiment called ole. This is difficult to translate by a single word but the nearest is perhaps "indignation." Ole is usually defined by Lugbara as the sentiment aroused by seeing a man eating rich food, with succulent relishes, and who does not invite one to share with him. Or the feeling of seeing a rival at a dance showing off his agility and impressing girls while one is standing at the edge of the circle alone. It is this same sentiment that motivates witches. . . . So that in this sense it might be translated as "envy." But "envy" is not sufficient for the sentiment that is supposed to be felt by an elder invoking the ghosts against a dependent. He does so because he is outraged, in his role as head of the kin group and not as an individual, at the anti-social behaviour of the offender. His authority as an elder has been flouted and the kinship relationship of which this is a part has been weakened. If the invoker is not an elder he is outraged at behaviour towards him that is unfitting from a kinsman. The sort of action that leads to ole is striking or fighting with a kinsman older than oneself—this is perhaps the worst offence possible, and although it is comparatively uncommon it is frequently given as the example of an offence that leads to ghost invocation; to swear or shout at a kinsman; to deceive a close kinsman by stealing or cheating or lying; to quarrel with a kinsman; for a woman to quarrel with her husband, or to strike him or deny him the exercise of the rights he holds in her; for a man to fail to carry out the duties of a guardian or heir. They are all offences which affect the social relations that are at the basis of orderly family and community life, and the non-observance of which brings a man "shame."

A person is said to have ghosts invoked against him because he "destroys, the words of the home" ('buru). 'Buru is the word for home or homestead in its social rather than physical sense. The purpose of ghost invocation may be seen in the statement that the work of an elder is "to purify the territory (of the lineage), so that the home may be all clean" (angu edezu, 'buru ma ovu alaru). I have been told

The work of an elder is to keep the territory without trouble, so that the home may be clean, so that death, sickness and "evil words" do not enter into the homesteads and people live peacefully and quietly. Then their wives will have children and they will be many there together.

"Evil words" (e'yo onzi) refer especially to witchcraft, part of the elders duty being to see that rancour and quarrels are controlled so that witchcraft does not appear. The statement continues

It is good that an elder invokes his ghosts against his disobedient "sons," who do not follow his words. A man stands in place of his (dead) father, and if a wife or child does him ill he will cry to that father and trouble will seize that child. This is good. This is what we call ole. Ole does not destroy the land. It is bad for a man to strike with his hand, or with his spear; now the ghosts strike on his behalf. These are the words of the lineage. . . . See, a client cannot invoke the ghosts; he has no clan. But I, and that elder there . . . we have our kinsmen, and it is good that we invoke the ghosts against our sons.

It seems correct to translate *ole* as a feeling of indignation or outrage at sins or immoral behaviour, using "immoral" in a limited sense to refer to behaviour directed against recognition of orderly ties of kinship and lineage.

. .

The lineage consists of both living and dead, and lineage authority is thought to be exercised by the dead as well as the living, their representatives. That the authority with which ghostly sickness is concerned is essentially lineage authority may be seen from the process of ghostly vengeance. This is the bringing of sickness by the ghosts on their own account, without invocation, if their living kin neglect them by not placing meat and beer at their shrines for a long time. The dead are said to murmur together "Our child is bad, he does not care for us now," and they cause sickness to visit him. It is said that the dead watch one anothers' offering jealously, "as our elders do"—the motives attributed to the dead are those attributed to the living too.

A ghost watches a man giving food at sacrifice to him. A brother of that ghost begs food of him. The other will laugh and say "Have you no sons?" Then he thinks "Why does my child not give me food? If he does not give me food soon I shall send sickness to him." Then later that man is seized by sickness, or his wife and his children. The sickness is that of the

ghosts, to grow thin and to ache throughout the body; these are the sicknesses of the dead. You go to the rubbing-stick oracle, and it says "Your father is sending sickness (ka). He wants to eat food of yours. For many days you have not given him food, now he is begging food from you." People do not grumble at the ghosts, because it is the living man who is selfish. He makes a sacrifice and the dead are joyful. He gives them beer, a he-goat, or a bull.

This is how Lugbara describe the process, but there is a difference between this account and actuality. Lugbara describe an ideal, in sociological isolation; but in reality the offerings made as a consequence of ghostly vengeance are made within a social context of disputes over lineage authority. A small offering is placed on the ghost shrines at every meal, a child usually being sent with a piece of the cooked food; and at a beer-drink beer may be poured on the stones also. This is not "sacrifice" (*owi*), and there is no congregation as there is at a proper sacrifice. A sacrifice is not made except for a specific purpose in response to a specific case of sickness of which the agent is said by the oracles to be a ghost. In fact it is the living members of the lineage who may grumble in this way ("as our elders do") and it is thought that the ghosts then hear them. This is not invocation, which is a deliberate and conscious "thinking" by a man near the shrines. In ghostly vengeance the living are thought merely to talk or to grumble among themselves about the behaviour of a kinsman, and the dead then hear them and take the decision to send sickness themselves, as a result of their own discussion and not at the specific request of the living. The point of the difference is that in ghost invocation a man takes the responsibility upon himself for causing sickness, even though indirectly. In ghostly vengeance it is the dead who are believed to be responsible for the decision, and they make it upon the grumbling of many people and not on the invocation of a single person: responsibility is thus shared both among the dead and among a group of living kin.

Ruth Bunzel

THE NATURE OF KATCINAS

One of the most common souvenirs bought by travelers in the American South-west is the small, brightly painted wooden doll called the "katcina." Often erroneously called an Indian "god" or "fetish," the dolls, in fact, serve as visual aids in educating Pueblo Indian children in the intricacies of the Katcina Cult found among these Indians. The katcina spirits, in part thought to be tribal ancestral spirits and in part the spirits of departed tribal members, are of many forms and fill many roles: Pautiwa is the chief of katcina village; Chakwena Woman aids in rabbit hunts; the Koyemshi are clowns. Katcina spirits are participants in, rather than the objects of, Pueblo ceremonials. Enacted by men in the masks and body decorations appropriate to particular spirits or types of spirits, katcinas take part in fertility ceremonies, rain dances, and many of the ceremonies involved in the yearly round. They mingle in the streets with the people, discipline unruly children in their homes, chide deviants publicly, and, in front of all the people during ceremonials in the plazas, they often dramatize the values and beliefs basic to Pueblo Indian culture.

Recalling that katcinas are thought to be, in part, the spirits of the dead, Zuni attitudes toward these "ghosts" stand in contrast to those of the Apaches and the Ifaluks cited in the previous articles.

Extracted with editorial modifications from "Zuni Katcinas," *47th Annual Report of the Bureau of American Ethnology*, pp. 837–1086 (Washington, D.C.: 1932), by permission of the author and the Bureau of American Ethnology.

The Katcina Cult is one of the six major cults of Zuni, and might indeed be called the dominant Zuni cult. It includes many of the most beautiful and spectacular ceremonies, and the ceremonies which attract the most popular attention Furthermore, it is the one cult which personally reaches all people, since all males belong to it and are required to participate in its ceremonies. Moreover, at the present time it is an ascendant cult. At a time when the societies are declining in membership, and the priesthoods experience difficulties in filling their ranks, when ceremonies lapse because no one competent to perform them survives, the Katcina Society is extending its activities. More katcina dances are held each year than in Mrs. Stevenson's time, and the dances last longer. It is true that some of the older dances are no longer performed, but on the other hand for each dance that lapses two new ones are introduced. It is the most vital, the most spectacular, and the most pervasive of Zuni cults; whatever foreign elements it may at one time or another have incorporated, its ideology and form are aboriginal and characteristic, and for the average Zuni it is the focal point of religious, social, and aesthetic experience.

The Katcina Cult is built upon the worship, principally through impersonation, of a group of supernaturals called in Zuni terminology *koko*. The koko live in a lake, *Hatin kaiakwi* (whispering spring), west of Zuni, near St. Johns, Arizona. In the bottom of this lake they have a village (*Koluwalawa*, katcina village) reached by ladders through the lake. Here they spend their time singing and dancing, and occasionally they come to Zuni to dance for their "daylight" fathers. They live on the spiritual essence of food sacrificed to them in the river, and clothe themselves with the feathers of prayer sticks. They turn into ducks when traveling back and forth to Zuni.

The first katcinas were the children of humans lost through contact with contamination, unwilling sacrifices to atone for sin. By origin and later association they are identified with the dead. Mortals on death join the katcinas at katcina village and become like them.

In addition to being identified with the dead the katcinas are especially associated with clouds and rain. When they come to dance they come in rain. They are equivalent to the Shiwana of Keresan pueblos.

In ancient times, the katcina used to come to Zuni to dance for their people in order that they might be gay. But always when they left someone "went with them," that is, died, and so they decided not to come any more. But they authorized masked dances and promised "to come and stand before them." So now when a katcina dance is held the katcinas come merely as rain, and no one dies. So the institution of masked dancing, originated according to legend to assuage the loneliness of parents for their lost children, has become a rain-making ceremony.

The power of katcina ceremonies resides in the masks which, whether ancient tribal property or individually owned modern masks, are believed to contain divine substance, by means of which the katcina whose representation is worn "makes himself into a person." Masks are treated with the utmost reverence. The awe which Zunis feel for all sacred and powerful objects is intensified in this case by the fact that masks are representations of the dead, and, indeed, the very substance of death. Therefore the use of masks is surrounded by special taboos. One must never try on a mask when not participating in a ceremony, else one will die. One must never use human hair or the hair of a live horse on a mask, else that person or horse will surely die. If one is incontinent during a katcina ceremony the mask will choke him or stick to his face during the dance.

The katcinas are very intimate and affectionate supernaturals. They like pretty clothes and feathers; they like to sing and dance, and to visit. Above all they like to come to Zuni to dance.

The folk tales about individual katcinas describe them at home in their kitchens, scrambling for their feathers at the solstices, quarreling amiably among themselves, meddling in one another's affairs. They have a village organization similar to that of Zuni. Pautiwa is "the boss," as Zunis say. His pekwin, who delivers his messages, is Kaklo. His principal administrative duties seem to be to keep his people quiet long enough to give a courteous welcome to visitors, to receive messages from Zuni, and to decide when to dance there and who shall go. Pautiwa "makes the New Year" at Zuni. His representative brings in the Ca'lako crook and crooks for other special ceremonies, such as the initiation and the dance of the Kanakwe, thus determining the calendar of katcina ceremonies for the year. Whenever the people at Zuni decide they want one of the regular katcina dances they send prayer sticks to katcina village (kiva chiefs plant prayer sticks four days before a dance) and Pautiwa decides whom to send.

Hamokatsik, the mother of the katcinas, looks after their clothing when they prepare for dances.

In addition to the official visits of the katcinas when invited with prayer sticks, they sometimes pay unexpected visits on missions of good will. They come to plant and harvest for deserted children, to affirm the supernatural power of the pious and despised. Pautiwa visits in disguise poor and despised maidens, and leaves wealth and blessing behind him. Katcinas in disguise bring proud girls to their senses by the amiable disciplinary methods so characteristically Zunian.

In reading these folk tales we cannot but be struck by their resemblance in feeling and tone to medieval tales of saints and angels—such tales as that of the amiable angel who turned off the wine tap left open by the monk who was so pious that he didn't even stop to turn off the tap when summoned for prayer. The particular situations in which katcinas prove helpful and their special techniques differ, of course, from those of saints and angels. Medieval saints do not ordinarily humble proud maids by contriving in spite of impossible tests to sleep with them and so instruct them in the delights of normal human association and the advantages of humility. But in spite of these differences the popular attitudes and feeling for the role of supernaturals in commonplace human affairs are curiously similar. Undoubtedly this modern folklore concerning katcinas has been strongly colored by Catholic influences.

But for all their generally amiable and benign character, there is a certain sinister undertone to all katcina ceremonies. It is said more often of the katcinas than of other supernaturals that they are "dangerous." The katcinas inflict the most direct and dramatic punishments for violation of their sanctity. If a priest fails in his duties, he does not get rain during his retreat, he may suffer from general bad luck, he may become sick and may even die if he does nothing to "save his life." But the katcina impersonator who fails in his trust may be choked to death by his mask during the ceremony. There is always a certain feeling of danger in wearing a mask. In putting on a mask the wearer always addresses it in prayer: "Do not cause me any serious trouble." A man wearing a mask or, in katcina dances without mask, one wearing katcina body paint, is untouchable. He is dangerous to others until his paint has been washed off. Zunis watching katcinas dance shrink from them as they pass through narrow passages, in order not to touch their bodies.

The first katcinas were children sacrificed to the water to atone for sin; afterwards when they came to dance, bringing their blessing of rain and fertility, "they took someone with them"; that is, they exacted a human life from the village. It was only when masks were substituted for the actual presence of the katcinas that this heavy toll was lightened.

There are hints in ritual that ideas of human sacrifice may lie but a little way beneath the surface in the concept of masked impersonation. The great ceremony of the Ca'lako opens with the appointment of a group of impersonators of the gods. For a year they are set apart. They do no work of their own. In the case of the Saiyataca party they even assume the names of the gods whom they are to impersonate. At the end of their term of office they have elaborate ceremonies in which they appear in mask; that is, in the regalia of death. After all-night ceremonies they depart for the home of the dead. "Everyone cries when they go," as a Zuni informant says. "It is very sad to see them go, because we always think that we shall never see them again." The final ceremony of the departure of the Ca'lako is especially suggestive of this interpretation. When out of sight of the village the Ca'lako are pursued by young men. When caught they are thrown down and killed, and the mask is treated like the body of a fallen deer—"for good luck in hunting." On returning the impersonators are met outside the village by their aunts and taken at once to their houses to be bathed before they are safe for human contact.

Identification with the god, and the killing of the god, for fecundity, as found in ancient Mexico, seem to be ideas in keeping with Zuni concepts. But Zuni temperament would repudiate the bloody sacrifice. It may well be that the particular technique of impersonation, with its atmosphere of the sinister and dangerous, is the symbolic representation of the extirpated fact. Tales of the former existence of human sacrifice in the pueblos continually crop up.

Frazer, quoting Bourke, gives an account of the sacrifice of a youth at the fire festival (tribal initiation) of the Hopi. Mrs. Stevenson refers to the report of human sacrifice at Zia. There are cases of human sacrifices for fertility among the Pawnee and the Sioux. The prevalence of all forms of human sacrifice among the Aztecs is too well known to require comment. Among the Aztecs, however, are found two striking features: The dancing of priests in the flayed skin of the sacrificial victim, and the identification of the sacrificial victim with god, as for example, in the sacrifice of Tezcatlipoca. In the battle with the katcinas at Acoma the katcinas are ritualistically slain so that their blood may fertilize the earth. In the prayers of the scalp dance there are frequent allusions to blood as a fertilizing medium, so possibly the whole complex of human sacrifice is not so remote historically or conceptually as might at first appear.

The persistent rumors of an early prevalence of human sacrifice in the pueblos may be without foundation, but the reworking of a cult that once included human sacrifice is quite in accord with pueblo tendency to absorb ritual from all sides and mitigate all its more violent features.

10
DYNAMICS
IN RELIGION

Introduction

Like other aspects of culture, religious systems are in constant process of alteration, either in response to internal pressures within the social system, to environmental changes, or to the impact of acculturation. Anthropologists have especially recently stressed the problems of change, in part because they wished to correct the common misconception that primitive religion does not undergo modification, in part because changes in the religious sphere have given us some of our most important data and insights on the general processes of culture change. The following selections focus upon these dynamic aspects of religion.

The first series of papers on "nativistic movements" has been included to show how these movements develop in response to stresses set up by the impact of Western culture upon non-Western cultures. Ralph Linton's paper is an early attempt to define the essence of the phenomena and to provide a workable typology of the movements. More recently Anthony Wallace has written what is becoming a classic paper on these movements in which he defines the concept of "revitalization" and outlines certainly uniformly found processes in revitalization movements. The

Barber, Hill, and Slotkin selections deal with problems connected with the Ghost Dance and the Peyote Cult, which are two of the most important movements of the nativistic type among North American Indians. Belshaw's contribution takes us to another part of the world and provides materials on similar cults that have developed in Melanesia. The cargo cults are still active in New Guinea and are continuing to be studied by anthropologists at the present time. Both here and in North America there is currently much interest in the concept of millenarism which is dealt with in Peter Worsley's interesting book *The Trumpet Shall Sound* (1957; reprinted in paperback in 1968) and in David Aberle's theoretical paper "A Note on Relative Deprivation Theory."

The final selection, "Ritual and Social Change: A Javanese Example," by Clifford Geertz, could have been placed in the section dealing with death and ghosts but has been included here because its real stress is on change in religion, especially the changes generated by internal pressures due to incongruities between the social and cultural dimensions of a society.

Ralph Linton

NATIVISTIC MOVEMENTS

The impact of European culture upon the small, primitive societies of the world during the past four centuries has frequently led to the appearance of what have come to be known as "nativistic movements," wherein the primitive societies have reacted, sometimes violently, against domination by the Europeans and engaged in organized attempts to revive or perpetuate certain aspects of their native cultures in the face of this pressure to change. Since the religious systems of the primitive societies typically embodied the central values of their cultures, these nativistic movements almost always involved some type of religious or magical procedures as their essential elements and hence have provided us with crucial data on dynamics in religion.

This general paper of Ralph Linton's is an attempt to define and classify the types of nativistic movements that have occurred in culture-contact situations and to identify the conditions under which these various types of movements arise. Linton makes it clear that nativism can appear in the dominant group as well as in the subordinate group in a culture-contact situation, although the more dramatic manifestations tend to occur in the subordinate society.

Reprinted from *American Anthropologist*, XLV (1943), 230–240, by permission of the American Anthropological Association.

At the time that the centennial meeting of the American Ethnological Society was planned, the writer was invited to contribute a paper on nativistic movements in North America. When he attempted to prepare this it soon became evident that there was a need for a systematic analysis of nativistic phenomena in general. Although the Social Science Research Council's Committee on Acculturation had made some progress in this direction much remained to be done. The present paper is an attempt to provide such a systematic analysis and is presented in the hope that its formulations may be modified and expanded by further research.

The first difficulty encountered in the study of nativistic movements was that of delimiting the field. The term "nativistic" has been loosely applied to a rather wide range of phenomena, resembling in this respect many other terms employed by the social sciences. For the writer to determine arbitrarily which of several established usages is to be considered correct and which incorrect is not only presumptuous but also one of the surest ways to promote misunderstanding of the theoretical contributions he hopes to make. The only satisfactory definition under such circumstances is one based upon the common denominators of the meanings which have come to be attached to the term through usage. With this as a guide, we may define a nativistic movement as "Any conscious, organized attempt on the part of a society's members to revive or perpetuate selected aspects of its culture."

Like all definitions, the above requires amplification to make its implications clear. Its crux lies in the phrase "conscious, organized effort." All societies seek to perpetuate their own cultures, but they usually do this unconsciously and as a part of the normal processes of individual training and socialization. Conscious, organized efforts to perpetuate a culture can arise only when a society becomes conscious that there are cultures other than its own and that the existence of its own culture is threatened. Such consciousness, in turn, is a by-product of close and continuous contact with other societies; an acculturation phenomenon under the definition developed by the above-mentioned committee.

The phrase "selected aspects of its culture" also requires elaboration. Nativistic movements concern themselves with particular elements of culture, never with cultures as wholes. This generalization holds true whether we regard cultures as continuums of long duration or follow the usual ethnographic practice of applying the term "a culture" to the content of such a continuum at a particular point in time. The avowed purpose of a nativistic movement may be either to revive the past culture or to perpetuate the current one, but it never really attempts to do either. Any attempt to revive a past phase of culture in its entirety is immediately blocked by the recognition that this phase was, in certain respects, inferior to the present one and by the incompatability of certain past culture patterns with current conditions. Even the current phase of a culture is never satisfactory at all points and also includes a multitude of elements which seem too trivial to deserve deliberate perpetuation. What really happens in all nativistic movements is that certain current or remembered elements of culture are selected for emphasis and given symbolic value. The more distinctive such elements are with respect to other cultures with which the society is in contact, the greater their potential value as symbols of the society's unique character.

The main considerations involved in this selective process seem to be those of distinctiveness and of the practicability of reviving or perpetuating the element under current conditions. Thus the Ghost Dance laid great stress on the revival of such distinctive elements of Indian culture as games and ceremonial observances, elements which could be revived under agency conditions. At the same time it allowed its adherents to continue the use of cloth, guns, kettles, and other objects of European manufacture which were obviously superior to their aboriginal equivalents. In fact, in many cases the converts were assured that when the dead returned and the whites were swept away, the houses, cattle and other valuable property of the whites would remain for the Indians to inherit.

All the phenomena to which the term "nativistic" has been applied have in common these factors of selection of culture elements and deliberate, conscious effort to perpetuate such elements. However, they differ so widely in other respects that they cannot be understood without further analysis. At the outset it is necessary to distinguish between those forms of nativism which involve an attempt to revive extinct or at least moribund elements of culture and those which merely seek to perpetuate current ones. For convenience we will refer to the first of these forms as *revivalistic nativism*, to the second as *perpetuative nativism*. These two forms are not completely exclusive. Thus a revivalistic nativistic movement will be almost certain to include in its selection of elements some of those which are current in the culture although derived from its past. Conversely a perpetuative nativistic movement may include elements which had been consciously revived at

an earlier date. However, the emphases of these two forms are distinct. The revivalistic type of nativism can be illustrated by such movements as the Celtic revival in Ireland, with its emphasis on the medieval Irish tradition in literature and its attempt to revive a moribund national language. The perpetuative type of nativism can be illustrated by the conditions existing in some of the Rio Grande Pueblos or in various Indian groups in Guatemala. Such groups are only vaguely conscious of their past culture and make no attempts to revive it, but they have developed elaborate and conscious techniques for the perpetuation of selected aspects of their current culture and are unalterably opposed to assimilation into the alien society which surrounds them.

There is a further necessity for distinguishing between what we may call *magical nativism* and *rational nativism*. It may well be questioned whether any sort of nativistic movement can be regarded as genuinely rational, since all such movements are, to some extent, unrealistic, but at least the movements of the latter order appear rational by contrast with those of the former.

Magical nativistic movements are often spectacular and always troublesome to administrators, facts which explain why they have received so much attention from anthropologists. Such movements are comparable in many respects to the messianic movements which have arisen in many societies in time of stress. They usually originate with some individual who assumes the role of prophet and is accepted by the people because they wish to believe. They always lean heavily on the supernatural and usually embody apocalyptic and millennial aspects. In such movements moribund elements of culture are not revived for their own sake or in anticipation of practical advantages from the elements themselves. Their revival is part of a magical formula designed to modify the society's environment in ways which will be favorable to it. The selection of elements from the past culture as tools for magical manipulation is easily explainable on the basis of their psychological associations. The society's members feel that by behaving as the ancestors did they will, in some usually undefined way, help to recreate the total situation in which the ancestors lived. Perhaps it would be more accurate to say that they are attempting to recreate those aspects of the ancestral situation which appear desirable in retrospect.

Such magical nativistic movements seem to differ from ordinary messianic and millennial movements in only two respects. In the nativistic movements the anticipated millennium is modeled directly on the past, usually with certain additions and modifications, and the symbols which are magically manipulated to bring it about are more or less familiar elements of culture to which new meanings have been attached. In non-nativistic messianic movements, the millennial condition is represented as something new and unique and the symbols manipulated to bring it about tend to be new and unfamiliar. Even in these respects the differences are none too clear. New elements of culture often emerge in connection with magical nativistic movements, as in the case of the distinctive Ghost Dance art. Conversely, messianic movements may lean heavily upon the familiar symbolism of the culture, as in the case of most Christian cults of this type. The basic feature of both messianic cults and magical nativistic movements is that they represent frankly irrational flights from reality. Their differences relate only to the ways in which such flights are implemented and are, from the point of view of their functions, matters of minor importance.

What we have chosen to call rational nativistic movements are a phenomenon of a quite different sort. While such movements resemble the magical ones in their conscious effort to revive or perpetuate selected elements of culture, they have different motivations. What these are can be understood more readily if we reintroduce at this point the distinction previously made between revivalistic and perpetuative nativistic movements. Rational revivalistic nativistic movements are, almost without exception, associated with frustrating situations and are primarily attempts to compensate for the frustrations of the society's members. The elements revived become symbols of a period when the society was free or, in retrospect, happy or great. Their usage is not magical but psychological. By keeping the past in mind, such elements help to re-establish and maintain the self-respect of the group's members in the face of adverse conditions. Rational perpetuative nativistic movements, on the other hand, find their main function in the maintenance of social solidarity. The elements selected for perpetuation become symbols of the society's existence as a unique entity. They provide the society's members with a fund of common knowledge and experience which is exclusively their own and which sets them off from the members of other societies. In both types of rational nativistic movement the culture elements selected for symbolic use are chosen realistically and with regard to the possibility of perpetuating them under current conditions.

It must be emphasized that the four forms of nativistic movement just discussed are not absolutes. Purely revivalistic or perpetuative, magical or rational movements form a very small minority of the observed cases. However, these forms represent the polar positions of series within which all or nearly all given nativistic movements can be placed. Moreover, it will usually be found that a given nativistic movement lies much closer to one end of such a scale than to the other if it is analyzed in terms of the criteria used to establish the polar positions. If we combine the polar positions in the two series, the result is a fourfold typology of nativistic movements, as follows:

1. Revivalistic-magical
2. Revivalistic-rational
3. Perpetuative-magical
4. Perpetuative-rational

Forms 1, 2, and 4 in this typology recur with great frequency, while form 3 is so rare that the writer has been unable to find any clearly recognizable example of it. The reason for this probably lies in the conditions which are usually responsible for magical nativistic movements. The inception of such movements can be traced almost without exception to conditions of extreme hardship or at least extreme dissatisfaction with the *status quo*. Since the current culture is associated with such conditions and has failed to ameliorate them, magical efficacy in modifying these conditions can scarcely be ascribed to any of its elements. Nevertheless, a perpetuative-magical movement might very well arise in the case of a society which currently occupies an advantageous position but sees itself threatened with an imminent loss of that position. It is highly probable that if we could canvass the whole range of nativistic movements examples of this type could be found.

An understanding of the various contact situations in which nativistic movements may arise is quite as necessary for the study of these phenomena as is a typology of such movements. There have been many cases of contact in which they have not arisen at all.

The reasons for this seem to be so variable and in many cases so obscure that nothing like a satisfactory analysis is possible. The most that we can say is that nativistic movements are unlikely to arise in situations where both societies are satisfied with their current relationship, or where societies which find themselves at a disadvantage can see that their condition is improving. However, such movements may always be initiated by particular individuals or groups who stand to gain by them and, if the prestige of such initiators is high enough, may achieve considerable followings even when there has been little previous dissatisfaction.

Although the immediate causes of nativistic movements are highly variable, most of them have as a common denominator a situation of inequality between the societies in contact. Such inequalities may derive either from the attitudes of the societies involved or from actual situations of dominance and submission. In order to understand the motives for nativistic movements the distinction between these two sources of inequality must be kept clearly in mind. Inequality based on attitudes of superiority and inferiority may exist in the absence of real dominance, although situations of dominance seem to be uniformly accompanied by the development of such attitudes. As regards attitudes of superiority and inferiority, two situations may exist. Each of the groups involved in the contact may consider itself superior or one group may consider itself superior with the other acquiescing in its own inferiority. There seem to be no cases in which each of the groups involved in a contact considers itself inferior. The nearest approach to such a condition is the recognition of mixed inferiority and superiority, i.e., the members of each group regard their own culture as superior in certain respects and inferior in others. Such a condition is especially favorable to the processes of culture exchange and ultimate assimilation of the two groups. It rarely if ever results in the development of nativistic movements.

The type of situation in which each society considers itself superior is well illustrated by the relations between Mexicans and Indians in our own Southwest. In this case factors of practical dominance are ruled out by the presence of a third group, the Anglo-American, which dominates Indian and Mexican alike. Although the two subject groups are in close contact, each of them feels that any assimilation would involve a loss of prestige. The transfer of individuals from one social-cultural continuum to the other is met by equal resistance on both sides and the processes of assimilation never have a chance to get under way. Under such circumstances the life of each of the societies is conscious of its own culture and consciously seeks to perpetuate its distinctive elements. At the same time this consciousness of difference is devoid of envy or frustration and produces no friction. The members of each group pursue their own goals with the aid of their own techniques and, although the situation does not preclude economic rivalries—witness the constant quarrels over water rights—it does preclude social rivalries. It seems that the establishment of such attitudes of mutual social exclusiveness, without hatred or dominance, provides the soundest basis for organizing symbiotic relationships between societies and should be encouraged in all cases where the attitudes of one or both of the groups in contact preclude assimilation.

Contact situations comparable to that just discussed are not infrequent, but they seem to be less common than those in which both groups agree on the superiority of one of the parties. It must be repeated that such attitudes are not necessarily linked with conditions of actual dominance. Thus the Japanese during the early period of European contact acquiesced in the European's estimate of his own superiority and borrowed European culture elements eagerly and indiscriminately although maintaining national independence. Again, the disunited German states of the eighteenth century acknowledged the superiority of French culture and were eager for French approval even when no political factors were involved.

When two groups stand in such a mutually recognized relationship of superiority and inferiority, but with no factors of actual dominance involved, the contact will rarely if ever give rise to nativistic movements of the magical type. The relationship cannot produce the extreme stresses which drive the members of a society into such flights from reality. On the other hand, the contact may well give rise to rational nativistic movements, but these will rarely if ever appear during the early contact period. At first the superior group is usually so sure of its position that it feels no reluctance toward borrowing convenient elements from the culture of the inferior one. Conversely, the inferior group borrows eagerly from the superior one and looks forward to full equality with it as soon as the cultural differences have been obliterated. During this period impecunious members of the superior group are likely to turn their prestige to practical advantage by marrying rich members of the inferior one and, for a time, genuine assimilation appears to be under way. In such a situation the nativistic trends will normally appear first in the superior group, which is naturally jealous of its prestige. The movements inaugurated will generally be of the perpetuative-rational type, designed to maintain the *status quo*, and will include increasing reluctance to borrow elements of culture from the inferior group and the increase of social discrimination against its members and those of the superior group who consort with them.

When such a nativistic movement gets well under way in the superior group, there will usually be a nativistic response from the inferior one. Finding themselves frustrated in their desire for equality, with or without actual assimilation, the inferiors will develop their own nativistic movements, acting on the well-known sour-grapes principle. However, these movements will be of the revivalistic-rational rather than the perpetuative-rational type. The culture elements selected for emphasis will tend to be drawn from the past rather than the present, since the attitudes of the superior group toward the current culture will have done much to devaluate it. In general, symbolic values will be attached, by preference, to culture elements which were already on the wane at the time of the first contact with the superior group, thus embodying in the movement a denial that the culture of the other group ever was considered superior.

We have already said that attitudes of superiority and inferiority seem to be present in all cases of contact involving actual dominance. Combining these two sets of factors we get the following possible situations for contact groups:

1. Dominant-superior
2. Dominant-inferior
3. Dominated-superior
4. Dominated-inferior

These situations assume agreement on the part of the groups involved not only with respect to dominance, readily demonstrable, but also with respect to attitudes. The frequent lack of such agreement makes it necessary to add a fifth situation, that in which the dominant and dominated group each considers itself superior. The other possible combinations, those involving attitudes of inferiority on the part of both dominant and dominated and those involving attitudes of mixed inferiority and superiority on both sides, may be ruled out from the present discussion. The first of these possible combinations simply does not occur. The second occurs rather frequently, but as in the cases where it occurs without domination, normally results in assimilation rather than the production of nativistic movements.

The idea that nativistic movements may arise in dominant as well as dominated groups appears strange to us, since most of our experience of such movements comes from the contact of Europeans with native peoples. However, we must not forget that Europeans have occupied a singularly favored position in such contacts. Even where the European settles permanently among a native population, he remains a mere outlier of white society and, thanks to modern means of transportation and communication, can keep close touch with the parent body. This parent body is shielded from contact and assimilation and is thus able to send out to its colonial ruling groups constant increments of individuals who are culturally unmixed. Moreover, the technological superiority of European culture has, until recently, rendered the dominance of colonial groups secure. The nativism of Europeans has, therefore, been largely unconscious and entirely of the perpetuative-rational type. It has manifested itself in such things as the practice of sending children back to Europe to be educated or the Englishman's insistence on dressing for dinner even when alone in a remote outpost of empire. Most dominant groups have been less fortunate. They have found themselves threatened, from the moment of their accession to power, not only by foreign invasion or domestic revolt but also by the insidious processes of assimilation which might, in the long run, destroy their distinctive powers and privileges. This threat was especially menacing when, as in most of the pre-machine age empires, the dominant and dominated groups differed little if at all in physical type. Among such rulers the frustrations which motivate nativistic movements in inferior or dominated groups were replaced by anxieties which produced very much the same results.

Returning to the contact situations previously tabulated, we find that dominant-superior groups tend to initiate perpetuative-rational forms of nativism as soon as they achieve power and to adhere to them with varying intensity as long as they remain in power. Thus the various groups of nomad invaders who conquered China all attempted to maintain much of their distinctive culture and at the height of their power they issued repressive measures directed not only against the Chinese but also against those of their own group who had begun to adopt Chinese culture. It seems probable that revivalist-rational forms of nativism will not arise in a dominant-superior group, at least as regards elements of culture which were moribund at the time of their accession to power, although this form of nativism might develop with respect to culture elements which had fallen into neglect during the period of power. It seems possible also that, under conditions of extreme threat, some form of brief revivalist-magical nativism might arise in such a group, but information that might verify these conjectures is lacking.

The situation in which a dominant group acknowledges its cultural inferiority to the dominated is one which must arise very infrequently. However, examples of it are provided by such cases as that of the Goths at the time of their conquest of Italy. Such a group immediately finds itself caught on the horns of a dilemma. It can remove its feelings of inferiority only by undergoing cultural if not society assimilation with the conquered society, while such assimilation is almost certain to cost it its dominant position. It seems probable that such a society might develop nativistic movements either when its desire for cultural assimilation with the conquered was frustrated or when it found its dominant position seriously threatened, but again information is lacking.

There is abundant information on nativistic movements among dominated groups and in discussing these we stand on firm ground. A dominated group which considers itself superior will normally develop patterns of rational nativism from the moment that it is brought under domination. These patterns may be either revivalist or perpetuative but are most likely to be a combination of both. One of the commonest rationalizations for loss of a dominant position is that it is due to a society's failure to adhere closely enough to its distinctive culture patterns. Very often

such nativism will acquire a semi-magical quality founded on the belief that if the group will only stand firm and maintain its individuality it will once again become dominant. Fully developed magical-revivalist nativism is also very likely to appear in groups of this sort since to the actual deprivations entailed by subjection there are added the frustrations involved by loss of dominance. These frustrations are somewhat mitigated in the cases where the dominant group recognizes the superiority of the dominated group's culture. Such attitudes strengthen the rational nativistic tendencies of the dominated group and diminish the probabilities for magical-revivalist nativism of the more extreme type. Lastly, in cases where the dominant group concurs with the dominated in considering certain aspects of the latter's culture superior but will not grant the superiority of the culture as a whole, this attitude will stimulate the dominated group to focus attention upon such aspects of its culture and endow them with added symbolic value.

A dominated group which considers itself inferior, a condition common among societies of low culture which have recently been brought under European domination, is extremely unlikely to develop any sort of rational nativism during the early period of its subjection. It may, however, develop nativism of the revivalist-magical type if it is subjected to sufficient hardships. The threshold of suffering at which such movements may develop will vary greatly from group to group and will be influenced not only by the degree of hardship but also by the society's patterns of reliance upon the supernatural. A devout society will turn to nativism of this sort long before a skeptical one will. If the hardships arising from subjection are not extreme, the inferior group will usually show great eagerness to assume the culture of the dominant society, this eagerness being accompanied by a devaluation of everything pertaining to its own. Nativistic movements tend to arise only when the members of the subject society find that their assumption of the culture of the dominant group is being effectively opposed by it, or that it is not improving their social position. The movements which originate under these circumstances are practically always rational with a combination of revivalist and perpetuative elements. In this respect they resemble the nativistic movements which originate in inferior groups which are not subject to domination and there can be little doubt that the primary causes are the same in both cases. These movements are a response to frustration rather than hardship and would not arise if the higher group were willing to assimilate the lower one.

Rational nativistic movements can readily be converted into mechanisms for aggression. Since the dominated society has been frustrated in its earlier desires to become acculturated and to achieve social equality, it can frustrate the dominant society in turn by refusing to accept even those elements of culture which the dominant group is eager to share with it. Dominated societies which have acquired these attitudes and developed conscious techniques for preventing further acculturation present one of the most difficult problems for administrators. Passive resistance requires much less energy than any of the techniques needed to break it down, especially if the culture patterns of the dominant group preclude the use of forcible methods.

One final aspect of nativistic movements remains to be considered. The generalizations so far developed have been based upon the hypothesis that societies are homogeneous and react as wholes to contact situations. Very frequently this is not the case, especially in societies which have a well-developed class organization. In such societies nativistic tendencies will be strongest in those classes or individuals who occupy a favored position and who feel this position threatened by culture change. This factor may produce a split in the society, the favored individuals or groups indulging in a rational nativism, either revivalistic or perpetuative, while those in less favored positions are eager for assimilation. This condition can be observed in many immigrant groups in America where individuals who enjoyed high status in the old European society attempt to perpetuate the patterns of that society while those who were of low status do their best to become Americanized.

In a rapidly shrinking world the study of nativistic movements, as of acculturation in general, has ceased to be a matter of purely academic interest. As contacts between societies become more frequent and more general, the need for an understanding of the potentialities of such contact situations becomes more urgent. The troubles which they usually involve can be traced, with few exceptions, to two factors: exploitation and frustration. The first of these is the easier to deal with and may well disappear with the spread of modern science and techniques to all parts of the world. The second is more difficult to deal with, since its removal entails fundamental changes in attitudes of superiority and inferiority. Without these there would be no bar to the assimilation of societies in contact situations or to the final creation of a world society. However, this seems to be one of those millennial visions mentioned elsewhere in this report. Failing assimilation, the happiest situation which can arise out of the contact of two societies seems to be that in which each society is firmly convinced of its own superiority. Rational revivalistic or perpetuative nativistic movements are the best mechanism which has so far been developed for establishing these attitudes in groups whose members suffer from feelings of inferiority. It would appear, therefore, that they should be encouraged rather than discouraged.

Anthony F. C. Wallace

REVITALIZATION MOVEMENTS

The publication of this paper by Anthony F. C. Wallace represents another landmark in anthropological attempts to formulate the general characteristics of major cultural-system innovations that typically involve religious patterns. Wallace suggests that these major innovations, variously called "nativistic movements," "cargo cults," "messianic movements," "revolutions," etc., are characterized by a uniform process which he calls "revitalization." He outlines the

Reprinted in abridged form from *American Anthropologist*, LVIII (1956), 264–281, by permission of the author and the American Anthropological Association.

structure of the process in terms of five somewhat overlapping stages: Steady State; Period of Individual Stress; Period of Cultural Distortion; Period of Revitalization; and finally a New Steady State again. In his sophisticated use of culture-pattern and psychological theory, Wallace has added important theoretical dimensions to our understandings of "revitalization movements" and has suggested that the historical origin of a great proportion of religious phenomena has been in such movements. Interested readers will find a full application of his ideas in his recently published book *The Death and Rebirth of the Seneca* (1970).

INTRODUCTION

Behavioral scientists have described many instances of attempted and sometimes successful innovation of whole cultural systems, or at least substantial portions of such systems. Various rubrics are employed, the rubric depending on the discipline and the theoretical orientation of the researcher, and on salient local characteristics of the cases he has chosen for study. "Nativistic movement," "reform movement," "cargo cult," "religious revival," "messianic movement," "utopian community," "sect formation," "mass movement," "social movement," "revolution," "charismatic movement," are some of the commonly used labels. This paper suggests that all these phenomena of major cultural-system innovation are characterized by a uniform process, for which I propose the term "revitalization." The body of the paper is devoted to two ends: (1) an introductory statement of the concept of revitalization, and (2) an outline of certain uniformly-found processual dimensions of revitalization movements.

THE CONCEPT OF REVITALIZATION

A revitalization movement is defined as a deliberate, organized, conscious effort by members of a society to construct a more satisfying culture. Revitalization is thus, from a cultural standpoint, a special kind of culture change phenomenon: the persons involved in the process of revitalization must perceive their culture, or some major areas of it, as a system (whether accurately or not); they must feel that this cultural system is unsatisfactory; and they must innovate not merely discrete items, but a new cultural system, specifying new relationships as well as, in some cases, new traits. The classic processes of culture change (evolution, drift, diffusion, historical change, acculturation) all produce changes in cultures as systems; however, they do not depend on deliberate intent by members of a society, but rather on a gradual chain-reaction effect: introducing A induces change in B; changing B affects C; when C shifts, A is modified; this involves D ... and so on *ad infinitum*. This process continues for years, generations, centuries, millennia, and its pervasiveness has led many cultural theorists to regard culture change as essentially a slow, chain-like, self-contained procession of superorganic inevitabilities. In revitalization move ments, however, A, B, C, D, E ... N are shifted into a new *Gestalt* abruptly and simultaneously in intent; and frequently within a few years the new plan is put into effect by the participants in the movement.

. .

The term "revitalization" implies an organismic analogy. This analogy is, in fact, an integral part of the concept of revitalization. A human society is here regarded as a definite kind of organism, and its culture is conceived as those patterns of learned behavior which certain "parts" of the social organism or system (individual persons and groups of persons) characteristically display. A corollary of the organismic analogy is the principle of homeostasis: that a society will work, by means of coordinated actions (including "cultural" actions) by all or some of its parts, to preserve its own integrity by maintaining a minimally fluctuating, life-supporting matrix for its individual members, and will, under stress, take emergency measures to preserve the constancy of this matrix. Stress is defined as a condition in which some part, or the whole, of the social organism is threatened with more or less serious damage. The perception of stress, particularly of increasing stress, can be viewed as the common denominator of the panel of "drives" or "instincts" in every psychological theory.

As I am using the organismic analogy, the total system which constitutes a society in cludes as significant parts not only persons and groups with their respective patterns of behavior, but also literally the cells and organs of which the persons are composed.

Indeed, one can argue that the system includes nonhuman as well as human subsystems. Stress on one level is stress on all levels. For example, lowering of sugar level (hunger) in the fluid matrix of the body cells of one group of persons in a society is a stress in the society as a whole. This holistic view of society as organism integrated from cell to nation depends on the assumption that society, as an organization of living matter, is definable as a network of intercommunication. Events on one subsystem level must affect other subsystems (cellular vis-à-vis institutional, personal vis-à-vis societal) at least as information; in this view, social organization exists to the degree that events in one subsystem are information to other subsystems.

There is one crucial difference between the principles of social organization and that of the individual person: a society's parts are very widely interchangeable, a person's only slightly so. The central nervous system cells, for example, perform many functions of coordinating information and executing adaptive action which other cells cannot do. A society, on the other hand, has a multiple-replacement capacity, such that many persons can perform the analogous information-coordination and executive functions on behalf of society-as-organism. Furthermore, that regularity of patterned behavior which we call culture depends relatively more on the ability of constituent units autonomously to perceive the system of which they are a part, to receive and transmit information, and to act in accordance with the necessities of the system, than on any all-embracing central administration which stimulates specialized parts to perform their function.

It is therefore functionally necessary for every person in society to maintain a mental image of the society and its culture, as well as of his own body and its behavioral regularities, in order to act in ways which reduce stress at all levels of the system. The person does, in fact, maintain such an image. This mental image I have called "the mazeway," since as a model of the cell-body-personality-nature-culture-society system or field, organized by the individual's own experience, it includes perceptions of both the maze of physical objects of the environment (internal and external, human and nonhuman) and also of the ways in which this maze can be manipulated by the self and others in order to minimize stress. The mazeway is nature,

society, culture, personality, and body image, as seen by one person. . . .

We may now see more clearly what "revitalization movements" revitalize. Whenever an individual who is under chronic, physiologically measurable stress, receives repeated information which indicates that his mazeway does not lead to action which reduces the level of stress, he must choose between maintaining his present mazeway and tolerating the stress, or changing the mazeway in an attempt to reduce the stress. Changing the mazeway involves changing the total *Gestalt* of his image of self, society, and culture, of nature and body, and of ways of action. It may also be necessary to make changes in the "real" system in order to bring mazeway and "reality" into congruence. The effort to work a change in mazeway and "real" system together so as to permit more effective stress reduction is the effort at revitalization; and the collaboration of a number of persons in such an effort is called a revitalization movement.

The term revitalization movement thus denotes a very large class of phenomena. Other terms are employed in the existing literature to denote what I would call subclasses, distinguished by a miscellany of criteria. "Nativistic movements," for example, are revitalization movements characterized by strong emphasis on the elimination of alien persons, customs, values, and/or material from the mazeway (Linton, 1943). "Revivalistic" movements emphasize the institution of customs, values, and even aspects of nature which are thought to have been in the mazeway of previous generations but are not now present (Mooney, 1892–1893). "Cargo cults" emphasize the importation of alien values, customs, and material into the mazeway, these things being expected to arrive as a ship's cargo as for example in the Vailala Madness (Williams, 1923, 1934). "Vitalistic movements" emphasize the importation of alien elements into the mazeway but do not necessarily invoke ship and cargo as the mechanism. "Millenarian movements" emphasize mazeway transformation in an apocalyptic world transformation engineered by the supernatural. "Messianic movements" emphasize the participation of a divine savior in human flesh in the mazeway transformation (Wallis, 1918, 1943). These and parallel terms do not denote mutually exclusive categories, for a given revitalization movement may be nativistic, millenarian, messianic, and revivalistic all at once; and it may (in fact, usually does) display ambivalence with respect to nativistic, revivalistic, and importation themes.

Revitalization movements are evidently not unusual phenomena, but are recurrent features in human history. Probably few men have lived who have not been involved in an instance of the revitalization process. They are, furthermore, of profound historical importance. Both Christianity and Mohammedanism, and possibly Buddhism as well, originated in revitalization movements. Most denominational and sectarian groups and orders budded or split off after failure to revitalize a traditional institution. One can ask whether a large proportion of religious phenomena have not originated in personality transformation dreams or visions characteristic of the revitalization process. Myths, legends, and rituals may be relics, either of the manifest content of vision-dreams or of the doctrines and history of revival and import cults, the circumstances of whose origin have been distorted and forgotten, and whose connection with dream states is now ignored. Myths in particular have long been noted to possess a dream-like quality, and have been more or less speculatively-interpreted according to the principles of symptomatic dream interpretation. It is tempting to suggest that myths and, often, even legends, read like dreams because they *were* dreams when they were first told. It is tempting to argue further that culture heroes represent a condensation of the figures of the prophet and of the supernatural being of whom he dreamed.

In fact, it can be argued that all organized religions are relics of old revitalization movements, surviving in routinized form in stabilized cultures, and that religious phenomena per se originated (if it is permissible still in this day and age to talk about the "origins" of major elements of culture) in the revitalization process—i.e., in visions of a new way of life by individuals under extreme stress.

THE PROCESSUAL STRUCTURE

A basic methodological principle employed in this study is that of event-analysis (Wallace, 1953). This approach employs a method of controlled comparison for the study of processes involving longer or shorter diachronic sequences (vide Eggan, 1954, and Steward, 1953). It is postulated that events or happenings of various types have genotypical structures independent of local cultural differences;

for example, that the sequence of happenings following a severe physical disaster in cities in Japan, the United States, and Germany will display a uniform pattern, colored but not obscured by local differences in culture. These types of events may be called behavioral units. Their uniformity is based on generic human attributes, both physical and psychological, but it requires extensive analytical and comparative study to elucidate the structure of any one. Revitalization movements constitute such a behavioral unit, and so also, on a lower level of abstraction, do various subtypes within the larger class, such as cargo and revival cults. We are therefore concerned with describing the generic structure of revitalization movements considered as a behavioral unit, and also of variation along the dimensions characteristic of the type.

The structure of the revitalization process, in cases where the full course is run, consists of five somewhat overlapping stages: (1) Steady State; (2) Period of Individual Stress; (3) Period of Cultural Distortion; (4) Period of Revitalization (in which occur the functions of mazeway reformulation, communication, organization, adaptation, cultural transformation, and routinization), and finally, (5) New Steady State. These stages are described briefly in the following sections.

I. Steady State. For the vast majority of the population, culturally recognized techniques for satisfying needs operate with such efficiency that chronic stress within the system varies within tolerable limits. Some severe but still tolerable stress may remain general in the population, and a fairly constant incidence of persons under, for them, intolerable stress may employ "deviant" techniques (e.g., psychotics). Gradual modification or even rapid substitution of techniques for satisfying some needs may occur without disturbing the steady state, as long as (1) the techniques for satisfying other needs are not seriously interfered with, and (2) abandonment of a given technique for reducing one need in favor of a more efficient technique does not leave other needs, which the first technique was also instrumental in satisfying, without any prospect of satisfaction.

II. The Period of Increased Individual Stress. Over a number of years, individual members of a population (which may be "primitive" or "civilized," either a whole society or a class, caste, religious, occupational, acculturational, or other definable social group) experience increasingly severe stress as a result of the decreasing efficiency of certain stress-reduction techniques. The culture may remain essentially unchanged or it may undergo considerable changes, but in either case there is continuous diminution in its efficiency in satisfying needs. The agencies responsible for interference with the efficiency of a cultural system are various: climatic, floral and faunal change; military defeat; political subordination; extreme pressure toward acculturation resulting in internal cultural conflict; economic distress; epidemics; and so on. The situation is often, but not necessarily, one of acculturation, and the acculturating agents may or may not be representatives of Western European cultures. While the individual can tolerate a moderate degree of increased stress and still maintain the habitual way of behavior, a point is reached at which some alternative way must be considered. Initial consideration of a substitute way is likely, however, to increase stress because it arouses anxiety over the possibility that the substitute way will be even less effective than the original, and that it may also actively interfere with the execution of other ways. In other words, it poses the threat of mazeway disintegration. Furthermore, admission that a major technique is worthless is extremely threatening because it implies that the whole mazeway system may be inadequate.

III. The Period of Cultural Distortion. The prolonged experience of stress, produced by failure of need satisfaction techniques and by anxiety over the prospect of changing behavior patterns, is responded to differently by different people. Rigid persons apparently prefer to tolerate high levels of chronic stress rather than make systematic adaptive changes in the mazeway. More flexible persons try out various limited mazeway changes in their personal lives, attempting to reduce stress by addition or substitution of mazeway elements with more or less concern for the *Gestalt* of the system. Some persons turn to psychodynamically regressive innovations; the regressive response empirically exhibits itself in increasing incidences of such things as alcoholism, extreme passivity and indolence, the development of highly ambivalent dependency relationships, intragroup violence, disregard of kinship and sexual mores, irresponsibility in public officials, states of depression and self-reproach, and probably a variety of psychosomatic and neurotic disorders. Some of these regressive action systems become, in effect, new cultural patterns.

In this phase, the culture is internally distorted; the elements are not harmoniously related but are mutually inconsistent and interfering. For this reason alone, stress continues to rise. "Regressive" behavior, as defined by the society, will arouse considerable guilt and hence increase stress level or at least maintain it at a high point; and the general process of piecemeal cultural substitution will multiply situations of mutual conflict and misunderstanding, which in turn increase stress-level again.

Finally, as the inadequacy of existing ways of acting to reduce stress becomes more and more evident, and as the internal incongruities of the mazeway are perceived, symptoms of anxiety over the loss of a meaningful way of life also become evident: disillusionment with the mazeway, and apathy toward problems of adaptation, set in.

IV. The Period of Revitalization. This process of deterioration can, if not checked, lead to the death of the society. Population may fall even to the point of extinction as a result of increasing death rates and decreasing birth rates; the society may be defeated in war, invaded, its population dispersed and its customs suppressed; factional disputes may nibble away areas and segments of the population. But these dire events are not infrequently forestalled, or at least postponed, by a revitalization movement. Many such movements are religious in character, and such religious revitalization movements must perform at least six major tasks:

1. *Mazeway Reformulation.* Whether the movement is religious or secular, the reformulation of the mazeway generally seems to depend on a restructuring of elements and subsystems which have already attained currency in the society and may even be in use, and which are known to the person who is to become the prophet or leader. The occasion of their combination in a form which constitutes an internally consistent structure, and of their acceptance by the prophet as a guide to action, is abrupt and dramatic, usually occurring as a moment of insight, a brief period of realization of relationships and opportunities. These moments are often called inspiration or revelation. The reformulation also seems normally to occur in its initial form in the mind of a single person rather than to grow directly out of group deliberations.

With a few exceptions, every religious revitalization movement with which I am acquainted has been originally conceived in one or several hallucinatory visions by a single individual. A supernatural being appears to the prophet-to-be, explains his own and his society's troubles as being entirely or partly a result of the violation of certain rules, and promises individual and social revitalization if the injunctions are followed and the rituals practiced, but personal and social catastrophe if they are not. These dreams express: (1) the dreamer's wish for a satisfying parental figure (the supernatural, guardian-spirit content), (2) world-destruction fantasies (the apocalyptic, millennial content), (2) feelings of guilt and anxiety (the moral content), and (4) longings for the establishment of an ideal state of stable and satisfying human and supernatural relations (the restitution fantasy or Utopian content). In a sense, such a dream also functions almost as a funeral ritual: the "dead" way of life is recognized as dead; interest shifts to a god, the community, and a new way. A new mazeway *Gestalt* is presented, with more or less innovation in details of content. The prophet feels a need to tell others of his experience, and may have definite feelings of missionary or messianic obligation. Generally he shows evidence of a radical inner change in personality soon after the vision experience: a remission of old and chronic physical complaints, a more active and purposeful way of life, greater confidence in interpersonal relations, the dropping of deep-seated habits like alcoholism. Hence we may call these visions "personality transformation dreams."

. . .

2. *Communication.* The dreamer undertakes to preach his revelations to people, in an evangelistic or messianic spirit; he becomes a prophet. The doctrinal and behavioral injunctions which he preaches carry two fundamental motifs: that the convert will come under the care and protection of certain supernatural beings; and that both he and his society will benefit materially from an identification with some definable new cultural system (whether a revived culture or a cargo culture, or a syncretism of both, as is usually the case). The preaching may take many forms (e.g., mass exhortation vs. quiet individual persuasion) and may be directed at various sorts of audiences (e.g., the elite vs. the down-trodden). As he gathers disciples, these assume much of the responsibility for communicating the "good word," and communication remains one of the primary activities of the movement during later phases of organization.

3. *Organization.* Converts are made by the prophet. Some undergo hysterical seizures induced by suggestion in a crowd situation; some experience an ecstatic vision in private circumstances; some are convinced by more or less rational arguments, some by considerations of expediency and opportunity. A small clique of special disciples (often including a few already influential men) clusters about the prophet and an embryonic campaign organization develops with three orders of personnel: the prophet; the disciples; and the followers. Frequently the action program from here on is effectively administered in large part by a political rather than a religious leadership. Like the prophet, many of the converts undergo a revitalizing personality transformation.

Max Weber's concept of "charismatic leadership" well describes the type of leader-follower relationship characteristic of revitalization movement organizations (1947). The fundamental element of the vision, as I have indicated above, is the entrance of the visionary into an intense relationship with a supernatural being. This relationship, furthermore, is one in which the prophet accepts the leadership, succor, and dominance of the supernatural. Many followers of a prophet, especially the disciples, also have ecstatic revelatory experiences; but they and all sincere followers who have not had a personal revelation also enter into a parallel relationship to the prophet: as God is to the prophet, so (almost) is the prophet to his followers. The relationship of the follower to the prophet is in all probability determined by the displacement of transference dependency wishes onto his image; he is regarded as an uncanny person, of unquestionable authority in one or more spheres of leadership, sanctioned by the supernatural. Max Weber denotes this quality of uncanny authority and moral ascendency in a leader as charisma. Followers defer to the charismatic leader not because of his status in an existing authority structure but because of a fascinating personal "power," often ascribed to supernatural sources and validated in successful performance, akin to the "mana" or "orenda" of ethnological literature. The charismatic leader thus is not merely permitted but expected to phrase his call for adherents as a demand to perform a duty to a power higher than human. Weber correctly points out that the "routinization" of charisma is a critical issue in movement organization, since unless this "power" is distributed to other personnel in a stable institutional structure, the movement itself is liable to die with the death or failure of individual prophet, king, or war lord.

. . .

4. *Adaptation.* The movement is a revolutionary organization and almost inevitably will encounter some resistance. Resistance may in some cases be slight and fleeting but more commonly is determined and resourceful, and is held either by a powerful faction within the society or by agents of a dominant foreign society. The movement may therefore have to use various strategies of adaptation: doctrinal modification; political and diplomatic maneuver; and force. These strategies are not mutually exclusive nor, once chosen, are they necessarily maintained through the life of the movement. In most instances the original doctrine is continuously modified by the prophet, who responds to various criticisms and affirmations by adding to, emphasizing, playing down, and eliminating selected elements of the original visions. This reworking makes the new doctrine more acceptable to special interest groups, may give it a better "fit" to the population's cultural and personality patterns, and may take account of the changes occurring in the general milieu. In instances where organized hostility to the movement develops, a crystallization of counter-hostility against unbelievers frequently occurs, and emphasis shifts from cultivation of the ideal to combat against the unbeliever.

5. *Cultural Transformation.* As the whole or a controlling portion of the population comes to accept the new religion with its various injunctions, a noticeable social revitalization occurs, signalized by the reduction of the personal deterioration symptoms of individuals, by extensive cultural changes, and by an enthusiastic embarkation on some organized program of group action. This group program may, however, be more or less realistic and more or less adaptive: some programs are literally suicidal; others represent well conceived and successful projects of further social, political, or economic reform; some fail, not through any deficiency in conception and execution, but because circumstances made defeat inevitable.

6. *Routinization.* If the group action program in nonritual spheres is effective in reducing stress-generating situations, it becomes established as normal in various economic, social, and political institutions and customs. Rarely does the movement organization assert or maintain a totalitarian control over all aspects of the transformed culture; more usually, once the desired transformation has occurred, the organization contracts and maintains responsibility only for the preservation of doctrine and the performance of ritual (i.e., it becomes a church). . . .

V. The New Steady State. Once cultural transformation has been accomplished and the new cultural system has proved itself viable, and once the movement organization has solved its problems of routinization, a new steady state may be said to exist. The culture of this state will probably be different in pattern, organization or *Gestalt*, as well as in traits, from the earlier steady state; it will be different from that of the period of cultural distortion.

VARIETIES AND DIMENSIONS OF VARIATION

I will discuss four of the many possible variations: the choice of identification; the choice of secular and religious means; nativism; and the success-failure continuum.

1. *Choice of Identification.* Three varieties have been distinguished already on the basis of differences in choice of identification: movements which profess to *revive* a traditional culture now fallen into desuetude; movements which profess to *import* a foreign cultural system; and movements which profess neither revival nor importation, but conceive that the desired cultural endstate, which has never been enjoyed by ancestors or foreigners, will be realized for the first time in a future *Utopia.* The Ghost Dance, the Xosa Revival, and the Boxer Rebellion are examples of professedly revivalistic movements; the Vailala Madness (and other cargo cults) and the Taiping Rebellion are examples of professedly importation movements. Some formulations like Ikhnaton's monotheistic cult in old Egypt and many Utopian programs, deny any substantial debt to the past or to the foreigner, but conceive their ideology to be something new under the sun, and its culture to belong to the future.

. .

Culture areas seem to have characteristic ways of handling the identification problem. The cargo fantasy, although it can be found outside the Melanesian area, seems to be particularly at home there; South American Indian prophets frequently preached of a migration to a heaven-on-earth free of Spaniards and other evils, but the promised-land fantasy is known elsewhere; North American Indian prophets most commonly emphasized the revival of the old culture by ritual and moral purification, but pure revival ideas exist in other regions too. Structural "necessity" or situational factors associated with culture area may be responsible. The contrast between native-white relationships in North America (a "revival" area) and Melanesia (an "importation" area) may be associated with the fact that American Indians north of Mexico were never enslaved on a large scale, forced to work on plantations, or levied for labor in lieu of taxes, whereas Melanesians were often subjected to more direct coercion by foreign police power. The Melanesian response has been an identification with the aggressor (vide Bettelheim, 1947). On the other hand, the American Indians have been less dominated as individuals by whites, even under defeat and injustice. Their response to this different situation has by and large been an identification with a happier past. This would suggest that an important variable in choice of identification is the degree of domination exerted by a foreign society, and that import-oriented revitalization movements will not develop until an extremely high degree of domination is reached.

2. *The Choice of Secular and Religious Means.* There are two variables involved here: the amount of secular action which takes place in a movement, and the amount of religious action. Secular action is here defined as the manipulation of human relationships; religious action as the manipulation of relationships between human and supernatural beings. No revitalization movement can, by definition, be truly nonsecular, but some can be relatively less religious than others, and movements can change in emphasis depending on changing circumstances. There is a tendency, which is implicit in the earlier discussion of stages, for movements to become more political in emphasis, and to act through secular rather than religious institutions, as problems of organization, adaptation, and routinization become more pressing. The Taiping Rebellion, for instance, began as religiously-preoccupied movements; opposition by the Manchu dynasty and by foreign powers forced it to become more and more political and military in orientation.

A few "purely" political movements like the Hebertist faction during the French Revolution, and the Russian communist movement and its derivatives, have been officially atheistic, but the quality of doctrine and of leader-follower relationships is so similar, at least on superficial inspection, to religious doctrine and human-supernatural relations, that one wonders whether it is not a distinction without a difference. Communist movements are commonly asserted to have the quality of religious movements, despite their failure to appeal to a supernatural community, and such things as the development of a Marxist gospel with elaborate exegesis, the embalming of Lenin, and the concern with conversion, confession, and moral purity (as defined by the movement) have the earmarks of religion. The Communist Revolution of 1917 in Russia was almost typical in structure of religious revitalization movements: there was a very sick society, prophets appealed to a revered authority (Marx), apocalyptic and Utopian fantasies were preached, and missionary fervor animated the leaders. Furthermore, many social and political reform movements, while not atheistic, act through secular rather than religious media and invoke religious sanction only in a perfunctory way. I do not wish to elaborate the discussion at this time, however, beyond the point of suggesting again that the obvious distinctions between religious and secular movements may conceal fundamental similarities of sociocultural process and of psychodynamics, and that while all secular prophets have not had personality transformation visions, some probably have, and others have had a similar experience in ideological conversion.

Human affairs around the world seem more and more commonly to be decided without reference to supernatural powers. It is an interesting question whether mankind can profitably dispense with the essential element of the religious revitalization process before reaching a Utopia without stress or strain. While religious movements may involve crude and powerful emotions and irrational fantasies of interaction with nonexistent beings, and can occasionally lead to unfortunate practical consequences in human relations, the same fantasies and emotions could lead to even more unfortunate practical consequences for world peace and human welfare when directed toward people improperly perceived and toward organs of political action and cultural ideologies. The answer would seem to be that as fewer and fewer men make use of the religious displacement process, there will have to be a corresponding reduction of the incidence and severity of transference neuroses, or human relationships will be increasingly contaminated by character disorders, neurotic acting out, and paranoid deification of political leaders and ideologies.

3. *Nativism.* Because a major part of the program of many revitalization movements has been to expel the persons or customs of foreign invaders or overlords, they have been widely called "nativistic movements." However, the amount of nativistic activity in movements is variable. Some movements— the cargo cults, for instance—are antinativistic from a cultural standpoint but nativistic from a personnel standpoint. Handsome Lake was only mildly nativistic; he sought for an accommodation of cultures and personalities rather than expulsion, and favored entry of certain types of white persons and culture-content. Still, many of the classic revivalistic movements have been vigorously nativistic, in the ambivalent way discussed earlier. Thus nativism is a dimension of variation rather than an elemental property of revitalization movements.

A further complication is introduced by the fact that the nativistic component of a revitalization movement not uncommonly is very low at the time of conception, but increases sharply after the movement enters the adaptation stage. Initial doctrinal formulations emphasize love, co-operation, understanding, and the prophet and his disciples expect the powers-that-be to be reasonable and accepting. When these powers interfere with the movement, the response is apt to take the form of an increased nativistic component in the doctrine. Here again, situational factors are important for an understanding of the course and character of the movement.

4. *Success and Failure.* The outline of stages as given earlier is properly applicable to a revitalization movement which is completely successful. Many movements are abortive; their progress is arrested at some intermediate point. This raises a taxonomic question: how many stages should the movement achieve in order to qualify for inclusion in the category? Logically, as long as the original conception is a doctrine of revitalization by culture change, there should be no requisite number of stages. Practically, we have selected only movements which passed the first three stages (conception, communication, and organization) and entered the fourth (adaptation). This means that the bulk of our information on success and failure will deal with circumstances of relatively late adaptation, rather than with such matters as initial blockage of communication and interference with organization.

Two major but not unrelated variables seem to be very important in determining the fate of any given movement: the relative "realism" of the doctrine; and the amount of force exerted against the organization by its opponents. "Realism" is a difficult concept to define without invoking the concept of success or failure, and unless it can be so defined, is of no use as a variable explanatory of success or failure. Nor can one use the criterion of conventionality of perception, since revitalization movements are by definition unconventional. While a great deal of doctrine in every movement (and, indeed, in every person's mazeway) is extremely unrealistic in that predictions of events made on the basis of its assumptions will prove to be more or less in error, there is only one sphere of behavior in which such error is fatal to the success of a revitalization movement: prediction of the outcome of conflict situations. If the organization cannot predict successfully the consequences of its own moves and of its opponents' moves in a power struggle, its demise is very likely. If, on the other hand, it is canny about conflict, or if the amount of resistance is low, it can be extremely "unrealistic" and extremely unconventional in other matters without running much risk of early collapse. In other words, probability of failure would seem to be negatively correlated with degree of realism in conflict situations, and directly correlated with amount of resistance. Where conflict-realism is high and resistance is low, the movement is bound to achieve the phase of routinization. Whether its culture will be viable for long beyond this point, however, will depend on whether its mazeway formulations lead to actions which maintain a low level of stress.

SUMMARY

This programmatic paper outlines the concepts, assumptions, and initial findings of a comparative study of religious revitalization movements. Revitalization movements are defined as deliberate, conscious, organized efforts by members of a society to create a more satisfying culture. The revitalization movement as a general type of event occurs under two conditions: high stress for individual members of the society, and disillusionment with a distorted cultural *Gestalt*. The movement follows a series of functional stages: mazeway reformulation, communication, organization, adaptation, cultural transformation, and routinization. Movements vary along several dimensions, of which choice of identification, relative degree of religious and secular emphasis, nativism, and success or failure are discussed here. The movement is usually conceived in a prophet's revelatory visions, which provide for him a satisfying relationship to the supernatural and outline a new way of life under divine sanction. Followers achieve similar satisfaction of dependency needs in the charismatic relationship. It is suggested that the historical origin of a great proportion of religious phenomena has been in revitalization movements.

Bernard Barber

ACCULTURATION AND MESSIANIC MOVEMENTS

Among the many nativistic movements that have been developed in the wake of the impact of white American culture upon the native Indian cultures of the United States, two have been selected for special treatment: the Ghost Dance and the Peyote Cult. The Ghost Dance was a classic example of Linton's magical-revivalistic type of movement and appeared in two waves, both originating among the Northern Paiute Indians in Nevada. The first Ghost Dance started in 1870 and spread mainly to Northern California; the second started in 1890 and spread mainly eastward to the Plains tribes. In this selection Barber develops the thesis that these differential spreads can be accounted for by the relative amounts of deprivation in the two areas.

He then goes on to describe the Peyote Cult as an alternative response to deprivation which, because it was essentially nonviolent and nonthreatening to white American culture and worked in Christian elements and symbols, could spread and survive in areas where the Ghost Dance was forcibly exterminated. We thus seem to have an understandable sequence of acculturation events and native Indian responses—severe deprivation following the extermination of the buffalo herds, and the displacement and resettlement of Indian tribes—setting the cultural stage for acceptance and development of the Ghost Dance, which was to bring back the ancestors driving immense herds of buffalo before them. When the Ghost Dance did not produce the hoped-for results, or was forcibly stamped out by Indian agents and soldiers, the same tribes began to accept the Peyote Cult, which crystallized around passive acceptance and resignation in the face of continuing deprivation.

The outstanding account of the Ghost Dance is found in James Mooney's "The Ghost-Dance Religion" (1896).

Reprinted from *American Sociological Review*, VI (1941), 663–669, by permission of the author and the American Sociological Association.

Robert H. Lowie has recently called our attention again to the problem of messianic movements among the American aborigines. Among the North American Indians one of the fundamental myths was the belief that a culture hero would one day appear and lead them to a terrestrial paradise. Under certain conditions, which this paper will describe and analyze, these myths have become the ideological basis for messianic movements. In the messianic movement, the ushering in of the "golden age" by the messiah is announced for the *immediate* future. Twenty such movements had been recorded in the United States alone prior to 1890.

The messianic doctrine is essentially a statement of hope. Through the intervention of the Great Spirit or of his emissary, the earth will shortly be transformed into a paradise, enjoyed by both the living and the resurrected dead. In anticipation of the happy return to the golden age, believers must immediately return to the aboriginal mode of life. Traits and customs which are symbolic of foreign influence must be put aside. All members of the community—men, women, and children—must participate. Besides reverting to the early folkways, believers must adopt special ritual practices until the millennium arrives. Thus in the American Ghost Dance movements ceremonial bathing and an elaborate dance were the chief ritual innovations. The doctrine always envisages a restoration of earthly values. These values will be enjoyed, however, in a transcendental setting, for in the age which is foretold there will be no sickness or death; there will be only eternal happiness. The messianic doctrine is peaceful. The exclusion of the whites from the golden age is not so much a reflection of hostility toward them as a symbolization of the fulfillment of the former way of life. The millennium is to be established through divine agency; believers need only watch and pray.

The general sociocultural situation that precipitates a messianic movement has been loosely described as one of "harsh times." Its specific characteristic is the widespread experience of "deprivation"—the despair caused by inability to obtain what the culture has defined as the ordinary satisfactions of life. The fantasy situation pictured in the messianic doctrine attracts adherents chiefly because it includes those things which formerly provided pleasure in life, the loss of which constitutes deprivation. The pervasiveness of the precipitating cultural crisis may be inferred from the broad range of sociocultural items to be restored in the golden age. For example, one of the Sioux participants in the Ghost Dance experienced a vision of an old-fashioned buffalo hunt, genuine in all details. He said that he had beheld the scouts dashing back to proclaim the sighting of a herd. Now, the killing off of the buffalo was probably the greatest blow to the Plains Indians. Another bitter grievance was the expropriation of the Indian lands and the segregation of the tribes

on reservations; removal to a new geographical setting had more or less direct repercussions on every phase of the culture. For example, the prophet Smohalla promised, among other things, the restoration of the original tribal lands.

Deprivation may arise from the destruction not only of physical objects but also of sociocultural activities. In the aboriginal Sioux culture, millions of buffalo furnished an unlimited supply of food. Buffaloes and their by-products were perhaps the most important commodity in the Sioux economy, being employed as articles of exchange, as material for tepees, bedding, war shields, and the like. In addition, the buffalo was the focal point of many ritual and social activities of the Sioux. When the buffaloes were destroyed, therefore, the Sioux were deprived not only of food, but also of culturally significant activities. The tribal societies concerned with war and hunting lost their function and atrophied. The arts and techniques surrounding the buffalo hunt, arts and techniques which had once been sources of social status and of pride in "workmanship," were now rendered useless.

The impact of the white culture, besides depriving the Indians of their customary satisfactions, adds to their suffering by introducing the effects of new diseases and intoxicating liquor. In 1889 the Sioux suffered decimating epidemics of measles, grippe, and whooping cough. It is significant that Tenskwatawa prophesied that there would be no smallpox in the golden age. Complaints about the evil influences of firewater were expressed by "Open Door"; by "Handsome Lake," the Iroquois Prophet; by the Delaware Prophet; and by Känakuk, among others.

The messianic movement served to "articulate the spiritual depression" of the Indians. Those groups which faced a cultural impasse were predisposed to accept a doctrine of hope. Correlatively, the tribes that rejected the doctrine were in a state in which the values of their old life still functioned. In a condition of anomie, where there is a disorganization of the "controlling normative structure," most of the members of the group are thrown out of adjustment with significant features of their social environment. The old set of social and cultural norms is undermined by the civilized culture. Expectations are frustrated, there is a "sense of confusion, a loss of orientation," there is no longer a foundation for security. At such a time, messianic prophecies are most likely to be accepted and made the basis of action. Messiahs preach the return to the old order, or rather, to a new order in which the old will be revived. Essentially, their function is to proclaim a *stable order*, one which will define the ends of action. Their doctrines describe men's former life, meaningful and satisfactory.

The stabilizing function of the messianic movement may be illustrated in specific cases. Investigation of the 1870 and 1890 North American Ghost Dance movements shows that they are correlated with widespread deprivation. The two movements, though they originated in the same tribe, the North Paiute of Nevada, spread over different areas, depending upon the presence or absence of a deprivation situation. A comparison of the two movements makes the relationship clear-cut. The Ghost Dance of 1870 spread only through northern California; the tribes in that area had "suffered as great a disintegration by 1870 . . . as the average tribe of the central United States had undergone by 1890." In 1890 the Ghost Dance once again spread from the North Paiute, but this time not to California. By 1875 the movement there had exhausted itself and was abandoned. All the dancing and adherence to the rules of conduct had failed to bring the golden age. Disillusionment supervened upon the discovery that the movement was an inadequate response. The alternative response seems to have been a despondent and relatively amorphous adaptation. The Indians "had long since given up all hope and wish of the old life and adapted themselves as best they might to the new civilization that engulfed them." The 1890 movement did spread to the Plains tribes because by 1890 their old life had virtually disappeared, and the doctrine of the Ghost Dance was eagerly adopted for the hope that it offered. The radical changes among the Plains tribes in the twenty-year period, 1870–1890, may best be traced by examining the history of the Teton Sioux. Up to 1868, they were the least affected by white contact of all the tribes of the Plains area. By 1890, however, they were experiencing an intense deprivation situation, the climax of a trend which had begun twenty years before. Especially severe were the years between 1885–1890, when crops failed, many cattle died of disease, and a large part of the population was carried off by epidemics.

Further corroboration of the positive correlation of the messianic movement with extended deprivation has been presented by Nash. In 1870 the Ghost Dance doctrine was presented to three tribes which had been brought together on the Klamath reservation six years before, the Klamath, the Modoc, and the Paviotso. Of the three tribes, the Modoc, who had experienced the greatest amount of deprivation, participated most intensely. The Paviotso, who had experienced minimal cultural changes, participated least of all. Moreover, Nash found that within the tribes the members participated differentially, in rough proportion to the deprivation experienced.

A case study of the Navaho furnishes still further support for our thesis. Until quite recently, the Navaho territory was relatively isolated; few roads crossed it and there were not more than two thousand white inhabitants. The Navaho had managed to maintain the essentials of their own culture; their economic life had remained favorable; and from 1869 to 1931 they increased in numbers from less than 10,000 to 45,000. In 1864, in retaliation for their marauding, the United States Government rounded up the Navaho and banished them to the Bosque Redondo on the Pecos River. This exile was an exception to the fact that in general they had not suffered deprivation. They could not adapt to the agricultural life imposed on them and begged for permission to go home. Many died during epidemics of smallpox, whooping cough, chicken pox, and pneumonia. After four years, they were given sheep, goats, and clothing by the Government and allowed to return to their own country.

The equilibrium of the Navaho culture was quickly restored. The tribe grew rich in herds and silver. The old way of life was resumed in its essentials, despite the greater emphasis on a pastoral economy. The deprivation situation of 1864–1868 was left behind; life was integrated around a stable culture pattern. In the winter of 1889–1890, when Paiute runners tried to spread the belief in the coming of the Ghost Dance Messiah, their mission was fruitless. "They preached and prophesied for a considerable time, but the Navaho were skeptical, laughed at the prophets, and paid but little attention to their prophecies." There was no social need of a redeemer.

Within the last fifteen years, however, the entire situation of the Navaho tribe has changed. There has been constantly increasing contact with the white culture. Automobiles and railroads have brought tourists. The number of trading stores has increased. The discovery of oil on the reservation has produced rapid changes. Children have been sent to Government schools, far from their homes. Since 1929, the depression has reduced the income from the sale of blankets and silver jewelry. By far the most important difficulty now confronting the Navaho is the problem of overgrazing and soil erosion. To avert disaster, a basic reorgnization of the economic activities of the tribe is necessary. Therefore the Government, to meet this *objective* condition, has introduced a soil-erosion and stock-reduction program, but it has been completely unsatisfactory to the Navaho. Stock-reduction not only threatens their economic interests, *as they see them*, but undermines the basis of important sentiments and activities in the Navaho society. To destroy in a wanton fashion the focus of so many of their day-to-day interests cuts the cultural ground from under them.

Thus at present the Navaho are experiencing widespread deprivation. Significantly enough, within the past few years there has been a marked emergence of anti-white sentiment. Revivalistic cults have appeared. There has also been a great increase in recourse to aboriginal ceremonials on all occasions. Long reports of Navaho revivalistic activities were carried recently in *The Farmington Times Hustler*, a weekly published in Farmington, New Mexico. These activities bear a detailed similarity to the Ghost Dance and other American Indian messianic doctrines.

Despite the positive correlation of the messianic movement and deprivation, there is no one-to-one relation between these variables. It is here suggested that the messianic movement is *only one of several alternative responses*. In the other direction, the relationship is more determinate; the messianic movement is comprehensible only as a response to widespread deprivation. The alternative response of armed rebellion and physical violence has already been suggested. The depopulation among the natives of the South Pacific Islands may be viewed as still another response. The moral depression which, it often has been held, is one of the "causes" of the decline of the native races may be construed as a mode of reaction to the loss of an overwhelming number of satisfactions.

The theory of alternative responses may be tentatively checked against another set of data. The Ghost Dance among the Plains tribes lasted little more than a year or two, coming to a sharp end as a result of the suppression of the so-called "Sioux outbreak" with which it adventitiously had become connected in the minds of the whites. The Government agents on the Indian reservations successfully complied with their instructions to exterminate the movement. However, the deprivation of the tribes remained as acute as ever. It is in this context that the Peyote Cult emerged and spread among the Indians *as an alternative response*. It became the focus of a marked increase of attention and activity after 1890, thus coming in approximate temporal succession to the Ghost Dance. Completely nonviolent and nonthreatening to the white culture, the Peyote Cult has been able to survive in an environment which was radically opposed to the messianic movements.

The general and specific sociocultural matrices of the Peyote Cult are the same as those of the messianic movements. The Indians

fifty years ago, when Peyote first became known to them . . . were experiencing . . . despair and hopelessness over their vanishing culture, over their defeats, over the past grandeur that could not be regained. They were facing a spiritual crisis. . . . Some turned to Peyotism, and as time has but intensified the antagonistic forces, more and more have become converted to the new religion which offers a means of escape . . . [V. Petrullo, The Diabolic Root, *p. 27].*

The Peyote Cult, like the messianic movement, was an "autistic" response, in Lasswell's terms, but the essential element of its doctrine was different. Whereas the Ghost Dance doctrine had graphically described a reversion to the aboriginal state, the Peyote Cult crystallized around passive acceptance and resignation in the face of the existing deprivation. It is an alternative response which seems to be better adapted to the existing phase of acculturation.

Thus we have tested the hypotheses that the primitive messianic movement is correlated with the occurrence of widespread deprivation and that it is only one of several alternative responses. There is a need for further studies, especially in regard to the specific sociocultural conditions which produce responses.

W. W. Hill

THE NAVAHO INDIANS AND THE GHOST DANCE OF 1890

In response to Barber's thesis that the Ghost Dance spread to California tribes in 1870 and to Plains tribes in 1890 because of widespread deprivation, but failed to be accepted by the Navaho Indians because their life was integrated around a stable culture pattern, Hill shows convincingly in his paper that although Barber's general hypothesis may be sound, special cultural patterns in a particular tribe can be crucial in leading a people to reject a movement that is embraced by neighboring tribes. In this case Hill demonstrates that the Navaho fear of the dead and ghosts, which is an underlying and pervasive pattern in Navaho culture, was the critical factor in their rejection of the Ghost Dance. As Hill expresses it, "The Navaho were frightened out of their wits for fear the tenets of the movement were true"—that is, that the ghosts would come back!

Reprinted from *American Anthropologist*, XLVI (1944), 523–527, by permission of the author and the American Anthropological Association.

For years it has been the custom for most anthropologists to revert to economic determinism for an explanation of messianic phenomena. Recently, however, Bernard Barber in his paper "Acculturation and Messianic Movements" called our attention to approaches other than economic, i.e., social, and during the past year Ralph Linton in his article "Nativistic Movements" has outlined a whole new field for researches in the dynamics associated with revivalistic and perpetuative aspects of cultures. Stimulated by these two works I examined my field material on the Ghost Dance of 1890 among the Navaho and, because the data therein varied so from accounts of other tribes, decided to present it for publication.

To those acquainted with Navaho Indians any mention of their association with the Ghost Dance of 1890 must seem anomalous. While strictly speaking no direct participation did occur, this messianic development reached the Navaho and the impact registered profoundly on the minds of the individuals of the period. According to Mooney, news of the movement was conveyed to the Navaho via the Paiute. This was confirmed by some Navaho. However, others assigned it to the Southern Ute, while still others were unable to give any provenience. Most, however, agreed that while it was known throughout the reservation, the focal point for the dissemination of the concepts was in the Shiprock, Nava [Newcomb] Tohatchi region, i.e., northwest New Mexico, a factor which lends weight to their probable diffusion from the Southern Ute.

Most of the familiar traits of the Ghost Dance complex, the resurrection of the dead, the removal of the whites, the reestablishment of the old order of life, and survival through compulsory belief and participation in the movement, were known to the Navaho. The most widespread and significant element was the reported return of the dead. This was variously expressed. Some informants simply state that the dead or ghosts were said to be returning. Elaboration on this theme included the statements that those who had died during the incarceration at Fort Sumner, and those who had been killed by enemies, were coming back, and that the headmen were leading the ghosts back to the reservation.

Other phases of the doctrine were also subject to individual elaboration. The vehicle for white elimination varied in its practical methods, some holding that they were to be exterminated, others that they would leave the Navaho area and return to their former habitat. It was thought that the arrival of the millennium would bring with it the return of the old order, social and religious, plentiful game, ample rainfall, and corn immune from disease. Those who believed in and participated in the movement were to live; those who were skeptical were to die.

It is clear that the Navaho were thoroughly cognizant of all the essential elements of the Ghost Dance of 1890. It has also been established that the movement failed to flourish or find acceptance. We have the testimony of informants alive during this period, the statement of Washington Matthews to Mooney, and Barber's conclusions to this effect. The reasons for this rejection pose some interesting problems in dynamics and configuration.

The question of why the Navaho failed to embrace a doctrine found palatable by so many Indian peoples of North America represents a situation probably unique in the history of messianic movements. Barber has suggested that the rejection was due to a lack of social and spiritual "deprivation." This corresponds to an idea expressed many years ago by Wissler, in connection with the spread of the Ghost Dance in the Plains, and termed by him the occurrence of a cultural vacuum. I should like to present, however, an alternative possibility for the rejection of the 1890 Ghost Dance by the Navaho other than Barber's "life was integrated around a stable culture pattern."

It appears that the lack of acceptance resulted from the functioning of phases of Navaho culture falling into categories described by Kluckhohn as belonging to a covert pattern or configuration. The appended accounts show Navaho attitudes toward the Ghost Dance to have been ones of extreme ambivalence. It is apparent that the acceptance or rejection, per se, on the basis of the benefits which the movement promised was absent from the minds of informants. The question of "life integrated around a stable culture pattern" (if such existed in 1890, it certainly did not in 1870 when according to informants a similar opportunity was rejected) was not a consideration in the decisions. In fact, the idea of rejection or acceptance was of minimum importance; the Navaho interest in the movement was a manifestation of anxiety as to whether or not the reports which reached them were true.

An underlying fear appears even in accounts of the most skeptical informants. It is expressed, according to Navaho pattern, in references to abnormal weather conditions which prevailed during the period, suspicion of witchcraft in connection with the purveyors of the movement, and post-factum rationalizations of dire consequences both to individuals and property. All these were secondary expressions. The real anxiety concern was with the one element which was the core of the movement, i.e., the return of the dead.

Had the "economic" or "social integration" factors been compulsive, a selective element could have been expected to operate; the Navaho might gladly have embraced parts of the complex—the restoration of the old life and the disappearance of the whites—while rejecting the tidings that the dead were to return. However, the compelling element for them was clearly their fear of the dead; so much so that all other tenets were infected by it, hence suspect and to be rejected.

For the Navaho with his almost psychotic fear of death, the dead, and all connected with them, no greater cataclysm than the return of the departed or ghosts could be envisaged. In short, the Navaho were frightened out of their wits for fear the tenets of the movement were true. Thus, a covert pattern or configuration, deep-seated in the unconscious psychology of that people, acted as a barrier to the diffusion of a complex embraced by most of the tribes in western United States.

APPENDIX

The Late Fat One's Son, Tohatchi, N.M.: "The ignorant Navaho like myself were saying at this time, 'Look over toward Nava. [Nava (Newcomb) is north of Tohatchi. The ghosts are thought to reside in the north.] They [ghosts] are there already at Nava and will soon appear on the high ridges between Nava and Cornfields.' Then they would mention the names of the different headmen who had died and who were leading the ghosts back. Among them they mentioned my own father. The majority of the people believed in this. Those who did not believe, would ask, 'What is the purpose of these ghosts coming back?' The believers would say, 'They are just coming back to live with us and to tell us of the things in the other world.' Some of the people were singing to prevent the ghosts from coming back; they were afraid of them. This lasted one whole summer but gradually died out because no ghosts appeared and because the unbelievers ridiculed the believers. They tried to find the source of this rumor but they could not find where it started. They decided that some woman must have started it." The informant said that he does not know how far the Ghost Dance spread but believes that it was known throughout the reservation. The ghosts were to bring with them much rain; there were to be quantities of game in the country again; they were to bring corn which was immune from all diseases; all the old customs were to be reinstated; everything was to be as it was in the beginning because these ghosts knew conditions on both sides [i.e., in life and death] and they were to combine things from both sides and make things perfect. Some of the men even told people that they should be thankful that their relatives were returning. "Old Manuelito, of Fort Sumner time, was the chief unbeliever. He said, 'It is our belief that if ghosts appear it is bad luck. If they do appear we will have to get rid of them.' I was living close to Manuelito so I did not believe in their return, but everyone was talking so strongly about it it was hard not to believe. A woman dreamed that in the future the ghosts would return to the land of the living. That seems to have been the start of it. Manuelito told all the leading men to try and discourage this ghost business. He said, 'We know that ghosts are bad.' He tried to get the people to think of beneficial things, like agriculture and sheep raising. He said, 'Why ask the ghosts to come back; some day you will get a chance to go there.' This ghost dance never caused any harm but this witch business did. Right after [the captivity at] Fort Sumner the Navaho were very poor."

Grey Hair, White Cone, Ariz.: "The people who were saying this were a kind of prophet people. After they had said this thing a number of girls and boys around eighteen years of age died." The informant says that he has heard this prediction of the return of the dead three times during his life. "The first time was when I was about twelve years old [1870]. I heard it again when I was about thirty years old [1890]. The last time I heard it was about fifteen years ago [about 1918]. These prophet men were thinking bad. They must have been thinking that all the Navaho were going to die. A few years after the first time I heard this [1870] there was an epidemic of measles and a great many people died. A few years after the second time [1890] an epidemic of mumps killed a great number of people. Nothing has happened as yet since the last prophecy but I am waiting to see what will."

Slim Curley, Crystal, Ariz.: "I was living at Lukachukai. I was a young man at the time. The days were just hazy and the sun was reddish. Everything looked peculiar. People began to say that the Utes and Paiutes were talking about the ghosts coming. Many of the people in the country did not believe this. You could tell because they ridiculed the idea. However, there were a number who did believe it. I remember at a gathering for gambling one night there was a man who did not believe it. This man asked another for some money, saying, 'I hear that the ghosts are coming back to this country. No doubt my mother is in the crowd and you can have intercourse with her when she returns.' Those who believed said, 'The Utes are sending word ahead that the

ghosts are coming.' In the last month Chi Dodge was giving a group of medicine men a talking to. In the course of the talk he said, 'You must not start all these rumors.' He said, 'Look what happened after Fort Sumner [days]; someone started this rumor that all the white men were to be exterminated and then later this business about the ghosts coming back was started.' One old man wanted to take a party to the west to visit Changing Woman and find out what this return of the ghosts meant."

Mr. Headman, Head Springs, Ariz.: "There were Holy Men among the Navaho who told the old men and women that the dead were coming back. However, the old men and women did not believe it. They said, 'No one is going to come back once they are dead. If they come back it will mean that they will bring back all kinds of sickness. Also, if they come back there will be no rains and no corn.' They told the prophets that they should not say that the dead were coming back. The prophets said, 'When the ghosts come back all the whites . . .'—it hurts an old man like me to say these kind of words [i.e., to talk about ghosts]."

Albert G. Sandoval, Lukachukai, Ariz.: "It was known all over the reservation but most of the people did not believe it. They never danced. The Gods have left the country and have visited the people for the last time. The dead do not come back. In 1920 a preacher on the San Juan predicted a flood. The people were frightened and the majority of them left for the mountains. There was a hell of a mess. Most of the Indians took all their possessions with them. The knowledge [of the Ghost Dance] does not seem to have come from any particular source. Everyone knew of it but it just seems to have been passed along."

Pete Price, Fort Defiance, Ariz.: "The wind and the weather were very unusual at that time. Then word came that the dead were coming back to the earth. However, the majority of the people did not take this very seriously. They used to joke about it."

Mr. Left-Handed, Crown Point, N.M.: "I heard that all the Navaho who had died at Fort Sumner and all those who had been killed by enemies were coming back to life. The Navaho were all to go back where they had been living before and all the whites would have to go back to their own country. This came from around Tohatchi. There was no dance connected with the coming of the ghosts. As a rule it was not believed by the majority. Most of the people thought that this was started by the witches."

The Late Little Smith's Son, Crown Point, N.M.: "When we first heard of it I was living along Tohatchi flat. We heard that the ghosts were moving in close to where we were. Some of the young scouts told me that my father was coming back and that I had better go over and meet him. They said that all those who did not believe that the ghosts were coming back were going to die; the rest of the people would live on. This ghost business started up near Shiprock. A man there started it."

J. S. Slotkin

THE PEYOTE WAY

Peyote (a name derived from the Nahuatl word *peyotl*) was used in the cere-monies of Indians in central and northern Mexico in pre-Columbian times. The Huichol Indians living in the Sierra Madre mountains of western Mexico still make long pilgrimages on foot to collect peyote for their ceremonies each year. From Mexico the custom of taking peyote spread to the United States Indians and by 1890 it had become an important form of religion among the Plains tribes. Today, as Slotkin points out, Peyote religion is the most widespread contem-porary religion among the Indians of the United States. It is organized as the Native American Church and has become a kind of Indian version of Christianity, having adopted white Christian theology, ethics, and eschatology and modified these features to make them more compatible with traditional Indian culture.

The following selection provides a brief but illuminating description of "the Peyote Way," written by an anthropologist who was a member and officer of the Native American Church. In addition to the other technical reports published by Slotkin and mentioned in the selection, there is also a monograph by Weston LaBarre, *The Peyote Cult* (1938), and a popular book by Aldous Huxley, *Doors to Perception* (1954), which describes Huxley's experiences in taking mescaline, the same drug that is found in peyote. An excellent recent monograph on the Peyote Cult is David Aberle's *The Peyote Religion Among the Navaho* (1965).

Reprinted from *Tomorrow*, IV, No. 3 (1955–1956), 64–70, by permission of the author and Garrett Publications.

Peyote (*Lophophora williamsi*) is a spineless cactus which grows in the northern half of Mexico and for a short distance north of the Texas border. It has attracted attention be-cause it is used as a sacrament in religious rites conducted by Indians in the United States and Canada belonging to the Native American Church. The Peyote Religion or Peyote Way, as it is called by members, is the most widespread contemporary religion among the Indians, and is continually spread-ing to additional tribes.

From the viewpoint of almost all Peyotists, the religion is an Indian version of Chris-tianity. White Christian theology, ethics, and eschatology have been adopted with modifi-cations which make them more compatible with traditional Indian culture. The religion probably originated among the Kiowa and Comanche in Oklahoma about 1885.

The Peyote rite is an all-night ceremony, lasting approximately from sunset to sunrise, characteristically held in a Plains type tipi. Essentially the rite has four major elements: prayer, singing, eating the sacramental Peyote, and contemplation. The ritual is well defined, being divided into four periods: from sunset to midnight, from midnight to three o'clock, from three o'clock to dawn, and from dawn to morning. Four fixed songs sung by the rite leader, analogous to the fixed songs in the Catholic Mass, mark most of these divisions.

The rite within the tipi begins with the Starting Song; the midnight period is marked by the Midnight Water Song; there is no special song at three o'clock; at dawn there is the Morning Water Song, and the rite ends with the Quitting Song. At midnight sacred water is drunk again and a communion meal eaten.

Usually five people officiate at the rite. Four are men: the leader, often referred to as the Roadman because he leads the group along the Peyote Road (that is, the Peyotist way of life) to salvation; the drum chief who accompanies the leader when he sings; the cedar chief who is in charge of the cedar incense; and the fire chief who maintains a ritual fire and acts as sergeant-at-arms. A close female relative of the leader, usually his wife, brings in, and prays over, the morning water.

In clockwise rotation, starting with the leader, each male participant sings a set of four solo songs; he is accompanied on a water drum by the man to his right. The singing continues from the time of the Starting Song to that of the Morning Water Song; the number of rounds of singing therefore depends upon the number of men present. On most occasions there are four rounds, so that each man sings a total of sixteen songs.

During the rite Peyote is taken in one of the following forms: the fresh whole plant except for roots (green Peyote), the dried top of the plant (Peyote button), or an infusion of the Peyote button in water (Peyote tea). Some people have no difficulty taking Peyote. But many find it bitter, inducing indigestion or nausea A common complaint is, "It's hard to take Peyote."

The amount taken depends upon the individual, and the solemnity of the ritual occasion. There is great tribal variability in amount used, and accurate figures are virtually impossible to obtain. But in general one might say that under ordinary circumstances the bulk of the people take less than a dozen Peyotes On the most serious occasions, such as rites held for someone mortally sick, those present take as much Peyote as they can; the capacity of most people seems to range from about four to forty Peyote buttons.

Peyotists have been organized into the Native American Church since 1918. These church groups run the gamut of comprehensiveness from the single local group on the one extreme, to the intertribal and international federation known as the Native American Church of North America, on the other extreme.

In a series of other publications I have discussed the early history of Peyotism ("Peyotism, 1521–1891," *American Anthropologist*, LVII [1955], pp. 202–230), presented an historical and generalized account of the religion (in a book to be published in 1956[1]), and given a detailed description of the Peyote Religion in a single tribe ("Menomini Peyotism," *Transactions of the American Philosophical Society*, XLII [1952], Part 4)—all from the viewpoint of a relatively detached anthropologist. The present essay is different. Here I concentrate on the contemporary uses of, and attitudes toward, sacramental Peyote, and write as a member and officer of the Native American Church of North America. Of course the presentation is mine, but I think substantially it represents the consensus of our membership.

Long ago God took pity on the Indian. (Opinions vary as to when this happened: when plants were created at the origin of the world, when Jesus lived, or after the white man had successfully invaded this continent.) So God created Peyote and put some of his power into it for the use of Indians. Therefore the Peyotist takes the sacramental Peyote to absorb God's power contained in it, in the same way that the white Christian takes the sacramental bread and wine.

Power is the English term used by Indians for the supernatural force called *mana* by anthropologists; it is equivalent to the New Testament *pneuma*, translated as Holy Spirit or Holy Ghost. Power is needed to live. As a Crow Indian once remarked to me as we were strolling near a highway, man is like an auto; if the car loses its power it cannot go. Physically, power makes a person healthy, and safe when confronted by danger. Spiritually, power gives a person knowledge of how to behave successfully in everyday life, and what to make of one's life as a whole. The Peyotist obtains power from the sacramental Peyote.

Physically, Peyote is used as a divine healer and amulet.

For sick people Peyote is used in various ways. In a mild illness Peyote is taken as a home remedy. Thus when a man has a cold, he drinks hot Peyote tea and goes to bed. In more serious illnesses Peyote is taken during the Peyote rite. Such an illness is due not only to lack of sufficient power, but also to a foreign object within the body. Therefore a

---

[1] ED. NOTE: *The Peyote Religion: A Study in Indian-White Relations* (Glencoe, Ill.: The Free Press, 1956).

seriously sick person who takes Peyote usually vomits, thus expelling the foreign object which is the precipitating cause of the illness; then more Peyote is taken in order to obtain the amount of power needed for health.

In cases of severe illness, the rite itself is held for the purpose of healing the patient; it is often referred to as a doctoring meeting. In addition to having the sick person take Peyote, as in less desperate cases, everyone else present prays to God to give the patient extra power so he or she will recover.

Members may keep a Peyote button at home, or on their person, to protect them from danger. The latter is particularly true of men in the armed forces. The power within the Peyote wards off harm from anything in the area of its influence. In cases of great danger, as when a young man is about to leave for military service, a prayer meeting is held at which everyone present beseeches God to give the man extra power to avoid harm.

Spiritually, Peyote is used to obtain knowledge. This is known as learning from Peynote. Used properly, Peyote is an inexhaustible teacher. A stock statement is, "You can use Peyote all your life, but you'll never get to the end of what there is to be known from Peyote. Peyote is always teaching you something new." Many Peyotists say that the educated white man obtains his knowledge from books —particularly the Bible; while the uneducated Indian has to obtain his knowledge from Peyote. But the Indian's means of achieving knowledge is superior to that of the white man. The latter learns from books merely what other people have to say; the former learns from Peyote by direct experience.

A Comanche once said, "The white man talks *about* Jesus; we talk *to* Jesus." Thus the individual has a vividly direct experience of what he learns, qualitatively different from inference or hearsay. Therefore the Peyotist, epistemologically speaking, is an individualist and empiricist; he believes only what he himself has experienced.

A Peyotist maxim is, "The only way to find out about Peyote is to take it and learn from Peyote yourself." It may be interesting to know what others have to say; but all that really matters is what one has directly experienced—what he has learned himself from Peyote. This conception of salvation by knowledge, to be achieved by revelation (in this case, through Peyote) rather than through verbal or written learning, is a doctrine similar to that of early Middle Eastern Gnosticism.

The mere act of eating Peyote does not itself bring knowledge. The proper ritual behavior has to be observed before one is granted knowledge through Peyote. Physically, one must be clean, having bathed and put on clean clothes. Spiritually, one must put away all evil thought. Psychologically, one must be conscious of his personal inadequacy, humble, sincere in wanting to obtain the benefits of Peyote, and concentrate on it.

Peyote teaches in a variety of ways.

One common way in which Peyote teaches is by heightening the sensibility of the Peyotist, either in reference to himself or to others.

Heightened sensibility to oneself manifests itself as increased powers of introspection. One aspect of introspection is very important in Peyotism. During the rite a good deal of time is spent in self-evaluation. Finally the individual engages in silent or vocal prayer to God, confessing his sins, repenting, and promising to follow the Peyote Road (that is, the Peyotist ethic) more carefully in the future. If he has spiritual evil within him, Peyote makes him vomit, thus purging him of sin.

Heightened sensibility to others manifests itself as what might be called mental telepathy. One either feels that he knows what others are thinking, or feels that he either influences, or is influenced by, the thoughts of others. In this connection a frequent phenomenon is speaking in tongues, which results from the fact that people from different tribes participate in a rite together, each using his own language; Peyote teaches one the meaning of otherwise unknown languages.

For example, during the rite each male participant in succession sings solo four songs at a time. Recently a Winnebago sitting next to me sang a song with what I heard as a Fox text (Fox is an Algonquian language closely related to Menomini, the language I use in the rite), sung so clearly and distinctly I understood every word.

When he was through, I leaned over and asked, "How come you sang that song in Fox rather than Winnebago (a Siouan language unintelligible to me)?"

"I did sing it in Winnebago," he replied. The afternoon following the rite he sat down next to me and asked me to listen while he repeated the song; this time it was completely unintelligible to me because the effects of Peyote had worn off.

A second common way in which Peyote teaches is by means of revelation, called a vision. The vision is obtained because one has eaten enough Peyote under the proper ritual conditions to obtain the power needed to commune with the spirit world. The vision provides a direct experience (visual, auditory, or a combination of both) of God or some intermediary spirit, such as Jesus, Peyote Spirit (the personification of Peyote), or Waterbird.

The nature of the vision depends upon the personality and problems of the individual. The following are typical: He may be comforted by seeing or hearing some previously unexperienced item of Peyotist belief, or departed loved ones now in a happy existence. He may be guided on the one hand by being shown the way to solve some problem in daily life; on the other hand, he may be reproved for evil thoughts or deeds, and warned to repent.

A third way in which Peyote teaches is by means of mystical experience. This is relatively uncommon. It is limited to Peyotists of a certain personality type among the more knowledgeable members of the church; roughly speaking, they have what white people would call a mystical temperament. These Peyotists, in turn, rarely have visions, and tend to look upon them as distractions. The mystical experience may be said to consist in the harmony of all immediate experience with whatever the individual conceives to be the highest good.

Peyote has the remarkable property of helping one to have a mystical experience for an indefinite period of time, as opposed to most forms of mystical discipline under which the mystical experience commonly lasts for a matter of minutes. Actually I have no idea of how long I could maintain such an experience with Peyote, for after about an hour or so it is invariably interrupted by some ritual detail I am required to perform.

What happens to the Peyotist phenomenologically that makes possible the extraordinary results I have described? It seems to depend on both the physiological and psychological effects of Peyote.

Physiologically, Peyote seems to have curative properties. Many times, after a variety of illnesses brought about by fieldwork conditions, I have left a Peyote meeting permanently well again.

Another physiological effect of Peyote is that it reduces the fatigue to an astonishing extent. For instance, I am not robust, but after taking Peyote I can participate in the rite with virtually no fatigue—a rite which requires me to sit on the ground, cross-legged, with no back rest, and without moving, for 10 to 14 hours at a stretch; all this in the absence of food and water.

Psychologically, Peyote increases one's sensitivity to relevant stimuli. This applies to both external and internal stimuli. Externally, for example, the ritual fire has more intense colors when I am under the influence of Peyote. Internally, I find it easier to introspect upon otherwise vague immediate experiences.

At the same time, Peyote decreases one's sensitivity to irrelevant external and internal stimuli. Very little concentration is needed for me to ignore distracting noises inside or outside the tipi. Similarly, extraneous internal sensations or ideas are easily ignored.

Thus, on one occasion I wrote in my field diary, "I could notice no internal sensations. If I paid very close attention, I could observe a vague and faint feeling that suggested that without Peyote my back would be sore from sitting up in one position all night; the same was true of my crossed legs. Also, my mouth might be dry, but I couldn't be sure."

The combination of such effects as absence of fatigue, heightened sensitivity to relevant stimuli, and lowered sensitivity to irrelevant stimuli, should make it easier to understand how the individual is disposed to learn from Peyote under especially created ritual conditions.

To any reader who becomes intrigued by Peyote, two warnings should be given. First, I have discussed the effects of Peyote on those who used it as a sacrament under ritual conditions. The described responses of white people to Peyote under experimental conditions are quite different; in fact, they tend to be psychologically traumatic. Second, Peyote is a sacrament in the Native American Church, which refuses to permit the presence of curiosity seekers at its rites, and vigorously opposes the sale or use of Peyote for non-sacramental purposes.

Cyril S. Belshaw

THE SIGNIFICANCE
OF MODERN CULTS IN
MELANESIAN DEVELOPMENT

This selection takes us to a description and analysis of nativistic cults in another part of the world, the Melanesian islands in the South Pacific. Belshaw provides a vivid summary of the main features of the modern nativistic cults that have occurred. He then goes on to show that the movements were widely separated in time and place and that their similarities must be due to similarities in local conditions which produce them. These local conditions are essentially ones in which the Melanesians are halfway between the old and the new way of living. The natives have been in contact with thriving European communities, but none of them have been able to participate in vigorous activity leading to a higher standard of life. Hence they are envious of the Europeans, but without effective means of achieving a European way of life. So like the Ghost Dance, Peyote Cult, and other movements among the North American Indians, these Melanesian cults appear to be triggered by the same kind of conditions among people who find themselves in a transitional state. The people respond by developing cults which explain European success, and attempt to achieve a method of parallel success by adopting and manipulating (in magical fashion) symbols of the European way of life: flags and flagpoles, chairs and rulers, and so on.

Reprinted in abridged form from *The Australian Outlook*, IV (1950), 116–125, by permission of the author and the Australian Institute of International Affairs.

Although we know that in New Caledonia and Fiji the Melanesian people have shown themselves capable of considerable political development, many of us who know the Melanesian in the New Hebrides, British Solomon Islands, and New Guinea are inclined to doubt the possibility, at least in the near future, of Melanesians organizing their own political movements. The "Fuzzy Wuzzy Angels" of the war, emerging from the bush with hardly-come-by garden produce, resisting many forms of agricultural innovation, chewing betel nut, wearing cast-off clothing, speaking seemingly mutilated forms of English, appear to be far removed from any form of modern organization. The British Solomon Island experiments in Native Courts and Councils, though a tremendously, promising innovation, have been temporarily arrested by a strange native cult. The suggestion that there might before long be a pan-Melanesian nationalist movement would evoke incredulous smiles from most European Island residents, who point to the impossibility of persuading laborers from different communities to work together in harmony, to the multifarious languages and cultures, and to the absence of anything approaching a centralized organization in traditional life.

It is the purpose of this article to suggest, however, that this is far too simple an inter-

pretation of Melanesian possibilities. An analysis of certain apparently isolated Melanesian cults, which have grown up in European times, will give an indication of some of these possibilities. We may begin by a brief summary of their features.

THE TUKA CULT OF FIJI

About 1885 a prophet arose among the hill tribes of Fiji. He claimed that it had been revealed to him that before long the whole world would be turned upside down, particularly that the whites would serve the natives, the chiefs would serve the common people, and his followers would have eternal life. Jehovah was subordinated to local gods, and through the use of supernatural powers derived from the gods, the prophet was enabled to secure the obedience of a large following. This following drilled in European style to repulse the expected advance of the Administration. The prophet was banished, but the belief in the *tuka* cult continued.

THE BAIGONA CULT OF PAPUA

The *Baigona* Snake Cult of the Northern Division of Papua operated for many years from 1911. The prophet had the secrets of sorcery and prophecy revealed to him by the *Baigona Snake*, and cultivated its good-will by special rites. He sold the secrets of the cult to those who wished to be initiated. The movement was characterized by trances. Its rise coincided with the attempt to bring the area under administrative control. An administrative patrol was endangered and administrative pressure to reduce the trances and abolish the sale of initiation in accordance with antisorcery policy was not completely successful.

THE LONTIS CULT OF BUKA

I have not been able to find details of this cult, which occurred in 1913 during the German administration. Numerous arrests were made.

THE GERMAN WISLIN
OF THE TORRES STRAITS

This is the first clear specimen of the genus now known as "Cargo Cult." It occurred in 1913 on the island of Saibai, Torres Straits. The prophet declared that his followers would see the *markai*, the spirits of the dead, who would come to them in a steamer, bringing all kinds of manufactured cargo, and who would kill all the whites. Those who disobeyed the prophet would lose all their money and would be unable to earn any more.

THE TARO CULT AND
ITS RELATIVES IN PAPUA

This cult, very much akin to the *Baigona*, but in which the native vegetable taro took the place of the *baigona* snake, was more vigorous in its proselytism and lasted from 1914 into the late twenties. Dreams, ritual, and shaking fits played a prominent part in it. Off-shoots were the *Kava Kava* and *Kekesi* cults in the same area (Northern Division).

THE VAILALA MADNESS OF PAPUA

The *Vailala Madness*, which swept the Gulf Division of Papua from 1919 to 1923, was in the hands of sorcerers who had the power of divination during trances, and who encouraged their followers to take part in orgies of shaking fits. The great bull-roarer ceremonies of the kinship groups were abandoned, and new ceremonies were created to take their place. A steamer was expected, bringing the deceased relatives who were to have white skins. The new ceremonies contained a Christian element, flagpoles were given names and treated as the media through whom messages from the dead were received, there was a certain element of military drill, and women were given equality. Public confessionals took place.

THE MURDER OF CLAPCOTT,
NEW HEBRIDES

In 1923 the inland people of Espiritu Santo, New Hebrides, were influenced by rumors of death-raising. The prophet concerned claimed that if all the Europeans were killed the dead would arise, with white skins. They would bring European goods with them, and a house was built to receive these. To join the movement, it was necessary to pay a pig, or a fee of 5/– to one pound. During a great feast the prophet's wife died, and a European, Clapcott, was immediately killed. It is stated that the same people killed some Europeans called Greig in 1908, but details do not seem to have been published. These are the only occasions in which Europeans have been assaulted during these movements, though resistance and threats have been offered on several occasions.

THE CARGO CULTS OF BUKA

In 1932 and 1933 a cargo cult arose which appeared to be related to the previously mentioned *Lontis* cult. The prophet claimed that a steamer would arrive, laden with good things, and that all Buka would be ruled from their village. A store was to be built to receive these goods, and the police to be resisted if they interfered. But the ship would not come while food was available, and hence gardens were abandoned for some time. The leaders were imprisoned, but the cult continued.

THE MARKHAM CARGO CULT, NEW GUINEA

In 1933 a prophet arose in this area who claimed that Jehovah was subordinate to Satan. Once again the spirits of the dead were expected to return, bringing goods; gardens lapsed; and séances took place. Villages were destroyed and community houses built, and it was erroneously believed that the Administration would be passive.

THE CHAIR AND RULE
MOVEMENT OF THE SOLOMONS

About 1939 a European missionary encouraged the Melanesians of Santa Ysabel, Gela, and Savo to agitate for a seat on the nominated Advisory Council. He emphasized the need for a chairman and rules of procedure. The movement got out of hand and was misinterpreted. The Melanesians elevated a flag, a wooden chair, and a wooden rule into positions of ritual importance. They wrote to friends in San Cristoval and agitated for higher wages. Those involved were punished and the missionary asked to leave the Protectorate. His memory was still revered in 1945 among some people. The Administration was prompted into plans for Native Courts and Councils by this movement.

THE JOHN FRUM MOVEMENT, NEW HEBRIDES

In 1940 a native of the island of Tanna declared himself to be the prophet of John Frum, a spirit which evidently took the place of the ancient spirit of Karaperamun, formerly of great power. John Frum declared that the whole island was shortly to change in nature—its volcanic cone to be replaced by fertile plains, its people to be eternally young and healthy, and to have everything that they could ever desire. In order to achieve this end, it was necessary to hunt and kill all Europeans, to rid themselves of the taint of European money, to rid themselves of immigrant natives, and to return to the old customs of polygyny, dancing, kava drinking, and so forth, which had been rigidly proscribed by the theocratic Presbyterian Church. Money was taken to the stores and a great spending spree indulged in. The Administration took action; arrests were made.

The movement continued, however, especially in 1942, 1943, and 1947, encouraged by letters from the former leaders, who had been banished to Malekula. A modern touch was added by the construction of an aerodrome for American Liberators. The imprisoned leaders succeeded in converting neighboring villages on Malekula. A similar movement arose on Ambryn, in which a house was built to receive goods from the Messageries Maritimes steamer "Le Polynésien."

THE NAKED CULT, ESPIRITU SANTO

This cult, seen from 1944 to 1948, appears to be connected with the Clapcott murder case mentioned previously. It has, however, rather different features. The followers of the prophet are to go naked and are to cohabit in public. Villages are to be destroyed and replaced by two communal houses, one for the men and one for the women. All animals and property received from the Europeans are to be destroyed. Old customs such as exogamy and marriage payments are to be scrapped. The people are no longer to work for the Europeans, but to wait for the arrival of the Americans, when they will receive all good things. The people are to have immortality.

THE MASINGA RULE MOVEMENT OF THE SOLOMONS

The *Masinga* rule movement first made its appearance at the end of 1945 and in 1946 and is the most political of any of the movements that have yet appeared. In its early stages it appeared to have connections with the earlier Chair and Rule movement, and with disaffection which was rife on Guadalcanal, following the presence of Allied troops. It soon took on its own form, however, with Malaita the center. Buildings were erected to warehouse the expected free gifts from American liberators; monetary contributions were exacted from the adherents of the movement; the leaders were reputed to have boundless wealth in dollars and to pay their followers twelve pounds a month; Melanesians were forbidden to work for Europeans unless a wage of twelve pounds a month was paid; missionary and administrative work was resisted; demonstrations of several thousand natives took place on Government stations demanding education, higher wages, political independence, and the removal of Europeans; "soldiers" were drilled; the central organization on Malaita established connections with Ulawa and San Cristoval and the movement was eventually copied in the Santa Cruz group and the Western Solomons. At first the Administration was prepared to tolerate the movement and wait for it to die out, but as resistance, and particularly drilling, grew in scale, several score of arrests were made. The movement still continues, and so do the arrests.

OTHER CONTEMPORARY MOVEMENTS

At the close of the recent war, Melanesia was left with three described movements, *Masinga* Rule, John Frum, and the Naked Cult. There appears, however, to have been a general revival of similar movements all over Melanesia, with the possible exception of New Caledonia, though we still await published details of them. There is the Apolisi prophet movement of Fiji, a cargo cult in the Loyalty Islands (the first reported) and in New Guinea, and a similar movement in the Purari Delta of Papua. This latter appears to have interesting possibilities, for it is reported that for the first time the Administration, while watching it carefully, is encouraging it and aiding it in its development program—including rebuilding of villages and reorganization of agriculture. (These two objectives were also part of the *Masinga* Rule movement, but neither Melanesian leadership nor Administration pursued them vigorously.)

These then are the principal details of about thirteen movements that have been described over the past fifty years. What is their significance?

The first point to notice is that the movements are widely separated in time and place, from the Torres Straits to Fiji, and that this effectively rules out the possibility that they are copies of each other. Their similarities must be due to similarities in local conditions which produce them.

The movements fall into two main groups, with borderline cases in between. The first of these is seen in its purest form in the *Baigona* and Taro cults in Papua. There is no hint here of conflict with the European until the European Administrator, from the Melanesian point of view, "butts in." In their essentials, the cults are similar to those found everywhere in Melanesia at the time of the arrival of the Europeans. They express the indigenous Melanesian animist interpretation of the world and his centuries-old traditional delight in ceremonial and cult practices. They are novel only in that their origins have been observed and not speculated about, and from this point of view they are of considerable interest to the sociologist.

The other cults are a modern modification of this phenomenon. But before we make this clear, a number of alternative hypotheses may be disposed of.

First, there is the understandable Administrative view that these are dangerous movements, interrupting Melanesian life, threatening good order, and evidencing the unhealthy despotic powers of sorcerers who, by trickery, have bullied the local people, and who make their fortune by the sale of their tricks. Of the political aspects of this view, I will speak later. But as a theory of origins it is most defective. No leader, it must be emphasized, in the absence of mechanical instruments or a police state, can force people to follow him or accept his doctrines. The traditional Melanesian method of avoiding unwanted leaders is simply to move somewhere else, found a new village, grow new gardens, or retaliate by counter-sorcery or murder. It must be accepted that the religious element in these cults is sufficiently near the Melanesian pattern to enable us to believe that their following is by and large popular. As for the sale of the tricks of the trade, that too is common to most

forms of Melanesian sorcery, and even the passing on of dance movements and songs. It is, as it were, payment for copyright.

Secondly, there is the view that the cults express a reaction to a particular event or organization. It is superficially possible, for instance, to blame the John Frum movement on to the rather rigid and narrow interpretations of recent Presbyterian proselytizing. Similarly, one could blame the Espiritu Santo movement on to the sale of liquor and to other abuses by the traders. And the *Masinga* Rule movement has been blamed on "Marxist elements" among American troops.

All these views possess an element of truth, but all lack conviction. Why should such diverse historical facts give rise to such unified movements? On the other hand, if we describe the position of these Melanesian communities in the modern world we can see that there is indeed a common element.

None of these communities is untouched by European influence; and none of them has been able to take full advantage of living under that influence. Moving roughly west to east, the Torres Straits have been the happy hunting grounds of pearl fishers and labor recruiters, but at the beginning of the century the island of Saibai was subject to no permanent European influences; the Gulf of Papua is not a favorite area of European exploitation, though there have been European planters there; Buka again is on the fringe of European activity; Gela it is true is very close to the pre-war Solomon Island capital of Tulagi—but here the movement was more definitely political rather than religious and it was stronger in the less developed north than in the more developed south; Malaita is a classic example, for here there was practically no European activity, while the almost overpopulated communities sent their sons to other islands for plantation work; inland Espiritu Santo has hardly been visited by Europeans, though there is a thriving community on the coast; Tanna is a small island well off the beaten track, again exporting a few of its people as seamen; and the Loyalty Islands, unattractive to European settlers, live by exporting produce to Noumea, the New Caledonian capital. Inland Fiji, at the time of the Tuka Cult, was quite primitive.

These people, then, have all been in contact with thriving European communities, but none of them have been able to participate in vigorous activity leading to a higher standard of life. I think it is most significant that the two extremes of Melanesian life do not appear so far to have succumbed to these cults, though they have problems of their own. On the one hand, we have the thriving native settlements in or near such towns as Port Moresby, Rabaul, Vila, and in New Caledonia, and areas of intensive missionary industrial work. Here the people are in the grip of modern life—and have little time or inclination to organize into cults. On the other hand, we have areas such as the interior of New Guinea and Malekula, where cults continue in their native form, unmodified by European intrusion.

If we accept this thesis, it is easy to understand that the similarities in the cults are due to the position of the communities halfway between the old and the new way of living; and that the differences are due almost solely to particular historical circumstances. The universals seem to be these. The "halfway" Melanesian sees other people who possess a way of living that he tends to envy. He has to find some explanation of European power in holding sway over multitudes; of the miraculous arrival of manufactured goods in ships and aeroplanes; of strange European behavior which sends away piles of raw materials; of the peculiar distaste with which Europeans treat him. On the one hand, this gives him an end of activity—he must strive to attain a similar power. On the other hand, it sets him an intellectual problem and gives him an emotional experience. His emotional experience is jealousy, sometimes hatred, of the

European, who neither gives him these things as a friend nor initiates him into the mysteries of the process of sale and production—indeed, tries to fob him off with Biblical education. His intellectual problem is, first, to explain European success, and, second, to achieve a method of parallel success.

This problem must be solved in terms of Melanesian experience. There is behind him the great tradition of cults such as the *Baigona*, and animism. It is natural that he should turn to find a superior cult. At first, it was Christianity in many parts, which was conceived as a superior, sometimes as a supplementary, animism. This fails, or is not understood, and is molded on to something new. The new cult endeavors to copy significant European activities. There is the belief in shipping, that is, in the origin of cargoes—for remember, most Melanesians have not seen or experienced the manufacturing process. There is a mystical significance in the revolting white skin of Europeans, and in money, which circulates so strangely; in flags and flagpoles, which the European treats with peculiar reverence; in towns and houses rather than villages; in soldiers and drilling—which *must* be mystical, for what use is there in it? And in later years, of course, there is the myth of American arrival, so obviously based upon the big-handedness and freedom of American troops. These things supplied the modern elements in the cargo myth, the myth which explained European successes and indicated the correct road to follow.

David Aberle

A NOTE ON RELATIVE DEPRIVATION THEORY AS APPLIED TO MILLENARIAN AND OTHER CULT MOVEMENTS

Many scholars have had the impression that cult movements labeled variously as "nativistic," "revitalistic," "messianic," "millenarian," and the like, have a certain unity, and have been dissatisfied with the inability of these terms to single out the common thread running through them all. They are not sufficiently

Reprinted from "Millenial Dreams in Action," in Sylvia L. Thrupp (ed.), *Comparative Studies in Society and History*, Supplement II (The Hague: Mouton & Co., 1962), pp. 209–214, by permission of the author and the Society for the Comparative Study of Society and History.

all-encompassing. To take one instance, the millenarian movements of the Middle Ages in Europe were not nativistic and certainly had none of the syncretistic, acculturative, or political overtones found among so many of the cults in question. Another example is provided by the cargo movements of the central New Guinea highlands, where cults have arisen without the natives ever having seen a white man. David Aberle has made a genuine contribution toward the solution of the dilemma by his suggestion that the theme running through these cults is one of relative deprivation. Thus, although he does not say so, he has shifted the emphasis from the reaction to the cause underlying the reaction, thus reaching into the heart of the matter, which after all concerns religion as a force providing hope and comfort where people perceive their lot as an unhappy one. He distinguishes three types of reference points for relative deprivation, as well as four kinds of deprivation, making twelve categories in all. No cult movement fits neatly into any one compartment alone, as becomes obvious if one draws up a table composed of these categories, eliminating, as does Aberle, purely personal deprivations as opposed to societal ones. Where, for example, would one fit in the Mau Mau of Kenya, or the Black Muslims of the United States?

I will not attempt to review the history of theories of deprivation and relative deprivation, especially since they enter, explicitly or implicitly, into so many explanations of specific religious and political movements and so many general theories in this area. I will rather attempt to supply a statement of my own viewpoint, recognizing that many parts of it can be found in the works of others.

Relative deprivation is defined as a negative discrepancy between legitimate expectation and actuality. Where an individual or a group has a particular expectation and furthermore where this expectation is considered to be a proper state of affairs, and where something less than that expectation is fulfilled, we may speak of relative deprivation. It is important to stress that deprivation *is* relative and not absolute. To a hunting and gathering group with an expectation of going hungry one out of four days, failure to find game is not a relative deprivation, although it may produce marked discomfort. It is a truism that for a multi-millionaire to lose all but his last million in a stock market crash *is* a major deprivation. The deprivation, then, is not a particular objective state of affairs, but a difference between an anticipated state of affairs and a less agreeable actuality. We must furthermore consider the expectations as *standards*, rather than merely as prophecies of what will happen tomorrow.

The discovery of what constitutes serious deprivation for particular groups or individuals is a difficult empirical problem. It requires careful attention to the reference points that people employ to judge their legitimate expectations, as well as to their actual circumstances. Among the obvious reference points that can

be, and are used for such judgments are: (1) one's past versus one's present circumstances; (2) one's present versus one's future circumstances; (3) one's own versus someone else's present circumstances.

The first and third types of judgment are easily illustrated. Any one who worked among the Navaho Indians in the 1940's was obliged to notice that for many Navahos the Government livestock reduction of the 1930's had created a situation where they viewed themselves as worse off than they had been, and as worse off than they should have been. And the impression one derives from Margaret Mead's account of the Manus, in *New Lives for Old*, is that these people regard themselves as worse off than they should be, by comparison with full participants in Western material culture.

Perhaps the second type of judgment requires some elucidation. If, let us say, a group of elderly pensioners have a particular standard of living, and have reason to believe that the shrinking dollar value of their pensions will not long permit this, then, with only a little strain they may be regarded as relatively deprived: their *prospective actuality* is worse than their standard of legitimate expectation.

The critical feature of these and subsequent examples is that they involve not only relative deprivation, but a deprivation which stems from *change*, actual or anticipated. It is where conditions decline by comparison with the past, where it is expected that they will decline, in the future by comparison with the present, and where shifts in the relative conditions of two groups occur, that the deprivation experience becomes significant for efforts at remedial action. Indeed it is change itself that creates discrepancies between *legitimate* expectations and actuality, either by worsening the conditions of a group, or by exposing a group to new standards.

The previous examples are very much concerned with material goods. It is not necessary, however, to assume that all deprivation experiences are primarily concerned with such goods. I have attempted a rough classification of types of deprivation. They fall into four groups: possessions, status, behavior, and worth. They may furthermore be classified as *personal* and *group* or *category* experiences. A man whose house is destroyed by fire experiences a personal deprivation of possessions—since this is *not* an experience most of us plan on. An American Indian tribe expropriated from its land, experiences group deprivation of possessions. Allowing for this, we have, in fact, at least three measuring points for deprivation, and at least four areas of deprivation, classified in each case as personal versus group (e.g., tribe) or category (e.g., Negro). This provides a 24-cell table of deprivations, one too large to illustrate in detail.

We can, however, eliminate the purely personal deprivations. If the individual does not find that there are others in like circumstances, their significance for social movements, millenarian or other, political or religious, would appear to be trivial. I will attempt to illustrate the others, using Navaho examples and only one frame of reference for comparison: present (undesirable) versus past (desirable). Navahos who had large herds in the 1920's lost them through livestock reduction in the 1930's. Those with such herds constituted a category, and their loss of stock adversely affected other Navahos who had benefitted from their generosity, so that the Navahos as a group or set of groups experienced deprivation of possessions, with respect to diet, trade goods procured through sale of animal products, etc. In addition, the large owners suffered deprivation of status. The society was reduced to far more egalitarian relationships; the man who had had followers to herd for him, gratitude for generosity, and standing because of his wealth now was almost as badly off as any other Navaho. His comparison here was to his past status in *his* group, not vis-à-vis the outside world. These were among the key deprivations experienced by Navahos during this period.

With the decline in livestock holdings came a necessary decline in certain types of behavior

viewed as desirable by Navahos. Kin did not fulfil their obligation to kin, neighbors to neighbors, "rich" to poor, because the wherewithal for reciprocity and generosity was no longer there. There was a pervasive feeling that people did not *behave* as they should, or as they once did, and this I would call a deprivation in the area of behavior. This particular type of deprivation can be equally well illustrated by a shift to a different frame of reference for deprivation. With continued exposure to Americans, under circumstances which make Americans a model, some Navahos have come to feel that they do not behave as they should, by comparison with Americans: they are dirty, or superstitious, or eat "bad" foods (e.g., prairie dogs).

Finally, I come to worth, which is to some degree a residual category. It refers to a person's experience of others' estimation of him on grounds over and above his alterable characteristics—of possessions, status, and behavior. It is best illustrated again by those Navahos who use the outside world as a point of reference. Navahos with most contact have come to realize that to some degree neither wealth, occupational status, nor "proper" behavior can alter the fact that they are Navahos, and that they are therefore regarded as inferior and undesirable. Their total worth, then, is not what they feel it should be, and they experience a sense of deprivation in this regard. Many Navahos are still sufficiently insulated from the larger world not to have this experience.

Now I conceive of any of these types of deprivation, measured by any of these reference points, to be the possible basis for efforts at remedial action to overcome the discrepancy between actuality and legitimate aspiration. (They can also be the basis for apathy disorganization, despair, or suicide.) Insofar as the actions are undertaken by individuals and not by groups they are not relevant for present considerations. But the face of deprivation is clearly an insufficient basis for predicting whether remedial efforts will occur, and, if they occur, whether they will have as aims changing the world, transcending it, or withdrawing from it, whether the remedy will be sought in direct action or ritual, and whether it will be sought with the aid of supernatural powers or without. The Navahos, have, for example, attempted to influence the Indian Service, hide their sheep, form political organizations, and protest to Congress. They have, in isolated instances, had visions of the total destruction of the whites, and in groups, Navaho members of the peyote cult have used the ritual of that cult both to attempt to foresee further Government plans and to seek new wealth through God's help.

I take it that the interest of the conference in millenarian movements was primarily in those movements which seek supernatural help, or which, at any rate, seek supernatural intervention in the affairs of men.

A sense of blockage—of the insufficiency of ordinary action—seems to me, as it has seemed to many others, the source of the more supernaturally based millenarian, nativistic, revitalistic, and cargo movements—to use terms applied to various types of movements which we somehow sense as belonging together in some respects. And, difficult as it may be to anticipate whether a group's aspiration will be to return to the past, achieve the standards of the outside world, or transcend earthly standards completely, there is usually no serious difficulty in deciding whether, at a particular time, a particular group faces obstacles which are empirically insurmountable in short-run terms. No one knew whether the Navahos would become violent over stock reduction, but everyone knew that in the 20th century the violence of a few tens of thousands of American Indians could be put down if it became necessary to do so. We then add to our focus on deprivation types, attention to the question whether direct action could be expected to solve the group's problems. If it could not, we expect a correspondingly large increment of religious and magical action, although we cannot outlaw the possibility that this may lead to violence.

If we now turn to types of deprivation, we can have some expectation that the ideology of the movement will be related to the type of deprivation—or at least that emphasis in the ideology will be so related. The Plains Ghost Dance, although it originated elsewhere, spread among the Plains when the buffalo were gone—and anticipated the marvelous removal of the white man and a life of abundant hunting and gathering. It was oriented to deprivation of possessions. The Handsome Lake cult, originating long after the conquest of the Iroquois, focussed vigorously on morality and thus had a strong component of reaction to deprivation in the behavioral area. Peyotism, one of the most viable of American Indian nativistic movements, contains in its beliefs and values: elements of magical aid, including assistance in gaining more wealth;

certain compensations for loss of status; a code of morality vigorously opposing drunkenness, adultery, and shiftlessness, three plagues of Reservation life; and hundreds of items designed to restore the self-respect of the Indian as an Indian. It is no accident that peyotism can therefore appeal to the traditional, who have suffered material deprivation, the formerly well-to-do, who have suffered status deprivation, the disorganized sufferers from deprivation in the behavioral area, and the marginal men with their ambivalence about being Indian in a white world. No one peyotist need come to peyotism for all of these, but a variety of sufferers can be accommodated.

This framework seems to me to be a profitable one for the inspection of various cults, including millenarian movements. It is not limited to absolute deprivation, nor to the assumption that the deprived are always those at the bottom of the status hierarchy. By the same token, it has a certain excessive flexibility. It is always possible after the fact to find deprivations. What is important is to be able to predict either the types of deprivations that lead to certain ideological formations, or the degree of deprivation which crystallizes a cult movement. To date neither of these goals is achieved, although we are closer to the first than to the second. It is more appealing to me, however, to attempt to work within this formula than to assume randomness of social behavior or an indefinite plurality of causes. At a minimum, it is fair to say that millenarian, revitalistic, and cargo cult movements do not arise under circumstances where the members of a group think that the world is so nearly perfect that transformation or translation must be just around the corner. There is sufficient evidence of abundant distress in many instances to make this approach at least valuable for exploration.

Lastly, we come to the millenarian movement itself, rather than to the family of movements of which it is a part. My own experience has been largely with other than millenarian movements, and my exposure to the millenarian materials presented at the conference was a new experience.

The question is, what good is relative deprivation theory for the analysis of such movements? First, I will give to the adherents of the boredom theory of millenarian movements as many specific instances as they choose to claim, provided it is not maintained that *most* millenarian *movements* involving some active participation of believers are inspired by boredom. Second, I grant nothing to the utility of theories which are based on supposedly pan-human experiences, since constants cannot be used to explain variables. Third, the fact that a movement is *millenarian* is a totally insufficient basis for deciding what type of deprivation is important (in cases not involving boredom); both inspection of the ideology and of the condition of the adherents is necessary for this purpose, as Cohn's paper amply demonstrates. There is no reason why only the deprivations of peasants, and why only hunger and landlessness need be considered as bases for deprivation, or why the proof that it wasn't the peasants (or the disoriented new urbanites) that were involved is any reason not to look further for the deprivations of groups that did participate. Fourth—and this is prejudice—I am willing to admit that pure existential unease or concern with spiritual discomfort dissociated from the social conditions of participants forms a useful basis for explaining these movements.

This all adds up to the assumption that millenarian movements are susceptible to analysis in terms of deprivation theory, in the same way as cargo cults, the Handsome Lake cult, the peyote cult, and so on. Furthermore, the tense expectation of the millennium is not a sufficient basis for classifying these movements, since the things their ideologies react against are diverse. Hence there is one sense in which they should be parcelled out with their nearest non-millenarian cognates, and

this we did not attempt. It is possible that the Tupi-Guarani movements, for example, belong in the family of ideologies of expansion, quite as much as in the family of millenarian movements. This position, however, also leaves something to be desired, since we have an uneasy sense that in one way or another the millenarian movements *do* share something besides tense expectation. I would suggest that many of them have one thing in common. The millenarian ideology often justifies the *removal* of the participants in the movement from the ordinary spheres of life. Indeed, this removal is frequently not only social but spatial, whether it takes the form of withdrawal or of wandering. I would suggest that the deprivations which form the background for the movement not only involve the sense of blockage to which I have referred earlier, which leads to resort to supernaturalism, but also the sense of a social order which cannot be reconstituted to yield the satisfactions desired. The millenarian ideology justifies the removal of the participants from that social order, by reassuring them that the order itself will not long continue, and frees them to indulge in phantasy about the ideal society, or to attempt to build it in isolation or through violent attempts against the existing order. Those who suffer from acute deprivation and cannot withdraw from the world can only constitute sects of the elect, or utilize devices to compensate for deprivation. The millenarian ideology justifies withdrawal, and that is its functional significance.

Clifford Geertz

RITUAL AND SOCIAL CHANGE: A JAVANESE EXAMPLE

The following article contains a suggested revision of "functional" sociocultural theory, centering the problem around a chronicle of a Javanese burial ceremony and the surrounding events. It also embodies an analysis of the cultural and social phenomena involved in the burial situation from the position of the suggested revision in theory. Actual cultural practice, contained in the ethnographic description, is seen in the diachronic context of changing political and social patterns.

Reprinted in abridged form from *American Anthropologist*, LIX (1957), 32–54, by permission of the author and the American Anthropological Association.

The point is made that any "functional" analysis must differentiate between the different systems to which each—cultural practice and social structure—belongs. Culture, Geertz states, exists in a system wherein the parts have consistency and unity on the basis of style, logical implication, meaning, and value. The social structure, on the other hand, is integrated into a "causal web"; each part is integral to the functioning of the whole. It is further suggested that, because of the differing ways in which the two systems are integrated, conflict between them is an inherent potential stemming from the basic independence of each dimension as far as the initiation of change is concerned, yet there is interdependence of each after change has taken place.

In the burial scene the kampong dwellers, adherents of a peasant or folk-like culture, find that the traditional beliefs and practices, integrated through "logico-meaningful" relationships, are in conflict with the "causal-functional" integration of the social structure, derived in part from the urban sphere. The conflict arises from the discontinuity that exists between the two dimensions because of their differing types of integration and their differing points of articulation with the urban sociocultural system.

Many elements found here among the Javanese have been previously cited as occurring in other groups: fear of the dead, concern for the welfare of the living who come into contact with the deceased, a desire to complete the burial as rapidly as possible, and the culturally approved, ritualized expression of emotion generated through the loss of a son, a friend, or a neighbor. The reader might join Geertz and the inhabitants of Modjokuto in pondering the question, "What direction will burial customs take when death next occurs in a Permai family?"

As in so many areas of anthropological concern, functionalism, either of the sociological sort associated with the name of Radcliffe-Brown or of the social-psychological sort associated with Malinowski, has tended to dominate recent theoretical discussions of the role of religion in society. Stemming originally from Durkheim's *The Elementary Forms of the Religious Life* and Robertson Smith's *Lectures on the Religion of the Semites*, the sociological approach (or, as the British anthropologists prefer to call it, the social anthropological approach) emphasizes the manner in which belief and particularly ritual reinforce the traditional social ties between individuals; it stresses the way in which the social structure of a group is strengthened and perpetuated through the ritualistic or mythic symbolization of the underlying social values upon which it rests. The social psychological approach, of which Frazer and Tylor were perhaps the pioneers but which found its clearest statement in Malinowski's classic *Magic, Science and Religion*, emphasizes what religion does for the individual—how it satisfies both his cognitive affective demands for a stable, comprehensible, and coercible world, and how it enables him to maintain an inner security in the face of natural contingency. Together the two approaches have given us an increasingly detailed understanding of the social and psychological "functions" of religion in a wide range of societies.

Where the functional approach has been least impressive, however, is in dealing with social change. As has been noted by several writers, the emphasis on systems in balance, on social homeostasis, and on timeless structural pictures leads to a bias in favor of "well-integrated" societies in a stable equilibrium and to a tendency to emphasize the functional aspects of a people's social usages and customs rather than their dysfunctional implications. In analyses of religion this static, ahistorical approach has led to a somewhat overconservative view of the role of ritual and belief in social life. Despite cautionary comments by Kluckhohn (1944) and others on the "gain and cost" of various religious practices such as witchcraft, the tendency has been consistently to stress the harmonizing, integrating, and psychologically supportive aspects of religious patterns rather than the disruptive, disintegrative, and psychologically disturbing aspects; to demonstrate the manner in which religion preserves social and psychological structure rather than the manner in which it destroys or transforms it. Where change has been treated, as in Redfield's work on Yucatán, it has largely been in terms of progressive disintegration: "The changes in culture that in Yucatán appear to 'go along with' lessening isolation and homogeneity are seen to be chiefly three: disorganization of the culture, secularization, and individualization." Yet even a passing knowledge of our own religious history makes us hesitate to affirm such a simply "positive" role for religion generally.

It is the thesis of this paper that one of the major reasons for the inability of functional theory to cope with change lies in its failure to treat sociological and cultural processes on equal terms; almost inevitably one of the two is either ignored or is sacrificed to become but a simple reflex, a "mirror image," of the other. Either culture is regarded as wholly derivative from the forms of social organization—the approach characteristic of the British structuralists as well as many American sociologists; or the forms of social organization are regarded as behavioral embodiments of cultural patterns—the approach of Malinowski and many American anthropologists. In either case, the lesser term tends to drop out as a dynamic factor and we are left either with an omnibus concept of culture ("that complex whole . . .") or else with a completely comprehensive concept of social structure ("social structure is not an aspect of culture, but the entire culture of a given people handled in a special frame of theory" [Fortes]. In such a situation, the dynamic elements in social change which arise from the failure of cultural patterns to be perfectly congruent with the forms of social organization are largely incapable of formulation. "We functionalists," E. R. Leach has recently remarked, "are not really 'anti-historical' by principle; it is simply that we do not know how to fit historical materials into our framework of concepts."

A revision of the concepts of functional theory so as to make them capable of dealing more effectively with "historical materials" might well begin with an attempt to distinguish analytically between the cultural and social aspects of human life, and to treat them as independently variable yet mutually interdependent factors. Though separable only conceptually, culture and social structure will then be seen to be capable of a wide range of modes of integration with one another, of which the simple isomorphic mode is but a limiting case—a case common only in societies which have been stable over such an extended time as to make possible a close adjustment between social and cultural aspects. In most societies, where change is a characteristic rather than an abnormal occurrence, we shall expect to find more or less radical discontinuities between the two. I would argue that it is in these very discontinuities that we shall find some of the primary driving forces in change.

One of the more useful ways—but far from the only one—of distinguishing between culture and social system is to see the former as an ordered system of meaning and of symbols, in terms of which social interaction takes place; and to see the latter as a pattern of social interaction itself. On the one level there is the framework of beliefs, expressive symbols, and values in terms of which individuals define their world, express their feelings, and make their judgments; on the other level there is the ongoing process of interactive behavior, whose persistent form we call social structure. Culture is the fabric of meaning in terms of which human beings interpret their experience and guide their action; social structure is the form that action takes, the actually existing network of social relations. Culture and social structure are then but different abstractions from the same phenomena. The one considers social action in respect to its meaning for those who carry it out, the other considers it in terms of its contribution to the functioning of some social system.

The nature of the distinction between culture and social system is brought out more clearly when one considers the contrasting sorts of integration characteristic of each of them. This contrast is between what Sorokin has called "logico-meaningful integration" and what he has called 'causal-functional integration.' By logico-meaningful integration, characteristic of culture, is meant the sort of integration one finds in a Bach fugue, in Catholic dogma, or in the general theory of relativity; it is a unity of style, of logical implication, of meaning and value. By causal-functional integration, characteristic of the social system, is meant the kind of integration one finds in an organism, where all the parts are units in a single causal web; each part is an element in a reverberating causal ring which "keeps the system going." And because these two types of integration are not identical, because the particular form one of them takes does not directly imply the form the other will take, there is an inherent incongruity and tension between the two and between both of them and a third element, the pattern of motivational integration within the individual which we usually call personality structure.

Thus conceived, a social system is only one of three aspects of the structuring of a completely concrete system of social action. The other two are the personality systems of the individual actors and the cultural system which is built into their action. Each of the three must be considered to be an independent focus of the organization of the elements of the action system in the sense that no one of them is theoretically reducible to terms of one or a combination of the other two. Each is indispensable to the other two in the sense that without personalities and culture there would be no social system and so on around the roster of logical possibilities. But this interdependence and interpenetration is a very different matter from reducibility, which would mean that the important properties and processes of one class of system could be theoretically derived from our theoretical knowledge of one or both of the other two. The action frame of reference is common to all three and this fact makes certain "transformations" between them possible. But on the level of theory here attempted they do not constitute a single system, however this might turn out to be on some other theoretical level [Parsons, The Social System].

I will attempt to demonstrate the utility of this more dynamic functionalist approach by applying it to a particular case of a ritual which failed to function properly. I shall try to show how an approach which does not distinguish the "logico-meaningful" cultural aspects of the ritual pattern from the "causal-functional" social structural aspects is unable to account adequately for this ritual failure, and how an approach which does so distinguish them is able to analyze more explicitly the cause of the trouble. It will further be argued that such an approach is able to avoid the simplistic view of the functional role of religion in society which sees that role merely as structure-conserving, and to substitute for it a more complex conception of the relations between religious belief and practice and secular social life. Historical materials can be fitted into such a conception, and the functional analysis of religion can therefore be widened to deal more adequately with processes of change

THE SETTING

The case to be described is that of a funeral held in Modjokuto, a small town in eastern Central Java. A young boy, about ten years of age, who was living with his uncle and aunt, died very suddenly but his death, instead of being followed by the usual hurried, subdued, yet methodically efficient Javanese funeral ceremony and burial routine, brought on an extended period of pronounced social strain and severe psychological tension. The complex of beliefs and rituals which had for generations brought countless Javanese safely through the difficult post-mortem period

suddenly failed to work with its accustomed effectiveness. To understand why it failed demands knowledge and understanding of a whole range of social and cultural changes which have taken place in Java since the first decades of this century. This disrupted funeral was in fact but a microcosmic example of the broader conflicts, structural dissolutions, and attempted reintegrations which, in one form or another, are characteristic of contemporary Indonesian society.

The religious tradition of Java, particularly of the peasantry, is a composite of Indian, Islamic, and indigenous Southeast Asian elements. The rise of large, militaristic kingdoms in the inland rice basins in the early centuries of the Christian era was associated with the diffusion of Hinduist and Buddhist culture patterns to the island; the expansion of international maritime trade in the port cities of the northern coast in the fifteenth and sixteenth centuries was associated with the diffusion of Islamic patterns. Working their way into the peasant mass, these two world religions became fused with the underlying animistic traditions characteristic of the whole Malaysian culture area. The result was a balanced syncretism of myth and ritual in which Hindu gods and goddesses, Moslem prophets and saints, and local place spirits and demons all found a proper place.

The central ritual form in this syncretism is a communal feast, called the *slametan*. Slametans, which are given with only slight variations in form and content on almost all occasions of religious significance—at passage points in the life cycle, on calendrical holidays, at certain stages of the crop cycle, on changing one's residence, etc.—are intended to be both offerings to the spirits and commensal mechanisms of social integration for the living. The meal, which consists of specially prepared dishes, each symbolic of a particular religious concept, is cooked by the female members of one nuclear family household and set out on mats in the middle of the living-room. The male head of the household invites the male heads of the eight or ten contiguous households to attend; no close neighbor is ignored in favor of one further away. After a speech by the host explaining the spiritual purpose of the feast and a short Arabic chant, each man takes a few hurried, almost furtive, gulps of food, wraps the remainder of the meal in a banana-leaf basket, and returns home to share it with his family. It is said that the spirits draw their sustenance from the odor of the food, the incense which is burned, and the Moslem prayer; the human participants draw theirs from the material substance of the food and from their social interaction. The result of this quiet, undramatic little ritual is two-fold: the spirits are appeased and neighborhood solidarity is strengthened.

The ordinary canons of functional theory are quite adequate for the analysis of such a pattern. It can rather easily be shown that the slametan is well designed both to "tune up the ultimate value attitudes" necessary to the effective integration of a territorially based social structure, and to fulfill the psychological needs for intellectual coherence and emotional stability characteristic of a peasant population. The Javanese village (once or twice a year, village-wide slametans are held) is essentially a set of geographically contiguous, but rather self-consciously autonomous, nuclear family households whose economic and political interdependence is of roughly the same circumscribed and explicitly defined sort as that demonstrated in the slametan. The demands of the labor-intensive rice and dry-crop agricultural process require the perpetuation of specific modes of technical cooperation and enforce a sense of community on the otherwise rather self-contained families—a sense of community which the slametan clearly reinforces. And when we consider the manner in which various conceptual and behavioral elements from Hindu-Buddhism, Islam, and "animism" are reinterpreted and balanced to form a distinctive and nearly homogeneous religious style, the close functional adjustment between the communal feast pattern and the conditions of Javanese rural life is even more readily apparent.

But the fact is that in all but the more isolated parts of Java, both the simple territorial basis of village social integration and the syncretic basis of its cultural homogeneity have been progressively undermined over the past fifty years. Population growth, urbanization, monetization, occupational differentiation, and the like have combined to weaken the traditional ties of peasant social structure; and the winds of doctrine which have accompanied the appearance of these structural changes have disturbed the simple uniformity of religious belief and practice characteristic of an earlier period. The rise of nationalism, Marxism and Islamic reform as ideologies, which resulted in part from the increasing complexity of Javanese society, has affected not only the large cities where these creeds first appeared and have always had their greatest strength, but has had a heavy impact on the smaller towns and villages as well. In fact, much of recent Javanese social change is perhaps most aptly characterized as a shift from a situation in which the primary integrative ties between individuals (or between families) are phrased in terms of geographical proximity to one in which they are phrased in terms of ideological like-mindedness.

In the villages and small towns these major ideological changes appeared largely in the guise of a widening split between those who emphasized the Islamic aspects of the indigenous religious syncretism and those who emphasized the Hinduist and animistic elements. It is true that some difference between these variant subtraditions has been present since the arrival of Islam; some individuals have always been particularly skilled in Arabic chanting or particularly learned in Moslem law, while others have been adept at more Hinduistic mystical practices or specialists in local curing techniques. But these contrasts were softened by the easy tolerance of the Javanese for a wide range of religious concepts, so long as basic ritual patterns—i.e., slametans—were faithfully supported; whatever social divisiveness they stimulated was largely obscured by the overriding commonalities of rural and small-town life.

However, the appearance after 1910 of Islamic modernism (as well as vigorous conservative reactions against it) and religious nationalism among the economically and politically sophisticated trading classes of the larger cities strengthened the feeling for Islam as an exclusivist, antisyncretic creed among the more orthodox element of the mass of the population. Similarly, secular nationalism and Marxism, appearing among the civil servants and the expanding proletariat of these cities, strengthened the pre-Islamic (i.e., Hinduist-animist) elements of the syncretic pattern, which these groups tended to prize as a counterweight to puristic Islam and which some of them adopted as a general religious framework in which to set their more specifically political ideas. On the one hand there arose a more self-conscious Moslem, basing his religious beliefs and practices more explicitly on the international and universalistic doctrines of Mohammed; on the other hand there arose a more self-conscious "nativist," attempting to evolve a generalized religious system out of the material—muting the more Islamic elements—of his inherited religious tradition. And the contrast between the first kind of man, called a *santri*, and the second, called an *abangan*, grew steadily more acute, until today it forms the major cultural distinction in the whole of the Modjokuto area.

It is especially in the town that this contrast has come to play a crucial role. The absence of pressures toward interfamilial cooperation exerted by the technical requirements of wet-rice growing, as well as lessened effectiveness of the traditional forms of village government in the face of the complexities of urban living, severely weaken the social supports of the syncretic village pattern. When each man makes his living—as chauffeur, trader, clerk, or laborer—more or less independently of how his neighbors make theirs, his sense of the importance of the neighborhood community naturally diminishes. A more differentiated class system, more bureaucratic and impersonal forms of government, greater heterogeneity of social background, all tend to lead to the same result: the de-emphasis of strictly geographical ties in favor of diffusely ideological ones. For the townsman, the distinction between santri and abangan becomes even sharper, for it emerges as his primary point of social reference; it becomes a symbol of his social identity, rather than a mere contrast in belief. The sort of friends he will have the sort of organizations he will join, the sort of political leadership he will follow, the sort of person he or his son will marry, will all be strongly influenced by the side of this ideological bifurcation which he adopts as his own.

There is thus emerging in the town—though not only in the town—a new pattern of social living organized in terms of an altered framework of cultural classification. Among the elite this new pattern has already become rather highly developed, but among the mass of the townspeople it is still in the process of formation. Particularly in the *kampongs*, the off-the-street neighborhoods in which the common Javanese townsmen live crowded together in a helter-skelter profusion of little bamboo houses, one finds a transitional society in which the traditional forms of rural living are being steadily dissolved and new forms steadily reconstructed. In these enclaves of peasants-come-to-town (or of sons and grandsons of peasants-come-to-town), Redfield's folk culture is being constantly converted into his urban culture, though this latter is not accurately characterized by such negative and residual terms as "secular," "individualized," and "culturally disorganized." What is occurring in the kampongs is not so much a destruction of traditional ways of life as a construction of a new one; the sharp social conflict characteristic of these lower-class neighborhoods is not simply indicative of a loss of cultural consensus, but rather indicative of a search, not yet entirely successful, for new, more generalized, and flexible patterns of belief and value.

In Modjokuto, as in most of Indonesia, this search is taking place largely within the social context of the mass political parties, as well as in the women's clubs, youth organizations, labor unions, and other sodalities formally or informally linked with them. There are several of these parties (though the recent general election severely reduced their number), each led by educated urban elites—civil servants, teachers, traders, students, and the like—and each competing with the others for the political allegiance of both the half rural, half urban kampong dwellers and of the mass of the peasantry. And almost without exception, they appeal to one or another side of the santri-abangan split. Of this complex of political parties and sodalities, only two are of immediate concern to us here: Masjumi, a huge, Islam-based political party; and Permai, a vigorously anti-Moslem politico-religious cult.

Masjumi is the more or less direct descendant of the pre-war Islamic reform movement. Led, at least in Modjokuto, by modernist santri intellectuals, it stands for a socially conscious, antischolastic, and somewhat puritanical version of back-to-the Koran Islam. In company with the other Moslem parties, it also supports the institution of an "Islamic State" in Indonesia in place of the present secular republic. However, the meaning of this ideal is not entirely clear. Masjumi's enemies accuse it of pressing for an intolerant, medievalist theocracy in which abangans and non-Moslems will be persecuted and forced to follow exactly the prescripts of the Moslem law, while Masjumi's leaders claim that Islam is intrinsically tolerant and that they only desire a government explicitly based on the Moslem creed, one whose laws will be in consonance with the teachings of the Koran and Hadith. In any case, Masjumi, the country's largest Moslem party, is one of the major spokesmen on both the national and the local levels for the values and aspirations of the santri community.

Permai is not so impressive on a national scale. Though it is a nation-wide party, it is a fairly small one, having strength only in a few fairly circumscribed regions. In the Modjokuto area, however, it happened to be of some importance, and what it lacked in national scope it made up in local intensity. Essentially, Permai is a fusion of Marxist politics with abangan religious patterns. It combines a fairly explicit anti-Westernism, anti-capitalism, and anti-imperialism with an attempt to formalize and generalize some of the more characteristic diffuse themes of the peasant religious syncretism. Permai meetings follow both the slametan pattern, complete with incense and symbolic food (but without Islamic chants), and modern parliamentary procedure; Permai pamphlets contain calendrical and numerological divinatory systems and mystical teachings as well as analyses of class conflict; and Permai speeches are concerned with elaborating both religious and political concepts. In Modjokuto, Permai is also a curing cult, with its own special medical practices and spells, a secret password, and cabalistic interpretations of passages in the leaders' social and political writings.

But Permai's most notable characteristic is its strong anti-Moslem stand. Charging that Islam is a foreign import, unsuited to the needs and values of the Javanese, the cult urges a return to "pure" and "original" Javanese beliefs, by which they seem to mean to the indigenous syncretism with the more Islamic elements removed. In line with this, the cult-party has initiated a drive, on both national and local levels, for secular (i.e., non-Islamic) marriage and funeral rites. As the situation stands now, all but Christians and Balinese Hindus must have their marriages legitimatized by means of the Moslem ritual. Funeral rites are an individual concern but, because of the long history of syncretism, they are so deeply involved with Islamic customs that a genuinely non-Islamic funeral tends to be a practical impossibility.

Permai's action on the local level in pursuit of non-Islamic marriage and funeral ceremonies took two forms. One was heavy pressure on local government officials to permit such practices, and the other was heavy pressure on its own members to follow, voluntarily, rituals purified of Islamic elements. In the case of marriage, success was more or less precluded because the local officials' hands were tied by Central Government ordinances, and even highly ideologized members of the cult would not dare an openly "illegitimate" marriage. Without a change in the law, Permai had little chance to alter marriage forms, though a few abortive attempts were made to conduct civil ceremonies under the aegis of abangan-minded village chiefs.

The case of funerals was somewhat different, for a matter of custom rather than law was involved. During the year I was in the field, the tension between Permai and Masjumi increased very sharply. This was due in part to the imminence of Indonesia's first general elections, and in part to the effects of the cold war. It was also influenced by various special occurrences—such as a report that the national head of Permai had publicly called Mohammed a false prophet; a speech in the nearby regional capital by a Masjumi leader in which he accused Permai of intending to raise a generation of bastards in Indonesia; and a bitter village-chief election largely fought out on santri vs. abangan grounds. As a result, the local subdistrict officer, a worried bureaucrat trapped in the middle, called a meeting of all the village religious officials, or *Modins*. Among many other duties, a Modin is traditionally responsible for conducting funerals. He directs the whole ritual, instructs the mourners in the technical details of burial, leads the Koran chanting, and reads a set speech to the deceased at the graveside. The subdistrict officer instructed the Modins—the majority of whom were village Masjumi leaders—that in case of the death of a member of Permai, they were merely to note the name and age of the deceased and return home; they were not to participate in the ritual. He warned that if they did not do as he advised, they would be responsible if trouble started and he would not come to their support.

This was the situation on July 17, 1954, when Paidjan, nephew of Karman, an active and ardent member of Permai, died suddenly in the Modjokuto kampong in which I was living.

THE FUNERAL

The mood of a Javanese funeral is not one of hysterical bereavement, unrestrained sobbing, or even of formalized cries of grief for the deceased's departure. Rather, it is a calm, undemonstrative, almost languid letting go, a brief ritualized relinquishment of a relationship no longer possible. Tears are not approved of and certainly not encouraged; the effort is to get the job done, not to linger over the pleasures of grief. The detailed busy-work of the funeral, the politely formal social intercourse with the neighbors pressing in from all sides, the series of commemorative slametans stretched out at intervals for almost three years—the whole momentum of the Javanese ritual system is supposed to carry one through grief without severe emotional disturbance. For the mourner, the funeral and postfuneral ritual is said to produce a feeling of *iklas*, a kind of willed affectlessness, a detached and static state of "not caring"; for the neighborhood group it is said to produce *rukun*, "communal harmony."

The actual service is in essence simply another version of the slametan, adapted to the special requirements of interment. When the news of a death is broadcast through the area, everyone in the neighborhood must drop what he is doing and go immediately to the home of the survivors. The women bring bowls of rice, which is cooked up into a slametan; the men begin to cut wooden grave markers and to dig a grave. Soon the Modin arrives and begins to direct activities. The corpse is washed in ceremonially prepared water by the relatives (who unflinchingly hold the body on their laps to demonstrate their affection for the deceased as well as their self-control); then it is wrapped in muslin. About a dozen santris, under the leadership of the Modin, chant Arabic prayers over the body for five or ten minutes; after this it is carried, amid various ritual acts, in a ceremonial procession to the graveyard where it is interred in prescribed ways. The Modin reads a grave-side speech to the deceased, reminding him of his duties as a believing Moslem; and the funeral is over, usually only two or three hours after death. The funeral proper is followed by commemorative slametans in the home of the survivors at three, seven, forty, and one hundred days after death; on the first and second anniversary of death; and, finally, on the thousandth day, when the corpse is considered to have turned to dust and the gap between the living and the dead to have become absolute.

This was the ritual pattern which was called into play when Paidjan died. As soon as dawn broke (death occurred in the early hours of the morning), Karman, the uncle, dispatched a telegram to the boy's parents in a nearby city, telling them in characteristic Javanese fashion that their son was ill. This evasion was intended to soften the impact of death by allowing them to become aware of it more gradually. Javanese feel that emotional damage results not from the severity of a frustration but from the suddenness with which it comes, the degree to which it "surprises" one unprepared for it. It is "shock," not suffering itself, which is feared. Next, in the expectation that the parents would arrive within a few hours, Karman sent for the Modin to begin the ceremony. This was done on the theory that by the time the parents had come little would be left to do but inter the body, and they would thus once more be spared unnecessary stress. By ten o'clock at the very latest it should all be over; a saddening incident, but a ritually muted one.

But when the Modin, as he later told me, arrived at Karman's house and saw the poster displaying Permai's political symbol, he told Karman that he could not perform the ritual. After all, Karman belonged to "another religion" and he, the Modin, did not know the correct burial rituals for it; all he knew was Islam. "I don't want to insult your religion," he said piously, "on the contrary, I hold it in the utmost regard, for there is no intolerance in Islam. But I don't know your ritual. The Christians have their own ritual and their own specialist (the local preacher), but what does Permai do? Do they burn the corpse or what?" (This is a sly allusion to Hindu burial practices; evidently the Modin enjoyed himself hugely in this interchange.) Karman was, the Modin told me, rather upset at all this and evidently surprised, for although he was an active member of Permai, he was a fairly unsophisticated one. It had evidently never occurred to him that the anti-Moslem-funeral agitation of the party would ever appear as a concrete problem, or that the Modin would actually refuse to officiate. Karman was actually not a bad fellow, the Modin concluded; he was but a dupe of his leaders.

After leaving the now highly agitated Karman, the Modin went directly to the subdistrict officer to ask if he had acted properly. The officer was morally bound to say that he had, and thus fortified the Modin returned home to find Karman and the village policeman, to whom he had gone in desperation, waiting for him. The policeman, a personal friend of Karman's, told the Modin that according to time-honored custom he was supposed to bury everyone with impartiality, never mind whether he happened to agree with their politics. But the Modin, having now been personally supported by the subdistrict officer, insisted that it was no longer his responsibility. However, he suggested if Karman wished, he could go to the village chief's office and sign a public statement, sealed with the Government stamp and countersigned by the village chief in the presence of two witnesses, declaring that he, Karman, was a true believing Moslem and that he wished the Modin to bury the boy according to Islamic custom. At this suggestion that he officially abandon his religious beliefs, Karman exploded into a rage and stormed from the house, rather uncharacteristic behavior for a Javanese. By the time he arrived home again, at his wit's end about what to do next, he found to his dismay that the news of the boy's death had been broadcast and the entire neighborhood was already gathering for the ceremony.

Like most of the kampongs in the town of Modjokuto, the one in which I lived consisted both of pious santris and ardent abangans (as well as a number of less intense adherents of either side), mixed together in a more or less random manner. In the town, people are forced to live where they can and take whomever they find for neighbors, in contrast to the rural areas where whole neighborhoods, even whole villages, still tend to be made up almost entirely of either abangans or santris. The majority of the santris in the kampong were members of Masjumi and most of the abangans were followers of Permai, and in daily life, social interaction between the two groups was minimal. The abangans, most of whom were either petty artisans or manual laborers, gathered each late afternoon at Karman's roadside coffee shop for the idle twilight conversations which are typical of small town and village life in Java; the santris—tailors, traders and storekeepers for the most part—usually gathered in one or another of the santri-run shops for the same purpose. But despite this lack of close social ties, the demonstration of territorial unity at a funeral was still felt by both groups to be an unavoidable duty; of all the Javanese rituals, the funeral probably carries the greatest obligation on attendance. Everyone who lives within a certain roughly defined radius of the survivor's home is expected to come to the ceremony; and on this occasion everyone did.

With this as background, it is not surprising that when I arrived at Karman's house about eight o'clock, I found two separate clusters of sullen men squatting disconsolately on either side of the yard, a nervous group of whispering women sitting idly inside the house near the still clothed body, and a general air of doubt and uneasiness in place of the usual quiet busyness of slametan preparing, body washing, and guest greeting. The abangans were grouped near the house where Karman was crouched, staring blankly off into space, and where Sudjoko and Sastro, the town Chairman and Secretary of Permai (the only nonresidents of the kampong present) sat on chairs, looking vaguely out of place. The santris were crowded together under the narrow shadow of a coconut palm about thirty yards away, chatting quietly to one another about everything but the problem at hand. The almost motionless scene suggested an unlooked-for intermission in a familiar drama, as when a motion picture stops in the mid-action.

After a half hour or so, a few of the abangans began to chip half-heartedly away at pieces of wood to make grave markers and a few women began to construct small flower offerings for want of anything better to do; but it was clear that the ritual was arrested and that no one quite knew what to do next. Tension slowly rose. People nervously watched the sun rise higher and higher in the sky, or glanced at the impassive Karman. Mutterings about the sorry state of affairs began to appear ("everything these days is a political problem," an old, traditionalistic man of about eighty grumbled to me, "you can't even die any more but what it becomes a political problem"). Finally, about 9:30, a young santri tailor named Abu decided to try to do something about the situation before it deteriorated entirely: he stood up and gestured to Karman, the first serious instrumental act which had occurred all morning. And Karman, roused from his meditation, crossed the no-man's-land to talk to him.

As a matter of fact, Abu occupied a rather special position in the kampong. Although he was a pious santri and a loyal Masjumi member, he had more contact with the Permai group because his tailor shop was located directly behind Karman's coffee shop. Though Abu, who stuck to his sewing machine night and day, was not properly a member of this group, he would often exchange comments with them from his work bench about twenty feet away. True, a certain amount of tension existed between him and the Permai people over religious issues. Once, when I was inquiring about their eschatological beliefs, they referred me sarcastically to Abu, saying he was an expert, and they teased him quite openly about what they considered the wholly ridiculous Islamic theories of the afterlife. Nevertheless, he had something of a social bond with them, and it was perhaps reasonable that he should be the one to try to break the deadlock.

"It is already nearly noon," Abu said, "things can't go straight on like this." He suggested that he send Umar, another of the santris, to see if the Modin could now be induced to come; perhaps things were cooler with him now. Meanwhile, he could get the washing and wrapping of the corpse started himself. Karman replied that he would think about it, and returned to the other side of the yard for a discussion with the two Permai leaders. After a few minutes of vigorous gesturing and nodding, Karman returned and said simply, "all right, that way." "I know how you feel," Abu said, "I'll just do what is absolutely necessary and keep the Islam out as much as possible." He gathered the santris together and they entered the house.

The first requisite was stripping the corpse (which was still lying on the floor, because no one could bring himself to move it). But by now the body was rigid, making it necessary to cut the clothes off with a knife, an unusual procedure which deeply disturbed everyone, especially the women clustered around. The santris finally managed to get the body outside and set up the bathing enclosure. Abu asked for volunteers for the washing; he reminded them that God would consider such an act a good work. But the relatives, who normally would be expected to undertake this task, were by now so deeply shaken and confused that they were unable to bring themselves to hold the boy on their laps in the customary fashion. There was another wait while people looked hopelessly at each other. Finally, Pak Sura, a member of Karman's group but no relative, took the boy on his lap, although he was clearly frightened and kept whispering a protective spell. One reason the Javanese give for their custom of rapid burial is that it is dangerous to have the spirit of the deceased hovering around the house.

Before the washing could begin, however, someone raised the question as to whether one person was enough—wasn't it usually three? No one was quite sure, including Abu; some thought three a necessary number. After about ten minutes of anxious discussion, a male cousin of the boy and a carpenter, un-

related to him, managed to work up the courage to join Pak Sura. Abu, attempting to act the Modin's role as best he could, sprinkled a few drops of water on the corpse and then it was washed, rather haphazardly and in unsacralized water. When this was finished, however, the procedure was again stalled, for no one knew exactly how to arrange the small cotton pads which, under Moslem law, should plug the body orifices. Karman's wife, sister of the deceased's mother, could evidently take no more, for she broke into a loud, unrestrained wailing, the only demonstration of this sort I witnessed among the dozen or so Javanese funerals I attended. Everyone was further upset by this development, and most of the kampong women made a frantic but unavailing effort to comfort her. Most of the men remained seated in the yard, outwardly calm and inexpressive, but the embarrassed uneasiness which had been present since the beginning seemed to be turning toward fearful desperation. "It is not nice for her to cry that way," several men said to me, "it isn't proper." At this point, the Modin arrived.

However, he was still adamant. Further, he warned Abu that he was courting eternal damnation by his actions. "You will have to answer to God on Judgment Day," he said, "if you make mistakes in the ritual. It will be your responsibility. For a Moslem, burial is a serious matter and must be carried out according to the Law by someone who knows what the Law is, not according to the will of the individual." He then suggested to Sodjoko and Sastro, the Permai leaders, that they take charge of the funeral, for as party "intellectuals" they must certainly know what kind of funeral customs Permai followed. The two leaders, who had not moved from their chairs, considered this as everyone watched expectantly, but they finally refused, with some chagrin, saying they really did not know how to go about it. The Modin shrugged and turned away. One of the bystanders, a friend of Karman's, then suggested that they just take the body out and bury it and forget about the whole ritual; it was extremely dangerous to leave things as they were much longer. I don't know whether this remarkable suggestion would have been followed, for at this juncture the mother and father of the dead child entered the kampong.

They seemed quite composed. They were not unaware of the death, for the father later told me he had suspected as much when he got the telegram; he and his wife had prepared themselves for the worst and were more or less resigned by the time they arrived. When they approached the kampong and saw the whole neighborhood gathered, they knew that their fears were well founded. When Karman's wife, whose weeping had subsided slightly, saw the dead boy's mother come into the yard, she burst free of those who were comforting her and with a shriek rushed to embrace her sister. In what seemed a split second, both women had dissolved into wild hysterics and the crowd had rushed in and pulled them apart, dragging them to houses at opposite sides of the kampong. Their wailing continued in undiminished volume, and nervous comments arose to the effect that they ought to get on with the burial in one fashion or another, before the boy's spirit possessed someone.

But the mother now insisted on seeing the body of her child before it was wrapped. The father at first forbade it, angrily ordering her to stop crying—didn't she know that such behavior would darken the boy's pathway to the other world? But she persisted and so they brought her, stumbling, to where he lay in Karman's house. The women tried to keep her from drawing too close, but she broke loose and began to kiss the boy about the genitals. She was snatched away almost immediately by her husband and the women, though she screamed that she had not yet finished; and they pulled her into the back room where she subsided into a daze. After a while—the body was finally being wrapped, the Modin having unbent enough to point out where the cotton pads went—she seemed to lose her bearings entirely and began to move about the yard shaking hands with everyone, all strangers to her, and saying, "forgive me my faults, forgive me my faults." Again she was forcibly restrained; people said, "calm yourself, think of your other children—do you want to follow your son to the grave?"

The corpse was now wrapped and new suggestions were made that it be taken off immediately to the graveyard. At this point, Abu approached the father, who, he evidently felt, had now displaced Karman as the man legally responsible for the proceedings. Abu explained that the Modin, being a Government official, did not feel free to approach the father himself, but he would like to know: how did he wish the boy to be buried—the Islamic way or what? The father, somewhat bewildered, said, "Of course, the Islamic way.

I don't have much of any religion, but I'm not a Christian, and when it comes to death the burial should be in the Islamic way. Completely Islamic." Abu explained again that the Modin could not approach the father directly, but that he, being "free," could do as he pleased. He said that he had tried to help as best he could but that he had been careful to do nothing Islamic before the father came. It was too bad, he apologized, about all the tension that was in the air, that political differences had to make so much trouble. But after all, everything had to be "clear" and "legal" about the funeral. It was important for the boy's soul. The santris, somewhat gleefully, now chanted their prayers over the corpse, and it was carried to the grave and buried in the usual manner. The Modin gave the usual graveyard speech, as amended for children, and the funeral was finally completed. None of the relatives or the women went to the graveyard; but when we returned to the house—it was now well after noon—the slametan was finally served, and Paidjan's spirit presumably left the kampong to begin its journey to the other world.

Three days later, in the evening, the first of the commemorative slametans was held, but it turned out that not only were no santris present but that it was as much a Permai political and religious cult meeting as a mourning ritual. Karman started off in the traditional fashion by announcing in high Javanese that this was a slametan in remembrance of the death of Paidjan. Sudjoko, the Permai leader, immediately burst in saying, "No, no, that is wrong. At a third-day slametan you just eat and give a long Islamic chant for the dead, and we are certainly not going to do that." Then he launched into a long, rambling speech. Everyone, he said, must know the philosophical-religious basis of the country. "Suppose this American (he pointed to me; he was not at all pleased by my presence) came up and asked you: what is the spiritual basis of the country? and you didn't know—wouldn't you be ashamed?"

He went on in this vein, building up a whole rationale for the present national political structure on the basis of a mystical interpretation of President Sukarno's "Five Points" (Monotheism, Social Justice, Humanitarianism, Democracy, and Nationalism) which are the official ideological foundation of the new republic. Aided by Karman and others, he worked out a micro-macrocosm correspondence theory in which the individual is seen to be but a small replica of the state, and the state but an enlarged image of the individual. If the state is to be ordered, then the individual must also be ordered; each implies the other. As the President's Five Points are at the basis of the state, so the five senses are at the basis of an individual. The processes of harmonizing both are the same, and it is this we must be sure we know. The discussion continued for nearly half an hour, ranging widely through religious, philosophical, and political issues (including, evidently for my benefit, a discussion of the Rosenbergs' execution).

We paused for coffee and as Sudjoko was about to begin again, Paidjan's father, who had been sitting quietly and expressionless began suddenly to talk, softly and with a curiously mechanical tonelessness, almost as if he were reasoning with himself but without much hope of success. "I am sorry for my rough city accent," he said, "but I very much want to say something." He hoped they would forgive him; they could continue their discussion in a moment. "I have been trying to be iklas ("detached," "resigned") about Paidjan's death. I'm convinced that everything that could have been done for him was done and that his death was just an event which simply happened." He said he was still in Modjokuto because he could not yet face the people where he lived, couldn't face having to tell each one of them what had occurred. His wife, he said, was a little more iklas now too. It was hard, though. He kept telling himself it was just the will of God, but it was so hard, for nowadays people didn't agree on things any more; one person tells you one thing and others tell you another. It's hard to know which is right, to know what to believe. He said he appreciated all the Modjokuto people coming to the funeral, and he was sorry it had been all mixed up. "I'm not very religious myself. I'm not Masjumi and I'm not Permai. But I wanted the boy to be buried in the old way. I hope no one's feelings were hurt." He said again he was trying to be iklas, to tell himself it was just the will of God, but it was hard, for things were so confused these days. It was hard to see why the boy should have died.

This sort of public expression of one's feelings is extremely unusual—in my experience unique—among Javanese, and in the formalized traditional slametan pattern there is simply no place for it (nor for philosophical or political discussion). Everyone present was rather shaken by the father's talk, and there was a painful silence. Sudjoko finally began to talk again, but this time he described in detail the boy's death. How Paidjan had first gotten a fever and Karman had called him, Sudjoko, to come and say a Permai spell. But the boy did not respond. They finally took him to a male nurse in the hospital, where he was given an injection. But still he worsened. He vomited blood and went into convulsions, which Sudjoko described rather graphically, and then he died. "I don't know why the Permai spell didn't work," he said, "it has worked before. This time it didn't. I don't know why; that sort of thing can't be explained no matter how much you think about it. Sometimes it just works and sometimes it just doesn't." There was another silence and then, after about ten minutes more of political discussion, we disbanded. The father returned the next day to his home and I was not invited to any of the later slametans. When I left the field about four months later, Karman's wife had still not entirely recovered from the experience, the tension between the santris and the abangans in the kampong had increased, and everyone wondered what would happen the next time a death occurred in a Permai family.

. . .

In sum, the disruption of Paidjan's funeral may be traced to a single source: an incongruity between the cultural framework of meaning and the patterning of social interaction, and incongruity due to the persistence in an urban environment of a religious symbol system adjusted to peasant social structure. Static functionalism, of either the sociological or social-psychological sort, is unable to isolate this kind of incongruity because it fails to discriminate between logico-meaningful integration and causal-functional integration; because it fails to realize that cultural structure and social structure are not mere reflexes of one another but independent, yet interdependent, variables. The driving forces in social change can be clearly formulated only by a more dynamic form of functionalist theory, one which takes into account the fact that man's need to live in a world to which he can attribute some significance, whose essential import he feels he can grasp, often diverges from his concurrent need to maintain a social organism. A diffuse concept of culture as "learned behavior," a static view of social structure as an equilibrated pattern of inter-action, and a stated or unstated assumption that the two must somehow (save in "disorganized" situations) be simple mirror images of one another, is rather too primitive a conceptual apparatus with which to attack such problems as those raised by Paidjan's unfortunate but instructive funeral.

BIOGRAPHIES
OF AUTHORS

DAVID FRIEND ABERLE (1918–) was born in Minnesota and obtained his doctor's degree from Columbia University. He is currently Professor of Anthropology at the University of British Columbia. He is a member of the executive board of the American Anthropological Association. Most of his field work has been done with the Navaho Indians, about whom he has written extensively. His relevant publications include *Navaho and Ute Peyotism* (with Omer C. Stewart; 1957), and *The Peyote Religion Among the Navaho* (1966).

BERNARD BARBER (1918–) is Professor of Sociology and chairman of the department at Barnard College, Columbia University. He received his education at Harvard, where he was granted his Ph.D. Professor Barber is the author of *Science and the Social Order* (1952), *Social Stratification* (1957), *Drugs and Society* (1967), and the editor of *L. J. Henderson on the Social System* (1970).

ROBERT NEELLY BELLAH (1927–) was born in Oklahoma and received his doctorate from Harvard in 1955. He is presently a Ford Professor of Sociology and Comparative Studies and chairman of the Center for Japanese and Korean Studies at the University of California, Berkeley. Interested in the sociology of religion, he is the author of *Tokugawa Religion* (1957), the editor of *Religion and Progress in Modern Asia* (1965), and the author of *Beyond Belief: Essays on Religion in a Post-Traditional World* (1970).

CYRIL SHIRLEY BELSHAW (1921–) was born in New Zealand and educated there and at the London School of Economics. He has done administrative work and field research in Melanesia. At present he is Professor of Anthropology at the University of British Columbia. He is the author of *The Great Village* (1957) and *Under the Ivi Tree* (1964).

WALDEMAR BOGORAS (VLADIMIR GERMANOVICH BOGORAZ) (1865–1936) was a Russian who was exiled in his youth to Siberia. At the invitation of his friend Waldemar Jochelson he joined the Jesup North Pacific Expedition, working with the Chukchee, Koryak, Yukaghir, and Lamut. For a while he lived in the United States and then returned to Russia, where he was associated with the Academy of Sciences Museum of Anthropology and Ethnography in Leningrad. He wrote novels under the pseudonym "Tan." Among his numerous monographs are *The Chukchee* (1904–1909), *Chukchee Mythology* (1910), and *Koryak Texts* (1917).

RUTH LEAH BUNZEL (1898–) was born in New York City and received her doctorate from Columbia in 1929, where she was trained under Franz Boas and where she is presently a Research Associate. During the war she was an analyst for the Office of War Information. Her main field research has been done in connection with Zuni ceremonialism, but she has had additional research experience in Middle America and is the author of "Introduction to Zuni Ceremonialism," "Zuni Origin Myths," "Zuni Katcinas," and "Zuni Ritual Poetry," all of which appeared in the *47th Report Bureau of American Ethnology, 1929–1930* (1932), as well as *Chichicastenango: A Guatemalan Village* (1952). She has also investigated American and Chinese national character.

WALTER BRADFORD CANNON (1871–1945) took his A.B. (1896), A.M. (1897), and M.D. (1900) at Harvard University and was the holder of numerous honorary degrees from universities throughout the world. He was George Higginson Professor of Physiology at Harvard from 1906 until his retirement in 1942. He was responsible for solving the acute World War I problem of traumatic shock, and he discovered the adrenalin-like hormone "sympathin." Many of his studies dealt with homeostasis, a term which he introduced to the literature. His publications include *Bodily Changes in Pain, Hunger, Fear and Rage* (1915; revised 1929), *Traumatic Shock* (1923), and *The Wisdom of the Body* (1932).

ELIZABETH FLORENCE COLSON (1917–   ) was trained in anthropology at Radcliffe, where *she received the doctorate. She is Professor of Anthropology at the University of California, Berkeley, having previously been director of the Rhodes-Livingstone Institute and associated with the African Studies Program at Boston University. Her field work was done in California, Washington, Zambia, and Australia. Among her publications are *Marriage and the Family Among the Plateau Tonga of Northern Rhodesia* (1958), *Social Organization of the Gwembe Tonga* (1960), and *The Plateau Tonga* (1962).

CLARK EDWARD CUNNINGHAM (1934–   ) was born in Kansas City, Missouri, and received his doctorate from Oxford in 1963. He is presently Associate Professor of Anthropology, Preventive Medicine, and Community Health at the University of Illinois at Champaign-Urbana. His field work was done in Indonesian Timor and Central and North Thailand.

MARY DOUGLAS (1921–   ) was born in Italy and received her doctorate from Oxford in 1951. She is presently a Professor of Anthropology at the University College, London. Her field work was done in the Kasai district of the former Belgian Congo. She is the author of *Purity and Danger* (1966) and *Natural Symbols* (1970).

LOUIS CHARLES JEAN DUMONT (1911–   ) was born in Salonica (Greece) and received his doctorate from the University of Paris in 1954. He was Lecturer in Indian Sociology at Oxford from 1951 to 1955 and is presently Directeur d'Études at the École Pratique des Hautes Études in Paris. His field work has been done in India. He is the author of *La Tarasque* (1951), *Une Sous-caste de l'Inde du Sud* (1957), *Homo Hierarchicus* (English edition 1970), and *Religion, Politics and History in India* (1970).

ALAN DUNDES (1934–   ) was born in New York City and received his doctorate from Indiana University in 1962. He is presently Professor of Anthropology and Folklore at the University of California, Berkeley, and a member of the executive board of the American Folklore Society. His field work was done with the Florida Seminole and the Potawatomi (Mayetta, Kansas). He is the author of *The Morphology of North American Indian Folktales* (1964).

ÉMILE DURKHEIM (1858–1917), a Frenchman by birth, was descended from a long line of rabbis and at an early age prepared for the rabbinate, but soon decided to become a teacher. He attended the École

Normale Supérieure, where he was much influenced by Fustel de Coulanges and Émile Boutroux. For a few years he taught philosophy at various lycées and then turned to sociology. To prepare himself for improving his doctoral dissertation, he spent a year in Paris and Germany. At the University of Bordeaux in 1887 he gave the first course in social science ever offered in France. Six years later he defended his two doctoral theses, one of them being his *De la division du travail social* (1893). He founded the *Année Sociologique* in 1898. He taught sociology for thirty years at Bordeaux and the University of Paris. He was a prolific writer and, in turn, has been the object of scores of expository and critical books and articles.

EDWARD EVAN EVANS-PRITCHARD (1902–   ) is Emeritus Professor of Social Anthropology at Oxford. He received his master's degree at Oxford and his doctorate at the University of London. He has taught and done research at the Egyptian University at Cairo the University of London, and Cambridge and was knighted in 1971. He has carried on field work in the Sudan, the Belgian Congo, Ethiopia, and Kenya. Among his books are *Witchcraft, Oracles and Magic Among the Azande* (1937), *Nuer Religion* (1956), and *Theories of Primitive Religion* (1966).

RAYMOND WILLIAM FIRTH (1901–   ) is Emeritus Professor of Anthropology at the University of London. Born in New Zealand, he first read Economics and later received his graduate training in anthropology under Malinowski in London. His major field research has been carried out on the island of Tikopia and in the Malay State of Kelantan. From 1953 to 1955 he was president of the Royal Anthropological Institute of Great Britain and Ireland. He is the author of *The Work of the Gods in Tikopia* (1940), *The Fate of the Soul: An Interpretation of Some Primitive Concepts* (1955), *Tikopia Ritual and Belief* (1967), and *Rank and Religion in Tikopia* (1970). Some of his papers have been republished in his *Essays on Social Organization and Values* (1964).

CHARLES OLIVER FRAKE (1930–   ) was born in Wyoming and received his doctorate from Yale in 1955. He was a Fellow of the Center for Advanced Study in the Behavioral Sciences in 1967–1968. He is presently Professor of Anthropology at Stanford, having taught previously at Harvard. Southeast Asia holds his principal regional interest, and he has done field work in the Philippines (Mindanao, Sulu).

JAMES GEORGE FRAZER (1854–1941) was born in Glasgow and educated at Glasgow University and Trinity College, Cambridge. He was called to the bar in 1879, and in 1907 became Professor of Social Anthropology at the University of Liverpool. He was knighted in 1914. Frazer had a strong interest in comparative religion, and it was in this field that he made his chief contributions to anthropological theory. Among his numerous writings the most famous is *The Golden Bough* (1st ed., 1890; 3d ed., 12 vols., 1911–1915). He also wrote *The Belief in Immortality and the Worship of the Dead* (1913–1924), *Folk-Lore in the Old Testament* (1918), *Myths of the Origin of Fire* (1930), and *The Fear of the Dead in Primitive Religion* (1933–1936).

NUMA-DENYS FUSTEL DE COULANGES (1830–1889) was a French historian who, after he lost his professorship in antiquities at the University of Strasbourg in 1870 when Strasbourg became German, turned to medieval history, where he exerted much influence in the reinterpretation of the history of the Middle Ages. However, he is best remembered for his effort at tracing the influence of early religion on the development of Greek and Roman society, publishing his ideas in his great book, *La Cité antique* (1864). While director of the École Normale Supérieure he attracted the admiration of a young student, Émile Durkheim.

CLIFFORD GEERTZ (1926–   ) is Professor of the Social Sciences at the Institute for Advanced Study, Princeton, New Jersey. He was born in San Francisco. After attending Antioch College he went to Harvard and there received his doctorate in social anthropology in 1956. He has carried on field research in Java, Bali, and Morocco. Among his publications is his book *The Religion of Java* (1960).

GARY HAMILTON GOSSEN (1942–   ) received his doctorate from Harvard in 1970. He is presently Assistant Professor of Anthropology at the University of California, Santa Cruz. His field research was done in Chamula (Chiapas, Mexico), Spain, Costa Rica, and the Prairie Potawatomi Reservation (Kansas).

WILLARD WILLIAMS HILL (1902–   ) was chairman of the Department of Anthropology at the University of New Mexico from 1948 to 1964 and is presently Professor Emeritus at the same institution. He received his doctorate from Yale. Most of his field research has been done among the Navaho, on whom he is one of the outstanding authorities, but he has also worked with the Pueblo, Ute, and Pomo Indians. He is the author of *Navaho Warfare* (1936), *The Agricultural and Hunting Methods of the Navaho Indians* (1938), and *Navaho Material Culture* (with Clyde Kluckhohn and Lucy Wales Kluckhohn; 1971). In preparation he has *The Ethnology of Santa Clara Pueblo*.

GEORGE CASPAR HOMANS (1910–   ) is a sociologist who was trained at Harvard, where he has taught since 1939 except for a period of military service. He is now Professor of Sociology and chairman of the Department of Sociology. He has served as president of the American Sociological Association (1963–1964). He is the author of *The Human Group* (1950), *Social Behavior* (1961), and *Sentiments and Activities* (1962).

ROBIN HORTON (1932–   ) is a Senior Research Fellow in the Institute of African Studies, University of Ibadan, Nigeria. His special interests are in the ethnography of the Ibo-speaking peoples of the Niger delta and in more general problems relating to the sociology of ideas. He is the author of *Kalabari Sculpture* (1966).

CLYDE KLUCKHOHN (1905–1960) was born in Iowa and did graduate work at the universities of Vienna, Oxford, and Harvard, where he received his doctorate and taught until his death. He served as chairman of the Department of Anthropology at Harvard and was one of the organizers of the Department of Social Relations at that institution, where he also served from 1947 to 1954 as director of the Russian Research Center. He was one of the outstanding authorities on the Navaho Indians, with whom he did extensive field work for a quarter of a century. He was active in the reorganization of the American Anthropological Association, being elected president of that body in 1947; but his dedication to his profession ranged beyond this and he was frequently called upon to serve in various administrative and advisory capacities. Of his numerous publications, those bearing on Navaho religion include *Navaho Classification of Their Song Ceremonials* (1938), *An Introduction to Navaho Chant Practice* (1940), both of which were written with Leland C. Wyman, and *Navaho Witchcraft* (1944).

ALFRED LOUIS KROEBER (1876–1960) was born in Hoboken, New Jersey, and trained in anthropology at Columbia by Boas, receiving his doctorate in 1901. From that year until his retirement in 1946 he taught at the University of California at Berkeley and was for many years curator of its museum of anthropology. He was not only one of the most prolific writers in his discipline (over 500 publications) but one of the most active in its various societies, having served as president of the American Folklore Society (1906), the American Anthropological Association (1917–1919), and the Linguistic Society of America (1940). He was also the recipient of several honorary degrees and awards. Most of his field research was done with the Indians of California. Of his publications, some of the most noteworthy were the *Handbook of the Indians of California* (1925), *Configurations of Culture Growth* (1944), and, especially, *Anthropology* (1923; revised 1948), which as a textbook exerted an important influence on generations of students.

EDMUND RONALD LEACH (1910–   ) was born in England and educated at Cambridge and the London School of Economics. His field work has been extensive, having been conducted in China, Formosa, Iraq, Burma, Borneo, and elsewhere. He is presently Provost of King's College, Cambridge, a position which he has held since 1966. He has been University Reader in Social Anthropology at Cambridge since 1957. He is the author of *Political Systems of Highland Burma* (1954; reprinted 1964),

Pul Eliya: A Village in Ceylon (1961), *Rethinking Anthropology* (1961), and editor of *The Structural Study of Myth and Totemism* (1967).

WILLIAM ARMAND LESSA (1908–   ) is Professor Emeritus of Anthropology and head of the Pacific Island Program at the University of California, Los Angeles. Born in Newark, he began his work in anthropology with Hooton as an undergraduate at Harvard and later received the doctorate in social anthropology from the University of Chicago. His field work began in Hawaii and has extended to China, Ulithi Atoll, and Samoa. Among his books and monographs the one most relevant to the field of religion is his *Tales from Ulithi Atoll: A Comparative Study in Oceanic Folklore* (1961). He is also the author of *Chinese Body Divination* (1968).

CLAUDE LÉVI-STRAUSS (1908–   ) is Directeur d'Études at the École Pratique des Hautes Études in Paris and has held this post since 1950. He has also been Professeur au Collège de France in Paris since 1959. He was born in Brussels and educated at the University of Paris, where he obtained his Agrégé de Philosophie in 1931 and his Docteur ès Lettres in 1949. Early in his career he taught at the University of São Paulo and the New School for Social Research, New York. Later he served as cultural attaché to the French embassy in the United States. His field work was done in South and Central Mato Grosso, Brazil (1935–1936), and North and West Mato Grosso and South Amazonas (1938–1939). He has gained world recognition in anthropology for his pursuit of what has been called the "structural method." Among his writings are *Tristes tropiques* (1955; trans. 1961), *Le Totémisme aujourd'hui* (1962; trans. 1963), *La Pensée sauvage* (1962; trans. 1966), *Structural Anthropology* (1963), *Mythologiques I: Le Cru et le cuit* (1964; trans. 1969), *Mythologiques II: Du Miel aux cendres* (1966), and *Mythologiques III: L'Origine des manières de table* (1968).

RALPH LINTON (1893–1953) studied anthropology for brief periods at Pennsylvania and Columbia but received his doctorate from Harvard. After serving as assistant curator of the Chicago Natural History Museum, he taught at Wisconsin and Columbia, and was Sterling Professor of Anthropology at Yale at the time of his death. From 1939 to 1945 he was editor of the *American Anthropologist*, and in 1946 was president of the American Anthropological Association. His field researches took him to various parts of the world, including the Marquesas, Madagascar, South Africa, Peru, and Brazil. He is the author of *The Study of Man* (1936), *The Cultural Background of Personality* (1945), and *The Tree of Culture* (1955, posthumous), as well as numerous monographs and articles.

ROBERT HARRY LOWIE (1883–1957) at the time of his death was Professor Emeritus of Anthropology at the University of California, Berkeley. He was born in Vienna and educated in the United States, receiving the doctorate in 1908 from Columbia,

where he studied under Boas. From 1907 to 1921 he was associated with the American Museum of Natural History and after that he went to Berkeley. He was editor of the *American Anthropologist* from 1924 to 1933, and president of the American Folklore Society, the American Ethnological Society, and the American Anthropological Association. He wrote numerous books, among them *Primitive Society* (1920), *Primitive Religion* (1924; revised, 1948), and *The History of Ethnological Theory* (1937).

BRONISLAW MALINOWSKI (1884–1942) was born and educated in Poland, where he took his Ph.D. in physics and mathematics. When ill health forced him to leave the University of Cracow in order to recuperate, he accidentally came across a copy of Frazer's *The Golden Bough*, which awakened his interest in the study of culture. He went to England in 1910 and studied under C. G. Seligman at the London School of Economics. Beginning in 1914 he spent two-and-a-half years doing research in the Pacific islands, chiefly in the Trobriands, which were made famous by his many books, including *Argonauts of the Western Pacific* (1928) and *Coral Gardens and Their Magic* (1935). In 1927 he was appointed to the first Chair in Anthropology at the University of London, where his weekly seminars became famous. At the time of his death he was a Visiting Professor at Yale University. An article written by S. F. Nadel, "Malinowski on Magic and Religion," appears in *Man and Culture—An Evaluation of the Work of Bronislaw Malinowski*, edited by Raymond Firth (1957).

DUANE GERALD METZGER (1930–   ) is Associate Professor of Social Science and Anthropology at the University of California, Irvine. He holds master's and doctor's degrees from the University of Chicago and was a Junior Fellow in the Society of Fellows at Harvard. He has done field work in Chiapas, Mexico.

JOHN FRANCIS MIDDLETON (1921–   ) was born in London and obtained his doctorate from Oxford in 1953. He is presently Professor of Anthropology and head of the Department of Anthropology at New York University. His field work was carried out in Uganda, Zanzibar, and Nigeria. He is the author of *Lugbara Religion* (1960), joint editor of *Witchcraft and Sorcery in East Africa* (1963), and co-editor of *Spirit Mediumship and Society in Africa* (1969).

OMAR KHAYYAM MOORE (1920–   ) was born in Utah and received his doctorate from Washington University in 1949. He is presently Professor of Social Psychology and director of the Clarifying Environments Program at the University of Pittsburgh. He is also president of the Responsive Environments Foundation. His publications include "Divination—A New Perspective," which appears in this volume.

RODNEY NEEDHAM (1923–   ) was born in England and received his doctorate from Oxford in 1953. He is presently Lecturer in Social Anthropology at the University of Oxford. He has written a number of articles, some of which are "The Left Hand of the Mugwe" (1960), "Blood, Thunder and Mockery of Animals" (1964), and "Right and Left in Nyoro Symbolic Classification" (1967). He is also the author of *Structure and Sentiment* (1962). His field work was done in the interior of Borneo, Malaya, and Sumba.

MORRIS EDWARD OPLER (1907–   ) is Professor of Anthropology at the University of Oklahoma. He was born in Buffalo and received his doctorate from the University of Chicago in 1933. His field research was carried out in the American Southwest and in India. Among his publications are *Myths and Tales of the Jicarilla Apache Indians* (1938), *Myths and Legends of the Lipan Apache Indians* (1940), *An Apache Life-Way* (1941), *Myths and Tales of the Chiricahua Apache Indians* (1942), *The Character and Derivation of the Jicarilla Holiness Rite* (1943), and *Apache Odyssey* (1969).

TALCOTT PARSONS (1902–   ) was born in Colorado. After attending the London School of Economics, where he studied with Ginsberg and Malinowski, he went to the University of Heidelberg and there received the doctorate in sociology and economics. He began teaching at Harvard in 1927, at first in economics and later in sociology, and is now Professor of Sociology. He was the first chairman of the Department of Social Relations at that institution (1946–1957), being one of its founders. From 1967 to 1971, he served as president of the American Academy of Arts and Sciences. He has translated and edited some of the works of Max Weber. Among his own writings are *The Structure of Social Action* (1937), *The Social System* (1951), and *Structure and Process in Modern Societies* (1960).

ALFRED REGINALD RADCLIFFE-BROWN (1881–1955) was born and educated in England, where he trained in anthropology under Haddon and Rivers at Cambridge University. His first field trip took him to the Andaman Islands from 1906 to 1908, and his fellowship thesis for Trinity College was a conventional reconstruction of Andaman culture history. But while teaching at the London School of Economics and at Cambridge he became aware of the French sociologists, especially Durkheim and Mauss, and eventually completely rewrote his Andamanese materials in terms of the meaning and function of their rites, myths, and institutions. From 1910 to 1912 he did field research in Australia. He spent a considerable part of his life abroad, being affiliated with the Pretoria Museum, the University of Cape Town, the University of Sydney, the University of Chicago, Yenching University, the University of São Paulo, Farouk I University, and Grahamstown. He was called to the newly created Chair of Social Anthropology at Oxford in 1937. Radcliffe-Brown is author of *The Andaman Islanders* (1922). Three collections of his essays, addresses, and seminar lectures have been published: *Structure and Function in Primitive Society* (1952), *A Natural Science of Society* (1957), and *Method in Social Anthropology* (1958).

KNUD RASMUSSEN (1879–1933) was born in Greenland, of partially Eskimo parentage. He learned to speak an Eskimo dialect before he was competent in Danish. He had as playmates during his childhood Eskimos who were entirely Christianized, and as a boy he dreamed of exploring and living in the unknown northland. He made the first of nearly a dozen major expeditions to the polar regions from 1902 to 1904, and this trip resulted in the publication of *The People of the Polar North* (1905), which established him as an authority on the Eskimos. Although particularly interested in folklore, he contributed greatly to knowledge about Greenland and the polar regions. He wrote on geography, natural history, language, general ethnology, and many other subjects, and in recognition of his research and writings he was awarded a Ph.D. from the University of Copenhagen. He was editor or author of several multivolume works on the Eskimo, of which *Report of the Fifth Thule Expedition, 1921–24* was one.

PETER JOHN ARTHUR RIGBY (1938–   ) was born in India and received his doctorate from Cambridge in 1964. He is presently Professor of Sociology and chairman of that department at Makerere University, Kampala, Uganda. His field work was done in Tanzania and Uganda. He is the author of *Cattle and Kinship Among the Gogo* (1969).

RENATO IGNACIO ROSALDO, JR. (1941–   ) was born in Champaign, Illinois, and did both his undergraduate and graduate studies at Harvard, receiving his doctorate in 1970. He is presently Assistant Professor of Anthropology at Stanford. His field research was done in Ecuador, Peru, Chiapas (Mexico), and with the Ilongot of Northern Luzon, Philippines.

RICHARD ALLAN SHWEDER (1945–   ) was born in New York and did his undergraduate studies at the University of Pittsburgh. He is presently a Ph.D. candidate at Harvard. His field research has been carried out in Chiapas, Mexico, and Orissa, India.

JAMES SYDNEY SLOTKIN (1913–1958) at the time of his death was Associate Professor in the Department of Social Sciences of the University of Chicago, at which institution he received his training in anthropology. His field research was conducted among the Menomini Indians. Among his pertinent publications are *The Peyote Religion* (1956) and *The Menomini Powwow Religion* (1957).

MELFORD ELLIOT SPIRO (1920–   ) was born in Cleveland and received his doctorate from Northwestern University in 1950. He is Professor of Anthropology and chairman of that department at the University of California, San Diego. His field work includes studies of the Ojibway, the natives of Ifaluk Atoll, an Israeli kibbutz, and the Burmese. He is the author of *An Atoll Culture: Ethnography of*

Ifaluk in the Caroline Islands (with E. G. Burrows; 1953), *Kibbutz: Venture in Utopia* (1956), *Burmese Supernaturalism: A Study in the Explanation and Resolution of Suffering* (1967), and *Buddhism and Society: A Great Tradition and Its Burmese Vicissitudes* (1970).

WILLIAM EDWARD HANLEY STANNER (1905–   ) was born in Sydney, Australia, and educated at Sydney University and the University of London, where he received his doctorate in 1938. He has done field research in Australia, New Guinea, Fiji, Western Samoa, and Kenya. He was director of the Makerere Institute in Uganda (1947–1949) and served on the South Pacific Commission (1953–1955). In 1950 he was appointed Reader in Comparative Social Institutions, and in 1964 Professor of Anthropology at the Australian National University, Canberra. In 1961 he was convener and chairman of a national conference which led to the formation of the Australian Institute of Aboriginal Studies and in 1967 was appointed a member of the Australian Commonwealth Council for Aboriginal Affairs. His publications include *The South Seas in Transition* (1953), *On Aboriginal Religion* (1963), *After the Dreaming* (1968), and *The Kitui Kamba* (1970).

MISCHA TITIEV (1901–   ) is Professor of Anthropology at the University of Michigan. He was born in Russia and educated at Harvard, where he received the doctorate in 1935. He is an authority on the Hopi Indians, having written *Notes on Hopi Witchcraft* (1942) and *Old Oraibi: A Study of the Hopi Indians of Third Mesa* (1944). In 1948 he did field research with the Araucanian Indians in Chile, and in 1951 with rural Japanese. He is the author of *The Science of Man* (1954; rev. 1963), *Introduction to Cultural Anthropology* (1959), and other works.

HUGH REDWALD TREVOR-ROPER (1914–   ) has been Regius Professor of Modern History at Oxford since 1957. Educated at Charterhouse and Christ Church, Oxford, he has written a number of books, some of which are *Archbishop Laud* (1940), *The Last Days of Hitler* (1947), *The Rise of Christian Europe* (1965), and *Religion, The Reformation and Social Change* (1967).

VICTOR W. TURNER (1920–   ) was born in Scotland and obtained his doctorate from the University of Manchester in 1955. He was chairman of the African Studies Committee at Cornell from 1964 to 1968 and is presently Professor of Social Thought and of Anthropology at the University of Chicago. His field research has been done in Zambia, Uganda, and Mexico. He is the author of *Ndembu Divination* (1961), *Chihamba the White Spirit* (1962), *The Forest of Symbols* (1967), *The Drums of Affliction* (1968), and *The Ritual Process* (1969).

EDWARD BURNETT TYLOR (1832–1917) was the foremost anthropologist of his time. Although not a university graduate, having been privately educated, he became Keeper of the University Museum at Oxford and a reader there from 1884 until 1896,

when he was given a professorship. He had an unusually wide range of interests. He went to Mexico in 1856 in the company of a prehistorian, and visited some Pueblo villages in 1884, but he was not a fieldworker. However, his critical appraisals and analyses of secondary materials were significant contributions to the nascent fund of anthropological knowledge. He was not strictly an evolutionist, for he insisted on the important part played in the development of culture by diffusion. His best-known works are *Researches in the Early History of Mankind and the Development of Civilization* (1865), *Primitive Culture: Researches into the Development of Mythology, Philosophy, Religion, Language, Art, and Custom* (1871), and *Anthropology: An Introduction to the Study of Man and Civilization* (1881).

EVON ZARTMAN VOGT (1918–   ) was born in Gallup, New Mexico, and educated at the University of Chicago, where he received his doctorate in 1948. Since then he has been teaching at Harvard, where he is now Professor of Social Anthropology, Curator of Middle American Ethnology, and currently serving as chairman of the Department of Anthropology. He has done extensive field work among the Navaho Indians of New Mexico and the Tzotzil Indians of Chiapas, Mexico. His publications include *Navaho Veterans* (1951), *Modern Homesteaders* (1955), *Water Witching U.S.A.* (with Ray Hyman; 1959), *Desarrollo Cultural de los Mayas* (with Alberto Ruz; 1964), *Zinacantan: A Maya Community in the Highlands of Chiapas* (1969), and *The Zinacantecos of Mexico: A Modern Maya Way of Life* (1970).

ANTHONY FRANCIS CLARKE WALLACE (1923–   ) was born in Toronto and studied at the University of Pennsylvania, where he obtained his doctorate in 1950. He is presently chairman and Professor of the Department of Anthropology at the University of Pennsylvania, as well as Medical Research Scientist at the Eastern Pennsylvania Psychiatric Institute. His field work was done with the Iroquois Indians. He is the author of *Religion: An Anthropological View* (1966) and *The Death and Rebirth of the Seneca* (1970).

GERALD E. WILLIAMS (1925–   ) is Associate Professor of Anthropology and presently serving as chairman of that Department at the University of Rochester. Born in Ohio, he did his graduate work in anthropology at the University of Chicago, his dissertation being on colloquial Minangkabau, a language of Western Sumatra. He has done field work as well in Java and Mexico.

ROY GEOFFREY WILLIS (1927–   ) was born in England and studied at Oxford, where he obtained his doctorate in 1966. He was Research Assistant at University College, London, from 1965 to 1967 and is presently Lecturer in Social Anthropology at the Centre of African Studies, University of Edinburgh, Scotland. His field research was done among the Fipa of southwest Tanzania from 1962 to 1964 and in 1966.

EDMUND WILSON (1895–   ) is a literary critic and writer with an interest in problems of comparative religion. After his graduation from Princeton in 1916 he served as managing editor of *Vanity Fair* from 1920 to 1921, as associate editor of the *New Republic* from 1926 to 1931, and as book review editor of the *New Yorker* from 1944 to 1948. He has published almost a score of books, including *The Scrolls from the Dead Sea* (1955), in connection with which he visited the Dead Sea site where the scrolls were found.

ERIC ROBERT WOLF (1923–   ) was born in Vienna and received his doctorate in anthropology from Columbia in 1951. He is Professor of Anthropology and chairman of that department at the University of Michigan. He has done field work in Puerto Rico, Mexico, and the Italian Alps. He is co-editor of *Comparative Studies in Society and History*. He is the author of *Sons of the Shaking Earth* (1959) and *Peasants* (1966).

SELECTED MONOGRAPHS ON NON-WESTERN RELIGIOUS SYSTEMS

BARTON, R. F. *The Religion of the Ifugaos*. ("Memoirs of the American Anthropological Association," No. 65.) Menasha, Wis., 1946.

This account of "the most extensive and pervasive religion that has yet been reported . . . outside of India" introduces the gods and describes their uses and some occasions on which they are invoked. Interesting features of the work are an attempt at quantification—for example, counting the times a particular benefit is sought in a sample of rites—and an examination of the historical development of the religion based on comparative data from related groups.

BATESON, GREGORY. *Naven: A Survey of the Problems Suggested by a Composite Picture of the Culture of a New Guinea Tribe Drawn from Three Points of View*. Stanford, Calif.: Stanford University Press, 1958.

The *naven* ceremony of the Iatmul of New Guinea is a celebration of important achievements, especially when accomplished for the first time. The ceremony is performed for a person by a classificatory mother's brother and marked by sex role reversals by the participants. Bateson attempts to explain the ceremony by placing it in its full cultural context, in which he distinguishes structure and function, and relating it to the ethos or emotional tone of the society.

BELLAH, ROBERT N. *Tokugawa Religion: The Values of Pre-Industrial Japan*. New York: The Free Press, 1957.

The author uses Max Weber's sociological frame of reference to demonstrate the influence of certain religious and political value orientations found in the feudal Tokugawa period which, he proposes, formed the matrix for the prodigious and vigorous later economic and political development of Japan into an industrial nation.

BOGORAS, WALDEMAR. *The Chukchee*, Vol. VII of Franz Boas (ed.), *The Jesup North Pacific Expedition*. ("Memoirs of the American Museum of Natural History," Vol. XI, Parts 2 and 3.) Leiden: E. J. Brill, 1904–1909.

Based on extensive field work among the reindeer-breeding peoples of Siberia, this monograph presents a wealth of detail on Chukchee cosmology and on the ritual means for securing the benefits of good spirits and warding off the effects of evil ones. (The sketches of these spirits by Chukchee are illuminating.) Seasonal sacrifices are associated with the life cycle of the reindeer, while other ritual centers around the hearth, each household having its own sacred objects and signs.

BOWERS, ALFRED W. *Mandan Social and Ceremonial Organization*. Chicago: The University of Chicago Press, 1950.

Although this book is concerned with ritual, describing a variety of ceremonies each built around a specific need (buffalo, eagles, rain), it is valuable also as mythology, since all the rites are dramatizations of myths. Each centers about a bundle of objects which represent the characters and incidents of the myth.

BUNZEL, RUTH. "Introduction to Zuni Ceremonialism," *47th Annual Report of the Bureau of American Ethnology*, pp. 467–545. Washington, D.C., 1932.

In this summary of the rich and varied ceremonialism of Zuni, the author points out that the apparent complexity is one of organization rather than content. She demonstrates this by abstracting a pattern of ritual elements common to all rites and by listing the major cults and their internal organization and interactions. Special emphasis is placed on the aesthetic functions of the ritual in Zuni life.

BUNZEL, RUTH. *Chichicastenango: A Guatemalan Village.* ("Publications of the American Ethnological Society," Vol. XXII.) Locust Valley, N.Y.: J. J. Augustin, 1952.

This study of a Guatemalan community contains a great deal of detail on the organizational aspects of the local religion—the selection and functioning of the rotating officials of the church—and on the *fiesta* round. In addition, consideration is given to the role of the ancestors as supplements to the Catholic saints, the use of the ancient calendar, divination by seeds, and the ideas of sin and penance.

CASO, ALFONSO. *The Aztecs: People of the Sun.* Norman: University of Oklahoma Press, 1960.

Caso sees the worship of the gods (especially the sun) and their maintenance by sacrifices as the central motivating force behind the Aztec nation. He examines the gods—their powers and their demands—and suggests that the requirements of the religion had a profound formative influence on the society. Illustrations in color from the codices contribute to the exposition and make this an attractive book.

EVANS, I. H. N. *The Religion of the Tempasuk Dusuns of North Borneo.* New York: Cambridge University Press, 1953.

The author gives a detailed account of Dusun religion and custom set in a background of daily life, pointing out the similarities to beliefs and practices found not only in other parts of Borneo but also in the Philippines, Indonesia, and Malaya. Among such similarities he cites the idea of multiple souls, soul wandering and capture, the importance of priestesses or mediums, as well as striking resemblances in ceremonial practice.

EVANS-PRITCHARD, E. E. *Witchcraft, Oracles and Magic Among the Azande.* Oxford: Clarendon Press, 1937.

Throughout this skillful account the author explores the dynamics of Zande belief—the balance between faith and skepticism and between empirical and mystical causes. To the Azande, witchcraft is the socially relevant cause of an illness and death; it is a purely psychical act, imputed to others (usually social deviants) and denied in oneself.

EVANS-PRITCHARD, E. E. *Nuer Religion.* Oxford: Clarendon Press, 1956.

In this study Evans-Pritchard describes a religion which is distinctive in its markedly monotheistic tendency, its strong sense of dependence on God, and the idea of punishment for sin and the consequent guilt, confession, and expiatory sacrifice. He suggests that Nuer religious thought, in which one spirit has many manifestations, is a reflection of the segmentary structure of the society.

FIRTH, RAYMOND. *The Work of the Gods in Tikopia.* ("London School of Economics and Political Science Monographs on Social Anthropology," Nos. 1 and 2.) London: Percy Lund, Humphries & Co., 1940.

Firth gives a step-by-step, eye-witness account, enriched by his closeness to the people and the vernacular, of the ritual cycle in this small Pacific society. He stresses the unity, perceived by the people themselves, of the series of rites—consecration of canoes and temples, harvest and planting, sacred dances, moral exhortation, and taboos on noise and amusement. Attention is given throughout to the sources of variation, by conscious innovation or error, in the tradition—the dynamics of ritual.

FLETCHER, ALICE, and LA FLESCHE, FRANCIS. "The Omaha Tribe," *27th Annual Report of the Bureau of American Ethnology*, pp. 15–672. Washington, D.C., 1911.

This study emphasizes ritual, both that of the secret societies and that performed by the clans for the tribe. The camp circle has two ritual divisions—the northern, the clans of which are responsible for rites concerned with creation and the cosmos, and the southern, whose clans perform the rites of war, maize, buffalo, and the sacred pole which "holds the tribe together."

FORTUNE, R. F. *Sorcerers of Dobu.* London: George Routledge & Sons, 1932.

The author sees jealousy of possession as a keynote to this culture and traces it in the attitudes toward, and uses of, the incantations which are the means of control over the supernatural. Both garden magic and spells for inflicting disease are privately owned and secret and are employed largely to protect one's property from others. Divination by watergazing is a technique for locating the sorcerer who has caused a particular illness.

FORTUNE, R. F. *Manus Religion.* ("Memoirs, American Philosophical Society," Vol. III.) Philadelphia, 1935.

Dr. Fortune presents an exhaustive account of every facet of Manus religion with a wealth of illustrative case material, native opinions, and so on. Due to his intimacy with the villagers, he describes their personalities and emotional reactions as accurately as the average individual could describe those of his European neighbor.

FOSTER, GEORGE M. *Empire's Children: The People of Tzintzuntzan.* ("Smithsonian Institution, Institute of Social Anthropology, Publications," No. 6.) Washington, D.C., 1948.

In this community, considered by the author as one of the least rural in all rural Mexico, Catholicism of a Mexican variety has replaced the old religion in its entirety. The Church, with its rotating offices, its associations, and its ceremonial calendar, is a social and spiritual focus for the community.

GEERTZ, CLIFFORD. *The Religion of Java.* New York: The Free Press, 1960.

Javanese religion is seen as having a Great and a Little tradition, each of which blends an animistic and a Hindu heritage. Their world view and social behavior are contrasted with a third element, *santri*, the more nearly orthodox Islamic tradition. The author links each with residence and occupation, but even more importantly with religious orientation and political alignments. The study emerges as an analysis of the Javanese value system.

GRINNELL, GEORGE B. *The Cheyenne Indians.* 2 vols. New Haven, Conn.: Yale University Press, 1923.

In an account reflecting several decades of acquaintance with the Cheyenne, the author describes in detail two of the four major ceremonies, pointing up the importance of the personal ordeal, private or public, in securing success and averting evil. Healing, also rich in ceremony, receives lengthy consideration.

GUSINDE, MARTIN. *Die Feuerland Indianer.* Band 2. *Die Yamana.* Mödling bei Wien: Verlag der Internationalen Zeitschrift "Anthropos," 1937.

This work contains an account of the religious concepts and practices of the primitive Yahgan of Tierra del Fuego. The author gives particular attention to the myths, which are concerned with the creation of the world and the invention (by a legendary family) of important parts of the social life.

HERSKOVITS, MELVILLE J. *Dahomey.* 2 vols. Locust Valley, N.Y.: J. J. Augustin, 1938.

The political complexity of this West African monarchy is here shown to be paralleled by an elaborate theology and a set of specialized religious institutions. In addition to ancestor worship carried on by extended families, there are rites for royal ancestors (at one time including human sacrifice), divination, and rituals performed by the highly trained priests of five separate cults.

JUNOD, HENRI A. *The Life of a South African Tribe.* 2d ed., revised and enlarged. London: Macmillan & Co., Ltd., 1927.

This missionary's work on the Thonga deals rather sympathetically with religious observances and gives explanations for them in native terms. The worship of ancestors is central, and divination with dice is used to determine the occasions for sacrifice; a great variety of the latter are employed for rain making and growth, purification after death, punishment and reconciliation of enemies, and, combined with magic, medicine.

LANTIS, MARGARET. *Alaskan Eskimo Ceremonialism.* ("Publications of the American Ethnological Society," Vol. XI.) Locust Valley, N.Y.: J. J. Augustin, 1947.

This survey draws together material on ceremonial from the various Eskimo groups of Alaska, pointing out the distribution and variation of ceremonies at life crises, memorial feasts for the dead, secret societies which impersonate devils to frighten the uninitiated, and hunting ritual (the latter most

highly developed). The author attempts a reconstruction of historical relationships on the basis of the distributional data.

LEÓN-PORTILLA, MIGUEL. *Tiempo y Realidad en el Pensamiento Maya: Ensayo de Acercamiento.* ("Instituto de Investigaciones Históricas, Serie de Culturas Mesoamericanas," 2.) Mexico: Universidad Nacional Autónoma de Mexico, 1968.

In this analysis of ancient Maya cosmology and religious symbolism, León-Portilla uses ethnohistoric documents, chronicles, and linguistic and archaeological data to support his basic hypothesis that religious belief and many aspects of cognitive reality for the ancient Maya were a part of an obsessive and all-encompassing vision of temporal cycles. The solar cycles were particularly important in this cosmological system and served to delimit not only temporal, but also spatial, categories. He demonstrates that many of the Mayas' artistic, literary, and intellectual achievements developed as expressions of their concern with the reckoning of time. Professor Alfonso Villa Rojas' appendix to this volume will orient the reader to temporal and spatial aspects of the cosmologies of contemporary Indian groups of Mexico and Guatemala who are descendants of the ancient Maya.

LIENHARDT, GODFREY. *Divinity and Experience: The Religion of the Dinka.* Oxford: Oxford University Press, 1961.

This analysis of the religion of the Dinka, a pastoral people of East Africa, is concerned principally with cosmology rather than ritual. The author discusses the Dinka concept of "Divinity" (connoting formlessness or event rather than the more substantive term "God"), the political and religious ascendance of the clans of spear-masters, and the part played by cattle sacrifices in the ceremonials, which he interprets as being social-symbolic dramas paralleling events, not altering them. Cattle are offered as foils for disaster and as substitutes for men who would otherwise be the victims.

LOWIE, ROBERT H. *The Crow Indians.* New York: Farrar & Rinehart, 1935.

Lowie's insight into Crow culture and his wide knowledge of others give both depth and perspective to this work. He sees the vision quest or guardian-spirit complex as the dominant pattern in Crow relations with the supernatural, and traces this and the idea of "medicine" in a variety of communal ceremonies.

MCILWRAITH, T. F. *The Bella Coola.* 2 vols. Toronto: University of Toronto Press, 1948.

This monograph on a vanishing Northwest Coast society presents a view of the world in which all the forces and beings in nature are conceived as persons. Religious belief and practice are consequently multifaceted and ubiquitous. Inheritance of myths and dances through sibs, shamanism, and a series of origin stories involving the ingenious Raven are features of considerable interest.

MALINOWSKI, BRONISLAW. *Coral Gardens and Their Magic*. 2 vols. London: George Allen & Unwin, Ltd., 1935.

Focusing on agriculture in the Trobriands, Malinowski here enlarges upon his ideas about magic with a coherent and colorful illustration of its nature, its role, and its relationship to technology and practical work. Although there are references to myths which underpin land tenure and the cultivation of gardens, this is primarily a book about practice and not about a system of beliefs.

MEAD, MARGARET. *The Mountain Arapesh*, Vol. II, *Supernaturalism*. ("Anthropological Papers of the American Museum of Natural History," Vol. XXXVII, Part 3, pp. 317–451.) New York, 1940.

In this monograph Mead describes the Arapesh world view, pointing out the absence of cosmology and the recurrence of the basic contrast between the physiological nature of men and women in ideas about human beings, spirits associated with the kin groups, life, and death. She traces this contrast in selected myths and rituals, primarily in rites of passage and harvest ceremonies.

MIDDLETON, JOHN. *Lugbara Religion: Ritual and Authority Among an East African People*. London: Oxford University Press, published for the International African Institute, 1960.

This book is more a sociological analysis of the place of ritual and belief in Lugbara social life than an exposition of their theology. It emphasizes the cult of the dead and its role in the maintenance of lineage authority. Competition for power within the lineage and household is shown to involve manipulation of this cult and, through it, the power of the ancestors.

MORLEY, SYLVANUS G. *The Ancient Maya*. 3d ed., revised by George W. Brainerd. Stanford, Calif.: Stanford University Press, 1956.

Morley draws on a lifetime of work in Maya archaeology and ethnology for this description of the Maya gods and the calendrical ritual directed to them. He traces the development of pantheon, priesthood, and ritual as this can be seen in the archaeological record.

MURPHY, ROBERT F. *Mundurucú Religion*. ("University of California Publications in American Archaeology and Ethnology," Vol. XLIX, No. 1.) Berkeley, 1958.

Murphy examines the transformations which the religion of the Mundurucú, an Indian tribe in Brazil, is undergoing today due to profound changes in their culture and social organization. Until very recently the core of their religious beliefs was the relationship between humans and game animals, now declining due to a different economic orientation. He also emphasizes the continued persistence and importance of sorcery.

NADEL, S. F. *Nupe Religion*. London: Routledge & Kegan Paul, Ltd., 1954.

Nadel's description and discussion of the theology, divination and other rituals, medicine, and witchcraft of this tribe of the Sudan reflects both anthropological sophistication and exhaustive field research. Consideration is given to the borrowing of elements of religion from other tribes and to conversion to Islam, both of which provide insight into the indigenous system.

NIMUENDAJÚ, CURT. *The Eastern Timbira*. Translated by Robert H. Lowie. ("University of California Publications in American Archaeology and Ethnology," Vol. XLI.) Berkeley, 1946.

The chief emphasis in this study of a Brazilian tribe is on ceremonial and its organization. The annual dry-season rites are the initiation of age classes or dances performed by hereditary men's societies. In the rainy season these societies and ceremonial moieties participate in planting, growth, and harvest ritual.

OPLER, MORRIS E. *An Apache Life-Way*. Chicago: The University of Chicago Press, 1941.

Seeking to convey the Apache's view of life in, as nearly as possible, the Apache's own terms, Opler arranges his material on religious beliefs and practices in the order of their introduction in the individual life cycle. To the same end, he makes extensive use of verbatim reports of his informants on ritual (girls' puberty ceremony, shamanistic ceremonies for curing, love, hunting, and war) and cosmology.

ORTIZ, ALFONSO. *The Tewa World: Space, Time, Being, and Becoming in a Pueblo Society*. Chicago: The University of Chicago Press, 1969.

The author, who was born a member of the pueblo studied, describes Tewa mythology, world view, and ritual in relation to the moiety system which divides society, for ceremonial purposes, into "Summer people" and "Winter people." Besides tracing the wide ramifications of the dual mode of classification at both the social and symbolic levels, he determines the mechanisms by which unity is maintained in the face of these divisions.

RADCLIFFE-BROWN, A. R. *The Andaman Islanders*. Cambridge: At the University Press, 1922.

After describing the customs and beliefs of the Andamanese, Radcliffe-Brown proceeds to interpret the ceremonies and some of the myths from the point of view of social anthropology. He suggests that both of these serve to maintain and transmit the sentiments on which the social system depends, and shows how certain features of the marriage, funeral, and puberty rites contribute to this end.

RADIN, PAUL. "The Winnebago Tribe," *37th Annual Report of the Bureau of American Ethnology*, pp. 35–550. Washington, D.C., 1923.

Radin discusses Winnebago religious concepts and describes the four major kinds of ceremony: the clan feast; the rites of four societies of individuals blessed by the same spirit; the Medicine dance, whose membership is voluntary; and the dance following success in war. He provides perspective by a consideration of the introduction of a modern cult, Peyote.

RASMUSSEN, KNUD. *Report of the Fifth Thule Expedition, 1921–24*, Vol. VII, No. 1, *Intellectual Culture of the Iglulik Eskimos*. Copenhagen: Gyldendalske Boghandel, Nordisk Forlag, 1929.

Rasmussen prefaces his work with a group of Eskimo autobiographies which bring out the difficulties of life in the far north. He proceeds, with the aid of myths and first-person statements from articulate informants, to show how the Eskimo views this life. Shamanism, amulets, and magic words as means of reducing the uncertainties of existence are described.

REDFIELD, ROBERT. *Tepoztlan: A Mexican Village*. Chicago: The University of Chicago Press, 1930.

With characteristic and appealing simplicity Redfield describes the fusion of Spanish and Aztec elements which constitutes the religion of these Mexican peasants. He follows the yearly round of *fiestas* and discusses the concepts of *santo* (saint) and *veterano* (military hero) as foci of the sentiments of the community.

REDFIELD, ROBERT, and VILLA ROJAS, ALFONSO. *Chan Kom: A Maya Village*. ("Carnegie Institution of Washington Publications," No. 448.) Washington, D.C., 1934.

In this Maya village the authors find two separate complexes of sacred ritual, each with its own practitioners and general sphere of operations. One uses prayers from the Catholic liturgy recited by professional *cantores*; this complex is usually chosen for baptism, marriage, and death. The other uses Maya priests and prayers to the spirits of the milpa, the village, and the rain, and is used for agriculture and illness.

REICHEL-DOLMATOFF, GERARDO. *Amazonian Cosmos; The Sexual and Religious Symbolism of the Tukano Indians*. Chicago: The University of Chicago Press, 1971.

Based upon sustained work with one informant who had left his tribe and was living in Bogotá, this recent volume provides an astonishingly intricate view of the cosmology and ceremonies of the Tukano Indians who live in Northwest Amazonia. The work contains data on the tribal creation myth, the cosmological beliefs, and the ceremonies which focus upon sexual symbolism and the intimate interrelationships between men and the natural world.

REINA, RUBEN E. *The Law of the Saints: A Pokomam Pueblo and Its Community Culture*. Indianapolis and New York: The Bobbs-Merrill Co., Inc., 1966.

Reina presents a thorough ethnography of Chinautla—a colorful Guatemalan community of modern Maya Indians, Spanish-speaking Ladinos and Mengalas, those of Spanish descent who have assumed the Indian life style. He integrates his description with the abstract concept of the "Law of the Saints," which is a kind of ideal model for the

customary, the good, and the desirable. Formally responsible for maintaining the community's adherence to ideal behavior are the members of the religious *cofradias*, the organizations in charge of the pueblo's fiestas and religious celebrations.

RIVERS, W. H. R. *The Todas*. London: Macmillan & Co., Ltd., 1906.

The core of the religious life of this people of India's Nilgiri hills is the care of the sacred water buffaloes. This work is done in village dairies, graded by degree of sanctity, by an ordained priesthood; the elaborateness of ritual and the personal requirements of the priests vary accordingly. Religious practices of the common people include rites of passage and the observance of taboos on periodic sacred days.

ROSCOE, JOHN. *The Bakitara*. Cambridge: At the University Press, 1923.

A major focus of this monograph from East Africa is the ritual surrounding the king, described as both "the great high priest of the nation" and "almost a deity himself." Supplementing the king were rain makers, diviners of many kinds, and priests devoted to each of the nineteen gods concerned with cattle raising.

SCHÄRER, HANS. *Ngaju Religion: The Conception of God Among a South Borneo People*. The Hague: Martinus Nijhoff, 1963.

The Ngaju cosmology is seen as expressing unity, at all levels, as the union of opposites, the divisions of the world created by a pervasive dualistic principle of classification. God, an ambivalent and bisexual deity, combines in himself the Hornbill and Watersnake (lesser deities), upperworld and underworld, man and woman, sun and moon, good and evil, life and death, hornbill and watersnake ceremonial moieties, etc. The basic social norms, *hadat*, are rooted in this divine order; thus transgressions of custom invite natural disaster.

SELIGMAN, C. G., and SELIGMAN, BRENDA Z. *The Veddas*. Cambridge: At the University Press, 1911.

The Seligmans present a detailed account of the culture and religions of the Veddas of Ceylon, who for many years served as a sort of stockpile of a "primitive people." Their religion centers around the ancestral spirits, who enter into the bodies of shamans or other persons in order to communicate with their descendants. Strikingly, belief in magic and sorcery appear to be lacking here.

SHIROKOGOROFF, S. M. *The Psychomental Complex of the Tungus*. London: Kegan Paul, 1935.

This monograph gives systematic treatment to the beliefs of a Siberian people in spirits residing in nature and in the dead and to the methods (most of them individual) of managing these spirits. Particular attention is given to shamanism—the rituals and paraphernalia, the psychological aspects of both performance and belief, the social position of the shaman, and the possible sources of the complex.

SPECK, FRANK G. *Naskapi*. Norman: University of Oklahoma Press, 1935.

This work on the religion of the hunting bands of Labrador stresses the individual nature of religious observance and links it with dispersed nomadic settlement; aside from feasts in celebration of hunting success, no religious assembly is known. The author discusses the spiritual guide and the ritual of hunting in which this spirit is invoked by sweat baths, songs, drumming, and divination.

SPENCER, BALDWIN, and GILLEN, F. J. *The Arunta*. 2 vols. London: Macmillan & Co., Ltd., 1927.

A major part of this monograph is concerned with totemism—the relationship between the individual and his totem and the associated *churinga* (sacred object); the traditions, in which totemic ancestors and local topography are linked; and the various rituals whereby the totem animal or plant is increased and the young are initiated into the secrets of the sacred.

STANNER, W. E. H. *On Aboriginal Religion*. ("Oceania Monographs," No. 11.) Sydney, 1963.

This is a masterful and unique effort to examine Australian religion, with the author endeavoring to study it in itself and not as a mirror of something else.

TITIEV, MISCHA. *Old Oraibi*. ("Papers of the Peabody Museum of American Archaeology and Ethnology," Vol. XXI, No. 1.) Cambridge, Mass., 1944.

Titiev describes Hopi ceremonialism in all its complexity and interprets the various rituals in terms of the basic concepts of continuity of life after death and the duality of the year. The colourful Katcina Cult, centering around the impersonation of the dead, displays these concepts as fundamentals, while other rituals, performed by secret societies, share them to some extent.

TOBING, PHILLIP ODER LUMBAN. *The Structure of the Toba-Batak Belief in the High God*. Amsterdam: Jacob van Campen, 1956.

The author, himself a Toba-Batak, presents the total cosmology of the Toba-Batak as a manifestation of their high god whose primary embodiment is the tree of life, a giant banyan tree whose branches form the upperworld, whose trunk is the middle-world of everyday life, and whose roots are the underworld where the yearly circling of a *naga* (dragon) around the cardinal points expresses the unity of time and space. This basic conception pervades Toba-Batak life, being symbolized in microcosm in the village, house, ritual space, and even the groups in the marriage exchange.

TSCHOPIK, HARRY, JR. *The Aymara of Chucuito, Peru*. I. *Magic* ("Anthropological Papers of the American Museum of Natural History," Vol. XLIV, Part 2, pp. 137–308.) New York, 1951.

The aim of this monograph is to suggest a relationship between a highly specialized system of magic (described in detail) and certain salient features of Aymara personality. The author suggests that the specialization of practitioners (six kinds, distinguished by the problems each handles), the proliferation of specific rites, and the private nature of most magic are compatible with the characteristic ways of expressing anxiety and hostility.

TURNER, VICTOR W. *Chihamba, the White Spirit: A Ritual Drama of the Ndembu*. Manchester: Manchester University Press, for the Rhodes-Livingstone Institute, 1962.

In this monograph Turner describes in detail the Chihamba ritual of the Ndembu of Zambia, which is designed to overcome attacks by an ancestress and a nature spirit, and he includes the native explanation of each step. This is followed by a discussion of symbolism in general and a comparative analysis of "white" color symbolism around the world.

TURNER, VICTOR W. *The Forest of Symbols: Aspects of Ndembu Ritual*. Ithaca: Cornell University Press, 1967.

This book is a collection of essays, both theoretical and descriptive, on the ritual system of the Ndembu of Zambia. The author analyzes the rites as systems of symbols whose meanings are revealed through native exegesis, their use in the ceremonies, and their relations within the ritual setting. Certain basic themes, such as the rivalry between male and female and the importance of red, white, and black as life forces, are revealed even in dissimilar rites.

TURNER, VICTOR W. *The Drums of Affliction: A Study of Religious Processes among the Ndembu of Zambia*. Oxford: Oxford University Press, 1968.

This more recent volume of Victor Turner's is not only important theoretically, but also contains additional detailed ethnographic descriptions and analyses of the meaning of symbolism in the rituals of affliction of the Ndembu. The volume includes a discussion of divination and of the rituals as social dramas in full cultural context.

UNDERHILL, RUTH. *Papago Indian Religion*. New York: Columbia University Press, 1946.

The author approaches the description of Papago ceremonies from the point of view of the contrast between two coexistent methods of contact with the supernatural—the communal and the individual. Whether of rain-making ceremony or guardian-spirit quest, the descriptions are well written and enhanced by the inclusion of poetic songs and texts.

VAILLANT, GEORGE C. *Aztecs of Mexico*. Garden City, N.Y.: Doubleday & Co., 1941.

On the basis of Conquest documents, Vaillant constructs a brief but vivid and discerning picture of Aztec religion. He describes some of the hierarchy of gods who gave their names to the days of the ritual year, and demonstrates with clarity how this ritual calendar set the times for ceremonies—often human sacrifices—performed by the priesthood, itself a hierarchy.

VOGT, EVON Z. *Zinacantan: A Maya Community in the Highlands of Chiapas.* Cambridge: Harvard University Press, 1969.

This ethnography on a contemporary Tzotzil-speaking tribe in southern Mexico provides data on the economic system and social structure followed by a full-length description of the religious system, including chapters on myths, ritual symbols, cosmological beliefs, shamanism, and the complex ceremonies of the cargo system attached to the cult of the saints. Not only is the syncretism between Maya and Catholic elements examined, but the monograph also suggests how contemporary Maya data may illuminate the social structure and religion of the ancient Maya as well as provide some general insights as to how the tribal society copes with the modern world that is just now reaching into the remote highlands of Chiapas.

WARNER, W. LLOYD. *A Black Civilization: A Social Study of an Australian Tribe.* Rev. ed. New York: Harper & Row, Publishers, Inc., 1958.

Totemism among the Murngin of Australia and its elaborate, myth-dramatizing ritual are carefully described and sociologically interpreted in this work. In addition, the role of magicians ("black" ones to cause illness and "white" ones to cure it) is examined, with special reference to arrangements in a northern subgroup which lacks this means of dealing with disease.

REFERENCES CITED

ABERLE, DAVID. "A Note on Relative Deprivation Theory as Applied to Millenarian and Other Cult Movements," in Sylvia L. Thrupp (ed.), *Millenial Dreams in Action*. ("Comparative Studies in Society and History," Supplement 2.) The Hague, 1962.

ABERLE, DAVID. *The Peyote Religion Among the Navaho*. Chicago: Aldine Publishing Co., 1965.

ABRAHAM, KARL. "Selected Papers on Psycho-analysis." *The International Psycho-Analytical Library*, No. 13. London: Hogarth Press, 1948.

BANTON, MICHAEL (ed.). *Anthropological Approaches to the Study of Religion*. ("Association of Social Anthropologists Monographs," No. 3.) London: Tavistock Publications, 1965; New York: Frederick A. Praeger, Inc. 1966.

BARBER, BERNARD. "Acculturation and Messianic Movements," *American Sociological Review*, VI (1941), 663–669.

BARNOUW, VICTOR. "A Psychological Interpretation of a Chippewa Origin Legend," *Journal of American Folklore*, LXVIII (1955), 73–85, 211–223, 341–355.

BASCOM, WILLIAM R. "The Sanctions of Ifa Divination," *Journal of the Royal Anthropological Institute*, LXXI (1941), 43–54.

BASCOM, WILLIAM R. "Folklore and Anthropology," *Journal of American Folklore*, LXVI (1953), 283–290.

BASCOM, WILLIAM R. "The Myth-Ritual Theory," *Journal of American Folklore*, LXX (1957), 103–114.

BEAUCLAIR, INEZ DE. "Black Magic on Ifaluk," *American Anthropologist*, LXV (1963), 388–389.

BEIDELMAN, T. O. "Right and Left Hand Among the Kaguru: A Note on Symbolic Classification," *Africa*, XXXI (1961), 250–257.

BEIDELMAN, T. O. "Kaguru Omens: An East African People's Concepts of the Unusual, Unnatural and Supernatural," *Anthropological Quarterly*, XXXVI (1963), 43–59.

BEIDELMAN, T. O. "Pig (Guluwe): An Essay on Ngulu Sexual Symbolism and Ceremony," *Southwestern Journal of Anthropology*, XX (1964), 359–392.

BEIDELMAN, T. O. "Swazi Royal Ritual," *Africa*, XXXVI (1966), 373–405.

BEIDELMAN, T. O. "Utani: Some Kaguru Notions of Death, Sexuality and Affinity," *Southwestern Journal of Anthropology*, XXII (1966), 354–380.

BELLAH, ROBERT N. *Tokugawa Religion: The Values of Pre-Industrial Japan*. New York: The Free Press, 1957.

BELLAH, ROBERT N. "Religious Evolution," *American Sociological Review*, XXIX (1964), 358–374.

BELSHAW, CYRIL S. "The Significance of Modern Cults in Melanesian Development," *The Australian Outlook*, IV (1950), 116–125.

BENEDICT, RUTH. *Zuni Mythology*. ("Columbia University Contributions to Anthropology," No. 21.) New York, 1935.

BERKELEY-HILL, OWEN. "The Anal-Erotic Factor in the Religion, Philosophy, and Character of the Hindus," *International Journal of Psycho-analysis* II (1921), 306–338.

BETTELHEIM, BRUNO. "Individual and Mass Behavior in Extreme Situations," in T. M. Newcomb *et al.* (eds.), *Readings in Social Psychology*. New York, Holt, Rinehart & Winston, Inc., 1947.

BETTELHEIM, BRUNO. *Symbolic Wounds, Puberty Rites and the Envious Male*. New York: The Free Press, 1954.

BOAS, FRANZ. "Indianische sagen von der nord-pacifischen küste Amerikas." Berlin: A. Asher & Co., 1895.

BOAS, FRANZ. *Kwakiutl Tales*. ("Columbia University Contributions to Anthropology," No. 2.) New York, 1910.

BOAS, FRANZ. "The Origin of Totemism," *Journal of American Folklore*, XXIII (1910), 392–393.

BOAS, FRANZ. "Psychological Problems in Anthropology," *American Journal of Psychology*, XXI (1910), 371–384.

BOAS, FRANZ. "Kwakiutl Culture as Reflected in Mythology," *Memoirs of the American Folklore Society*, No. 28. 1935.

BOEHM, FELIX. "The Femininity-Complex in Men," *International Journal of Psycho-analysis*, XI (1930), 444–469.

BOGORAS, WALDEMAR. *The Chukchee*, Vol. VII of Franz Boas (ed.), *The Jesup North Pacific Expedition*. ("Memoirs of the American Museum of Natural History," Vol. XI, Parts 2 and 3.) Leiden: E. J. Brill, 1904–1909.

BOGORAS, WALDEMAR. *Chuckchee Mythology*. ("Jesup North Pacific Expedition," Publication 8.) "Memoirs of the American Museum of Natural History," Vol. XII. Leiden, 1910.

BOURKE, JOHN G. *Scatalogic Rites of All Nations*. Washington, D.C.: W. H. Lowerdermilk & Co., 1891.

BROWN, J. "A Cross Cultural Study of Female Initiation Rites," *American Anthropologist*, LXV (1963), 837–855.

BRYANT, A. T. *The Zulu People*. Pietermaritzburg: Shuter and Shooter, 1949.

BÜCHER, A. *Arbeit und Rhythmus*. 2d ed. Leipzig, 1899.

BUNZEL, RUTH L. "Introduction to Zuni Ceremonialism," *47th Annual Report of the Bureau of American Ethnology*, pp. 467–545. Washington, D.C., 1932.

BUNZEL RUTH L. "Zuni Katcinas," *47th Annual Report of the Bureau of American Ethnology*, pp. 837–1086. Washington, D.C., 1932.

BUNZEL RUTH L. *Chichicastenango: A Guatemalan Village*. ("Publications of the American Ethnological Society," Vol. XXII.) Locust Valley, N.Y.: J. J. Augustin, 1952.

BURRIDGE, K. O. L. "Lévi-Strauss and Myth," in E. R. Leach (ed.), *The Structural Study of Myth and Totemism*. ("Association of Social Anthropologists Monographs," No. 5.) London: Tavistock Publications, 1967.

CAMPBELL, JOSEPH. *The Hero with a Thousand Faces*. New York: Meridian, 1956.

CANCIAN, FRANK. "Some Aspects of the Social and Religious Organization of a Maya Society," *XXXV Congreso Internacional de Americanistas, Actas y Memorias*, I (1962), 336–343.

CANCIAN, FRANK. *Economics and Prestige in a Maya Community: The Religious Cargo System in Zinacantan*. Stanford, Calif.: Stanford University Press, 1965.

CANNON, WALTER B. *The Wisdom of the Body*. (1932). Paperback edition, New York: W. W. Norton & Co., 1963.

CANNON, WALTER B. "'Voodoo' Death," *American Anthropologist*, XVIV (1942), 169–181.

CARROLL, JOHN B. *Language, Thought, and Reality: Selected Writings of Benjamin Lee Whorf*. Cambridge, Mass.: The M.I.T. Press; and New York: John Wiley & Sons, 1956.

CAWTE, J. E. "Further Comment on the Australian Subincision Ceremony" (letter to the editor), *American Anthropologist*, LXX (1968), 961–964.

CHAMBERLAIN, ALEXANDER F. "American Bells," *Encyclopedia of Religious Ethics*, VI (1913), 316–318.

CICERO, M. TULLIUS. *De Legibus*. Edited by Georges de Plinval. Paris: Les Belles lettres, 1959.

COHEN, PERCY. "Theories of Myth," *Man*, IV (1969), No. 3, 337–353.

COLSON, ELIZABETH. "Ancestral Spirits and Social Structure Among the Plateau Tonga," *International Archives of Ethnography*, XLVII, Part 1 (1954), 21–68.

COMTE, AUGUSTE. *Cours de philosophie positive*. Paris: Borrani et Droz, 1835–1852.

CORY, H. "Gogo Law and Custom." Dar es Salaam, 1951.

COUNT, EARL W. "The Earth-Diver and the Rival Twins: A Clue to Time Correlation in North-Eurasiatic and North American Mythology," in Sol Tax (ed.), *Indian Tribes of Aboriginal America*. Selected Papers of the 19th International Congress of Americanists. Chicago: The University of Chicago Press, 1952.

CRAWLEY, A. E. "Drums and Cymbals," *Encyclopedia of Religious Ethics*, V (1912), 89–94.

CRAWLEY, A. E. *Dress, Drinks and Drums: Further Studies of Savages and Sex*. Edited by T. Besterman. London: Methuen & Co., Ltd., 1931.

CUNNINGHAM, CLARK E. "Order in the Atoni House," *Bijdragen tot de Taal-, Land- en Volkenkunde*, Deel 120, 1e Aflevering (1964), 34–68.

DEVEREUX, GEORGE. "Cultural and Characterological Traits of the Mohave Related to the Anal Stage of Psychosexual Development," *Psychoanalytic Quarterly*, XX (1951), 398–422.

DE WAAL MALEFIJT, ANNEMARIE. *Religion and Culture: An Introduction to Anthropology of Religion*. New York: The Macmillan Company, 1968.

DORSON, RICHARD. "The Eclipse of Solar Mythology," *Journal of American Folklore*, LXVIII (1955), 393–416. Reprinted in Alan Dundes (ed.), *The Study of Folklore*. Englewood Cliffs, N.J.: Prentice-Hall, Inc., 1965.

DOUGLAS, MARY. *Purity and Danger*. London: Routledge & Kegan Paul, Ltd., 1966.

DOUGLAS, MARY. "The Meaning of Myth," in E. R. Leach (ed.), *The Structural Study of Myth and Totemism*. ("Association of Social Anthropologists Monographs," No. 5.) London: Tavistock Publications, 1967.

DOUGLAS, MARY. "Pollution," *Encyclopedia of the Social Sciences*, XII (1968), 336–341

DRAGOMANOV, MIXAILO PETROVIC. "Notes on the Slavic Religio-Ethical Legends: The Dualistic Creation of the World," *Russian and East European Series*, XXIII (1961). Bloomington: Indiana University Publications.

DUMONT, LOUIS. *Une Sous-Caste de l'Inde du Sud.* Paris–The Hague: Mouton & Co., 1957.

DUMONT, LOUIS. "A Structural Definition of a Folk Deity of Tamil Nad: Aiyanar, the Lord," in *Religion, Politics and History in India*, Collected Papers in Indian Sociology, Sec. 2. Paris–The Hague: Mouton & Co., 1970.

DUNDES, ALAN. "Earth-Diver: Creation of the Mythopoeic Male," *American Anthropologist*, LXIV (1962), 1032–1051.

DUNDES, ALAN. "From Etic to Emic Units in the Structural Study of Folktales," *Journal of American Folklore*, LXXV (1963), 95–105.

DUNDES, ALAN (ed.) *The Study of Folklore.* Englewood Cliffs, N.J.: Prentice-Hall, Inc., 1965.

DURKHEIM, ÉMILE. *The Elementary Forms of the Religious Life.* Translated from the French by Joseph Ward Swain. London: George Allen & Unwin, Ltd., 1915. Paperback edition, New York: The Free Press, 1954.

DURKHEIM, ÉMILE. *Les Règles de la Méthode Sociologique.* Paris: Presses Universitaires de France, 1967.

DURKHEIM, ÉMILE, and MAUSS, MARCEL. *Primitive Classification.* Translated by Rodney Needham. London: Cohen & West, Ltd.; Chicago: University of Chicago Press, 1963.

DWORAKOWSKA, M. "The Origin of Bell and Drum," *Pr. Etnol. Warsaw 5.* Warsaw: Nakladem Towarzystwa Nankowego Warszawskiego, 1938.

EARLY, JOHN D. *The Sons of San Lorenzo in Zinacantan.* Ph.D. dissertation, Harvard University, 1965.

EARLY, JOHN D. "El Ritual Zinacanteco en Honor del Señor Esquipulas," in Evon Z. Vogt (ed.), *Los Zinacantecos: Un Pueblo de los Altos de Chiapas.* Mexico, D. F.: Instituto Nacional Indigenista, 1966, pp. 337–354.

EGGAN, FRED. "Social Anthropology and the Method of Controlled Comparison," *American Anthropologist*, LVI (1954), 743–763.

EISLER, MICHAEL JOSEPH. "A Man's Unconscious Phantasy of Pregnancy in the Guise of Traumatic Hysteria: A Clinical Contribution to Anal Erotism," *International Journal of Psychoanalysis*, II (1921), 255–286.

ELIADE, MIRCEA. *The Sacred and the Profane: The Nature of Religion.* New York: Harcourt Brace Jovanovich, 1959. [German edition, 1957.] Paperback edition, New York: Harper & Row, Publishers, Inc., 1961.

ELIADE, MIRCEA. *Shamanism: Archaic Techniques of Ecstasy.* Rev. ed. Translated by W. T. Trask. (Bollingen Series 76.) New York: Pantheon Books, Inc., 1964.

ELWIN, VERRIER. *Myths of Middle India.* Madras: Oxford University Press, 1949.

ELWIN, VERRIER. *Tribal Myths of Orissa.* Bombay: Oxford University Press, 1954.

ELWIN, VERRIER. *The Religion of an Indian Tribe.* London: Geoffrey Cumberlege, 1955.

EVANS-PRITCHARD, E. E. *Witchcraft, Oracles and Magic Among the Azande.* Oxford: Clarendon Press, 1937.

EVANS-PRITCHARD, E. E. *Nuer Religion.* Oxford: Clarendon Press, 1956.

EVANS-PRITCHARD, E. E. "Religion," in E. E. Evans-Pritchard *et al.*, *The Institutions of Primitive Society.* Oxford: Basil Blackwell, 1956.

FERENCZI, SANDOR. "Further Contributions to the Theory and Technique of Psycho-analysis," *The International Psycho-analytical Library*, No. 11. London: Hogarth Press, 1950.

FERENCZI, SANDOR. *Sex in Psycho-analysis.* New York: Dover Publications, Inc., 1956.

FESTINGER, LEON. *A Theory of Cognitive Dissonance.* New York: Harper & Row, Publishers, Inc., 1957.

FIRTH, RAYMOND. *The Work of the Gods in Tikopia.* ("London School of Economics and Political Science Monographs on Social Anthropology," Nos. 1 and 2.) London: Percy Lund, Humphries & Co., 1940.

FIRTH, RAYMOND. *Elements of Social Organization.* London: Watts & Co., 1951.

FIRTH, RAYMOND (ed.). *Man and Culture: An Evaluation of the Work of Bronislaw Malinowski.* London: Routledge & Kegan Paul, Ltd., 1957.

FIRTH, RAYMOND. *History and Traditions of Tikopia.* ("The Polynesian Society," Memoir No. 33.) Wellington, New Zealand, 1961.

FIRTH, RAYMOND. "Offering and Sacrifice: Prob¹ of Organization," *Journal of the Royal Anthro pological Institute*, XCIII (1963), 12–24

FISCHER, J. L. "The Sociopsychological Analysis of Folktales," *Current Anthropology*, IV (1963), 235–295.

FORTES, MEYER. "Totem and Taboo," in *Proceedings of the Royal Anthropological Institute* (1966), pp. 5–22

FRAKE, CHARLES O. "The Diagnosis of Disease Among the Subanun of Mindanao," *American Anthropologist*, LXIII (1961), 113–132.

FRAKE, CHARLES O. "A Structural Description of Subanun 'Religious Behavior,'" in W. H. Goodenough (ed.), *Explorations in Honor of George Peter Murdock.* New York: McGraw-Hill Book Co., 1964.

FRAZER, JAMES G. *Psyche's Task: A Discourse Concerning the Influence of Superstition on the Growth of Institutions.* London: Macmillan & Co., Ltd., 1909.

FRAZER, JAMES G. *The Golden Bough: A Study in Magic and Religion.* 12 vols. 3d ed., revised and enlarged. London: Macmillan & Co., Ltd., 1911–1915. Abridged edition, 1922; reprinted New York: St. Martins Press, Inc., 1955.

FRAZER, JAMES G. *Sir Roger de Coverley, and Other Literary Pieces*. London: Macmillan & Co., Ltd., 1920.

FRAZER, JAMES G. *The Fear of the Dead in Primitive Religion*. 3 vols. London: Macmillan & Co., Ltd., 1933–1936.

FRAZER, JAMES G. *Creation and Evolution in Primitive Cosmogonies*. London: Macmillan & Co., Ltd., 1935.

FREEDMAN, MAURICE. *Rites and Duties, or: Chinese Marriage* London: G. Bell & Sons, Ltd., 1967.

FRENKEL-BRUNSWIK, ELSE. "Intolerance of Ambiguity as an Emotional and Perceptual Personality Variable," *Journal of Personality*, XVIII (1949), 108–143.

FREUD, SIGMUND. *Totem and Taboo: Resemblances Between the Psychic Life of Savages and Neurotics*. Authorized English translation, with Introduction, by A. A. Brill. New York: Moffat Yard & Co., 1918. Paperback edition, New York: Vintage Books, 1952.

FREUD, SIGMUND. *The Basic Writings of Sigmund Freud*. New York: Modern Library, 1938.

FREUD, SIGMUND. "Obsessive Acts and Religious Practices," *Collected Papers*, Vol. II. Translated by Joan Rivière. 5 vols. London: Hogarth Press and the Institute of Psycho-Analysis, 1948–1950.

FREUD, SIGMUND. *A General Introduction to Psycho-Analysis*. New York: Permabooks, 1953.

FREUD, SIGMUND, and OPPENHEIM, D. E. *Dreams in Folklore*. New York: International Universities Press, 1958.

FROMM, ERICH. *Escape from Freedom*. New York: Rinehart & Co., 1941.

FROMM, ERICH. *The Forgotten Language*. New York: Grove Press, 1951.

FUNG, YU-LAN. *A History of Chinese Philosophy*. Translated by Derk Bodde. Peiping: H. Vetch, 1937.

FUSTEL DE COULANGES, N. D. *La Cité antique*. Paris: Durand, 1864. [Also published in English translation as *The Ancient City*, various editions, including paperback by Doubleday & Co., 1963.]

GEERTZ, CLIFFORD. "Ritual and Social Change: A Javanese Example," *American Anthropologist*, LIX (1957), 32–54.

GEERTZ, CLIFFORD. *The Religion of Java*. New York: The Free Press, 1960.

GEERTZ, CLIFFORD. "Religion as a Cultural System," in Michael Banton (ed.), *Anthropological Approaches to the Study of Religion*. ("Association of Social Anthropologists Monographs," No. 3.) London: Tavistock Publications, 1965; New York: Frederick A. Praeger, Inc., 1966.

GENNEP, ARNOLD L. VAN. "Essai d'une théorie des langues spéciales," *Rev. Étud. Ethnogr. Sociol.*, I (1908), 276–277.

GENNEP, ARNOLD L. VAN. *The Rites of Passage*. London: Routledge and Kegan Paul, Ltd.; Chicago: The University of Chicago Press, 1960. [French edition, *Les Rites de Passage*. Paris: E. Nourry, 1909.]

GEORGES, ROBERT (ed.). *Studies on Mythology*. Homewood, Ill.: The Dorsey Press, 1968.

GINZBERG, LOUIS. *The Legends of the Jews*, I. Philadelphia: Jewish Publication Society of America, 1925.

GLUCKMAN, MAX. *Rituals of Rebellion in South-East Africa*. Manchester: Manchester University Press, 1954.

GOLDENWEISER, ALEXANDER A. "Totemism: An Analytical Study," *Journal of American Folklore*, XXIII (1910), 179–293.

GOLDENWEISER, ALEXANDER A. "Religion and Society: A Critique of Émile Durkheim's Theory of the Origin and Nature of Religion," *The Journal of Philosophy, Psychology, and Scientific Methods*, XIV (1917), 113–124.

GOLDENWEISER, ALEXANDER A. "Totemism. An Essay on Religion and Society," in V. F. Calverton (ed.), *The Making of Man: An Outline of Anthropology*. New York: Modern Library, 1931.

GOODE, WILLIAM J. *Religion Among the Primitives*. New York: The Free Press, 1951.

GOODY, JACK. "Religion and Ritual: The Definitional Problem," *British Journal of Sociology*, XII (1961), 142–164.

GOSSEN, GARY H. *Time and Space in Chamula Oral Tradition*. Ph.D. dissertation, Department of Anthropology, Harvard University, 1970.

GREY, GEORGE. *Polynesian Mythology and Ancient Traditional History of the New Zealand Race*. London: John Murray, 1855.

GUIRAND, FELIX. "Assyro-Babylonian Mythology," in *Larousse Encyclopedia of Mythology*. New York: Prometheus Press, 1959.

HALLOWELL, A. IRVING. "Freudian Symbolism in the Dream of a Salteaux Indian," *Man*, XXXVIII (1938), 47–48.

HALLOWELL, A. IRVING. "Myth, Culture and Personality," *American Anthropologist*, XLIX (1947), 544–556.

HALLOWELL, A. IRVING. *Culture and Experience*. Philadelphia: University of Pennsylvania Press, 1955.

HARRIES, L. "The Initiation Rites of the Makonde Tribe." ("Rhodes-Livingstone Communications," No. 3.). Lusaka, 1944.

HARRISON, JANE. *Prolegomena to the Study of Greek Religion*. London: Cambridge University Press, 1903.

HARRISON, JANE. *Themis: A Study of the Social Origins of Greek Religion*. Cambridge: At the University Press, 1912.

HAYES, E. NELSON, and HAYES, TANYA (eds.). *Claude Lévi-Strauss: The Anthropologist as Hero*. Cambridge, Mass., and London: The M.I.T. Press, 1970.

HEBB, DONALD O. *The Organization of Behavior: A Neuro-Psychological Theory*. New York: John Wiley & Sons, Inc., 1949.

HEBB, DONALD O. *A Textbook of Psychology*. Philadelphia: W. B. Saunders Co., 1958.

HERTZ, R. *Death and the Right Hand.* Translated by Rodney and Claudia Needham. London: Cohen & West, Ltd.; New York: The Free Press, 1960. (First published in 1909.)

HILL, W. W. "The Navaho Indians and the Ghost Dance of 1890," *American Anthropologist,* XLVI (1944), 523–527.

HOAGLAND, HUDSON. "Some Comments on Science and Faith," in "Conference on Science, Philosophy, and Religion." New York, 1941. (Mimeographed.)

HOCART, A. M. *Kings and Councillors.* Cairo: Egyptian University, Faculty of Arts, 1936.

HOCART, A. M. *The Life-Giving Myth.* London: Methuen & Co., Ltd., 1952.

HOCART, A. M. *Social Origins.* London: Methuen & Co., Ltd., 1954.

HOMANS, GEORGE C. "Anxiety and Ritual: The Theories of Malinowski and Radcliffe-Brown," *American Anthropologist,* XLIII (1941), 164–172.

HORTON, ROBIN. "A Definition of Religion, and Its Uses," *Journal of the Royal Anthropological Institute,* XC (1960), 201–226.

HORTON, ROBIN. "The Kalabari World View: An Outline and Interpretation," *Africa,* XXXII (1962), No. 3, 197–220.

HORTON, ROBIN. "Ritual Man in Africa," *Africa,* XXXIV (1964), No. 2, 85–104.

HOWELLS, W. W. *The Heathens: Primitive Man and His Religions.* Garden City, N.Y.: Doubleday & Co., 1948. Paperback edition, New York: Natural History Press.

HUBERT, HENRI, and MAUSS, MARCEL. *Sacrifice: Its Nature and Function.* Translated by W. D. Halls. Chicago: University of Chicago Press, 1964.

HUCKEL, HELEN. "Vicarious Creativity," *Psychoanalysis,* II (1953), 44–50.

HUME, DAVID. *Four Dissertations. I, The Natural History of Religion. . . .* London: A. Millar, 1757.

HUXLEY, ALDOUS. *Doors to Perception.* New York: Harper & Row, Publishers, Inc., 1954.

HUXLEY, FRANCIS. "Anthropology and ESP," in J. R. Smythies (ed.), *Science and ESP.* London: Routledge & Kegan Paul, Ltd., 1967.

HYMAN, STANLEY EDGAR. "The Ritual View of Myth and the Mythic," *Journal of American Folklore,* LXVIII (1955), 462–472.

JAKOBSON, ROMAN, and HALLE, MORRIS. *Fundamentals of Language.* The Hague: Mouton & Co., 1956.

JAMES, E. O. *Comparative Religion: An Introductory and Historical Study.* London: Methuen & Co., Ltd., 1938.

JAMES, WILLIAM. *Principles of Psychology.* Vol. I. New York: H. Holt, 1918.

JONES, ERNEST. "Essays in Applied Psycho-analysis, II." *The International Psycho-analytical Library,* No. 41. London: Hogarth Press, 1951.

JONES, ERNEST. "How to Tell Your Friends from Geniuses," *Saturday Review,* XL (August 10, 1957), 9–10, 39–40.

JUNG, CARL GUSTAV. *Psychology of the Unconscious.* New York: Moffat Yard & Co., 1916.

KANT, IMMANUEL. *Kritik der reunen Vernunft.* 2d ed. Riga, 1787.

KARDINER, ABRAM. *The Individual and His Society.* New York: Columbia University Press, 1939.

KARDINER, ABRAM. *The Psychological Frontiers of Society.* New York: Columbia University Press, 1945.

KIELL, NORMAN (ed.). *Psychoanalysis, Psychology and Literature.* Madison: University of Wisconsin Press, 1963.

KITAGAWA, JOSEPH M. "The Nature and Program of the History of Religions Field," *Divinity School News* (November, 1957), 13–25.

KLUCKHOHN, CLYDE. "Myths and Rituals: A General Theory," *Harvard Theological Review,* XXXV (January, 1942), 45–79.

KLUCKHOHN, CLYDE. *Navaho Witchcraft.* ("Peabody Museum Papers," No. 22.) Cambridge, Mass., 1944.

KLUCKHOHN, CLYDE. "Universal Categories of Culture," in *Anthropology Today: An Encyclopedic Inventory,* prepared under the chairmanship of A. L. Kroeber. Chicago: The University of Chicago Press, 1953.

KLUCKHOHN, CLYDE. "Recurrent Themes in Myths and Mythmaking," *Proceedings of the American Academy of Arts and Sciences,* LXXXVIII (1959), 268–279.

KÖNGAS, ELLI KAIJA. "The Earth-Diver," *Ethnohistory,* VII (1960), 151–180.

KROEBER, ALFRED L. "Totem and Taboo: An Ethnologic Psychoanalysis," *American Anthropologist,* XXII (1920), 48–55.

KROEBER, ALFRED L. "Totem and Taboo in Retrospect," *American Journal of Sociology,* XLV (1939), 446–451.

KROEBER, ALFRED L. *Anthropology.* New ed., revised. New York: Harcourt, Brace & World, 1948.

KROEBER, ALFRED L. *The Nature of Culture.* Chicago: The University of Chicago Press, 1952.

KUPER, HILDA. *An African Aristocracy.* London: Oxford University Press, for the International African Institute, 1947.

LA BARRE, WESTON. *The Peyote Cult.* ("Yale University Publications in Anthropology," No. 13.) New Haven, Conn., 1938.

LANG, ANDREW. *The Making of Religion.* London: Longmans, Green & Co., 1898.

LANG, ANDREW. *Myth, Ritual and Religion.* Vol. I. London: Longmans, Green & Co., 1899.

LANGER, SUZANNE K. *Feeling and Form: A Theory of Art.* New York: Charles Scribner's Sons, 1953.

LAROMIGUIÈRE, P. *Leçons de philosophie sur les principes de l'intelligence, ou sur les causes et su les origines des idées.* 4th ed. 3 vols. Paris Brunot-Labbe, 1826.

LEACH, E. R. "Magical Hair," *Journal of the Roya Anthropological Institute (Man),* LXXVV (1958), 147–164

LEACH, E. R. "Lévi-Strauss in the Garden of Eden: An Examination of Some Recent Developments in the Analysis of Myth," *Transactions of the New York Academy of Sciences*, Ser. II, XXIII (1961), 386–396.

LEACH, E. R. *Pul Eliya: A Village in Ceylon.* Cambridge: Cambridge University Press, 1961.

LEACH, E. R. "Two Essays on the Symbolic Representation of Time," in *Rethinking Anthropology.* London: Athlone Press, University of London, 1961.

LEACH, E. R. "Genesis as Myth," *Discovery*, XXIII (1962), 30–35.

LEACH, E. R. "Pulleyar and the Lord Buddha: An Aspect of Religious Syncretism in Ceylon," *Psychoanalysis and the Psychoanalytic Review*, XLIX (1962), No. 2, 80–102.

LEACH, E. R. "Anthropological Aspects of Language: Animal Categories and Verbal Abuse," in Eric H. Lenneberg, *New Directions in the Study of Language.* Cambridge, Mass.: The M.I.T. Press, 1964, pp. 23–63.

LEACH, E. R. *Political Systems of Highland Burma.* London: G. Bell & Sons, Ltd., 1954. Reprinted, Boston: Beacon Press, 1964.

LEACH, E. R. "Ritualization in Man in Relation to Conceptual and Social Development," *Philosophical Transactions of the Royal Society of London*, CCLI (1966), Ser. B, No. 772, 403–408.

LEACH, E. R. (ed.). *The Structural Study of Myth and Totemism.* ("Association of Social Anthropologists," Monograph 5.) London: Tavistock Publications, 1967.

LEACH, E. R. *Claude Lévi-Strauss.* New York: The Viking Press, 1970.

LEEUW, G. VAN DER. *Phänomenologie der Religion.* 2d ed. Tübingen: J. C. B. Mohr (Paul Siebeck), 1933.

LEIGHTON, ALEXANDER H., and LEIGHTON, DOROTHEA C. "Elements of Psychotherapy in Navaho Religion," *Psychiatry*, IV (1941), 515–524.

LEIGHTON, ALEXANDER H., and LEIGHTON, DOROTHEA C. "Some Types of Uneasiness and Fear in a Navaho Indian Community," *American Anthropologist*, XLIV (1942), 194–209.

LENNEBERG, ERIC H. *New Directions in the Study of Language.* Cambridge, Mass.: The M.I.T. Press, 1964.

LEÓN-PORTILLA, MIGUEL. *Tiempo y Realidad en el Pensamiento Maya.* Instituto de Investigaciones Históricas. Mexico: Universidad Nacional Autónoma de Mexico, 1968.

LESSA, WILLIAM A. "Oedipus-Type Tales in Oceania," *Journal of American Folklore*, LXIX (1956), 63–73.

LESSA, WILLIAM A. "Sorcery on Ifaluk," *American Anthropologist*, LXIII (1961), 817–820.

LESSA, WILLIAM A. *Tales from Ulithi Atoll: A Comparative Study in Oceanic Folklore.* ("University of California Publications: Folklore Studies," No. 13). Berkeley and Los Angeles, 1961.

LESSA, WILLIAM A. "The Decreasing Power of Myth on Ulithi," *Journal of American Folklore*, LXXV (1962), 153–159.

LESSA, WILLIAM A. "Discoverer-of-the-Sun," *Journal of American Folklore*, LXXIX (1966), 3–51.

LESSA, WILLIAM, and SPIEGELMAN, MARVIN. "Ulithian Personality As Seen Through Ethnographic Materials and Thematic Test Analysis." ("University of California Publications in Culture and Society," Vol. II, No. 2.) Berkeley, 1954.

LÉVI-STRAUSS, CLAUDE. "La Geste d'Asdiwal," *École Pratique des Hautes Études, Section des Sciences Religieuses.* Extr. Annuaire, 1958–1959, pp. 3–43.

LÉVI-STRAUSS, CLAUDE. "The Bear and the Barber," *Journal of the Royal Anthropological Institute*, XCIII (1963), 1–11.

LÉVI-STRAUSS, CLAUDE. "The Structural Study of Myth," in *Structural Anthropology.* New York: Basic Books, Inc., 1963.

LÉVI-STRAUSS, CLAUDE. *Totemism.* Boston: Beacon Press, 1963. [French edition, *Le Totémisme aujourd'hui.* Paris: Presses Universitaires de France, 1962.]

LÉVI-STRAUSS, CLAUDE. *Mythologiques II: Du Miel aux cendres.* Paris: Libraire Plon, 1966.

LÉVI-STRAUSS, CLAUDE. *The Savage Mind.* London: Weidenfeld and Nicolson, 1966. [French edition, *La Pensée sauvage.* Paris: Libraire Plon, 1962.]

LÉVI-STRAUSS, CLAUDE. *Mythologiques III: L'Origine des manières de table.* Paris: Libraire Plon, 1968.

LÉVI-STRAUSS, CLAUDE. *The Elementary Structures of Kinship.* Boston: Beacon Press, 1969. [French edition, *Les Structures élémentaires de la parenté.* Paris: Les Presses Universitaires, 1949.]

LÉVI-STRAUSS, CLAUDE. *The Raw and the Cooked.* New York: Harper & Row, Publishers, Inc., 1969. [French edition, *Mythologiques I: Le Cru et le cuit.* Paris: Plon, 1964.]

LÉVY-BRUHL, LUCIEN. *How Natives Think.* London: George Allen & Unwin, Ltd., 1926. [French edition, *Les Fonctions mentales dans les sociétés primitives.* Paris: F. Alcan, 1910.] Paperback edition, New York: Washington Square Press, 1966.

LÉVY-BRUHL, LUCIEN. *Primitive Mentality.* London: Macmillan & Co., Ltd., 1923. [French edition, 1922.]

LÉVY-BRUHL, LUCIEN. *Les Carnets de Lucien Lévy-Bruhl.* Paris: Libraire Plon, 1949.

LEWIS, OSCAR. "Comparisons in Cultural Anthropology," in *Yearbook of Anthropology, 1955*, William L. Thomas, Jr. (ed.). New York: Wenner-Gren Foundation for Anthropological Research, Inc., 1955.

LIENHARDT, GODFREY. *Divinity and Experience: The Religion of the Dinka.* Oxford: Clarendon Press, 1961.

LIENHARDT, GODFREY. *Social Anthropology.* London and New York: Oxford University Press, 1964.

LINTON, RALPH. "Nativistic Movements," *American Anthropologist*, XLV (1943), 230–240.

LOMBROSO, CESARE. *The Man of Genius*. London: Walter Scott, 1895.

LOWIE, ROBERT H. *Primitive Society*. New York: Liveright Publishing Corp., 1920.

LOWIE, ROBERT H. *The Crow Indians*. New York: Farrar & Rinehart, 1935.

LOWIE, ROBERT H. *Primitive Religion*. Enl. ed. New York: Liveright Publishing Corp., 1948.

LOWIE, ROBERT H. *Indians of the Plains*. ("American Museum of Natural History, Anthropological Handbooks," No. 1.) New York: McGraw-Hill Book Co., 1954.

LOWIE, ROBERT H. "Religion in Human Life," *American Anthropologist*, LXV (1963), 532–542.

LUKAS, FRANZ. "Das ei als kosmogonische vorsellung," *Zeitschrift des Vereins für Volkskunde*, IV (1894), 227–243.

McCLELLAND, DAVID C., and FRIEDMAN, G. A. "A Cross-Cultural Study of the Relationship Between Child-Training Practices and Achievement Motivation Appearing in Folk Tales," in G. E. Swanson, T. M. Newcomb, and E. L. Hartley (eds.), *Readings in Social Psychology*. New York: Holt, Rinehart & Winston, Inc., 1952.

McCULLOCH, J. A. "Monsters," in *Hastings Encyclopaedia of Religion and Ethics*. Edinburgh: T. & T. Clark, 1913.

McLUHAN, MARSHALL. *Understanding Media: The Extensions of Man*. London: Routledge & Kegan Paul, Ltd., 1964.

MAIR, LUCY. *Witchcraft*. New York: McGraw-Hill Book Co., 1969.

MALINOWSKI, BRONISLAW. *Myth in Primitive Psychology*. New York: W. W. Norton & Co., 1926.

MALINOWSKI, BRONISLAW. *Sex and Repression in Savage Society*. London: Routledge & Kegan Paul, Ltd., 1927.

MALINOWSKI, BRONISLAW. "Culture," in *Encyclopaedia of the Social Sciences*, IV (1931), 621–646.

MALINOWSKI, BRONISLAW. *Coral Gardens and Their Magic*. 2 vols. London: George Allen & Unwin, Ltd., 1935.

MALINOWSKI, BRONISLAW. *Magic, Science and Religion, and Other Essays*. Boston: Beacon Press, 1948; and New York: The Free Press, 1948. Paperback edition, Garden City, N.Y.: Doubleday Anchor Books, 1954.

MANN, JOHN. *The Folktale as a Reflector of Individual and Social Structure*. Ph.D. dissertation, Columbia University, 1958.

MARETT, ROBERT RANULPH. *The Threshold of Religion*. London: Methuen & Co., Ltd., 1909.

MATTHEWS, WASHINGTON. *The Night Chant: A Navaho Ceremony*. ("Memoirs of the American Museum of Natural History," No. 6.) New York, 1902.

MATTHEWS, WASHINGTON. "Myths of Gestation and Parturition," *American Anthropologist*, IV (1902), 737–742.

MAUSS, MARCEL. *The Gift*. London: Cohen & West, Ltd., 1954. First published 1925. Paperback edition, New York: W. W. Norton & Co., 1967.

MERTON, ROBERT K. "Social Structure and Anomie," *American Sociological Review*, III (1938), 672–682.

METZGER, DUANE, and WILLIAMS, GERALD. "Tenejapa Medicine I: The Curer," *Southwestern Journal of Anthropology*, XIX (1963), 216–234.

MIDDELKOOP, P. *Curse Retribution Enmity: As Data in Natural Religion, Especially on Timor, Confronted with the Scriptures*. Amsterdam: Jacob van Campen, 1960.

MIDDLETON, JOHN. "The Cult of the Dead: Ancestors of Ghosts," in *Lugbara Religion: Ritual and Authority Among an East African People*. London: Oxford University Press, 1960.

MIDDLETON, JOHN. *Gods and Rituals*. ("American Museum of Natural History Sourcebooks in Anthropology.") New York: The Natural History Press, 1967.

MIDDLETON, JOHN. *Magic, Witchcraft, and Curing*. ("American Museum of Natural History Sourcebooks in Anthropology.") New York: The Natural History Press, 1967.

MIDDLETON, JOHN. *Myth and Cosmos*. ("American Museum of Natural History Sourcebooks in Anthropology.") New York: The Natural History Press, 1967.

MIDDLETON, JOHN, and WINTER, EDWARD (eds.). *Witchcraft and Sorcery in East Africa*. London: Routledge, 1963. New York: Frederick A. Praeger, 1963.

MONEY-KYRLE, R. *The Meaning of Sacrifice*. ("The International Psycho-Analytic Library," No. 16.) London: Hogarth Press, 1930.

MOONEY, JAMES. "The Ghost-Dance Religion and the Sioux Outbreak of 1890," *14th Annual Report of the Bureau of American Ethnology, 1892–93*, Part 2. Washington, D.C.: 1896.

MOORE, OMAR K. "Divination—A New Perspective," *American Anthropologist*, LIX (1957), 69–74.

MORGAN, WILLIAM. "Navaho Dreams," *American Anthropologist*, XXXIV (1932), 390–405.

MORGAN, WILLIAM. *Human Wolves Among the Navaho*. ("Yale University Publications in Anthropology," No. 11.) New Haven, Conn., 1936.

MÜLLER, F. MAX (trans.). *Rig-Veda-Sanhita: The Sacred Hymns of the Brahmans*. London: Trübner & Co., 1869.

MURDOCK, GEORGE P. *Social Structure*. New York: The Macmillan Co., 1949.

NADEL, S. F. "A Field Experiment in Racial Psychology," *British Journal of Psychology*, XXVIII (1937), 195–211.

NADEL, S. F. "A Study of Shamanism in the Nuba Mountains," *Journal of the Royal Anthropological Institute*, LXXVI (1946), 25–37.

NADEL, S. F. *Nupe Religion*. London: Routledge & Kegan Paul, Ltd., 1954.

NEEDHAM, JAMES (ed.). *Science, Religion and Reality.* New York: The Macmillan Co., 1925.

NEEDHAM, RODNEY. "A Structural Analysis of Purum Society," *American Anthropologist*, LX (1958), 75–101.

NEEDHAM, RODNEY. "The Left Hand of the Mugwe: An Analytical Note on the Structure of Meru Symbolism," *Africa*, XXXI (1961), 28–33.

NEEDHAM, RODNEY. "Blood, Thunder, and Mockery of Animals." *Sociologus*, 14 (1964), 136–149.

NEEDHAM, RODNEY. "Percussion and Transition," *Journal of the Royal Anthropological Institute (Man)*, II (1967), No. 4, 606–614.

NEEDHAM, RODNEY. "Right and Left in Nyoro Symbolic Classification," *Africa*, XXXVII, (1967), No. 4, 425–452.

NEHER, ANDREW. "A Physiological Explanation of Unusual Behavior in Ceremonies Involving Drums," *Human Biology*, XXXIV (1962), No. 2, 151–160.

NORBECK, EDWARD. *Religion in Primitive Society.* New York: Harper & Row, Publishers, Inc., 1961.

NORBECK, E., WALKER, D., and COHEN, M. "The Interpretation of Data: Puberty Rites," *American Anthropologist*, LXIV (1962), 463–485.

OGDEN, C. K., and RICHARDS, I. A. *The Meaning of Meaning.* New York: Harcourt, Brace & World, 1923.

OPLER, MORRIS E. "An Interpretation of Ambivalence of Two American Indian Tribes," *Journal of Social Psychology*, VIII, No. 1 (February, 1936), 82–115.

OPLER, MORRIS E. "Further Comparative Anthropological Data Bearing on the Solution of a Psychological Problem," *Journal of Social Psychology*, IX (1938), 477–483.

OPLER, MORRIS E. *An Apache Life-Way.* Chicago: The University of Chicago Press, 1941.

OSGOOD, C., and SEBEOK, T. (eds.). *Psycholinguistics: A Survey of Theory and Research Problems.* Bloomington: Indiana University Press, 1965.

PARSONS, TALCOTT. *Essays in Sociological Theory: Pure and Applied.* New York: The Free Press, 1949.

PARSONS, TALCOTT. *The Social System.* New York: The Free Press, 1951.

PARSONS, TALCOTT. "Religious Perspectives in Sociology and Social Psychology," in Hoxie N. Fairchild (ed.), *Religious Perspectives in College Teaching.* New York: The Ronald Press Co., 1952.

PARSONS, TALCOTT, BALES, R. F., and SHILS, E. S. *Working Papers in the Theory of Action.* New York: The Free Press, 1953.

PARTRIDGE, E. *A Dictionary of Slang and Unconventional English.* 3d ed. London: Routledge & Kegan Paul, Ltd., 1949.

PERRY, RALPH BARTON. *General Theory of Value: Its Meaning and Basic Principles Construed in Terms of Interest.* New York: Longmans, Green & Co., 1926.

PETRULLO, VICENZO. *The Diabolic Root: A Study of Peyotism, the New Indian Religion, Among the Delawares.* Philadelphia: University of Pennsylvania Press, 1934.

POSINSKY, S. H. "The Problem of Yurok Anality," *American Imago*, XIV (1957), 3–31.

POSTMAN, L. "The Present Status of Inference Theory," in Charles N. Cofer (ed.), *Verbal Learning and Verbal Behavior.* New York: McGraw-Hill Book Co., 1961, pp. 152–196.

POUILLON, JEAN, and MARANDA, PIERRE. *Échanges et Communications.* Mélanges Offert à Claude Lévi-Strauss. The Hague: Mouton & Co., 1970.

POZAS, RICARDO. *Chamula: Un Pueblo Indio de los Altos de Chiapas.* ("Memorias del Instituto Nacional Indigenista," VII.) Mexico, 1959.

POZAS, RICARDO. *Juan the Chamula: An Ethnological Re-creation of the Life of a Mexican Indian.* Translated from the Spanish by Lysander Kemp. Berkeley and Los Angeles: University of California Press, 1962.

RADCLIFFE-BROWN, A. R. *The Andaman Islanders.* Cambridge: At the University Press, 1922.

RADCLIFFE-BROWN, A. R. "The Sociological Theory of Totemism," *Proceedings of the Fourth Pacific Science Congress* (Java, 1929). Batavia, 1930.

RADCLIFFE-BROWN, A. R. *Taboo.* ("The Frazer Lecture," 1939.) Cambridge: University Press, 1939.

RADCLIFFE-BROWN, A. R. "Religion and Society," *Journal of the Royal Anthropological Institute*, LXXV (1945), 33–43.

RADCLIFFE-BROWN, A. R. "The Comparative Method in Social Anthropology." Huxley Memorial Lecture for 1951. *Journal of the Royal Anthropological Institute*, LXXXI (1951), 15–22. [Republished in *Method in Social Anthropology*, edited by M. N. Srinivas. Chicago: The University of Chicago Press, 1958.]

RADCLIFFE-BROWN, A. R. *Structure and Function in Primitive Society.* New York: The Free Press, 1952.

RADIN, PAUL. *Primitive Religion: Its Nature and Origin.* New York: The Viking Press, Inc., 1937.

RADIN, PAUL. *The Trickster.* New York: Philosophical Library, 1956.

RAGLAN, FITZ ROY RICHARD SOMERSET (LORD). *The Hero: A Study in Tradition, Myth, and Drama.* London: Methuen & Co., Ltd., 1936.

RANK, OTTO. "Die Symbolschichtung im Wecktraum und ihre Wiederkehr im mythischen Denken," *Jahrbuch für Psychoanalytische Forschungen*, IV (1912), 51–115.

RANK, OTTO. *Psychoanalytische Beiträge zur Mythenforschung.* 2d ed. Leipzig: Internationaler Psychoanalytischer Verlag, 1922.

RASMUSSEN, KNUD. *Report of the Fifth Thule Expedition, 1921–24*, Vol. VII, No. 1, *Intellectual Culture of the Iglulik Eskimos.* Copenhagen: Gyldendalske Boghandel, Nordisk Forlag, 1929.

REICHEL-DOLMATOFF, GERARDO. *Amazonian Cosmos: The Sexual and Religious Symbolism of the Tukano Indians*. Chicago: University of Chicago Press, 1971.

REIK, THEODOR. "Gold und Kot," *International Zeitschrift für Psychoanalyse*, III (1951), 183.

REINACH, SALOMON. *Orpheus: A History of Religions*. Translated by Florence Simmonds. Enl. New York: Liveright Publishing Corp., 1930.

RICHARDS, A. *Chisungu*. London: Faber & Faber, Ltd., 1956.

RIGBY, PETER. "The Gogo of Central Tanganyika: Cattle and Kinship in a Semi-Pastoral Society." Ph.D. dissertation, King's College, Cambridge University, 1964.

RIGBY, PETER. "Dual Symbolic Classification Among the Gogo of Central Tanzania," *Africa*, XXXVI (1966), No. 1, 1–17.

RIGBY, PETER. "Some Gogo Rituals of 'Purification': An Essay on Social and Moral Categories," in E. R. Leach (ed.), *Dialectic in Practical Religion*. Cambridge: Cambridge University Press, 1968, pp. 153–178.

RÓHEIM, GÉZA. "Primitive Man and Environment," *International Journal of Psycho-Analysis*, II (1921), 157–178.

RÓHEIM, GÉZA. "Psycho-analysis and the Folk-Tale," *International Journal of Psycho-Analysis*, III (1922), 180–186.

RÓHEIM, GÉZA. "Heiliges Geld in Melanesien," *Internationale Zeitschrift für Psychoanalyse*, IX (1923), 384–401.

RÓHEIM, GÉZA. "Psycho-analysis of Primitive Culture Types," *International Journal of Psycho-Analysis*, XIII (1932), 1–221. (Róheim Australasian Research number.)

RÓHEIM, GÉZA. "Society and the Individual," *Psychoanalytic Quarterly*, IX (1940), 526–545.

RÓHEIM, GÉZA. "Myth and Folk-Tale," *American Imago*, II (1941), 266–279.

RÓHEIM, GÉZA. *The Gates of the Dream*. New York: International Universities Press, 1951.

RÓHEIM, GÉZA. "Fairy Tale and Dream," *The Psychoanalytic Study of the Child*, VIII (1953), 394–403.

RÓHEIM, GÉZA. "Dame Holle: Dream and Folk Tale (Grimm No. 24)," in Robert Lindner (ed.), *Explorations in Psychoanalysis*. New York: Julian Press, 1953.

ROOTH, ANNA BIRGITTA. "The Creation Myths of the North American Indians," *Anthropos*, LII (1957), 497–508.

ROSALDO, RENATO I., JR. "Metaphors of Hierarchy in a Mayan Ritual," *American Anthropologist*, LXX (1968), 524–536.

ROSCOE, JOHN. *The Bakitara*. Cambridge: the University Press, 1923.

SAHAGÚN, BERNARDINO DE. *The Florentine Codex: General History of the Things of New Spain*, Book II, *The Ceremonies*. Translated by A. J. O. Anderson and C. E. Dibble. ("Monographs of the School of American Research," No. 14, Part 3.) Santa Fe, N.M.: Museum of New Mexico, 1951.

SANTAYANA, GEORGE. *Reason in Religion*. New York: Collier Books, 1906.

SAPIR, EDWARD. "Conceptual Categories in Primitive Languages," *Science*, LXXIV (1931), 578.

SAVILLE, MARSHALL H. "The Goldsmith's Art in Ancient Mexico." ("Indian Notes and Monographs.") New York: Heye Foundation, 1920.

SCHMIDT, WILHELM. *The Origin and Growth of Religion: Facts and Theories*. Translated by H. J. Rose. New York: Lincoln MacVeagh, 1931.

SCHUTZ, A. *The Problem of Social Reality. Collected Papers*, Vol. I. The Hague: Martinus Nijhoff, 1962.

SCHWARTZ, EMANUEL K. "A Psychoanalytic Study of the Fairy Tale," *American Journal of Psychotherapy*, X (1956), 740–762.

SCHWARTZBAUM, HAIM. "Jewish and Moslem Sources of a Falasha Creation Myth," in Raphael Patai, Francis Lee Utley, and Dov Noy (eds.), *Studies in Biblical and Jewish Folklore*. ("American Folklore Society," Memoir 51.) Bloomington: Indiana University Press, 1960.

SELIGMAN, C. G., and SELIGMAN, BRENDA Z. *The Veddas*. Cambridge: At the University Press, 1911.

SILBERER, HERBERT. "A Pregnancy Phantasy in a Man," *Psychoanalytic Review*, XII (1925), 377–396.

SILVER, DANIEL. *Zinacanteco Shamanism*. Unpublished Ph.D. dissertation, Department of Social Relations, Harvard University, 1966.

SINGER, MILTON. "The Cultural Pattern of Indian Civilization," *Far Eastern Quarterly*, XV (1955), 23–36.

SINGER, PHILIP, and DESOLE, DANIEL E. "The Australian Subincision Ceremony Reconsidered: Vaginal Envy or Kangaroo Bifid Penis Envy," *American Anthropologist*, LXIX (1967), 355–358.

SLOTKIN, J. S. "Menomini Peyotism," *Transactions of the American Philosophical Society*, XLII, Part 4 (1952).

SLOTKIN, J. S. "Peyotism, 1521–1891," *American Anthropologist*, LVII (1955), 202–230.

SLOTKIN, J. S. "The Peyote Way," *Tomorrow*, IV, No. 3 (1955–1956), 64–70.

SLOTKIN, J. S. *The Peyote Religion: A Study in Indian-White Relations*. New York: The Free Press, 1956.

SLOTKIN, J. S. *The Menomini Powwow Religion*. Milwaukee, Wis.: Milwaukee Public Museum, 1957.

SMITH, W. ROBERTSON. *Lectures on the Religion of the Semites*. New York: D. Appleton & Co., 1889. Paperback edition, New York: Meridian Books, 1957.

SPECK, FRANK G. *Naskapi*. Norman: University of Oklahoma Press, 1935.

SPENCE, LEWIS. *An Introduction to Mythology*. New York: Farrar & Rinehart, 1921.

SPENCER, BALDWIN, and GILLEN, F. J. *The Arunta*. 2 vols. London: Macmillan & Co., Ltd., 1927.

SPENCER, KATHERINE. "Reflection of Social Life in the Navaho Origin Myth." ("University of New Mexico Publications in Anthropology," No. 3.) 1947.

SPIRO, MELFORD E. "Ghosts, Ifaluk, and Teleological Functionalism," *American Anthropologist*, LIV (1952), 497–503.

SPIRO, MELFORD E. "Sorcery, Evil Spirits, and Functional Analysis: A Rejoinder," *American Anthropologist*, LXIII (1961), 820–824.

STANNER, W. E. H. "The Dreaming," in T. A. G. Hungerford (ed.), *Australian Signpost*. Melbourne: F. W. Chesire, 1956.

STANNER, W. E. H. *On Aboriginal Religion*. ("Oceania Monographs," No. 11.) Sydney, 1963.

STANNER, W. E. H. "Religion, Totemism, and Symbolism," in R. M. and C. H. Berndt (eds.), *Aboriginal Man in Australia*. Sydney: Angus and Robertson, 1965.

STEARN, G. E. "Conversations with McLuhan," *Encounter*, XXVIII (1967), 50–58.

STEINER, FRANZ. *Taboo*. New York: Philosophical Library, 1956. Paperback edition, Baltimore: Penguin Books, 1968.

STEKEL, WILHELM. *Patterns of Psychosexual Infantilism*. New York: Grove Press, 1959.

STEWARD, JULIAN N. "Evolution and Process," in A. L. Kroeber (ed.), *Anthropology Today*. Chicago: The University of Chicago Press, 1953.

STURTEVANT, WILLIAM C. "Categories, Percussion and Physiology," *Journal of the Royal Anthropological Institute (Man)*, III (1968), No. 1, 133–134.

TAX, SOL, *et al.* (eds.). *An Appraisal of Anthropology Today*. Chicago: The University of Chicago Press, 1953.

THOMPSON, J. ERIC S. *Maya History and Religion*. Norman: University of Oklahoma Press, 1970.

THOMPSON, STITH. *Tales of the North American Indians*. Cambridge, Mass.: Harvard University Press, 1929.

THOMPSON, STITH. *Motif-Index of Folk-Literature*. Bloomington: Indiana University Press, 1955.

TITIEV, MISCHA. "A Fresh Approach to the Problem of Magic and Religion," *Southwestern Journal of Anthropology*, XVI (1960), 292–298.

TREVOR-ROPER, H. R. "The European Witch-Craze of the Sixteenth and Seventeenth Centuries," in *The Crisis of the Seventeenth Century*. New York: Harper & Row, Publishers, Inc., 1968.

TURNER, VICTOR. *Ndembu Divination: Its Symbolism and Techniques*. ("Rhodes-Livingstone Papers," No. 31.) Manchester, 1961.

TURNER, VICTOR. "Ritual Symbolism, Morality and Social Structure Among the Ndembu," *Rhodes-Livingstone Journal*, XXX (1961), 1–10.

TURNER, VICTOR. *Chihamba the White Spirit*. ("Rhodes-Livingstone Papers," No. 33.) Manchester, 1962.

TURNER, VICTOR. "Three Symbols of *Passage* in Ndembu Circumcision Ritual," in M. Gluckman (ed.), *Essays in the Ritual of Social Relations*. Manchester: Manchester University Press, 1962, pp. 124–173.

TURNER, VICTOR. "Betwixt and Between: The Liminal Period in *Rites de Passage*," in the *Proceedings of the American Ethnological Society*, Symposium on New Approaches to the Study of Religion, 1964, pp. 4–20.

TURNER, VICTOR. "Symbols in Ndembu Ritual," in M. Gluckman (ed.), *Closed Systems and Open Minds: The Limits of Naivety in Social Anthropology*. London: Manchester University Press, 1964.

TURNER, VICTOR. "Colour Classification in Ndembu Ritual: A Problem in Primitive Classification," in *Anthropological Approaches to the Study of Religion*. ("Association of Social Anthropologists," Monograph 3.) London: Tavistock Publications, 1966.

TURNER, VICTOR. *The Forest of Symbols*. Ithaca and London: Cornell University Press, 1967.

TURNER, VICTOR. *The Drums of Affliction*. Oxford: Oxford University Press, 1968.

TURNER, VICTOR. *The Ritual Process*. Chicago: Aldine Publishing Co. 1969.

TYLER, STEPHEN A. (ed.). *Cognitive Anthropology*. New York: Holt, Rinehart & Winston, Inc., 1969.

TYLOR, EDWARD B. *Primitive Culture: Researches into the Development of Mythology, Philosophy, Religion, Language, Art, and Custom*. 2d ed. 2 vols. London: John Murray, 1873.

VOGT, EVON Z. "Water Witching: An Interpretation of a Ritual Pattern in a Rural American Community," *Scientific Monthly*, LXXV (September, 1952), 175–186.

VOGT, EVON Z. *Modern Homesteaders: The Life of a Twentieth-Century Frontier Community*. Cambridge: Harvard University Press, 1955.

VOGT, EVON Z. "Structural and Conceptual Replication in Zinacantan Culture," *American Anthropologist*, LXVII (1965), 342–353.

VOGT, EVON Z. "Ceremonial Organization in Zinacantan," *Ethnology*, IV (1965), 39–52.

VOGT, EVON Z. *Zinacantan: A Maya Community in the Highlands of Chiapas*. Cambridge, Mass.: Belknap Press of the Harvard University Press, 1969.

VOGT, EVON Z. and HYMAN, RAY. *Water Witching U.S.A.* Chicago: The University of Chicago Press, 1959.

VOGT, EVON Z., and VOGT, CATHERINE C. "Lévi-Strauss Among the Maya," *Journal of the Royal Anthropological Institute (Man)*, V (1970), 379–392.

VOLTAIRE, FRANÇOIS MARIE AROUET DE. *Dictionnaire philosophique, portatif*. Nouv. éd., rev. Londres, 1765.

WALLACE, ANTHONY F. C. "Revitalization Movements," *American Anthropologist*, LVIII (1956), 264–281.

WALLACE, ANTHONY F. C. *Culture and Personality*. New York: Random House, Inc., 1961.

WALLACE, ANTHONY F. C. *Religion: An Anthropological View.* New York: Random House, Inc., 1966.

WALLACE, ANTHONY F. C. *The Death and Rebirth of the Seneca.* New York: Alfred A. Knopf, Inc., 1970.

WALLIS, WILSON D. *Messiahs—Christian and Pagan.* Boston: R. G. Badger, 1918.

WALLIS, WILSON D. *Religion in Primitive Society.* New York: F. S. Crofts & Co., 1939.

WALLIS, WILSON D. *Messiahs—Their Role in Civilization.* Washington, D.C.: American Council on Public Affairs, 1943.

WARNER, W. LLOYD. *A Black Civilization: A Social Study of an Australian Tribe.* New York: Harper & Row, Publishers, Inc., 1937.

WARNER, W. LLOYD. *American Life: Dream and Reality.* Chicago: The University of Chicago Press, 1953.

WARNER, W. LLOYD. *The Living and the Dead: A Study of the Symbolic Life of Americans.* New Haven, Conn.: Yale University Press, 1959.

WARNER, W. LLOYD. *The Family of God.* New Haven, Conn.: Yale University Press, 1961.

WASSERSTROM, ROBERT. *Our Lady of the Salt.* A.B. honors thesis, Harvard College, 1970.

WAX, MURRAY, and WAX, ROSALIE. "The Notion of Magic," *Current Anthropology,* IV (1963), 495–518.

WAX, ROSALIE, and WAX, MURRAY. "The Magical World View," *Journal for the Scientific Study of Religion,* I (1962), 179–188.

WEBER, MAX. *The Theory of Social and Economic Organization.* New York: The Free Press, 1947.

WENTWORTH, H., and FLEXNER, S. B. *Dictionary of American Slang.* New York: Thomas Y. Crowell Co., 1961.

WHEELER, ADDISON J. "Gongs and Bells," *Encyclopedia of Religious Ethics,* VI (1913), 313–316.

WHEELER-VOEGELIN, ERMINIE. "Earth Diver," in Maria Leach (ed.), *Standard Dictionary of Folklore, Mythology, and Legend,* Vol. I. New York: Funk & Wagnalls, 1949.

WHEELER-VOEGELIN, ERMINIE, and MOORE, REMEDIOS W. "The Emergence Myth in Native North America," in W. Edson Richmond (ed.), *Studies in Folklore.* Bloomington: Indiana University Press, 1957.

WHITEHEAD, ALFRED N. *Symbolism.* New York: G. P. Putnam's Sons, 1927.

WHITING, JOHN W. M. "The Cross-Cultural METHOD," in Gardner Lindzey (ed.), *Handbook of Social Psychology.* Vol. I, pp. 523–531. Cambridge: Addison-Wesley, 1954.

WHITING, JOHN W. M., KLUCKHOHN, RICHARD, and ANTHONY, ALBERT. "The Function of Male Initiation Ceremonies at Puberty," in Eleanor E. Maccoby, T. M. Newcomb, and E. L. Hartley (eds.), *Readings in Social Psychology.* New York: Holt, Rinehart & Winston, Inc. 1958.

WILBUR, GEORGE B., and MUENSTERBERGER, WARNER (eds.). *Psychoanalysis and Culture.* New York: International Universities Press, 1951.

WILKEN, G. A. "Het shamanisme bij de volken van den Indischen Archipel," *Bijdragen tot de Taal-, Land- en Volkenkunde,* XXXVI (1887), 427–497.

WILLIAMS, F. E. *The Vailala Madness and the Destruction of Native Ceremonies in the Gulf Division.* ("Anthropology Report," No. 4.) Port Moresby: Territory of Papua, 1923.

WILLIAMS, F. E. "The Vailala Madness in Retrospect," in *Essays Presented to C. G. Seligman,* edited by E. E. Evans-Pritchard, *et al.* London: Kegan, Paul, Trench, Trubner & Co., 1934.

WILLIS, R. G. "Traditional History and Social Structure in Ufipa," *Africa,* XXXIV (1964), 340–352.

WILLIS, R. G. "The Head and the Loins: Lévi-Strauss and Beyond," *Journal of the Royal Anthropological Institute (Man),* II (1967), No. 4, 519–534.

WILLOUGHBY, R. R. "Magic and Cognate Phenomena: An Hypothesis," in C. Murchison (ed.), *Handbook of Social Psychology.* Worcester, Mass. Clark University Press, 1935, pp. 461–519.

WILSON, EDMUND. *Red, Black, Blond and Olive.* New York: Oxford University Press, 1956.

WILSON, MONICA. "Nyakyusa Ritual and Symbolism," *American Anthropologist,* LVI (1954), 228–241.

WILSON, MONICA. *Rituals of Kinship Among the Nyakyusa.* London: Oxford University Press, 1957.

WILSON, MONICA. *Divine Kings and the Breath of Men.* London: Cambridge University Press, 1959.

WOLF, ERIC. "The Virgin of Gaudalupe: A Mexican National Symbol," *Journal of American Folklore,* LXXI (1958), 34–39.

WOLFENSTEIN, MARTHA. "'Jack and the Beanstalk': An American Version," in Margaret Mead and Martha Wolfenstein (eds.), *Childhood in Contemporary Cultures.* Chicago: The University of Chicago Press, 1955.

WORSLEY, PETER. *The Trumpet Shall Sound.* London: MacGibbon & Kee, 1957.

WYCOCO (MOORE), REMEDIOS. *The Types of North-American Indian Tales.* Unpublished Ph.D. dissertation, Indiana University, 1951.

YALMAN, NUR. "The Raw: the Cooked: Nature: Culture," in E. R. Leach (ed.), *The Structural Study of Myth and Totemism.* ("Association of Social Anthropologists," Monograph No 5.) London. Tavistock Publications, 1967.

YINGER, J. MILTON. *Religion, Society and the Individual.* New York. The Macmillan Co., 1957.

YINGER, J. MILTON. *The Scientific Study of Religion.* New York: The Macmillan Co., 1970.

ZIMMER, H. R. *Myths and Symbols in Indian Art and Literature.* New York: Pantheon Books, Inc. 1946.

ZIMMER, H. R. *Philosophies of India*. Edited by Joseph Campbell. New York: Pantheon Books, Inc., 1951.

ZIMMER, H. R. *The Art of Indian Asia: Its Mythology and Transformations*. Edited by Joseph Campbell. New York: Pantheon Books, Inc., 1955.

INDEX OF AUTHORS AND TITLES

73 74 75 76   9 8 7 6 5 4 3